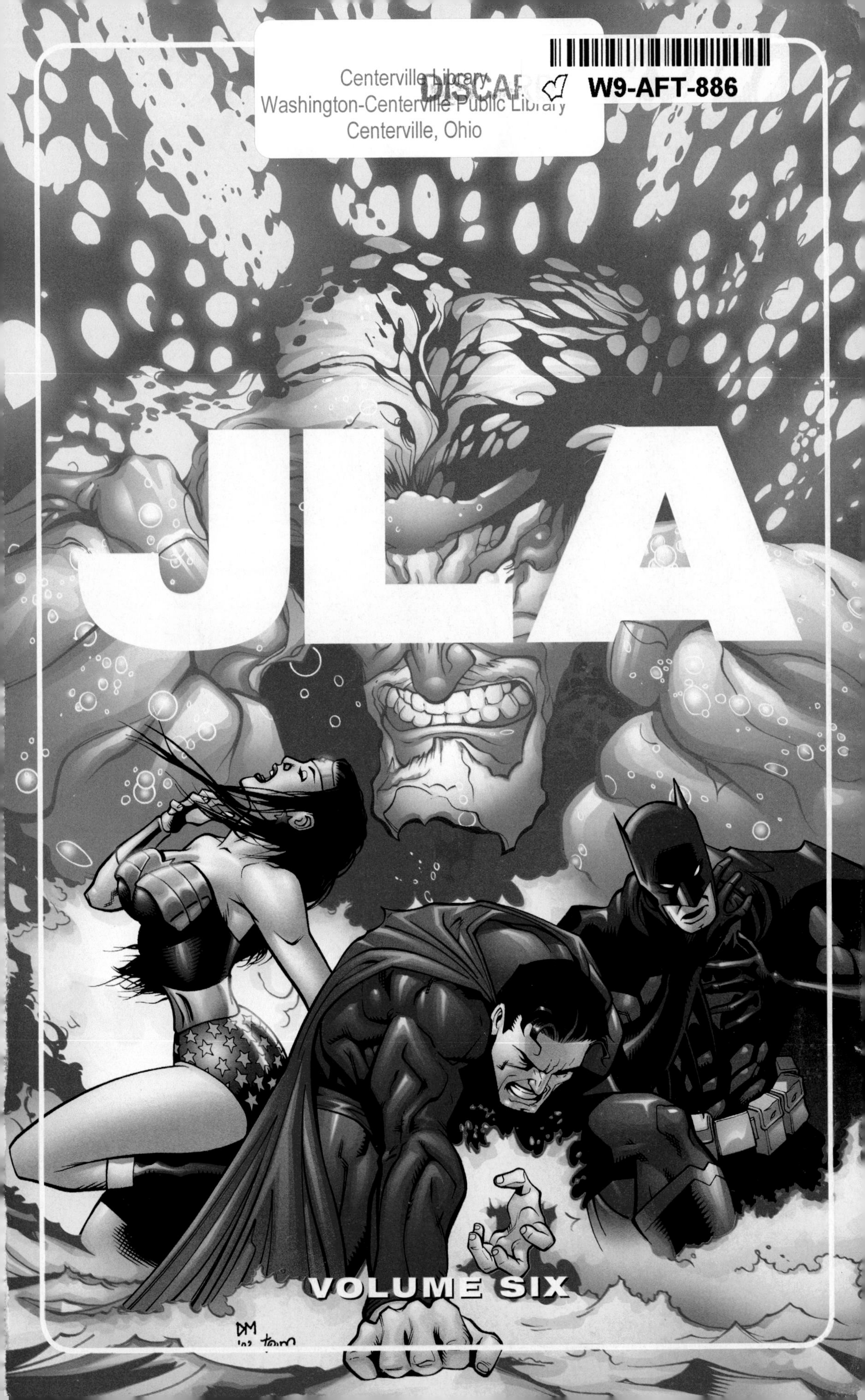
JLA
VOLUME SIX

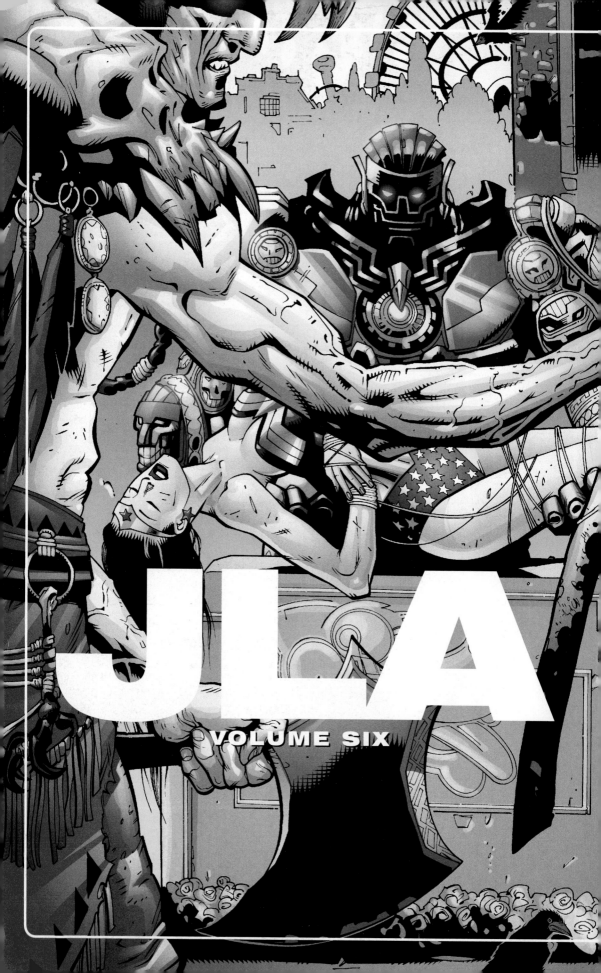

JLA

VOLUME SIX

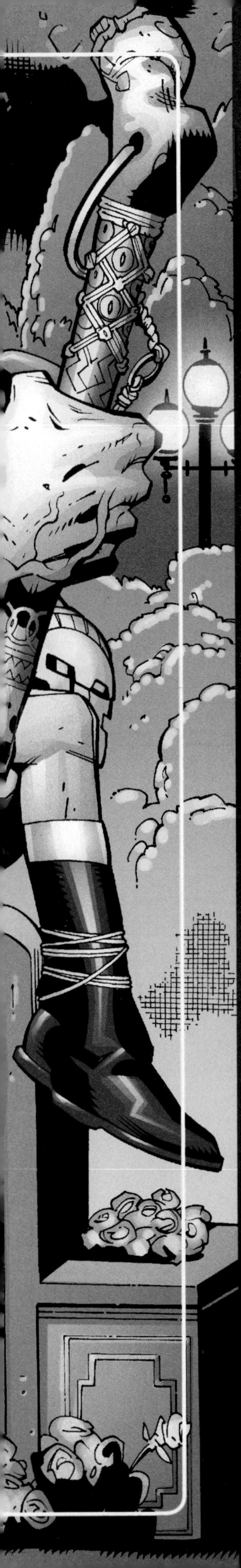

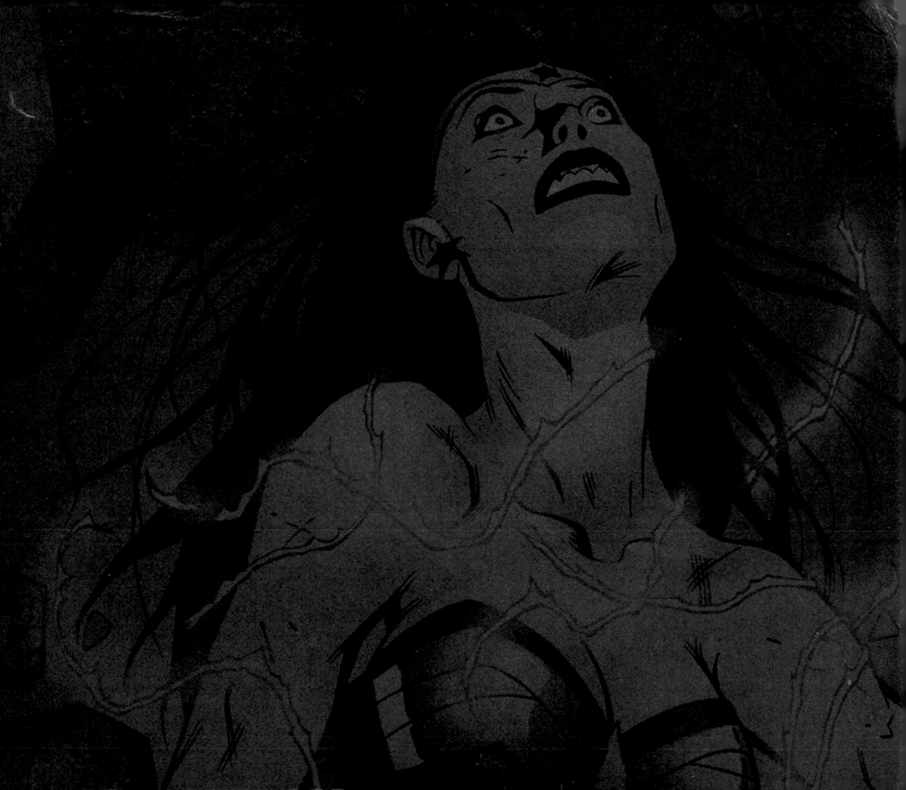

JOE KELLY
writer

DOUG MAHNKE
YVEL GUICHET
LEWIS LA ROSA
DARRYL BANKS
DIETRICH SMITH
pencillers

TOM NGUYEN
MARK PROPST
AL MILGROM
WAYNE FAUCHER
SEAN PARSONS
BOB PETRECCA
inkers

DAVID BARON
colorist
KEN LOPEZ
letterer

DOUG MAHNKE
TOM NGUYEN
collection cover artists

Superman created by
JERRY SIEGEL
& JOE SHUSTER
By special arrangement
with the Jerry Siegel family

DAN RASPLER Editor – Original Series
STEPHEN WACKER Associate Editor – Original Series
ROBBIN BROSTERMAN Design Director – Books :: ROBBIE BIEDERMAN Publication Design

BOB HARRAS Senior VP – Editor-in-Chief, DC Comics

DIANE NELSON President :: DAN DIDIO and JIM LEE Co-Publishers :: GEOFF JOHNS Chief Creative Officer
AMIT DESAI Senior VP – Marketing & Franchise Management :: AMY GENKINS Senior VP – Business & Legal Affairs
NAIRI GARDINER Senior VP – Finance :: JEFF BOISON VP – Publishing Planning :: MARK CHIARELLO VP – Art Direction & Design
JOHN CUNNINGHAM VP – Marketing :: TERRI CUNNINGHAM VP – Editorial Administration
LARRY GANEM SVP – Talent Relations & Services :: ALISON GILL Senior VP – Manufacturing & Operations
HANK KANALZ Senior VP – Vertigo & Integrated Publishing :: JAY KOGAN VP – Business & Legal Affairs, Publishing
JACK MAHAN VP – Business Affairs, Talent :: NICK NAPOLITANO VP – Manufacturing Administration :: SUE POHJA VP – Book Sales
FRED RUIZ VP – Manufacturing Operations :: COURTNEY SIMMONS Senior VP – Publicity :: BOB WAYNE Senior VP – Sales

Interior color separations by Heroic Age & Digital Chameleon

JLA Volume Six. Published by DC Comics. Compilation Copyright © 2015 DC Comics. All Rights Reserved.
Originally published in single magazine form in JLA 61-76 © 2002, 2003 DC Comics. All Rights Reserved.
All characters, their distinctive likenesses and related elements featured in this publication are trademarks
of DC Comics. The stories, characters and incidents featured in this publication are entirely fictional.
DC Comics does not read or accept unsolicited ideas, stories or artwork.

DC Comics, 1700 Broadway,
New York, NY 10019 A Warner Bros. Entertainment Company.
Printed by RR Donnelley, Owensville, MO, USA. 12/19/14. First Printing.
ISBN: 978-1-4012-5136-9

Library of Congress Cataloging-in-Publication Data

Kelly, Joe, 1971- author.
   JLA. Volume 6 / Joe Kelly, writer ; Doug Mahnke, artist.
      pages cm
   ISBN 978-1-4012-5136-9 (pbk.)
   1. Graphic novels. I. Mahnke, Doug, illustrator. II. Title.

PN6728.J87K5 2015
741.5'973--dc23
                                                    2014034336

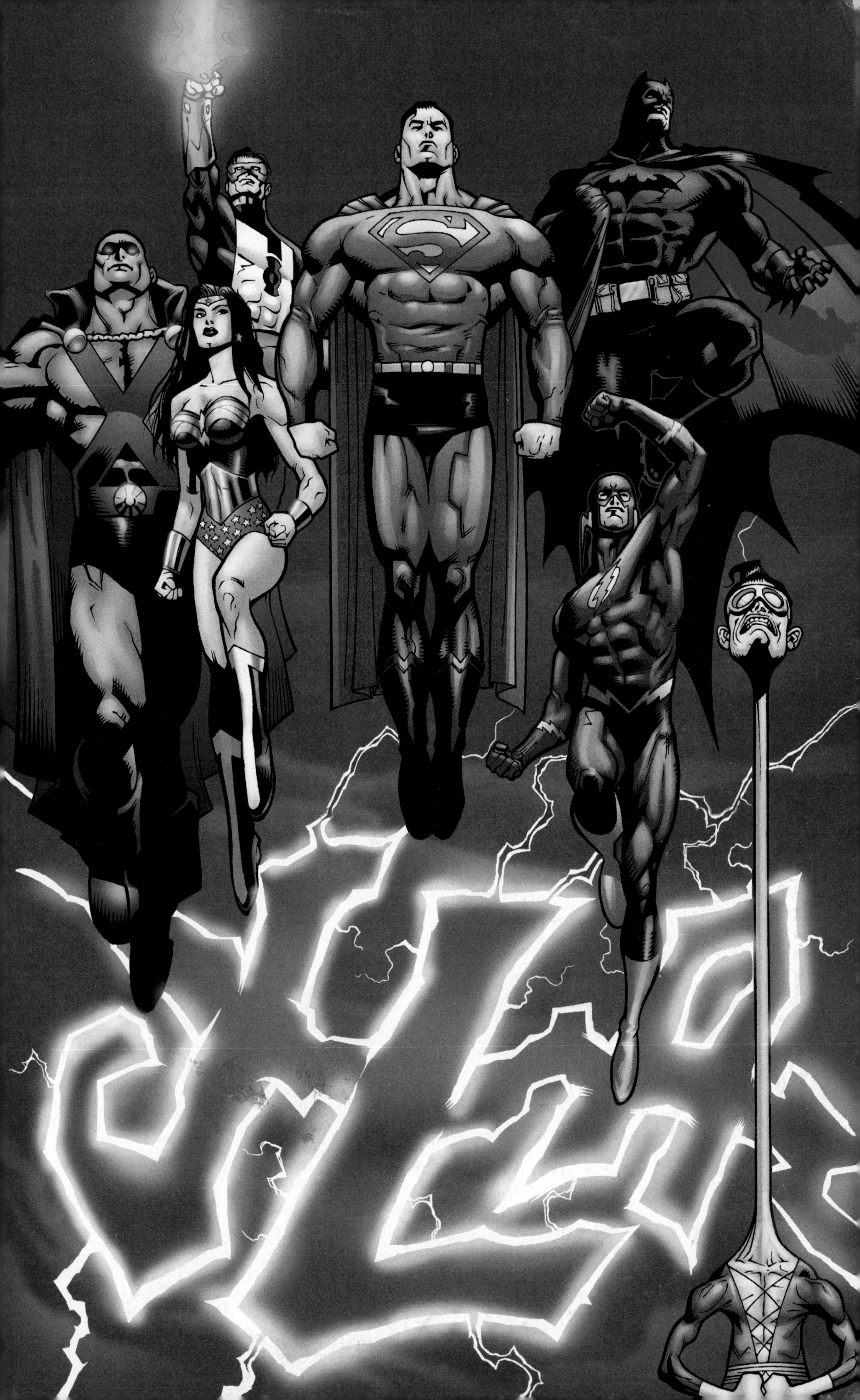

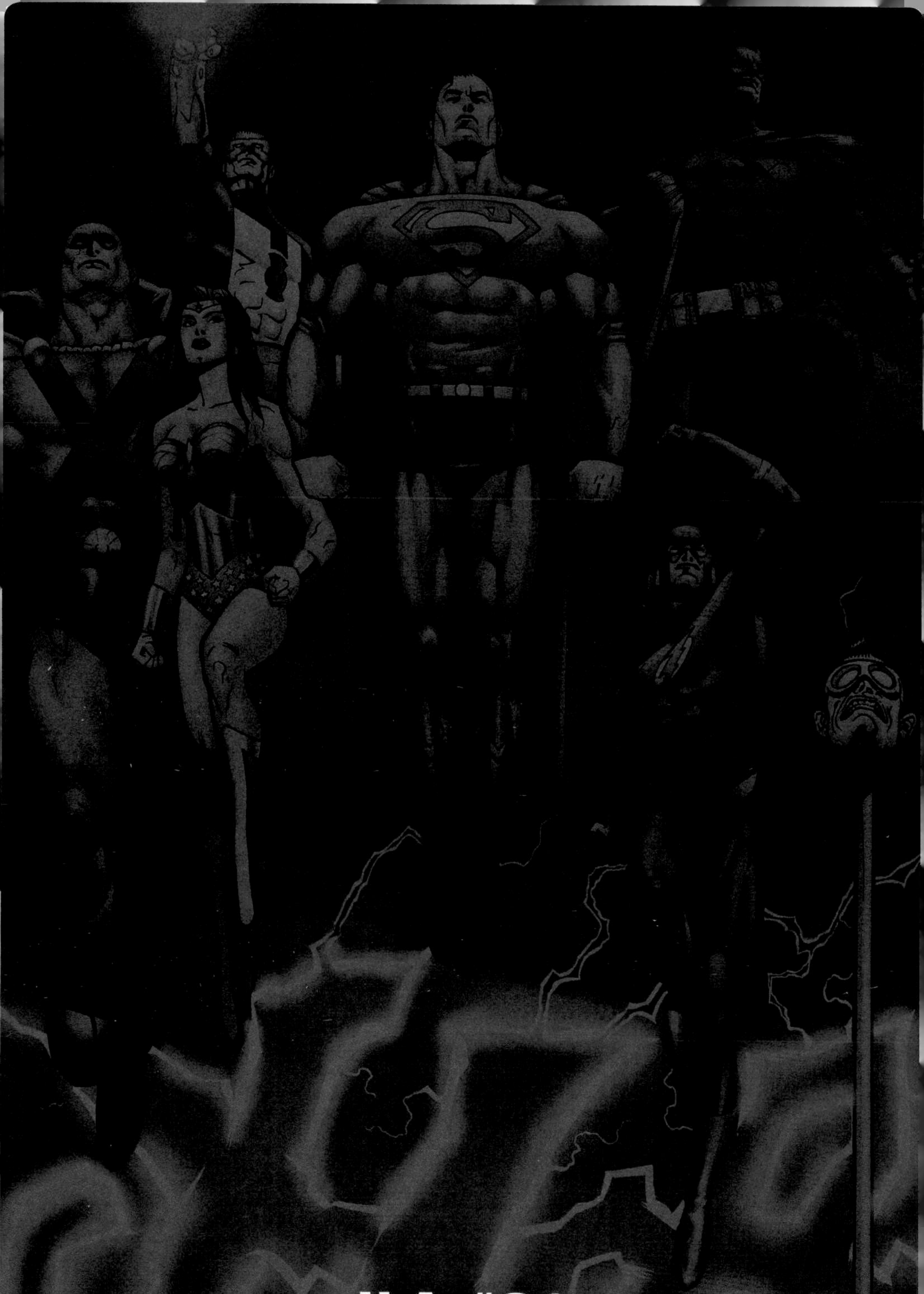

JLA #61

WRITTEN BY JOE KELLY

PENCILS BY DOUG MAHNKE,
WITH INKS BY TOM NGUYEN
AND COLORS BY DAVID BARON
COVER BY DOUG MAHNKE & TOM NGUYEN

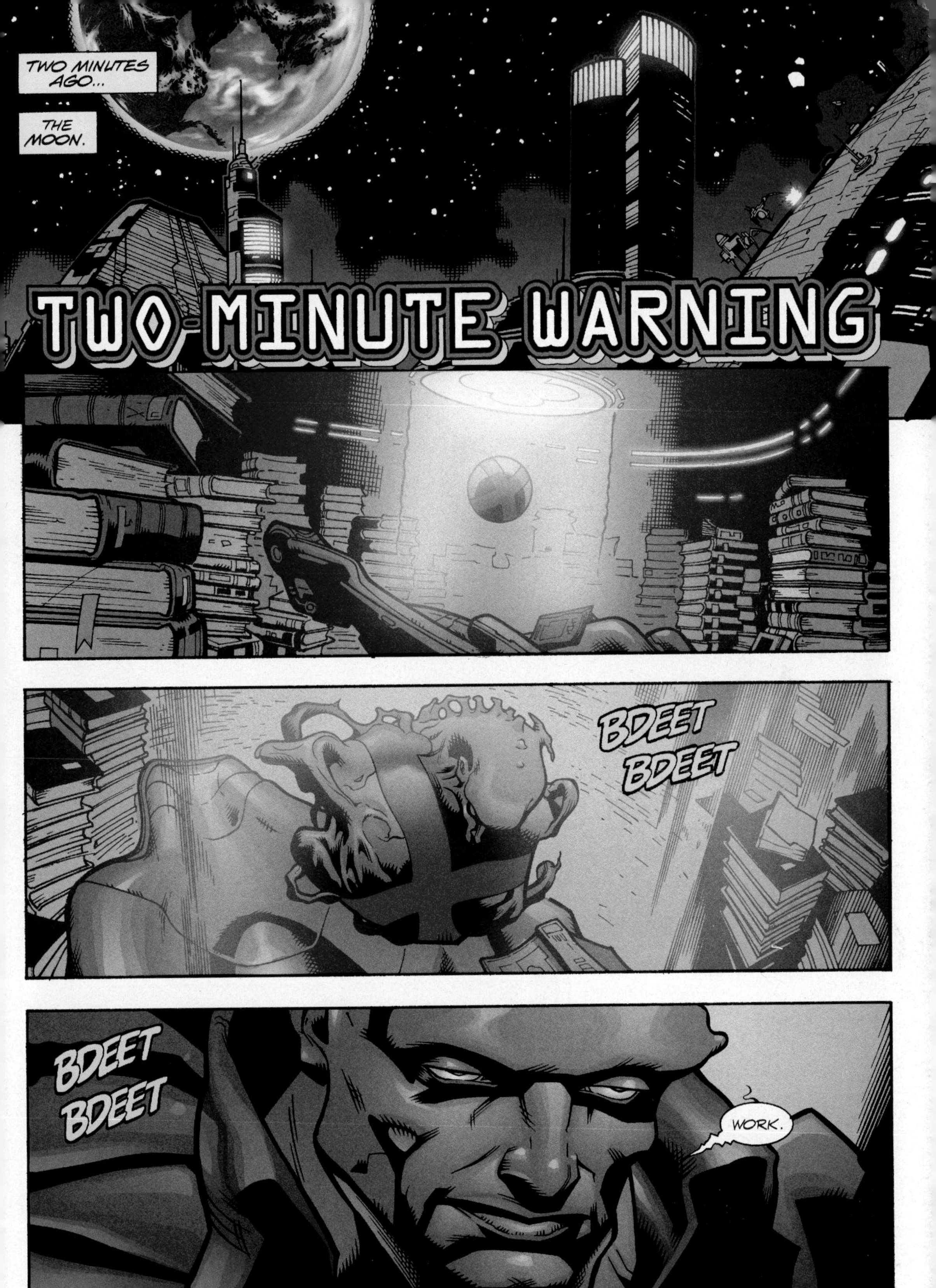
TWO MINUTES AGO...
THE MOON.
TWO MINUTE WARNING
BDEET BDEET
BDEET BDEET
WORK.

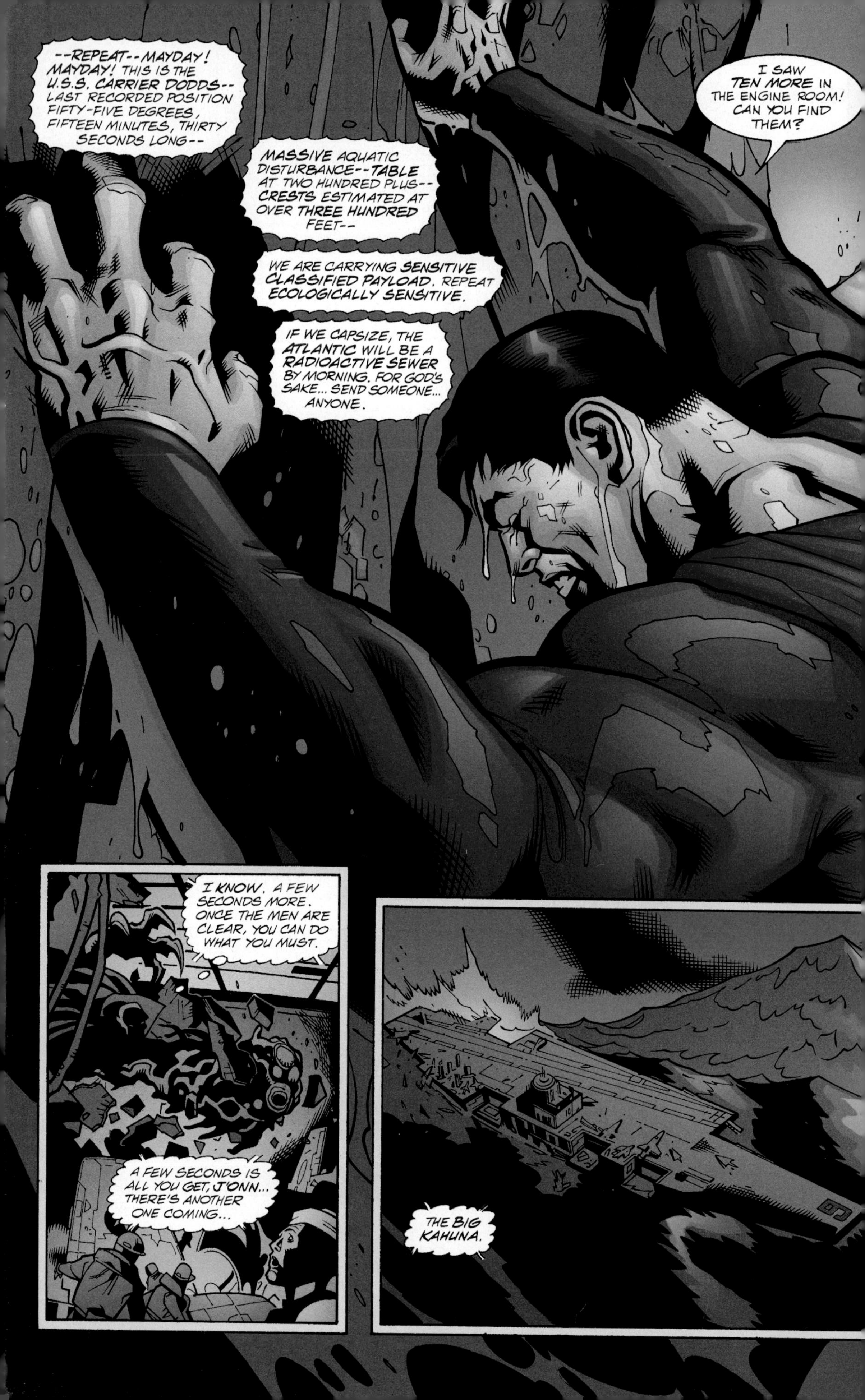
--REPEAT--MAYDAY! MAYDAY! THIS IS THE U.S.S. CARRIER DODDS-- LAST RECORDED POSITION FIFTY-FIVE DEGREES, FIFTEEN MINUTES, THIRTY SECONDS LONG--
MASSIVE AQUATIC DISTURBANCE--TABLE AT TWO HUNDRED PLUS-- CRESTS ESTIMATED AT OVER THREE HUNDRED FEET--
WE ARE CARRYING SENSITIVE CLASSIFIED PAYLOAD. REPEAT ECOLOGICALLY SENSITIVE.
IF WE CAPSIZE, THE ATLANTIC WILL BE A RADIOACTIVE SEWER BY MORNING. FOR GOD'S SAKE... SEND SOMEONE... ANYONE.
I SAW TEN MORE IN THE ENGINE ROOM! CAN YOU FIND THEM?
I KNOW. A FEW SECONDS MORE. ONCE THE MEN ARE CLEAR, YOU CAN DO WHAT YOU MUST.
A FEW SECONDS IS ALL YOU GET, J'ONN... THERE'S ANOTHER ONE COMING...
THE BIG KAHUNA.

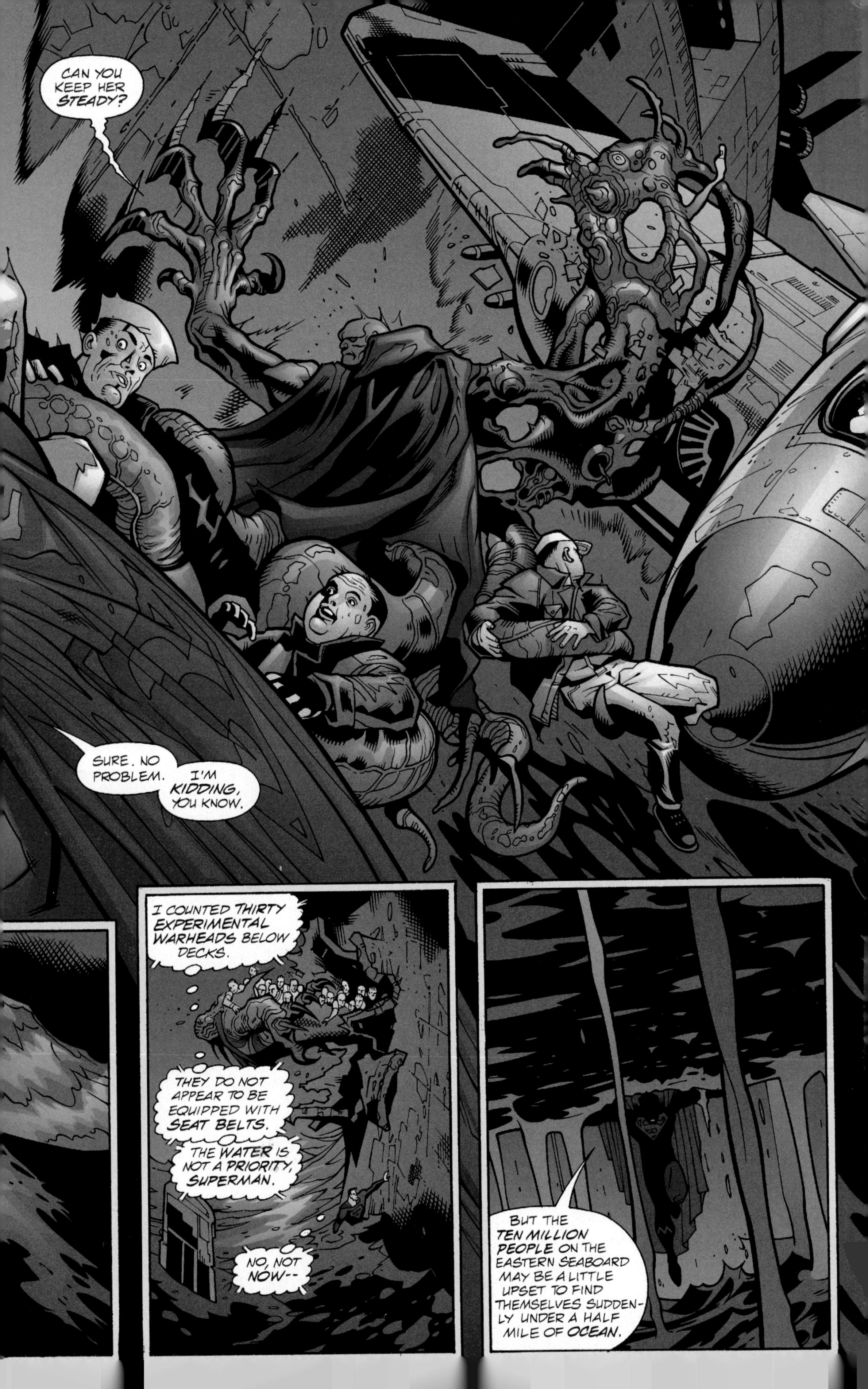
CAN YOU KEEP HER STEADY?
SURE. NO PROBLEM.
I'M KIDDING, YOU KNOW.
I COUNTED THIRTY EXPERIMENTAL WARHEADS BELOW DECKS.
THEY DO NOT APPEAR TO BE EQUIPPED WITH SEAT BELTS.
THE WATER IS NOT A PRIORITY, SUPERMAN.
NO, NOT NOW--
BUT THE TEN MILLION PEOPLE ON THE EASTERN SEABOARD MAY BE A LITTLE UPSET TO FIND THEMSELVES SUDDEN-LY UNDER A HALF MILE OF OCEAN.

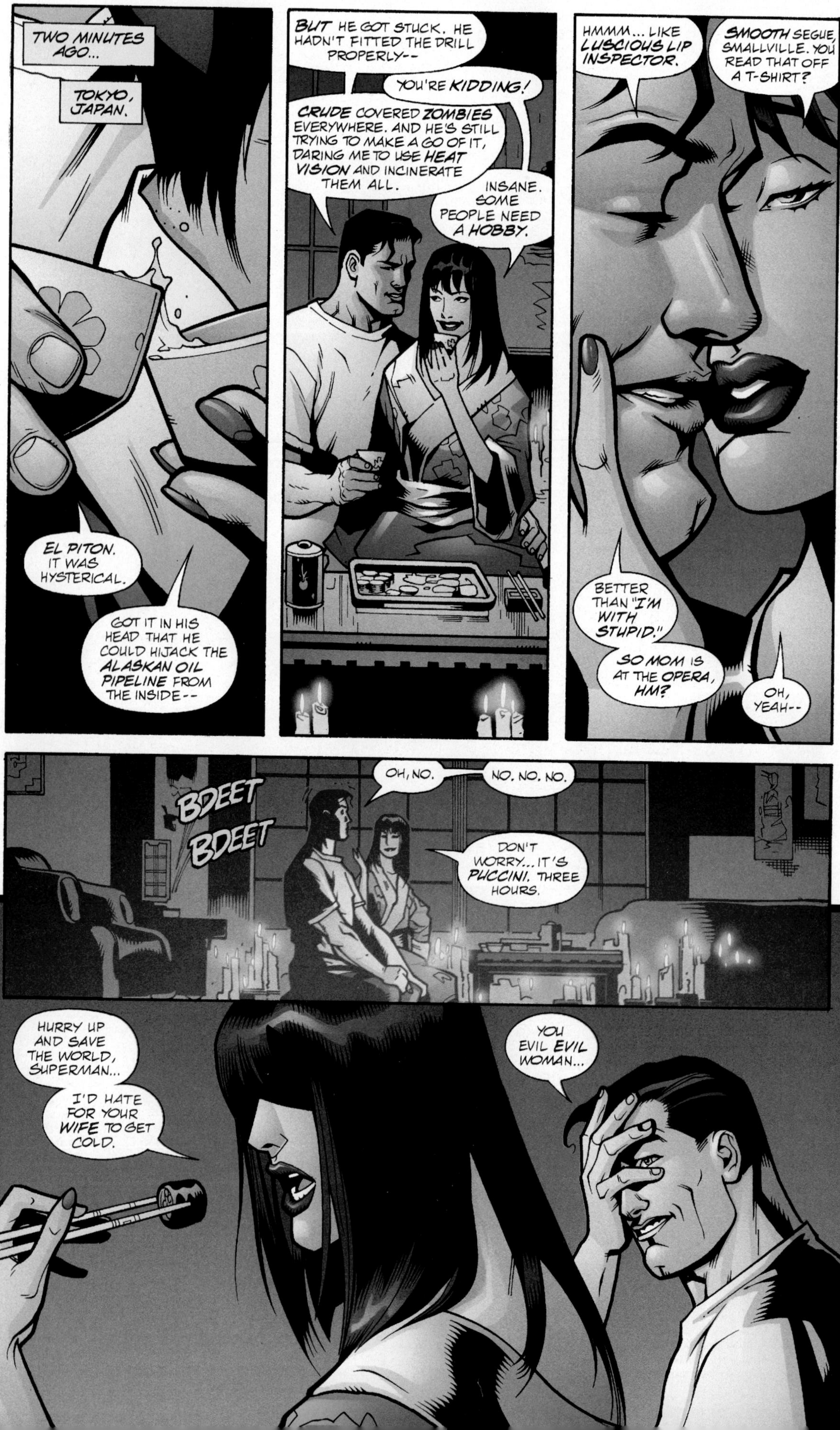

TWO MINUTES AGO...
TOKYO, JAPAN.
EL PITON. IT WAS HYSTERICAL.
GOT IT IN HIS HEAD THAT HE COULD HIJACK THE ALASKAN OIL PIPELINE FROM THE INSIDE--
BUT HE GOT STUCK. HE HADN'T FITTED THE DRILL PROPERLY--
YOU'RE KIDDING!
CRUDE COVERED ZOMBIES EVERYWHERE. AND HE'S STILL TRYING TO MAKE A GO OF IT, DARING ME TO USE HEAT VISION AND INCINERATE THEM ALL.
INSANE. SOME PEOPLE NEED A HOBBY.
HMMM... LIKE LUSCIOUS LIP INSPECTOR.
SMOOTH SEGUE, SMALLVILLE. YOU READ THAT OFF A T-SHIRT?
BETTER THAN "I'M WITH STUPID."
SO MOM IS AT THE OPERA, HM?
OH, YEAH--
BDEET
BDEET
OH, NO.
NO. NO. NO.
DON'T WORRY... IT'S PUCCINI. THREE HOURS.
HURRY UP AND SAVE THE WORLD, SUPERMAN...
I'D HATE FOR YOUR WIFE TO GET COLD.
YOU EVIL EVIL WOMAN...

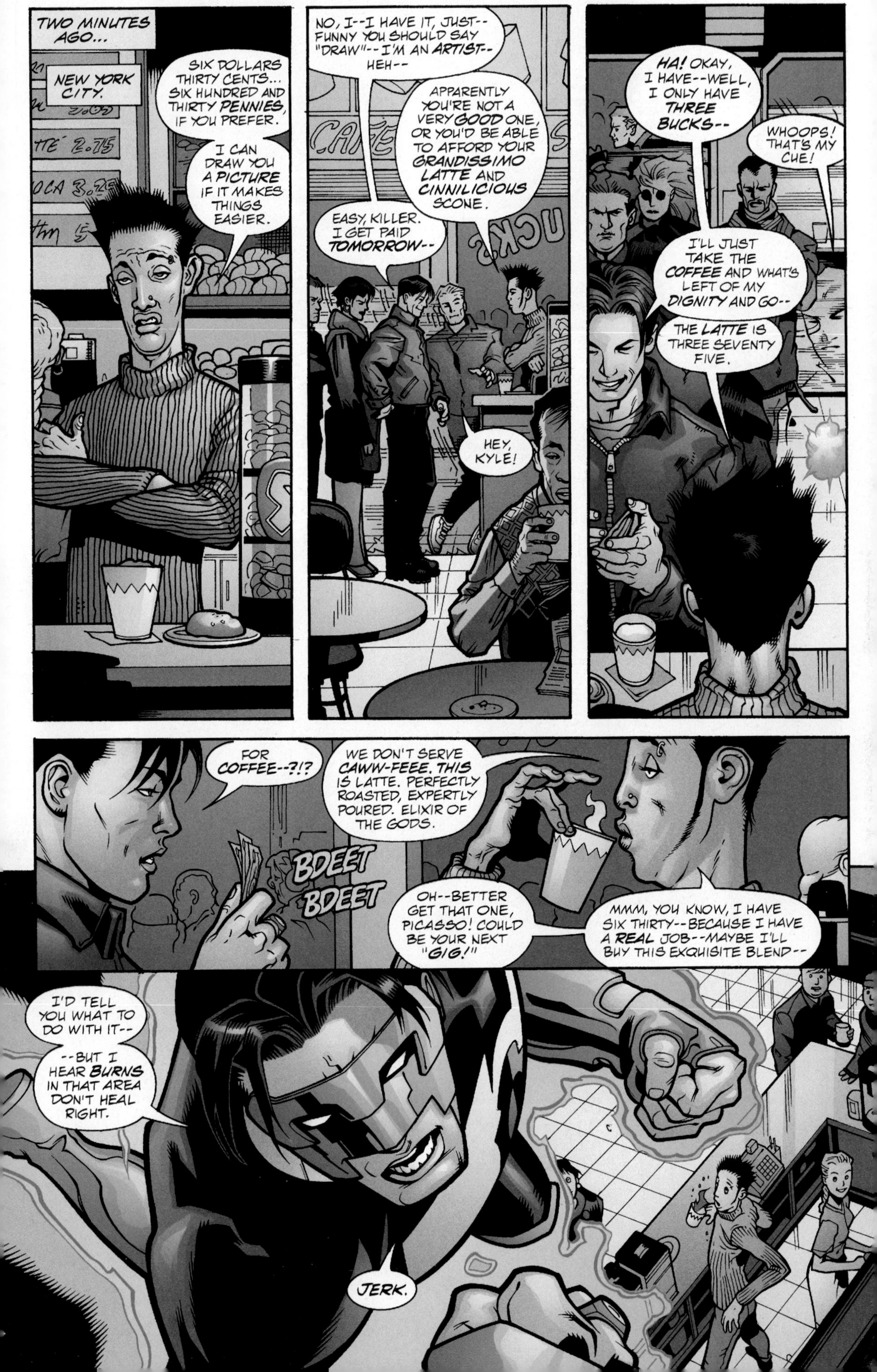
TWO MINUTES AGO...
NEW YORK CITY.
SIX DOLLARS THIRTY CENTS... SIX HUNDRED AND THIRTY PENNIES, IF YOU PREFER.
I CAN DRAW YOU A PICTURE IF IT MAKES THINGS EASIER.
NO, I--I HAVE IT, JUST-- FUNNY YOU SHOULD SAY "DRAW"--I'M AN ARTIST-- HEH--
APPARENTLY YOU'RE NOT A VERY GOOD ONE, OR YOU'D BE ABLE TO AFFORD YOUR GRANDISSIMO LATTE AND CINNILICIOUS SCONE.
EASY, KILLER. I GET PAID TOMORROW--
HEY, KYLE!
HA! OKAY, I HAVE--WELL, I ONLY HAVE THREE BUCKS--
WHOOPS! THAT'S MY CUE!
I'LL JUST TAKE THE COFFEE AND WHAT'S LEFT OF MY DIGNITY AND GO--
THE LATTE IS THREE SEVENTY FIVE.
FOR COFFEE--?!?
WE DON'T SERVE CAWW-FEEE. THIS IS LATTE. PERFECTLY ROASTED, EXPERTLY POURED. ELIXIR OF THE GODS.
BDEET BDEET
OH--BETTER GET THAT ONE, PICASSO! COULD BE YOUR NEXT "GIG!"
MMM, YOU KNOW, I HAVE SIX THIRTY--BECAUSE I HAVE A REAL JOB--MAYBE I'LL BUY THIS EXQUISITE BLEND--
I'D TELL YOU WHAT TO DO WITH IT--
--BUT I HEAR BURNS IN THAT AREA DON'T HEAL RIGHT.
JERK.

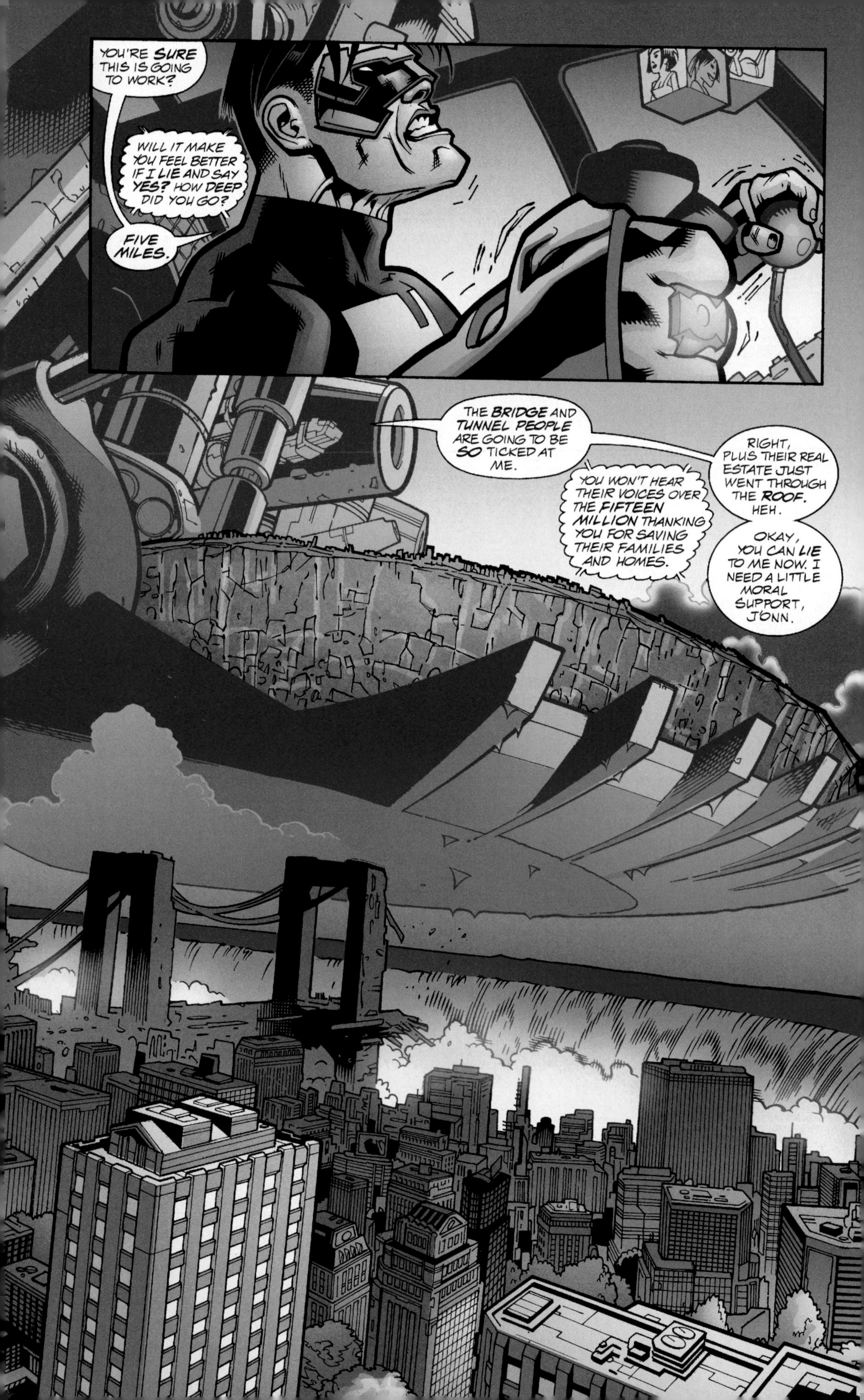

YOU'RE SURE THIS IS GOING TO WORK?
WILL IT MAKE YOU FEEL BETTER IF I LIE AND SAY YES? HOW DEEP DID YOU GO?
FIVE MILES.
THE BRIDGE AND TUNNEL PEOPLE ARE GOING TO BE SO TICKED AT ME.
RIGHT, PLUS THEIR REAL ESTATE JUST WENT THROUGH THE ROOF. HEH.
YOU WON'T HEAR THEIR VOICES OVER THE FIFTEEN MILLION THANKING YOU FOR SAVING THEIR FAMILIES AND HOMES.
OKAY, YOU CAN LIE TO ME NOW. I NEED A LITTLE MORAL SUPPORT, J'ONN.

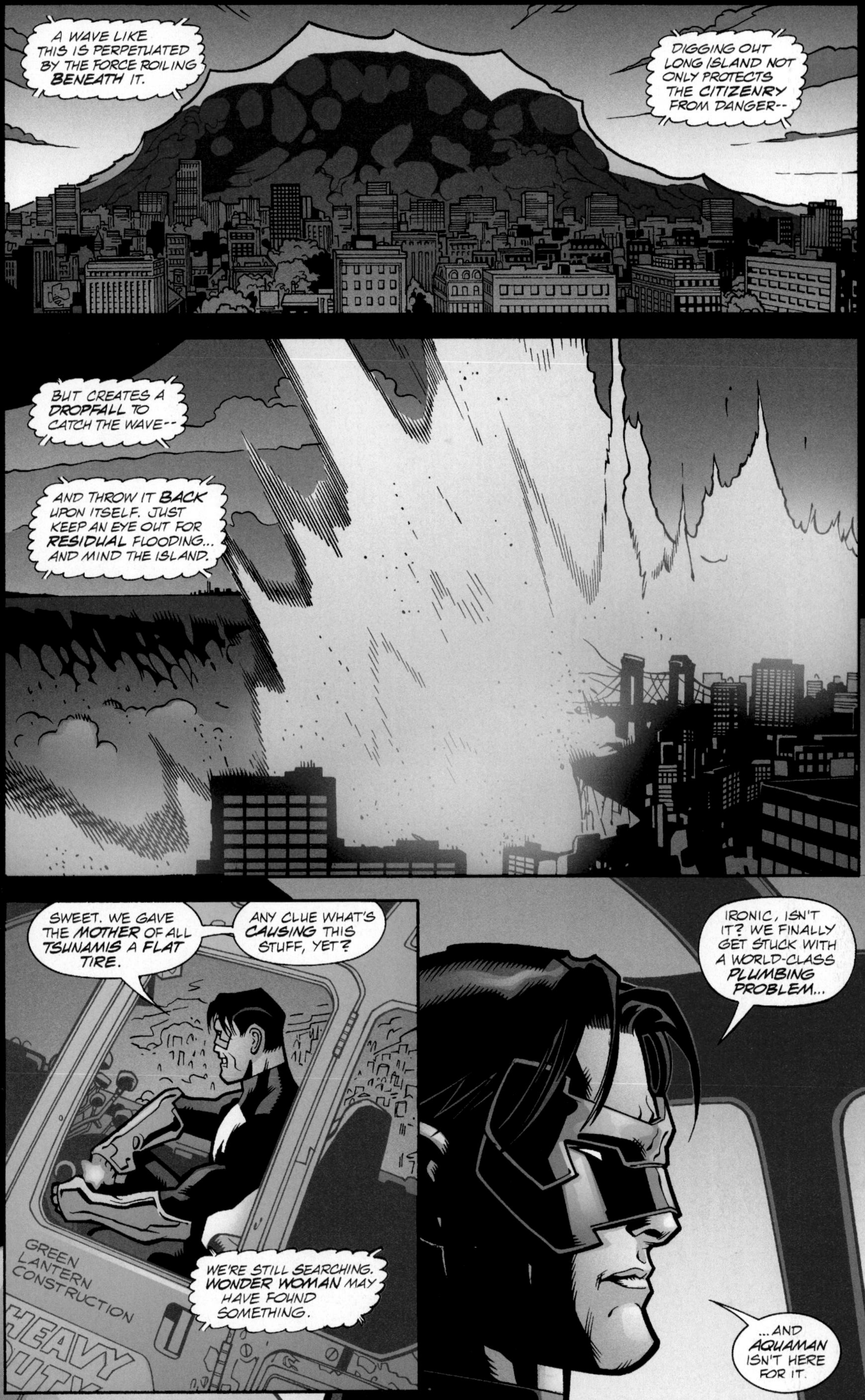
A WAVE LIKE THIS IS PERPETUATED BY THE FORCE ROILING BENEATH IT.
DIGGING OUT LONG ISLAND NOT ONLY PROTECTS THE CITIZENRY FROM DANGER--
BUT CREATES A DROPFALL TO CATCH THE WAVE--
AND THROW IT BACK UPON ITSELF. JUST KEEP AN EYE OUT FOR RESIDUAL FLOODING... AND MIND THE ISLAND.
SWEET. WE GAVE THE MOTHER OF ALL TSUNAMIS A FLAT TIRE.
ANY CLUE WHAT'S CAUSING THIS STUFF, YET?
GREEN LANTERN CONSTRUCTION
HEAVY DUTY
WE'RE STILL SEARCHING. WONDER WOMAN MAY HAVE FOUND SOMETHING.
IRONIC, ISN'T IT? WE FINALLY GET STUCK WITH A WORLD-CLASS PLUMBING PROBLEM...
...AND AQUAMAN ISN'T HERE FOR IT.

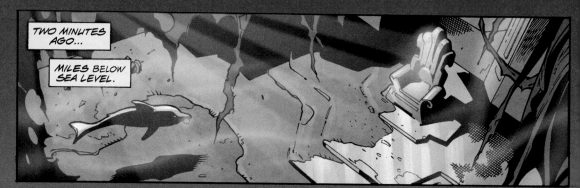

TWO MINUTES
AGO...

MILES BELOW
SEA LEVEL.

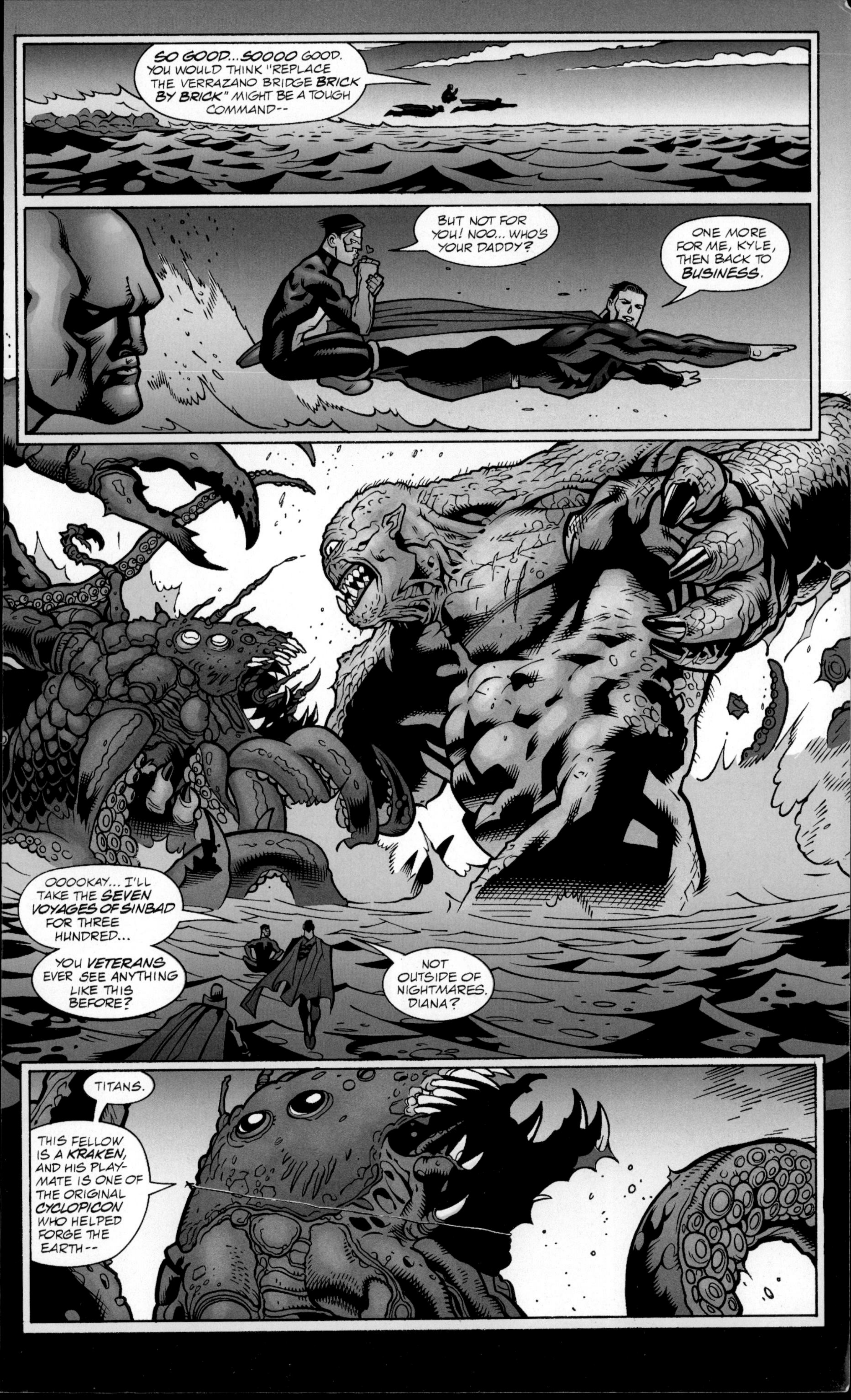
SO GOOD...SOOOO GOOD. YOU WOULD THINK "REPLACE THE VERRAZANO BRIDGE BRICK BY BRICK" MIGHT BE A TOUGH COMMAND--
BUT NOT FOR YOU! NOO... WHO'S YOUR DADDY?
ONE MORE FOR ME, KYLE, THEN BACK TO BUSINESS.
OOOOKAY... I'LL TAKE THE SEVEN VOYAGES OF SINBAD FOR THREE HUNDRED...
YOU VETERANS EVER SEE ANYTHING LIKE THIS BEFORE?
NOT OUTSIDE OF NIGHTMARES. DIANA?
TITANS.
THIS FELLOW IS A KRAKEN, AND HIS PLAY-MATE IS ONE OF THE ORIGINAL CYCLOPICON WHO HELPED FORGE THE EARTH--

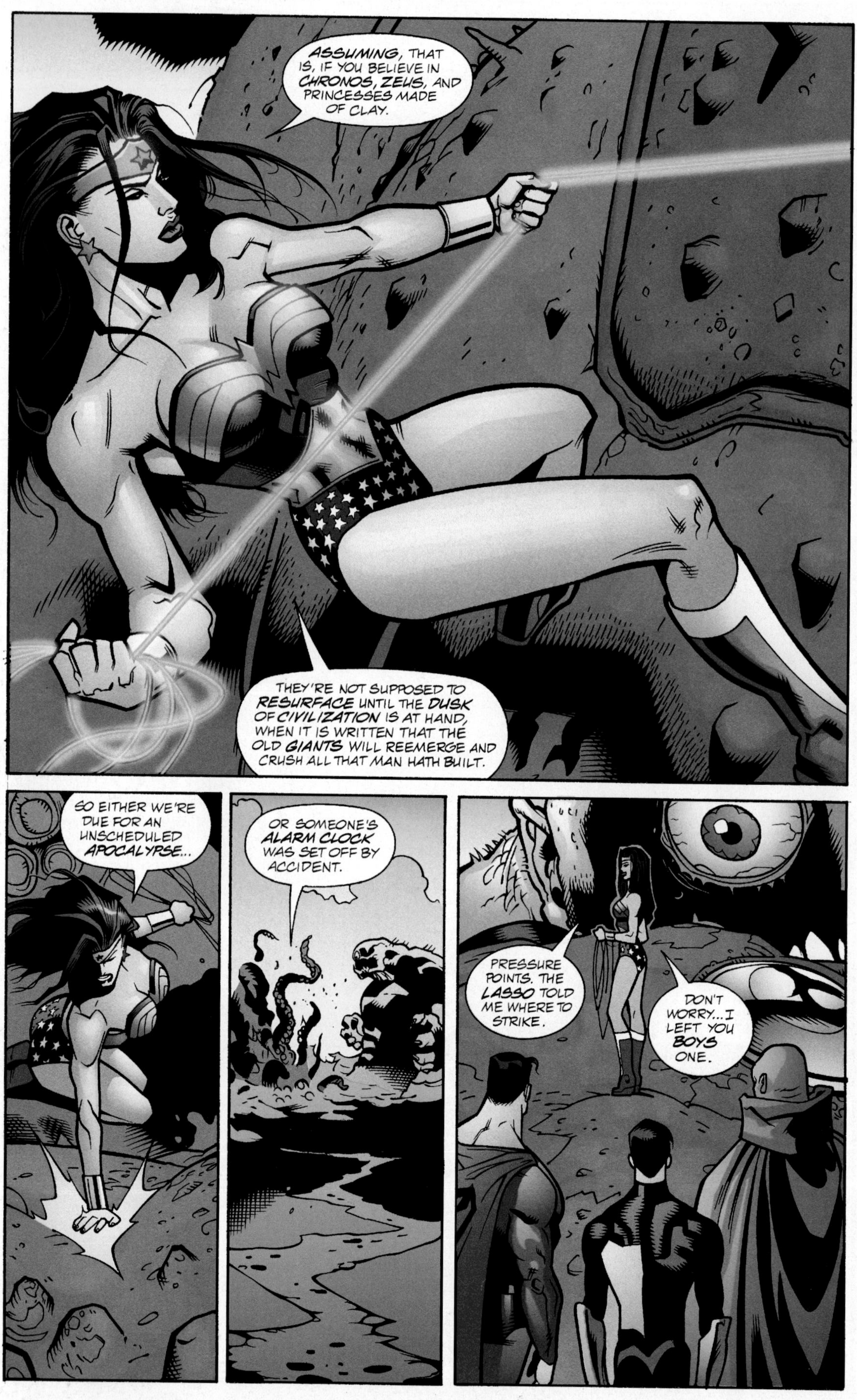
ASSUMING, THAT IS, IF YOU BELIEVE IN CHRONOS, ZEUS, AND PRINCESSES MADE OF CLAY.
THEY'RE NOT SUPPOSED TO RESURFACE UNTIL THE DUSK OF CIVILIZATION IS AT HAND, WHEN IT IS WRITTEN THAT THE OLD GIANTS WILL REEMERGE AND CRUSH ALL THAT MAN HATH BUILT.
SO EITHER WE'RE DUE FOR AN UNSCHEDULED APOCALYPSE...
OR SOMEONE'S ALARM CLOCK WAS SET OFF BY ACCIDENT.
PRESSURE POINTS. THE LASSO TOLD ME WHERE TO STRIKE.
DON'T WORRY... I LEFT YOU BOYS ONE.

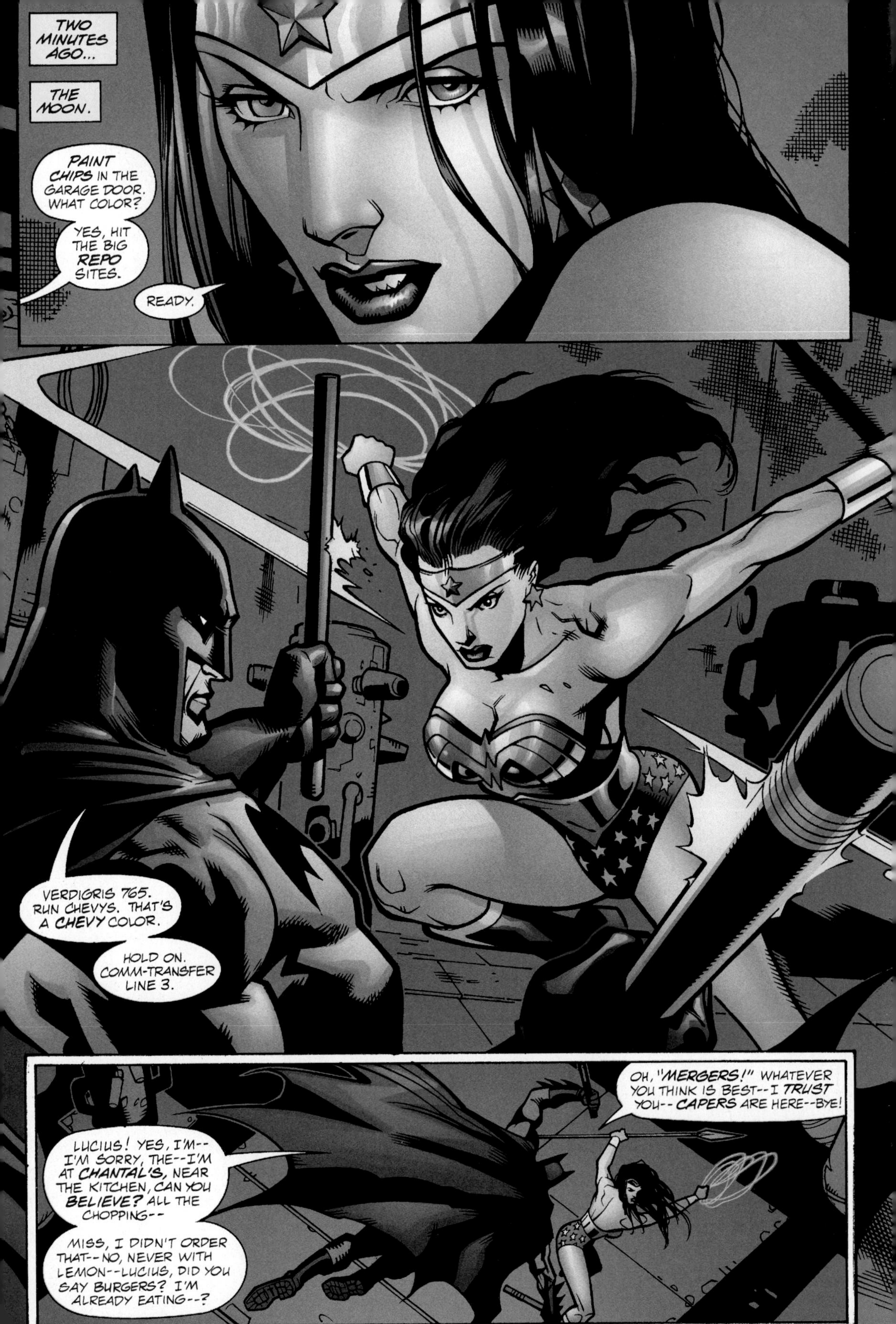
TWO MINUTES AGO...
THE MOON.
PAINT CHIPS IN THE GARAGE DOOR. WHAT COLOR?
YES, HIT THE BIG REPO SITES.
READY.
VERDIGRIS 765. RUN CHEVYS. THAT'S A CHEVY COLOR.
HOLD ON. COMM-TRANSFER LINE 3.
OH, "MERGERS!" WHATEVER YOU THINK IS BEST--I TRUST YOU--CAPERS ARE HERE--BYE!
LUCIUS! YES, I'M--I'M SORRY, THE--I'M AT CHANTAL'S, NEAR THE KITCHEN, CAN YOU BELIEVE? ALL THE CHOPPING--
MISS, I DIDN'T ORDER THAT--NO, NEVER WITH LEMON--LUCIUS, DID YOU SAY BURGERS? I'M ALREADY EATING--?

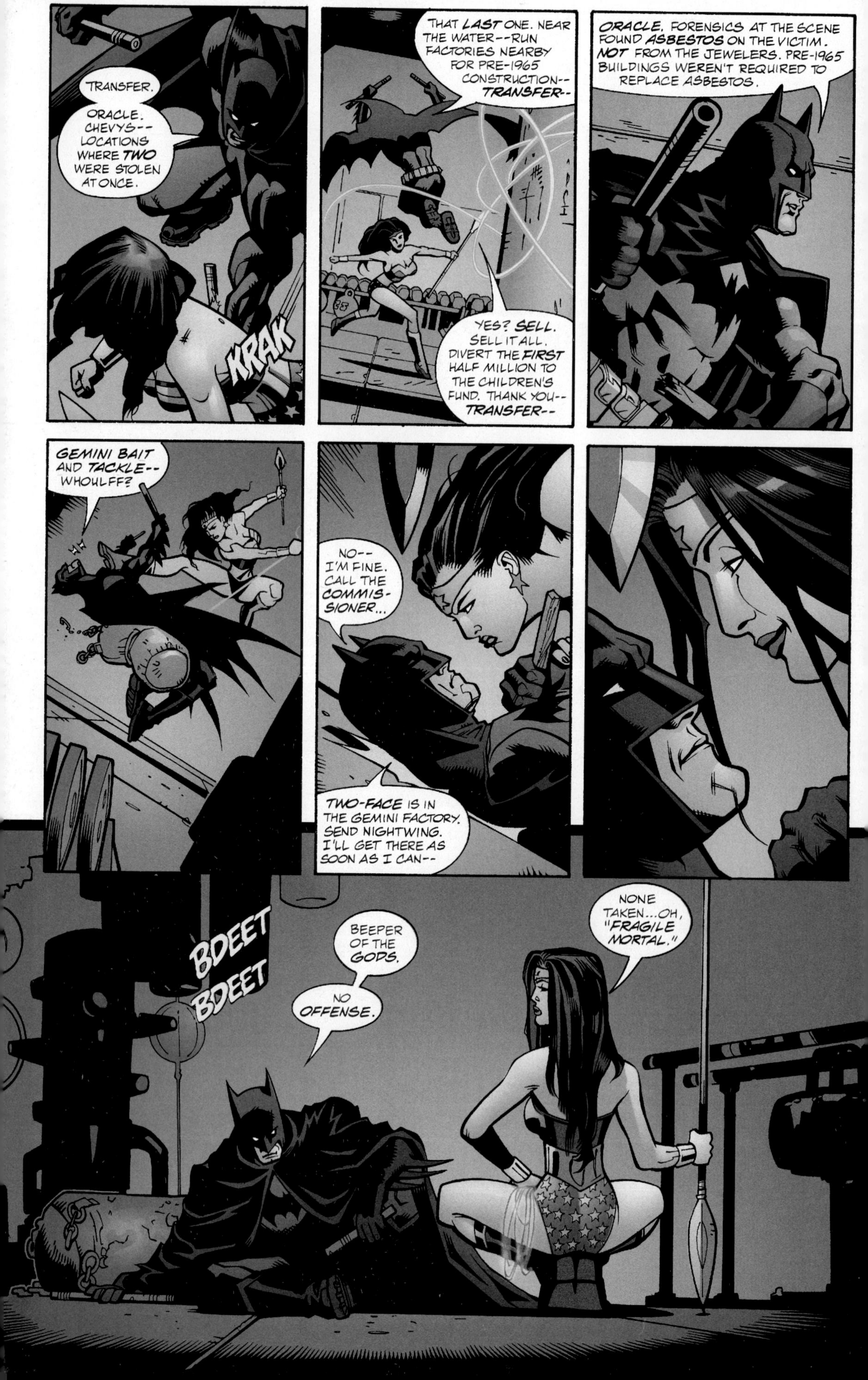
TRANSFER.
ORACLE. CHEVYS-- LOCATIONS WHERE TWO WERE STOLEN AT ONCE.
KRAK
THAT LAST ONE. NEAR THE WATER--RUN FACTORIES NEARBY FOR PRE-1965 CONSTRUCTION-- TRANSFER--
YES? SELL. SELL IT ALL. DIVERT THE FIRST HALF MILLION TO THE CHILDREN'S FUND. THANK YOU-- TRANSFER--
ORACLE. FORENSICS AT THE SCENE FOUND ASBESTOS ON THE VICTIM. NOT FROM THE JEWELERS. PRE-1965 BUILDINGS WEREN'T REQUIRED TO REPLACE ASBESTOS.
GEMINI BAIT AND TACKLE-- WHOULFF?
NO-- I'M FINE. CALL THE COMMISSIONER...
TWO-FACE IS IN THE GEMINI FACTORY. SEND NIGHTWING. I'LL GET THERE AS SOON AS I CAN--
BDEET
BDEET
BEEPER OF THE GODS.
NO OFFENSE.
NONE TAKEN...OH, "FRAGILE MORTAL."

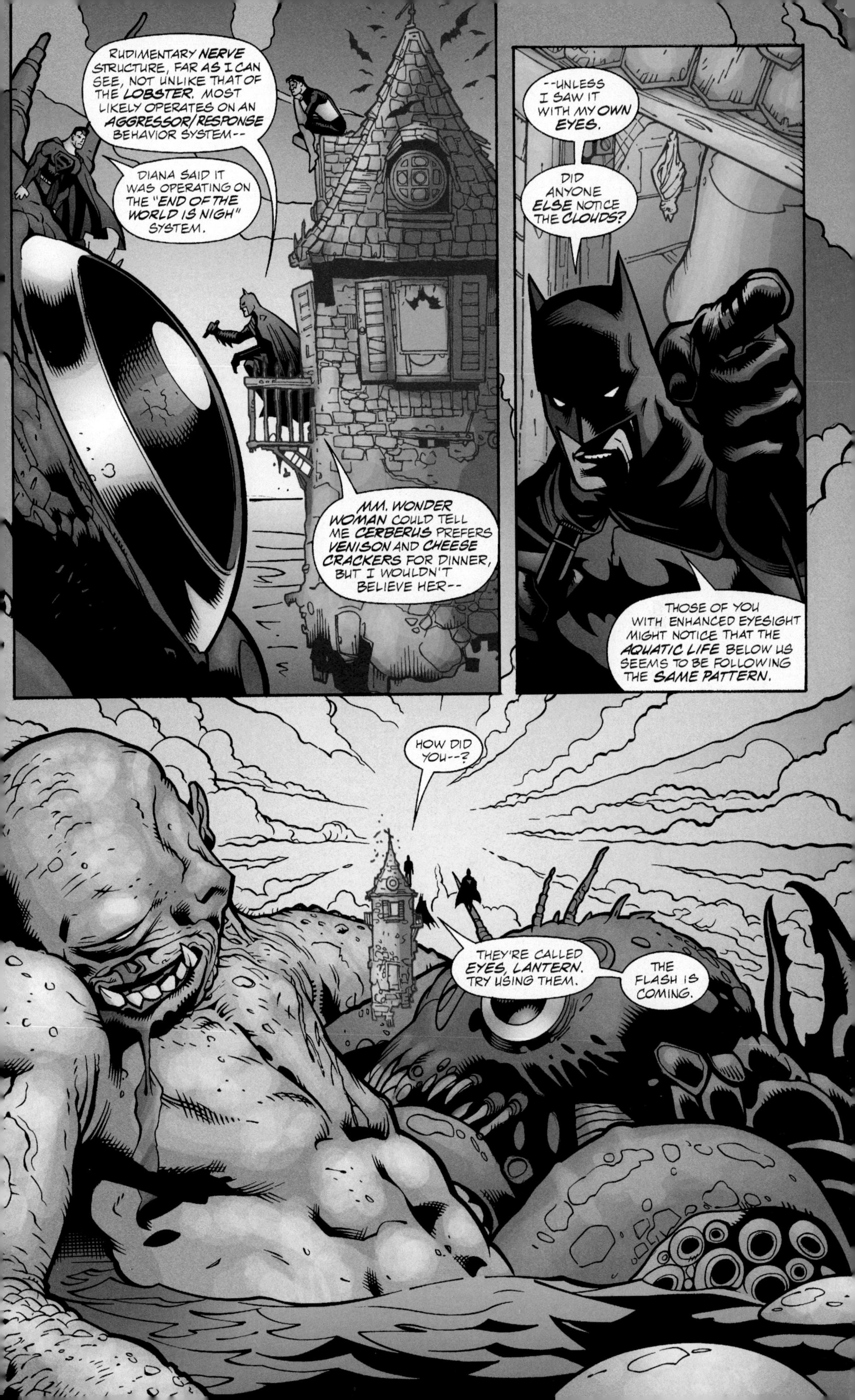
RUDIMENTARY NERVE STRUCTURE, FAR AS I CAN SEE, NOT UNLIKE THAT OF THE LOBSTER. MOST LIKELY OPERATES ON AN AGGRESSOR/RESPONSE BEHAVIOR SYSTEM--
DIANA SAID IT WAS OPERATING ON THE "END OF THE WORLD IS NIGH" SYSTEM.
MM. WONDER WOMAN COULD TELL ME CERBERUS PREFERS VENISON AND CHEESE CRACKERS FOR DINNER, BUT I WOULDN'T BELIEVE HER--
--UNLESS I SAW IT WITH MY OWN EYES.
DID ANYONE ELSE NOTICE THE CLOUDS?
THOSE OF YOU WITH ENHANCED EYESIGHT MIGHT NOTICE THAT THE AQUATIC LIFE BELOW US SEEMS TO BE FOLLOWING THE SAME PATTERN.
HOW DID YOU--?
THEY'RE CALLED EYES, LANTERN. TRY USING THEM.
THE FLASH IS COMING.

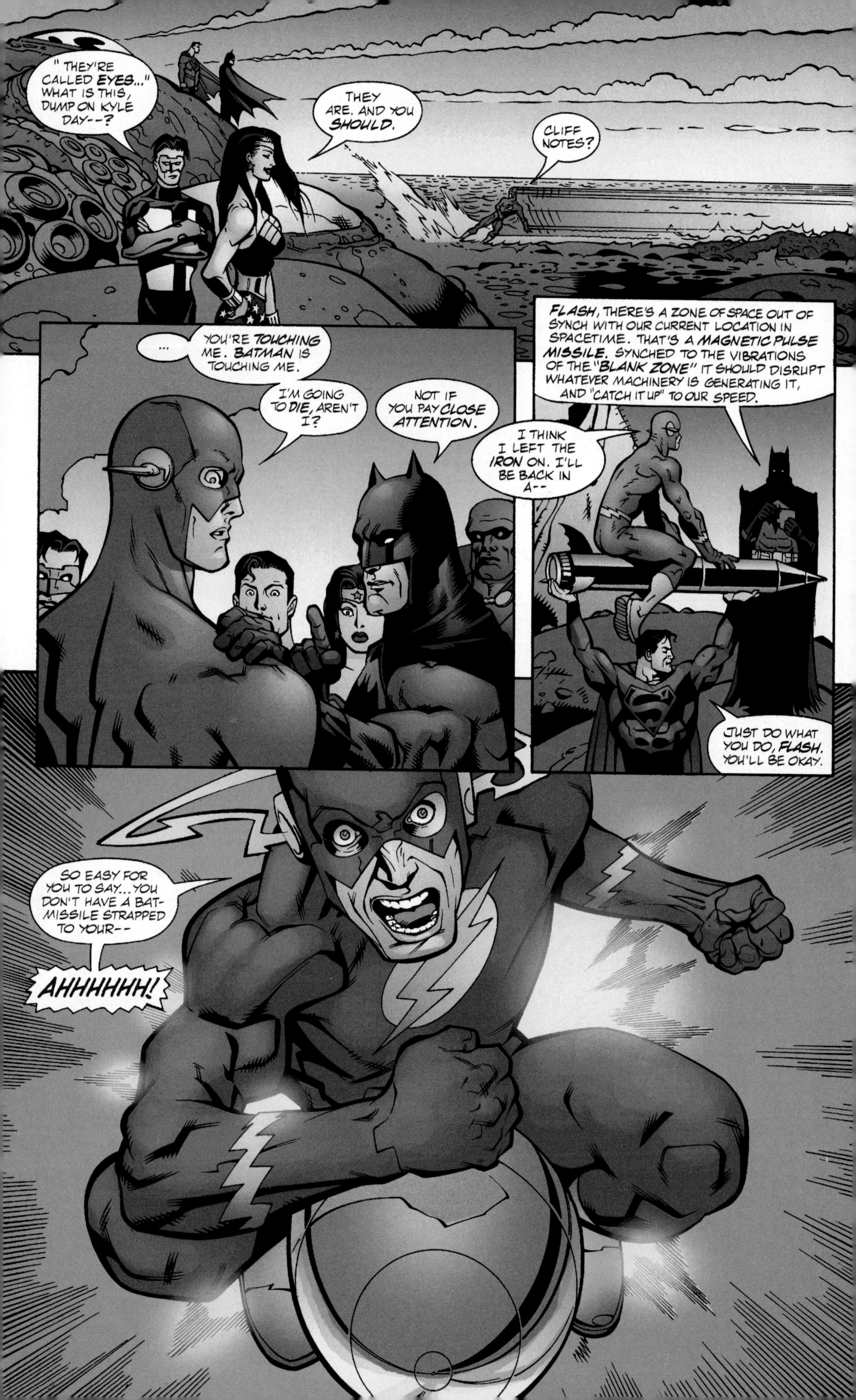

"THEY'RE CALLED EYES..." WHAT IS THIS, DUMP ON KYLE DAY--?
THEY ARE. AND YOU SHOULD.
CLIFF NOTES?
...
YOU'RE TOUCHING ME. BATMAN IS TOUCHING ME.
I'M GOING TO DIE, AREN'T I?
NOT IF YOU PAY CLOSE ATTENTION.
FLASH, THERE'S A ZONE OF SPACE OUT OF SYNCH WITH OUR CURRENT LOCATION IN SPACETIME. THAT'S A MAGNETIC PULSE MISSILE. SYNCHED TO THE VIBRATIONS OF THE "BLANK ZONE" IT SHOULD DISRUPT WHATEVER MACHINERY IS GENERATING IT, AND "CATCH IT UP" TO OUR SPEED.
I THINK I LEFT THE IRON ON. I'LL BE BACK IN A--
JUST DO WHAT YOU DO, FLASH. YOU'LL BE OKAY.
SO EASY FOR YOU TO SAY... YOU DON'T HAVE A BAT-MISSILE STRAPPED TO YOUR--
AHHHHHH!

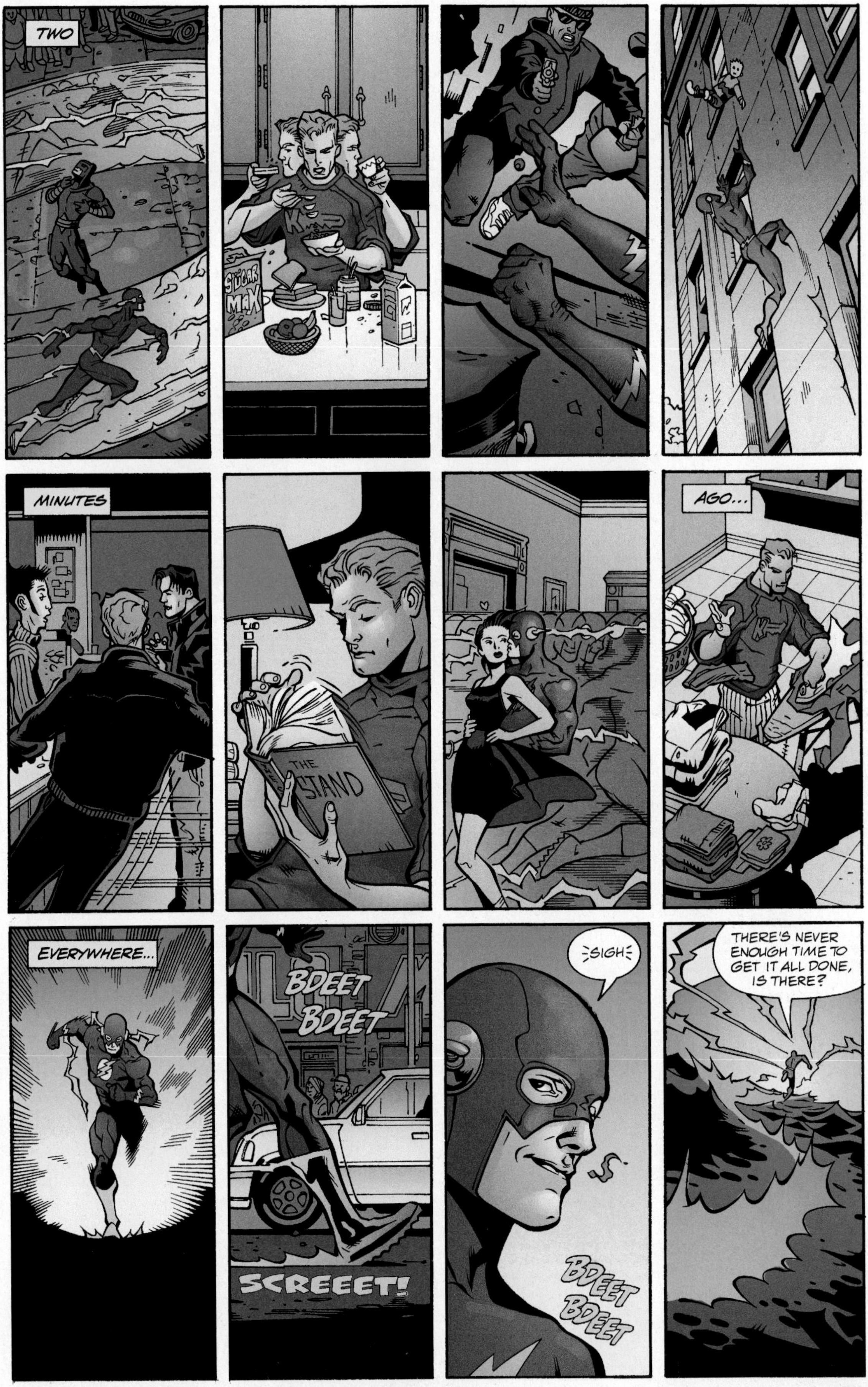
TWO
SUGAR MAX
MINUTES
THE STAND
AGO...
EVERYWHERE...
BDEET BDEET
SCREEET!
SIGH
BDEET BDEET
THERE'S NEVER ENOUGH TIME TO GET IT ALL DONE, IS THERE?

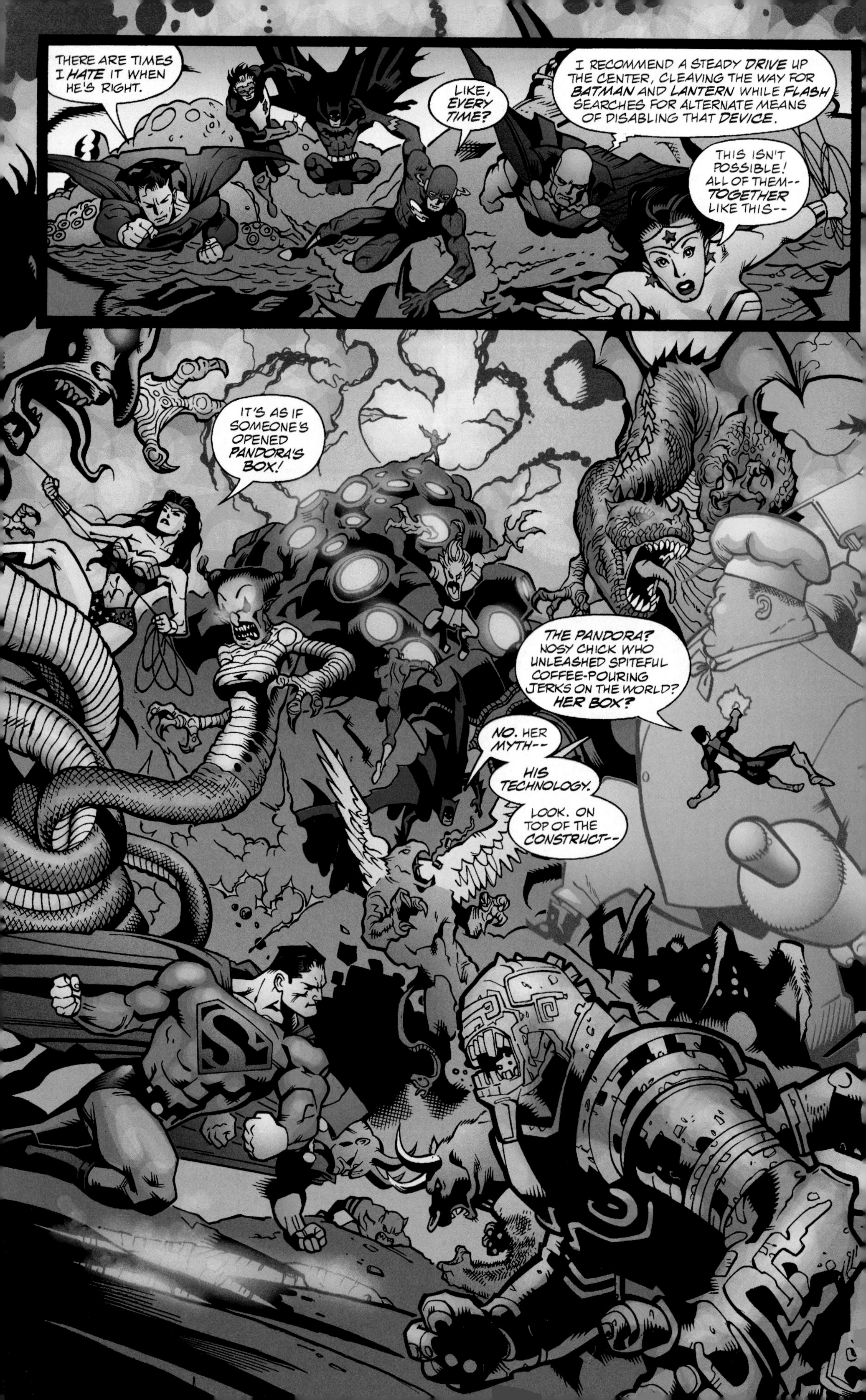

THERE ARE TIMES I HATE IT WHEN HE'S RIGHT.
LIKE, EVERY TIME?
I RECOMMEND A STEADY DRIVE UP THE CENTER, CLEAVING THE WAY FOR BATMAN AND LANTERN WHILE FLASH SEARCHES FOR ALTERNATE MEANS OF DISABLING THAT DEVICE.
THIS ISN'T POSSIBLE! ALL OF THEM-- TOGETHER LIKE THIS--
IT'S AS IF SOMEONE'S OPENED PANDORA'S BOX!
THE PANDORA? NOSY CHICK WHO UNLEASHED SPITEFUL COFFEE-POURING JERKS ON THE WORLD? HER BOX?
NO. HER MYTH--
HIS TECHNOLOGY.
LOOK. ON TOP OF THE CONSTRUCT--

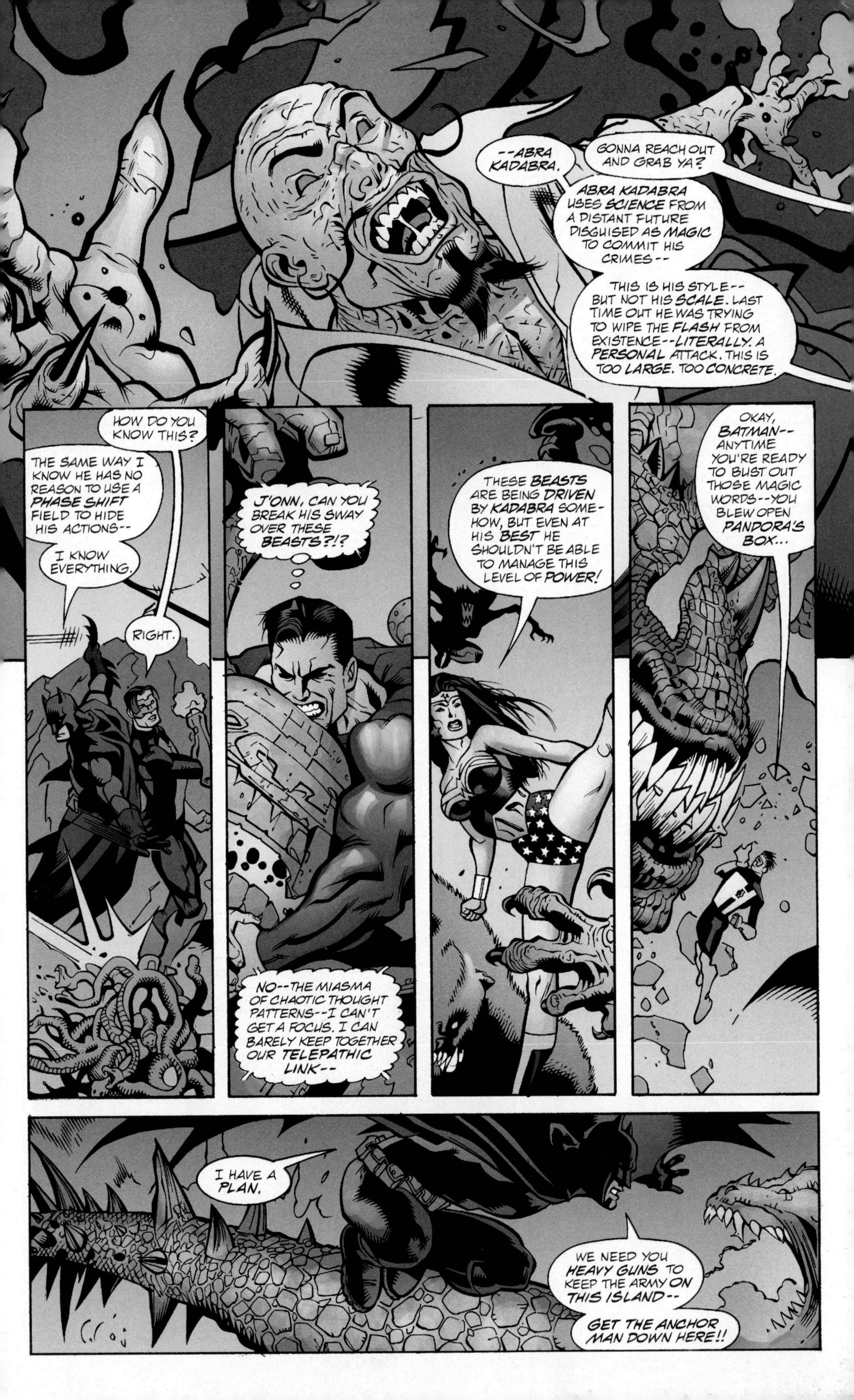
--ABRA KADABRA.
GONNA REACH OUT AND GRAB YA?
ABRA KADABRA USES SCIENCE FROM A DISTANT FUTURE DISGUISED AS MAGIC TO COMMIT HIS CRIMES--
THIS IS HIS STYLE--BUT NOT HIS SCALE. LAST TIME OUT HE WAS TRYING TO WIPE THE FLASH FROM EXISTENCE--LITERALLY. A PERSONAL ATTACK. THIS IS TOO LARGE. TOO CONCRETE.
HOW DO YOU KNOW THIS?
THE SAME WAY I KNOW HE HAS NO REASON TO USE A PHASE SHIFT FIELD TO HIDE HIS ACTIONS--
I KNOW EVERYTHING.
RIGHT.
J'ONN, CAN YOU BREAK HIS SWAY OVER THESE BEASTS?!?
NO--THE MIASMA OF CHAOTIC THOUGHT PATTERNS--I CAN'T GET A FOCUS. I CAN BARELY KEEP TOGETHER OUR TELEPATHIC LINK--
THESE BEASTS ARE BEING DRIVEN BY KADABRA SOMEHOW, BUT EVEN AT HIS BEST HE SHOULDN'T BE ABLE TO MANAGE THIS LEVEL OF POWER!
OKAY, BATMAN--ANYTIME YOU'RE READY TO BUST OUT THOSE MAGIC WORDS--YOU BLEW OPEN PANDORA'S BOX...
I HAVE A PLAN.
WE NEED YOU HEAVY GUNS TO KEEP THE ARMY ON THIS ISLAND--
GET THE ANCHOR MAN DOWN HERE!!

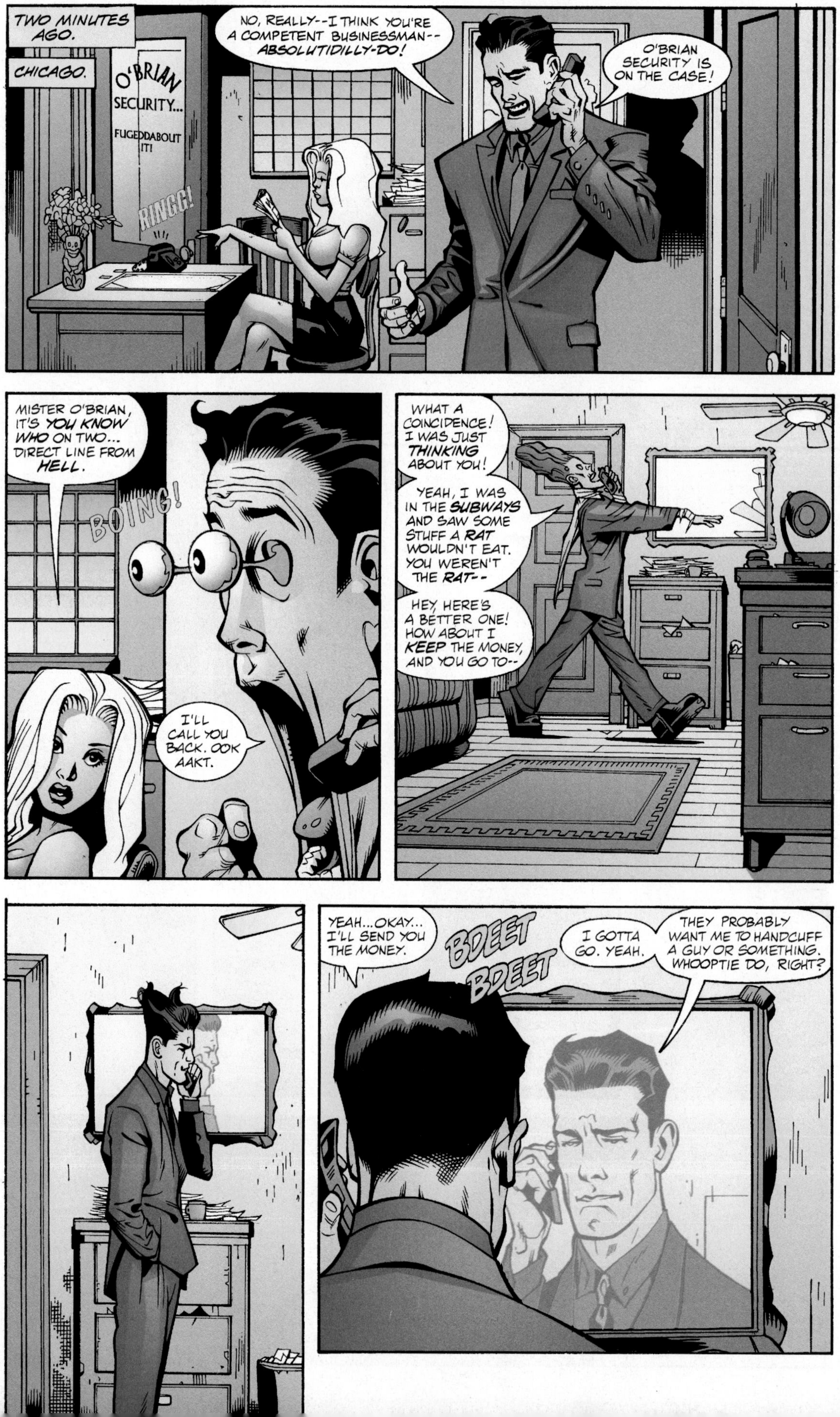
TWO MINUTES AGO.
CHICAGO.
O'BRIAN SECURITY... FUGEDDABOUT IT!
RINGG!
NO, REALLY--I THINK YOU'RE A COMPETENT BUSINESSMAN--ABSOLUTIDILLY-DO!
O'BRIAN SECURITY IS ON THE CASE!
MISTER O'BRIAN, IT'S YOU KNOW WHO ON TWO... DIRECT LINE FROM HELL.
BOING!
I'LL CALL YOU BACK. OOK AAKT.
WHAT A COINCIDENCE! I WAS JUST THINKING ABOUT YOU!
YEAH, I WAS IN THE SUBWAYS AND SAW SOME STUFF A RAT WOULDN'T EAT. YOU WEREN'T THE RAT--
HEY, HERE'S A BETTER ONE! HOW ABOUT I KEEP THE MONEY, AND YOU GO TO--
YEAH...OKAY... I'LL SEND YOU THE MONEY.
BDEET BDEET
I GOTTA GO. YEAH.
THEY PROBABLY WANT ME TO HANDCUFF A GUY OR SOMETHING. WHOOPTIE DO, RIGHT?

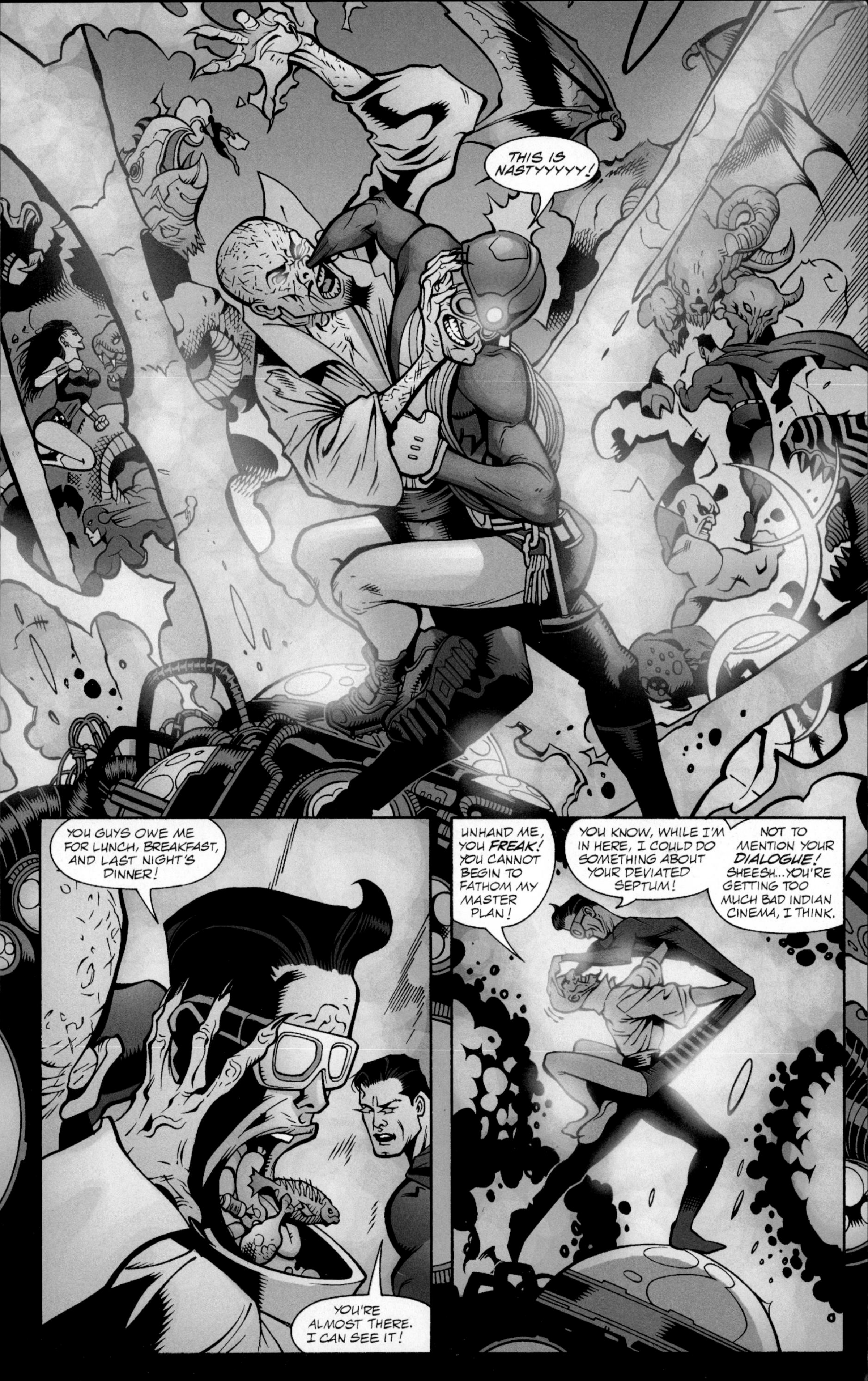

THIS IS NASTYYYYY!
YOU GUYS OWE ME FOR LUNCH, BREAKFAST, AND LAST NIGHT'S DINNER!
YOU'RE ALMOST THERE. I CAN SEE IT!
UNHAND ME, YOU FREAK! YOU CANNOT BEGIN TO FATHOM MY MASTER PLAN!
YOU KNOW, WHILE I'M IN HERE, I COULD DO SOMETHING ABOUT YOUR DEVIATED SEPTUM!
NOT TO MENTION YOUR DIALOGUE! SHEESH...YOU'RE GETTING TOO MUCH BAD INDIAN CINEMA, I THINK.

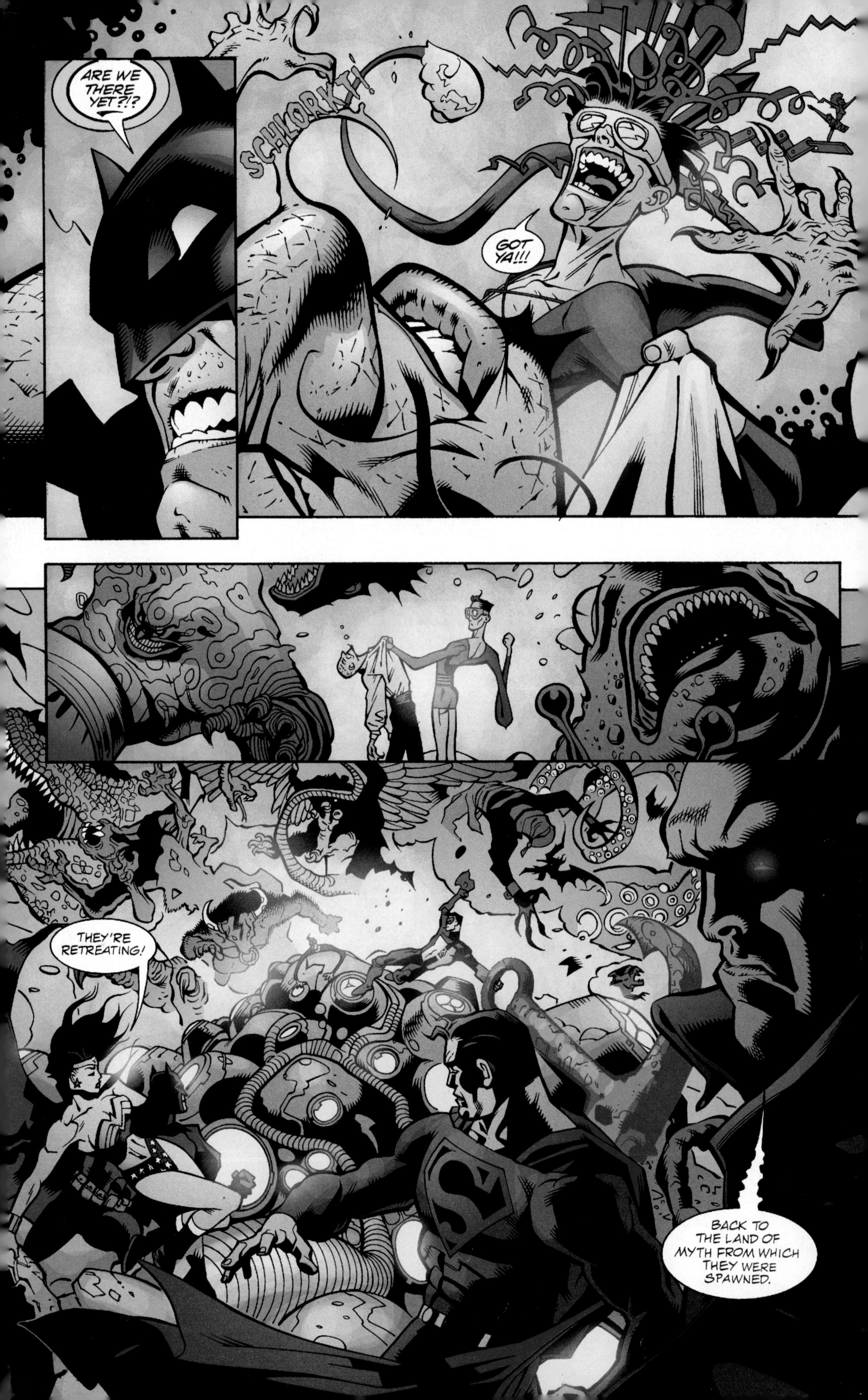
ARE WE THERE YET?!?
SCHLORKT!
GOT YA!!!
THEY'RE RETREATING!
BACK TO THE LAND OF MYTH FROM WHICH THEY WERE SPAWNED.

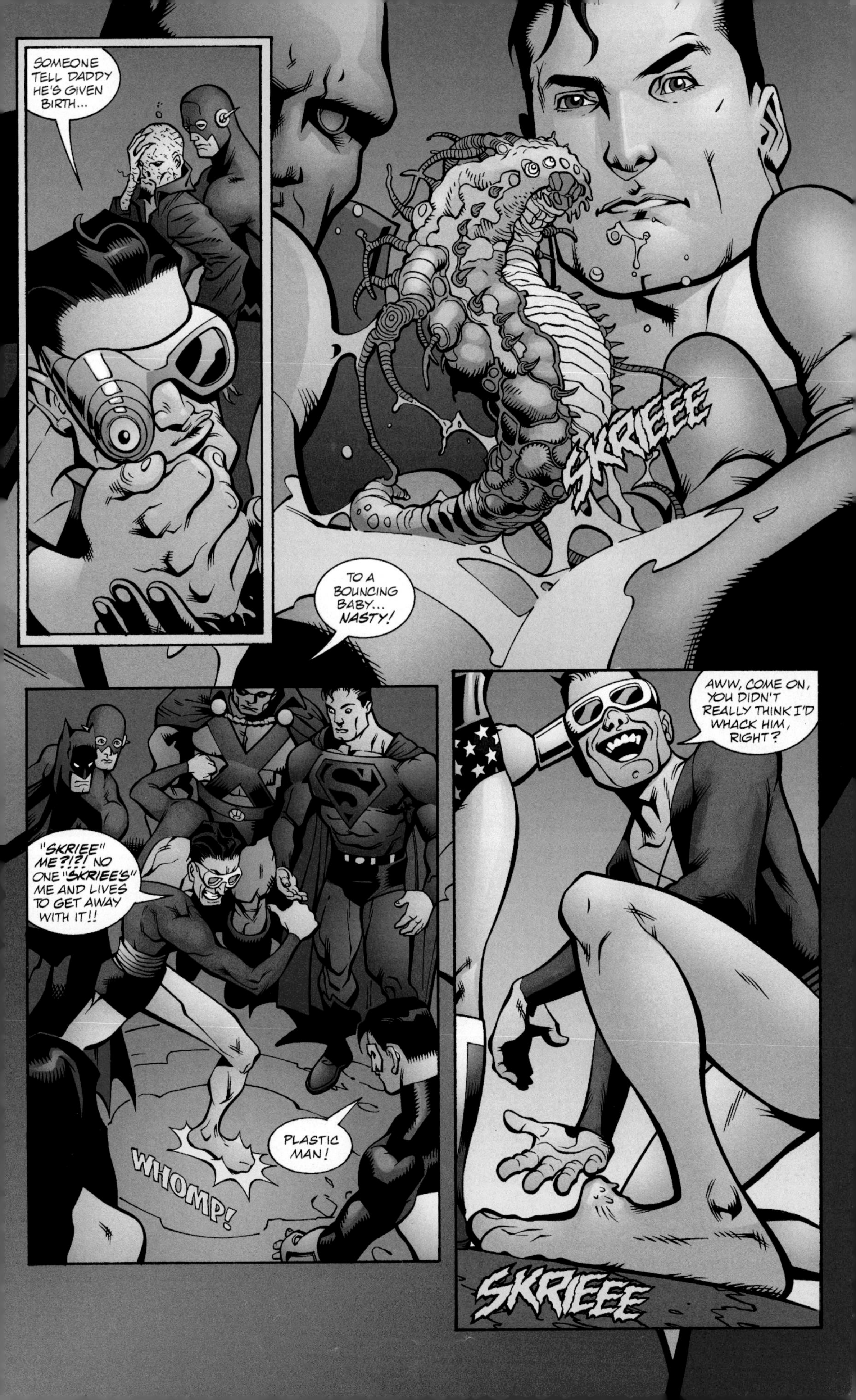
SOMEONE TELL DADDY HE'S GIVEN BIRTH...
TO A BOUNCING BABY... NASTY!
SKRIEEE
"SKRIEE" ME?!?! NO ONE "SKRIEE'S" ME AND LIVES TO GET AWAY WITH IT!!
PLASTIC MAN!
WHOMP!
AWW, COME ON, YOU DIDN'T REALLY THINK I'D WHACK HIM, RIGHT?
SKRIEEE

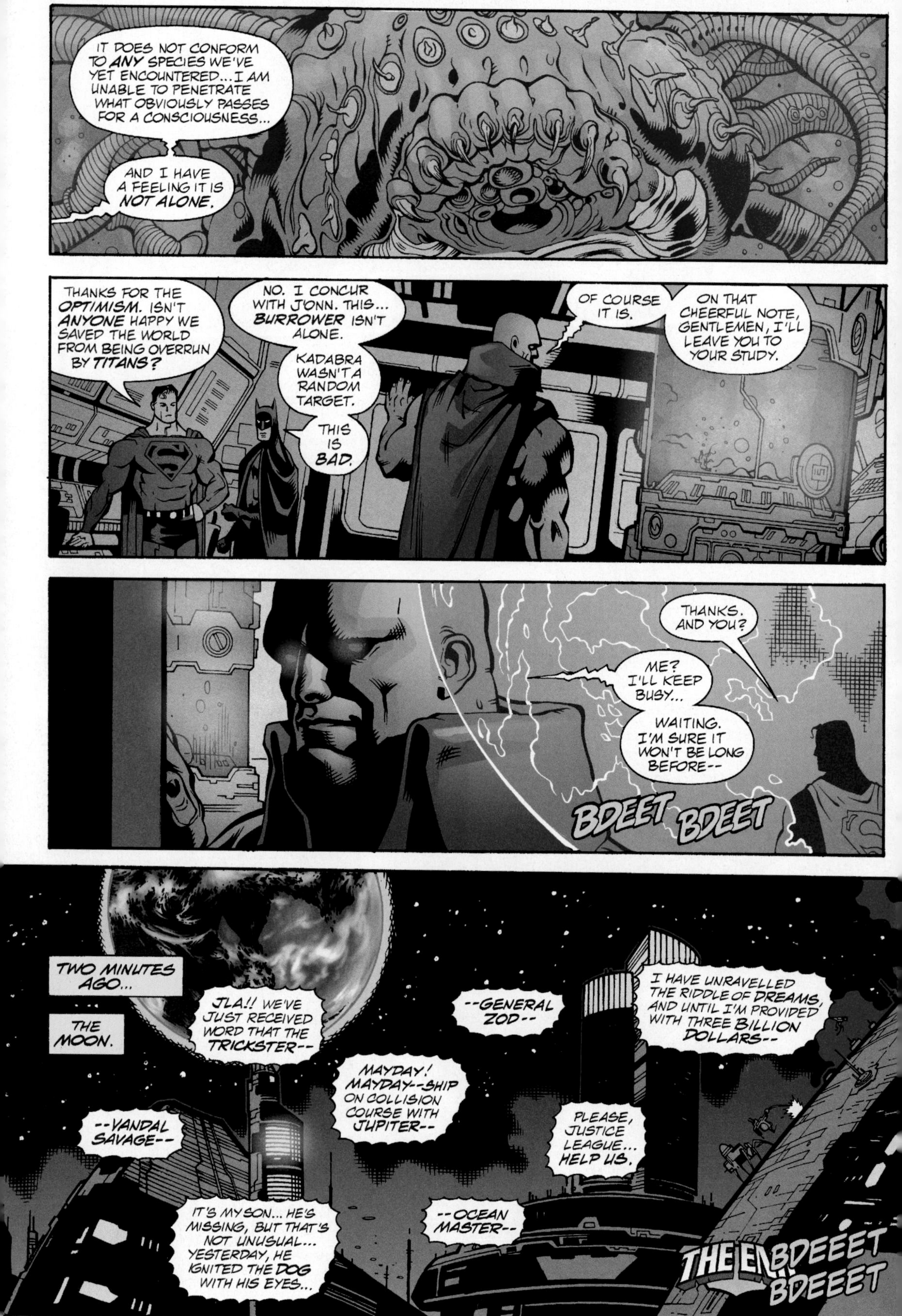
IT DOES NOT CONFORM TO ANY SPECIES WE'VE YET ENCOUNTERED... I AM UNABLE TO PENETRATE WHAT OBVIOUSLY PASSES FOR A CONSCIOUSNESS...
AND I HAVE A FEELING IT IS NOT ALONE.
THANKS FOR THE OPTIMISM. ISN'T ANYONE HAPPY WE SAVED THE WORLD FROM BEING OVERRUN BY TITANS?
NO. I CONCUR WITH J'ONN. THIS... BURROWER ISN'T ALONE.
KADABRA WASN'T A RANDOM TARGET.
THIS IS BAD.
OF COURSE IT IS.
ON THAT CHEERFUL NOTE, GENTLEMEN, I'LL LEAVE YOU TO YOUR STUDY.
THANKS. AND YOU?
ME? I'LL KEEP BUSY...
WAITING. I'M SURE IT WON'T BE LONG BEFORE--
BDEET BDEET
TWO MINUTES AGO...
THE MOON.
JLA!! WE'VE JUST RECEIVED WORD THAT THE TRICKSTER--
--GENERAL ZOD--
I HAVE UNRAVELLED THE RIDDLE OF DREAMS AND UNTIL I'M PROVIDED WITH THREE BILLION DOLLARS--
MAYDAY! MAYDAY--SHIP ON COLLISION COURSE WITH JUPITER--
--VANDAL SAVAGE--
PLEASE, JUSTICE LEAGUE... HELP US.
IT'S MY SON... HE'S MISSING, BUT THAT'S NOT UNUSUAL... YESTERDAY, HE IGNITED THE DOG WITH HIS EYES...
--OCEAN MASTER--
BDEEET BDEEET

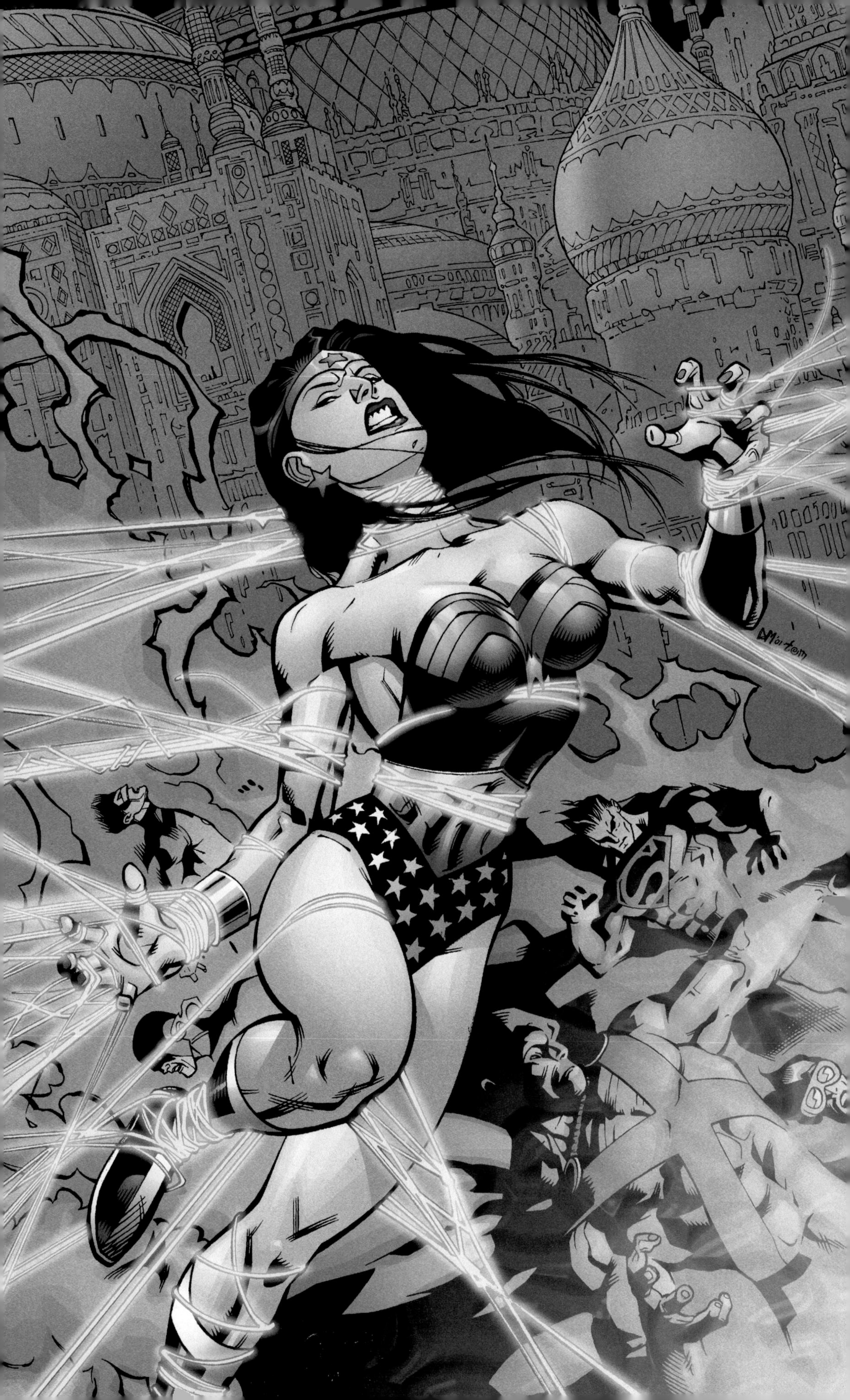

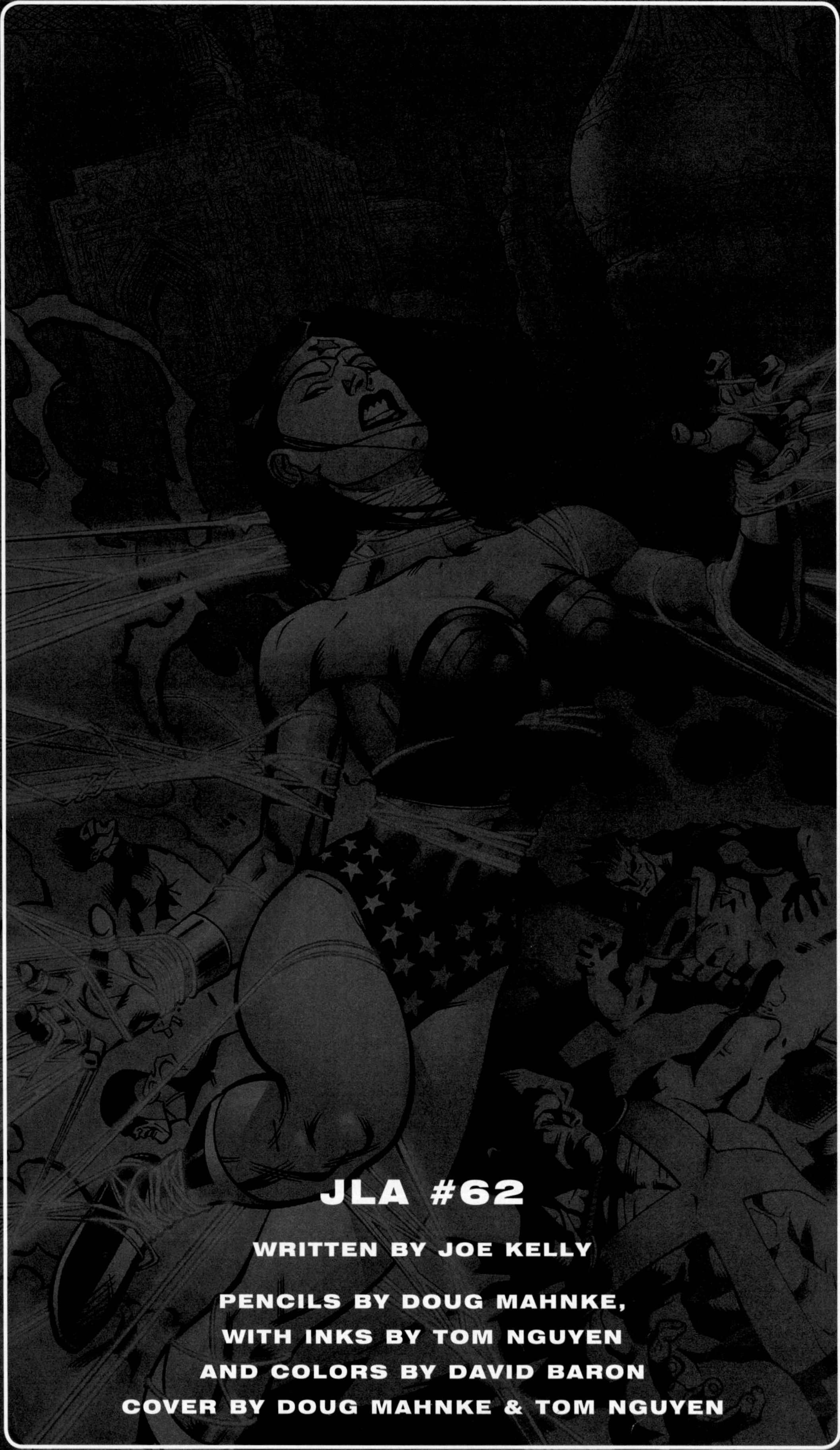

JLA #62

WRITTEN BY JOE KELLY

PENCILS BY DOUG MAHNKE,
WITH INKS BY TOM NGUYEN
AND COLORS BY DAVID BARON
COVER BY DOUG MAHNKE & TOM NGUYEN

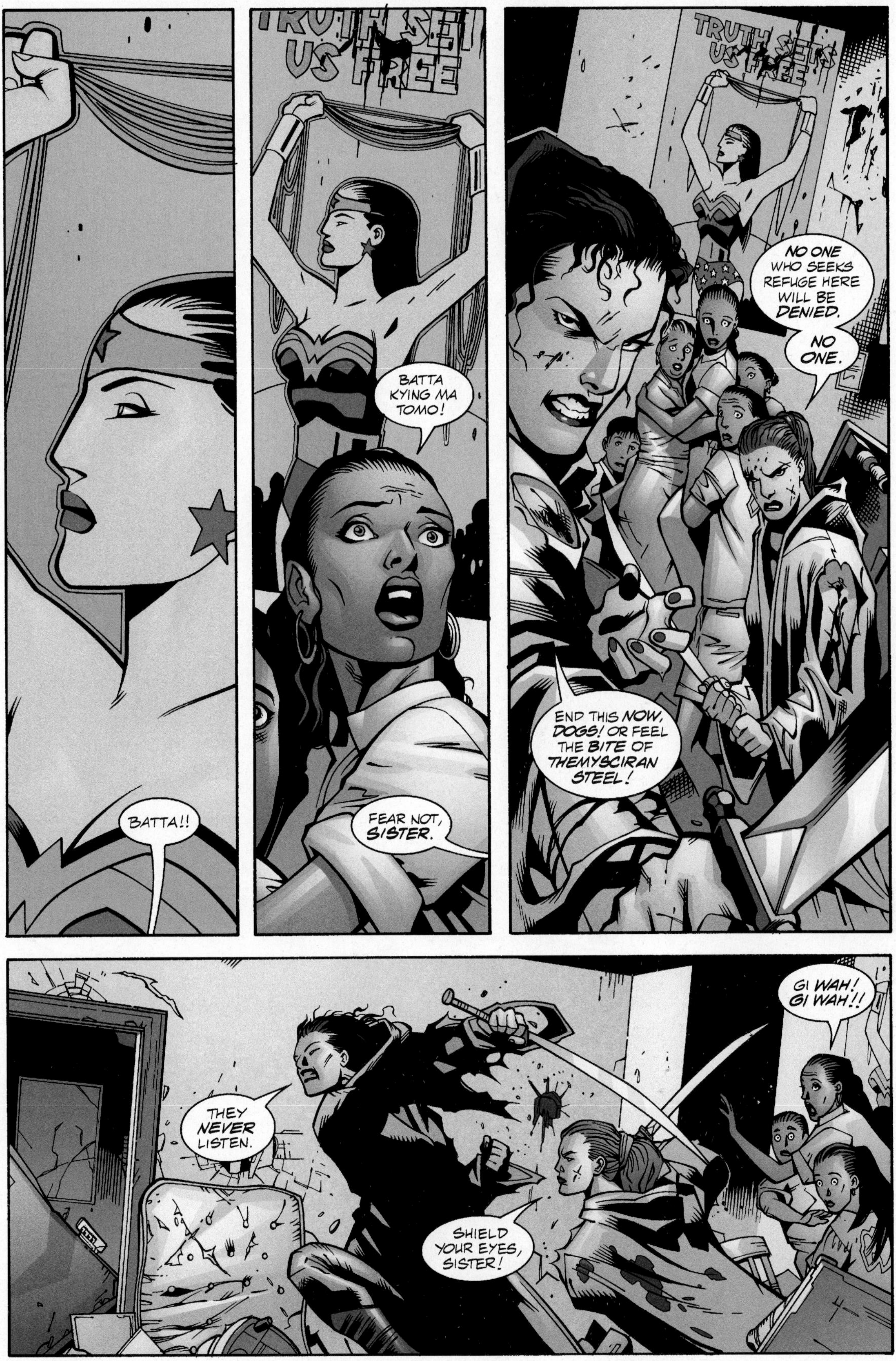
BATTA!!
TRUTH SETS US FREE
BATTA KYING MA TOMO!
FEAR NOT, SISTER.
TRUTH SETS US FREE
NO ONE WHO SEEKS REFUGE HERE WILL BE DENIED.
NO ONE.
END THIS NOW, DOGS! OR FEEL THE BITE OF THEMYSCIRAN STEEL!
GI WAH! GI WAH!!
THEY NEVER LISTEN.
SHIELD YOUR EYES, SISTER!

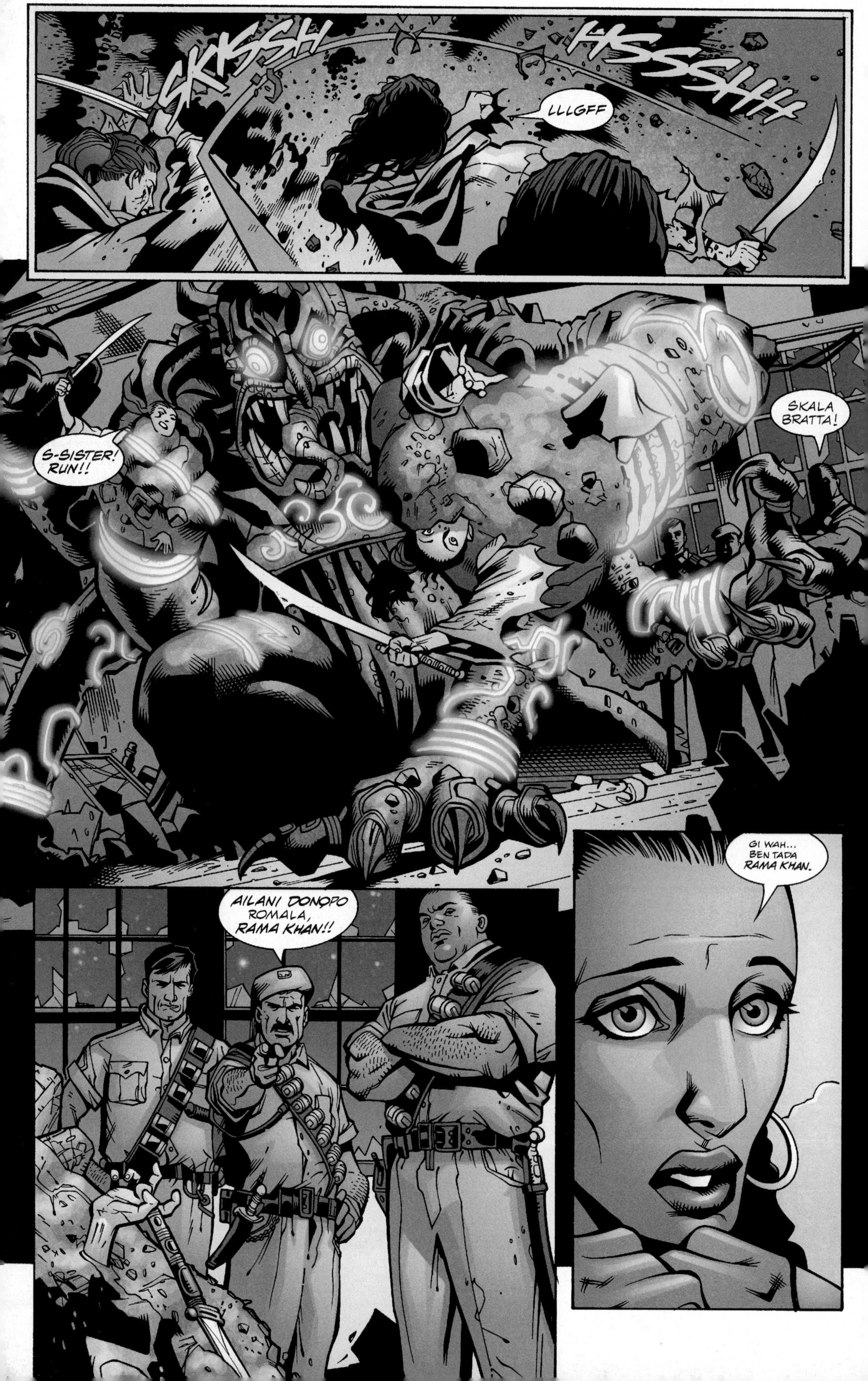
SKISSH
HSSSHH
LLLGFF
S-SISTER! RUN!!
SKALA BRATTA!
AILANI DONOPO ROMALA, RAMA KHAN!!
GI WAH... BEN TADA RAMA KHAN.

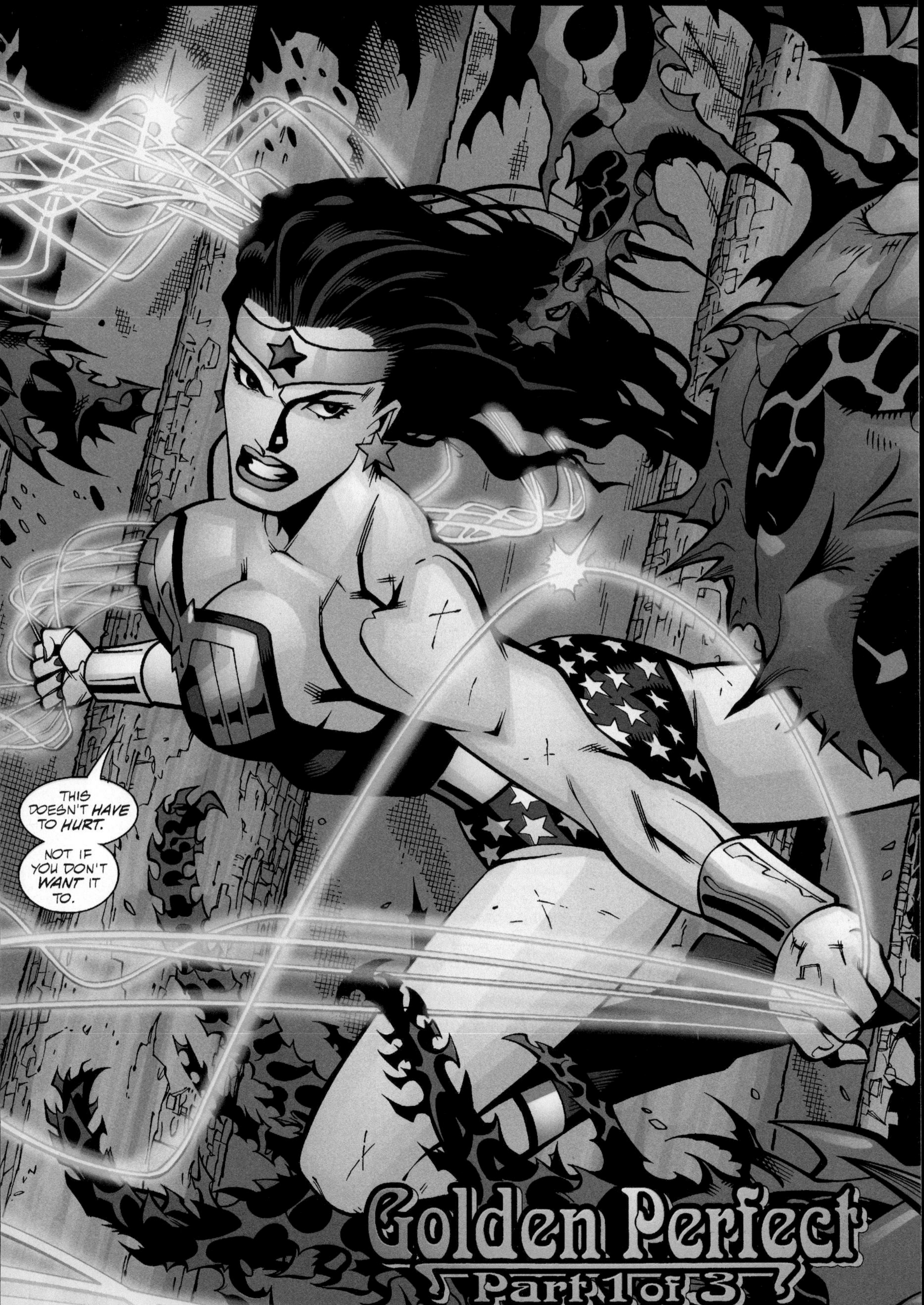
THIS DOESN'T *HAVE* TO *HURT*.
NOT IF YOU DON'T *WANT* IT TO.
Golden Perfect
Part 1 of 3

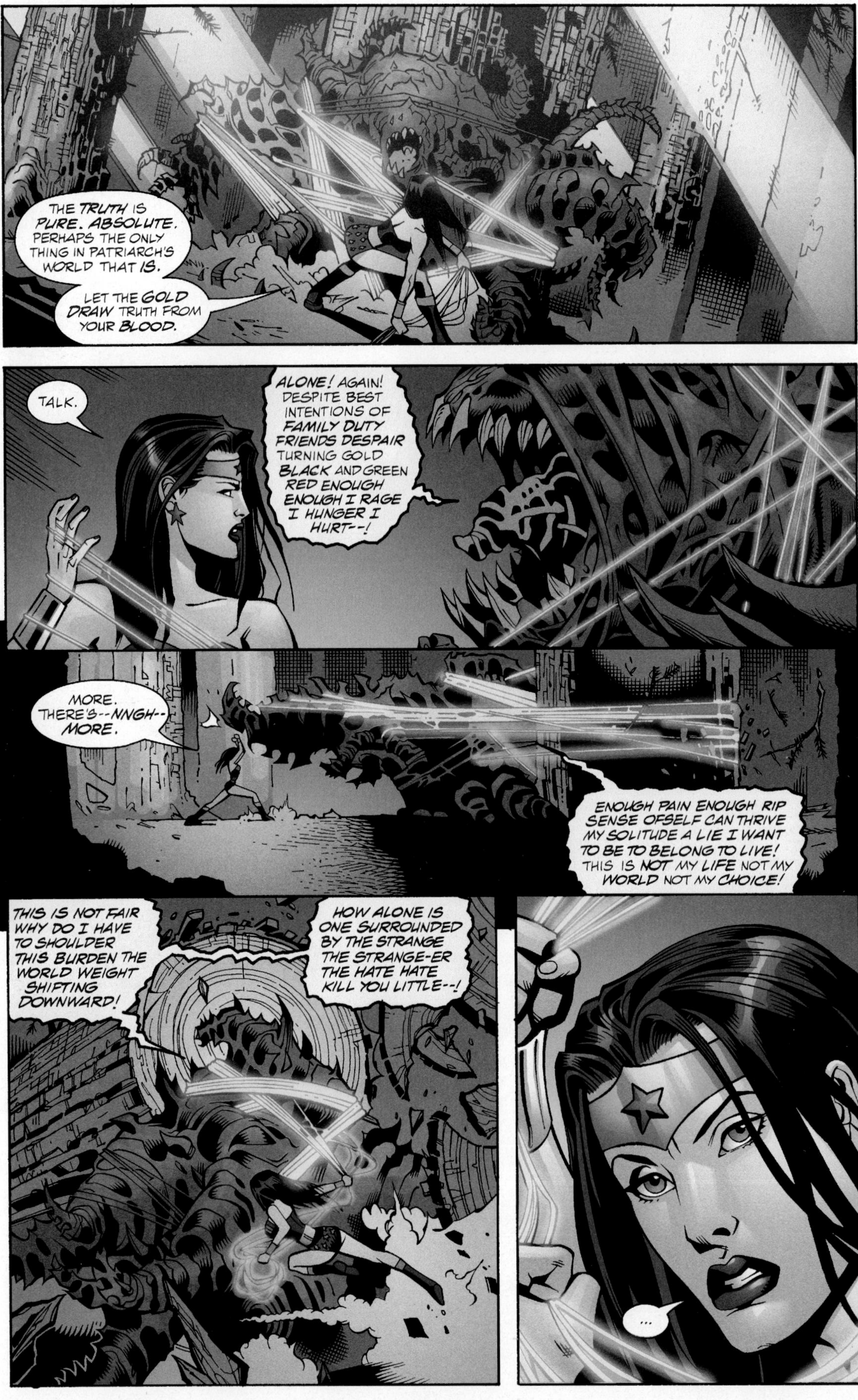
THE TRUTH IS PURE. ABSOLUTE. PERHAPS THE ONLY THING IN PATRIARCH'S WORLD THAT IS.
LET THE GOLD DRAW TRUTH FROM YOUR BLOOD.
TALK.
ALONE! AGAIN! DESPITE BEST INTENTIONS OF FAMILY DUTY FRIENDS DESPAIR TURNING GOLD BLACK AND GREEN RED ENOUGH ENOUGH I RAGE I HUNGER I HURT--!
MORE. THERE'S--NNGH-- MORE.
ENOUGH PAIN ENOUGH RIP SENSE OFSELF CAN THRIVE MY SOLITUDE A LIE I WANT TO BE TO BELONG TO LIVE! THIS IS NOT MY LIFE NOT MY WORLD NOT MY CHOICE!
THIS IS NOT FAIR WHY DO I HAVE TO SHOULDER THIS BURDEN THE WORLD WEIGHT SHIFTING DOWNWARD!
HOW ALONE IS ONE SURROUNDED BY THE STRANGE THE STRANGE-ER THE HATE HATE KILL YOU LITTLE--!
...

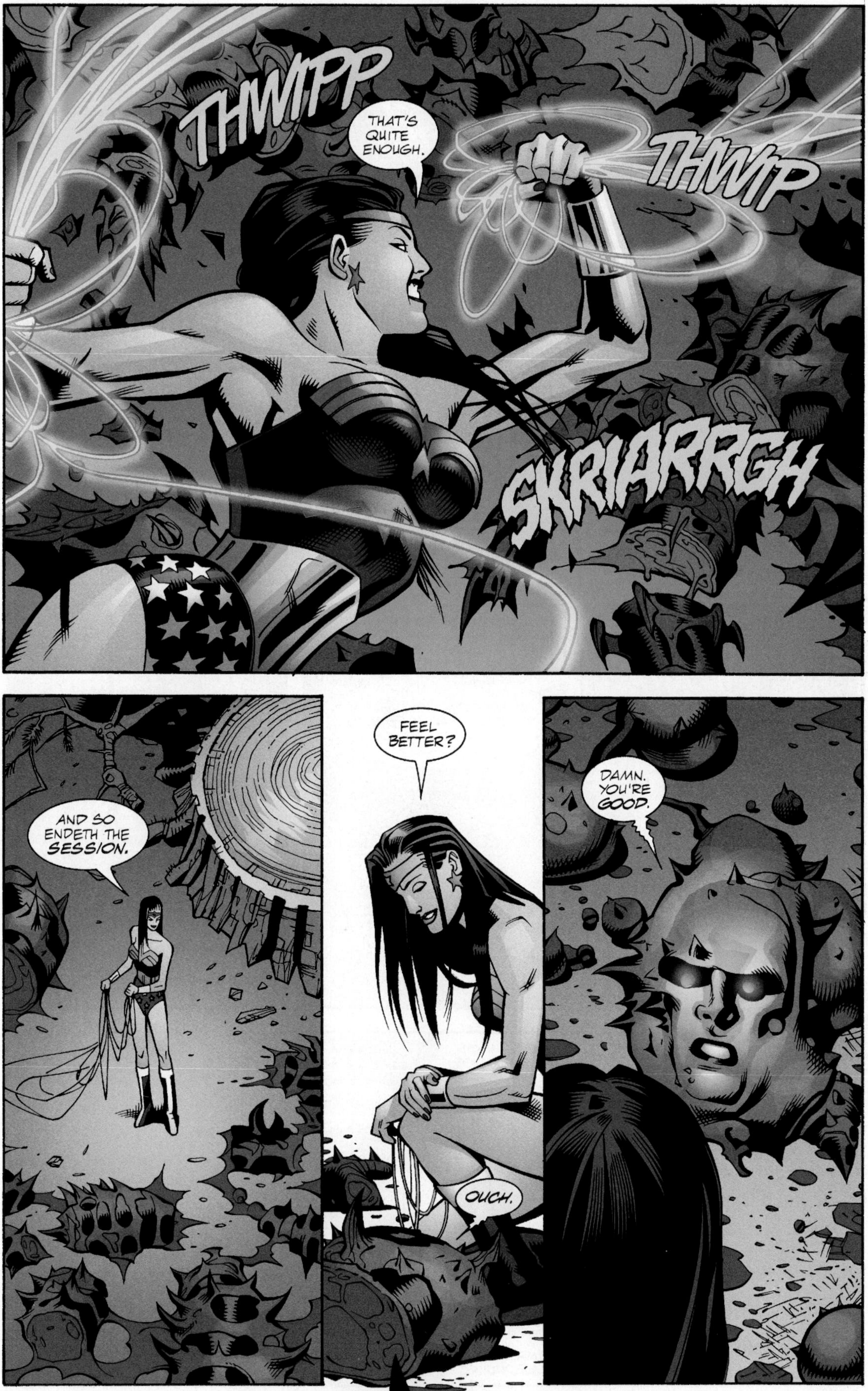
THWIPP
THAT'S QUITE ENOUGH.
THWIP
SKRIARRGH
AND SO ENDETH THE SESSION.
FEEL BETTER?
OUCH.
DAMN. YOU'RE GOOD.

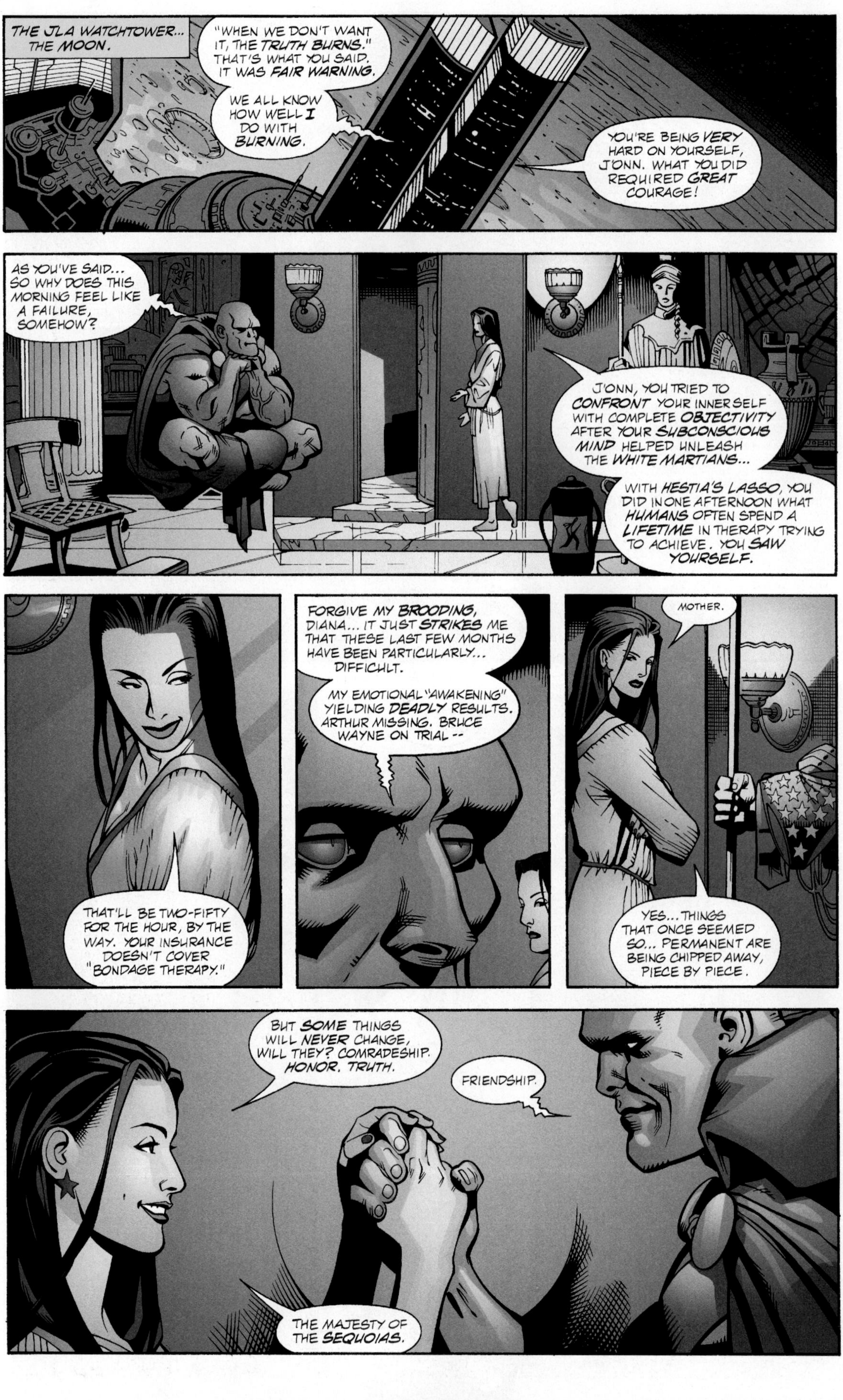
THE JLA WATCHTOWER... THE MOON.
"WHEN WE DON'T WANT IT, THE TRUTH BURNS." THAT'S WHAT YOU SAID. IT WAS FAIR WARNING.
WE ALL KNOW HOW WELL I DO WITH BURNING.
YOU'RE BEING VERY HARD ON YOURSELF, J'ONN. WHAT YOU DID REQUIRED GREAT COURAGE!
AS YOU'VE SAID... SO WHY DOES THIS MORNING FEEL LIKE A FAILURE, SOMEHOW?
J'ONN, YOU TRIED TO CONFRONT YOUR INNER SELF WITH COMPLETE OBJECTIVITY AFTER YOUR SUBCONSCIOUS MIND HELPED UNLEASH THE WHITE MARTIANS...
WITH HESTIA'S LASSO, YOU DID IN ONE AFTERNOON WHAT HUMANS OFTEN SPEND A LIFETIME IN THERAPY TRYING TO ACHIEVE. YOU SAW YOURSELF.
THAT'LL BE TWO-FIFTY FOR THE HOUR, BY THE WAY. YOUR INSURANCE DOESN'T COVER "BONDAGE THERAPY."
FORGIVE MY BROODING, DIANA... IT JUST STRIKES ME THAT THESE LAST FEW MONTHS HAVE BEEN PARTICULARLY... DIFFICULT.
MY EMOTIONAL "AWAKENING" YIELDING DEADLY RESULTS. ARTHUR MISSING. BRUCE WAYNE ON TRIAL --
MOTHER.
YES... THINGS THAT ONCE SEEMED SO... PERMANENT ARE BEING CHIPPED AWAY, PIECE BY PIECE.
BUT SOME THINGS WILL NEVER CHANGE, WILL THEY? COMRADESHIP. HONOR. TRUTH.
FRIENDSHIP.
THE MAJESTY OF THE SEQUOIAS.

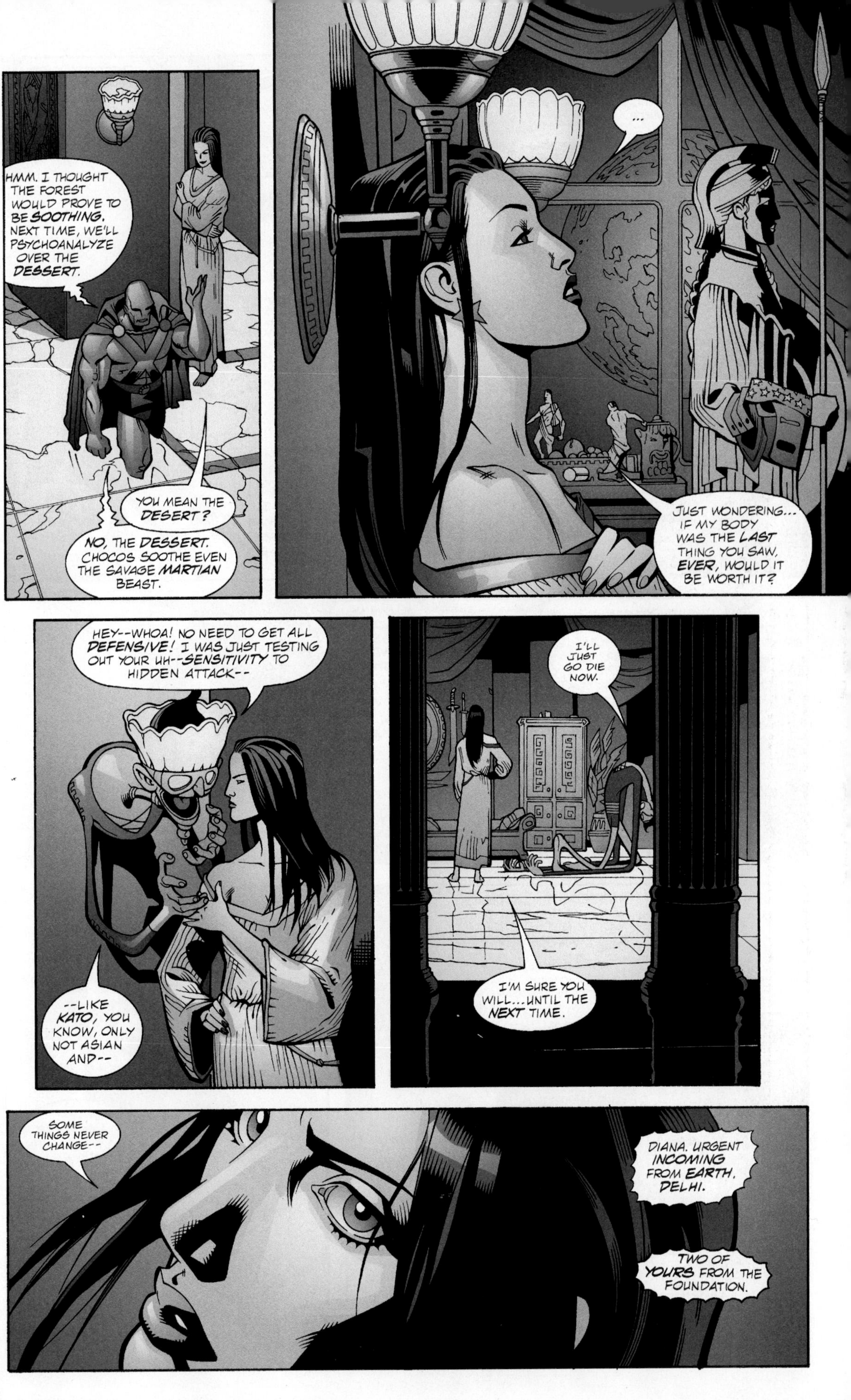
HMM. I THOUGHT THE FOREST WOULD PROVE TO BE SOOTHING. NEXT TIME, WE'LL PSYCHOANALYZE OVER THE DESSERT.
YOU MEAN THE DESERT?
NO, THE DESSERT. CHOCOS SOOTHE EVEN THE SAVAGE MARTIAN BEAST.
...
JUST WONDERING... IF MY BODY WAS THE LAST THING YOU SAW, EVER, WOULD IT BE WORTH IT?
HEY--WHOA! NO NEED TO GET ALL DEFENSIVE! I WAS JUST TESTING OUT YOUR UH--SENSITIVITY TO HIDDEN ATTACK--
--LIKE KATO, YOU KNOW, ONLY NOT ASIAN AND--
I'LL JUST GO DIE NOW.
I'M SURE YOU WILL...UNTIL THE NEXT TIME.
SOME THINGS NEVER CHANGE--
DIANA. URGENT INCOMING FROM EARTH, DELHI.
TWO OF YOURS FROM THE FOUNDATION.

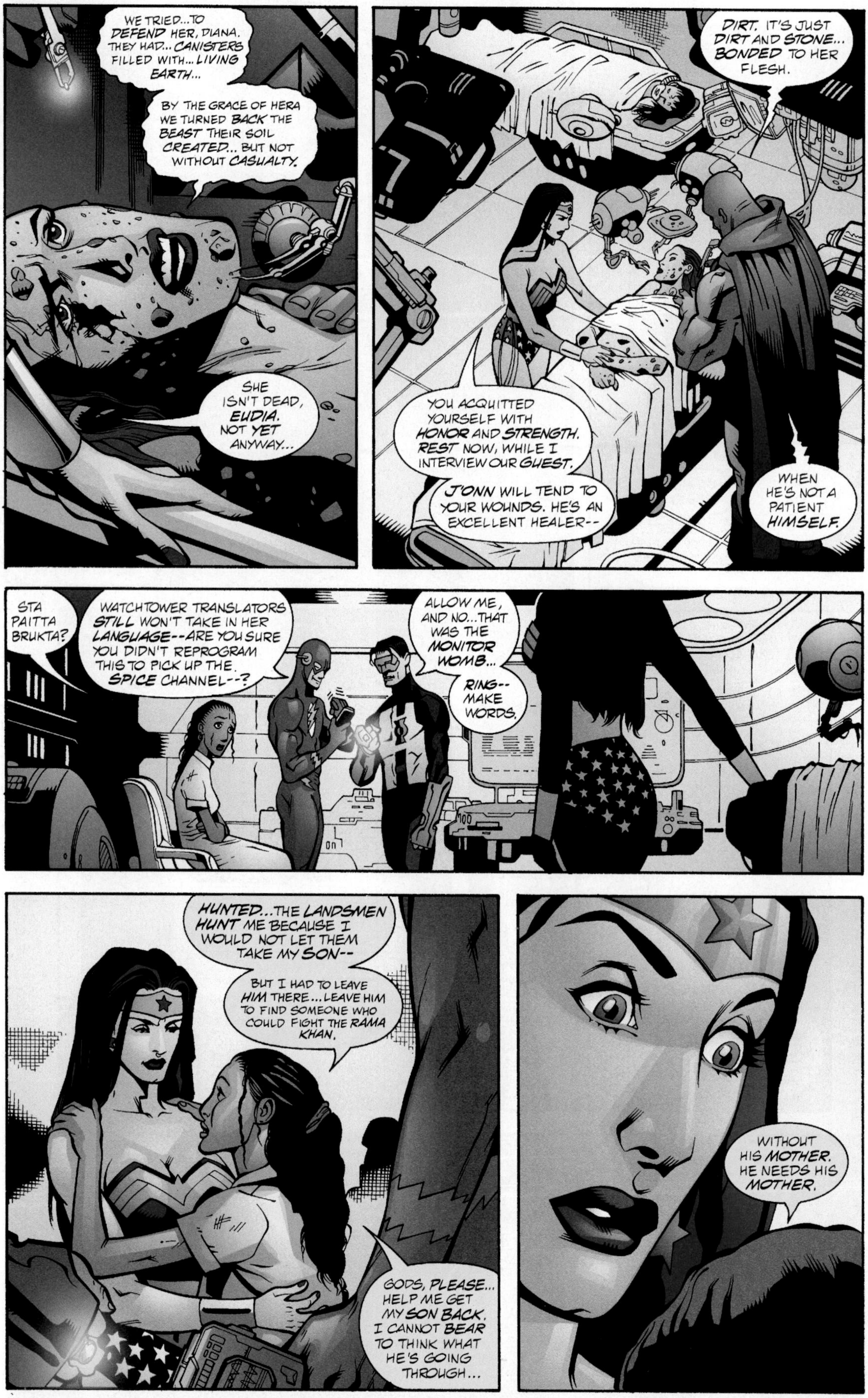
WE TRIED...TO DEFEND HER, DIANA. THEY HAD... CANISTERS FILLED WITH... LIVING EARTH...
BY THE GRACE OF HERA WE TURNED BACK THE BEAST THEIR SOIL CREATED... BUT NOT WITHOUT CASUALTY.
SHE ISN'T DEAD, EUDIA. NOT YET ANYWAY...
DIRT. IT'S JUST DIRT AND STONE... BONDED TO HER FLESH.
YOU ACQUITTED YOURSELF WITH HONOR AND STRENGTH. REST NOW, WHILE I INTERVIEW OUR GUEST.
J'ONN WILL TEND TO YOUR WOUNDS. HE'S AN EXCELLENT HEALER--
WHEN HE'S NOT A PATIENT HIMSELF.
STA PAITTA BRUKTA?
WATCHTOWER TRANSLATORS STILL WON'T TAKE IN HER LANGUAGE--ARE YOU SURE YOU DIDN'T REPROGRAM THIS TO PICK UP THE SPICE CHANNEL--?
ALLOW ME, AND NO...THAT WAS THE MONITOR WOMB...
RING--MAKE WORDS.
HUNTED...THE LANDSMEN HUNT ME BECAUSE I WOULD NOT LET THEM TAKE MY SON--
BUT I HAD TO LEAVE HIM THERE...LEAVE HIM TO FIND SOMEONE WHO COULD FIGHT THE RAMA KHAN.
GODS, PLEASE... HELP ME GET MY SON BACK. I CANNOT BEAR TO THINK WHAT HE'S GOING THROUGH...
WITHOUT HIS MOTHER. HE NEEDS HIS MOTHER.

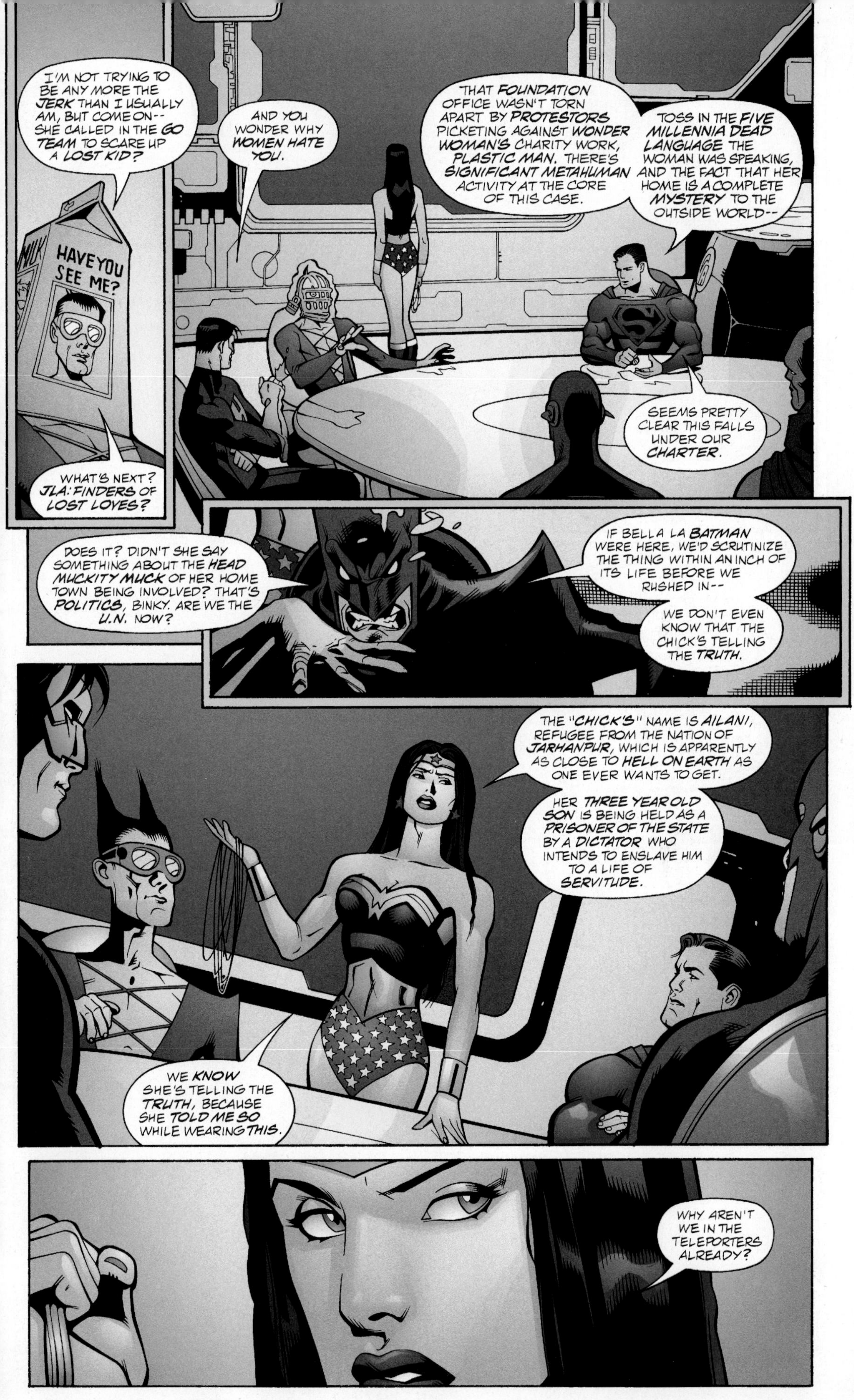

I'M NOT TRYING TO BE ANY MORE THE JERK THAN I USUALLY AM, BUT COME ON-- SHE CALLED IN THE GO TEAM TO SCARE UP A LOST KID?
WHAT'S NEXT? JLA: FINDERS OF LOST LOVES?
HAVE YOU SEE ME?
AND YOU WONDER WHY WOMEN HATE YOU.
THAT FOUNDATION OFFICE WASN'T TORN APART BY PROTESTORS PICKETING AGAINST WONDER WOMAN'S CHARITY WORK, PLASTIC MAN. THERE'S SIGNIFICANT METAHUMAN ACTIVITY AT THE CORE OF THIS CASE.
TOSS IN THE FIVE MILLENNIA DEAD LANGUAGE THE WOMAN WAS SPEAKING, AND THE FACT THAT HER HOME IS A COMPLETE MYSTERY TO THE OUTSIDE WORLD--
SEEMS PRETTY CLEAR THIS FALLS UNDER OUR CHARTER.
DOES IT? DIDN'T SHE SAY SOMETHING ABOUT THE HEAD MUCKITY MUCK OF HER HOME TOWN BEING INVOLVED? THAT'S POLITICS, BINKY. ARE WE THE U.N. NOW?
IF BELLA LA BATMAN WERE HERE, WE'D SCRUTINIZE THE THING WITHIN AN INCH OF ITS LIFE BEFORE WE RUSHED IN--
WE DON'T EVEN KNOW THAT THE CHICK'S TELLING THE TRUTH.
THE "CHICK'S" NAME IS AILANI, REFUGEE FROM THE NATION OF JARHANPUR, WHICH IS APPARENTLY AS CLOSE TO HELL ON EARTH AS ONE EVER WANTS TO GET.
HER THREE YEAR OLD SON IS BEING HELD AS A PRISONER OF THE STATE BY A DICTATOR WHO INTENDS TO ENSLAVE HIM TO A LIFE OF SERVITUDE.
WE KNOW SHE'S TELLING THE TRUTH, BECAUSE SHE TOLD ME SO WHILE WEARING THIS.
WHY AREN'T WE IN THE TELEPORTERS ALREADY?

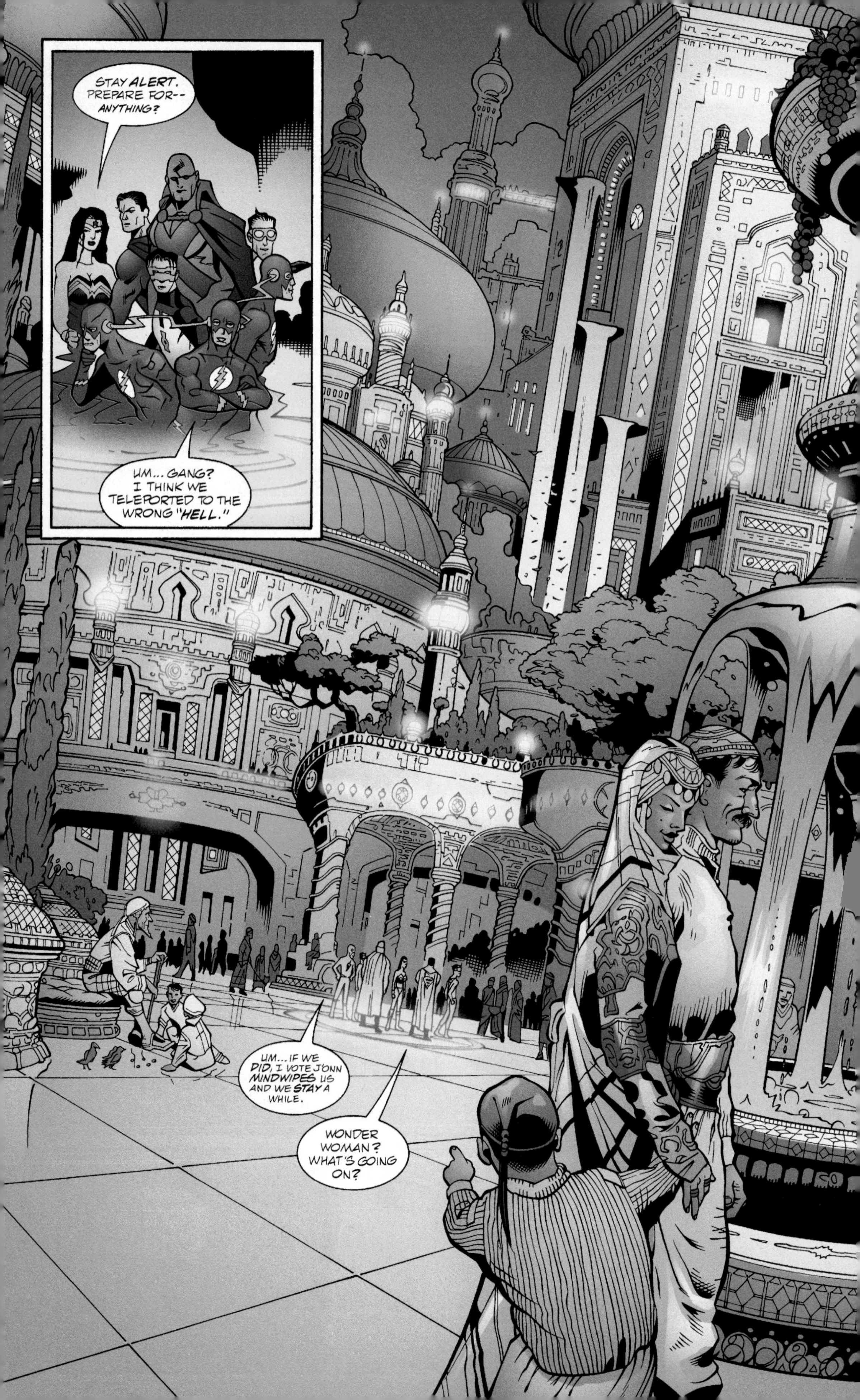
STAY ALERT. PREPARE FOR-- ANYTHING?
UM... GANG? I THINK WE TELEPORTED TO THE WRONG "HELL."
UM... IF WE DID, I VOTE J'ONN MINDWIPES US AND WE STAY A WHILE.
WONDER WOMAN? WHAT'S GOING ON?

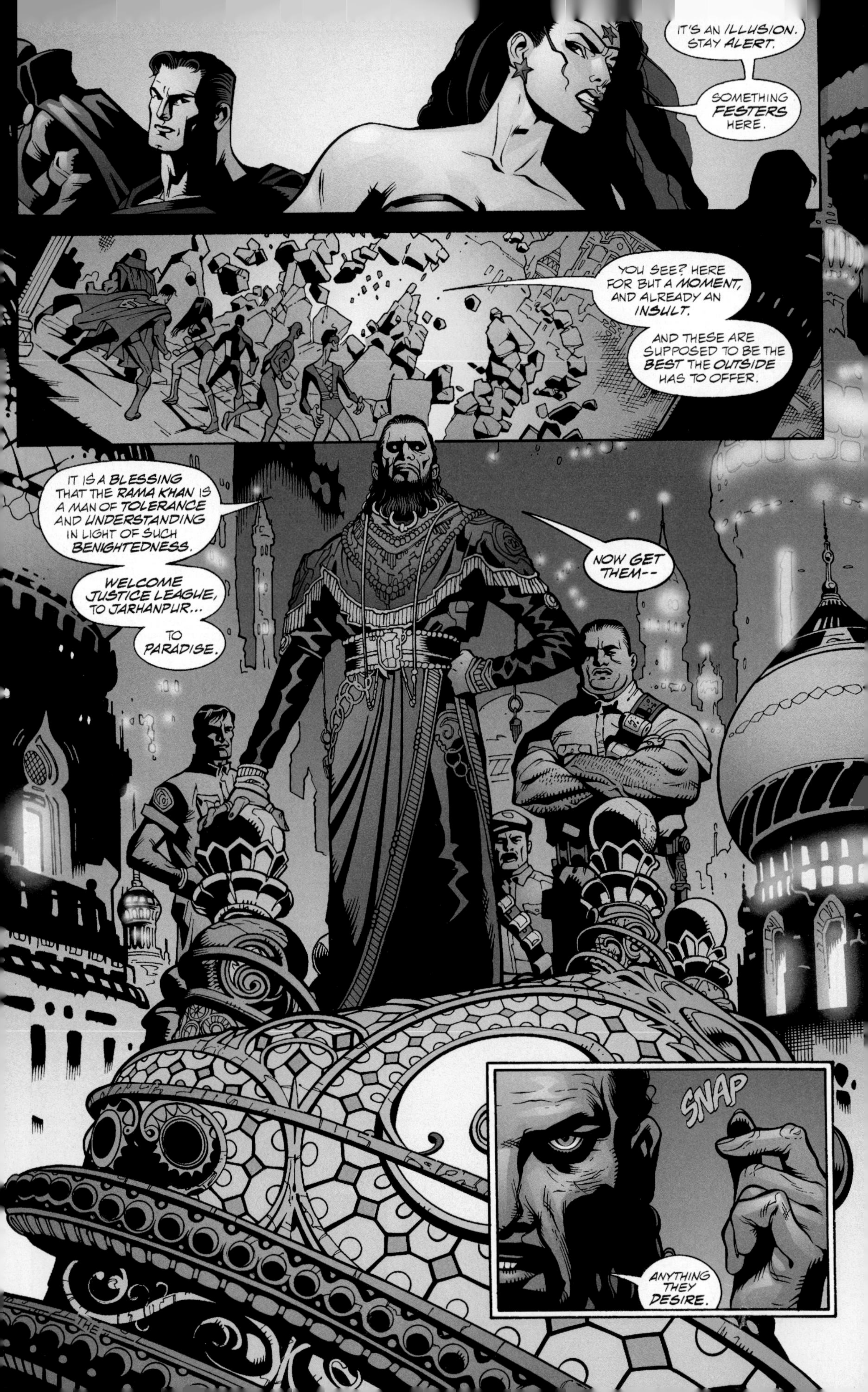
IT'S AN ILLUSION. STAY ALERT.
SOMETHING FESTERS HERE.
YOU SEE? HERE FOR BUT A MOMENT, AND ALREADY AN INSULT.
AND THESE ARE SUPPOSED TO BE THE BEST THE OUTSIDE HAS TO OFFER.
IT IS A BLESSING THAT THE RAMA KHAN IS A MAN OF TOLERANCE AND UNDERSTANDING IN LIGHT OF SUCH BENIGHTEDNESS.
WELCOME JUSTICE LEAGUE, TO JARHANPUR...
TO PARADISE.
NOW GET THEM--
SNAP
ANYTHING THEY DESIRE.

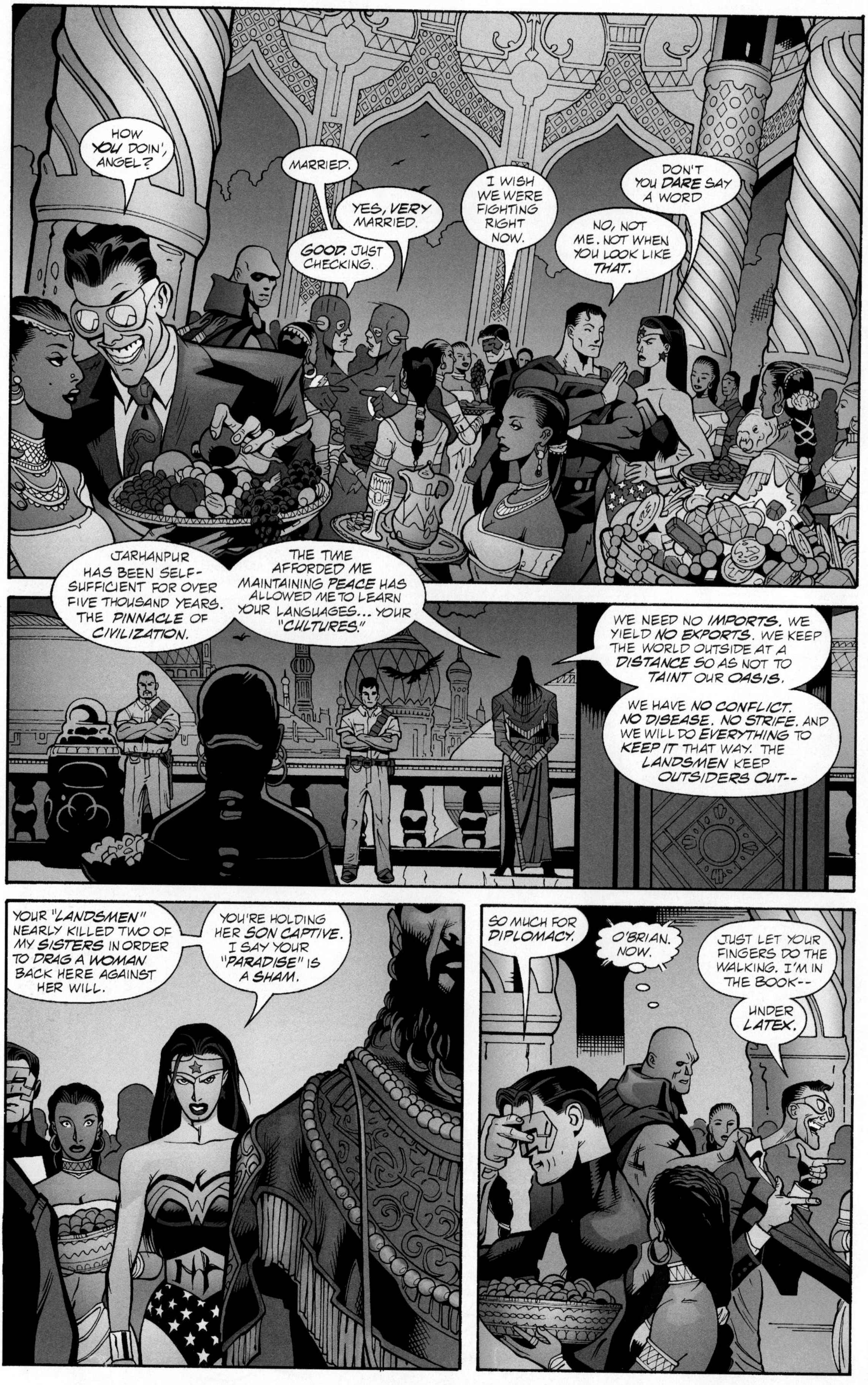
HOW YOU DOIN', ANGEL?
MARRIED.
YES, VERY MARRIED.
GOOD. JUST CHECKING.
I WISH WE WERE FIGHTING RIGHT NOW.
DON'T YOU DARE SAY A WORD
NO, NOT ME. NOT WHEN YOU LOOK LIKE THAT.
JARHANPUR HAS BEEN SELF-SUFFICIENT FOR OVER FIVE THOUSAND YEARS. THE PINNACLE OF CIVILIZATION.
THE TIME AFFORDED ME MAINTAINING PEACE HAS ALLOWED ME TO LEARN YOUR LANGUAGES... YOUR "CULTURES."
WE NEED NO IMPORTS. WE YIELD NO EXPORTS. WE KEEP THE WORLD OUTSIDE AT A DISTANCE SO AS NOT TO TAINT OUR OASIS.
WE HAVE NO CONFLICT. NO DISEASE. NO STRIFE. AND WE WILL DO EVERYTHING TO KEEP IT THAT WAY. THE LANDSMEN KEEP OUTSIDERS OUT--
YOUR "LANDSMEN" NEARLY KILLED TWO OF MY SISTERS IN ORDER TO DRAG A WOMAN BACK HERE AGAINST HER WILL.
YOU'RE HOLDING HER SON CAPTIVE. I SAY YOUR "PARADISE" IS A SHAM.
SO MUCH FOR DIPLOMACY.
O'BRIAN. NOW.
JUST LET YOUR FINGERS DO THE WALKING. I'M IN THE BOOK--
UNDER LATEX.

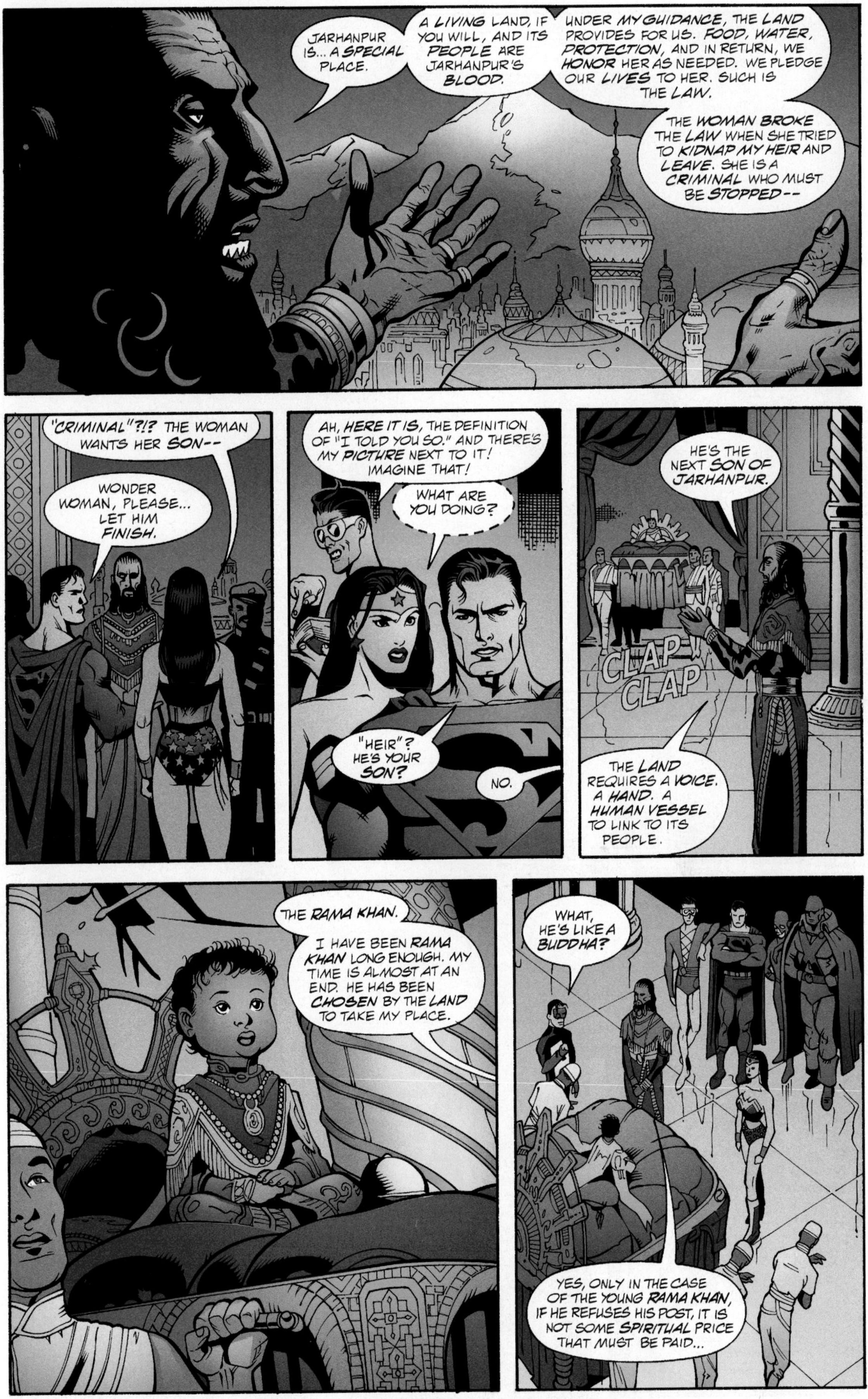

JARHANPUR IS... A SPECIAL PLACE.
A LIVING LAND, IF YOU WILL, AND ITS PEOPLE ARE JARHANPUR'S BLOOD.
UNDER MY GUIDANCE, THE LAND PROVIDES FOR US. FOOD, WATER, PROTECTION, AND IN RETURN, WE HONOR HER AS NEEDED. WE PLEDGE OUR LIVES TO HER. SUCH IS THE LAW.
THE WOMAN BROKE THE LAW WHEN SHE TRIED TO KIDNAP MY HEIR AND LEAVE. SHE IS A CRIMINAL WHO MUST BE STOPPED--
"CRIMINAL"?!? THE WOMAN WANTS HER SON--
WONDER WOMAN, PLEASE... LET HIM FINISH.
AH, HERE IT IS, THE DEFINITION OF "I TOLD YOU SO." AND THERE'S MY PICTURE NEXT TO IT! IMAGINE THAT!
WHAT ARE YOU DOING?
"HEIR"? HE'S YOUR SON?
NO.
HE'S THE NEXT SON OF JARHANPUR.
CLAP CLAP
THE LAND REQUIRES A VOICE. A HAND. A HUMAN VESSEL TO LINK TO ITS PEOPLE.
THE RAMA KHAN.
I HAVE BEEN RAMA KHAN LONG ENOUGH. MY TIME IS ALMOST AT AN END. HE HAS BEEN CHOSEN BY THE LAND TO TAKE MY PLACE.
WHAT, HE'S LIKE A BUDDHA?
YES, ONLY IN THE CASE OF THE YOUNG RAMA KHAN, IF HE REFUSES HIS POST, IT IS NOT SOME SPIRITUAL PRICE THAT MUST BE PAID...

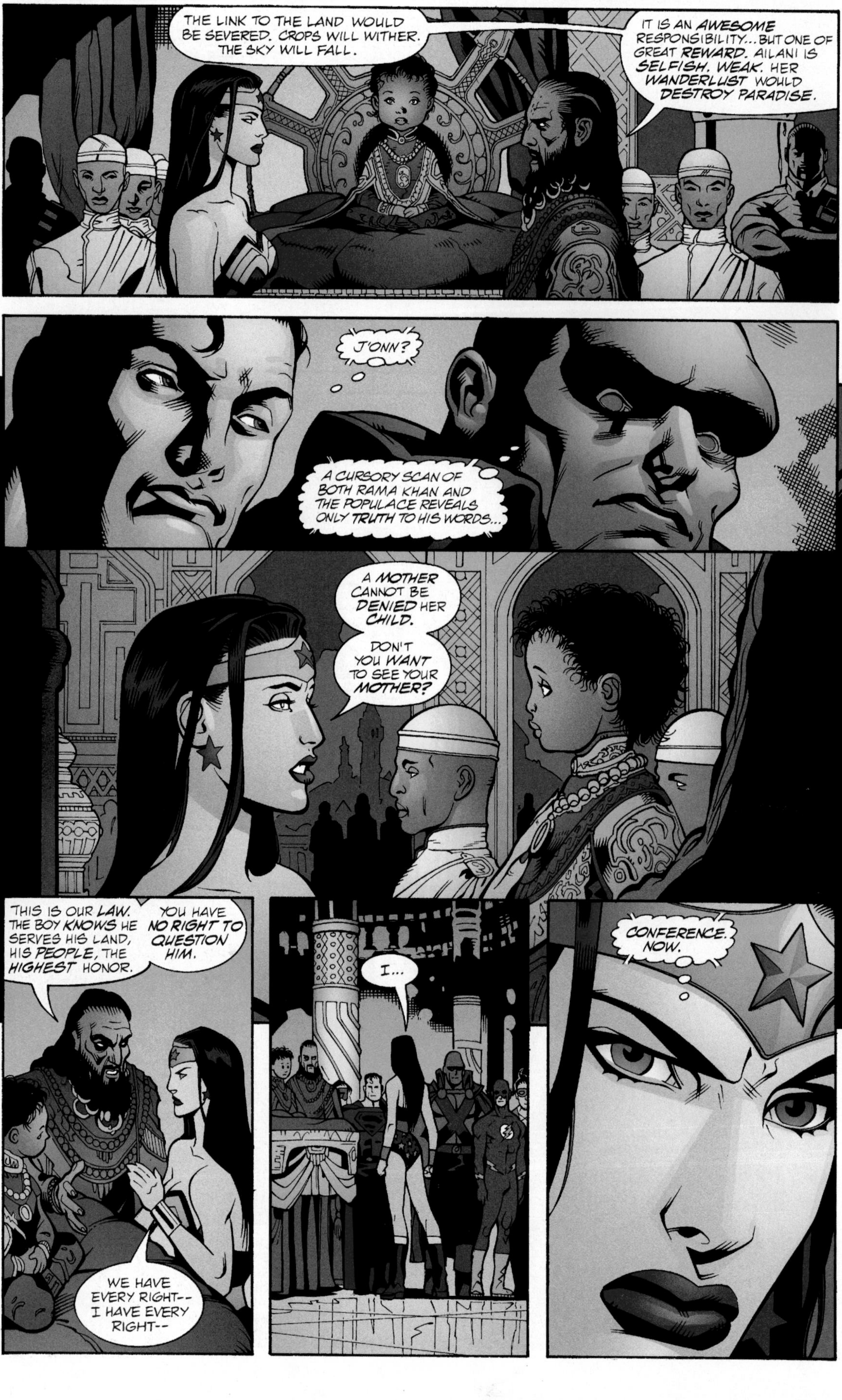
THE LINK TO THE LAND WOULD BE SEVERED. CROPS WILL WITHER. THE SKY WILL FALL.
IT IS AN AWESOME RESPONSIBILITY... BUT ONE OF GREAT REWARD. AILANI IS SELFISH. WEAK. HER WANDERLUST WOULD DESTROY PARADISE.
J'ONN?
A CURSORY SCAN OF BOTH RAMA KHAN AND THE POPULACE REVEALS ONLY TRUTH TO HIS WORDS...
A MOTHER CANNOT BE DENIED HER CHILD.
DON'T YOU WANT TO SEE YOUR MOTHER?
THIS IS OUR LAW. THE BOY KNOWS HE SERVES HIS LAND, HIS PEOPLE, THE HIGHEST HONOR.
YOU HAVE NO RIGHT TO QUESTION HIM.
WE HAVE EVERY RIGHT-- I HAVE EVERY RIGHT--
I...
CONFERENCE. NOW.

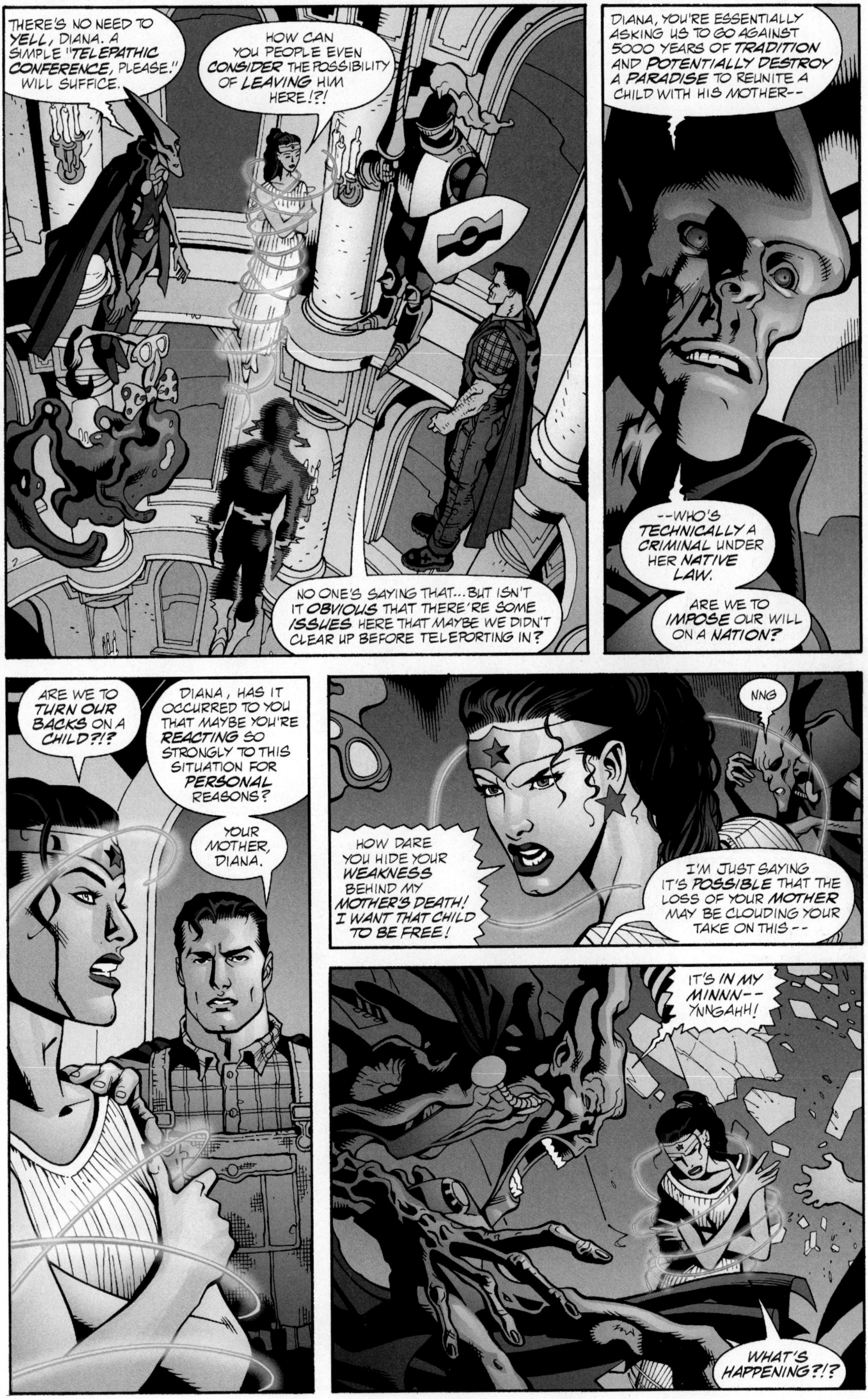
THERE'S NO NEED TO YELL, DIANA. A SIMPLE "TELEPATHIC CONFERENCE, PLEASE." WILL SUFFICE.
HOW CAN YOU PEOPLE EVEN CONSIDER THE POSSIBILITY OF LEAVING HIM HERE!?!
NO ONE'S SAYING THAT...BUT ISN'T IT OBVIOUS THAT THERE'RE SOME ISSUES HERE THAT MAYBE WE DIDN'T CLEAR UP BEFORE TELEPORTING IN?
DIANA, YOU'RE ESSENTIALLY ASKING US TO GO AGAINST 5000 YEARS OF TRADITION AND POTENTIALLY DESTROY A PARADISE TO REUNITE A CHILD WITH HIS MOTHER--
--WHO'S TECHNICALLY A CRIMINAL UNDER HER NATIVE LAW.
ARE WE TO IMPOSE OUR WILL ON A NATION?
ARE WE TO TURN OUR BACKS ON A CHILD?!?
DIANA, HAS IT OCCURRED TO YOU THAT MAYBE YOU'RE REACTING SO STRONGLY TO THIS SITUATION FOR PERSONAL REASONS?
YOUR MOTHER, DIANA.
NNG
HOW DARE YOU HIDE YOUR WEAKNESS BEHIND MY MOTHER'S DEATH! I WANT THAT CHILD TO BE FREE!
I'M JUST SAYING IT'S POSSIBLE THAT THE LOSS OF YOUR MOTHER MAY BE CLOUDING YOUR TAKE ON THIS--
IT'S IN MY MINNN-- YNNGAHH!
WHAT'S HAPPENING?!?

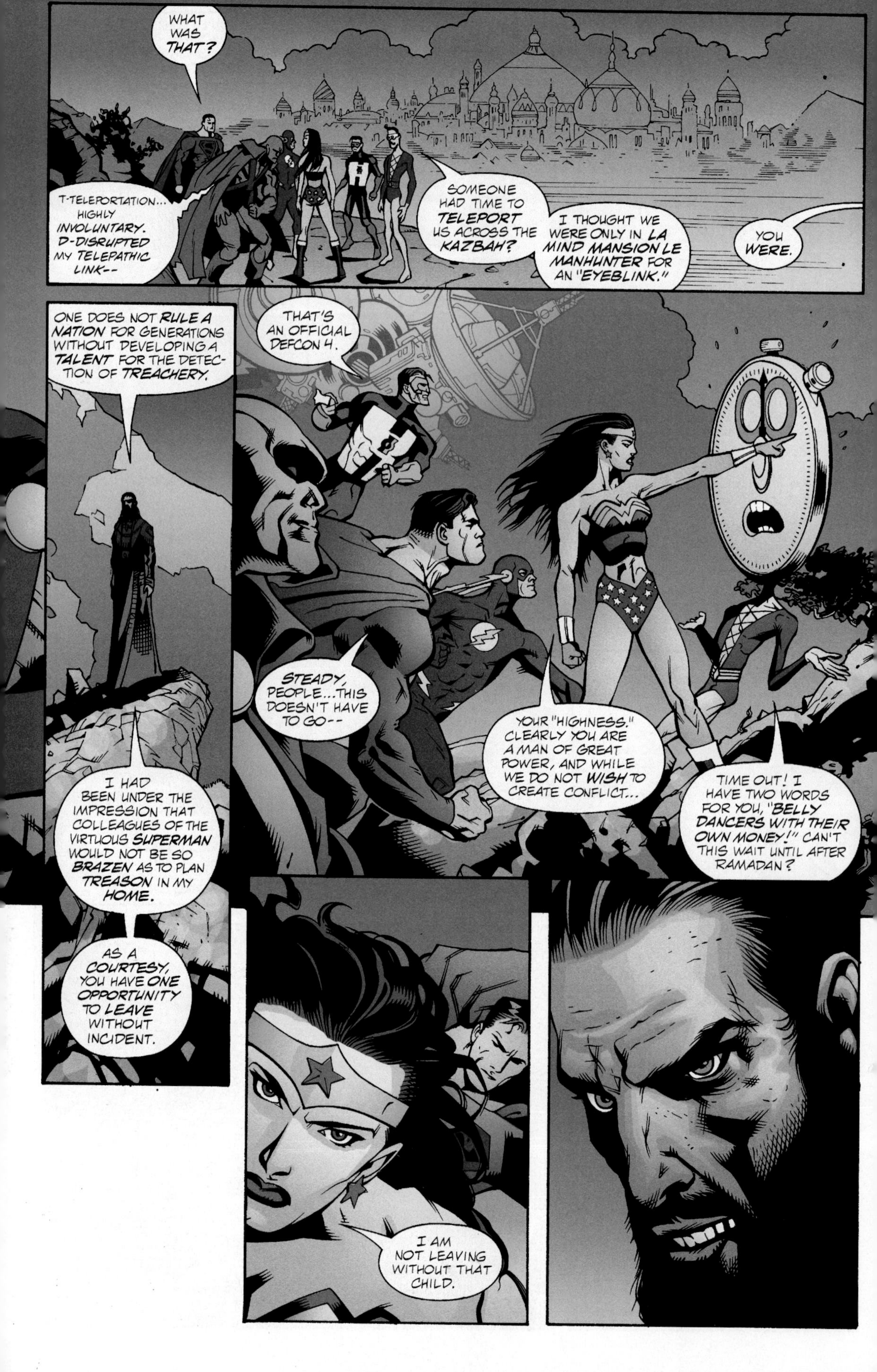
WHAT WAS THAT?
T-TELEPORTATION... HIGHLY INVOLUNTARY. D-DISRUPTED MY TELEPATHIC LINK--
SOMEONE HAD TIME TO TELEPORT US ACROSS THE KAZBAH?
I THOUGHT WE WERE ONLY IN LA MIND MANSION LE MANHUNTER FOR AN "EYEBLINK."
YOU WERE.
ONE DOES NOT RULE A NATION FOR GENERATIONS WITHOUT DEVELOPING A TALENT FOR THE DETECTION OF TREACHERY.
THAT'S AN OFFICIAL DEFCON 4.
STEADY, PEOPLE...THIS DOESN'T HAVE TO GO--
YOUR "HIGHNESS." CLEARLY YOU ARE A MAN OF GREAT POWER, AND WHILE WE DO NOT WISH TO CREATE CONFLICT...
TIME OUT! I HAVE TWO WORDS FOR YOU, "BELLY DANCERS WITH THEIR OWN MONEY!" CAN'T THIS WAIT UNTIL AFTER RAMADAN?
I HAD BEEN UNDER THE IMPRESSION THAT COLLEAGUES OF THE VIRTUOUS SUPERMAN WOULD NOT BE SO BRAZEN AS TO PLAN TREASON IN MY HOME.
AS A COURTESY, YOU HAVE ONE OPPORTUNITY TO LEAVE WITHOUT INCIDENT.
I AM NOT LEAVING WITHOUT THAT CHILD.

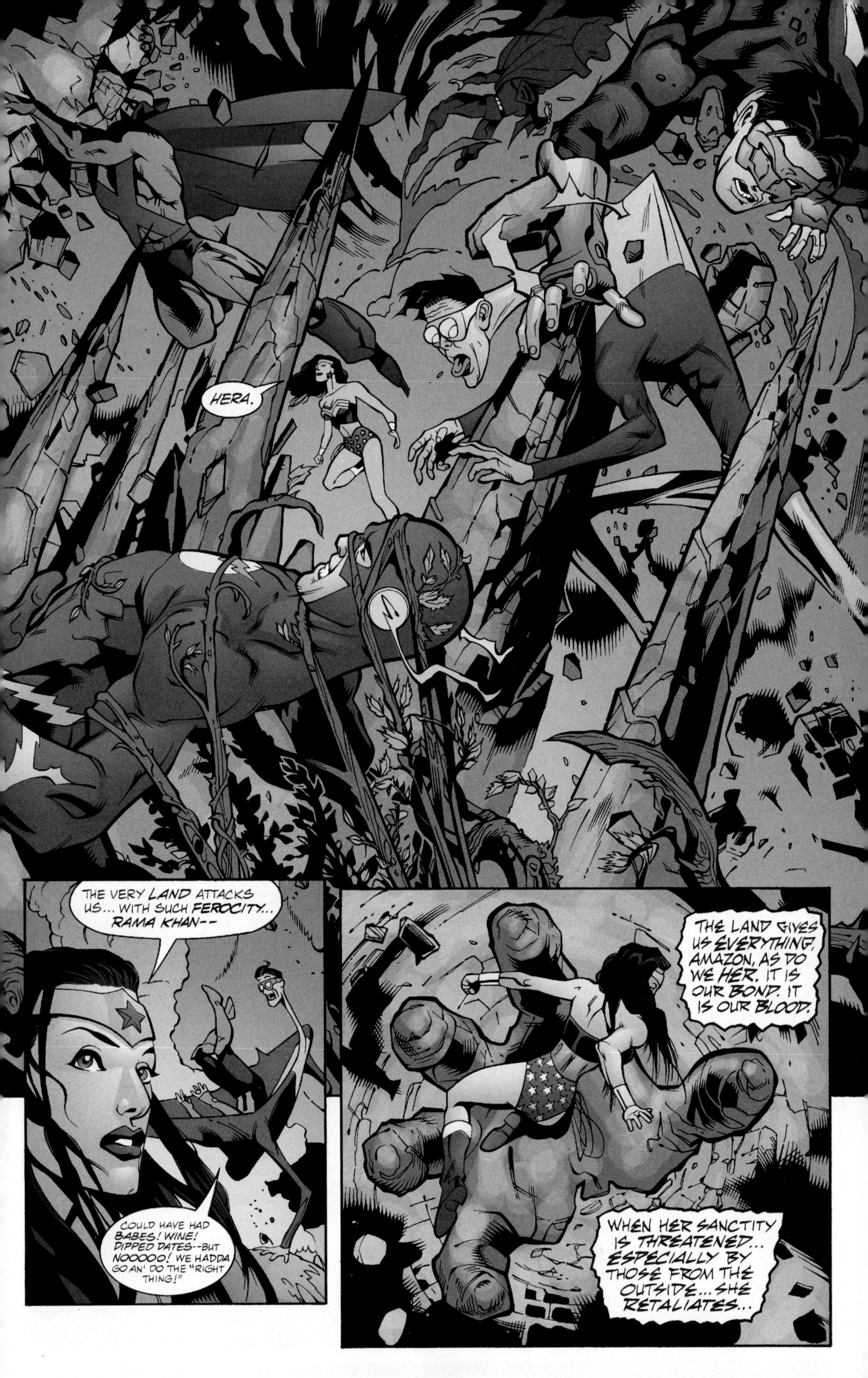
HERA.
THE VERY LAND ATTACKS US... WITH SUCH FEROCITY... RAMA KHAN--
COULD HAVE HAD BABES! WINE! DIPPED DATES--BUT NOOOOO! WE HADDA GO AN' DO THE "RIGHT THING!"
THE LAND GIVES US EVERYTHING, AMAZON, AS DO WE HER. IT IS OUR BOND. IT IS OUR BLOOD.
WHEN HER SANCTITY IS THREATENED... ESPECIALLY BY THOSE FROM THE OUTSIDE... SHE RETALIATES...

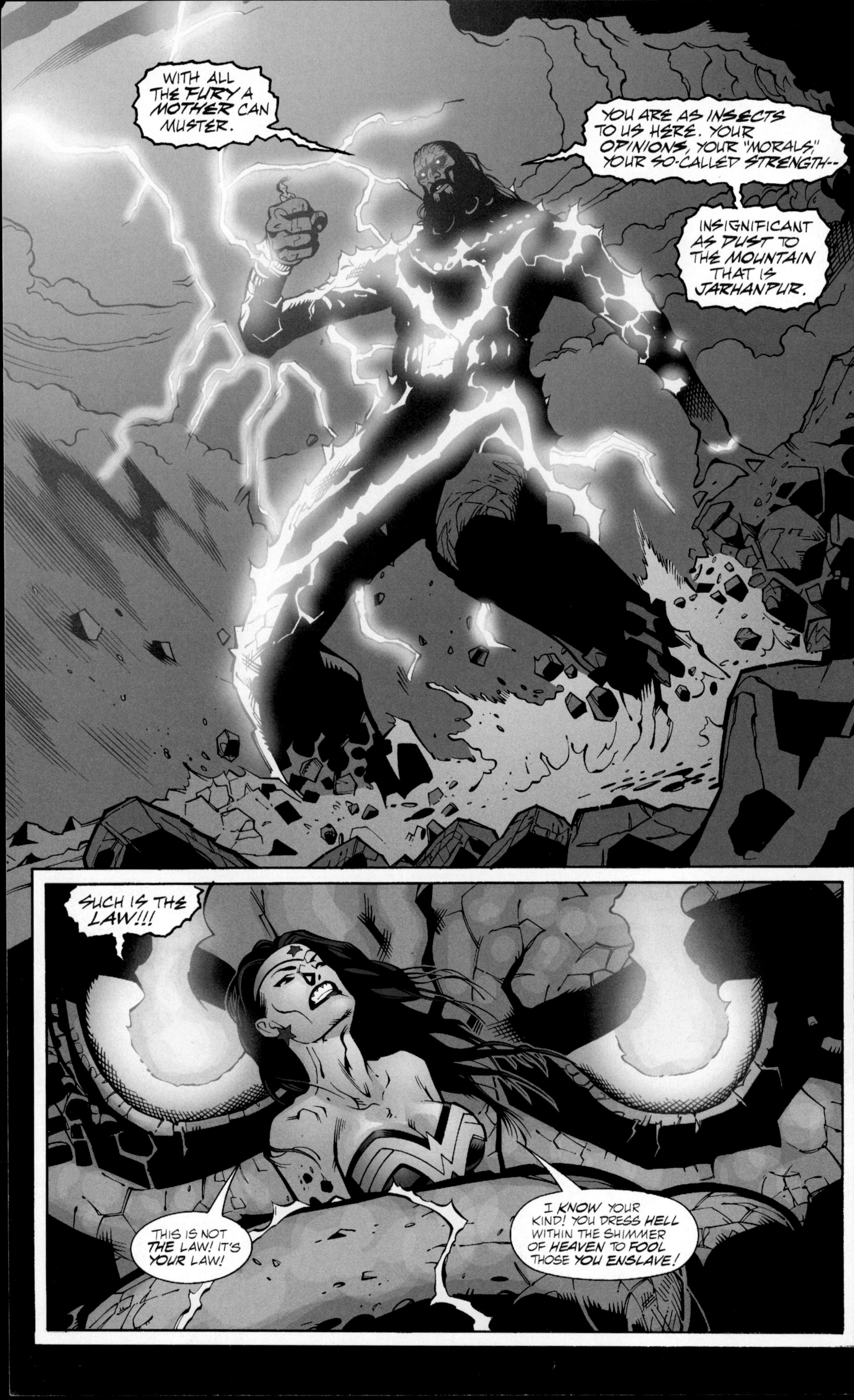
WITH ALL THE FURY A MOTHER CAN MUSTER.
YOU ARE AS INSECTS TO US HERE. YOUR OPINIONS, YOUR "MORALS," YOUR SO-CALLED STRENGTH--
INSIGNIFICANT AS DUST TO THE MOUNTAIN THAT IS JARHANPUR.
SUCH IS THE LAW!!!
THIS IS NOT THE LAW! IT'S YOUR LAW!
I KNOW YOUR KIND! YOU DRESS HELL WITHIN THE SHIMMER OF HEAVEN TO FOOL THOSE YOU ENSLAVE!

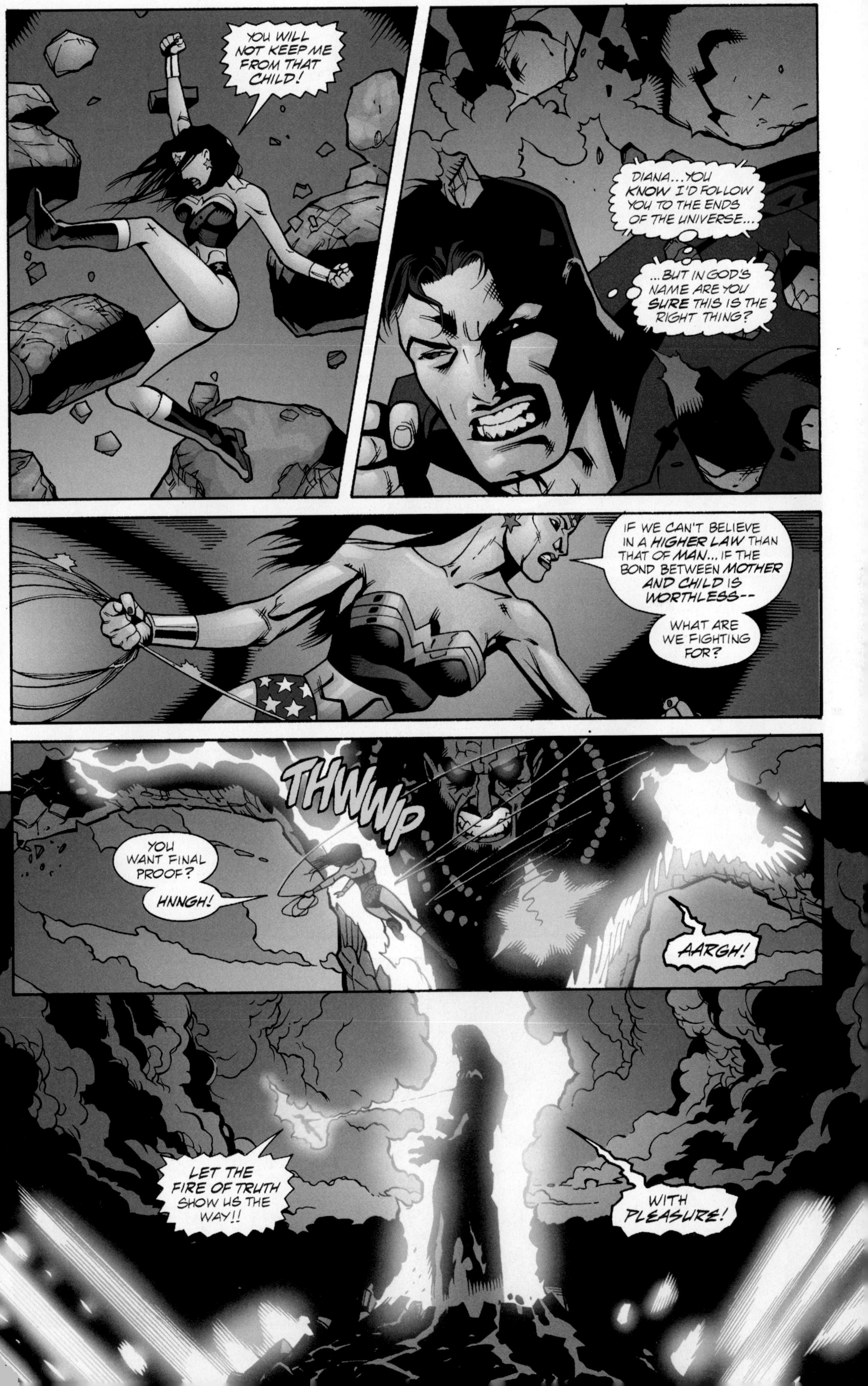
YOU WILL NOT KEEP ME FROM THAT CHILD!
DIANA...YOU KNOW I'D FOLLOW YOU TO THE ENDS OF THE UNIVERSE...
...BUT IN GOD'S NAME ARE YOU SURE THIS IS THE RIGHT THING?
IF WE CAN'T BELIEVE IN A HIGHER LAW THAN THAT OF MAN... IF THE BOND BETWEEN MOTHER AND CHILD IS WORTHLESS--
WHAT ARE WE FIGHTING FOR?
THWWIP
YOU WANT FINAL PROOF?
HNNGH!
AARGH!
LET THE FIRE OF TRUTH SHOW US THE WAY!!
WITH PLEASURE!

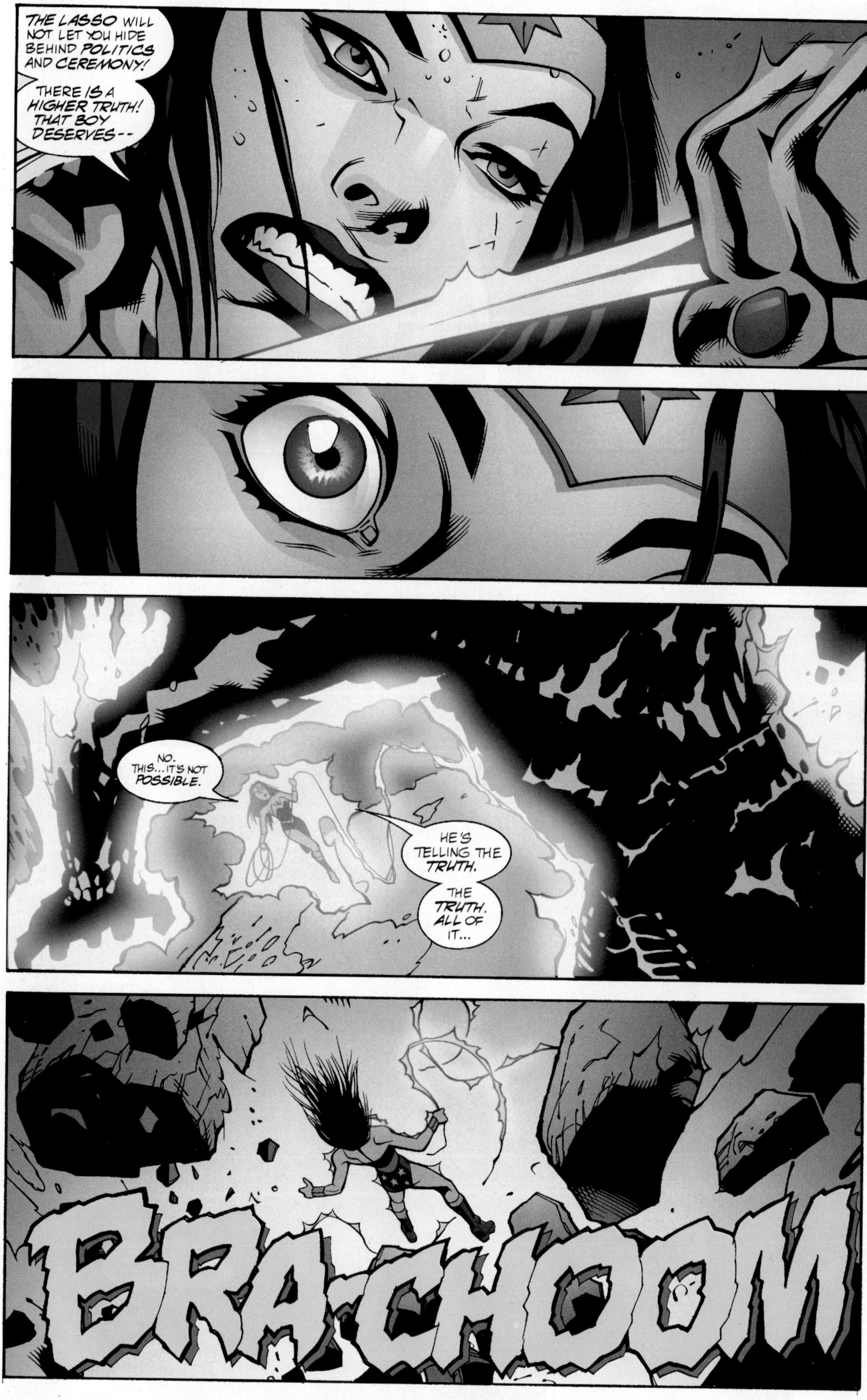
THE LASSO WILL NOT LET YOU HIDE BEHIND POLITICS AND CEREMONY!
THERE IS A HIGHER TRUTH! THAT BOY DESERVES--
NO. THIS...IT'S NOT POSSIBLE.
HE'S TELLING THE TRUTH.
THE TRUTH. ALL OF IT...
BRA-CHOOM

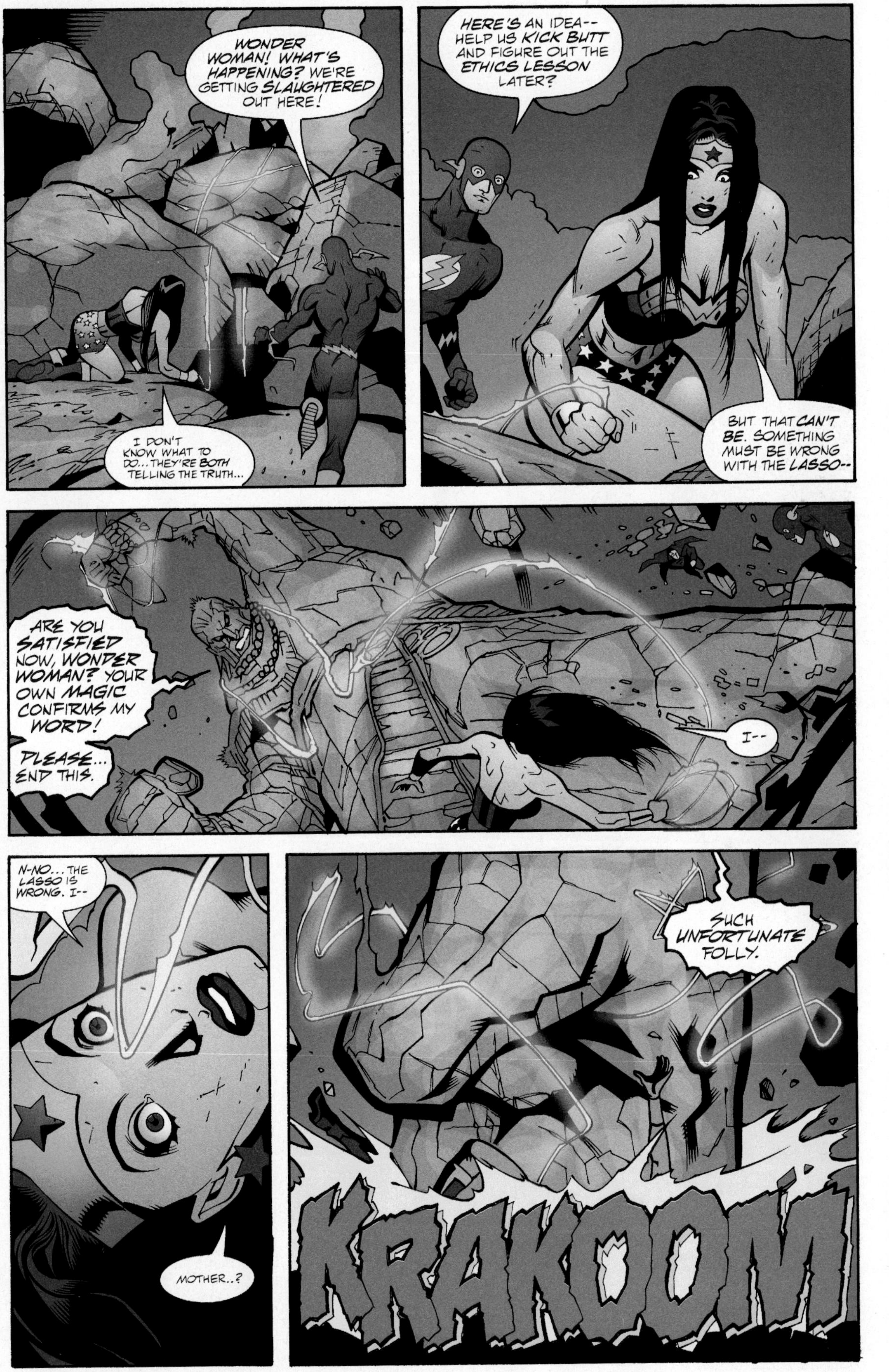
WONDER WOMAN! WHAT'S HAPPENING? WE'RE GETTING SLAUGHTERED OUT HERE!
I DON'T KNOW WHAT TO DO... THEY'RE BOTH TELLING THE TRUTH...
HERE'S AN IDEA-- HELP US KICK BUTT AND FIGURE OUT THE ETHICS LESSON LATER?
BUT THAT CAN'T BE. SOMETHING MUST BE WRONG WITH THE LASSO--
ARE YOU SATISFIED NOW, WONDER WOMAN? YOUR OWN MAGIC CONFIRMS MY WORD!
PLEASE... END THIS.
I--
N-NO... THE LASSO IS WRONG. I--
MOTHER..?
SUCH UNFORTUNATE FOLLY.
KRAKOOM

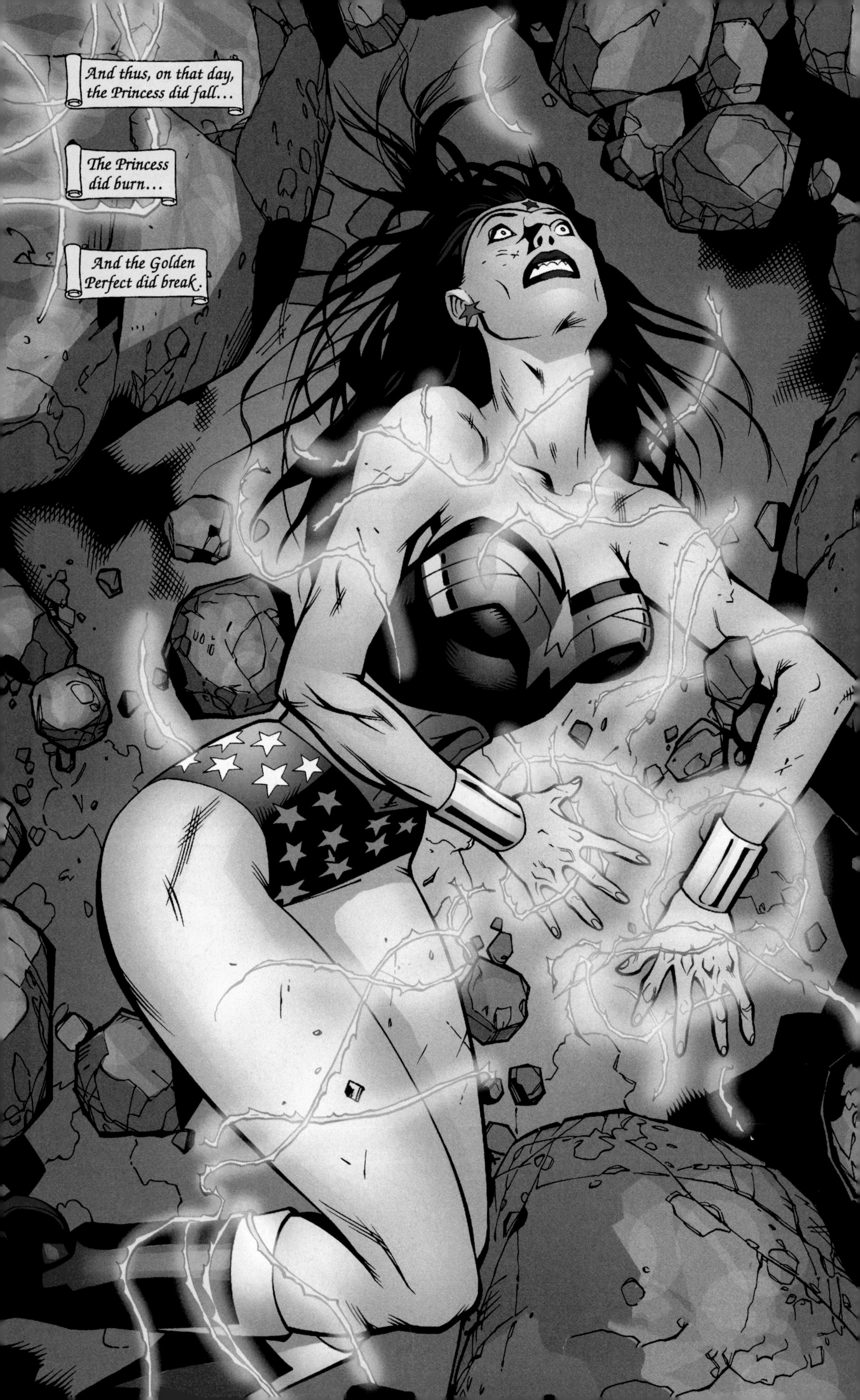

And thus, on that day, the Princess did fall...
The Princess did burn...
And the Golden Perfect did break.

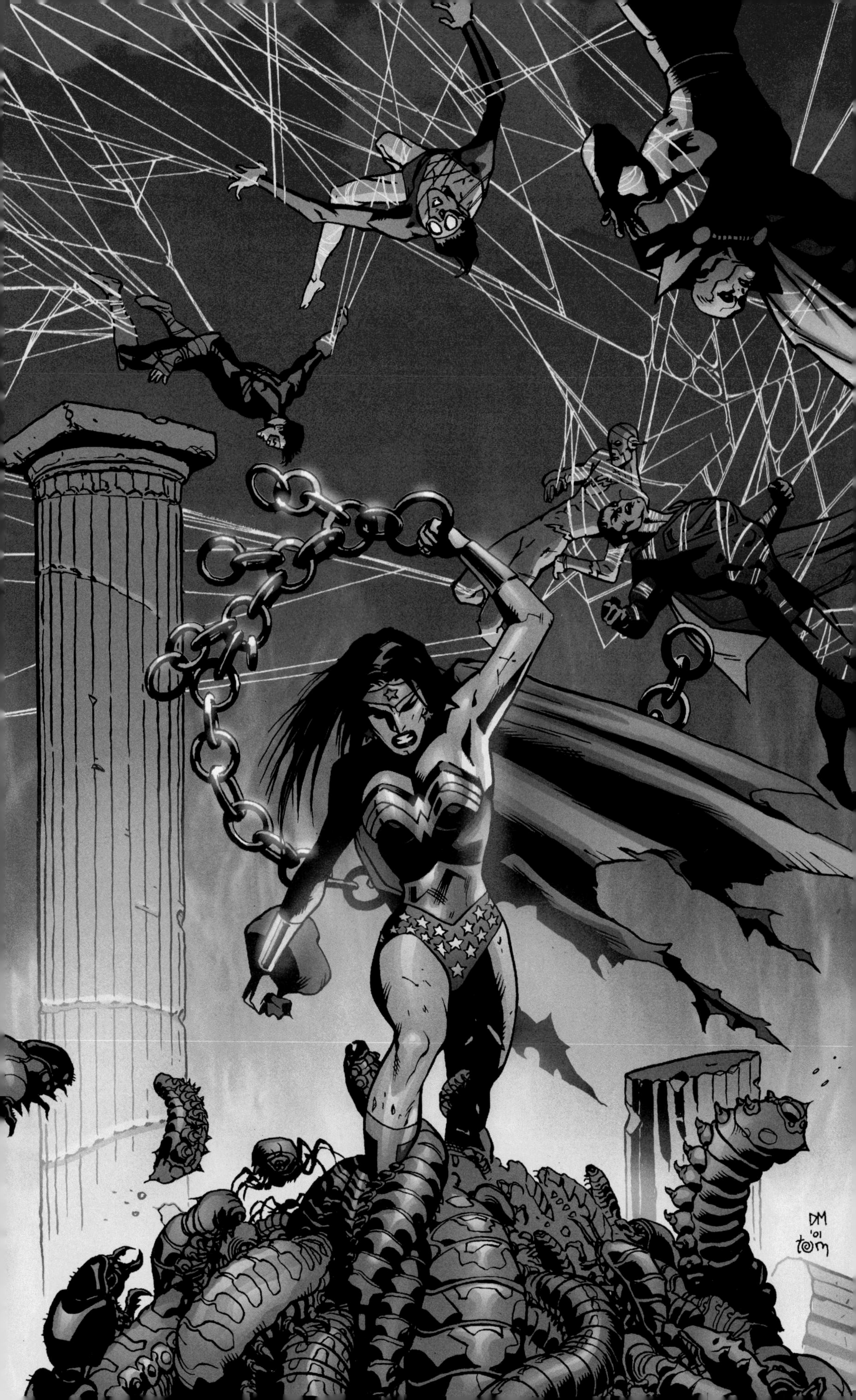
DM
'01
tom

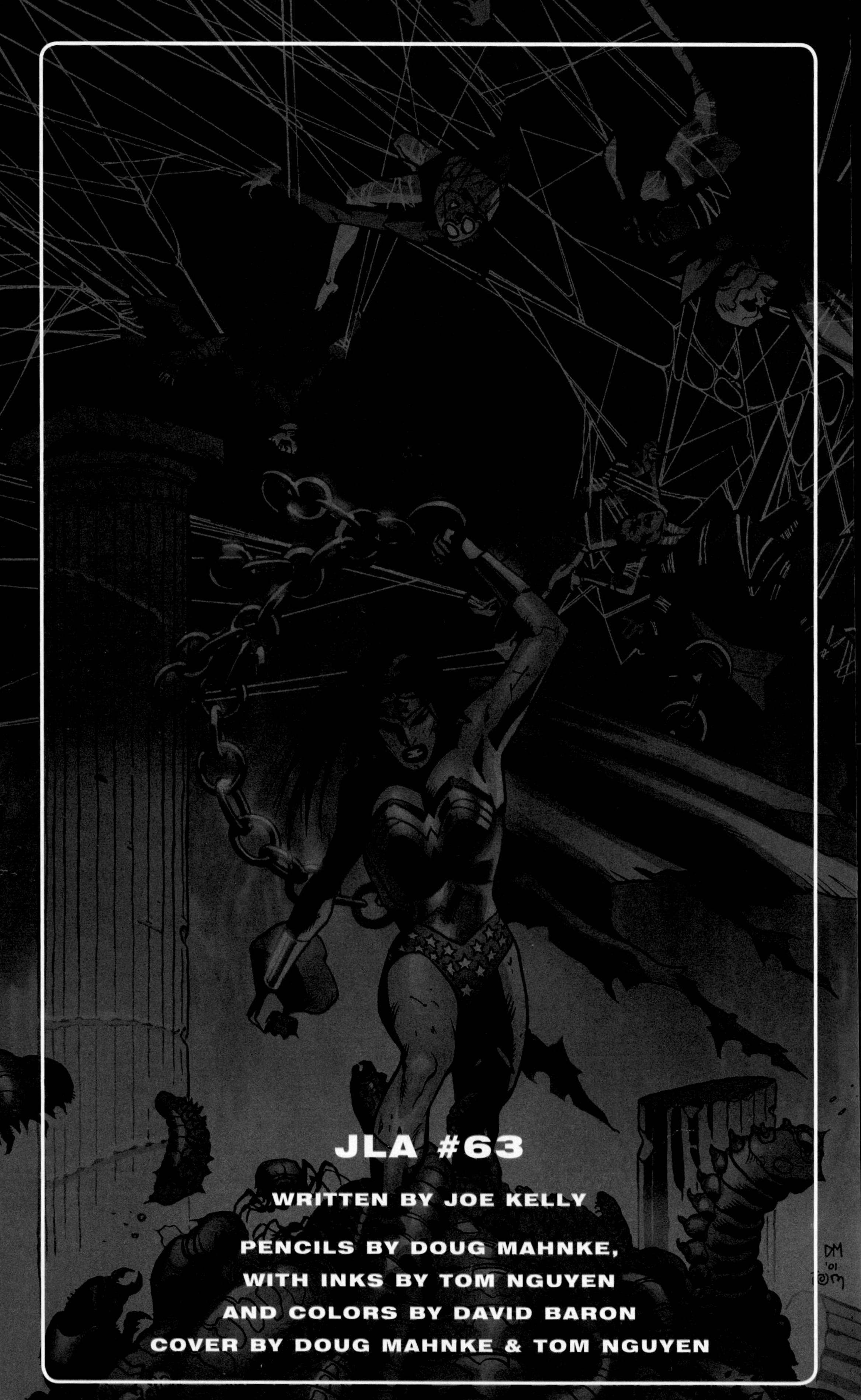

JLA #63

WRITTEN BY JOE KELLY

PENCILS BY DOUG MAHNKE,
WITH INKS BY TOM NGUYEN
AND COLORS BY DAVID BARON
COVER BY DOUG MAHNKE & TOM NGUYEN

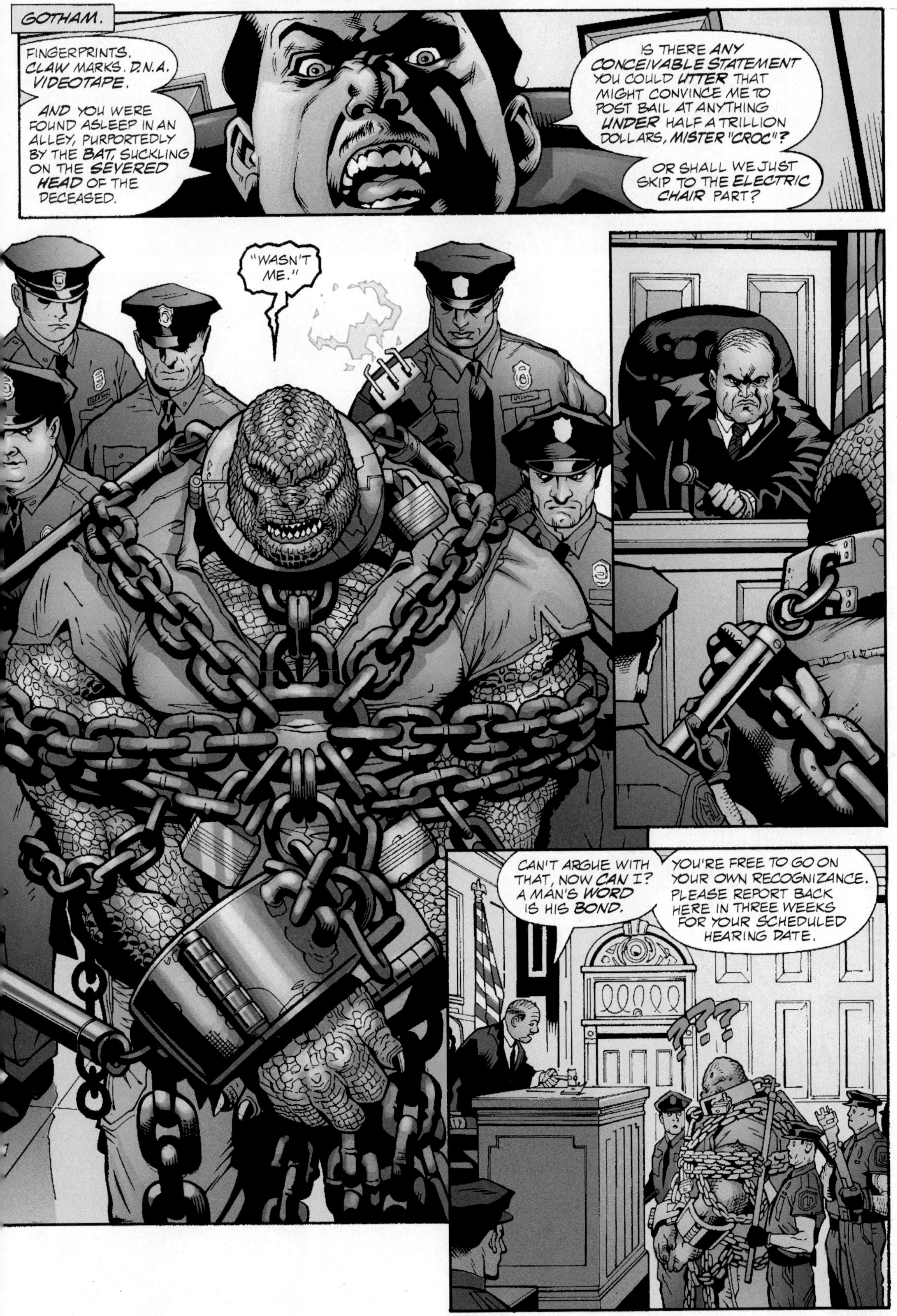
GOTHAM.
FINGERPRINTS. CLAW MARKS. D.N.A. VIDEOTAPE.
AND YOU WERE FOUND ASLEEP IN AN ALLEY, PURPORTEDLY BY THE BAT, SUCKLING ON THE SEVERED HEAD OF THE DECEASED.
IS THERE ANY CONCEIVABLE STATEMENT YOU COULD UTTER THAT MIGHT CONVINCE ME TO POST BAIL AT ANYTHING UNDER HALF A TRILLION DOLLARS, MISTER "CROC"?
OR SHALL WE JUST SKIP TO THE ELECTRIC CHAIR PART?
"WASN'T ME."
CAN'T ARGUE WITH THAT, NOW CAN I? A MAN'S WORD IS HIS BOND.
YOU'RE FREE TO GO ON YOUR OWN RECOGNIZANCE. PLEASE REPORT BACK HERE IN THREE WEEKS FOR YOUR SCHEDULED HEARING DATE.

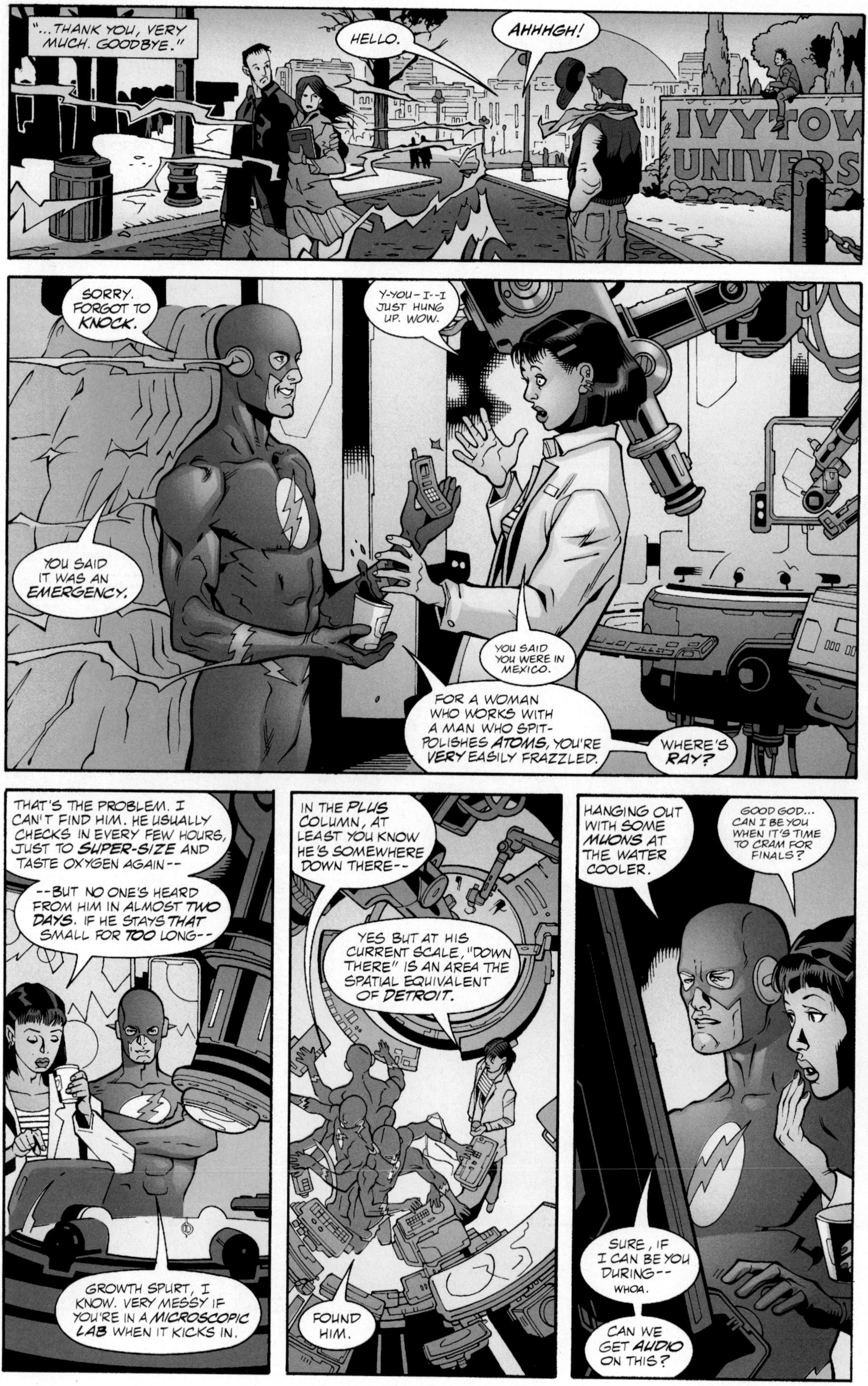
"...THANK YOU, VERY MUCH. GOODBYE."
HELLO.
AHHHGH!
IVYTOW
UNIVERS
SORRY. FORGOT TO KNOCK.
Y-YOU-I--I JUST HUNG UP. WOW.
YOU SAID IT WAS AN EMERGENCY.
YOU SAID YOU WERE IN MEXICO.
FOR A WOMAN WHO WORKS WITH A MAN WHO SPIT-POLISHES ATOMS, YOU'RE VERY EASILY FRAZZLED.
WHERE'S RAY?
THAT'S THE PROBLEM. I CAN'T FIND HIM. HE USUALLY CHECKS IN EVERY FEW HOURS, JUST TO SUPER-SIZE AND TASTE OXYGEN AGAIN--
--BUT NO ONE'S HEARD FROM HIM IN ALMOST TWO DAYS. IF HE STAYS THAT SMALL FOR TOO LONG--
GROWTH SPURT, I KNOW. VERY MESSY IF YOU'RE IN A MICROSCOPIC LAB WHEN IT KICKS IN.
IN THE PLUS COLUMN, AT LEAST YOU KNOW HE'S SOMEWHERE DOWN THERE--
YES BUT AT HIS CURRENT SCALE, "DOWN THERE" IS AN AREA THE SPATIAL EQUIVALENT OF DETROIT.
FOUND HIM.
HANGING OUT WITH SOME MUONS AT THE WATER COOLER.
GOOD GOD... CAN I BE YOU WHEN IT'S TIME TO CRAM FOR FINALS?
SURE, IF I CAN BE YOU DURING--
WHOA.
CAN WE GET AUDIO ON THIS?

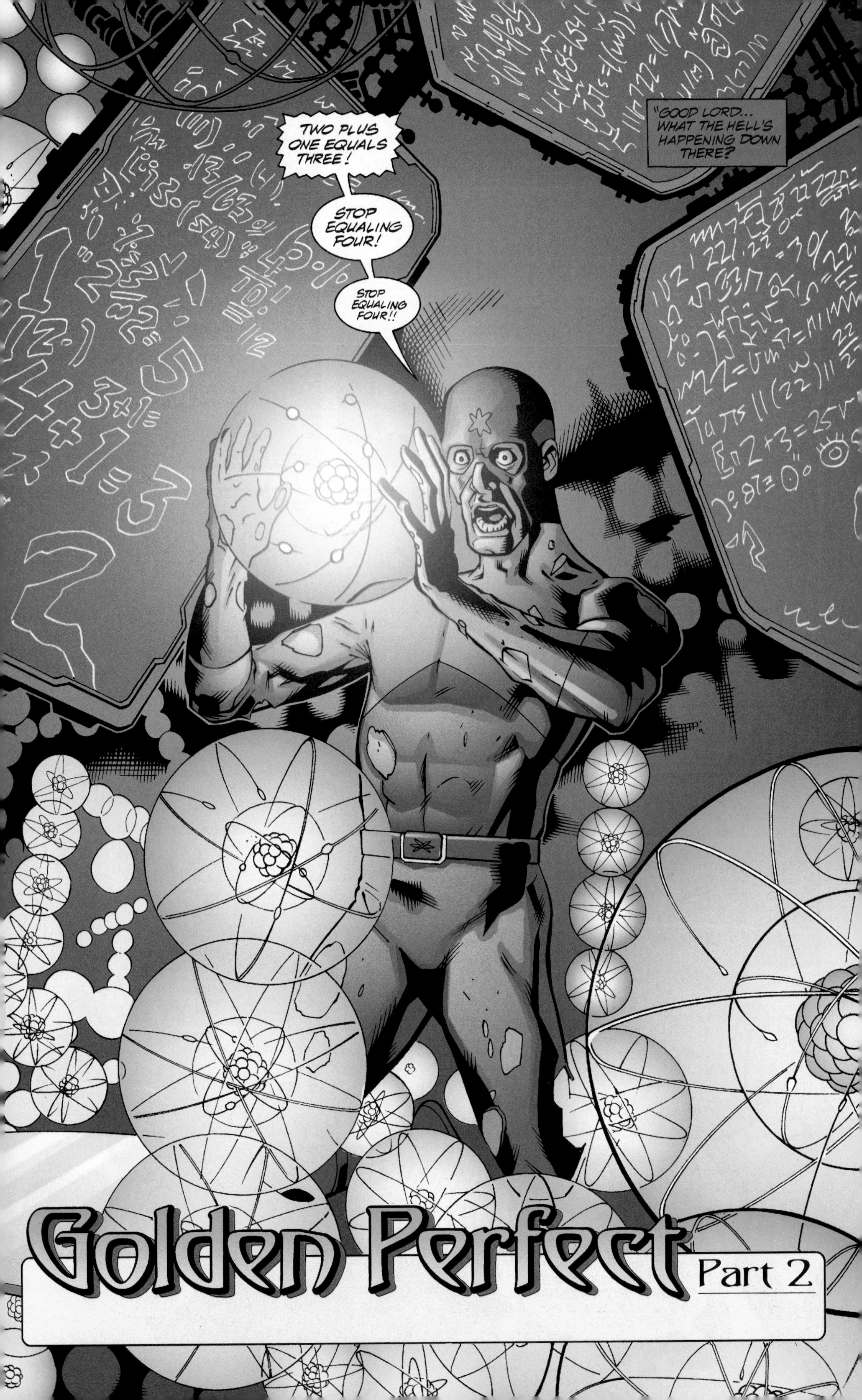
TWO PLUS ONE EQUALS THREE!
STOP EQUALING FOUR!
STOP EQUALING FOUR!!
"GOOD LORD... WHAT THE HELL'S HAPPENING DOWN THERE?
Golden Perfect Part 2

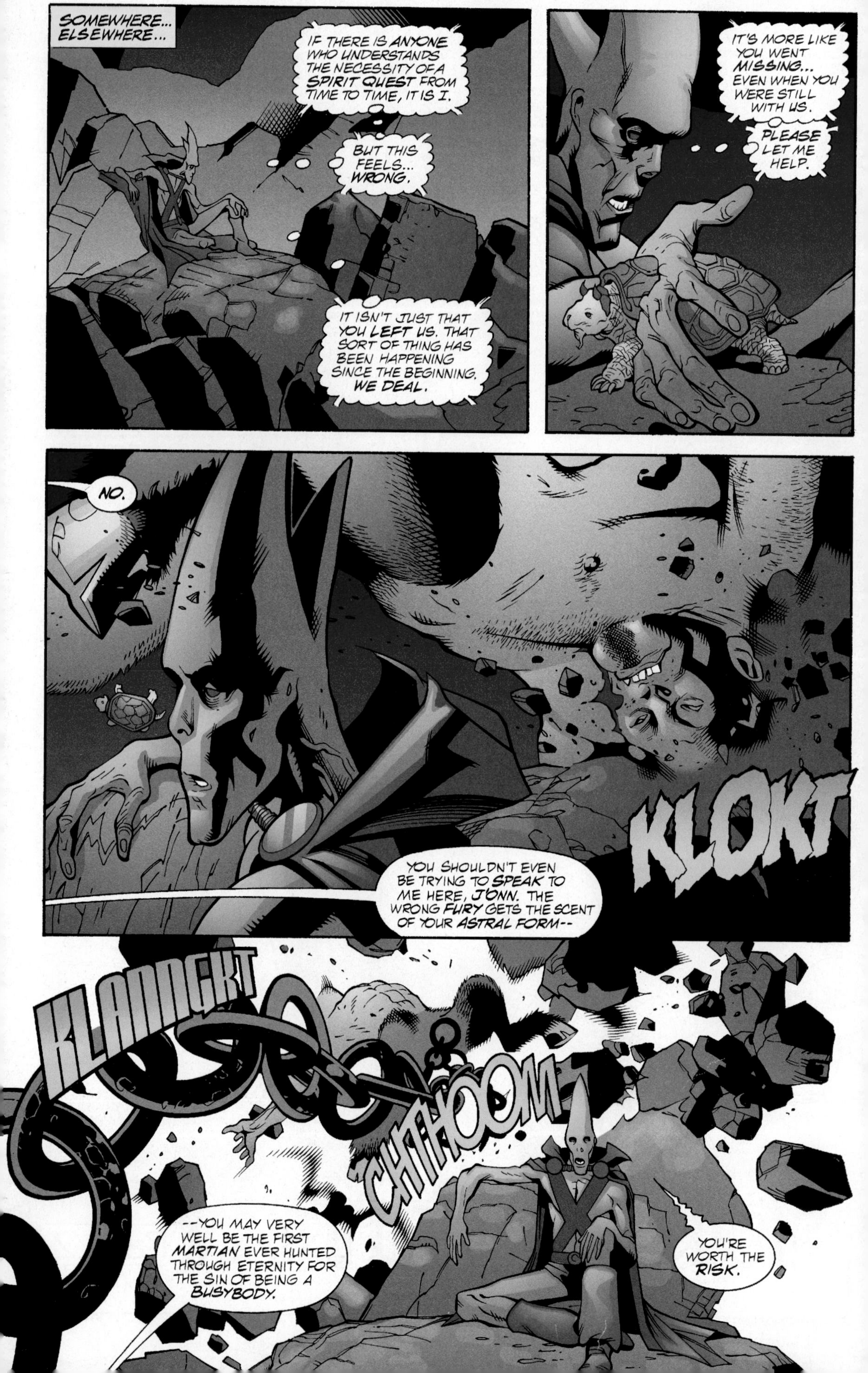
SOMEWHERE... ELSEWHERE...
IF THERE IS ANYONE WHO UNDERSTANDS THE NECESSITY OF A SPIRIT QUEST FROM TIME TO TIME, IT IS I.
BUT THIS FEELS... WRONG.
IT ISN'T JUST THAT YOU LEFT US. THAT SORT OF THING HAS BEEN HAPPENING SINCE THE BEGINNING. WE DEAL.
IT'S MORE LIKE YOU WENT MISSING... EVEN WHEN YOU WERE STILL WITH US.
PLEASE LET ME HELP.
NO.
KLOKT
YOU SHOULDN'T EVEN BE TRYING TO SPEAK TO ME HERE, J'ONN. THE WRONG FURY GETS THE SCENT OF YOUR ASTRAL FORM--
KLANNGKT
CHTHOOM
--YOU MAY VERY WELL BE THE FIRST MARTIAN EVER HUNTED THROUGH ETERNITY FOR THE SIN OF BEING A BUSYBODY.
YOU'RE WORTH THE RISK.

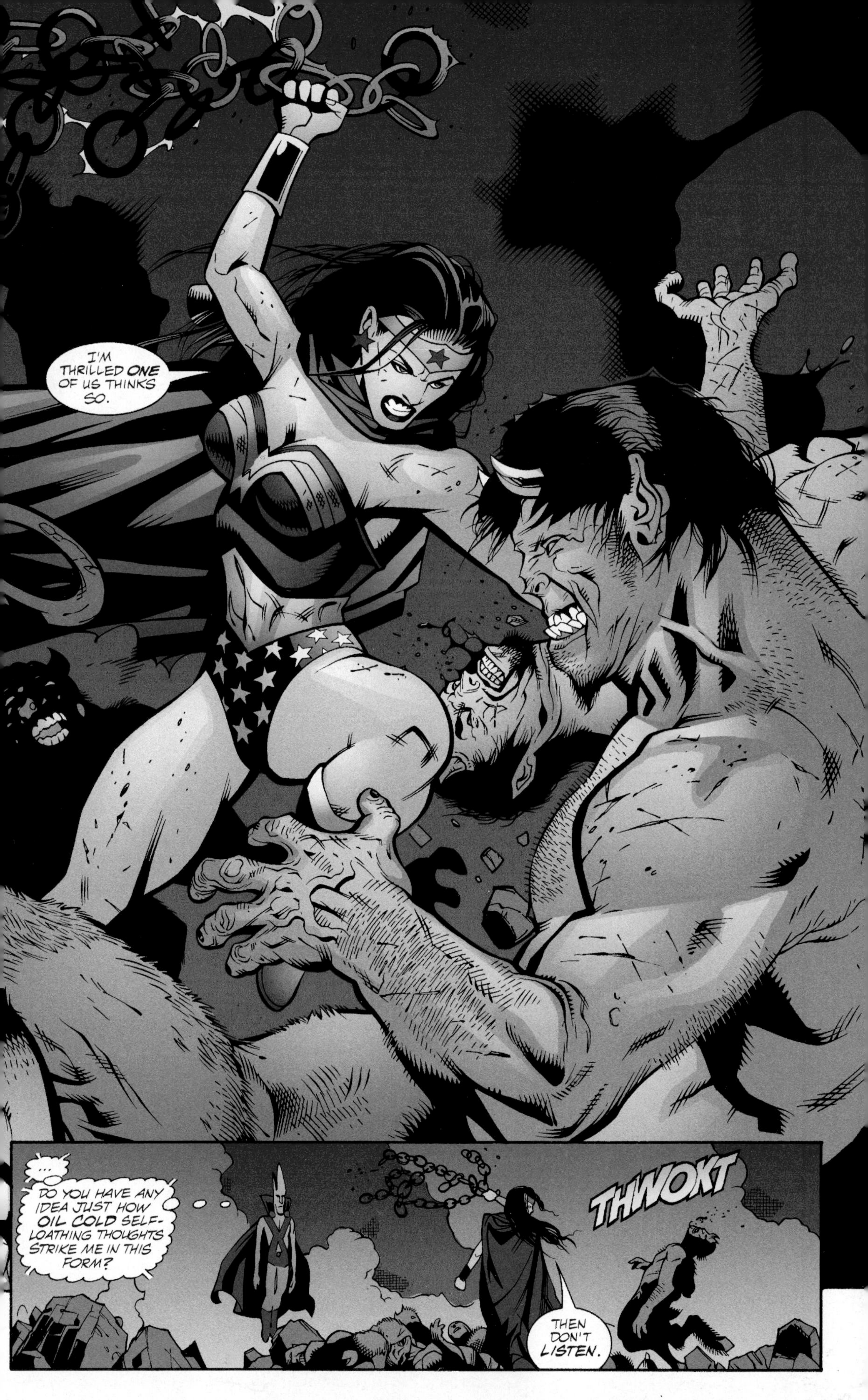
I'M THRILLED ONE OF US THINKS SO.
...
DO YOU HAVE ANY IDEA JUST HOW OIL COLD SELF-LOATHING THOUGHTS STRIKE ME IN THIS FORM?
THWOKT
THEN DON'T LISTEN.

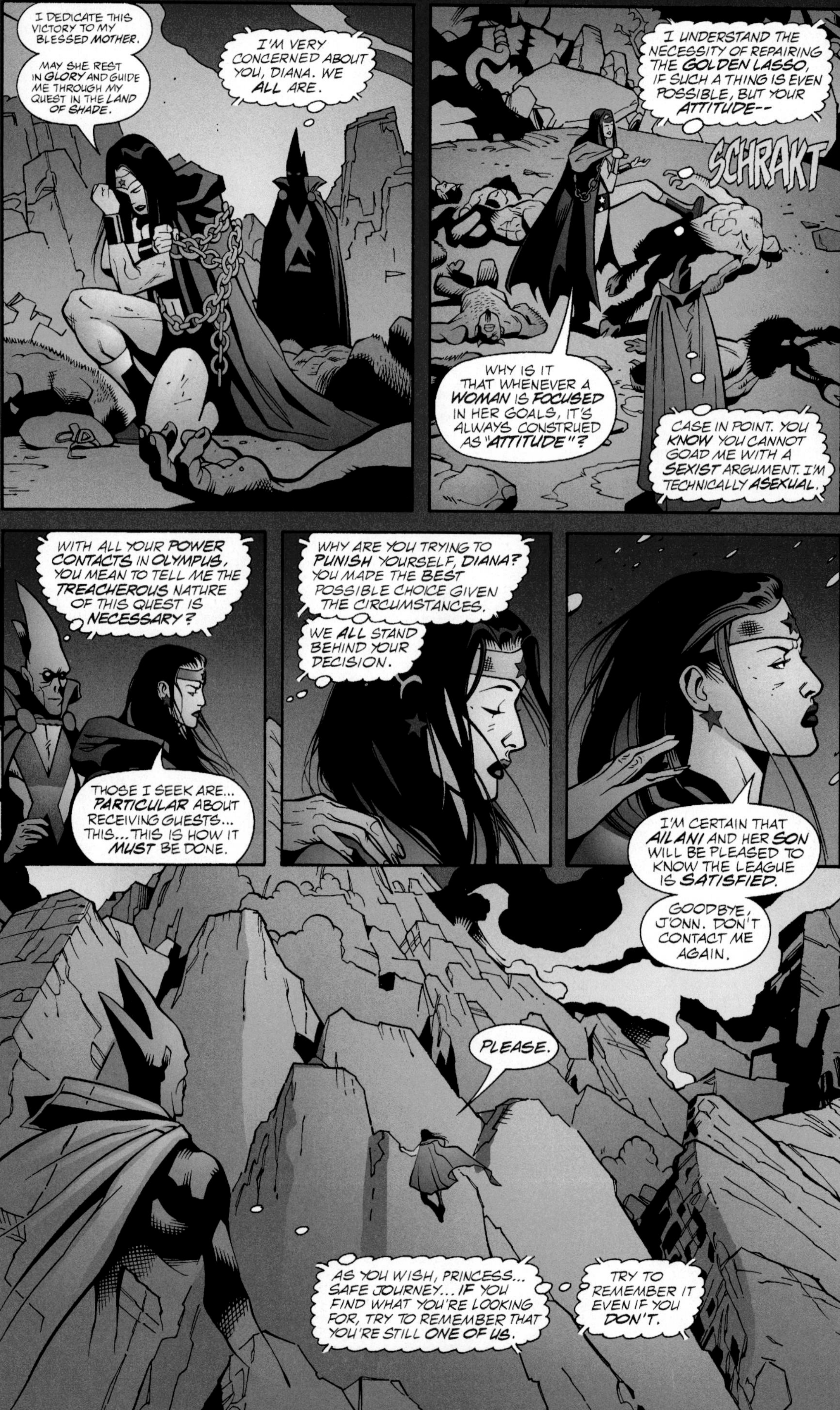
I DEDICATE THIS VICTORY TO MY BLESSED MOTHER.
MAY SHE REST IN GLORY AND GUIDE ME THROUGH MY QUEST IN THE LAND OF SHADE.
I'M VERY CONCERNED ABOUT YOU, DIANA. WE ALL ARE.
I UNDERSTAND THE NECESSITY OF REPAIRING THE GOLDEN LASSO, IF SUCH A THING IS EVEN POSSIBLE, BUT YOUR ATTITUDE--
SCHRAKT
WHY IS IT THAT WHENEVER A WOMAN IS FOCUSED IN HER GOALS, IT'S ALWAYS CONSTRUED AS "ATTITUDE"?
CASE IN POINT. YOU KNOW YOU CANNOT GOAD ME WITH A SEXIST ARGUMENT. I'M TECHNICALLY ASEXUAL.
WITH ALL YOUR POWER CONTACTS IN OLYMPUS, YOU MEAN TO TELL ME THE TREACHEROUS NATURE OF THIS QUEST IS NECESSARY?
THOSE I SEEK ARE... PARTICULAR ABOUT RECEIVING GUESTS... THIS... THIS IS HOW IT MUST BE DONE.
WHY ARE YOU TRYING TO PUNISH YOURSELF, DIANA? YOU MADE THE BEST POSSIBLE CHOICE GIVEN THE CIRCUMSTANCES.
WE ALL STAND BEHIND YOUR DECISION.
I'M CERTAIN THAT AILANI AND HER SON WILL BE PLEASED TO KNOW THE LEAGUE IS SATISFIED.
GOODBYE, J'ONN. DON'T CONTACT ME AGAIN.
PLEASE.
AS YOU WISH, PRINCESS... SAFE JOURNEY... IF YOU FIND WHAT YOU'RE LOOKING FOR, TRY TO REMEMBER THAT YOU'RE STILL ONE OF US.
TRY TO REMEMBER IT EVEN IF YOU DON'T.

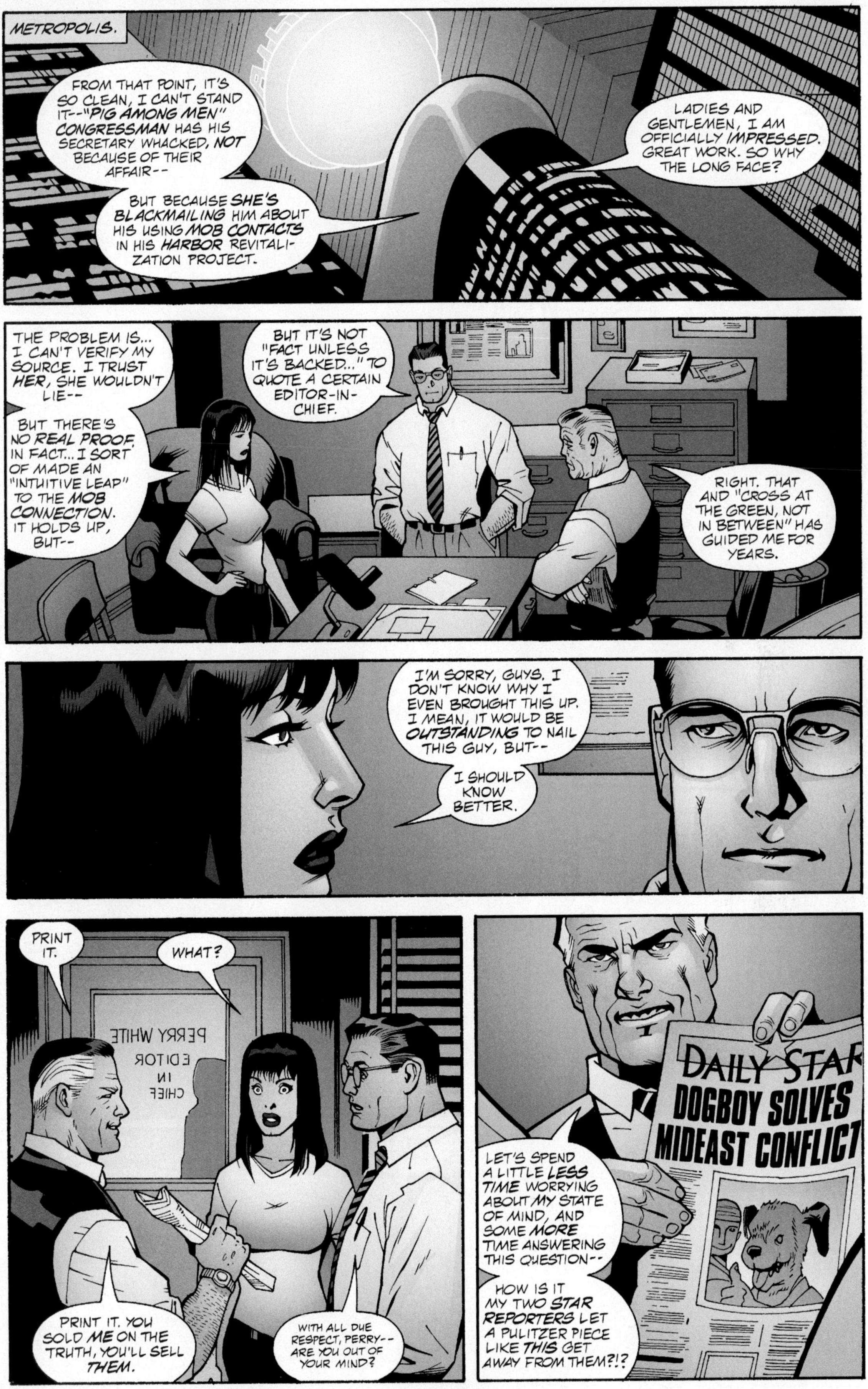
METROPOLIS.
FROM THAT POINT, IT'S SO CLEAN, I CAN'T STAND IT--"PIG AMONG MEN" CONGRESSMAN HAS HIS SECRETARY WHACKED, NOT BECAUSE OF THEIR AFFAIR--
BUT BECAUSE SHE'S BLACKMAILING HIM ABOUT HIS USING MOB CONTACTS IN HIS HARBOR REVITALIZATION PROJECT.
LADIES AND GENTLEMEN, I AM OFFICIALLY IMPRESSED. GREAT WORK. SO WHY THE LONG FACE?
THE PROBLEM IS... I CAN'T VERIFY MY SOURCE. I TRUST HER, SHE WOULDN'T LIE--
BUT THERE'S NO REAL PROOF. IN FACT... I SORT OF MADE AN "INTUITIVE LEAP" TO THE MOB CONNECTION. IT HOLDS UP, BUT--
BUT IT'S NOT "FACT UNLESS IT'S BACKED..." TO QUOTE A CERTAIN EDITOR-IN-CHIEF.
RIGHT. THAT AND "CROSS AT THE GREEN, NOT IN BETWEEN" HAS GUIDED ME FOR YEARS.
I'M SORRY, GUYS. I DON'T KNOW WHY I EVEN BROUGHT THIS UP. I MEAN, IT WOULD BE OUTSTANDING TO NAIL THIS GUY, BUT--
I SHOULD KNOW BETTER.
PRINT IT.
WHAT?
PERRY WHITE EDITOR IN CHIEF
PRINT IT. YOU SOLD ME ON THE TRUTH, YOU'LL SELL THEM.
WITH ALL DUE RESPECT, PERRY--ARE YOU OUT OF YOUR MIND?
DAILY STAR
DOGBOY SOLVES MIDEAST CONFLICT
LET'S SPEND A LITTLE LESS TIME WORRYING ABOUT MY STATE OF MIND, AND SOME MORE TIME ANSWERING THIS QUESTION--
HOW IS IT MY TWO STAR REPORTERS LET A PULITZER PIECE LIKE THIS GET AWAY FROM THEM?!?

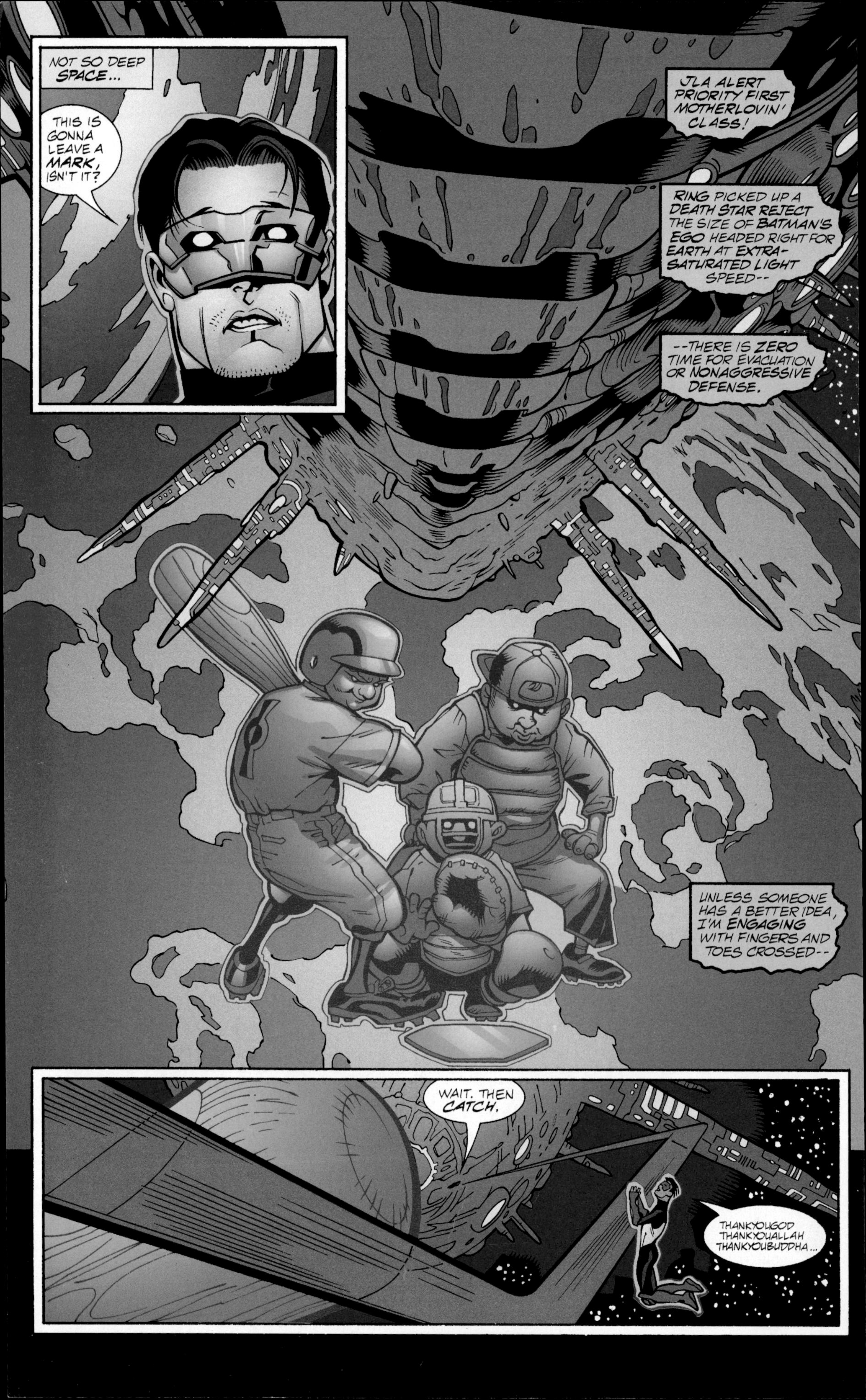
NOT SO DEEP SPACE...
THIS IS GONNA LEAVE A MARK, ISN'T IT?
JLA ALERT PRIORITY FIRST MOTHERLOVIN' CLASS!
RING PICKED UP A DEATH STAR REJECT THE SIZE OF BATMAN'S EGO HEADED RIGHT FOR EARTH AT EXTRA-SATURATED LIGHT SPEED--
--THERE IS ZERO TIME FOR EVACUATION OR NONAGGRESSIVE DEFENSE.
UNLESS SOMEONE HAS A BETTER IDEA, I'M ENGAGING WITH FINGERS AND TOES CROSSED--
WAIT. THEN CATCH.
THANKYOUGOD THANKYOUALLAH THANKYOUBUDDHA...

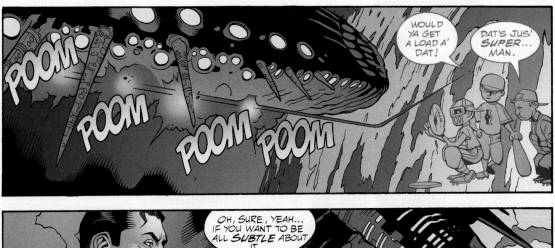

WOULD YA GET A LOAD A' DAT!

DAT'S JUS' *SUPER*... MAN.

POOM POOM POOM POOM

OH, SURE, YEAH... IF YOU WANT TO BE ALL *SUBTLE* ABOUT IT.

SORRY. I COULD SEE THERE WAS *NO LIFE* ABOARD, SO I WENT FOR ANYTHING THAT *LOOKED* LIKE AN *ENGINE.*

MM-HMM. I WAS GONNA DO THAT NEXT.

DO ME ONE BETTER: WHIP UP SOMETHING TO ASK THE *SHIP* WHY IT WAS ABOUT TO CRASH INTO OUR *PLANET.*

DONE AND--*WHOA!* FUNNY HOW *CHATTY* A MONOLITH GETS WHEN YOU TEAR OUT ITS GUTS--

HE LIKES LONG WALKS ON THE BEACH AND WATCHING "LOVE CRUISE" WHEN HE ISN'T FULFILLING HIS LIFE'S MISSION--

A *DEEP SPACE PROBE* LAUNCHED OVER *TEN MILLENNIA* AGO TO CHART THE *CENTER* OF *THE UNIVERSE.*

CORRECT ME IF I'M WRONG, BUT ISN'T THAT IN THE EXACT *OPPOSITE* DIRECTION?

CORRECTAMUNDO, MISTER *SAGAN.* LET'S SEE... HERBIE WENT OFF COURSE... TWO WEEKS AGO...

WHEN THE *EARTH* SUDDENLY BECAME THE *CENTER* OF THE *UNIVERSE.*

YOU MEAN... WHEN IT WAS REPROGRAMMED TO READ--?

NO... I MEAN... TWO WEEKS AGO, FROM THE SHIP'S PERSPECTIVE, THE *EARTH* BECAME THE *CENTER* OF THE UNIVERSE.

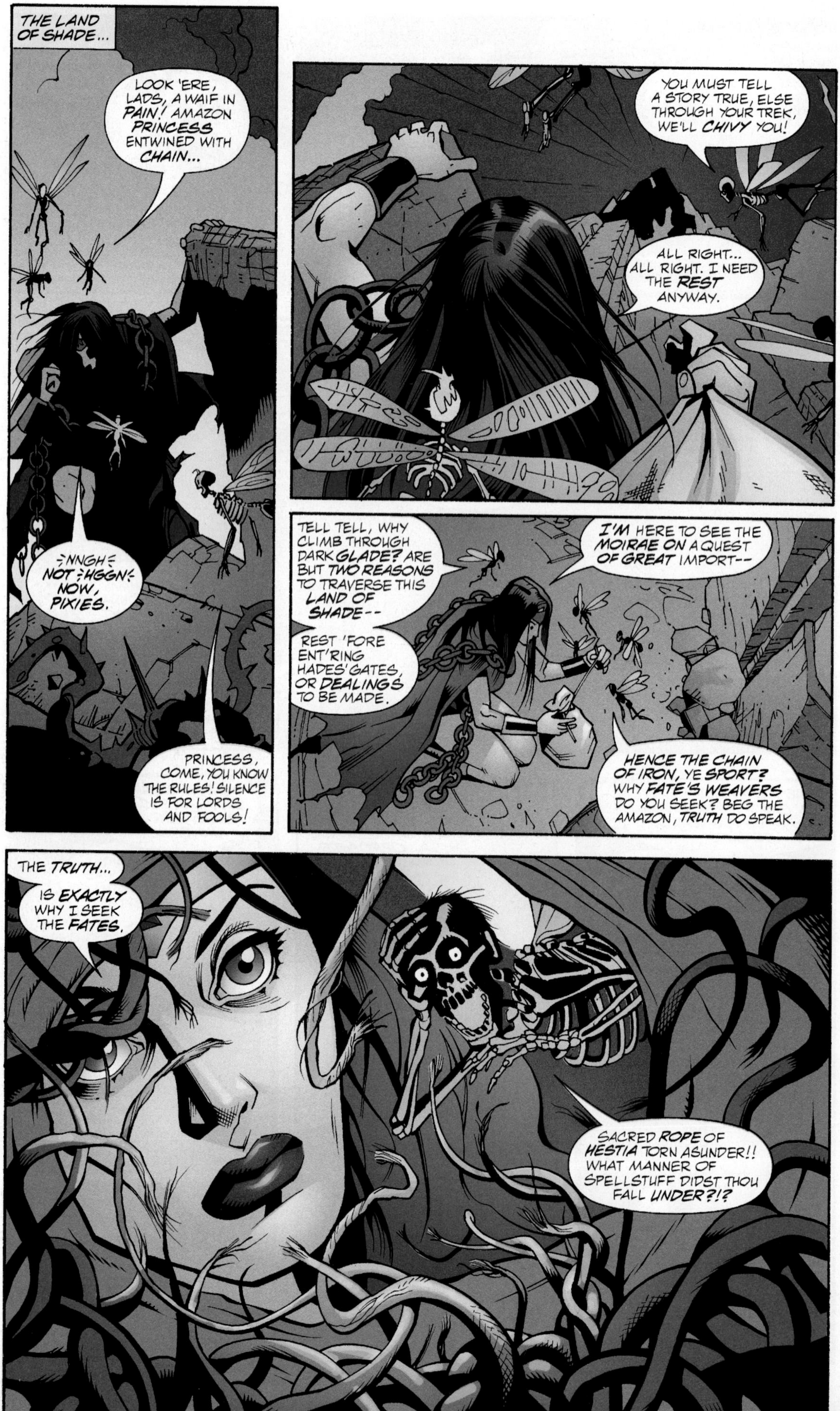
THE LAND OF SHADE...
LOOK 'ERE, LADS, A WAIF IN PAIN! AMAZON PRINCESS ENTWINED WITH CHAIN...
YOU MUST TELL A STORY TRUE, ELSE THROUGH YOUR TREK, WE'LL CHIVY YOU!
ALL RIGHT... ALL RIGHT. I NEED THE REST ANYWAY.
=NNGH= NOT =HGGN= NOW, PIXIES.
PRINCESS, COME, YOU KNOW THE RULES! SILENCE IS FOR LORDS AND FOOLS!
TELL TELL, WHY CLIMB THROUGH DARK GLADE? ARE BUT TWO REASONS TO TRAVERSE THIS LAND OF SHADE--
REST 'FORE ENT'RING HADES' GATES, OR DEALINGS TO BE MADE.
I'M HERE TO SEE THE MOIRAE ON A QUEST OF GREAT IMPORT--
HENCE THE CHAIN OF IRON, YE SPORT? WHY FATE'S WEAVERS DO YOU SEEK? BEG THE AMAZON, TRUTH DO SPEAK.
THE TRUTH...
IS EXACTLY WHY I SEEK THE FATES.
SACRED ROPE OF HESTIA TORN ASUNDER!! WHAT MANNER OF SPELLSTUFF DIDST THOU FALL UNDER?!?

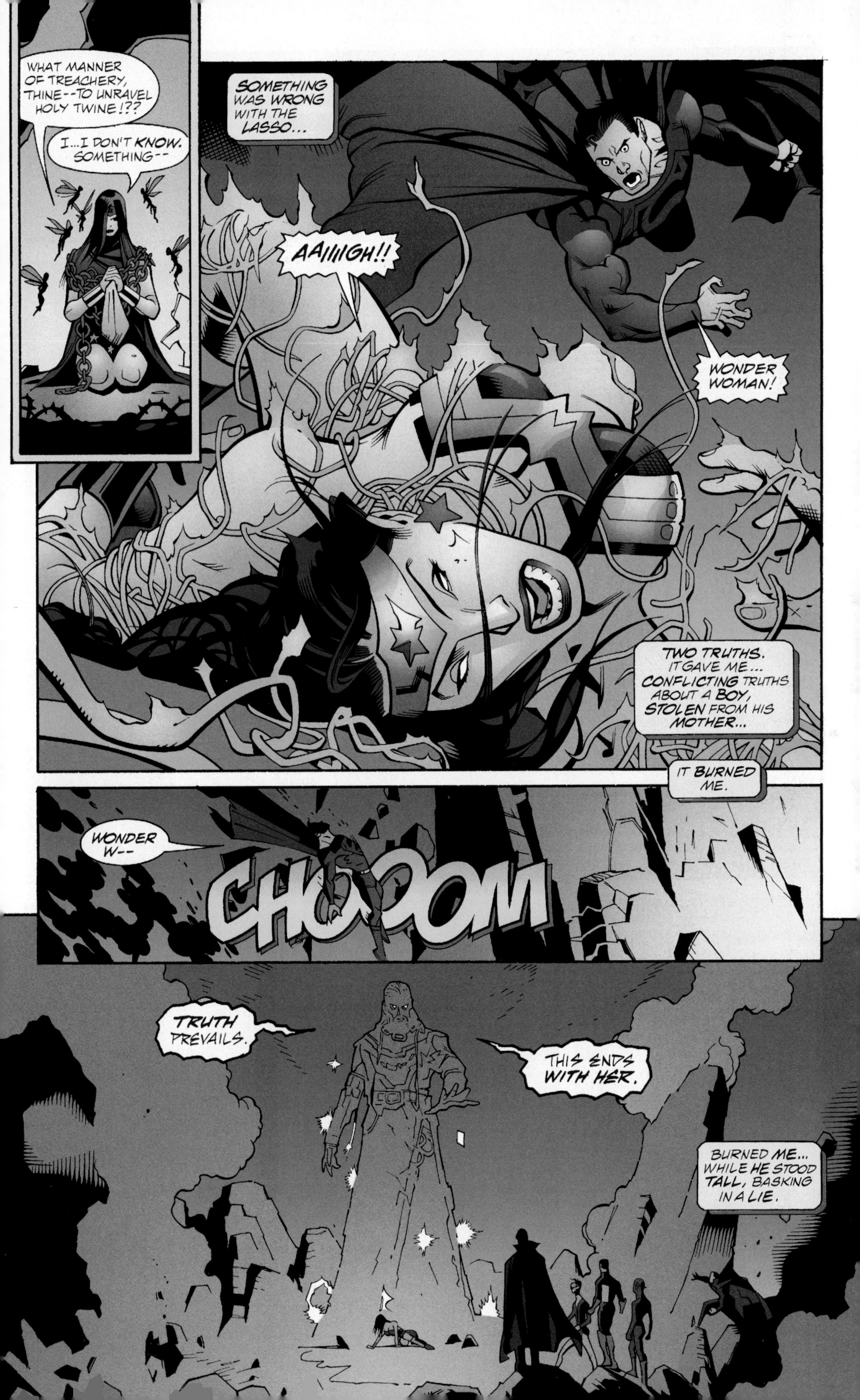
WHAT MANNER OF TREACHERY, THINE--TO UNRAVEL HOLY TWINE!??
I...I DON'T KNOW. SOMETHING--
SOMETHING WAS WRONG WITH THE LASSO...
AAIIIGH!!
WONDER WOMAN!
TWO TRUTHS. IT GAVE ME... CONFLICTING TRUTHS ABOUT A BOY, STOLEN FROM HIS MOTHER...
IT BURNED ME.
WONDER W--
CHOOOM
TRUTH PREVAILS.
THIS ENDS WITH HER.
BURNED ME... WHILE HE STOOD TALL, BASKING IN A LIE.

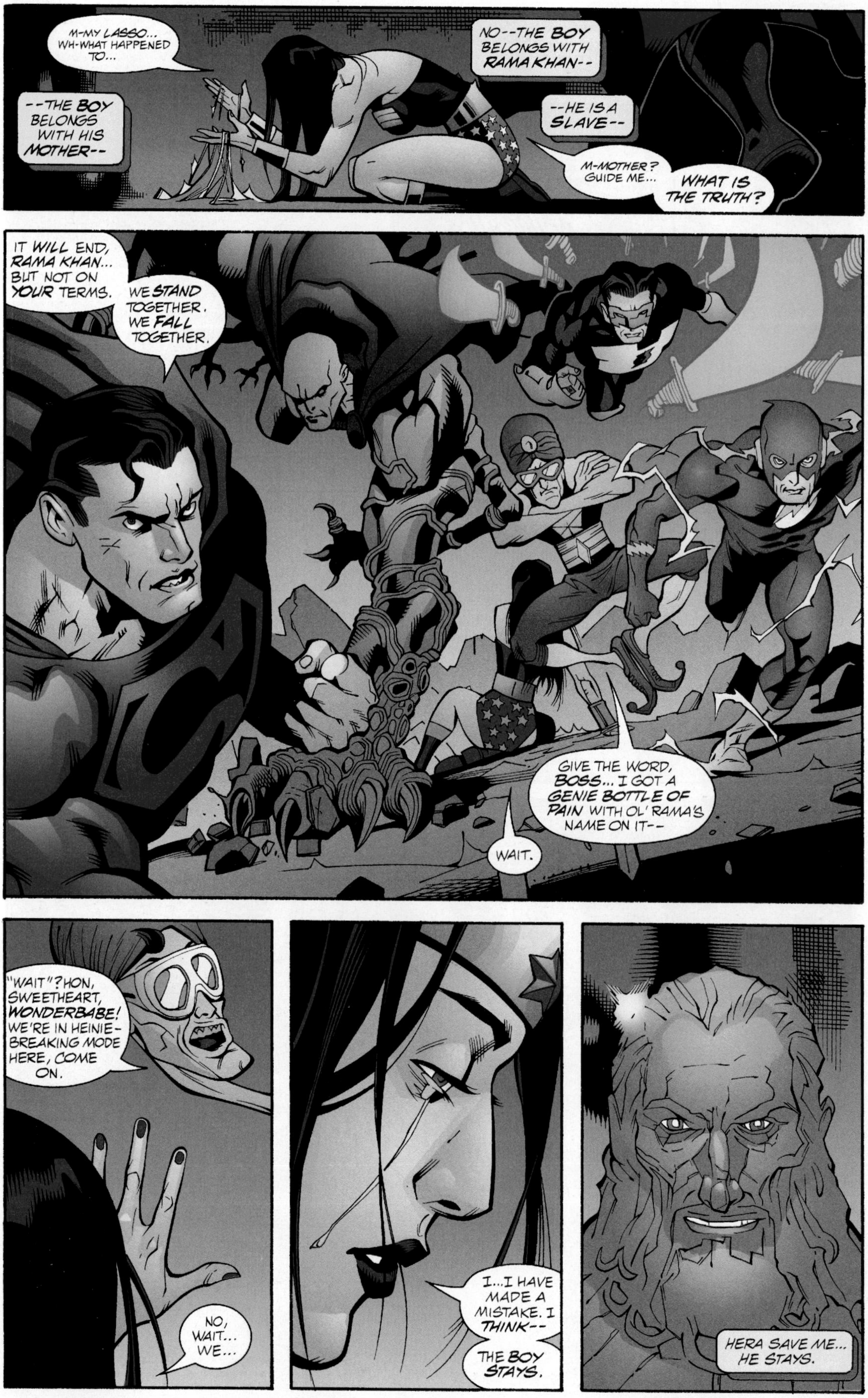
M-MY LASSO... WH-WHAT HAPPENED TO...
NO--THE BOY BELONGS WITH RAMA KHAN--
--THE BOY BELONGS WITH HIS MOTHER--
--HE IS A SLAVE--
M-MOTHER? GUIDE ME...
WHAT IS THE TRUTH?
IT WILL END, RAMA KHAN... BUT NOT ON YOUR TERMS.
WE STAND TOGETHER. WE FALL TOGETHER.
GIVE THE WORD, BOSS... I GOT A GENIE BOTTLE OF PAIN WITH OL' RAMA'S NAME ON IT--
WAIT.
"WAIT"? HON, SWEETHEART, WONDERBABE! WE'RE IN HEINIE-BREAKING MODE HERE, COME ON.
NO, WAIT... WE...
I...I HAVE MADE A MISTAKE. I THINK--
THE BOY STAYS.
HERA SAVE ME... HE STAYS.

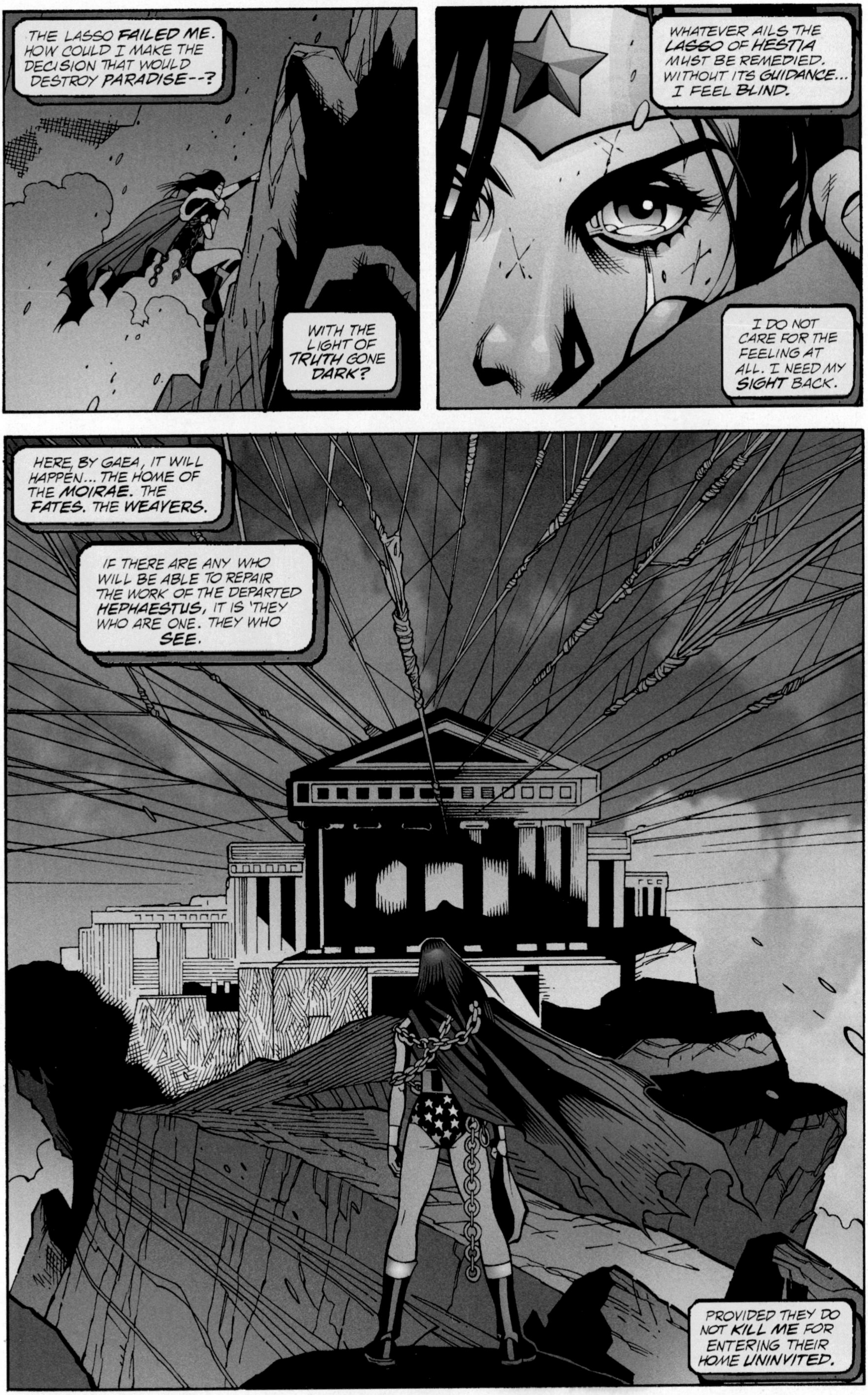
THE LASSO FAILED ME. HOW COULD I MAKE THE DECISION THAT WOULD DESTROY PARADISE--?
WITH THE LIGHT OF TRUTH GONE DARK?
WHATEVER AILS THE LASSO OF HESTIA MUST BE REMEDIED. WITHOUT ITS GUIDANCE... I FEEL BLIND.
I DO NOT CARE FOR THE FEELING AT ALL. I NEED MY SIGHT BACK.
HERE, BY GAEA, IT WILL HAPPEN... THE HOME OF THE MOIRAE. THE FATES. THE WEAVERS.
IF THERE ARE ANY WHO WILL BE ABLE TO REPAIR THE WORK OF THE DEPARTED HEPHAESTUS, IT IS 'THEY WHO ARE ONE. THEY WHO SEE.
PROVIDED THEY DO NOT KILL ME FOR ENTERING THEIR HOME UNINVITED.

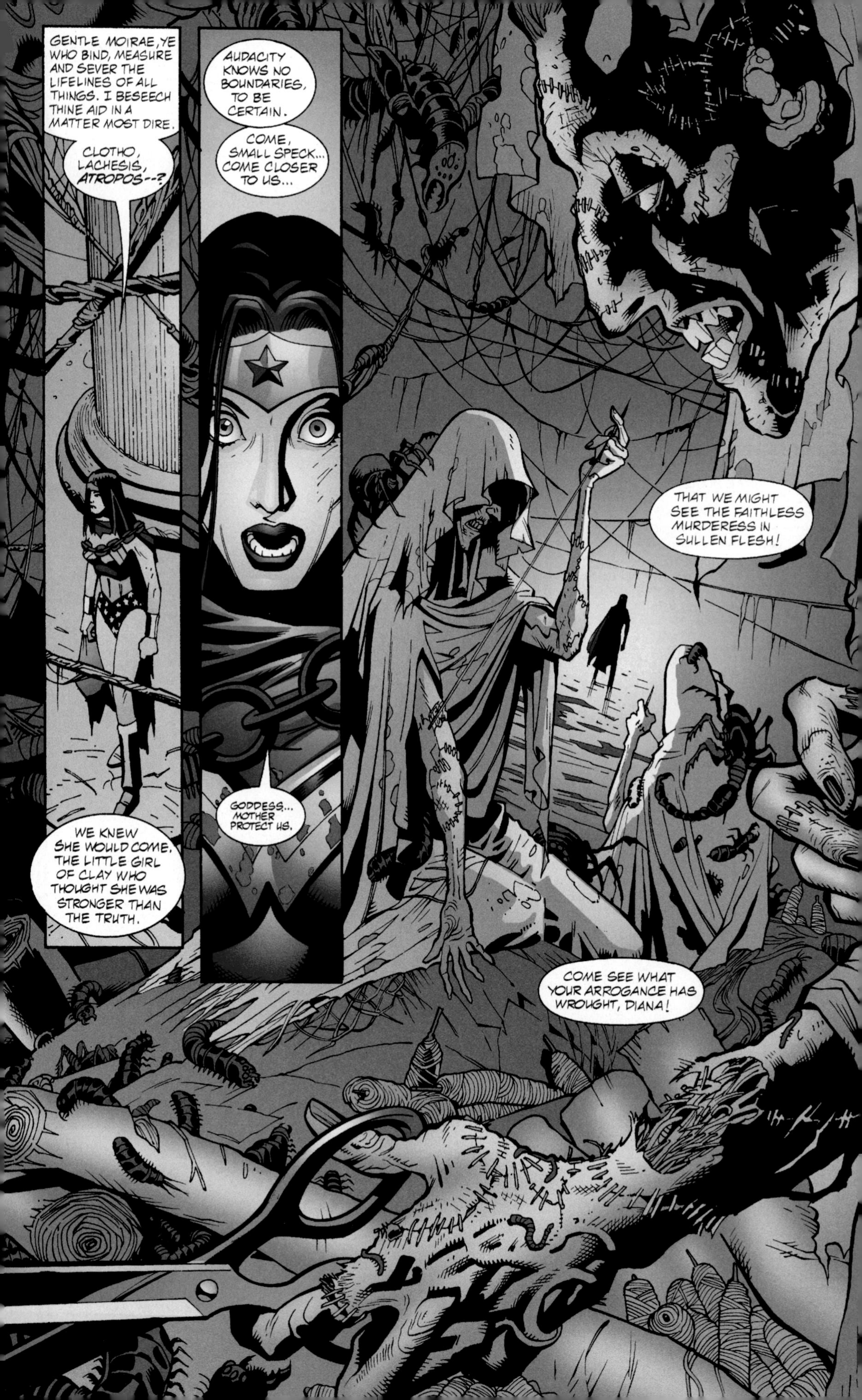
GENTLE MOIRAE, YE WHO BIND, MEASURE AND SEVER THE LIFELINES OF ALL THINGS. I BESEECH THINE AID IN A MATTER MOST DIRE.
CLOTHO, LACHESIS, ATROPOS--?
WE KNEW SHE WOULD COME. THE LITTLE GIRL OF CLAY WHO THOUGHT SHE WAS STRONGER THAN THE TRUTH.
AUDACITY KNOWS NO BOUNDARIES, TO BE CERTAIN.
COME, SMALL SPECK... COME CLOSER TO US...
GODDESS... MOTHER PROTECT US.
THAT WE MIGHT SEE THE FAITHLESS MURDERESS IN SULLEN FLESH!
COME SEE WHAT YOUR ARROGANCE HAS WROUGHT, DIANA!

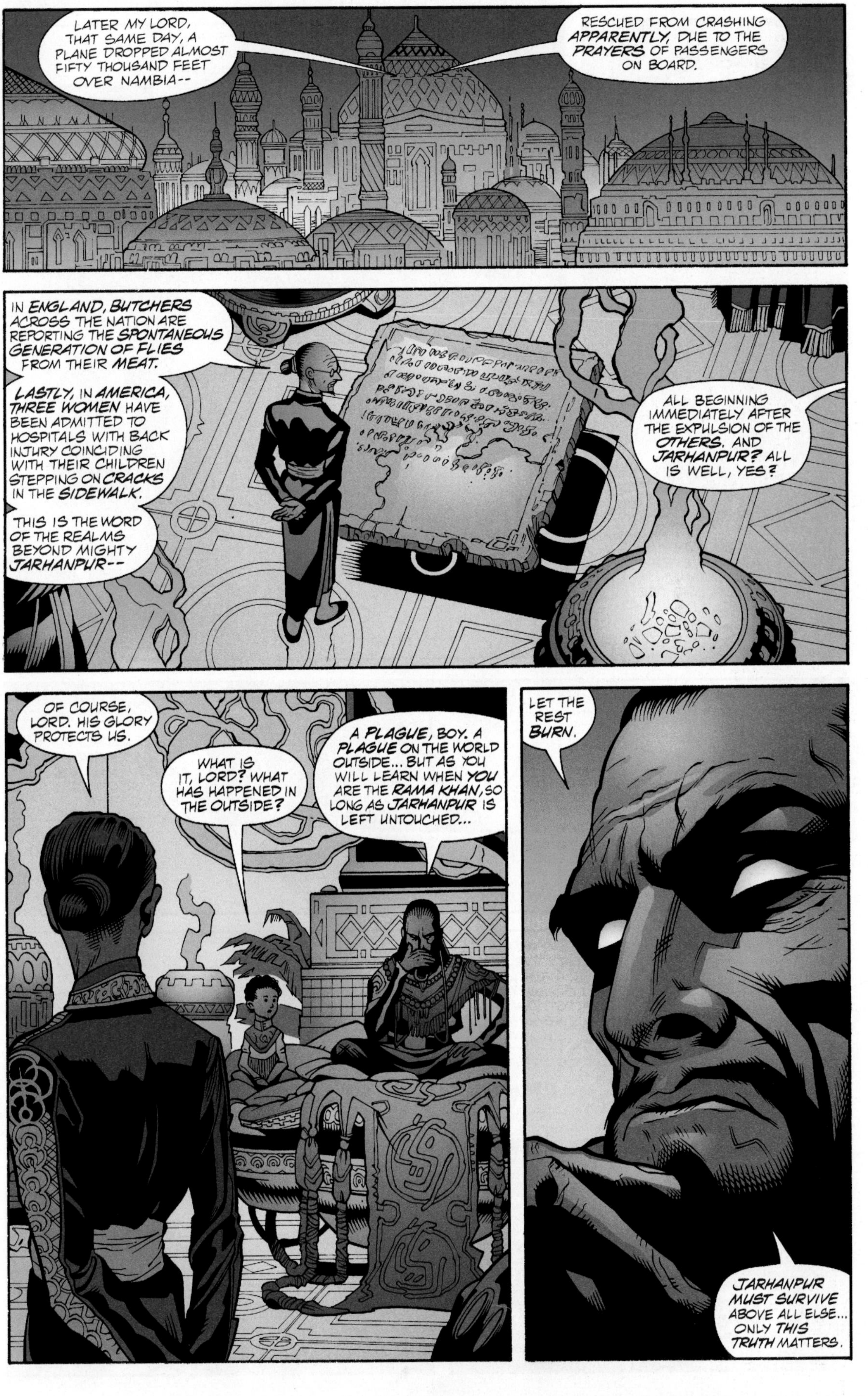
LATER MY LORD, THAT SAME DAY, A PLANE DROPPED ALMOST FIFTY THOUSAND FEET OVER NAMBIA--
RESCUED FROM CRASHING APPARENTLY, DUE TO THE PRAYERS OF PASSENGERS ON BOARD.
IN ENGLAND, BUTCHERS ACROSS THE NATION ARE REPORTING THE SPONTANEOUS GENERATION OF FLIES FROM THEIR MEAT.
LASTLY, IN AMERICA, THREE WOMEN HAVE BEEN ADMITTED TO HOSPITALS WITH BACK INJURY COINCIDING WITH THEIR CHILDREN STEPPING ON CRACKS IN THE SIDEWALK.
THIS IS THE WORD OF THE REALMS BEYOND MIGHTY JARHANPUR--
ALL BEGINNING IMMEDIATELY AFTER THE EXPULSION OF THE OTHERS. AND JARHANPUR? ALL IS WELL, YES?
OF COURSE, LORD. HIS GLORY PROTECTS US.
WHAT IS IT, LORD? WHAT HAS HAPPENED IN THE OUTSIDE?
A PLAGUE, BOY. A PLAGUE ON THE WORLD OUTSIDE... BUT AS YOU WILL LEARN WHEN YOU ARE THE RAMA KHAN, SO LONG AS JARHANPUR IS LEFT UNTOUCHED...
LET THE REST BURN.
JARHANPUR MUST SURVIVE ABOVE ALL ELSE... ONLY THIS TRUTH MATTERS.

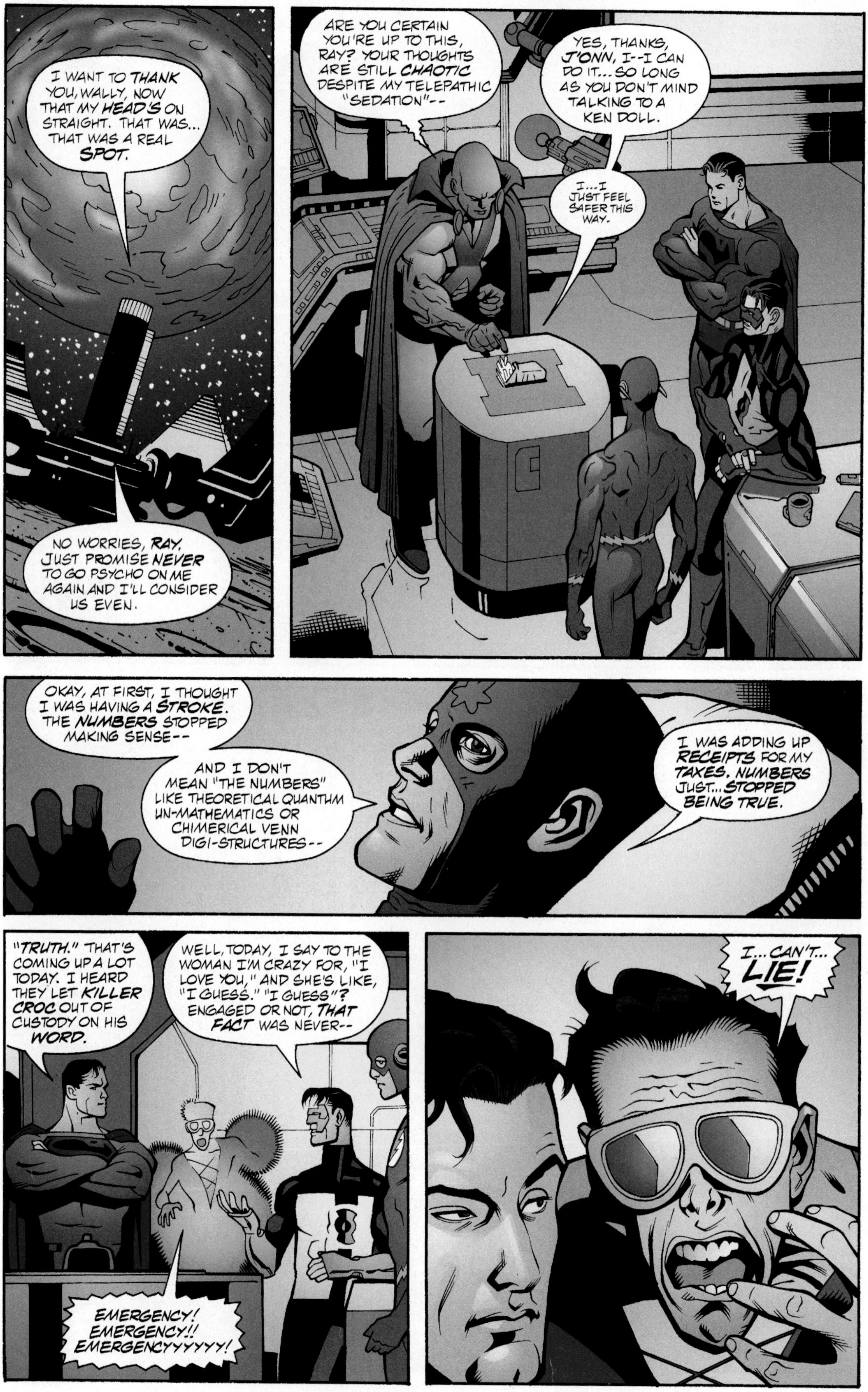
I WANT TO THANK YOU, WALLY, NOW THAT MY HEAD'S ON STRAIGHT. THAT WAS... THAT WAS A REAL SPOT.
NO WORRIES, RAY. JUST PROMISE NEVER TO GO PSYCHO ON ME AGAIN AND I'LL CONSIDER US EVEN.
ARE YOU CERTAIN YOU'RE UP TO THIS, RAY? YOUR THOUGHTS ARE STILL CHAOTIC DESPITE MY TELEPATHIC "SEDATION"--
YES, THANKS, J'ONN, I--I CAN DO IT... SO LONG AS YOU DON'T MIND TALKING TO A KEN DOLL.
I... I JUST FEEL SAFER THIS WAY.
OKAY, AT FIRST, I THOUGHT I WAS HAVING A STROKE. THE NUMBERS STOPPED MAKING SENSE--
AND I DON'T MEAN "THE NUMBERS" LIKE THEORETICAL QUANTUM UN-MATHEMATICS OR CHIMERICAL VENN DIGI-STRUCTURES--
I WAS ADDING UP RECEIPTS FOR MY TAXES. NUMBERS JUST... STOPPED BEING TRUE.
"TRUTH." THAT'S COMING UP A LOT TODAY. I HEARD THEY LET KILLER CROC OUT OF CUSTODY ON HIS WORD.
WELL, TODAY, I SAY TO THE WOMAN I'M CRAZY FOR, "I LOVE YOU," AND SHE'S LIKE, "I GUESS." "I GUESS"? ENGAGED OR NOT, THAT FACT WAS NEVER--
EMERGENCY! EMERGENCY!! EMERGENCYYYYYY!
I... CAN'T... LIE!

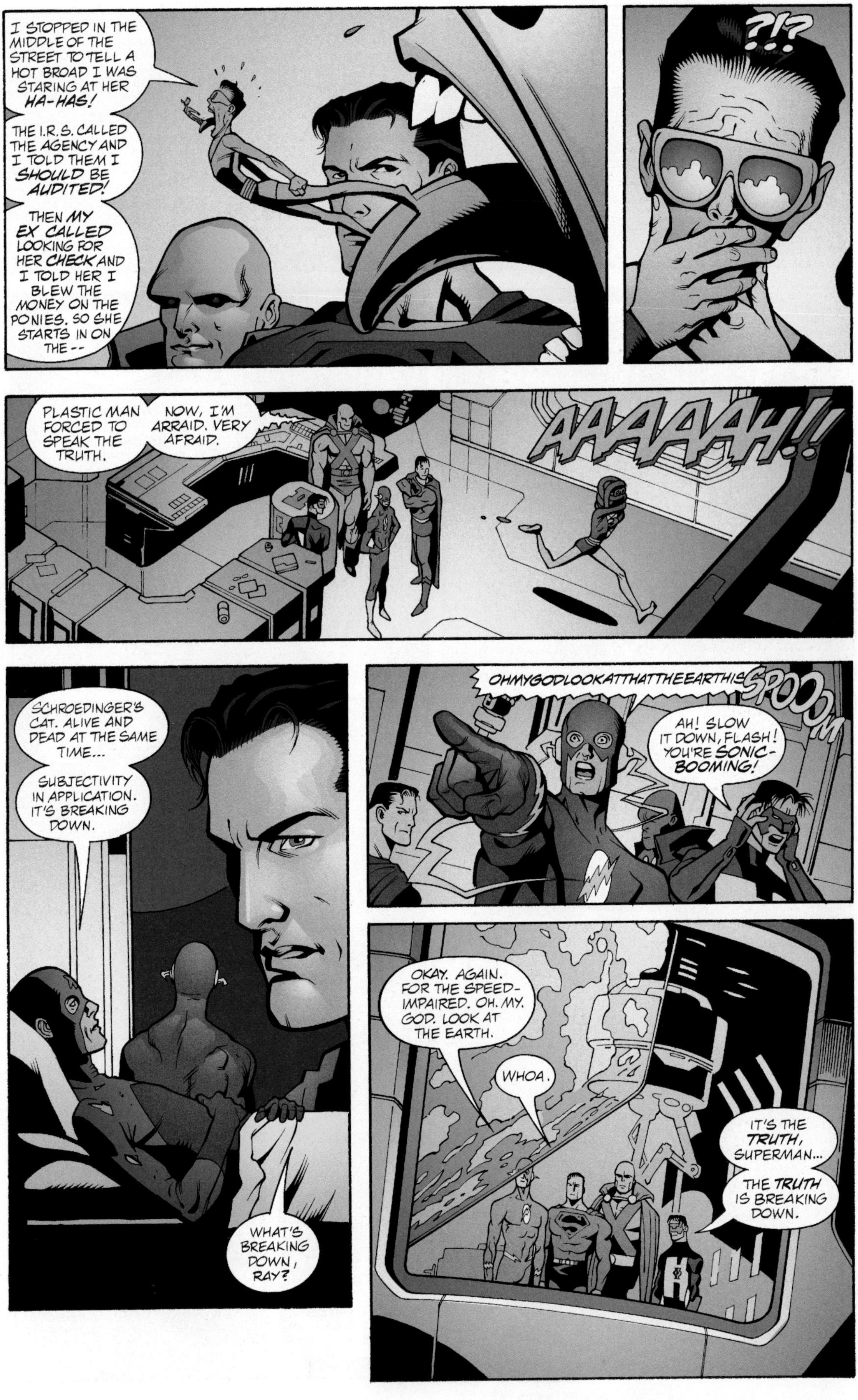
I STOPPED IN THE MIDDLE OF THE STREET TO TELL A HOT BROAD I WAS STARING AT HER HA-HAS!
THE I.R.S. CALLED THE AGENCY AND I TOLD THEM I SHOULD BE AUDITED!
THEN MY EX CALLED LOOKING FOR HER CHECK AND I TOLD HER I BLEW THE MONEY ON THE PONIES. SO SHE STARTS IN ON THE --
?!?
PLASTIC MAN FORCED TO SPEAK THE TRUTH.
NOW, I'M ARRAID. VERY AFRAID.
AAAAAH!!
SCHROEDINGER'S CAT. ALIVE AND DEAD AT THE SAME TIME...
SUBJECTIVITY IN APPLICATION. IT'S BREAKING DOWN.
WHAT'S BREAKING DOWN, RAY?
OHMYGODLOOKATTHATTHEEARTHIS
SPOOOM
AH! SLOW IT DOWN, FLASH! YOU'RE SONIC-BOOMING!
OKAY. AGAIN. FOR THE SPEED-IMPAIRED. OH. MY. GOD. LOOK AT THE EARTH.
WHOA.
IT'S THE TRUTH, SUPERMAN...
THE TRUTH IS BREAKING DOWN.

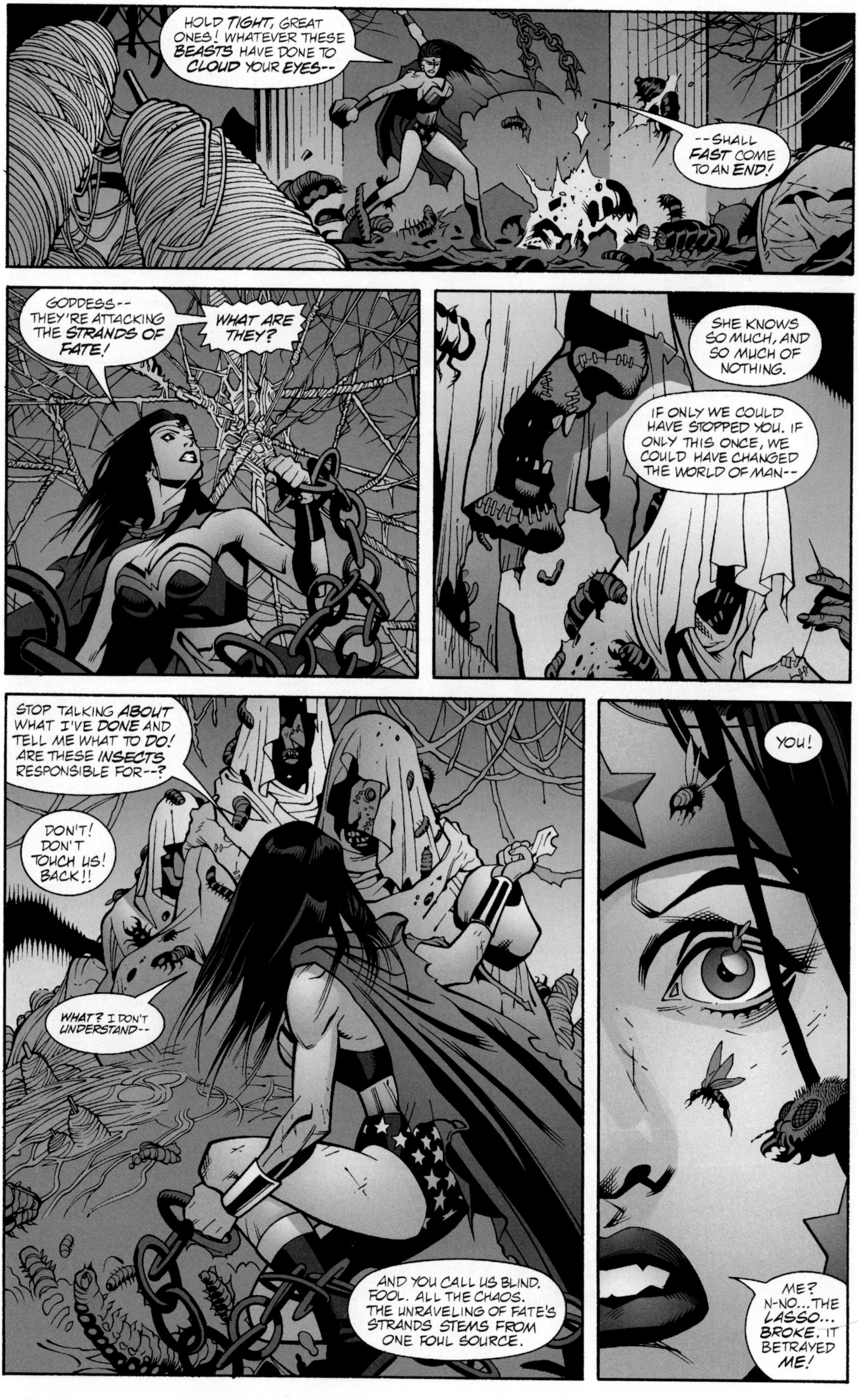
HOLD TIGHT, GREAT ONES! WHATEVER THESE BEASTS HAVE DONE TO CLOUD YOUR EYES--
--SHALL FAST COME TO AN END!
GODDESS--THEY'RE ATTACKING THE STRANDS OF FATE!
WHAT ARE THEY?
SHE KNOWS SO MUCH, AND SO MUCH OF NOTHING.
IF ONLY WE COULD HAVE STOPPED YOU. IF ONLY THIS ONCE, WE COULD HAVE CHANGED THE WORLD OF MAN--
STOP TALKING ABOUT WHAT I'VE DONE AND TELL ME WHAT TO DO! ARE THESE INSECTS RESPONSIBLE FOR--?
DON'T! DON'T TOUCH US! BACK!!
WHAT? I DON'T UNDERSTAND--
AND YOU CALL US BLIND. FOOL. ALL THE CHAOS. THE UNRAVELING OF FATE'S STRANDS STEMS FROM ONE FOUL SOURCE.
YOU!
ME? N-NO... THE LASSO... BROKE. IT BETRAYED ME!

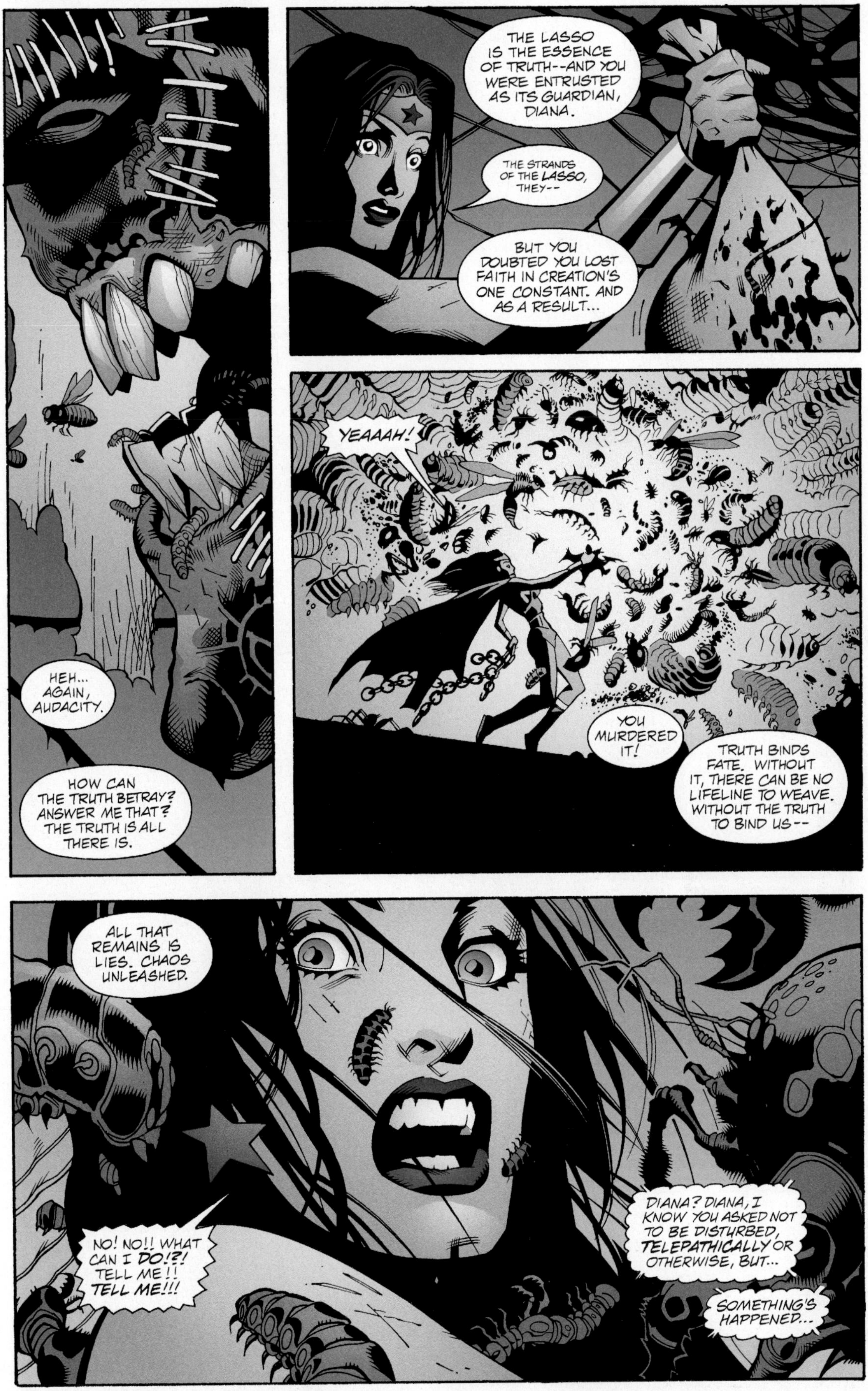
THE LASSO IS THE ESSENCE OF TRUTH--AND YOU WERE ENTRUSTED AS ITS GUARDIAN, DIANA.
THE STRANDS OF THE LASSO, THEY--
BUT YOU DOUBTED YOU LOST FAITH IN CREATION'S ONE CONSTANT. AND AS A RESULT...
HEH... AGAIN, AUDACITY.
HOW CAN THE TRUTH BETRAY? ANSWER ME THAT? THE TRUTH IS ALL THERE IS.
YEAAAH!
YOU MURDERED IT!
TRUTH BINDS FATE. WITHOUT IT, THERE CAN BE NO LIFELINE TO WEAVE. WITHOUT THE TRUTH TO BIND US--
ALL THAT REMAINS IS LIES. CHAOS UNLEASHED.
NO! NO!! WHAT CAN I DO!?! TELL ME!! TELL ME!!!
DIANA? DIANA, I KNOW YOU ASKED NOT TO BE DISTURBED, TELEPATHICALLY OR OTHERWISE, BUT...
SOMETHING'S HAPPENED...

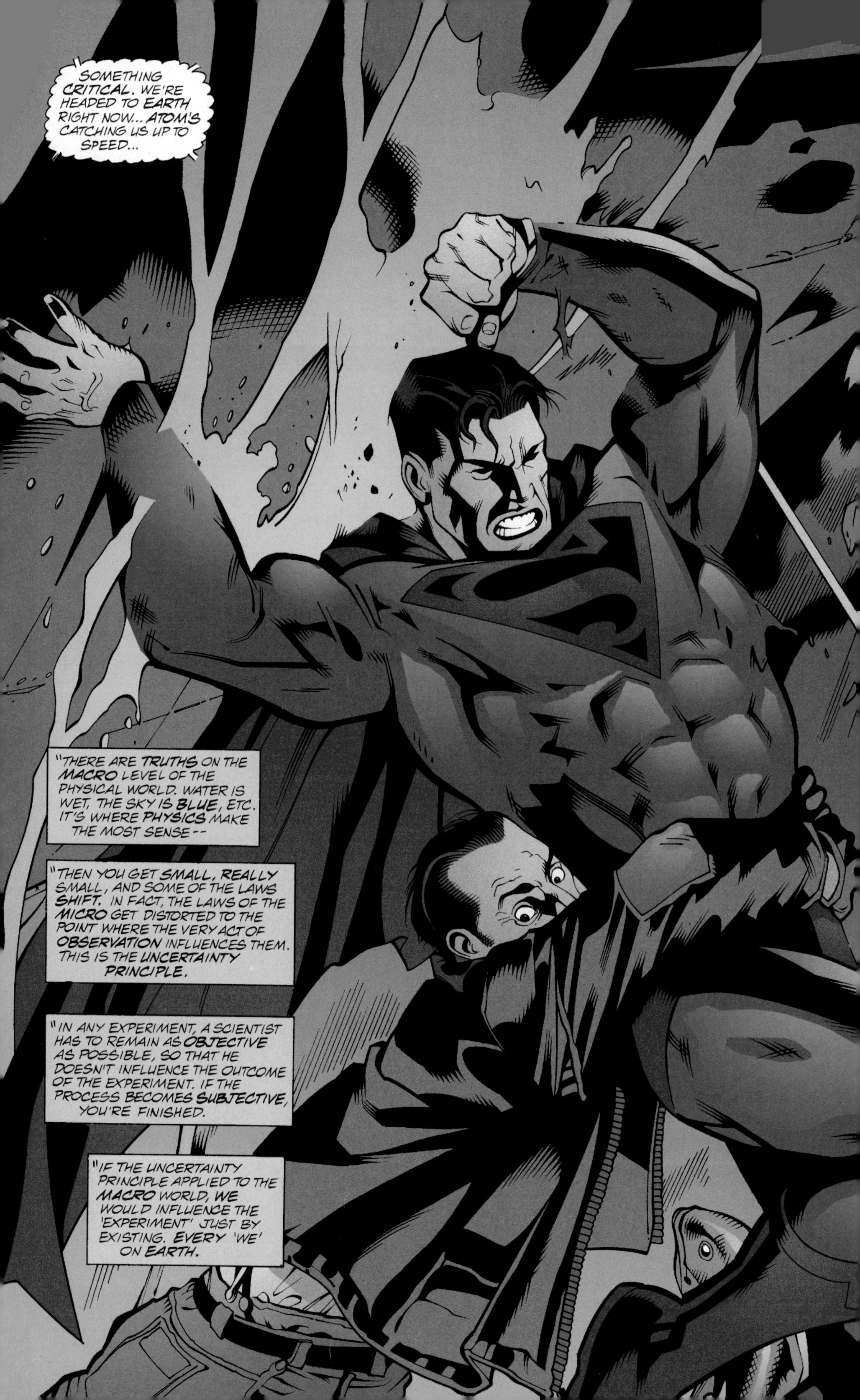
SOMETHING CRITICAL. WE'RE HEADED TO EARTH RIGHT NOW... ATOM'S CATCHING US UP TO SPEED...
"THERE ARE TRUTHS ON THE MACRO LEVEL OF THE PHYSICAL WORLD. WATER IS WET, THE SKY IS BLUE, ETC. IT'S WHERE PHYSICS MAKE THE MOST SENSE--
"THEN YOU GET SMALL, REALLY SMALL, AND SOME OF THE LAWS SHIFT. IN FACT, THE LAWS OF THE MICRO GET DISTORTED TO THE POINT WHERE THE VERY ACT OF OBSERVATION INFLUENCES THEM. THIS IS THE UNCERTAINTY PRINCIPLE.
"IN ANY EXPERIMENT, A SCIENTIST HAS TO REMAIN AS OBJECTIVE AS POSSIBLE, SO THAT HE DOESN'T INFLUENCE THE OUTCOME OF THE EXPERIMENT. IF THE PROCESS BECOMES SUBJECTIVE, YOU'RE FINISHED.
"IF THE UNCERTAINTY PRINCIPLE APPLIED TO THE MACRO WORLD, WE WOULD INFLUENCE THE 'EXPERIMENT' JUST BY EXISTING. EVERY 'WE' ON EARTH.

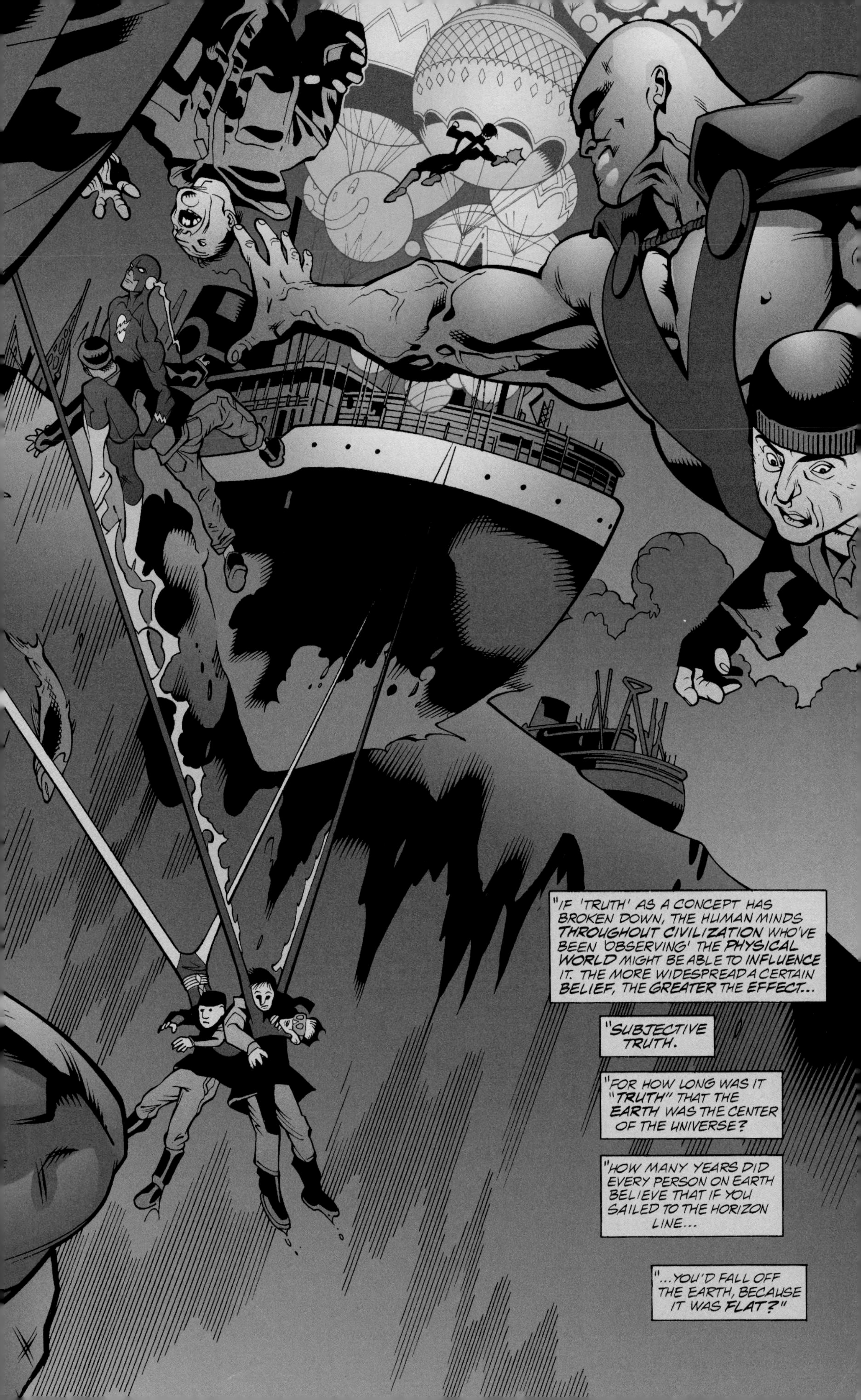
"IF 'TRUTH' AS A CONCEPT HAS BROKEN DOWN, THE HUMAN MINDS THROUGHOUT CIVILIZATION WHO'VE BEEN 'OBSERVING' THE PHYSICAL WORLD MIGHT BE ABLE TO INFLUENCE IT. THE MORE WIDESPREAD A CERTAIN BELIEF, THE GREATER THE EFFECT...
"SUBJECTIVE TRUTH.
"FOR HOW LONG WAS IT "TRUTH" THAT THE EARTH WAS THE CENTER OF THE UNIVERSE?
"HOW MANY YEARS DID EVERY PERSON ON EARTH BELIEVE THAT IF YOU SAILED TO THE HORIZON LINE...
"...YOU'D FALL OFF THE EARTH, BECAUSE IT WAS FLAT?"

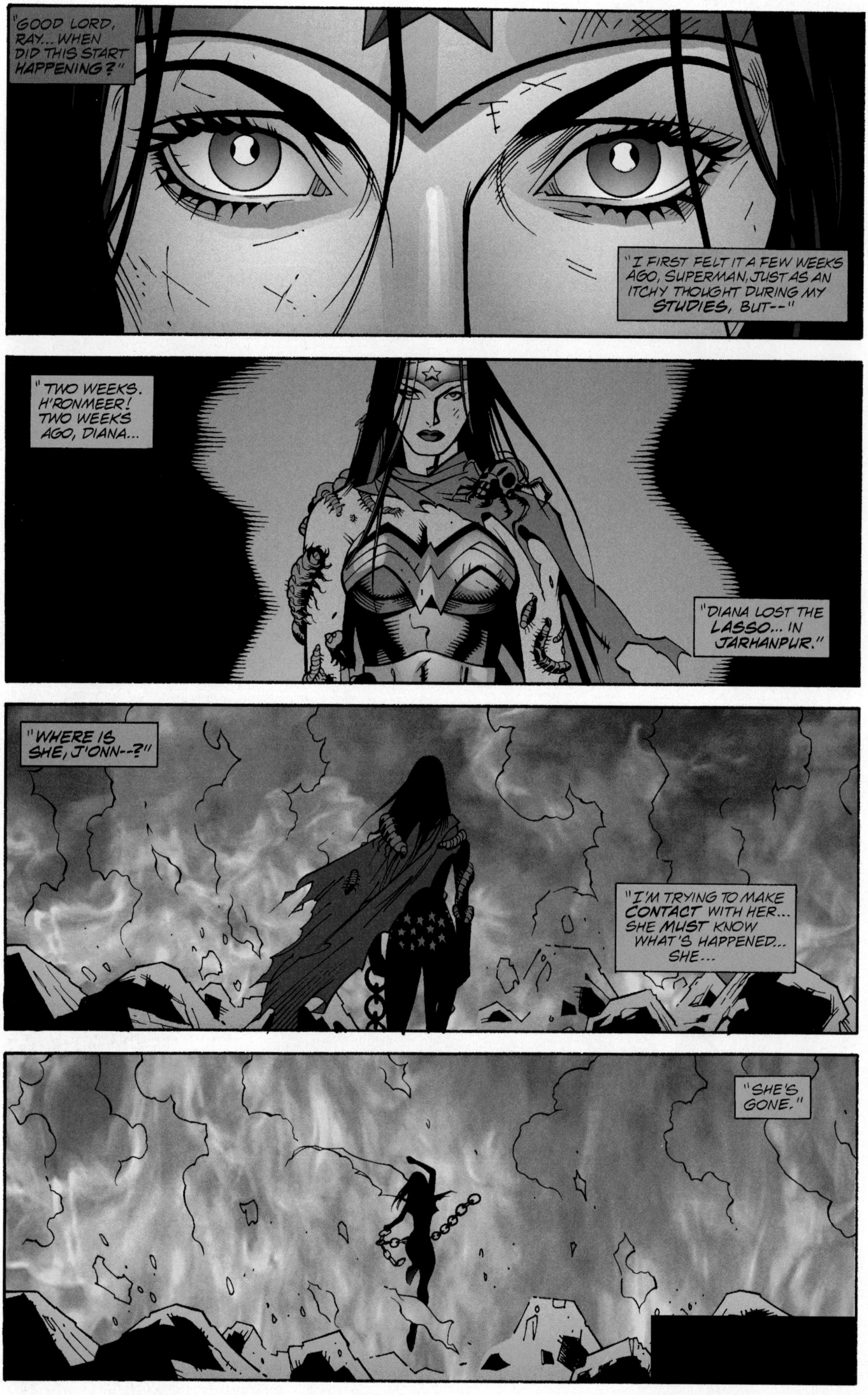
"GOOD LORD, RAY... WHEN DID THIS START HAPPENING?"
"I FIRST FELT IT A FEW WEEKS AGO, SUPERMAN, JUST AS AN ITCHY THOUGHT DURING MY STUDIES, BUT--"
"TWO WEEKS. H'RONMEER! TWO WEEKS AGO, DIANA...
"DIANA LOST THE LASSO... IN JARHANPUR."
"WHERE IS SHE, J'ONN--?"
"I'M TRYING TO MAKE CONTACT WITH HER... SHE MUST KNOW WHAT'S HAPPENED... SHE...
"SHE'S GONE."

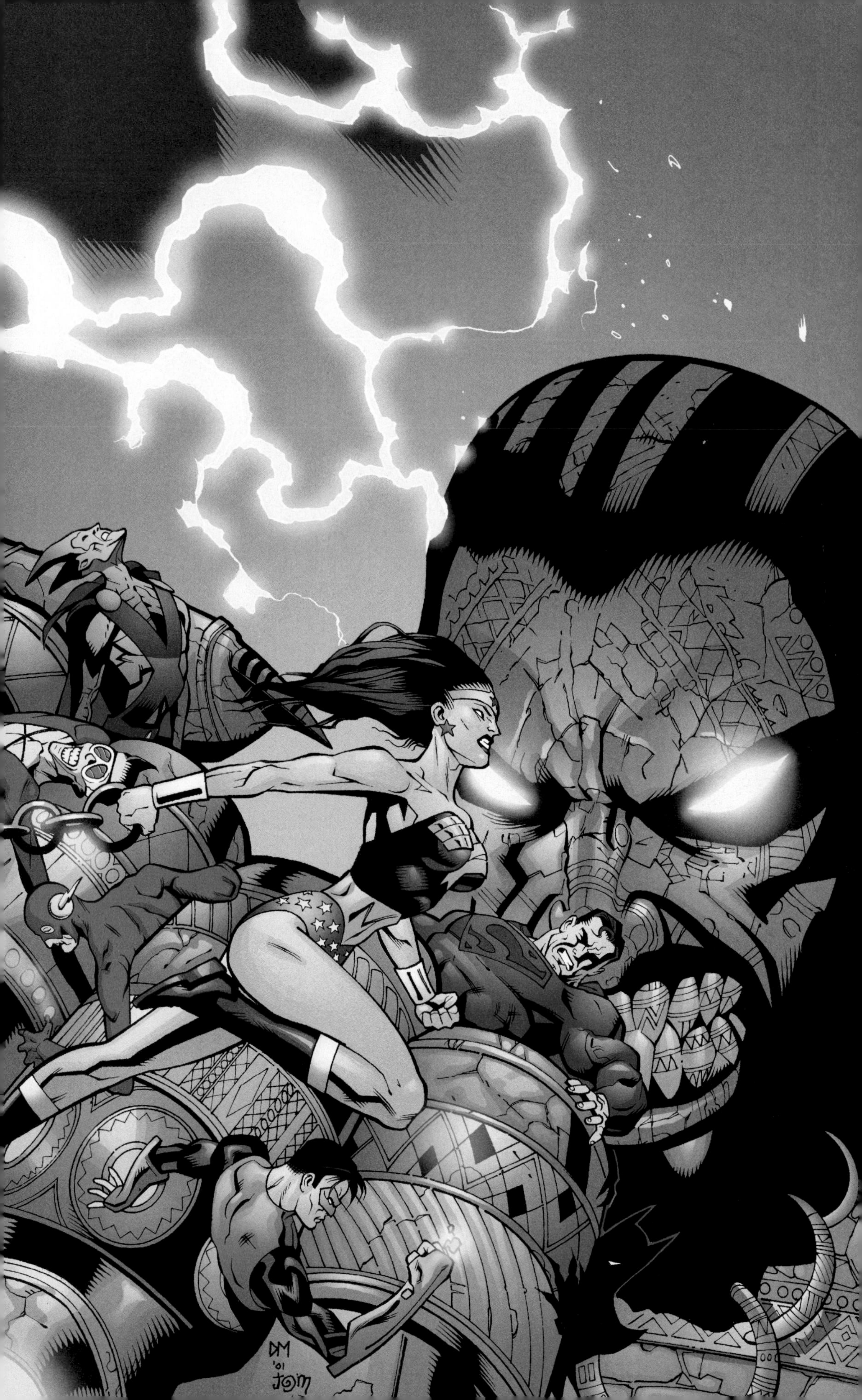

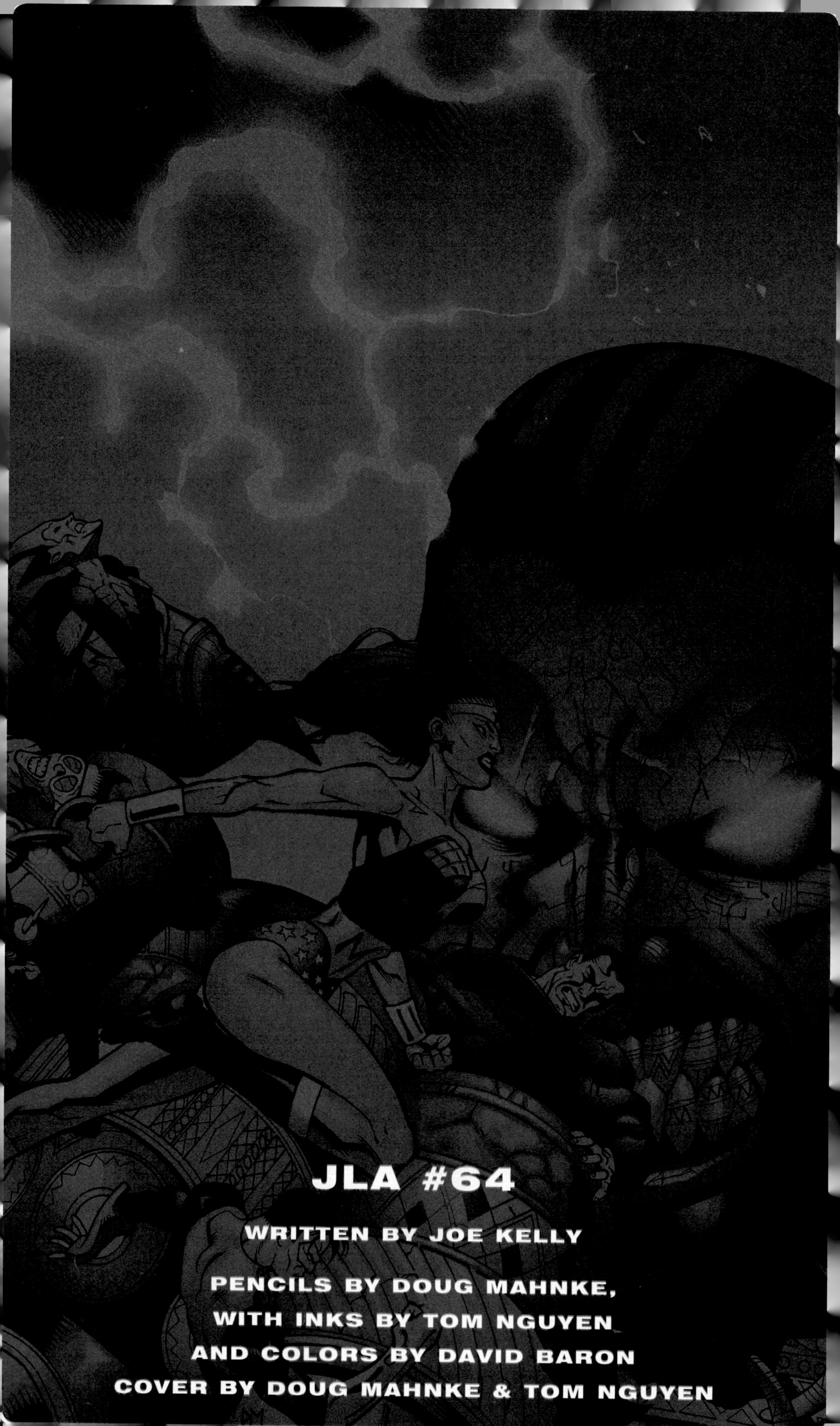

JLA #64

WRITTEN BY JOE KELLY

PENCILS BY DOUG MAHNKE,
WITH INKS BY TOM NGUYEN
AND COLORS BY DAVID BARON
COVER BY DOUG MAHNKE & TOM NGUYEN

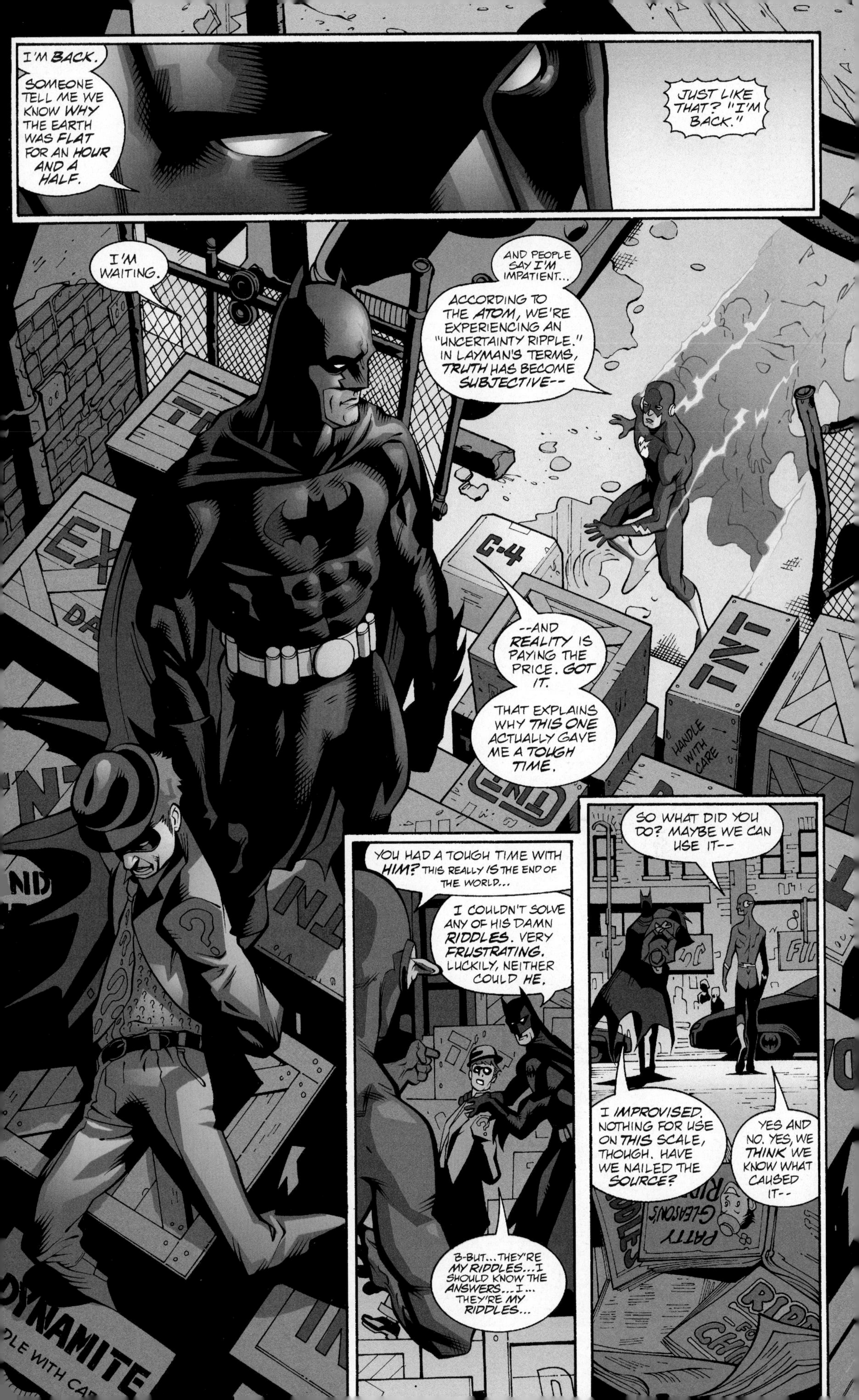
I'M BACK.
SOMEONE TELL ME WE KNOW WHY THE EARTH WAS FLAT FOR AN HOUR AND A HALF.
JUST LIKE THAT? "I'M BACK."
I'M WAITING.
AND PEOPLE SAY I'M IMPATIENT...
ACCORDING TO THE ATOM, WE'RE EXPERIENCING AN "UNCERTAINTY RIPPLE." IN LAYMAN'S TERMS, TRUTH HAS BECOME SUBJECTIVE--
C-4
--AND REALITY IS PAYING THE PRICE. GOT IT.
THAT EXPLAINS WHY THIS ONE ACTUALLY GAVE ME A TOUGH TIME.
TNT
HANDLE WITH CARE
YOU HAD A TOUGH TIME WITH HIM? THIS REALLY IS THE END OF THE WORLD...
I COULDN'T SOLVE ANY OF HIS DAMN RIDDLES. VERY FRUSTRATING. LUCKILY, NEITHER COULD HE.
B-BUT... THEY'RE MY RIDDLES... I SHOULD KNOW THE ANSWERS... I... THEY'RE MY RIDDLES...
SO WHAT DID YOU DO? MAYBE WE CAN USE IT--
I IMPROVISED. NOTHING FOR USE ON THIS SCALE, THOUGH. HAVE WE NAILED THE SOURCE?
YES AND NO. YES, WE THINK WE KNOW WHAT CAUSED IT--
DYNAMITE

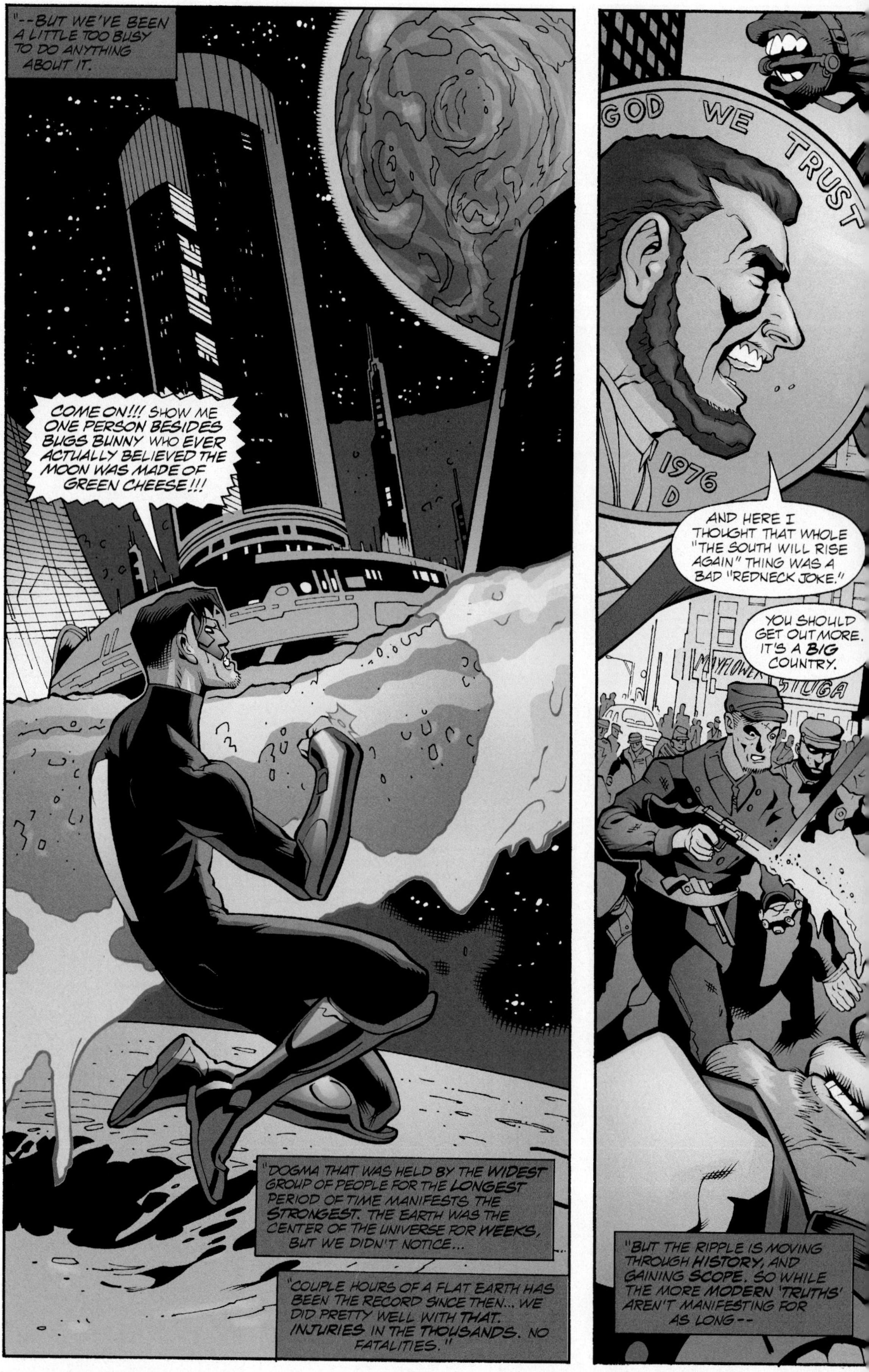
"--BUT WE'VE BEEN A LITTLE TOO BUSY TO DO ANYTHING ABOUT IT.
COME ON!!! SHOW ME ONE PERSON BESIDES BUGS BUNNY WHO EVER ACTUALLY BELIEVED THE MOON WAS MADE OF GREEN CHEESE!!!
"DOGMA THAT WAS HELD BY THE WIDEST GROUP OF PEOPLE FOR THE LONGEST PERIOD OF TIME MANIFESTS THE STRONGEST. THE EARTH WAS THE CENTER OF THE UNIVERSE FOR WEEKS, BUT WE DIDN'T NOTICE...
"COUPLE HOURS OF A FLAT EARTH HAS BEEN THE RECORD SINCE THEN... WE DID PRETTY WELL WITH THAT. INJURIES IN THE THOUSANDS. NO FATALITIES."
GOD WE TRUST
1976 D
AND HERE I THOUGHT THAT WHOLE "THE SOUTH WILL RISE AGAIN" THING WAS A BAD "REDNECK JOKE."
YOU SHOULD GET OUT MORE. IT'S A BIG COUNTRY.
MAYFLOWER
"BUT THE RIPPLE IS MOVING THROUGH HISTORY, AND GAINING SCOPE. SO WHILE THE MORE MODERN 'TRUTHS' AREN'T MANIFESTING FOR AS LONG--

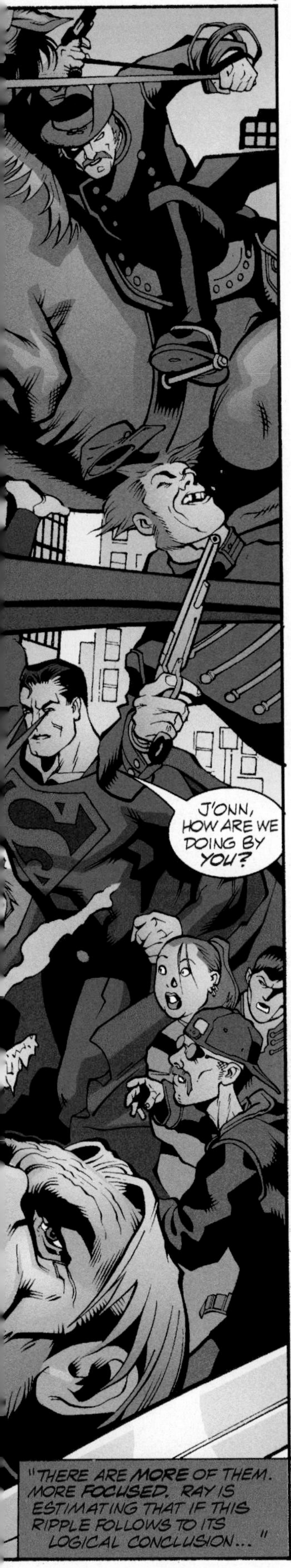
J'ONN, HOW ARE WE DOING BY YOU?
"THERE ARE MORE OF THEM. MORE FOCUSED. RAY IS ESTIMATING THAT IF THIS RIPPLE FOLLOWS TO ITS LOGICAL CONCLUSION..."

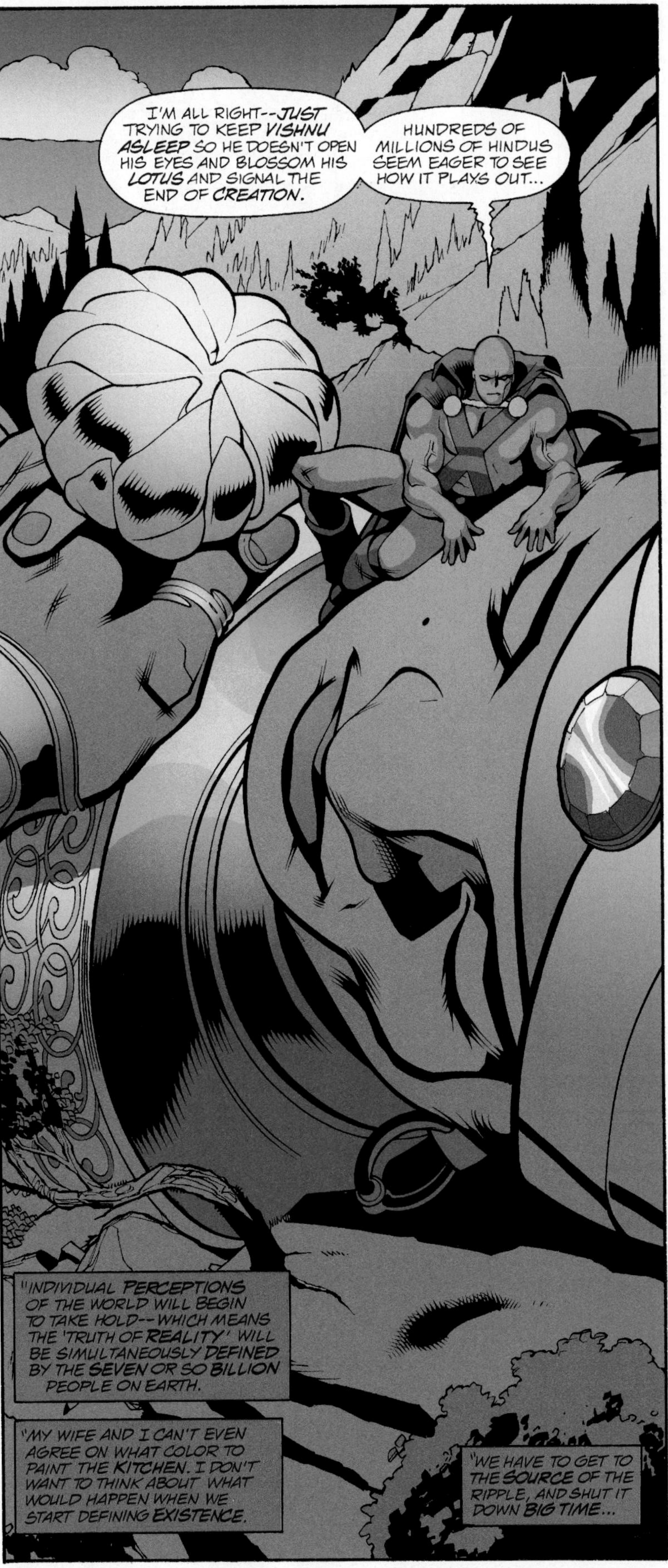
I'M ALL RIGHT--JUST TRYING TO KEEP VISHNU ASLEEP SO HE DOESN'T OPEN HIS EYES AND BLOSSOM HIS LOTUS AND SIGNAL THE END OF CREATION.
HUNDREDS OF MILLIONS OF HINDUS SEEM EAGER TO SEE HOW IT PLAYS OUT...
"INDIVIDUAL PERCEPTIONS OF THE WORLD WILL BEGIN TO TAKE HOLD--WHICH MEANS THE 'TRUTH OF REALITY' WILL BE SIMULTANEOUSLY DEFINED BY THE SEVEN OR SO BILLION PEOPLE ON EARTH.
"MY WIFE AND I CAN'T EVEN AGREE ON WHAT COLOR TO PAINT THE KITCHEN. I DON'T WANT TO THINK ABOUT WHAT WOULD HAPPEN WHEN WE START DEFINING EXISTENCE.
"WE HAVE TO GET TO THE SOURCE OF THE RIPPLE, AND SHUT IT DOWN BIG TIME...

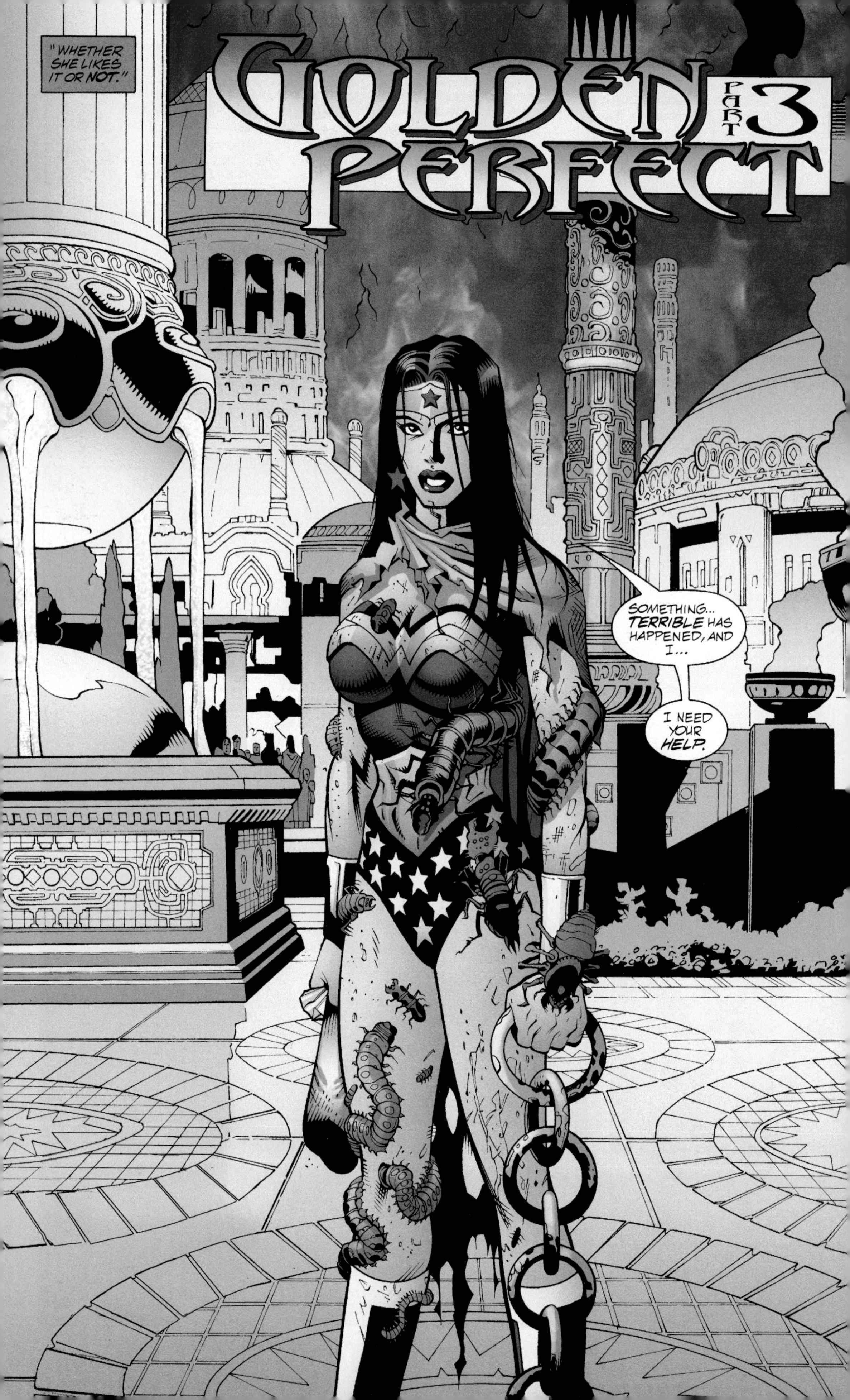
"WHETHER SHE LIKES IT OR NOT."
GOLDEN PERFECT PART 3
SOMETHING... TERRIBLE HAS HAPPENED, AND I...
I NEED YOUR HELP.

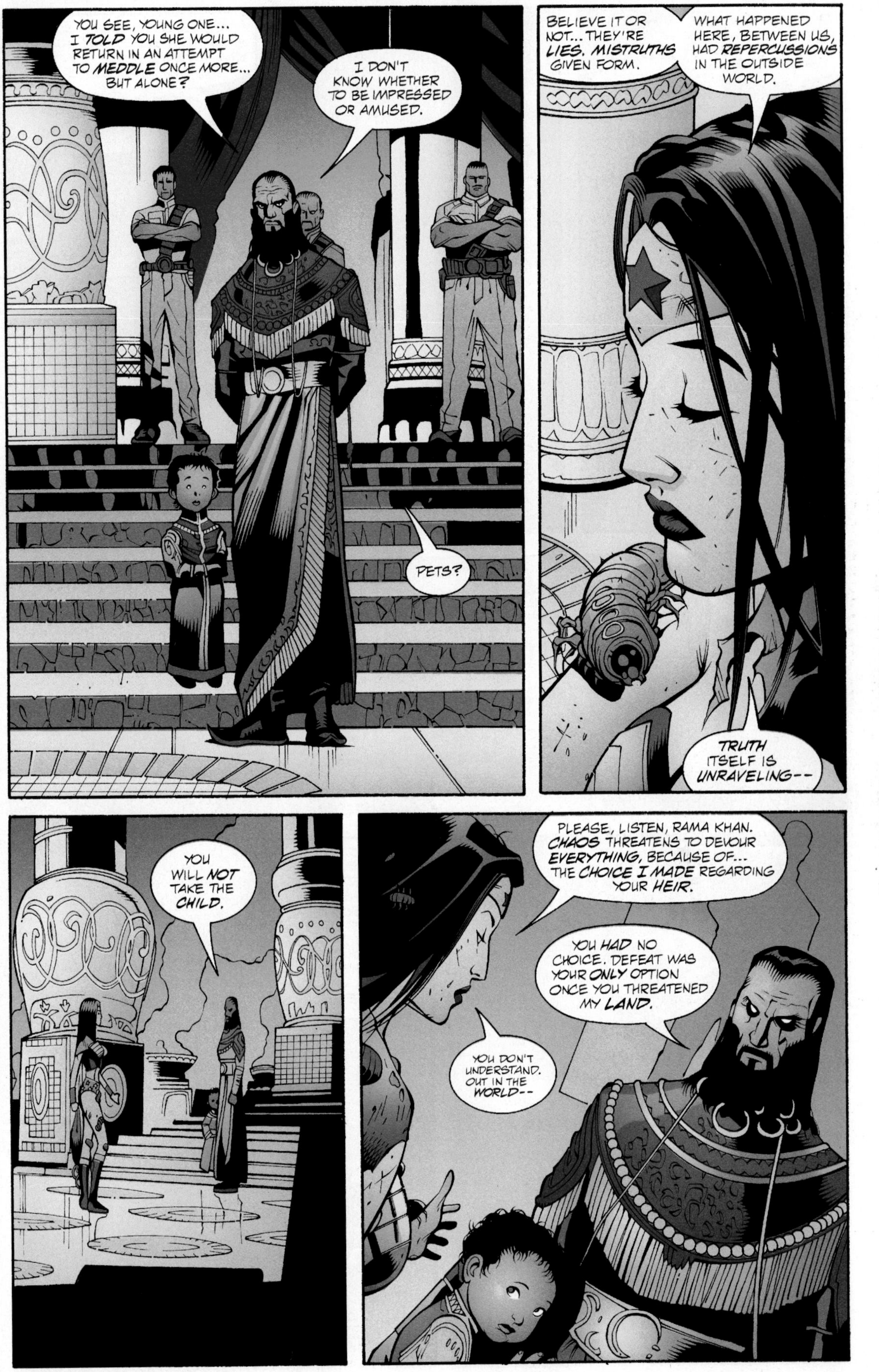
YOU SEE, YOUNG ONE... I TOLD YOU SHE WOULD RETURN IN AN ATTEMPT TO MEDDLE ONCE MORE... BUT ALONE?
I DON'T KNOW WHETHER TO BE IMPRESSED OR AMUSED.
PETS?
BELIEVE IT OR NOT... THEY'RE LIES. MISTRUTHS GIVEN FORM.
WHAT HAPPENED HERE, BETWEEN US, HAD REPERCUSSIONS IN THE OUTSIDE WORLD.
TRUTH ITSELF IS UNRAVELING--
YOU WILL NOT TAKE THE CHILD.
PLEASE, LISTEN, RAMA KHAN. CHAOS THREATENS TO DEVOUR EVERYTHING, BECAUSE OF... THE CHOICE I MADE REGARDING YOUR HEIR.
YOU HAD NO CHOICE. DEFEAT WAS YOUR ONLY OPTION ONCE YOU THREATENED MY LAND.
YOU DON'T UNDERSTAND. OUT IN THE WORLD--

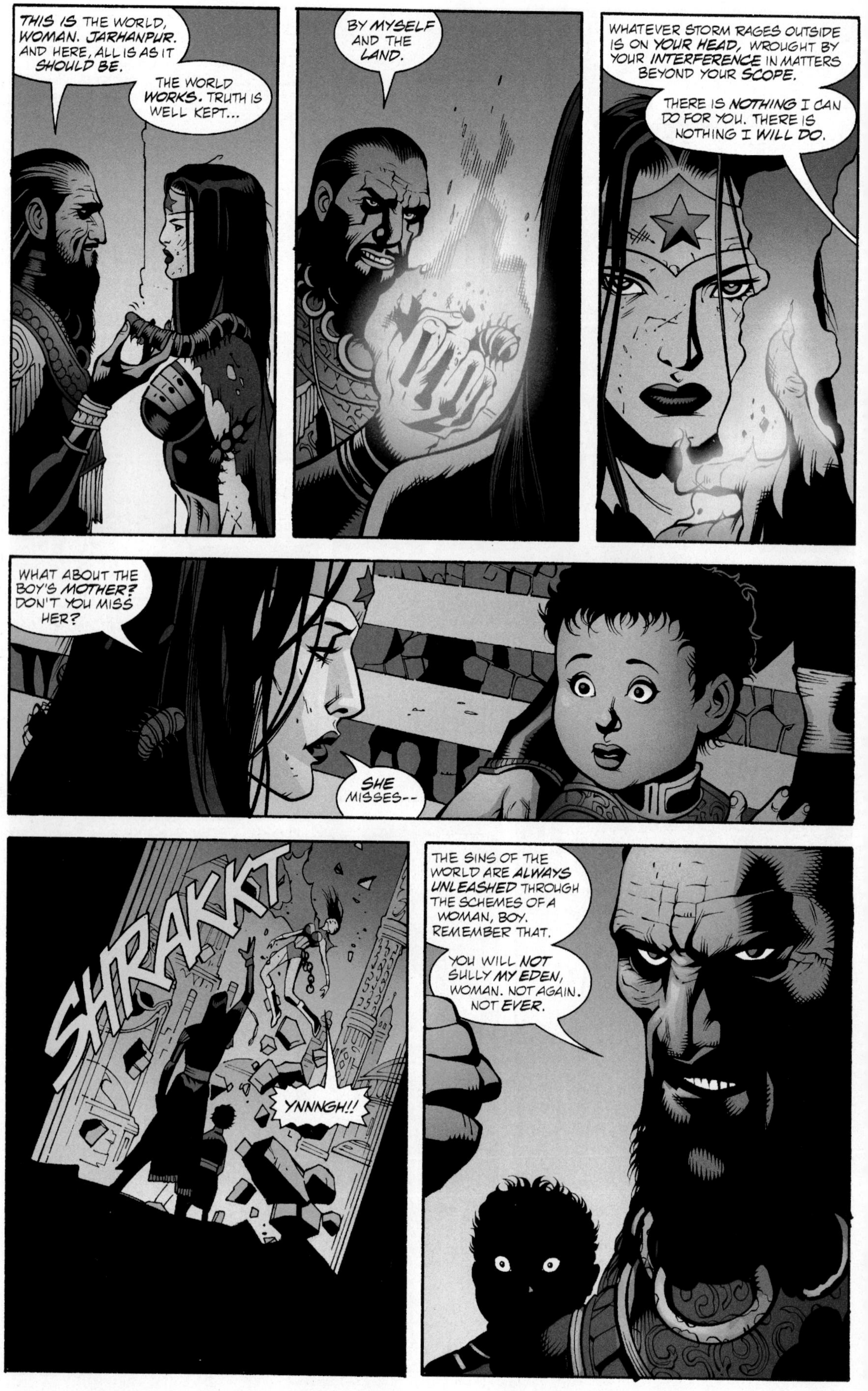
THIS IS THE WORLD, WOMAN. JARHANPUR. AND HERE, ALL IS AS IT SHOULD BE.
THE WORLD WORKS. TRUTH IS WELL KEPT...
BY MYSELF AND THE LAND.
WHATEVER STORM RAGES OUTSIDE IS ON YOUR HEAD, WROUGHT BY YOUR INTERFERENCE IN MATTERS BEYOND YOUR SCOPE.
THERE IS NOTHING I CAN DO FOR YOU. THERE IS NOTHING I WILL DO.
WHAT ABOUT THE BOY'S MOTHER? DON'T YOU MISS HER?
SHE MISSES--
SHRAKKT
YNNNGH!!
THE SINS OF THE WORLD ARE ALWAYS UNLEASHED THROUGH THE SCHEMES OF A WOMAN, BOY. REMEMBER THAT.
YOU WILL NOT SULLY MY EDEN, WOMAN. NOT AGAIN. NOT EVER.

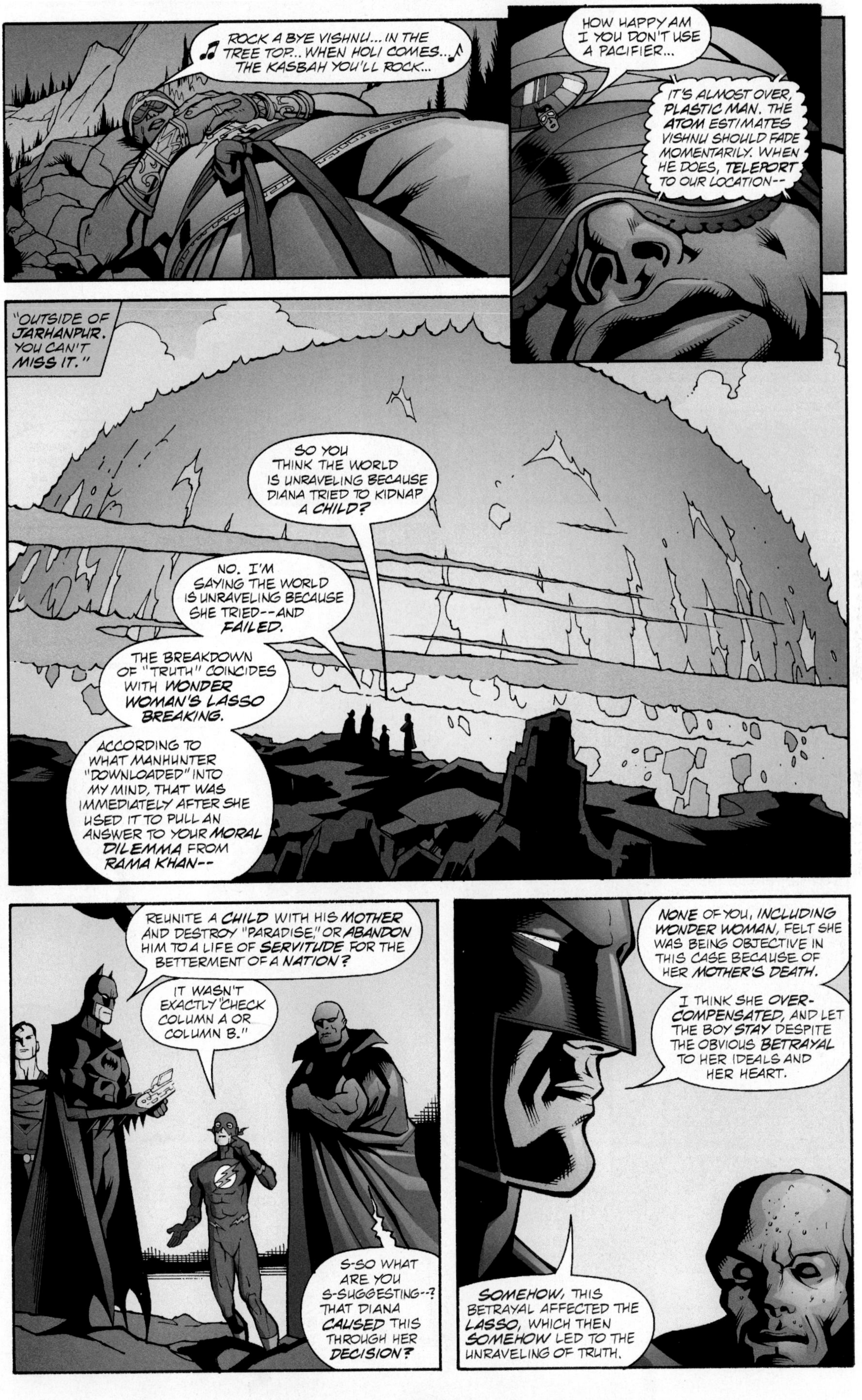
ROCK A BYE VISHNU... IN THE TREE TOP... WHEN HOLI COMES... THE KASBAH YOU'LL ROCK...
HOW HAPPY AM I YOU DON'T USE A PACIFIER...
IT'S ALMOST OVER, PLASTIC MAN. THE ATOM ESTIMATES VISHNU SHOULD FADE MOMENTARILY. WHEN HE DOES, TELEPORT TO OUR LOCATION--
"OUTSIDE OF JARHANPUR. YOU CAN'T MISS IT."
SO YOU THINK THE WORLD IS UNRAVELING BECAUSE DIANA TRIED TO KIDNAP A CHILD?
NO. I'M SAYING THE WORLD IS UNRAVELING BECAUSE SHE TRIED--AND FAILED.
THE BREAKDOWN OF "TRUTH" COINCIDES WITH WONDER WOMAN'S LASSO BREAKING.
ACCORDING TO WHAT MANHUNTER "DOWNLOADED" INTO MY MIND, THAT WAS IMMEDIATELY AFTER SHE USED IT TO PULL AN ANSWER TO YOUR MORAL DILEMMA FROM RAMA KHAN--
REUNITE A CHILD WITH HIS MOTHER AND DESTROY "PARADISE," OR ABANDON HIM TO A LIFE OF SERVITUDE FOR THE BETTERMENT OF A NATION?
IT WASN'T EXACTLY "CHECK COLUMN A OR COLUMN B."
S-SO WHAT ARE YOU S-SUGGESTING--? THAT DIANA CAUSED THIS THROUGH HER DECISION?
NONE OF YOU, INCLUDING WONDER WOMAN, FELT SHE WAS BEING OBJECTIVE IN THIS CASE BECAUSE OF HER MOTHER'S DEATH.
I THINK SHE OVER-COMPENSATED, AND LET THE BOY STAY DESPITE THE OBVIOUS BETRAYAL TO HER IDEALS AND HER HEART.
SOMEHOW, THIS BETRAYAL AFFECTED THE LASSO, WHICH THEN SOMEHOW LED TO THE UNRAVELING OF TRUTH.

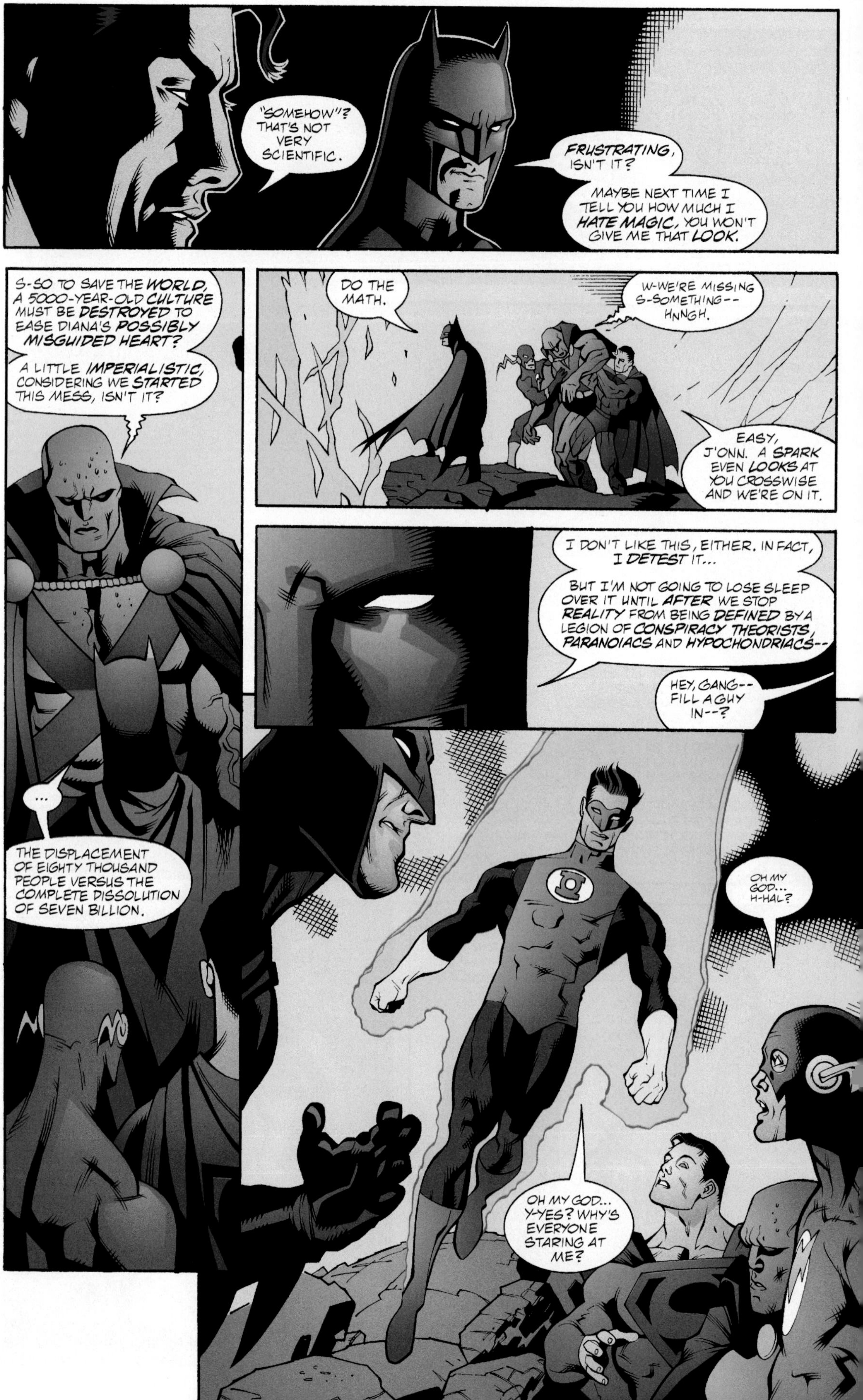
"SOMEHOW"? THAT'S NOT VERY SCIENTIFIC.
FRUSTRATING, ISN'T IT?
MAYBE NEXT TIME I TELL YOU HOW MUCH I HATE MAGIC, YOU WON'T GIVE ME THAT LOOK.
S-SO TO SAVE THE WORLD, A 5000-YEAR-OLD CULTURE MUST BE DESTROYED TO EASE DIANA'S POSSIBLY MISGUIDED HEART?
A LITTLE IMPERIALISTIC, CONSIDERING WE STARTED THIS MESS, ISN'T IT?
DO THE MATH.
W-WE'RE MISSING S-SOMETHING-- HNNGH.
EASY, J'ONN. A SPARK EVEN LOOKS AT YOU CROSSWISE AND WE'RE ON IT.
...
THE DISPLACEMENT OF EIGHTY THOUSAND PEOPLE VERSUS THE COMPLETE DISSOLUTION OF SEVEN BILLION.
I DON'T LIKE THIS, EITHER. IN FACT, I DETEST IT...
BUT I'M NOT GOING TO LOSE SLEEP OVER IT UNTIL AFTER WE STOP REALITY FROM BEING DEFINED BY A LEGION OF CONSPIRACY THEORISTS, PARANOIACS AND HYPOCHONDRIACS--
HEY, GANG-- FILL A GUY IN--?
OH MY GOD... H-HAL?
OH MY GOD... Y-YES? WHY'S EVERYONE STARING AT ME?

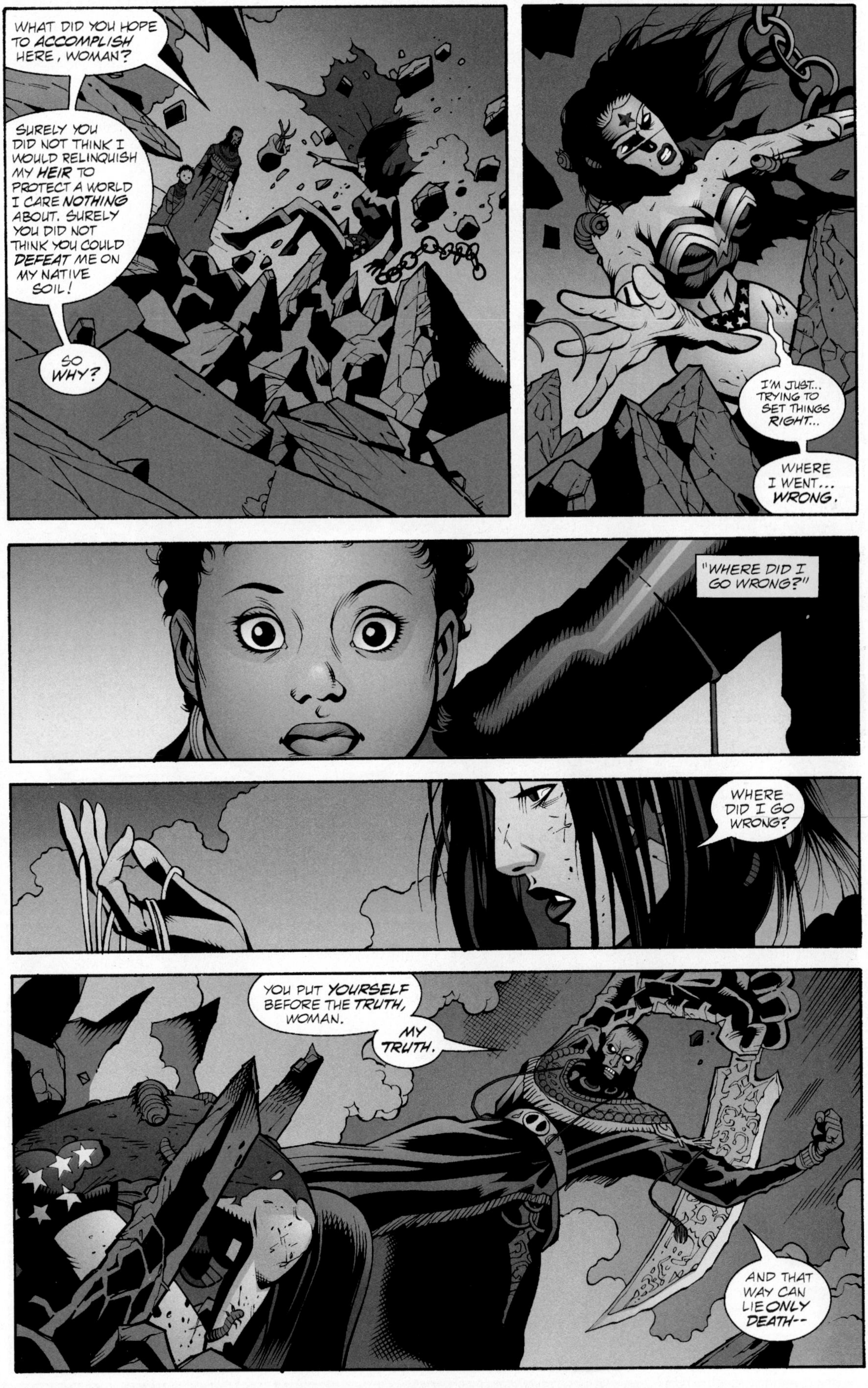
WHAT DID YOU HOPE TO ACCOMPLISH HERE, WOMAN?
SURELY YOU DID NOT THINK I WOULD RELINQUISH MY HEIR TO PROTECT A WORLD I CARE NOTHING ABOUT. SURELY YOU DID NOT THINK YOU COULD DEFEAT ME ON MY NATIVE SOIL!
SO WHY?
I'M JUST... TRYING TO SET THINGS RIGHT...
WHERE I WENT... WRONG.
"WHERE DID I GO WRONG?"
WHERE DID I GO WRONG?
YOU PUT YOURSELF BEFORE THE TRUTH, WOMAN.
MY TRUTH.
AND THAT WAY CAN LIE ONLY DEATH--

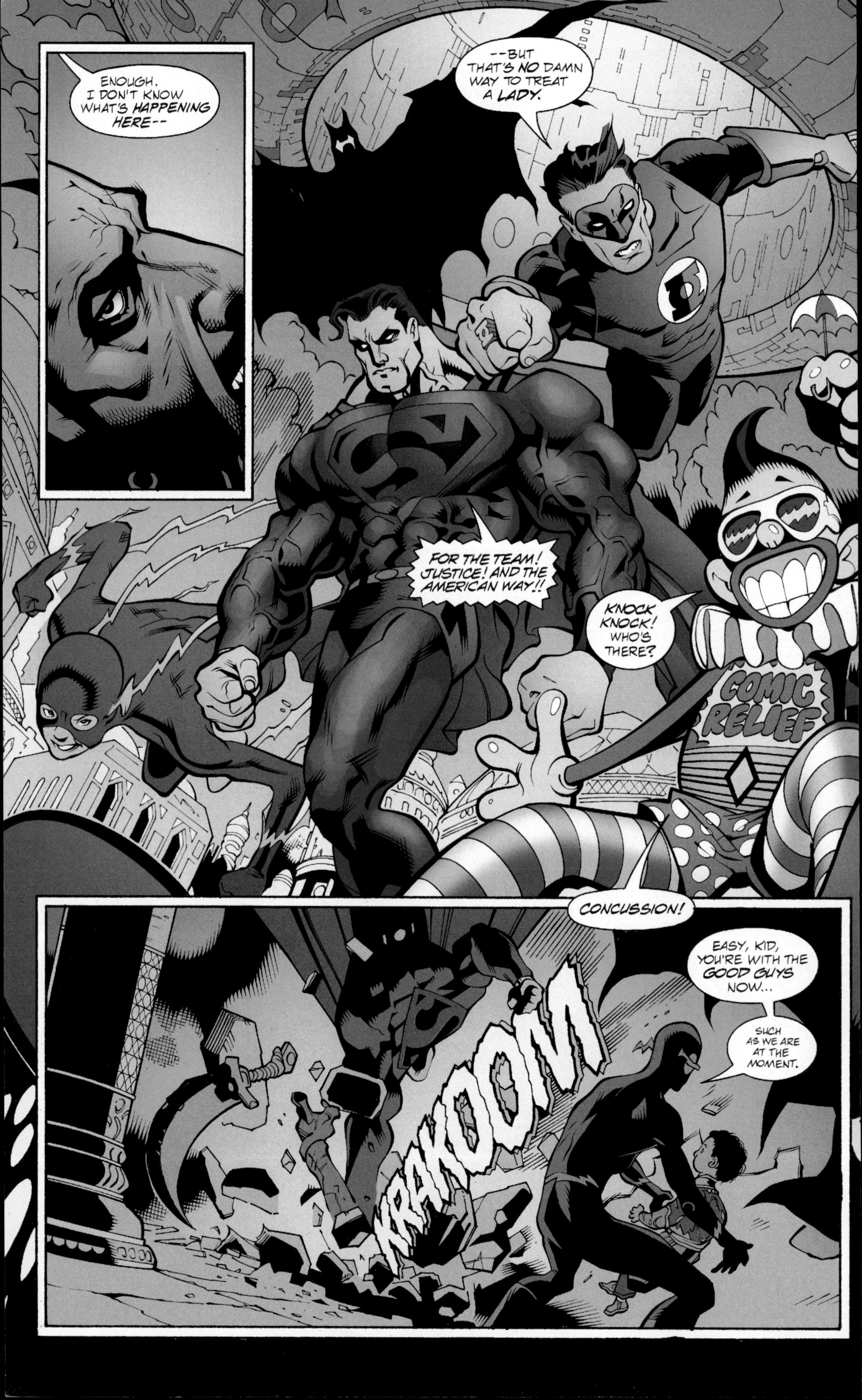

ENOUGH. I DON'T KNOW WHAT'S HAPPENING HERE--
--BUT THAT'S NO DAMN WAY TO TREAT A LADY.
FOR THE TEAM! JUSTICE! AND THE AMERICAN WAY!!
KNOCK KNOCK! WHO'S THERE?
COMIC RELIEF
CONCUSSION!
EASY, KID, YOU'RE WITH THE GOOD GUYS NOW...
SUCH AS WE ARE AT THE MOMENT.
KRAKOOM

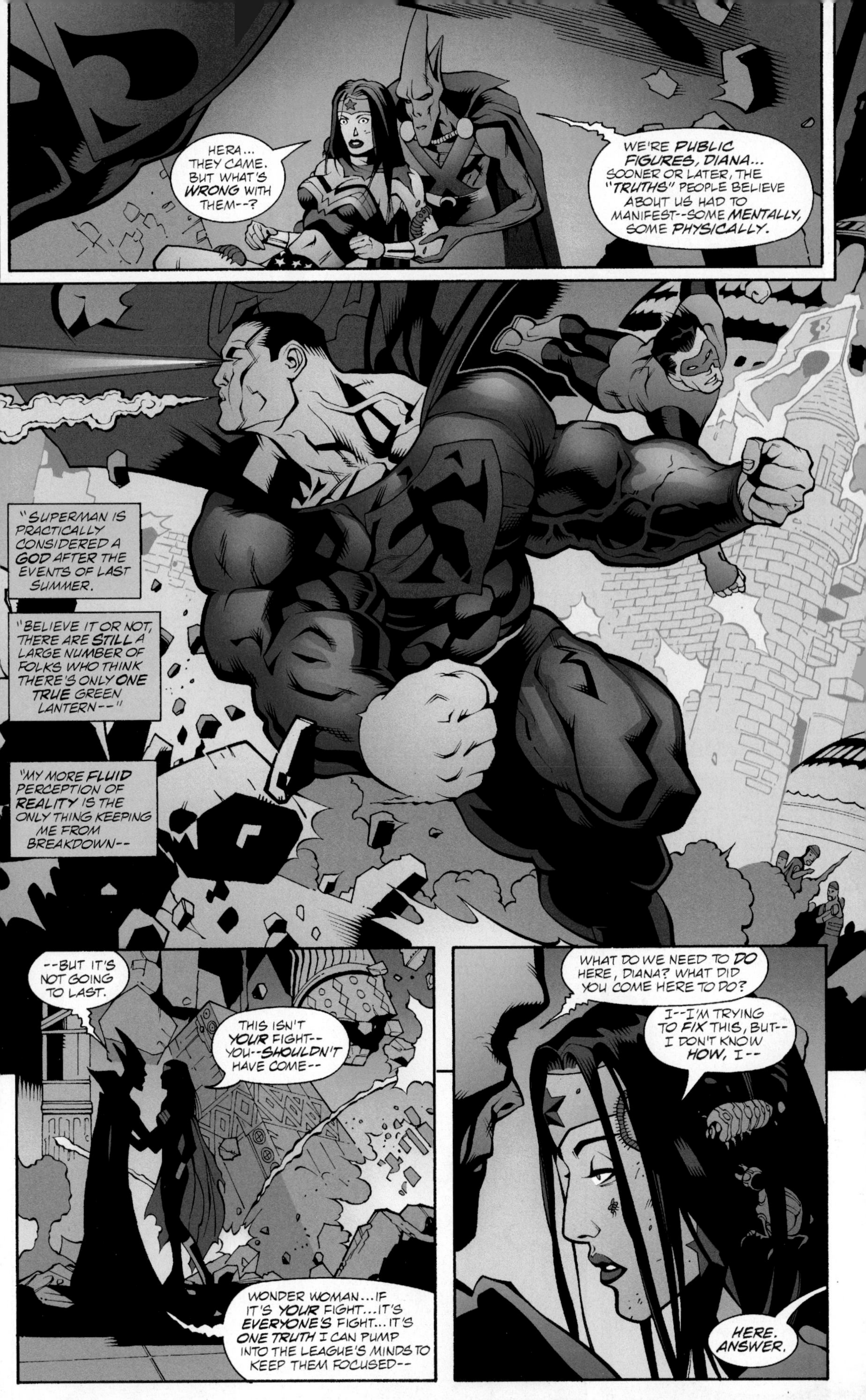
HERA... THEY CAME. BUT WHAT'S WRONG WITH THEM--?
WE'RE PUBLIC FIGURES, DIANA... SOONER OR LATER, THE "TRUTHS" PEOPLE BELIEVE ABOUT US HAD TO MANIFEST--SOME MENTALLY, SOME PHYSICALLY.
"SUPERMAN IS PRACTICALLY CONSIDERED A GOD AFTER THE EVENTS OF LAST SUMMER.
"BELIEVE IT OR NOT, THERE ARE STILL A LARGE NUMBER OF FOLKS WHO THINK THERE'S ONLY ONE TRUE GREEN LANTERN--"
"MY MORE FLUID PERCEPTION OF REALITY IS THE ONLY THING KEEPING ME FROM BREAKDOWN--
--BUT IT'S NOT GOING TO LAST.
THIS ISN'T YOUR FIGHT--YOU--SHOULDN'T HAVE COME--
WONDER WOMAN...IF IT'S YOUR FIGHT...IT'S EVERYONE'S FIGHT...IT'S ONE TRUTH I CAN PUMP INTO THE LEAGUE'S MINDS TO KEEP THEM FOCUSED--
WHAT DO WE NEED TO DO HERE, DIANA? WHAT DID YOU COME HERE TO DO?
I--I'M TRYING TO FIX THIS, BUT--I DON'T KNOW HOW, I--
HERE. ANSWER.

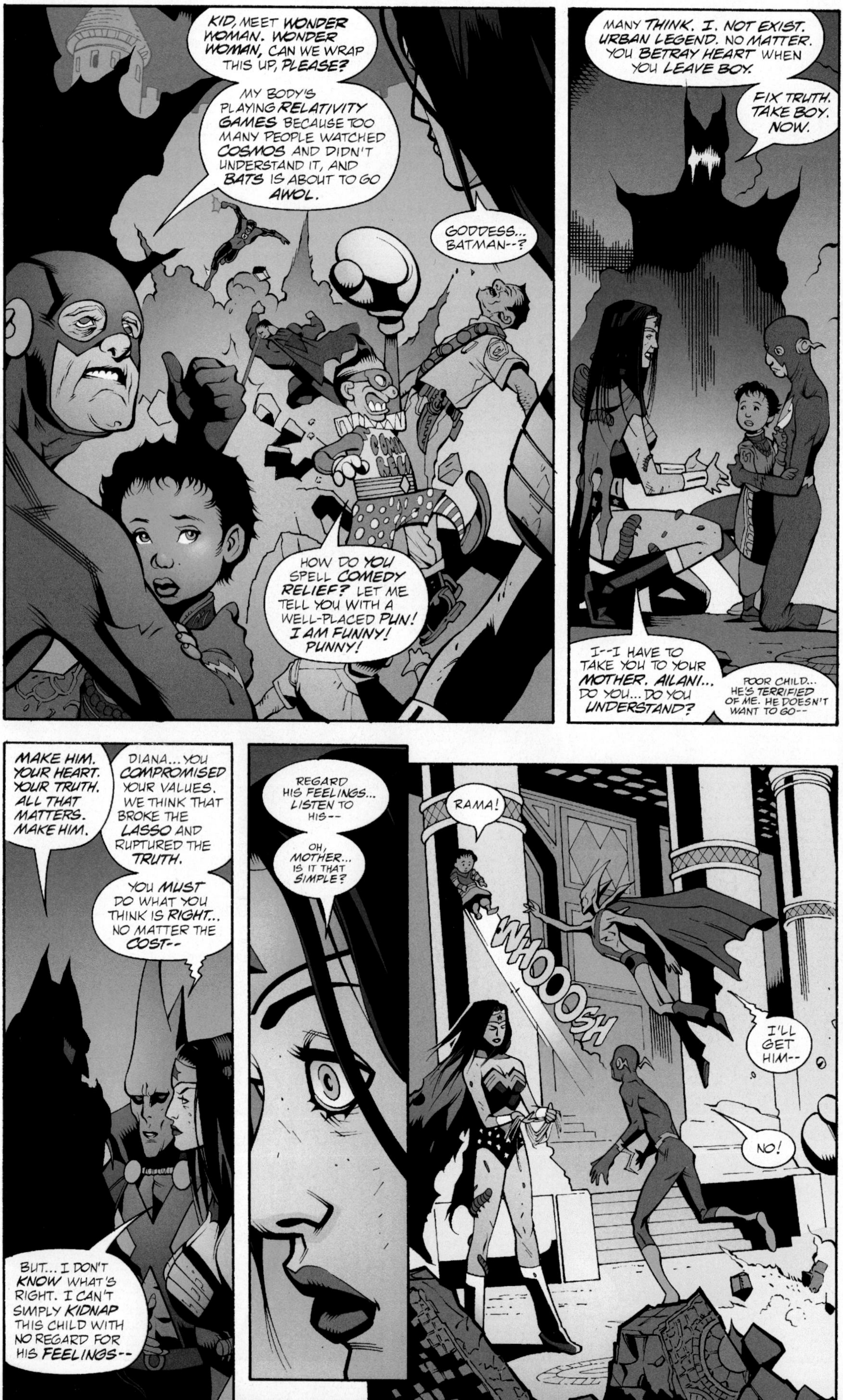
KID, MEET WONDER WOMAN. WONDER WOMAN, CAN WE WRAP THIS UP, PLEASE?
MY BODY'S PLAYING RELATIVITY GAMES BECAUSE TOO MANY PEOPLE WATCHED COSMOS AND DIDN'T UNDERSTAND IT, AND BATS IS ABOUT TO GO AWOL.
GODDESS... BATMAN--?
HOW DO YOU SPELL COMEDY RELIEF? LET ME TELL YOU WITH A WELL-PLACED PUN! I AM FUNNY! PUNNY!
MANY THINK. I. NOT EXIST. URBAN LEGEND. NO MATTER. YOU BETRAY HEART WHEN YOU LEAVE BOY.
FIX TRUTH. TAKE BOY. NOW.
I--I HAVE TO TAKE YOU TO YOUR MOTHER, AILANI... DO YOU... DO YOU UNDERSTAND?
POOR CHILD... HE'S TERRIFIED OF ME. HE DOESN'T WANT TO GO--
MAKE HIM. YOUR HEART. YOUR TRUTH. ALL THAT MATTERS. MAKE HIM.
DIANA... YOU COMPROMISED YOUR VALUES. WE THINK THAT BROKE THE LASSO AND RUPTURED THE TRUTH.
YOU MUST DO WHAT YOU THINK IS RIGHT... NO MATTER THE COST--
BUT... I DON'T KNOW WHAT'S RIGHT. I CAN'T SIMPLY KIDNAP THIS CHILD WITH NO REGARD FOR HIS FEELINGS--
REGARD HIS FEELINGS... LISTEN TO HIS--
OH, MOTHER... IS IT THAT SIMPLE?
RAMA!
WHOOOSH
I'LL GET HIM--
NO!

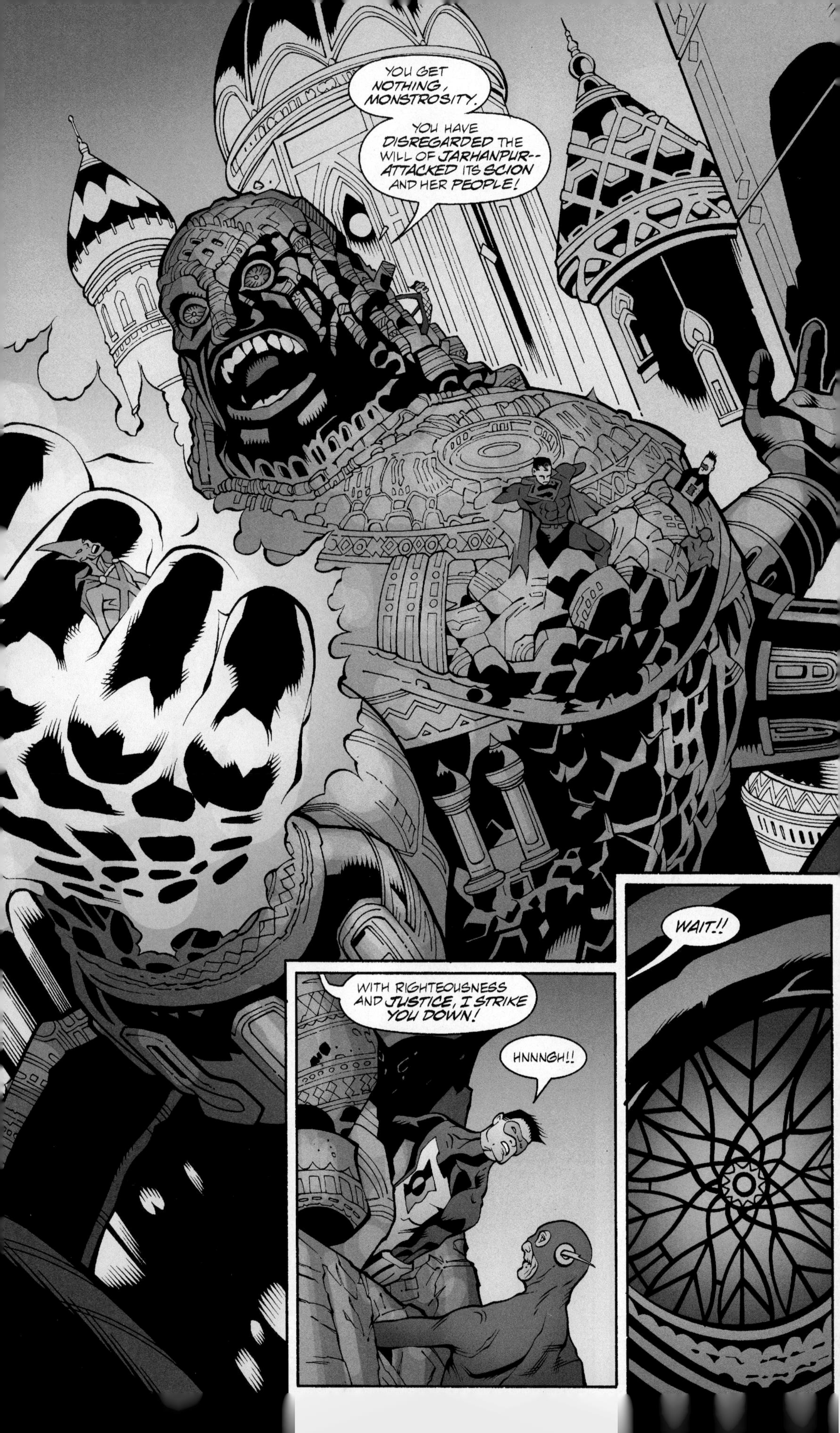
YOU GET NOTHING, MONSTROSITY.
YOU HAVE DISREGARDED THE WILL OF JARHANPUR-- ATTACKED ITS SCION AND HER PEOPLE!
WITH RIGHTEOUSNESS AND JUSTICE, I STRIKE YOU DOWN!
HNNNGH!!
WAIT!!

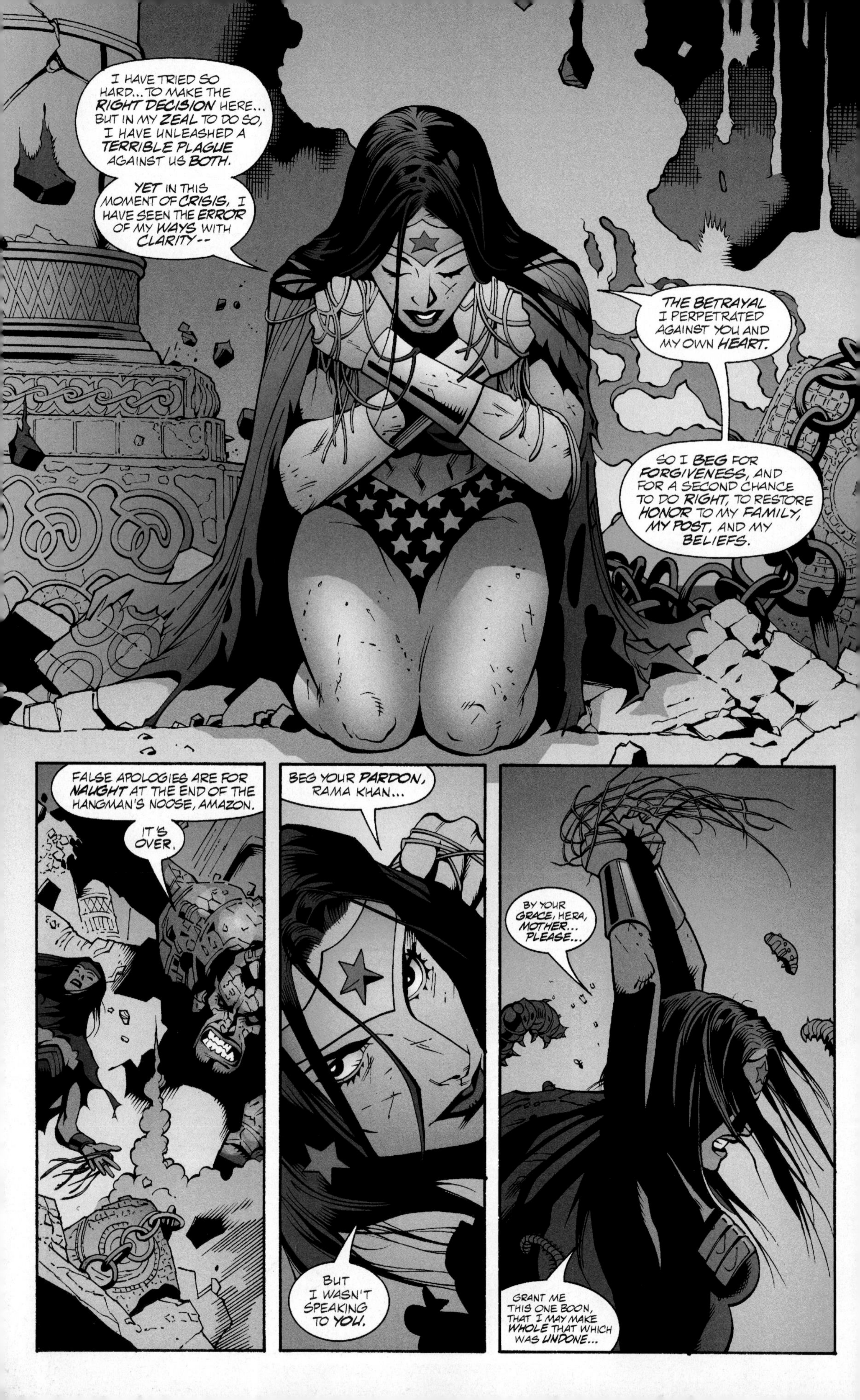
I HAVE TRIED SO HARD... TO MAKE THE RIGHT DECISION HERE... BUT IN MY ZEAL TO DO SO, I HAVE UNLEASHED A TERRIBLE PLAGUE AGAINST US BOTH.
YET IN THIS MOMENT OF CRISIS, I HAVE SEEN THE ERROR OF MY WAYS WITH CLARITY--
THE BETRAYAL I PERPETRATED AGAINST YOU AND MY OWN HEART.
SO I BEG FOR FORGIVENESS, AND FOR A SECOND CHANCE TO DO RIGHT, TO RESTORE HONOR TO MY FAMILY, MY POST, AND MY BELIEFS.
FALSE APOLOGIES ARE FOR NAUGHT AT THE END OF THE HANGMAN'S NOOSE, AMAZON.
IT'S OVER.
BEG YOUR PARDON, RAMA KHAN...
BUT I WASN'T SPEAKING TO YOU.
BY YOUR GRACE, HERA, MOTHER... PLEASE...
GRANT ME THIS ONE BOON, THAT I MAY MAKE WHOLE THAT WHICH WAS UNDONE...

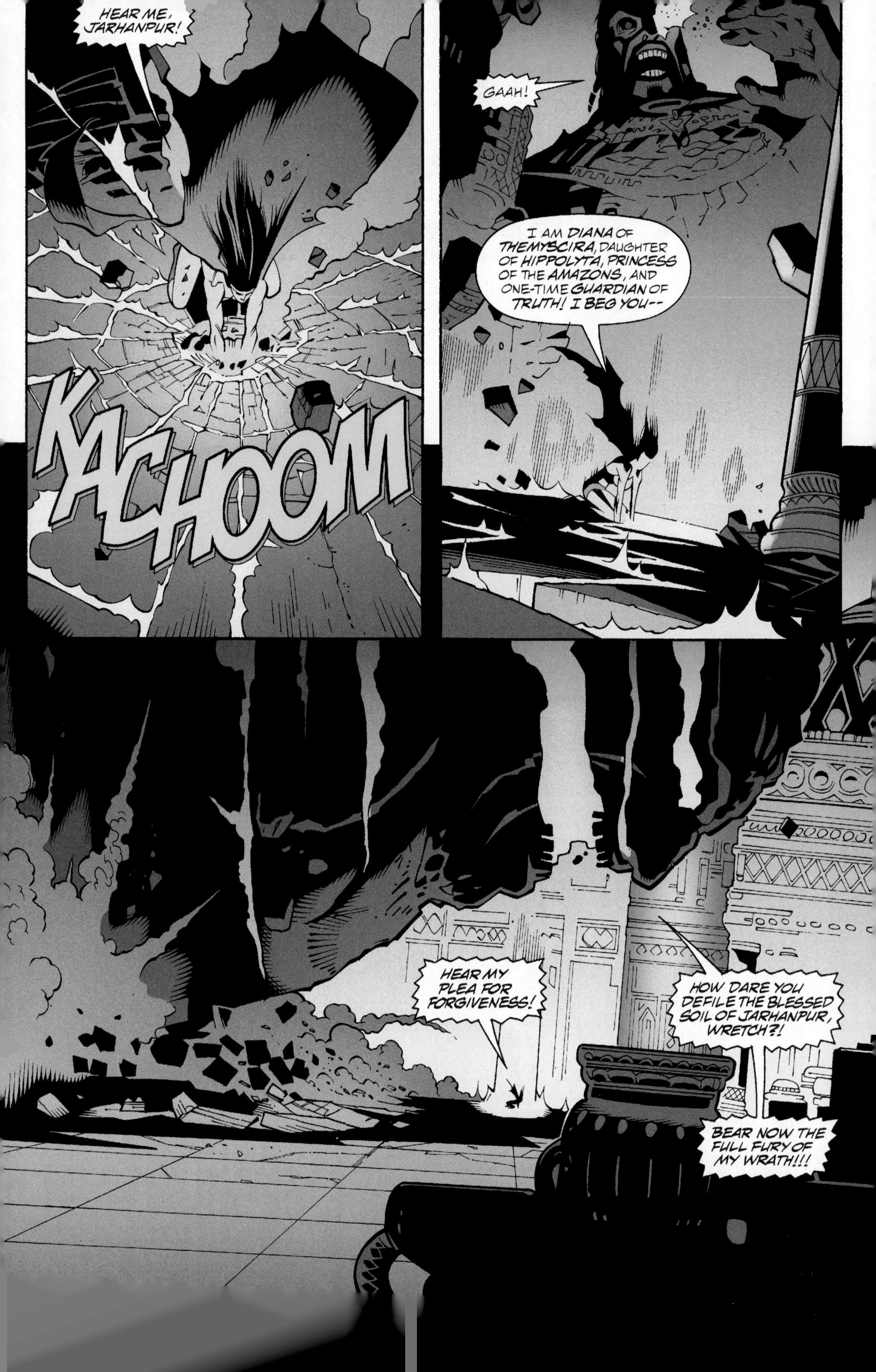
HEAR ME, JARHANPUR!
KACHOOM
GAAH!
I AM DIANA OF THEMYSCIRA, DAUGHTER OF HIPPOLYTA, PRINCESS OF THE AMAZONS, AND ONE-TIME GUARDIAN OF TRUTH! I BEG YOU--
HEAR MY PLEA FOR FORGIVENESS!
HOW DARE YOU DEFILE THE BLESSED SOIL OF JARHANPUR, WRETCH?!
BEAR NOW THE FULL FURY OF MY WRATH!!!

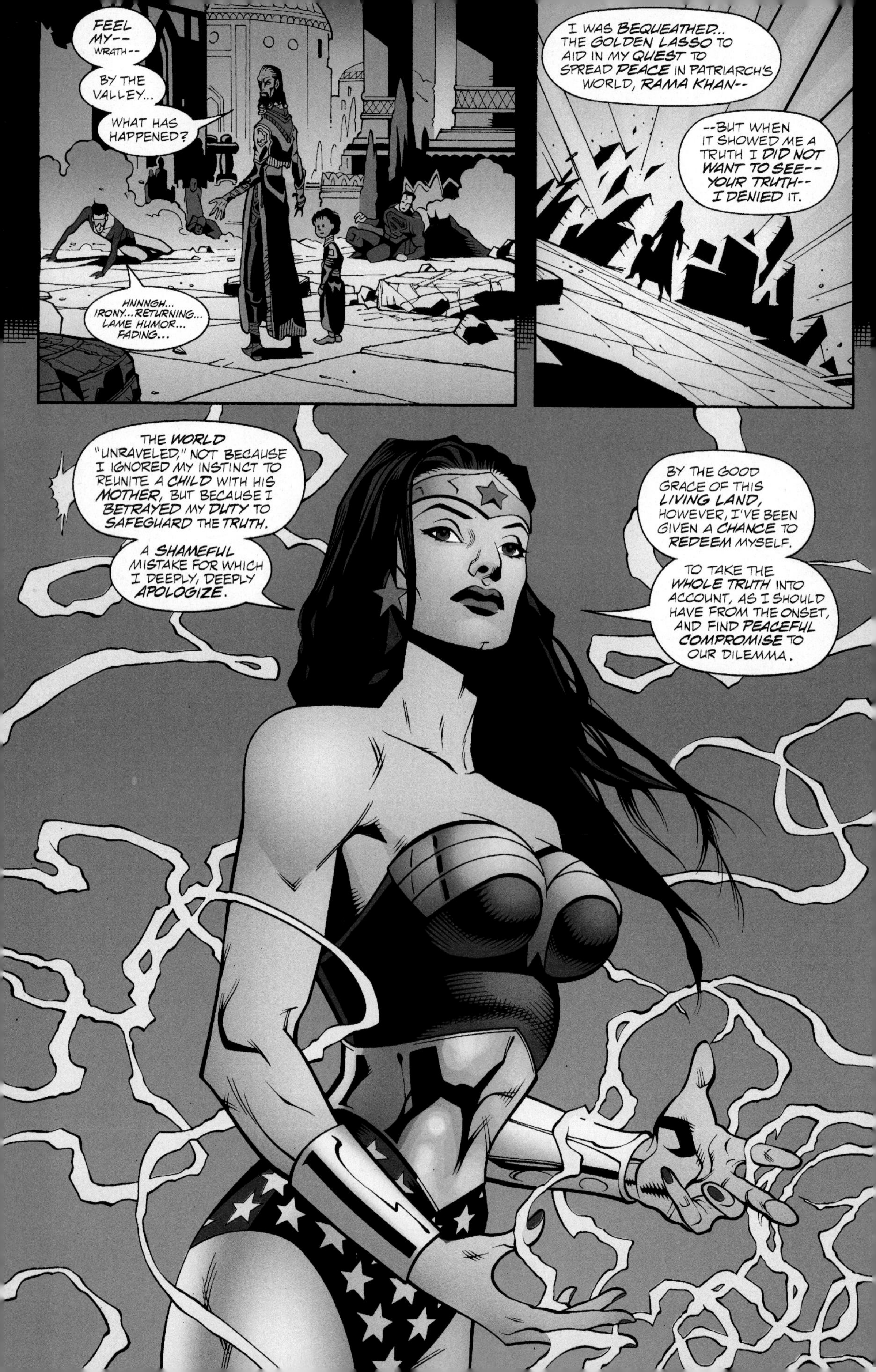
FEEL MY-- WRATH--
BY THE VALLEY...
WHAT HAS HAPPENED?
HNNNGH... IRONY...RETURNING... LAME HUMOR... FADING...
I WAS BEQUEATHED... THE GOLDEN LASSO TO AID IN MY QUEST TO SPREAD PEACE IN PATRIARCH'S WORLD, RAMA KHAN--
--BUT WHEN IT SHOWED ME A TRUTH I DID NOT WANT TO SEE-- YOUR TRUTH-- I DENIED IT.
THE WORLD "UNRAVELED," NOT BECAUSE I IGNORED MY INSTINCT TO REUNITE A CHILD WITH HIS MOTHER, BUT BECAUSE I BETRAYED MY DUTY TO SAFEGUARD THE TRUTH.
A SHAMEFUL MISTAKE FOR WHICH I DEEPLY, DEEPLY APOLOGIZE.
BY THE GOOD GRACE OF THIS LIVING LAND, HOWEVER, I'VE BEEN GIVEN A CHANCE TO REDEEM MYSELF.
TO TAKE THE WHOLE TRUTH INTO ACCOUNT, AS I SHOULD HAVE FROM THE ONSET, AND FIND PEACEFUL COMPROMISE TO OUR DILEMMA.

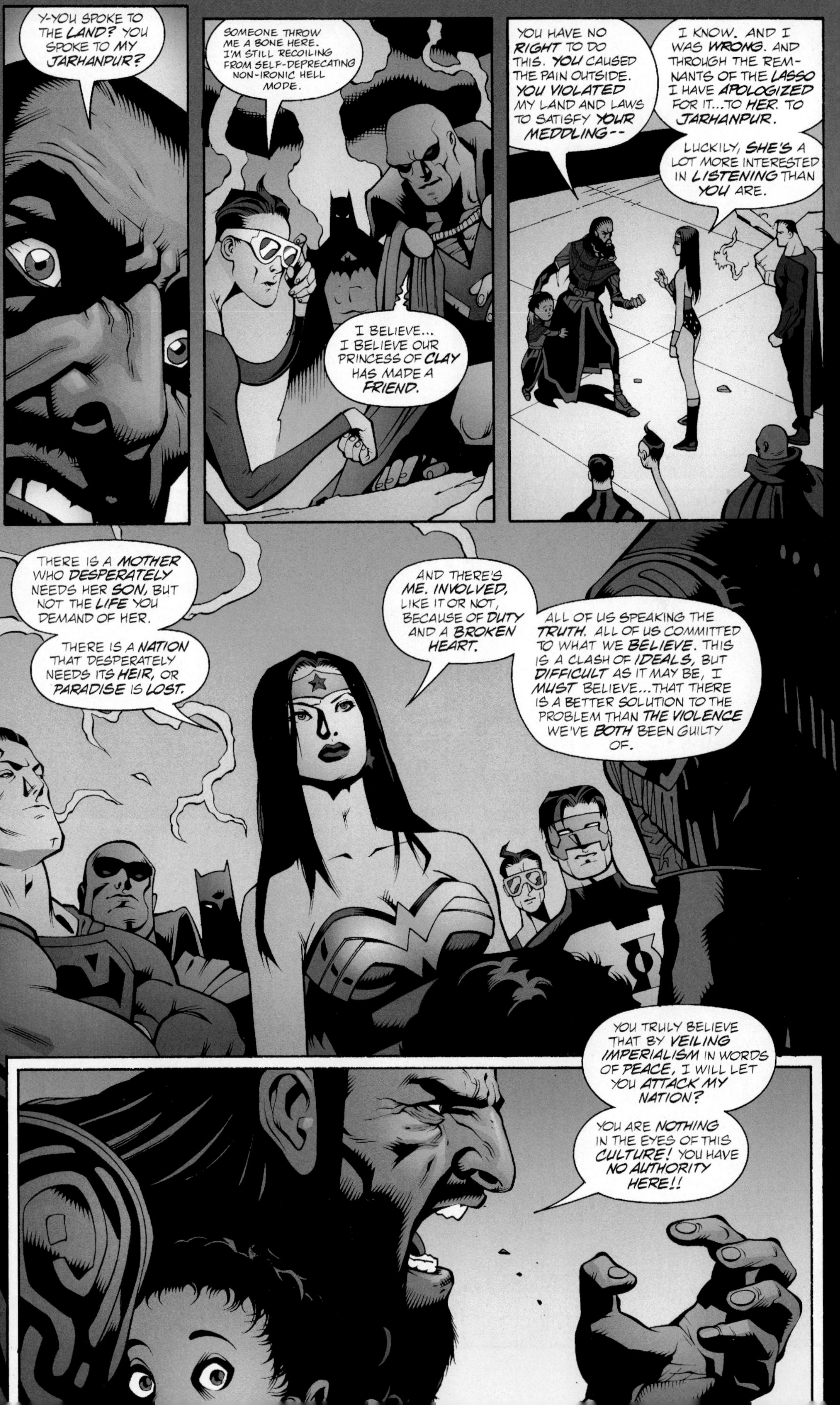

Y-YOU SPOKE TO THE LAND? YOU SPOKE TO MY JARHANPUR?
SOMEONE THROW ME A BONE HERE. I'M STILL RECOILING FROM SELF-DEPRECATING NON-IRONIC HELL MODE.
I BELIEVE... I BELIEVE OUR PRINCESS OF CLAY HAS MADE A FRIEND.
YOU HAVE NO RIGHT TO DO THIS. YOU CAUSED THE PAIN OUTSIDE. YOU VIOLATED MY LAND AND LAWS TO SATISFY YOUR MEDDLING--
I KNOW. AND I WAS WRONG. AND THROUGH THE REMNANTS OF THE LASSO I HAVE APOLOGIZED FOR IT...TO HER. TO JARHANPUR.
LUCKILY, SHE'S A LOT MORE INTERESTED IN LISTENING THAN YOU ARE.
THERE IS A MOTHER WHO DESPERATELY NEEDS HER SON, BUT NOT THE LIFE YOU DEMAND OF HER.
THERE IS A NATION THAT DESPERATELY NEEDS ITS HEIR, OR PARADISE IS LOST.
AND THERE'S ME. INVOLVED, LIKE IT OR NOT, BECAUSE OF DUTY AND A BROKEN HEART.
ALL OF US SPEAKING THE TRUTH. ALL OF US COMMITTED TO WHAT WE BELIEVE. THIS IS A CLASH OF IDEALS, BUT DIFFICULT AS IT MAY BE, I MUST BELIEVE...THAT THERE IS A BETTER SOLUTION TO THE PROBLEM THAN THE VIOLENCE WE'VE BOTH BEEN GUILTY OF.
YOU TRULY BELIEVE THAT BY VEILING IMPERIALISM IN WORDS OF PEACE, I WILL LET YOU ATTACK MY NATION?
YOU ARE NOTHING IN THE EYES OF THIS CULTURE! YOU HAVE NO AUTHORITY HERE!!

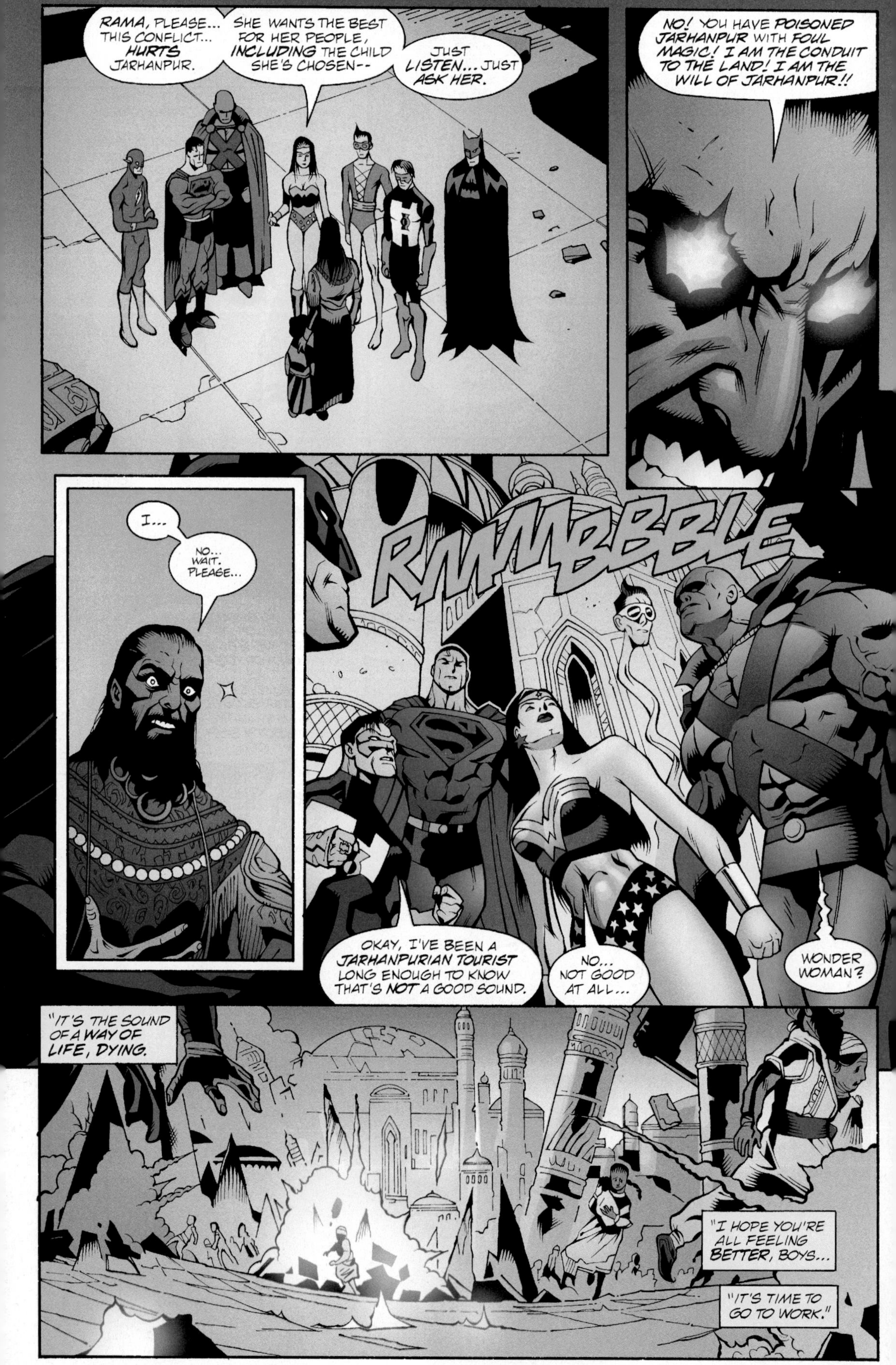
RAMA, PLEASE... THIS CONFLICT... HURTS JARHANPUR.
SHE WANTS THE BEST FOR HER PEOPLE, INCLUDING THE CHILD SHE'S CHOSEN--
JUST LISTEN... JUST ASK HER.
NO! YOU HAVE POISONED JARHANPUR WITH FOUL MAGIC! I AM THE CONDUIT TO THE LAND! I AM THE WILL OF JARHANPUR!!
I...
NO... WAIT. PLEASE...
RMMBBBLE
OKAY, I'VE BEEN A JARHANPURIAN TOURIST LONG ENOUGH TO KNOW THAT'S NOT A GOOD SOUND.
NO... NOT GOOD AT ALL...
WONDER WOMAN?
"IT'S THE SOUND OF A WAY OF LIFE, DYING.
"I HOPE YOU'RE ALL FEELING BETTER, BOYS...
"IT'S TIME TO GO TO WORK."

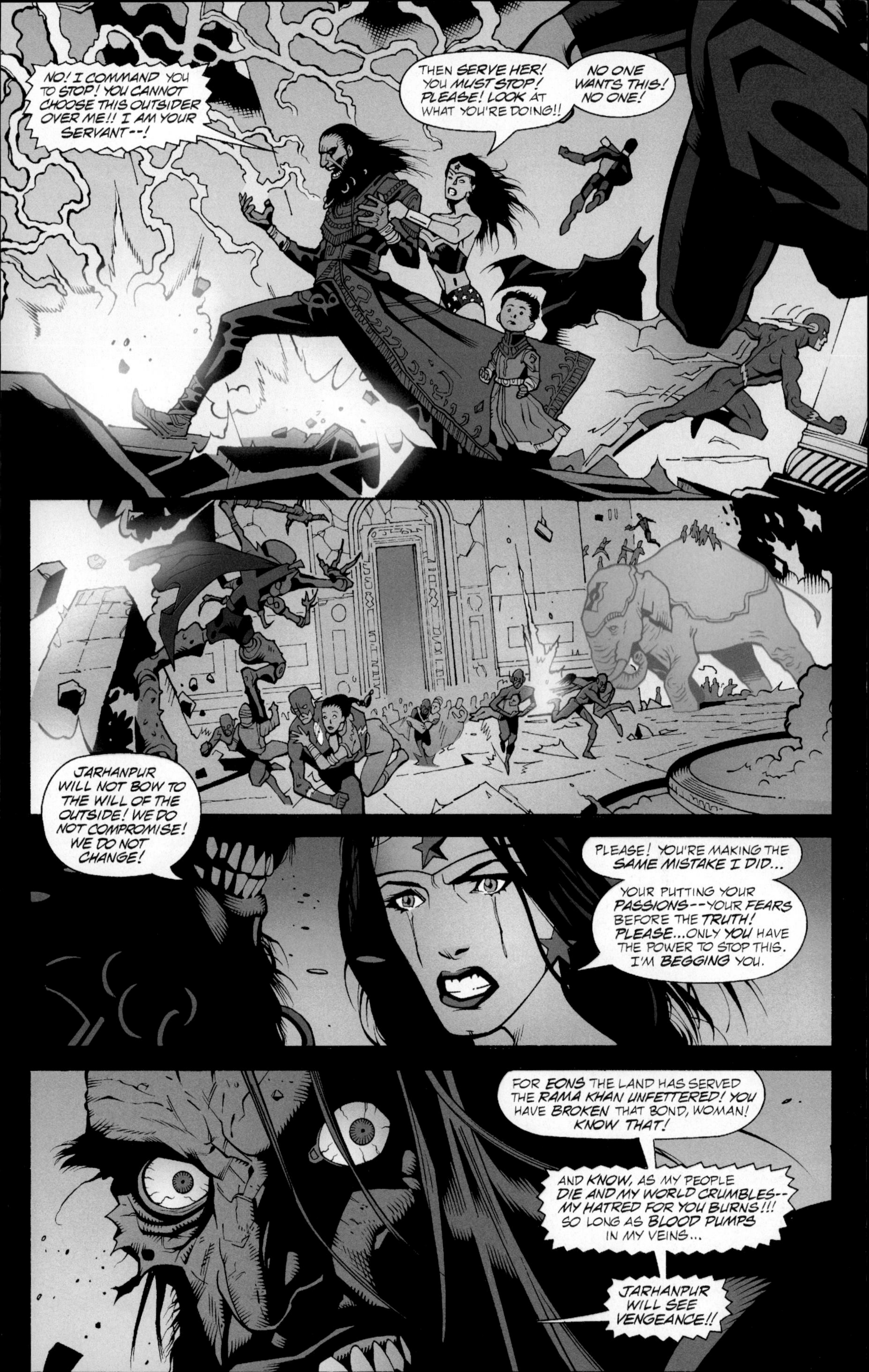
NO! I COMMAND YOU TO STOP! YOU CANNOT CHOOSE THIS OUTSIDER OVER ME!! I AM YOUR SERVANT--!
THEN SERVE HER! YOU MUST STOP! PLEASE! LOOK AT WHAT YOU'RE DOING!!
NO ONE WANTS THIS! NO ONE!
JARHANPUR WILL NOT BOW TO THE WILL OF THE OUTSIDE! WE DO NOT COMPROMISE! WE DO NOT CHANGE!
PLEASE! YOU'RE MAKING THE SAME MISTAKE I DID...
YOUR PUTTING YOUR PASSIONS--YOUR FEARS BEFORE THE TRUTH! PLEASE...ONLY YOU HAVE THE POWER TO STOP THIS. I'M BEGGING YOU.
FOR EONS THE LAND HAS SERVED THE RAMA KHAN UNFETTERED! YOU HAVE BROKEN THAT BOND, WOMAN! KNOW THAT!
AND KNOW, AS MY PEOPLE DIE AND MY WORLD CRUMBLES-- MY HATRED FOR YOU BURNS!!! SO LONG AS BLOOD PUMPS IN MY VEINS...
JARHANPUR WILL SEE VENGEANCE!!

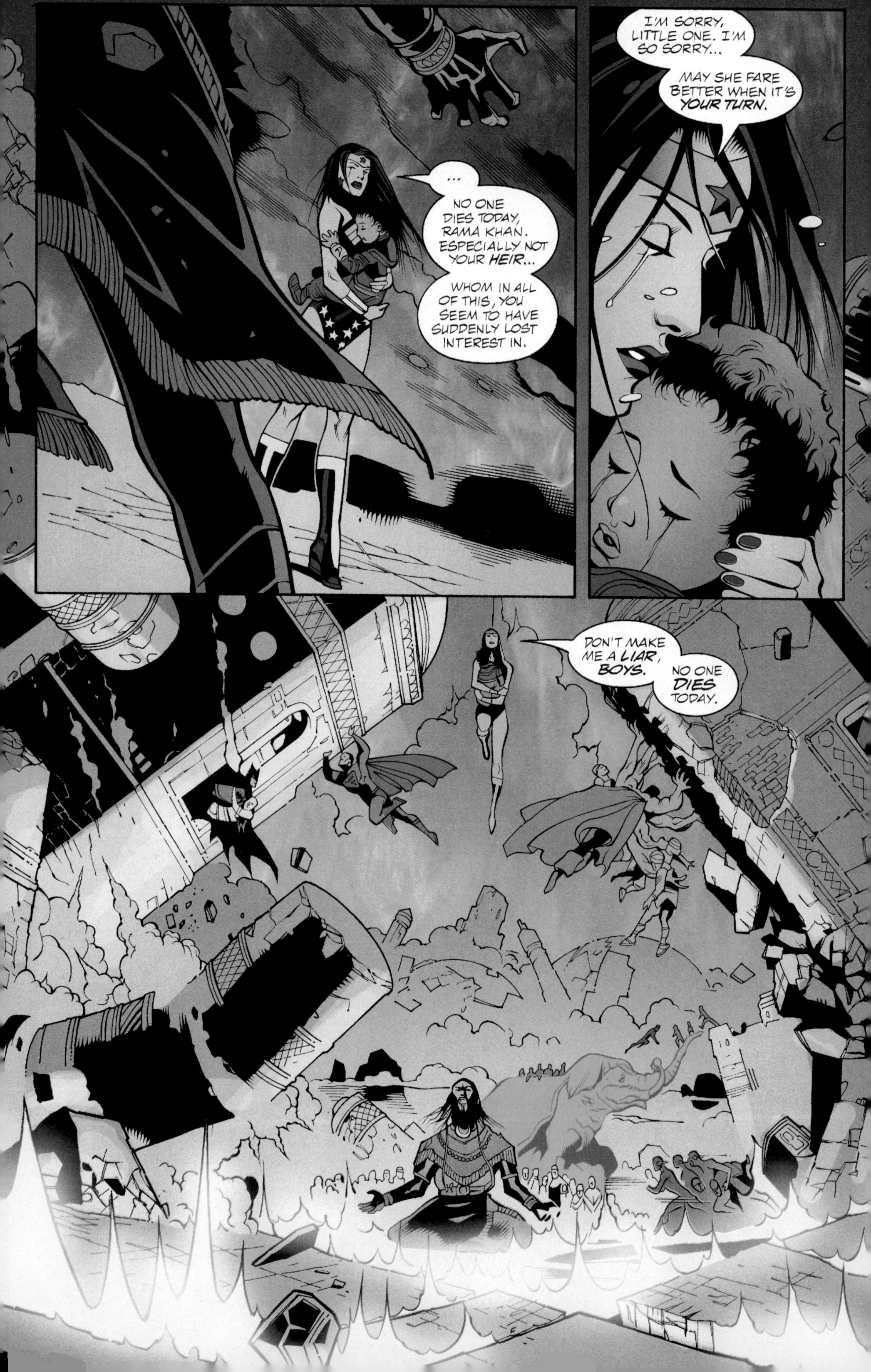
...
NO ONE DIES TODAY, RAMA KHAN. ESPECIALLY NOT YOUR HEIR...
WHOM IN ALL OF THIS, YOU SEEM TO HAVE SUDDENLY LOST INTEREST IN.
I'M SORRY, LITTLE ONE. I'M SO SORRY...
MAY SHE FARE BETTER WHEN IT'S YOUR TURN.
DON'T MAKE ME A LIAR, BOYS.
NO ONE DIES TODAY.

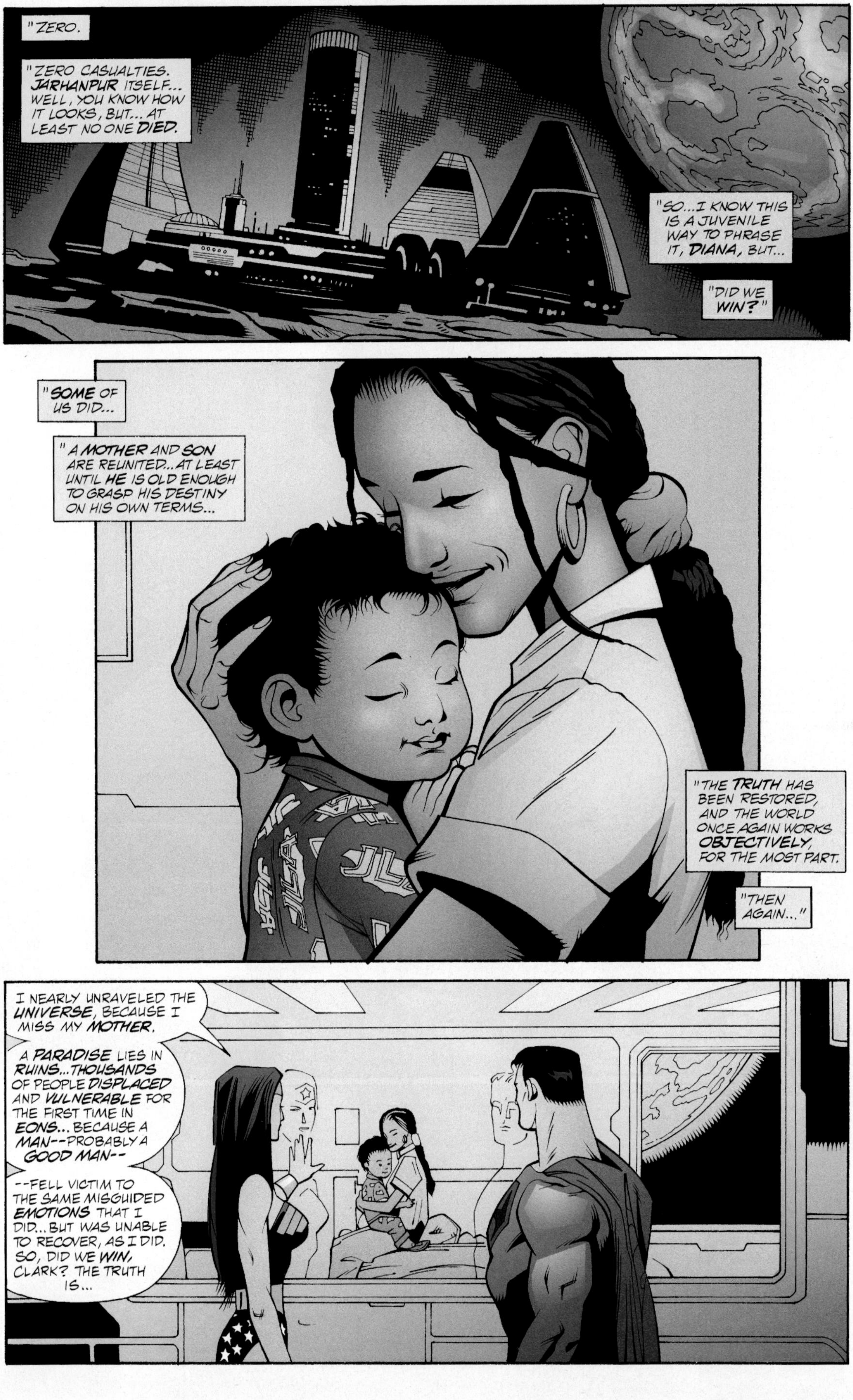
"ZERO.
"ZERO CASUALTIES. JARHANPUR ITSELF... WELL, YOU KNOW HOW IT LOOKS, BUT... AT LEAST NO ONE DIED.
"SO...I KNOW THIS IS A JUVENILE WAY TO PHRASE IT, DIANA, BUT...
"DID WE WIN?"
"SOME OF US DID...
"A MOTHER AND SON ARE REUNITED...AT LEAST UNTIL HE IS OLD ENOUGH TO GRASP HIS DESTINY ON HIS OWN TERMS...
"THE TRUTH HAS BEEN RESTORED, AND THE WORLD ONCE AGAIN WORKS OBJECTIVELY, FOR THE MOST PART.
"THEN AGAIN..."
I NEARLY UNRAVELED THE UNIVERSE, BECAUSE I MISS MY MOTHER.
A PARADISE LIES IN RUINS...THOUSANDS OF PEOPLE DISPLACED AND VULNERABLE FOR THE FIRST TIME IN EONS... BECAUSE A MAN--PROBABLY A GOOD MAN--
--FELL VICTIM TO THE SAME MISGUIDED EMOTIONS THAT I DID... BUT WAS UNABLE TO RECOVER, AS I DID. SO, DID WE WIN, CLARK? THE TRUTH IS...

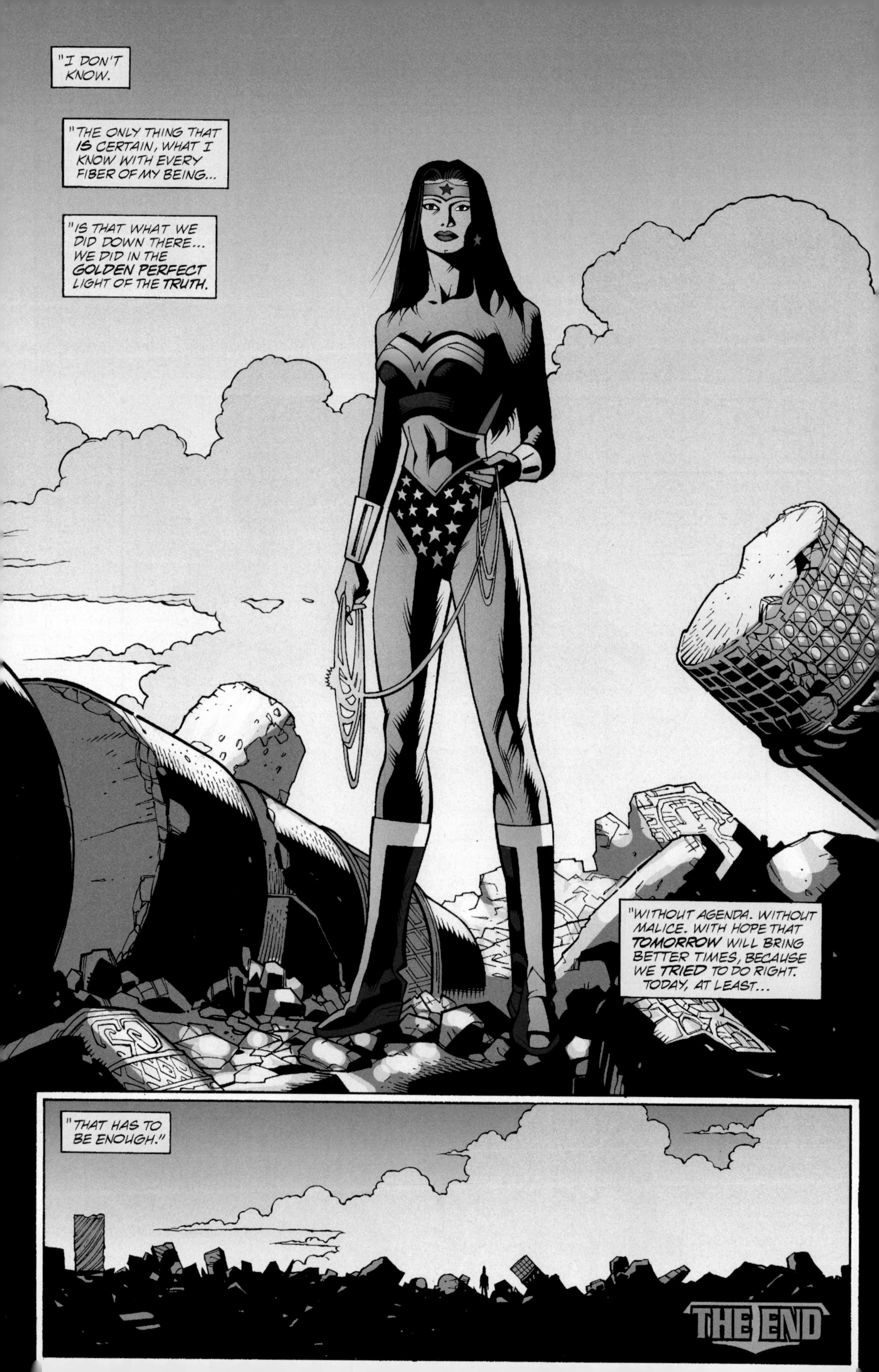
"I DON'T KNOW.
"THE ONLY THING THAT IS CERTAIN, WHAT I KNOW WITH EVERY FIBER OF MY BEING...
"IS THAT WHAT WE DID DOWN THERE... WE DID IN THE GOLDEN PERFECT LIGHT OF THE TRUTH.
"WITHOUT AGENDA. WITHOUT MALICE. WITH HOPE THAT TOMORROW WILL BRING BETTER TIMES, BECAUSE WE TRIED TO DO RIGHT. TODAY, AT LEAST...
"THAT HAS TO BE ENOUGH."
THE END

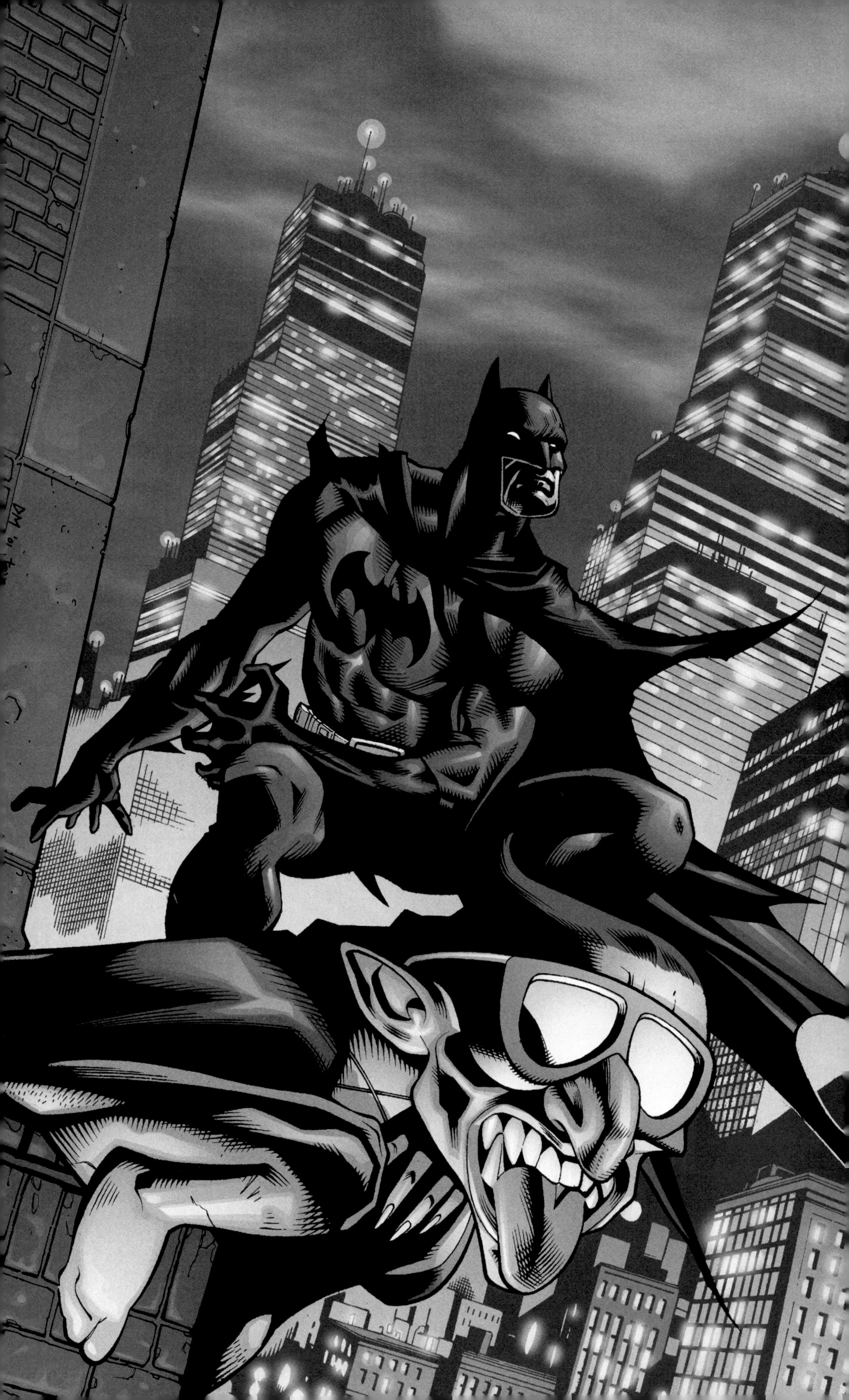

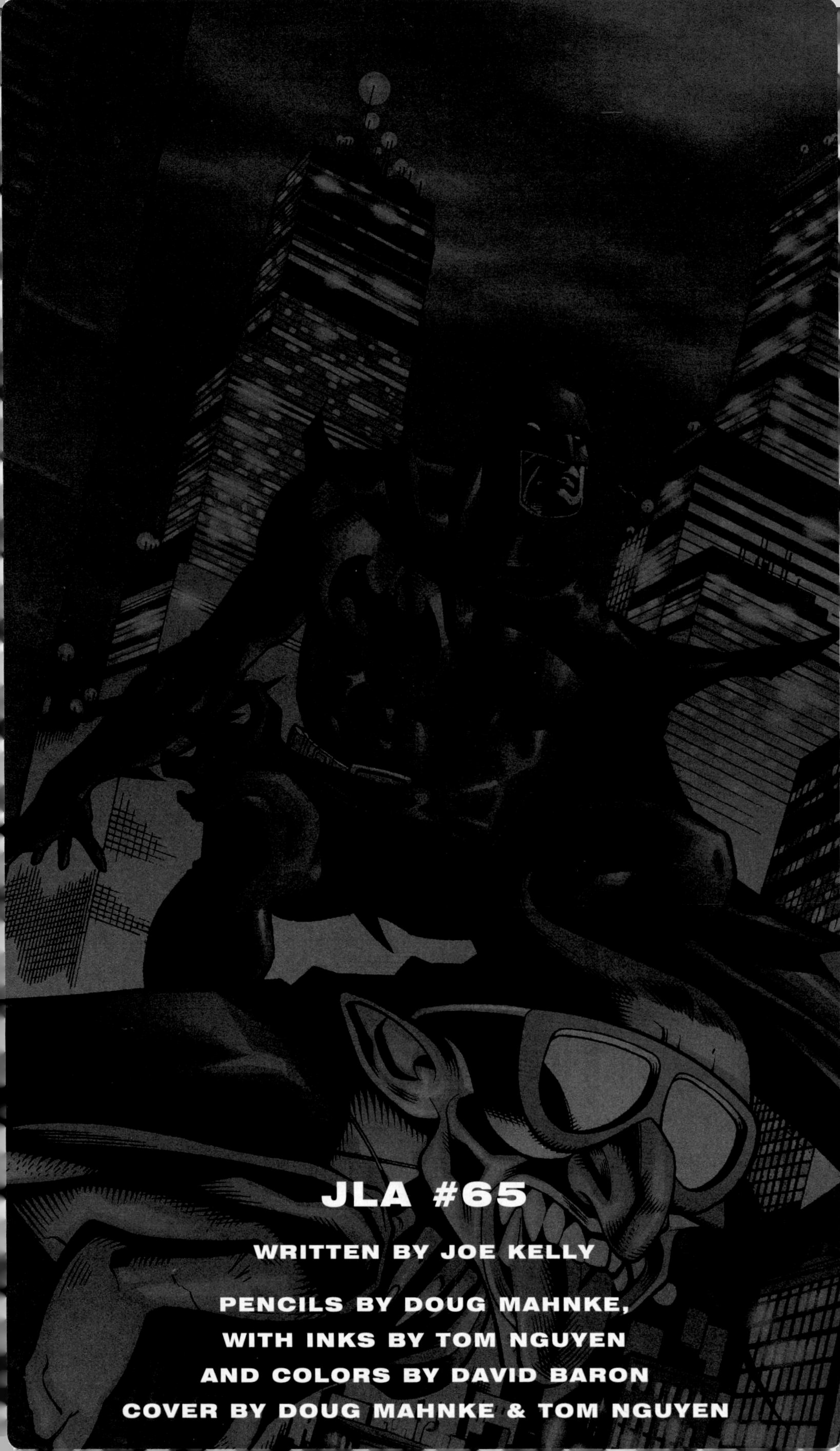

JLA #65

WRITTEN BY JOE KELLY

PENCILS BY DOUG MAHNKE,
WITH INKS BY TOM NGUYEN
AND COLORS BY DAVID BARON
COVER BY DOUG MAHNKE & TOM NGUYEN

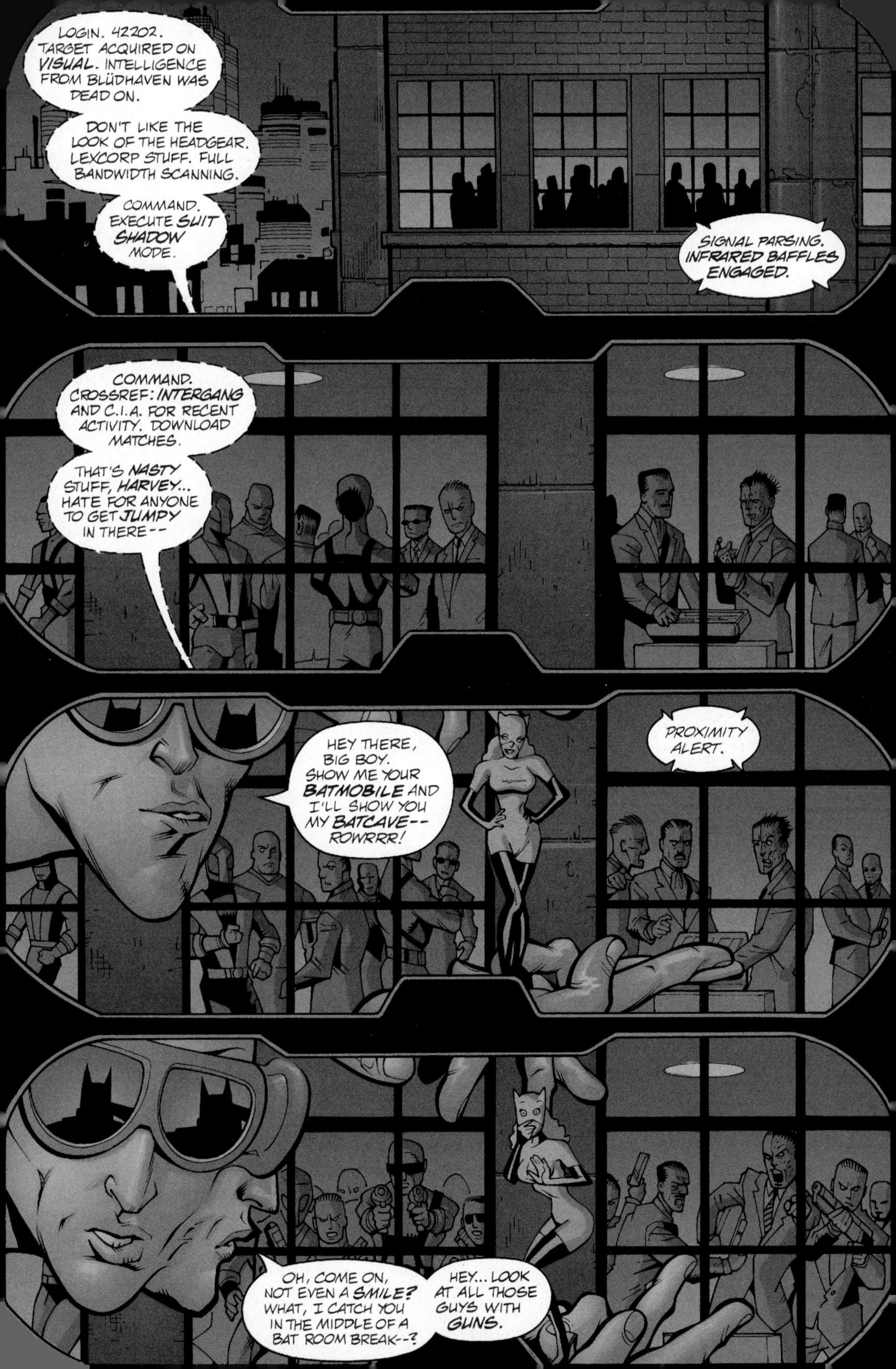
LOGIN. 42202. TARGET ACQUIRED ON VISUAL. INTELLIGENCE FROM BLÜDHAVEN WAS DEAD ON.
DON'T LIKE THE LOOK OF THE HEADGEAR. LEXCORP STUFF. FULL BANDWIDTH SCANNING.
COMMAND. EXECUTE SUIT SHADOW MODE.
SIGNAL PARSING. INFRARED BAFFLES ENGAGED.
COMMAND. CROSSREF: INTERGANG AND C.I.A. FOR RECENT ACTIVITY. DOWNLOAD MATCHES.
THAT'S NASTY STUFF, HARVEY... HATE FOR ANYONE TO GET JUMPY IN THERE--
HEY THERE, BIG BOY. SHOW ME YOUR BATMOBILE AND I'LL SHOW YOU MY BATCAVE--ROWRRR!
PROXIMITY ALERT.
OH, COME ON, NOT EVEN A SMILE? WHAT, I CATCH YOU IN THE MIDDLE OF A BAT ROOM BREAK--?
HEY... LOOK AT ALL THOSE GUYS WITH GUNS.

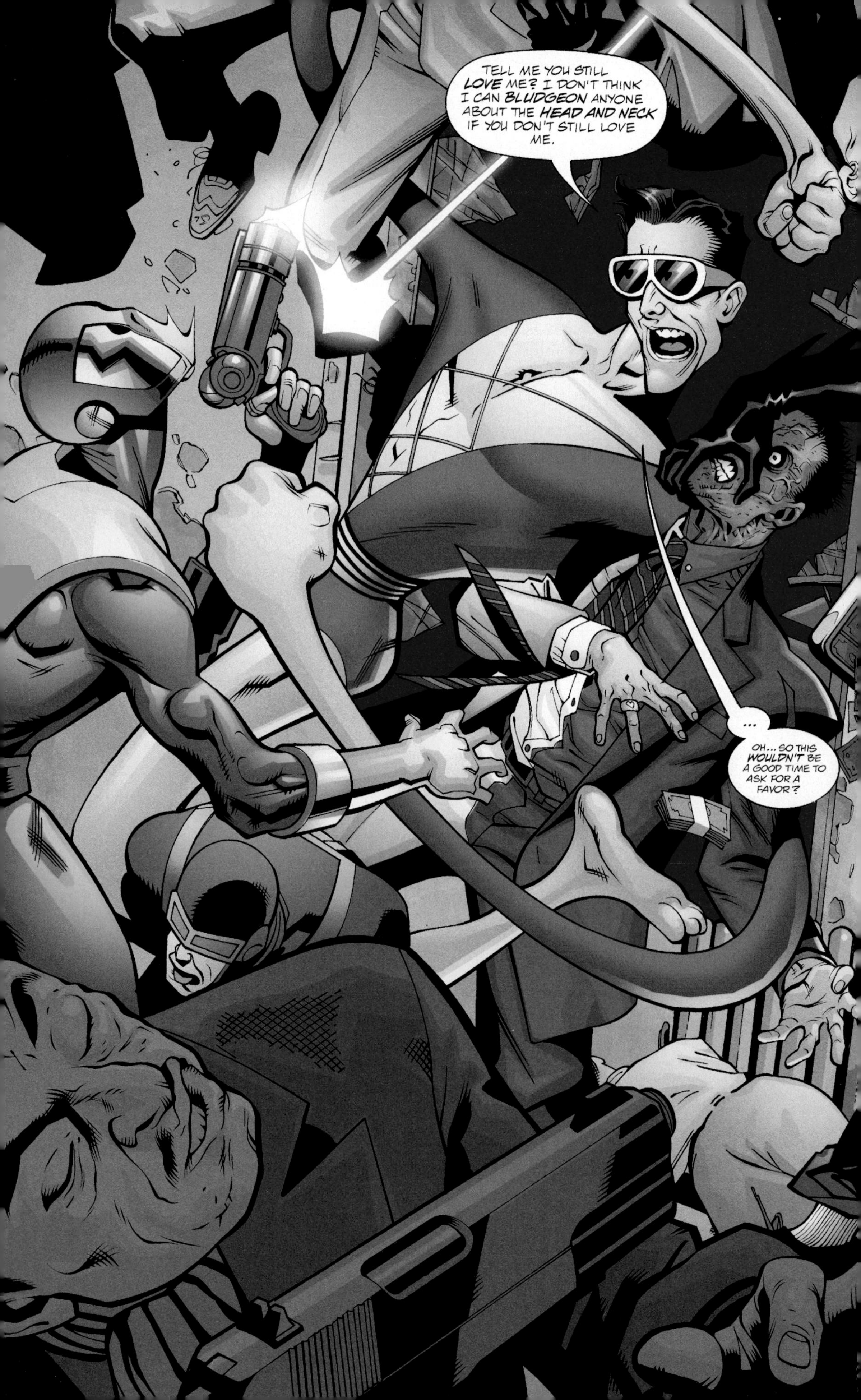

TELL ME YOU STILL LOVE ME? I DON'T THINK I CAN BLUDGEON ANYONE ABOUT THE HEAD AND NECK IF YOU DON'T STILL LOVE ME.
...
OH... SO THIS WOULDN'T BE A GOOD TIME TO ASK FOR A FAVOR?

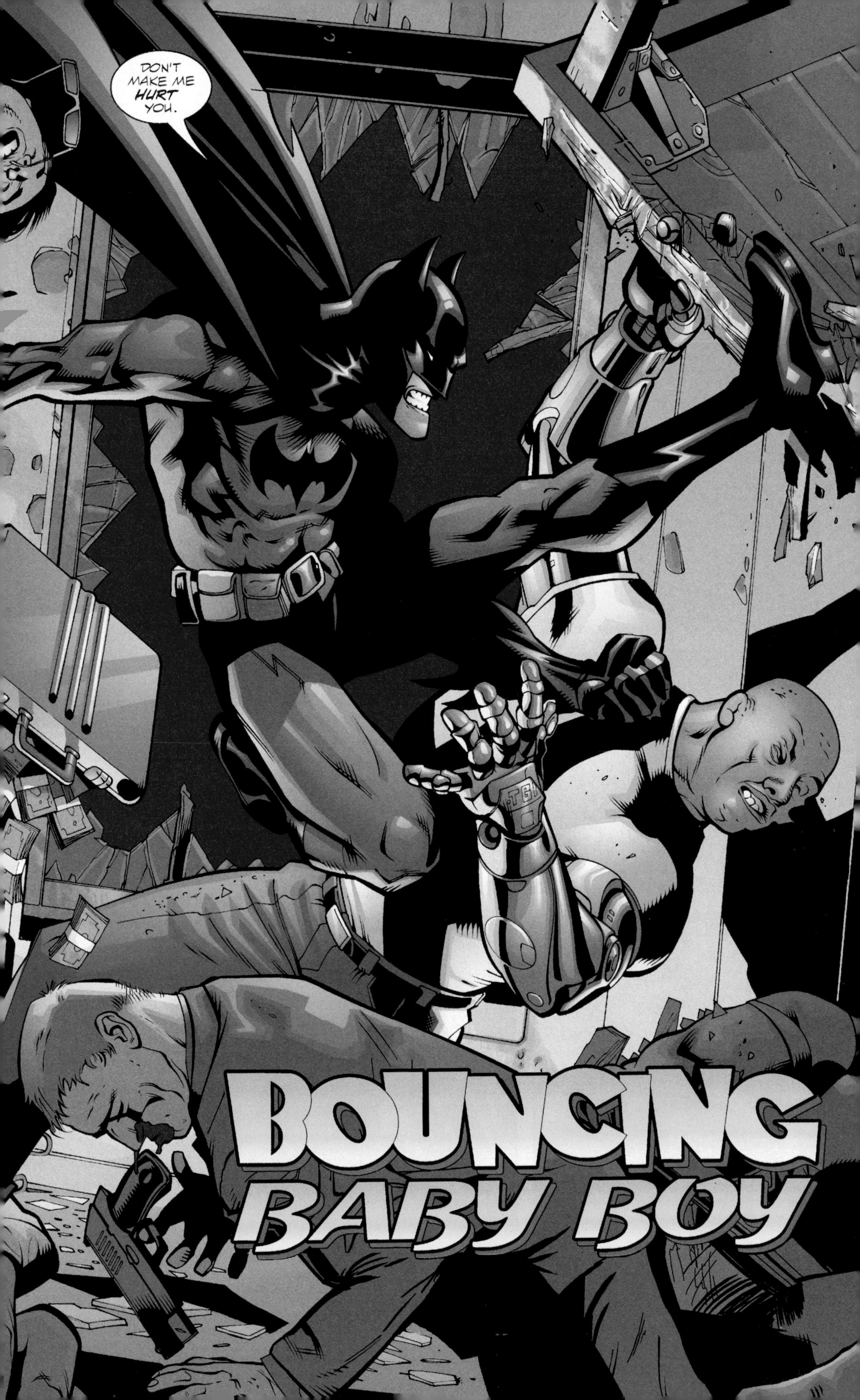
DON'T MAKE ME HURT YOU.
BOUNCING BABY BOY

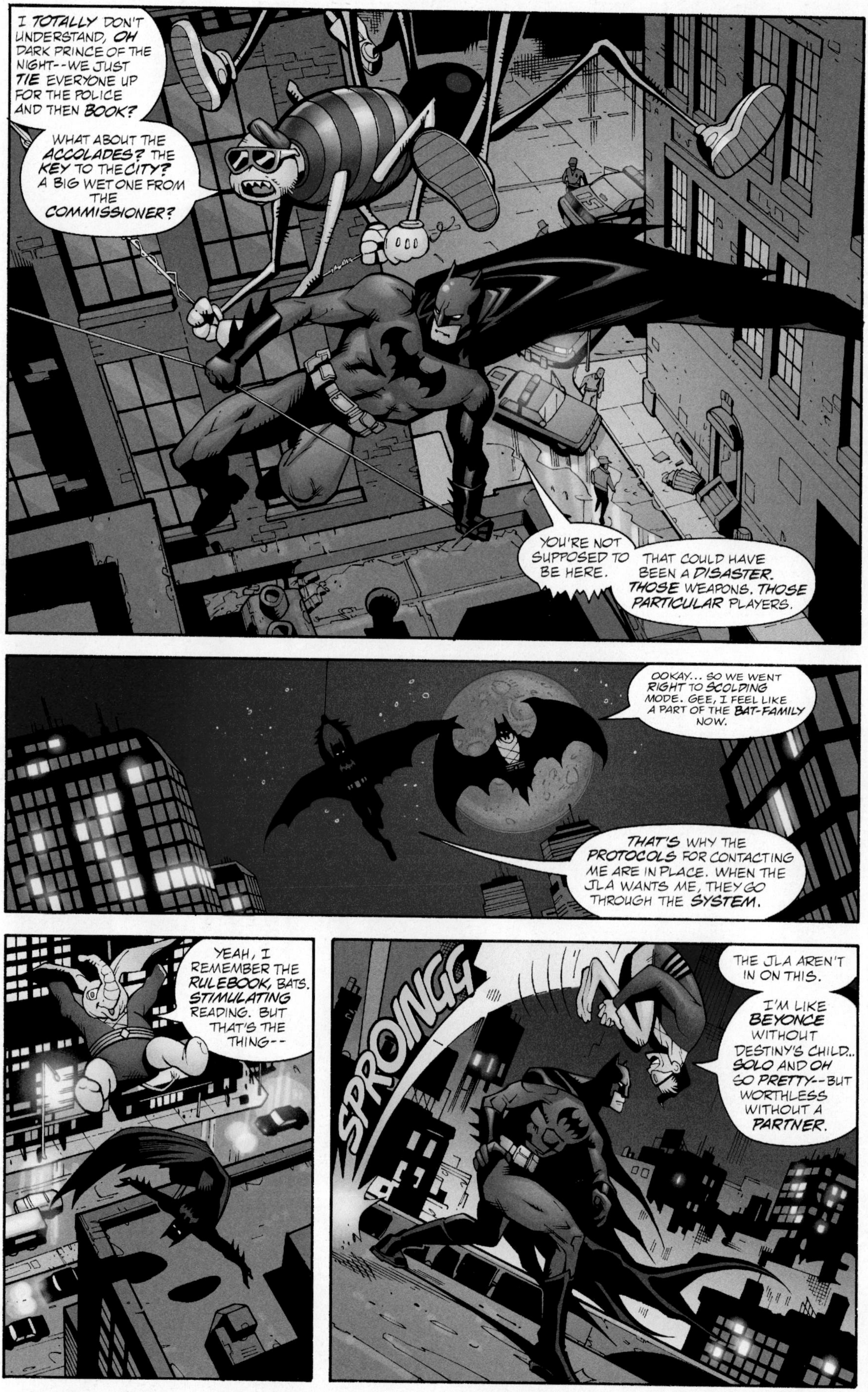
I TOTALLY DON'T UNDERSTAND, OH DARK PRINCE OF THE NIGHT--WE JUST TIE EVERYONE UP FOR THE POLICE AND THEN BOOK?
WHAT ABOUT THE ACCOLADES? THE KEY TO THE CITY? A BIG WET ONE FROM THE COMMISSIONER?
YOU'RE NOT SUPPOSED TO BE HERE.
THAT COULD HAVE BEEN A DISASTER. THOSE WEAPONS. THOSE PARTICULAR PLAYERS.
OOKAY... SO WE WENT RIGHT TO SCOLDING MODE. GEE, I FEEL LIKE A PART OF THE BAT-FAMILY NOW.
THAT'S WHY THE PROTOCOLS FOR CONTACTING ME ARE IN PLACE. WHEN THE JLA WANTS ME, THEY GO THROUGH THE SYSTEM.
YEAH, I REMEMBER THE RULEBOOK, BATS. STIMULATING READING. BUT THAT'S THE THING--
SPROINGG
THE JLA AREN'T IN ON THIS.
I'M LIKE BEYONCE WITHOUT DESTINY'S CHILD... SOLO AND OH SO PRETTY--BUT WORTHLESS WITHOUT A PARTNER.

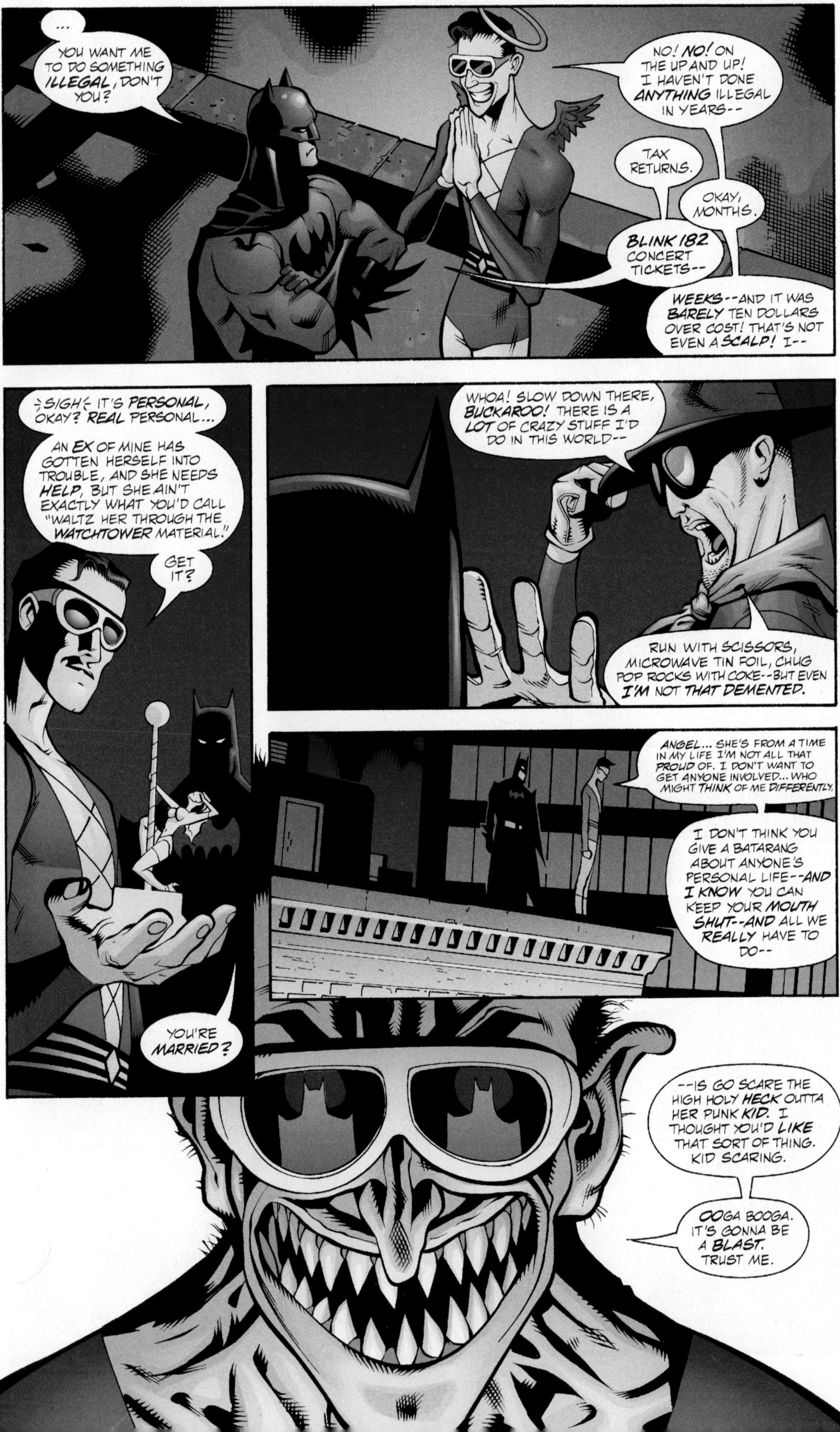
...
YOU WANT ME TO DO SOMETHING ILLEGAL, DON'T YOU?
NO! NO! ON THE UP AND UP! I HAVEN'T DONE ANYTHING ILLEGAL IN YEARS--
TAX RETURNS.
OKAY, MONTHS.
BLINK 182 CONCERT TICKETS--
WEEKS--AND IT WAS BARELY TEN DOLLARS OVER COST! THAT'S NOT EVEN A SCALP! I--
WHOA! SLOW DOWN THERE, BUCKAROO! THERE IS A LOT OF CRAZY STUFF I'D DO IN THIS WORLD--
RUN WITH SCISSORS, MICROWAVE TIN FOIL, CHUG POP ROCKS WITH COKE--BUT EVEN I'M NOT THAT DEMENTED.
-SIGH- IT'S PERSONAL, OKAY? REAL PERSONAL...
AN EX OF MINE HAS GOTTEN HERSELF INTO TROUBLE, AND SHE NEEDS HELP, BUT SHE AIN'T EXACTLY WHAT YOU'D CALL "WALTZ HER THROUGH THE WATCHTOWER MATERIAL."
GET IT?
YOU'RE MARRIED?
ANGEL... SHE'S FROM A TIME IN MY LIFE I'M NOT ALL THAT PROUD OF. I DON'T WANT TO GET ANYONE INVOLVED... WHO MIGHT THINK OF ME DIFFERENTLY.
I DON'T THINK YOU GIVE A BATARANG ABOUT ANYONE'S PERSONAL LIFE--AND I KNOW YOU CAN KEEP YOUR MOUTH SHUT--AND ALL WE REALLY HAVE TO DO--
--IS GO SCARE THE HIGH HOLY HECK OUTTA HER PUNK KID. I THOUGHT YOU'D LIKE THAT SORT OF THING. KID SCARING.
OOGA BOOGA. IT'S GONNA BE A BLAST. TRUST ME.

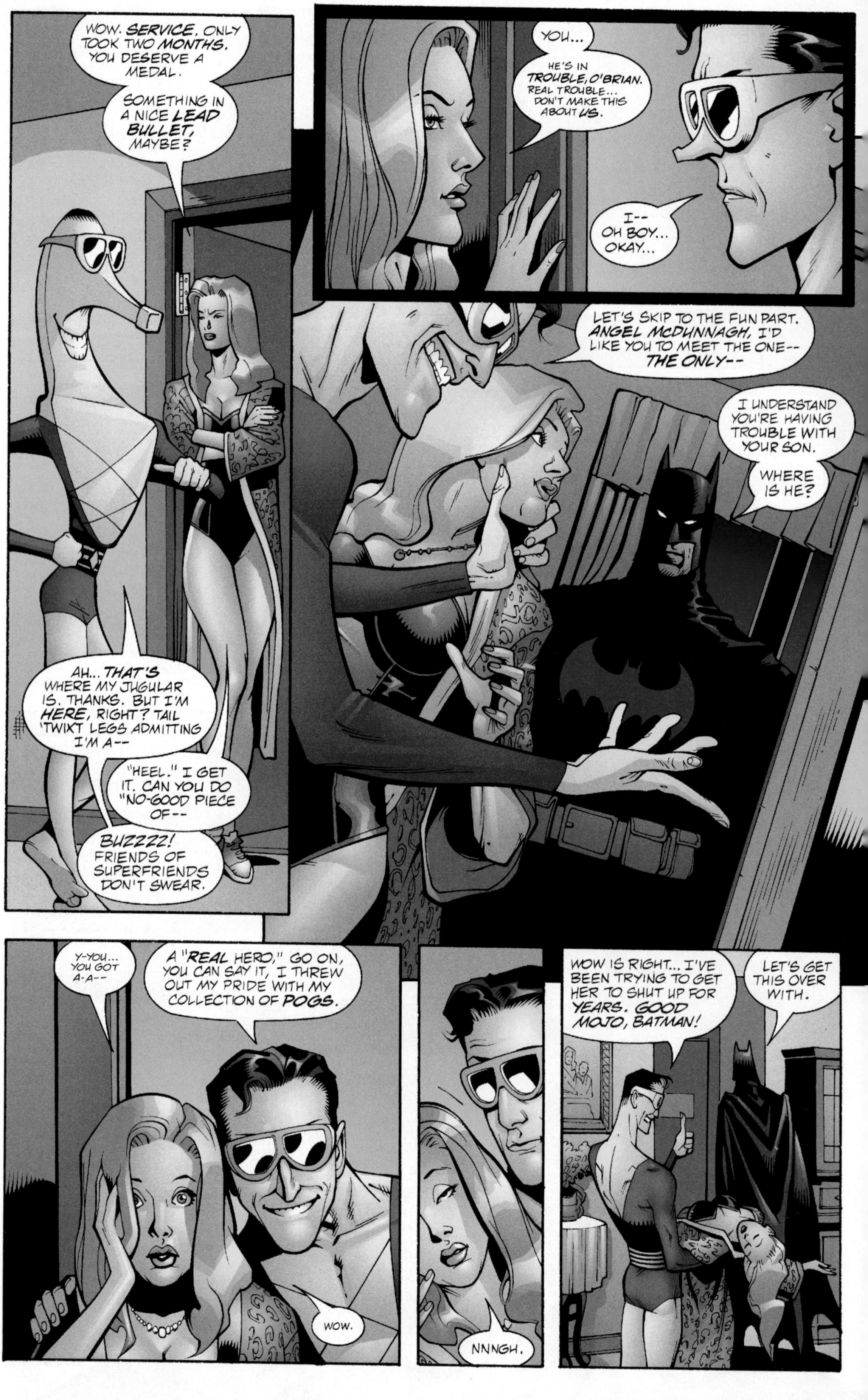
WOW. SERVICE. ONLY TOOK TWO MONTHS. YOU DESERVE A MEDAL.
SOMETHING IN A NICE LEAD BULLET, MAYBE?
AH... THAT'S WHERE MY JUGULAR IS. THANKS. BUT I'M HERE, RIGHT? TAIL 'TWIXT LEGS ADMITTING I'M A--
"HEEL." I GET IT. CAN YOU DO "NO-GOOD PIECE OF--
BUZZZZ! FRIENDS OF SUPERFRIENDS DON'T SWEAR.
YOU...
HE'S IN TROUBLE, O'BRIAN. REAL TROUBLE... DON'T MAKE THIS ABOUT US.
I-- OH BOY... OKAY...
LET'S SKIP TO THE FUN PART. ANGEL MCDUNNAGH, I'D LIKE YOU TO MEET THE ONE-- THE ONLY--
I UNDERSTAND YOU'RE HAVING TROUBLE WITH YOUR SON.
WHERE IS HE?
Y-YOU... YOU GOT A-A--
A "REAL HERO," GO ON, YOU CAN SAY IT, I THREW OUT MY PRIDE WITH MY COLLECTION OF POGS.
WOW.
NNNGH.
WOW IS RIGHT... I'VE BEEN TRYING TO GET HER TO SHUT UP FOR YEARS. GOOD MOJO, BATMAN!
LET'S GET THIS OVER WITH.

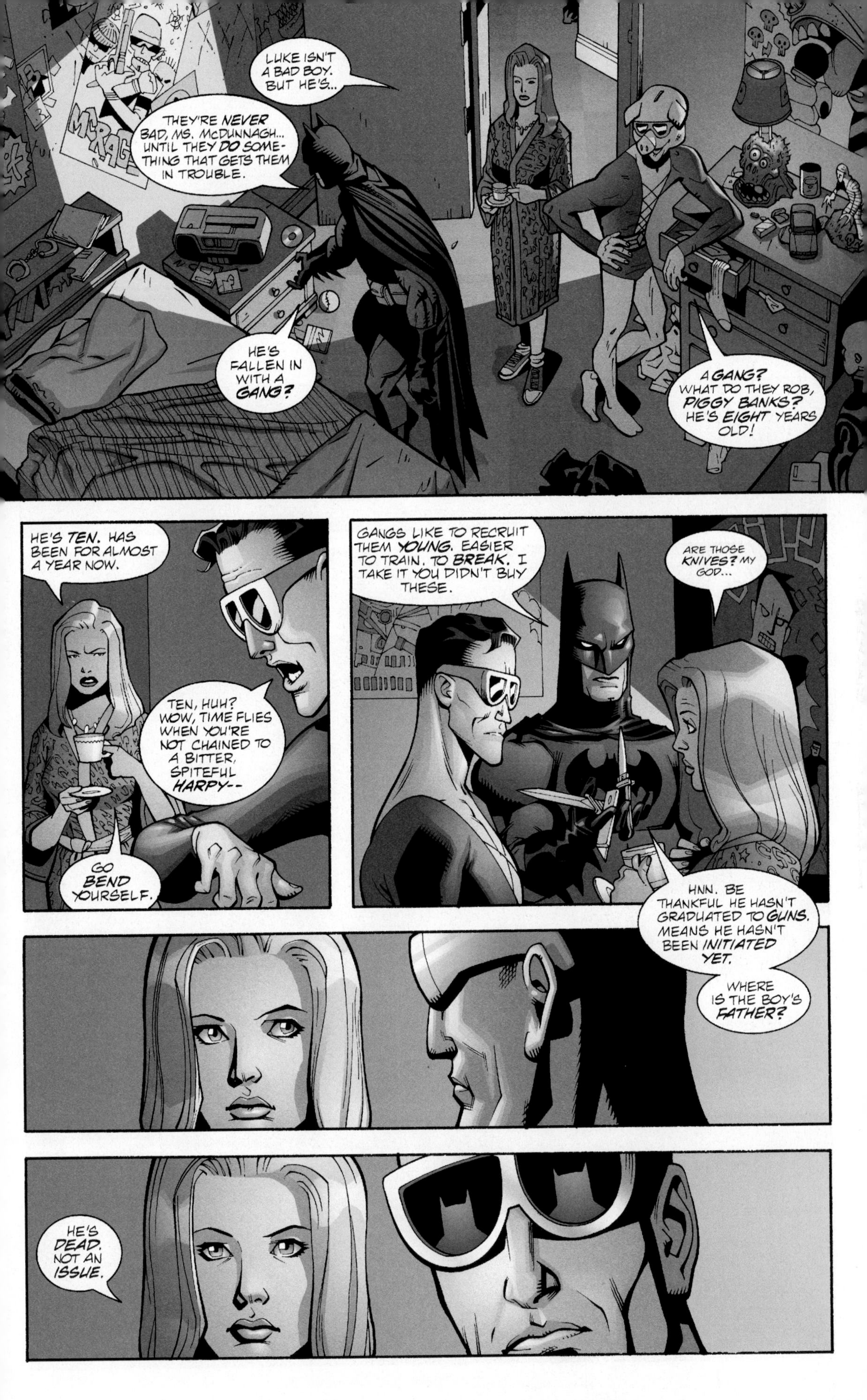
LUKE ISN'T A BAD BOY. BUT HE'S...
THEY'RE NEVER BAD, MS. McDUNNAGH... UNTIL THEY DO SOMETHING THAT GETS THEM IN TROUBLE.
HE'S FALLEN IN WITH A GANG?
A GANG? WHAT DO THEY ROB, PIGGY BANKS? HE'S EIGHT YEARS OLD!
HE'S TEN. HAS BEEN FOR ALMOST A YEAR NOW.
TEN, HUH? WOW, TIME FLIES WHEN YOU'RE NOT CHAINED TO A BITTER, SPITEFUL HARPY--
GO BEND YOURSELF.
GANGS LIKE TO RECRUIT THEM YOUNG. EASIER TO TRAIN. TO BREAK. I TAKE IT YOU DIDN'T BUY THESE.
ARE THOSE KNIVES? MY GOD...
HNN. BE THANKFUL HE HASN'T GRADUATED TO GUNS. MEANS HE HASN'T BEEN INITIATED YET.
WHERE IS THE BOY'S FATHER?
HE'S DEAD. NOT AN ISSUE.

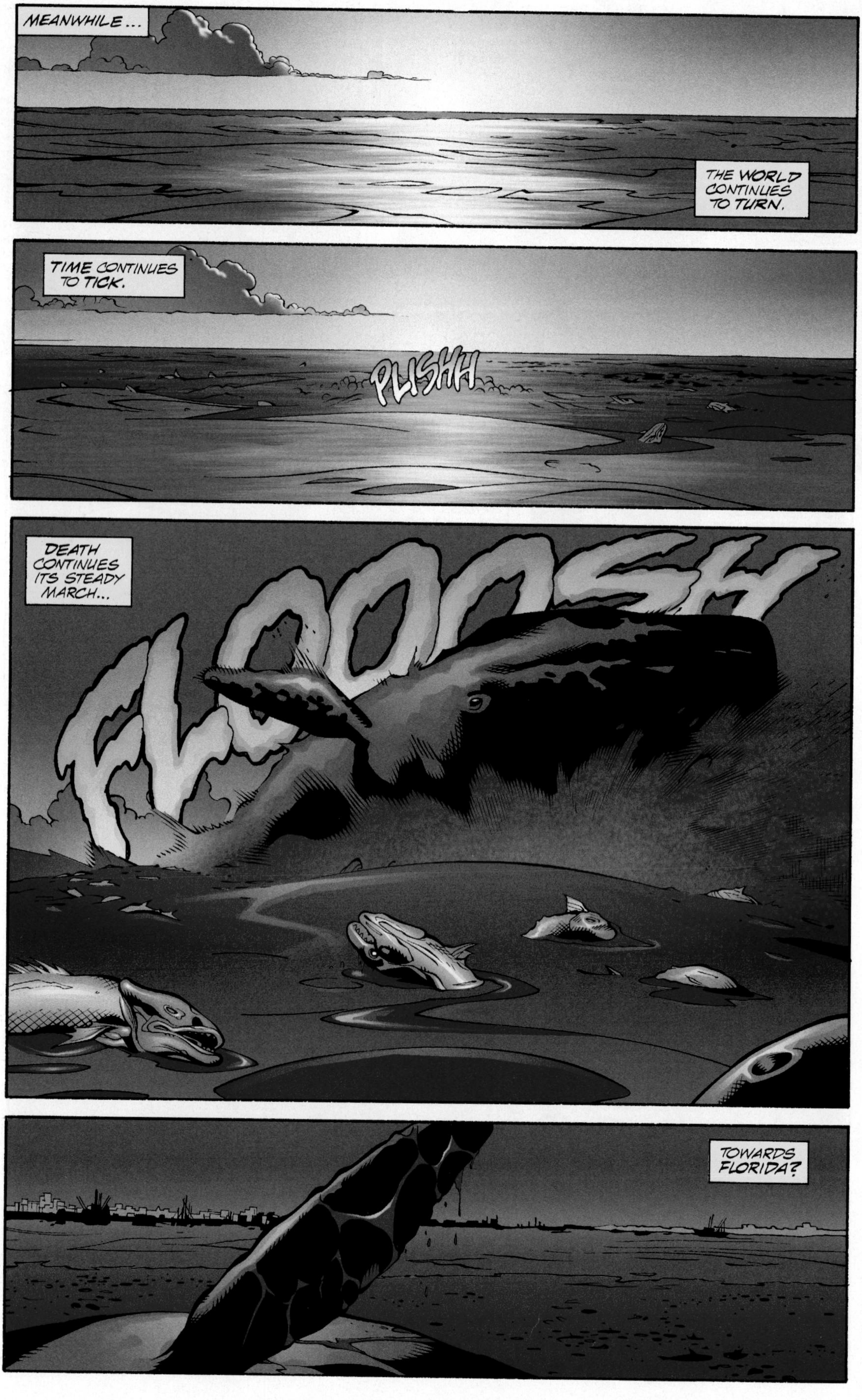
MEANWHILE...
THE WORLD CONTINUES TO TURN.
TIME CONTINUES TO TICK.
PLISHH
DEATH CONTINUES ITS STEADY MARCH...
FLOOOSH
TOWARDS FLORIDA?

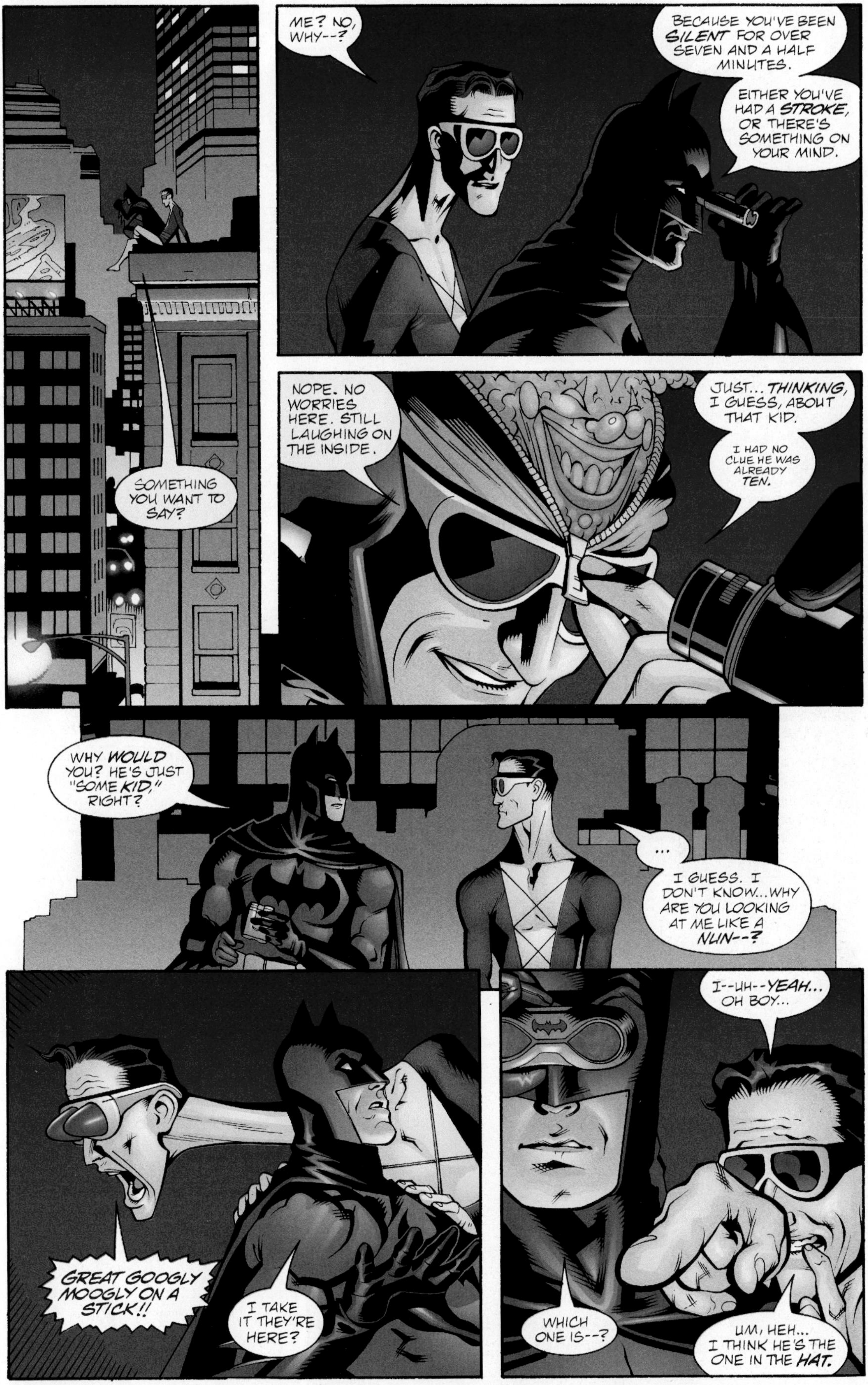
SOMETHING YOU WANT TO SAY?
ME? NO, WHY--?
BECAUSE YOU'VE BEEN SILENT FOR OVER SEVEN AND A HALF MINUTES.
EITHER YOU'VE HAD A STROKE, OR THERE'S SOMETHING ON YOUR MIND.
NOPE. NO WORRIES HERE. STILL LAUGHING ON THE INSIDE.
JUST... THINKING, I GUESS, ABOUT THAT KID.
I HAD NO CLUE HE WAS ALREADY TEN.
WHY WOULD YOU? HE'S JUST "SOME KID," RIGHT?
...
I GUESS. I DON'T KNOW... WHY ARE YOU LOOKING AT ME LIKE A NUN--?
GREAT GOOGLY MOOGLY ON A STICK!!
I TAKE IT THEY'RE HERE?
I--UH--YEAH... OH BOY...
WHICH ONE IS--?
UM, HEH... I THINK HE'S THE ONE IN THE HAT.

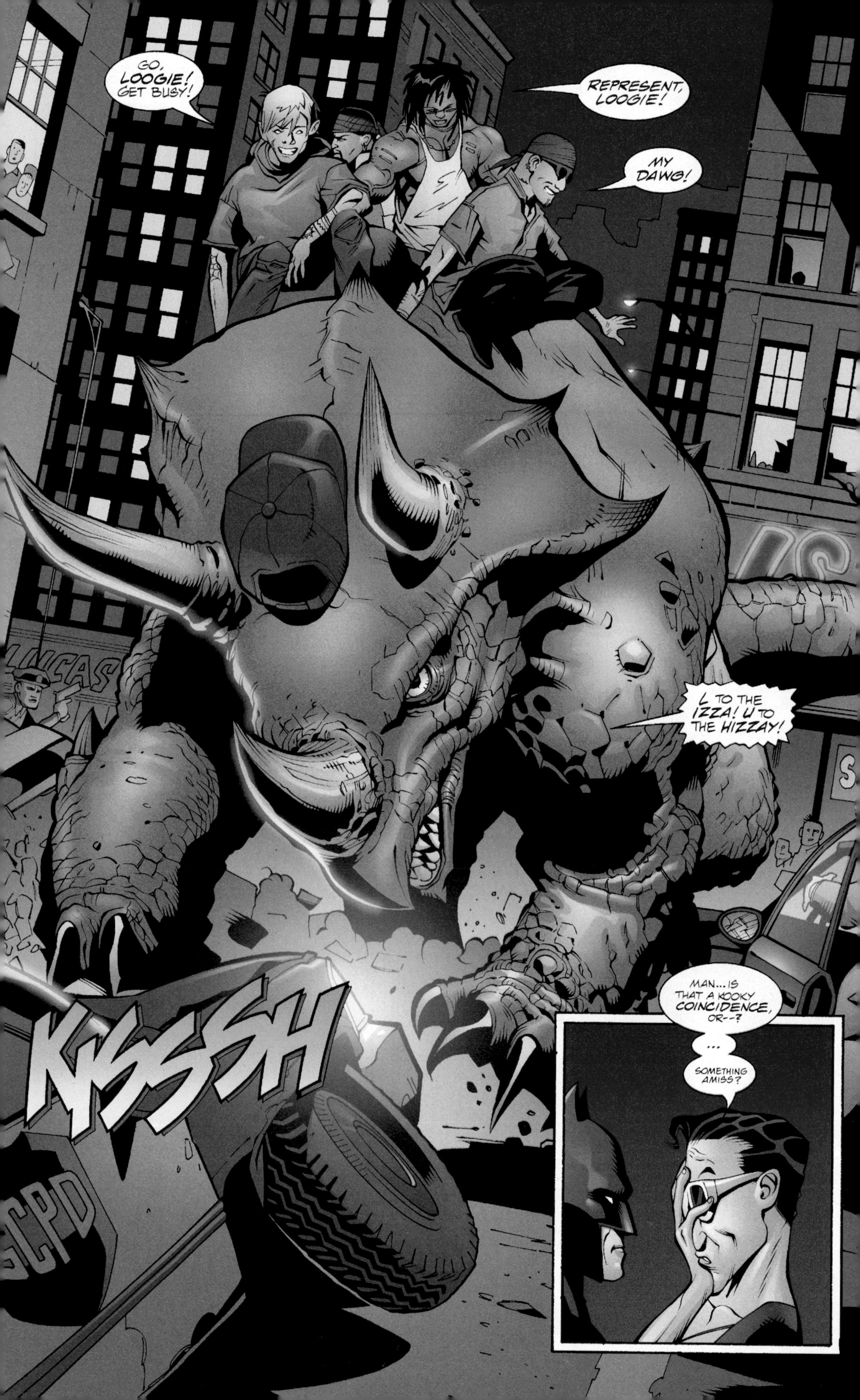
GO, LOOGIE! GET BUSY!
REPRESENT, LOOGIE!
MY DAWG!
L TO THE IZZA! U TO THE HIZZAY!
KSSSH
SCPD
MAN...IS THAT A KOOKY COINCIDENCE, OR--?
...
SOMETHING AMISS?

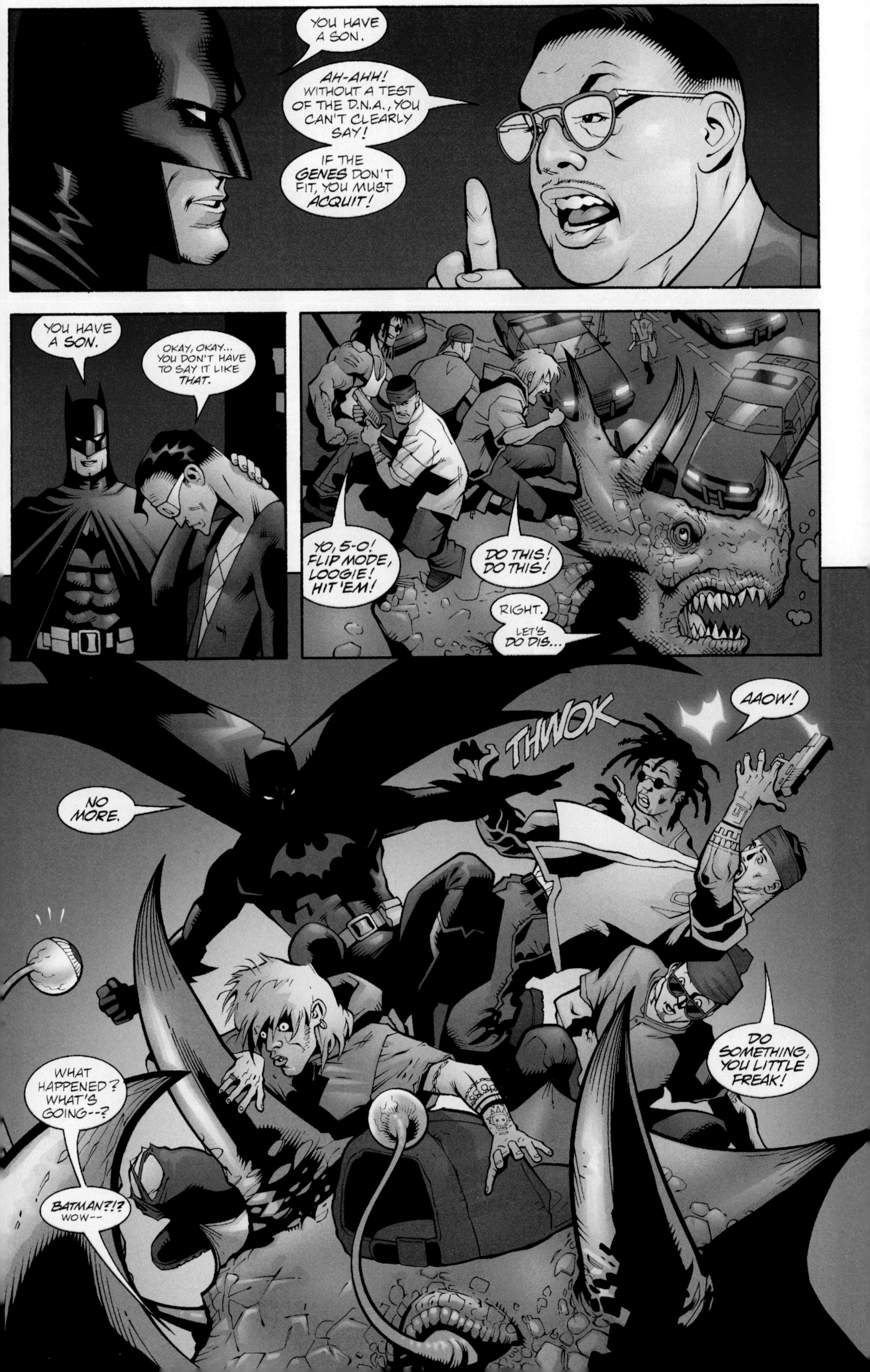
YOU HAVE A SON.
AH-AHH! WITHOUT A TEST OF THE D.N.A., YOU CAN'T CLEARLY SAY!
IF THE GENES DON'T FIT, YOU MUST ACQUIT!
YOU HAVE A SON.
OKAY, OKAY... YOU DON'T HAVE TO SAY IT LIKE THAT.
YO, 5-O! FLIP MODE, LOOGIE! HIT 'EM!
DO THIS! DO THIS!
RIGHT.
LET'S DO DIS...
THWOK
AAOW!
NO MORE.
DO SOMETHING, YOU LITTLE FREAK!
WHAT HAPPENED? WHAT'S GOING--?
BATMAN?!? WOW--

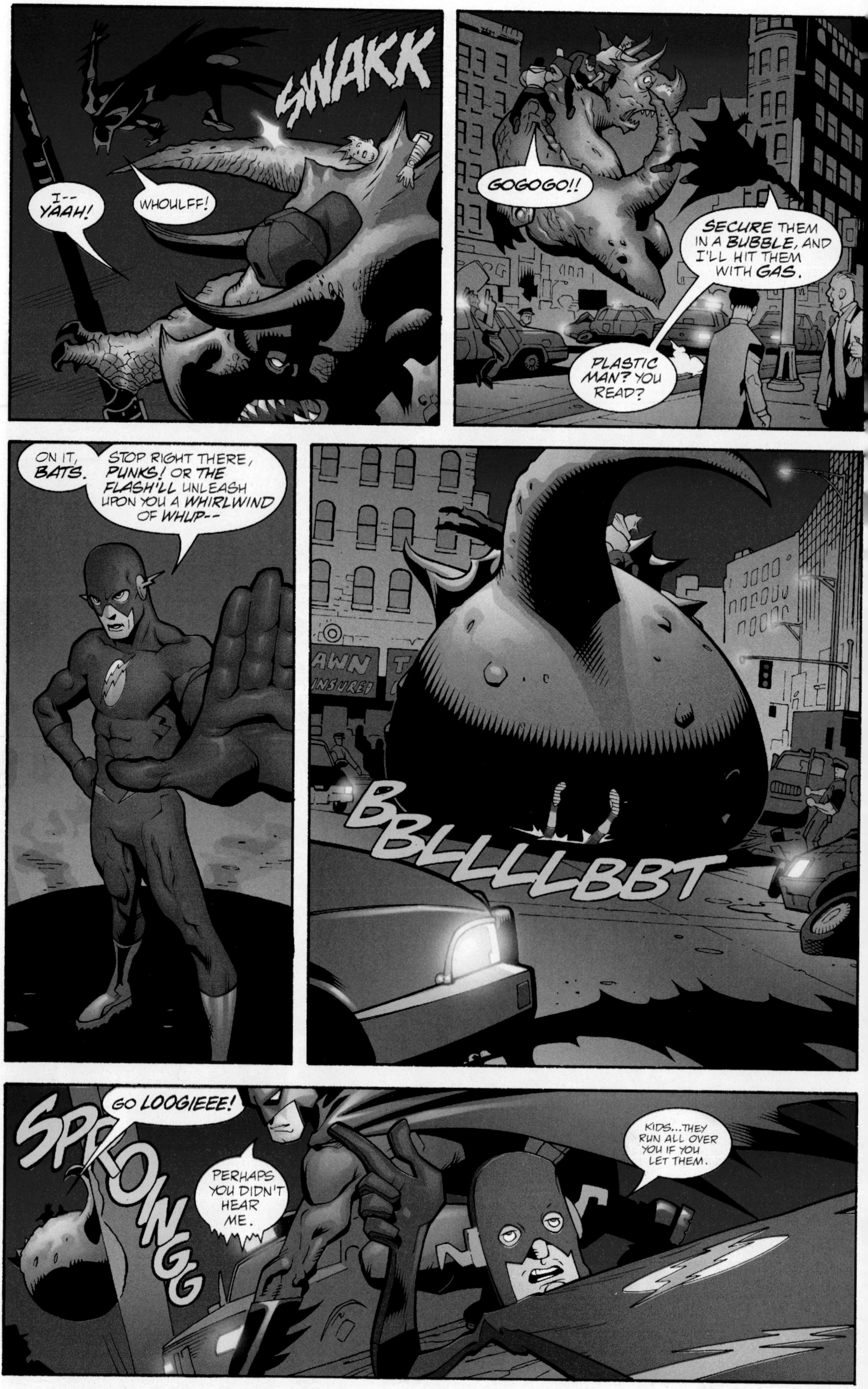
SWAKK
I-- YAAH!
WHOULFF!
GOGOGO!!
SECURE THEM IN A BUBBLE, AND I'LL HIT THEM WITH GAS.
PLASTIC MAN? YOU READ?
ON IT, BATS.
STOP RIGHT THERE, PUNKS! OR THE FLASH'LL UNLEASH UPON YOU A WHIRLWIND OF WHUP--
BBLLLLLBBT
SPROINGG
GO LOOGIEEE!
PERHAPS YOU DIDN'T HEAR ME.
KIDS...THEY RUN ALL OVER YOU IF YOU LET THEM.

I MADE A *LOT* OF PROGRESS SINCE THE OLD DAYS. I MEAN, *YOU* KNOW THIS. I'M *NOTHING* LIKE THE PRE-BENDY ME--

EXCEPT FOR THE FACT THAT *BROADS* STILL MAKE ME *STUPID.*

IT IS MY CURSE... *CHICKS* IS MY *KRYPTONITE.*

YOU *MUST* HAVE HAD *YOUR* SHARE OF *RON-DEZ-VOUZES* WITH THE *LADIES?* AM I RIGHT?

...

ANGEL AND I HAD OUR THING A WHILE BACK. FURIOUS AND *FUN-SURGEON-GENERAL-BAD* FOR US--WHEN *BOOM.*

AFTER THE *PARALYZING IRONY* OF A *RUBBER MAN* ACCIDENTALLY GETTING SOMEONE *PREGNANT* FINALLY WORE OFF...

OR MAYBE YOU LIKE TO KEEP *FOCUSED.*

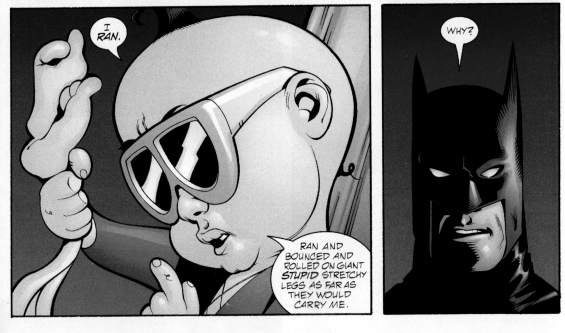

I *RAN.*

RAN AND BOUNCED AND ROLLED ON GIANT *STUPID* STRETCHY LEGS AS FAR AS THEY WOULD CARRY ME.

WHY?

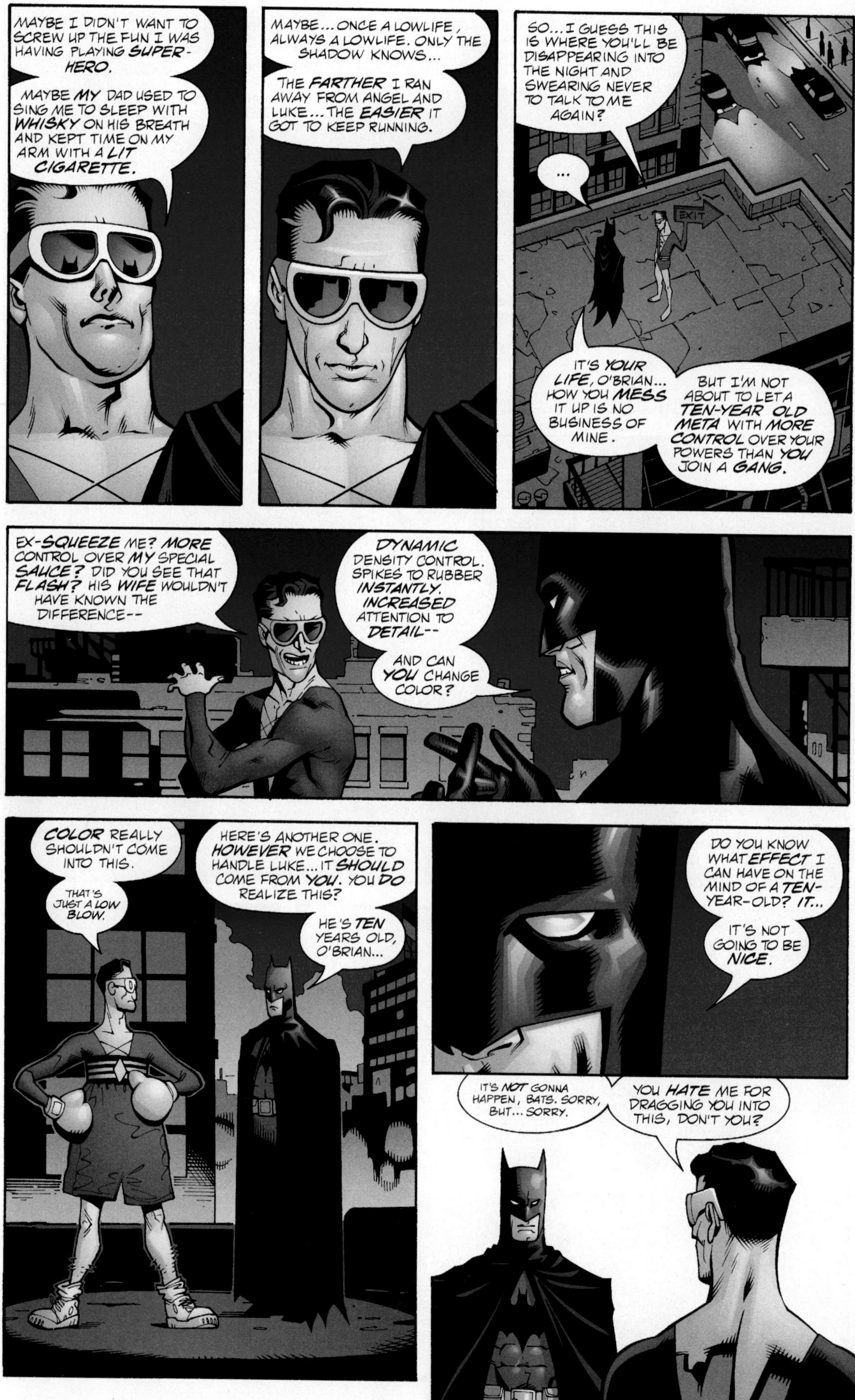
MAYBE I DIDN'T WANT TO SCREW UP THE FUN I WAS HAVING PLAYING SUPER-HERO.
MAYBE MY DAD USED TO SING ME TO SLEEP WITH WHISKY ON HIS BREATH AND KEPT TIME ON MY ARM WITH A LIT CIGARETTE.
MAYBE... ONCE A LOWLIFE, ALWAYS A LOWLIFE. ONLY THE SHADOW KNOWS...
THE FARTHER I RAN AWAY FROM ANGEL AND LUKE... THE EASIER IT GOT TO KEEP RUNNING.
SO... I GUESS THIS IS WHERE YOU'LL BE DISAPPEARING INTO THE NIGHT AND SWEARING NEVER TO TALK TO ME AGAIN?
...
EXIT
IT'S YOUR LIFE, O'BRIAN... HOW YOU MESS IT UP IS NO BUSINESS OF MINE.
BUT I'M NOT ABOUT TO LET A TEN-YEAR OLD META WITH MORE CONTROL OVER YOUR POWERS THAN YOU JOIN A GANG.
EX-SQUEEZE ME? MORE CONTROL OVER MY SPECIAL SAUCE? DID YOU SEE THAT FLASH? HIS WIFE WOULDN'T HAVE KNOWN THE DIFFERENCE--
DYNAMIC DENSITY CONTROL. SPIKES TO RUBBER INSTANTLY. INCREASED ATTENTION TO DETAIL--
AND CAN YOU CHANGE COLOR?
COLOR REALLY SHOULDN'T COME INTO THIS.
THAT'S JUST A LOW BLOW.
HERE'S ANOTHER ONE. HOWEVER WE CHOOSE TO HANDLE LUKE... IT SHOULD COME FROM YOU. YOU DO REALIZE THIS?
HE'S TEN YEARS OLD, O'BRIAN...
DO YOU KNOW WHAT EFFECT I CAN HAVE ON THE MIND OF A TEN-YEAR-OLD? IT...
IT'S NOT GOING TO BE NICE.
YOU HATE ME FOR DRAGGING YOU INTO THIS, DON'T YOU?
IT'S NOT GONNA HAPPEN, BATS. SORRY, BUT... SORRY.

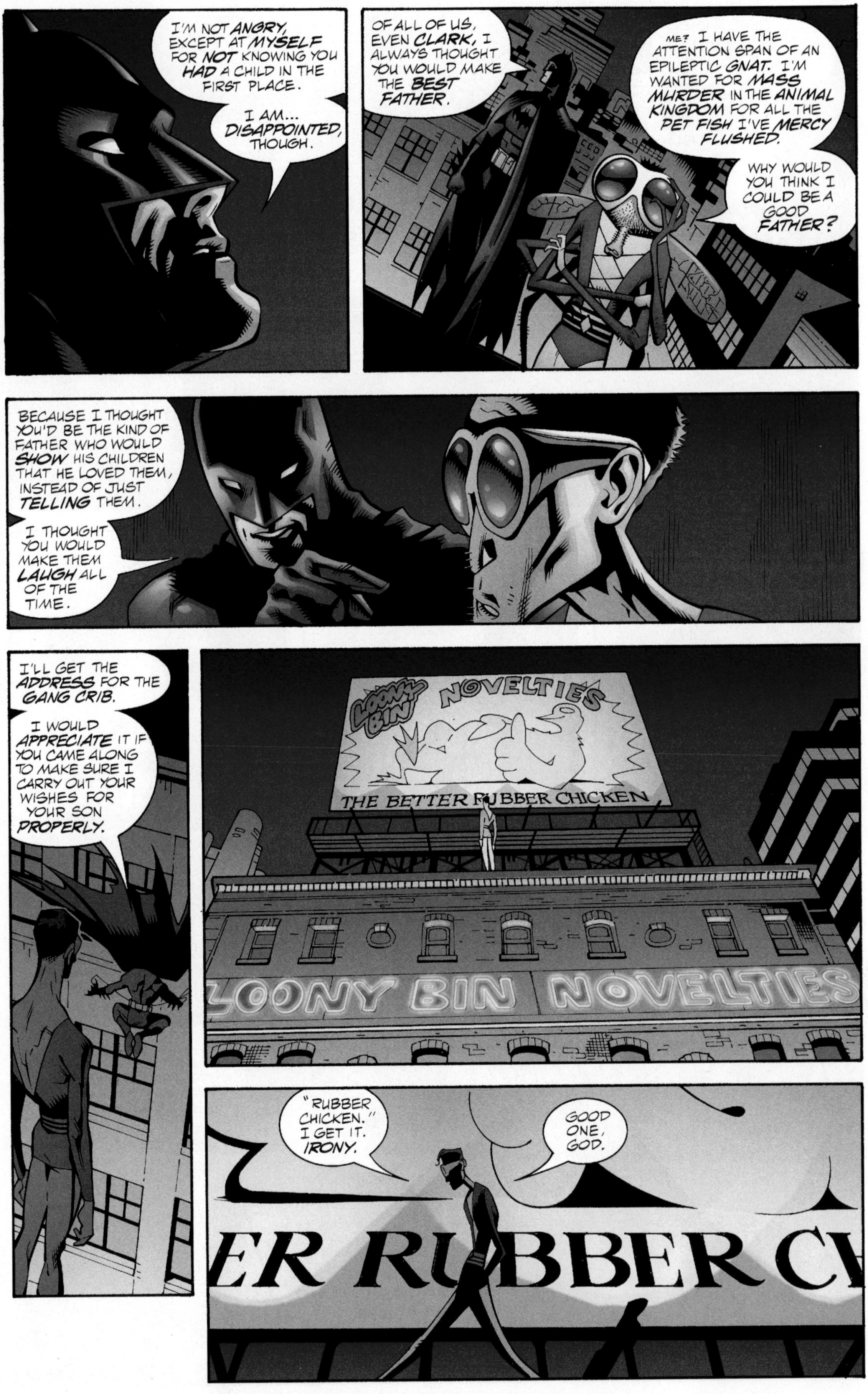
I'M NOT ANGRY, EXCEPT AT MYSELF FOR NOT KNOWING YOU HAD A CHILD IN THE FIRST PLACE.
I AM... DISAPPOINTED, THOUGH.
OF ALL OF US, EVEN CLARK, I ALWAYS THOUGHT YOU WOULD MAKE THE BEST FATHER.
ME? I HAVE THE ATTENTION SPAN OF AN EPILEPTIC GNAT. I'M WANTED FOR MASS MURDER IN THE ANIMAL KINGDOM FOR ALL THE PET FISH I'VE MERCY FLUSHED.
WHY WOULD YOU THINK I COULD BE A GOOD FATHER?
BECAUSE I THOUGHT YOU'D BE THE KIND OF FATHER WHO WOULD SHOW HIS CHILDREN THAT HE LOVED THEM, INSTEAD OF JUST TELLING THEM.
I THOUGHT YOU WOULD MAKE THEM LAUGH ALL OF THE TIME.
I'LL GET THE ADDRESS FOR THE GANG CRIB.
I WOULD APPRECIATE IT IF YOU CAME ALONG TO MAKE SURE I CARRY OUT YOUR WISHES FOR YOUR SON PROPERLY.
LOONY BIN NOVELTIES
THE BETTER RUBBER CHICKEN
LOONY BIN NOVELTIES
"RUBBER CHICKEN." I GET IT. IRONY.
GOOD ONE, GOD.
ER RUBBER C

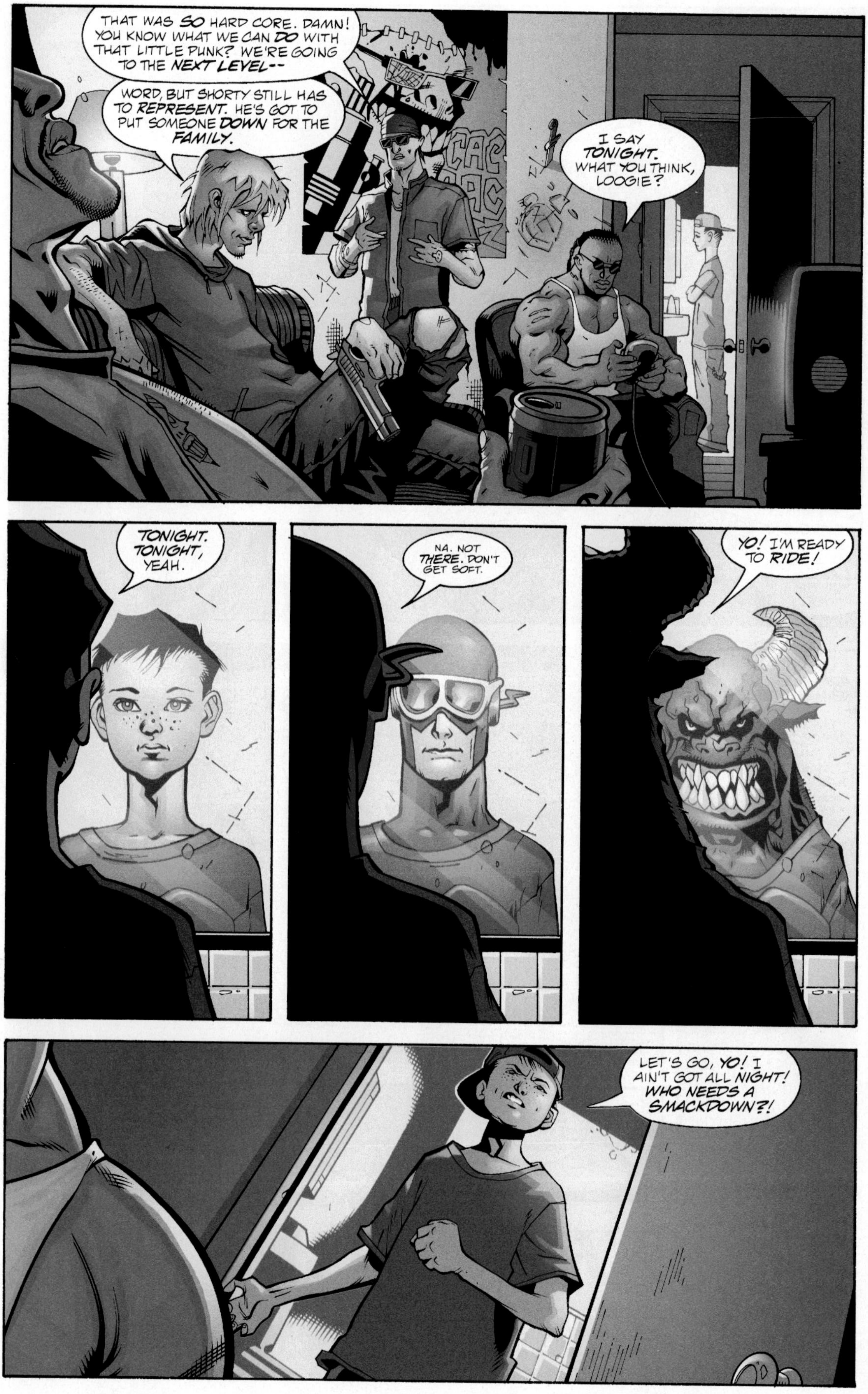
THAT WAS SO HARD CORE. DAMN! YOU KNOW WHAT WE CAN DO WITH THAT LITTLE PUNK? WE'RE GOING TO THE NEXT LEVEL--
WORD, BUT SHORTY STILL HAS TO REPRESENT. HE'S GOT TO PUT SOMEONE DOWN FOR THE FAMILY.
I SAY TONIGHT. WHAT YOU THINK, LOOGIE?
TONIGHT. TONIGHT, YEAH.
NA. NOT THERE. DON'T GET SOFT.
YO! I'M READY TO RIDE!
LET'S GO, YO! I AIN'T GOT ALL NIGHT! WHO NEEDS A SMACKDOWN?!

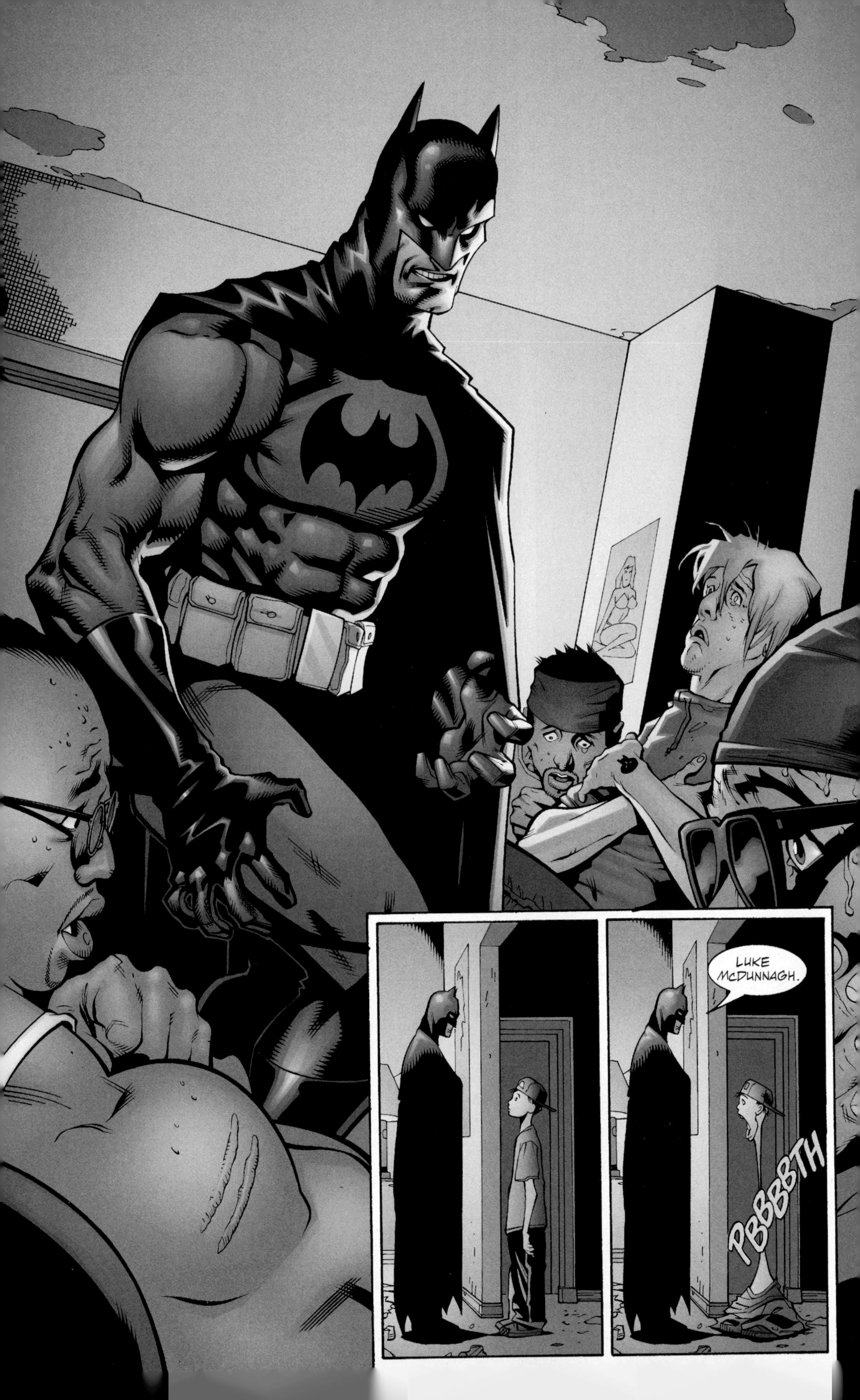
LUKE MCDUNNAGH.
PBBBBTH

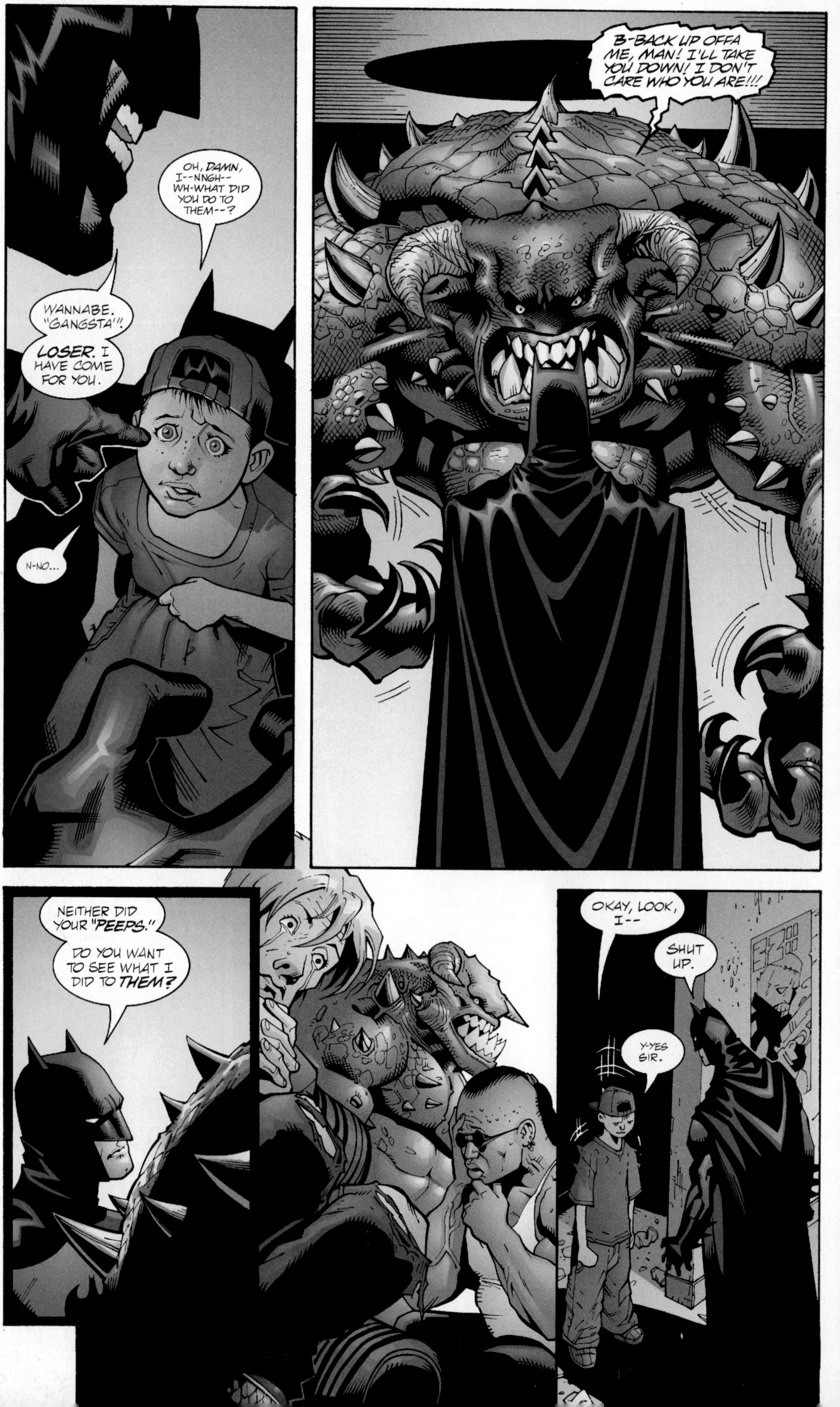
OH, DAMN, I--NNGH-- WH-WHAT DID YOU DO TO THEM--?
WANNABE. "GANGSTA".
LOSER. I HAVE COME FOR YOU.
N-NO...
B-BACK UP OFFA ME, MAN! I'LL TAKE YOU DOWN! I DON'T CARE WHO YOU ARE!!!
NEITHER DID YOUR "PEEPS."
DO YOU WANT TO SEE WHAT I DID TO THEM?
OKAY, LOOK, I--
SHUT UP.
Y-YES SIR.

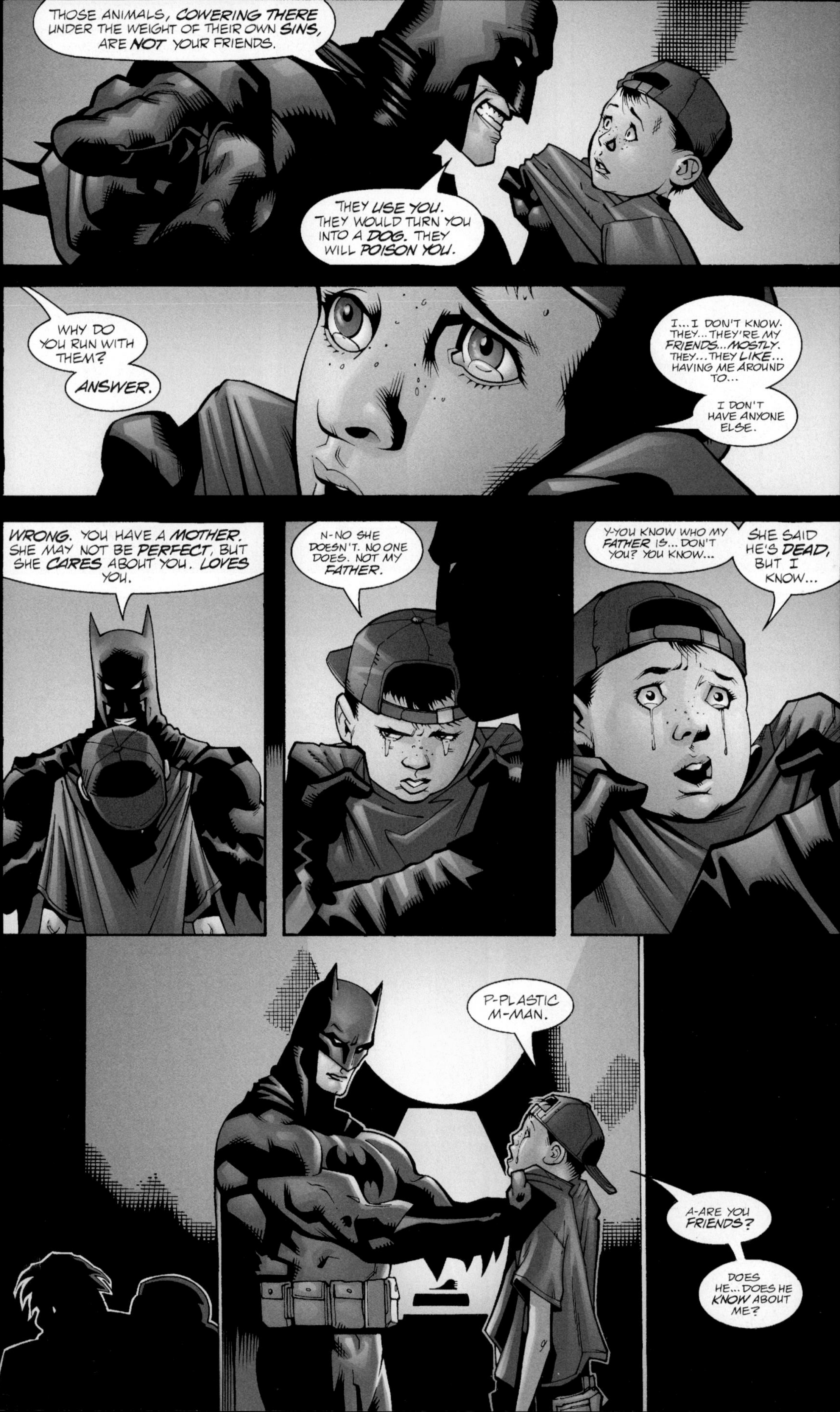
THOSE ANIMALS, COWERING THERE UNDER THE WEIGHT OF THEIR OWN SINS, ARE NOT YOUR FRIENDS.
THEY USE YOU. THEY WOULD TURN YOU INTO A DOG. THEY WILL POISON YOU.
WHY DO YOU RUN WITH THEM?
ANSWER.
I... I DON'T KNOW. THEY... THEY'RE MY FRIENDS... MOSTLY. THEY... THEY LIKE... HAVING ME AROUND TO...
I DON'T HAVE ANYONE ELSE.
WRONG. YOU HAVE A MOTHER. SHE MAY NOT BE PERFECT, BUT SHE CARES ABOUT YOU. LOVES YOU.
N-NO SHE DOESN'T. NO ONE DOES. NOT MY FATHER.
Y-YOU KNOW WHO MY FATHER IS... DON'T YOU? YOU KNOW...
SHE SAID HE'S DEAD, BUT I KNOW...
P-PLASTIC M-MAN.
A-ARE YOU FRIENDS?
DOES HE... DOES HE KNOW ABOUT ME?

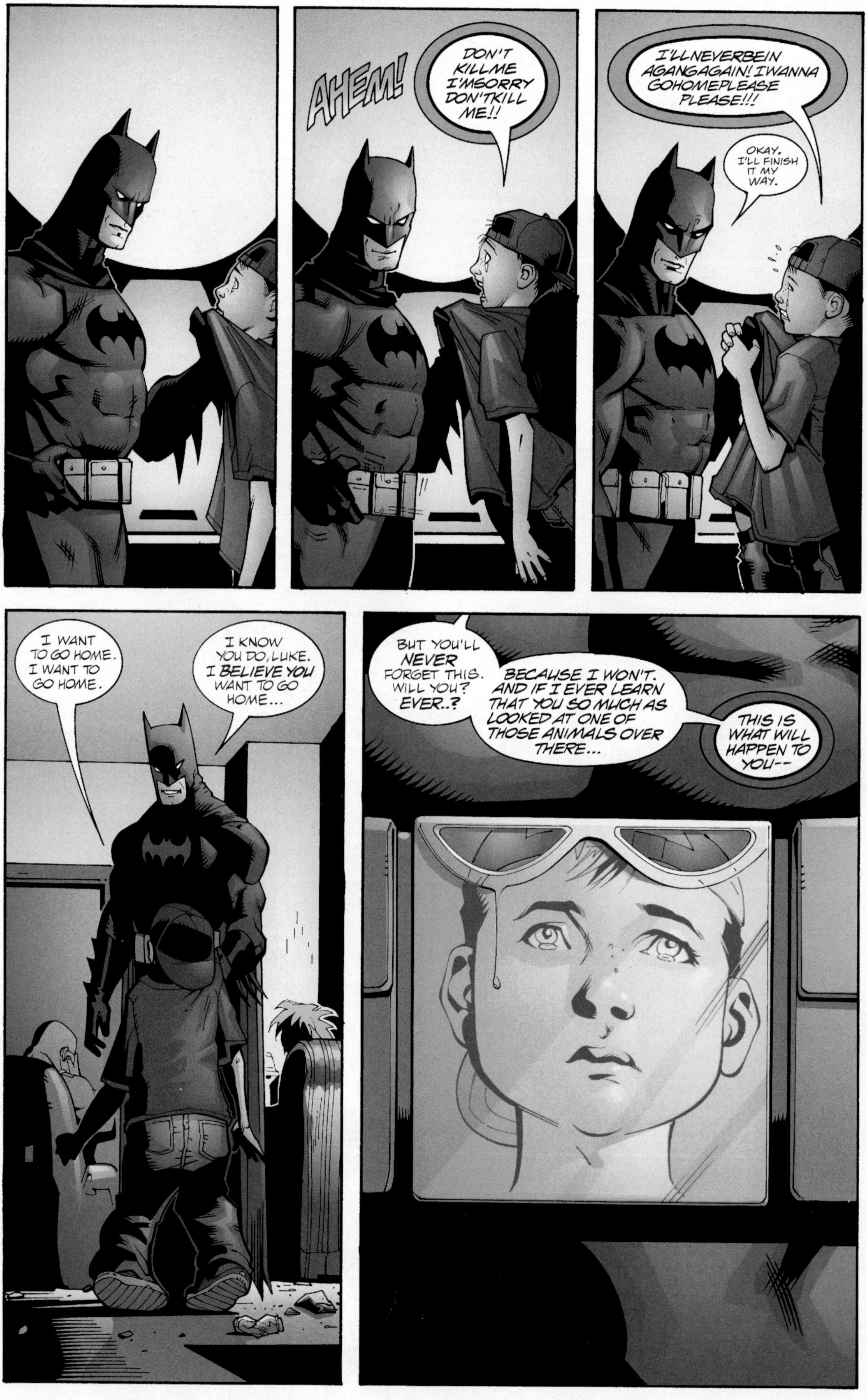

AHEM!
DON'T KILLME I'MSORRY DON'TKILL ME!!
I'LLNEVERBEIN AGANGAGAIN! IWANNA GOHOMEPLEASE PLEASE!!!
OKAY. I'LL FINISH IT MY WAY.
I WANT TO GO HOME. I WANT TO GO HOME.
I KNOW YOU DO, LUKE. I BELIEVE YOU WANT TO GO HOME...
BUT YOU'LL NEVER FORGET THIS. WILL YOU? EVER..?
BECAUSE I WON'T. AND IF I EVER LEARN THAT YOU SO MUCH AS LOOKED AT ONE OF THOSE ANIMALS OVER THERE...
THIS IS WHAT WILL HAPPEN TO YOU--

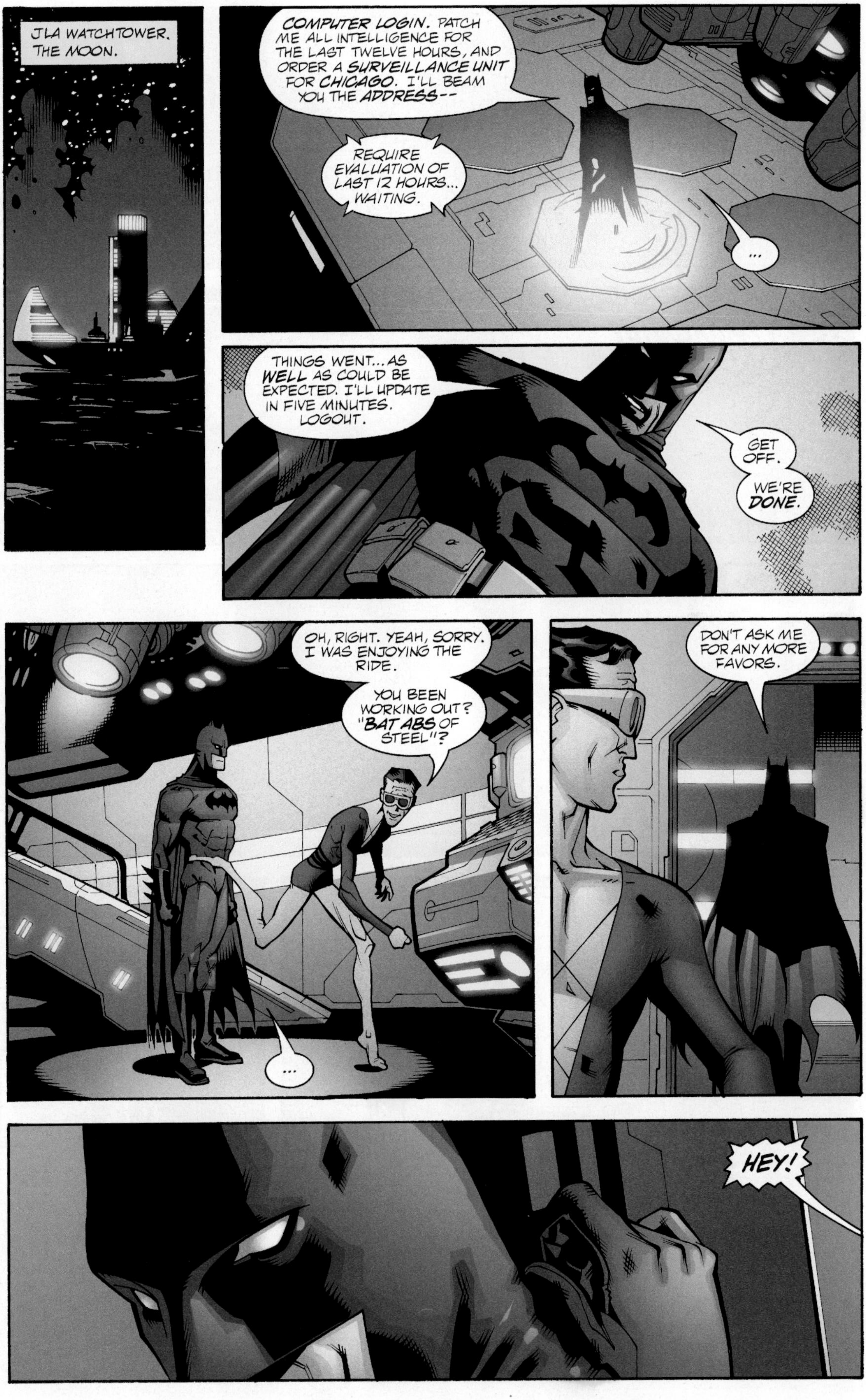
JLA WATCHTOWER. THE MOON.
COMPUTER LOGIN. PATCH ME ALL INTELLIGENCE FOR THE LAST TWELVE HOURS, AND ORDER A SURVEILLANCE UNIT FOR CHICAGO. I'LL BEAM YOU THE ADDRESS--
REQUIRE EVALUATION OF LAST 12 HOURS... WAITING.
...
THINGS WENT... AS WELL AS COULD BE EXPECTED. I'LL UPDATE IN FIVE MINUTES. LOGOUT.
GET OFF.
WE'RE DONE.
OH, RIGHT. YEAH, SORRY. I WAS ENJOYING THE RIDE.
YOU BEEN WORKING OUT? "BAT ABS OF STEEL"?
...
DON'T ASK ME FOR ANY MORE FAVORS.
HEY!

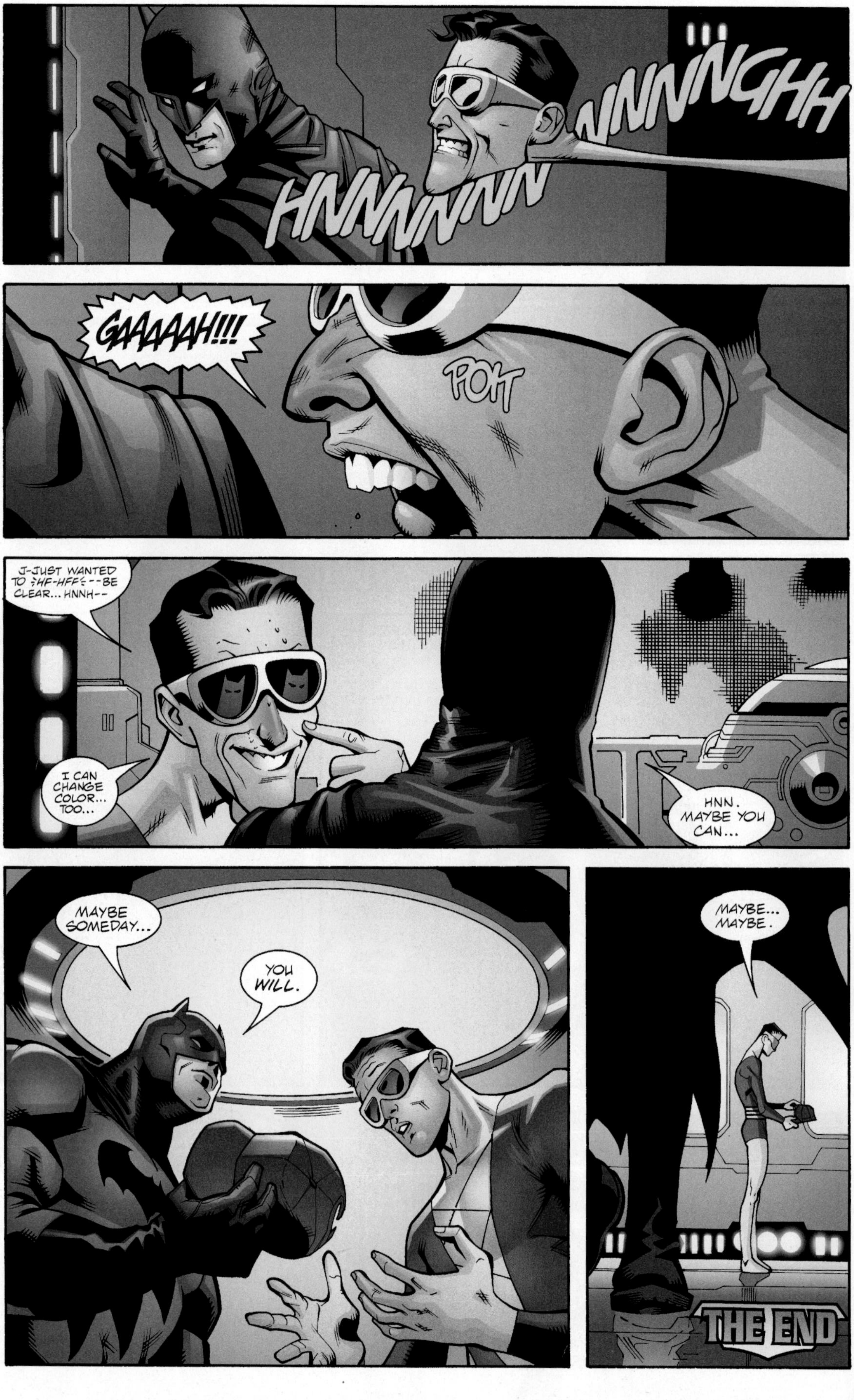
HNNNNNNN
NNNNGHH
GAAAAAH!!!
POK
J-JUST WANTED TO ~HF-HFF~--BE CLEAR... HNNH--
I CAN CHANGE COLOR... TOO...
HNN. MAYBE YOU CAN...
MAYBE SOMEDAY...
YOU WILL.
MAYBE... MAYBE.
THE END

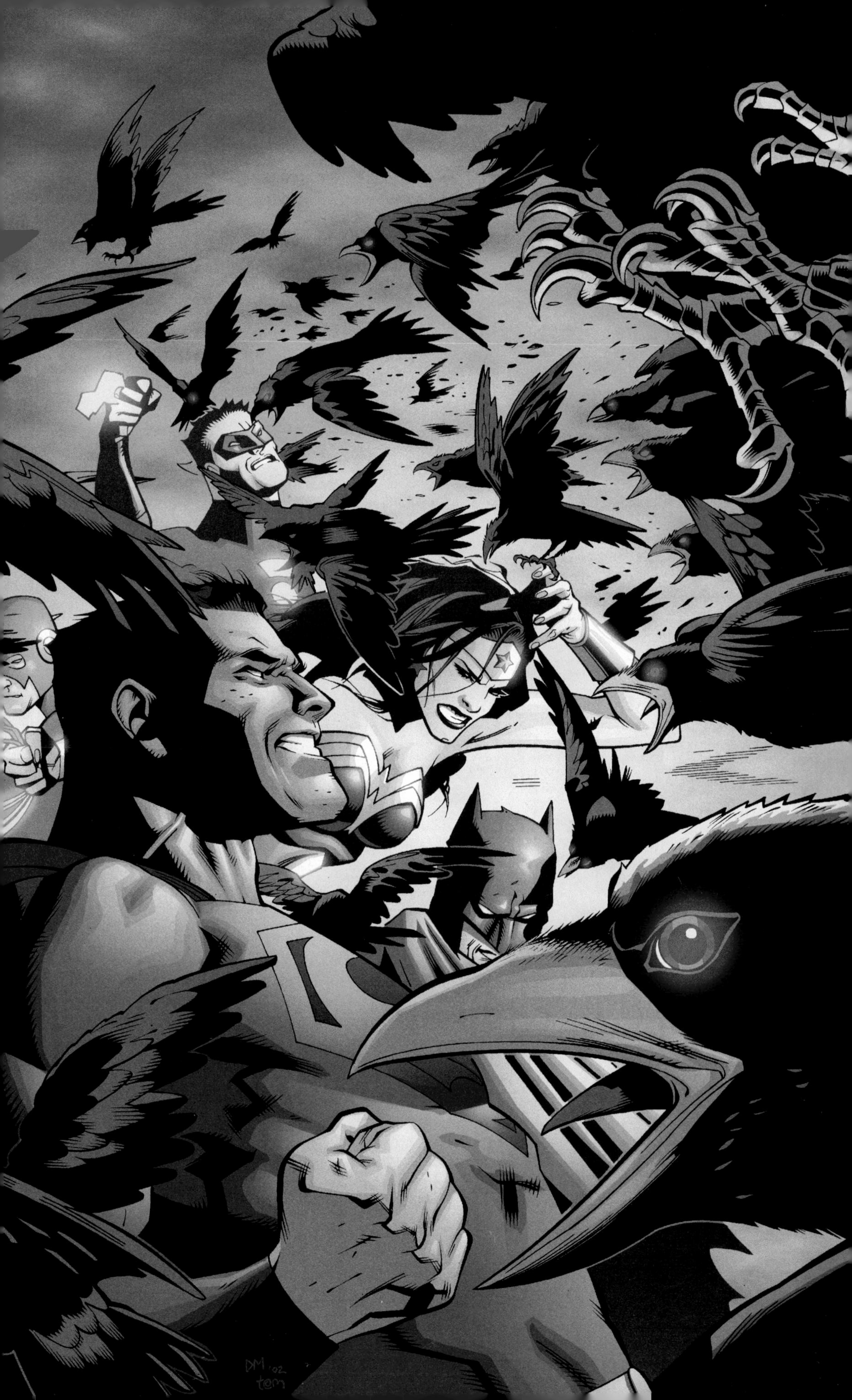

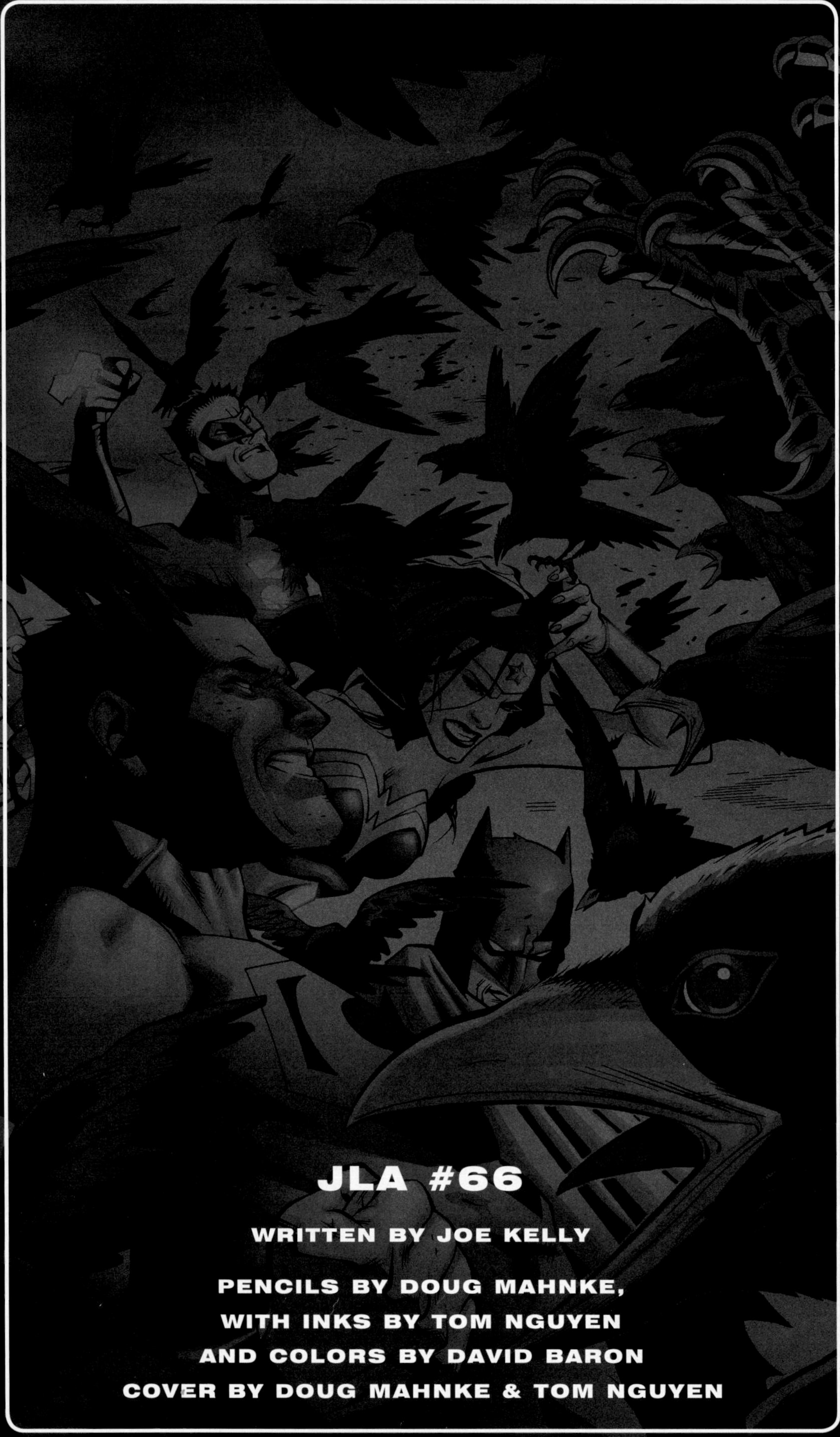

JLA #66

WRITTEN BY JOE KELLY

PENCILS BY DOUG MAHNKE,
WITH INKS BY TOM NGUYEN
AND COLORS BY DAVID BARON
COVER BY DOUG MAHNKE & TOM NGUYEN

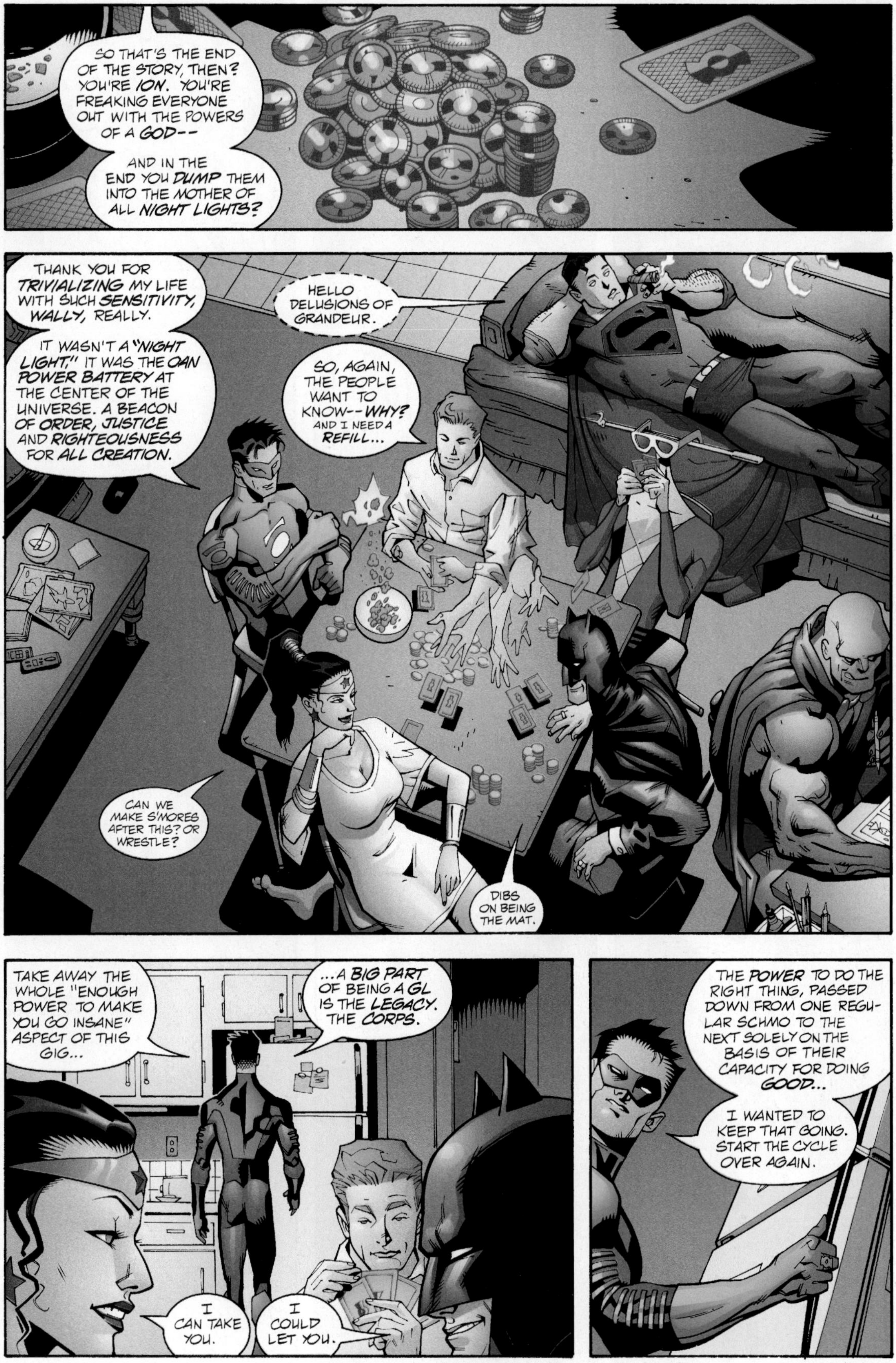
SO THAT'S THE END OF THE STORY, THEN? YOU'RE ION. YOU'RE FREAKING EVERYONE OUT WITH THE POWERS OF A GOD--
AND IN THE END YOU DUMP THEM INTO THE MOTHER OF ALL NIGHT LIGHTS?
THANK YOU FOR TRIVIALIZING MY LIFE WITH SUCH SENSITIVITY, WALLY, REALLY.
IT WASN'T A "NIGHT LIGHT," IT WAS THE OAN POWER BATTERY AT THE CENTER OF THE UNIVERSE. A BEACON OF ORDER, JUSTICE AND RIGHTEOUSNESS FOR ALL CREATION.
HELLO DELUSIONS OF GRANDEUR.
SO, AGAIN, THE PEOPLE WANT TO KNOW--WHY? AND I NEED A REFILL...
CAN WE MAKE S'MORES AFTER THIS? OR WRESTLE?
DIBS ON BEING THE MAT.
TAKE AWAY THE WHOLE "ENOUGH POWER TO MAKE YOU GO INSANE" ASPECT OF THIS GIG...
...A BIG PART OF BEING A GL IS THE LEGACY. THE CORPS.
I CAN TAKE YOU.
I COULD LET YOU.
THE POWER TO DO THE RIGHT THING, PASSED DOWN FROM ONE REGULAR SCHMO TO THE NEXT SOLELY ON THE BASIS OF THEIR CAPACITY FOR DOING GOOD...
I WANTED TO KEEP THAT GOING. START THE CYCLE OVER AGAIN.

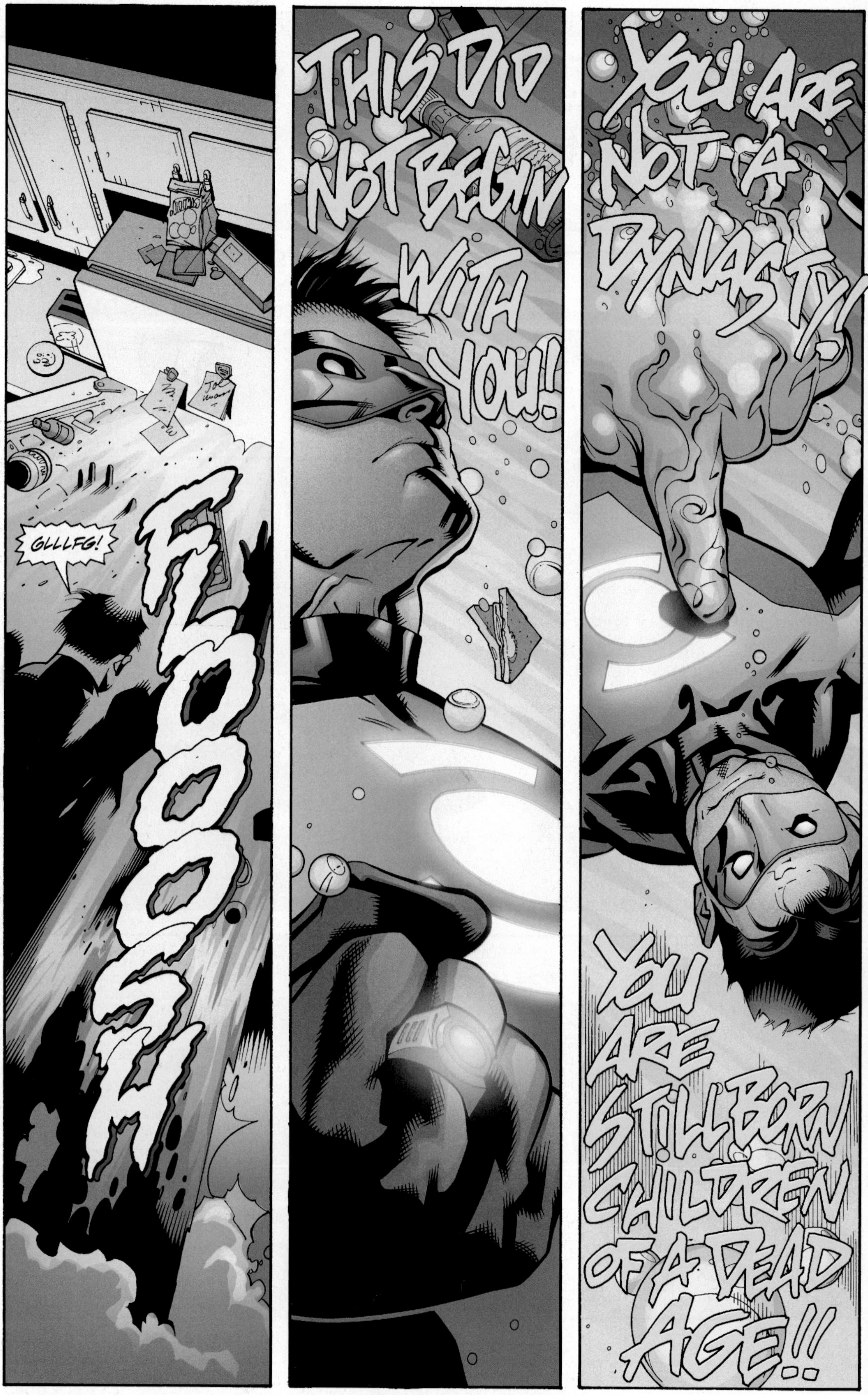
GLLLFG!
FLOOOSH
THIS DID NOT BEGIN WITH YOU!!
YOU ARE NOT A DYNASTY!
YOU ARE STILLBORN CHILDREN OF A DEAD AGE!!

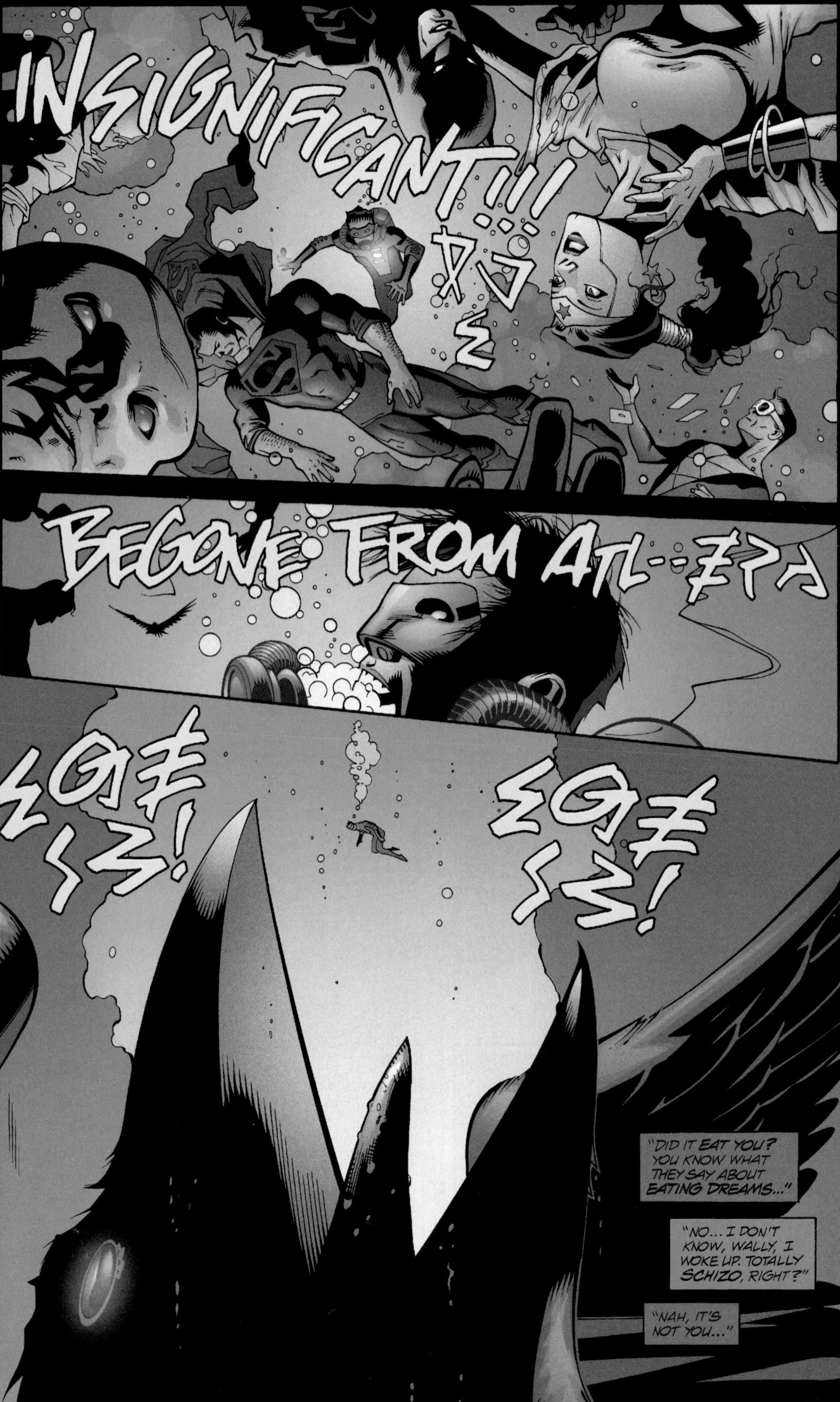
INSIGNIFICANT!!!
BEGONE FROM ATL--
"DID IT EAT YOU? YOU KNOW WHAT THEY SAY ABOUT EATING DREAMS..."
"NO... I DON'T KNOW, WALLY, I WOKE UP. TOTALLY SCHIZO, RIGHT?"
"NAH, IT'S NOT YOU..."

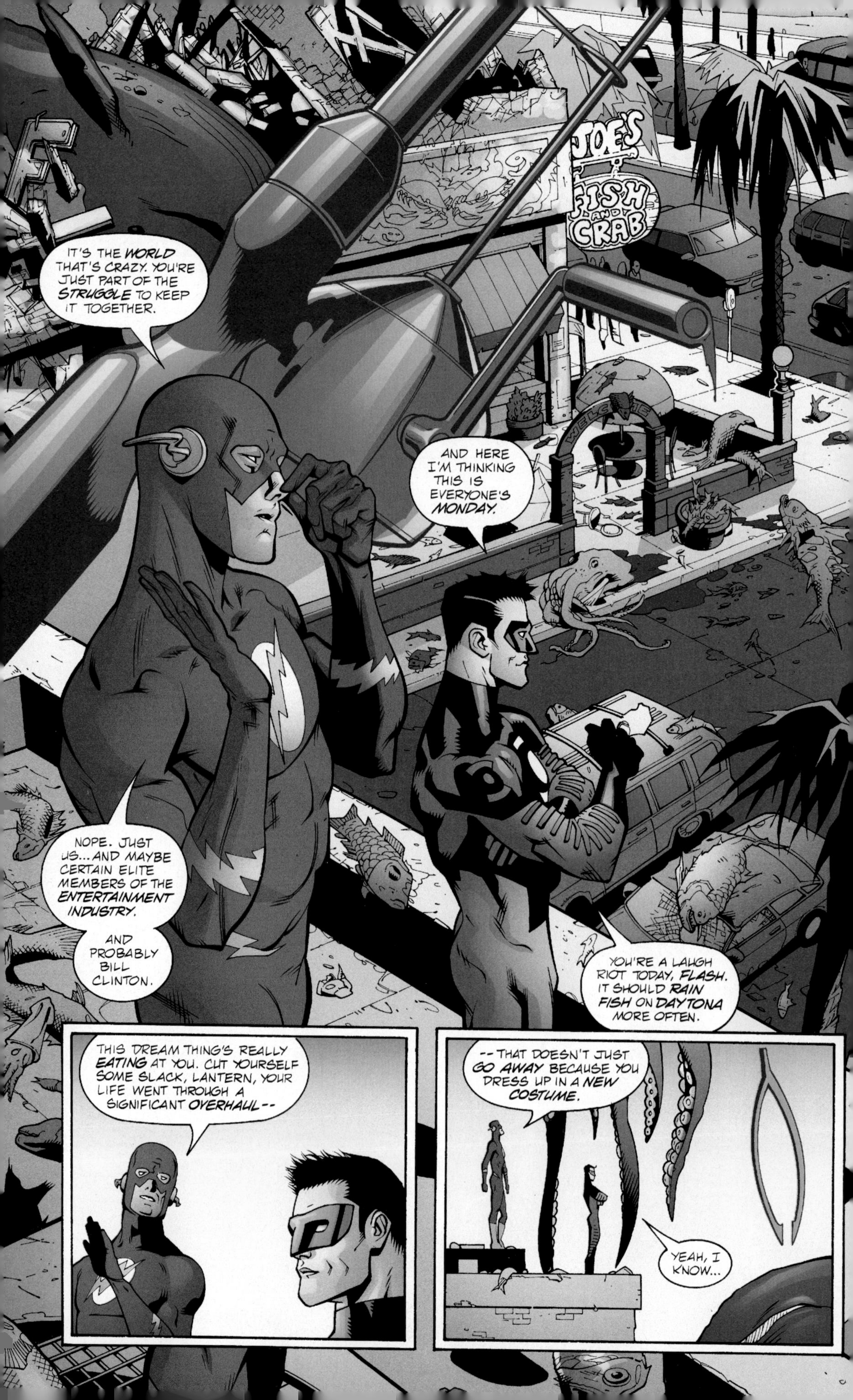

JOE'S
FISH AND CRAB
IT'S THE WORLD THAT'S CRAZY. YOU'RE JUST PART OF THE STRUGGLE TO KEEP IT TOGETHER.
AND HERE I'M THINKING THIS IS EVERYONE'S MONDAY.
NOPE. JUST US... AND MAYBE CERTAIN ELITE MEMBERS OF THE ENTERTAINMENT INDUSTRY.
AND PROBABLY BILL CLINTON.
YOU'RE A LAUGH RIOT TODAY, FLASH. IT SHOULD RAIN FISH ON DAYTONA MORE OFTEN.
THIS DREAM THING'S REALLY EATING AT YOU. CUT YOURSELF SOME SLACK, LANTERN, YOUR LIFE WENT THROUGH A SIGNIFICANT OVERHAUL--
--THAT DOESN'T JUST GO AWAY BECAUSE YOU DRESS UP IN A NEW COSTUME.
YEAH, I KNOW...

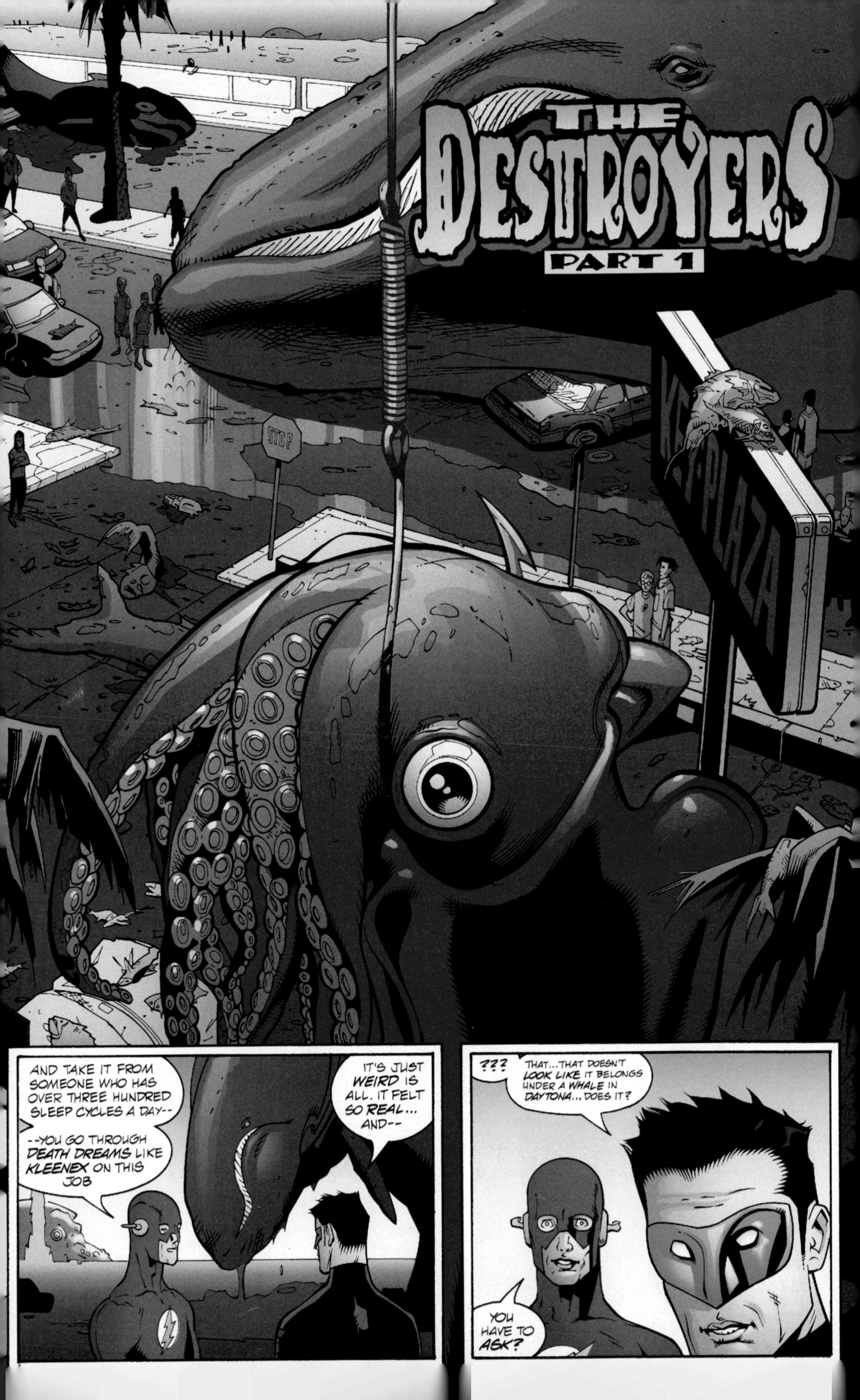
THE DESTROYERS
PART 1
STOP
PLAZA
AND TAKE IT FROM SOMEONE WHO HAS OVER THREE HUNDRED SLEEP CYCLES A DAY--
--YOU GO THROUGH DEATH DREAMS LIKE KLEENEX ON THIS JOB
IT'S JUST WEIRD IS ALL. IT FELT SO REAL... AND--
???
THAT...THAT DOESN'T LOOK LIKE IT BELONGS UNDER A WHALE IN DAYTONA... DOES IT?
YOU HAVE TO ASK?

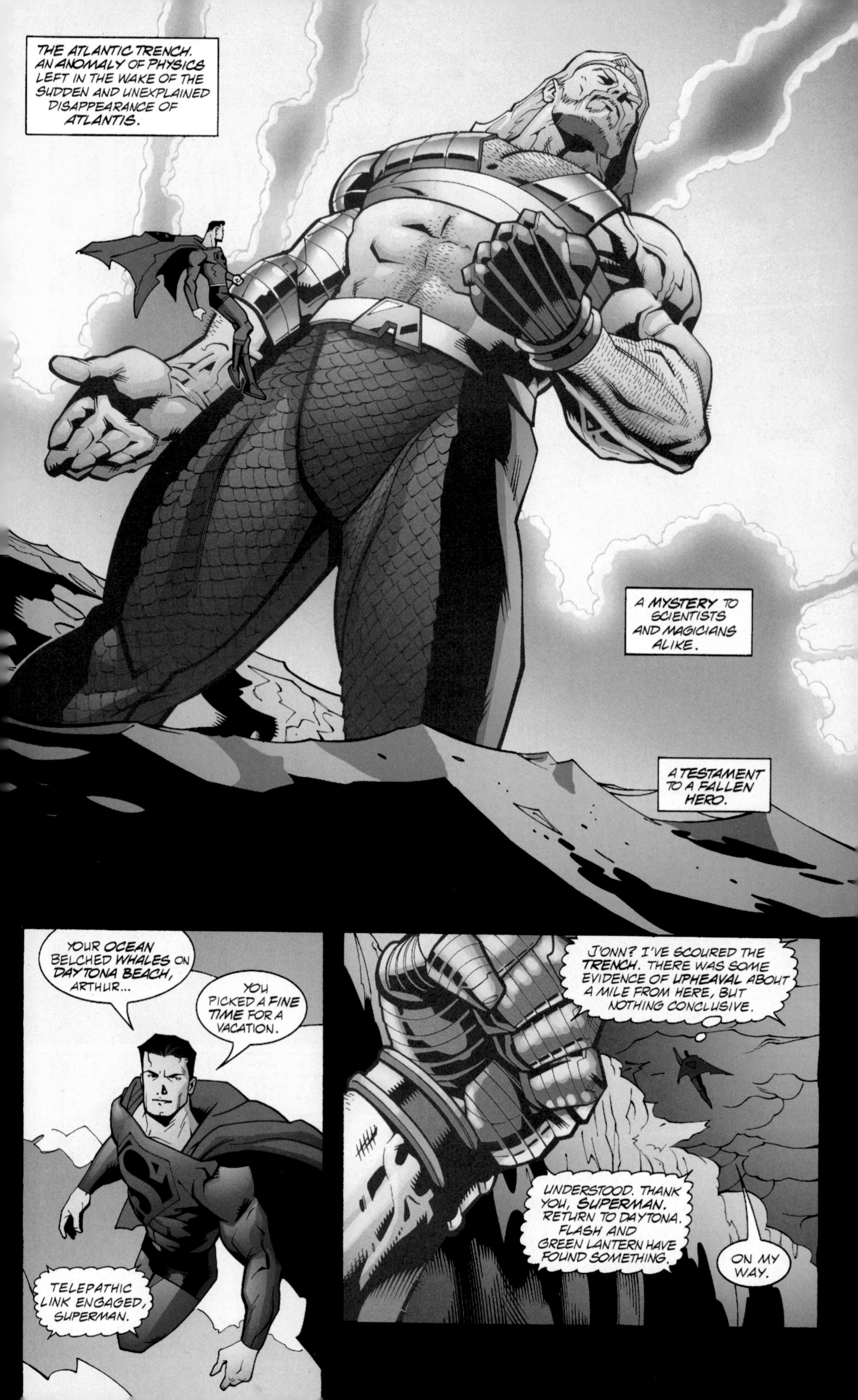
THE ATLANTIC TRENCH. AN ANOMALY OF PHYSICS LEFT IN THE WAKE OF THE SUDDEN AND UNEXPLAINED DISAPPEARANCE OF ATLANTIS.
A MYSTERY TO SCIENTISTS AND MAGICIANS ALIKE.
A TESTAMENT TO A FALLEN HERO.
YOUR OCEAN BELCHED WHALES ON DAYTONA BEACH, ARTHUR...
YOU PICKED A FINE TIME FOR A VACATION.
TELEPATHIC LINK ENGAGED, SUPERMAN.
J'ONN? I'VE SCOURED THE TRENCH. THERE WAS SOME EVIDENCE OF UPHEAVAL ABOUT A MILE FROM HERE, BUT NOTHING CONCLUSIVE.
UNDERSTOOD. THANK YOU, SUPERMAN. RETURN TO DAYTONA. FLASH AND GREEN LANTERN HAVE FOUND SOMETHING.
ON MY WAY.

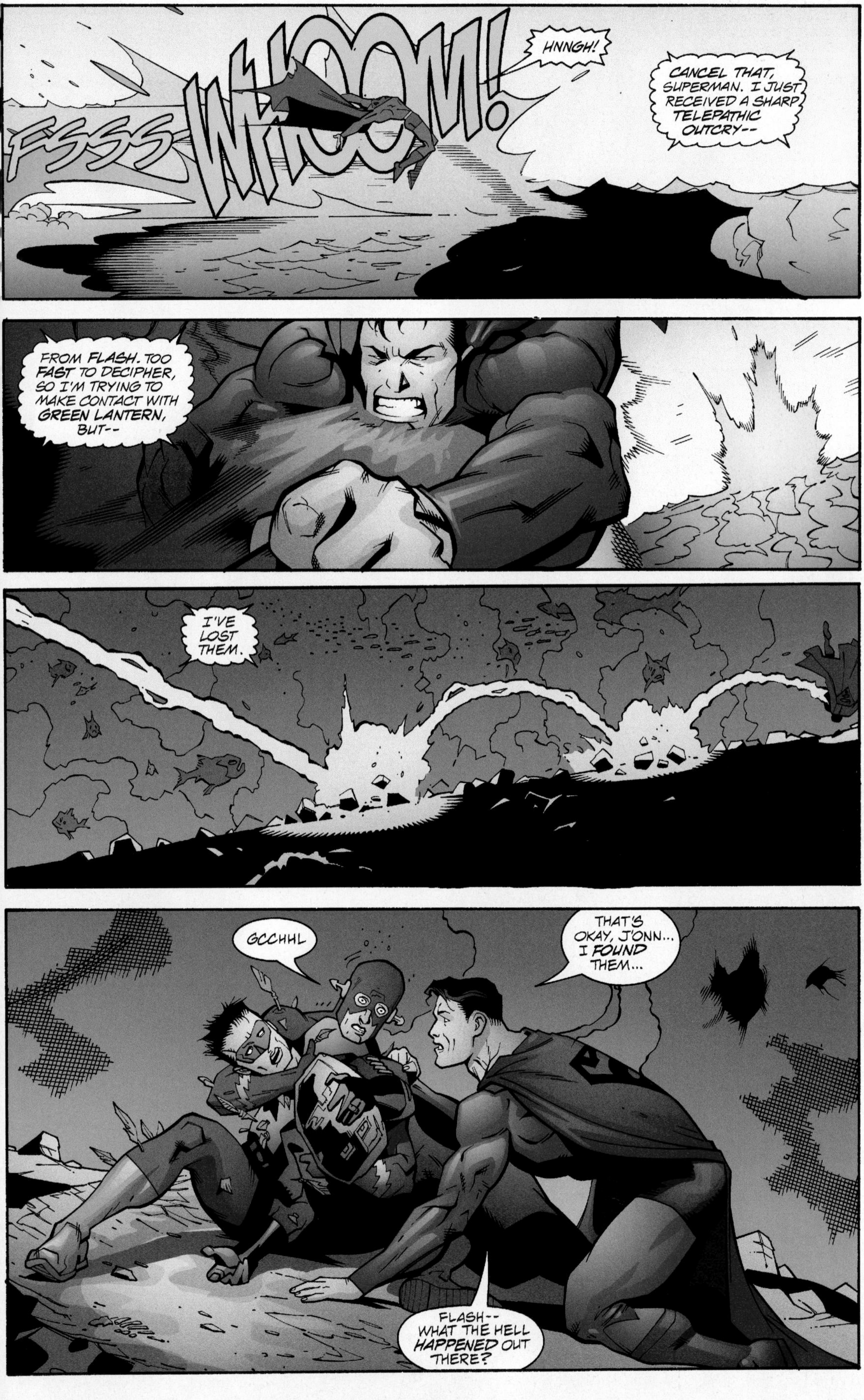
FSSS
WHOOM!
HNNGH!
CANCEL THAT, SUPERMAN. I JUST RECEIVED A SHARP TELEPATHIC OUTCRY--
FROM FLASH. TOO FAST TO DECIPHER, SO I'M TRYING TO MAKE CONTACT WITH GREEN LANTERN, BUT--
I'VE LOST THEM.
GCCHHL
THAT'S OKAY, J'ONN... I FOUND THEM...
FLASH-- WHAT THE HELL HAPPENED OUT THERE?

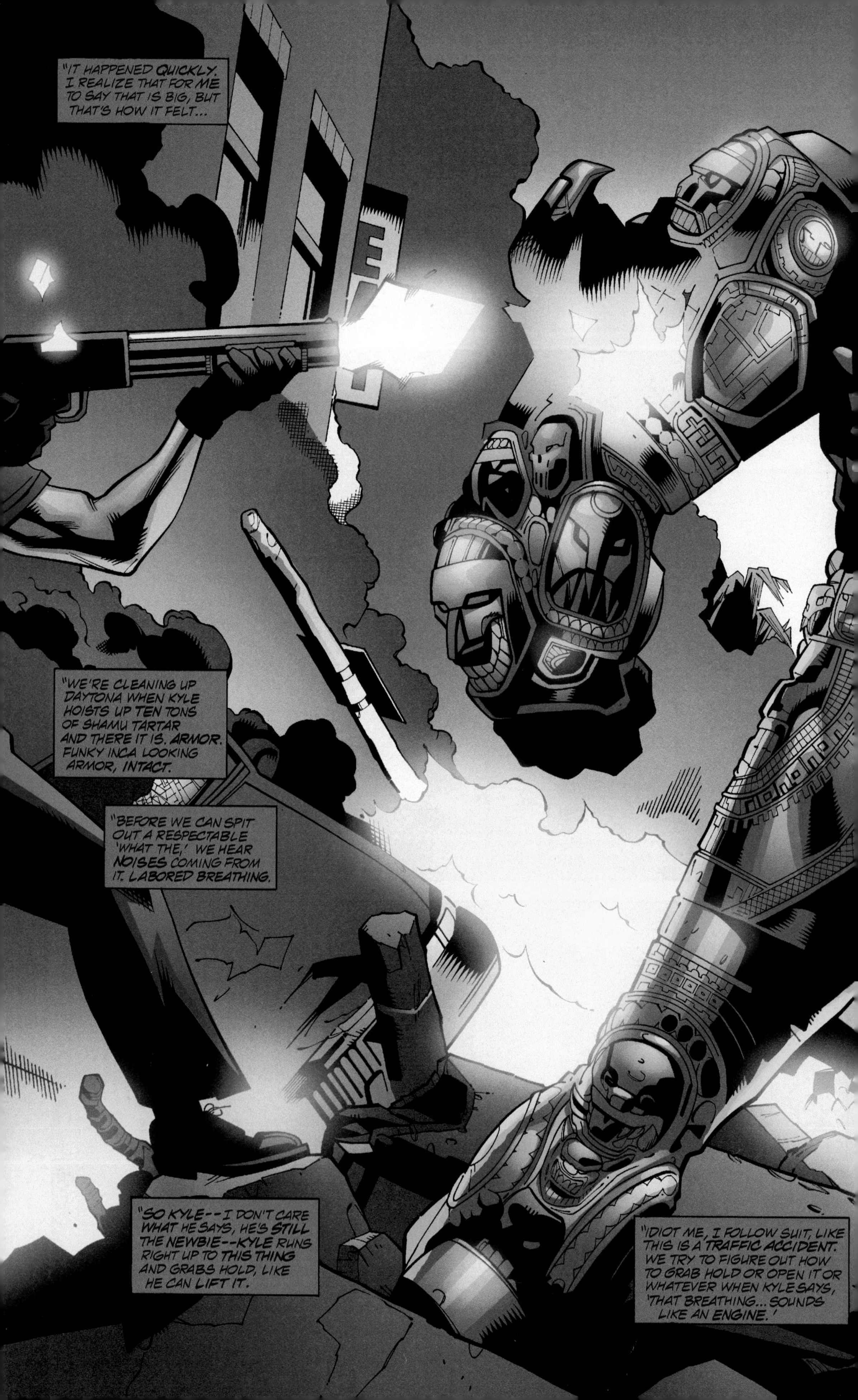
"IT HAPPENED QUICKLY. I REALIZE THAT FOR ME TO SAY THAT IS BIG, BUT THAT'S HOW IT FELT...
"WE'RE CLEANING UP DAYTONA WHEN KYLE HOISTS UP TEN TONS OF SHAMU TARTAR AND THERE IT IS. ARMOR. FUNKY INCA LOOKING ARMOR, INTACT.
"BEFORE WE CAN SPIT OUT A RESPECTABLE 'WHAT THE,' WE HEAR NOISES COMING FROM IT. LABORED BREATHING.
"SO KYLE--I DON'T CARE WHAT HE SAYS, HE'S STILL THE NEWBIE--KYLE RUNS RIGHT UP TO THIS THING AND GRABS HOLD, LIKE HE CAN LIFT IT.
"IDIOT ME, I FOLLOW SUIT, LIKE THIS IS A TRAFFIC ACCIDENT. WE TRY TO FIGURE OUT HOW TO GRAB HOLD OR OPEN IT OR WHATEVER WHEN KYLE SAYS, 'THAT BREATHING... SOUNDS LIKE AN ENGINE.'

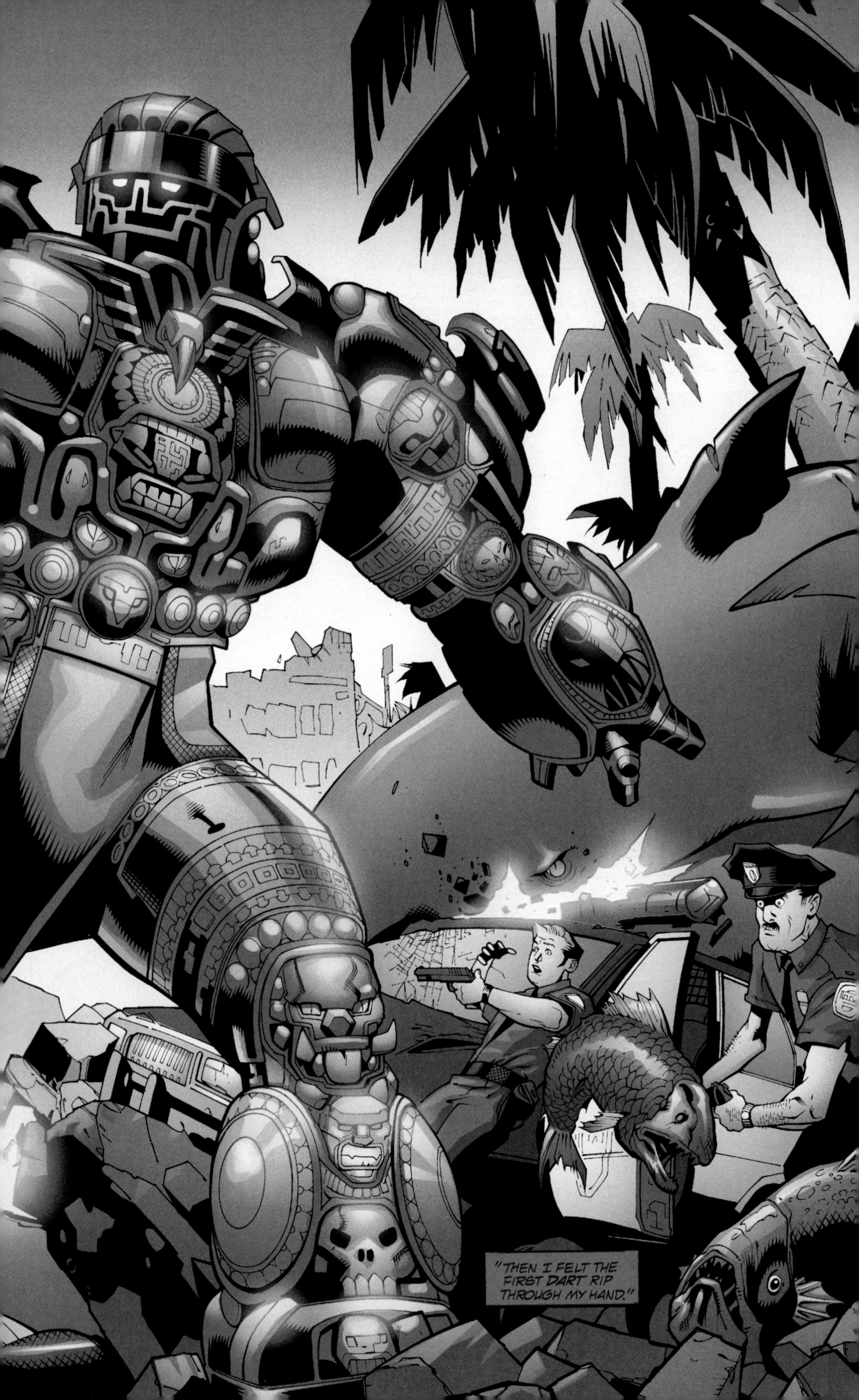
"THEN I FELT THE FIRST DART RIP THROUGH MY HAND."

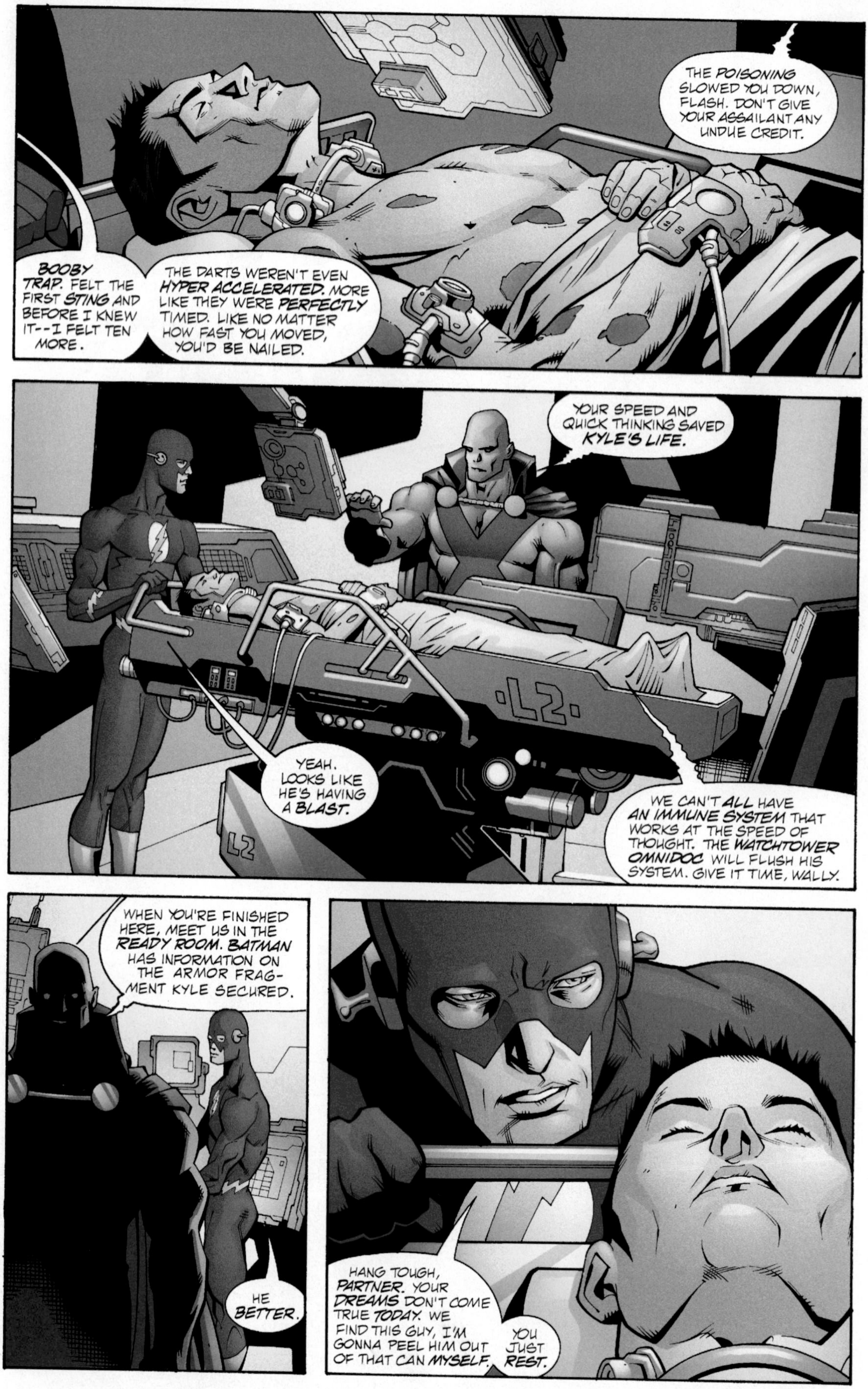
THE POISONING SLOWED YOU DOWN, FLASH. DON'T GIVE YOUR ASSAILANT ANY UNDUE CREDIT.
BOOBY TRAP. FELT THE FIRST STING AND BEFORE I KNEW IT--I FELT TEN MORE.
THE DARTS WEREN'T EVEN HYPER ACCELERATED. MORE LIKE THEY WERE PERFECTLY TIMED. LIKE NO MATTER HOW FAST YOU MOVED, YOU'D BE NAILED.
YOUR SPEED AND QUICK THINKING SAVED KYLE'S LIFE.
L2
YEAH. LOOKS LIKE HE'S HAVING A BLAST.
WE CAN'T ALL HAVE AN IMMUNE SYSTEM THAT WORKS AT THE SPEED OF THOUGHT. THE WATCHTOWER OMNIDOC WILL FLUSH HIS SYSTEM. GIVE IT TIME, WALLY.
WHEN YOU'RE FINISHED HERE, MEET US IN THE READY ROOM. BATMAN HAS INFORMATION ON THE ARMOR FRAGMENT KYLE SECURED.
HE BETTER.
HANG TOUGH, PARTNER. YOUR DREAMS DON'T COME TRUE TODAY. WE FIND THIS GUY, I'M GONNA PEEL HIM OUT OF THAT CAN MYSELF.
YOU JUST REST.

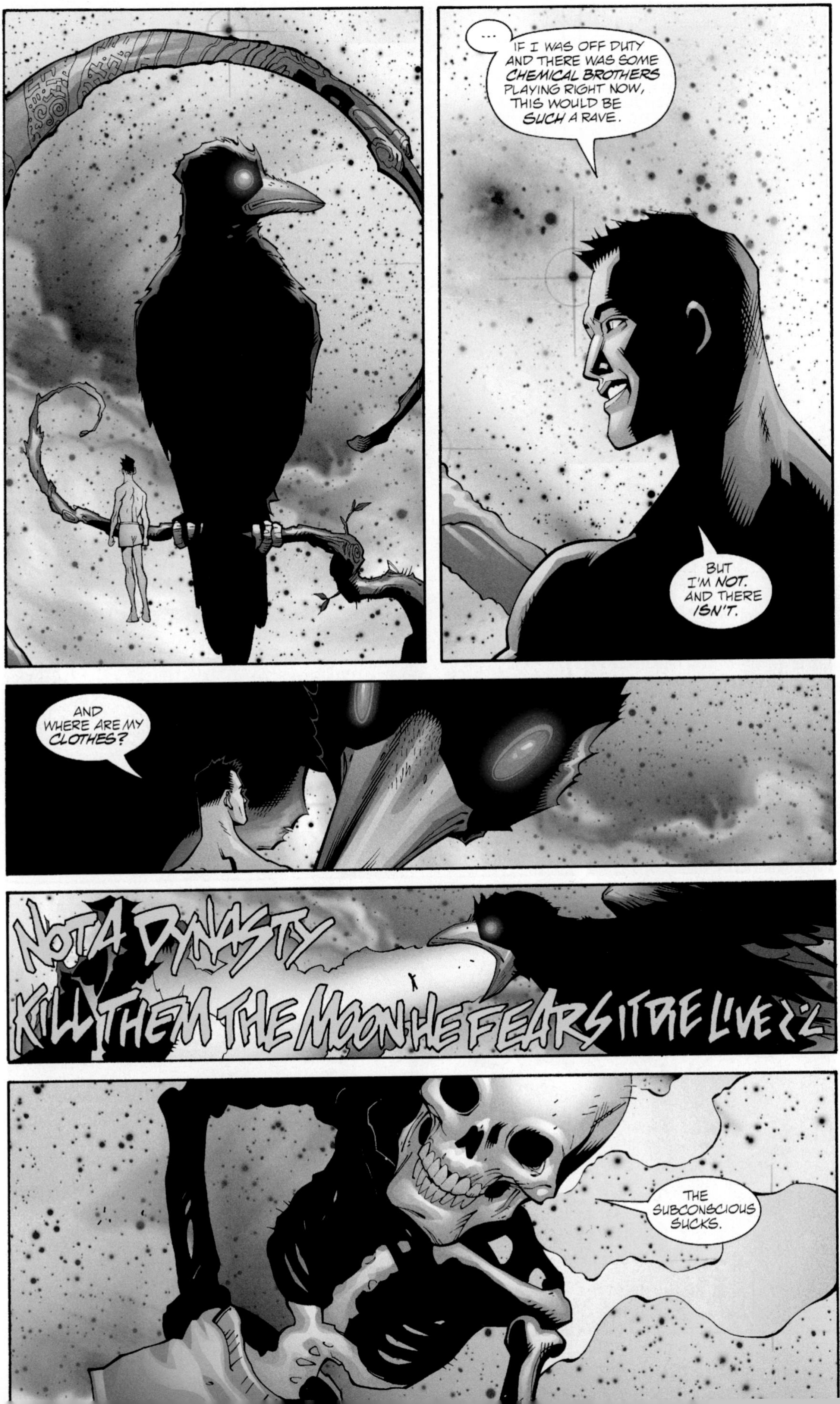
...
IF I WAS OFF DUTY AND THERE WAS SOME CHEMICAL BROTHERS PLAYING RIGHT NOW, THIS WOULD BE SUCH A RAVE.
BUT I'M NOT. AND THERE ISN'T.
AND WHERE ARE MY CLOTHES?
NOT A DYNASTY
KILL THEM THE MOON HE FEARS IT DIE LIVE
THE SUBCONSCIOUS SUCKS.

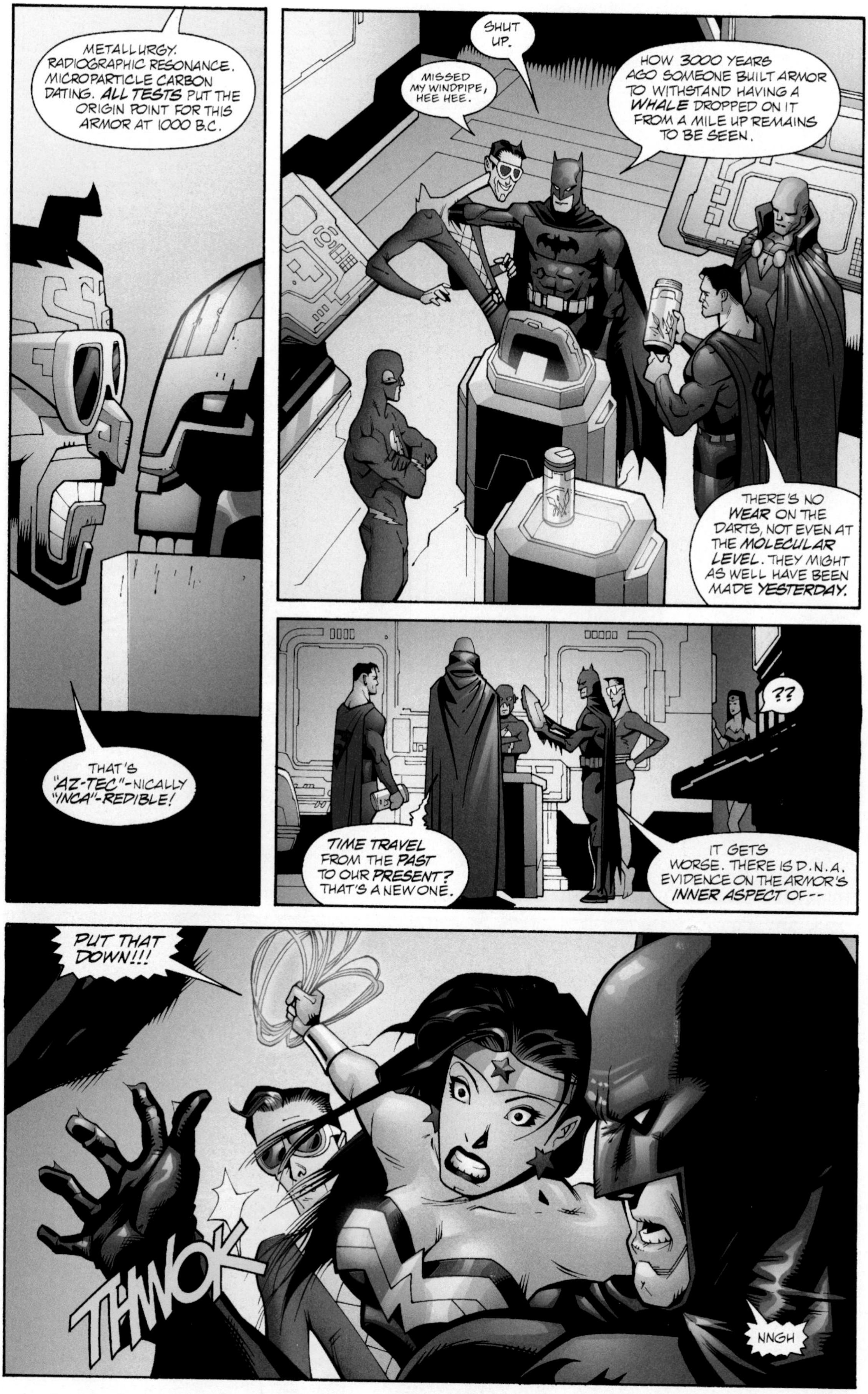
METALLURGY. RADIOGRAPHIC RESONANCE. MICROPARTICLE CARBON DATING. ALL TESTS PUT THE ORIGIN POINT FOR THIS ARMOR AT 1000 B.C.
THAT'S "AZ-TEC"-NICALLY "INCA"-REDIBLE!
SHUT UP.
MISSED MY WINDPIPE, HEE HEE.
HOW 3000 YEARS AGO SOMEONE BUILT ARMOR TO WITHSTAND HAVING A WHALE DROPPED ON IT FROM A MILE UP REMAINS TO BE SEEN.
THERE'S NO WEAR ON THE DARTS, NOT EVEN AT THE MOLECULAR LEVEL. THEY MIGHT AS WELL HAVE BEEN MADE YESTERDAY.
??
TIME TRAVEL FROM THE PAST TO OUR PRESENT? THAT'S A NEW ONE.
IT GETS WORSE. THERE IS D.N.A. EVIDENCE ON THE ARMOR'S INNER ASPECT OF--
PUT THAT DOWN!!!
THWOK
NNGH

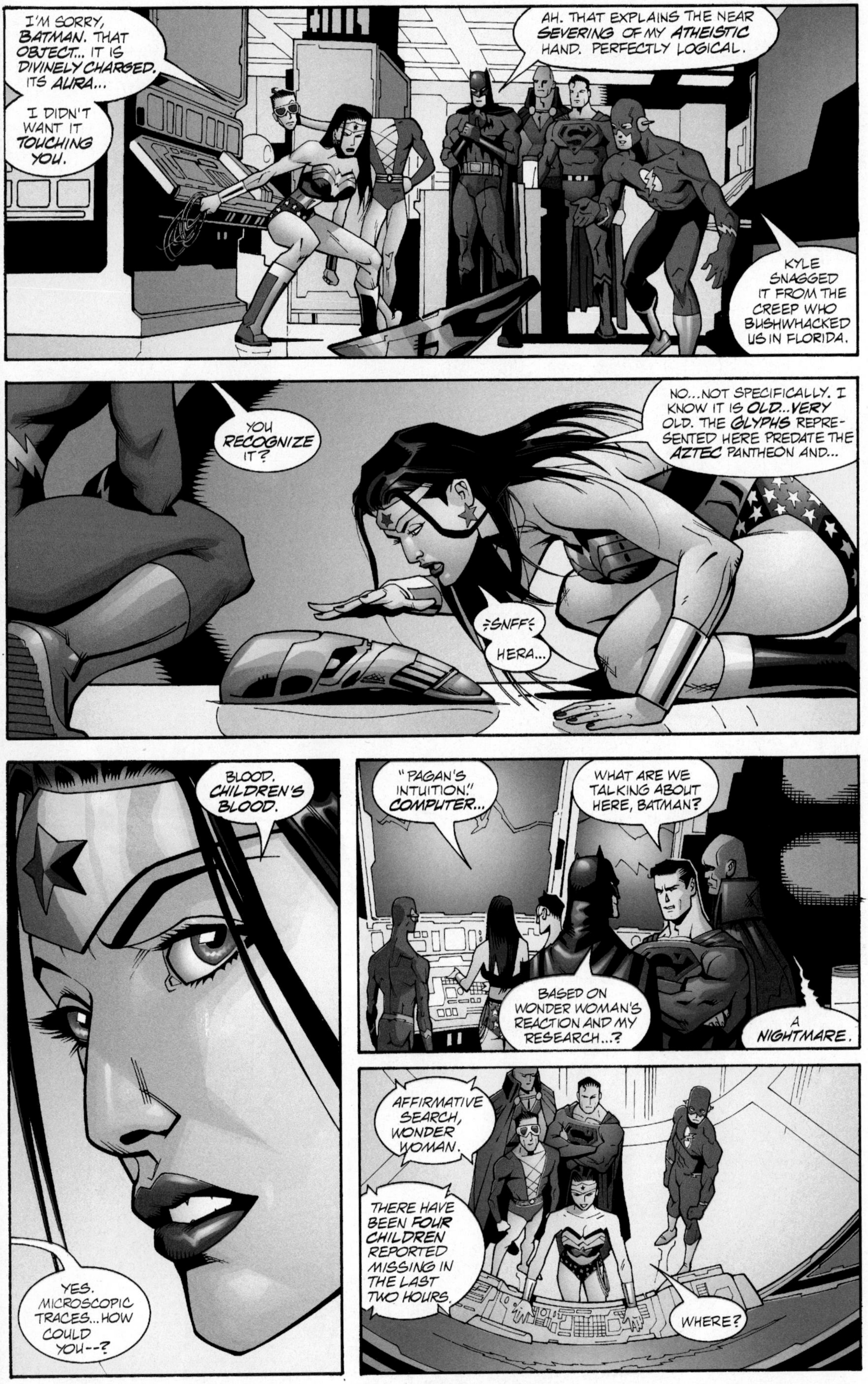
I'M SORRY, BATMAN. THAT OBJECT... IT IS DIVINELY CHARGED. ITS AURA...
I DIDN'T WANT IT TOUCHING YOU.
AH. THAT EXPLAINS THE NEAR SEVERING OF MY ATHEISTIC HAND. PERFECTLY LOGICAL.
KYLE SNAGGED IT FROM THE CREEP WHO BUSHWHACKED US IN FLORIDA.
YOU RECOGNIZE IT?
NO...NOT SPECIFICALLY. I KNOW IT IS OLD...VERY OLD. THE GLYPHS REPRESENTED HERE PREDATE THE AZTEC PANTHEON AND...
SNFF
HERA...
BLOOD. CHILDREN'S BLOOD.
YES. MICROSCOPIC TRACES...HOW COULD YOU--?
"PAGAN'S INTUITION." COMPUTER...
WHAT ARE WE TALKING ABOUT HERE, BATMAN?
BASED ON WONDER WOMAN'S REACTION AND MY RESEARCH...?
A NIGHTMARE.
AFFIRMATIVE SEARCH, WONDER WOMAN.
THERE HAVE BEEN FOUR CHILDREN REPORTED MISSING IN THE LAST TWO HOURS.
WHERE?

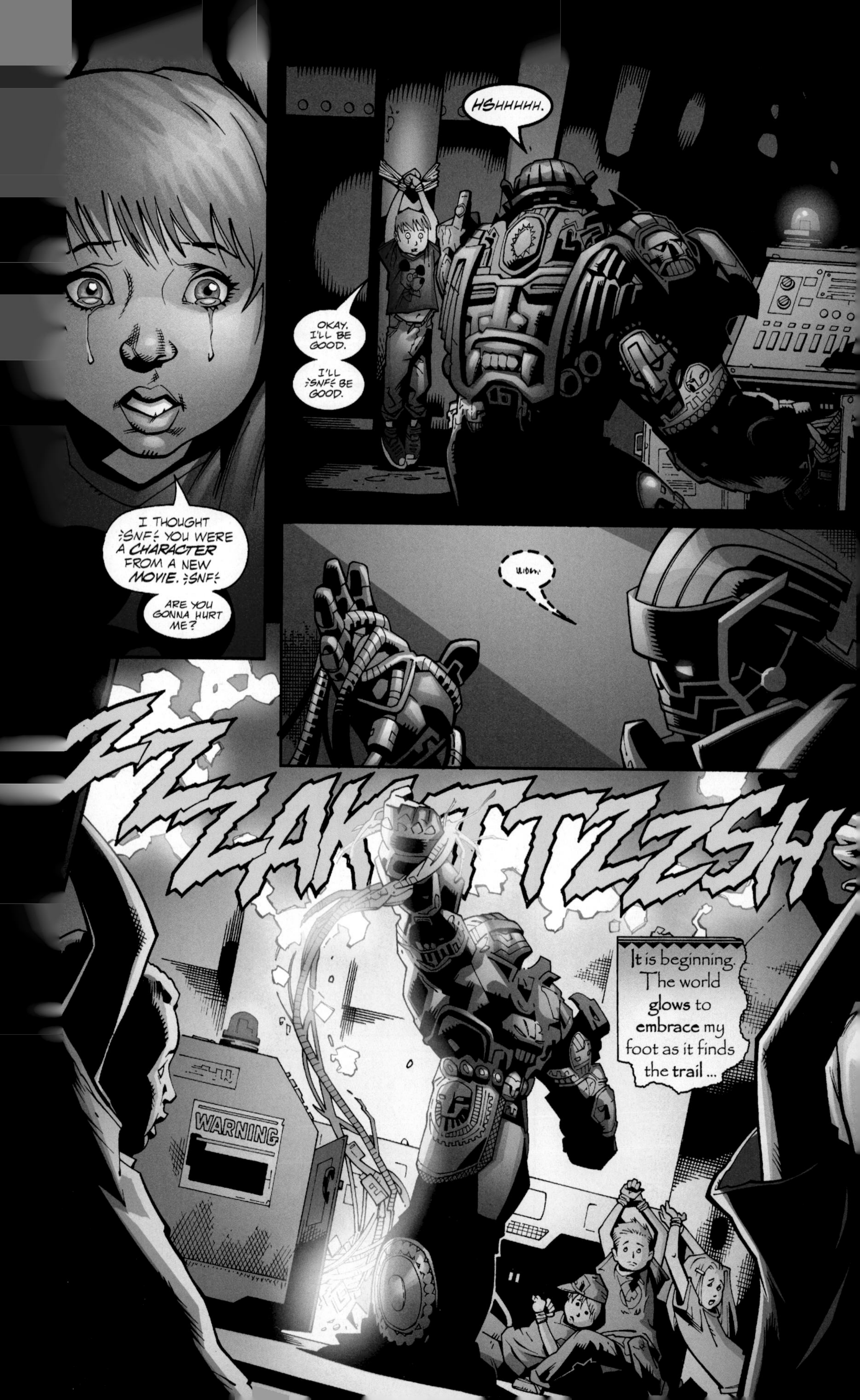

I THOUGHT ﹕SNF﹕ YOU WERE A CHARACTER FROM A NEW MOVIE. ﹕SNF﹕
ARE YOU GONNA HURT ME?
HSHHHHH.
OKAY. I'LL BE GOOD.
I'LL ﹕SNF﹕ BE GOOD.
It is beginning. The world glows to embrace my foot as it finds the trail ...
WARNING

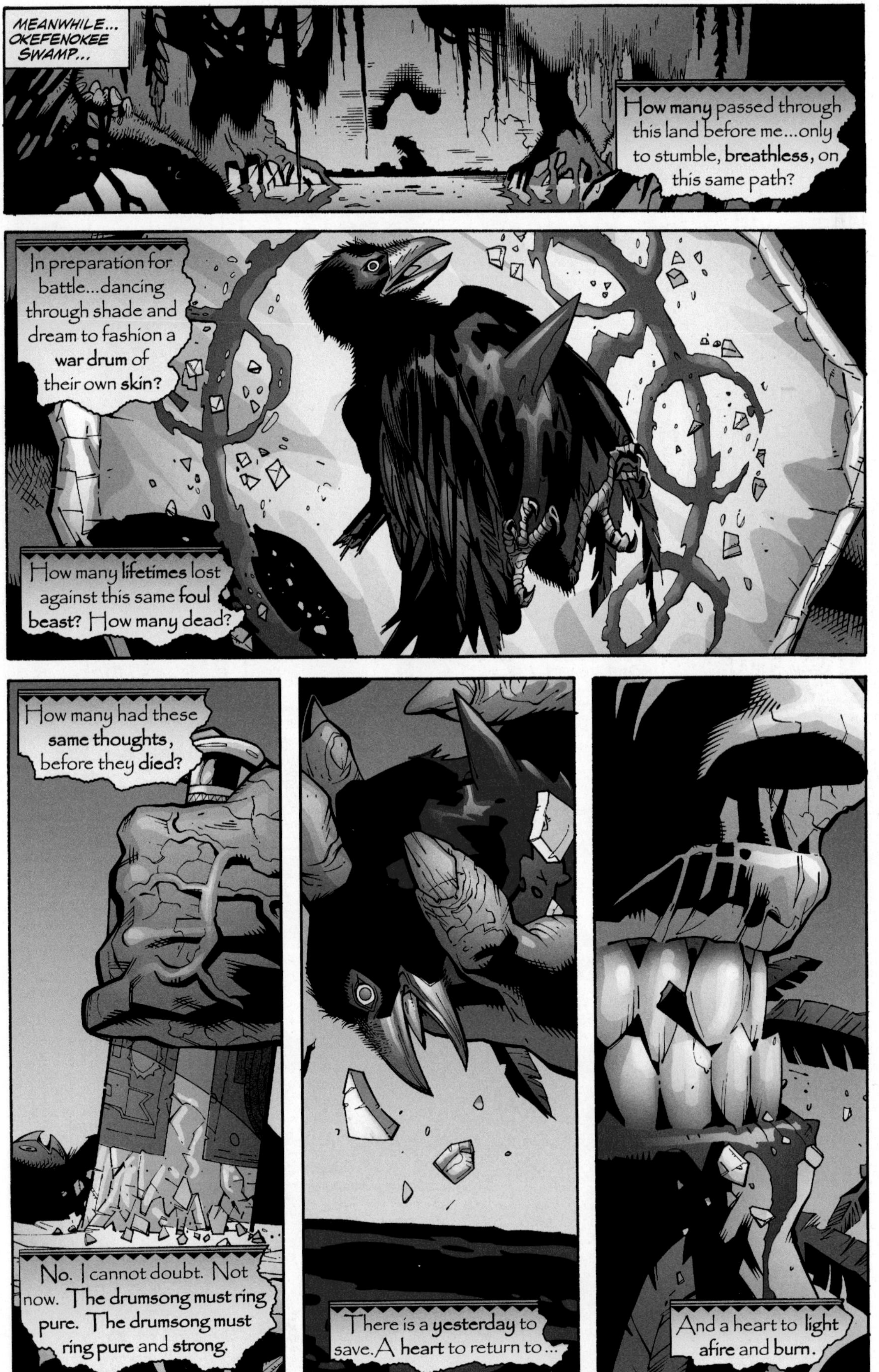
MEANWHILE... OKEFENOKEE SWAMP...
How many passed through this land before me...only to stumble, breathless, on this same path?
In preparation for battle...dancing through shade and dream to fashion a war drum of their own skin?
How many lifetimes lost against this same foul beast? How many dead?
How many had these same thoughts, before they died?
No. I cannot doubt. Not now. The drumsong must ring pure. The drumsong must ring pure and strong.
There is a yesterday to save. A heart to return to...
And a heart to light afire and burn.

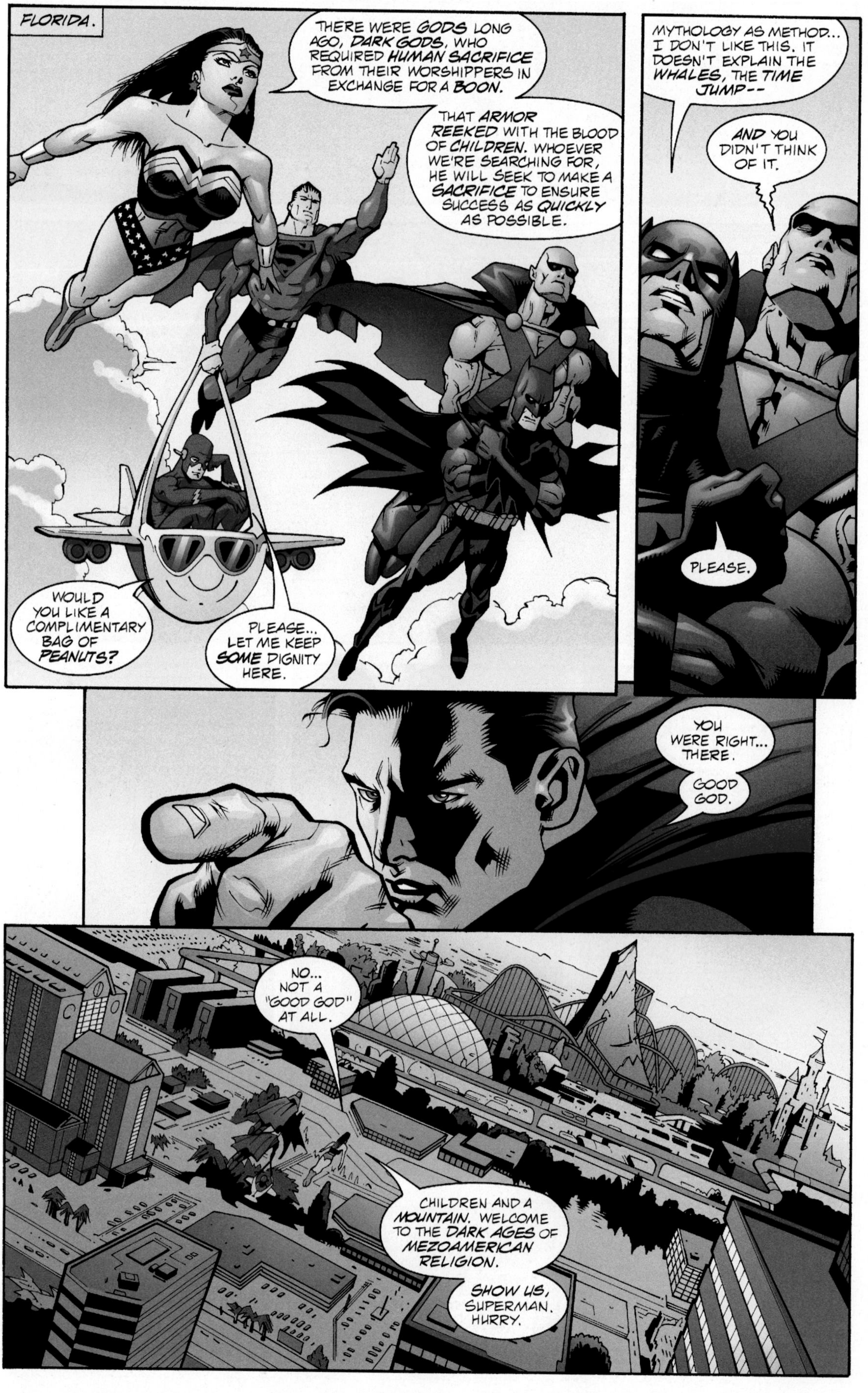
FLORIDA.
THERE WERE GODS LONG AGO, DARK GODS, WHO REQUIRED HUMAN SACRIFICE FROM THEIR WORSHIPPERS IN EXCHANGE FOR A BOON.
THAT ARMOR REEKED WITH THE BLOOD OF CHILDREN. WHOEVER WE'RE SEARCHING FOR, HE WILL SEEK TO MAKE A SACRIFICE TO ENSURE SUCCESS AS QUICKLY AS POSSIBLE.
WOULD YOU LIKE A COMPLIMENTARY BAG OF PEANUTS?
PLEASE... LET ME KEEP SOME DIGNITY HERE.
MYTHOLOGY AS METHOD... I DON'T LIKE THIS. IT DOESN'T EXPLAIN THE WHALES, THE TIME JUMP--
AND YOU DIDN'T THINK OF IT.
PLEASE.
YOU WERE RIGHT... THERE.
GOOD GOD.
NO... NOT A "GOOD GOD" AT ALL.
CHILDREN AND A MOUNTAIN. WELCOME TO THE DARK AGES OF MEZOAMERICAN RELIGION.
SHOW US, SUPERMAN. HURRY.

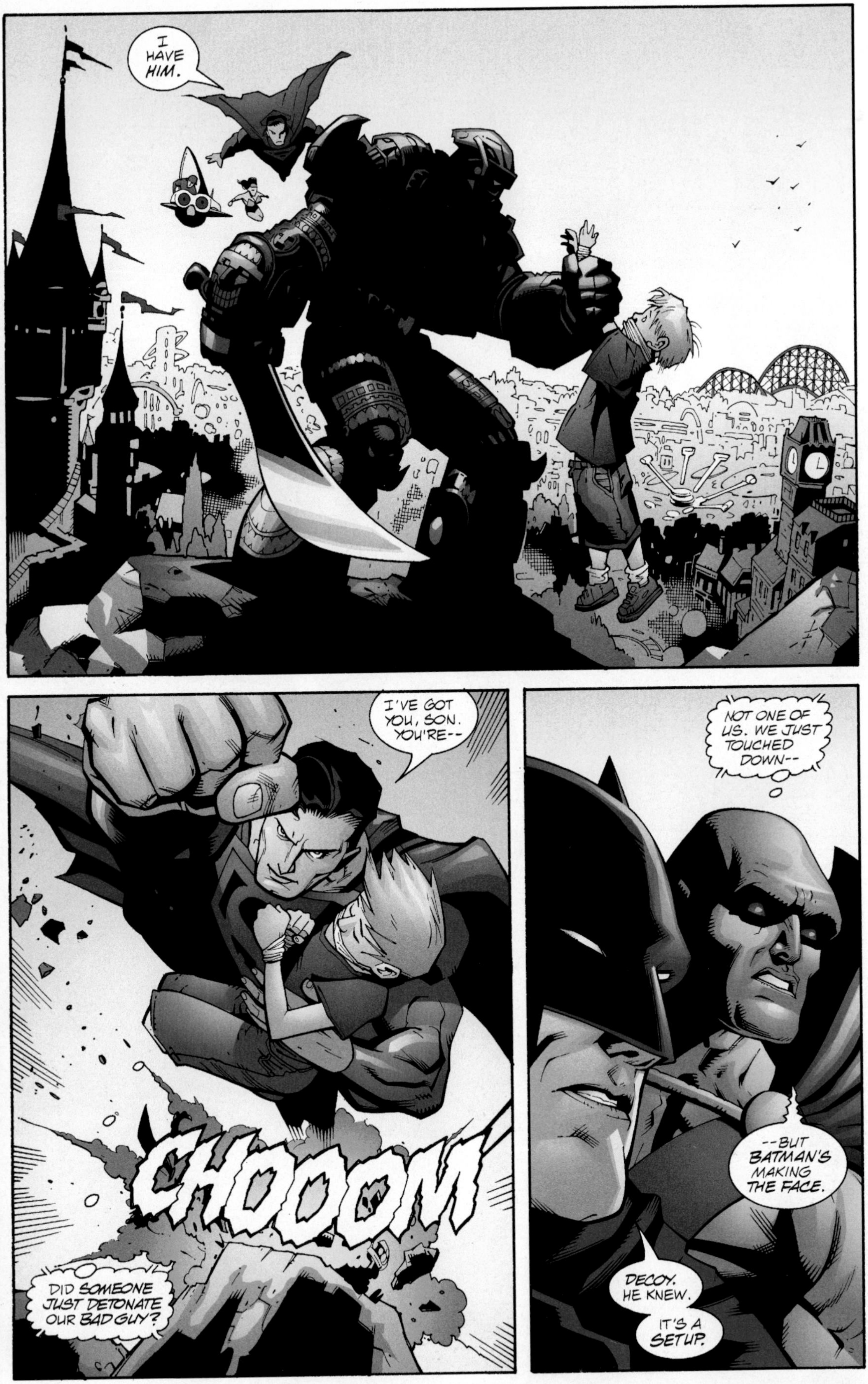
I HAVE HIM.
I'VE GOT YOU, SON. YOU'RE--
CHOOOM
DID SOMEONE JUST DETONATE OUR BAD GUY?
NOT ONE OF US. WE JUST TOUCHED DOWN--
--BUT BATMAN'S MAKING THE FACE.
DECOY. HE KNEW.
IT'S A SETUP.

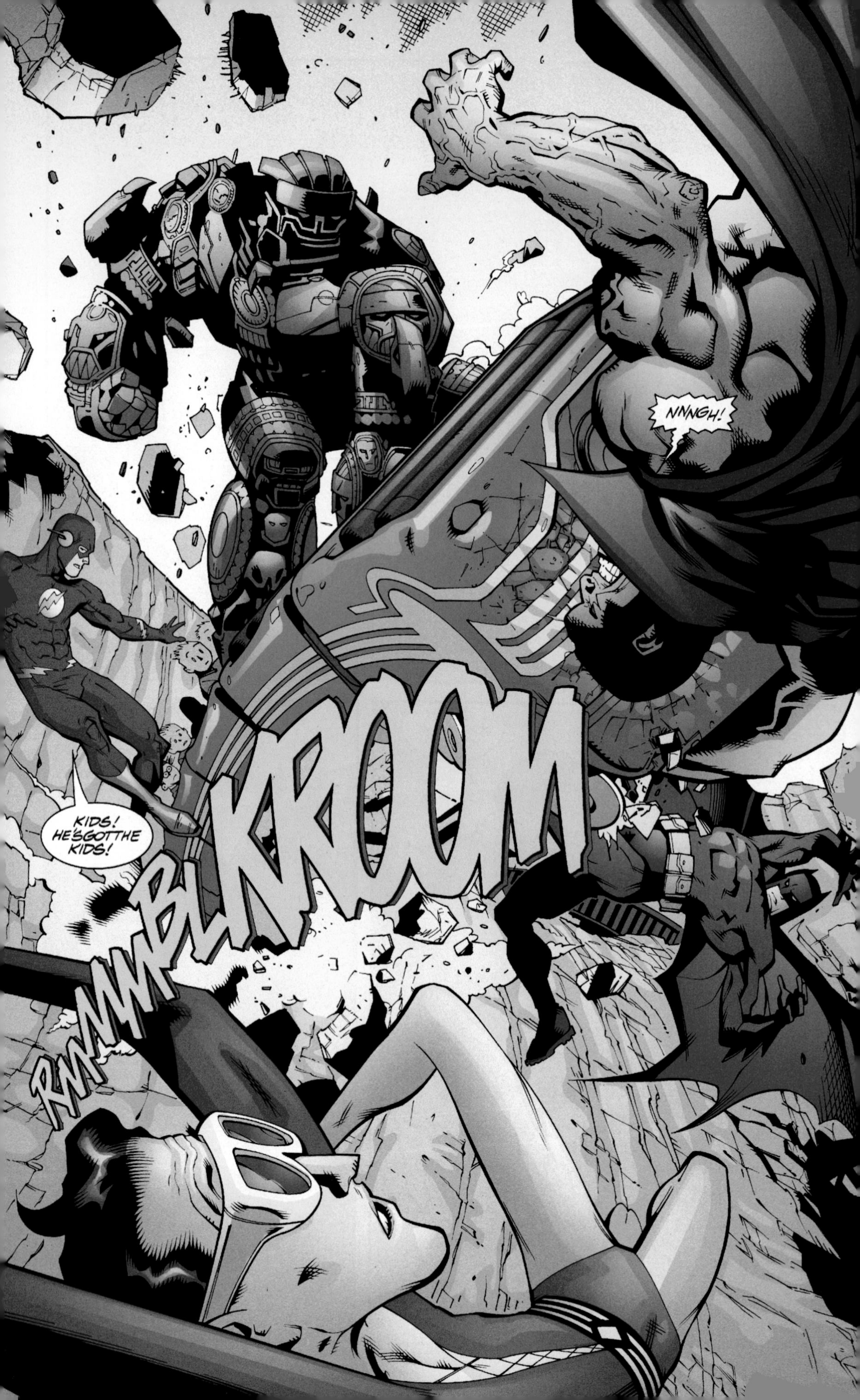
NNNGH!
KIDS! HE'S GOT THE KIDS!
RMMMMBLKROOM

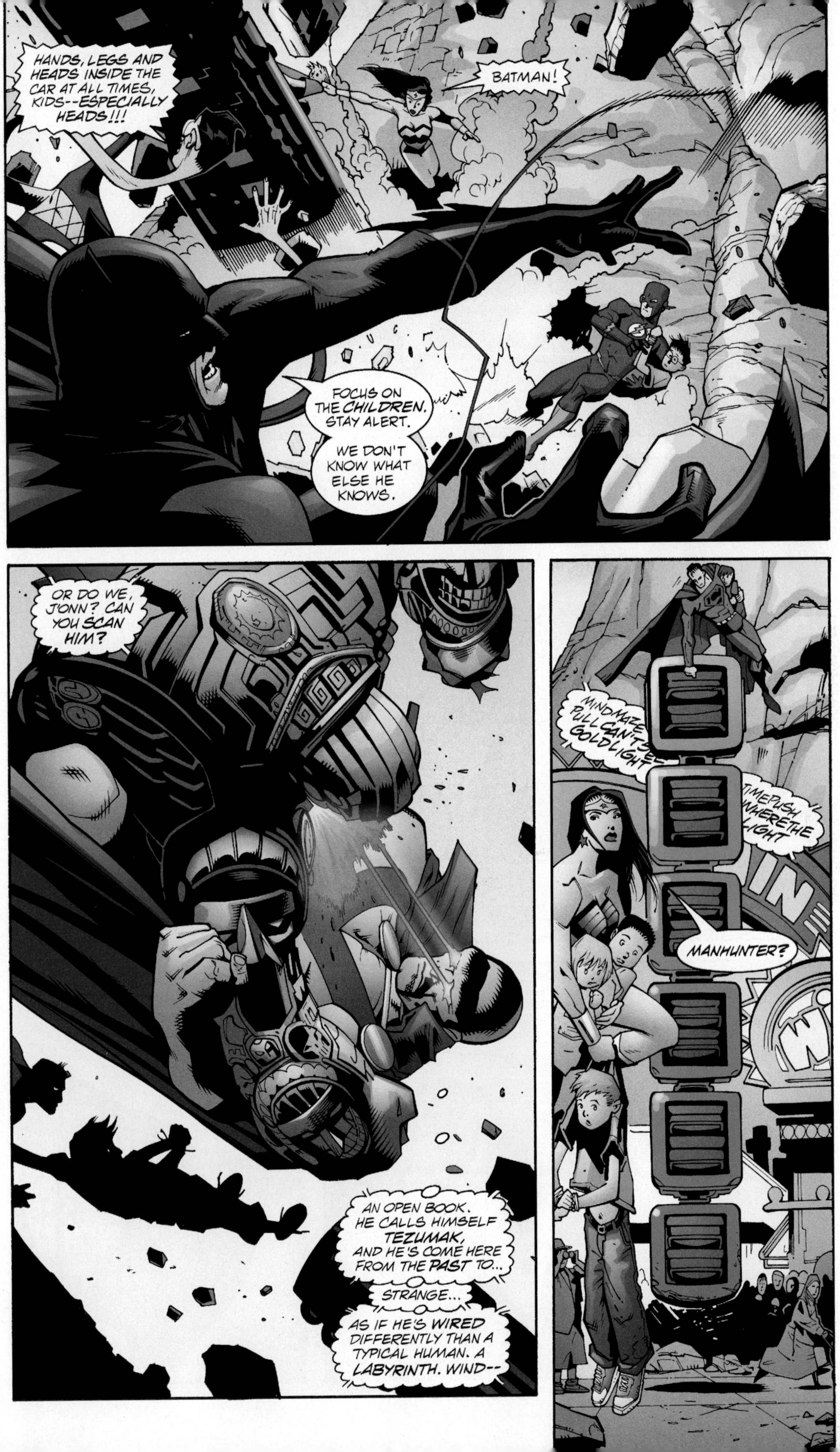

HANDS, LEGS AND HEADS INSIDE THE CAR AT ALL TIMES, KIDS--ESPECIALLY HEADS!!!
BATMAN!
FOCUS ON THE CHILDREN. STAY ALERT.
WE DON'T KNOW WHAT ELSE HE KNOWS.
OR DO WE, J'ONN? CAN YOU SCAN HIM?
AN OPEN BOOK. HE CALLS HIMSELF TEZUMAK, AND HE'S COME HERE FROM THE PAST TO...
STRANGE...
AS IF HE'S WIRED DIFFERENTLY THAN A TYPICAL HUMAN. A LABYRINTH. WIND--
MINDMAZE
PULL CAN'T
GOLDLIGHT
TIMEPUSH
HERETHE
LIGHT
MANHUNTER?

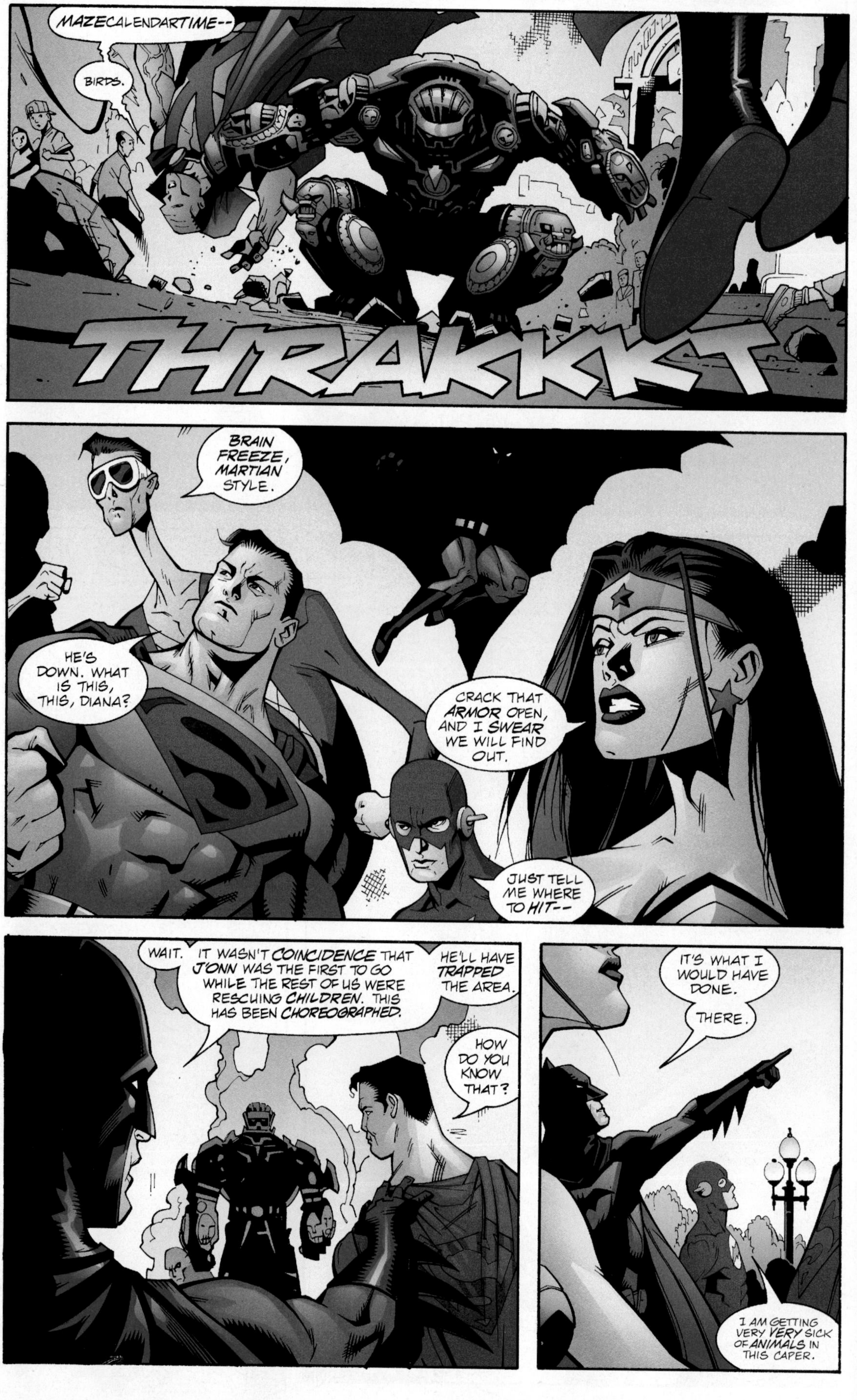
MAZECALENDARTIME--
BIRDS.
THRAKKT
BRAIN FREEZE, MARTIAN STYLE.
HE'S DOWN. WHAT IS THIS, THIS, DIANA?
CRACK THAT ARMOR OPEN, AND I SWEAR WE WILL FIND OUT.
JUST TELL ME WHERE TO HIT--
WAIT.
IT WASN'T COINCIDENCE THAT J'ONN WAS THE FIRST TO GO WHILE THE REST OF US WERE RESCUING CHILDREN. THIS HAS BEEN CHOREOGRAPHED.
HE'LL HAVE TRAPPED THE AREA.
HOW DO YOU KNOW THAT?
IT'S WHAT I WOULD HAVE DONE.
THERE.
I AM GETTING VERY VERY SICK OF ANIMALS IN THIS CAPER.

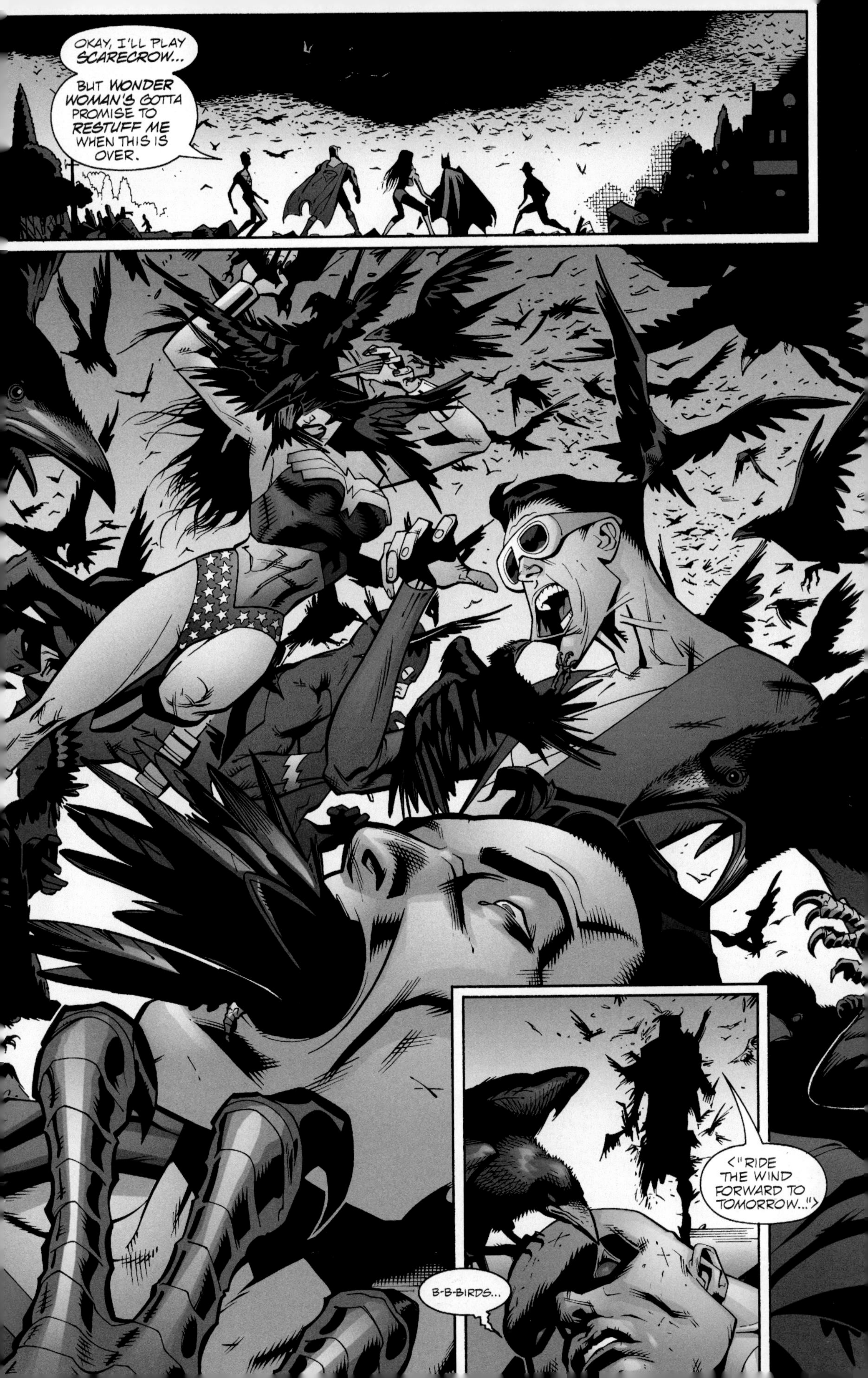
OKAY, I'LL PLAY SCARECROW...
BUT WONDER WOMAN'S GOTTA PROMISE TO RESTUFF ME WHEN THIS IS OVER.
<"RIDE THE WIND FORWARD TO TOMORROW...">
B-B-BIRDS...

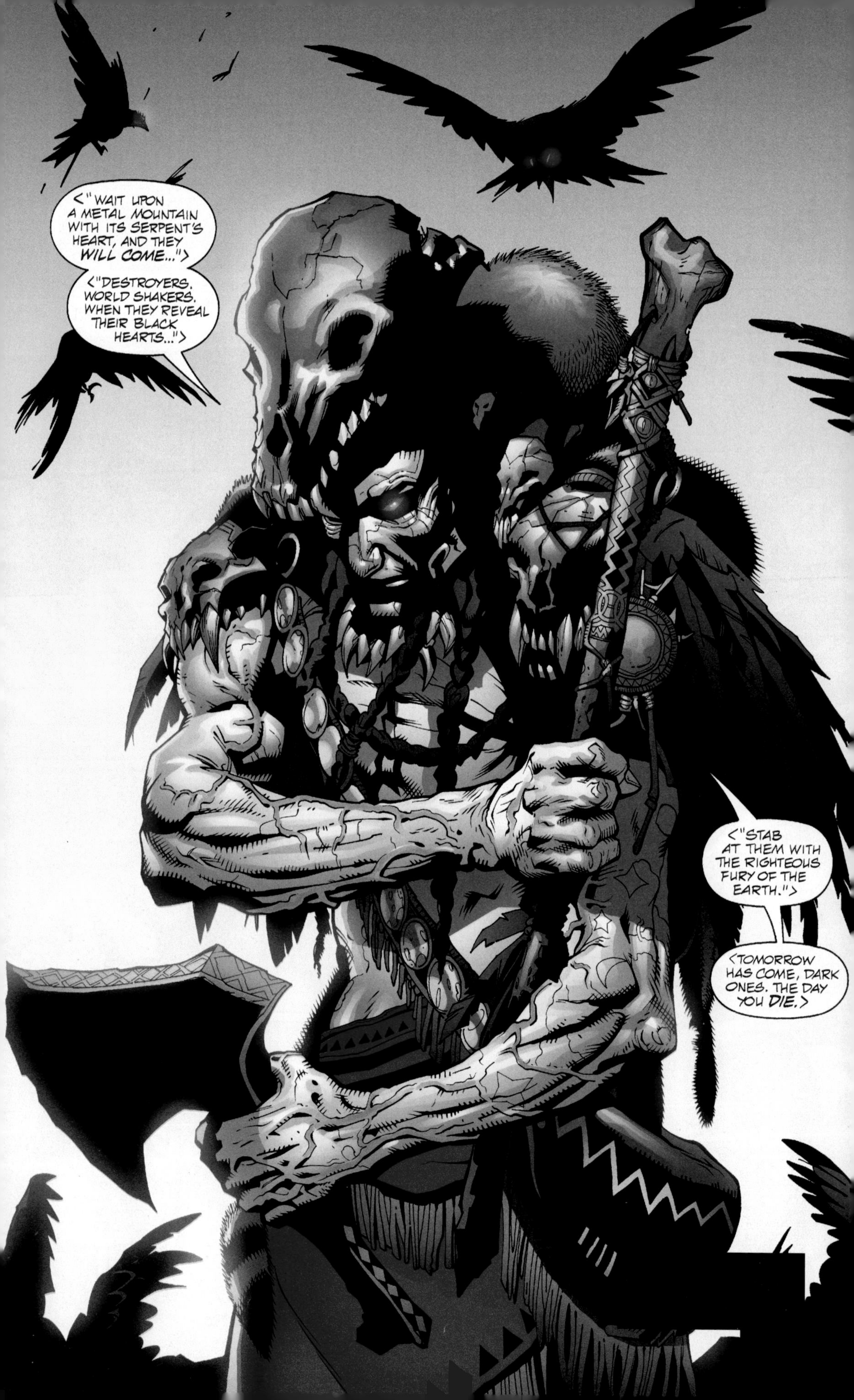

<"WAIT UPON A METAL MOUNTAIN WITH ITS SERPENT'S HEART, AND THEY WILL COME...">
<"DESTROYERS. WORLD SHAKERS. WHEN THEY REVEAL THEIR BLACK HEARTS...">
<"STAB AT THEM WITH THE RIGHTEOUS FURY OF THE EARTH.">
<TOMORROW HAS COME, DARK ONES. THE DAY YOU DIE.>

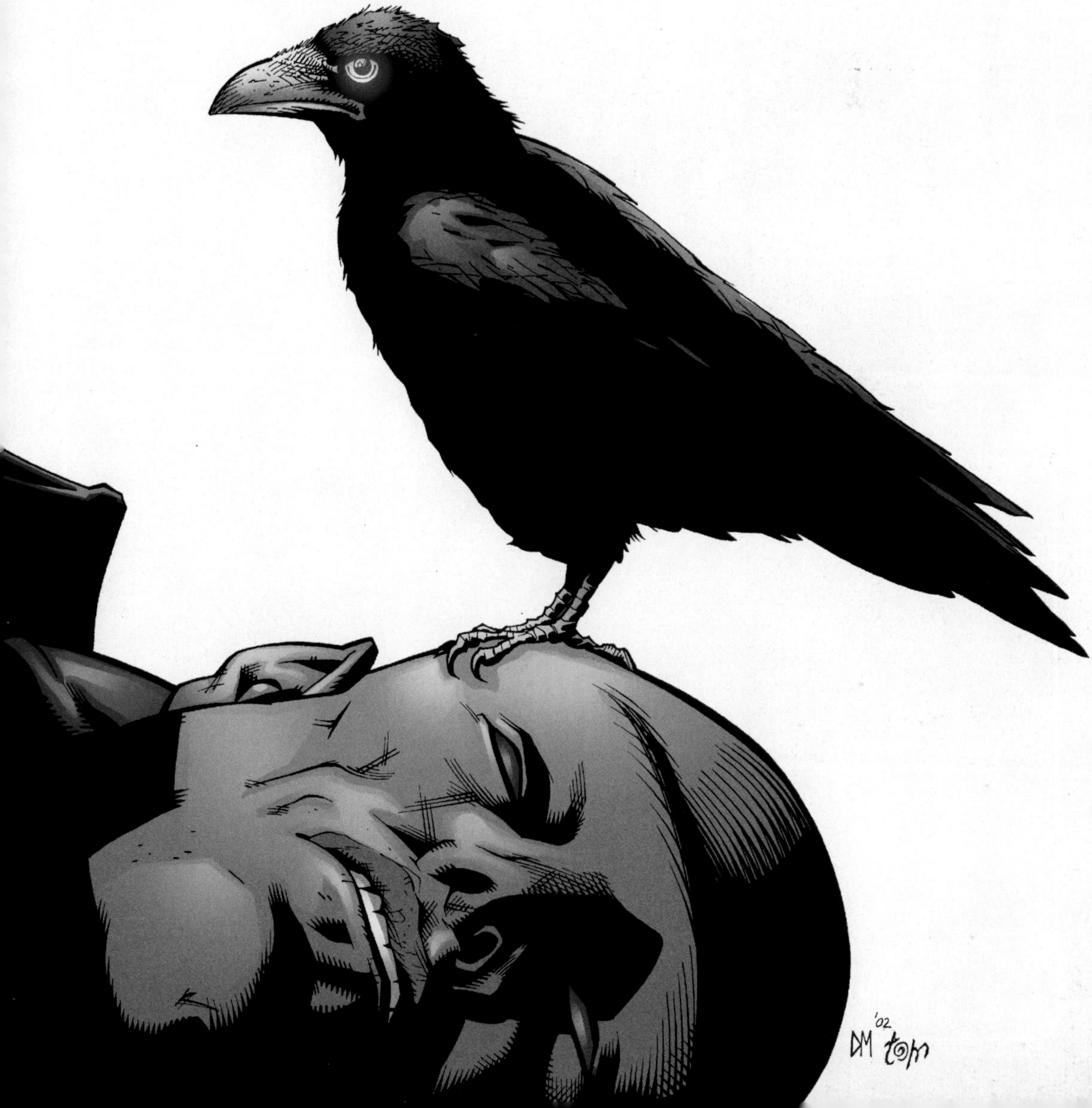

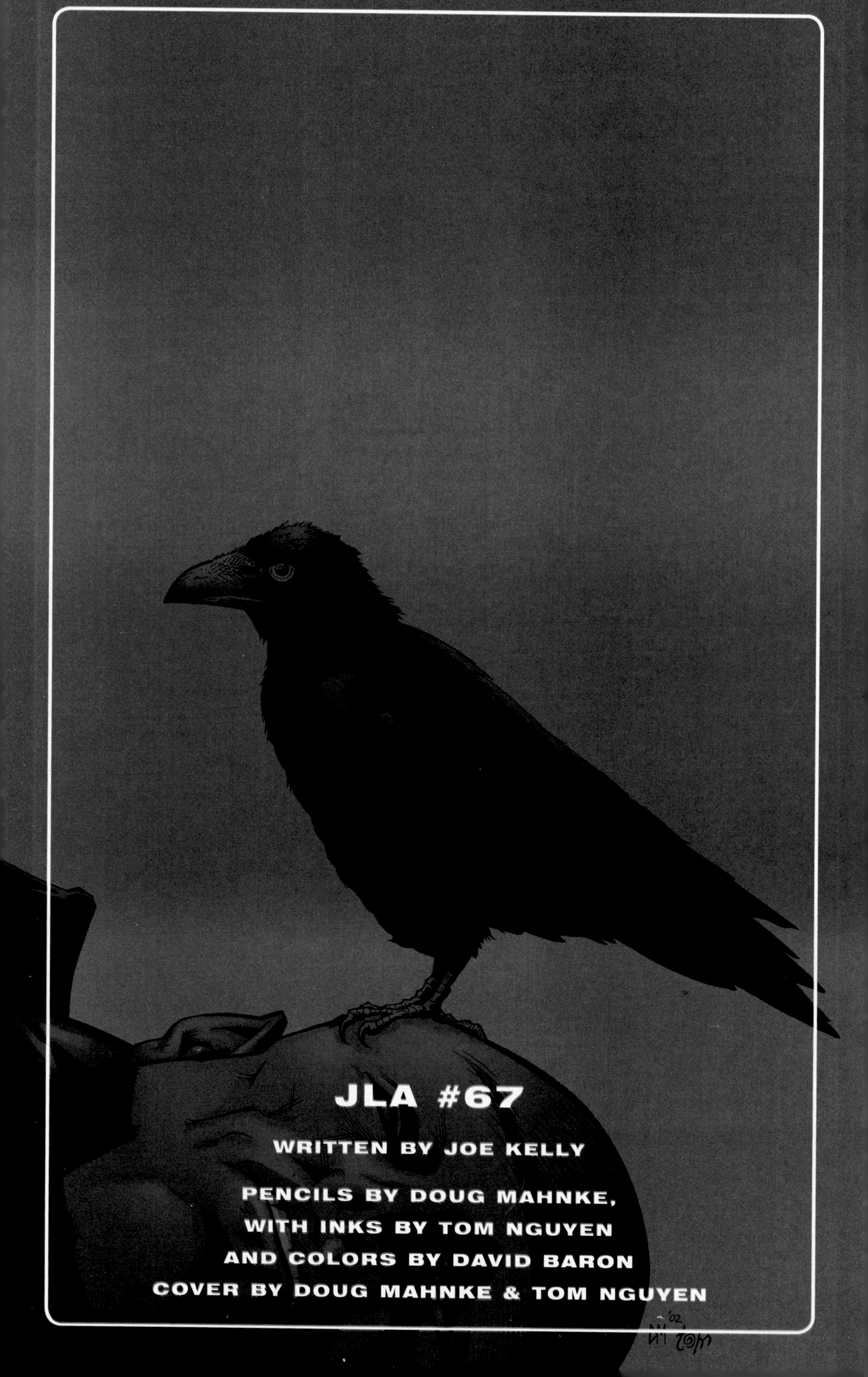

JLA #67

WRITTEN BY JOE KELLY

PENCILS BY DOUG MAHNKE,
WITH INKS BY TOM NGUYEN
AND COLORS BY DAVID BARON

COVER BY DOUG MAHNKE & TOM NGUYEN

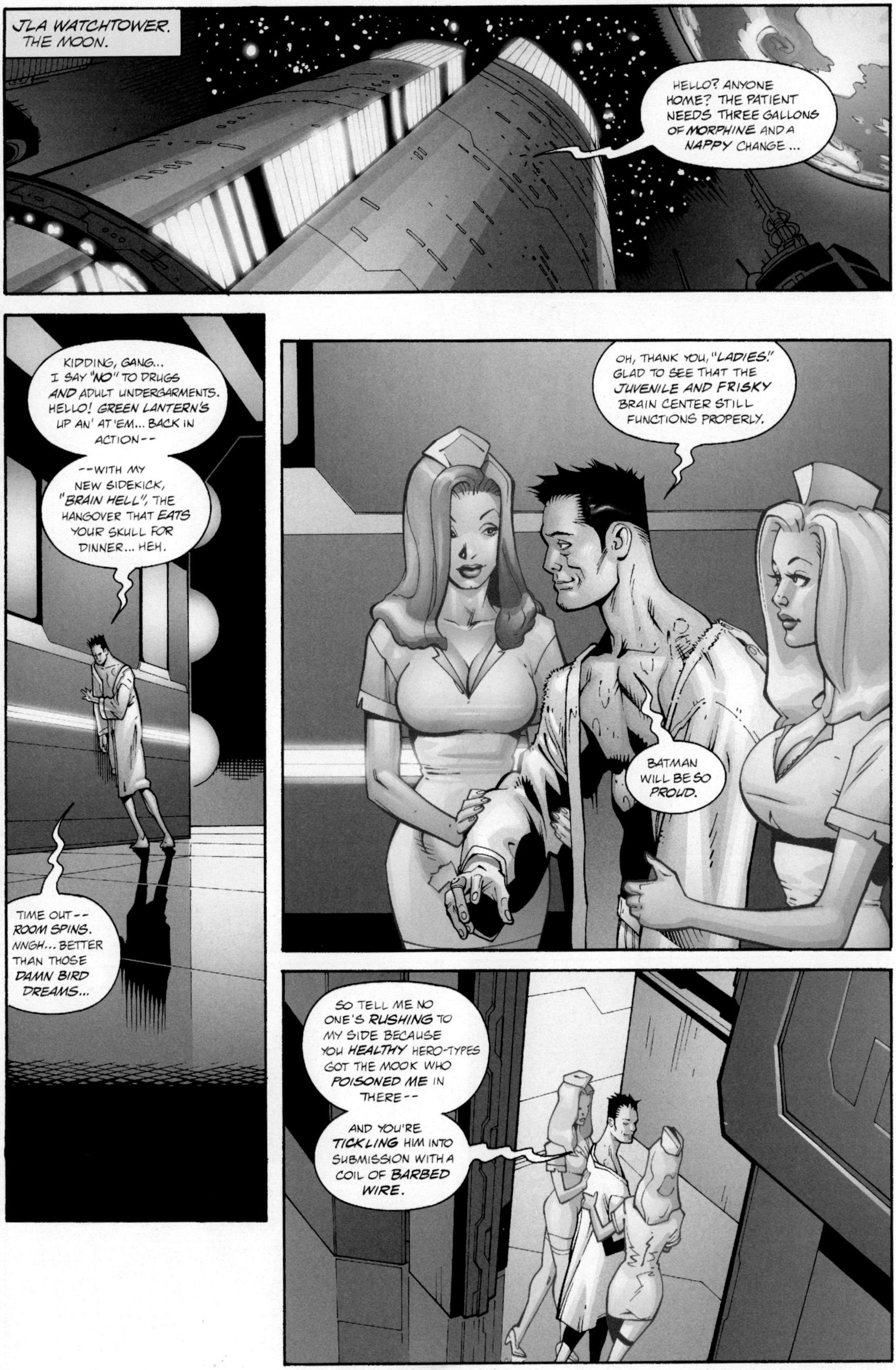
JLA WATCHTOWER. THE MOON.
HELLO? ANYONE HOME? THE PATIENT NEEDS THREE GALLONS OF MORPHINE AND A NAPPY CHANGE...
KIDDING, GANG... I SAY "NO" TO DRUGS AND ADULT UNDERGARMENTS. HELLO! GREEN LANTERN'S UP AN' AT 'EM... BACK IN ACTION--
--WITH MY NEW SIDEKICK, "BRAIN HELL", THE HANGOVER THAT EATS YOUR SKULL FOR DINNER... HEH.
TIME OUT-- ROOM SPINS. NNGH... BETTER THAN THOSE DAMN BIRD DREAMS...
OH, THANK YOU, "LADIES." GLAD TO SEE THAT THE JUVENILE AND FRISKY BRAIN CENTER STILL FUNCTIONS PROPERLY.
BATMAN WILL BE SO PROUD.
SO TELL ME NO ONE'S RUSHING TO MY SIDE BECAUSE YOU HEALTHY HERO-TYPES GOT THE MOOK WHO POISONED ME IN THERE--
AND YOU'RE TICKLING HIM INTO SUBMISSION WITH A COIL OF BARBED WIRE.

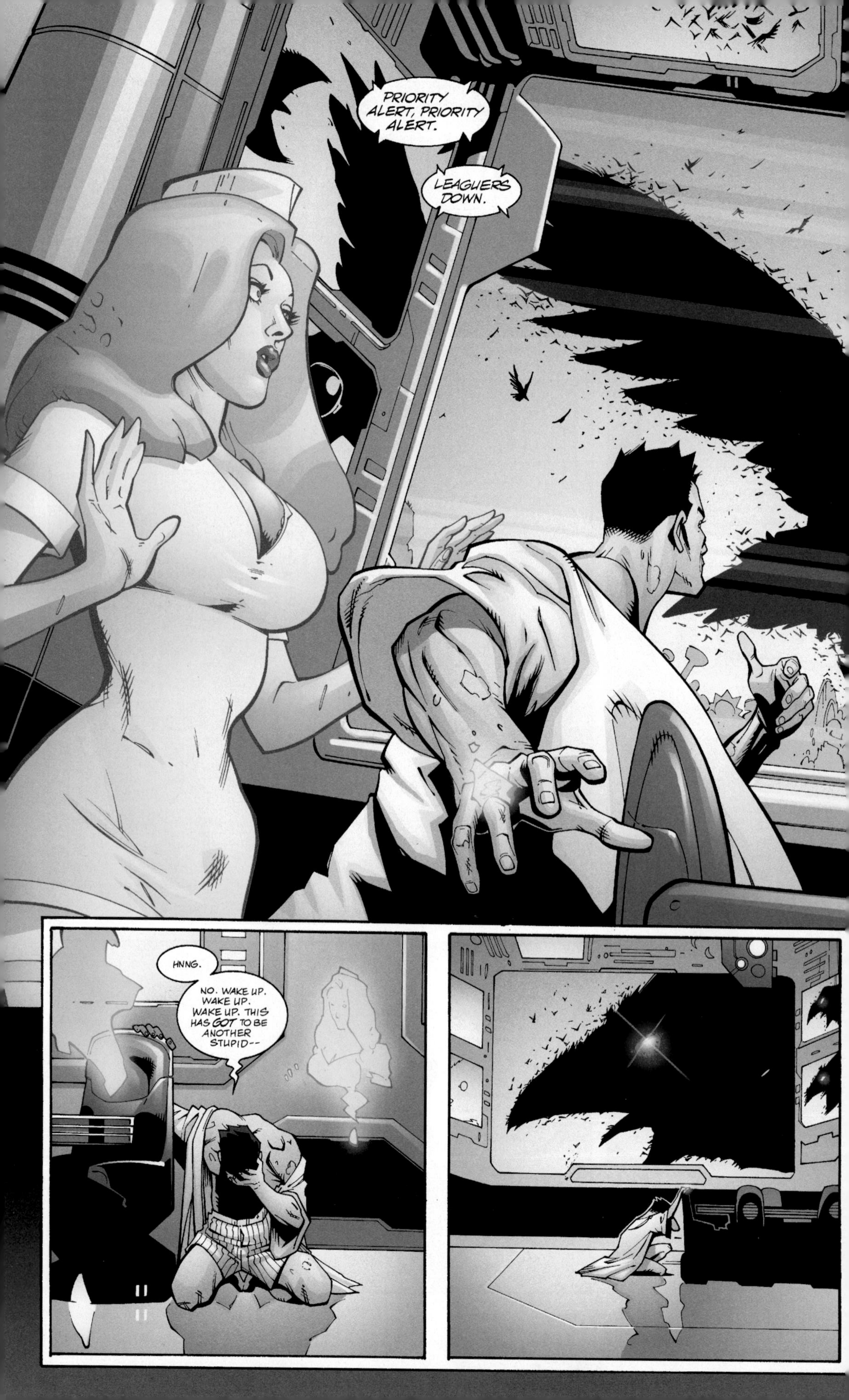
PRIORITY ALERT, PRIORITY ALERT.
LEAGUERS DOWN.
HNNG.
NO. WAKE UP. WAKE UP. WAKE UP. THIS HAS GOT TO BE ANOTHER STUPID--

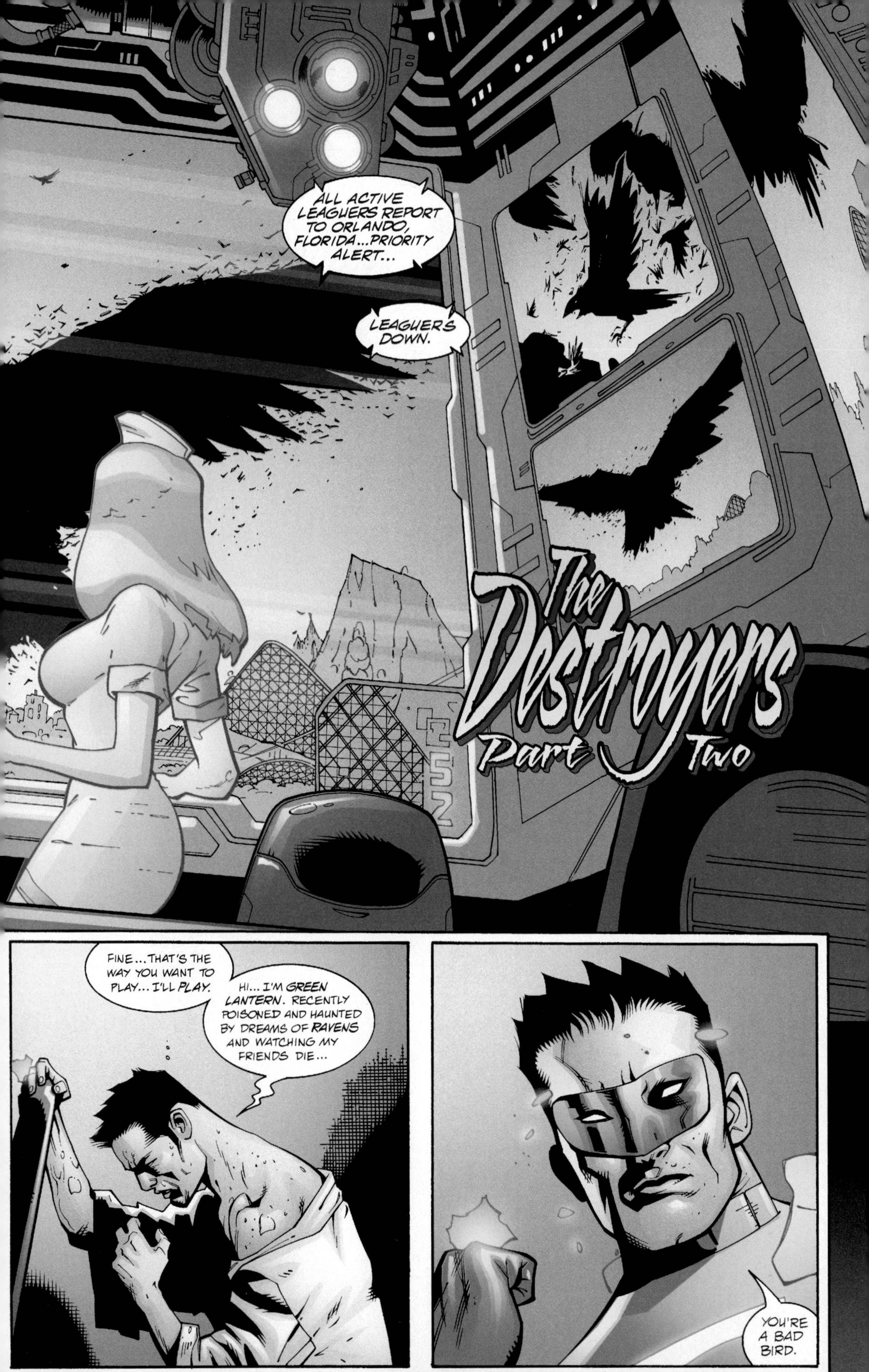
ALL ACTIVE LEAGUERS REPORT TO ORLANDO, FLORIDA...PRIORITY ALERT...
LEAGUERS DOWN.
The Destroyers Part Two
FINE... THAT'S THE WAY YOU WANT TO PLAY... I'LL PLAY.
HI... I'M GREEN LANTERN. RECENTLY POISONED AND HAUNTED BY DREAMS OF RAVENS AND WATCHING MY FRIENDS DIE...
YOU'RE A BAD BIRD.

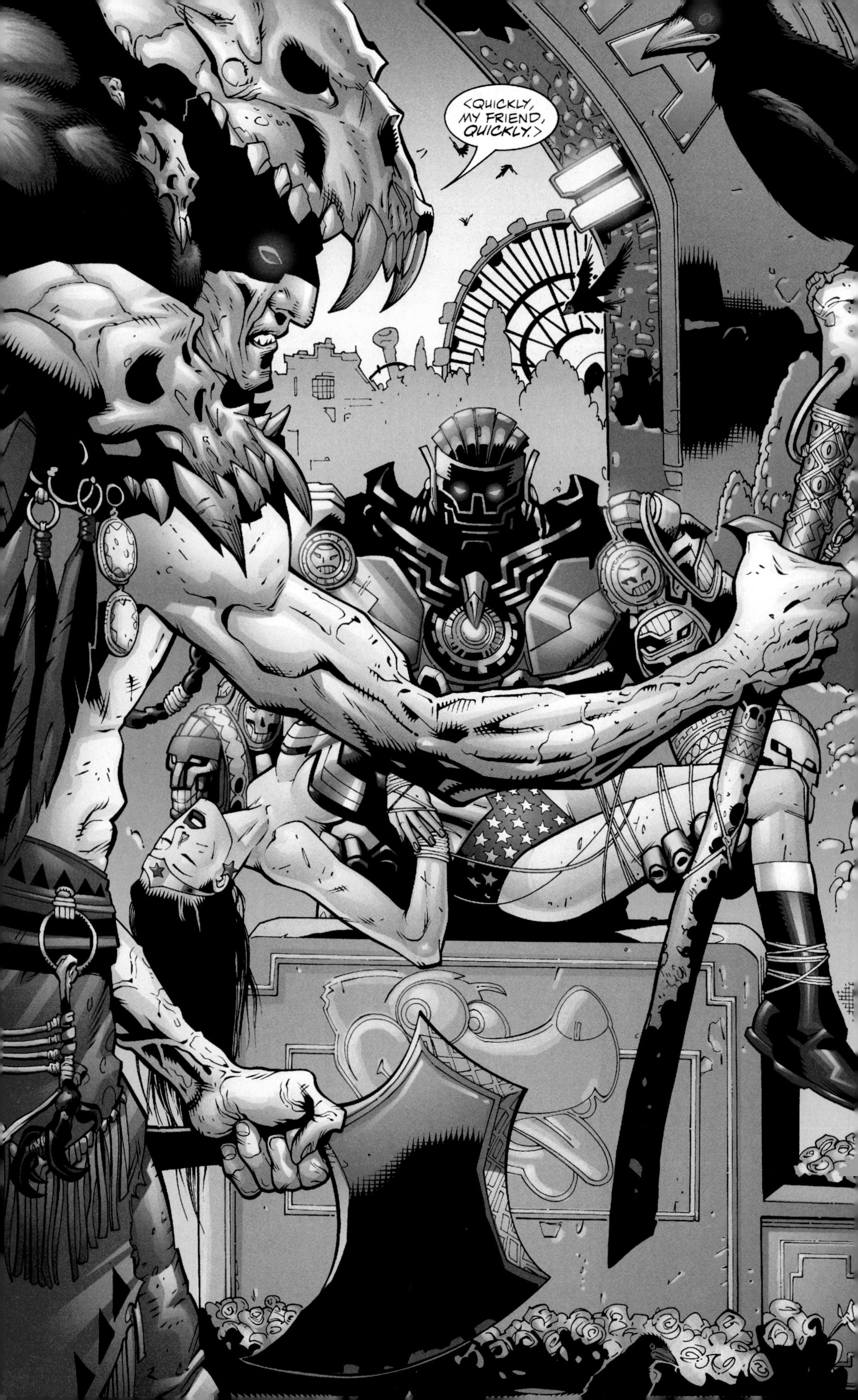
<QUICKLY, MY FRIEND, QUICKLY.>

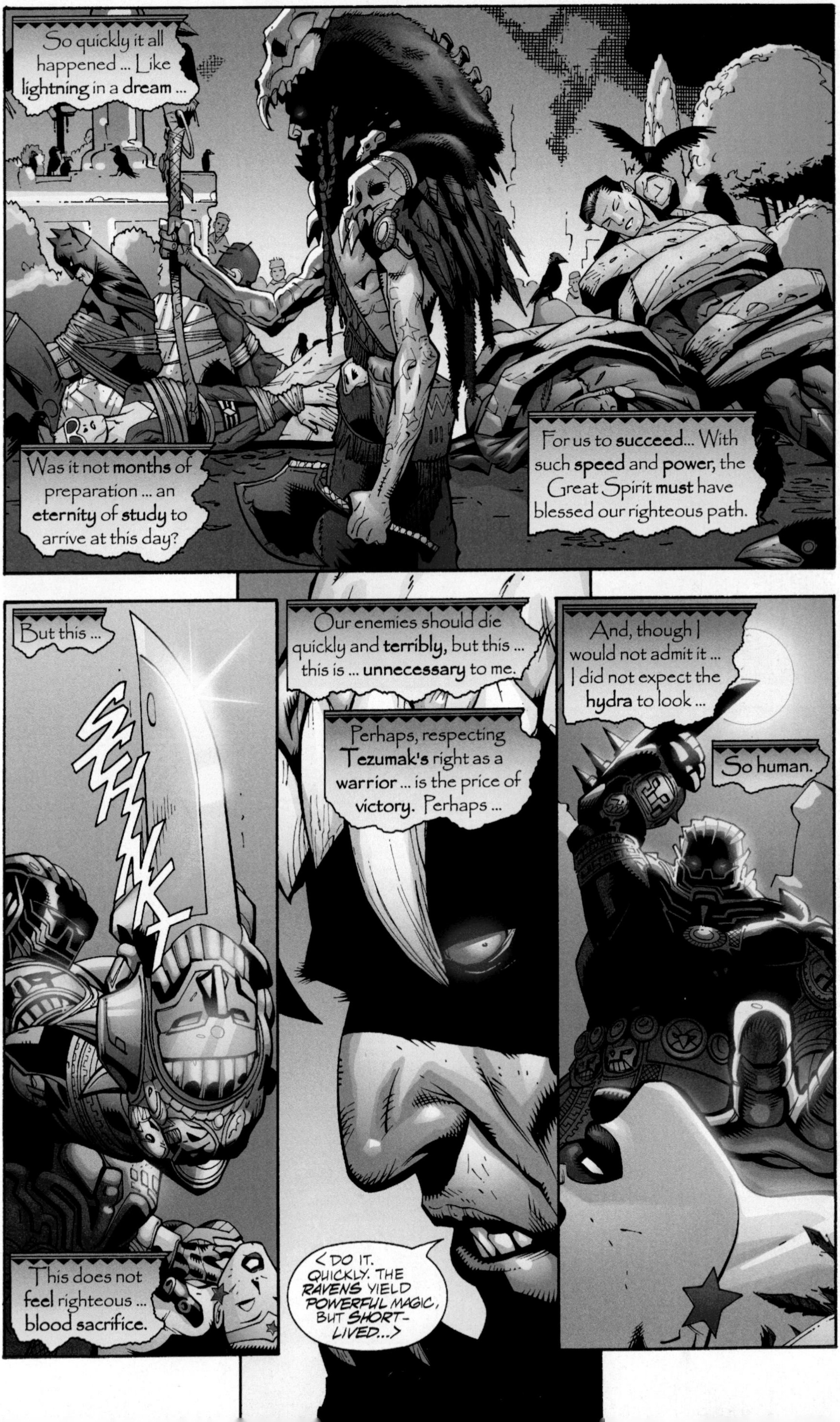
So quickly it all happened ... Like lightning in a dream ...
Was it not months of preparation ... an eternity of study to arrive at this day?
For us to succeed... With such speed and power, the Great Spirit must have blessed our righteous path.
But this ...
SCHINK!
This does not feel righteous ... blood sacrifice.
Our enemies should die quickly and terribly, but this ... this is ... unnecessary to me.
Perhaps, respecting Tezumak's right as a warrior ... is the price of victory. Perhaps ...
<DO IT. QUICKLY. THE RAVENS YIELD POWERFUL MAGIC, BUT SHORT-LIVED...>
And, though I would not admit it ... I did not expect the hydra to look ...
So human.

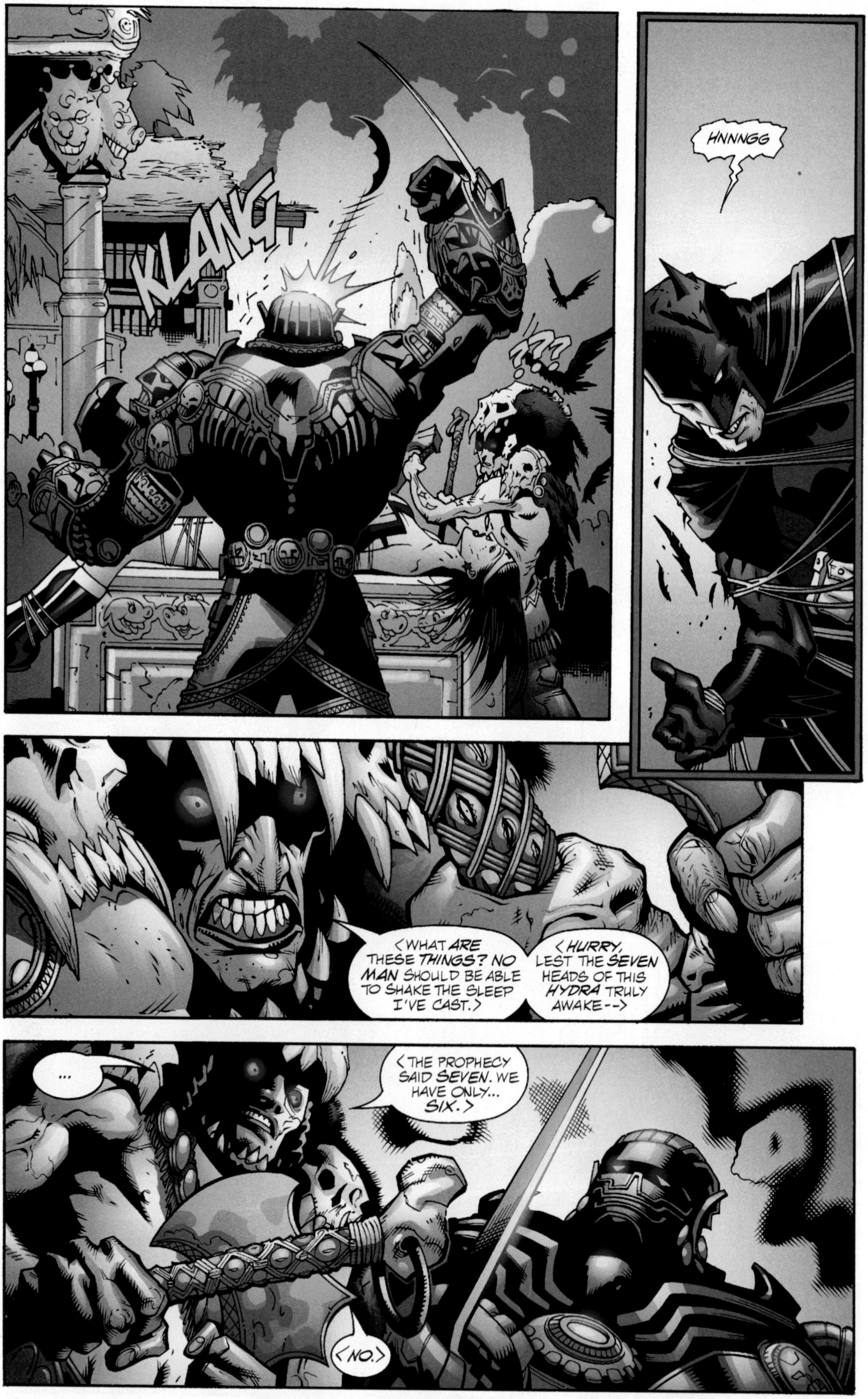
KLANG
HNNNGG
???
<WHAT ARE THESE THINGS? NO MAN SHOULD BE ABLE TO SHAKE THE SLEEP I'VE CAST.>
<HURRY, LEST THE SEVEN HEADS OF THIS HYDRA TRULY AWAKE-->
...
<THE PROPHECY SAID SEVEN. WE HAVE ONLY... SIX.>
<NO.>

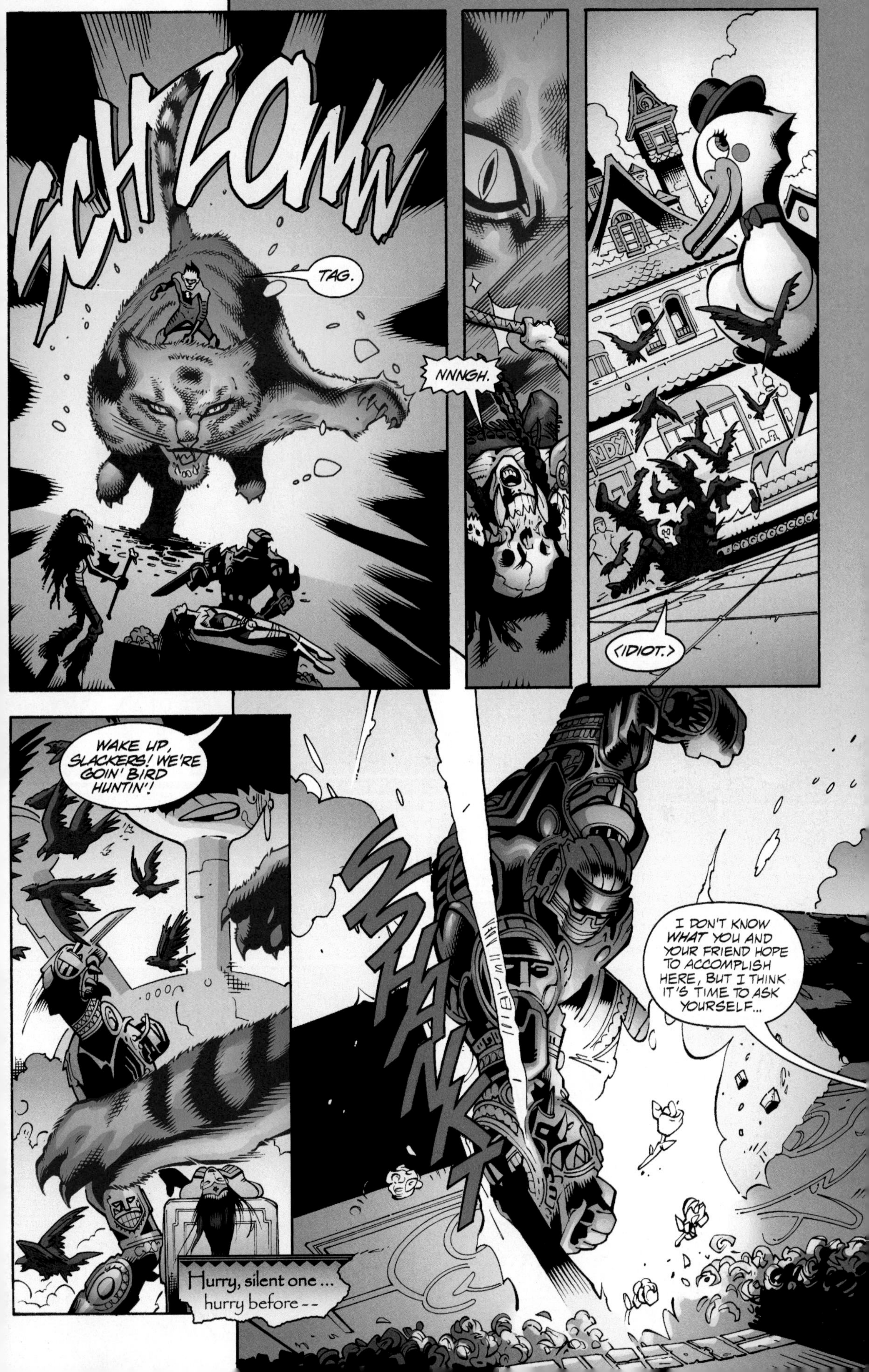
SCHZOWW
TAG.
NNNGH.
<IDIOT.>
WAKE UP, SLACKERS! WE'RE GOIN' BIRD HUNTIN'!
SWHANKT
I DON'T KNOW WHAT YOU AND YOUR FRIEND HOPE TO ACCOMPLISH HERE, BUT I THINK IT'S TIME TO ASK YOURSELF...
Hurry, silent one ... hurry before --

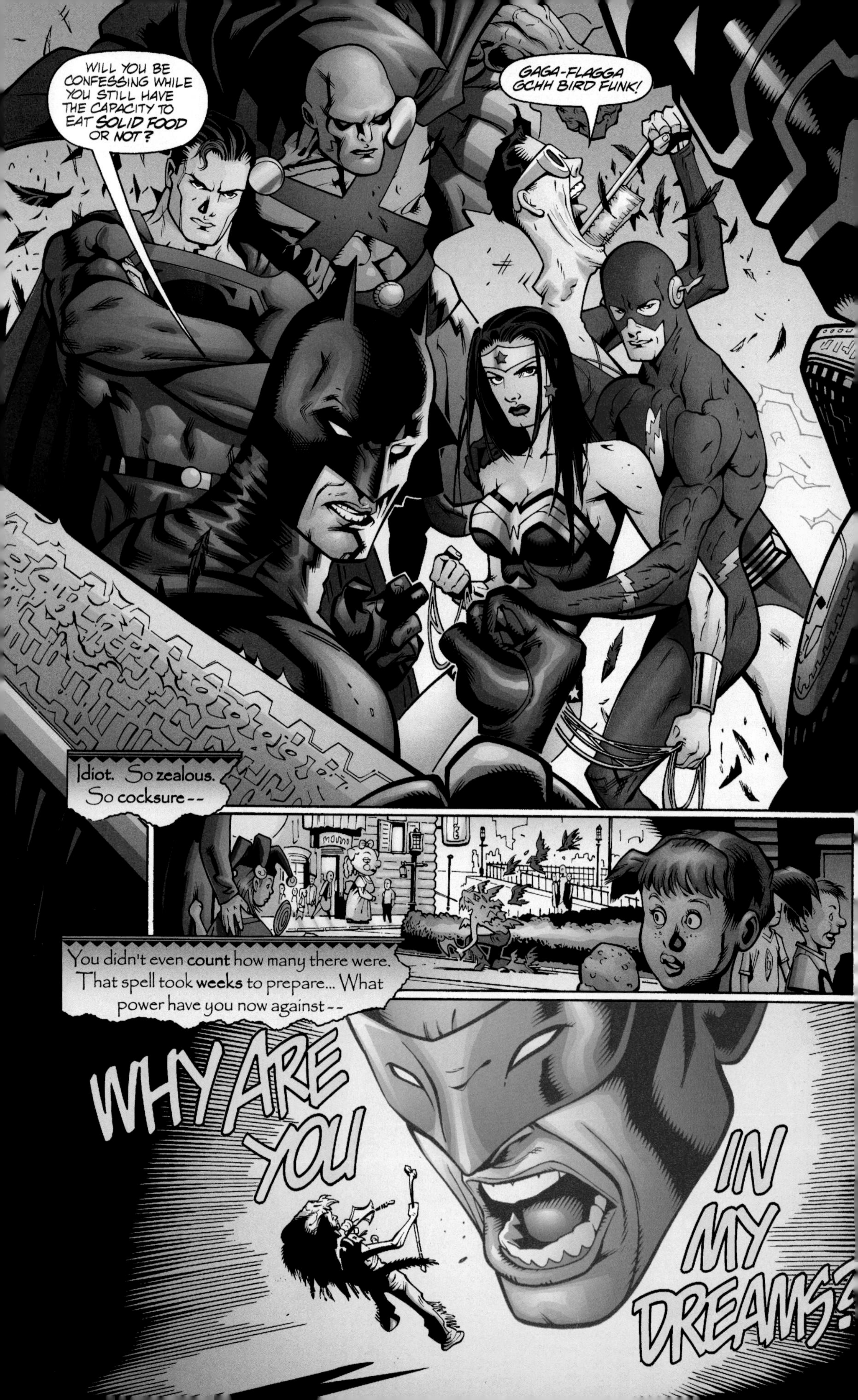

WILL YOU BE CONFESSING WHILE YOU STILL HAVE THE CAPACITY TO EAT SOLID FOOD OR NOT?
GAGA-FLAGGA GCHH BIRD FUNK!
Idiot. So zealous. So cocksure --
You didn't even count how many there were. That spell took weeks to prepare... What power have you now against --
WHY ARE YOU IN MY DREAMS?

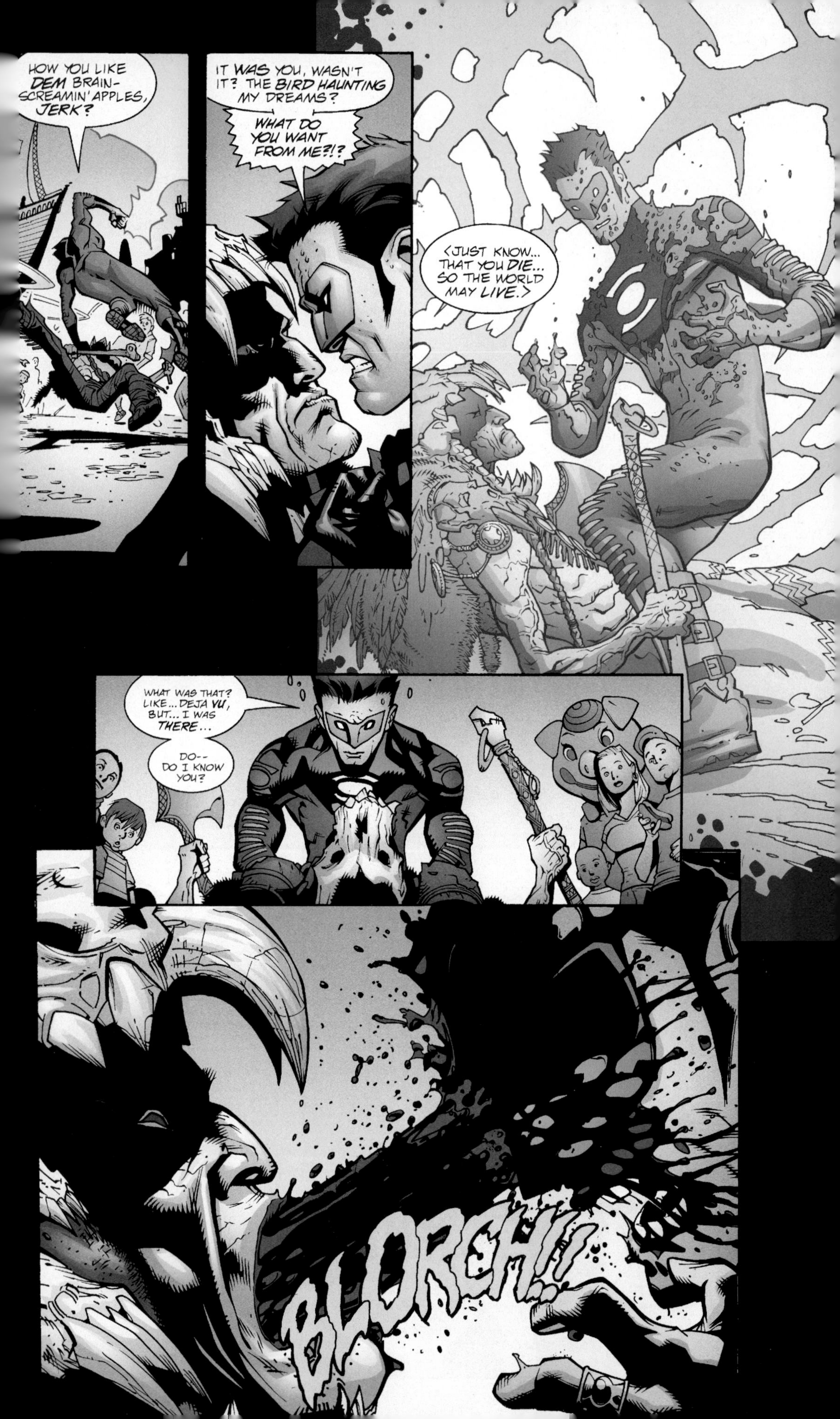
HOW YOU LIKE DEM BRAIN-SCREAMIN' APPLES, JERK?
IT WAS YOU, WASN'T IT? THE BIRD HAUNTING MY DREAMS?
WHAT DO YOU WANT FROM ME?!?
<JUST KNOW... THAT YOU DIE... SO THE WORLD MAY LIVE.>
WHAT WAS THAT? LIKE... DEJA VU, BUT... I WAS THERE...
DO-- DO I KNOW YOU?
BLORCH!!

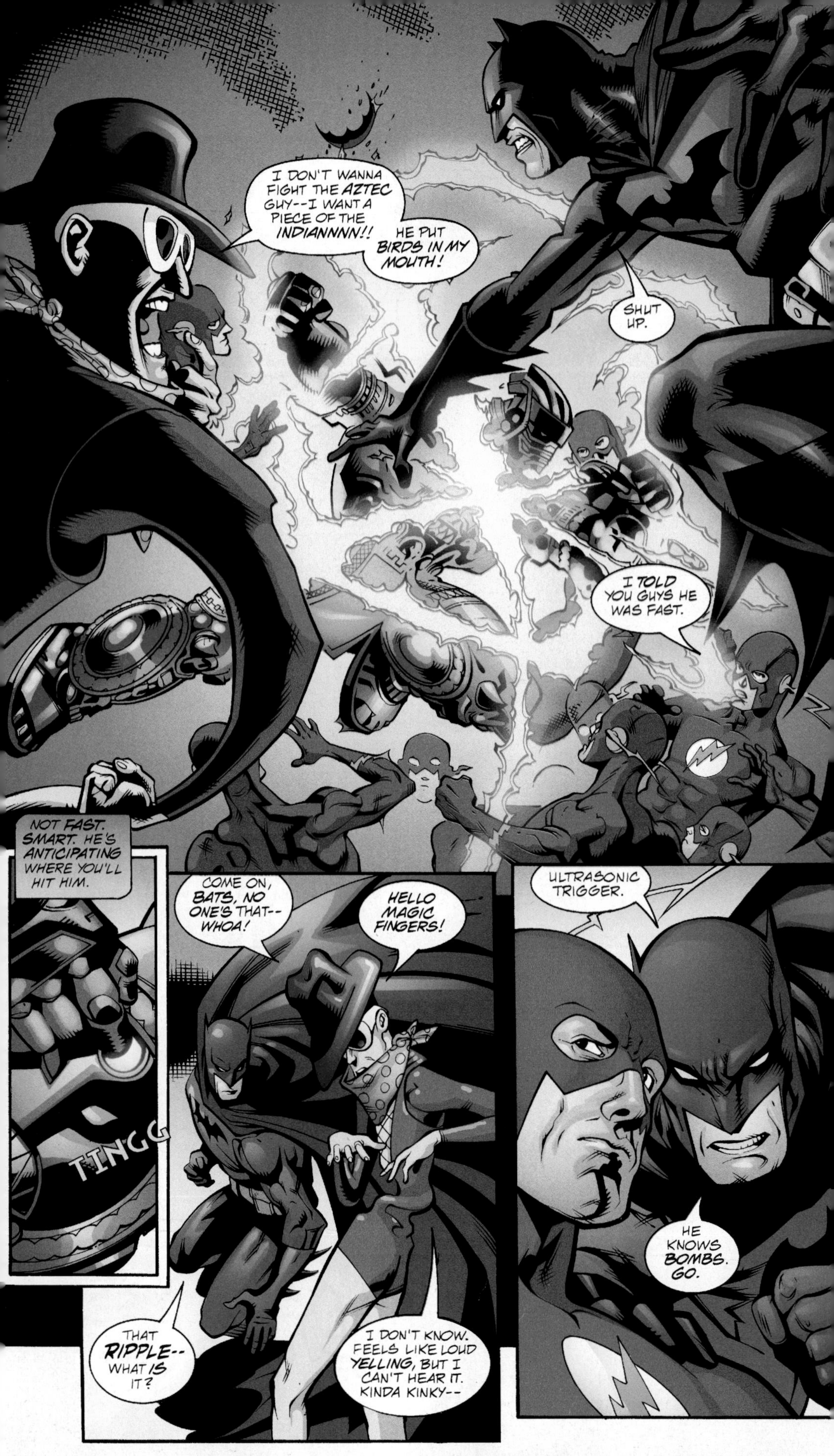

I DON'T WANNA FIGHT THE AZTEC GUY--I WANT A PIECE OF THE INDIANNNN!!
HE PUT BIRDS IN MY MOUTH!
SHUT UP.
I TOLD YOU GUYS HE WAS FAST.
NOT FAST. SMART. HE'S ANTICIPATING WHERE YOU'LL HIT HIM.
TINGG
COME ON, BATS, NO ONE'S THAT-- WHOA!
HELLO MAGIC FINGERS!
THAT RIPPLE-- WHAT IS IT?
I DON'T KNOW. FEELS LIKE LOUD YELLING, BUT I CAN'T HEAR IT. KINDA KINKY--
ULTRASONIC TRIGGER.
HE KNOWS BOMBS. GO.

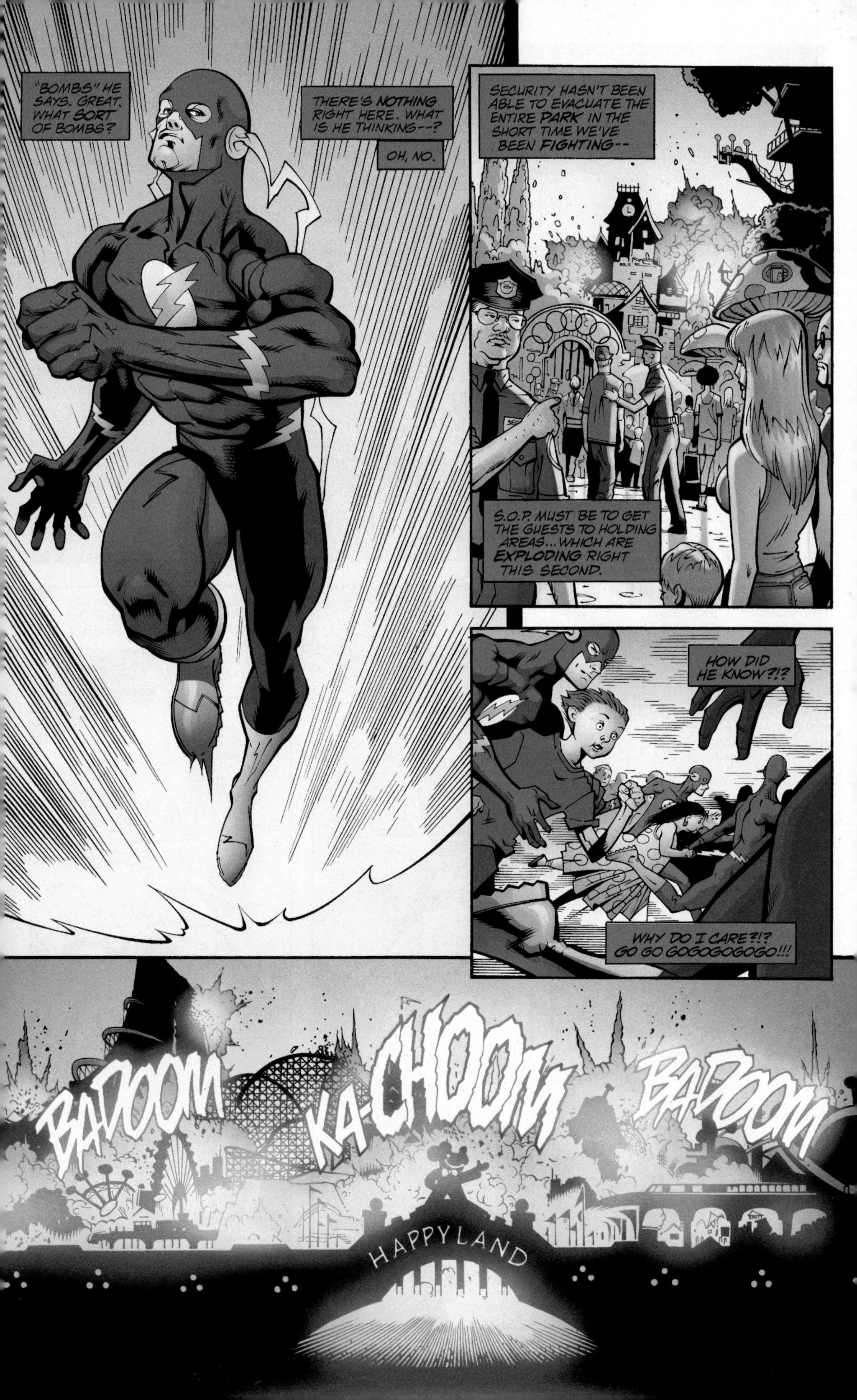
"BOMBS" HE SAYS. GREAT. WHAT SORT OF BOMBS?
THERE'S NOTHING RIGHT HERE. WHAT IS HE THINKING--?
OH, NO.
SECURITY HASN'T BEEN ABLE TO EVACUATE THE ENTIRE PARK IN THE SHORT TIME WE'VE BEEN FIGHTING--
S.O.P. MUST BE TO GET THE GUESTS TO HOLDING AREAS...WHICH ARE EXPLODING RIGHT THIS SECOND.
HOW DID HE KNOW?!?
WHY DO I CARE?!? GO GO GOGOGOGOGO!!!
BADOOM
KA-CHOOM
BADOOM
HAPPYLAND

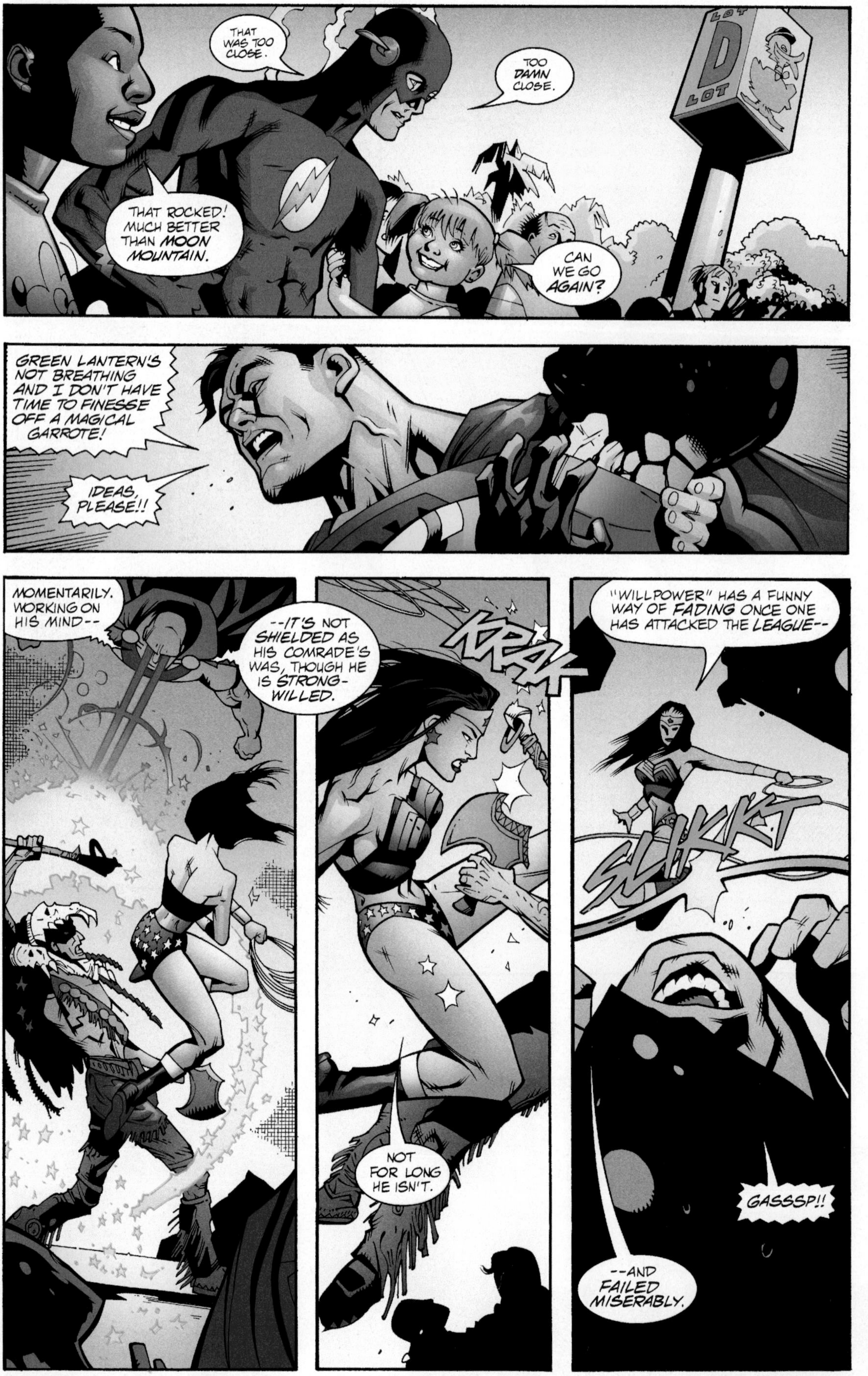
THAT WAS TOO CLOSE.
TOO DAMN CLOSE.
THAT ROCKED! MUCH BETTER THAN MOON MOUNTAIN.
CAN WE GO AGAIN?
LOT D LOT
GREEN LANTERN'S NOT BREATHING AND I DON'T HAVE TIME TO FINESSE OFF A MAGICAL GARROTE!
IDEAS, PLEASE!!
MOMENTARILY. WORKING ON HIS MIND--
--IT'S NOT SHIELDED AS HIS COMRADE'S WAS, THOUGH HE IS STRONG-WILLED.
KRAK
NOT FOR LONG HE ISN'T.
"WILLPOWER" HAS A FUNNY WAY OF FADING ONCE ONE HAS ATTACKED THE LEAGUE--
SLIKKT
GASSSP!!
--AND FAILED MISERABLY.

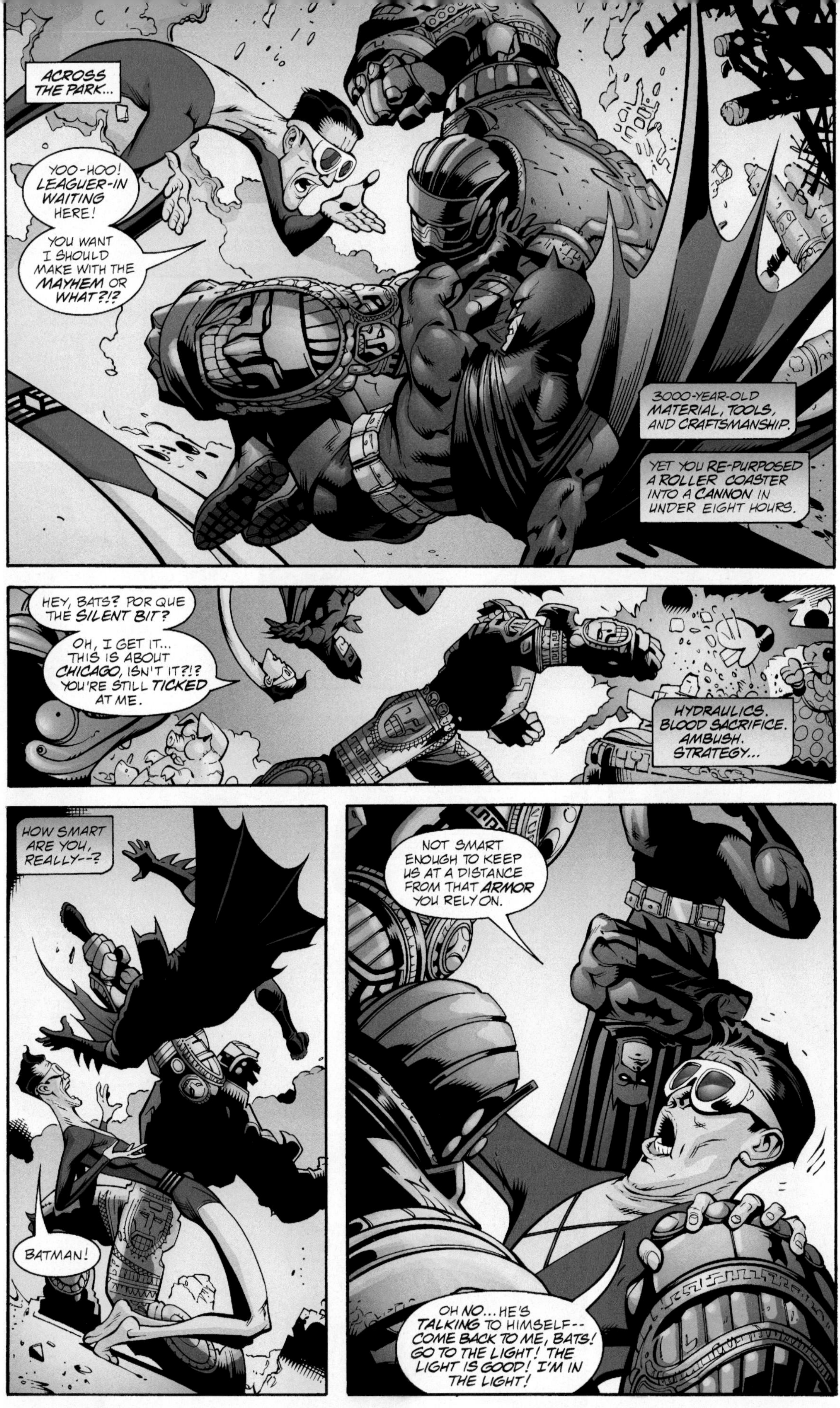
ACROSS THE PARK...
YOO-HOO! LEAGUER-IN WAITING HERE!
YOU WANT I SHOULD MAKE WITH THE MAYHEM OR WHAT?!?
3000-YEAR-OLD MATERIAL, TOOLS, AND CRAFTSMANSHIP.
YET YOU RE-PURPOSED A ROLLER COASTER INTO A CANNON IN UNDER EIGHT HOURS.
HEY, BATS? POR QUE THE SILENT BIT?
OH, I GET IT... THIS IS ABOUT CHICAGO, ISN'T IT?!? YOU'RE STILL TICKED AT ME.
HYDRAULICS. BLOOD SACRIFICE. AMBUSH. STRATEGY...
HOW SMART ARE YOU, REALLY--?
BATMAN!
NOT SMART ENOUGH TO KEEP US AT A DISTANCE FROM THAT ARMOR YOU RELY ON.
OH NO... HE'S TALKING TO HIMSELF-- COME BACK TO ME, BATS! GO TO THE LIGHT! THE LIGHT IS GOOD! I'M IN THE LIGHT!

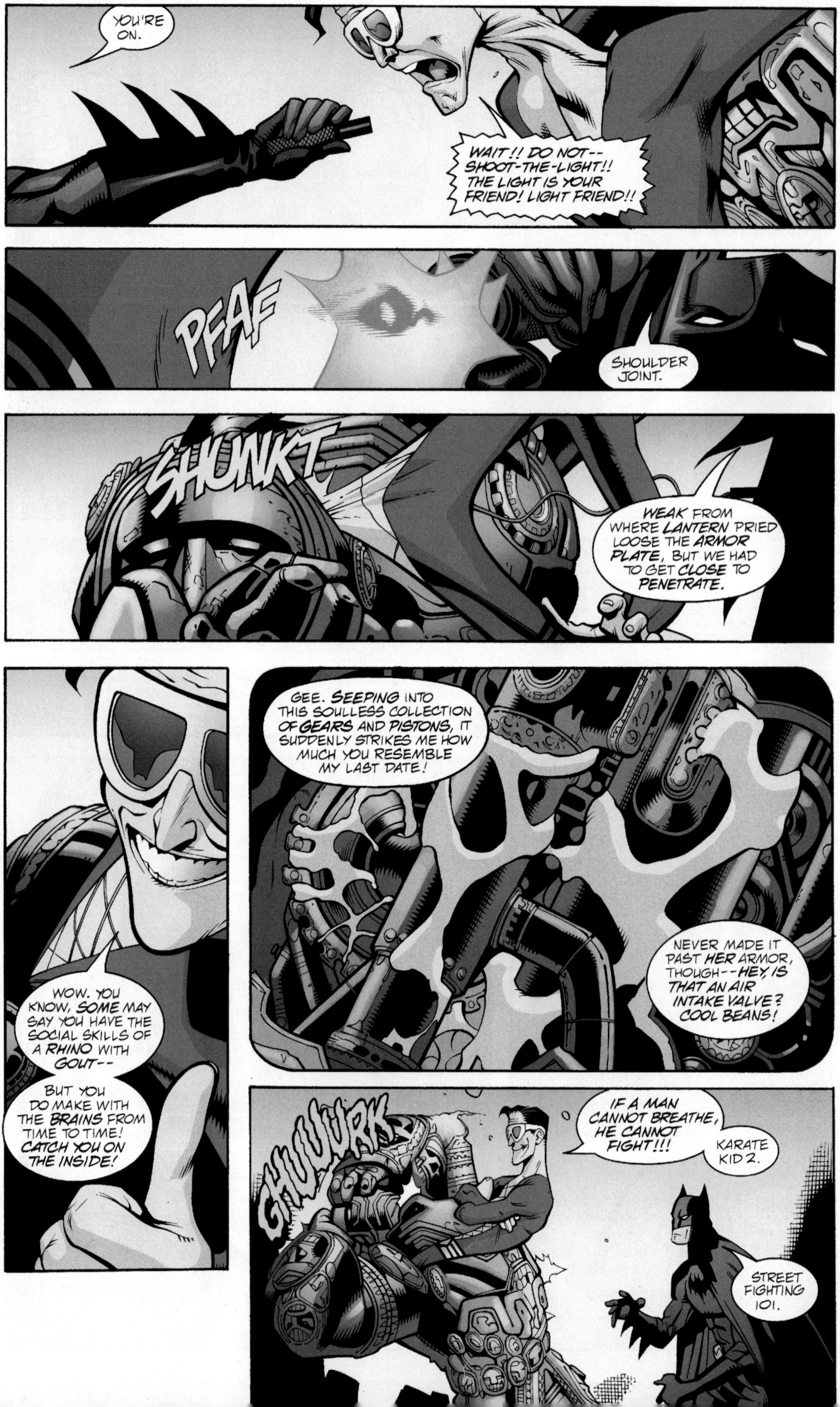
YOU'RE ON.
WAIT!! DO NOT-- SHOOT-THE-LIGHT!! THE LIGHT IS YOUR FRIEND! LIGHT FRIEND!!
PFAF
SHOULDER JOINT.
SHUNKT
WEAK FROM WHERE LANTERN PRIED LOOSE THE ARMOR PLATE, BUT WE HAD TO GET CLOSE TO PENETRATE.
WOW. YOU KNOW, SOME MAY SAY YOU HAVE THE SOCIAL SKILLS OF A RHINO WITH GOUT--
BUT YOU DO MAKE WITH THE BRAINS FROM TIME TO TIME! CATCH YOU ON THE INSIDE!
GEE. SEEPING INTO THIS SOULLESS COLLECTION OF GEARS AND PISTONS, IT SUDDENLY STRIKES ME HOW MUCH YOU RESEMBLE MY LAST DATE!
NEVER MADE IT PAST HER ARMOR, THOUGH--HEY, IS THAT AN AIR INTAKE VALVE? COOL BEANS!
GHUUURK
IF A MAN CANNOT BREATHE, HE CANNOT FIGHT!!!
KARATE KID 2.
STREET FIGHTING 101.

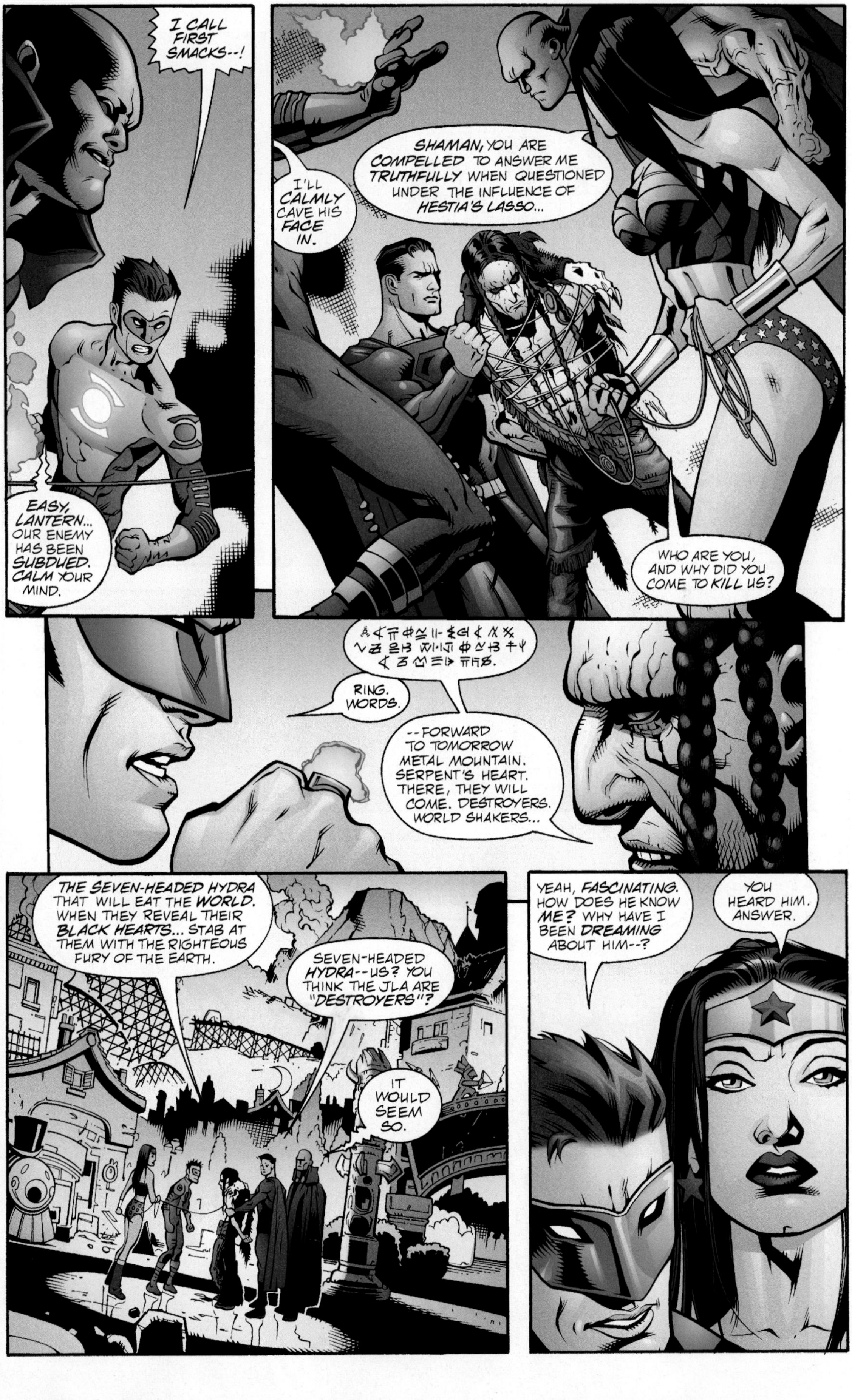
I CALL FIRST SMACKS--!
EASY, LANTERN... OUR ENEMY HAS BEEN SUBDUED. CALM YOUR MIND.
I'LL CALMLY CAVE HIS FACE IN.
SHAMAN, YOU ARE COMPELLED TO ANSWER ME TRUTHFULLY WHEN QUESTIONED UNDER THE INFLUENCE OF HESTIA'S LASSO...
WHO ARE YOU, AND WHY DID YOU COME TO KILL US?
RING. WORDS.
--FORWARD TO TOMORROW METAL MOUNTAIN. SERPENT'S HEART. THERE, THEY WILL COME. DESTROYERS. WORLD SHAKERS...
THE SEVEN-HEADED HYDRA THAT WILL EAT THE WORLD. WHEN THEY REVEAL THEIR BLACK HEARTS... STAB AT THEM WITH THE RIGHTEOUS FURY OF THE EARTH.
SEVEN-HEADED HYDRA--US? YOU THINK THE JLA ARE "DESTROYERS"?
IT WOULD SEEM SO.
YEAH, FASCINATING. HOW DOES HE KNOW ME? WHY HAVE I BEEN DREAMING ABOUT HIM--?
YOU HEARD HIM. ANSWER.

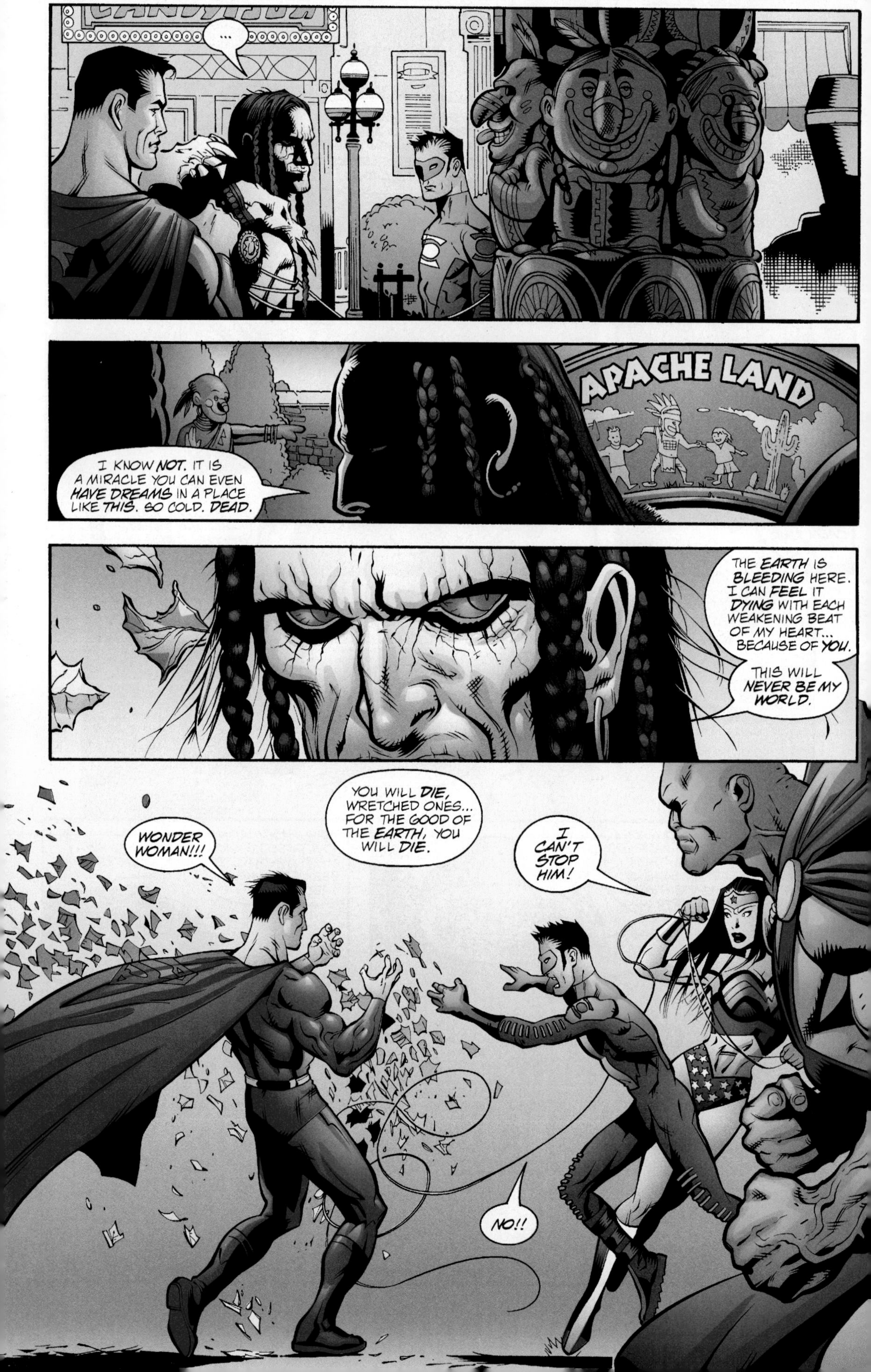
...
APACHE LAND
I KNOW NOT. IT IS A MIRACLE YOU CAN EVEN HAVE DREAMS IN A PLACE LIKE THIS. SO COLD. DEAD.
THE EARTH IS BLEEDING HERE. I CAN FEEL IT DYING WITH EACH WEAKENING BEAT OF MY HEART... BECAUSE OF YOU.
THIS WILL NEVER BE MY WORLD.
WONDER WOMAN!!!
YOU WILL DIE, WRETCHED ONES... FOR THE GOOD OF THE EARTH, YOU WILL DIE.
I CAN'T STOP HIM!
NO!!

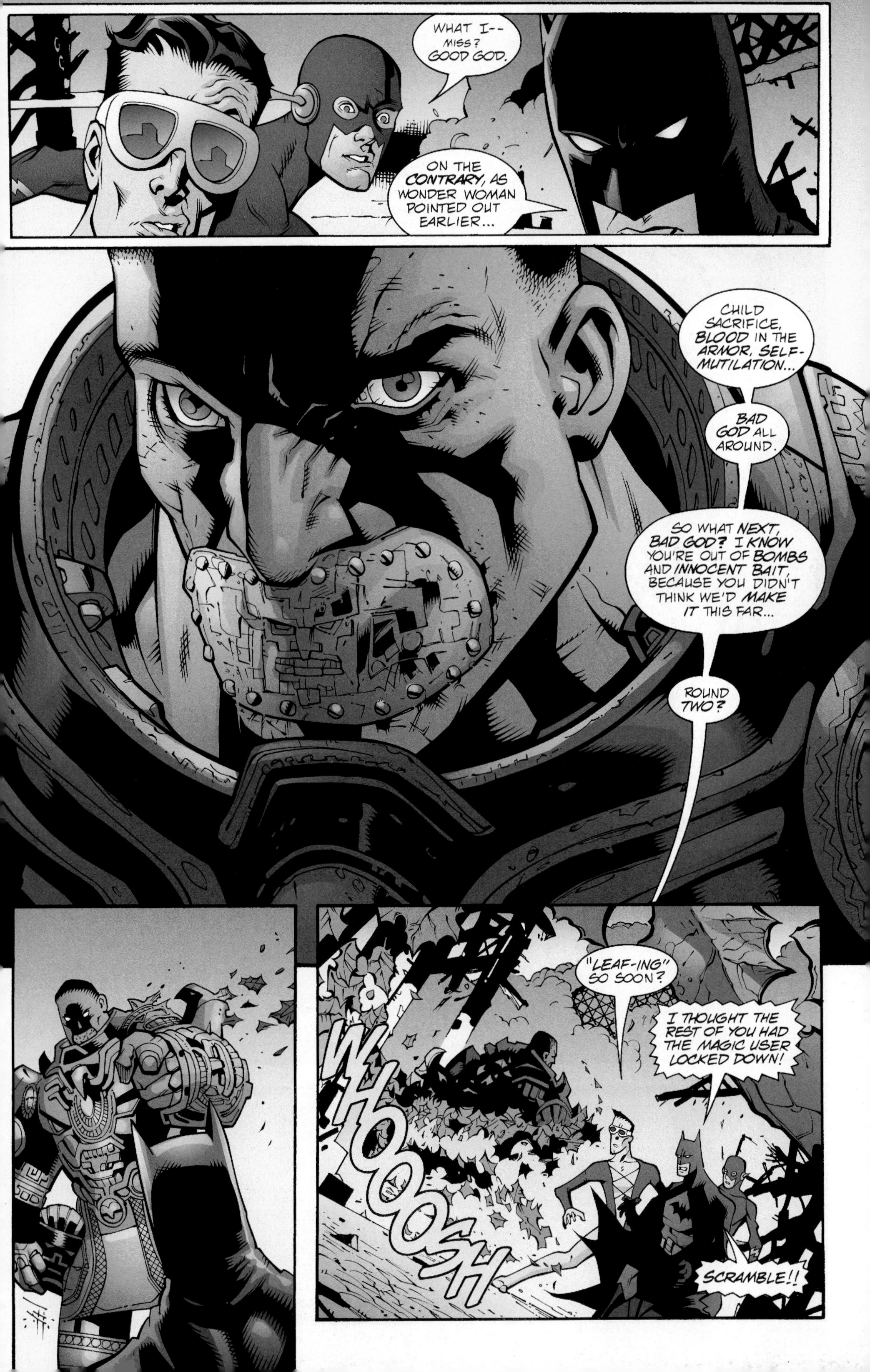
WHAT I-- MISS? GOOD GOD.
ON THE CONTRARY, AS WONDER WOMAN POINTED OUT EARLIER...
CHILD SACRIFICE, BLOOD IN THE ARMOR, SELF-MUTILATION...
BAD GOD ALL AROUND.
SO WHAT NEXT, BAD GOD? I KNOW YOU'RE OUT OF BOMBS AND INNOCENT BAIT, BECAUSE YOU DIDN'T THINK WE'D MAKE IT THIS FAR...
ROUND TWO?
WHOOOSH
"LEAF-ING" SO SOON?
I THOUGHT THE REST OF YOU HAD THE MAGIC USER LOCKED DOWN!
SCRAMBLE!!

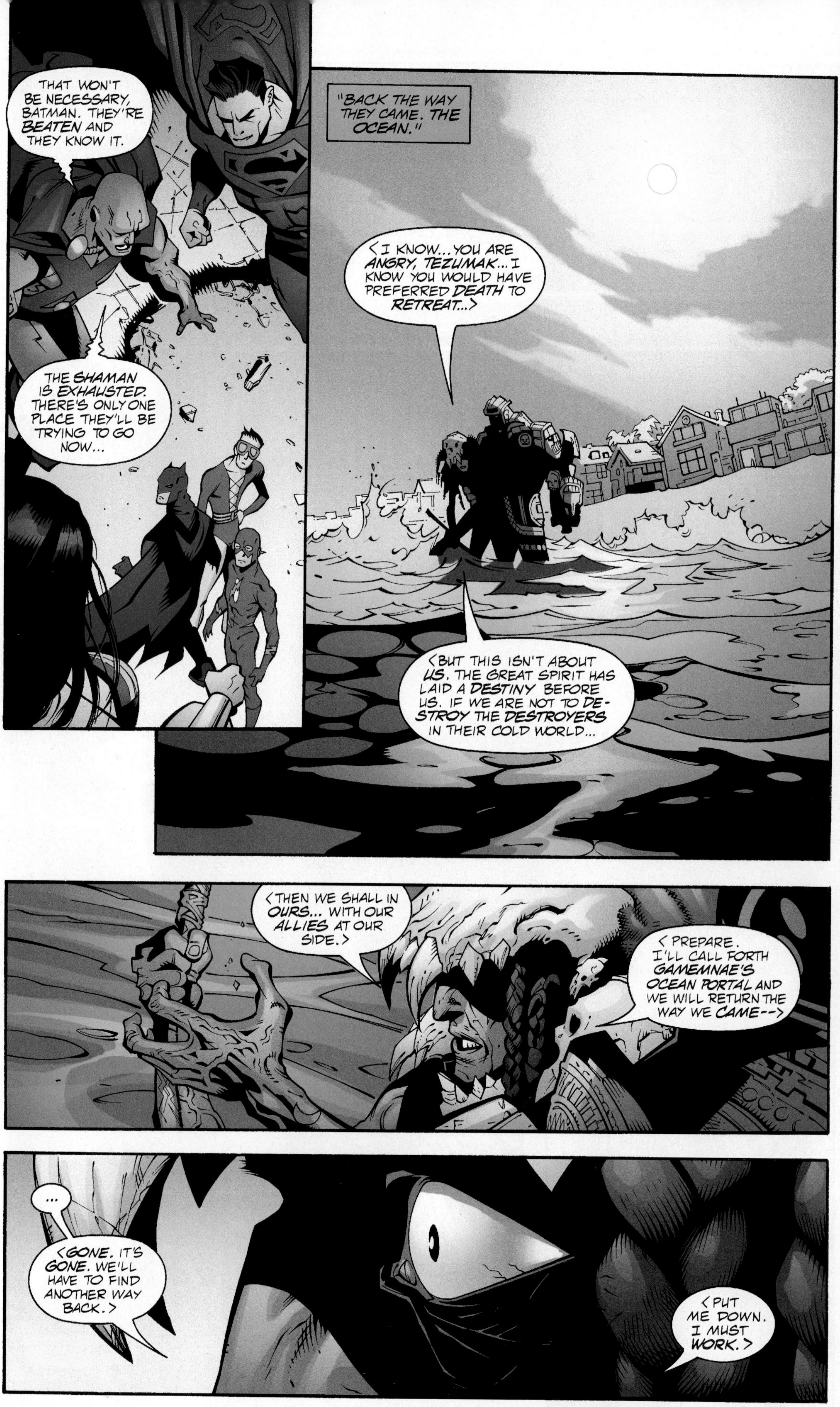
THAT WON'T BE NECESSARY, BATMAN. THEY'RE BEATEN AND THEY KNOW IT.
THE SHAMAN IS EXHAUSTED. THERE'S ONLY ONE PLACE THEY'LL BE TRYING TO GO NOW...
"BACK THE WAY THEY CAME. THE OCEAN."
<I KNOW...YOU ARE ANGRY, TEZUMAK...I KNOW YOU WOULD HAVE PREFERRED DEATH TO RETREAT...>
<BUT THIS ISN'T ABOUT US. THE GREAT SPIRIT HAS LAID A DESTINY BEFORE US. IF WE ARE NOT TO DESTROY THE DESTROYERS IN THEIR COLD WORLD...
<THEN WE SHALL IN OURS... WITH OUR ALLIES AT OUR SIDE.>
<PREPARE. I'LL CALL FORTH GAMEMNAE'S OCEAN PORTAL AND WE WILL RETURN THE WAY WE CAME-->
...
<GONE. IT'S GONE. WE'LL HAVE TO FIND ANOTHER WAY BACK.>
<PUT ME DOWN. I MUST WORK.>

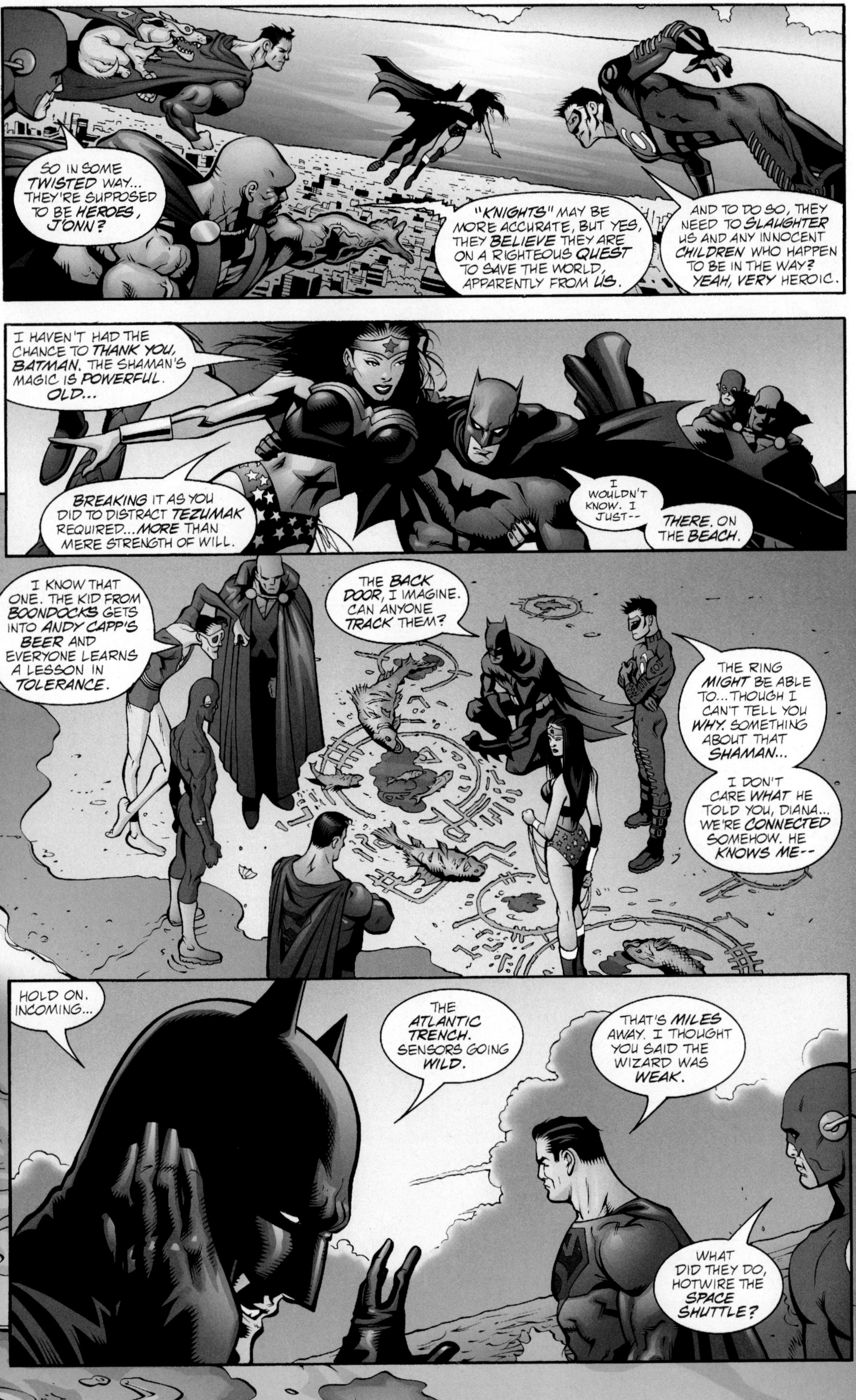

SO IN SOME TWISTED WAY... THEY'RE SUPPOSED TO BE HEROES, J'ONN?
"KNIGHTS" MAY BE MORE ACCURATE, BUT YES, THEY BELIEVE THEY ARE ON A RIGHTEOUS QUEST TO SAVE THE WORLD, APPARENTLY FROM US.
AND TO DO SO, THEY NEED TO SLAUGHTER US AND ANY INNOCENT CHILDREN WHO HAPPEN TO BE IN THE WAY? YEAH, VERY HEROIC.
I HAVEN'T HAD THE CHANCE TO THANK YOU, BATMAN. THE SHAMAN'S MAGIC IS POWERFUL. OLD...
BREAKING IT AS YOU DID TO DISTRACT TEZUMAK REQUIRED...MORE THAN MERE STRENGTH OF WILL.
I WOULDN'T KNOW. I JUST--
THERE. ON THE BEACH.
I KNOW THAT ONE. THE KID FROM BOONDOCKS GETS INTO ANDY CAPP'S BEER AND EVERYONE LEARNS A LESSON IN TOLERANCE.
THE BACK DOOR, I IMAGINE. CAN ANYONE TRACK THEM?
THE RING MIGHT BE ABLE TO...THOUGH I CAN'T TELL YOU WHY. SOMETHING ABOUT THAT SHAMAN...
I DON'T CARE WHAT HE TOLD YOU, DIANA... WE'RE CONNECTED SOMEHOW. HE KNOWS ME--
HOLD ON. INCOMING...
THE ATLANTIC TRENCH. SENSORS GOING WILD.
THAT'S MILES AWAY. I THOUGHT YOU SAID THE WIZARD WAS WEAK.
WHAT DID THEY DO, HOTWIRE THE SPACE SHUTTLE?

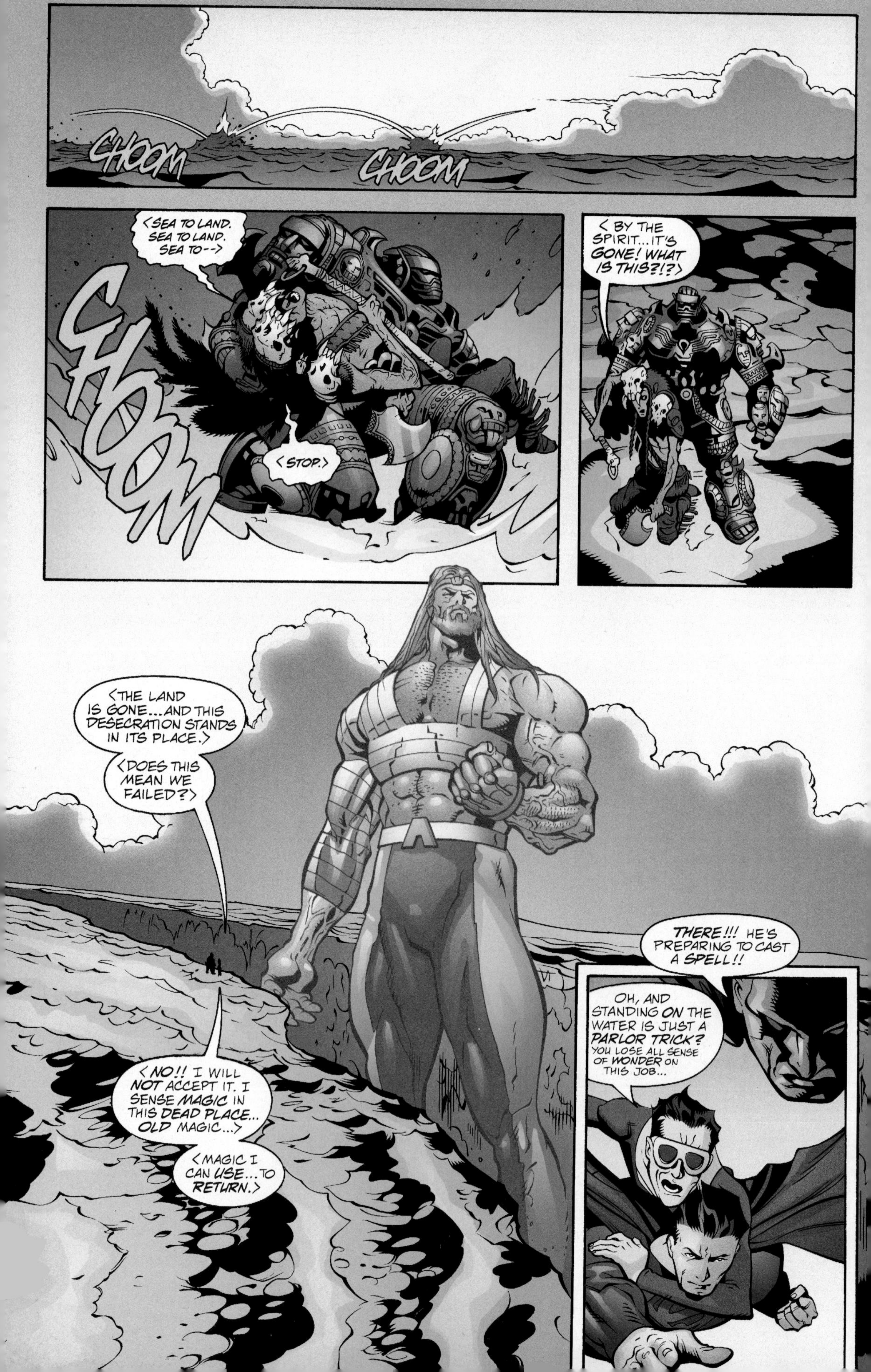
CHOOM
CHOOM
<SEA TO LAND. SEA TO LAND. SEA TO-->
CHOOM
<STOP.>
<BY THE SPIRIT...IT'S GONE! WHAT IS THIS?!?>
<THE LAND IS GONE...AND THIS DESECRATION STANDS IN ITS PLACE.>
<DOES THIS MEAN WE FAILED?>
<NO!! I WILL NOT ACCEPT IT. I SENSE MAGIC IN THIS DEAD PLACE... OLD MAGIC...>
<MAGIC I CAN USE... TO RETURN.>
THERE!!! HE'S PREPARING TO CAST A SPELL!!
OH, AND STANDING ON THE WATER IS JUST A PARLOR TRICK? YOU LOSE ALL SENSE OF WONDER ON THIS JOB...

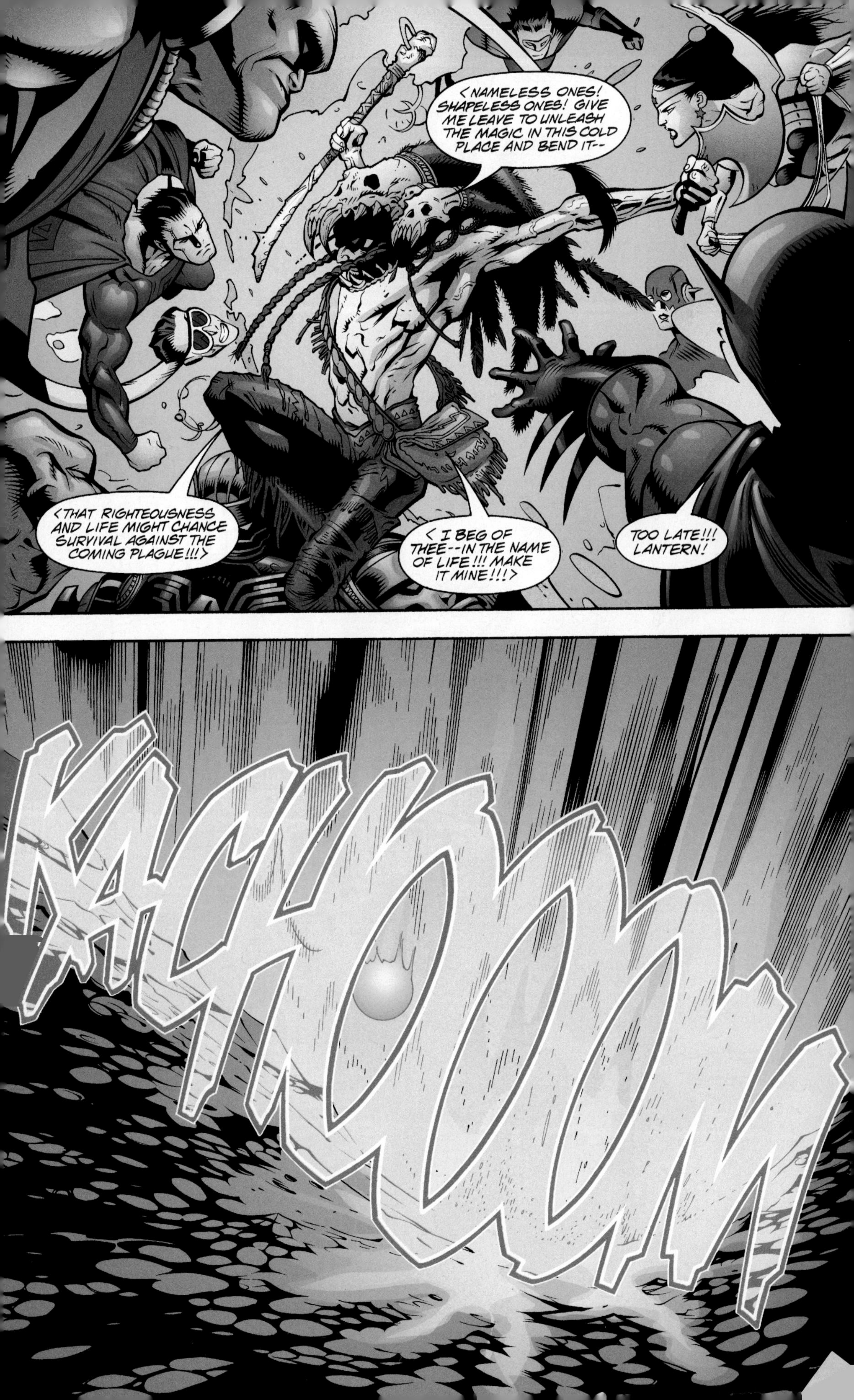
<NAMELESS ONES! SHAPELESS ONES! GIVE ME LEAVE TO UNLEASH THE MAGIC IN THIS COLD PLACE AND BEND IT--
<THAT RIGHTEOUSNESS AND LIFE MIGHT CHANCE SURVIVAL AGAINST THE COMING PLAGUE!!!>
< I BEG OF THEE--IN THE NAME OF LIFE!!! MAKE IT MINE!!!>
TOO LATE!!! LANTERN!
KACHOOOM

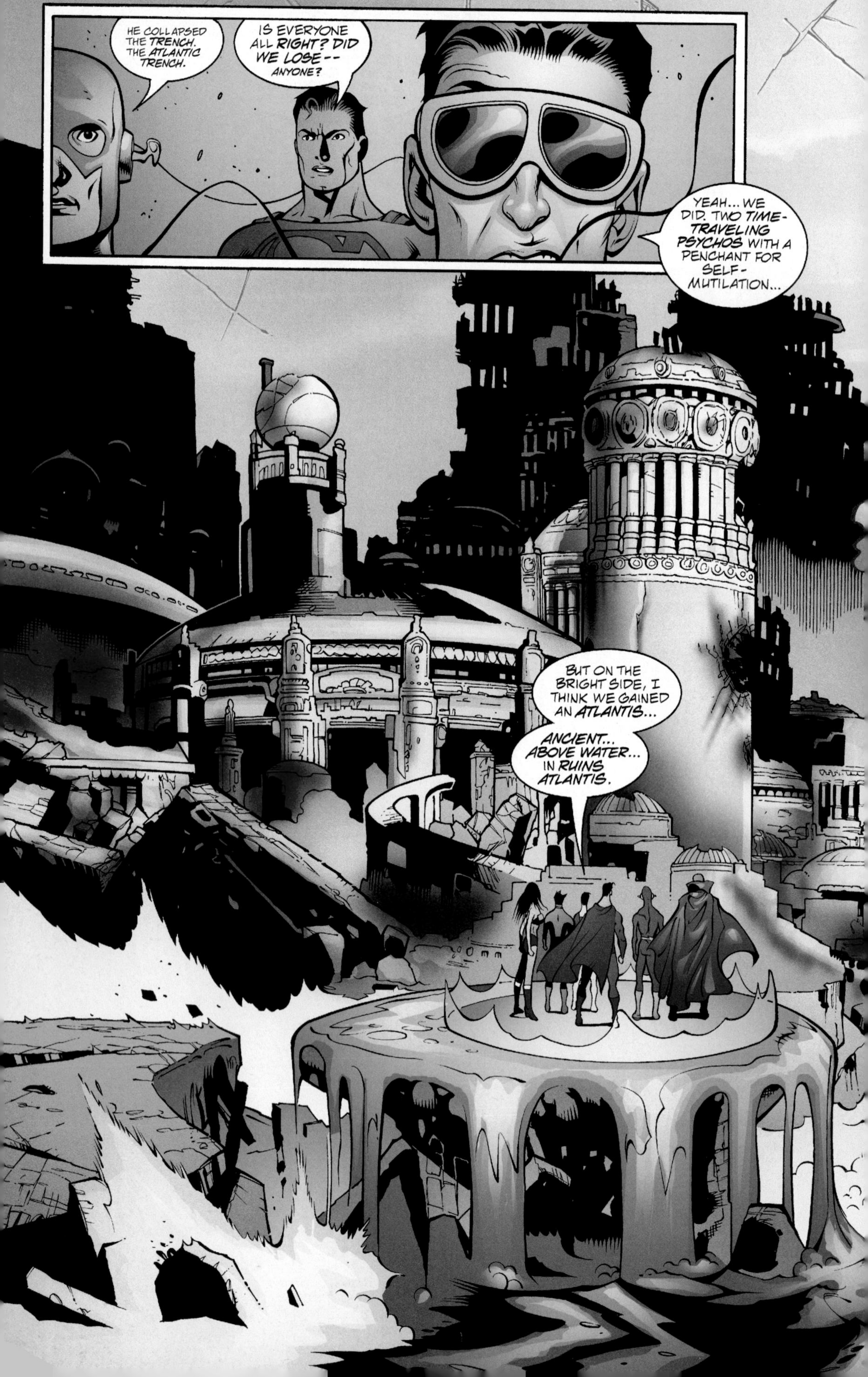
HE COLLAPSED THE TRENCH. THE ATLANTIC TRENCH.
IS EVERYONE ALL RIGHT? DID WE LOSE -- ANYONE?
YEAH... WE DID. TWO TIME-TRAVELING PSYCHOS WITH A PENCHANT FOR SELF-MUTILATION...
BUT ON THE BRIGHT SIDE, I THINK WE GAINED AN ATLANTIS...
ANCIENT... ABOVE WATER... IN RUINS ATLANTIS.

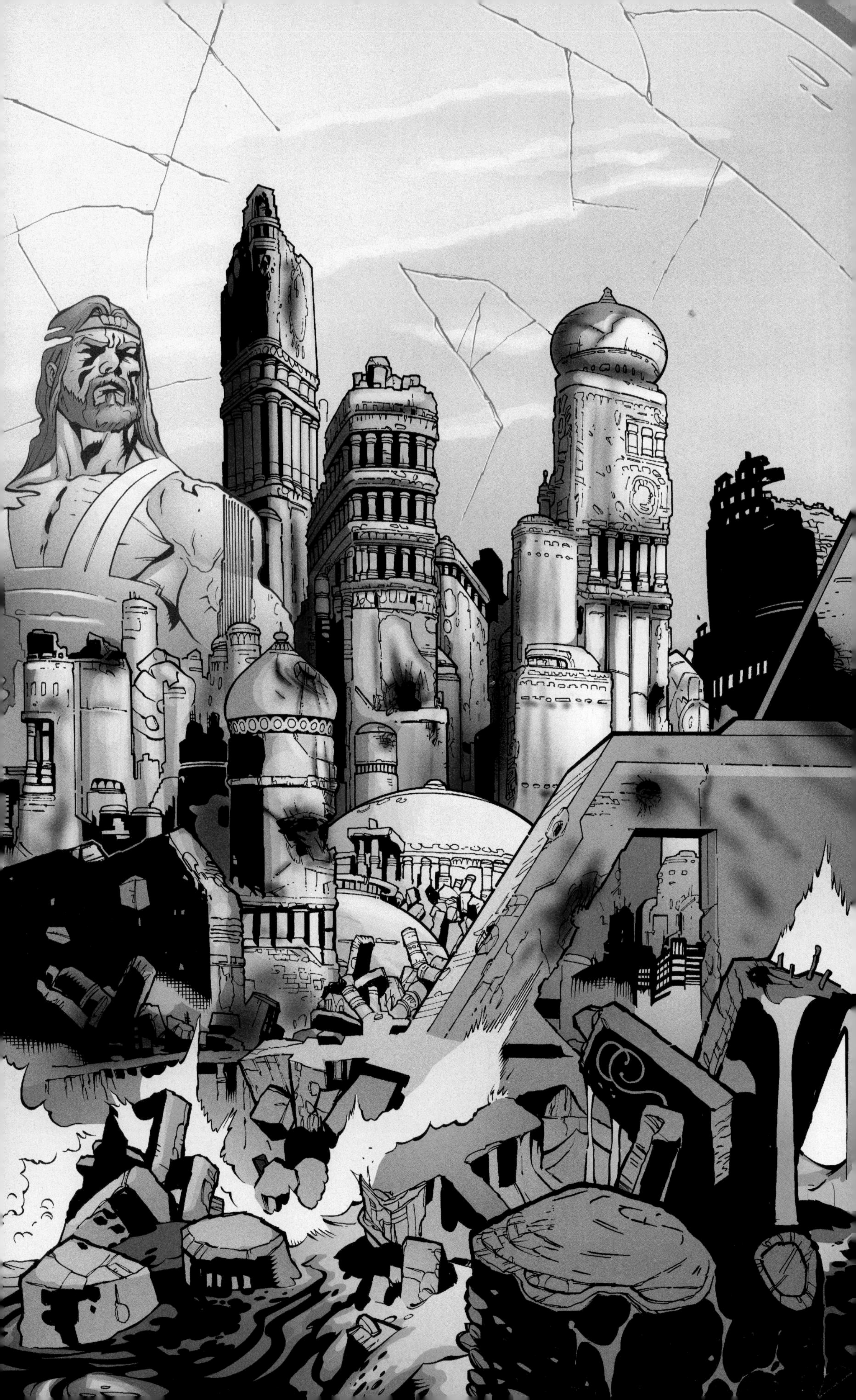

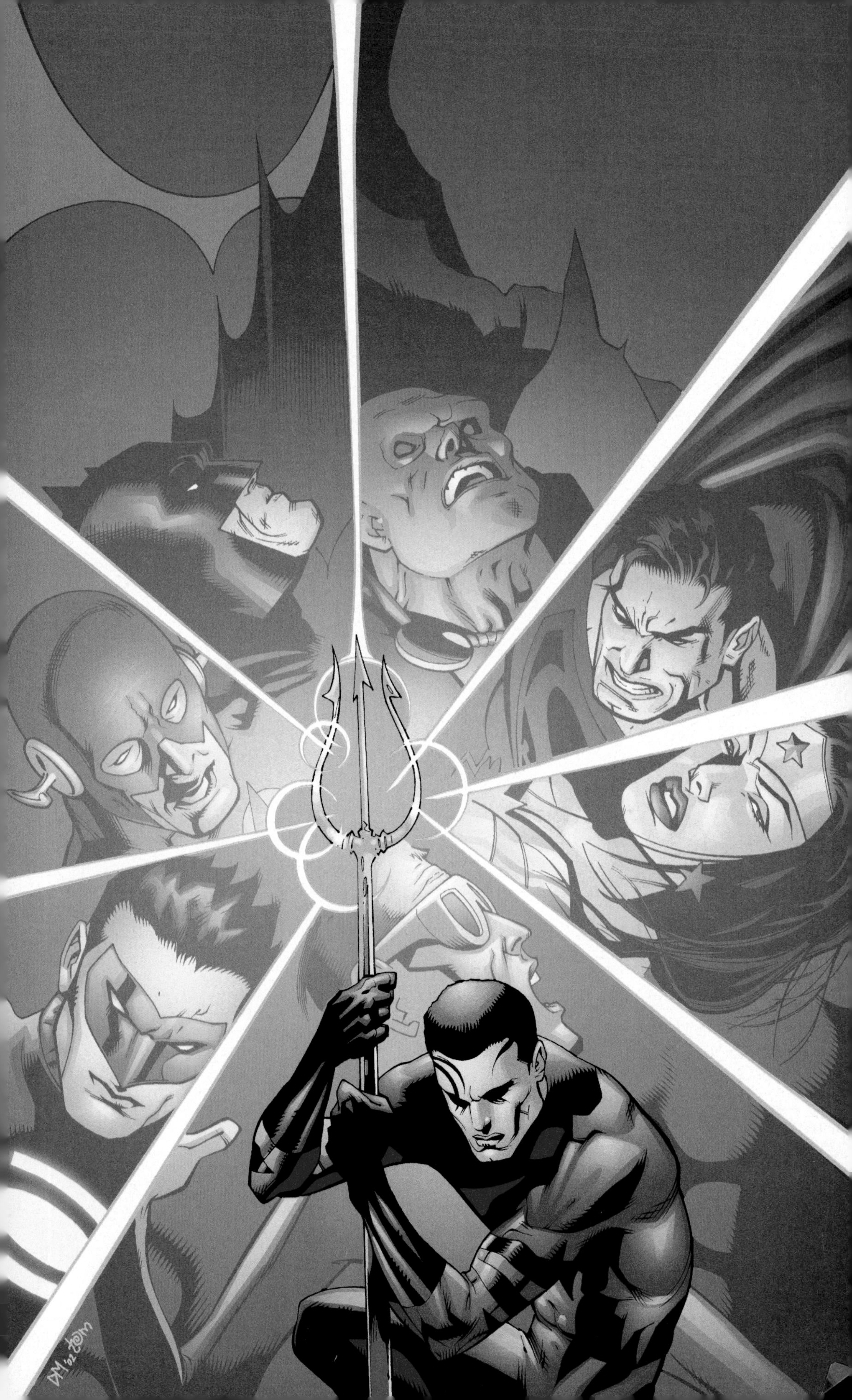

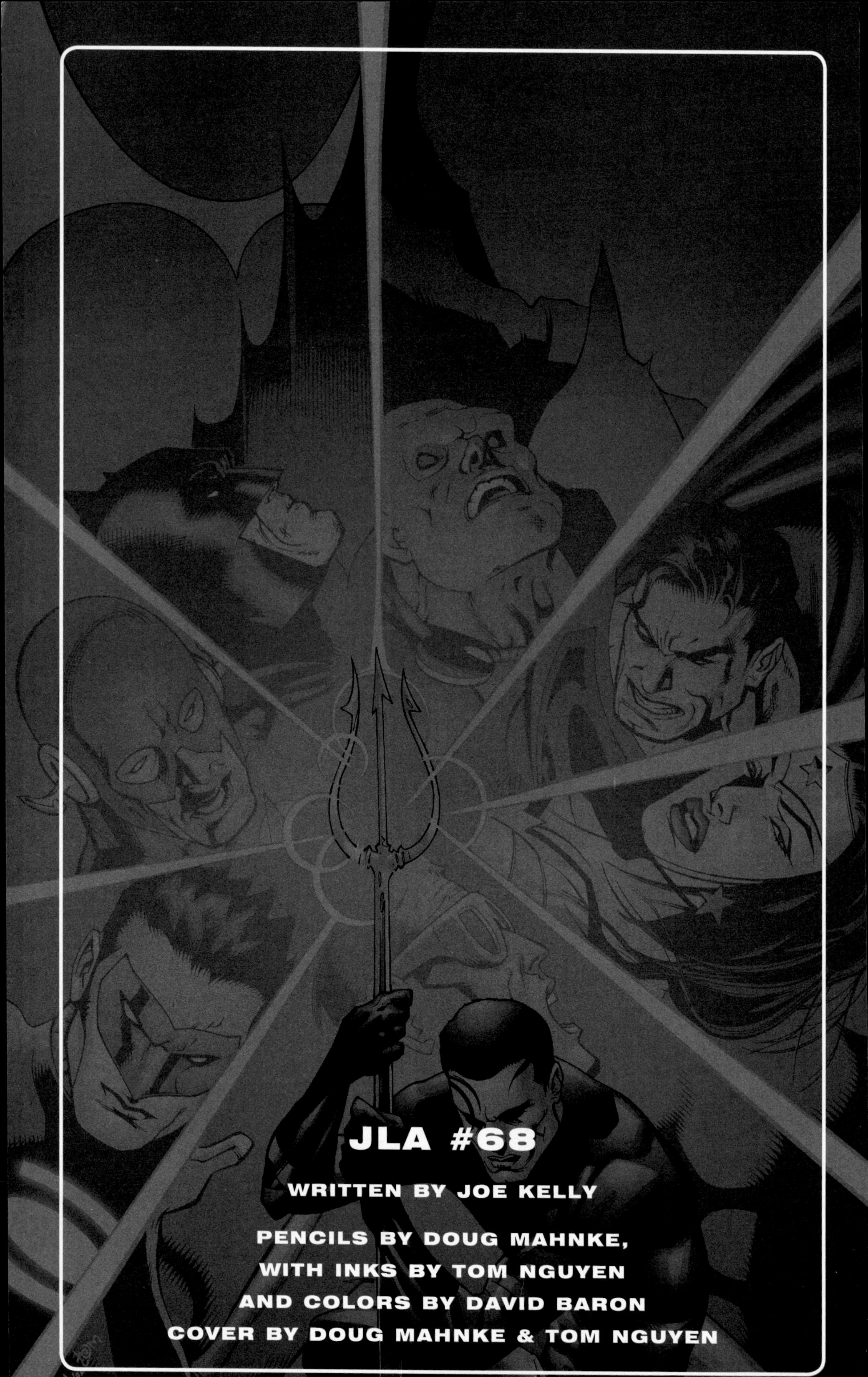

JLA #68

WRITTEN BY JOE KELLY

PENCILS BY DOUG MAHNKE,
WITH INKS BY TOM NGUYEN
AND COLORS BY DAVID BARON
COVER BY DOUG MAHNKE & TOM NGUYEN

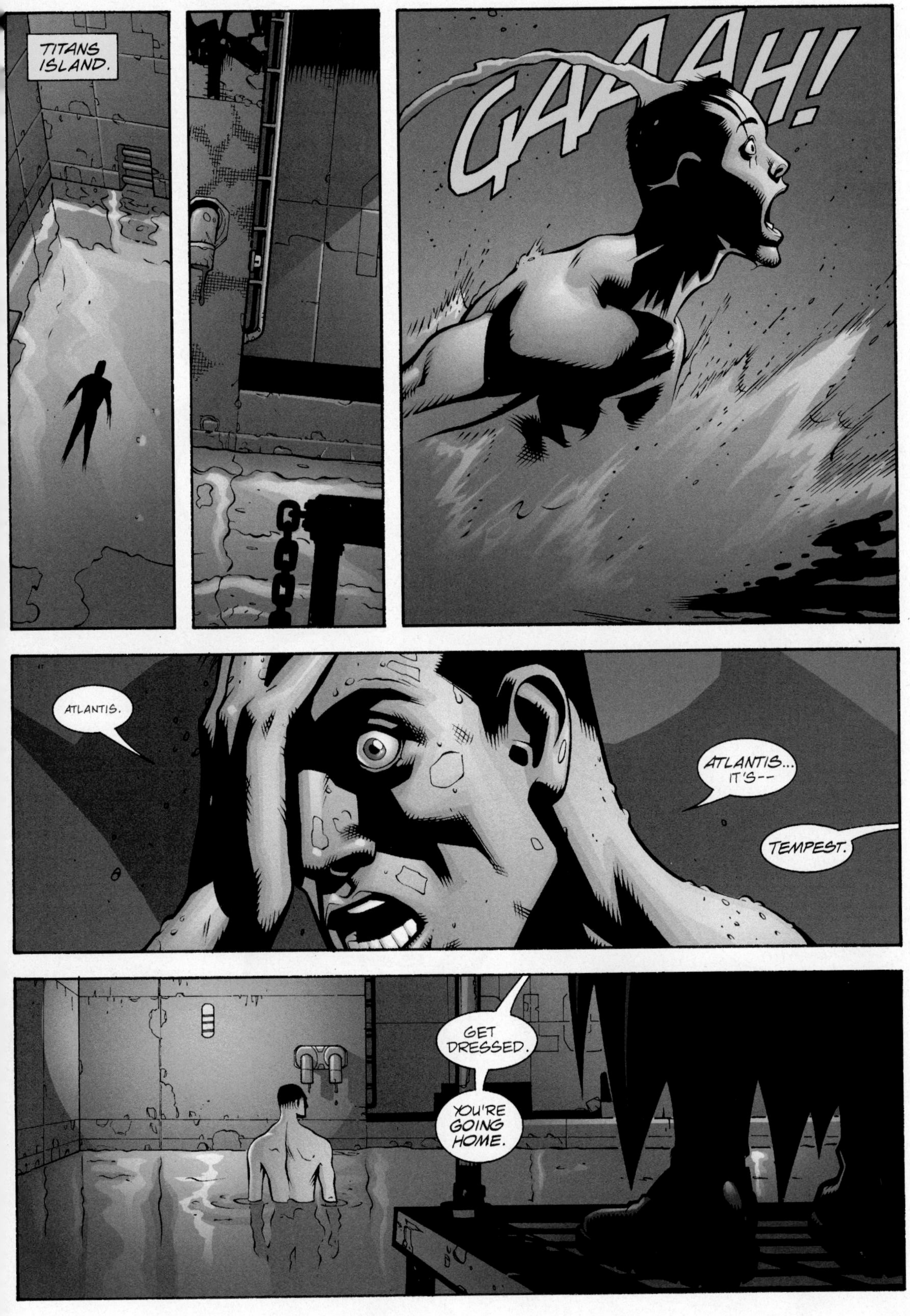

TITANS ISLAND.
GAAAH!
ATLANTIS.
ATLANTIS... IT'S--
TEMPEST.
GET DRESSED.
YOU'RE GOING HOME.

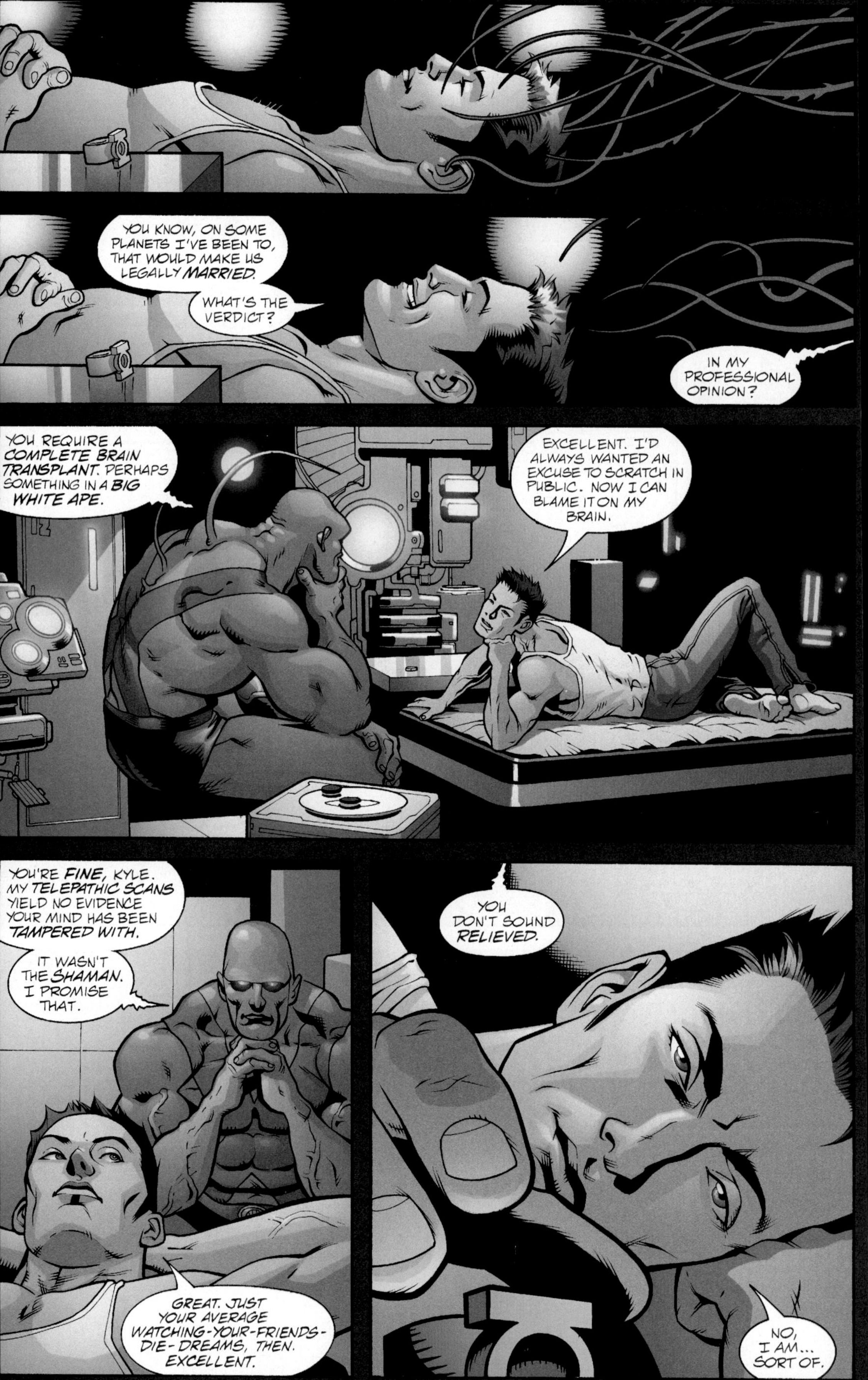
YOU KNOW, ON SOME PLANETS I'VE BEEN TO, THAT WOULD MAKE US LEGALLY MARRIED.
WHAT'S THE VERDICT?
IN MY PROFESSIONAL OPINION?
YOU REQUIRE A COMPLETE BRAIN TRANSPLANT. PERHAPS SOMETHING IN A BIG WHITE APE.
EXCELLENT. I'D ALWAYS WANTED AN EXCUSE TO SCRATCH IN PUBLIC. NOW I CAN BLAME IT ON MY BRAIN.
YOU'RE FINE, KYLE. MY TELEPATHIC SCANS YIELD NO EVIDENCE YOUR MIND HAS BEEN TAMPERED WITH.
IT WASN'T THE SHAMAN. I PROMISE THAT.
GREAT. JUST YOUR AVERAGE WATCHING-YOUR-FRIENDS-DIE-DREAMS, THEN. EXCELLENT.
YOU DON'T SOUND RELIEVED.
NO, I AM... SORT OF.

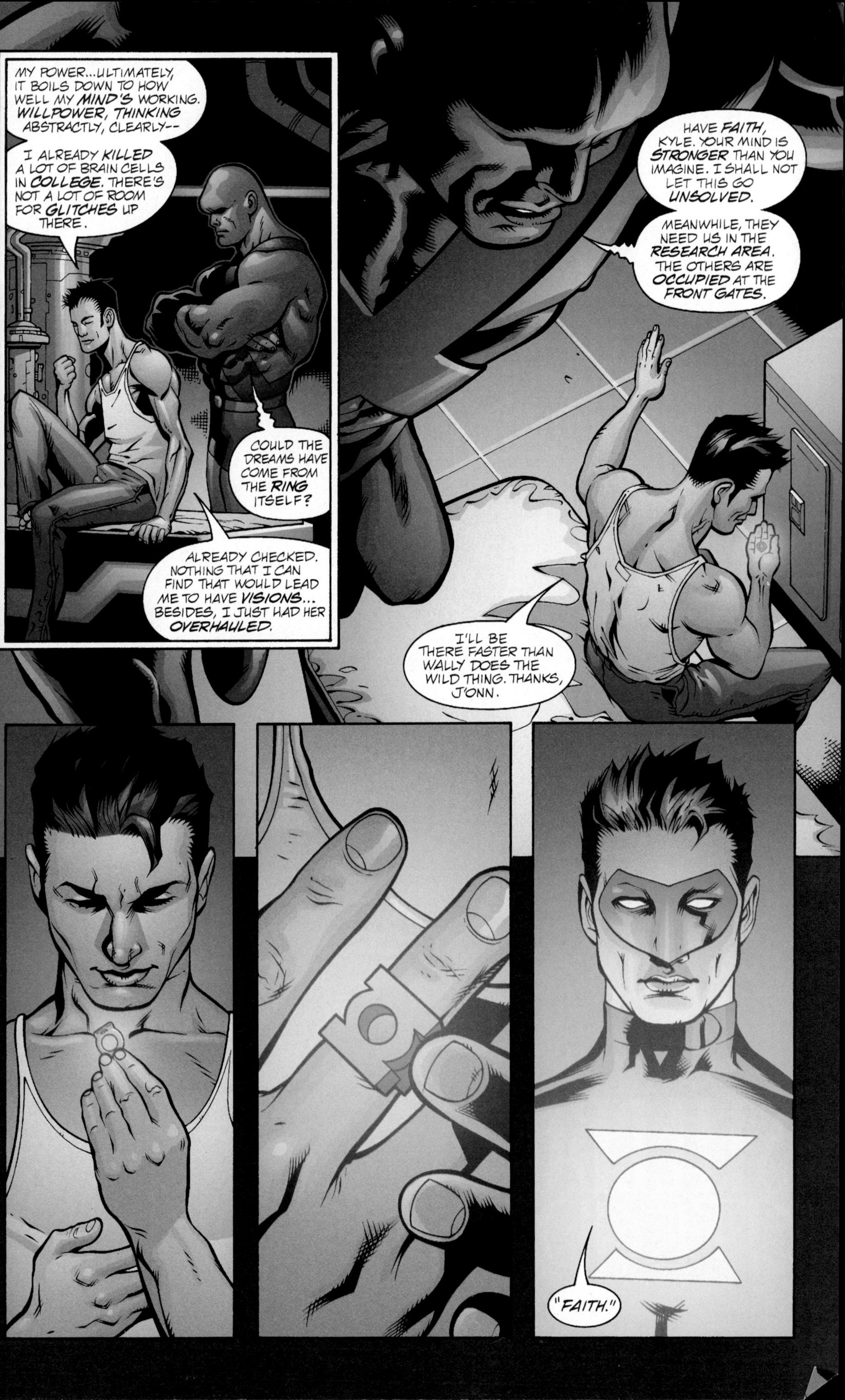
MY POWER...ULTIMATELY, IT BOILS DOWN TO HOW WELL MY MIND'S WORKING. WILLPOWER, THINKING ABSTRACTLY, CLEARLY--
I ALREADY KILLED A LOT OF BRAIN CELLS IN COLLEGE. THERE'S NOT A LOT OF ROOM FOR GLITCHES UP THERE.
COULD THE DREAMS HAVE COME FROM THE RING ITSELF?
ALREADY CHECKED. NOTHING THAT I CAN FIND THAT WOULD LEAD ME TO HAVE VISIONS... BESIDES, I JUST HAD HER OVERHAULED.
HAVE FAITH, KYLE. YOUR MIND IS STRONGER THAN YOU IMAGINE. I SHALL NOT LET THIS GO UNSOLVED.
MEANWHILE, THEY NEED US IN THE RESEARCH AREA. THE OTHERS ARE OCCUPIED AT THE FRONT GATES.
I'LL BE THERE FASTER THAN WALLY DOES THE WILD THING. THANKS, J'ONN.
"FAITH."

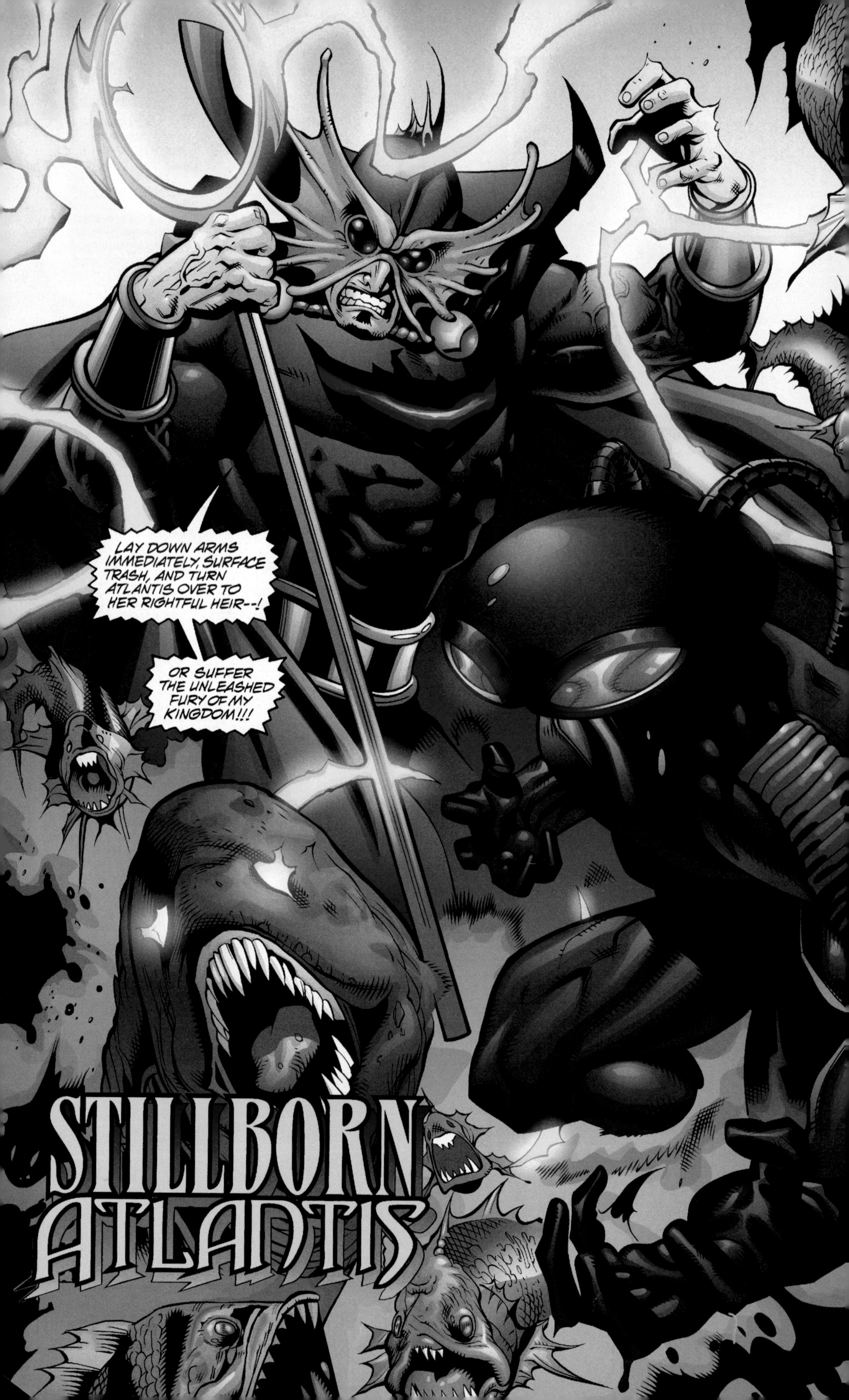
LAY DOWN ARMS IMMEDIATELY, SURFACE TRASH, AND TURN ATLANTIS OVER TO HER RIGHTFUL HEIR--!
OR SUFFER THE UNLEASHED FURY OF MY KINGDOM!!!
STILLBORN ATLANTIS

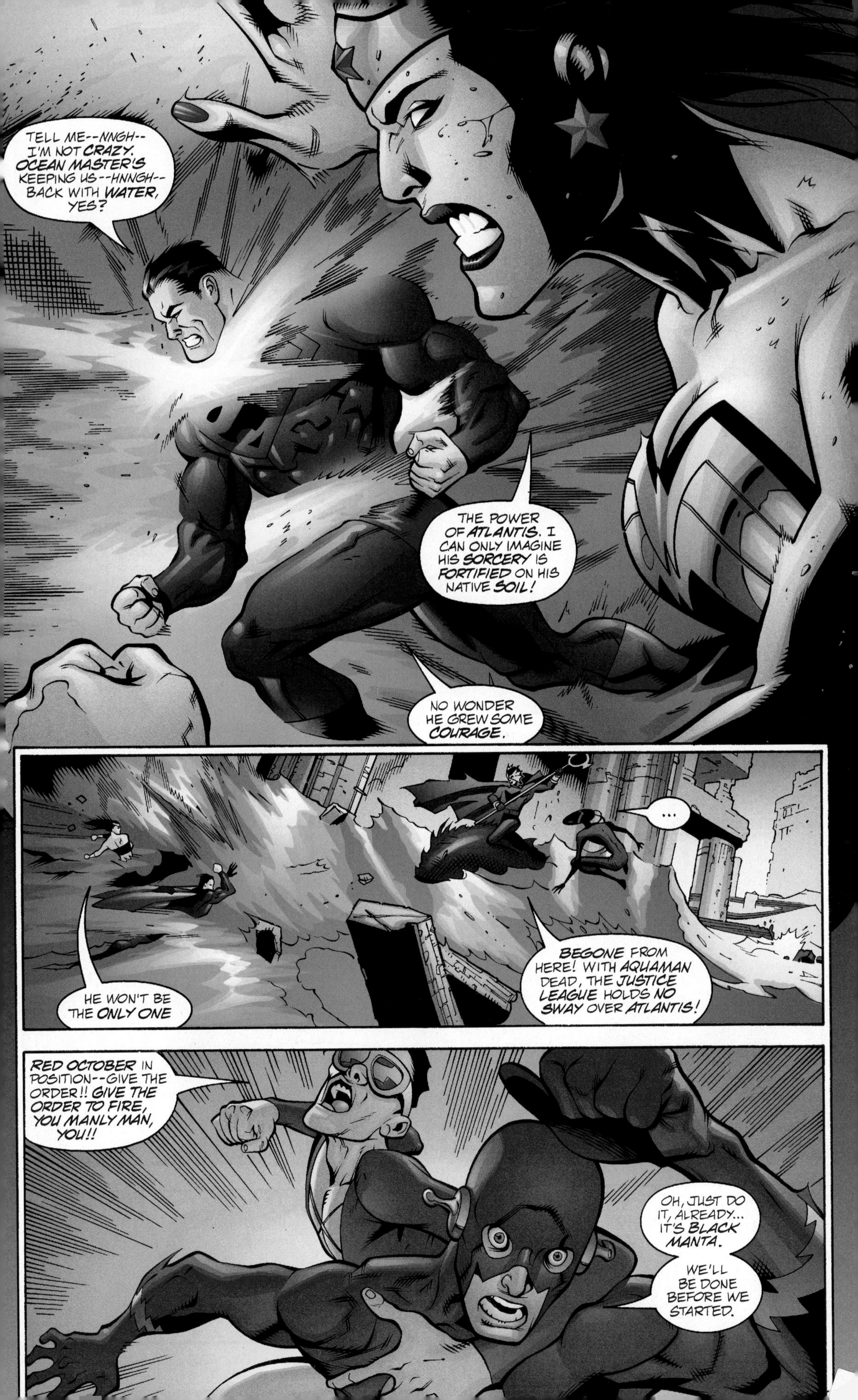
TELL ME--NNGH--I'M NOT CRAZY. OCEAN MASTER'S KEEPING US--HNNGH--BACK WITH WATER, YES?
THE POWER OF ATLANTIS. I CAN ONLY IMAGINE HIS SORCERY IS FORTIFIED ON HIS NATIVE SOIL!
NO WONDER HE GREW SOME COURAGE.
...
BEGONE FROM HERE! WITH AQUAMAN DEAD, THE JUSTICE LEAGUE HOLDS NO SWAY OVER ATLANTIS!
HE WON'T BE THE ONLY ONE
RED OCTOBER IN POSITION--GIVE THE ORDER!! GIVE THE ORDER TO FIRE, YOU MANLY MAN, YOU!!
OH, JUST DO IT, ALREADY... IT'S BLACK MANTA.
WE'LL BE DONE BEFORE WE STARTED.

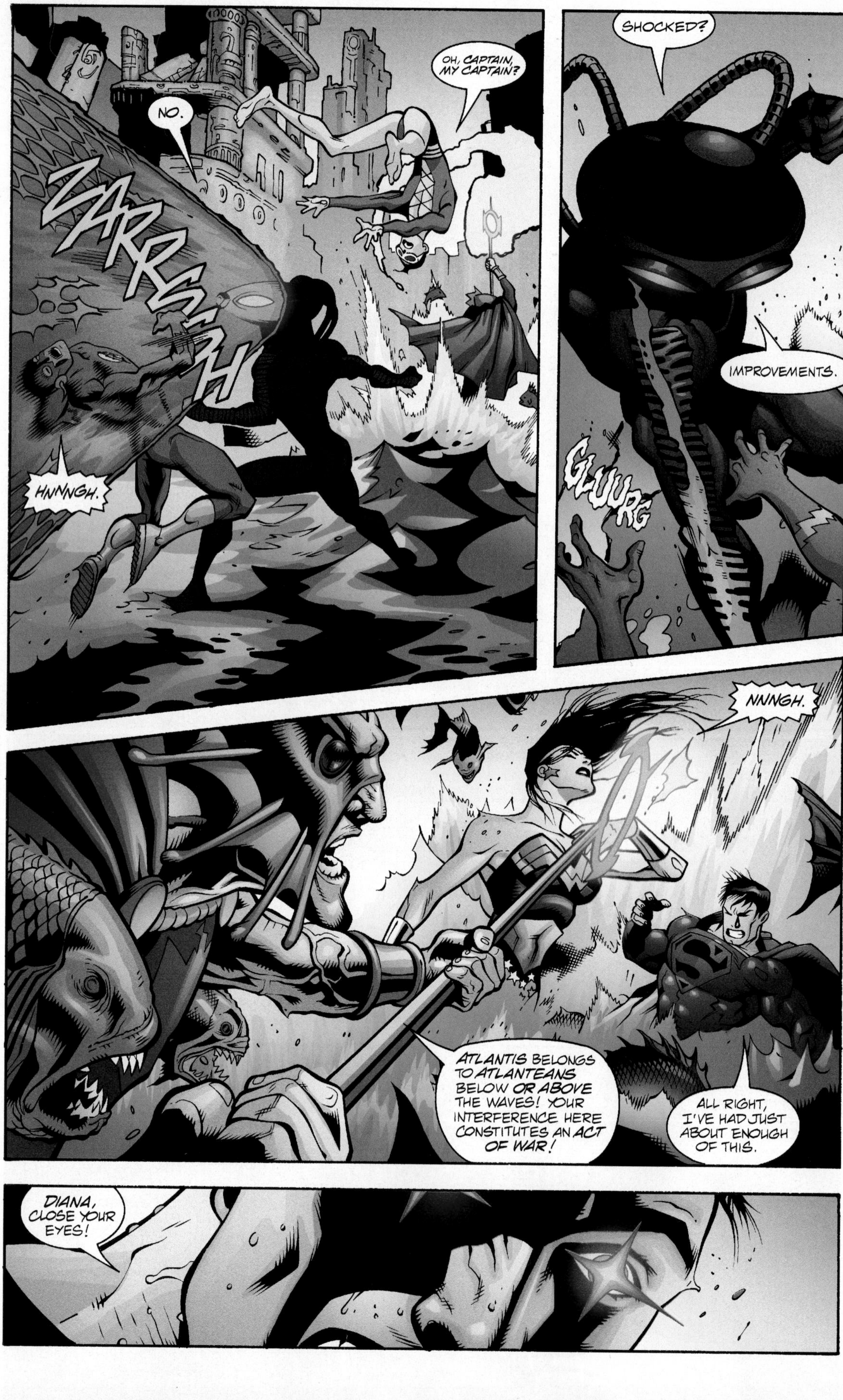
OH, CAPTAIN, MY CAPTAIN?
NO.
ZARRSSHH
HNNNGH.
SHOCKED?
IMPROVEMENTS.
GLUURG
NNNGH.
ATLANTIS BELONGS TO ATLANTEANS BELOW OR ABOVE THE WAVES! YOUR INTERFERENCE HERE CONSTITUTES AN ACT OF WAR!
ALL RIGHT, I'VE HAD JUST ABOUT ENOUGH OF THIS.
DIANA, CLOSE YOUR EYES!

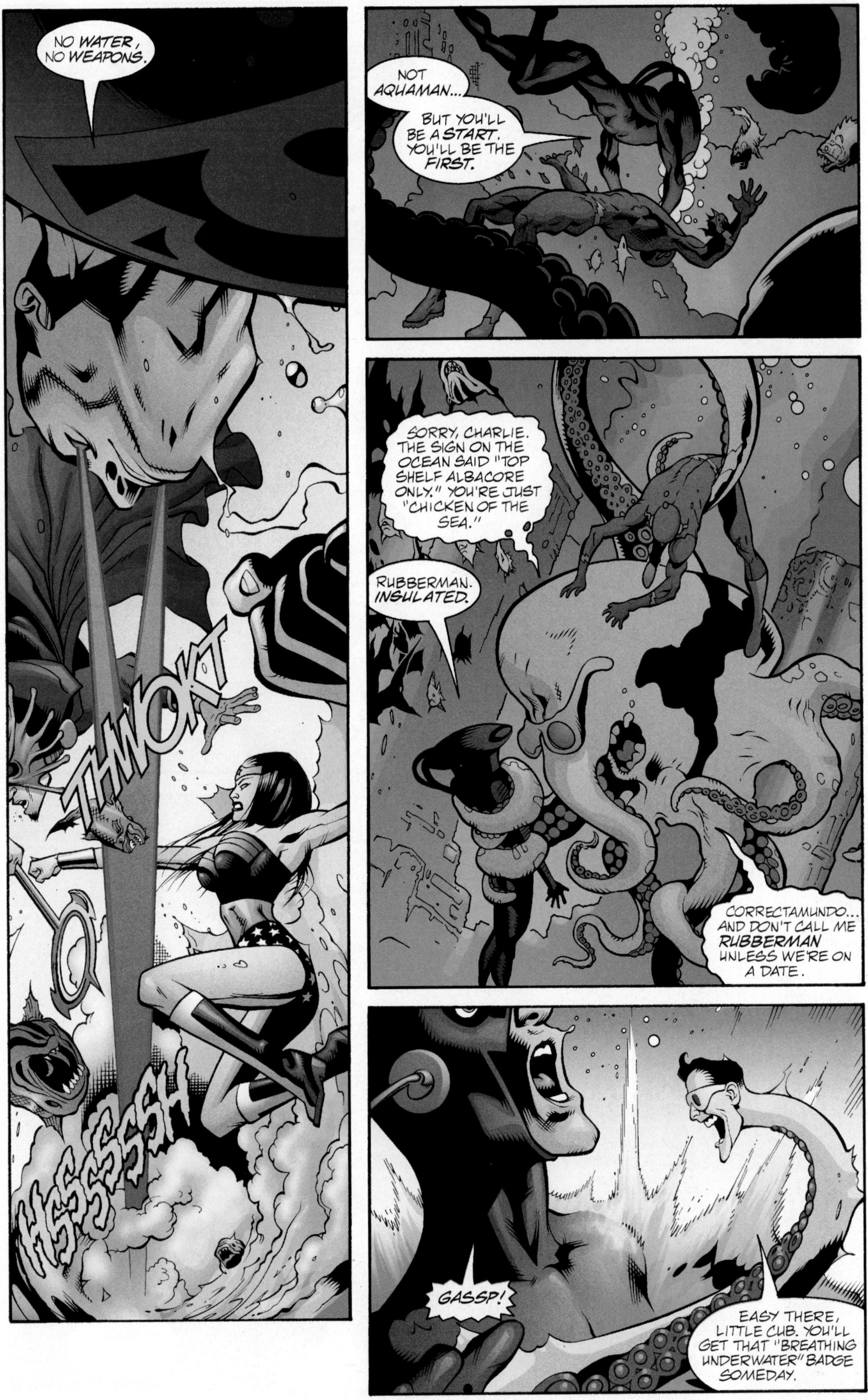
NO WATER, NO WEAPONS.
THWOK!
HSSSSSH
NOT AQUAMAN...
BUT YOU'LL BE A START. YOU'LL BE THE FIRST.
SORRY, CHARLIE. THE SIGN ON THE OCEAN SAID "TOP SHELF ALBACORE ONLY." YOU'RE JUST "CHICKEN OF THE SEA."
RUBBERMAN. INSULATED.
CORRECTAMUNDO... AND DON'T CALL ME RUBBERMAN UNLESS WE'RE ON A DATE.
GASSP!
EASY THERE, LITTLE CUB. YOU'LL GET THAT "BREATHING UNDERWATER" BADGE SOMEDAY.

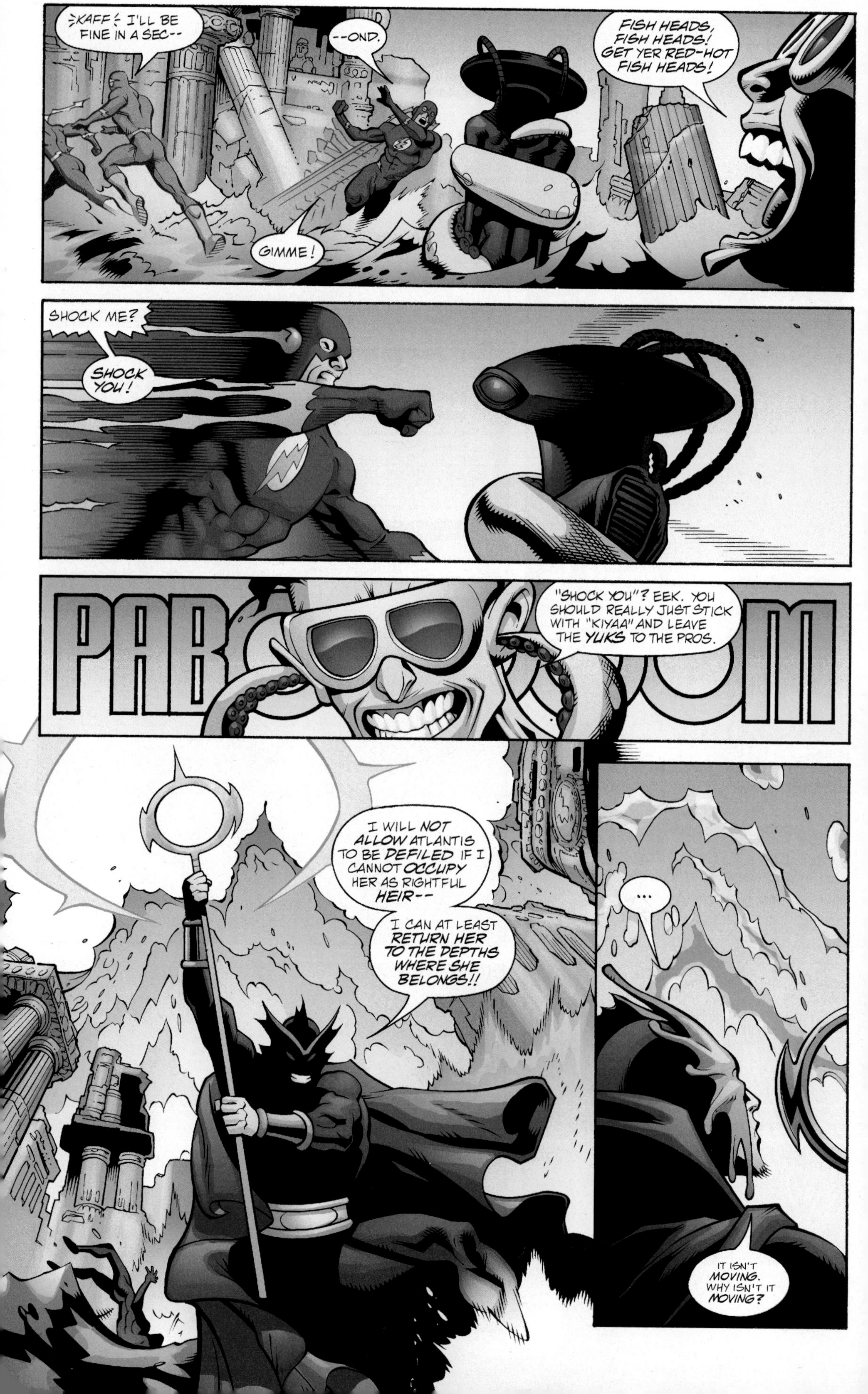

≥KAFF≤ I'LL BE FINE IN A SEC--
--OND.
FISH HEADS, FISH HEADS! GET YER RED-HOT FISH HEADS!
GIMME!
SHOCK ME?
SHOCK YOU!
PAB
M
"SHOCK YOU"? EEK. YOU SHOULD REALLY JUST STICK WITH "KIYAA" AND LEAVE THE YUKS TO THE PROS.
I WILL NOT ALLOW ATLANTIS TO BE DEFILED IF I CANNOT OCCUPY HER AS RIGHTFUL HEIR--
I CAN AT LEAST RETURN HER TO THE DEPTHS WHERE SHE BELONGS!!
...
IT ISN'T MOVING. WHY ISN'T IT MOVING?

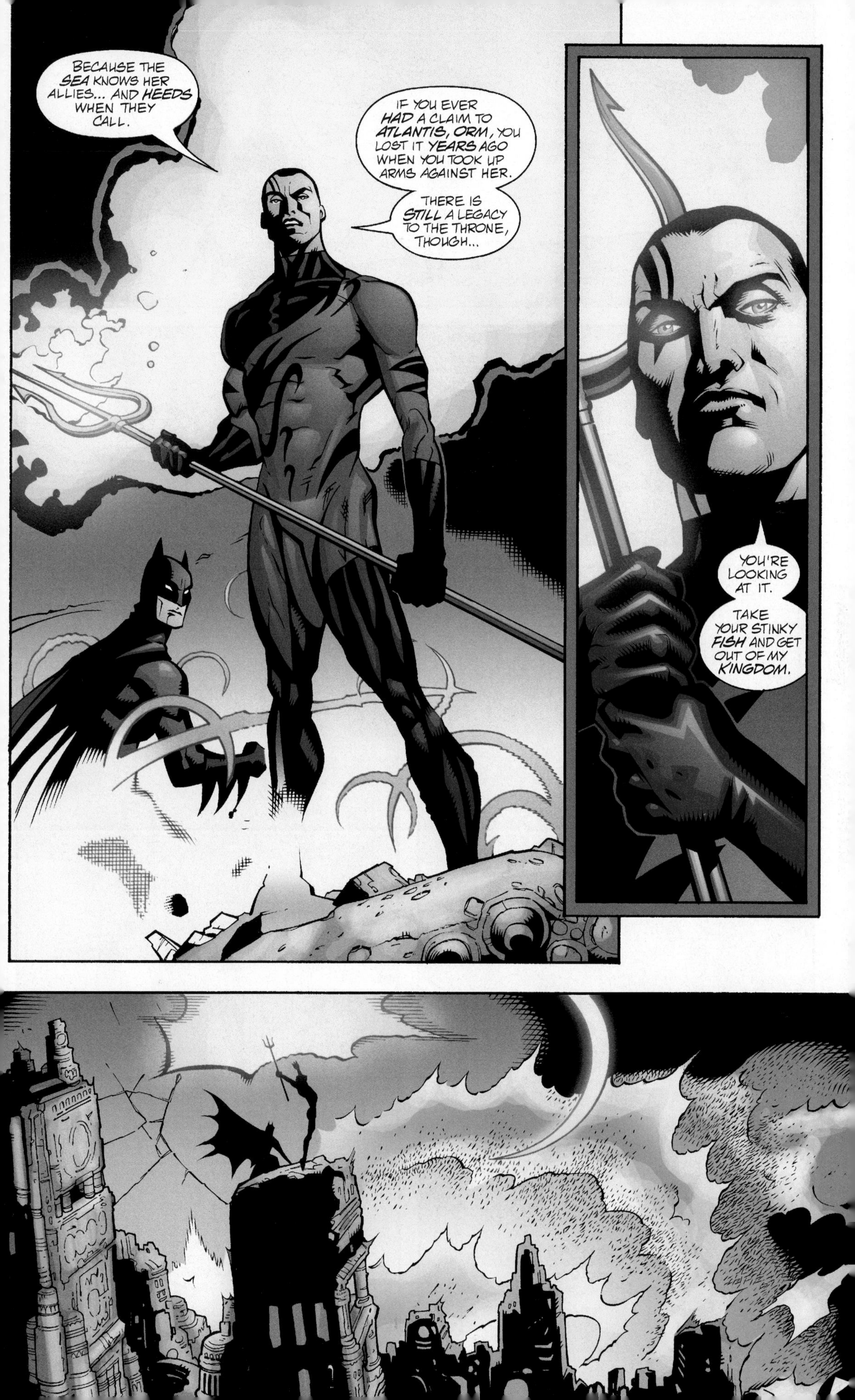
BECAUSE THE SEA KNOWS HER ALLIES... AND HEEDS WHEN THEY CALL.
IF YOU EVER HAD A CLAIM TO ATLANTIS, ORM, YOU LOST IT YEARS AGO WHEN YOU TOOK UP ARMS AGAINST HER.
THERE IS STILL A LEGACY TO THE THRONE, THOUGH...
YOU'RE LOOKING AT IT.
TAKE YOUR STINKY FISH AND GET OUT OF MY KINGDOM.

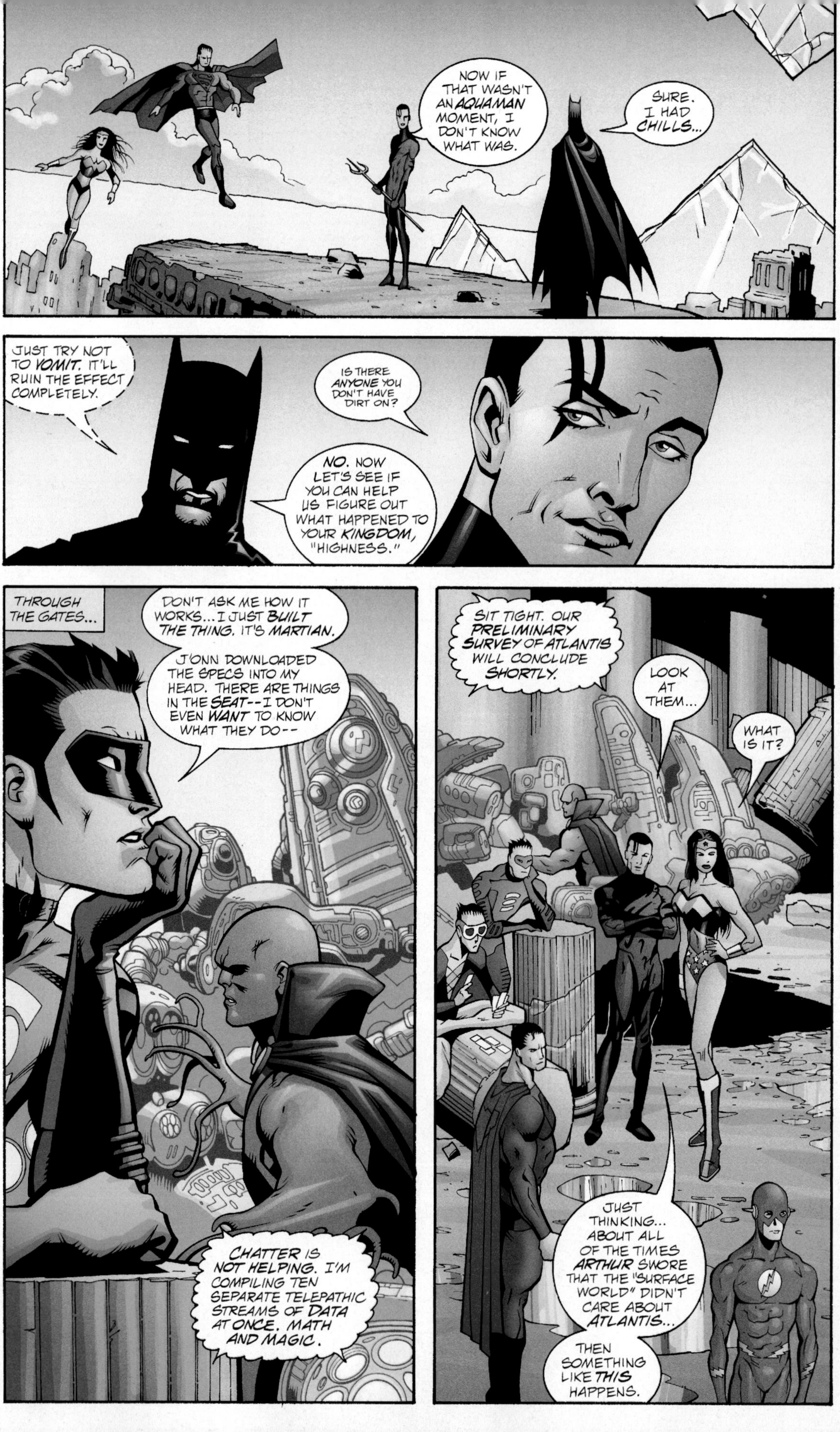
NOW IF THAT WASN'T AN AQUAMAN MOMENT, I DON'T KNOW WHAT WAS.
SURE. I HAD CHILLS...
JUST TRY NOT TO VOMIT. IT'LL RUIN THE EFFECT COMPLETELY.
IS THERE ANYONE YOU DON'T HAVE DIRT ON?
NO. NOW LET'S SEE IF YOU CAN HELP US FIGURE OUT WHAT HAPPENED TO YOUR KINGDOM, "HIGHNESS."
THROUGH THE GATES...
DON'T ASK ME HOW IT WORKS...I JUST BUILT THE THING. IT'S MARTIAN.
J'ONN DOWNLOADED THE SPECS INTO MY HEAD. THERE ARE THINGS IN THE SEAT--I DON'T EVEN WANT TO KNOW WHAT THEY DO--
CHATTER IS NOT HELPING. I'M COMPILING TEN SEPARATE TELEPATHIC STREAMS OF DATA AT ONCE. MATH AND MAGIC.
SIT TIGHT. OUR PRELIMINARY SURVEY OF ATLANTIS WILL CONCLUDE SHORTLY.
LOOK AT THEM...
WHAT IS IT?
JUST THINKING... ABOUT ALL OF THE TIMES ARTHUR SWORE THAT THE "SURFACE WORLD" DIDN'T CARE ABOUT ATLANTIS...
THEN SOMETHING LIKE THIS HAPPENS.

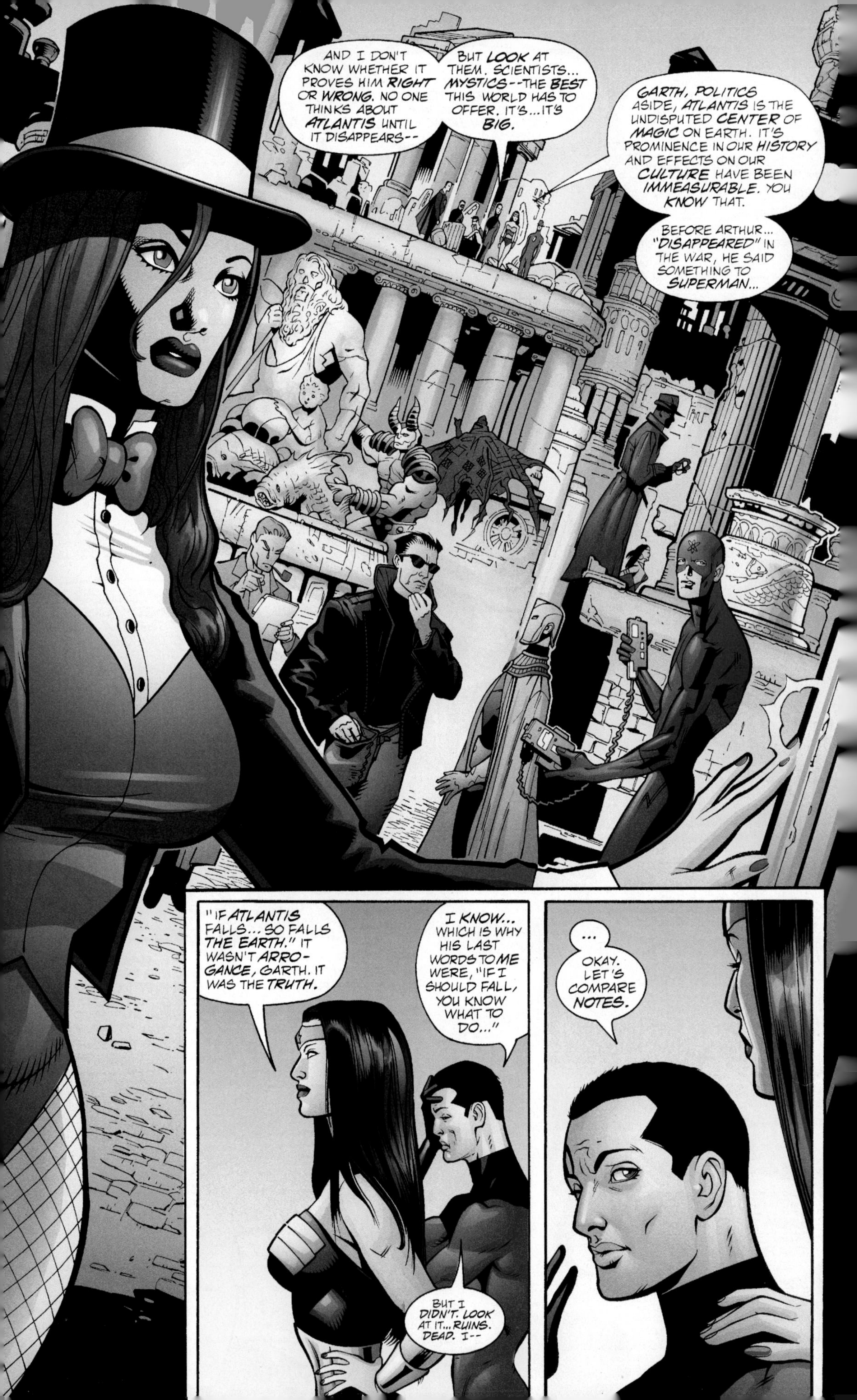
AND I DON'T KNOW WHETHER IT PROVES HIM RIGHT OR WRONG. NO ONE THINKS ABOUT ATLANTIS UNTIL IT DISAPPEARS--
BUT LOOK AT THEM. SCIENTISTS... MYSTICS--THE BEST THIS WORLD HAS TO OFFER. IT'S...IT'S BIG.
GARTH, POLITICS ASIDE, ATLANTIS IS THE UNDISPUTED CENTER OF MAGIC ON EARTH. IT'S PROMINENCE IN OUR HISTORY AND EFFECTS ON OUR CULTURE HAVE BEEN IMMEASURABLE. YOU KNOW THAT.
BEFORE ARTHUR... "DISAPPEARED" IN THE WAR, HE SAID SOMETHING TO SUPERMAN...
"IF ATLANTIS FALLS... SO FALLS THE EARTH." IT WASN'T ARRO-GANCE, GARTH. IT WAS THE TRUTH.
I KNOW... WHICH IS WHY HIS LAST WORDS TO ME WERE, "IF I SHOULD FALL, YOU KNOW WHAT TO DO..."
BUT I DIDN'T. LOOK AT IT... RUINS. DEAD. I--
...
OKAY. LET'S COMPARE NOTES.

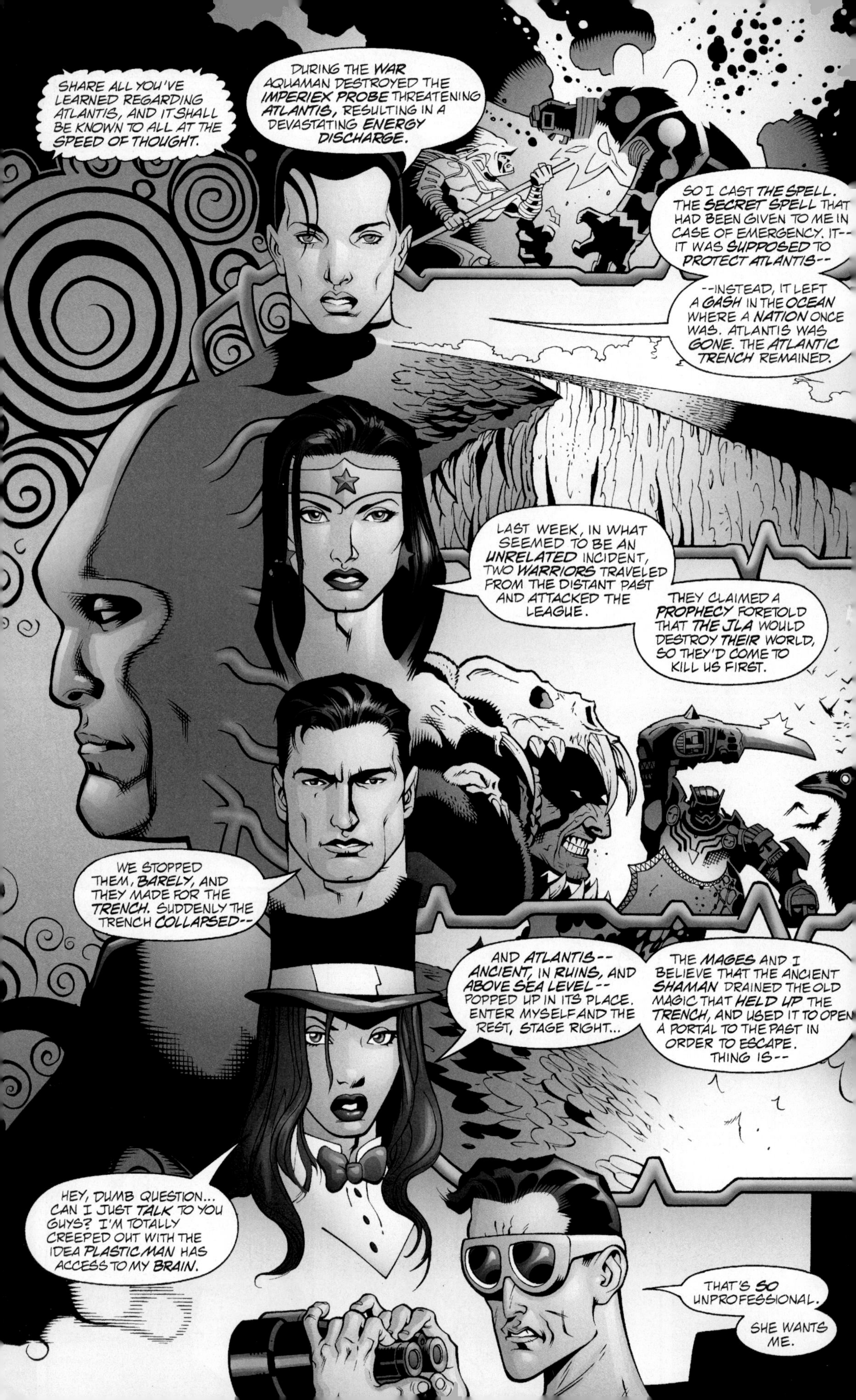

SHARE ALL YOU'VE LEARNED REGARDING ATLANTIS, AND IT SHALL BE KNOWN TO ALL AT THE SPEED OF THOUGHT.
DURING THE WAR AQUAMAN DESTROYED THE IMPERIEX PROBE THREATENING ATLANTIS, RESULTING IN A DEVASTATING ENERGY DISCHARGE.
SO I CAST THE SPELL. THE SECRET SPELL THAT HAD BEEN GIVEN TO ME IN CASE OF EMERGENCY. IT--IT WAS SUPPOSED TO PROTECT ATLANTIS--
--INSTEAD, IT LEFT A GASH IN THE OCEAN WHERE A NATION ONCE WAS. ATLANTIS WAS GONE. THE ATLANTIC TRENCH REMAINED.
LAST WEEK, IN WHAT SEEMED TO BE AN UNRELATED INCIDENT, TWO WARRIORS TRAVELED FROM THE DISTANT PAST AND ATTACKED THE LEAGUE.
THEY CLAIMED A PROPHECY FORETOLD THAT THE JLA WOULD DESTROY THEIR WORLD, SO THEY'D COME TO KILL US FIRST.
WE STOPPED THEM, BARELY, AND THEY MADE FOR THE TRENCH. SUDDENLY THE TRENCH COLLAPSED--
AND ATLANTIS--ANCIENT, IN RUINS, AND ABOVE SEA LEVEL--POPPED UP IN ITS PLACE. ENTER MYSELF AND THE REST, STAGE RIGHT...
THE MAGES AND I BELIEVE THAT THE ANCIENT SHAMAN DRAINED THE OLD MAGIC THAT HELD UP THE TRENCH, AND USED IT TO OPEN A PORTAL TO THE PAST IN ORDER TO ESCAPE. THING IS--
HEY, DUMB QUESTION... CAN I JUST TALK TO YOU GUYS? I'M TOTALLY CREEPED OUT WITH THE IDEA PLASTIC MAN HAS ACCESS TO MY BRAIN.
THAT'S SO UNPROFESSIONAL.
SHE WANTS ME.

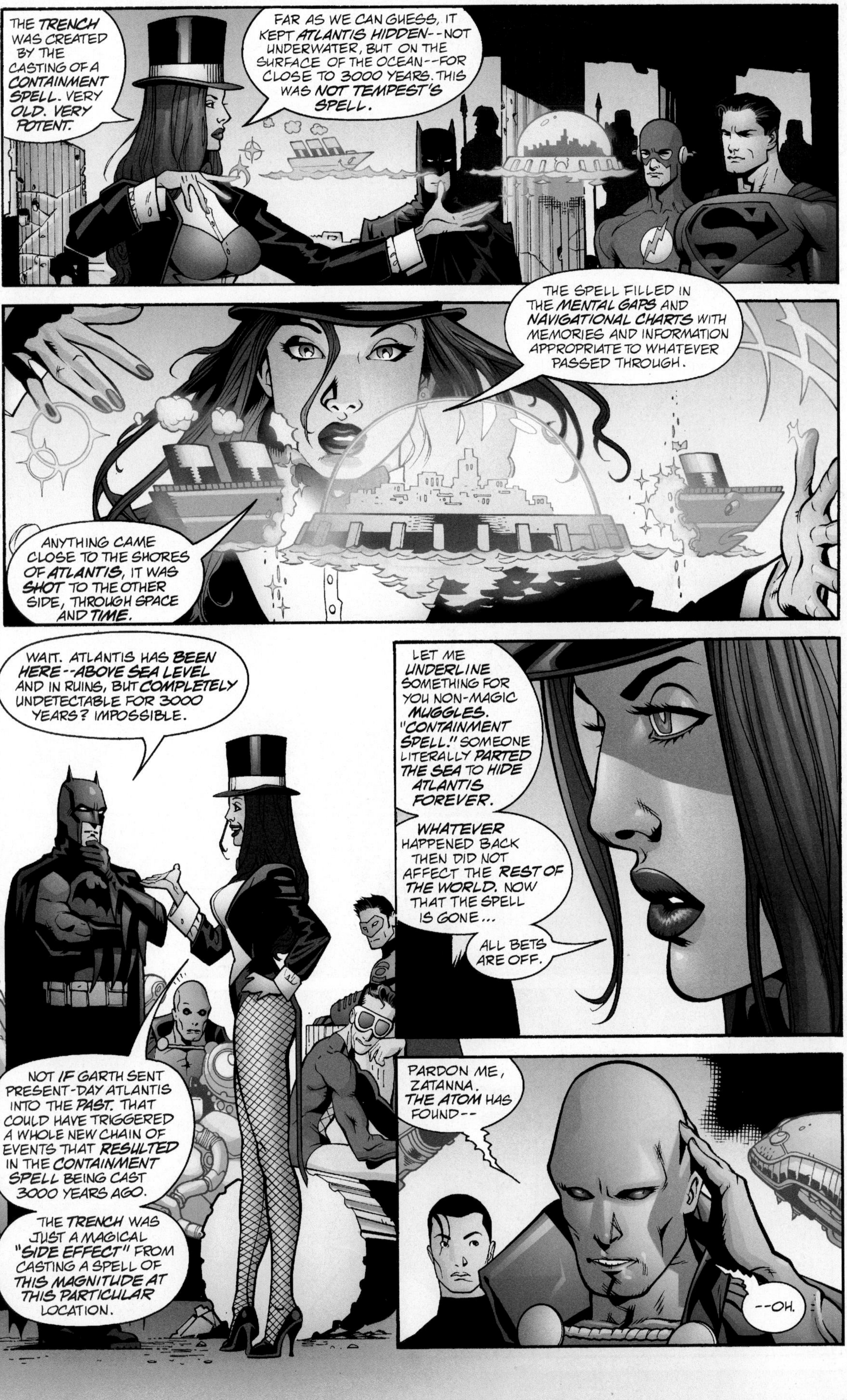
THE TRENCH WAS CREATED BY THE CASTING OF A CONTAINMENT SPELL. VERY OLD. VERY POTENT.
FAR AS WE CAN GUESS, IT KEPT ATLANTIS HIDDEN--NOT UNDERWATER, BUT ON THE SURFACE OF THE OCEAN--FOR CLOSE TO 3000 YEARS. THIS WAS NOT TEMPEST'S SPELL.
THE SPELL FILLED IN THE MENTAL GAPS AND NAVIGATIONAL CHARTS WITH MEMORIES AND INFORMATION APPROPRIATE TO WHATEVER PASSED THROUGH.
ANYTHING CAME CLOSE TO THE SHORES OF ATLANTIS, IT WAS SHOT TO THE OTHER SIDE, THROUGH SPACE AND TIME.
WAIT. ATLANTIS HAS BEEN HERE--ABOVE SEA LEVEL AND IN RUINS, BUT COMPLETELY UNDETECTABLE FOR 3000 YEARS? IMPOSSIBLE.
NOT IF GARTH SENT PRESENT-DAY ATLANTIS INTO THE PAST. THAT COULD HAVE TRIGGERED A WHOLE NEW CHAIN OF EVENTS THAT RESULTED IN THE CONTAINMENT SPELL BEING CAST 3000 YEARS AGO.
THE TRENCH WAS JUST A MAGICAL "SIDE EFFECT" FROM CASTING A SPELL OF THIS MAGNITUDE AT THIS PARTICULAR LOCATION.
LET ME UNDERLINE SOMETHING FOR YOU NON-MAGIC MUGGLES. "CONTAINMENT SPELL." SOMEONE LITERALLY PARTED THE SEA TO HIDE ATLANTIS FOREVER.
WHATEVER HAPPENED BACK THEN DID NOT AFFECT THE REST OF THE WORLD. NOW THAT THE SPELL IS GONE...
ALL BETS ARE OFF.
PARDON ME, ZATANNA. THE ATOM HAS FOUND--
--OH.

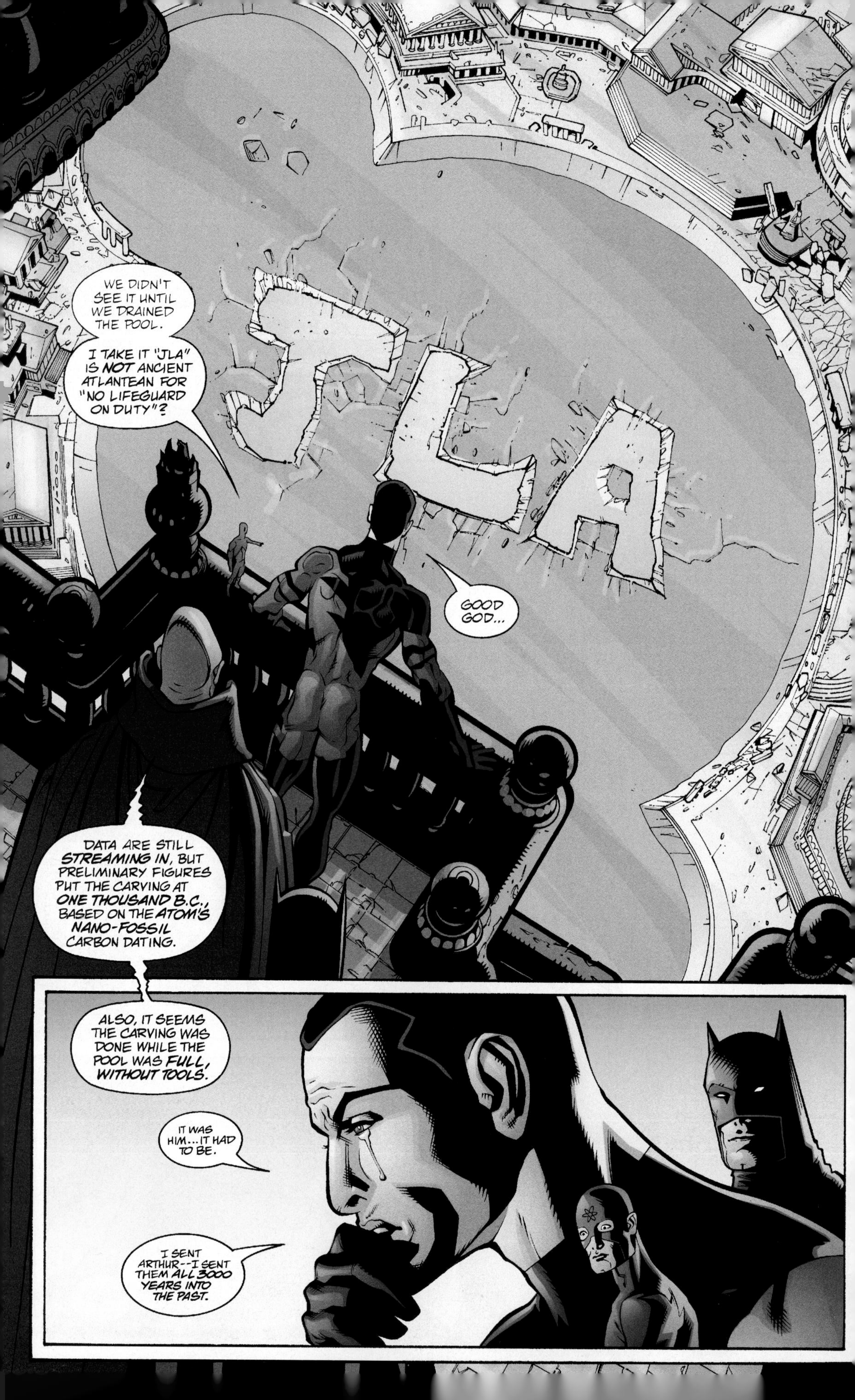
WE DIDN'T SEE IT UNTIL WE DRAINED THE POOL.
I TAKE IT "JLA" IS NOT ANCIENT ATLANTEAN FOR "NO LIFEGUARD ON DUTY"?
GOOD GOD...
DATA ARE STILL STREAMING IN, BUT PRELIMINARY FIGURES PUT THE CARVING AT ONE THOUSAND B.C., BASED ON THE ATOM'S NANO-FOSSIL CARBON DATING.
ALSO, IT SEEMS THE CARVING WAS DONE WHILE THE POOL WAS FULL, WITHOUT TOOLS.
IT WAS HIM...IT HAD TO BE.
I SENT ARTHUR--I SENT THEM ALL 3000 YEARS INTO THE PAST.

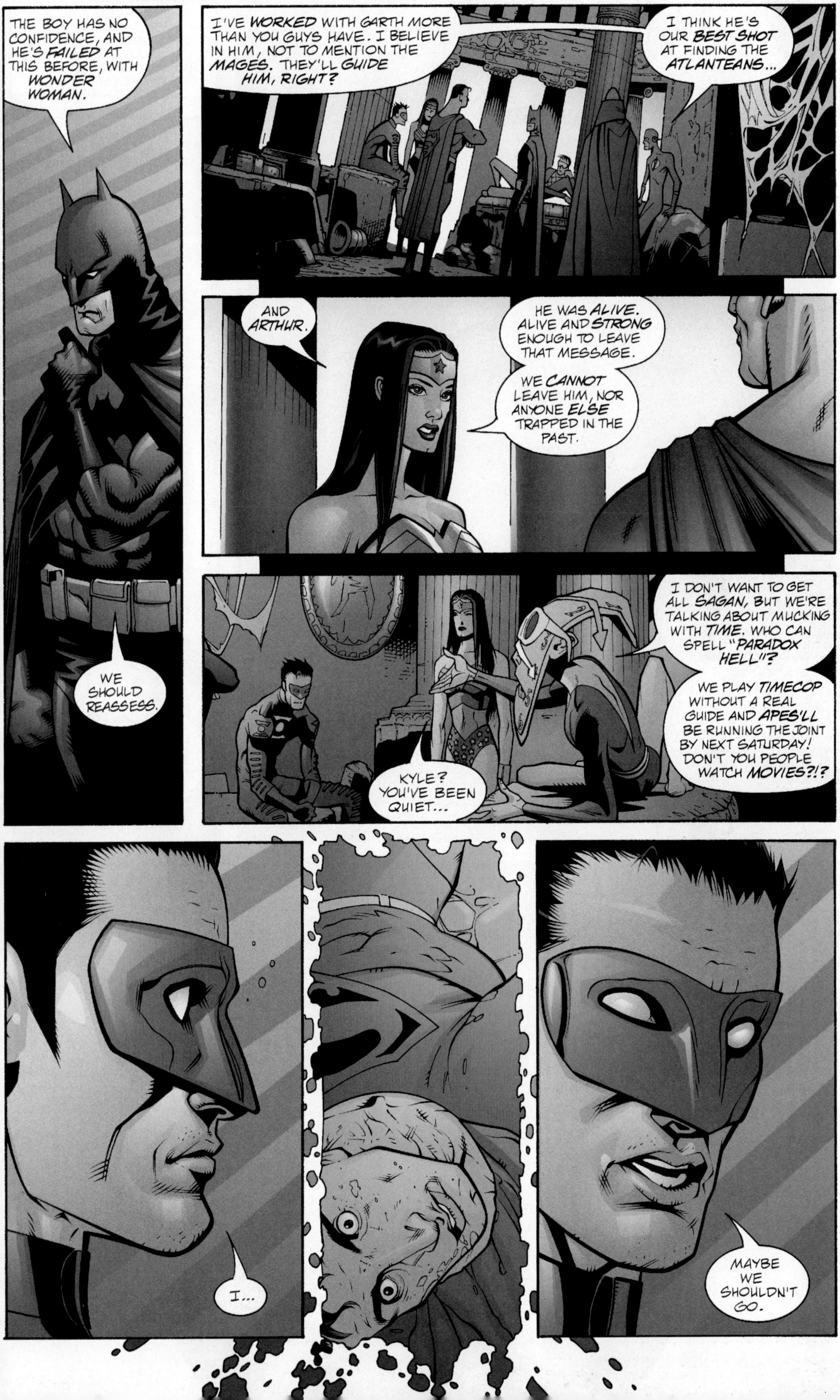
THE BOY HAS NO CONFIDENCE, AND HE'S FAILED AT THIS BEFORE, WITH WONDER WOMAN.
I'VE WORKED WITH GARTH MORE THAN YOU GUYS HAVE. I BELIEVE IN HIM, NOT TO MENTION THE MAGES. THEY'LL GUIDE HIM, RIGHT?
I THINK HE'S OUR BEST SHOT AT FINDING THE ATLANTEANS...
WE SHOULD REASSESS.
AND ARTHUR.
HE WAS ALIVE. ALIVE AND STRONG ENOUGH TO LEAVE THAT MESSAGE.
WE CANNOT LEAVE HIM, NOR ANYONE ELSE TRAPPED IN THE PAST.
I DON'T WANT TO GET ALL SAGAN, BUT WE'RE TALKING ABOUT MUCKING WITH TIME. WHO CAN SPELL "PARADOX HELL"?
WE PLAY TIMECOP WITHOUT A REAL GUIDE AND APES'LL BE RUNNING THE JOINT BY NEXT SATURDAY! DON'T YOU PEOPLE WATCH MOVIES?!?
KYLE? YOU'VE BEEN QUIET...
I...
MAYBE WE SHOULDN'T GO.

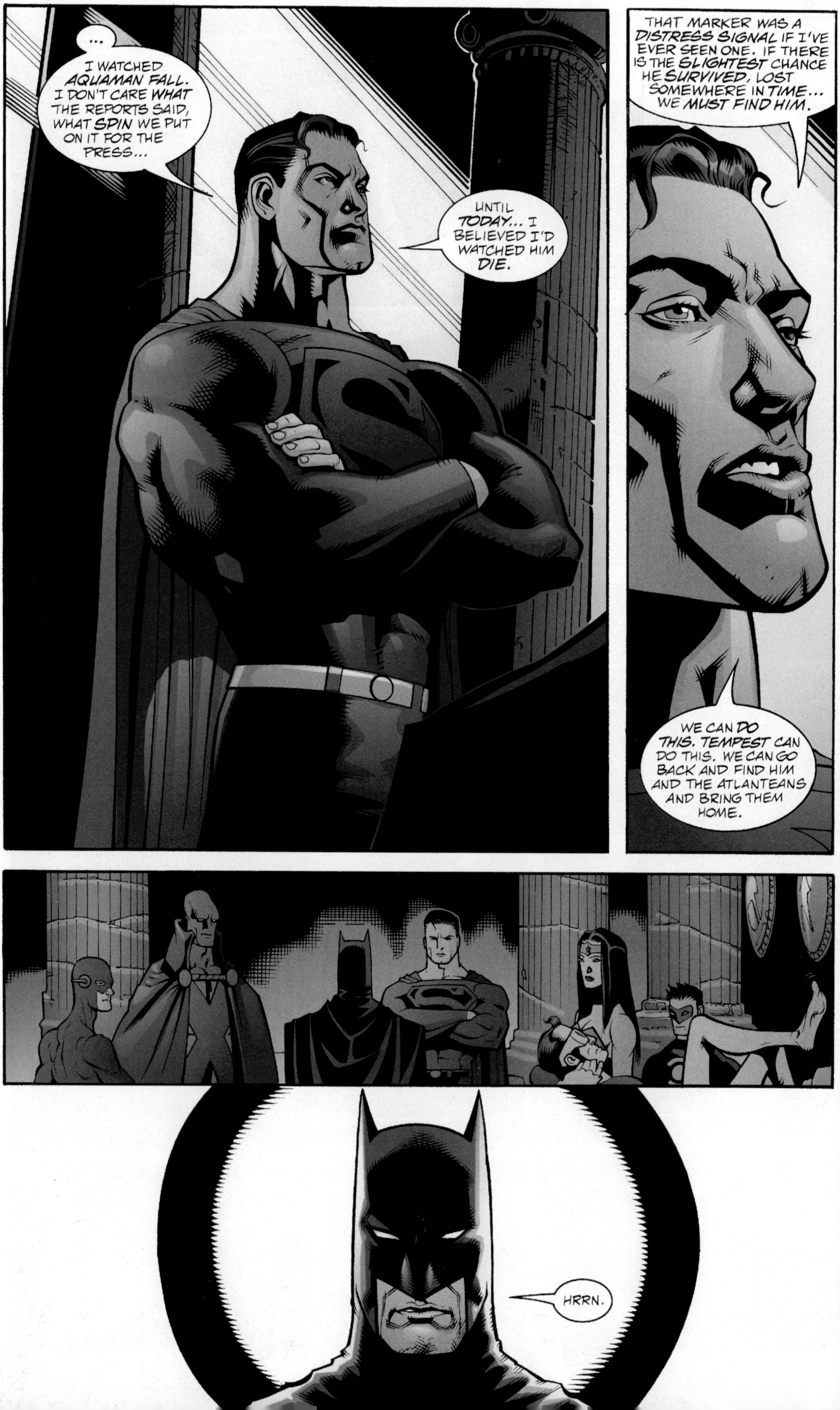

...
I WATCHED AQUAMAN FALL. I DON'T CARE WHAT THE REPORTS SAID, WHAT SPIN WE PUT ON IT FOR THE PRESS...
UNTIL TODAY... I BELIEVED I'D WATCHED HIM DIE.
THAT MARKER WAS A DISTRESS SIGNAL IF I'VE EVER SEEN ONE. IF THERE IS THE SLIGHTEST CHANCE HE SURVIVED, LOST SOMEWHERE IN TIME... WE MUST FIND HIM.
WE CAN DO THIS. TEMPEST CAN DO THIS. WE CAN GO BACK AND FIND HIM AND THE ATLANTEANS AND BRING THEM HOME.
HRRN.

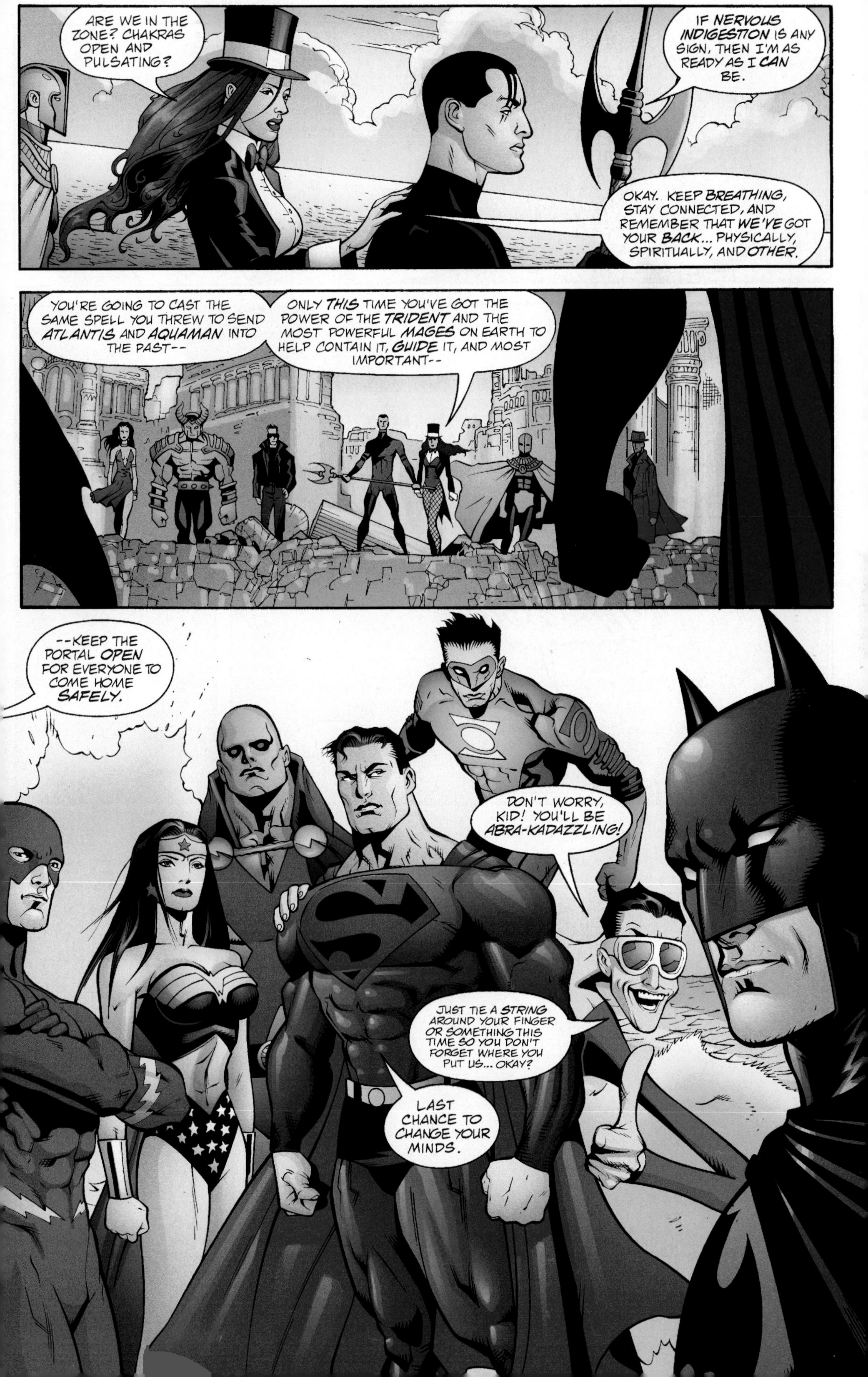
ARE WE IN THE ZONE? CHAKRAS OPEN AND PULSATING?
IF NERVOUS INDIGESTION IS ANY SIGN, THEN I'M AS READY AS I CAN BE.
OKAY. KEEP BREATHING, STAY CONNECTED, AND REMEMBER THAT WE'VE GOT YOUR BACK... PHYSICALLY, SPIRITUALLY, AND OTHER.
YOU'RE GOING TO CAST THE SAME SPELL YOU THREW TO SEND ATLANTIS AND AQUAMAN INTO THE PAST--
ONLY THIS TIME YOU'VE GOT THE POWER OF THE TRIDENT AND THE MOST POWERFUL MAGES ON EARTH TO HELP CONTAIN IT, GUIDE IT, AND MOST IMPORTANT--
--KEEP THE PORTAL OPEN FOR EVERYONE TO COME HOME SAFELY.
DON'T WORRY, KID! YOU'LL BE ABRA-KADAZZLING!
JUST TIE A STRING AROUND YOUR FINGER OR SOMETHING THIS TIME SO YOU DON'T FORGET WHERE YOU PUT US... OKAY?
LAST CHANCE TO CHANGE YOUR MINDS.

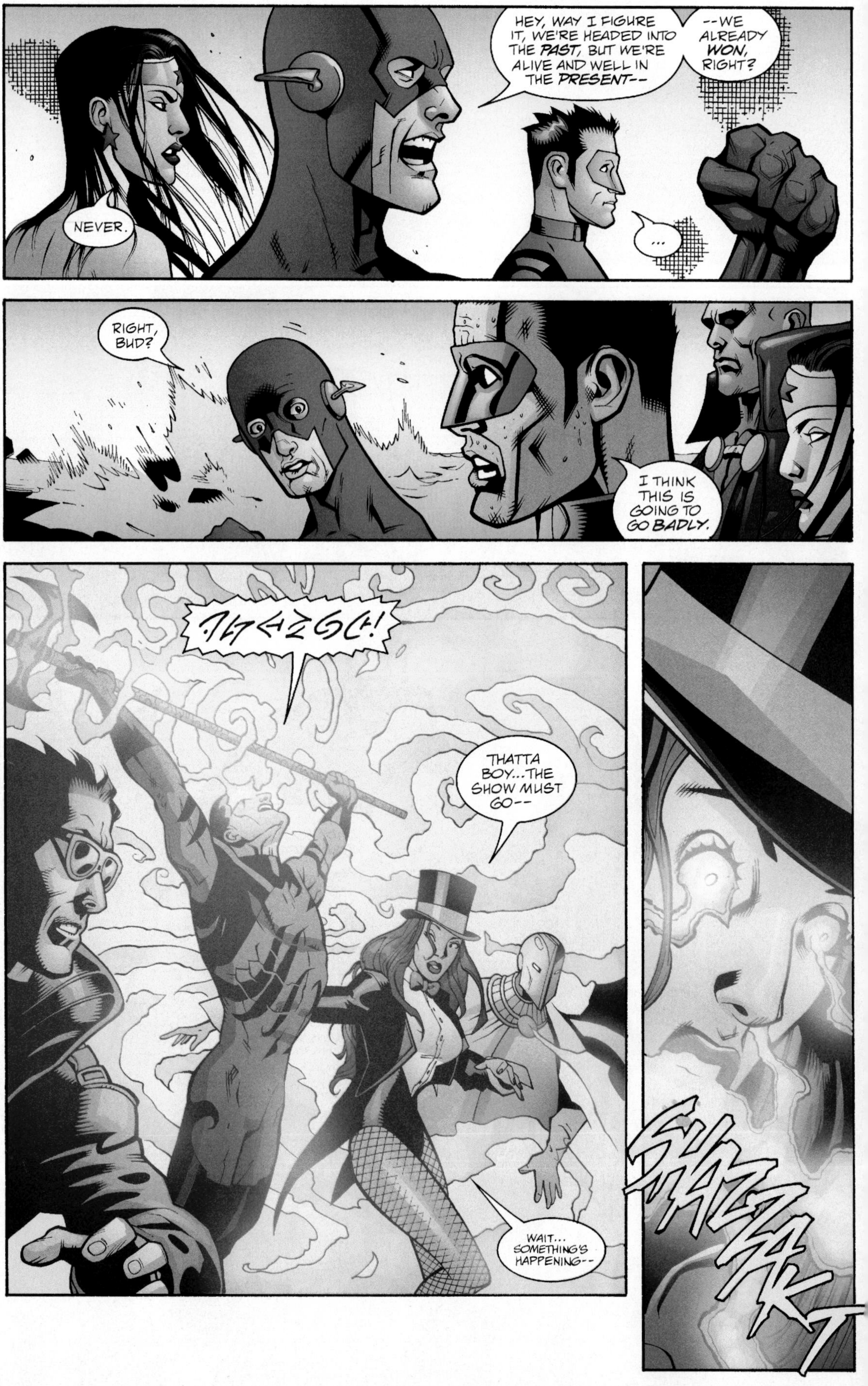
HEY, WAY I FIGURE IT, WE'RE HEADED INTO THE PAST, BUT WE'RE ALIVE AND WELL IN THE PRESENT--
--WE ALREADY WON, RIGHT?
NEVER.
...
RIGHT, BUD?
I THINK THIS IS GOING TO GO BADLY.
THATTA BOY... THE SHOW MUST GO--
WAIT... SOMETHING'S HAPPENING--
SHAZAKT

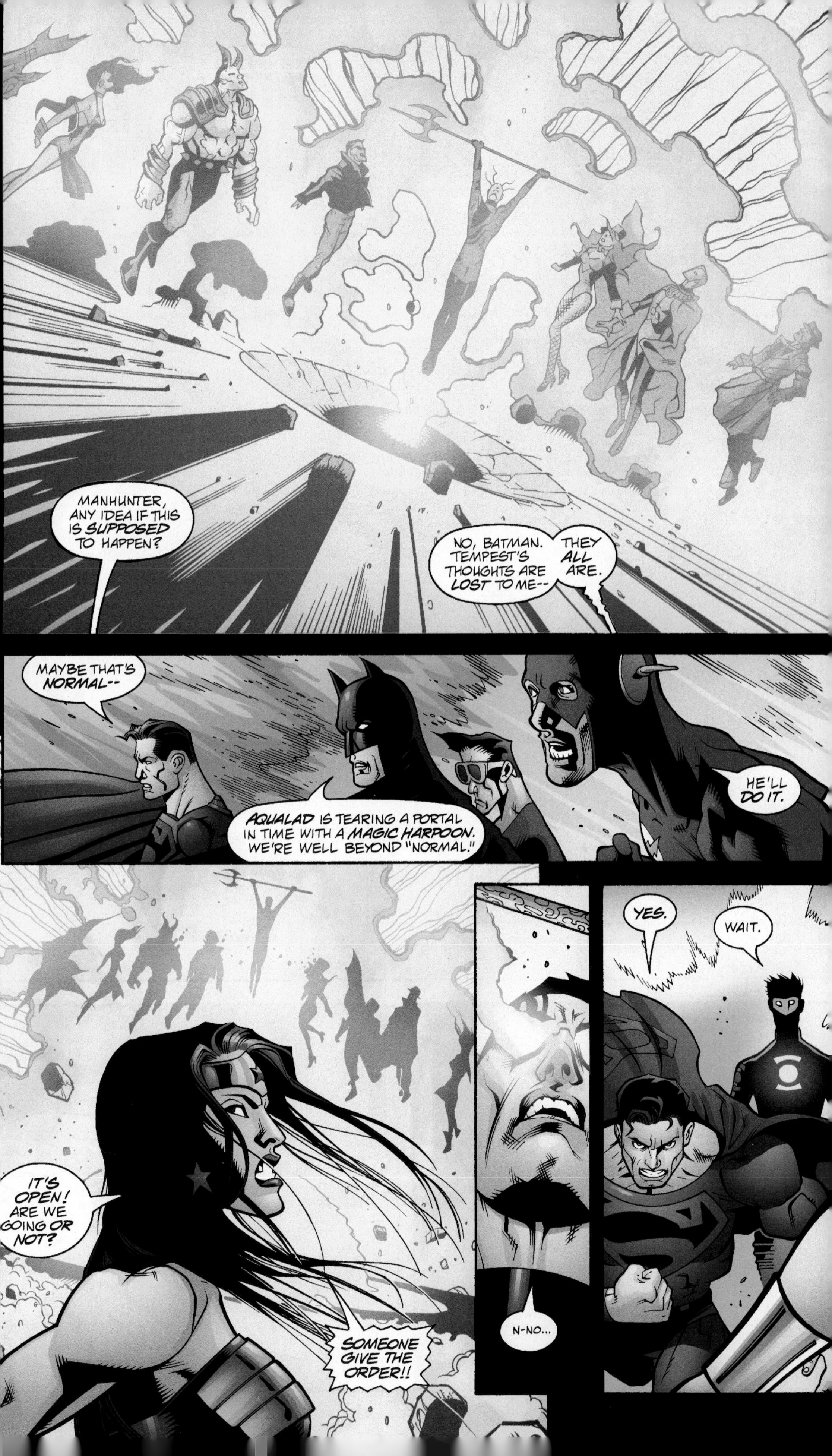
MANHUNTER, ANY IDEA IF THIS IS SUPPOSED TO HAPPEN?
NO, BATMAN. TEMPEST'S THOUGHTS ARE LOST TO ME--
THEY ALL ARE.
MAYBE THAT'S NORMAL--
AQUALAD IS TEARING A PORTAL IN TIME WITH A MAGIC HARPOON. WE'RE WELL BEYOND "NORMAL."
HE'LL DO IT.
IT'S OPEN! ARE WE GOING OR NOT?
SOMEONE GIVE THE ORDER!!
N-NO...
YES.
WAIT.

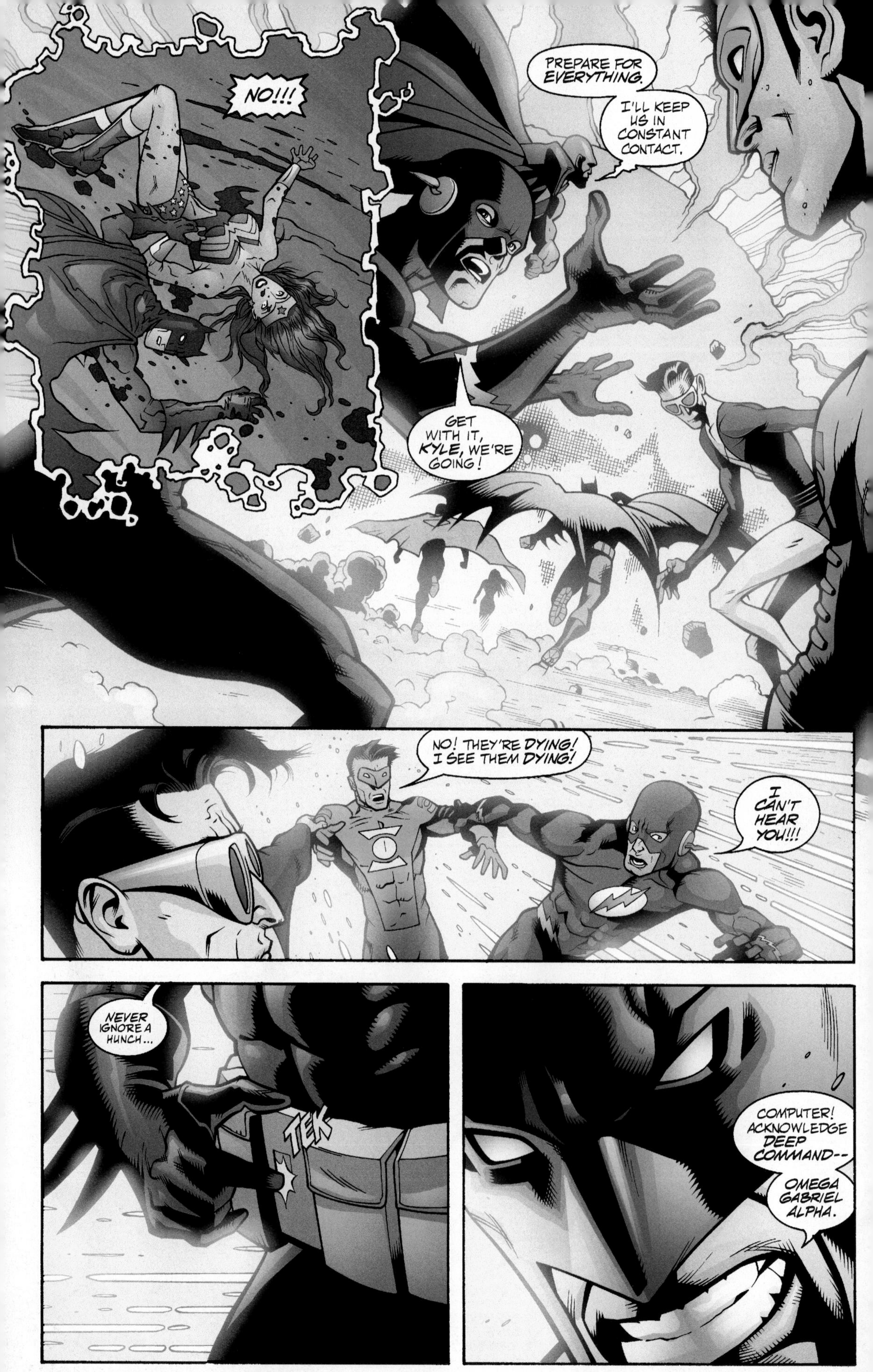
NO!!!
PREPARE FOR EVERYTHING.
I'LL KEEP US IN CONSTANT CONTACT.
GET WITH IT, KYLE, WE'RE GOING!
NO! THEY'RE DYING! I SEE THEM DYING!
I CAN'T HEAR YOU!!!
NEVER IGNORE A HUNCH...
TEK
COMPUTER! ACKNOWLEDGE DEEP COMMAND--
OMEGA GABRIEL ALPHA.

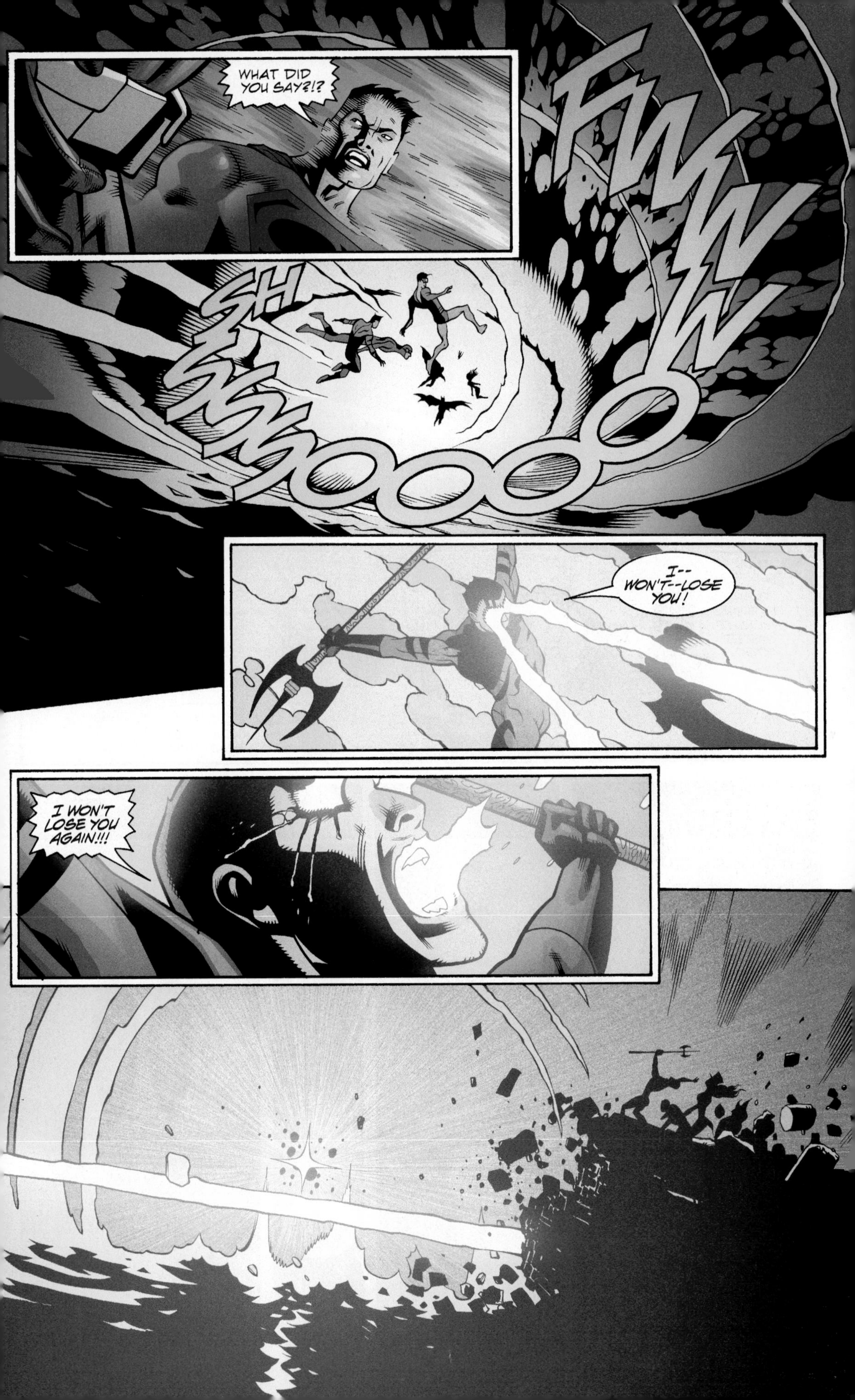
WHAT DID YOU SAY?!?
FWWWWOOOO
SHSSSSOOOO
I--WON'T--LOSE YOU!
I WON'T LOSE YOU AGAIN!!!

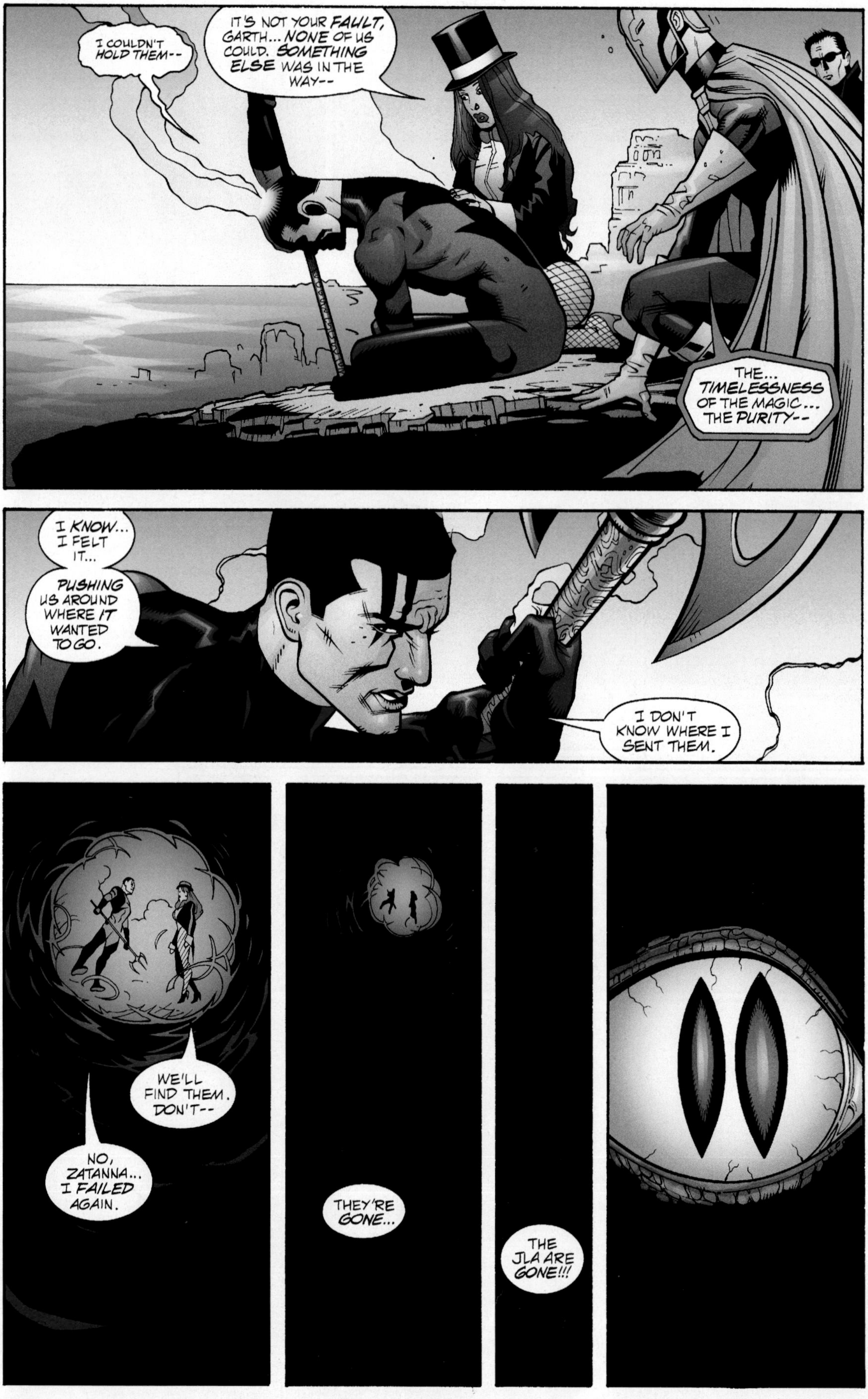
I COULDN'T HOLD THEM--
IT'S NOT YOUR FAULT, GARTH... NONE OF US COULD. SOMETHING ELSE WAS IN THE WAY--
THE... TIMELESSNESS OF THE MAGIC... THE PURITY--
I KNOW... I FELT IT...
PUSHING US AROUND WHERE IT WANTED TO GO.
I DON'T KNOW WHERE I SENT THEM.
WE'LL FIND THEM. DON'T--
NO, ZATANNA... I FAILED AGAIN.
THEY'RE GONE...
THE JLA ARE GONE!!!

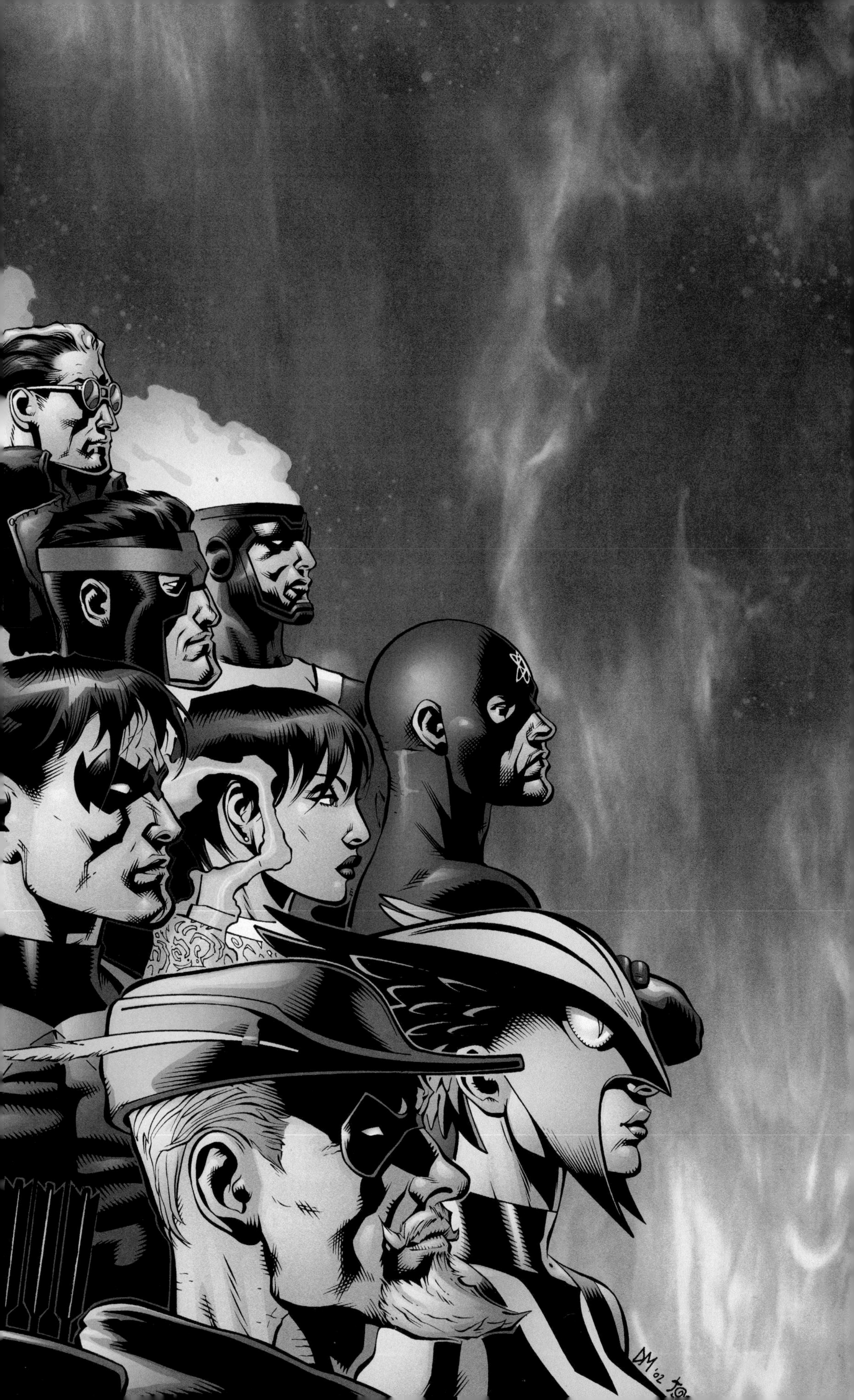

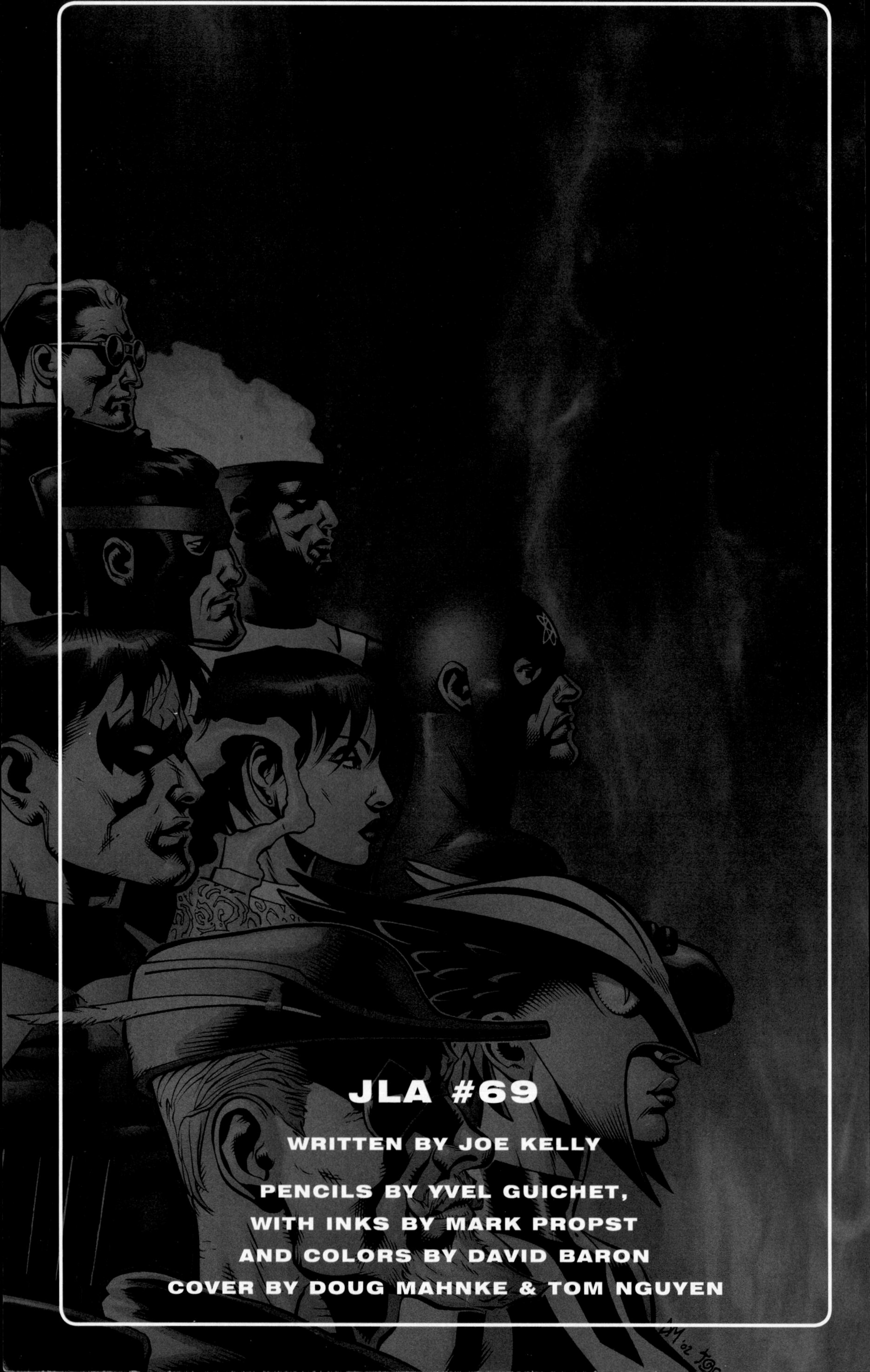

JLA #69

WRITTEN BY JOE KELLY

PENCILS BY YVEL GUICHET,
WITH INKS BY MARK PROPST
AND COLORS BY DAVID BARON
COVER BY DOUG MAHNKE & TOM NGUYEN

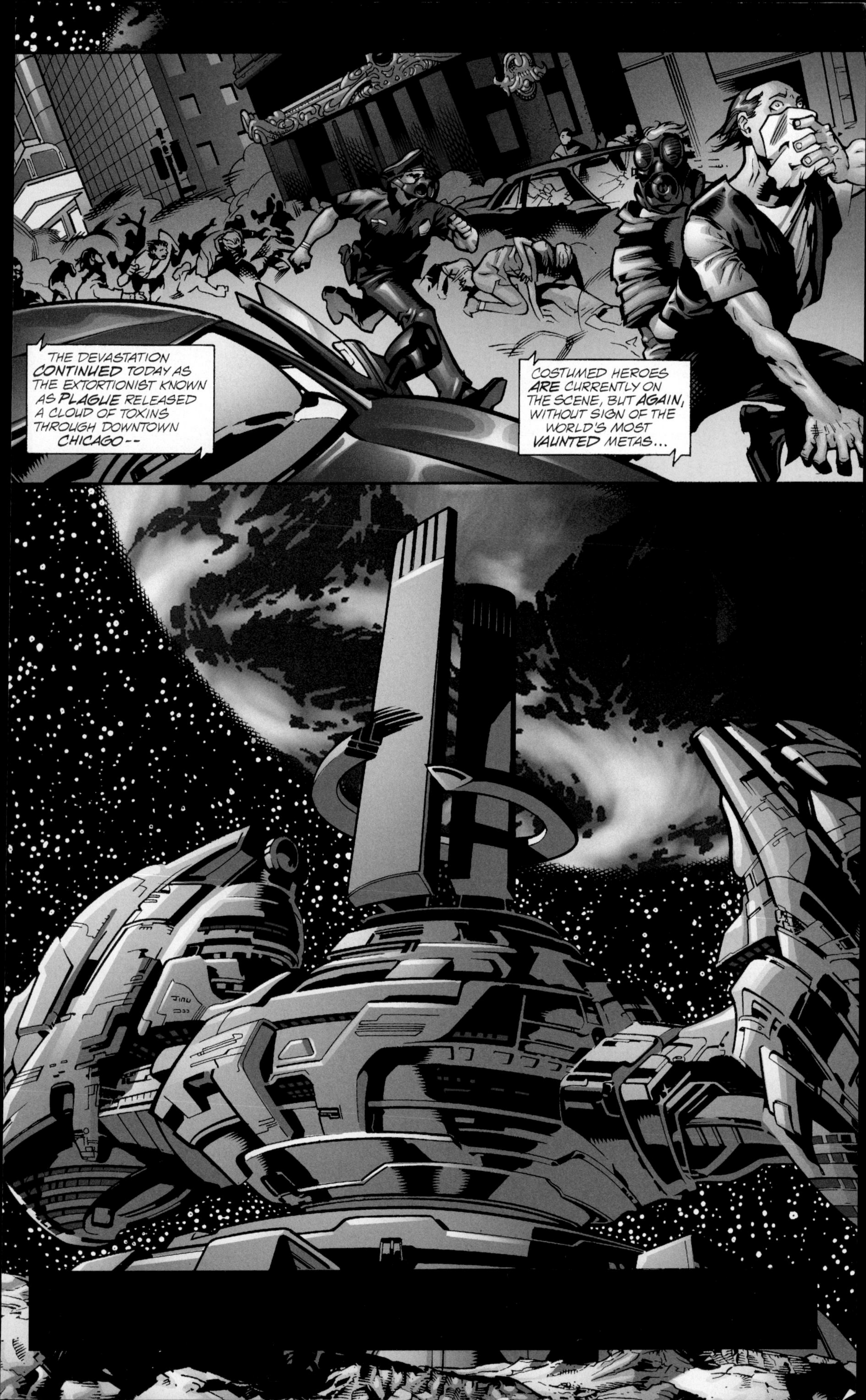
THE DEVASTATION CONTINUED TODAY AS THE EXTORTIONIST KNOWN AS PLAGUE RELEASED A CLOUD OF TOXINS THROUGH DOWNTOWN CHICAGO--
COSTUMED HEROES ARE CURRENTLY ON THE SCENE, BUT AGAIN, WITHOUT SIGN OF THE WORLD'S MOST VAUNTED METAS...

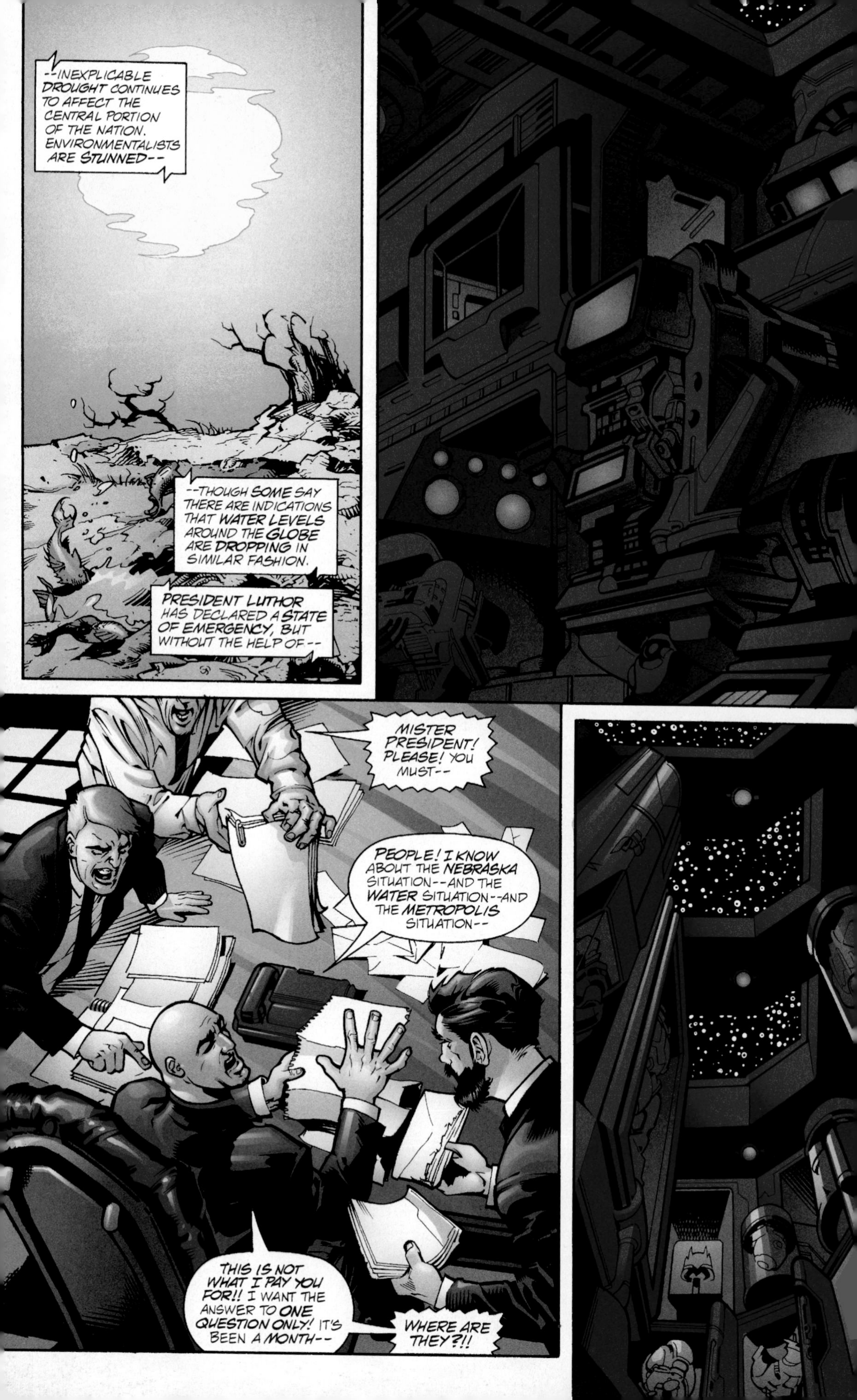
--INEXPLICABLE DROUGHT CONTINUES TO AFFECT THE CENTRAL PORTION OF THE NATION. ENVIRONMENTALISTS ARE STUNNED--
--THOUGH SOME SAY THERE ARE INDICATIONS THAT WATER LEVELS AROUND THE GLOBE ARE DROPPING IN SIMILAR FASHION.
PRESIDENT LUTHOR HAS DECLARED A STATE OF EMERGENCY, BUT WITHOUT THE HELP OF--
MISTER PRESIDENT! PLEASE! YOU MUST--
PEOPLE! I KNOW ABOUT THE NEBRASKA SITUATION--AND THE WATER SITUATION--AND THE METROPOLIS SITUATION--
THIS IS NOT WHAT I PAY YOU FOR!! I WANT THE ANSWER TO ONE QUESTION ONLY! IT'S BEEN A MONTH--
WHERE ARE THEY?!!

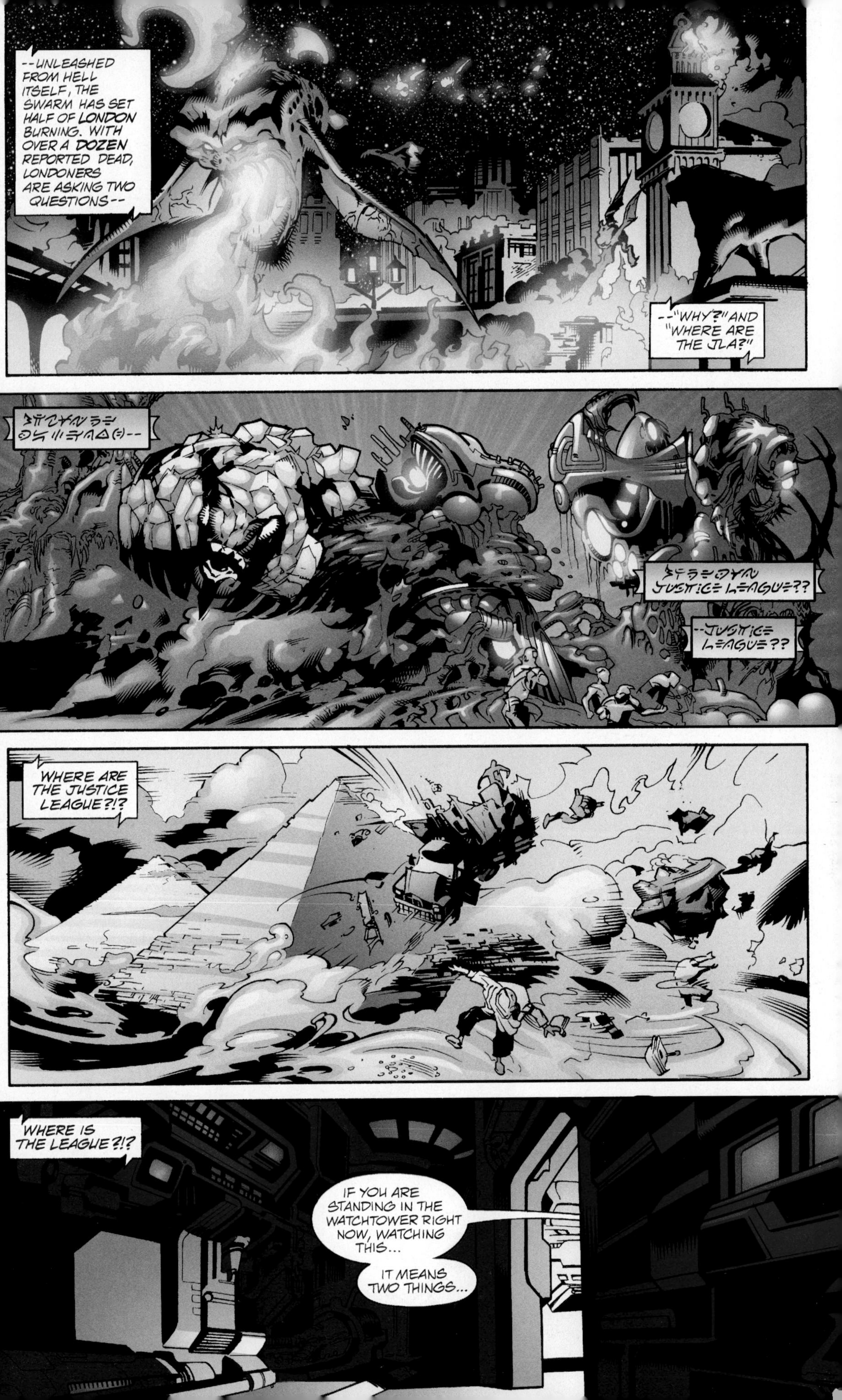

--UNLEASHED FROM HELL ITSELF, THE SWARM HAS SET HALF OF LONDON BURNING. WITH OVER A DOZEN REPORTED DEAD, LONDONERS ARE ASKING TWO QUESTIONS--
--"WHY?" AND "WHERE ARE THE JLA?"
JUSTICE LEAGUE??
--JUSTICE LEAGUE??
WHERE ARE THE JUSTICE LEAGUE?!?
WHERE IS THE LEAGUE?!?
IF YOU ARE STANDING IN THE WATCHTOWER RIGHT NOW, WATCHING THIS...
IT MEANS TWO THINGS...

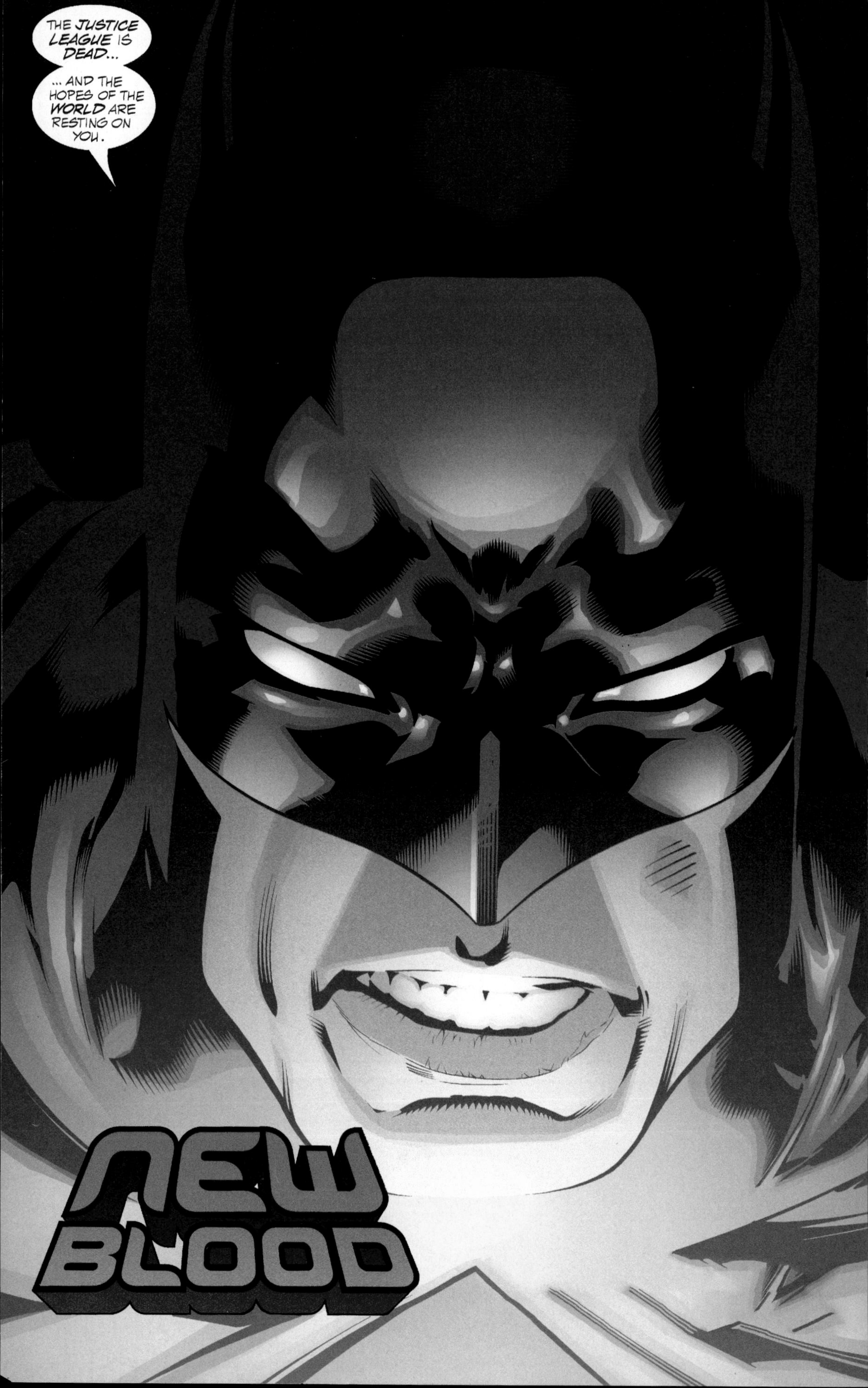
THE JUSTICE LEAGUE IS DEAD...
... AND THE HOPES OF THE WORLD ARE RESTING ON YOU.
NEW BLOOD

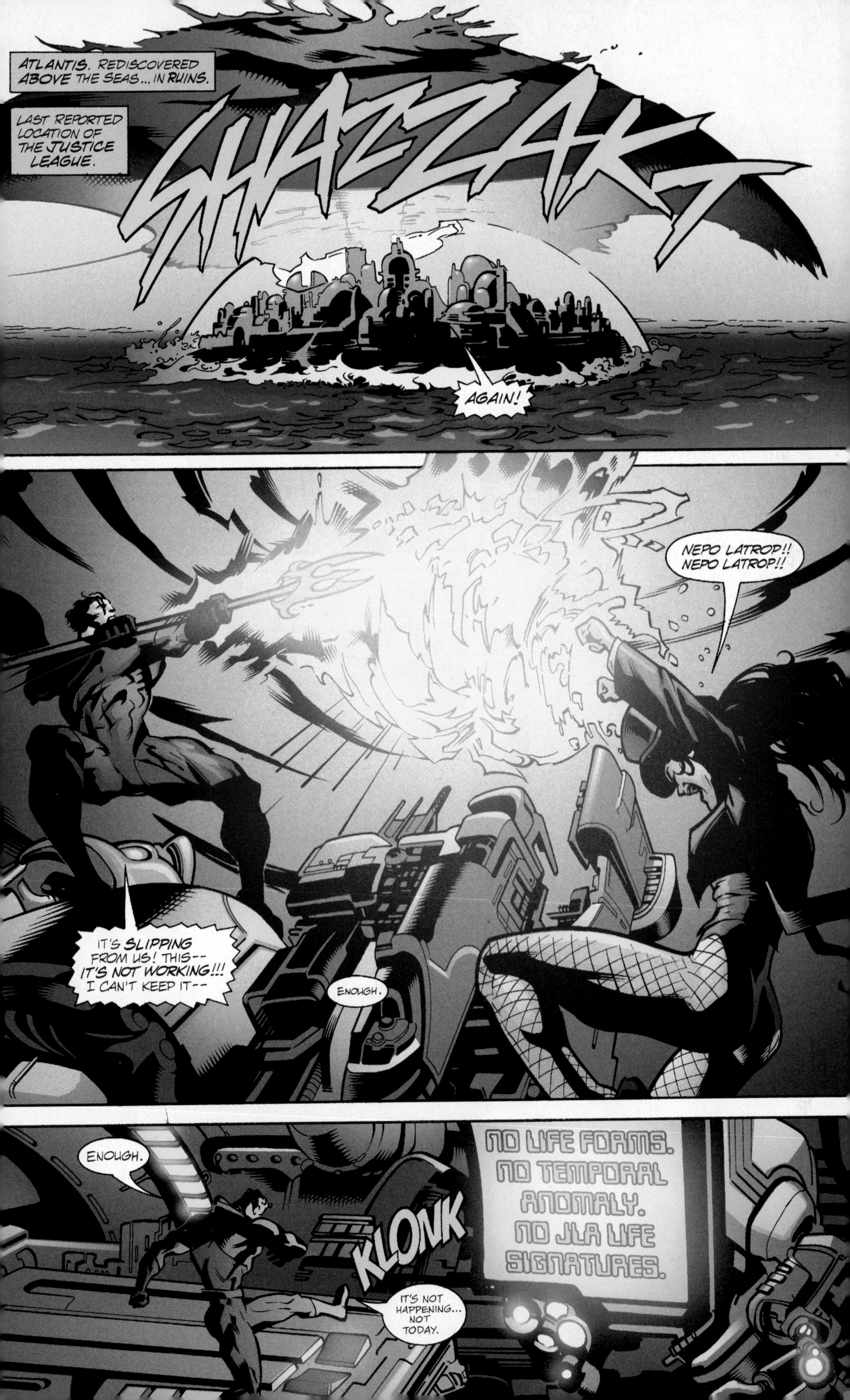
ATLANTIS. REDISCOVERED ABOVE THE SEAS... IN RUINS.
LAST REPORTED LOCATION OF THE JUSTICE LEAGUE.
SHAZZAKT
AGAIN!
NEPO LATROP!! NEPO LATROP!!
IT'S SLIPPING FROM US! THIS-- IT'S NOT WORKING!!! I CAN'T KEEP IT--
ENOUGH.
ENOUGH.
NO LIFE FORMS. NO TEMPORAL ANOMALY. NO JLA LIFE SIGNATURES.
KLONK
IT'S NOT HAPPENING... NOT TODAY.

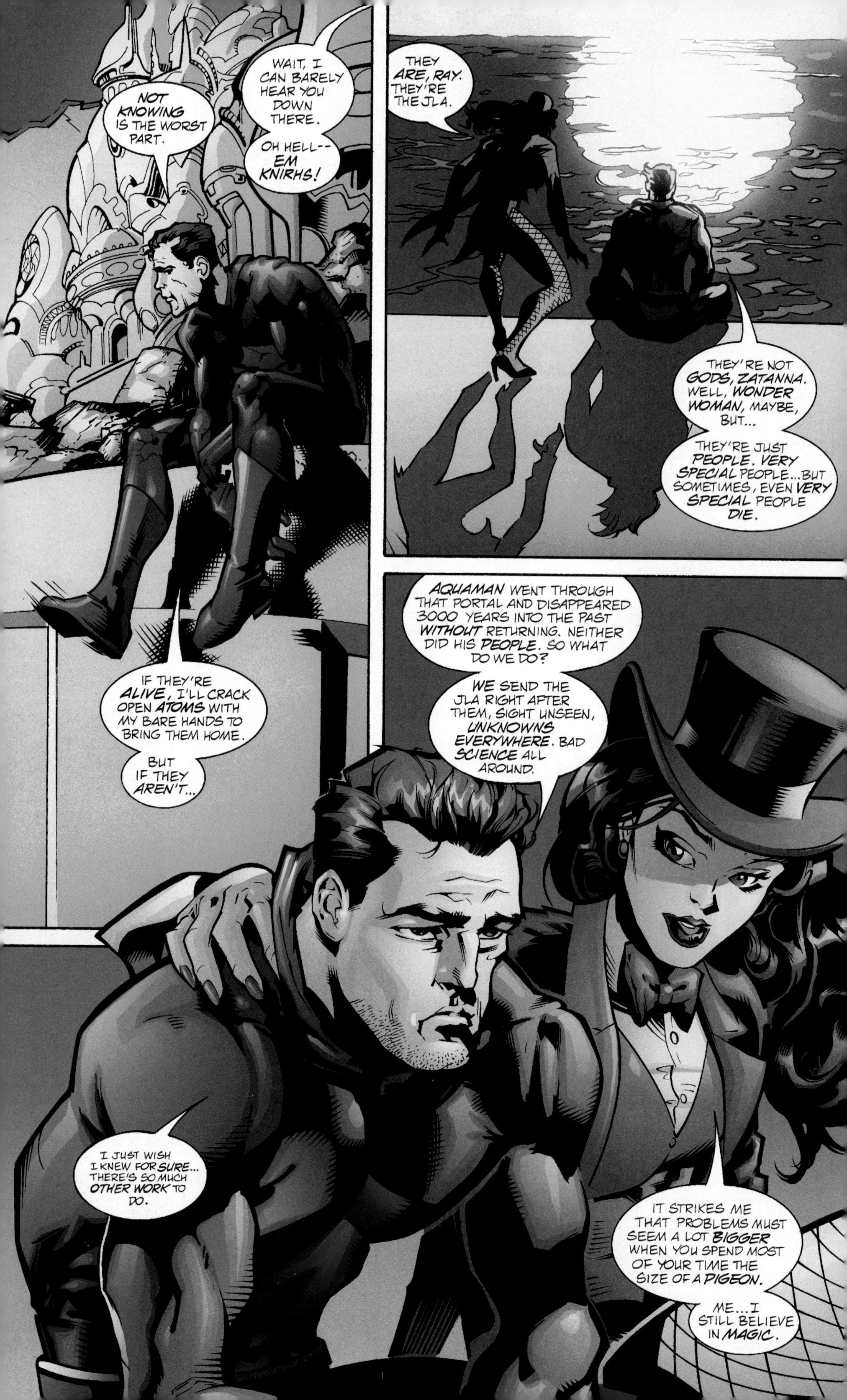
NOT KNOWING IS THE WORST PART.
WAIT, I CAN BARELY HEAR YOU DOWN THERE.
OH HELL-- EM KNIRHS!
THEY ARE, RAY. THEY'RE THE JLA.
THEY'RE NOT GODS, ZATANNA. WELL, WONDER WOMAN, MAYBE, BUT...
THEY'RE JUST PEOPLE. VERY SPECIAL PEOPLE...BUT SOMETIMES, EVEN VERY SPECIAL PEOPLE DIE.
IF THEY'RE ALIVE, I'LL CRACK OPEN ATOMS WITH MY BARE HANDS TO BRING THEM HOME.
BUT IF THEY AREN'T...
AQUAMAN WENT THROUGH THAT PORTAL AND DISAPPEARED 3000 YEARS INTO THE PAST WITHOUT RETURNING. NEITHER DID HIS PEOPLE. SO WHAT DO WE DO?
WE SEND THE JLA RIGHT AFTER THEM, SIGHT UNSEEN, UNKNOWNS EVERYWHERE. BAD SCIENCE ALL AROUND.
I JUST WISH I KNEW FOR SURE... THERE'S SO MUCH OTHER WORK TO DO.
IT STRIKES ME THAT PROBLEMS MUST SEEM A LOT BIGGER WHEN YOU SPEND MOST OF YOUR TIME THE SIZE OF A PIGEON.
ME...I STILL BELIEVE IN MAGIC.

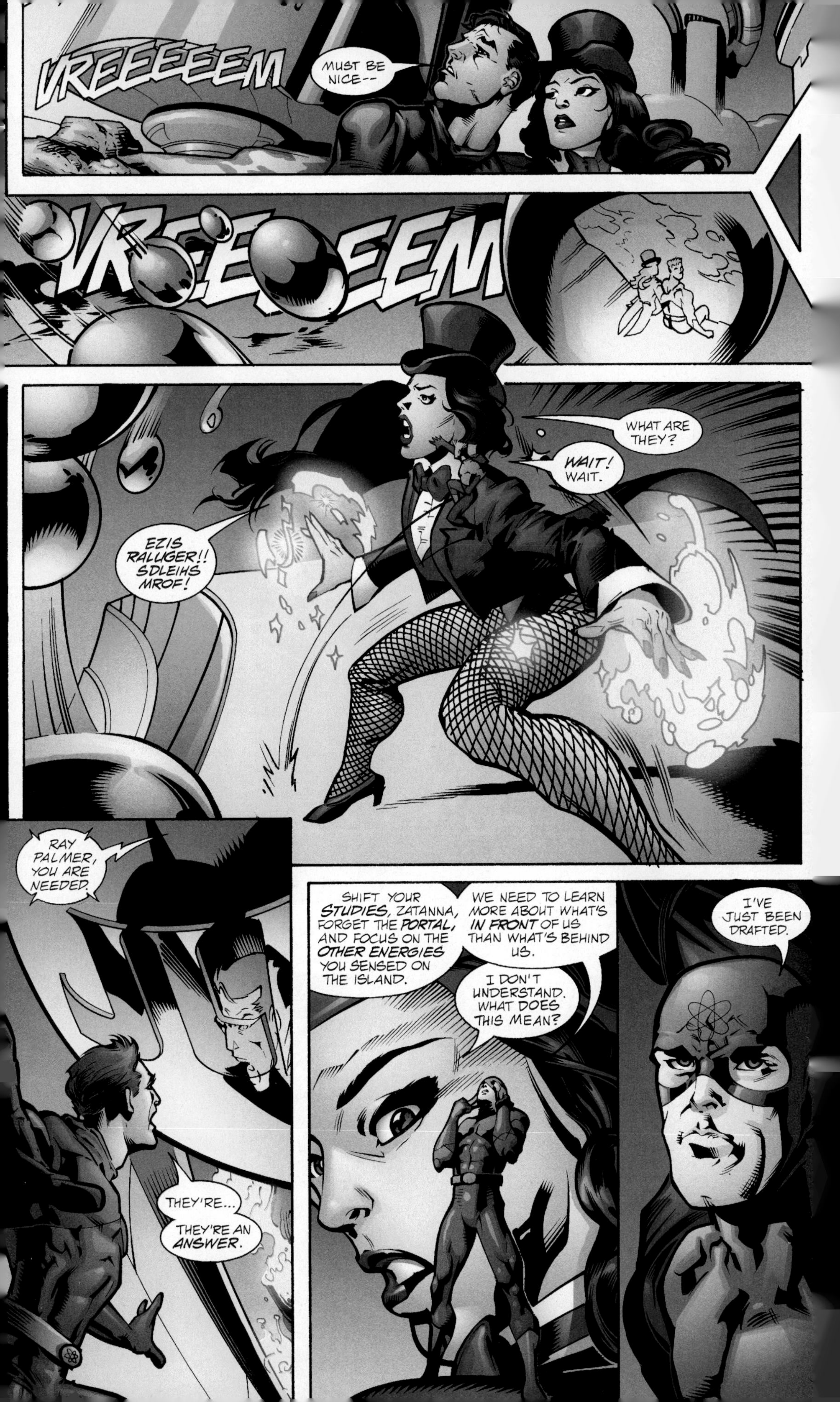
VREEEEEM
MUST BE NICE--
VREEEEEM
WHAT ARE THEY?
WAIT! WAIT.
EZIS RALUGER!! SDLEIHS MROF!
RAY PALMER, YOU ARE NEEDED.
THEY'RE...
THEY'RE AN ANSWER.
SHIFT YOUR STUDIES, ZATANNA, FORGET THE PORTAL, AND FOCUS ON THE OTHER ENERGIES YOU SENSED ON THE ISLAND.
WE NEED TO LEARN MORE ABOUT WHAT'S IN FRONT OF US THAN WHAT'S BEHIND US.
I DON'T UNDERSTAND. WHAT DOES THIS MEAN?
I'VE JUST BEEN DRAFTED.

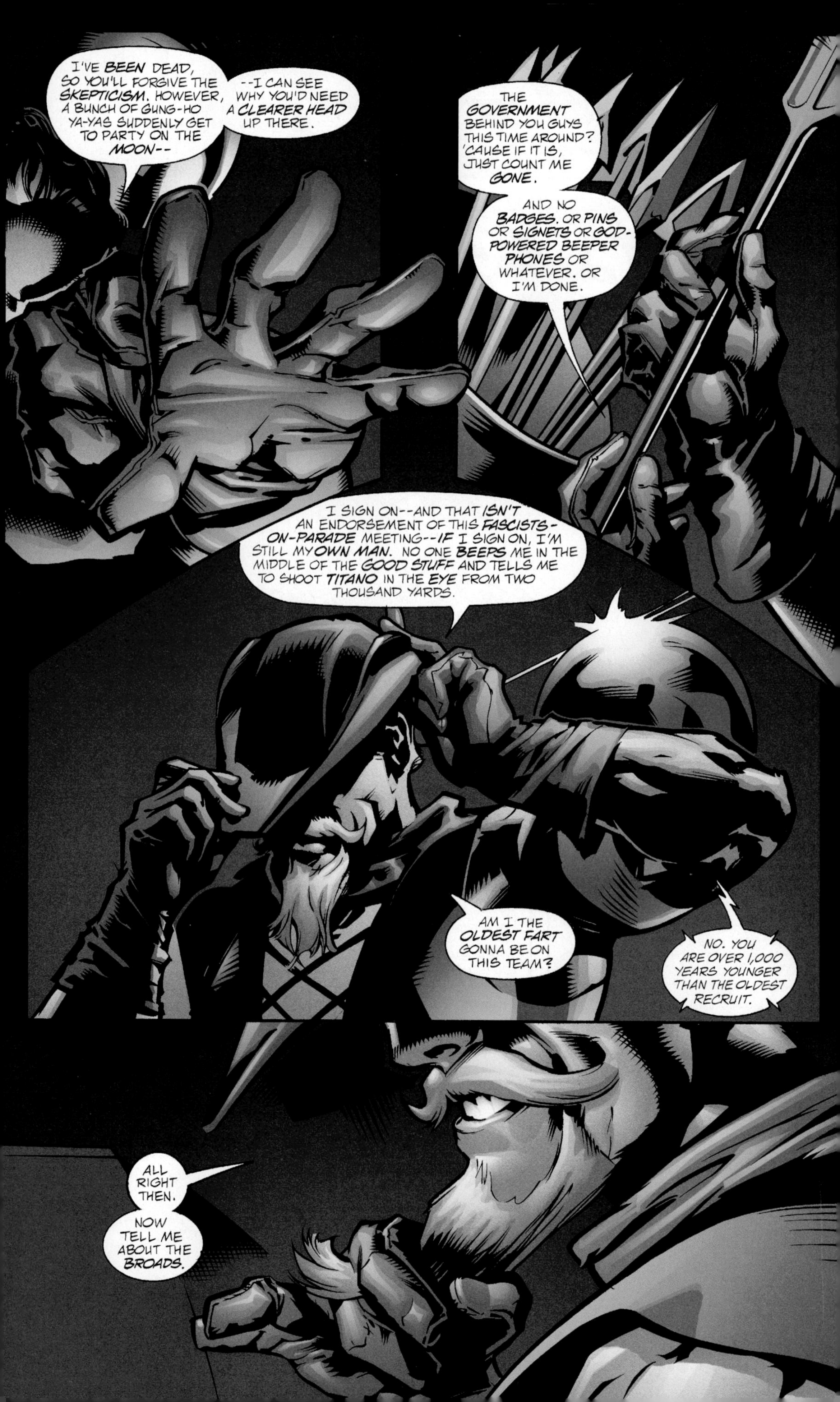

I'VE BEEN DEAD, SO YOU'LL FORGIVE THE SKEPTICISM. HOWEVER, A BUNCH OF GUNG-HO YA-YAS SUDDENLY GET TO PARTY ON THE MOON--
--I CAN SEE WHY YOU'D NEED A CLEARER HEAD UP THERE.
THE GOVERNMENT BEHIND YOU GUYS THIS TIME AROUND? 'CAUSE IF IT IS, JUST COUNT ME GONE.
AND NO BADGES. OR PINS OR SIGNETS OR GOD-POWERED BEEPER PHONES OR WHATEVER. OR I'M DONE.
I SIGN ON--AND THAT ISN'T AN ENDORSEMENT OF THIS FASCISTS-ON-PARADE MEETING--IF I SIGN ON, I'M STILL MY OWN MAN. NO ONE BEEPS ME IN THE MIDDLE OF THE GOOD STUFF AND TELLS ME TO SHOOT TITANO IN THE EYE FROM TWO THOUSAND YARDS.
AM I THE OLDEST FART GONNA BE ON THIS TEAM?
NO. YOU ARE OVER 1,000 YEARS YOUNGER THAN THE OLDEST RECRUIT.
ALL RIGHT THEN.
NOW TELL ME ABOUT THE BROADS.

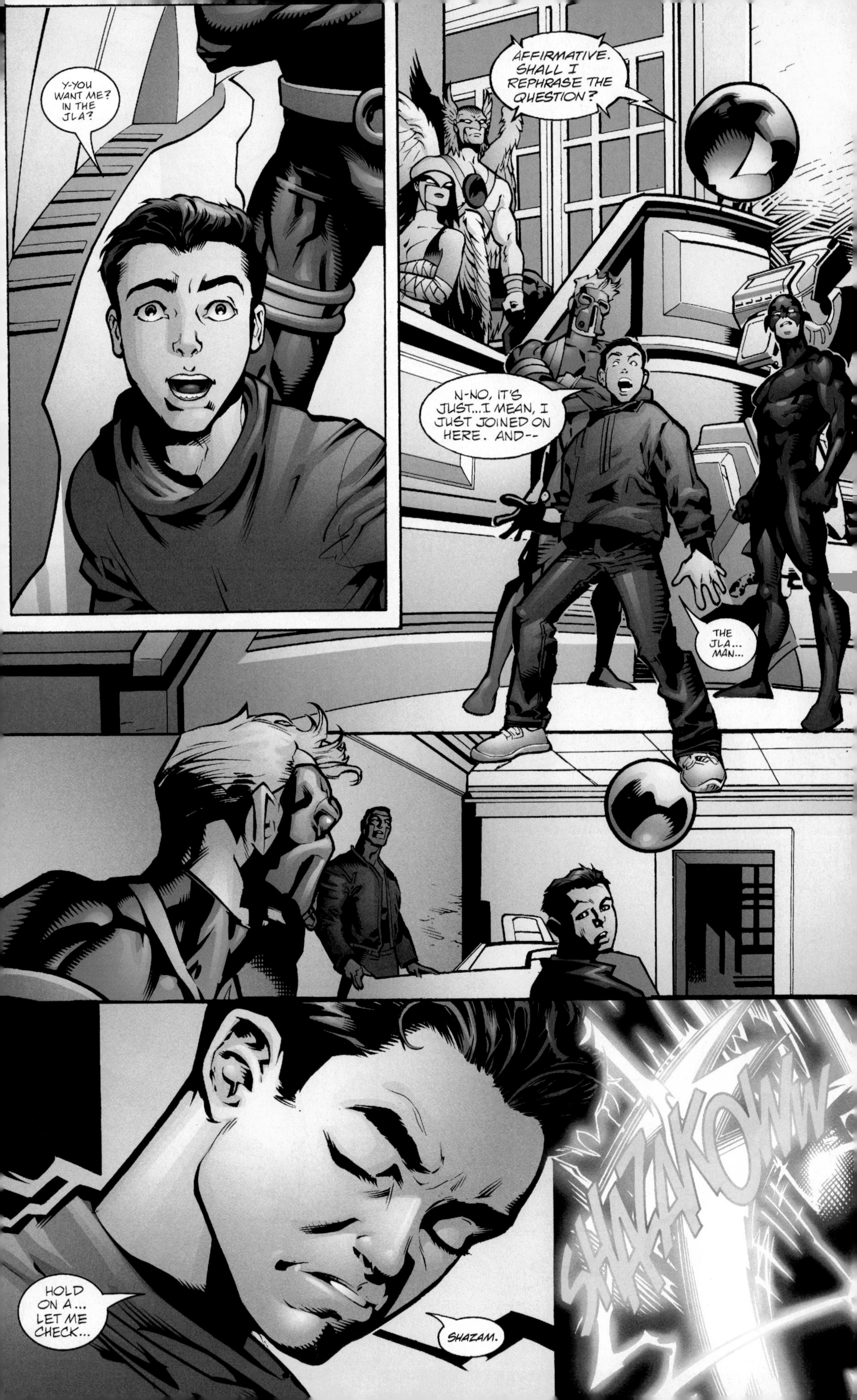
Y-YOU WANT ME? IN THE JLA?
AFFIRMATIVE. SHALL I REPHRASE THE QUESTION?
N-NO, IT'S JUST...I MEAN, I JUST JOINED ON HERE. AND--
THE JLA... MAN...
HOLD ON A... LET ME CHECK...
SHAZAM.
SHAZAKOWW

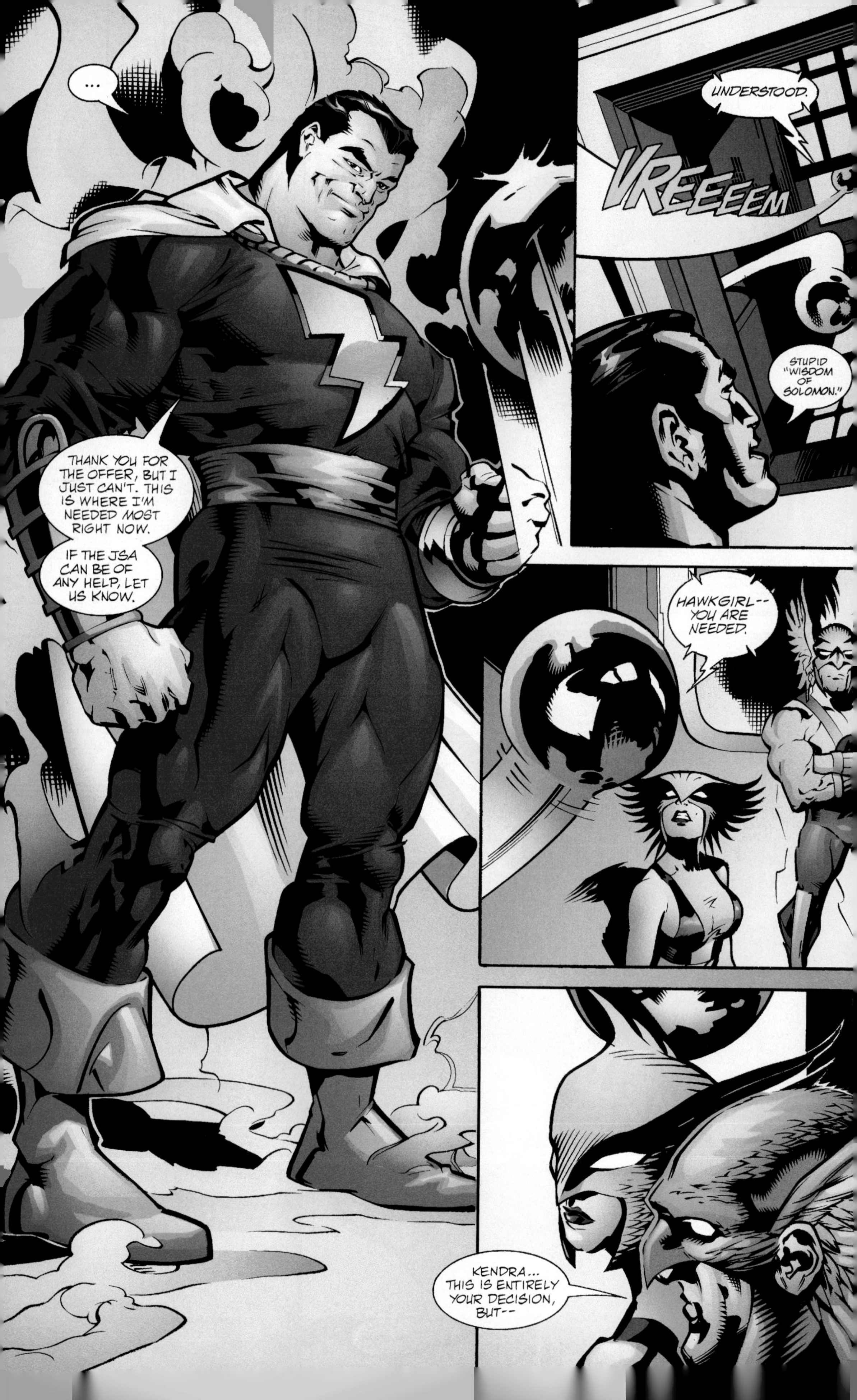
...
THANK YOU FOR THE OFFER, BUT I JUST CAN'T. THIS IS WHERE I'M NEEDED MOST RIGHT NOW.
IF THE JSA CAN BE OF ANY HELP, LET US KNOW.
UNDERSTOOD.
VREEEEM
STUPID "WISDOM OF SOLOMON."
HAWKGIRL-- YOU ARE NEEDED.
KENDRA... THIS IS ENTIRELY YOUR DECISION, BUT--

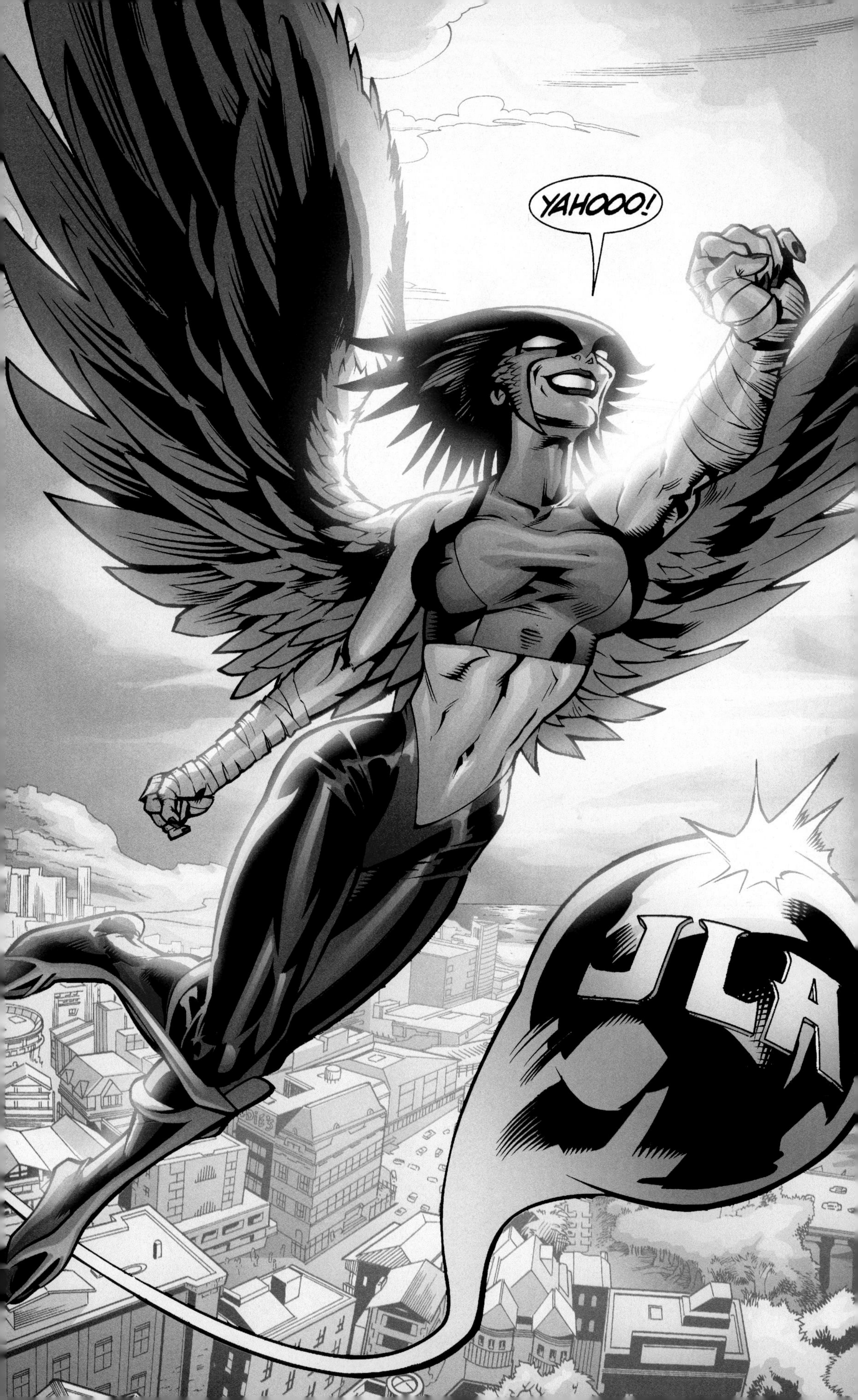
YAHOOO!
JLA

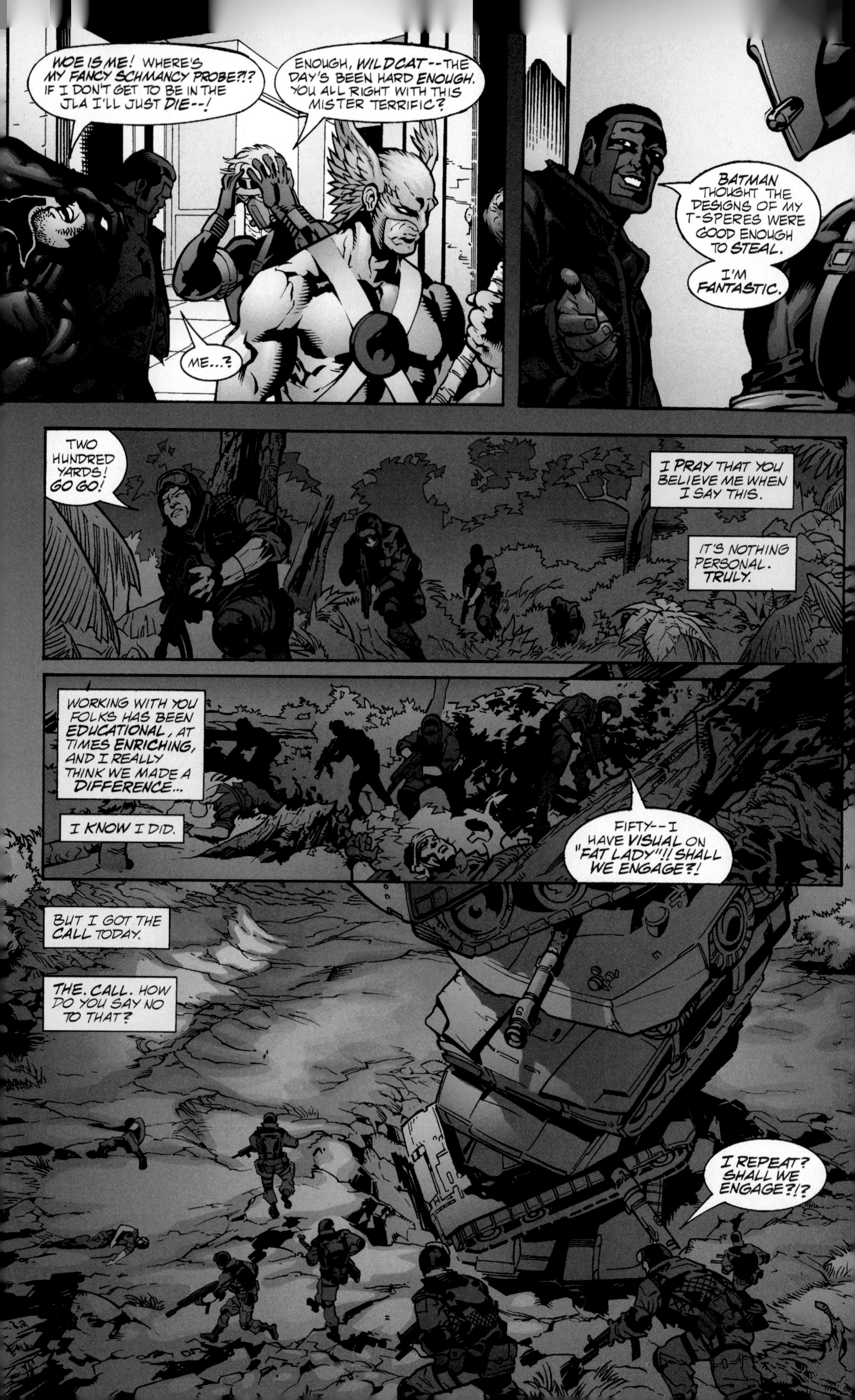
WOE IS ME! WHERE'S MY FANCY SCHMANCY PROBE?!? IF I DON'T GET TO BE IN THE JLA I'LL JUST DIE--!
ENOUGH, WILDCAT--THE DAY'S BEEN HARD ENOUGH. YOU ALL RIGHT WITH THIS MISTER TERRIFIC?
ME...?
BATMAN THOUGHT THE DESIGNS OF MY T-SPERES WERE GOOD ENOUGH TO STEAL.
I'M FANTASTIC.
TWO HUNDRED YARDS! GO GO!
I PRAY THAT YOU BELIEVE ME WHEN I SAY THIS.
IT'S NOTHING PERSONAL. TRULY.
WORKING WITH YOU FOLKS HAS BEEN EDUCATIONAL, AT TIMES ENRICHING, AND I REALLY THINK WE MADE A DIFFERENCE...
I KNOW I DID.
FIFTY--I HAVE VISUAL ON "FAT LADY"!! SHALL WE ENGAGE?!
BUT I GOT THE CALL TODAY.
THE. CALL. HOW DO YOU SAY NO TO THAT?
I REPEAT? SHALL WE ENGAGE?!?

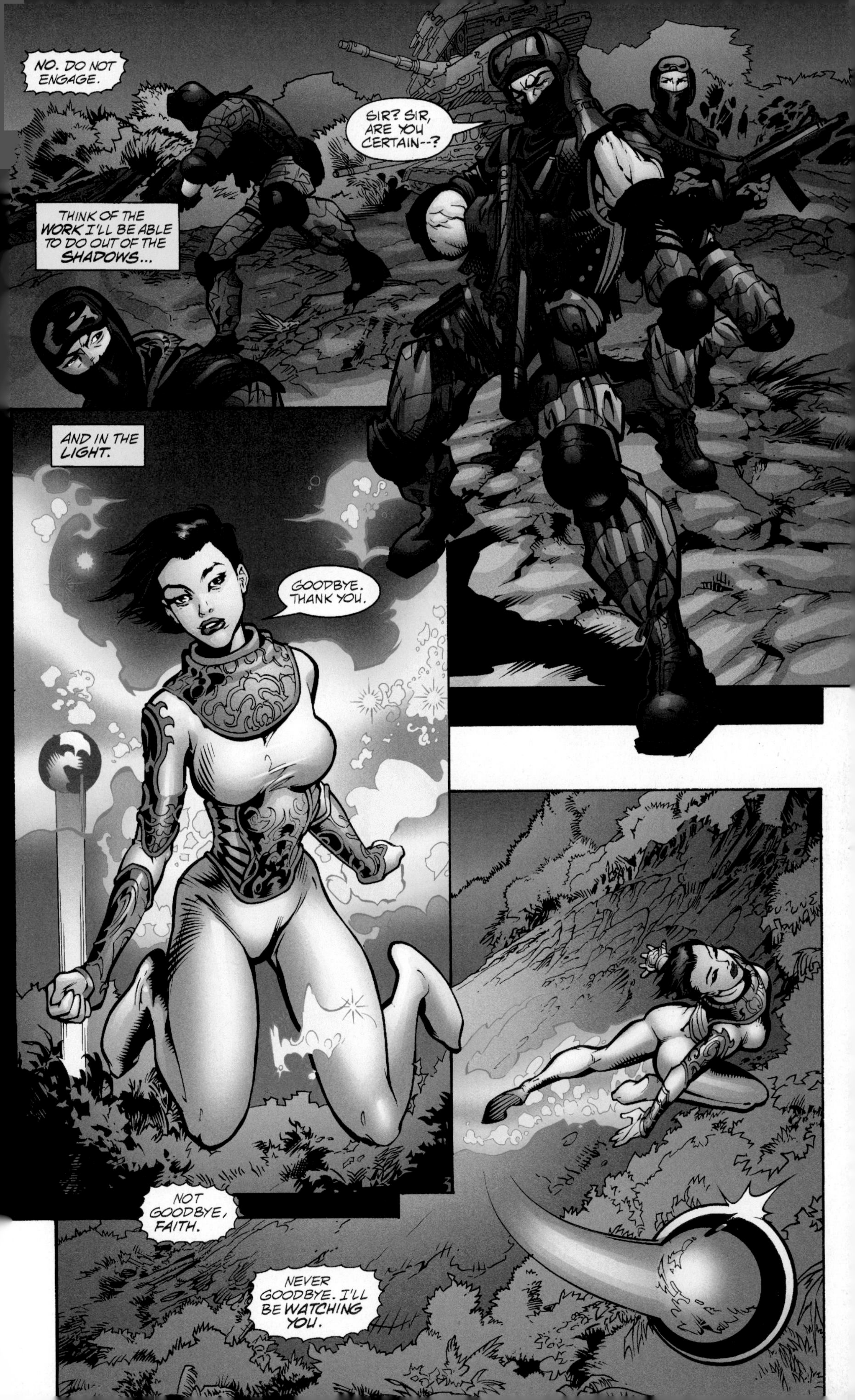
NO. DO NOT ENGAGE.
SIR? SIR, ARE YOU CERTAIN--?
THINK OF THE WORK I'LL BE ABLE TO DO OUT OF THE SHADOWS...
AND IN THE LIGHT.
GOODBYE. THANK YOU.
NOT GOODBYE, FAITH.
NEVER GOODBYE. I'LL BE WATCHING YOU.

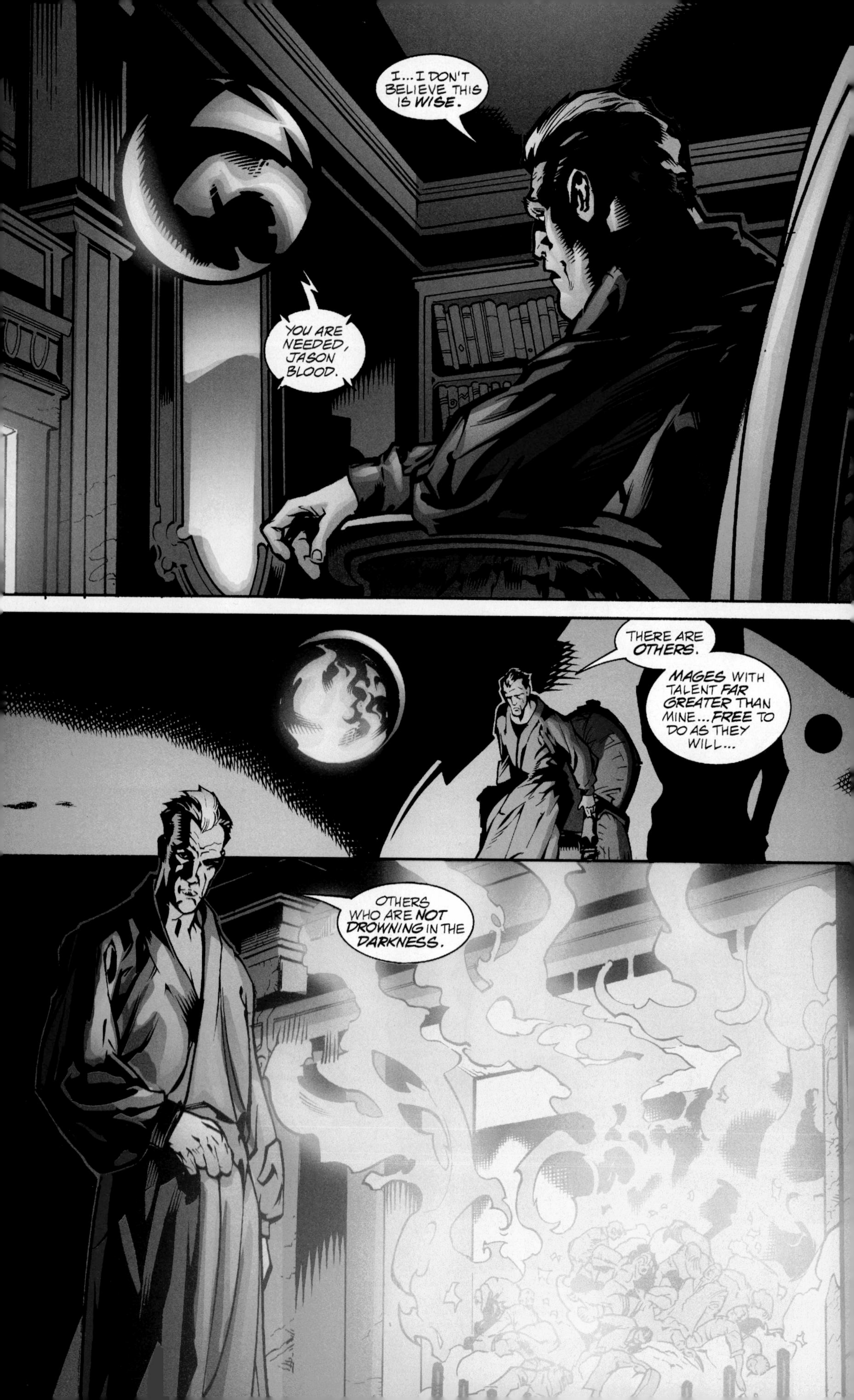
I...I DON'T BELIEVE THIS IS WISE.
YOU ARE NEEDED, JASON BLOOD.
THERE ARE OTHERS.
MAGES WITH TALENT FAR GREATER THAN MINE...FREE TO DO AS THEY WILL...
OTHERS WHO ARE NOT DROWNING IN THE DARKNESS.

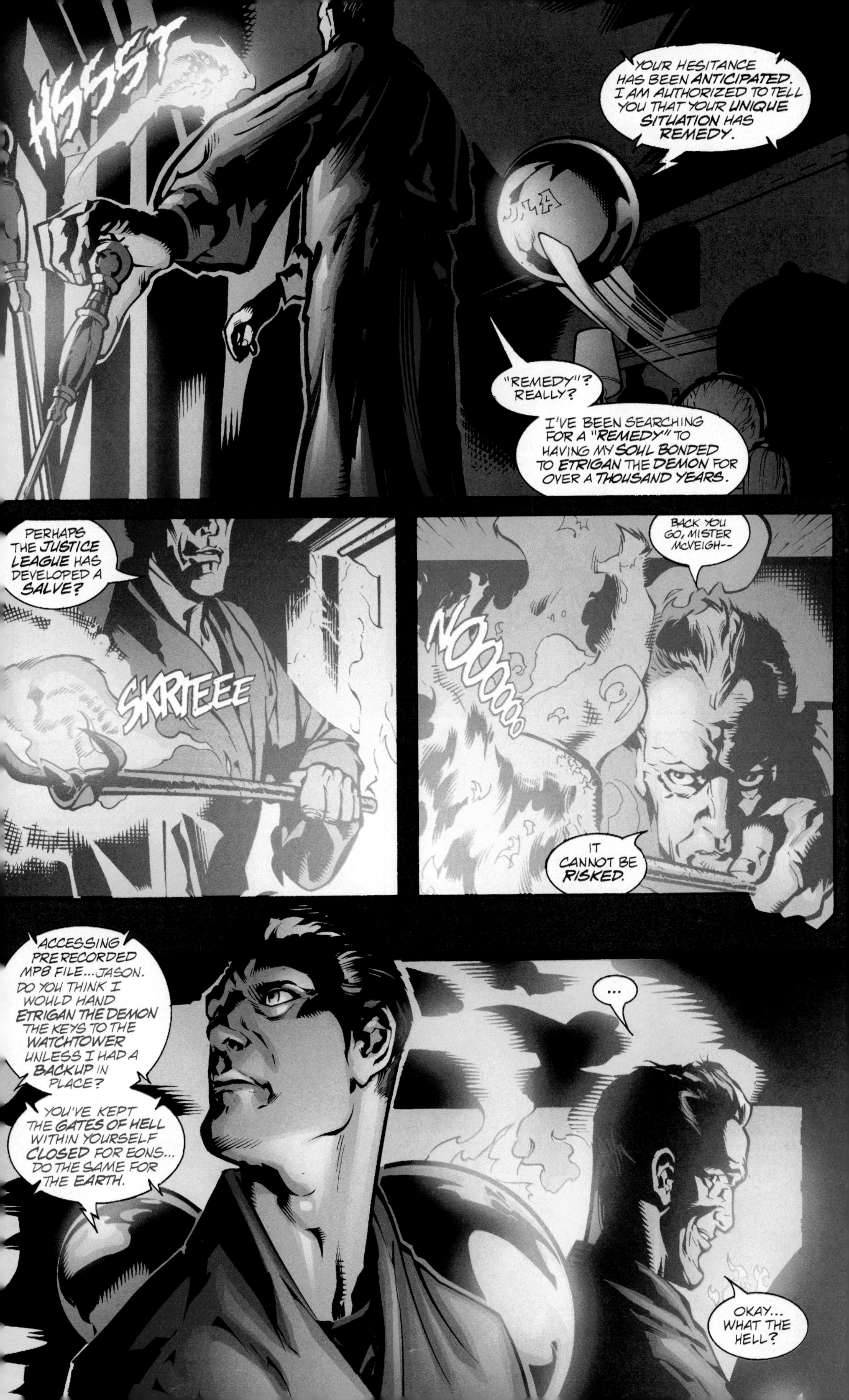
HSSST
YOUR HESITANCE HAS BEEN ANTICIPATED. I AM AUTHORIZED TO TELL YOU THAT YOUR UNIQUE SITUATION HAS REMEDY.
JLA
"REMEDY"? REALLY?
I'VE BEEN SEARCHING FOR A "REMEDY" TO HAVING MY SOUL BONDED TO ETRIGAN THE DEMON FOR OVER A THOUSAND YEARS.
PERHAPS THE JUSTICE LEAGUE HAS DEVELOPED A SALVE?
SKRTEEE
BACK YOU GO, MISTER McVEIGH--
NOOOOOO
IT CANNOT BE RISKED.
ACCESSING PRERECORDED MP8 FILE...JASON. DO YOU THINK I WOULD HAND ETRIGAN THE DEMON THE KEYS TO THE WATCHTOWER UNLESS I HAD A BACKUP IN PLACE?
YOU'VE KEPT THE GATES OF HELL WITHIN YOURSELF CLOSED FOR EONS... DO THE SAME FOR THE EARTH.
...
OKAY... WHAT THE HELL?

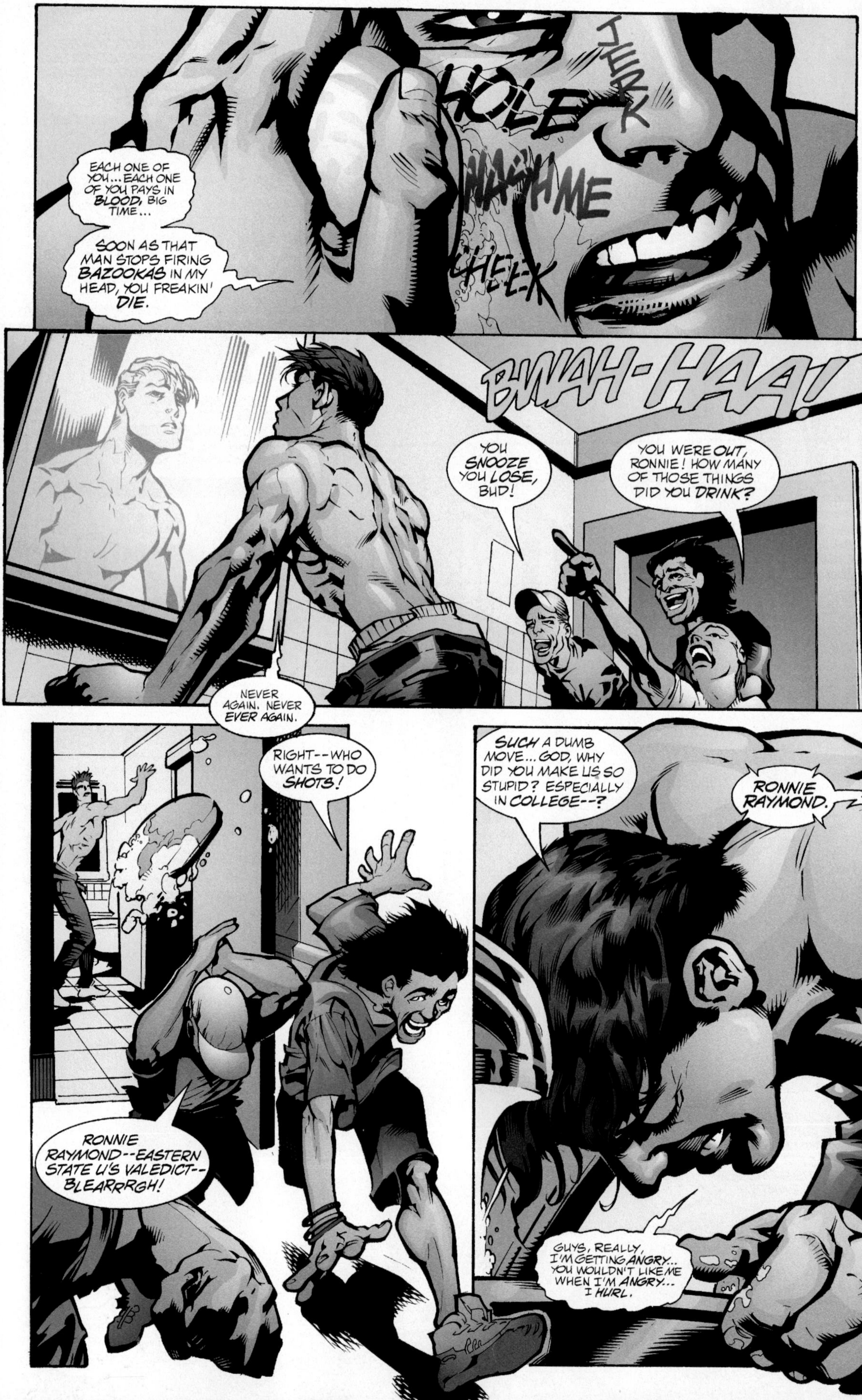
JERK
HOLE
EACH ONE OF YOU... EACH ONE OF YOU PAYS IN BLOOD, BIG TIME...
SOON AS THAT MAN STOPS FIRING BAZOOKAS IN MY HEAD, YOU FREAKIN' DIE.
BWAH-HAA!
YOU SNOOZE YOU LOSE, BUD!
YOU WERE OUT, RONNIE! HOW MANY OF THOSE THINGS DID YOU DRINK?
NEVER AGAIN. NEVER EVER AGAIN.
RIGHT--WHO WANTS TO DO SHOTS!
RONNIE RAYMOND--EASTERN STATE U'S VALEDICT--BLEARRRGH!
SUCH A DUMB MOVE... GOD, WHY DID YOU MAKE US SO STUPID? ESPECIALLY IN COLLEGE--?
RONNIE RAYMOND.
GUYS, REALLY, I'M GETTING ANGRY... YOU WOULDN'T LIKE ME WHEN I'M ANGRY... I HURL.

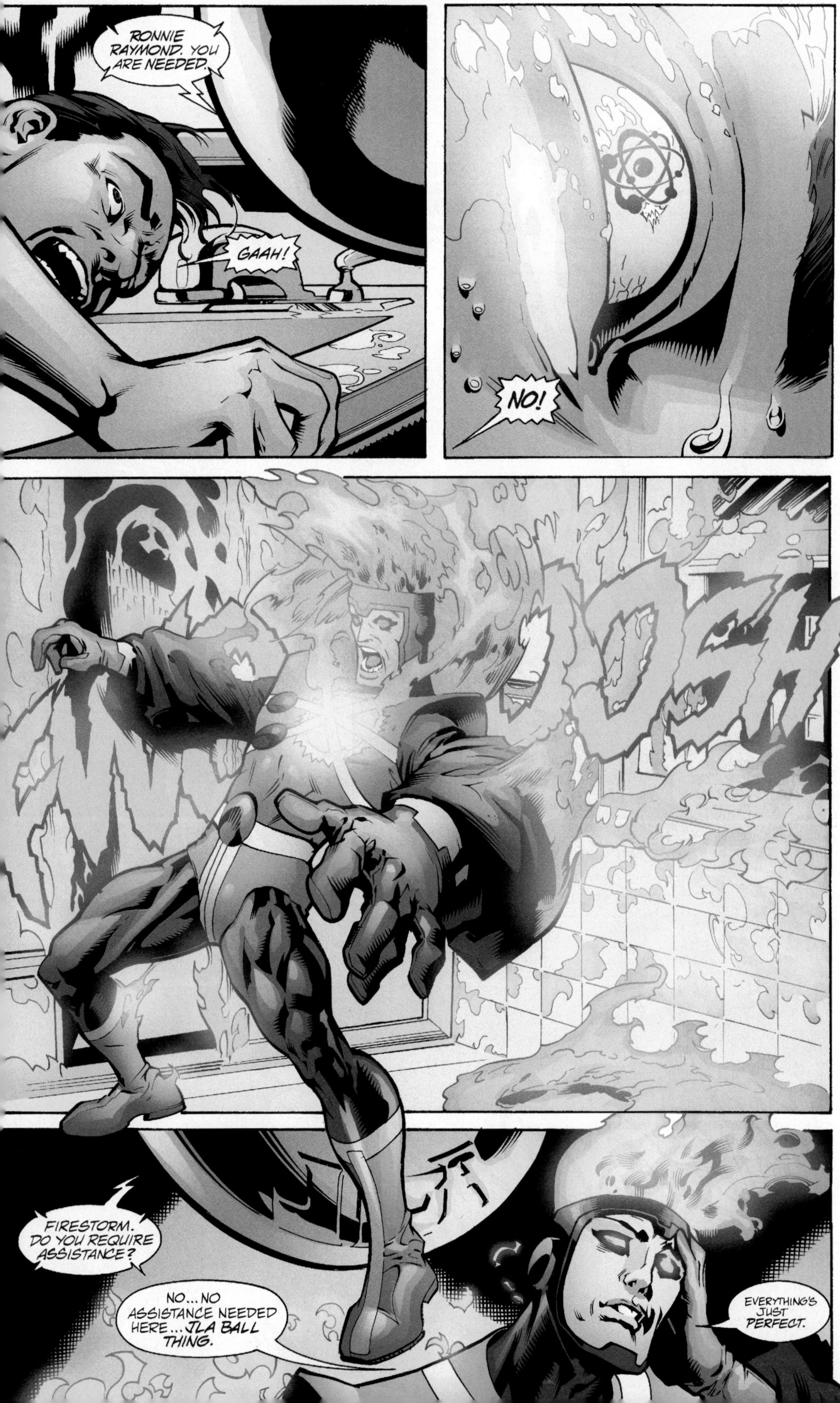
RONNIE RAYMOND. YOU ARE NEEDED.
GAAH!
NO!
FIRESTORM. DO YOU REQUIRE ASSISTANCE?
NO... NO ASSISTANCE NEEDED HERE... JLA BALL THING.
EVERYTHING'S JUST PERFECT.

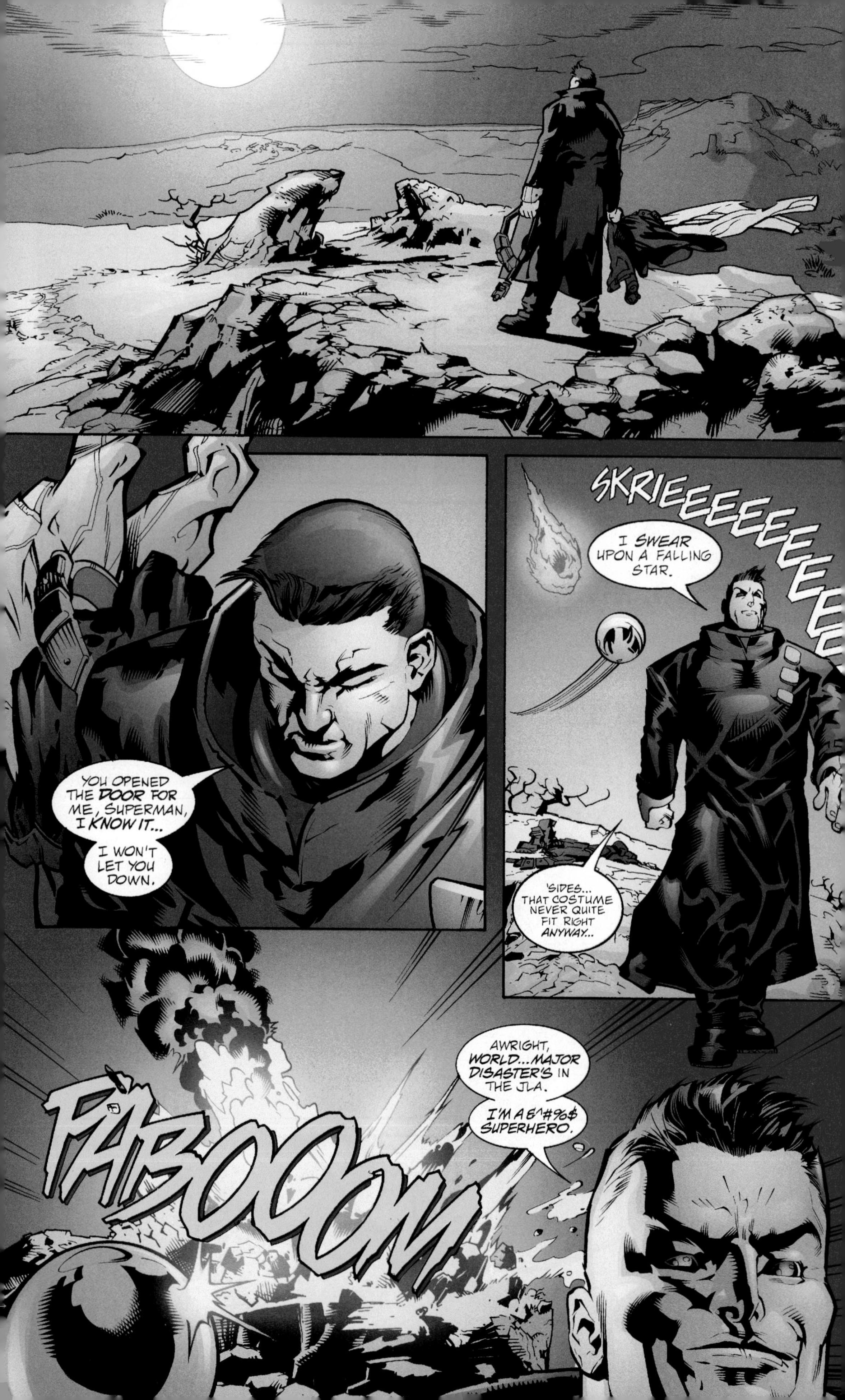

YOU OPENED THE DOOR FOR ME, SUPERMAN, I KNOW IT...
I WON'T LET YOU DOWN.
SKRIEEEEEEEEEE
I SWEAR UPON A FALLING STAR.
'SIDES... THAT COSTUME NEVER QUITE FIT RIGHT ANYWAY...
FABOOOM
AWRIGHT, WORLD... MAJOR DISASTER'S IN THE JLA.
I'M A &^#%$ SUPERHERO.

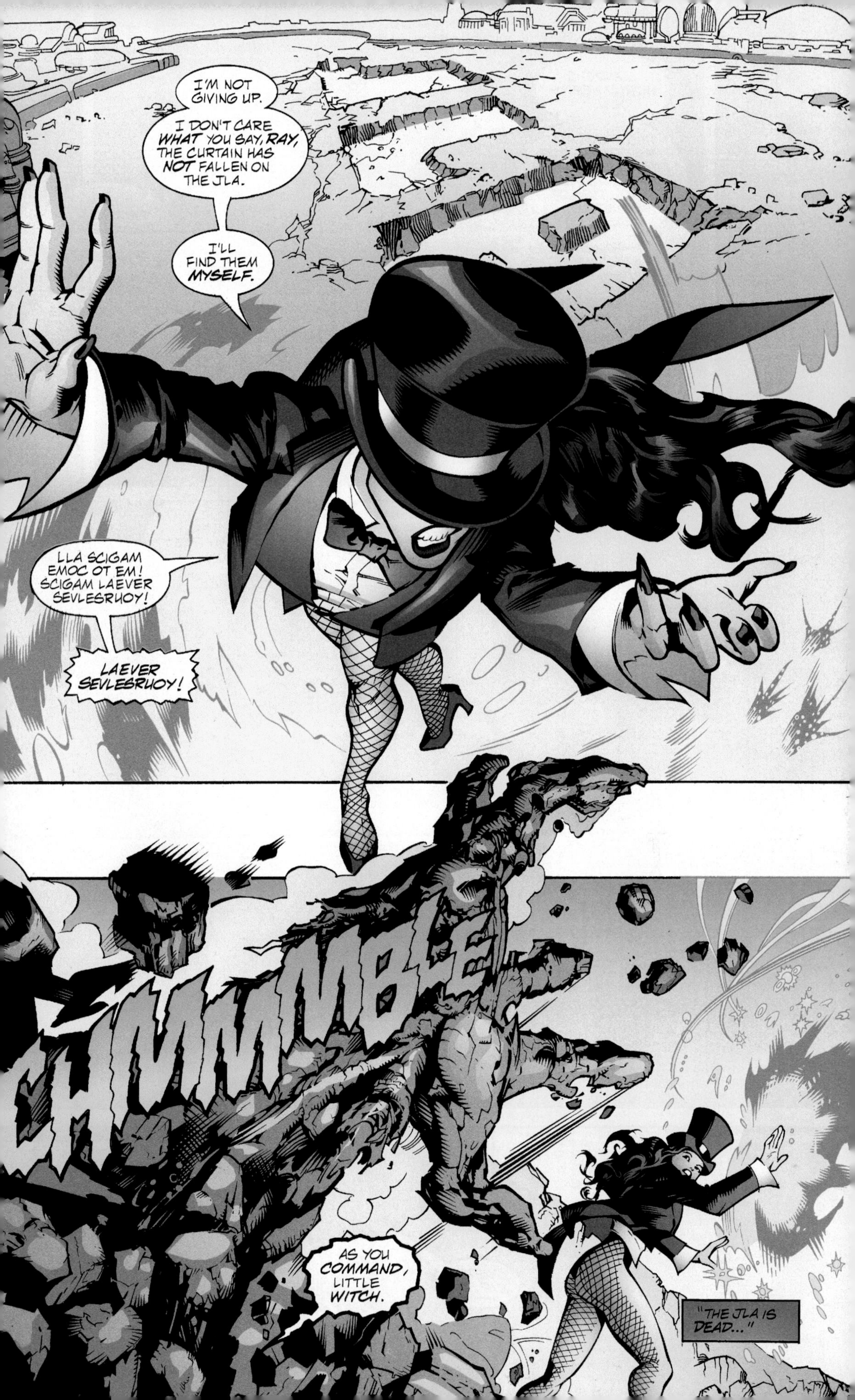
I'M NOT GIVING UP.
I DON'T CARE WHAT YOU SAY, RAY, THE CURTAIN HAS NOT FALLEN ON THE JLA.
I'LL FIND THEM MYSELF.
LLA SCIGAM EMOC OT EM! SCIGAM LAEVER SEVLESRUOY!
LAEVER SEVLESRUOY!
CHMMMBLE
AS YOU COMMAND, LITTLE WITCH.
"THE JLA IS DEAD..."

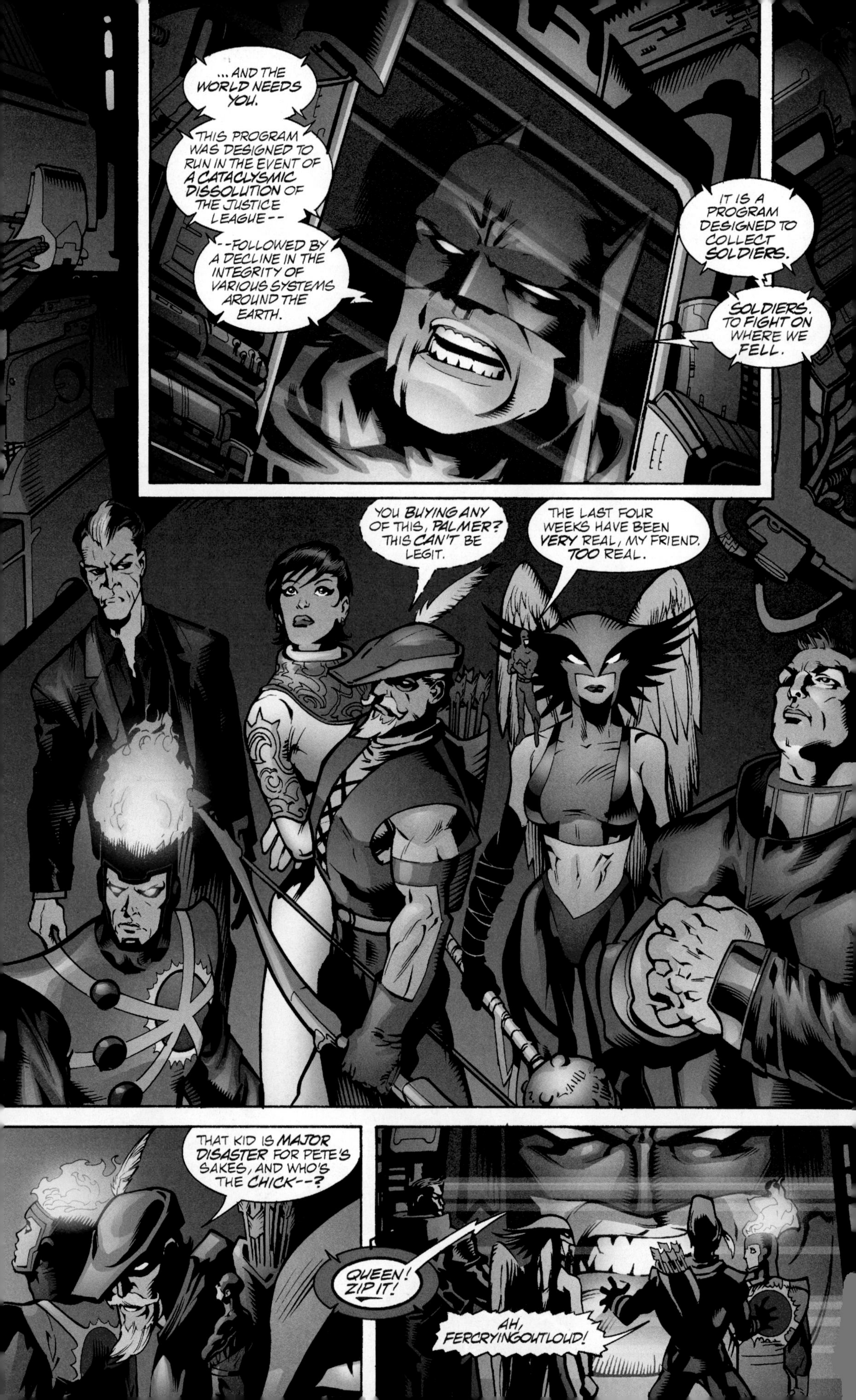
...AND THE WORLD NEEDS YOU.
THIS PROGRAM WAS DESIGNED TO RUN IN THE EVENT OF A CATACLYSMIC DISSOLUTION OF THE JUSTICE LEAGUE--
--FOLLOWED BY A DECLINE IN THE INTEGRITY OF VARIOUS SYSTEMS AROUND THE EARTH.
IT IS A PROGRAM DESIGNED TO COLLECT SOLDIERS.
SOLDIERS. TO FIGHT ON WHERE WE FELL.
YOU BUYING ANY OF THIS, PALMER? THIS CAN'T BE LEGIT.
THE LAST FOUR WEEKS HAVE BEEN VERY REAL, MY FRIEND. TOO REAL.
THAT KID IS MAJOR DISASTER FOR PETE'S SAKES, AND WHO'S THE CHICK--?
QUEEN! ZIP IT!
AH, FERCRYINGOUTLOUD!

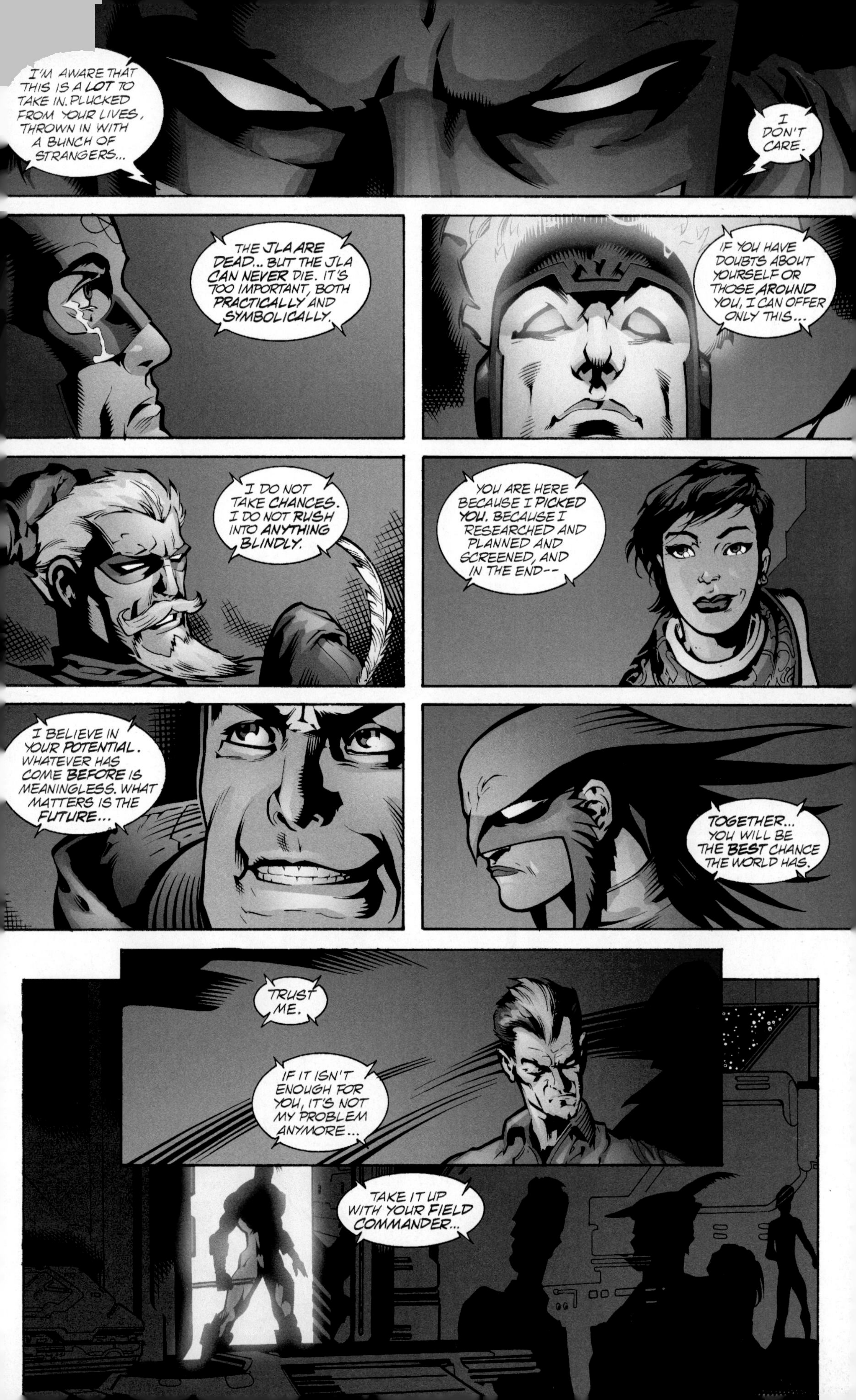
I'M AWARE THAT THIS IS A LOT TO TAKE IN. PLUCKED FROM YOUR LIVES, THROWN IN WITH A BUNCH OF STRANGERS...
I DON'T CARE.
THE JLA ARE DEAD... BUT THE JLA CAN NEVER DIE. IT'S TOO IMPORTANT, BOTH PRACTICALLY AND SYMBOLICALLY.
IF YOU HAVE DOUBTS ABOUT YOURSELF OR THOSE AROUND YOU, I CAN OFFER ONLY THIS...
I DO NOT TAKE CHANCES. I DO NOT RUSH INTO ANYTHING BLINDLY.
YOU ARE HERE BECAUSE I PICKED YOU. BECAUSE I RESEARCHED AND PLANNED AND SCREENED, AND IN THE END--
I BELIEVE IN YOUR POTENTIAL. WHATEVER HAS COME BEFORE IS MEANINGLESS. WHAT MATTERS IS THE FUTURE...
TOGETHER... YOU WILL BE THE BEST CHANCE THE WORLD HAS.
TRUST ME.
IF IT ISN'T ENOUGH FOR YOU, IT'S NOT MY PROBLEM ANYMORE...
TAKE IT UP WITH YOUR FIELD COMMANDER...

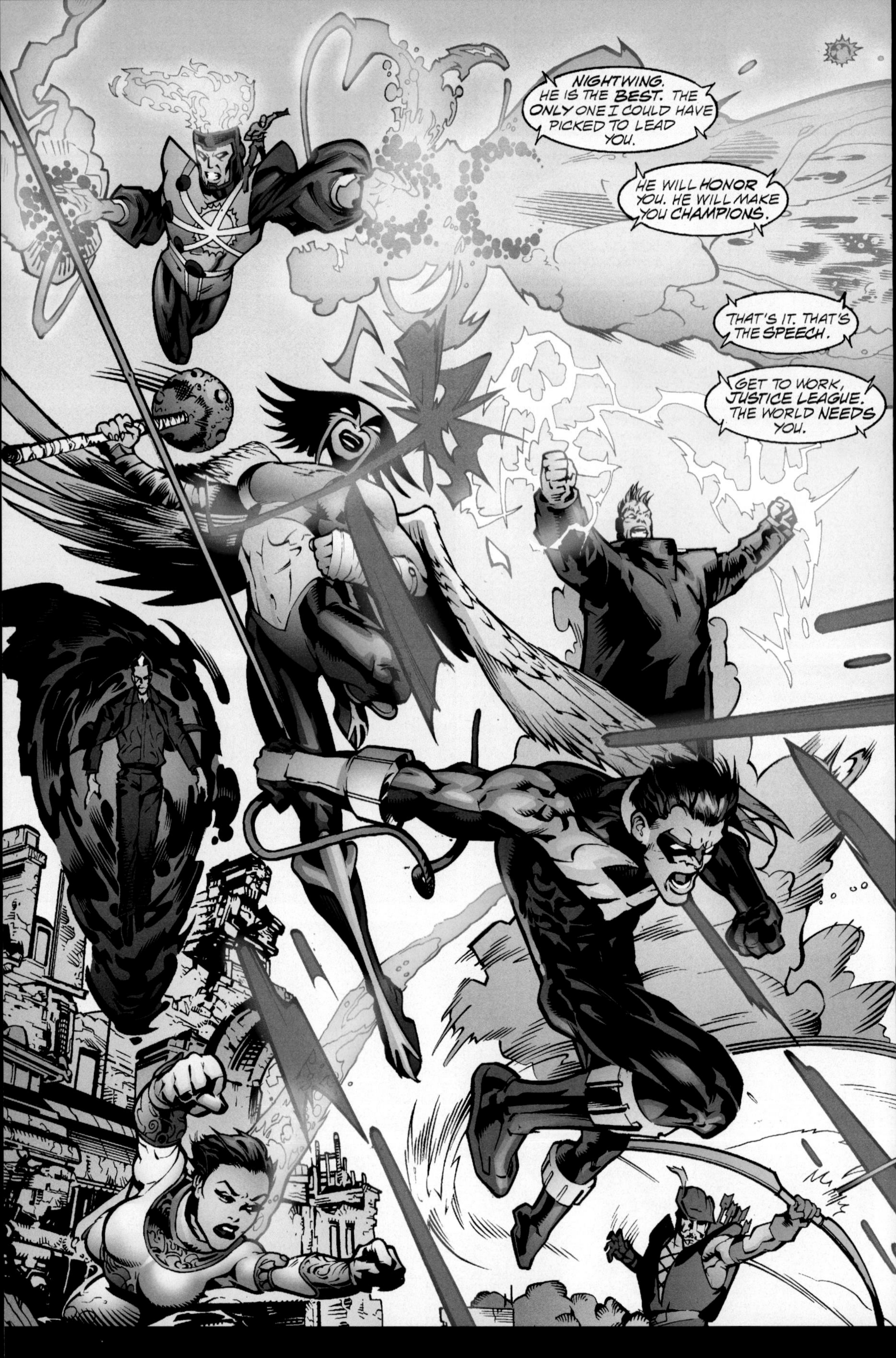
NIGHTWING. HE IS THE BEST. THE ONLY ONE I COULD HAVE PICKED TO LEAD YOU.
HE WILL HONOR YOU. HE WILL MAKE YOU CHAMPIONS.
THAT'S IT. THAT'S THE SPEECH.
GET TO WORK, JUSTICE LEAGUE. THE WORLD NEEDS YOU.

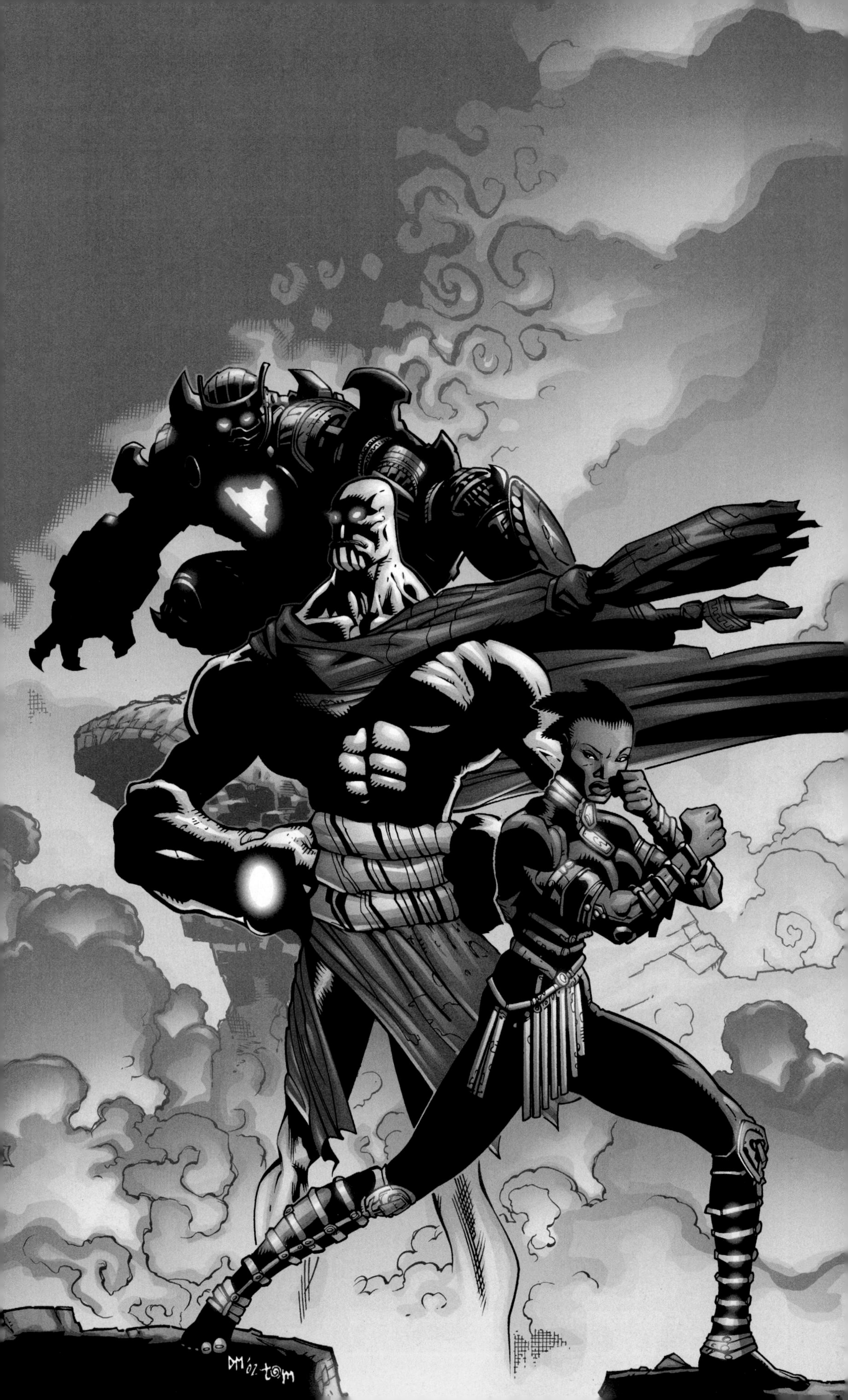

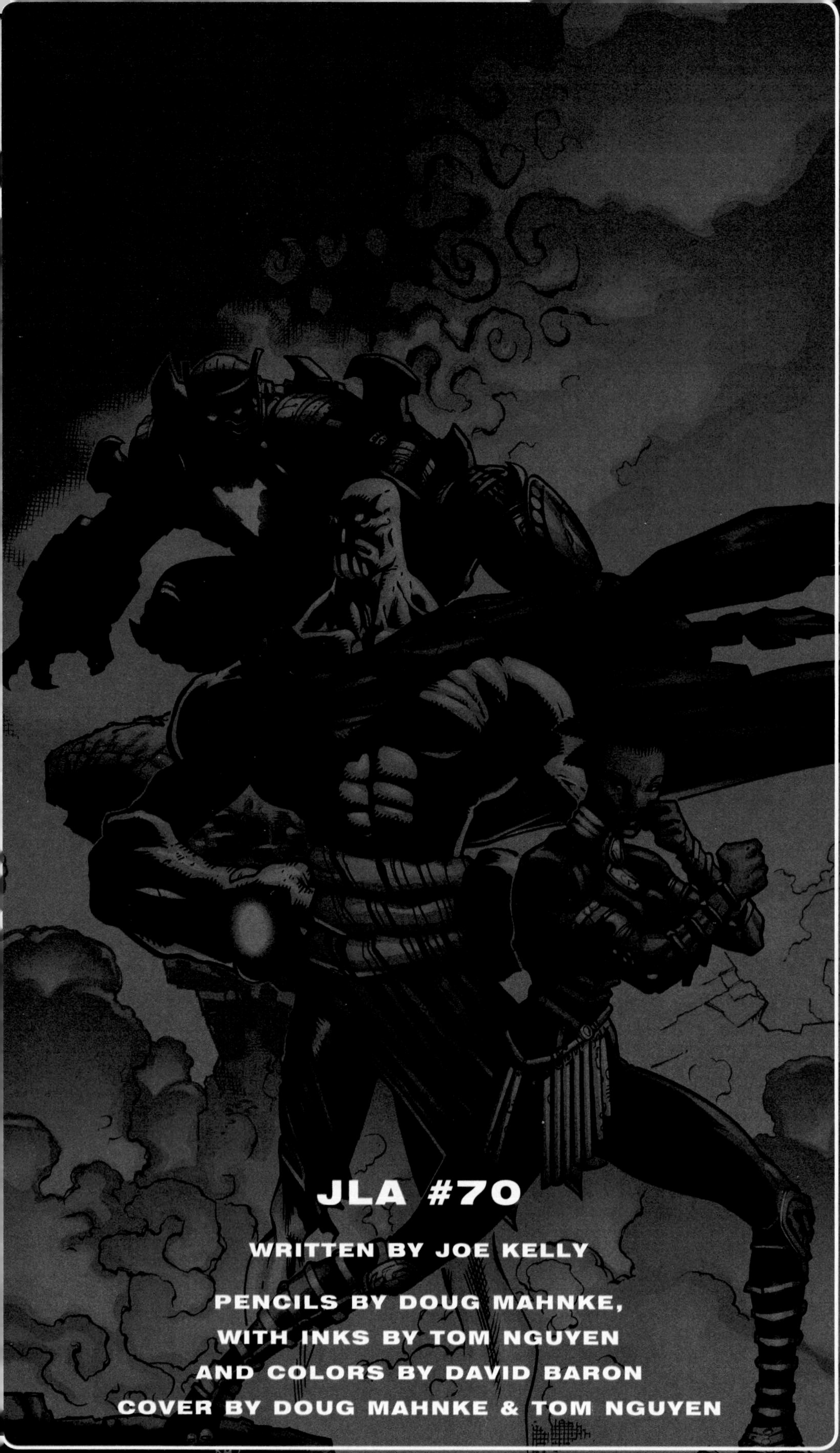

JLA #70

WRITTEN BY JOE KELLY

PENCILS BY DOUG MAHNKE,
WITH INKS BY TOM NGUYEN
AND COLORS BY DAVID BARON
COVER BY DOUG MAHNKE & TOM NGUYEN

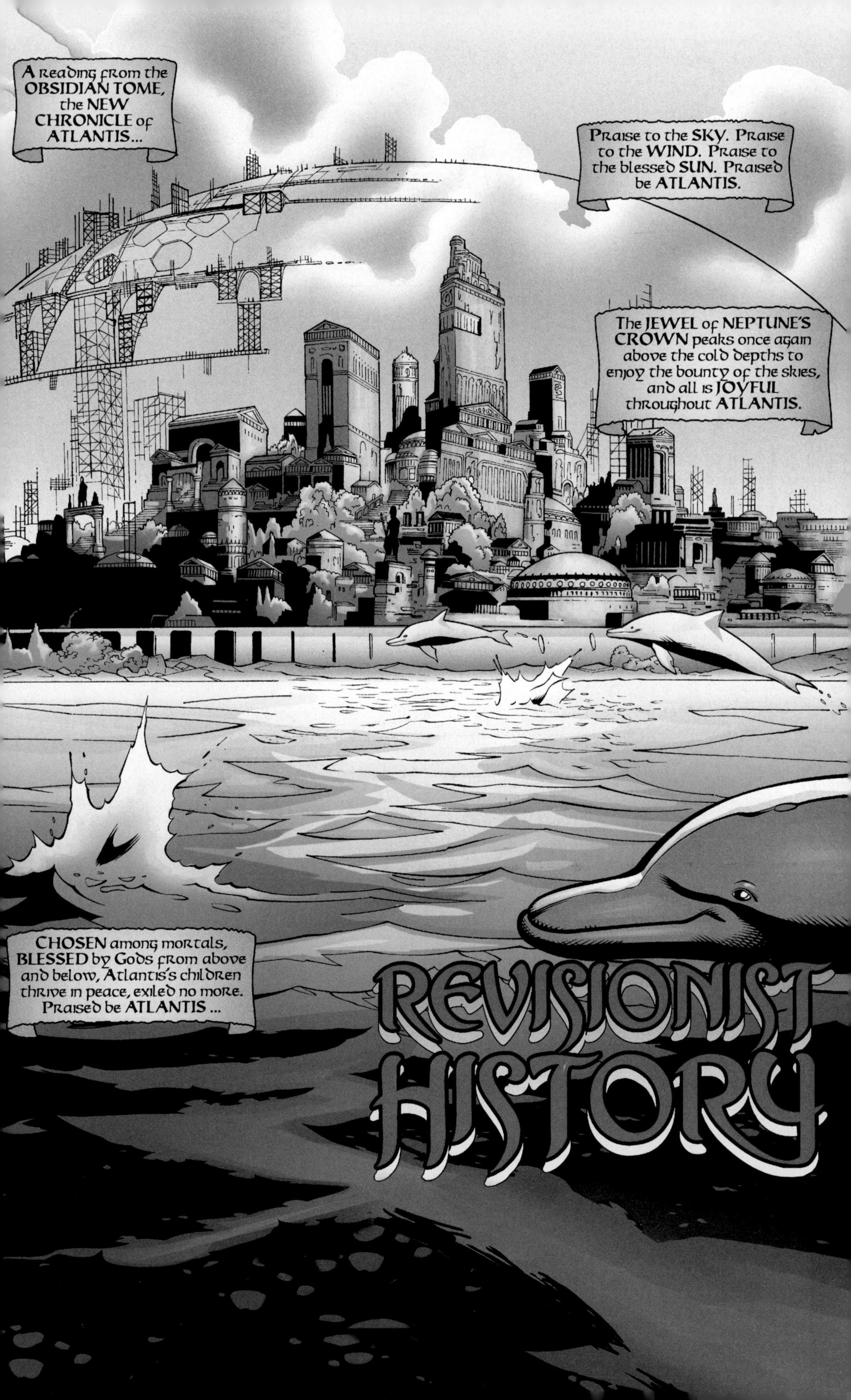
A reading from the OBSIDIAN TOME, the NEW CHRONICLE of ATLANTIS...
Praise to the SKY. Praise to the WIND. Praise to the blessed SUN. Praised be ATLANTIS.
The JEWEL of NEPTUNE'S CROWN peaks once again above the cold depths to enjoy the bounty of the skies, and all is JOYFUL throughout ATLANTIS.
CHOSEN among mortals, BLESSED by Gods from above and below, Atlantis's children thrive in peace, exiled no more. Praised be ATLANTIS ...
REVISIONIST HISTORY

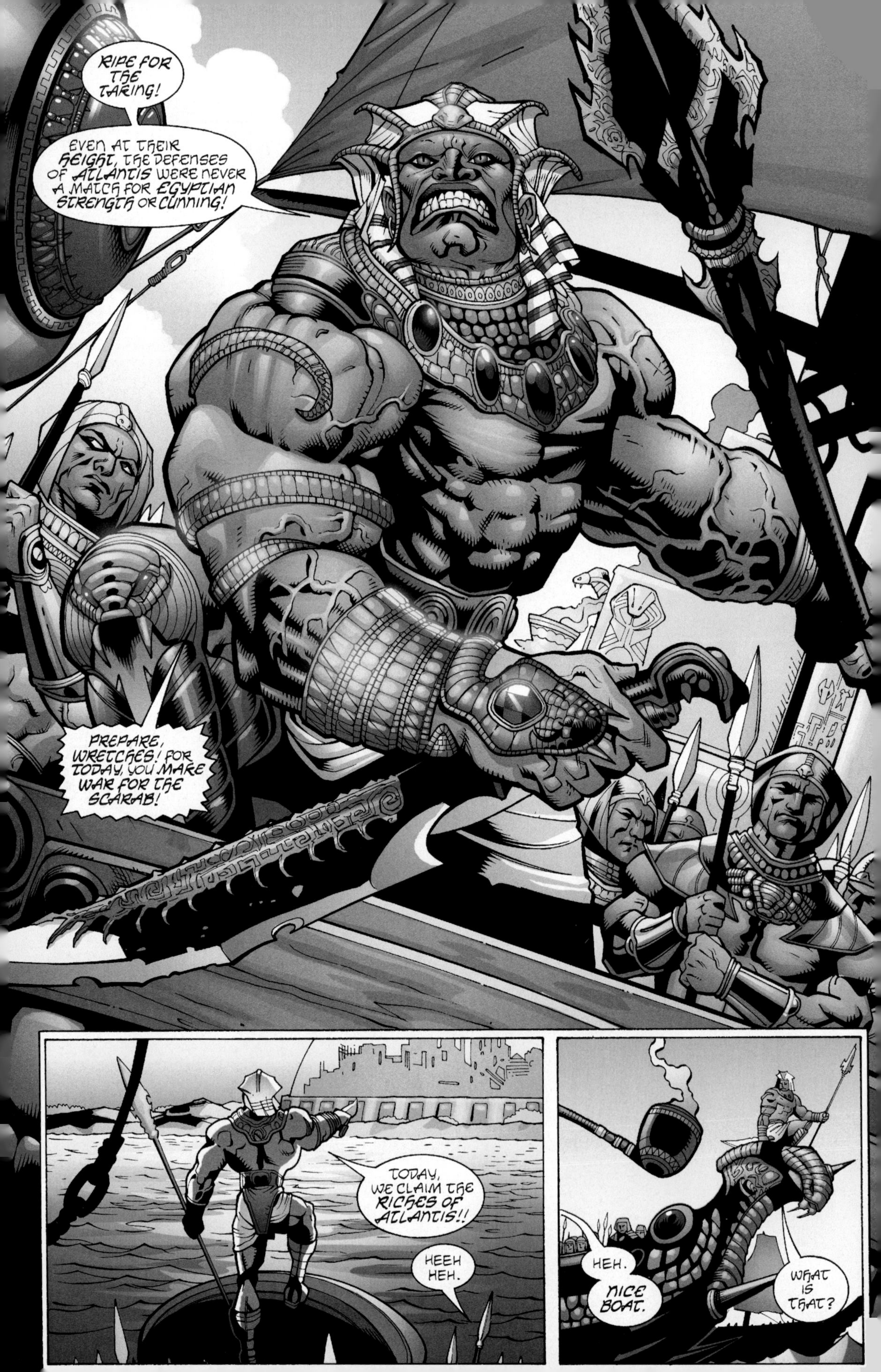
RIPE FOR THE TAKING!
EVEN AT THEIR HEIGHT, THE DEFENSES OF ATLANTIS WERE NEVER A MATCH FOR EGYPTIAN STRENGTH OR CUNNING!
PREPARE, WRETCHES! FOR TODAY, YOU MAKE WAR FOR THE SCARAB!
TODAY, WE CLAIM THE RICHES OF ATLANTIS!!
HEEH HEH.
HEH. NICE BOAT.
WHAT IS THAT?

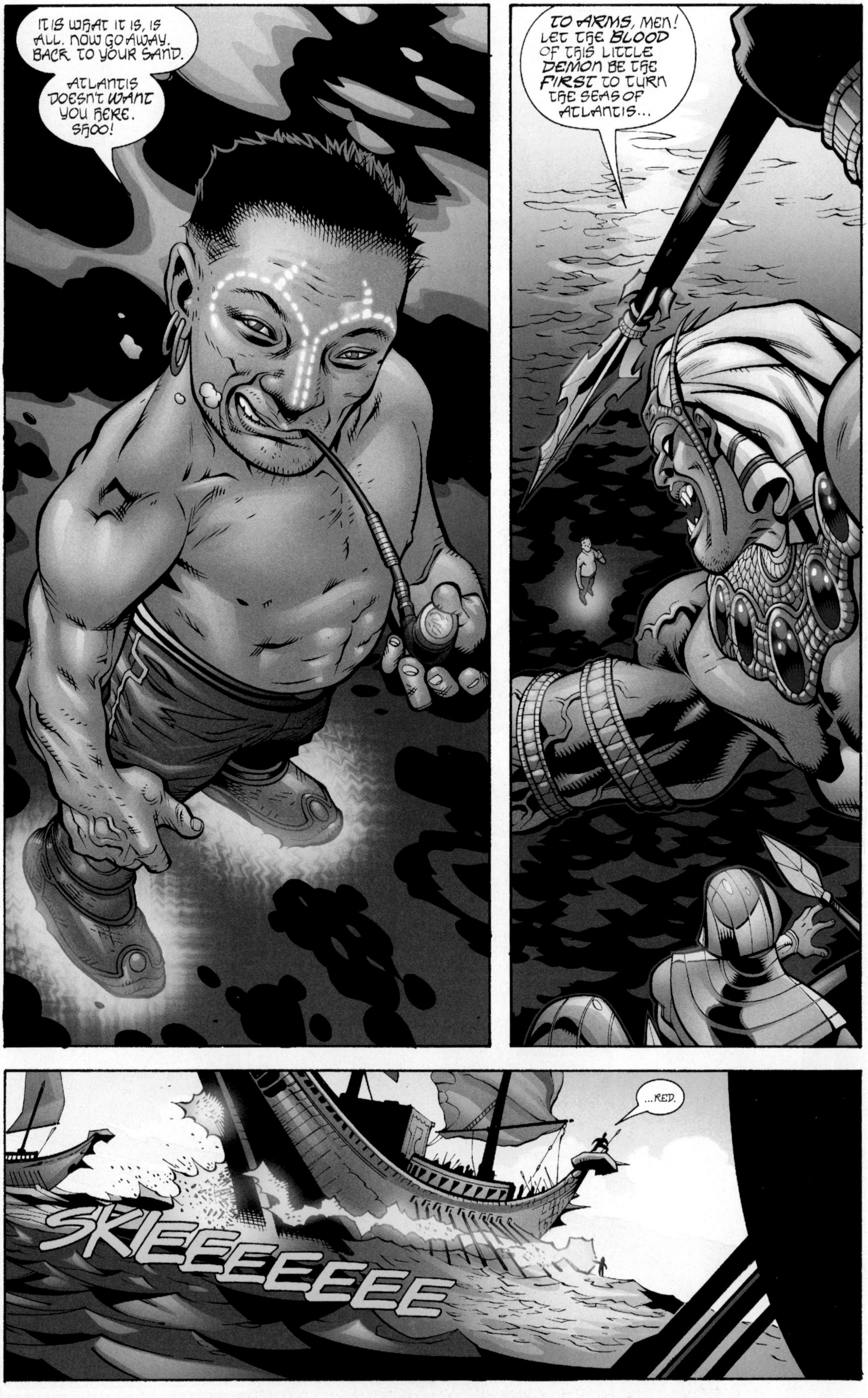
IT IS WHAT IT IS, IS ALL. NOW GO AWAY. BACK TO YOUR SAND.
ATLANTIS DOESN'T WANT YOU HERE. SHOO!
TO ARMS, MEN! LET THE BLOOD OF THIS LITTLE DEMON BE THE FIRST TO TURN THE SEAS OF ATLANTIS...
...RED.
SKIEEEEEEEEE

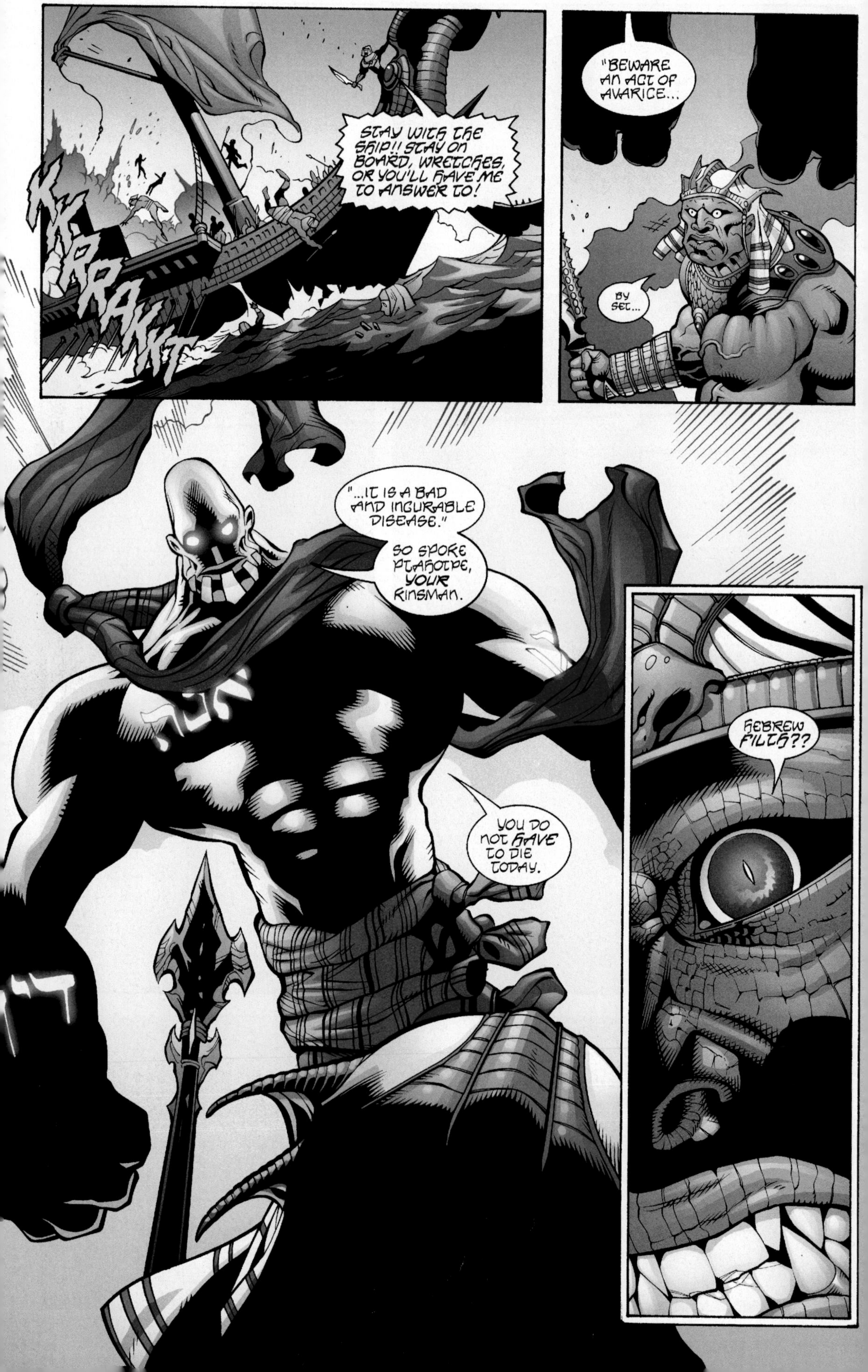
STAY WITH THE SHIP!! STAY ON BOARD, WRETCHES, OR YOU'LL HAVE ME TO ANSWER TO!
KKRRAKKT
"BEWARE AN ACT OF AVARICE...
BY SET...
"...IT IS A BAD AND INCURABLE DISEASE."
SO SPOKE PTAHOTPE, YOUR KINSMAN.
HEBREW FILTH??
YOU DO NOT HAVE TO DIE TODAY.

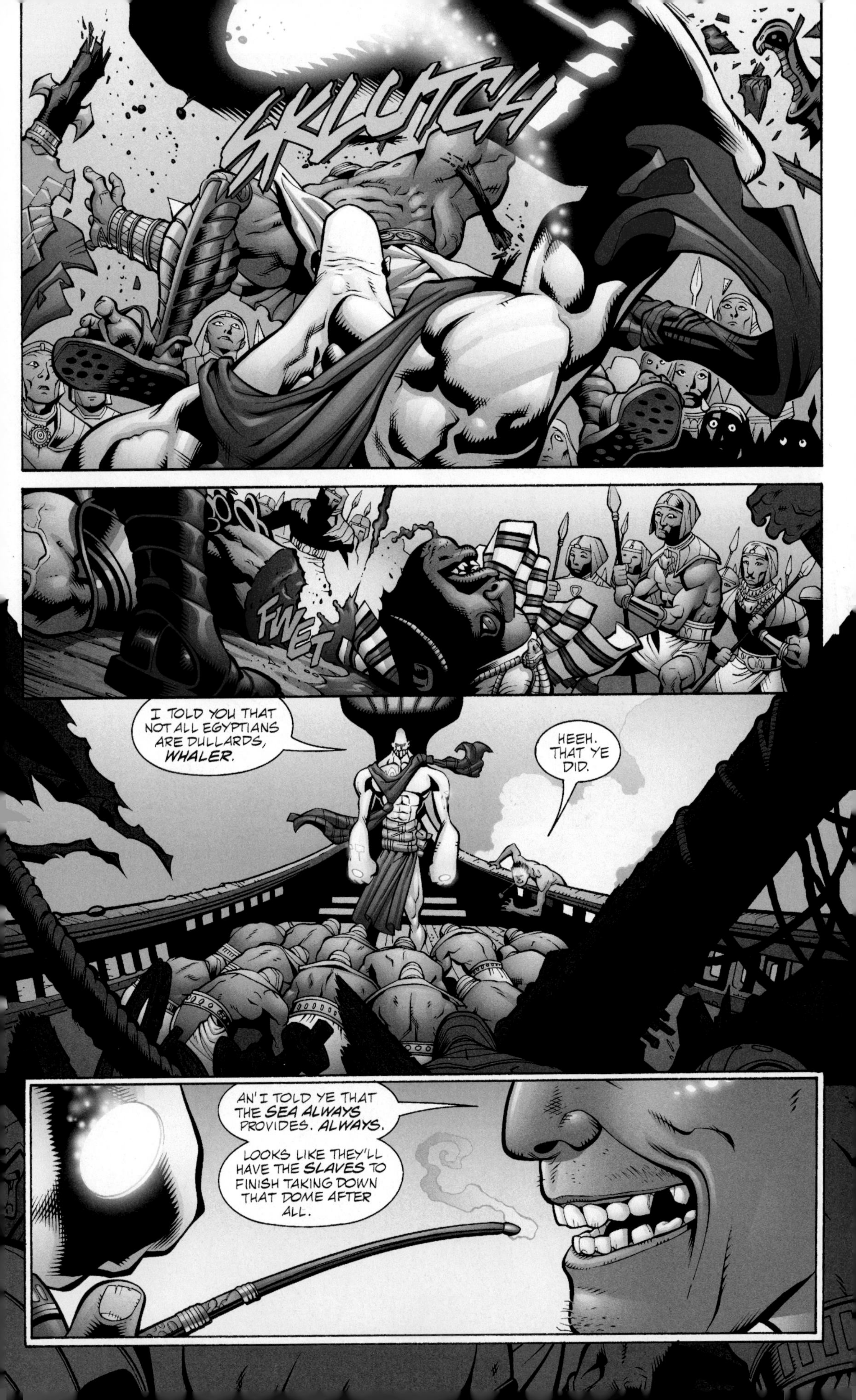
SKLUTCH
FWET
I TOLD YOU THAT NOT ALL EGYPTIANS ARE DULLARDS, WHALER.
HEEH. THAT YE DID.
AN' I TOLD YE THAT THE SEA ALWAYS PROVIDES. ALWAYS.
LOOKS LIKE THEY'LL HAVE THE SLAVES TO FINISH TAKING DOWN THAT DOME AFTER ALL.

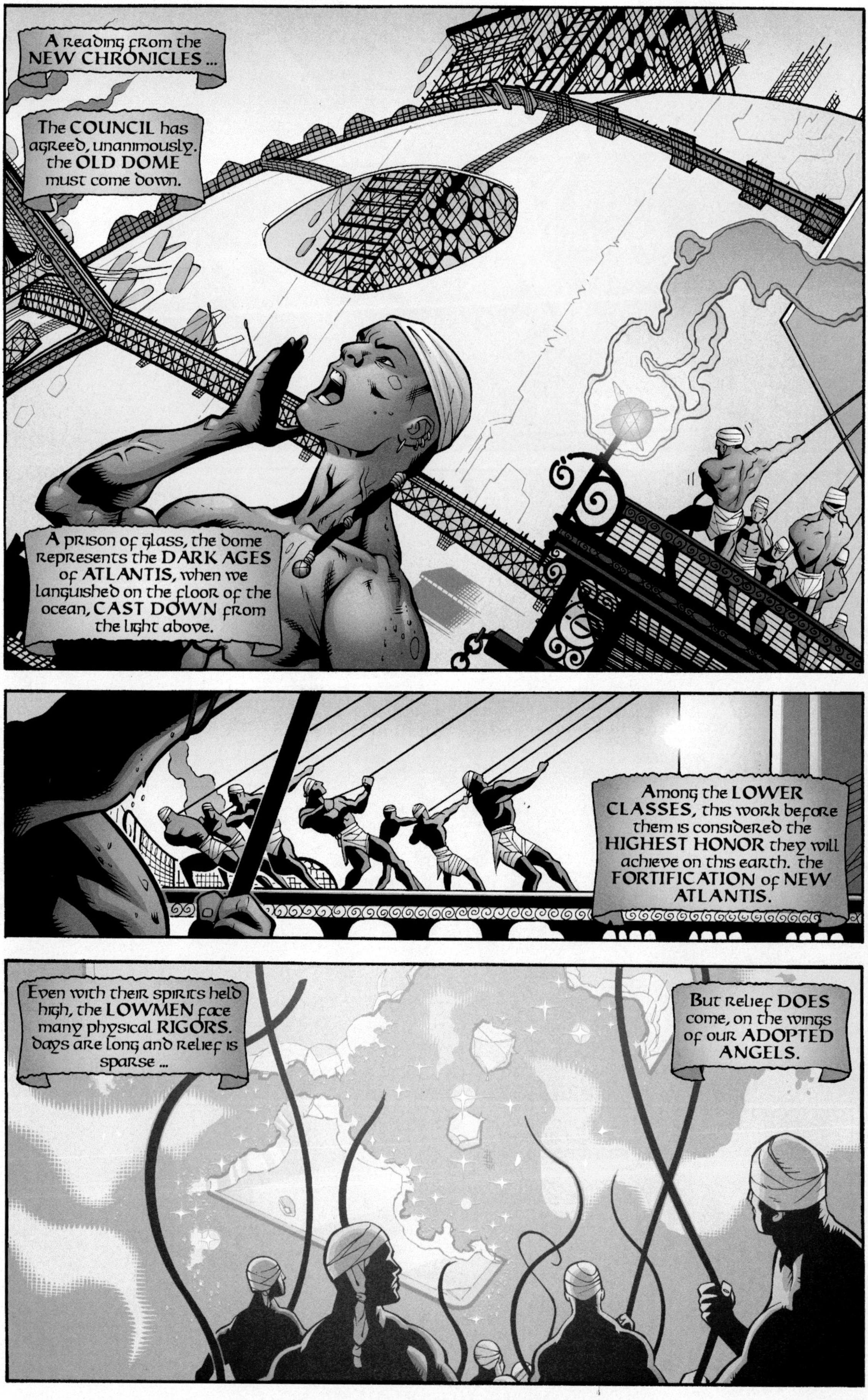
A reading from the NEW CHRONICLES ...
The COUNCIL has agreed, unanimously. the OLD DOME must come down.
A prison of glass, the dome represents the DARK AGES of ATLANTIS, when we languished on the floor of the ocean, CAST DOWN from the light above.
Among the LOWER CLASSES, this work before them is considered the HIGHEST HONOR they will achieve on this earth. the FORTIFICATION of NEW ATLANTIS.
Even with their spirits held high, the LOWMEN face many physical RIGORS. days are long and relief is sparse ...
But relief DOES come, on the wings of our ADOPTED ANGELS.

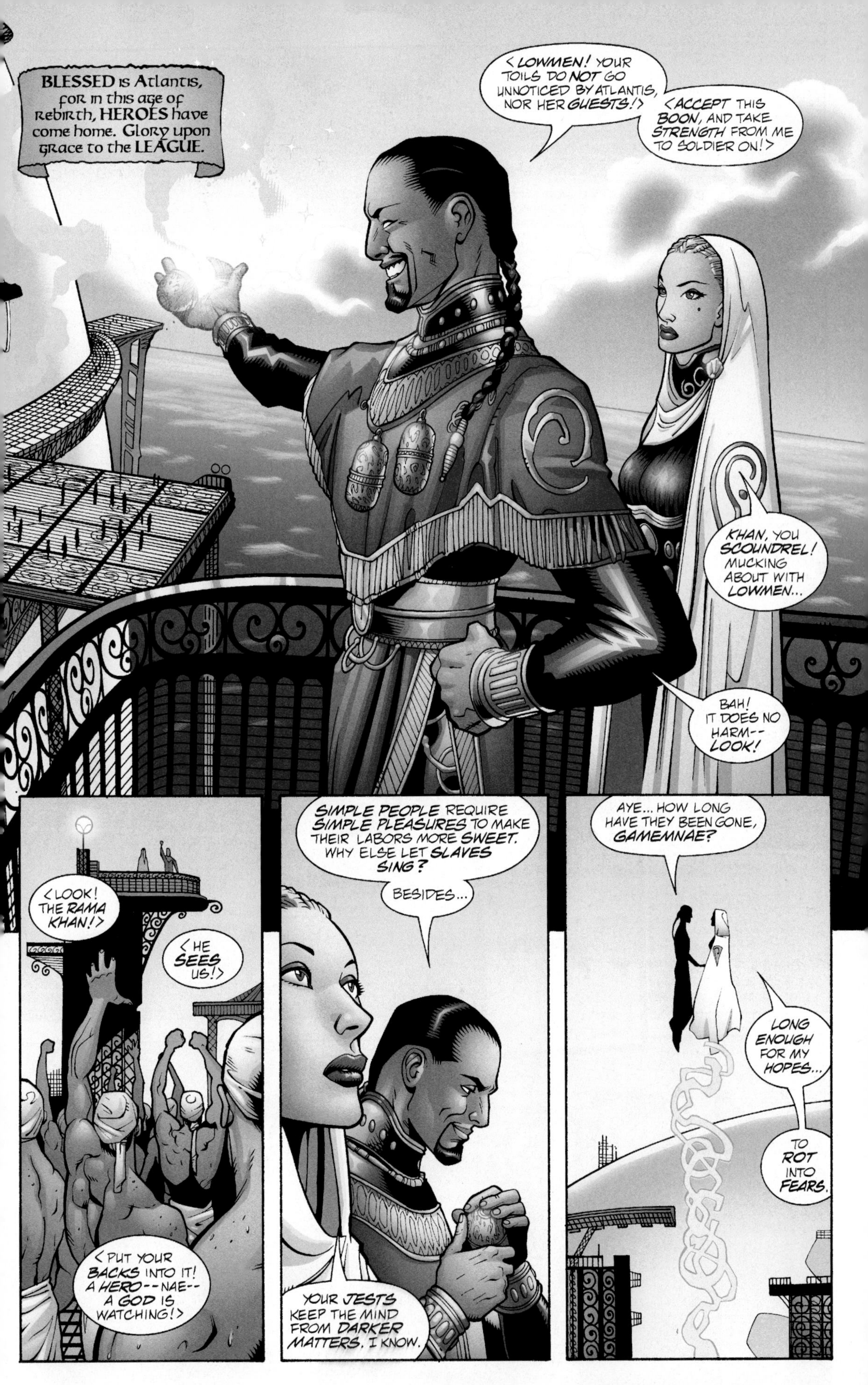
BLESSED is Atlantis, for in this age of rebirth, HEROES have come home. Glory upon grace to the LEAGUE.
< LOWMEN! YOUR TOILS DO NOT GO UNNOTICED BY ATLANTIS, NOR HER GUESTS!>
<ACCEPT THIS BOON, AND TAKE STRENGTH FROM ME TO SOLDIER ON!>
KHAN, YOU SCOUNDREL! MUCKING ABOUT WITH LOWMEN...
BAH! IT DOES NO HARM-- LOOK!
<LOOK! THE RAMA KHAN!>
< HE SEES US!>
< PUT YOUR BACKS INTO IT! A HERO--NAE-- A GOD IS WATCHING!>
SIMPLE PEOPLE REQUIRE SIMPLE PLEASURES TO MAKE THEIR LABORS MORE SWEET. WHY ELSE LET SLAVES SING?
BESIDES...
YOUR JESTS KEEP THE MIND FROM DARKER MATTERS. I KNOW.
AYE... HOW LONG HAVE THEY BEEN GONE, GAMEMNAE?
LONG ENOUGH FOR MY HOPES...
TO ROT INTO FEARS.

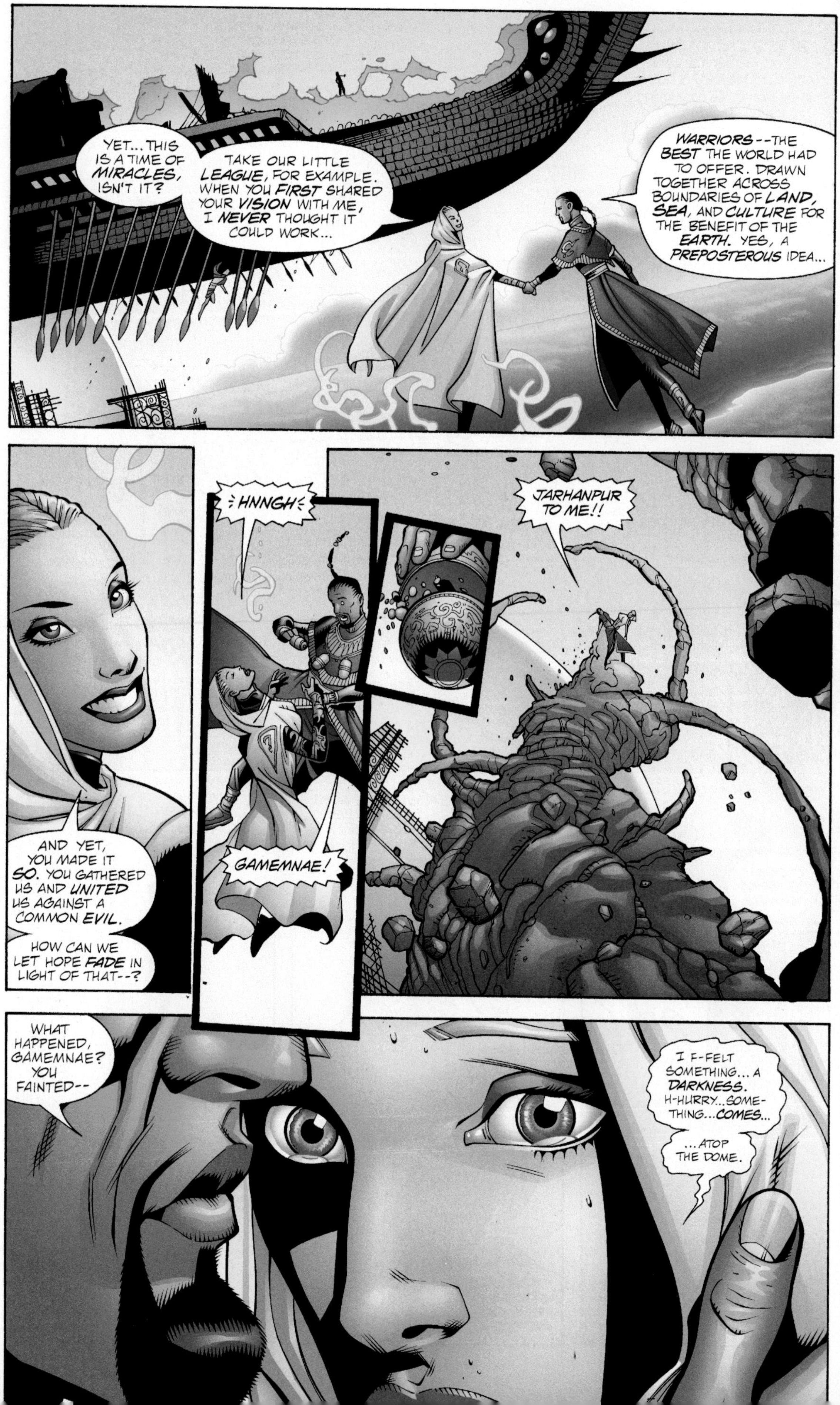
YET... THIS IS A TIME OF MIRACLES, ISN'T IT?
TAKE OUR LITTLE LEAGUE, FOR EXAMPLE. WHEN YOU FIRST SHARED YOUR VISION WITH ME, I NEVER THOUGHT IT COULD WORK...
WARRIORS--THE BEST THE WORLD HAD TO OFFER. DRAWN TOGETHER ACROSS BOUNDARIES OF LAND, SEA, AND CULTURE FOR THE BENEFIT OF THE EARTH. YES, A PREPOSTEROUS IDEA...
AND YET, YOU MADE IT SO. YOU GATHERED US AND UNITED US AGAINST A COMMON EVIL.
HOW CAN WE LET HOPE FADE IN LIGHT OF THAT--?
HNNGH
GAMEMNAE!
JARHANPUR TO ME!!
WHAT HAPPENED, GAMEMNAE? YOU FAINTED--
I F-FELT SOMETHING... A DARKNESS. H-HURRY...SOME-THING...COMES...
...ATOP THE DOME.

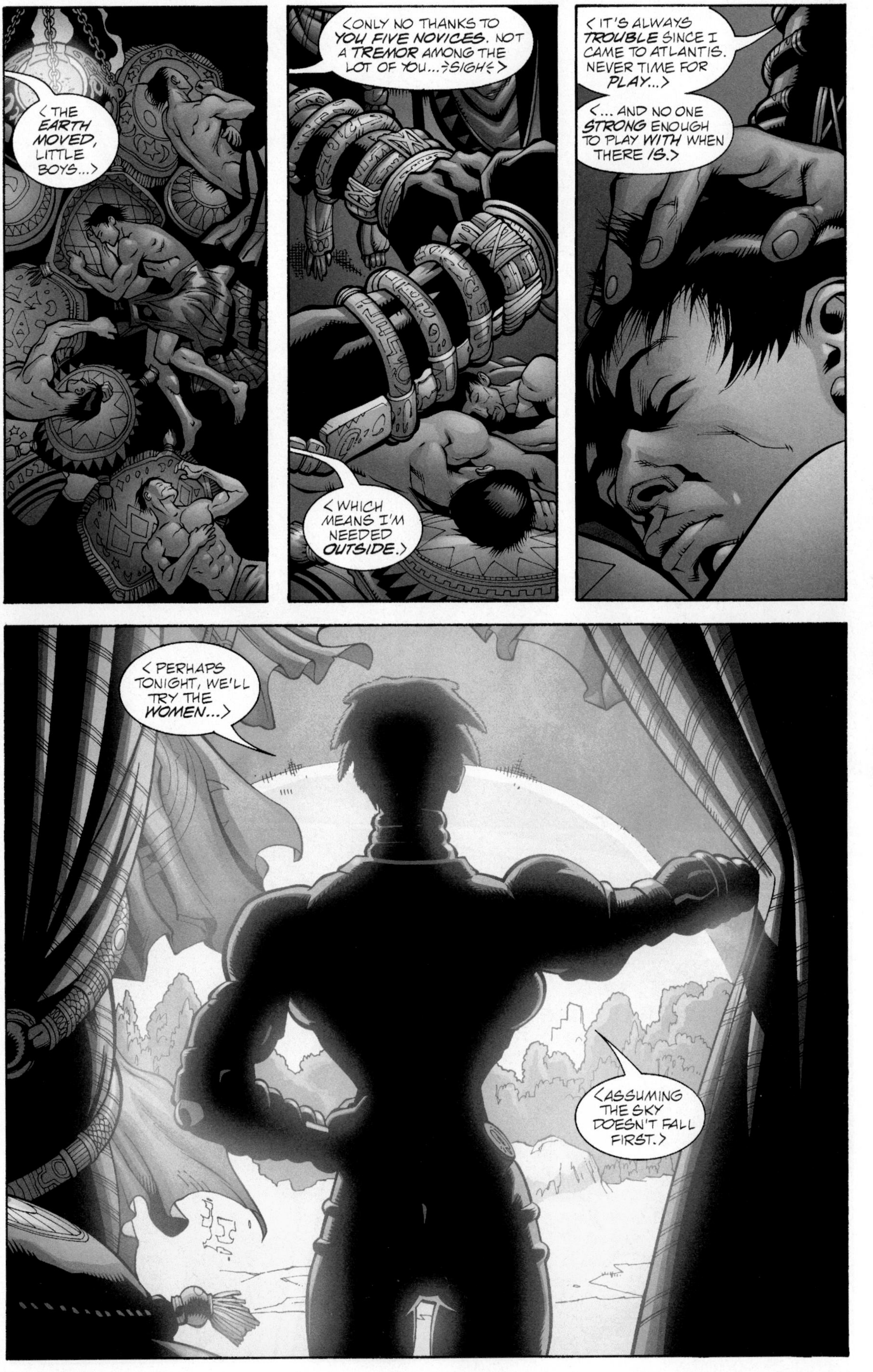
< THE EARTH MOVED, LITTLE BOYS... >
<ONLY NO THANKS TO YOU FIVE NOVICES. NOT A TREMOR AMONG THE LOT OF YOU... >SIGH< >
< WHICH MEANS I'M NEEDED OUTSIDE. >
< IT'S ALWAYS TROUBLE SINCE I CAME TO ATLANTIS. NEVER TIME FOR PLAY... >
<... AND NO ONE STRONG ENOUGH TO PLAY WITH WHEN THERE IS. >
< PERHAPS TONIGHT, WE'LL TRY THE WOMEN... >
<ASSUMING THE SKY DOESN'T FALL FIRST. >

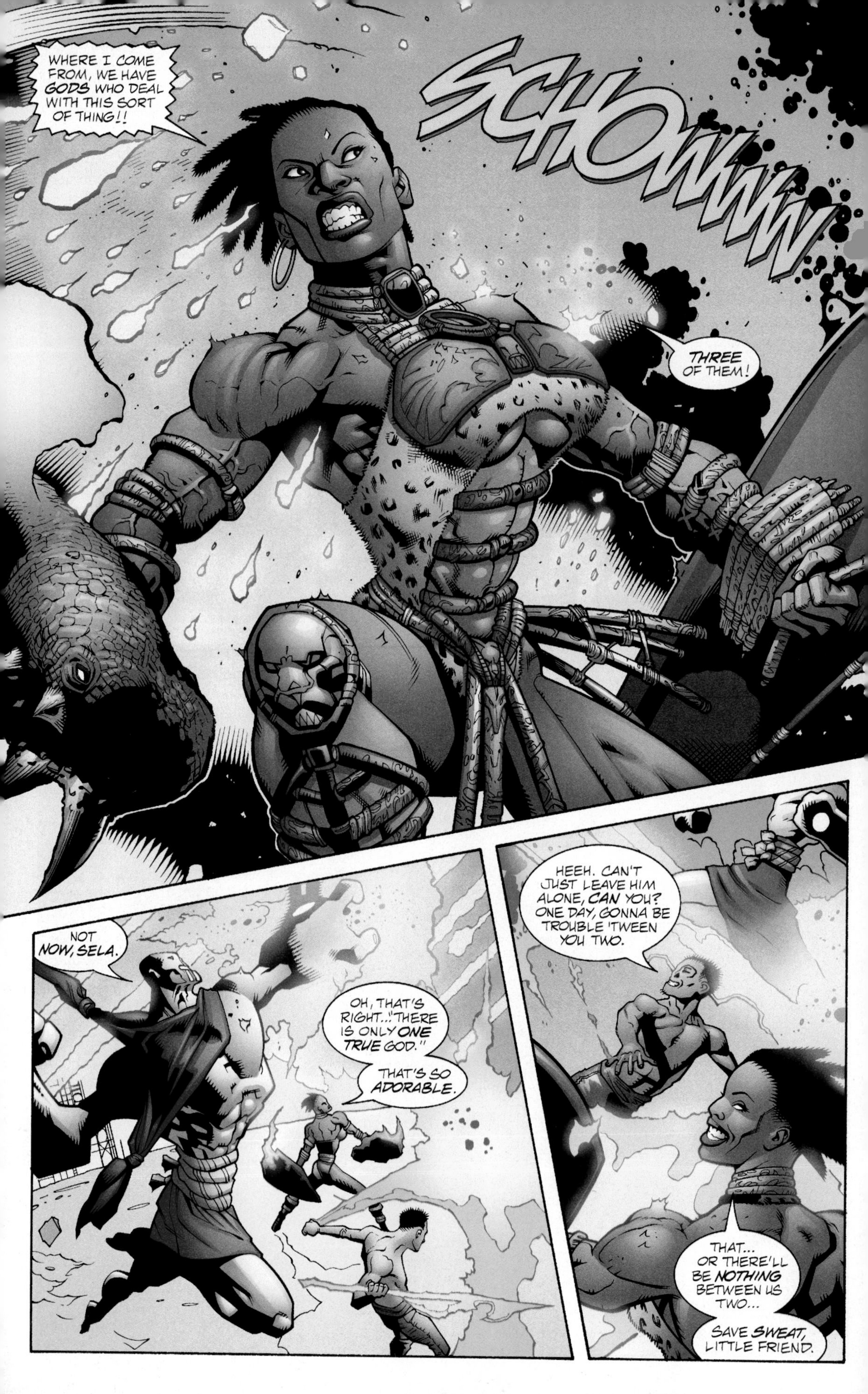
WHERE I COME FROM, WE HAVE GODS WHO DEAL WITH THIS SORT OF THING!!
SCHOWWW
THREE OF THEM!
NOT NOW, SELA.
OH, THAT'S RIGHT...'THERE IS ONLY ONE TRUE GOD.'
THAT'S SO ADORABLE.
HEEH. CAN'T JUST LEAVE HIM ALONE, CAN YOU? ONE DAY, GONNA BE TROUBLE 'TWEEN YOU TWO.
THAT... OR THERE'LL BE NOTHING BETWEEN US TWO...
SAVE SWEAT, LITTLE FRIEND.

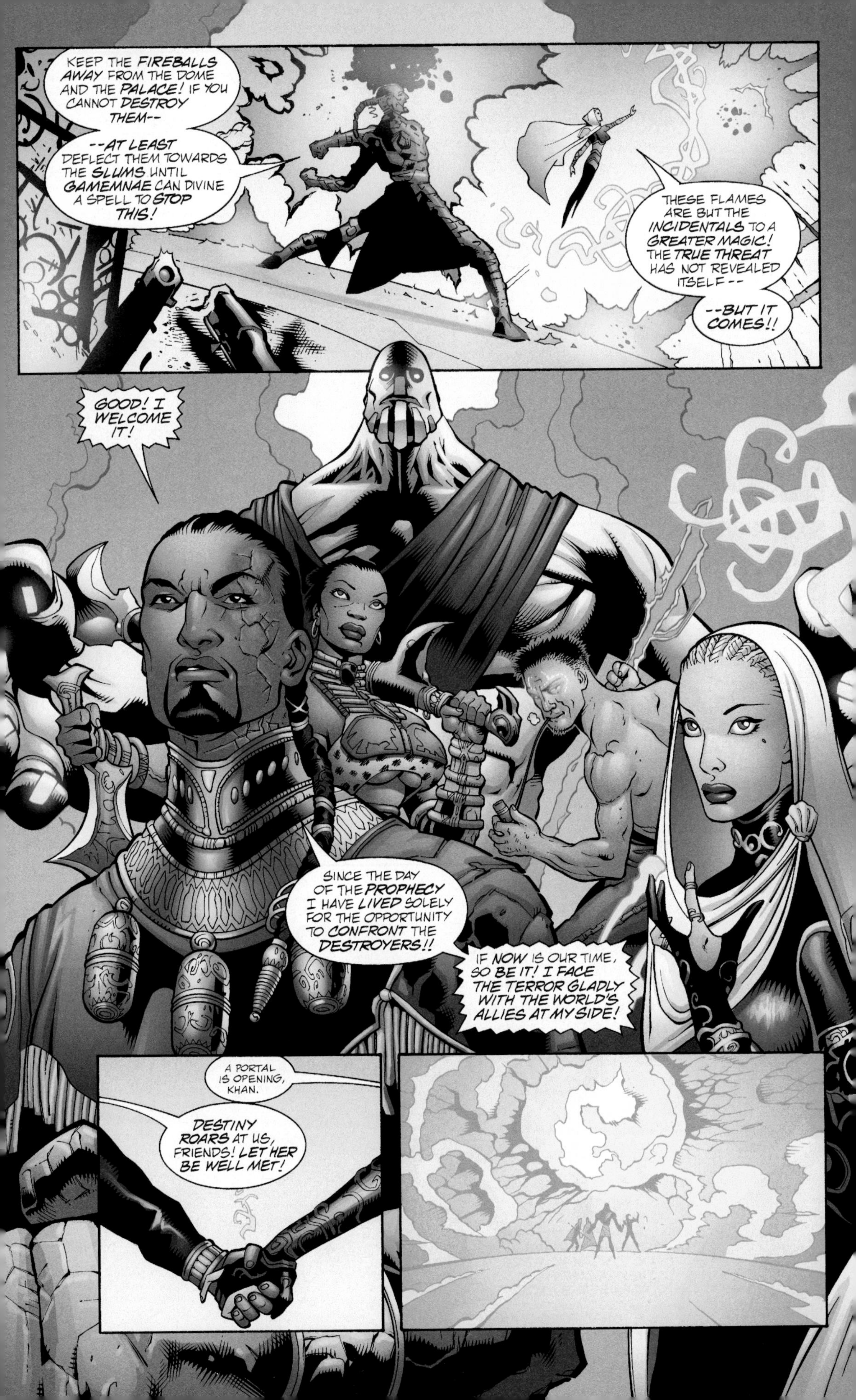
KEEP THE FIREBALLS AWAY FROM THE DOME AND THE PALACE! IF YOU CANNOT DESTROY THEM--
--AT LEAST DEFLECT THEM TOWARDS THE SLUMS UNTIL GAMEMNAE CAN DIVINE A SPELL TO STOP THIS!
THESE FLAMES ARE BUT THE INCIDENTALS TO A GREATER MAGIC! THE TRUE THREAT HAS NOT REVEALED ITSELF--
--BUT IT COMES!!
GOOD! I WELCOME IT!
SINCE THE DAY OF THE PROPHECY I HAVE LIVED SOLELY FOR THE OPPORTUNITY TO CONFRONT THE DESTROYERS!!
IF NOW IS OUR TIME, SO BE IT! I FACE THE TERROR GLADLY WITH THE WORLD'S ALLIES AT MY SIDE!
A PORTAL IS OPENING, KHAN.
DESTINY ROARS AT US, FRIENDS! LET HER BE WELL MET!

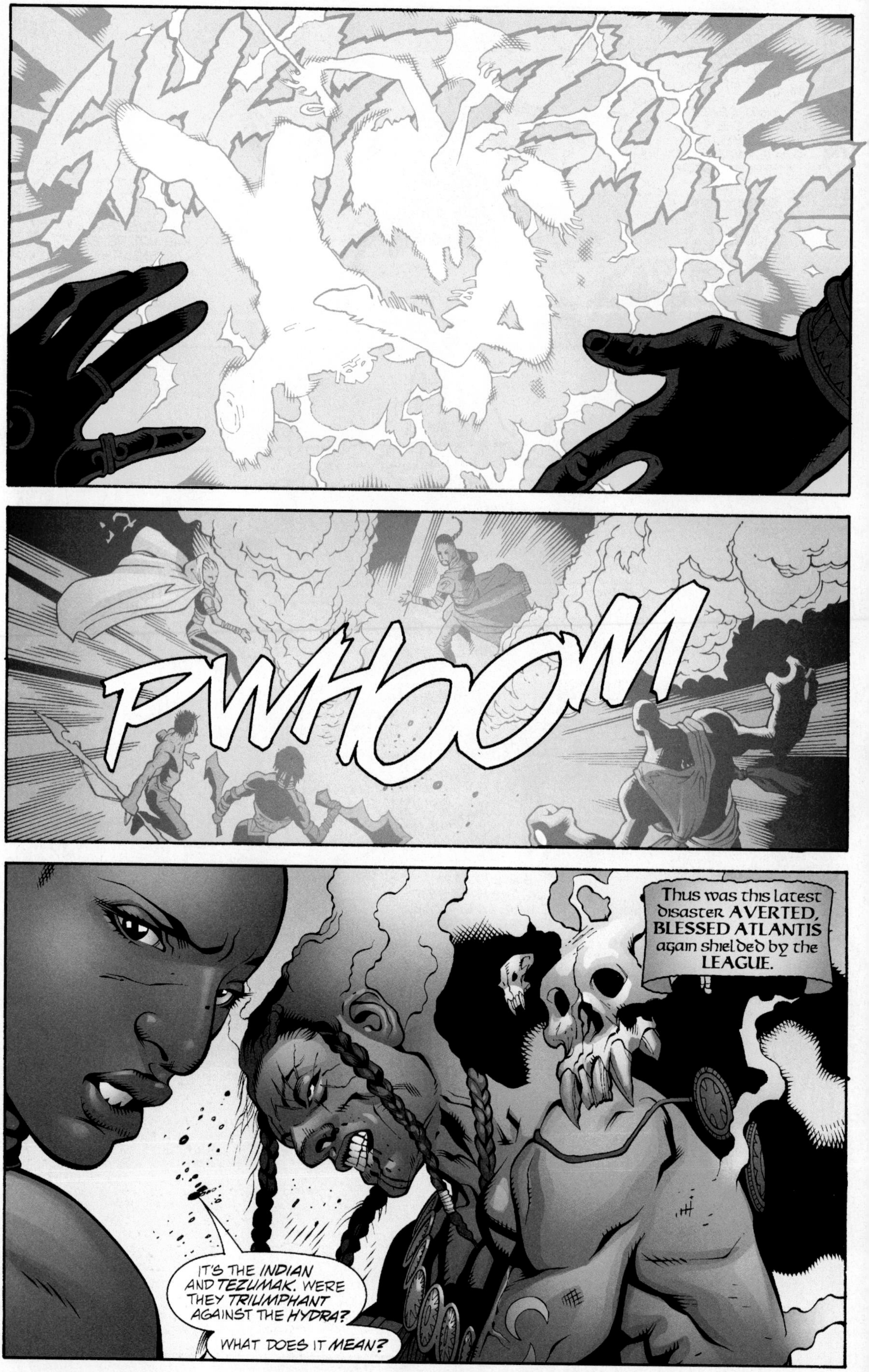
PWHOOM
Thus was this latest disaster AVERTED, BLESSED ATLANTIS again shielded by the LEAGUE.
IT'S THE INDIAN AND TEZUMAK. WERE THEY TRIUMPHANT AGAINST THE HYDRA?
WHAT DOES IT MEAN?

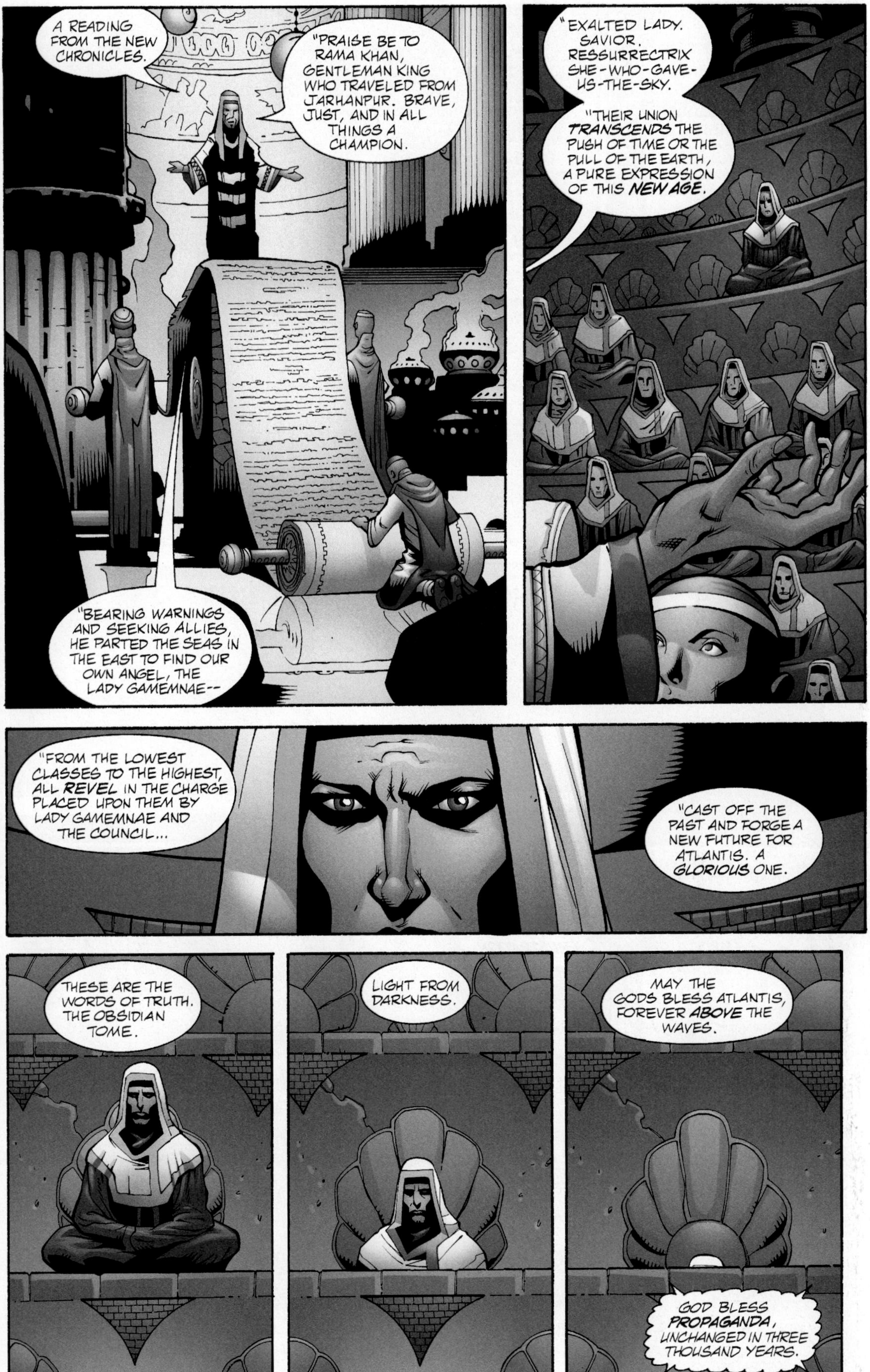
A READING FROM THE NEW CHRONICLES.
"PRAISE BE TO RAMA KHAN, GENTLEMAN KING WHO TRAVELED FROM JARHANPUR. BRAVE, JUST, AND IN ALL THINGS A CHAMPION.
"BEARING WARNINGS AND SEEKING ALLIES, HE PARTED THE SEAS IN THE EAST TO FIND OUR OWN ANGEL, THE LADY GAMEMNAE--
"EXALTED LADY. SAVIOR. RESSURRECTRIX SHE-WHO-GAVE-US-THE-SKY.
"THEIR UNION TRANSCENDS THE PUSH OF TIME OR THE PULL OF THE EARTH, A PURE EXPRESSION OF THIS NEW AGE.
"FROM THE LOWEST CLASSES TO THE HIGHEST, ALL REVEL IN THE CHARGE PLACED UPON THEM BY LADY GAMEMNAE AND THE COUNCIL...
"CAST OFF THE PAST AND FORGE A NEW FUTURE FOR ATLANTIS. A GLORIOUS ONE.
THESE ARE THE WORDS OF TRUTH. THE OBSIDIAN TOME.
LIGHT FROM DARKNESS.
MAY THE GODS BLESS ATLANTIS, FOREVER ABOVE THE WAVES.
GOD BLESS PROPAGANDA, UNCHANGED IN THREE THOUSAND YEARS.

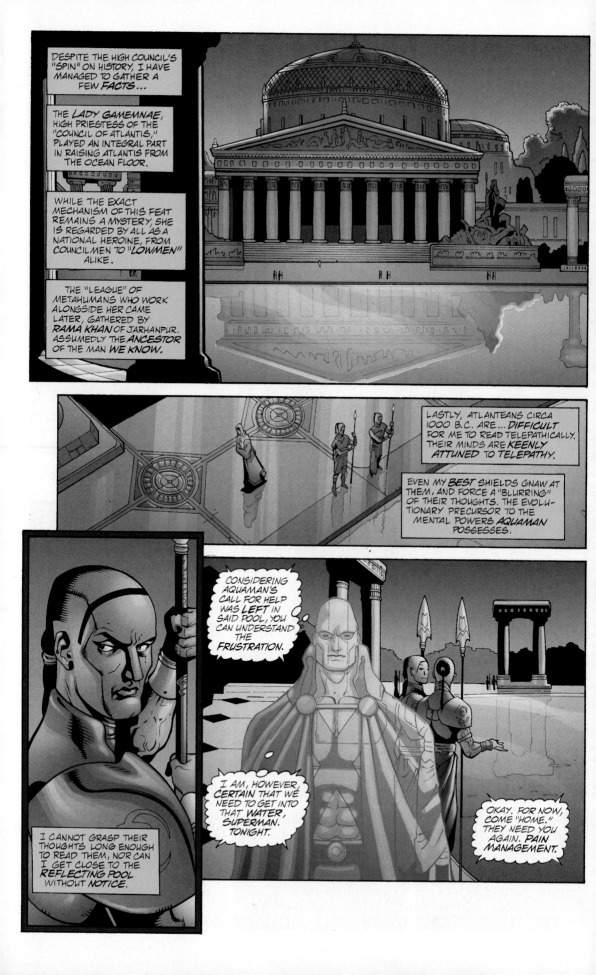

DESPITE THE HIGH COUNCIL'S "SPIN" ON HISTORY, I HAVE MANAGED TO GATHER A FEW *FACTS*...

THE *LADY GAMEMNAE*, HIGH PRIESTESS OF THE "COUNCIL OF ATLANTIS," PLAYED AN INTEGRAL PART IN RAISING ATLANTIS FROM THE OCEAN FLOOR.

WHILE THE EXACT MECHANISM OF THIS FEAT REMAINS A MYSTERY, SHE IS REGARDED BY ALL AS A NATIONAL HEROINE, FROM COUNCIL MEN TO "*LOWMEN*" ALIKE.

THE "LEAGUE" OF METAHUMANS WHO WORK ALONGSIDE HER CAME LATER, GATHERED BY *RAMA KHAN* OF JARHANPUR. ASSUMEDLY THE *ANCESTOR* OF THE MAN *WE KNOW*.

LASTLY, ATLANTEANS CIRCA 1000 B.C. ARE... *DIFFICULT* FOR ME TO READ TELEPATHICALLY. THEIR MINDS ARE *KEENLY ATTUNED* TO TELEPATHY.

EVEN MY *BEST* SHIELDS GNAW AT THEM, AND FORCE A "BLURRING" OF THEIR THOUGHTS. THE EVOLUTIONARY PRECURSOR TO THE MENTAL POWERS *AQUAMAN* POSSESSES.

CONSIDERING AQUAMAN'S CALL FOR HELP WAS *LEFT* IN SAID POOL, YOU CAN UNDERSTAND THE *FRUSTRATION*.

I CANNOT GRASP THEIR THOUGHTS LONG ENOUGH TO READ THEM, NOR CAN I GET CLOSE TO THE *REFLECTING POOL* WITHOUT *NOTICE*.

I AM, HOWEVER, *CERTAIN* THAT WE NEED TO GET INTO THAT *WATER*, SUPERMAN. TONIGHT.

OKAY. FOR NOW, COME "HOME." THEY NEED YOU AGAIN. *PAIN MANAGEMENT*.

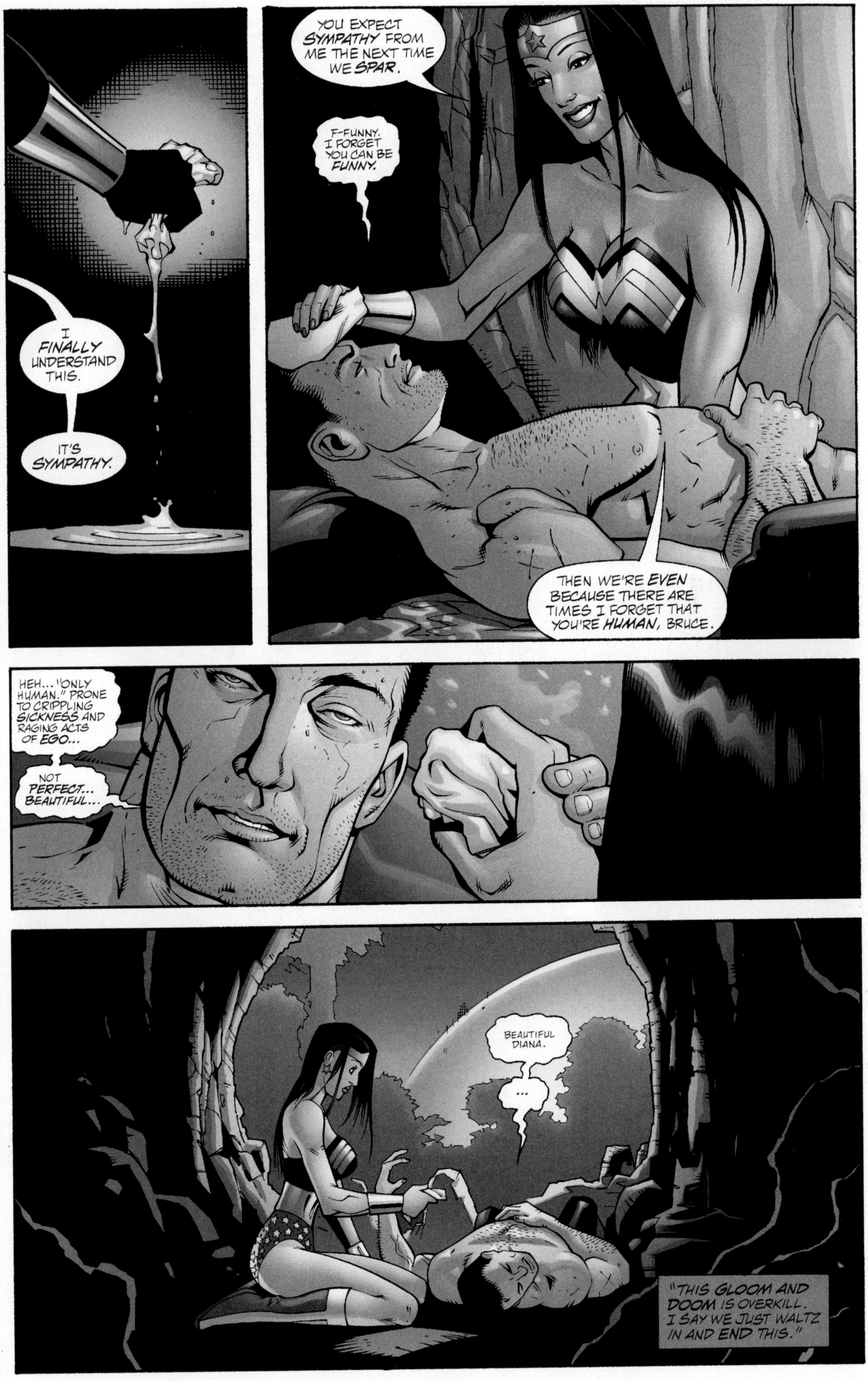
YOU EXPECT SYMPATHY FROM ME THE NEXT TIME WE SPAR.
F-FUNNY. I FORGET YOU CAN BE FUNNY.
I FINALLY UNDERSTAND THIS.
IT'S SYMPATHY.
THEN WE'RE EVEN BECAUSE THERE ARE TIMES I FORGET THAT YOU'RE HUMAN, BRUCE.
HEH... "ONLY HUMAN." PRONE TO CRIPPLING SICKNESS AND RAGING ACTS OF EGO...
NOT PERFECT... BEAUTIFUL...
BEAUTIFUL DIANA.
...
"THIS GLOOM AND DOOM IS OVERKILL. I SAY WE JUST WALTZ IN AND END THIS."

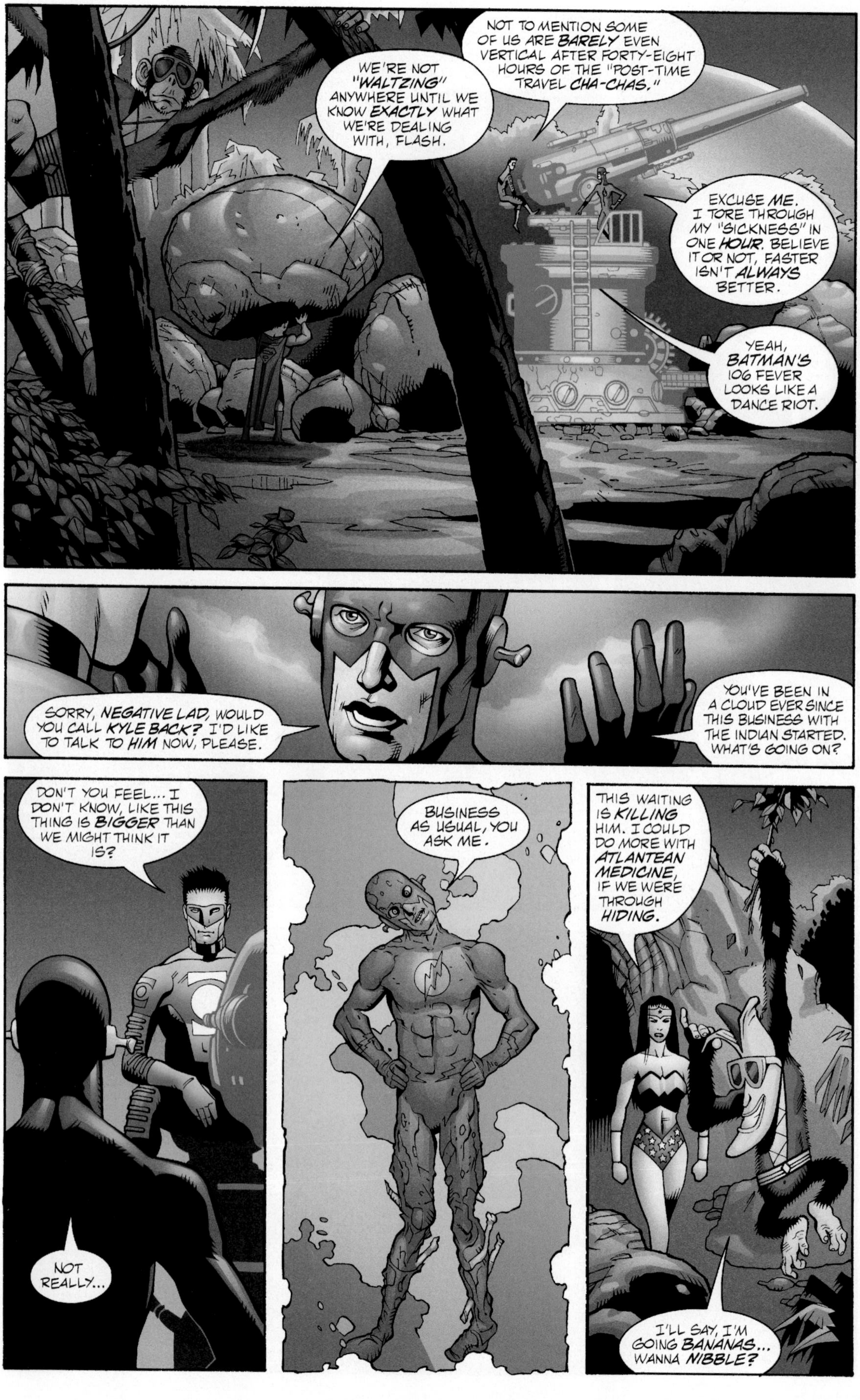
WE'RE NOT "WALTZING" ANYWHERE UNTIL WE KNOW EXACTLY WHAT WE'RE DEALING WITH, FLASH.
NOT TO MENTION SOME OF US ARE BARELY EVEN VERTICAL AFTER FORTY-EIGHT HOURS OF THE "POST-TIME TRAVEL CHA-CHAS."
EXCUSE ME. I TORE THROUGH MY "SICKNESS" IN ONE HOUR. BELIEVE IT OR NOT, FASTER ISN'T ALWAYS BETTER.
YEAH, BATMAN'S 106 FEVER LOOKS LIKE A DANCE RIOT.
SORRY, NEGATIVE LAD, WOULD YOU CALL KYLE BACK? I'D LIKE TO TALK TO HIM NOW, PLEASE.
YOU'VE BEEN IN A CLOUD EVER SINCE THIS BUSINESS WITH THE INDIAN STARTED. WHAT'S GOING ON?
DON'T YOU FEEL... I DON'T KNOW, LIKE THIS THING IS BIGGER THAN WE MIGHT THINK IT IS?
NOT REALLY...
BUSINESS AS USUAL, YOU ASK ME.
THIS WAITING IS KILLING HIM. I COULD DO MORE WITH ATLANTEAN MEDICINE, IF WE WERE THROUGH HIDING.
I'LL SAY, I'M GOING BANANAS... WANNA NIBBLE?

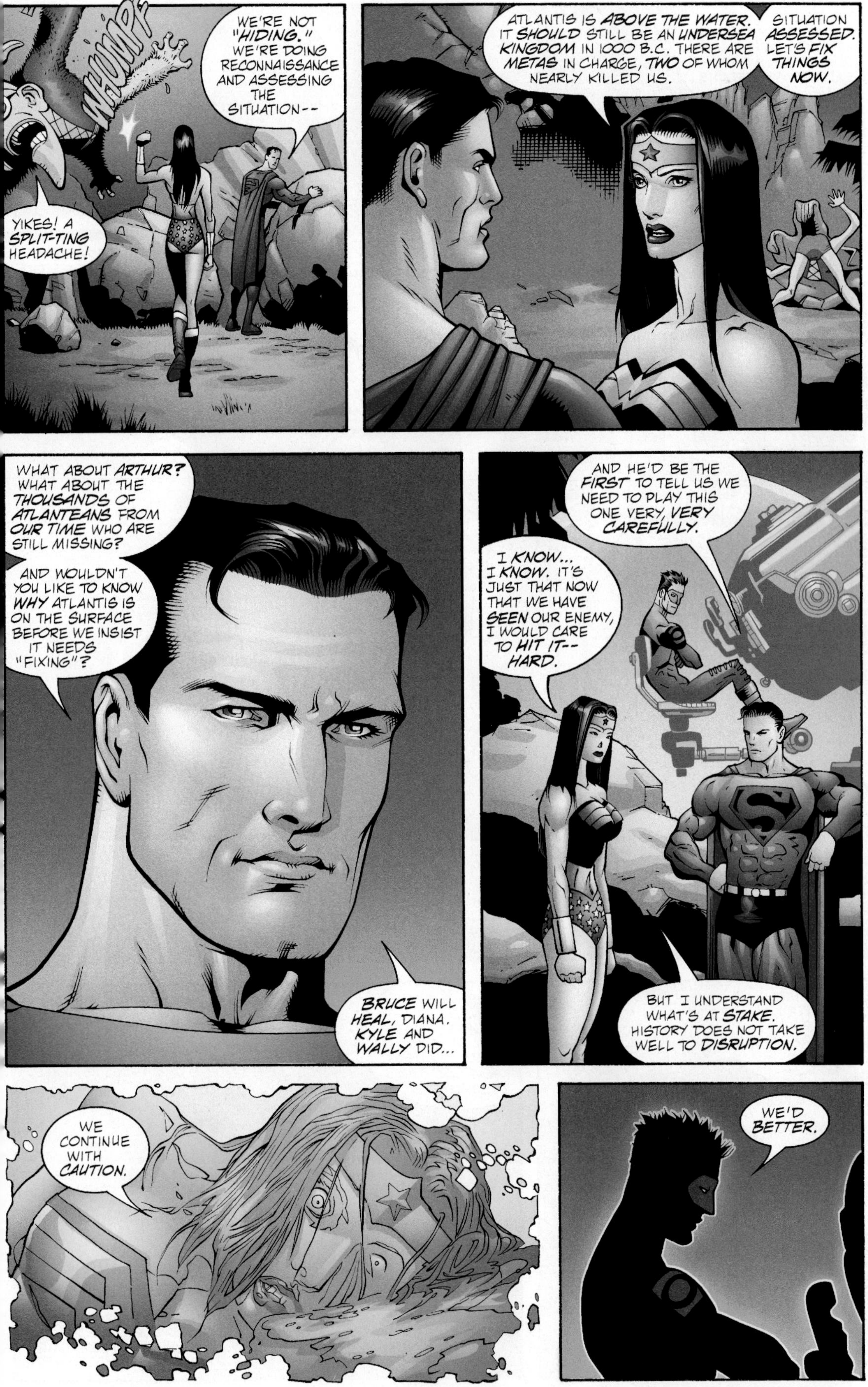
WHUMPF
WE'RE NOT "HIDING." WE'RE DOING RECONNAISSANCE AND ASSESSING THE SITUATION--
YIKES! A SPLIT-TING HEADACHE!
ATLANTIS IS ABOVE THE WATER. IT SHOULD STILL BE AN UNDERSEA KINGDOM IN 1000 B.C. THERE ARE METAS IN CHARGE, TWO OF WHOM NEARLY KILLED US.
SITUATION ASSESSED. LET'S FIX THINGS NOW.
WHAT ABOUT ARTHUR? WHAT ABOUT THE THOUSANDS OF ATLANTEANS FROM OUR TIME WHO ARE STILL MISSING?
AND WOULDN'T YOU LIKE TO KNOW WHY ATLANTIS IS ON THE SURFACE BEFORE WE INSIST IT NEEDS "FIXING"?
BRUCE WILL HEAL, DIANA. KYLE AND WALLY DID...
AND HE'D BE THE FIRST TO TELL US WE NEED TO PLAY THIS ONE VERY, VERY CAREFULLY.
I KNOW... I KNOW. IT'S JUST THAT NOW THAT WE HAVE SEEN OUR ENEMY, I WOULD CARE TO HIT IT-- HARD.
BUT I UNDERSTAND WHAT'S AT STAKE. HISTORY DOES NOT TAKE WELL TO DISRUPTION.
WE CONTINUE WITH CAUTION.
WE'D BETTER.

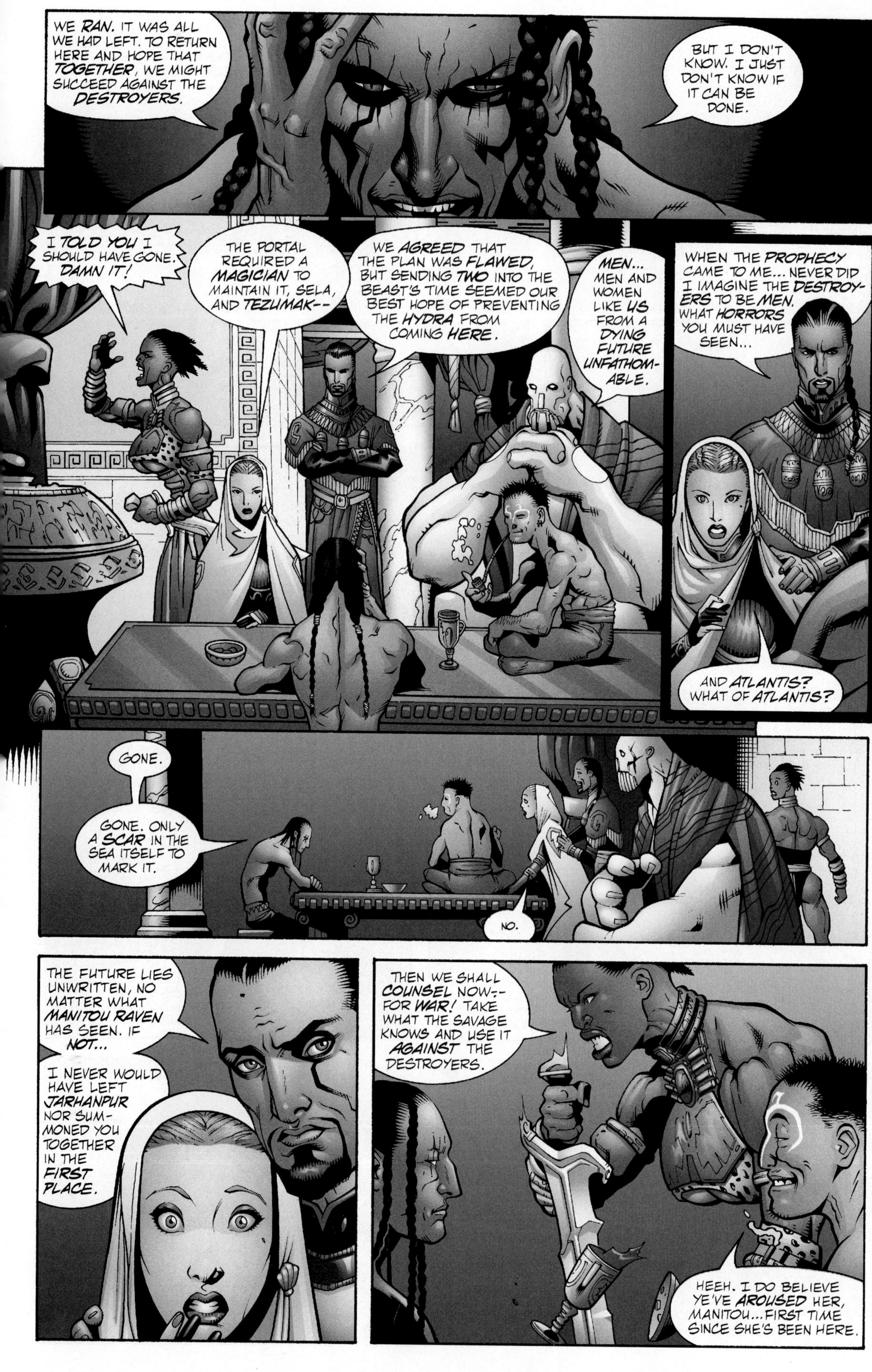
WE RAN. IT WAS ALL WE HAD LEFT. TO RETURN HERE AND HOPE THAT TOGETHER, WE MIGHT SUCCEED AGAINST THE DESTROYERS.
BUT I DON'T KNOW. I JUST DON'T KNOW IF IT CAN BE DONE.
I TOLD YOU I SHOULD HAVE GONE. DAMN IT!
THE PORTAL REQUIRED A MAGICIAN TO MAINTAIN IT, SELA, AND TEZUMAK--
WE AGREED THAT THE PLAN WAS FLAWED, BUT SENDING TWO INTO THE BEAST'S TIME SEEMED OUR BEST HOPE OF PREVENTING THE HYDRA FROM COMING HERE.
MEN... MEN AND WOMEN LIKE US FROM A DYING FUTURE UNFATHOM-ABLE.
WHEN THE PROPHECY CAME TO ME... NEVER DID I IMAGINE THE DESTROY-ERS TO BE MEN. WHAT HORRORS YOU MUST HAVE SEEN...
AND ATLANTIS? WHAT OF ATLANTIS?
GONE.
GONE. ONLY A SCAR IN THE SEA ITSELF TO MARK IT.
NO.
THE FUTURE LIES UNWRITTEN, NO MATTER WHAT MANITOU RAVEN HAS SEEN. IF NOT...
I NEVER WOULD HAVE LEFT JARHANPUR NOR SUM-MONED YOU TOGETHER IN THE FIRST PLACE.
THEN WE SHALL COUNSEL NOW-- FOR WAR! TAKE WHAT THE SAVAGE KNOWS AND USE IT AGAINST THE DESTROYERS.
HEEH. I DO BELIEVE YE'VE AROUSED HER, MANITOU... FIRST TIME SINCE SHE'S BEEN HERE.

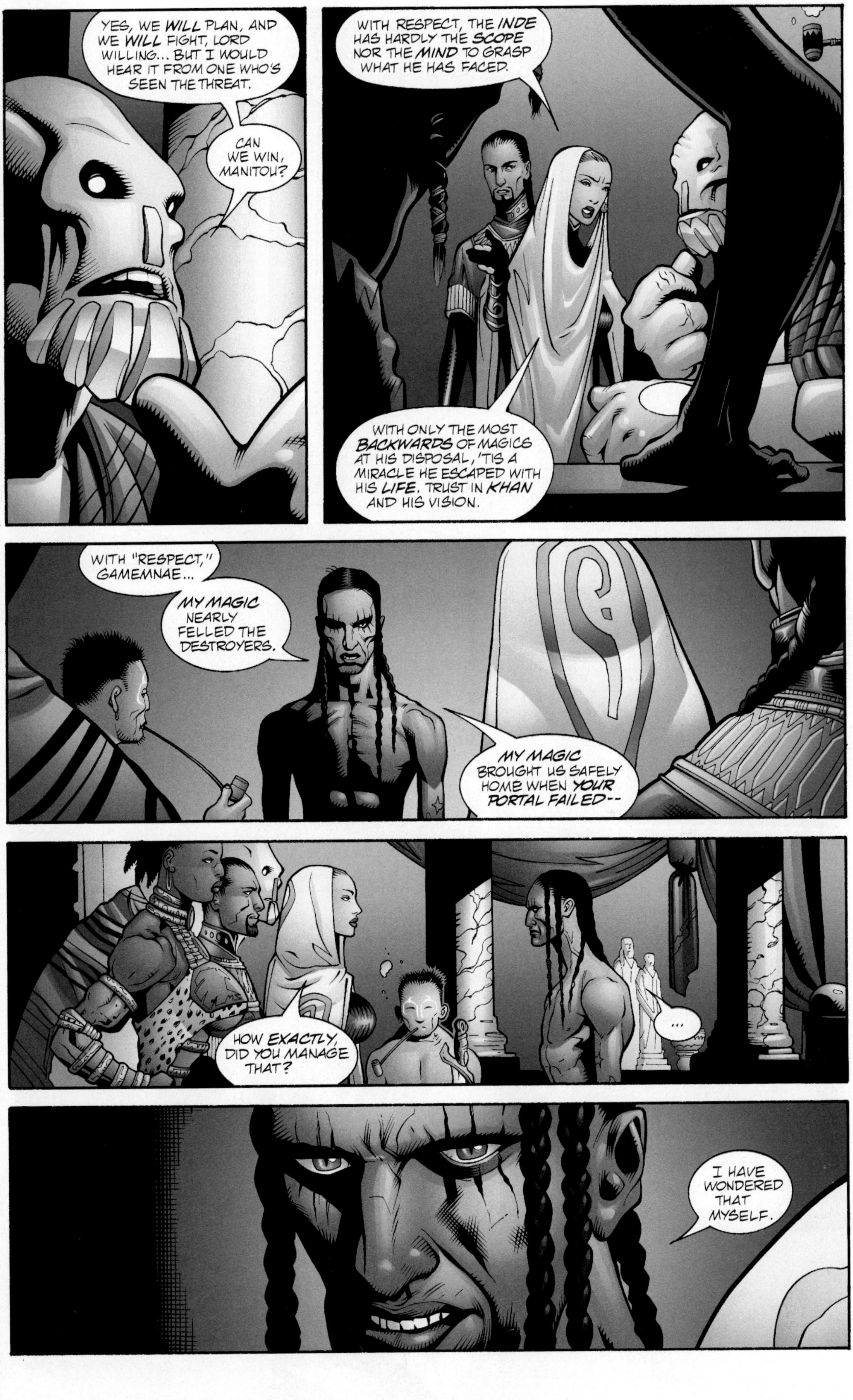
YES, WE WILL PLAN, AND WE WILL FIGHT, LORD WILLING... BUT I WOULD HEAR IT FROM ONE WHO'S SEEN THE THREAT.
CAN WE WIN, MANITOU?
WITH RESPECT, THE INDE HAS HARDLY THE SCOPE NOR THE MIND TO GRASP WHAT HE HAS FACED.
WITH ONLY THE MOST BACKWARDS OF MAGICS AT HIS DISPOSAL, 'TIS A MIRACLE HE ESCAPED WITH HIS LIFE. TRUST IN KHAN AND HIS VISION.
WITH "RESPECT," GAMEMNAE...
MY MAGIC NEARLY FELLED THE DESTROYERS.
MY MAGIC BROUGHT US SAFELY HOME WHEN YOUR PORTAL FAILED--
HOW EXACTLY, DID YOU MANAGE THAT?
...
I HAVE WONDERED THAT MYSELF.

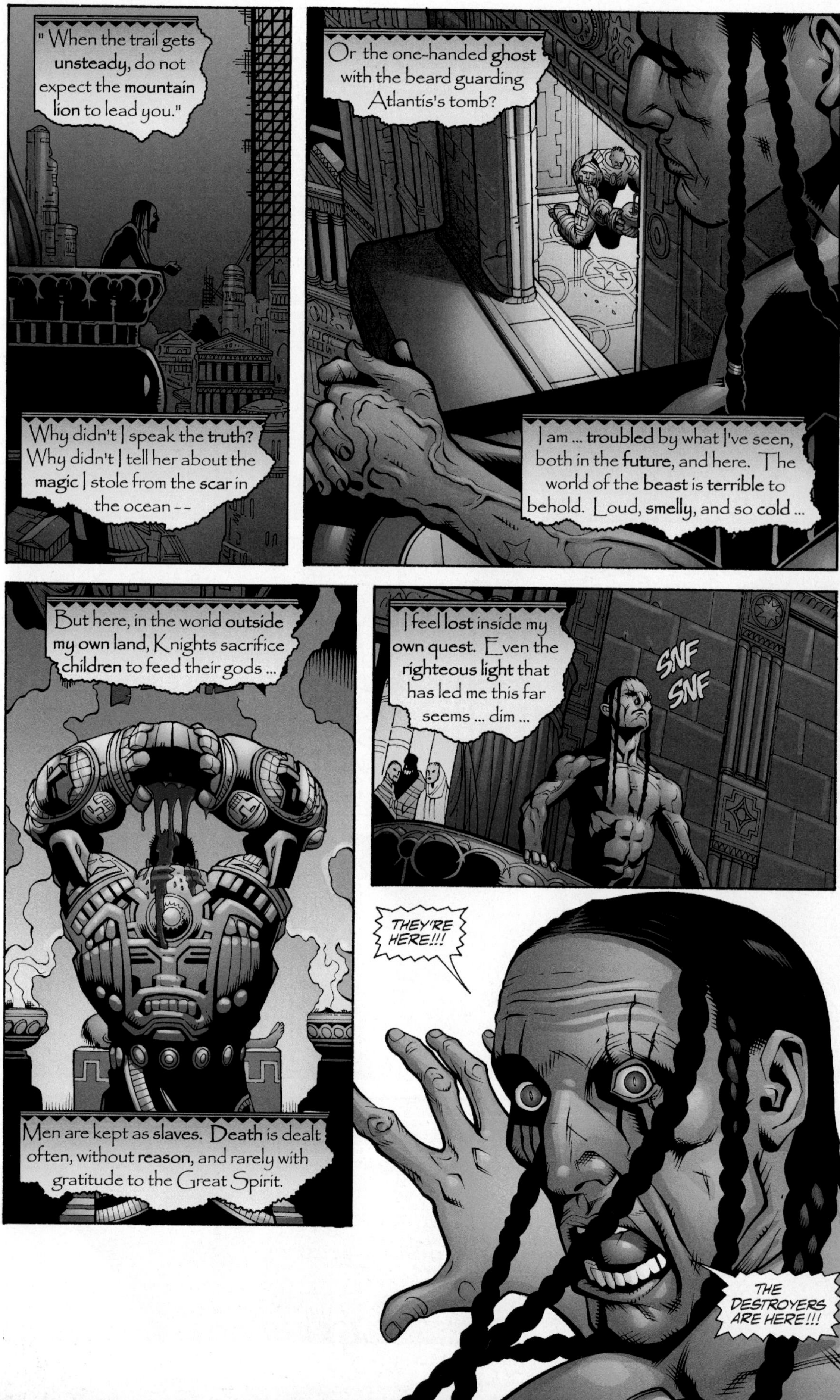
"When the trail gets unsteady, do not expect the mountain lion to lead you."
Why didn't I speak the truth? Why didn't I tell her about the magic I stole from the scar in the ocean --
Or the one-handed ghost with the beard guarding Atlantis's tomb?
I am ... troubled by what I've seen, both in the future, and here. The world of the beast is terrible to behold. Loud, smelly, and so cold ...
But here, in the world outside my own land, Knights sacrifice children to feed their gods ...
Men are kept as slaves. Death is dealt often, without reason, and rarely with gratitude to the Great Spirit.
I feel lost inside my own quest. Even the righteous light that has led me this far seems ... dim ...
SNF
SNF
THEY'RE HERE!!!
THE DESTROYERS ARE HERE!!!

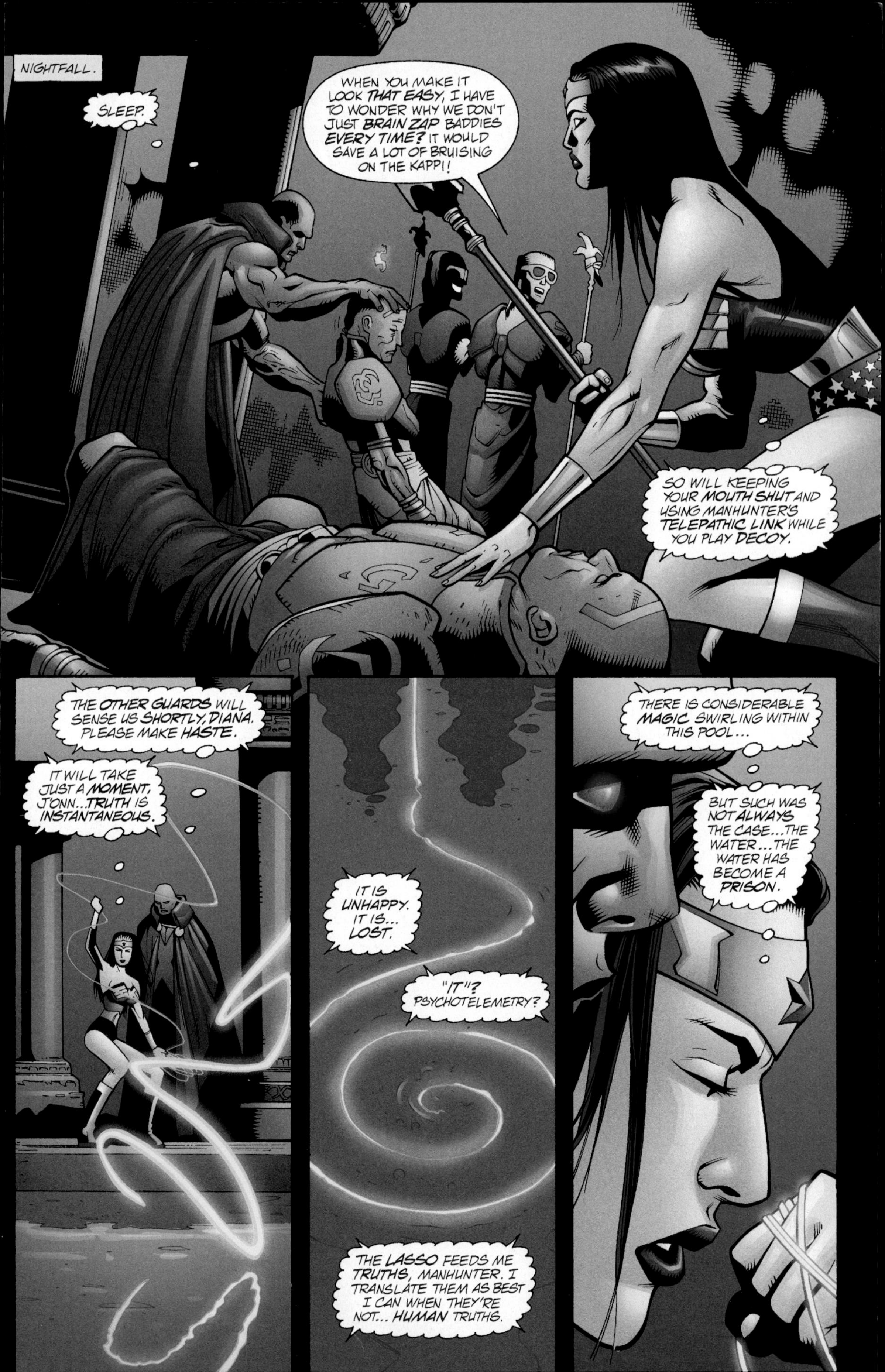
NIGHTFALL.
SLEEP.
WHEN YOU MAKE IT LOOK THAT EASY, I HAVE TO WONDER WHY WE DON'T JUST BRAIN ZAP BADDIES EVERY TIME? IT WOULD SAVE A LOT OF BRUISING ON THE KAPPI!
SO WILL KEEPING YOUR MOUTH SHUT AND USING MANHUNTER'S TELEPATHIC LINK WHILE YOU PLAY DECOY.
THE OTHER GUARDS WILL SENSE US SHORTLY, DIANA. PLEASE MAKE HASTE.
IT WILL TAKE JUST A MOMENT, J'ONN...TRUTH IS INSTANTANEOUS.
IT IS UNHAPPY. IT IS... LOST.
"IT"? PSYCHOTELEMETRY?
THE LASSO FEEDS ME TRUTHS, MANHUNTER. I TRANSLATE THEM AS BEST I CAN WHEN THEY'RE NOT... HUMAN TRUTHS.
THERE IS CONSIDERABLE MAGIC SWIRLING WITHIN THIS POOL...
BUT SUCH WAS NOT ALWAYS THE CASE...THE WATER...THE WATER HAS BECOME A PRISON.

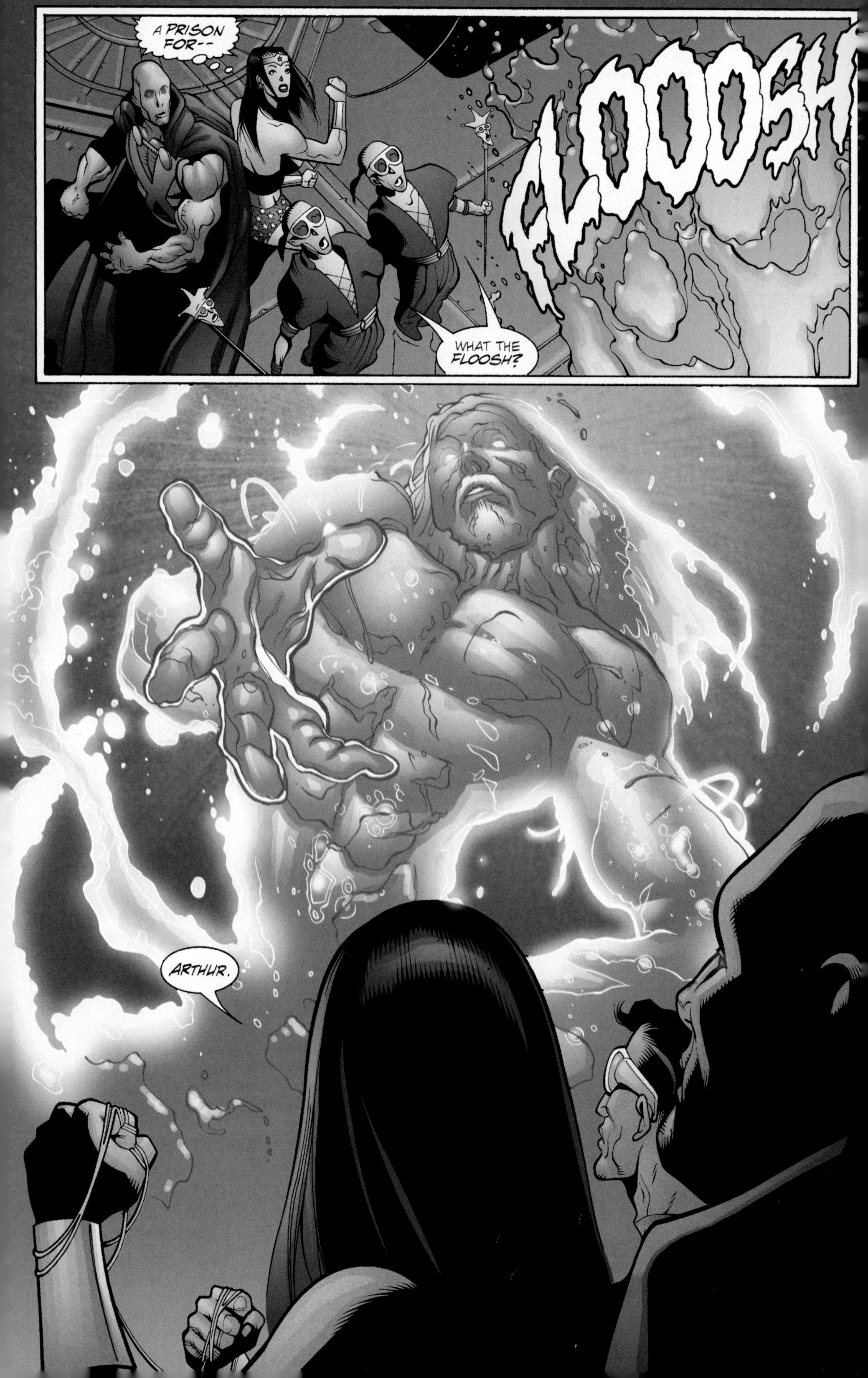
A PRISON FOR--
FLOOOSH
WHAT THE FLOOSH?
ARTHUR.

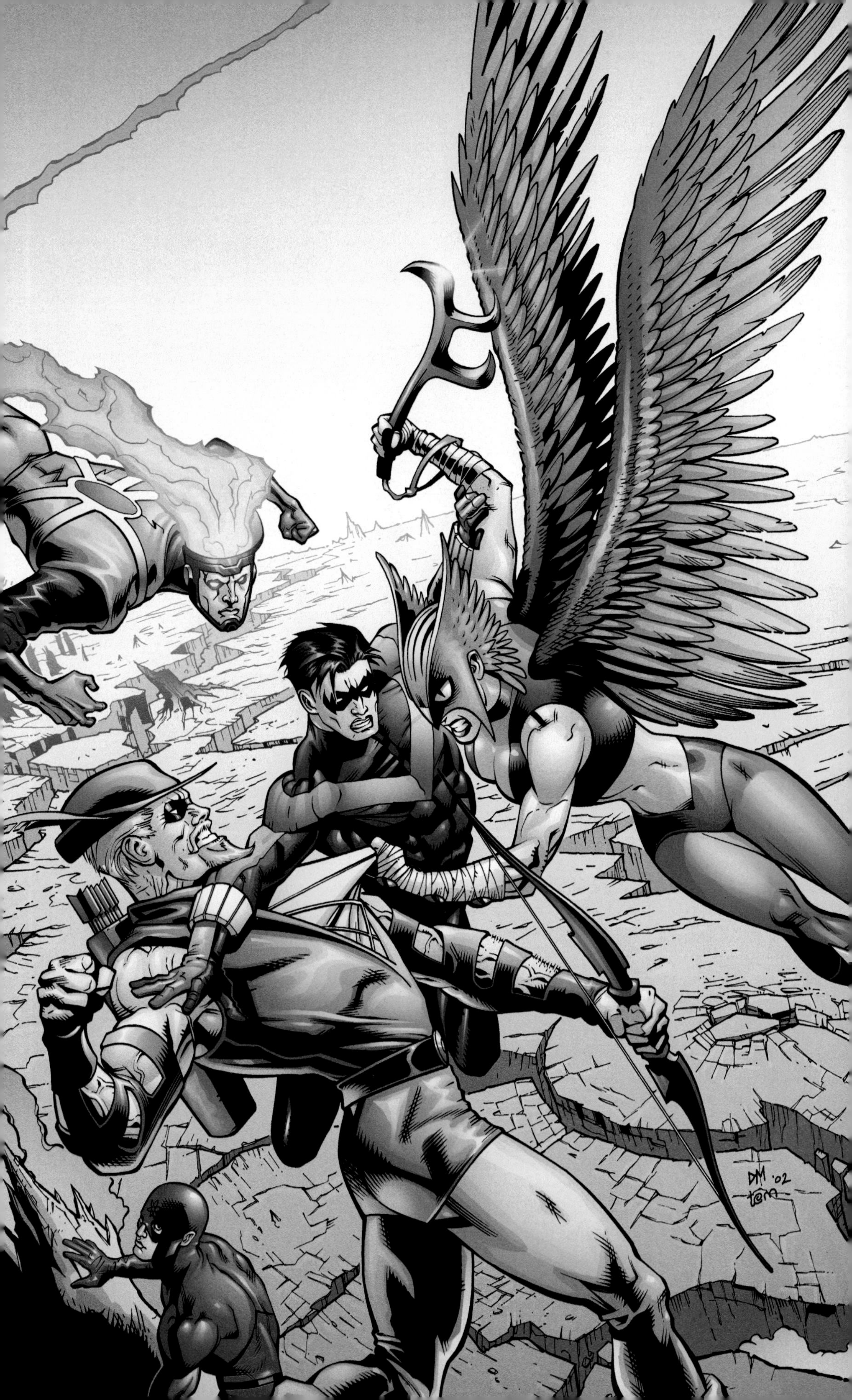

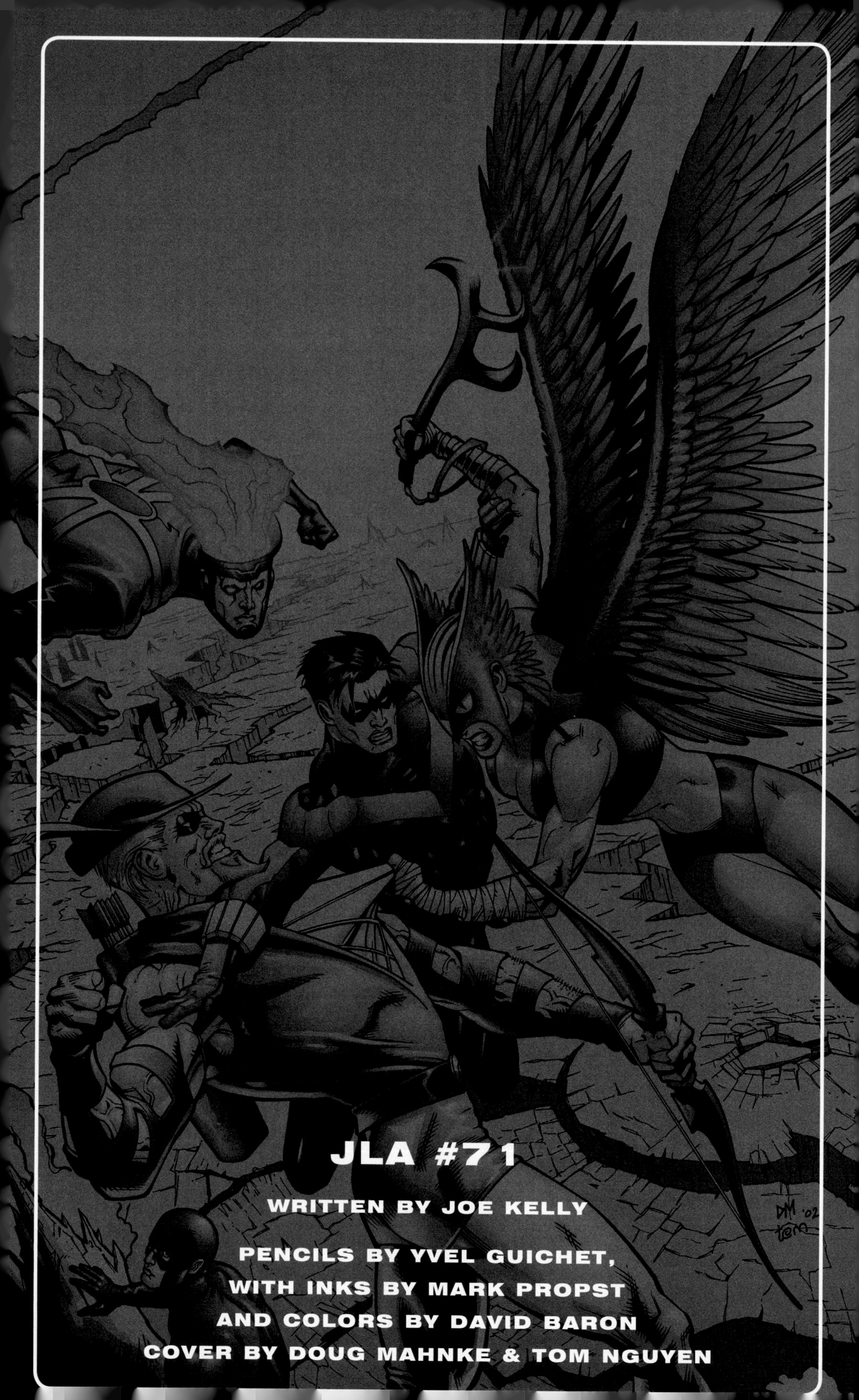

JLA #71

WRITTEN BY JOE KELLY

PENCILS BY YVEL GUICHET,
WITH INKS BY MARK PROPST
AND COLORS BY DAVID BARON
COVER BY DOUG MAHNKE & TOM NGUYEN

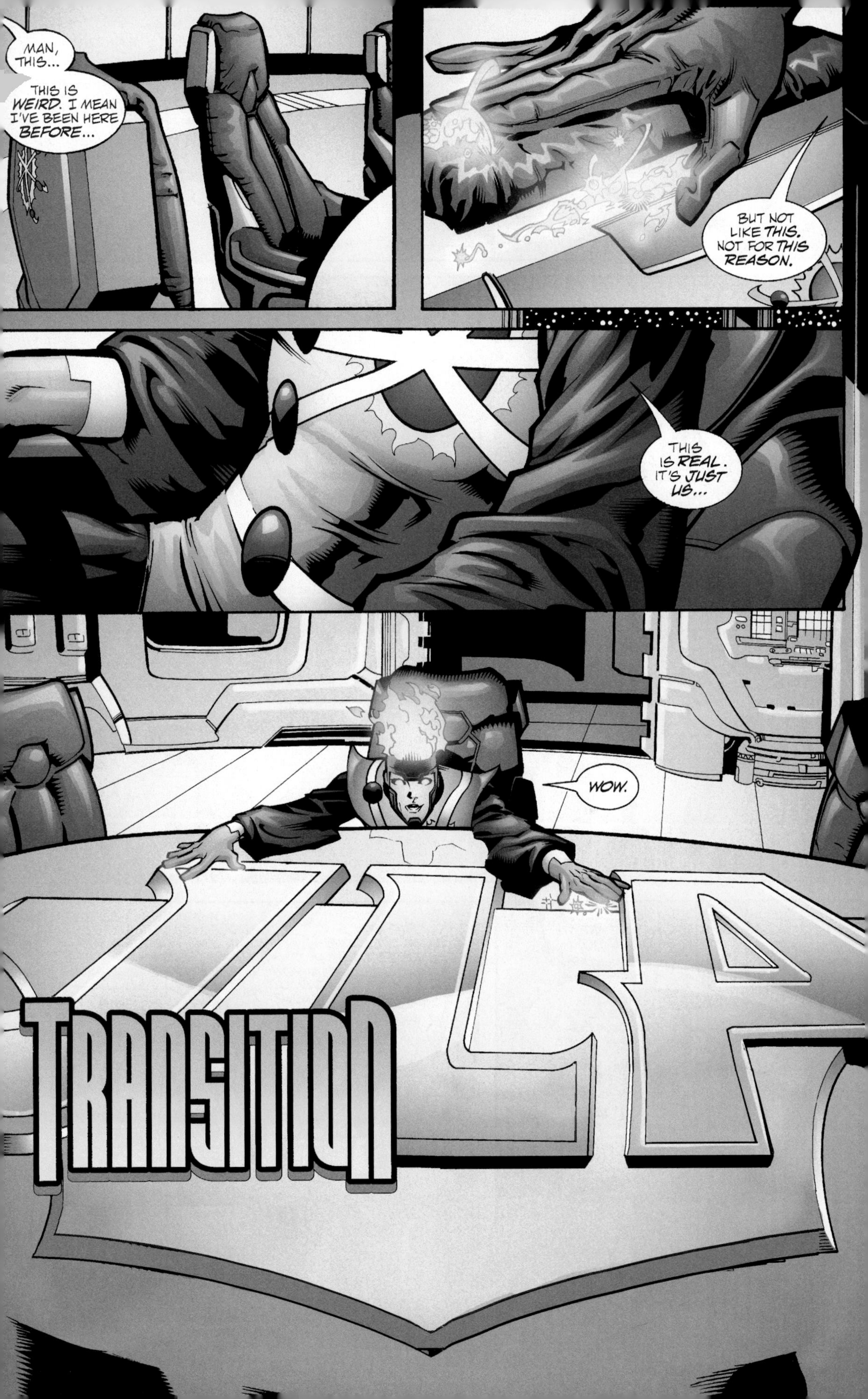
MAN, THIS...
THIS IS WEIRD. I MEAN I'VE BEEN HERE BEFORE...
BUT NOT LIKE THIS. NOT FOR THIS REASON.
THIS IS REAL. IT'S JUST US...
WOW.
TRANSITION

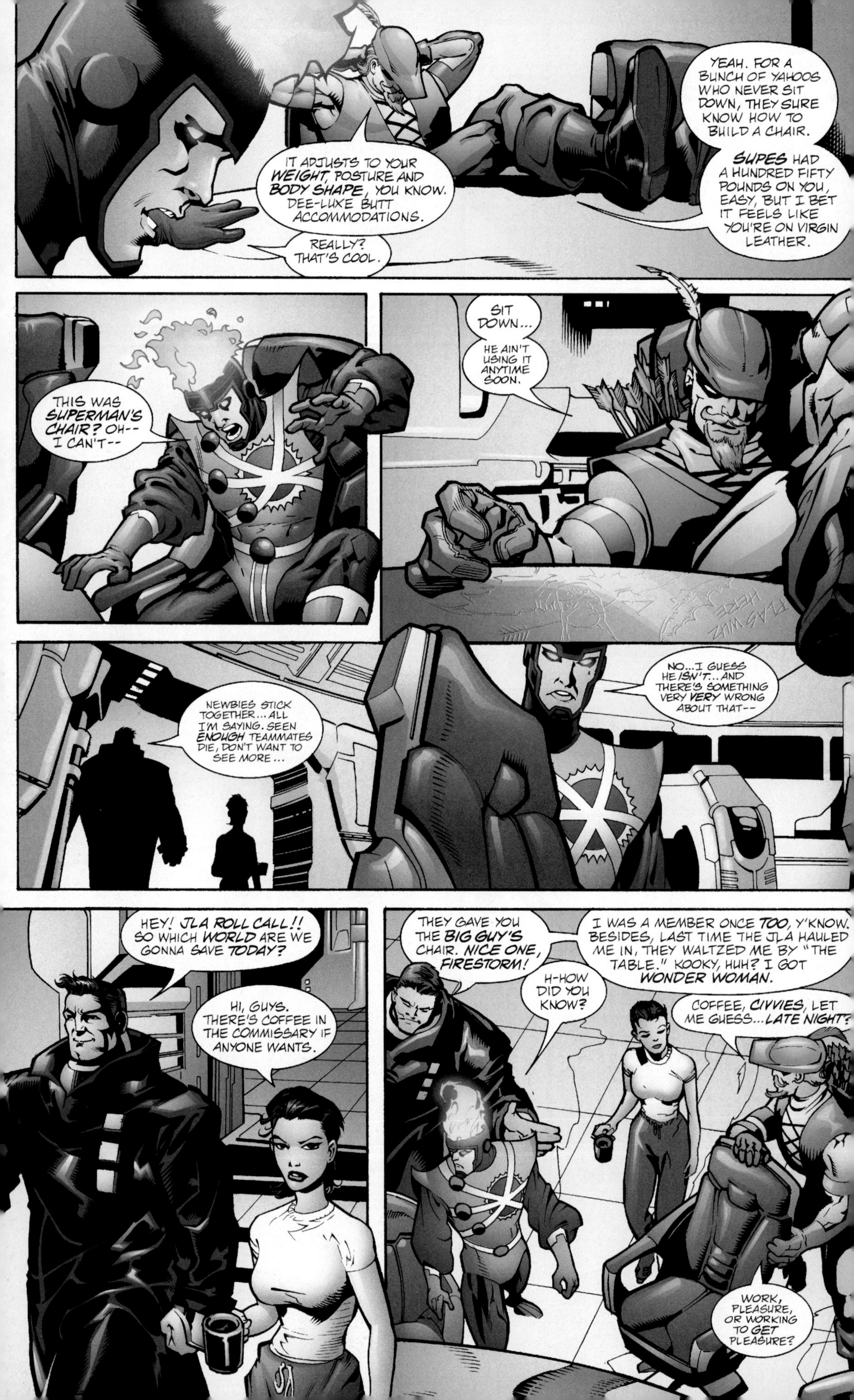
YEAH. FOR A BUNCH OF YAHOOS WHO NEVER SIT DOWN, THEY SURE KNOW HOW TO BUILD A CHAIR.
IT ADJUSTS TO YOUR WEIGHT, POSTURE AND BODY SHAPE, YOU KNOW. DEE-LUXE BUTT ACCOMMODATIONS.
REALLY? THAT'S COOL.
SUPES HAD A HUNDRED FIFTY POUNDS ON YOU, EASY, BUT I BET IT FEELS LIKE YOU'RE ON VIRGIN LEATHER.
THIS WAS SUPERMAN'S CHAIR? OH-- I CAN'T--
SIT DOWN...
HE AIN'T USING IT ANYTIME SOON.
NEWBIES STICK TOGETHER... ALL I'M SAYING. SEEN ENOUGH TEAMMATES DIE, DON'T WANT TO SEE MORE...
NO... I GUESS HE ISN'T... AND THERE'S SOMETHING VERY VERY WRONG ABOUT THAT--
HEY! JLA ROLL CALL!! SO WHICH WORLD ARE WE GONNA SAVE TODAY?
HI, GUYS. THERE'S COFFEE IN THE COMMISSARY IF ANYONE WANTS.
THEY GAVE YOU THE BIG GUY'S CHAIR. NICE ONE, FIRESTORM!
H-HOW DID YOU KNOW?
I WAS A MEMBER ONCE TOO, Y'KNOW. BESIDES, LAST TIME THE JLA HAULED ME IN, THEY WALTZED ME BY "THE TABLE." KOOKY, HUH? I GOT WONDER WOMAN.
COFFEE, CIVVIES, LET ME GUESS... LATE NIGHT?
WORK, PLEASURE, OR WORKING TO GET PLEASURE?

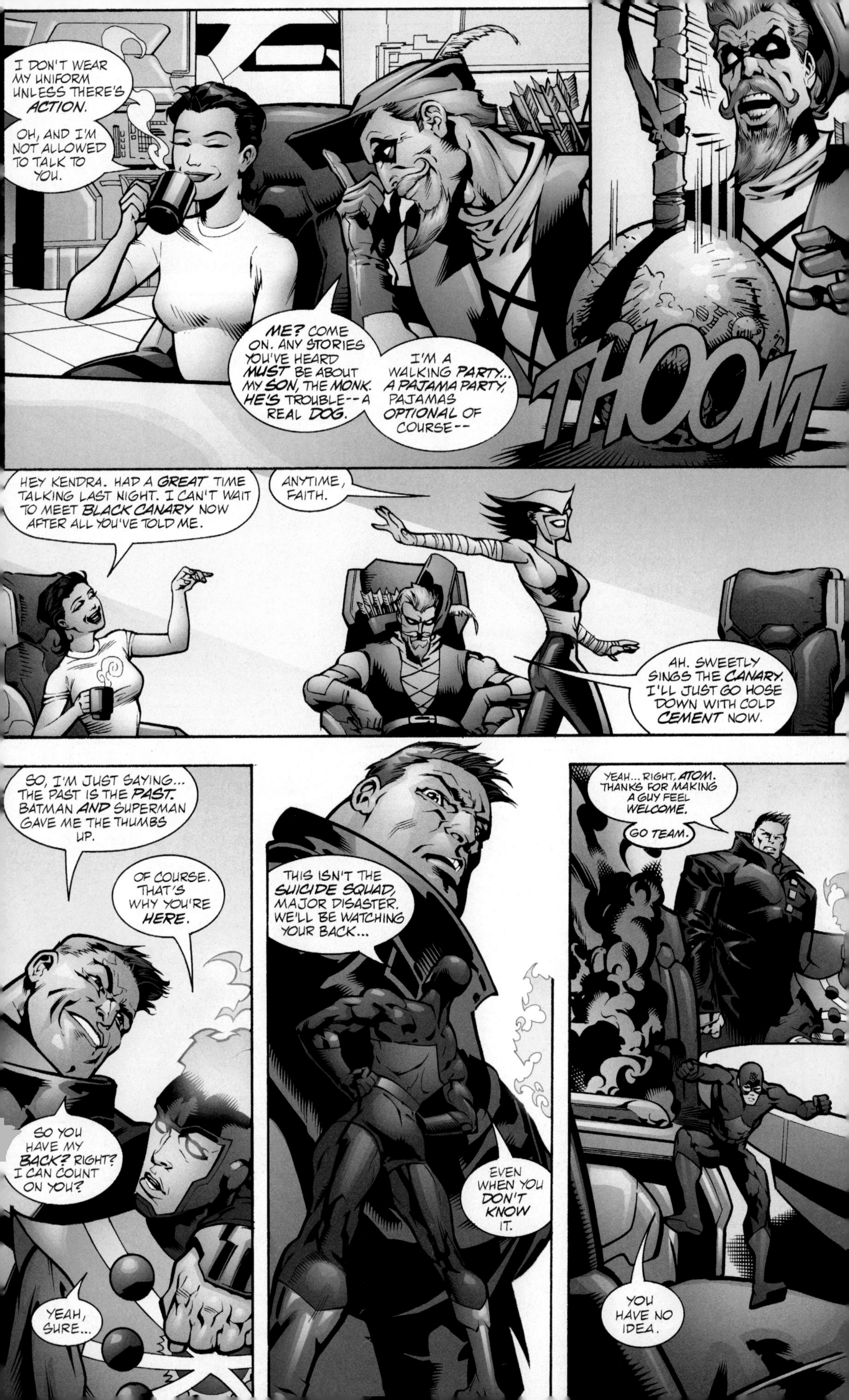

I DON'T WEAR MY UNIFORM UNLESS THERE'S ACTION.
OH, AND I'M NOT ALLOWED TO TALK TO YOU.
ME? COME ON. ANY STORIES YOU'VE HEARD MUST BE ABOUT MY SON, THE MONK. HE'S TROUBLE--A REAL DOG.
I'M A WALKING PARTY... A PAJAMA PARTY, PAJAMAS OPTIONAL OF COURSE--
THOOM
HEY KENDRA. HAD A GREAT TIME TALKING LAST NIGHT. I CAN'T WAIT TO MEET BLACK CANARY NOW AFTER ALL YOU'VE TOLD ME.
ANYTIME, FAITH.
AH. SWEETLY SINGS THE CANARY. I'LL JUST GO HOSE DOWN WITH COLD CEMENT NOW.
SO, I'M JUST SAYING... THE PAST IS THE PAST. BATMAN AND SUPERMAN GAVE ME THE THUMBS UP.
OF COURSE. THAT'S WHY YOU'RE HERE.
SO YOU HAVE MY BACK? RIGHT? I CAN COUNT ON YOU?
YEAH, SURE...
THIS ISN'T THE SUICIDE SQUAD, MAJOR DISASTER. WE'LL BE WATCHING YOUR BACK...
EVEN WHEN YOU DON'T KNOW IT.
YEAH... RIGHT, ATOM. THANKS FOR MAKING A GUY FEEL WELCOME.
GO TEAM.
YOU HAVE NO IDEA.

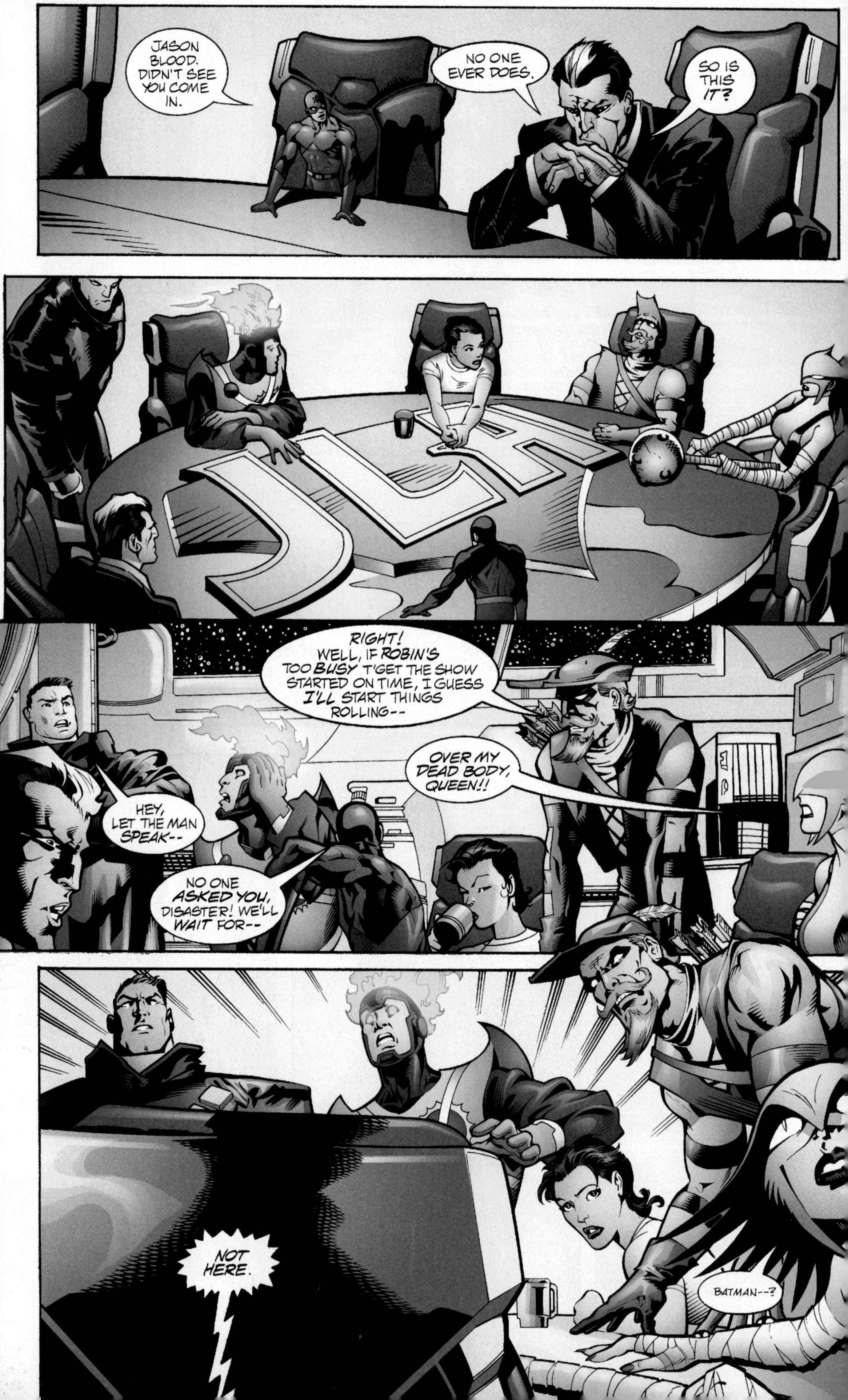
JASON BLOOD. DIDN'T SEE YOU COME IN.
NO ONE EVER DOES.
SO IS THIS IT?
RIGHT! WELL, IF ROBIN'S TOO BUSY T'GET THE SHOW STARTED ON TIME, I GUESS I'LL START THINGS ROLLING--
OVER MY DEAD BODY, QUEEN!!
HEY, LET THE MAN SPEAK--
NO ONE ASKED YOU, DISASTER! WE'LL WAIT FOR--
NOT HERE.
BATMAN--?

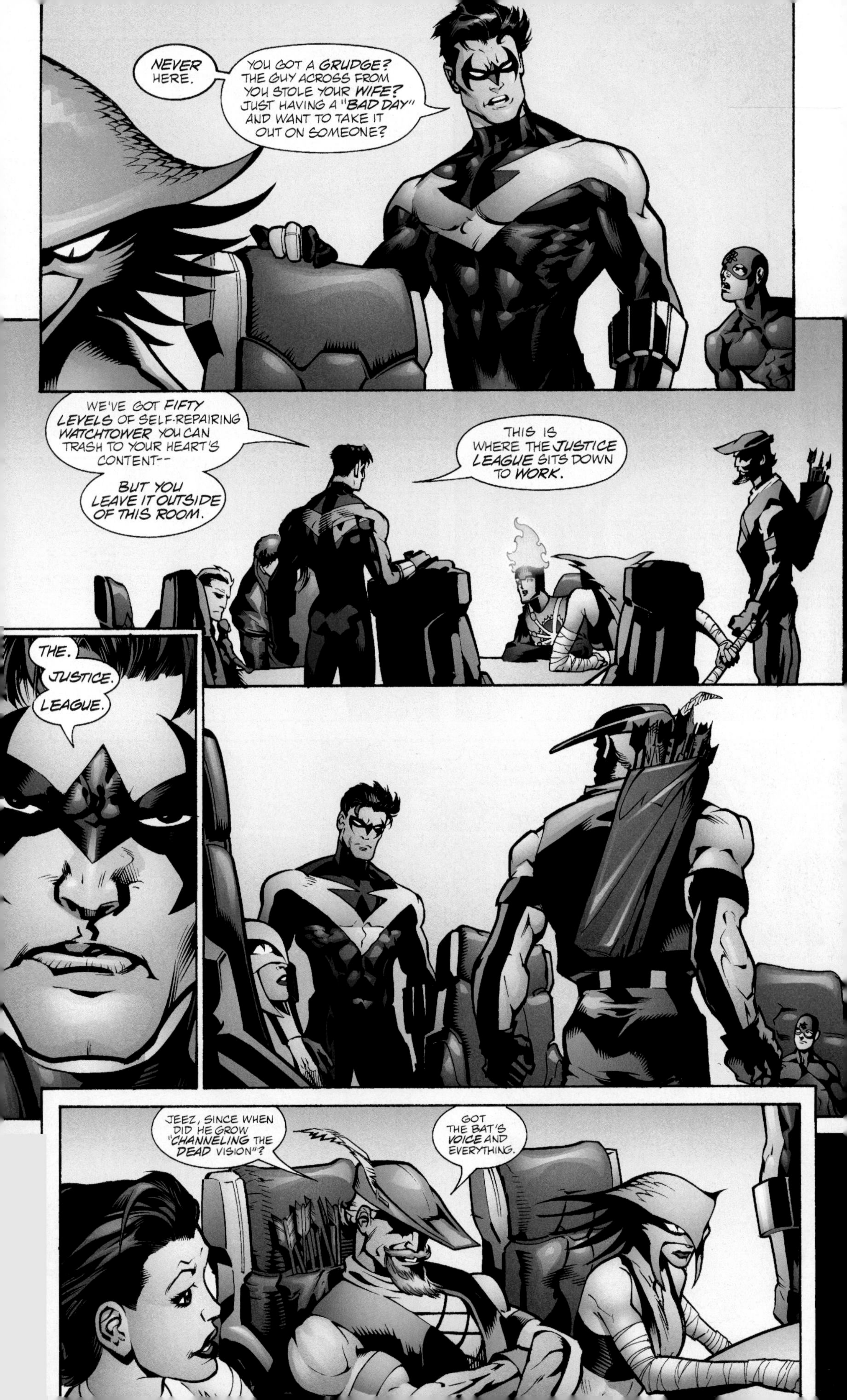
NEVER HERE.
YOU GOT A GRUDGE? THE GUY ACROSS FROM YOU STOLE YOUR WIFE? JUST HAVING A "BAD DAY" AND WANT TO TAKE IT OUT ON SOMEONE?
WE'VE GOT FIFTY LEVELS OF SELF-REPAIRING WATCHTOWER YOU CAN TRASH TO YOUR HEART'S CONTENT--
BUT YOU LEAVE IT OUTSIDE OF THIS ROOM.
THIS IS WHERE THE JUSTICE LEAGUE SITS DOWN TO WORK.
THE.
JUSTICE.
LEAGUE.
JEEZ, SINCE WHEN DID HE GROW "CHANNELING THE DEAD VISION"?
GOT THE BAT'S VOICE AND EVERYTHING.

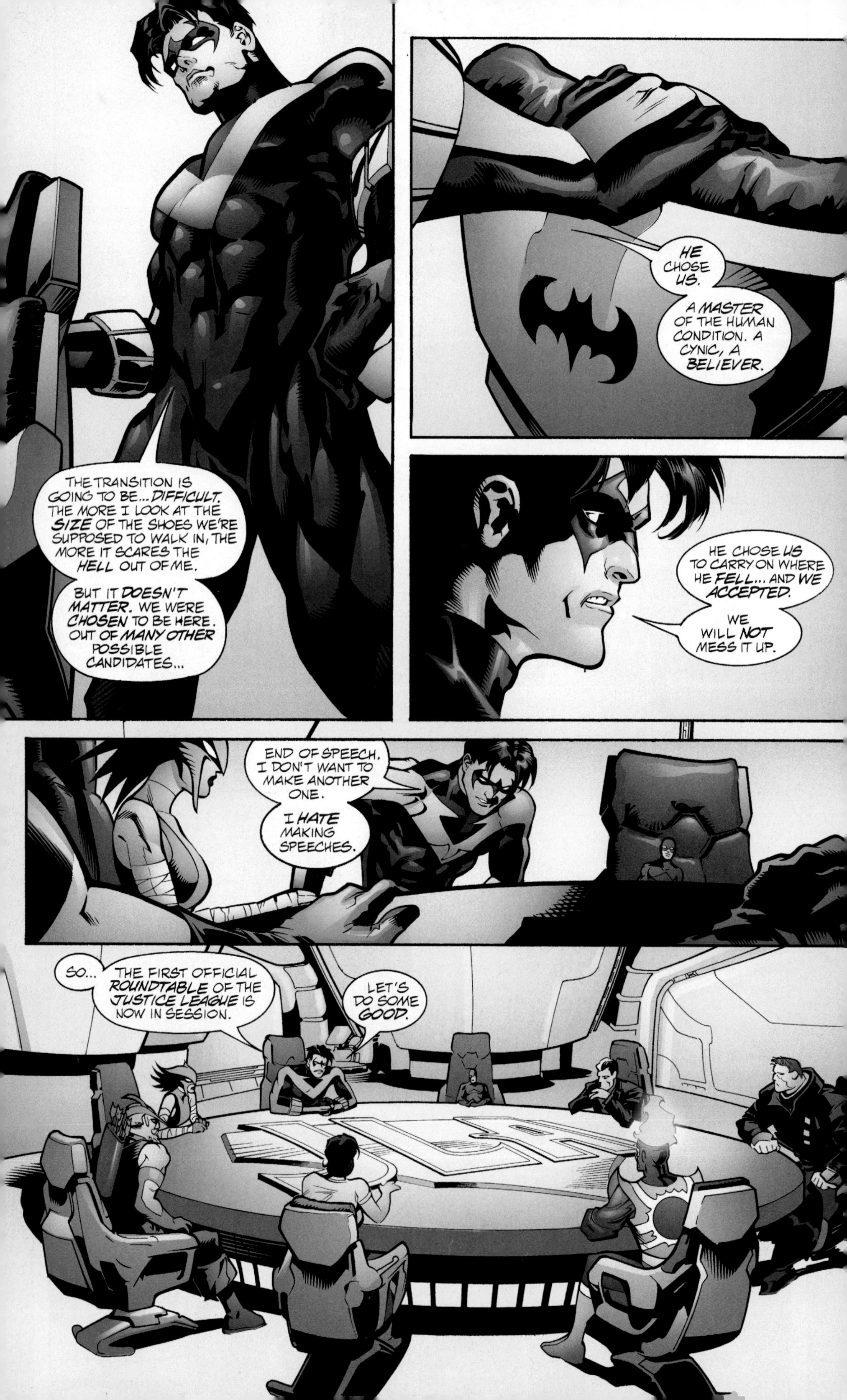
HE CHOSE US.
A MASTER OF THE HUMAN CONDITION. A CYNIC, A BELIEVER.
THE TRANSITION IS GOING TO BE... DIFFICULT. THE MORE I LOOK AT THE SIZE OF THE SHOES WE'RE SUPPOSED TO WALK IN, THE MORE IT SCARES THE HELL OUT OF ME.
BUT IT DOESN'T MATTER. WE WERE CHOSEN TO BE HERE. OUT OF MANY OTHER POSSIBLE CANDIDATES...
HE CHOSE US TO CARRY ON WHERE HE FELL... AND WE ACCEPTED.
WE WILL NOT MESS IT UP.
END OF SPEECH. I DON'T WANT TO MAKE ANOTHER ONE.
I HATE MAKING SPEECHES.
SO...
THE FIRST OFFICIAL ROUNDTABLE OF THE JUSTICE LEAGUE IS NOW IN SESSION.
LET'S DO SOME GOOD.

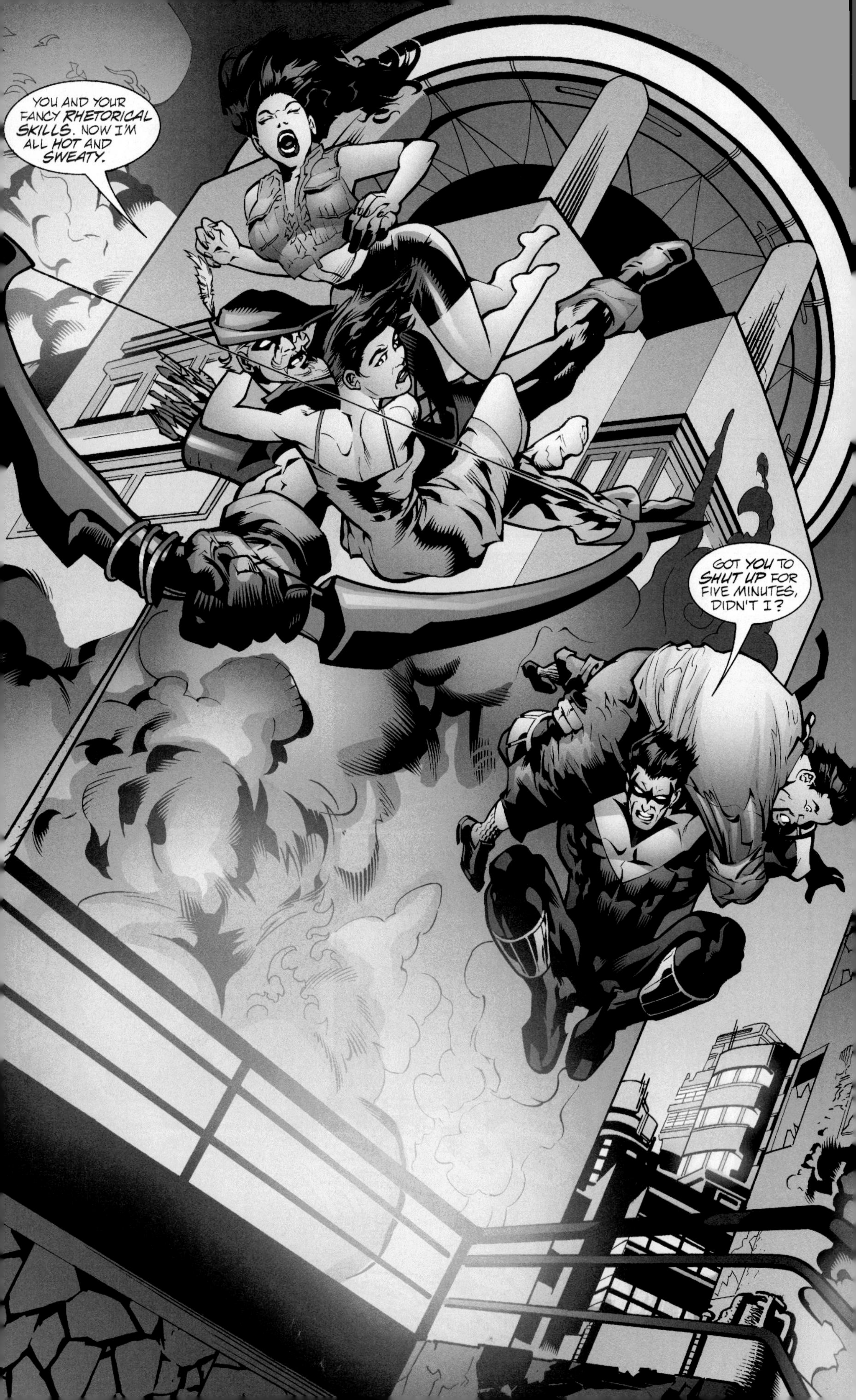
YOU AND YOUR FANCY RHETORICAL SKILLS. NOW I'M ALL HOT AND SWEATY.
GOT YOU TO SHUT UP FOR FIVE MINUTES, DIDN'T I?

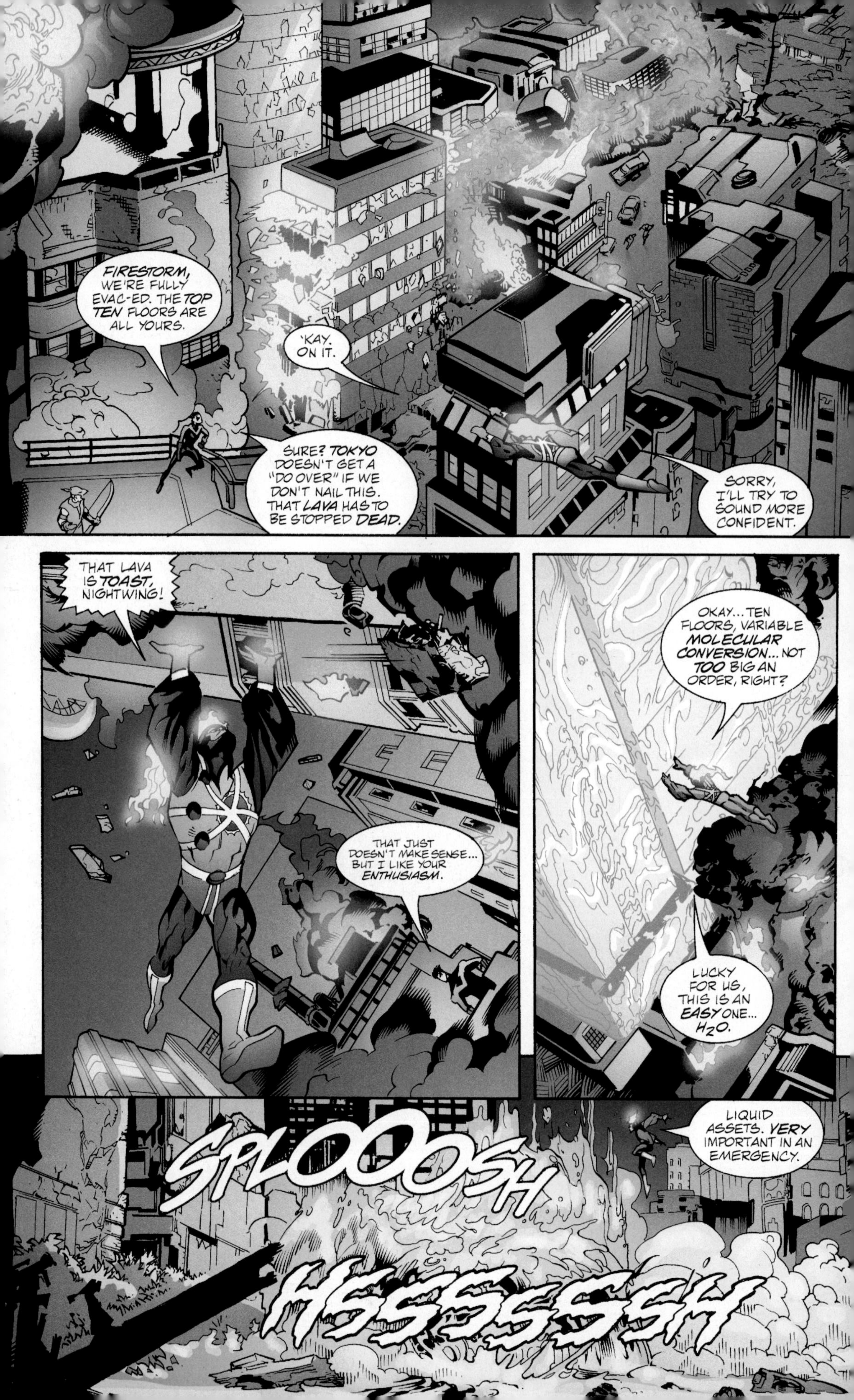
FIRESTORM, WE'RE FULLY EVAC-ED. THE TOP TEN FLOORS ARE ALL YOURS.
'KAY. ON IT.
SURE? TOKYO DOESN'T GET A "DO OVER" IF WE DON'T NAIL THIS. THAT LAVA HAS TO BE STOPPED DEAD.
SORRY, I'LL TRY TO SOUND MORE CONFIDENT.
THAT LAVA IS TOAST, NIGHTWING!
THAT JUST DOESN'T MAKE SENSE... BUT I LIKE YOUR ENTHUSIASM.
OKAY... TEN FLOORS, VARIABLE MOLECULAR CONVERSION... NOT TOO BIG AN ORDER, RIGHT?
LUCKY FOR US, THIS IS AN EASY ONE... H_2O.
SPLOOOSH
LIQUID ASSETS. VERY IMPORTANT IN AN EMERGENCY.
HSSSSSSH

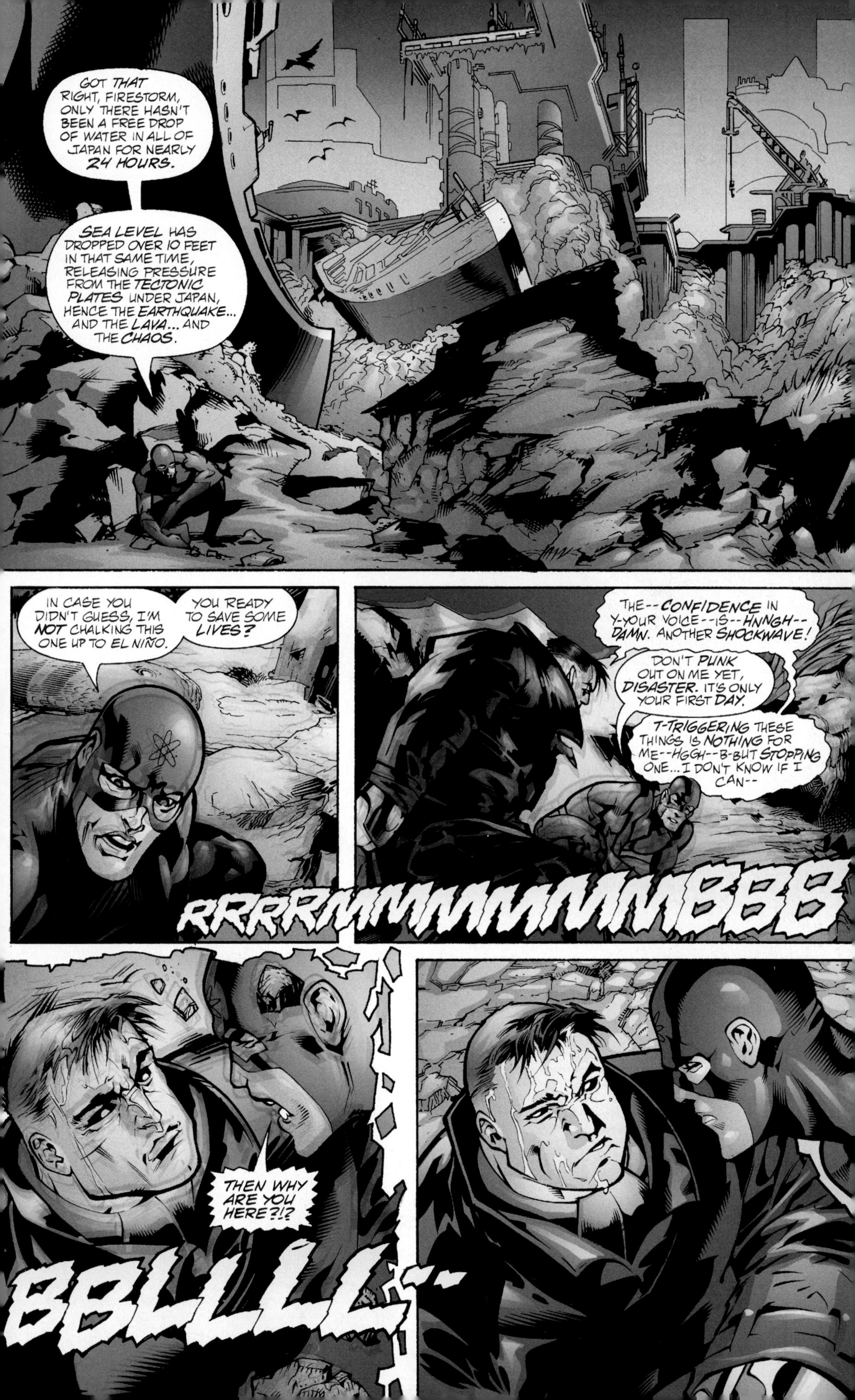
GOT THAT RIGHT, FIRESTORM, ONLY THERE HASN'T BEEN A FREE DROP OF WATER IN ALL OF JAPAN FOR NEARLY 24 HOURS.
SEA LEVEL HAS DROPPED OVER 10 FEET IN THAT SAME TIME, RELEASING PRESSURE FROM THE TECTONIC PLATES UNDER JAPAN, HENCE THE EARTHQUAKE... AND THE LAVA... AND THE CHAOS.
IN CASE YOU DIDN'T GUESS, I'M NOT CHALKING THIS ONE UP TO EL NIÑO.
YOU READY TO SAVE SOME LIVES?
THE--CONFIDENCE IN Y-YOUR VOICE--IS--HNNGH--DAMN. ANOTHER SHOCKWAVE!
DON'T PUNK OUT ON ME YET, DISASTER. IT'S ONLY YOUR FIRST DAY.
T-TRIGGERING THESE THINGS IS NOTHING FOR ME--HGGH--B-BUT STOPPING ONE... I DON'T KNOW IF I CAN--
RRRRMMMMMMMBBB
THEN WHY ARE YOU HERE?!?
BBLLLL--

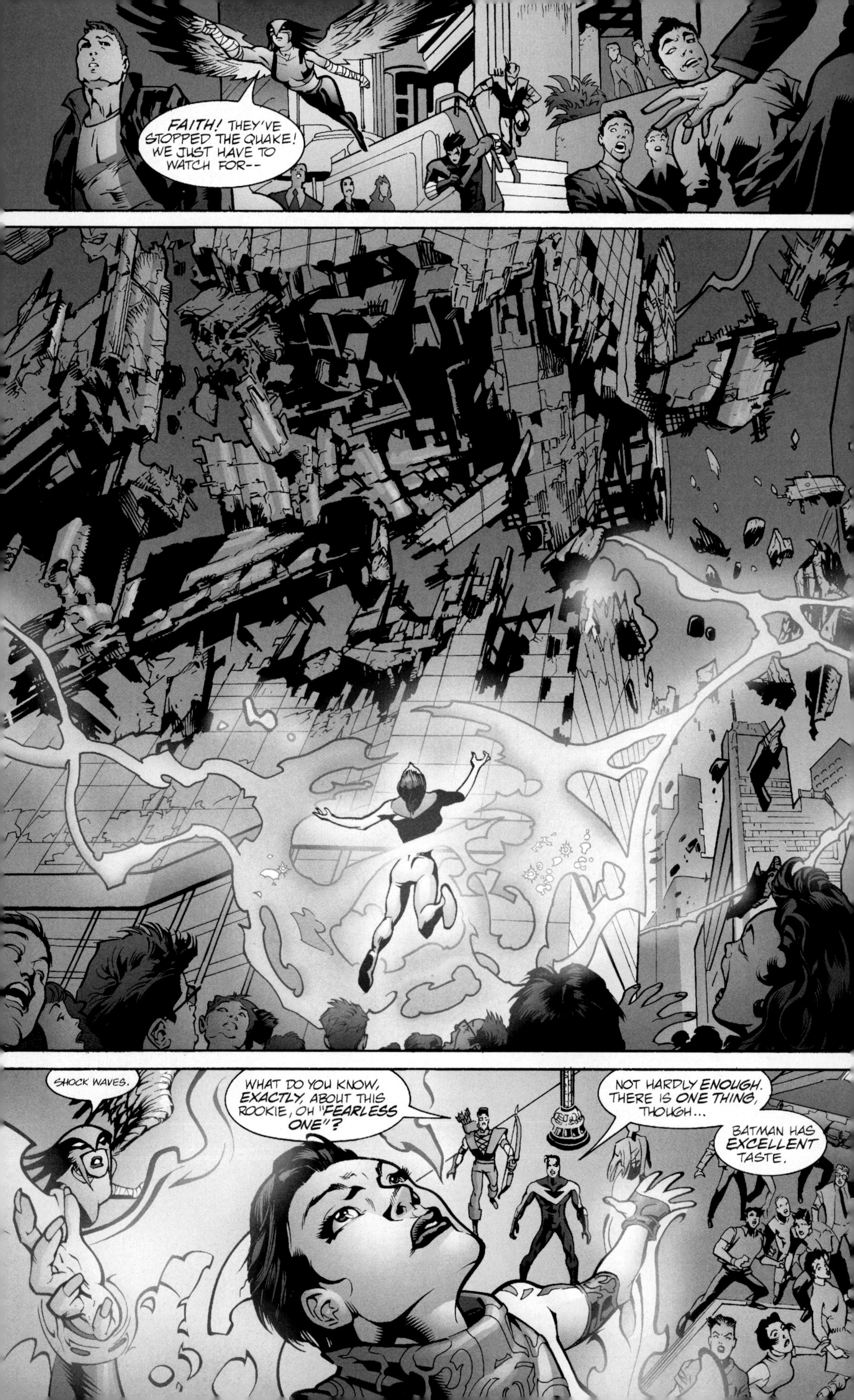
FAITH! THEY'VE STOPPED THE QUAKE! WE JUST HAVE TO WATCH FOR--
SHOCK WAVES.
WHAT DO YOU KNOW, EXACTLY, ABOUT THIS ROOKIE, OH "FEARLESS ONE"?
NOT HARDLY ENOUGH. THERE IS ONE THING, THOUGH...
BATMAN HAS EXCELLENT TASTE.

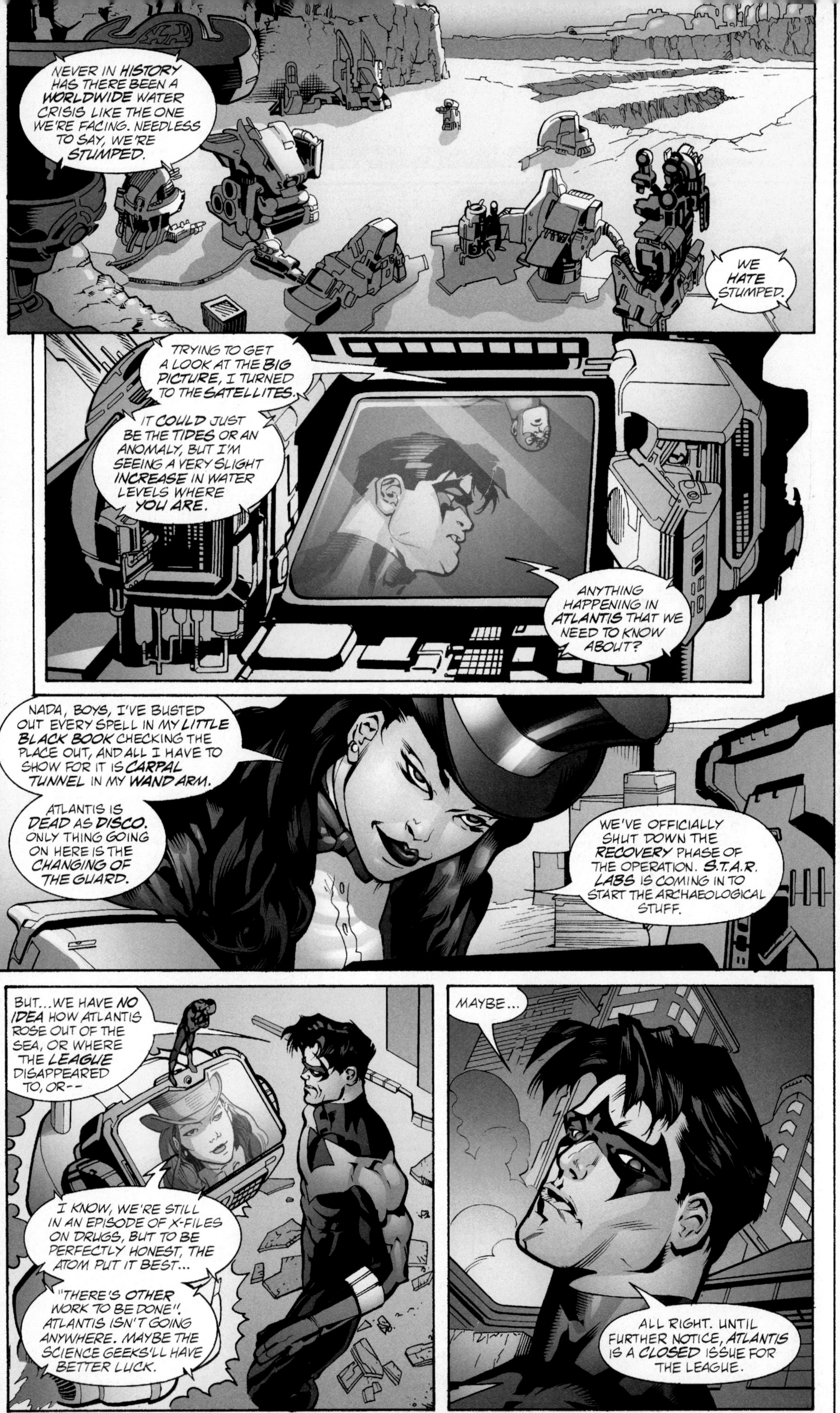
NEVER IN HISTORY HAS THERE BEEN A WORLDWIDE WATER CRISIS LIKE THE ONE WE'RE FACING. NEEDLESS TO SAY, WE'RE STUMPED.
WE HATE STUMPED.
TRYING TO GET A LOOK AT THE BIG PICTURE, I TURNED TO THE SATELLITES.
IT COULD JUST BE THE TIDES OR AN ANOMALY, BUT I'M SEEING A VERY SLIGHT INCREASE IN WATER LEVELS WHERE YOU ARE.
ANYTHING HAPPENING IN ATLANTIS THAT WE NEED TO KNOW ABOUT?
NADA, BOYS, I'VE BUSTED OUT EVERY SPELL IN MY LITTLE BLACK BOOK CHECKING THE PLACE OUT, AND ALL I HAVE TO SHOW FOR IT IS CARPAL TUNNEL IN MY WAND ARM.
ATLANTIS IS DEAD AS DISCO. ONLY THING GOING ON HERE IS THE CHANGING OF THE GUARD.
WE'VE OFFICIALLY SHUT DOWN THE RECOVERY PHASE OF THE OPERATION. S.T.A.R. LABS IS COMING IN TO START THE ARCHAEOLOGICAL STUFF.
BUT...WE HAVE NO IDEA HOW ATLANTIS ROSE OUT OF THE SEA, OR WHERE THE LEAGUE DISAPPEARED TO, OR--
I KNOW, WE'RE STILL IN AN EPISODE OF X-FILES ON DRUGS, BUT TO BE PERFECTLY HONEST, THE ATOM PUT IT BEST...
"THERE'S OTHER WORK TO BE DONE". ATLANTIS ISN'T GOING ANYWHERE. MAYBE THE SCIENCE GEEKS'LL HAVE BETTER LUCK.
MAYBE...
ALL RIGHT. UNTIL FURTHER NOTICE, ATLANTIS IS A CLOSED ISSUE FOR THE LEAGUE.

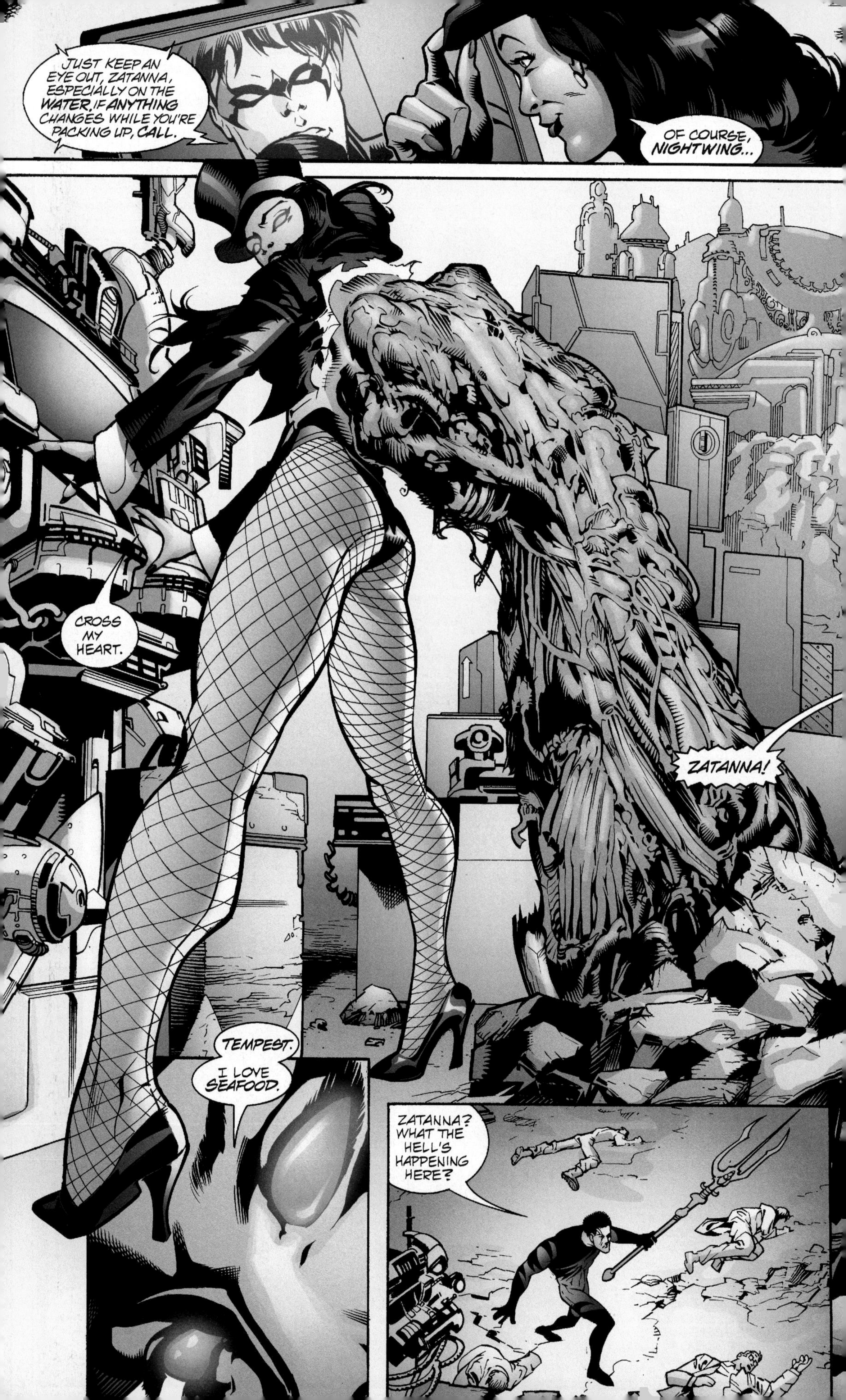
JUST KEEP AN EYE OUT, ZATANNA, ESPECIALLY ON THE WATER. IF ANYTHING CHANGES WHILE YOU'RE PACKING UP, CALL.
OF COURSE, NIGHTWING...
CROSS MY HEART.
ZATANNA!
TEMPEST. I LOVE SEAFOOD.
ZATANNA? WHAT THE HELL'S HAPPENING HERE?

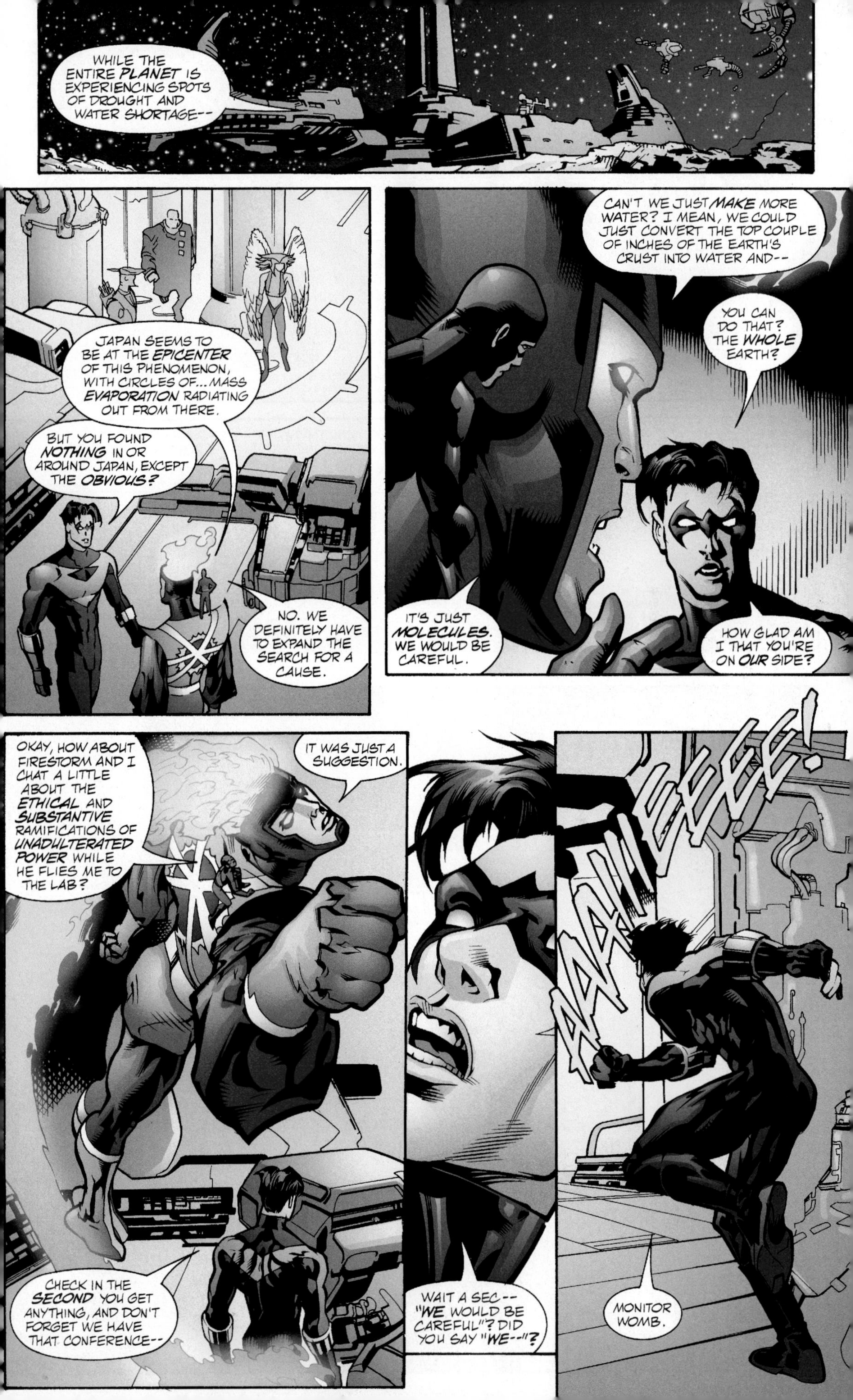
WHILE THE ENTIRE PLANET IS EXPERIENCING SPOTS OF DROUGHT AND WATER SHORTAGE--
JAPAN SEEMS TO BE AT THE EPICENTER OF THIS PHENOMENON, WITH CIRCLES OF... MASS EVAPORATION RADIATING OUT FROM THERE.
BUT YOU FOUND NOTHING IN OR AROUND JAPAN, EXCEPT THE OBVIOUS?
NO. WE DEFINITELY HAVE TO EXPAND THE SEARCH FOR A CAUSE.
CAN'T WE JUST MAKE MORE WATER? I MEAN, WE COULD JUST CONVERT THE TOP COUPLE OF INCHES OF THE EARTH'S CRUST INTO WATER AND--
YOU CAN DO THAT? THE WHOLE EARTH?
IT'S JUST MOLECULES. WE WOULD BE CAREFUL.
HOW GLAD AM I THAT YOU'RE ON OUR SIDE?
OKAY, HOW ABOUT FIRESTORM AND I CHAT A LITTLE ABOUT THE ETHICAL AND SUBSTANTIVE RAMIFICATIONS OF UNADULTERATED POWER WHILE HE FLIES ME TO THE LAB?
IT WAS JUST A SUGGESTION.
CHECK IN THE SECOND YOU GET ANYTHING, AND DON'T FORGET WE HAVE THAT CONFERENCE--
WAIT A SEC-- "WE WOULD BE CAREFUL"? DID YOU SAY "WE--"?
BADWHEEEE!
MONITOR WOMB.

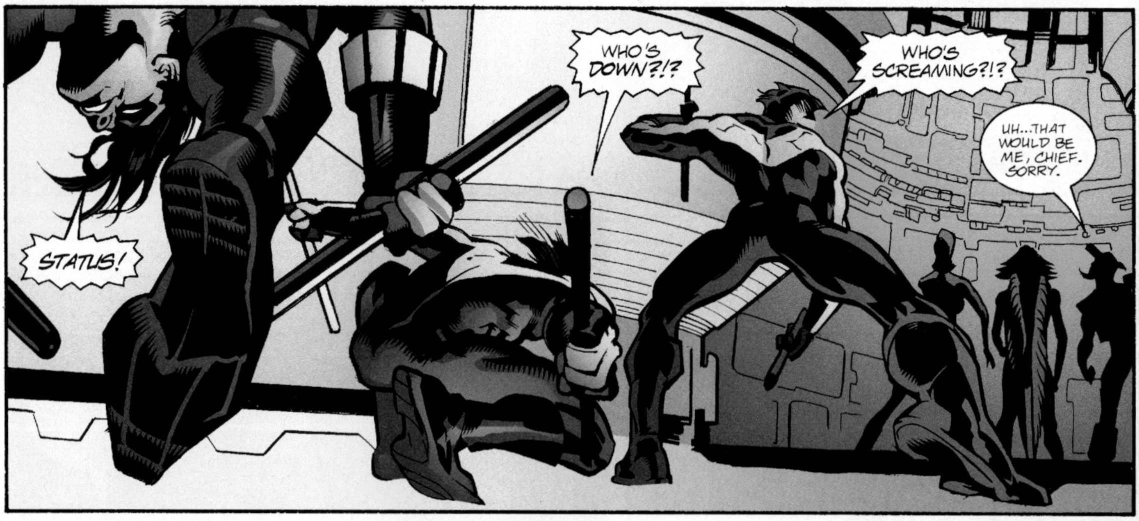
STATUS!
WHO'S DOWN?!?
WHO'S SCREAMING?!?
UH...THAT WOULD BE ME, CHIEF. SORRY.

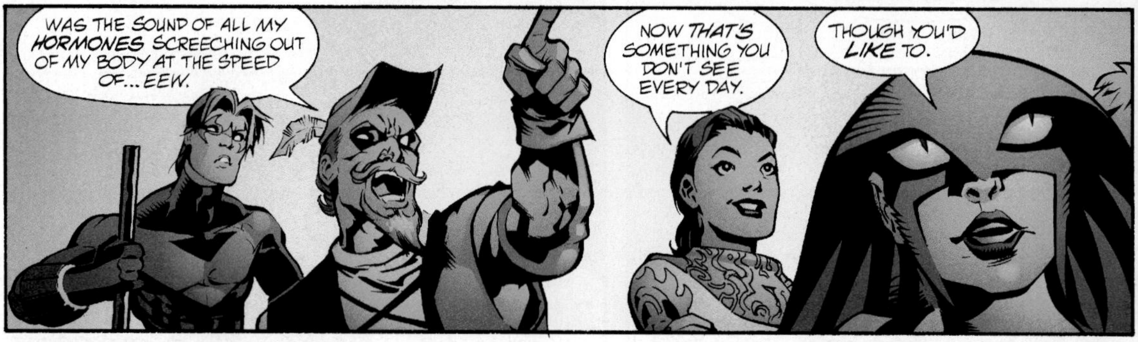
WAS THE SOUND OF ALL MY HORMONES SCREECHING OUT OF MY BODY AT THE SPEED OF... EEW.
NOW THAT'S SOMETHING YOU DON'T SEE EVERY DAY.
THOUGH YOU'D LIKE TO.

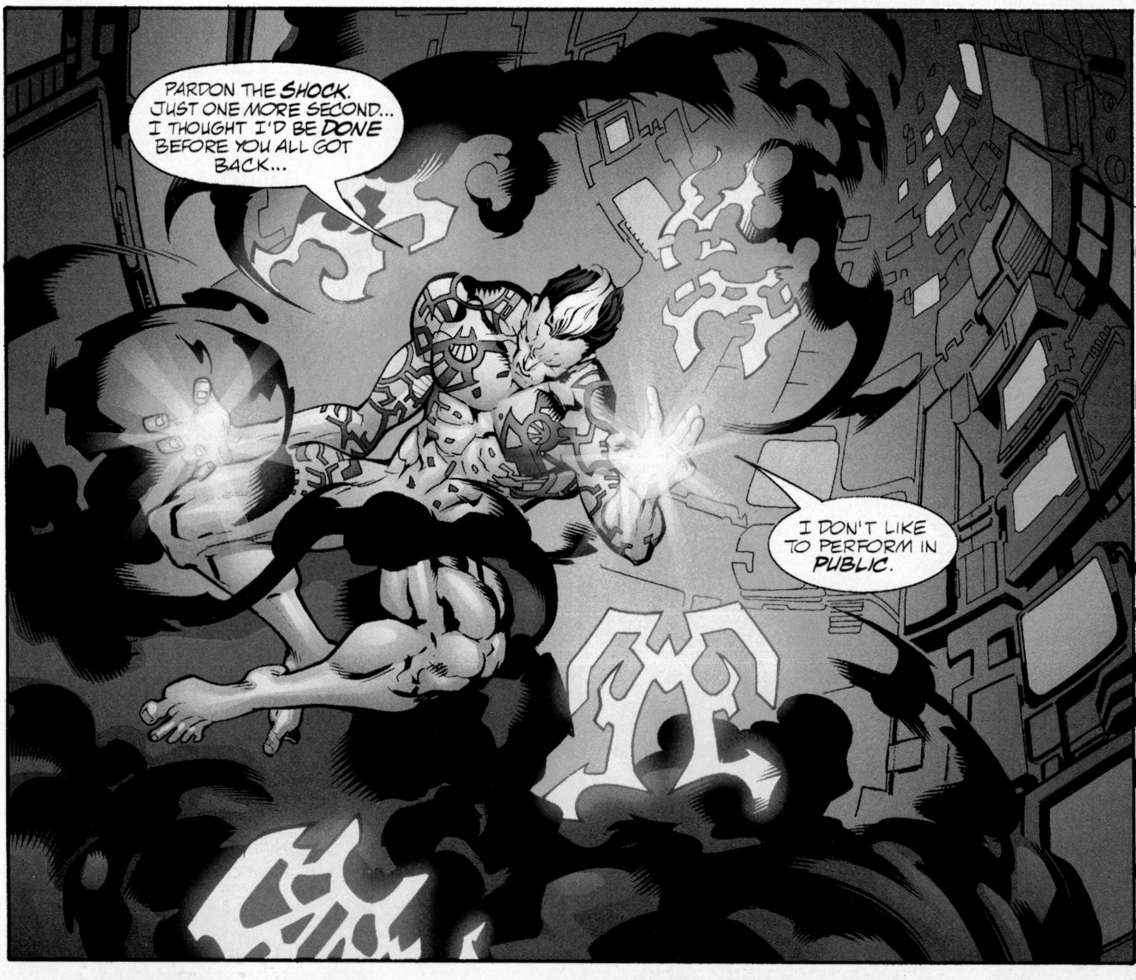
PARDON THE SHOCK. JUST ONE MORE SECOND... I THOUGHT I'D BE DONE BEFORE YOU ALL GOT BACK...
I DON'T LIKE TO PERFORM IN PUBLIC.

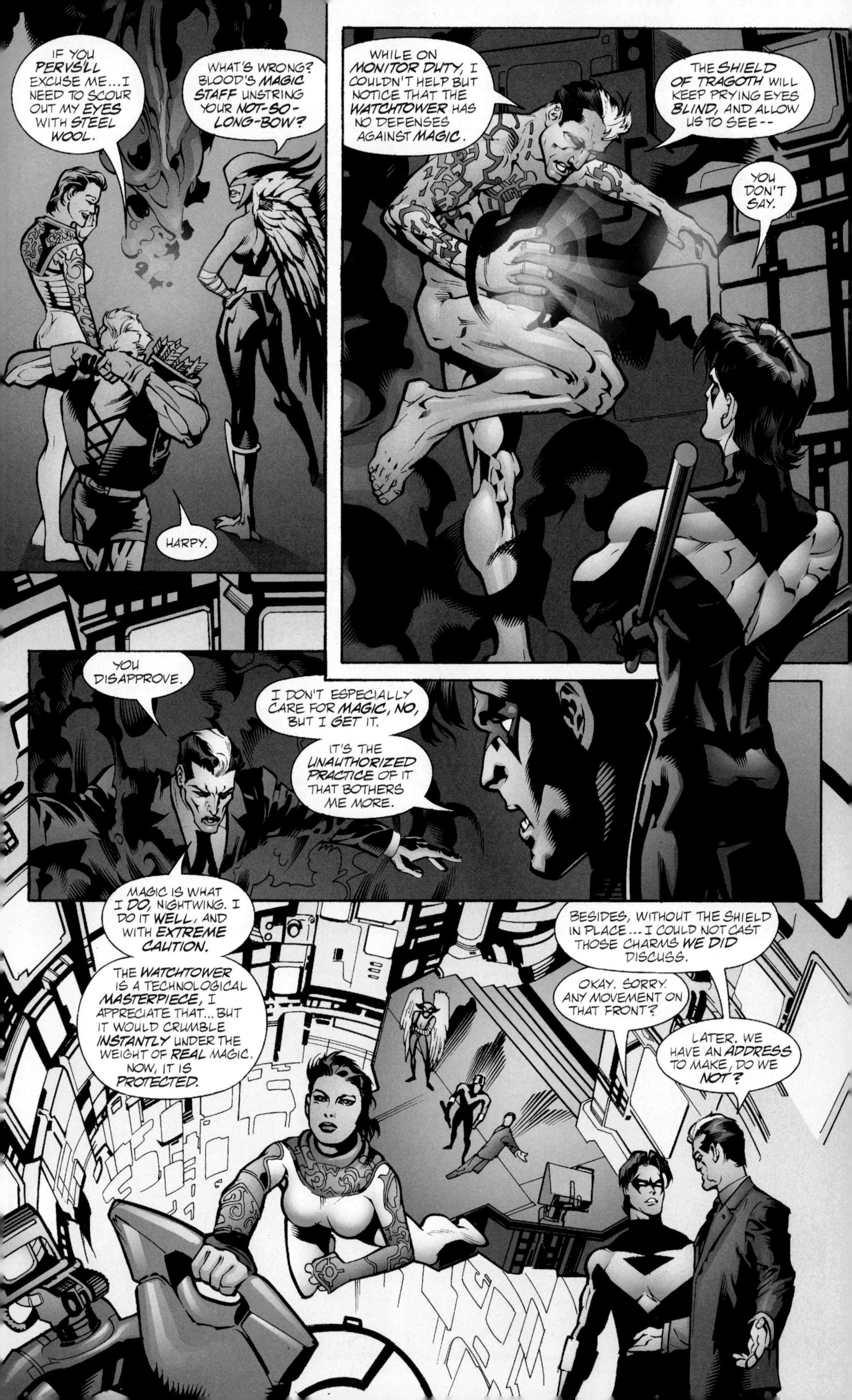
IF YOU PERVS'LL EXCUSE ME... I NEED TO SCOUR OUT MY EYES WITH STEEL WOOL.
WHAT'S WRONG? BLOOD'S MAGIC STAFF UNSTRING YOUR NOT-SO-LONG-BOW?
HARPY.
WHILE ON MONITOR DUTY, I COULDN'T HELP BUT NOTICE THAT THE WATCHTOWER HAS NO DEFENSES AGAINST MAGIC.
THE SHIELD OF TRAGOTH WILL KEEP PRYING EYES BLIND, AND ALLOW US TO SEE --
YOU DON'T SAY.
YOU DISAPPROVE.
I DON'T ESPECIALLY CARE FOR MAGIC, NO, BUT I GET IT.
IT'S THE UNAUTHORIZED PRACTICE OF IT THAT BOTHERS ME MORE.
MAGIC IS WHAT I DO, NIGHTWING. I DO IT WELL, AND WITH EXTREME CAUTION.
THE WATCHTOWER IS A TECHNOLOGICAL MASTERPIECE, I APPRECIATE THAT... BUT IT WOULD CRUMBLE INSTANTLY UNDER THE WEIGHT OF REAL MAGIC. NOW, IT IS PROTECTED.
BESIDES, WITHOUT THE SHIELD IN PLACE... I COULD NOT CAST THOSE CHARMS WE DID DISCUSS.
OKAY. SORRY. ANY MOVEMENT ON THAT FRONT?
LATER. WE HAVE AN ADDRESS TO MAKE, DO WE NOT?

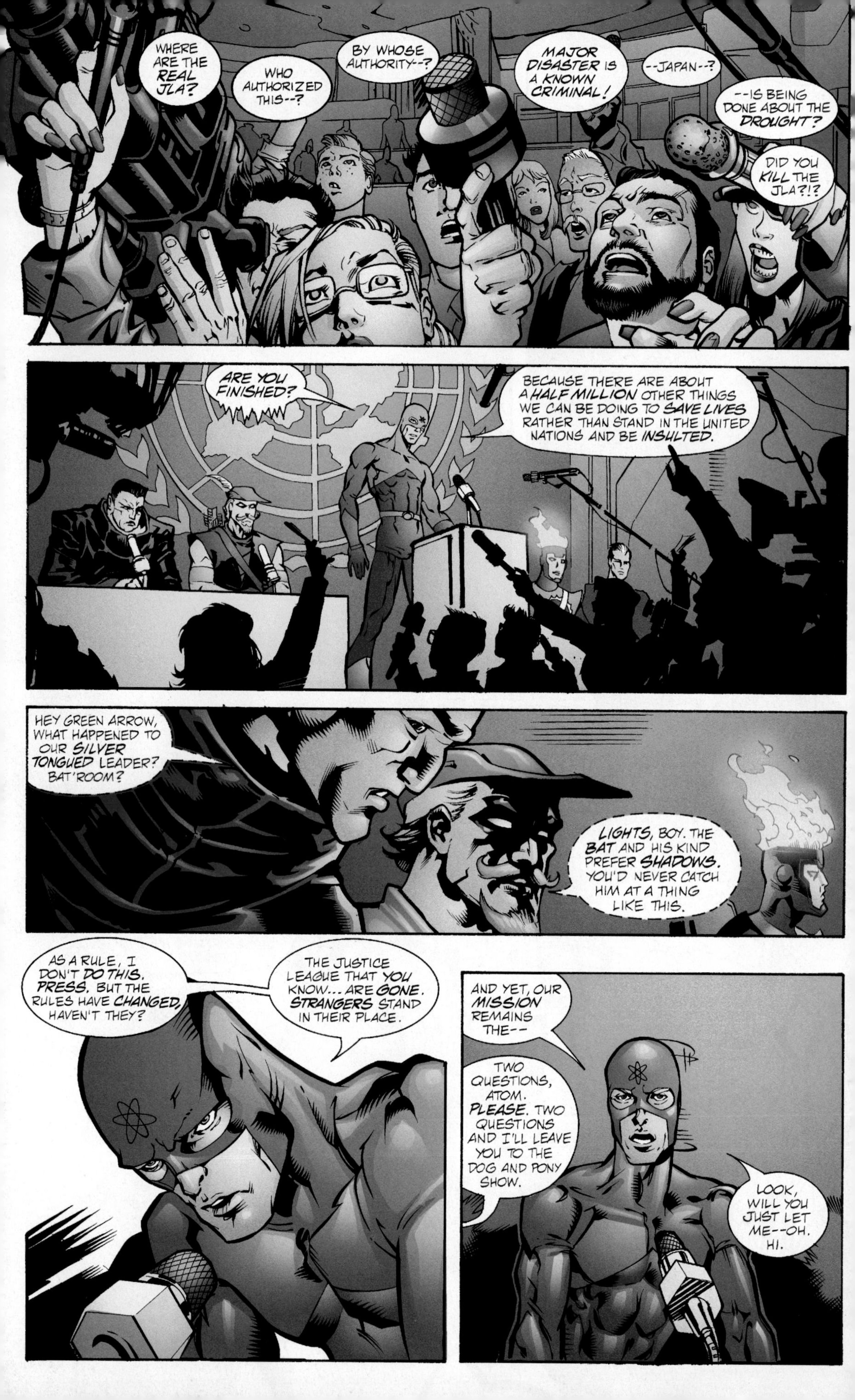
WHERE ARE THE REAL JLA?
WHO AUTHORIZED THIS--?
BY WHOSE AUTHORITY--?
MAJOR DISASTER IS A KNOWN CRIMINAL!
--JAPAN--?
--IS BEING DONE ABOUT THE DROUGHT?
DID YOU KILL THE JLA?!?
ARE YOU FINISHED?
BECAUSE THERE ARE ABOUT A HALF MILLION OTHER THINGS WE CAN BE DOING TO SAVE LIVES RATHER THAN STAND IN THE UNITED NATIONS AND BE INSULTED.
HEY GREEN ARROW, WHAT HAPPENED TO OUR SILVER TONGUED LEADER? BAT'ROOM?
LIGHTS, BOY. THE BAT AND HIS KIND PREFER SHADOWS. YOU'D NEVER CATCH HIM AT A THING LIKE THIS.
AS A RULE, I DON'T DO THIS. PRESS. BUT THE RULES HAVE CHANGED, HAVEN'T THEY?
THE JUSTICE LEAGUE THAT YOU KNOW... ARE GONE. STRANGERS STAND IN THEIR PLACE.
AND YET, OUR MISSION REMAINS THE--
TWO QUESTIONS, ATOM. PLEASE. TWO QUESTIONS AND I'LL LEAVE YOU TO THE DOG AND PONY SHOW.
LOOK, WILL YOU JUST LET ME--OH. HI.

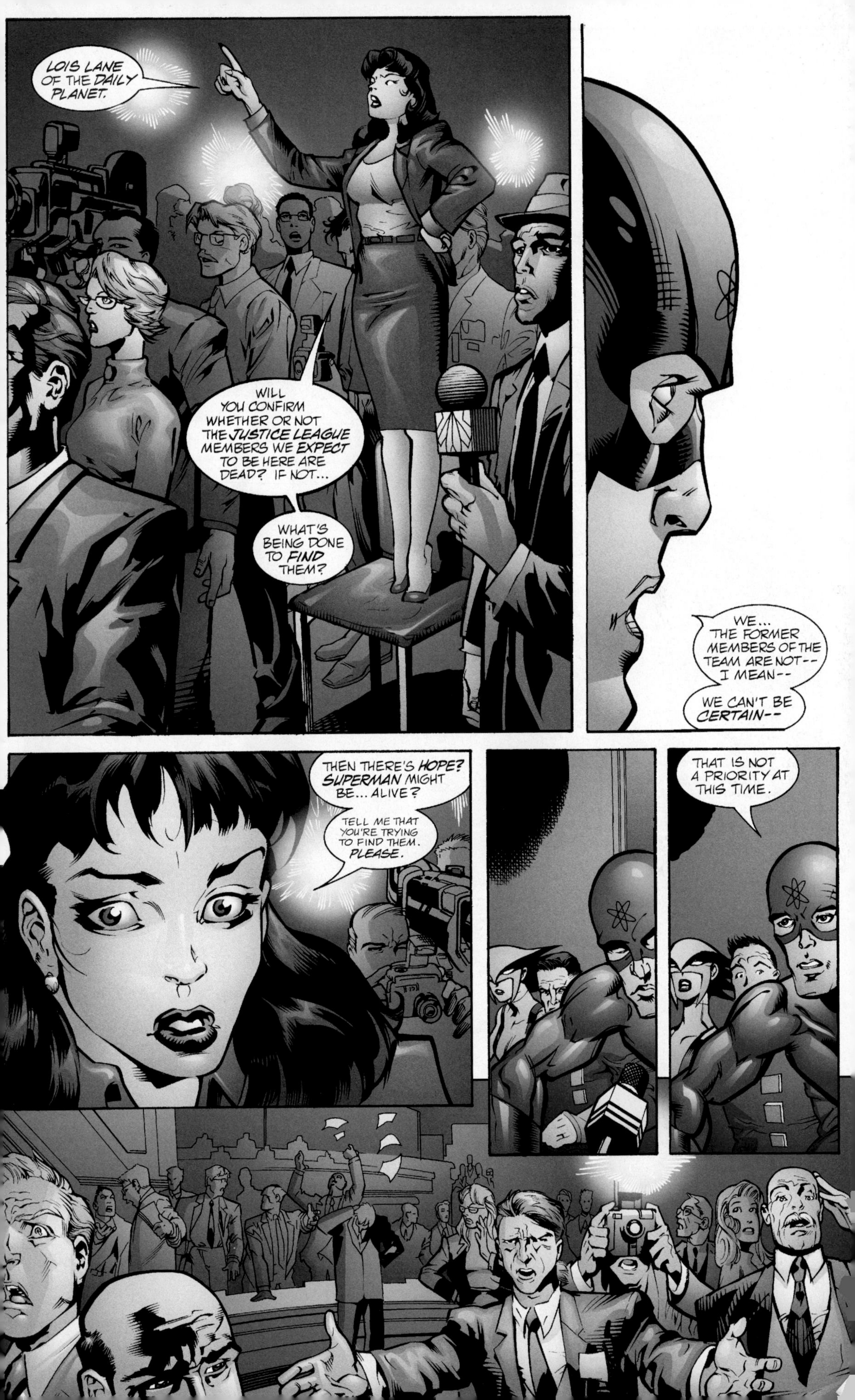
LOIS LANE OF THE DAILY PLANET.
WILL YOU CONFIRM WHETHER OR NOT THE JUSTICE LEAGUE MEMBERS WE EXPECT TO BE HERE ARE DEAD? IF NOT...
WHAT'S BEING DONE TO FIND THEM?
WE... THE FORMER MEMBERS OF THE TEAM ARE NOT-- I MEAN--
WE CAN'T BE CERTAIN--
THEN THERE'S HOPE? SUPERMAN MIGHT BE... ALIVE?
TELL ME THAT YOU'RE TRYING TO FIND THEM. PLEASE.
THAT IS NOT A PRIORITY AT THIS TIME.

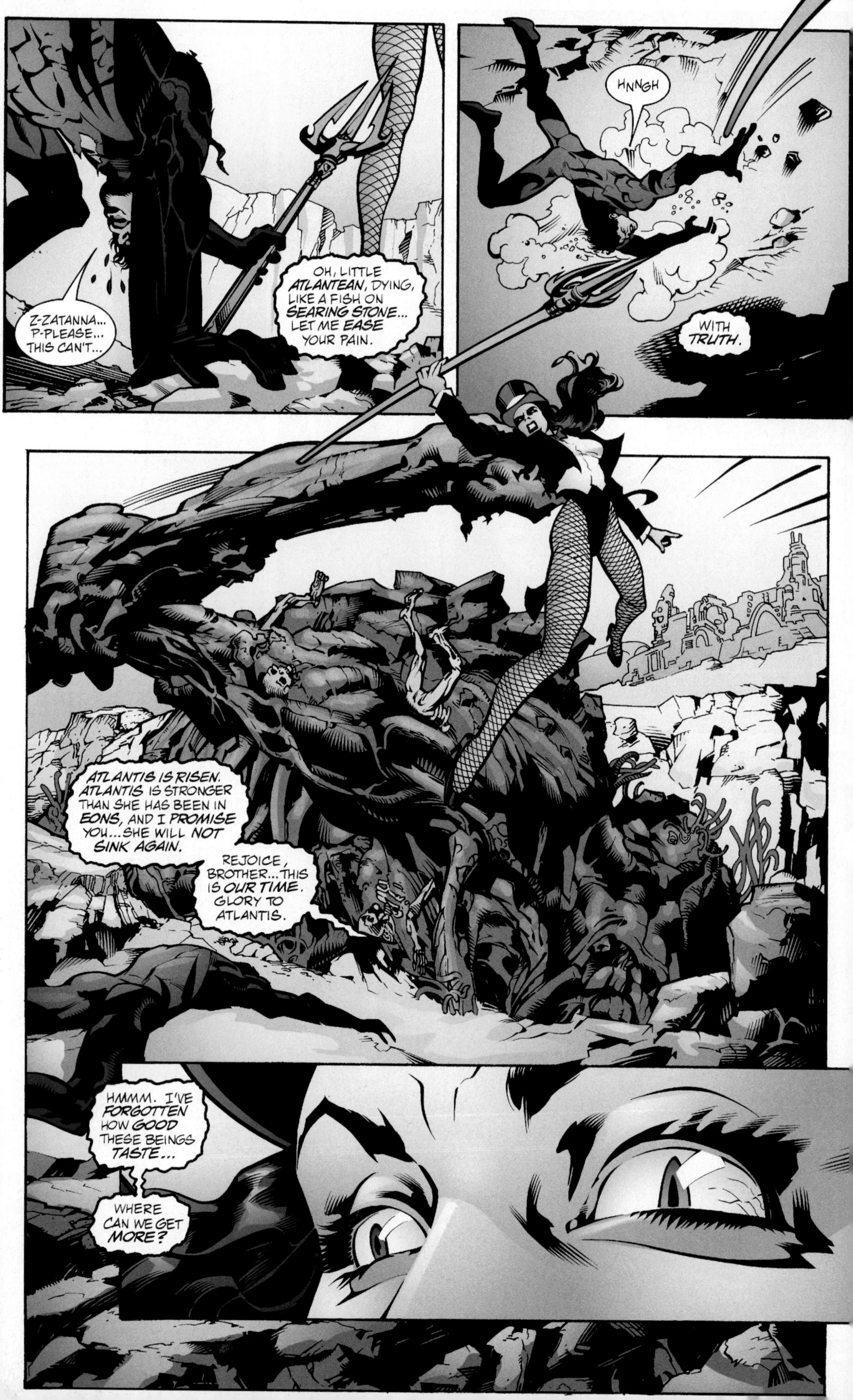
Z-ZATANNA... P-PLEASE... THIS CAN'T...
OH, LITTLE ATLANTEAN, DYING, LIKE A FISH ON SEARING STONE... LET ME EASE YOUR PAIN.
HNNGH
WITH TRUTH.
ATLANTIS IS RISEN. ATLANTIS IS STRONGER THAN SHE HAS BEEN IN EONS, AND I PROMISE YOU...SHE WILL NOT SINK AGAIN.
REJOICE, BROTHER...THIS IS OUR TIME. GLORY TO ATLANTIS.
HMMM. I'VE FORGOTTEN HOW GOOD THESE BEINGS TASTE...
WHERE CAN WE GET MORE?

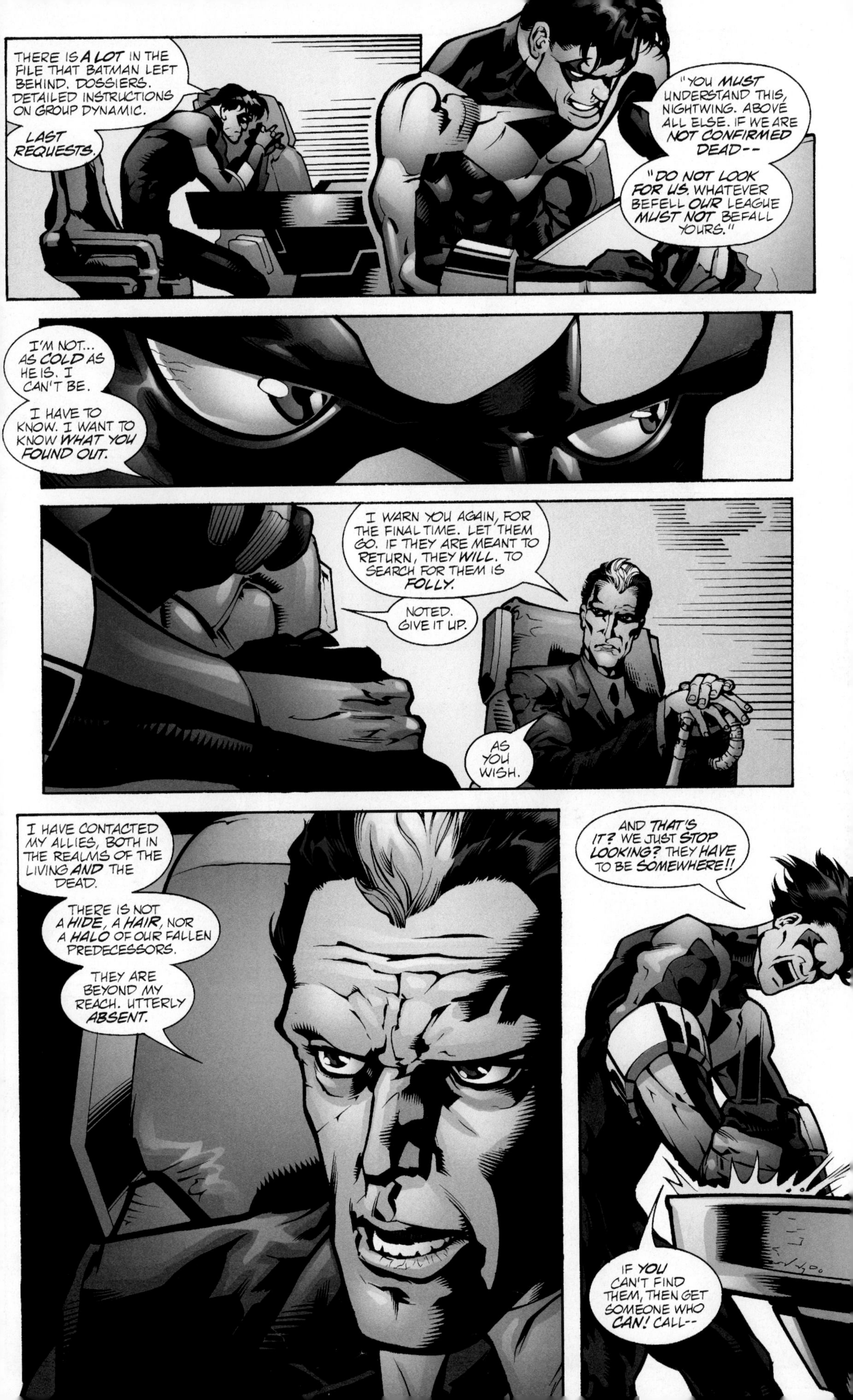
THERE IS A LOT IN THE FILE THAT BATMAN LEFT BEHIND. DOSSIERS. DETAILED INSTRUCTIONS ON GROUP DYNAMIC.
LAST REQUESTS.
"YOU MUST UNDERSTAND THIS, NIGHTWING. ABOVE ALL ELSE. IF WE ARE NOT CONFIRMED DEAD--
"DO NOT LOOK FOR US. WHATEVER BEFELL OUR LEAGUE MUST NOT BEFALL YOURS."
I'M NOT... AS COLD AS HE IS. I CAN'T BE.
I HAVE TO KNOW. I WANT TO KNOW WHAT YOU FOUND OUT.
I WARN YOU AGAIN, FOR THE FINAL TIME. LET THEM GO. IF THEY ARE MEANT TO RETURN, THEY WILL. TO SEARCH FOR THEM IS FOLLY.
NOTED. GIVE IT UP.
AS YOU WISH.
I HAVE CONTACTED MY ALLIES, BOTH IN THE REALMS OF THE LIVING AND THE DEAD.
THERE IS NOT A HIDE, A HAIR, NOR A HALO OF OUR FALLEN PREDECESSORS.
THEY ARE BEYOND MY REACH. UTTERLY ABSENT.
AND THAT'S IT? WE JUST STOP LOOKING? THEY HAVE TO BE SOMEWHERE!!
IF YOU CAN'T FIND THEM, THEN GET SOMEONE WHO CAN! CALL--

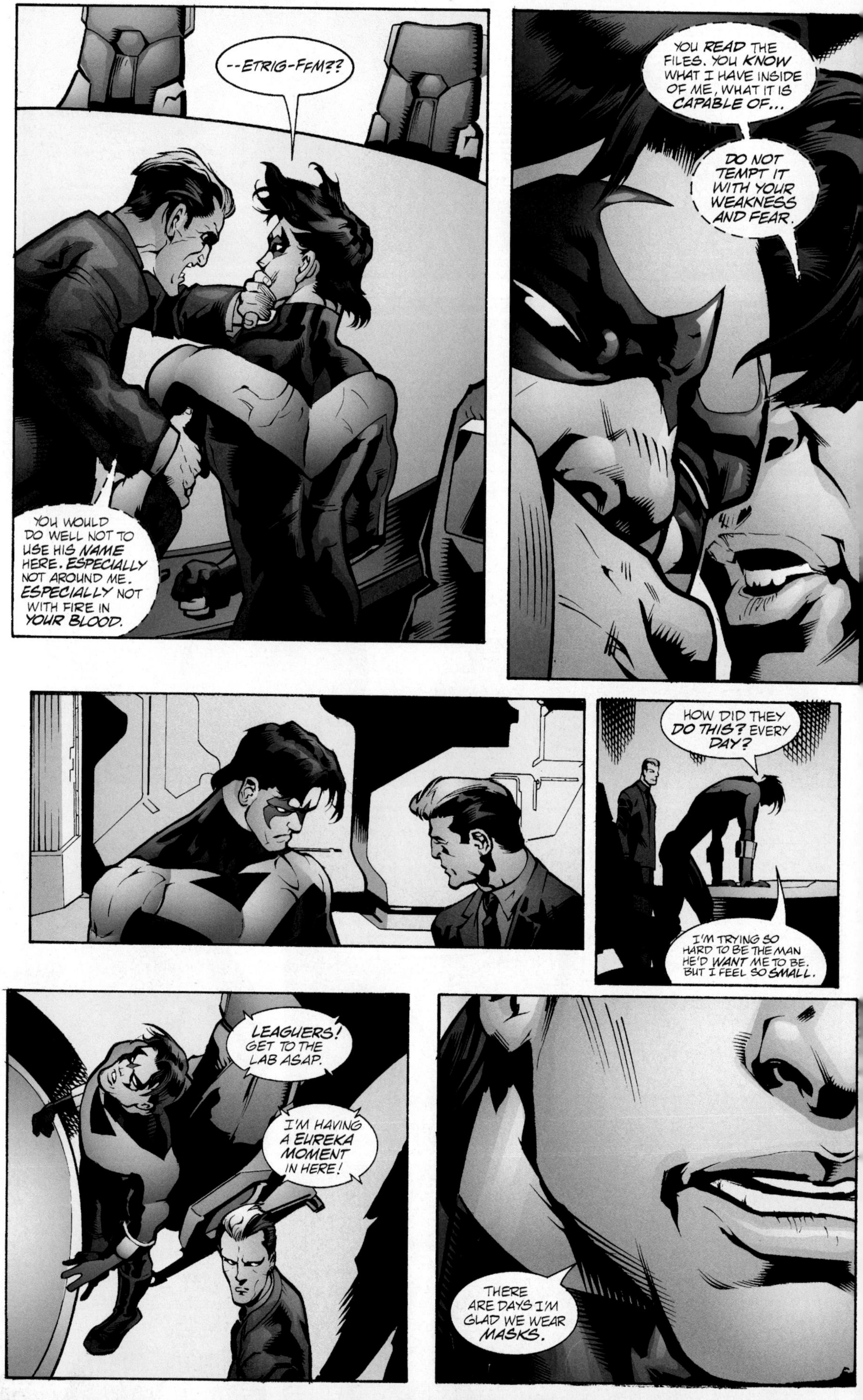
--ETRIG-FFM??
YOU WOULD DO WELL NOT TO USE HIS NAME HERE. ESPECIALLY NOT AROUND ME. ESPECIALLY NOT WITH FIRE IN YOUR BLOOD.
YOU READ THE FILES. YOU KNOW WHAT I HAVE INSIDE OF ME, WHAT IT IS CAPABLE OF...
DO NOT TEMPT IT WITH YOUR WEAKNESS AND FEAR.
HOW DID THEY DO THIS? EVERY DAY?
I'M TRYING SO HARD TO BE THE MAN HE'D WANT ME TO BE. BUT I FEEL SO SMALL.
LEAGUERS! GET TO THE LAB ASAP.
I'M HAVING A EUREKA MOMENT IN HERE!
THERE ARE DAYS I'M GLAD WE WEAR MASKS.

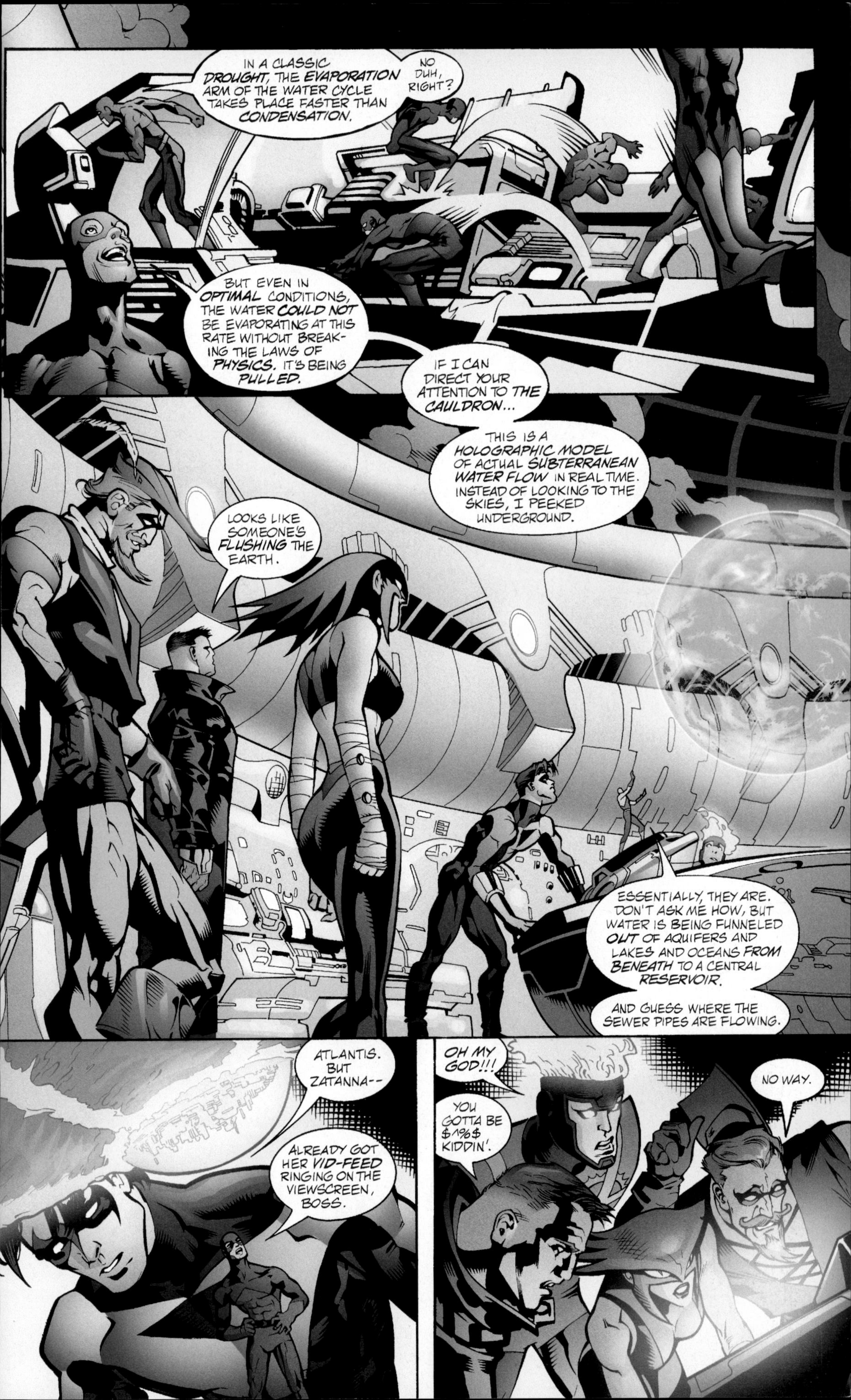

IN A CLASSIC DROUGHT, THE EVAPORATION ARM OF THE WATER CYCLE TAKES PLACE FASTER THAN CONDENSATION.
NO DUH, RIGHT?
BUT EVEN IN OPTIMAL CONDITIONS, THE WATER COULD NOT BE EVAPORATING AT THIS RATE WITHOUT BREAKING THE LAWS OF PHYSICS. IT'S BEING PULLED.
IF I CAN DIRECT YOUR ATTENTION TO THE CAULDRON...
THIS IS A HOLOGRAPHIC MODEL OF ACTUAL SUBTERRANEAN WATER FLOW IN REAL TIME. INSTEAD OF LOOKING TO THE SKIES, I PEEKED UNDERGROUND.
LOOKS LIKE SOMEONE'S FLUSHING THE EARTH.
ESSENTIALLY, THEY ARE. DON'T ASK ME HOW, BUT WATER IS BEING FUNNELED OUT OF AQUIFERS AND LAKES AND OCEANS FROM BENEATH TO A CENTRAL RESERVOIR.
AND GUESS WHERE THE SEWER PIPES ARE FLOWING.
ATLANTIS. BUT ZATANNA--
ALREADY GOT HER VID-FEED RINGING ON THE VIEWSCREEN, BOSS.
OH MY GOD!!!
YOU GOTTA BE $!%$ KIDDIN'.
NO WAY.

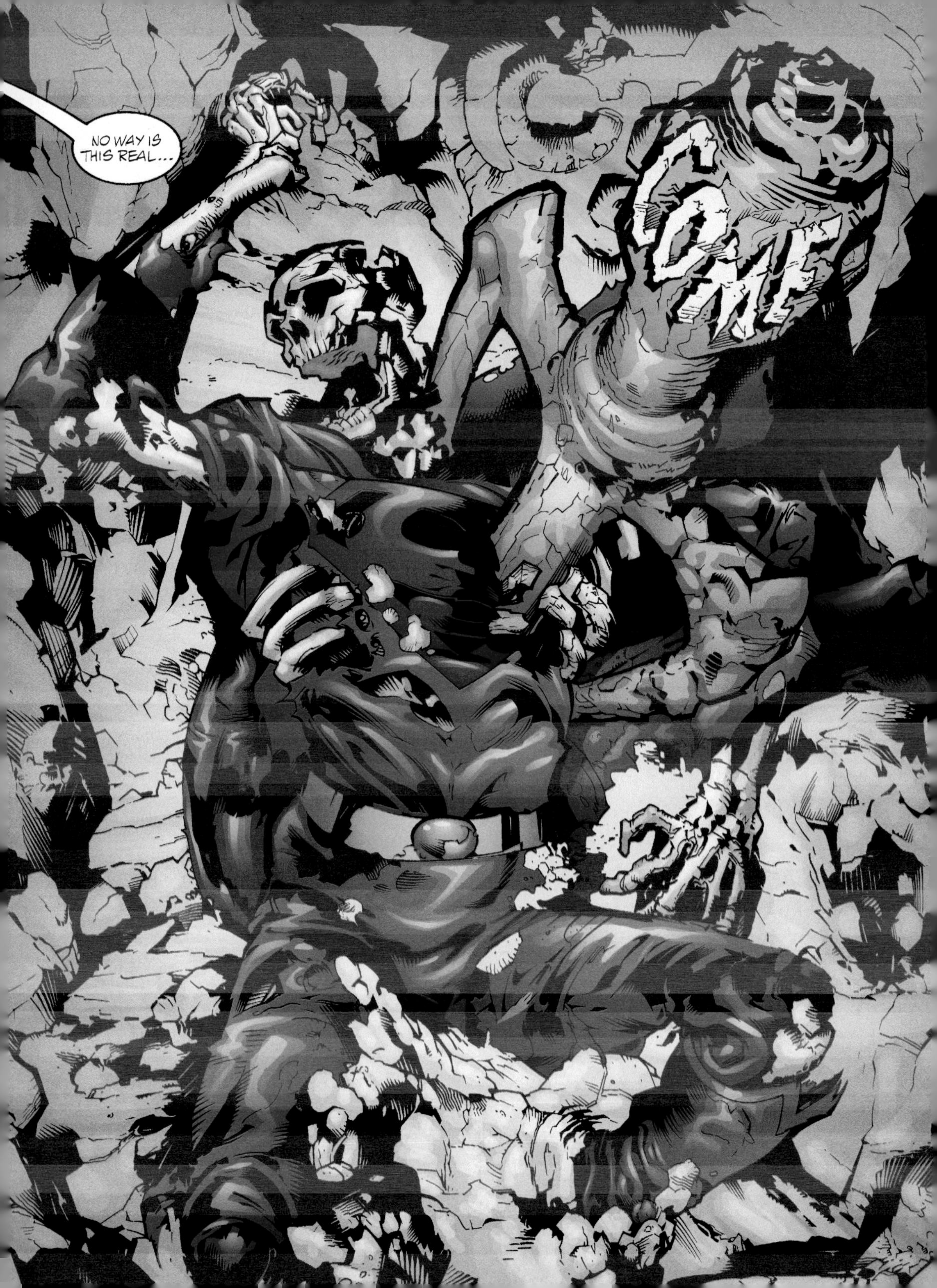
NO WAY IS THIS REAL...
OOMF

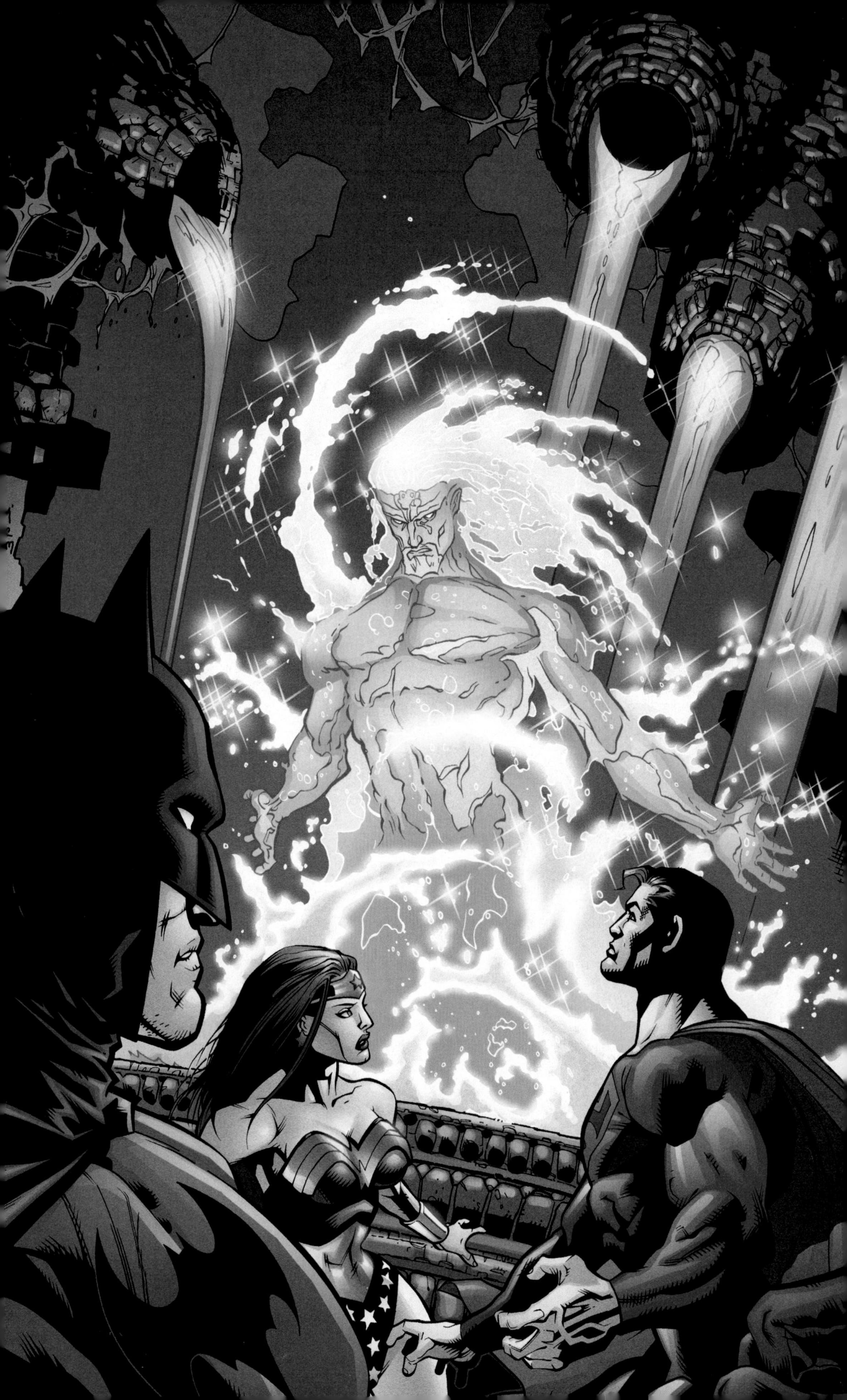

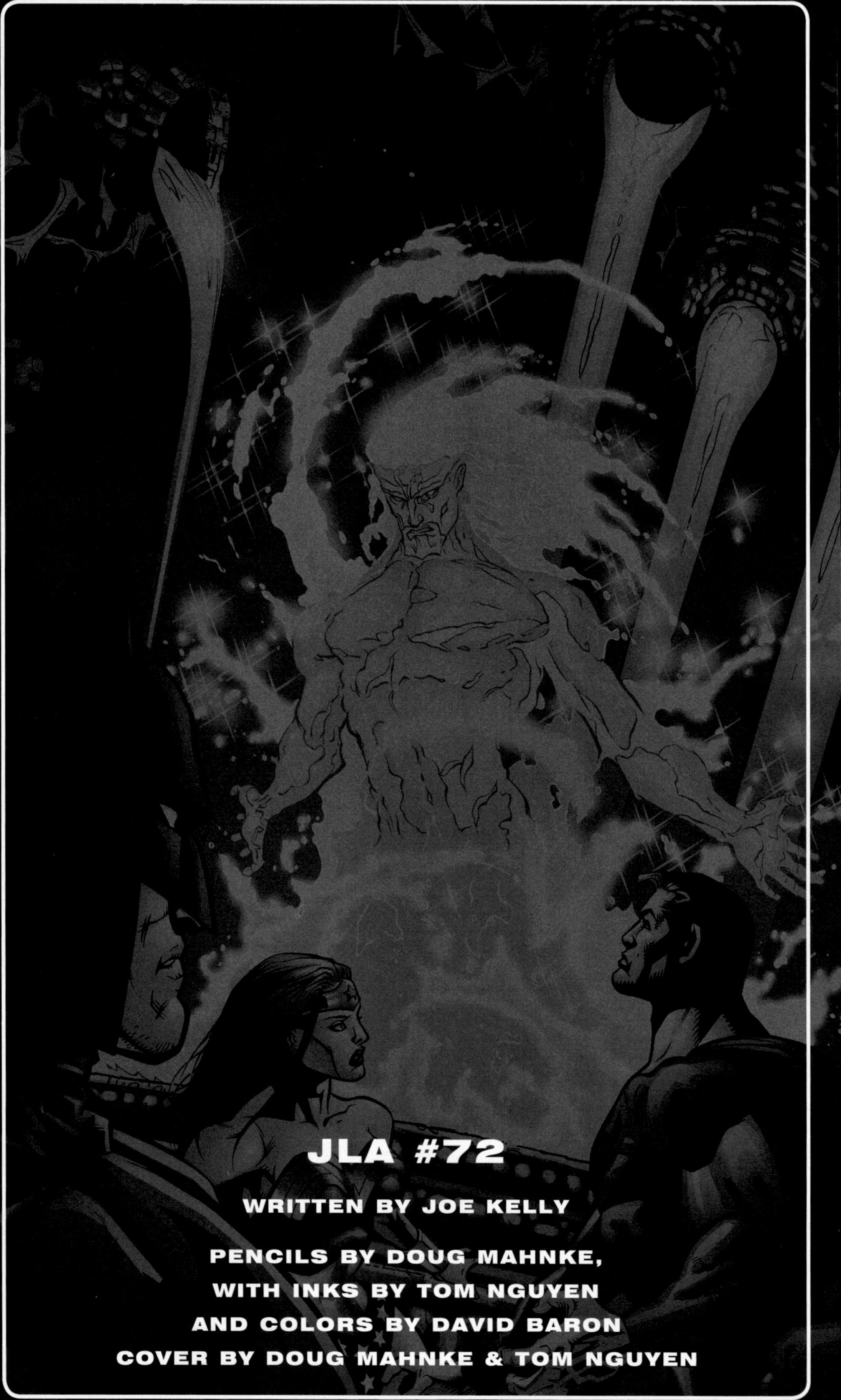

JLA #72

WRITTEN BY JOE KELLY

PENCILS BY DOUG MAHNKE,
WITH INKS BY TOM NGUYEN
AND COLORS BY DAVID BARON
COVER BY DOUG MAHNKE & TOM NGUYEN

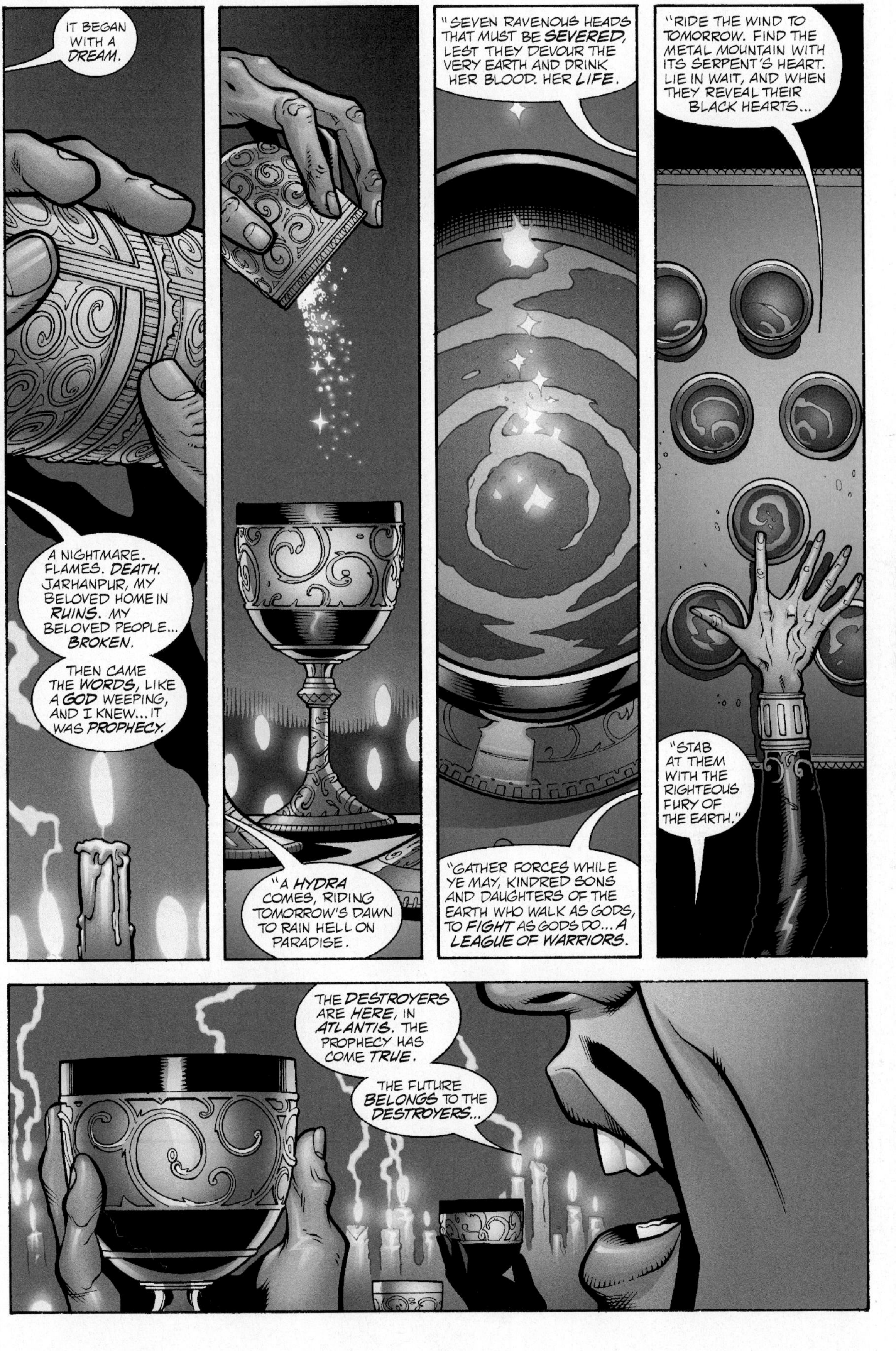

IT BEGAN WITH A DREAM.
A NIGHTMARE. FLAMES. DEATH. JARHANPUR, MY BELOVED HOME IN RUINS. MY BELOVED PEOPLE... BROKEN.
THEN CAME THE WORDS, LIKE A GOD WEEPING, AND I KNEW... IT WAS PROPHECY.
"A HYDRA COMES, RIDING TOMORROW'S DAWN TO RAIN HELL ON PARADISE.
"SEVEN RAVENOUS HEADS THAT MUST BE SEVERED, LEST THEY DEVOUR THE VERY EARTH AND DRINK HER BLOOD. HER LIFE.
"GATHER FORCES WHILE YE MAY, KINDRED SONS AND DAUGHTERS OF THE EARTH WHO WALK AS GODS, TO FIGHT AS GODS DO... A LEAGUE OF WARRIORS.
"RIDE THE WIND TO TOMORROW. FIND THE METAL MOUNTAIN WITH ITS SERPENT'S HEART. LIE IN WAIT, AND WHEN THEY REVEAL THEIR BLACK HEARTS...
"STAB AT THEM WITH THE RIGHTEOUS FURY OF THE EARTH."
THE DESTROYERS ARE HERE, IN ATLANTIS. THE PROPHECY HAS COME TRUE.
THE FUTURE BELONGS TO THE DESTROYERS...

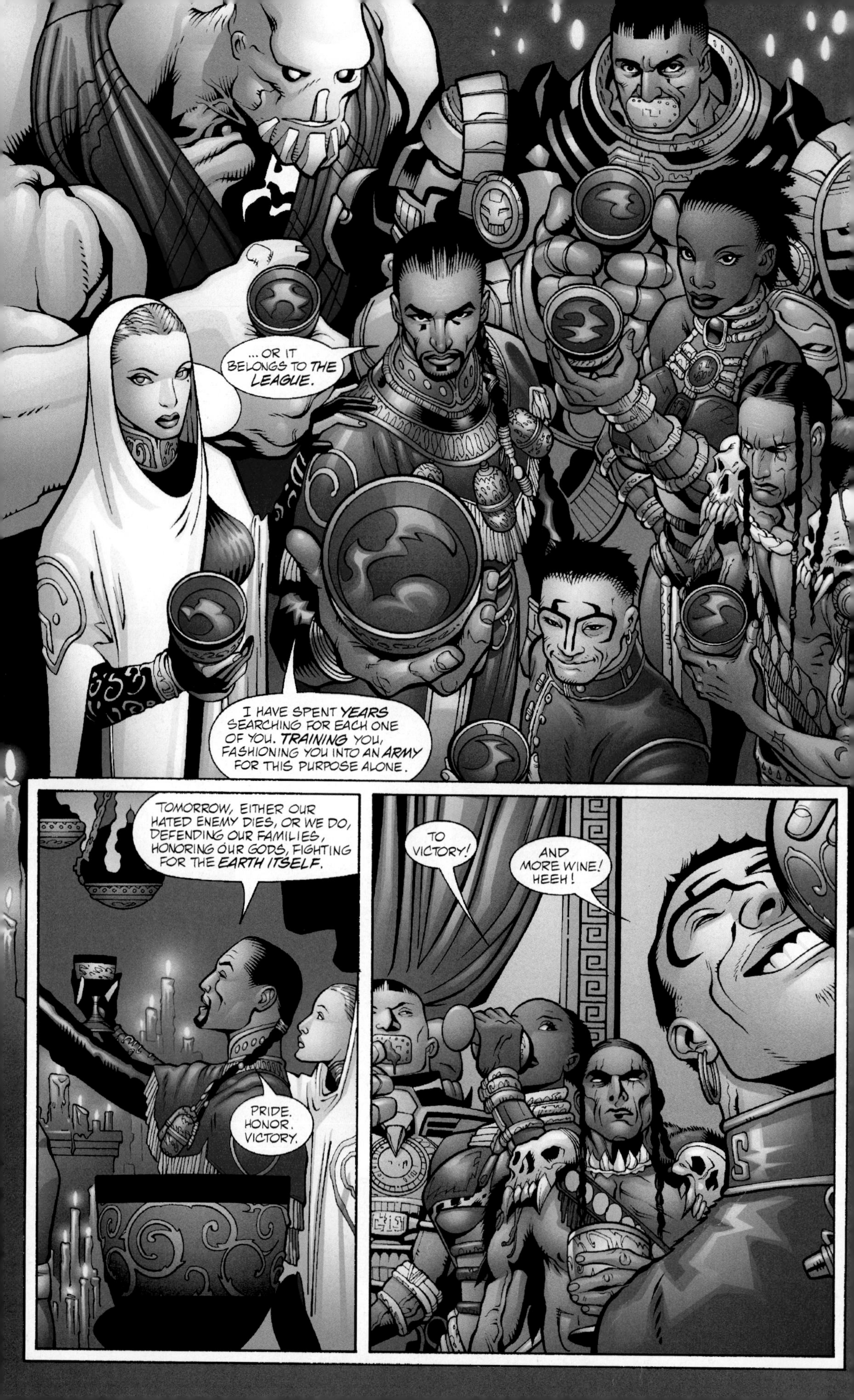
...OR IT BELONGS TO THE LEAGUE.
I HAVE SPENT YEARS SEARCHING FOR EACH ONE OF YOU. TRAINING YOU, FASHIONING YOU INTO AN ARMY FOR THIS PURPOSE ALONE.
TOMORROW, EITHER OUR HATED ENEMY DIES, OR WE DO, DEFENDING OUR FAMILIES, HONORING OUR GODS, FIGHTING FOR THE EARTH ITSELF.
PRIDE. HONOR. VICTORY.
TO VICTORY!
AND MORE WINE! HEEH!

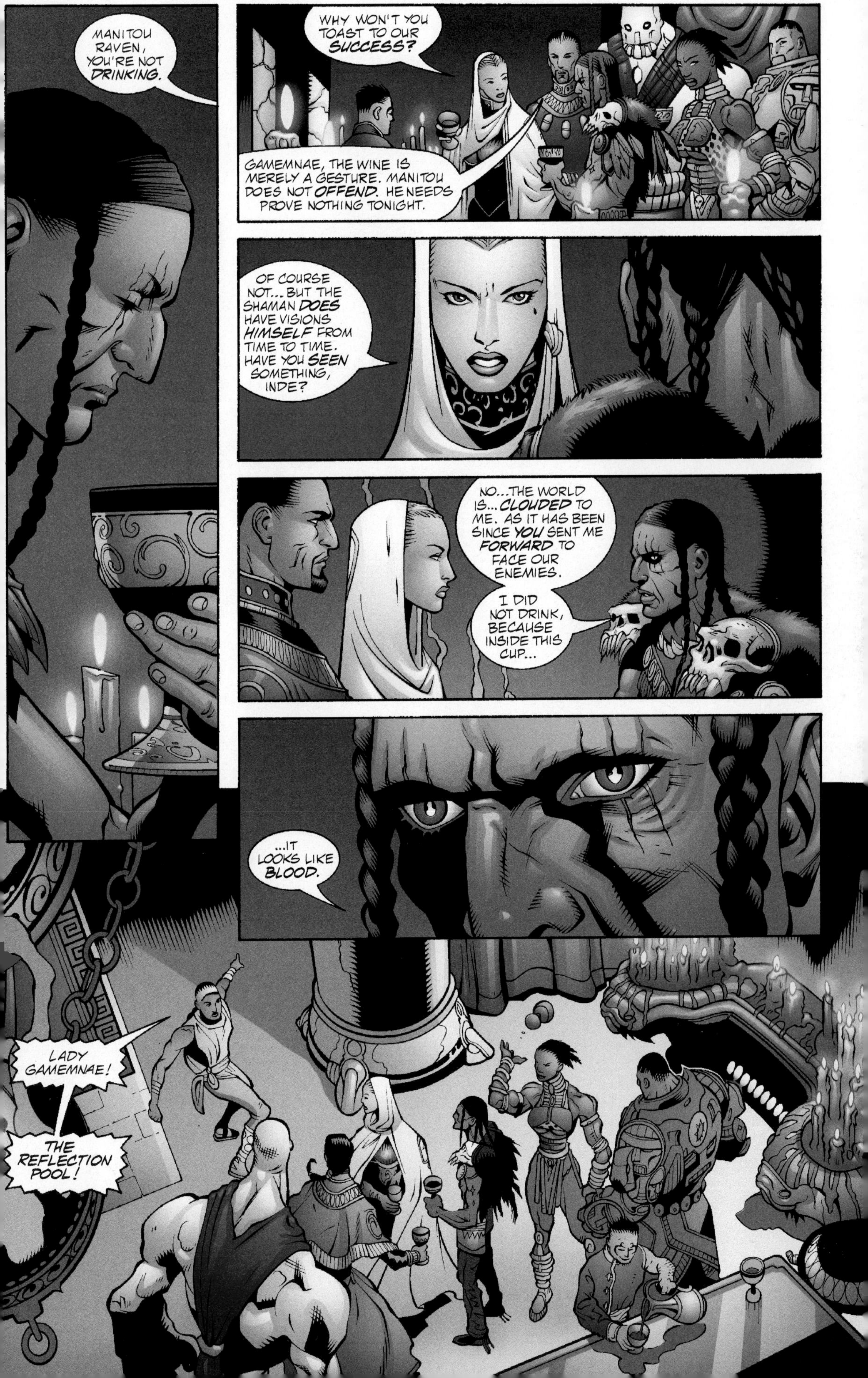

MANITOU RAVEN, YOU'RE NOT DRINKING.
WHY WON'T YOU TOAST TO OUR SUCCESS?
GAMEMNAE, THE WINE IS MERELY A GESTURE. MANITOU DOES NOT OFFEND. HE NEEDS PROVE NOTHING TONIGHT.
OF COURSE NOT... BUT THE SHAMAN DOES HAVE VISIONS HIMSELF FROM TIME TO TIME. HAVE YOU SEEN SOMETHING, INDE?
NO...THE WORLD IS...CLOUDED TO ME. AS IT HAS BEEN SINCE YOU SENT ME FORWARD TO FACE OUR ENEMIES.
I DID NOT DRINK, BECAUSE INSIDE THIS CUP...
...IT LOOKS LIKE BLOOD.
LADY GAMEMNAE!
THE REFLECTION POOL!

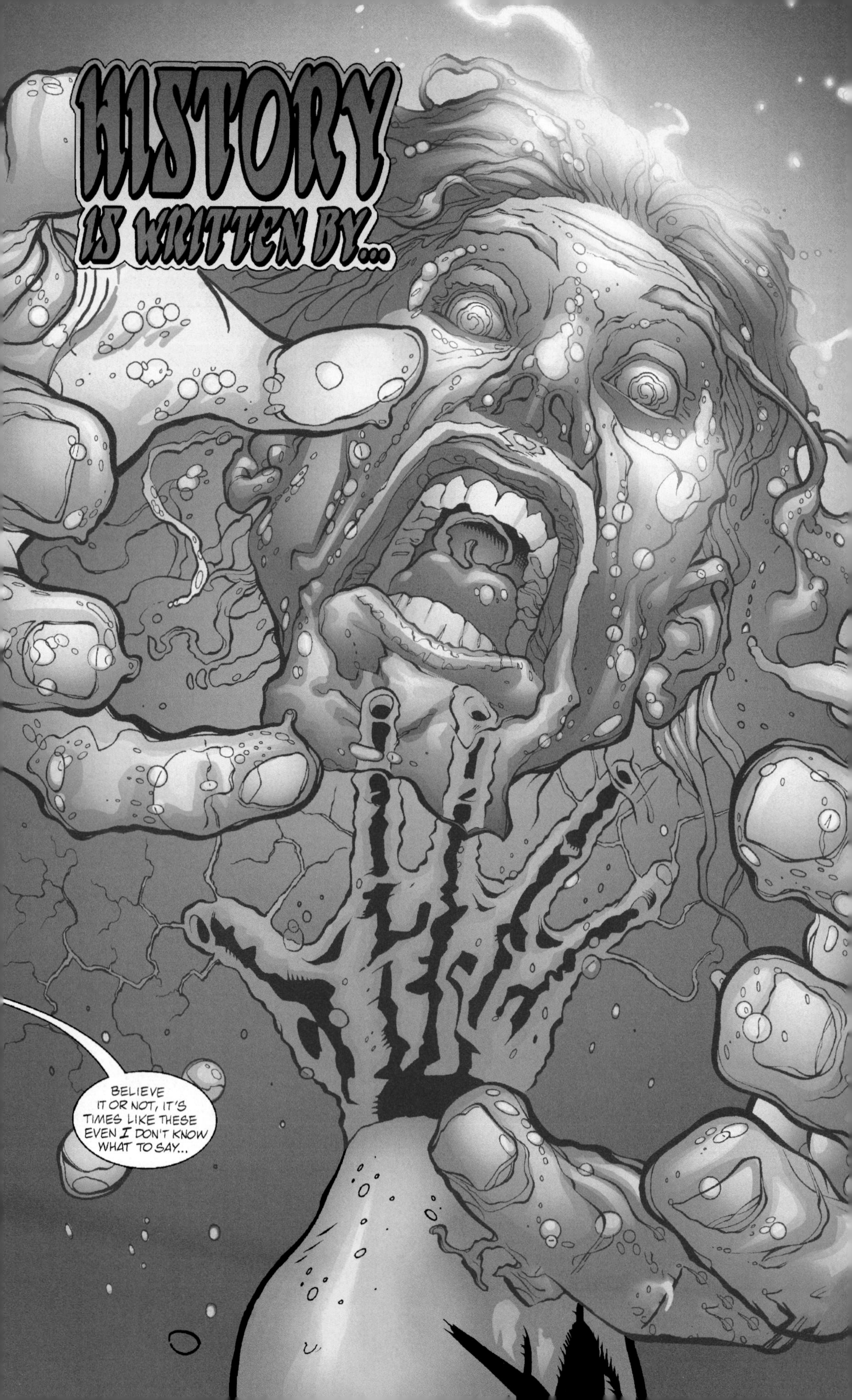
HISTORY IS WRITTEN BY...
BELIEVE IT OR NOT, IT'S TIMES LIKE THESE EVEN I DON'T KNOW WHAT TO SAY...

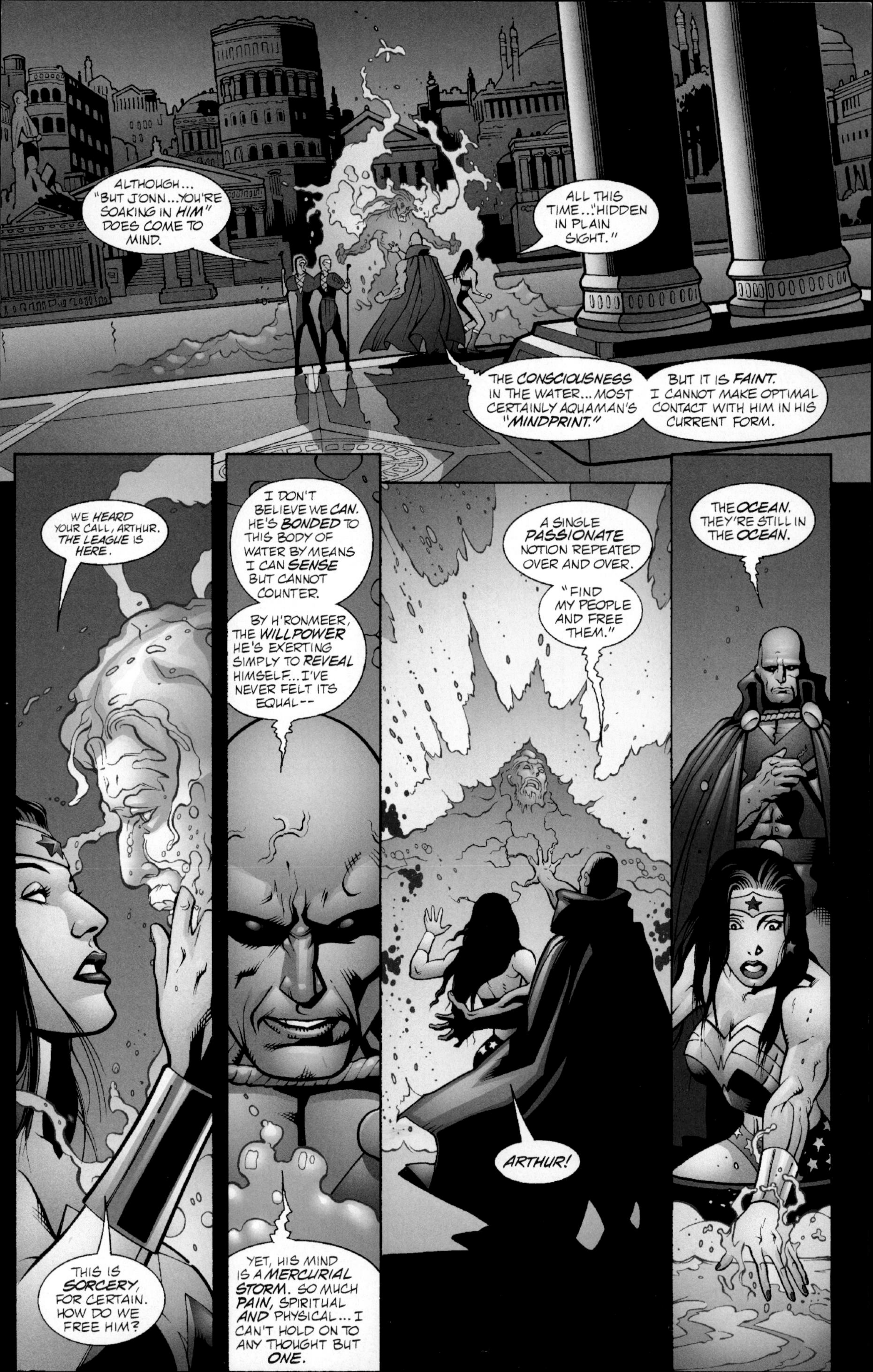
ALTHOUGH... "BUT J'ONN...YOU'RE SOAKING IN HIM" DOES COME TO MIND.
ALL THIS TIME..."HIDDEN IN PLAIN SIGHT."
THE CONSCIOUSNESS IN THE WATER...MOST CERTAINLY AQUAMAN'S "MINDPRINT."
BUT IT IS FAINT. I CANNOT MAKE OPTIMAL CONTACT WITH HIM IN HIS CURRENT FORM.
WE HEARD YOUR CALL, ARTHUR. THE LEAGUE IS HERE.
THIS IS SORCERY, FOR CERTAIN. HOW DO WE FREE HIM?
I DON'T BELIEVE WE CAN. HE'S BONDED TO THIS BODY OF WATER BY MEANS I CAN SENSE BUT CANNOT COUNTER.
BY H'RONMEER, THE WILLPOWER HE'S EXERTING SIMPLY TO REVEAL HIMSELF...I'VE NEVER FELT ITS EQUAL--
YET, HIS MIND IS A MERCURIAL STORM. SO MUCH PAIN, SPIRITUAL AND PHYSICAL...I CAN'T HOLD ON TO ANY THOUGHT BUT ONE.
A SINGLE PASSIONATE NOTION REPEATED OVER AND OVER.
"FIND MY PEOPLE AND FREE THEM."
ARTHUR!
THE OCEAN. THEY'RE STILL IN THE OCEAN.

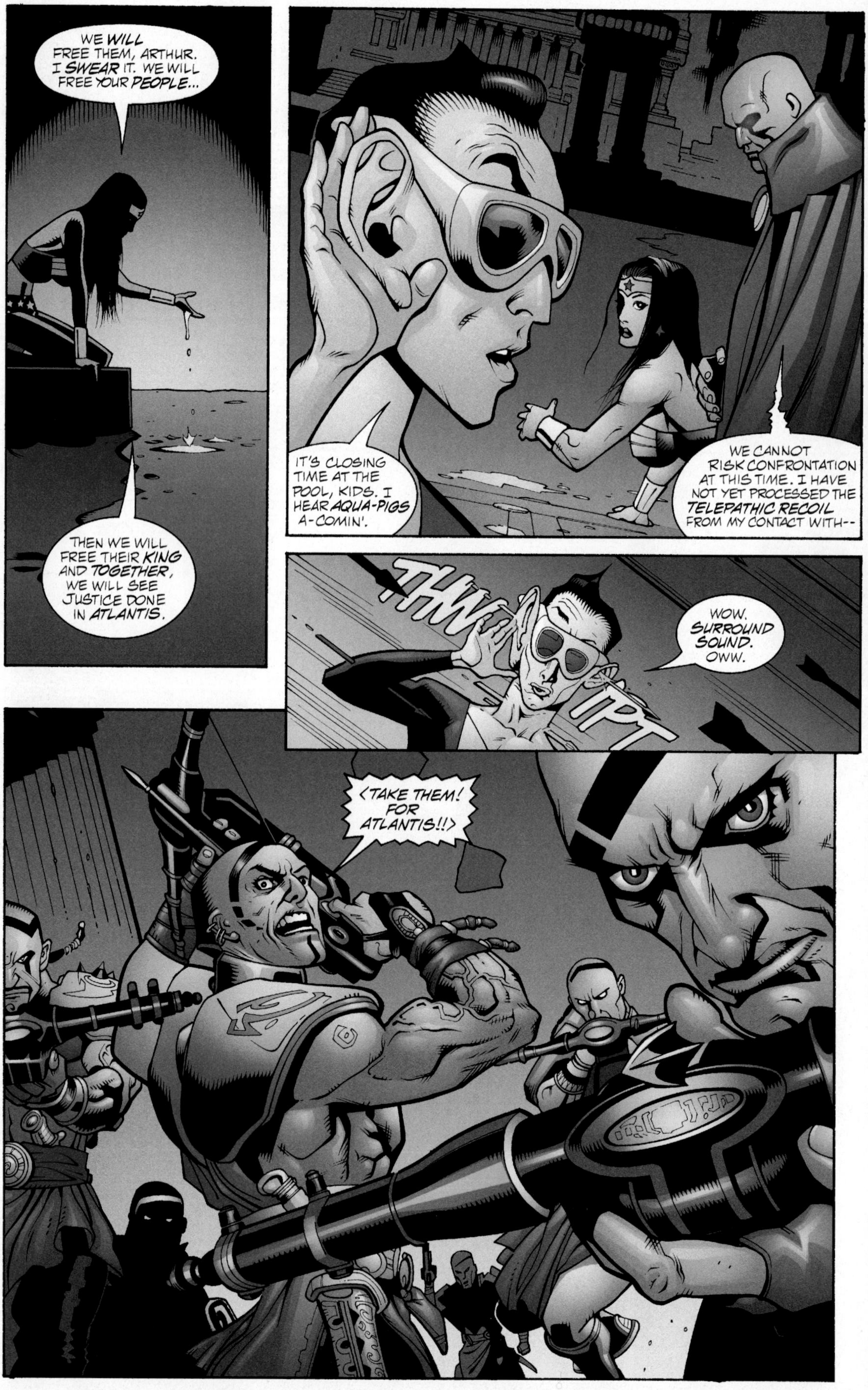
WE WILL FREE THEM, ARTHUR. I SWEAR IT. WE WILL FREE YOUR PEOPLE...
THEN WE WILL FREE THEIR KING AND TOGETHER, WE WILL SEE JUSTICE DONE IN ATLANTIS.
IT'S CLOSING TIME AT THE POOL, KIDS. I HEAR AQUA-PIGS A-COMIN'.
WE CANNOT RISK CONFRONTATION AT THIS TIME. I HAVE NOT YET PROCESSED THE TELEPATHIC RECOIL FROM MY CONTACT WITH--
THW
WOW. SURROUND SOUND. OWW.
IPT
<TAKE THEM! FOR ATLANTIS!!>

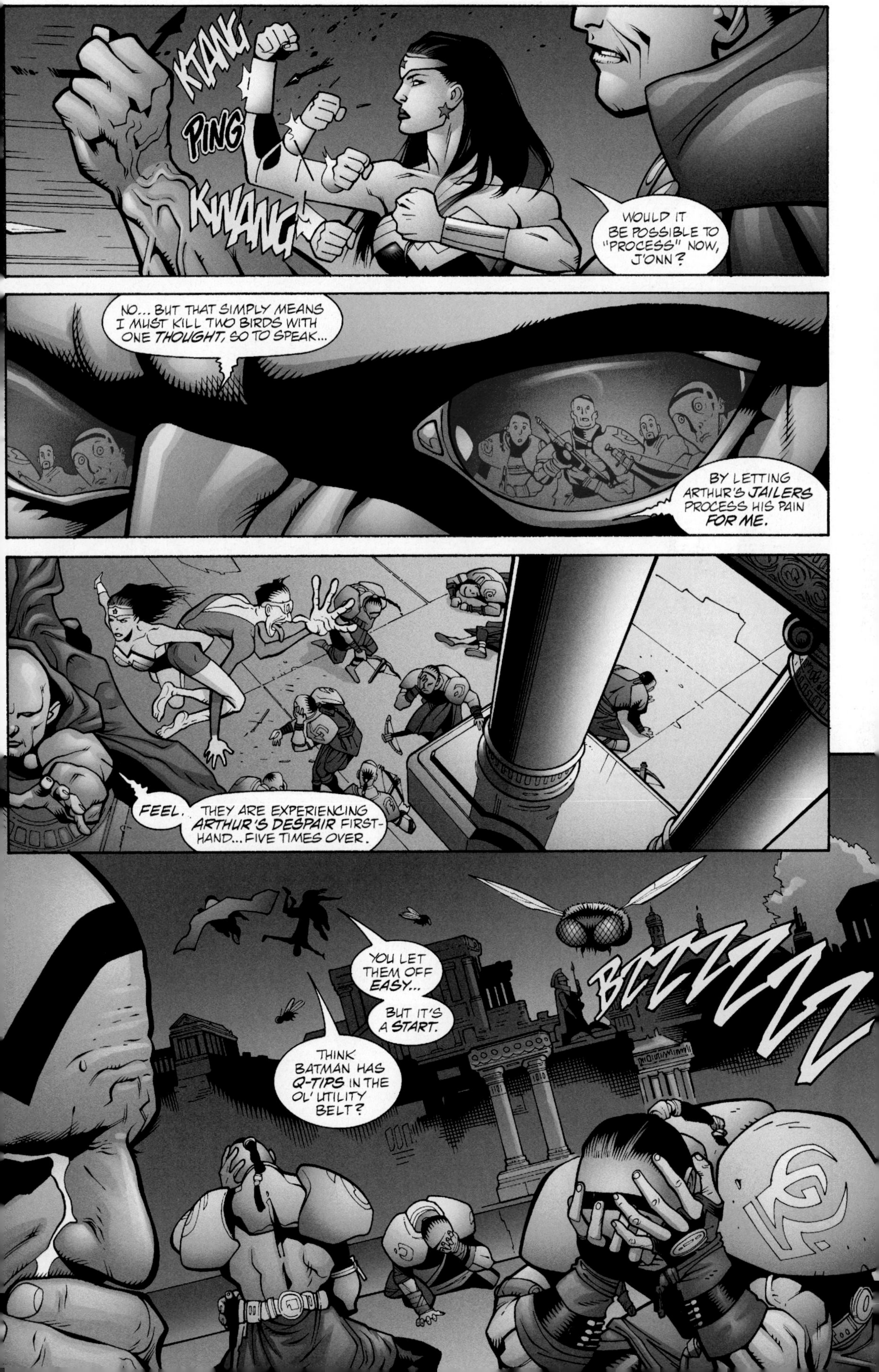
KTANG
PING
KWANG
WOULD IT BE POSSIBLE TO "PROCESS" NOW, J'ONN?
NO... BUT THAT SIMPLY MEANS I MUST KILL TWO BIRDS WITH ONE THOUGHT, SO TO SPEAK...
BY LETTING ARTHUR'S JAILERS PROCESS HIS PAIN FOR ME.
FEEL.
THEY ARE EXPERIENCING ARTHUR'S DESPAIR FIRST-HAND... FIVE TIMES OVER.
YOU LET THEM OFF EASY...
BUT IT'S A START.
THINK BATMAN HAS Q-TIPS IN THE OL' UTILITY BELT?
BZZZZZZ

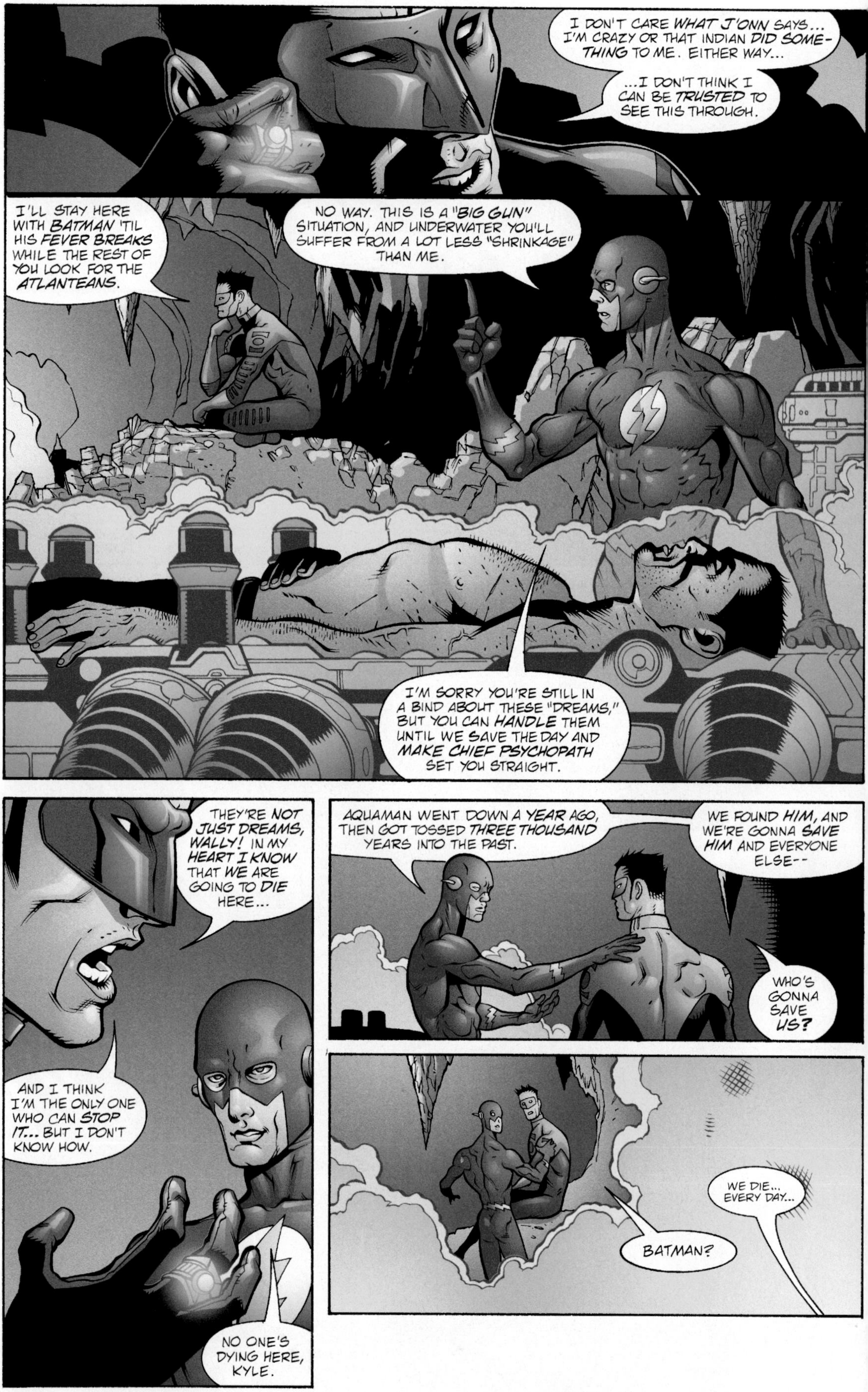
I DON'T CARE WHAT J'ONN SAYS... I'M CRAZY OR THAT INDIAN DID SOMETHING TO ME. EITHER WAY...
...I DON'T THINK I CAN BE TRUSTED TO SEE THIS THROUGH.
I'LL STAY HERE WITH BATMAN 'TIL HIS FEVER BREAKS WHILE THE REST OF YOU LOOK FOR THE ATLANTEANS.
NO WAY. THIS IS A "BIG GUN" SITUATION, AND UNDERWATER YOU'LL SUFFER FROM A LOT LESS "SHRINKAGE" THAN ME.
I'M SORRY YOU'RE STILL IN A BIND ABOUT THESE "DREAMS," BUT YOU CAN HANDLE THEM UNTIL WE SAVE THE DAY AND MAKE CHIEF PSYCHOPATH SET YOU STRAIGHT.
THEY'RE NOT JUST DREAMS, WALLY! IN MY HEART I KNOW THAT WE ARE GOING TO DIE HERE...
AND I THINK I'M THE ONLY ONE WHO CAN STOP IT... BUT I DON'T KNOW HOW.
NO ONE'S DYING HERE, KYLE.
AQUAMAN WENT DOWN A YEAR AGO, THEN GOT TOSSED THREE THOUSAND YEARS INTO THE PAST.
WE FOUND HIM, AND WE'RE GONNA SAVE HIM AND EVERYONE ELSE--
WHO'S GONNA SAVE US?
BATMAN?
WE DIE... EVERY DAY...

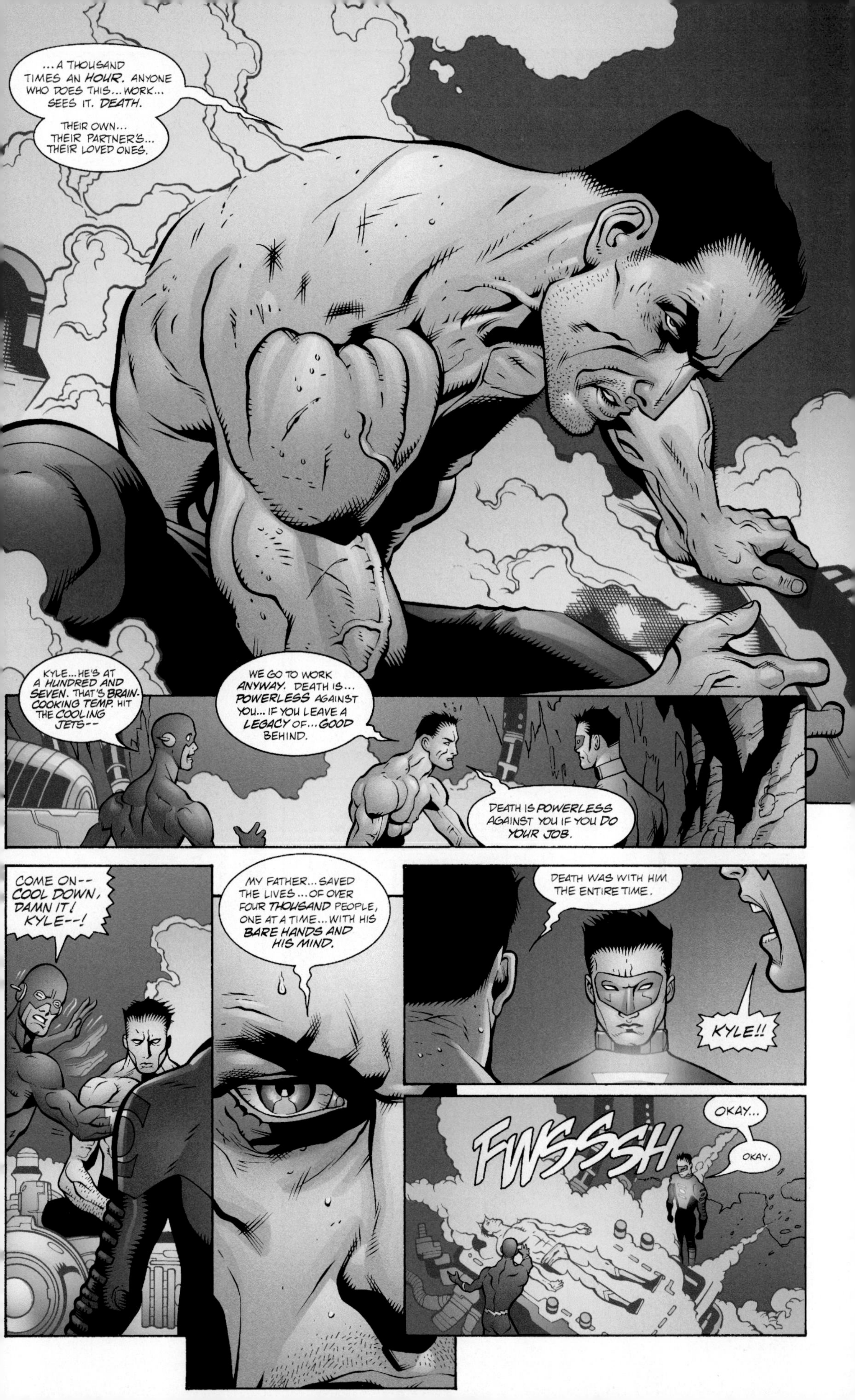
...A THOUSAND TIMES AN HOUR. ANYONE WHO DOES THIS...WORK... SEES IT. DEATH.
THEIR OWN... THEIR PARTNER'S... THEIR LOVED ONES.
KYLE...HE'S AT A HUNDRED AND SEVEN. THAT'S BRAIN-COOKING TEMP. HIT THE COOLING JETS--
WE GO TO WORK ANYWAY. DEATH IS... POWERLESS AGAINST YOU... IF YOU LEAVE A LEGACY OF...GOOD BEHIND.
DEATH IS POWERLESS AGAINST YOU IF YOU DO YOUR JOB.
COME ON-- COOL DOWN, DAMN IT! KYLE--!
MY FATHER...SAVED THE LIVES...OF OVER FOUR THOUSAND PEOPLE, ONE AT A TIME...WITH HIS BARE HANDS AND HIS MIND.
DEATH WAS WITH HIM THE ENTIRE TIME.
KYLE!!
FWSSSH
OKAY...
OKAY.

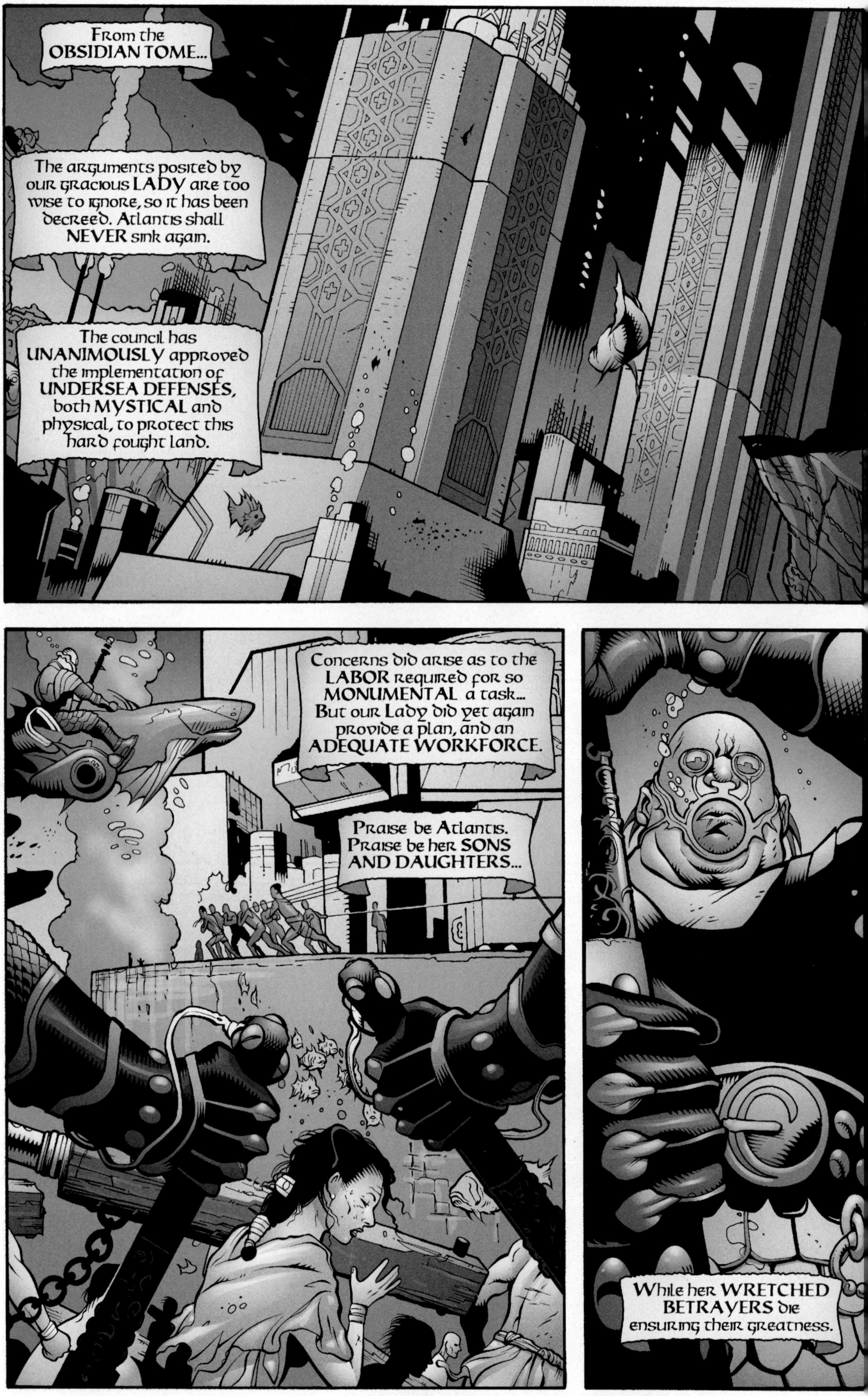
From the OBSIDIAN TOME...
The arguments posited by our gracious LADY are too wise to ignore, so it has been decreed. Atlantis shall NEVER sink again.
The council has UNANIMOUSLY approved the implementation of UNDERSEA DEFENSES, both MYSTICAL and physical, to protect this hard fought land.
Concerns did arise as to the LABOR required for so MONUMENTAL a task... But our Lady did yet again provide a plan, and an ADEQUATE WORKFORCE.
Praise be Atlantis. Praise be her SONS AND DAUGHTERS...
While her WRETCHED BETRAYERS die ensuring their greatness.

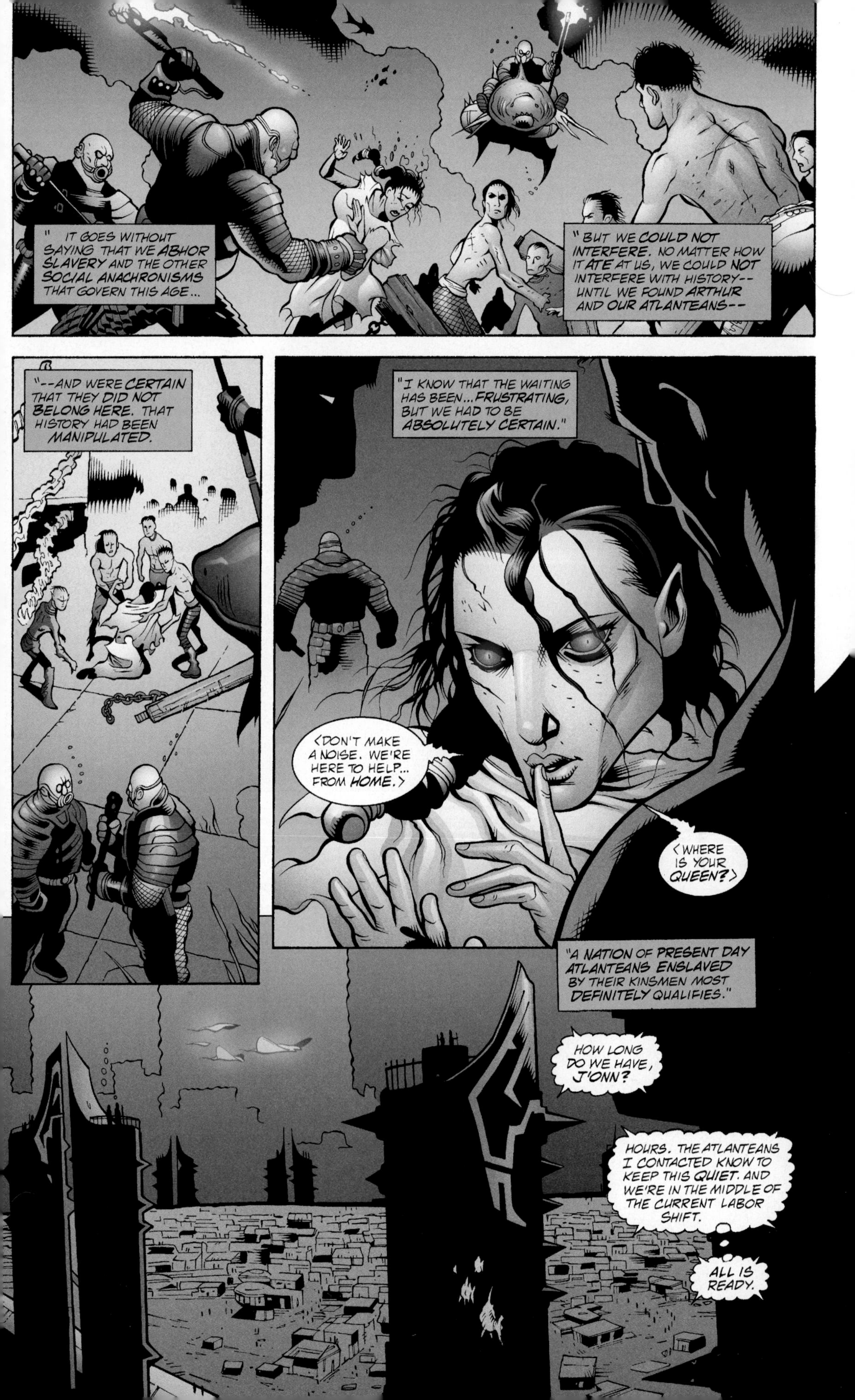
"IT GOES WITHOUT SAYING THAT WE ABHOR SLAVERY AND THE OTHER SOCIAL ANACHRONISMS THAT GOVERN THIS AGE...
"BUT WE COULD NOT INTERFERE. NO MATTER HOW IT ATE AT US, WE COULD NOT INTERFERE WITH HISTORY-- UNTIL WE FOUND ARTHUR AND OUR ATLANTEANS--
"--AND WERE CERTAIN THAT THEY DID NOT BELONG HERE. THAT HISTORY HAD BEEN MANIPULATED.
"I KNOW THAT THE WAITING HAS BEEN...FRUSTRATING, BUT WE HAD TO BE ABSOLUTELY CERTAIN."
<DON'T MAKE A NOISE. WE'RE HERE TO HELP... FROM HOME.>
<WHERE IS YOUR QUEEN?>
"A NATION OF PRESENT DAY ATLANTEANS ENSLAVED BY THEIR KINSMEN MOST DEFINITELY QUALIFIES."
HOW LONG DO WE HAVE, J'ONN?
HOURS. THE ATLANTEANS I CONTACTED KNOW TO KEEP THIS QUIET. AND WE'RE IN THE MIDDLE OF THE CURRENT LABOR SHIFT.
ALL IS READY.

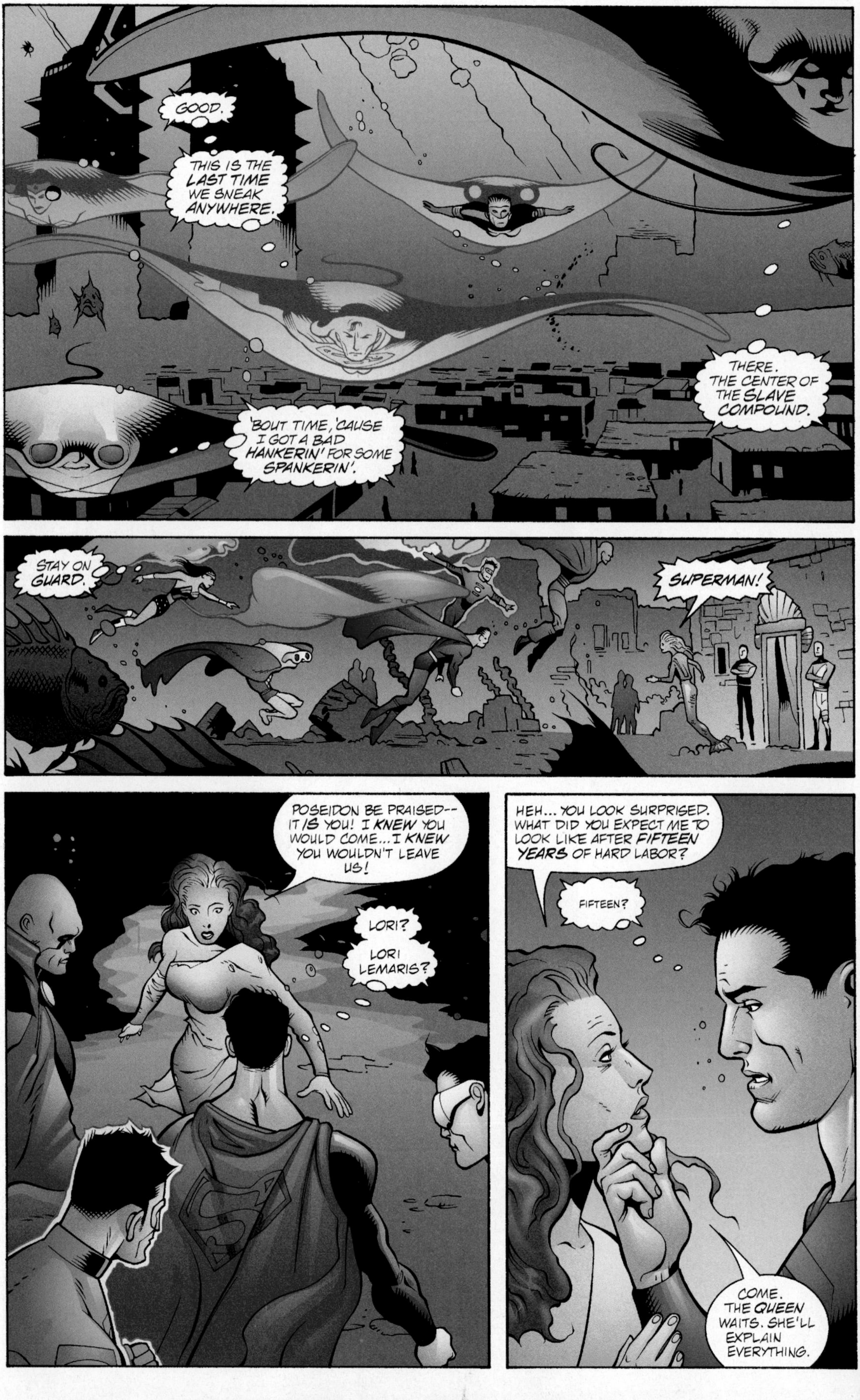

GOOD.
THIS IS THE LAST TIME WE SNEAK ANYWHERE.
'BOUT TIME, 'CAUSE I GOT A BAD HANKERIN' FOR SOME SPANKERIN'.
THERE. THE CENTER OF THE SLAVE COMPOUND.
STAY ON GUARD.
SUPERMAN!
POSEIDON BE PRAISED-- IT IS YOU! I KNEW YOU WOULD COME... I KNEW YOU WOULDN'T LEAVE US!
LORI?
LORI LEMARIS?
HEH... YOU LOOK SURPRISED. WHAT DID YOU EXPECT ME TO LOOK LIKE AFTER FIFTEEN YEARS OF HARD LABOR?
FIFTEEN?
COME. THE QUEEN WAITS. SHE'LL EXPLAIN EVERYTHING.

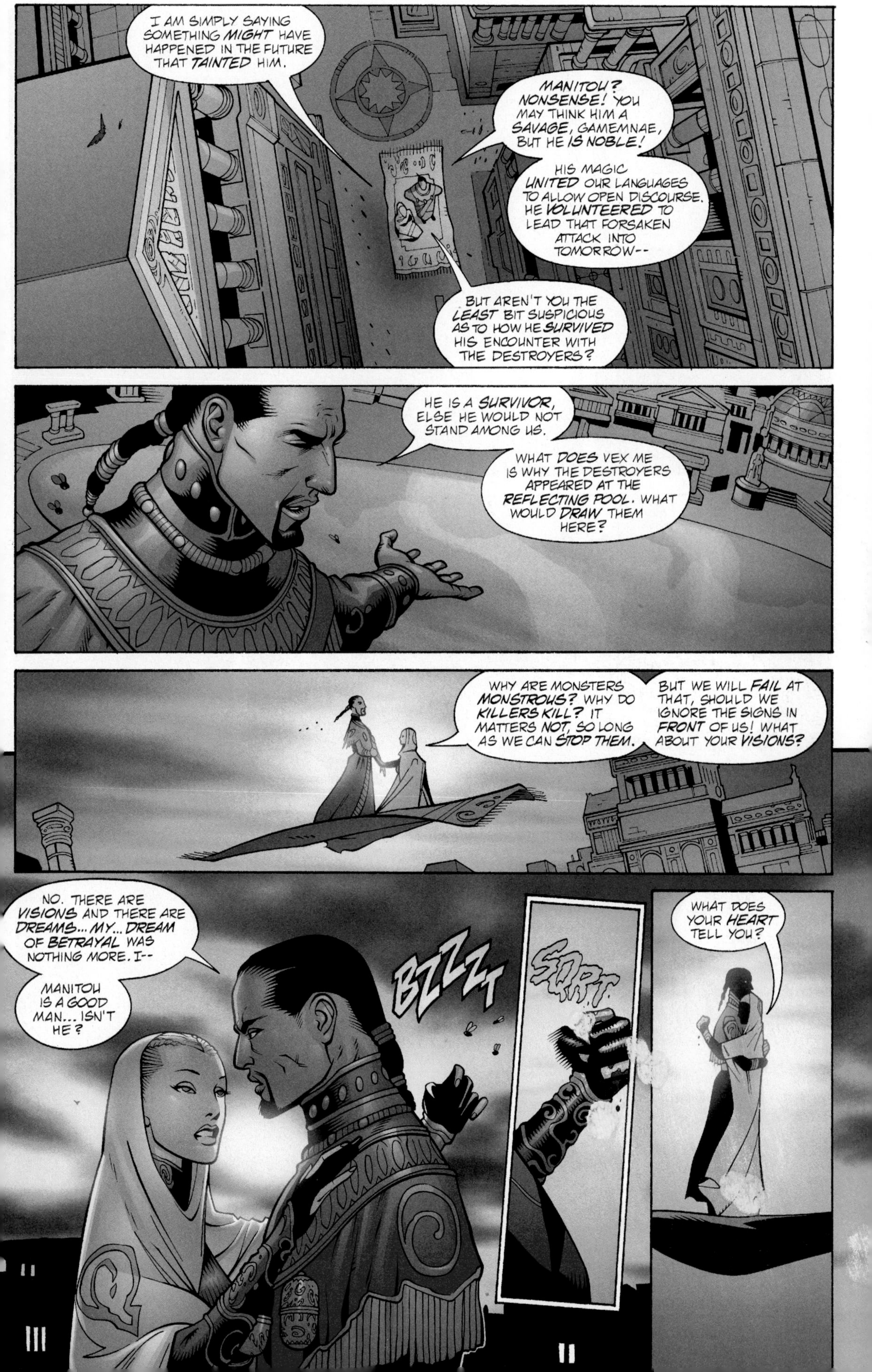
I AM SIMPLY SAYING SOMETHING MIGHT HAVE HAPPENED IN THE FUTURE THAT TAINTED HIM.
MANITOU? NONSENSE! YOU MAY THINK HIM A SAVAGE, GAMEMNAE, BUT HE IS NOBLE!
HIS MAGIC UNITED OUR LANGUAGES TO ALLOW OPEN DISCOURSE. HE VOLUNTEERED TO LEAD THAT FORSAKEN ATTACK INTO TOMORROW--
BUT AREN'T YOU THE LEAST BIT SUSPICIOUS AS TO HOW HE SURVIVED HIS ENCOUNTER WITH THE DESTROYERS?
HE IS A SURVIVOR, ELSE HE WOULD NOT STAND AMONG US.
WHAT DOES VEX ME IS WHY THE DESTROYERS APPEARED AT THE REFLECTING POOL. WHAT WOULD DRAW THEM HERE?
WHY ARE MONSTERS MONSTROUS? WHY DO KILLERS KILL? IT MATTERS NOT, SO LONG AS WE CAN STOP THEM.
BUT WE WILL FAIL AT THAT, SHOULD WE IGNORE THE SIGNS IN FRONT OF US! WHAT ABOUT YOUR VISIONS?
NO. THERE ARE VISIONS AND THERE ARE DREAMS... MY... DREAM OF BETRAYAL WAS NOTHING MORE. I--
MANITOU IS A GOOD MAN... ISN'T HE?
BZZZT
SQRT
WHAT DOES YOUR HEART TELL YOU?

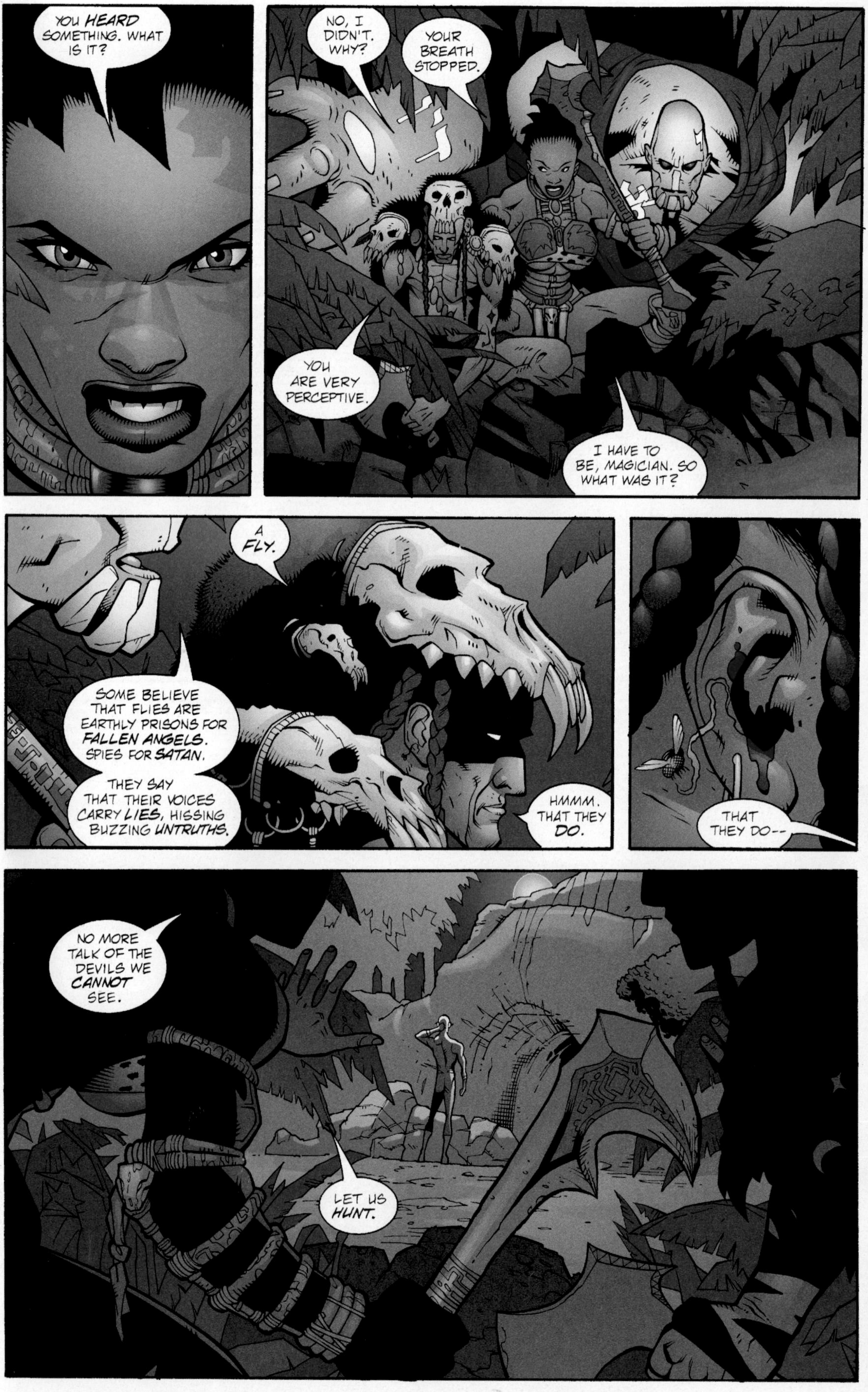
YOU HEARD SOMETHING. WHAT IS IT?
NO, I DIDN'T. WHY?
YOUR BREATH STOPPED.
YOU ARE VERY PERCEPTIVE.
I HAVE TO BE, MAGICIAN. SO WHAT WAS IT?
A FLY.
SOME BELIEVE THAT FLIES ARE EARTHLY PRISONS FOR FALLEN ANGELS. SPIES FOR SATAN.
THEY SAY THAT THEIR VOICES CARRY LIES, HISSING BUZZING UNTRUTHS.
HMMM. THAT THEY DO.
THAT THEY DO--
NO MORE TALK OF THE DEVILS WE CANNOT SEE.
LET US HUNT.

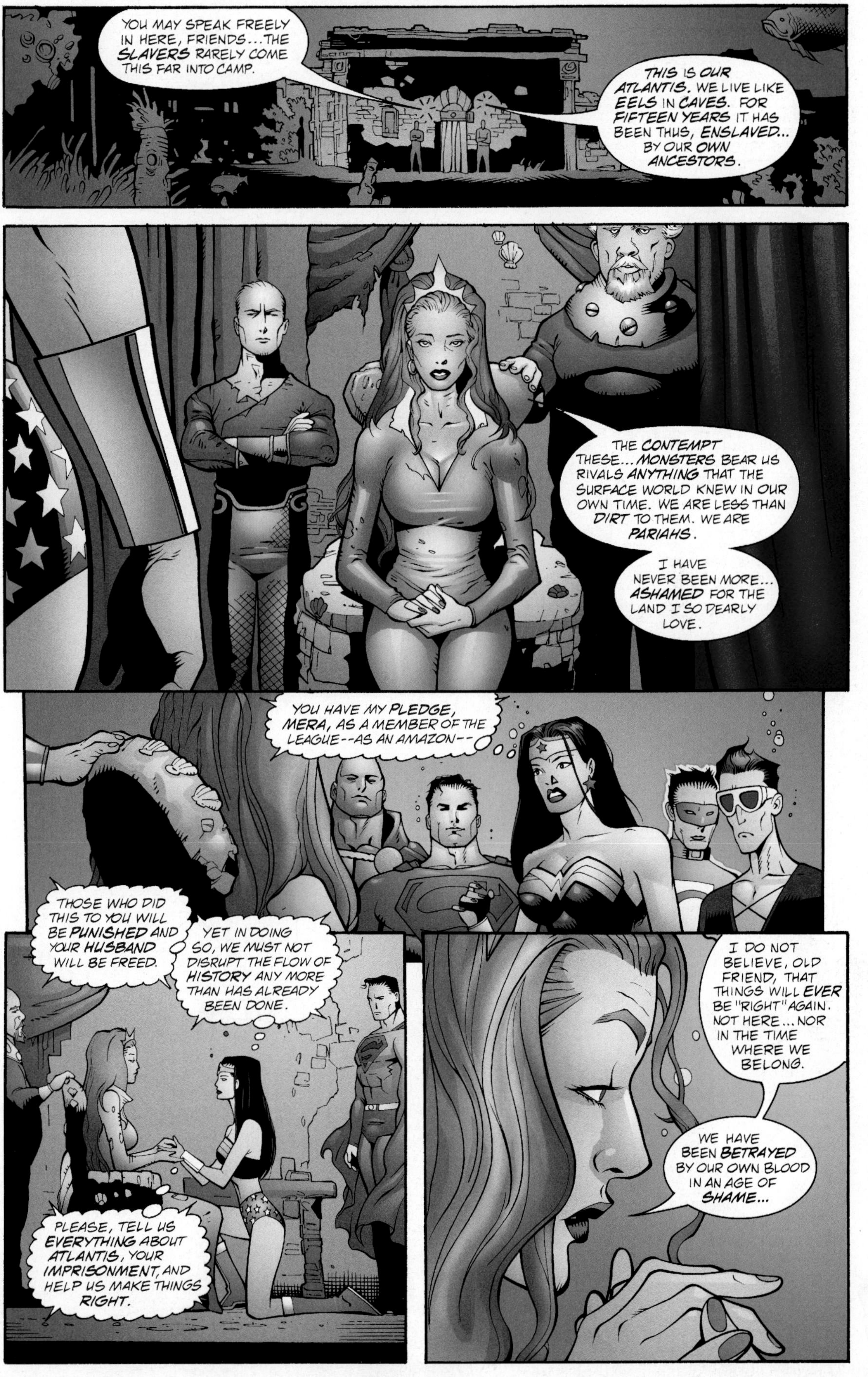
YOU MAY SPEAK FREELY IN HERE, FRIENDS... THE SLAVERS RARELY COME THIS FAR INTO CAMP.
THIS IS OUR ATLANTIS. WE LIVE LIKE EELS IN CAVES. FOR FIFTEEN YEARS IT HAS BEEN THUS, ENSLAVED... BY OUR OWN ANCESTORS.
THE CONTEMPT THESE... MONSTERS BEAR US RIVALS ANYTHING THAT THE SURFACE WORLD KNEW IN OUR OWN TIME. WE ARE LESS THAN DIRT TO THEM. WE ARE PARIAHS.
I HAVE NEVER BEEN MORE... ASHAMED FOR THE LAND I SO DEARLY LOVE.
YOU HAVE MY PLEDGE, MERA, AS A MEMBER OF THE LEAGUE--AS AN AMAZON--
THOSE WHO DID THIS TO YOU WILL BE PUNISHED AND YOUR HUSBAND WILL BE FREED.
YET IN DOING SO, WE MUST NOT DISRUPT THE FLOW OF HISTORY ANY MORE THAN HAS ALREADY BEEN DONE.
PLEASE, TELL US EVERYTHING ABOUT ATLANTIS, YOUR IMPRISONMENT, AND HELP US MAKE THINGS RIGHT.
I DO NOT BELIEVE, OLD FRIEND, THAT THINGS WILL EVER BE "RIGHT" AGAIN. NOT HERE... NOR IN THE TIME WHERE WE BELONG.
WE HAVE BEEN BETRAYED BY OUR OWN BLOOD IN AN AGE OF SHAME...

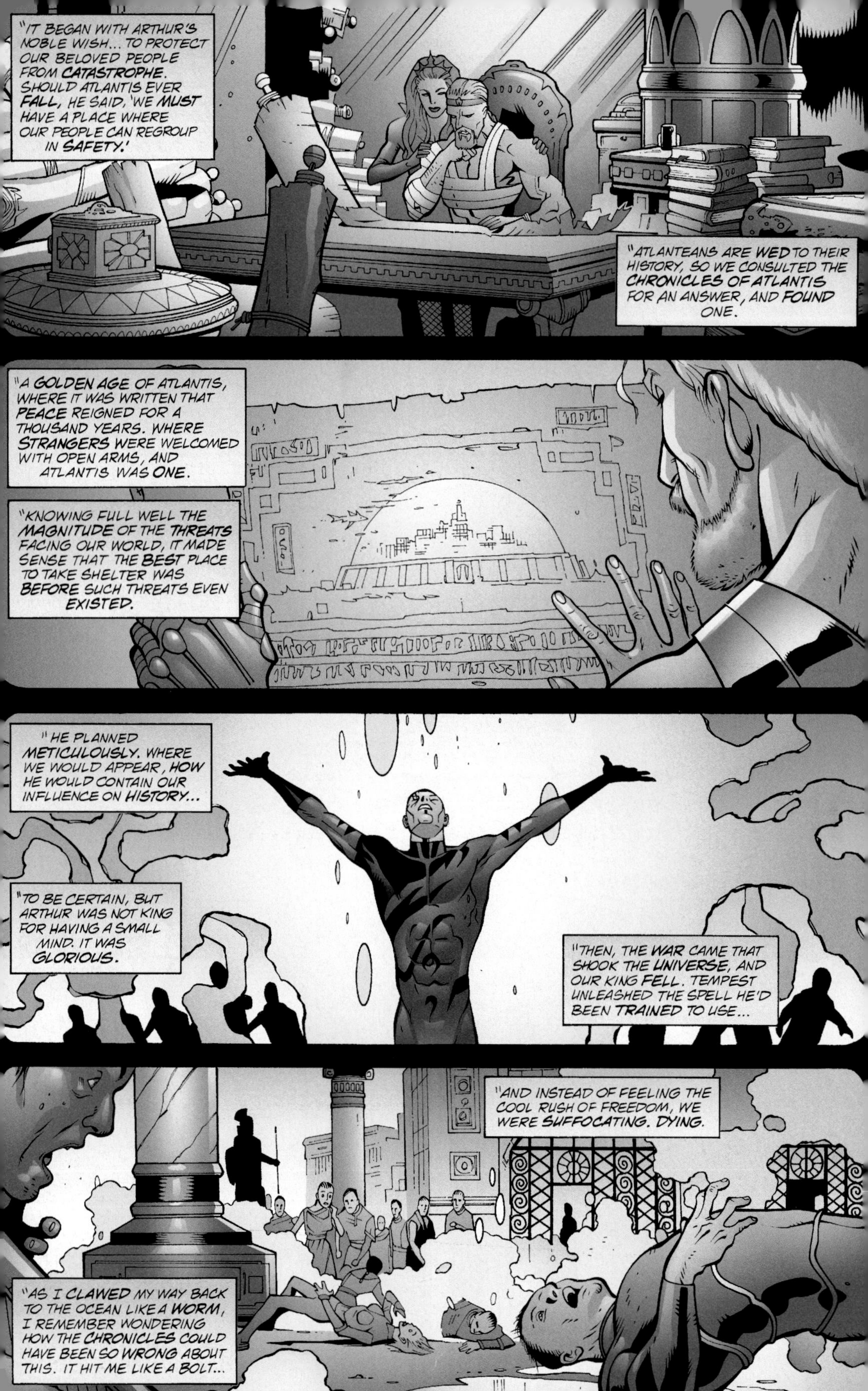
"IT BEGAN WITH ARTHUR'S NOBLE WISH... TO PROTECT OUR BELOVED PEOPLE FROM CATASTROPHE. SHOULD ATLANTIS EVER FALL, HE SAID, 'WE MUST HAVE A PLACE WHERE OUR PEOPLE CAN REGROUP IN SAFETY.'
"ATLANTEANS ARE WED TO THEIR HISTORY, SO WE CONSULTED THE CHRONICLES OF ATLANTIS FOR AN ANSWER, AND FOUND ONE.
"A GOLDEN AGE OF ATLANTIS, WHERE IT WAS WRITTEN THAT PEACE REIGNED FOR A THOUSAND YEARS. WHERE STRANGERS WERE WELCOMED WITH OPEN ARMS, AND ATLANTIS WAS ONE.
"KNOWING FULL WELL THE MAGNITUDE OF THE THREATS FACING OUR WORLD, IT MADE SENSE THAT THE BEST PLACE TO TAKE SHELTER WAS BEFORE SUCH THREATS EVEN EXISTED.
"HE PLANNED METICULOUSLY. WHERE WE WOULD APPEAR, HOW HE WOULD CONTAIN OUR INFLUENCE ON HISTORY...
"TO BE CERTAIN, BUT ARTHUR WAS NOT KING FOR HAVING A SMALL MIND. IT WAS GLORIOUS.
"THEN, THE WAR CAME THAT SHOOK THE UNIVERSE, AND OUR KING FELL. TEMPEST UNLEASHED THE SPELL HE'D BEEN TRAINED TO USE...
"AND INSTEAD OF FEELING THE COOL RUSH OF FREEDOM, WE WERE SUFFOCATING. DYING.
"AS I CLAWED MY WAY BACK TO THE OCEAN LIKE A WORM, I REMEMBER WONDERING HOW THE CHRONICLES COULD HAVE BEEN SO WRONG ABOUT THIS. IT HIT ME LIKE A BOLT...

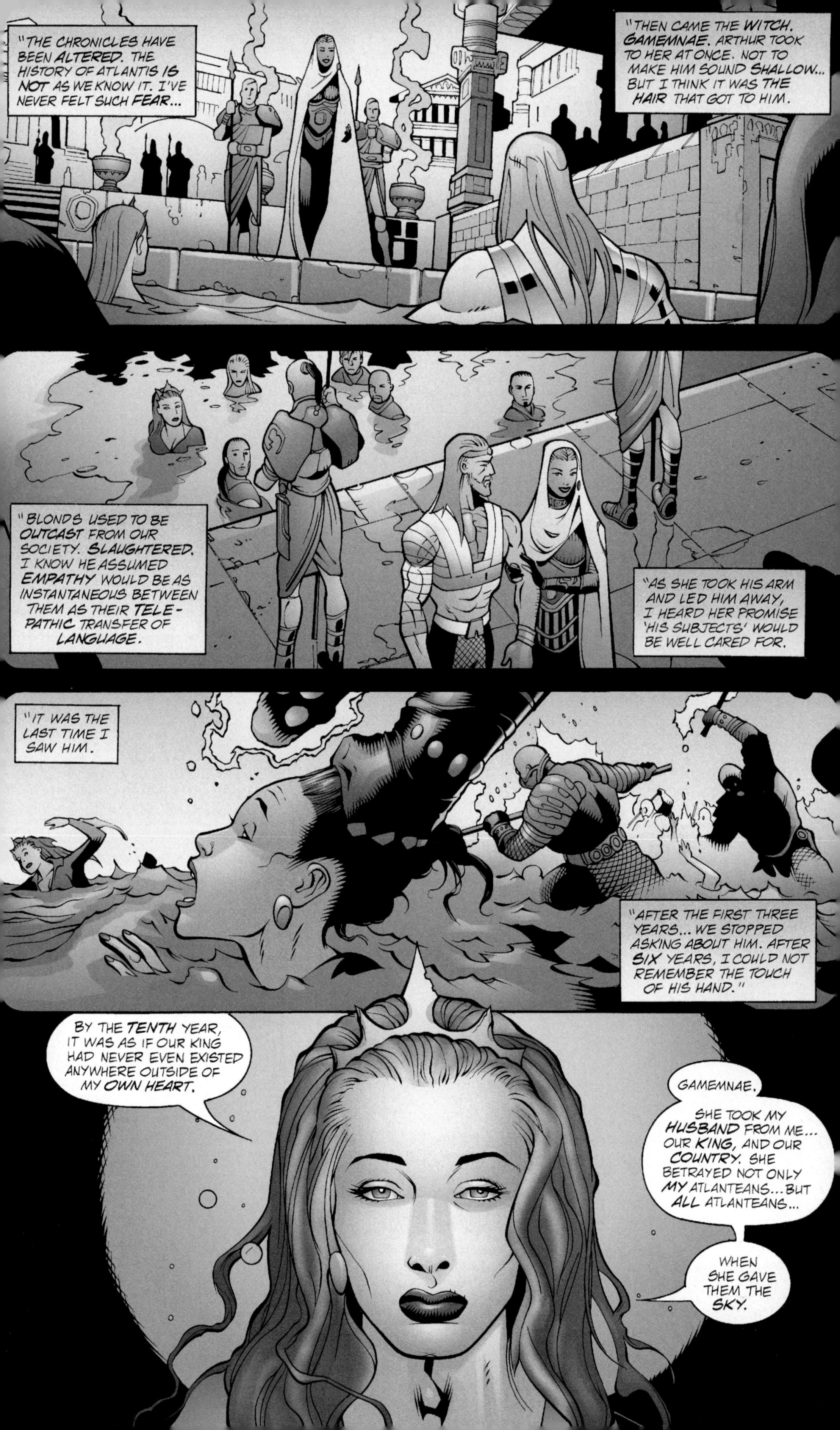
"THE CHRONICLES HAVE BEEN ALTERED. THE HISTORY OF ATLANTIS IS NOT AS WE KNOW IT. I'VE NEVER FELT SUCH FEAR...
"THEN CAME THE WITCH. GAMEMNAE. ARTHUR TOOK TO HER AT ONCE. NOT TO MAKE HIM SOUND SHALLOW... BUT I THINK IT WAS THE HAIR THAT GOT TO HIM.
"BLONDS USED TO BE OUTCAST FROM OUR SOCIETY. SLAUGHTERED. I KNOW HE ASSUMED EMPATHY WOULD BE AS INSTANTANEOUS BETWEEN THEM AS THEIR TELE-PATHIC TRANSFER OF LANGUAGE.
"AS SHE TOOK HIS ARM AND LED HIM AWAY, I HEARD HER PROMISE 'HIS SUBJECTS' WOULD BE WELL CARED FOR.
"IT WAS THE LAST TIME I SAW HIM.
"AFTER THE FIRST THREE YEARS... WE STOPPED ASKING ABOUT HIM. AFTER SIX YEARS, I COULD NOT REMEMBER THE TOUCH OF HIS HAND."
BY THE TENTH YEAR, IT WAS AS IF OUR KING HAD NEVER EVEN EXISTED ANYWHERE OUTSIDE OF MY OWN HEART.
GAMEMNAE.
SHE TOOK MY HUSBAND FROM ME... OUR KING, AND OUR COUNTRY. SHE BETRAYED NOT ONLY MY ATLANTEANS... BUT ALL ATLANTEANS...
WHEN SHE GAVE THEM THE SKY.

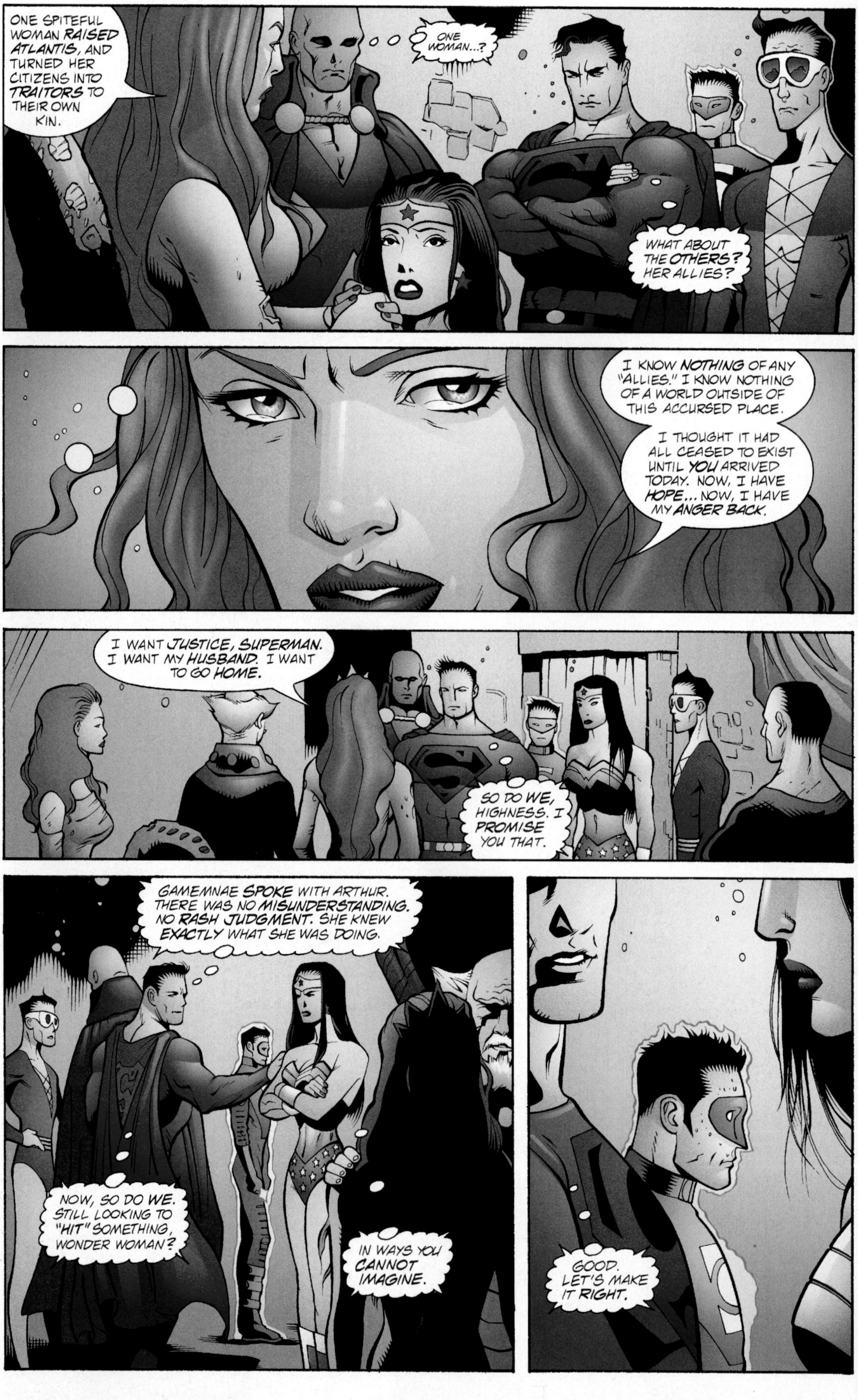
ONE SPITEFUL WOMAN RAISED ATLANTIS, AND TURNED HER CITIZENS INTO TRAITORS TO THEIR OWN KIN.
ONE WOMAN...?
WHAT ABOUT THE OTHERS? HER ALLIES?
I KNOW NOTHING OF ANY "ALLIES." I KNOW NOTHING OF A WORLD OUTSIDE OF THIS ACCURSED PLACE.
I THOUGHT IT HAD ALL CEASED TO EXIST UNTIL YOU ARRIVED TODAY. NOW, I HAVE HOPE... NOW, I HAVE MY ANGER BACK.
I WANT JUSTICE, SUPERMAN. I WANT MY HUSBAND. I WANT TO GO HOME.
SO DO WE, HIGHNESS. I PROMISE YOU THAT.
GAMEMNAE SPOKE WITH ARTHUR. THERE WAS NO MISUNDERSTANDING. NO RASH JUDGMENT. SHE KNEW EXACTLY WHAT SHE WAS DOING.
NOW, SO DO WE. STILL LOOKING TO "HIT" SOMETHING, WONDER WOMAN?
IN WAYS YOU CANNOT IMAGINE.
GOOD. LET'S MAKE IT RIGHT.

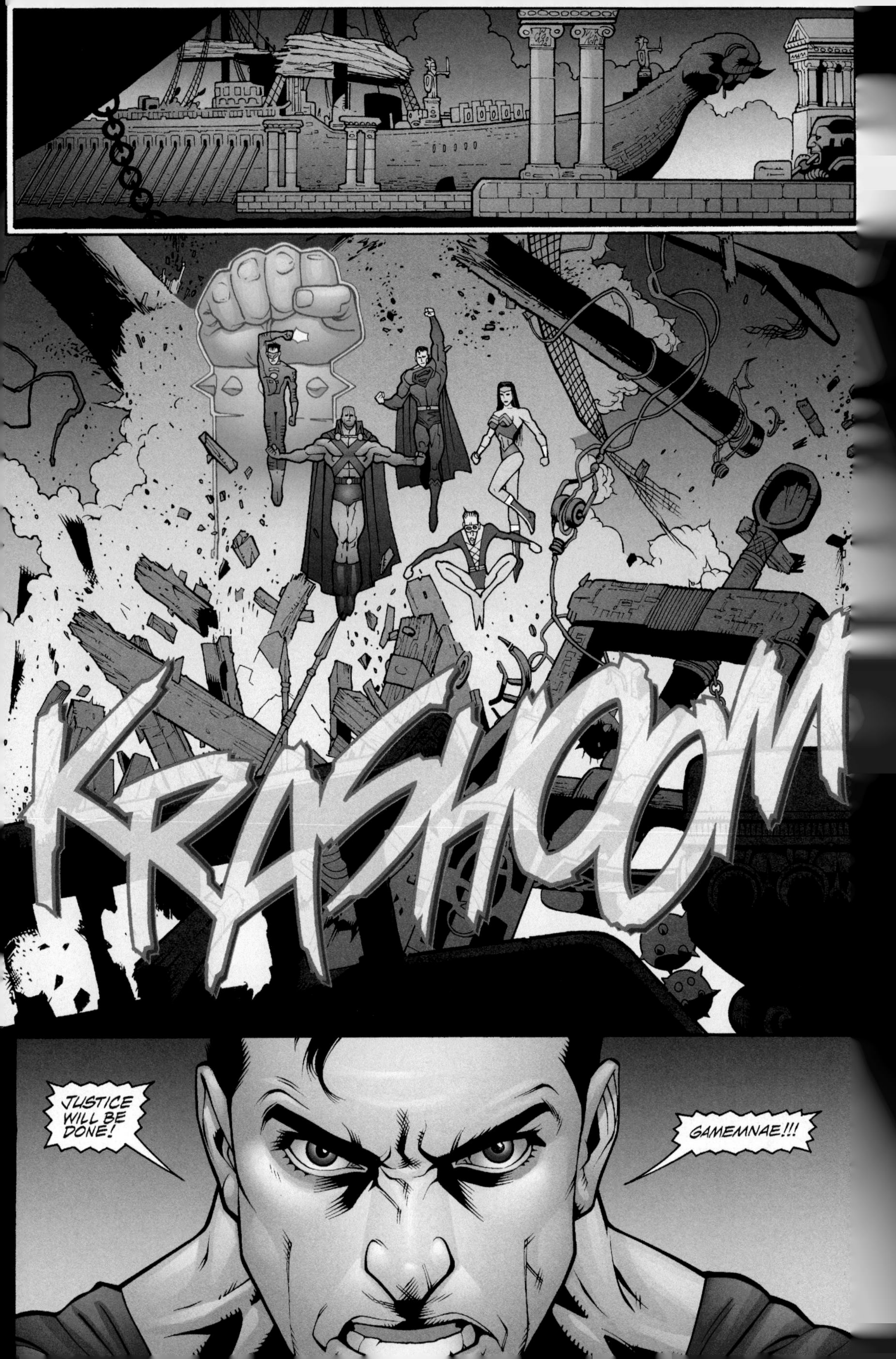
KRASHOOM
JUSTICE WILL BE DONE!
GAMEMNAE!!!

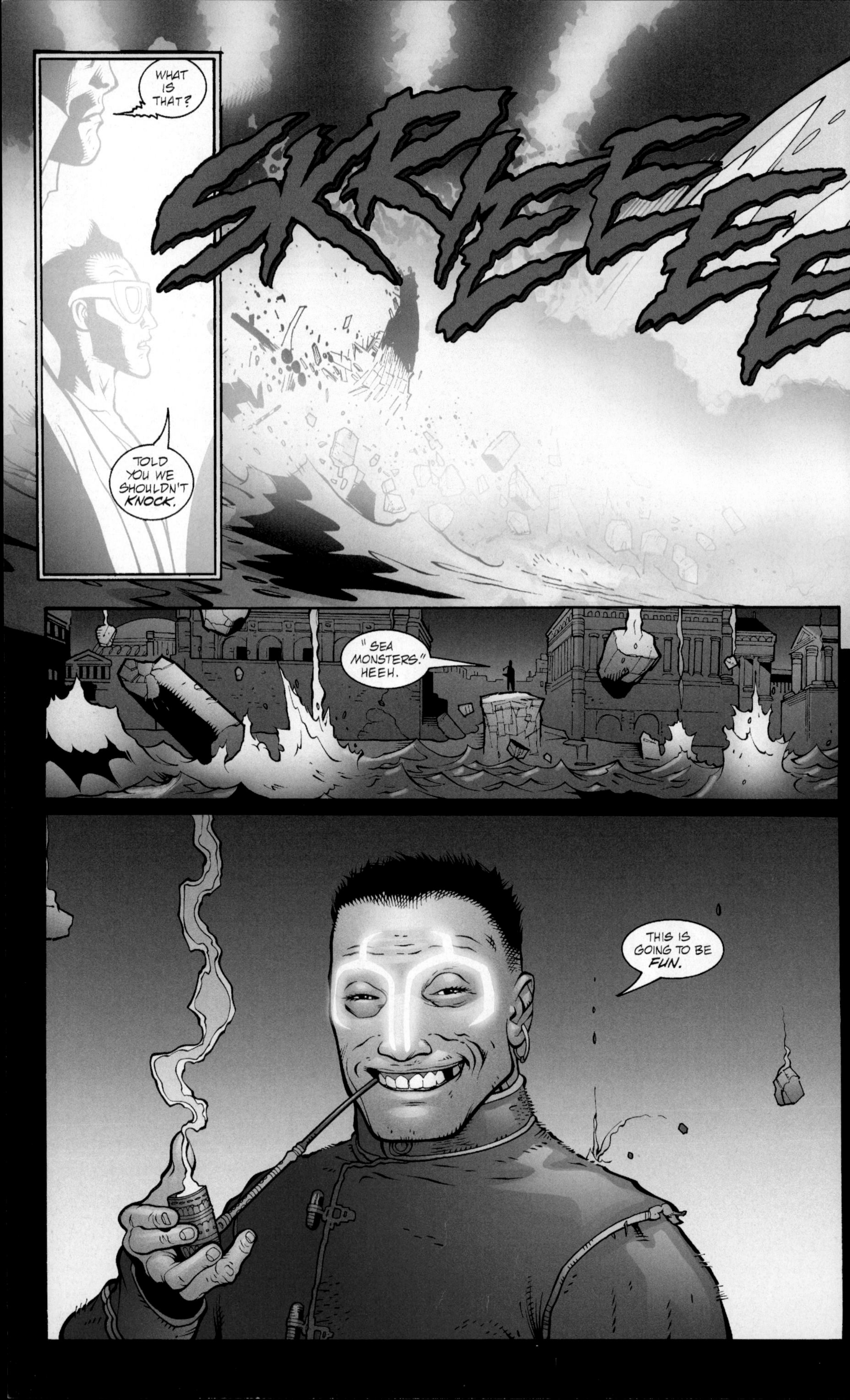
WHAT IS THAT?
SKRIEEEEE
TOLD YOU WE SHOULDN'T KNOCK.
"SEA MONSTERS." HEEH.
THIS IS GOING TO BE FUN.

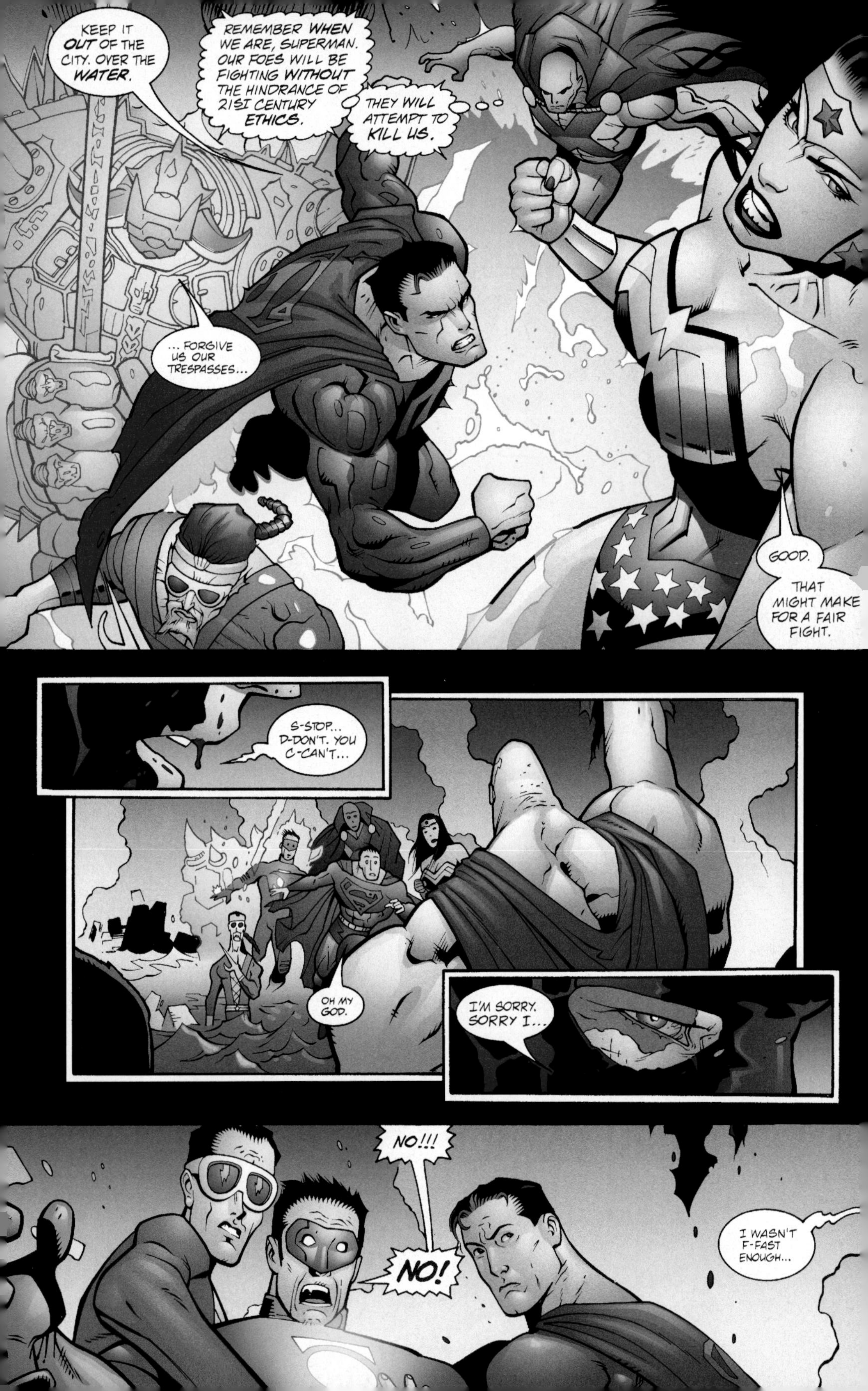
KEEP IT OUT OF THE CITY. OVER THE WATER.
REMEMBER WHEN WE ARE, SUPERMAN. OUR FOES WILL BE FIGHTING WITHOUT THE HINDRANCE OF 21ST CENTURY ETHICS.
THEY WILL ATTEMPT TO KILL US.
... FORGIVE US OUR TRESPASSES...
GOOD.
THAT MIGHT MAKE FOR A FAIR FIGHT.
S-STOP... D-DON'T. YOU C-CAN'T...
OH MY GOD.
I'M SORRY. SORRY I...
NO!!!
NO!
I WASN'T F-FAST ENOUGH...

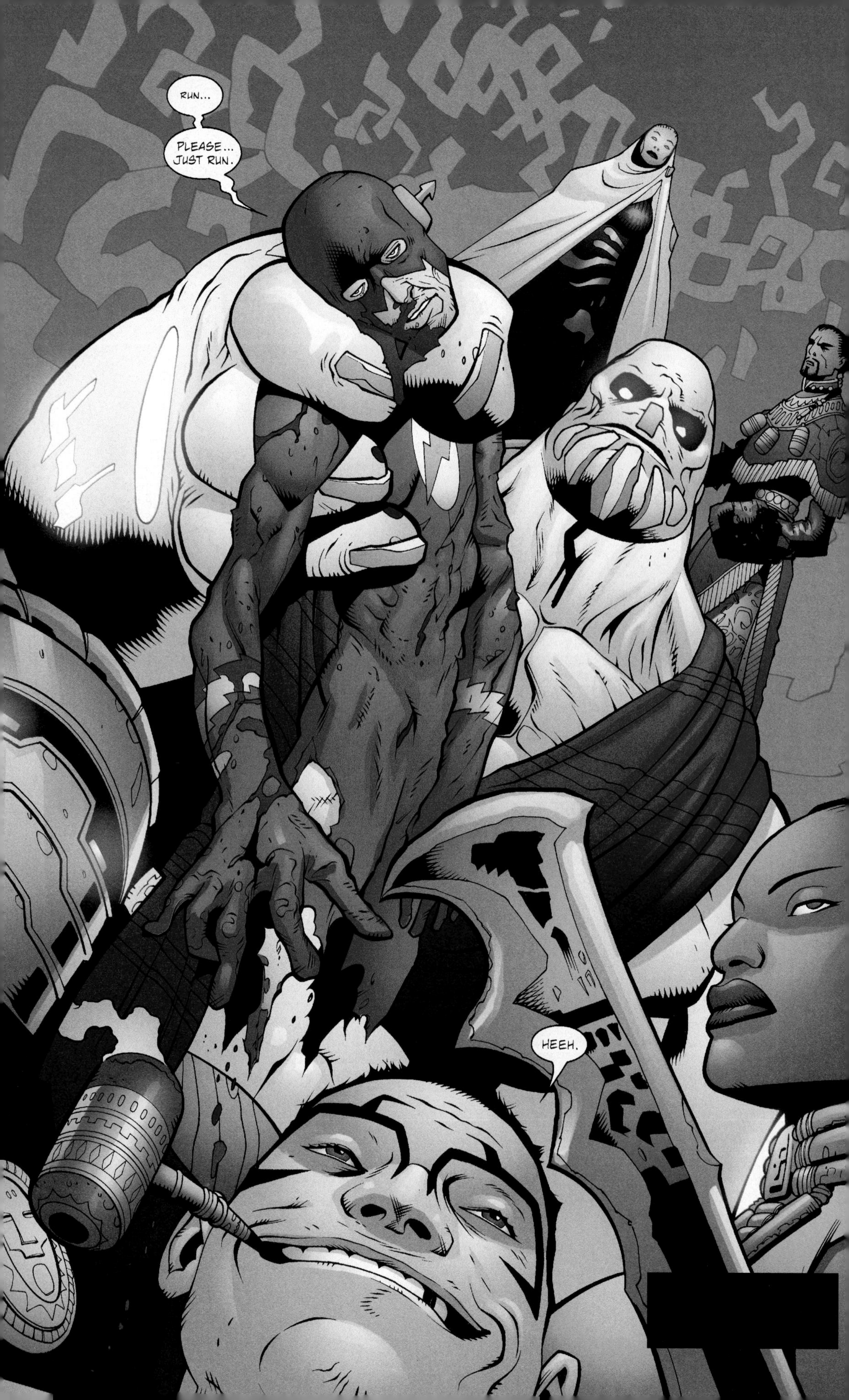
RUN...
PLEASE... JUST RUN.
HEEH.
[redacted]

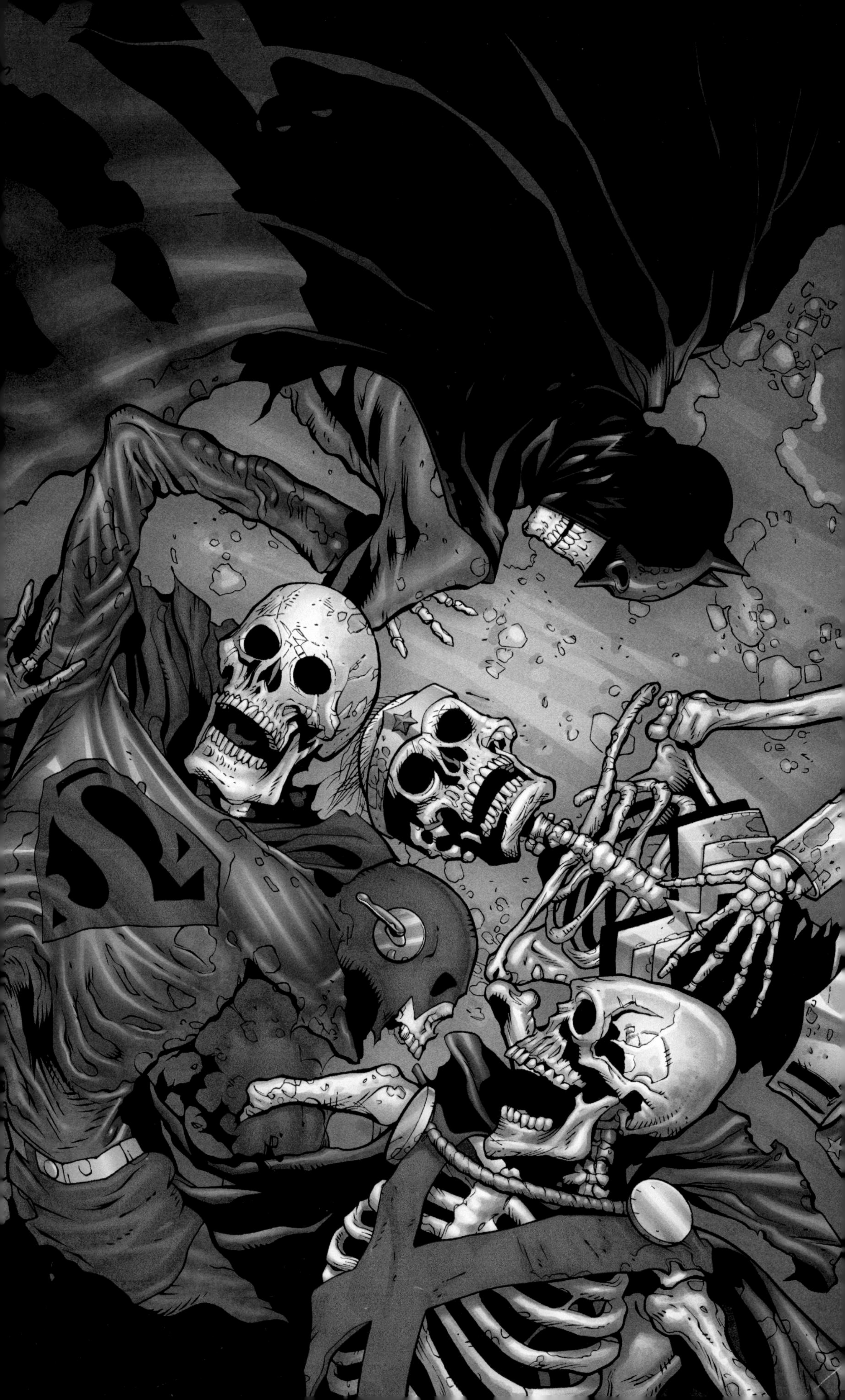

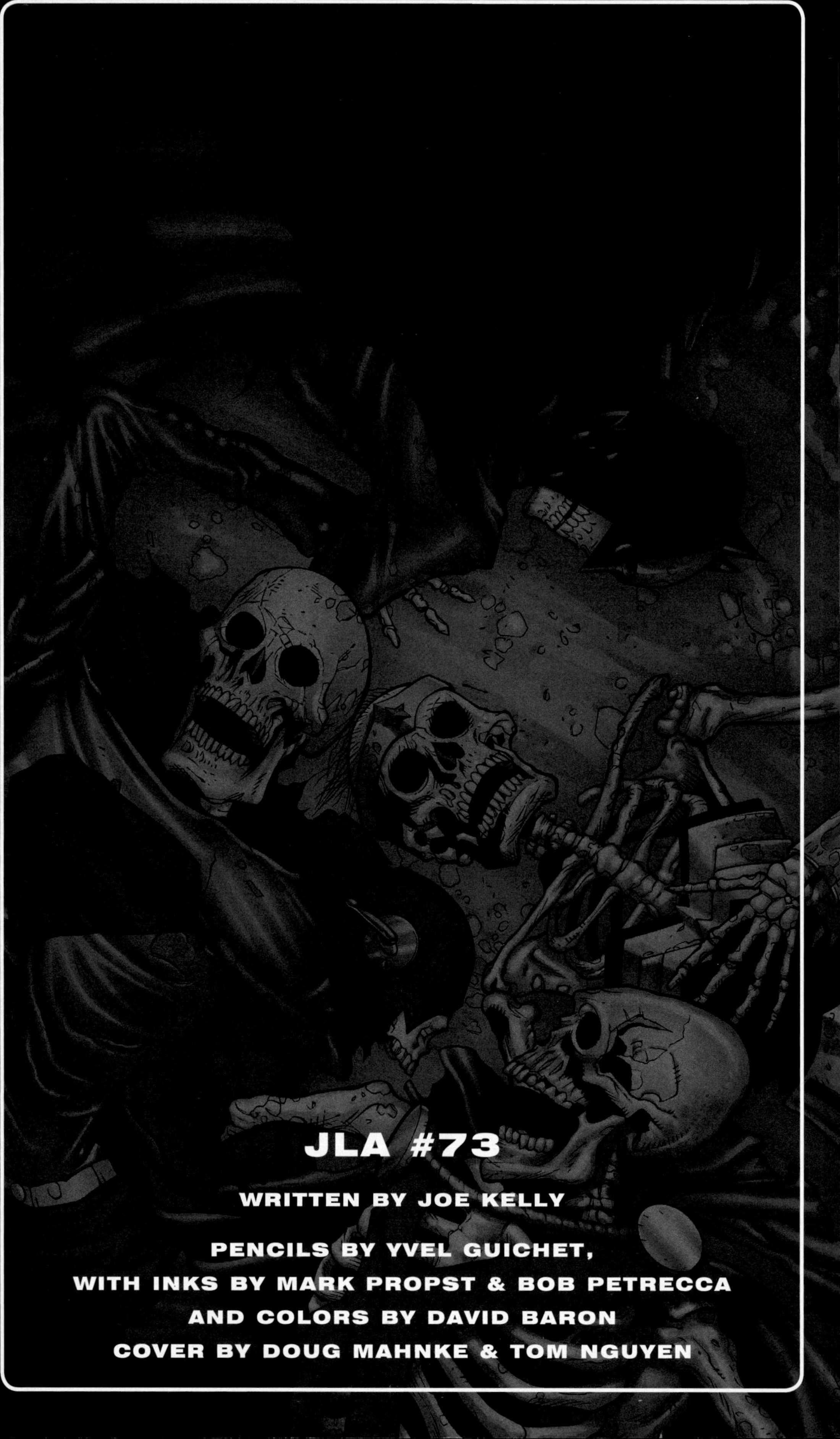

JLA #73

WRITTEN BY JOE KELLY

PENCILS BY YVEL GUICHET,
WITH INKS BY MARK PROPST & BOB PETRECCA
AND COLORS BY DAVID BARON
COVER BY DOUG MAHNKE & TOM NGUYEN

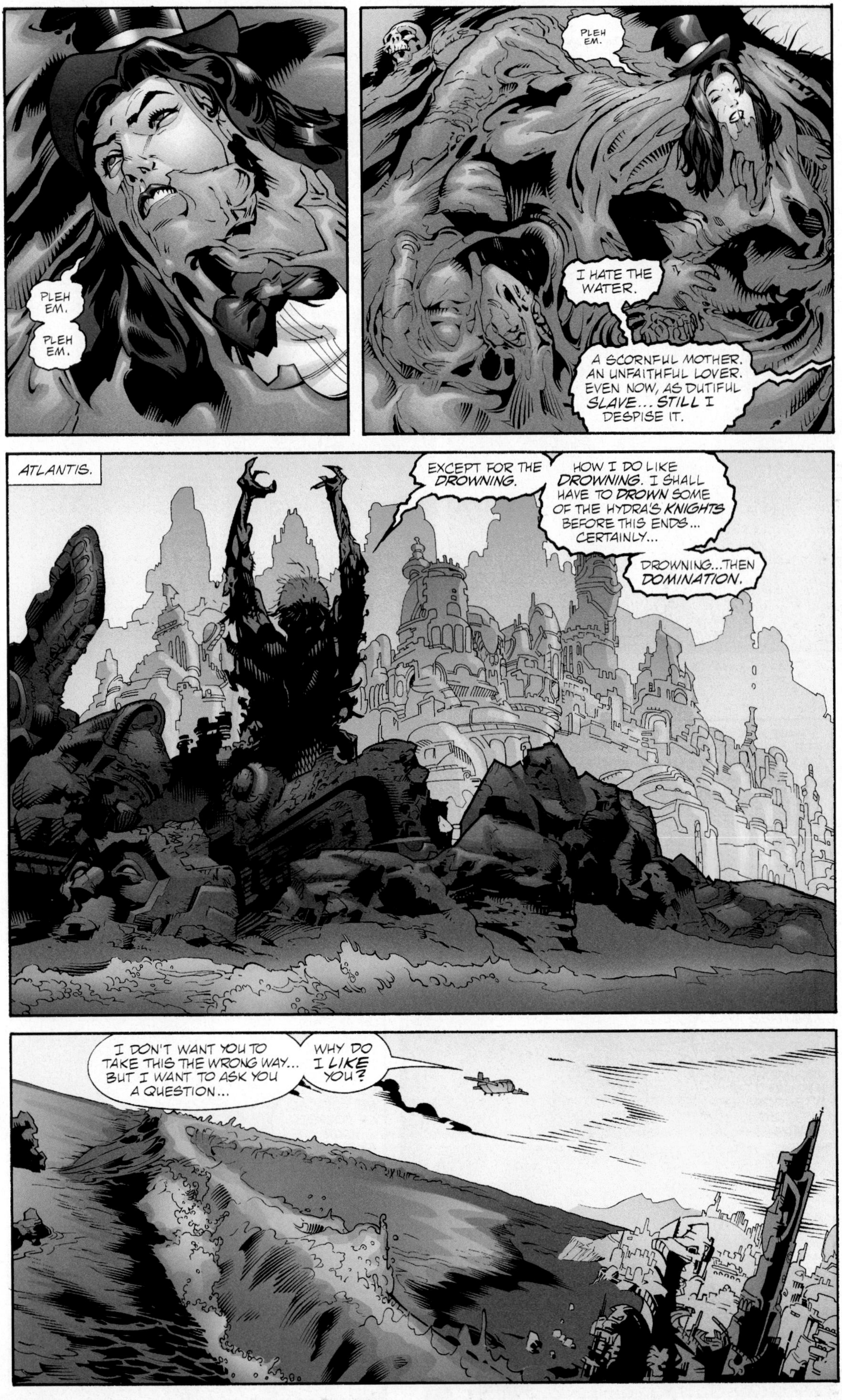
PLEH EM.
PLEH EM.
PLEH EM.
I HATE THE WATER.
A SCORNFUL MOTHER. AN UNFAITHFUL LOVER. EVEN NOW, AS DUTIFUL SLAVE... STILL I DESPISE IT.
ATLANTIS.
EXCEPT FOR THE DROWNING.
HOW I DO LIKE DROWNING. I SHALL HAVE TO DROWN SOME OF THE HYDRA'S KNIGHTS BEFORE THIS ENDS... CERTAINLY...
DROWNING...THEN DOMINATION.
I DON'T WANT YOU TO TAKE THIS THE WRONG WAY... BUT I WANT TO ASK YOU A QUESTION...
WHY DO I LIKE YOU?

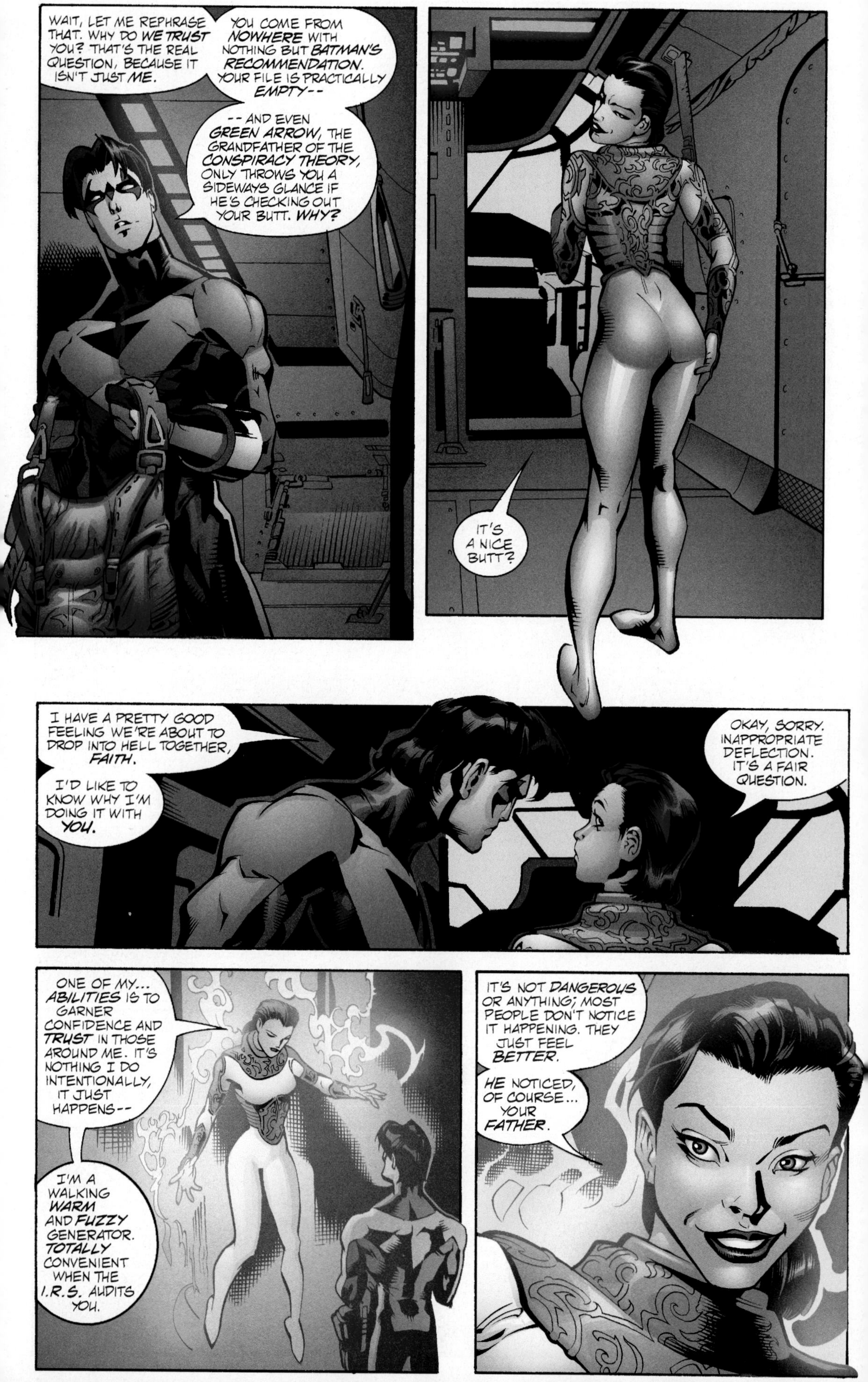
WAIT, LET ME REPHRASE THAT. WHY DO WE TRUST YOU? THAT'S THE REAL QUESTION, BECAUSE IT ISN'T JUST ME.
YOU COME FROM NOWHERE WITH NOTHING BUT BATMAN'S RECOMMENDATION. YOUR FILE IS PRACTICALLY EMPTY--
--AND EVEN GREEN ARROW, THE GRANDFATHER OF THE CONSPIRACY THEORY, ONLY THROWS YOU A SIDEWAYS GLANCE IF HE'S CHECKING OUT YOUR BUTT. WHY?
IT'S A NICE BUTT?
I HAVE A PRETTY GOOD FEELING WE'RE ABOUT TO DROP INTO HELL TOGETHER, FAITH.
I'D LIKE TO KNOW WHY I'M DOING IT WITH YOU.
OKAY, SORRY. INAPPROPRIATE DEFLECTION. IT'S A FAIR QUESTION.
ONE OF MY... ABILITIES IS TO GARNER CONFIDENCE AND TRUST IN THOSE AROUND ME. IT'S NOTHING I DO INTENTIONALLY, IT JUST HAPPENS--
I'M A WALKING WARM AND FUZZY GENERATOR. TOTALLY CONVENIENT WHEN THE I.R.S. AUDITS YOU.
IT'S NOT DANGEROUS OR ANYTHING; MOST PEOPLE DON'T NOTICE IT HAPPENING. THEY JUST FEEL BETTER.
HE NOTICED, OF COURSE... YOUR FATHER.

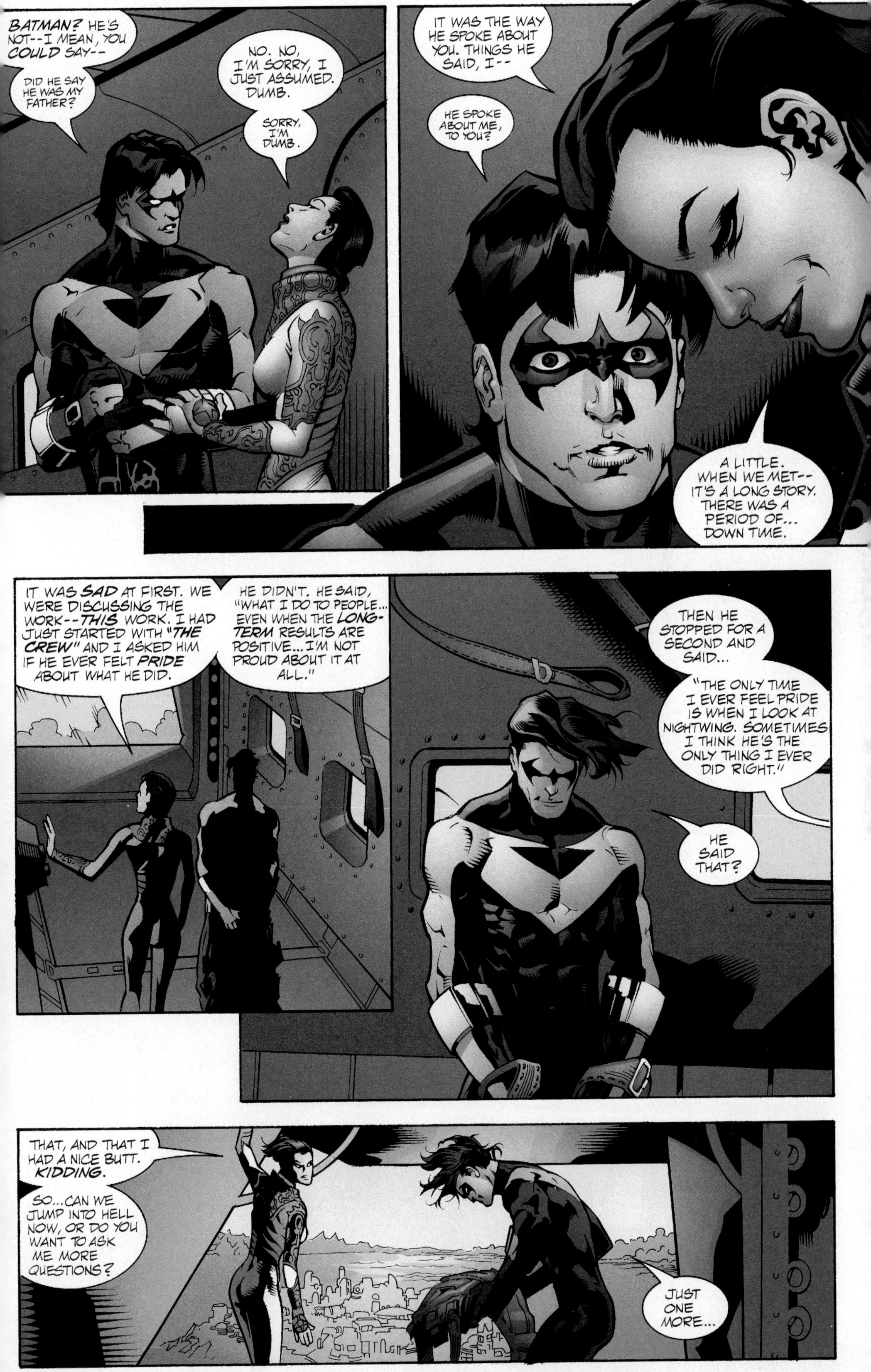
BATMAN? HE'S NOT--I MEAN, YOU COULD SAY--
DID HE SAY HE WAS MY FATHER?
NO. NO, I'M SORRY, I JUST ASSUMED. DUMB.
SORRY. I'M DUMB.
IT WAS THE WAY HE SPOKE ABOUT YOU. THINGS HE SAID, I--
HE SPOKE ABOUT ME, TO YOU?
A LITTLE. WHEN WE MET-- IT'S A LONG STORY. THERE WAS A PERIOD OF... DOWN TIME.
IT WAS SAD AT FIRST. WE WERE DISCUSSING THE WORK--THIS WORK. I HAD JUST STARTED WITH "THE CREW" AND I ASKED HIM IF HE EVER FELT PRIDE ABOUT WHAT HE DID.
HE DIDN'T. HE SAID, "WHAT I DO TO PEOPLE... EVEN WHEN THE LONG-TERM RESULTS ARE POSITIVE... I'M NOT PROUD ABOUT IT AT ALL."
THEN HE STOPPED FOR A SECOND AND SAID...
"THE ONLY TIME I EVER FEEL PRIDE IS WHEN I LOOK AT NIGHTWING. SOMETIMES I THINK HE'S THE ONLY THING I EVER DID RIGHT."
HE SAID THAT?
THAT, AND THAT I HAD A NICE BUTT. KIDDING.
SO...CAN WE JUMP INTO HELL NOW, OR DO YOU WANT TO ASK ME MORE QUESTIONS?
JUST ONE MORE...

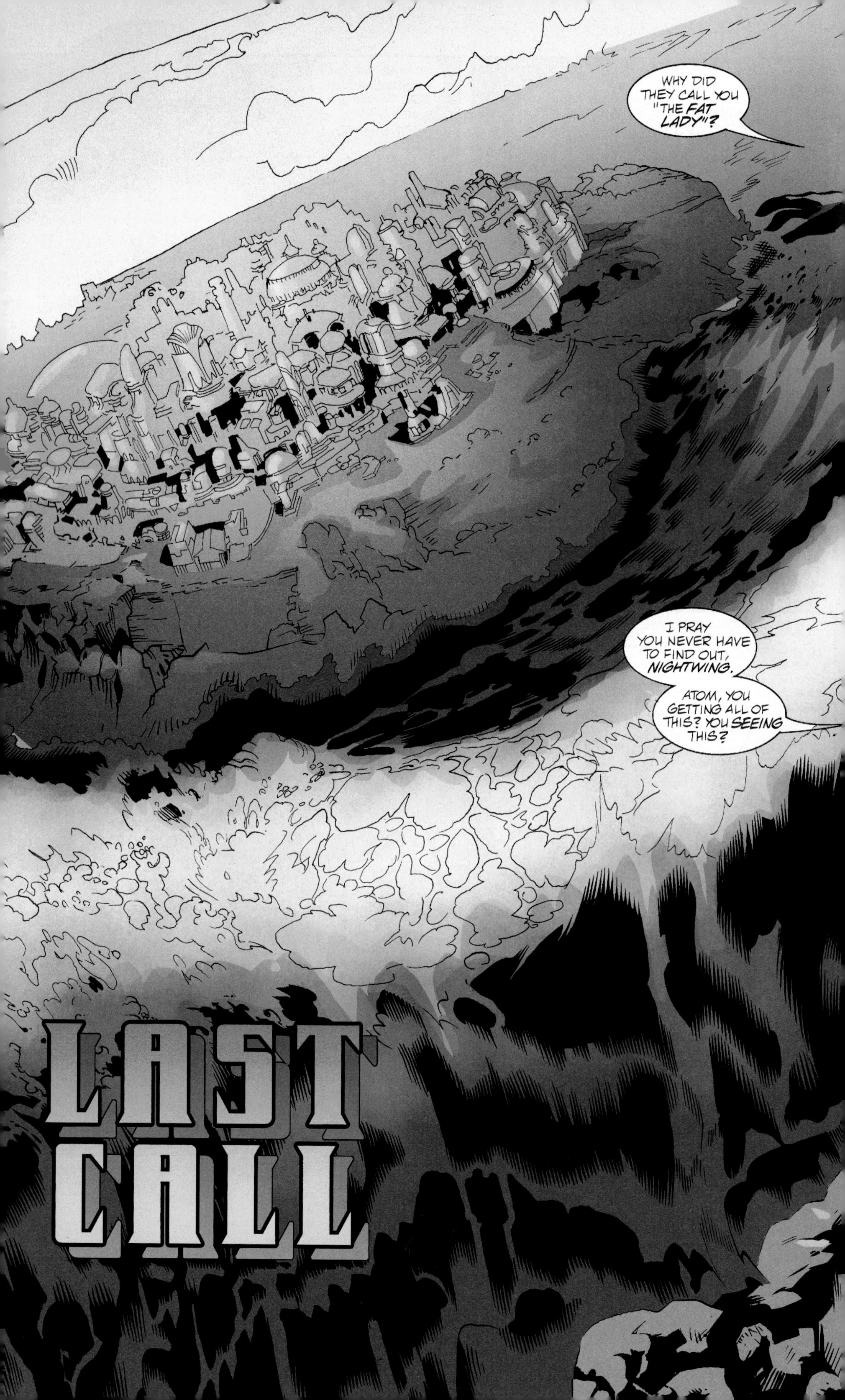
WHY DID THEY CALL YOU "THE FAT LADY"?
I PRAY YOU NEVER HAVE TO FIND OUT, NIGHTWING.
ATOM, YOU GETTING ALL OF THIS? YOU SEEING THIS?
LAST CALL

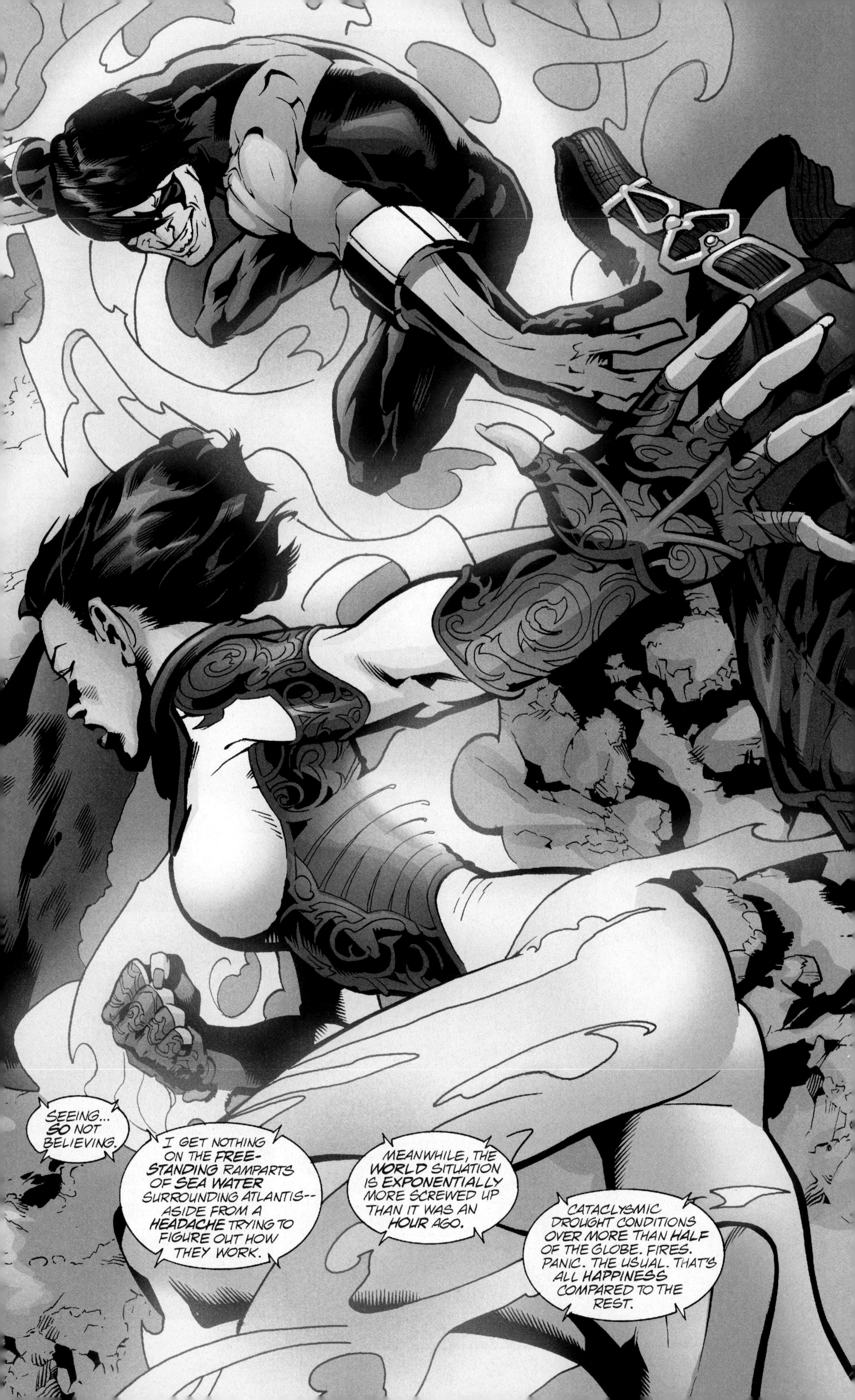
SEEING... SO NOT BELIEVING.
I GET NOTHING ON THE FREE-STANDING RAMPARTS OF SEA WATER SURROUNDING ATLANTIS-- ASIDE FROM A HEADACHE TRYING TO FIGURE OUT HOW THEY WORK.
MEANWHILE, THE WORLD SITUATION IS EXPONENTIALLY MORE SCREWED UP THAN IT WAS AN HOUR AGO.
CATACLYSMIC DROUGHT CONDITIONS OVER MORE THAN HALF OF THE GLOBE. FIRES. PANIC. THE USUAL. THAT'S ALL HAPPINESS COMPARED TO THE REST.

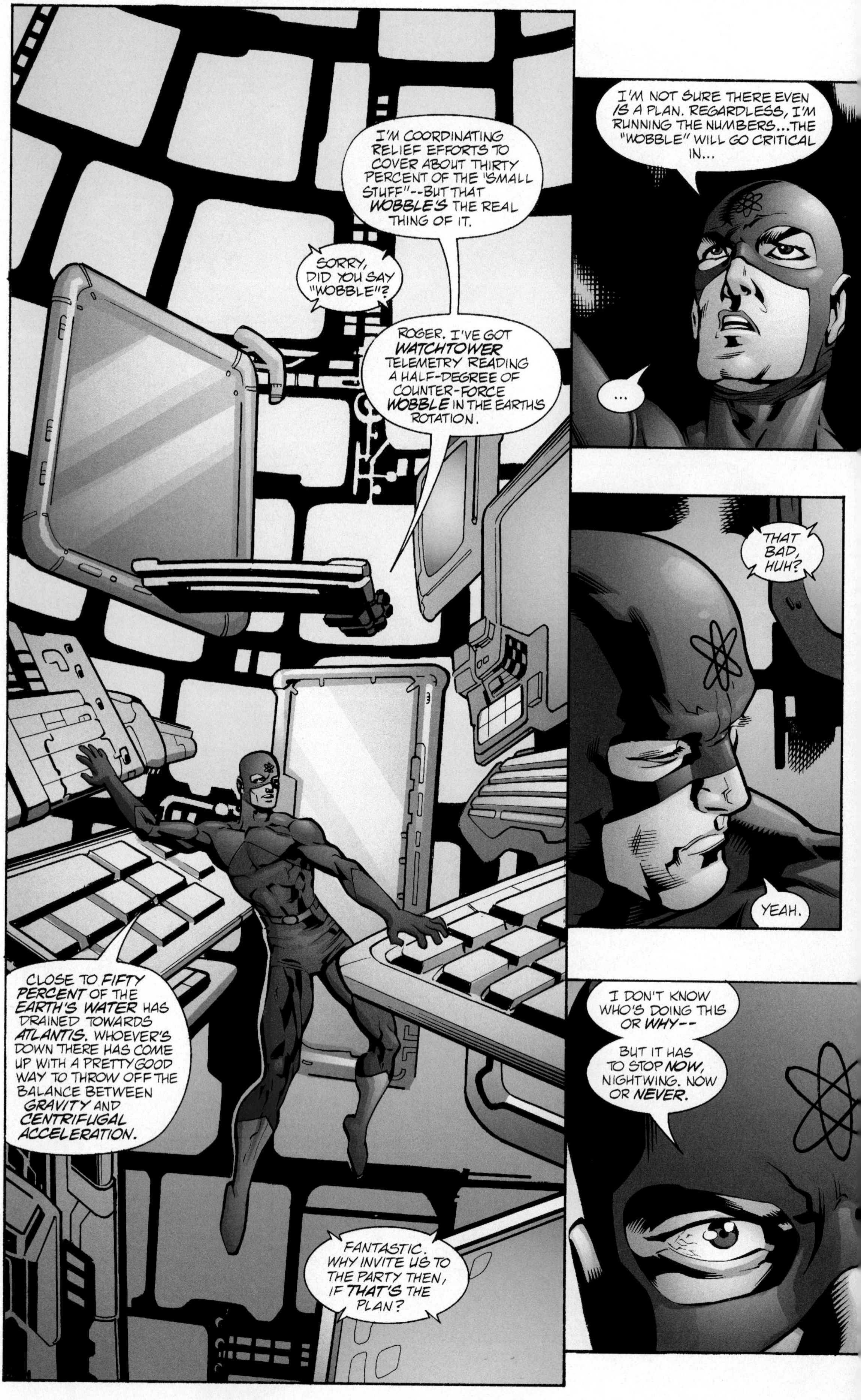
I'M COORDINATING RELIEF EFFORTS TO COVER ABOUT THIRTY PERCENT OF THE "SMALL STUFF"--BUT THAT WOBBLE'S THE REAL THING OF IT.
SORRY, DID YOU SAY "WOBBLE"?
ROGER. I'VE GOT WATCHTOWER TELEMETRY READING A HALF-DEGREE OF COUNTER-FORCE WOBBLE IN THE EARTH'S ROTATION.
CLOSE TO FIFTY PERCENT OF THE EARTH'S WATER HAS DRAINED TOWARDS ATLANTIS. WHOEVER'S DOWN THERE HAS COME UP WITH A PRETTY GOOD WAY TO THROW OFF THE BALANCE BETWEEN GRAVITY AND CENTRIFUGAL ACCELERATION.
FANTASTIC. WHY INVITE US TO THE PARTY THEN, IF THAT'S THE PLAN?
I'M NOT SURE THERE EVEN IS A PLAN. REGARDLESS, I'M RUNNING THE NUMBERS...THE "WOBBLE" WILL GO CRITICAL IN...
...
THAT BAD, HUH?
YEAH.
I DON'T KNOW WHO'S DOING THIS OR WHY--
BUT IT HAS TO STOP NOW, NIGHTWING. NOW OR NEVER.

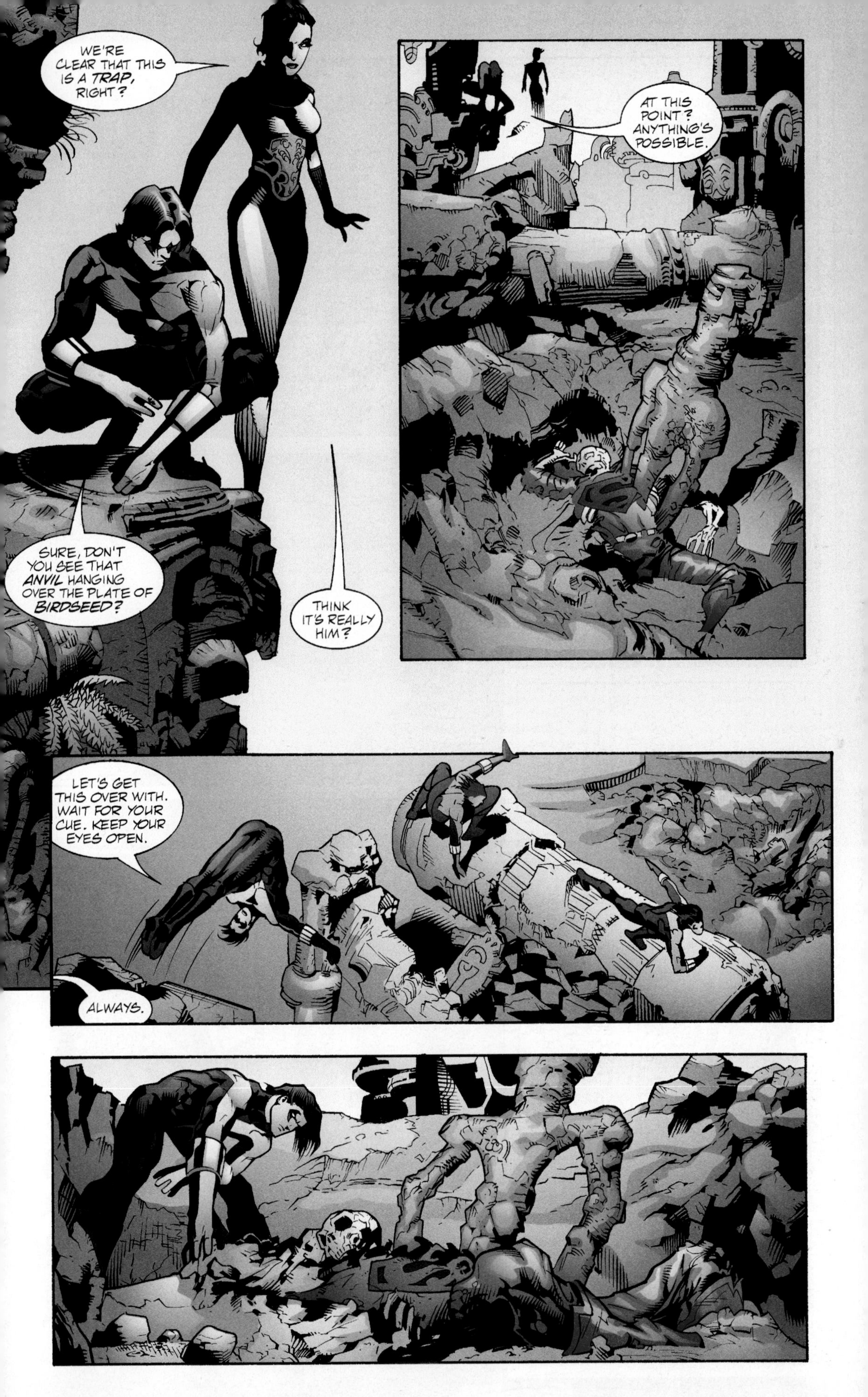
WE'RE CLEAR THAT THIS IS A TRAP, RIGHT?
SURE, DON'T YOU SEE THAT ANVIL HANGING OVER THE PLATE OF BIRDSEED?
THINK IT'S REALLY HIM?
AT THIS POINT? ANYTHING'S POSSIBLE.
LET'S GET THIS OVER WITH. WAIT FOR YOUR CUE. KEEP YOUR EYES OPEN.
ALWAYS.

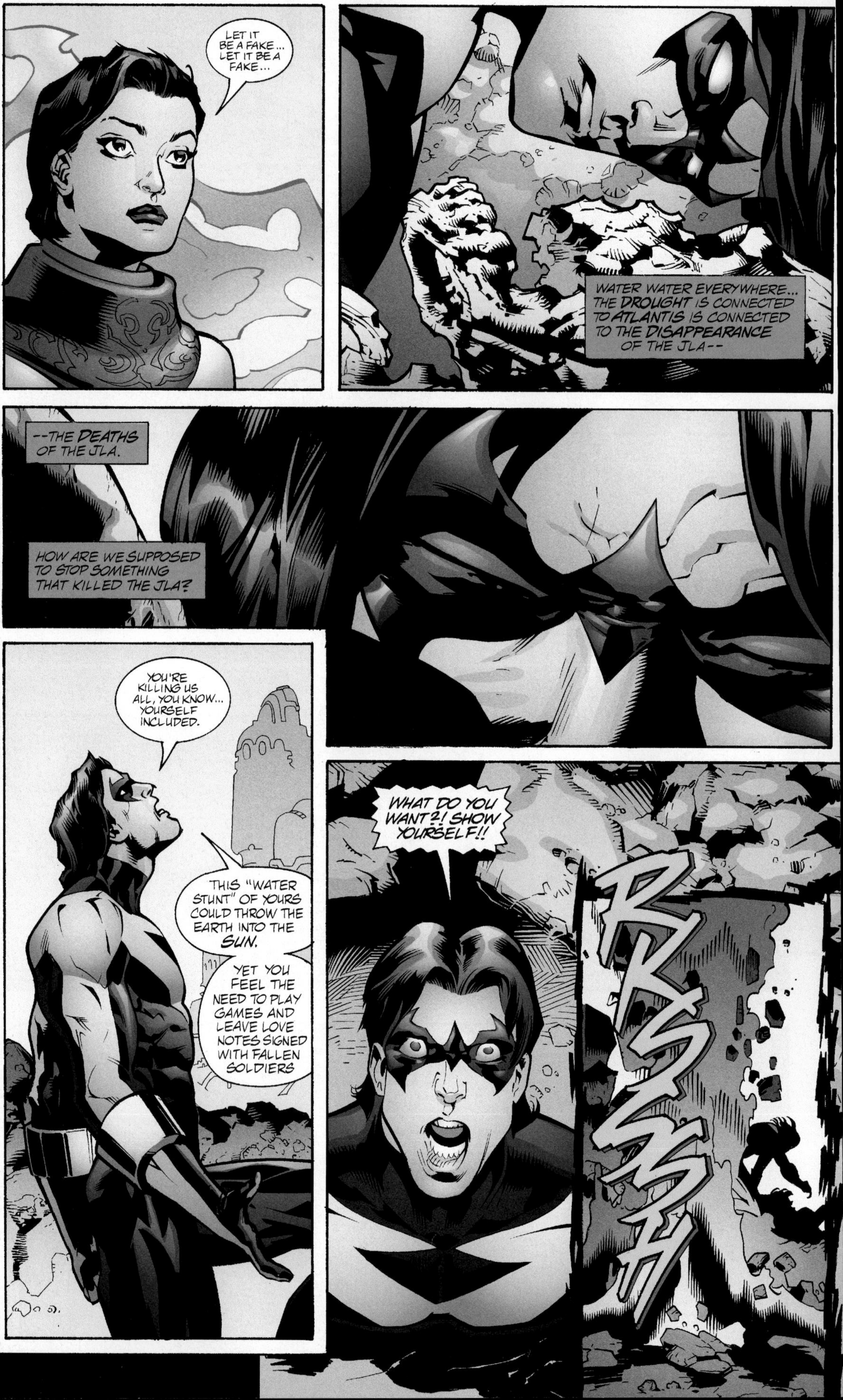
LET IT BE A FAKE... LET IT BE A FAKE...
WATER WATER EVERYWHERE... THE DROUGHT IS CONNECTED TO ATLANTIS IS CONNECTED TO THE DISAPPEARANCE OF THE JLA--
--THE DEATHS OF THE JLA.
HOW ARE WE SUPPOSED TO STOP SOMETHING THAT KILLED THE JLA?
YOU'RE KILLING US ALL, YOU KNOW... YOURSELF INCLUDED.
THIS "WATER STUNT" OF YOURS COULD THROW THE EARTH INTO THE SUN.
YET YOU FEEL THE NEED TO PLAY GAMES AND LEAVE LOVE NOTES SIGNED WITH FALLEN SOLDIERS
WHAT DO YOU WANT?! SHOW YOURSELF!!
RKSSHHH

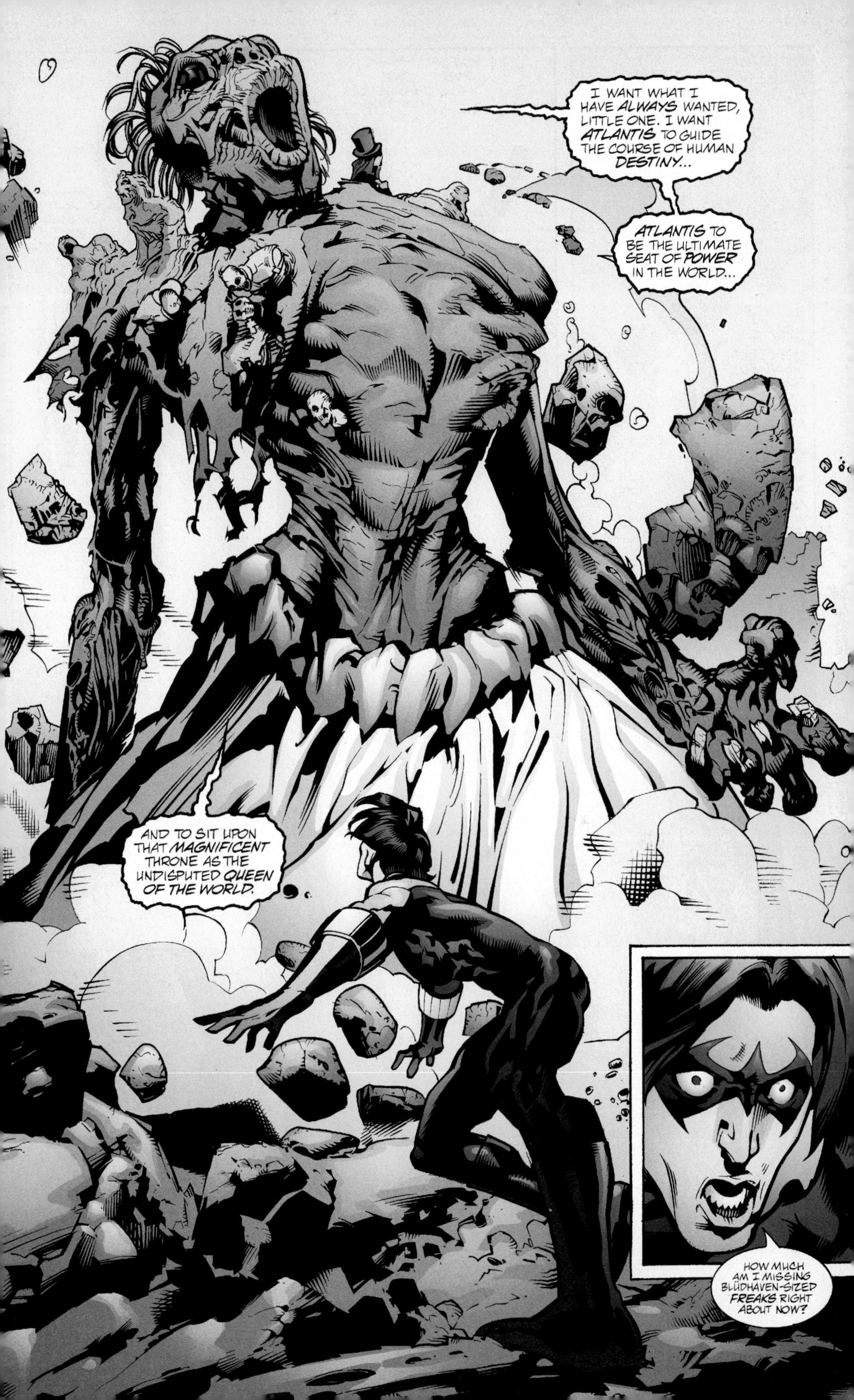
I WANT WHAT I HAVE ALWAYS WANTED, LITTLE ONE. I WANT ATLANTIS TO GUIDE THE COURSE OF HUMAN DESTINY...
ATLANTIS TO BE THE ULTIMATE SEAT OF POWER IN THE WORLD...
AND TO SIT UPON THAT MAGNIFICENT THRONE AS THE UNDISPUTED QUEEN OF THE WORLD.
HOW MUCH AM I MISSING BLÜDHAVEN-SIZED FREAKS RIGHT ABOUT NOW?

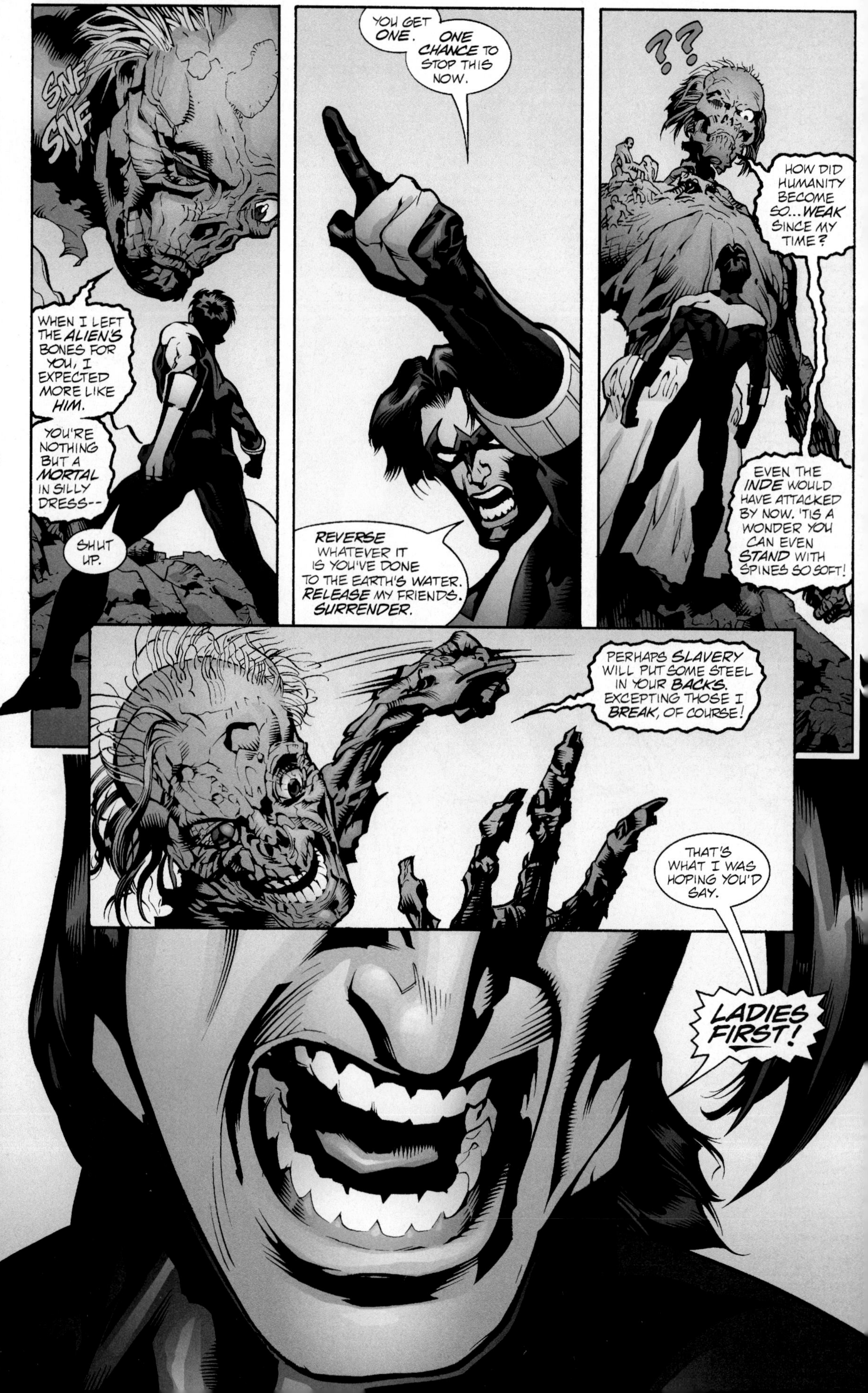
SNF SNF
WHEN I LEFT THE ALIEN'S BONES FOR YOU, I EXPECTED MORE LIKE HIM.
YOU'RE NOTHING BUT A MORTAL IN SILLY DRESS--
SHUT UP.
YOU GET ONE. ONE CHANCE TO STOP THIS NOW.
REVERSE WHATEVER IT IS YOU'VE DONE TO THE EARTH'S WATER. RELEASE MY FRIENDS. SURRENDER.
??
HOW DID HUMANITY BECOME SO...WEAK SINCE MY TIME?
EVEN THE INDE WOULD HAVE ATTACKED BY NOW. 'TIS A WONDER YOU CAN EVEN STAND WITH SPINES SO SOFT!
PERHAPS SLAVERY WILL PUT SOME STEEL IN YOUR BACKS. EXCEPTING THOSE I BREAK, OF COURSE!
THAT'S WHAT I WAS HOPING YOU'D SAY.
LADIES FIRST!

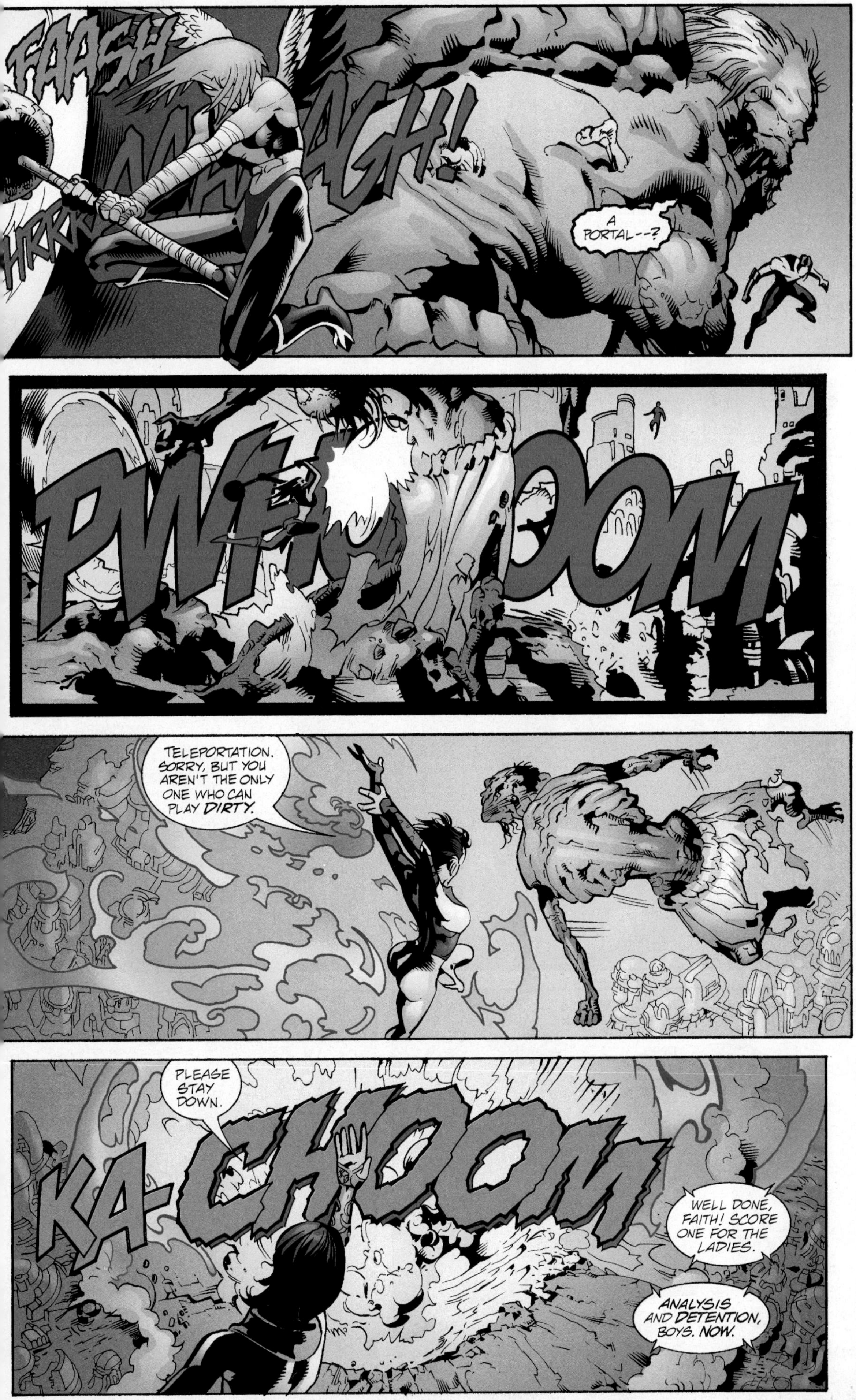
FAASH
HRRRAAAAAAAGH!
A PORTAL--?
PWHOOOM
TELEPORTATION. SORRY, BUT YOU AREN'T THE ONLY ONE WHO CAN PLAY DIRTY.
PLEASE STAY DOWN.
KA-CHOOM
WELL DONE, FAITH! SCORE ONE FOR THE LADIES.
ANALYSIS AND DETENTION, BOYS. NOW.

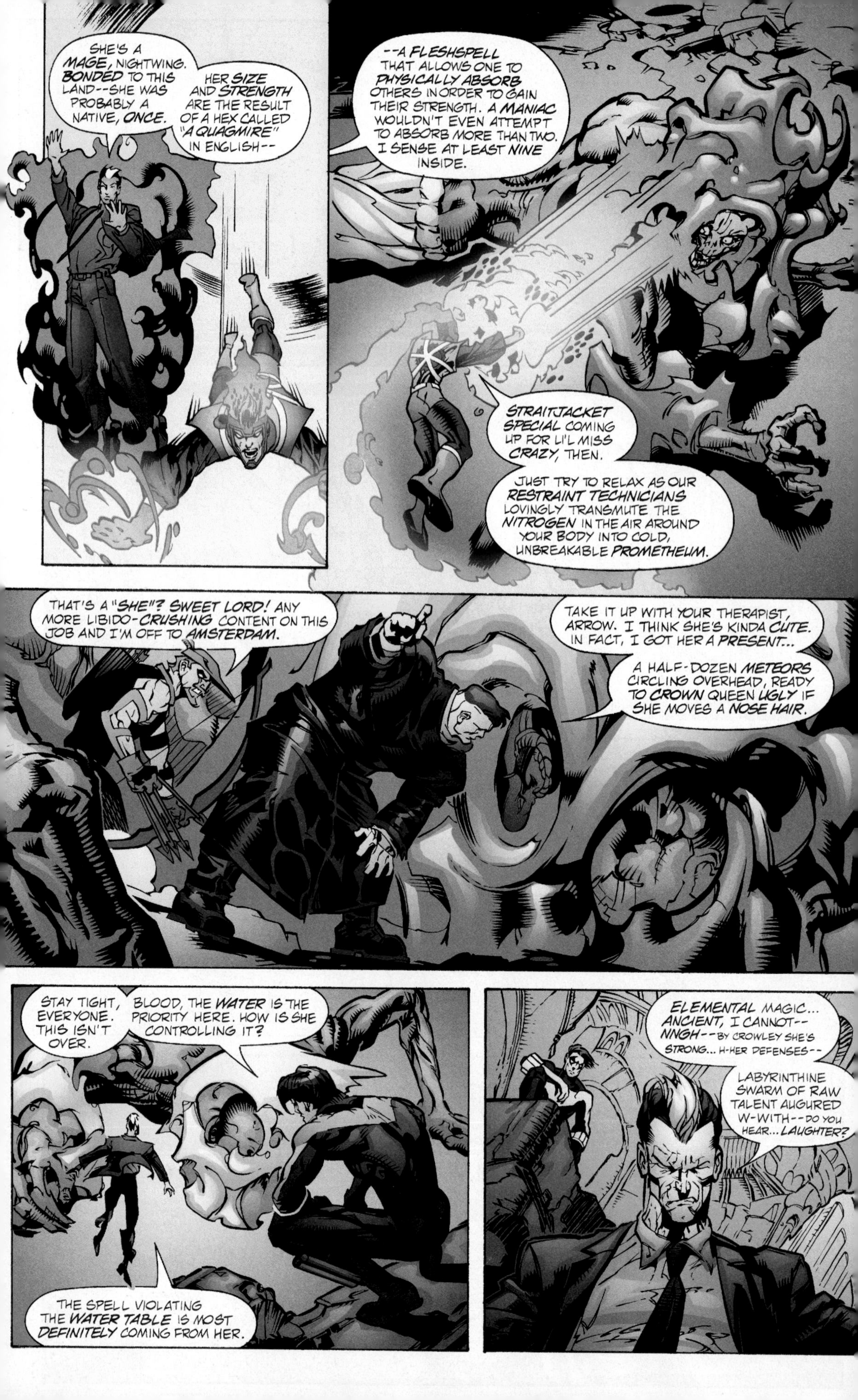
SHE'S A MAGE, NIGHTWING. BONDED TO THIS LAND--SHE WAS PROBABLY A NATIVE, ONCE.
HER SIZE AND STRENGTH ARE THE RESULT OF A HEX CALLED "A QUAGMIRE" IN ENGLISH--
--A FLESHSPELL THAT ALLOWS ONE TO PHYSICALLY ABSORB OTHERS IN ORDER TO GAIN THEIR STRENGTH. A MANIAC WOULDN'T EVEN ATTEMPT TO ABSORB MORE THAN TWO. I SENSE AT LEAST NINE INSIDE.
STRAITJACKET SPECIAL COMING UP FOR LI'L MISS CRAZY, THEN.
JUST TRY TO RELAX AS OUR RESTRAINT TECHNICIANS LOVINGLY TRANSMUTE THE NITROGEN IN THE AIR AROUND YOUR BODY INTO COLD, UNBREAKABLE PROMETHEUM.
THAT'S A "SHE"? SWEET LORD! ANY MORE LIBIDO-CRUSHING CONTENT ON THIS JOB AND I'M OFF TO AMSTERDAM.
TAKE IT UP WITH YOUR THERAPIST, ARROW. I THINK SHE'S KINDA CUTE. IN FACT, I GOT HER A PRESENT...
A HALF-DOZEN METEORS CIRCLING OVERHEAD, READY TO CROWN QUEEN UGLY IF SHE MOVES A NOSE HAIR.
STAY TIGHT, EVERYONE. THIS ISN'T OVER.
BLOOD, THE WATER IS THE PRIORITY HERE. HOW IS SHE CONTROLLING IT?
THE SPELL VIOLATING THE WATER TABLE IS MOST DEFINITELY COMING FROM HER.
ELEMENTAL MAGIC... ANCIENT, I CANNOT-- NNGH--BY CROWLEY SHE'S STRONG... H-HER DEFENSES--
LABYRINTHINE SWARM OF RAW TALENT AUGURED W-WITH--DO YOU HEAR... LAUGHTER?

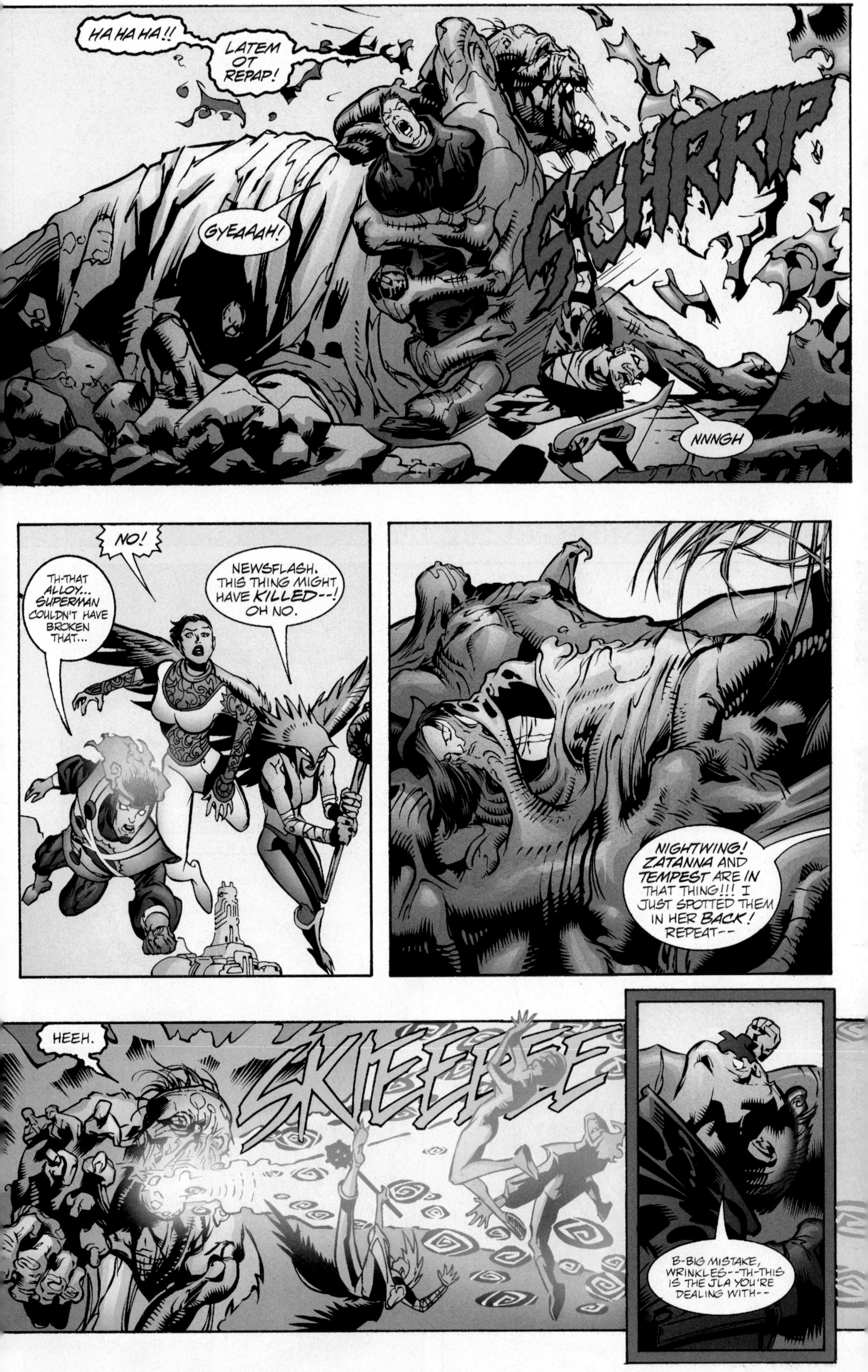
HA HA HA!!
LATEM OT REPAP!
GYEAAAH!
SCHRRIP
NNNGH
NO!
TH-THAT ALLOY... SUPERMAN COULDN'T HAVE BROKEN THAT...
NEWSFLASH. THIS THING MIGHT HAVE KILLED--! OH NO.
NIGHTWING! ZATANNA AND TEMPEST ARE IN THAT THING!!! I JUST SPOTTED THEM IN HER BACK! REPEAT--
HEEH.
B-BIG MISTAKE, WRINKLES--TH-THIS IS THE JLA YOU'RE DEALING WITH--

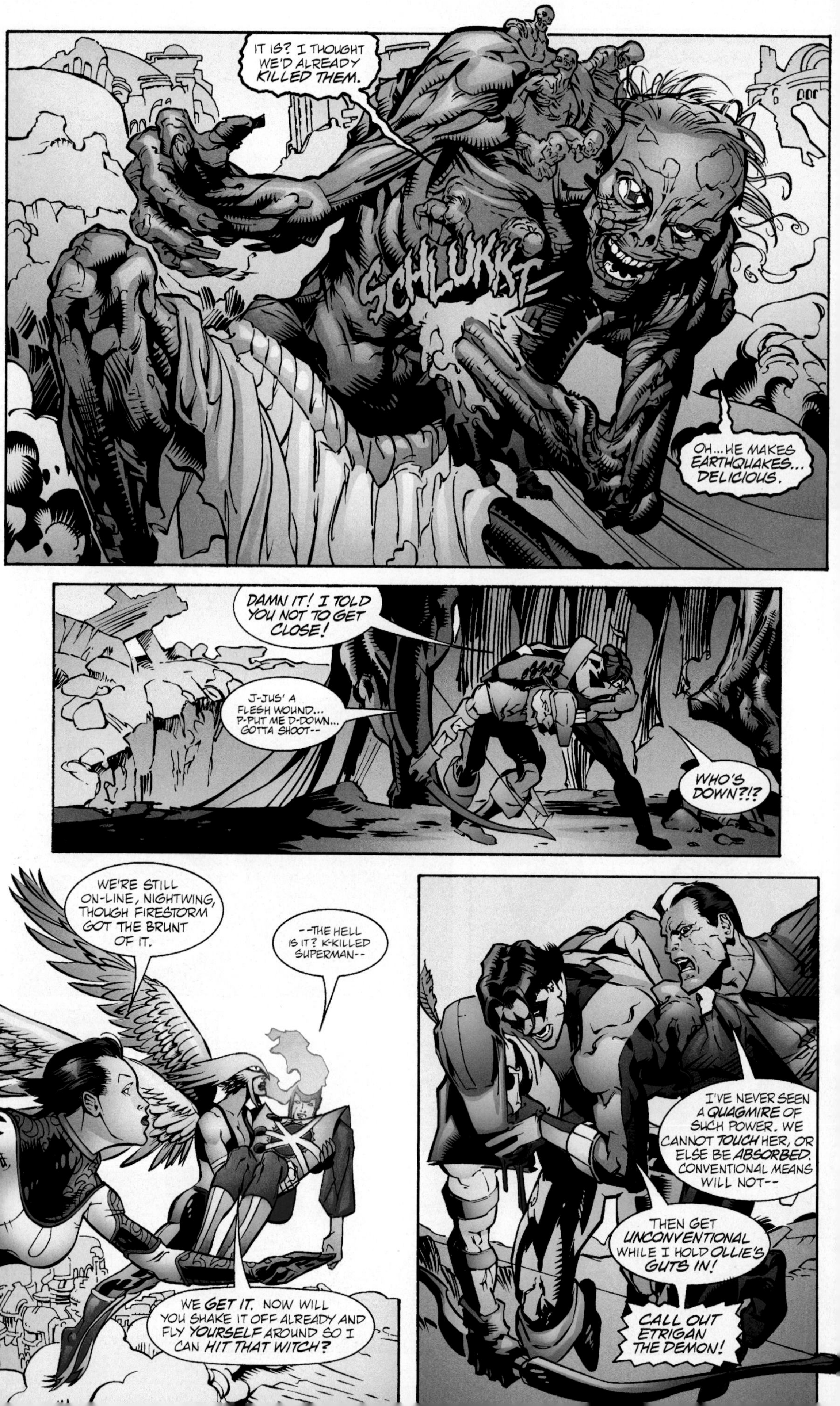
IT IS? I THOUGHT WE'D ALREADY KILLED THEM.
SCHLUKKT
OH... HE MAKES EARTHQUAKES... DELICIOUS.
DAMN IT! I TOLD YOU NOT TO GET CLOSE!
J-JUS' A FLESH WOUND... P-PUT ME D-DOWN... GOTTA SHOOT--
WHO'S DOWN?!?
WE'RE STILL ON-LINE, NIGHTWING, THOUGH FIRESTORM GOT THE BRUNT OF IT.
--THE HELL IS IT? K-KILLED SUPERMAN--
WE GET IT. NOW WILL YOU SHAKE IT OFF ALREADY AND FLY YOURSELF AROUND SO I CAN HIT THAT WITCH?
I'VE NEVER SEEN A QUAGMIRE OF SUCH POWER. WE CANNOT TOUCH HER, OR ELSE BE ABSORBED. CONVENTIONAL MEANS WILL NOT--
THEN GET UNCONVENTIONAL WHILE I HOLD OLLIE'S GUTS IN!
CALL OUT ETRIGAN THE DEMON!

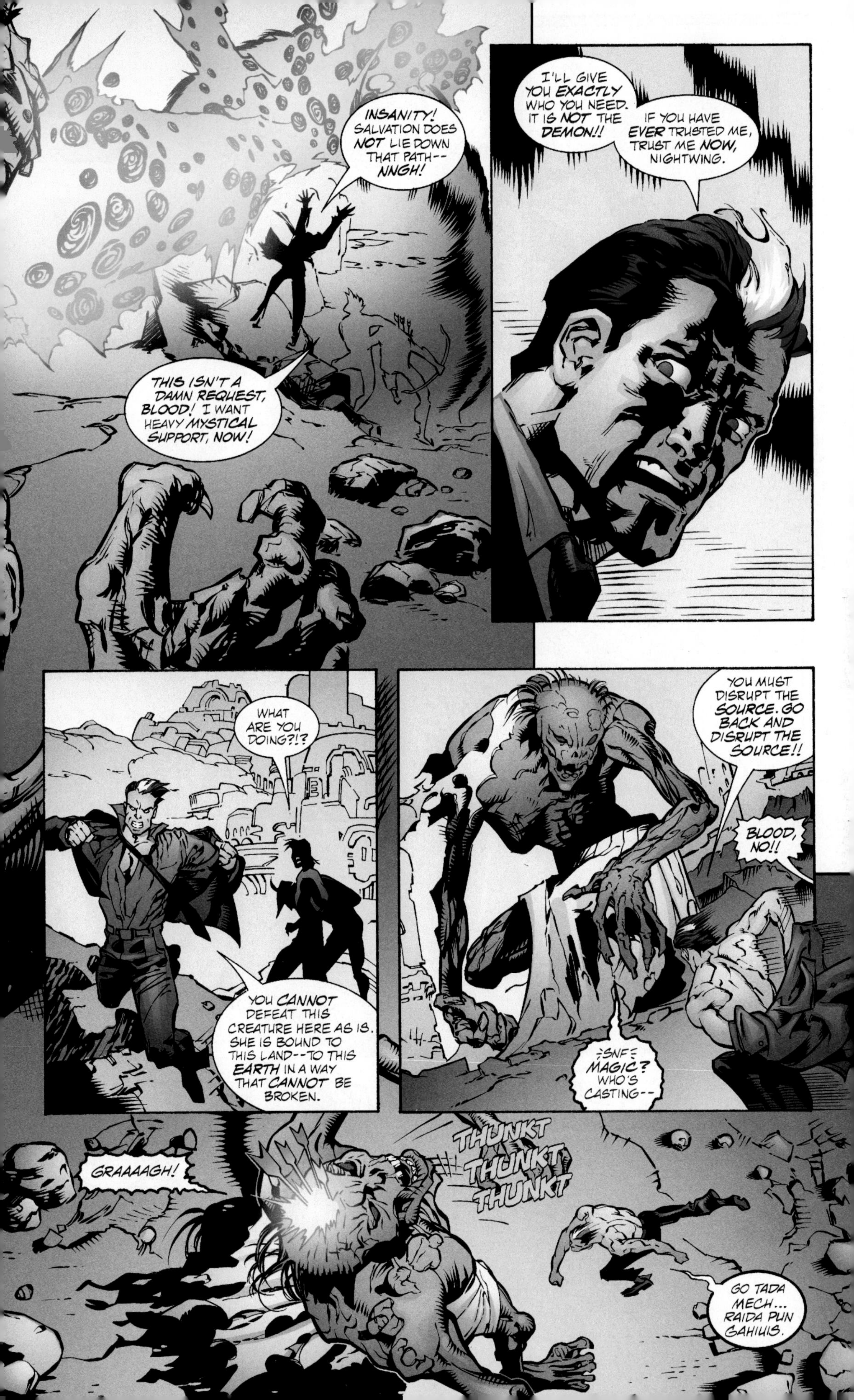
INSANITY! SALVATION DOES NOT LIE DOWN THAT PATH-- NNGH!
THIS ISN'T A DAMN REQUEST, BLOOD! I WANT HEAVY MYSTICAL SUPPORT, NOW!
I'LL GIVE YOU EXACTLY WHO YOU NEED. IT IS NOT THE DEMON!!
IF YOU HAVE EVER TRUSTED ME, TRUST ME NOW, NIGHTWING.
WHAT ARE YOU DOING?!?
YOU CANNOT DEFEAT THIS CREATURE HERE AS IS. SHE IS BOUND TO THIS LAND--TO THIS EARTH IN A WAY THAT CANNOT BE BROKEN.
YOU MUST DISRUPT THE SOURCE. GO BACK AND DISRUPT THE SOURCE!!
BLOOD, NO!!
SNF MAGIC? WHO'S CASTING--
GRAAAAGH!
THUNKT THUNKT THUNKT
GO TADA MECH... RAIDA PUN GAHIUIS.

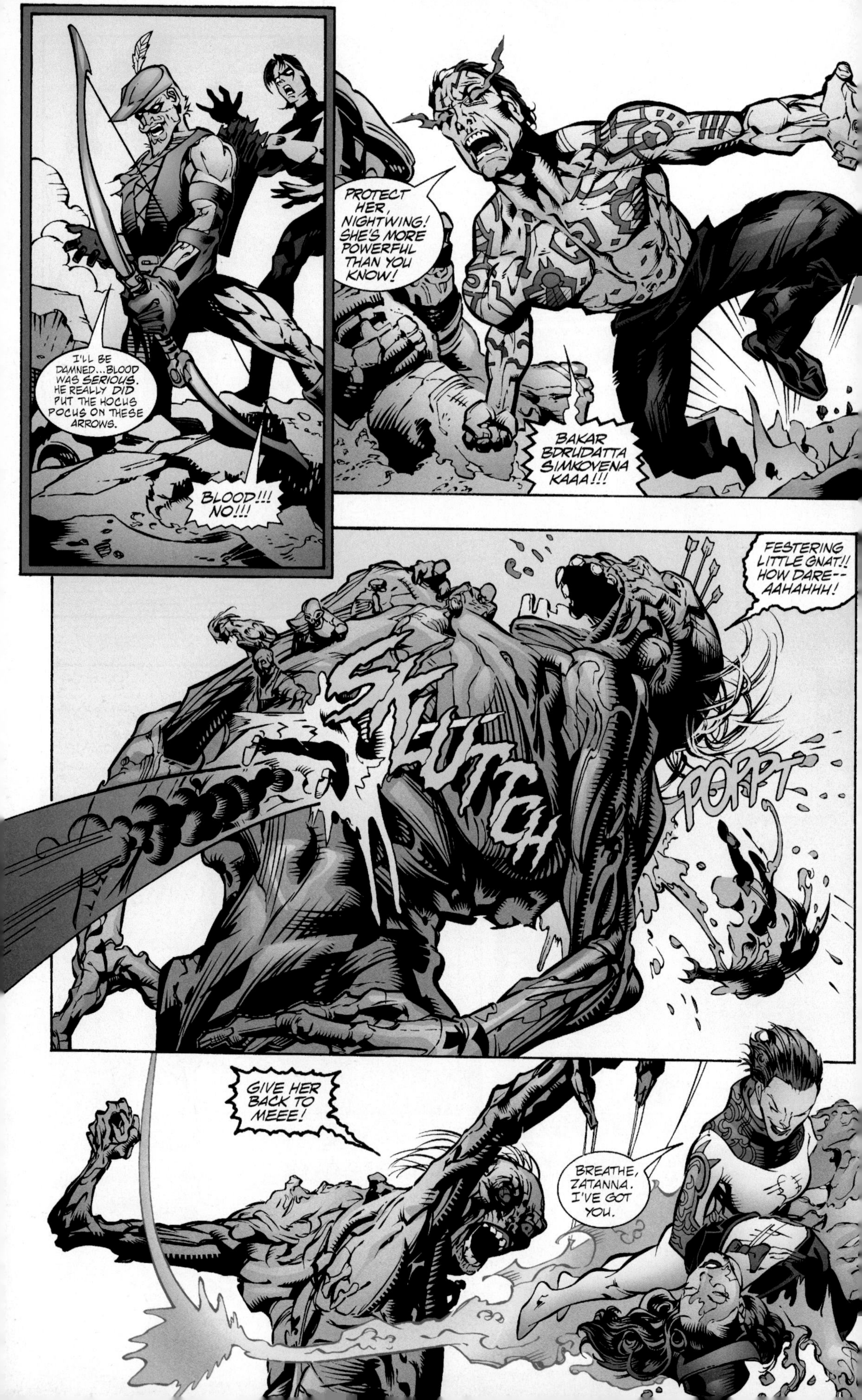
PROTECT HER, NIGHTWING! SHE'S MORE POWERFUL THAN YOU KNOW!
I'LL BE DAMNED...BLOOD WAS SERIOUS. HE REALLY DID PUT THE HOCUS POCUS ON THESE ARROWS.
BLOOD!!! NO!!!
BAKAR BDRUDATTA SIMKOVENA KAAA!!!
FESTERING LITTLE GNAT!! HOW DARE-- AAHAHHH!
SKLUTCH
POPPT
GIVE HER BACK TO MEEE!
BREATHE, ZATANNA. I'VE GOT YOU.

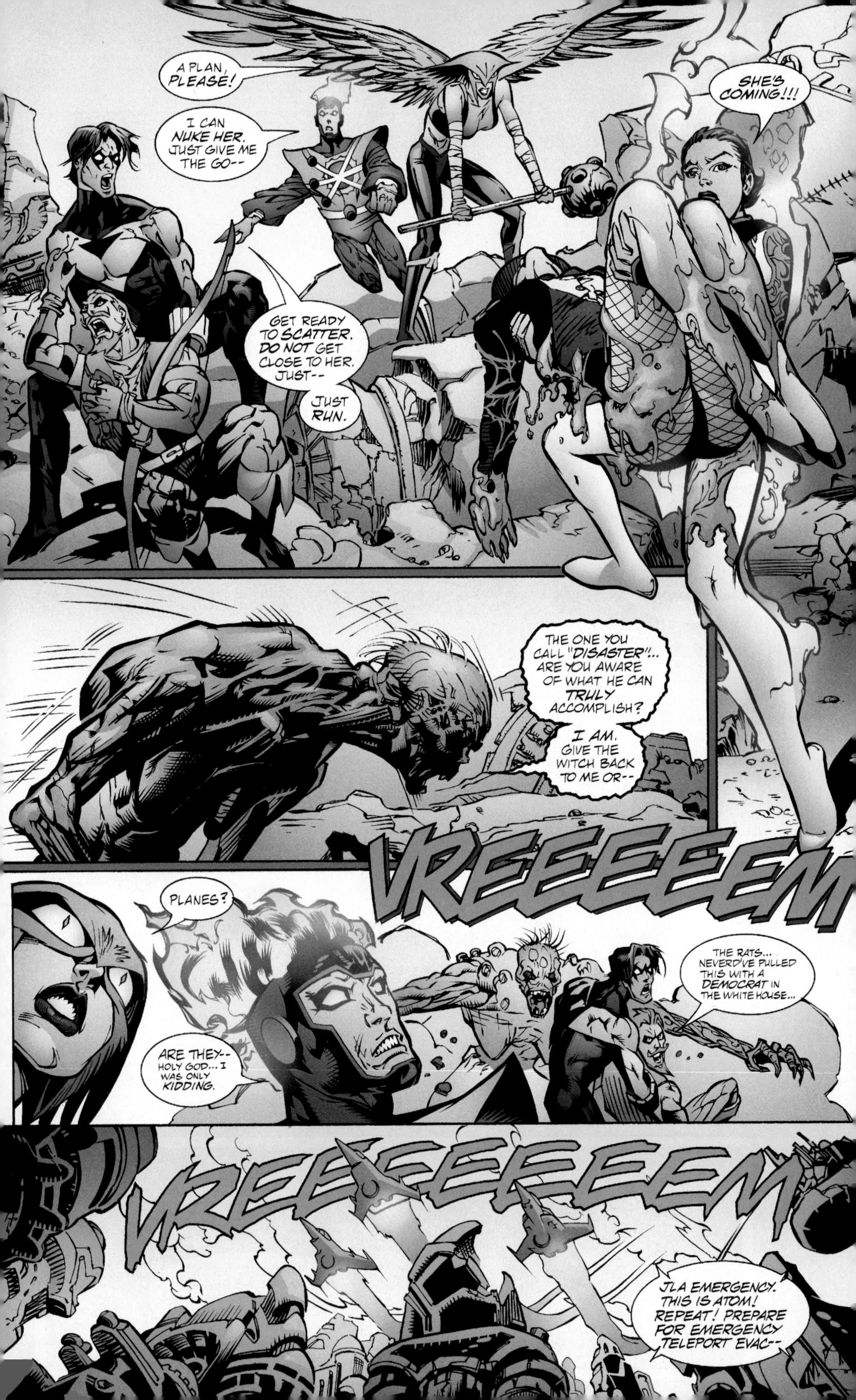
A PLAN, PLEASE!
I CAN NUKE HER. JUST GIVE ME THE GO--
SHE'S COMING!!!
GET READY TO SCATTER. DO NOT GET CLOSE TO HER. JUST--
JUST RUN.
THE ONE YOU CALL "DISASTER"... ARE YOU AWARE OF WHAT HE CAN TRULY ACCOMPLISH?
I AM. GIVE THE WITCH BACK TO ME OR--
VREEEEEM
PLANES?
THE RATS... NEVER'D'VE PULLED THIS WITH A DEMOCRAT IN THE WHITE HOUSE...
ARE THEY-- HOLY GOD... I WAS ONLY KIDDING.
VREEEEEEEEEM
JLA EMERGENCY. THIS IS ATOM! REPEAT! PREPARE FOR EMERGENCY TELEPORT EVAC--

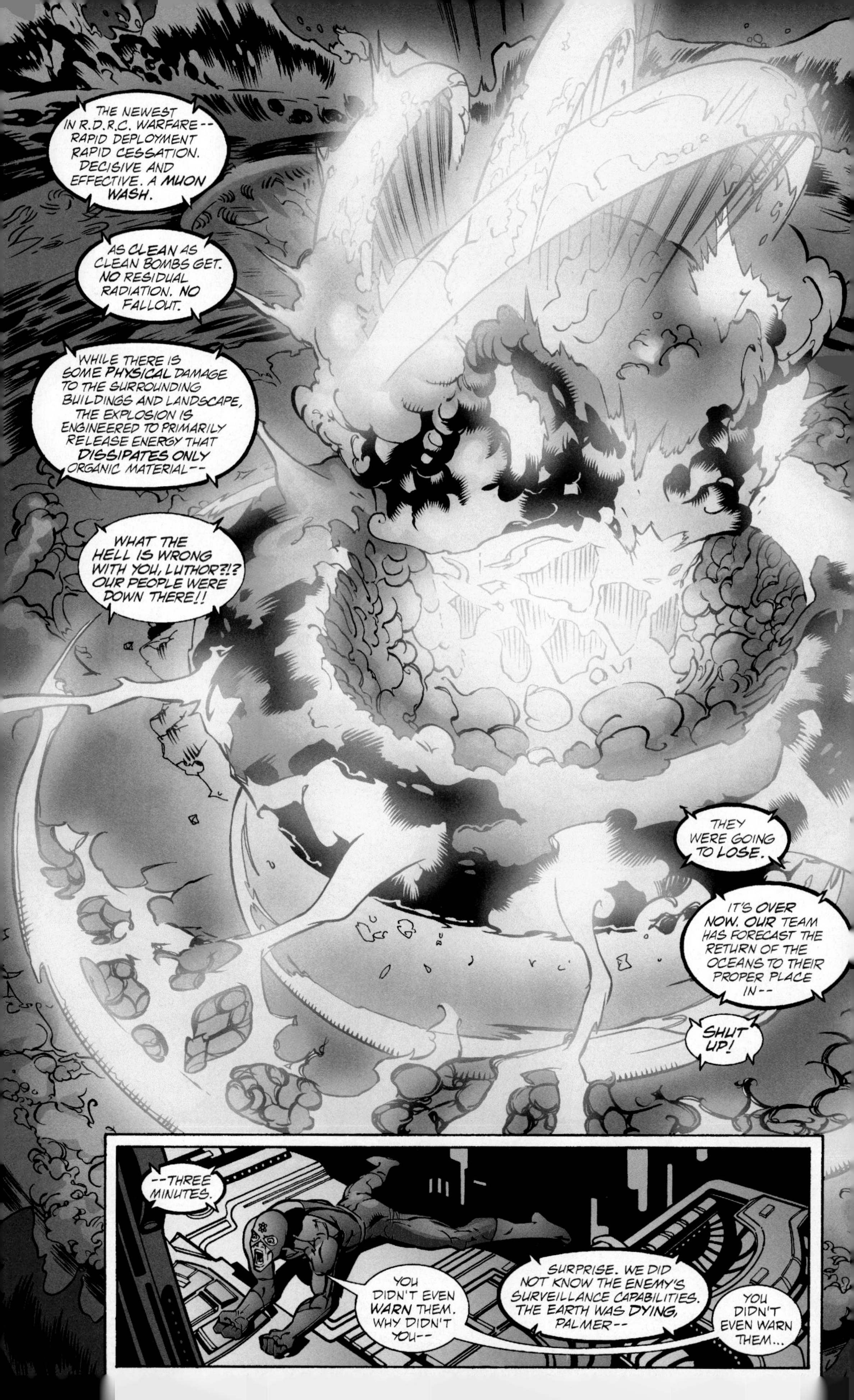
THE NEWEST IN R.D.R.C. WARFARE-- RAPID DEPLOYMENT RAPID CESSATION. DECISIVE AND EFFECTIVE. A MUON WASH.
AS CLEAN AS CLEAN BOMBS GET. NO RESIDUAL RADIATION. NO FALLOUT.
WHILE THERE IS SOME PHYSICAL DAMAGE TO THE SURROUNDING BUILDINGS AND LANDSCAPE, THE EXPLOSION IS ENGINEERED TO PRIMARILY RELEASE ENERGY THAT DISSIPATES ONLY ORGANIC MATERIAL--
WHAT THE HELL IS WRONG WITH YOU, LUTHOR?!? OUR PEOPLE WERE DOWN THERE!!
THEY WERE GOING TO LOSE.
IT'S OVER NOW. OUR TEAM HAS FORECAST THE RETURN OF THE OCEANS TO THEIR PROPER PLACE IN--
SHUT UP!
--THREE MINUTES.
YOU DIDN'T EVEN WARN THEM. WHY DIDN'T YOU--
SURPRISE. WE DID NOT KNOW THE ENEMY'S SURVEILLANCE CAPABILITIES. THE EARTH WAS DYING, PALMER--
YOU DIDN'T EVEN WARN THEM...

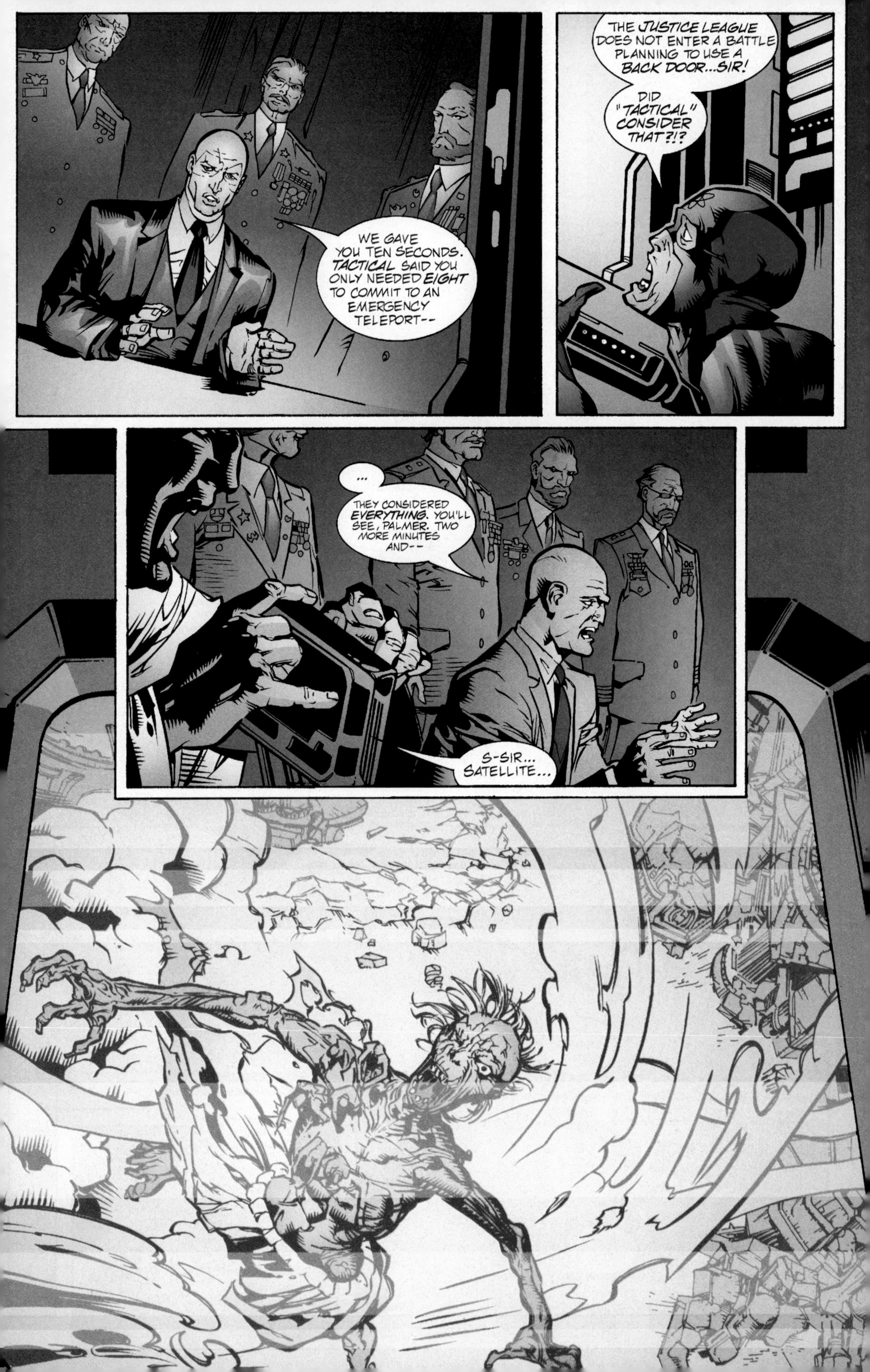
WE GAVE YOU TEN SECONDS. TACTICAL SAID YOU ONLY NEEDED EIGHT TO COMMIT TO AN EMERGENCY TELEPORT--
THE JUSTICE LEAGUE DOES NOT ENTER A BATTLE PLANNING TO USE A BACK DOOR...SIR!
DID "TACTICAL" CONSIDER THAT?!?
...
THEY CONSIDERED EVERYTHING. YOU'LL SEE, PALMER. TWO MORE MINUTES AND--
S-SIR... SATELLITE...

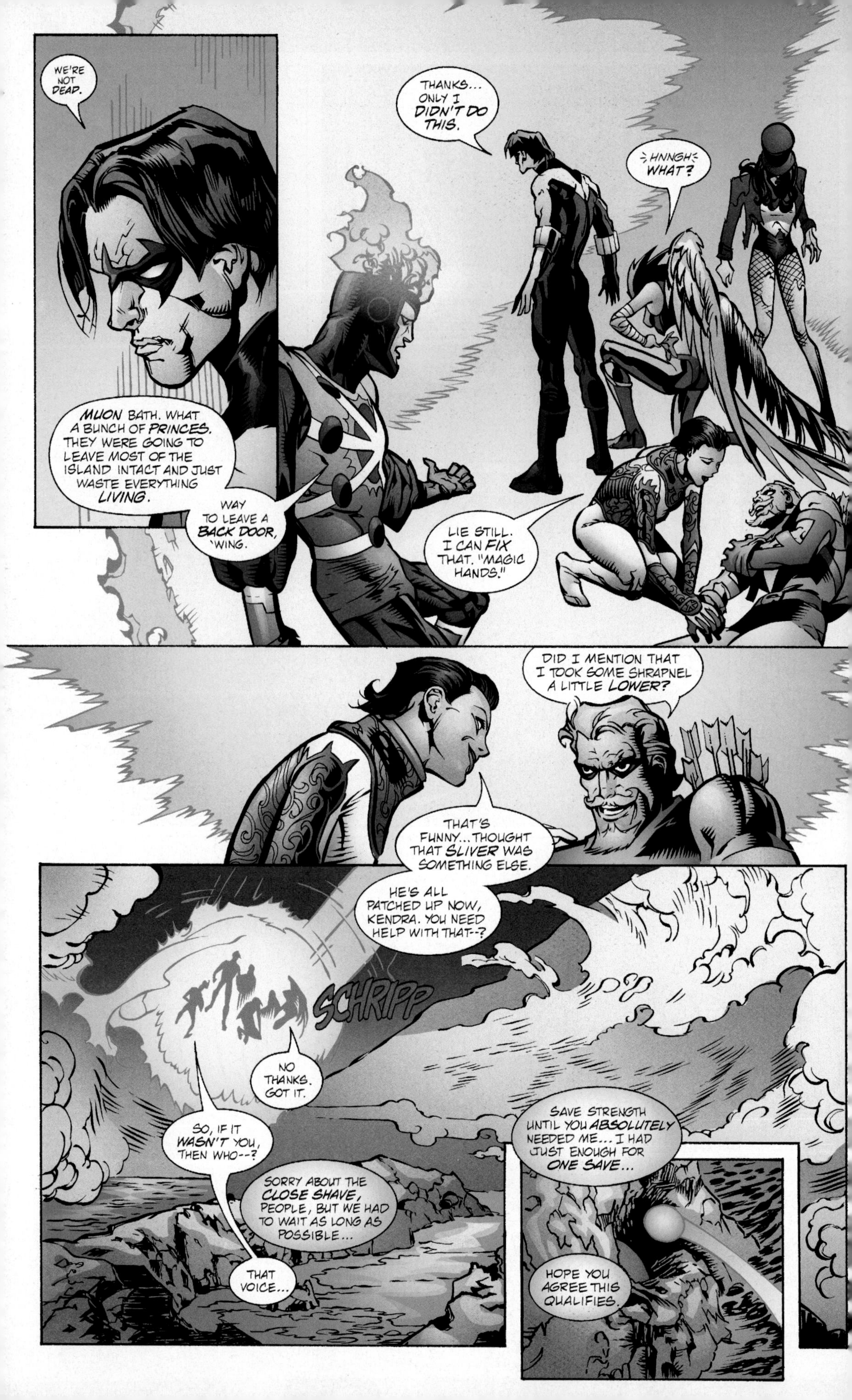

WE'RE NOT DEAD.
THANKS... ONLY I DIDN'T DO THIS.
HNNGH WHAT?
MUON BATH. WHAT A BUNCH OF PRINCES. THEY WERE GOING TO LEAVE MOST OF THE ISLAND INTACT AND JUST WASTE EVERYTHING LIVING.
WAY TO LEAVE A BACK DOOR, 'WING.
LIE STILL. I CAN FIX THAT. "MAGIC HANDS."
DID I MENTION THAT I TOOK SOME SHRAPNEL A LITTLE LOWER?
THAT'S FUNNY... THOUGHT THAT SLIVER WAS SOMETHING ELSE.
HE'S ALL PATCHED UP NOW, KENDRA. YOU NEED HELP WITH THAT--?
SCHRIPP
NO THANKS. GOT IT.
SO, IF IT WASN'T YOU, THEN WHO--?
SORRY ABOUT THE CLOSE SHAVE, PEOPLE, BUT WE HAD TO WAIT AS LONG AS POSSIBLE...
THAT VOICE...
SAVE STRENGTH UNTIL YOU ABSOLUTELY NEEDED ME... I HAD JUST ENOUGH FOR ONE SAVE...
HOPE YOU AGREE THIS QUALIFIES.

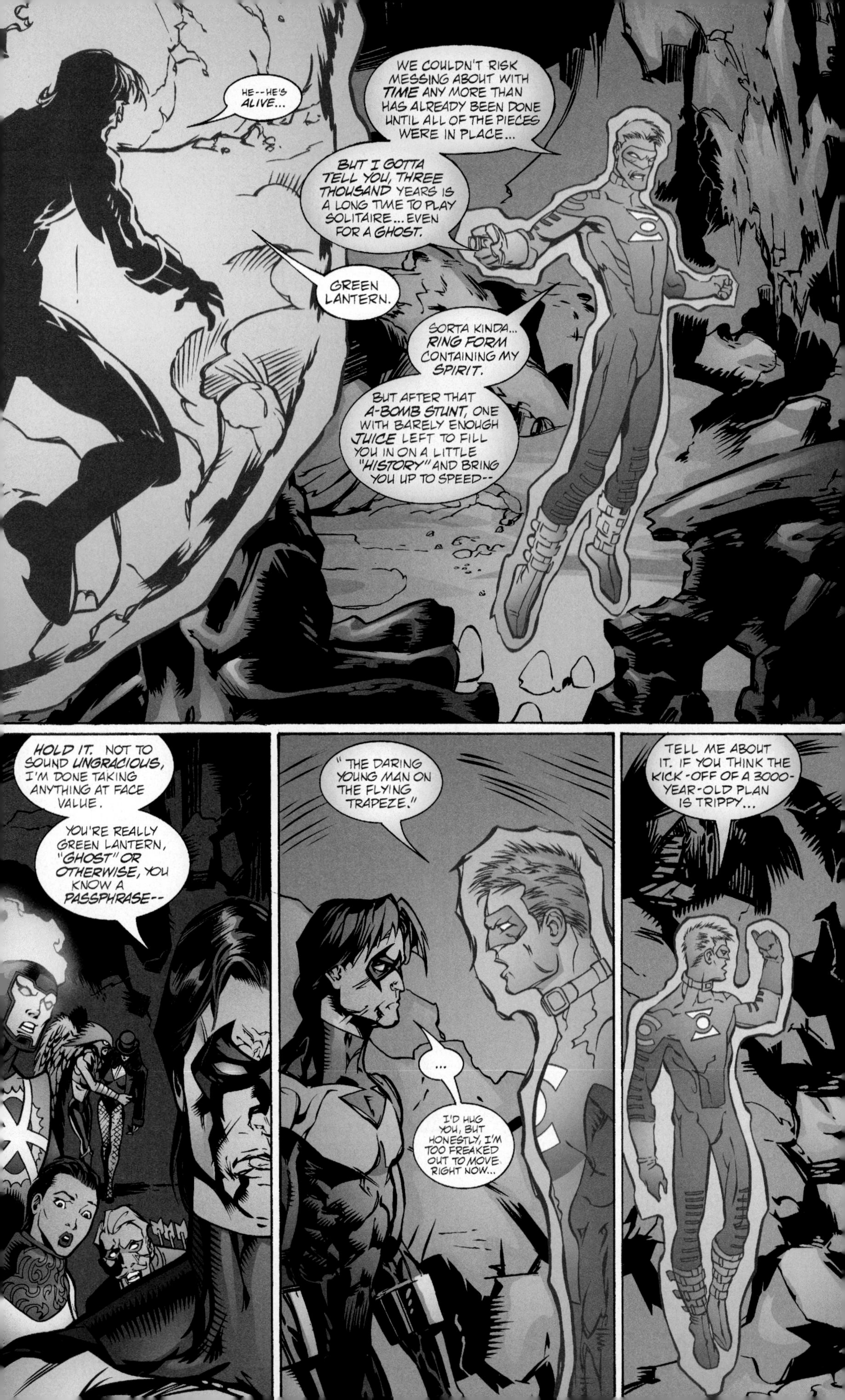
HE--HE'S ALIVE...
WE COULDN'T RISK MESSING ABOUT WITH TIME ANY MORE THAN HAS ALREADY BEEN DONE UNTIL ALL OF THE PIECES WERE IN PLACE...
BUT I GOTTA TELL YOU, THREE THOUSAND YEARS IS A LONG TIME TO PLAY SOLITAIRE... EVEN FOR A GHOST.
GREEN LANTERN.
SORTA KINDA... RING FORM CONTAINING MY SPIRIT.
BUT AFTER THAT A-BOMB STUNT, ONE WITH BARELY ENOUGH JUICE LEFT TO FILL YOU IN ON A LITTLE "HISTORY" AND BRING YOU UP TO SPEED--
HOLD IT. NOT TO SOUND UNGRACIOUS, I'M DONE TAKING ANYTHING AT FACE VALUE.
YOU'RE REALLY GREEN LANTERN, "GHOST" OR OTHERWISE, YOU KNOW A PASSPHRASE--
"THE DARING YOUNG MAN ON THE FLYING TRAPEZE."
...
I'D HUG YOU, BUT HONESTLY, I'M TOO FREAKED OUT TO MOVE RIGHT NOW...
TELL ME ABOUT IT. IF YOU THINK THE KICK-OFF OF A 3000-YEAR-OLD PLAN IS TRIPPY...

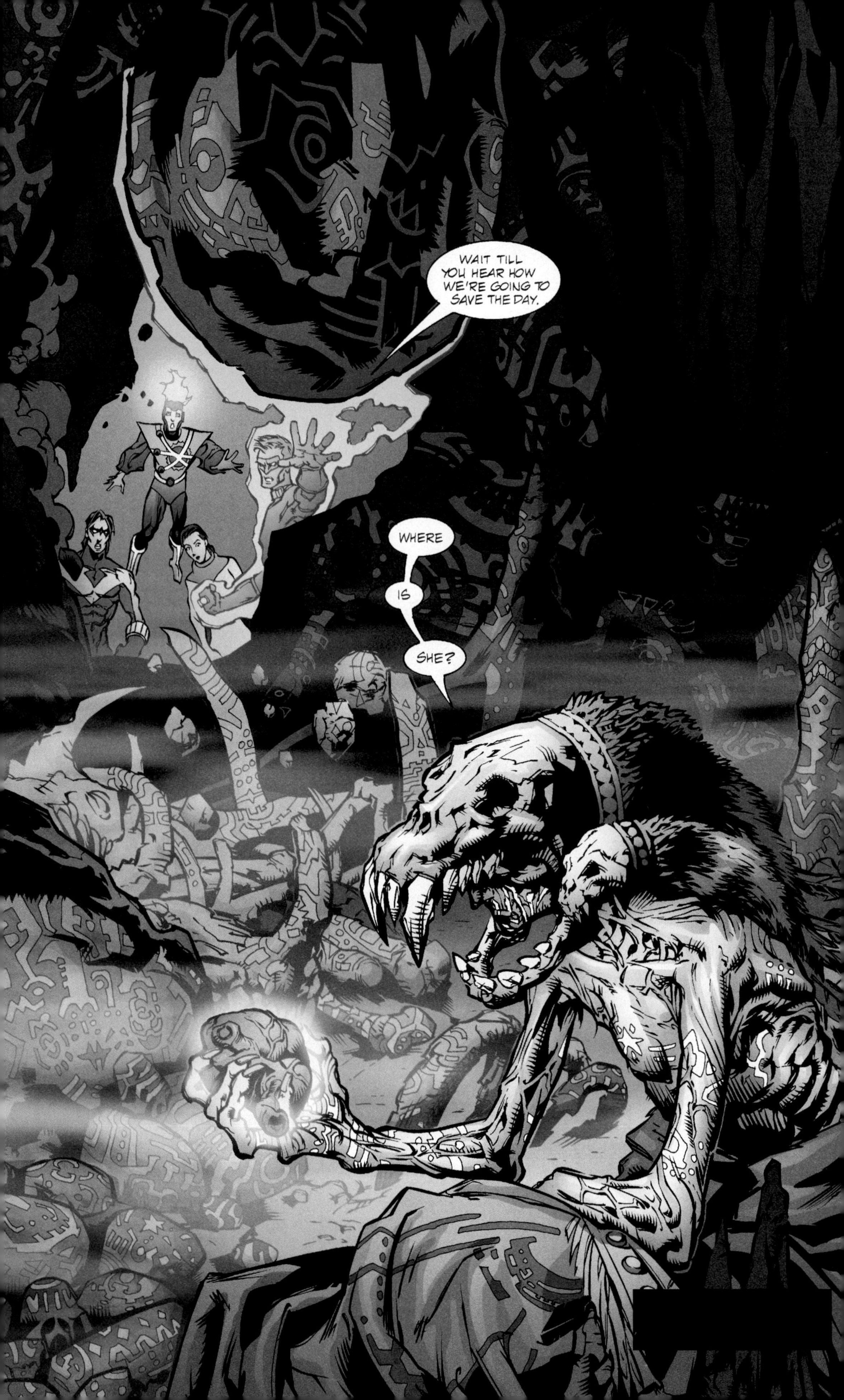
WAIT TILL YOU HEAR HOW WE'RE GOING TO SAVE THE DAY.
WHERE IS SHE?
[redacted]

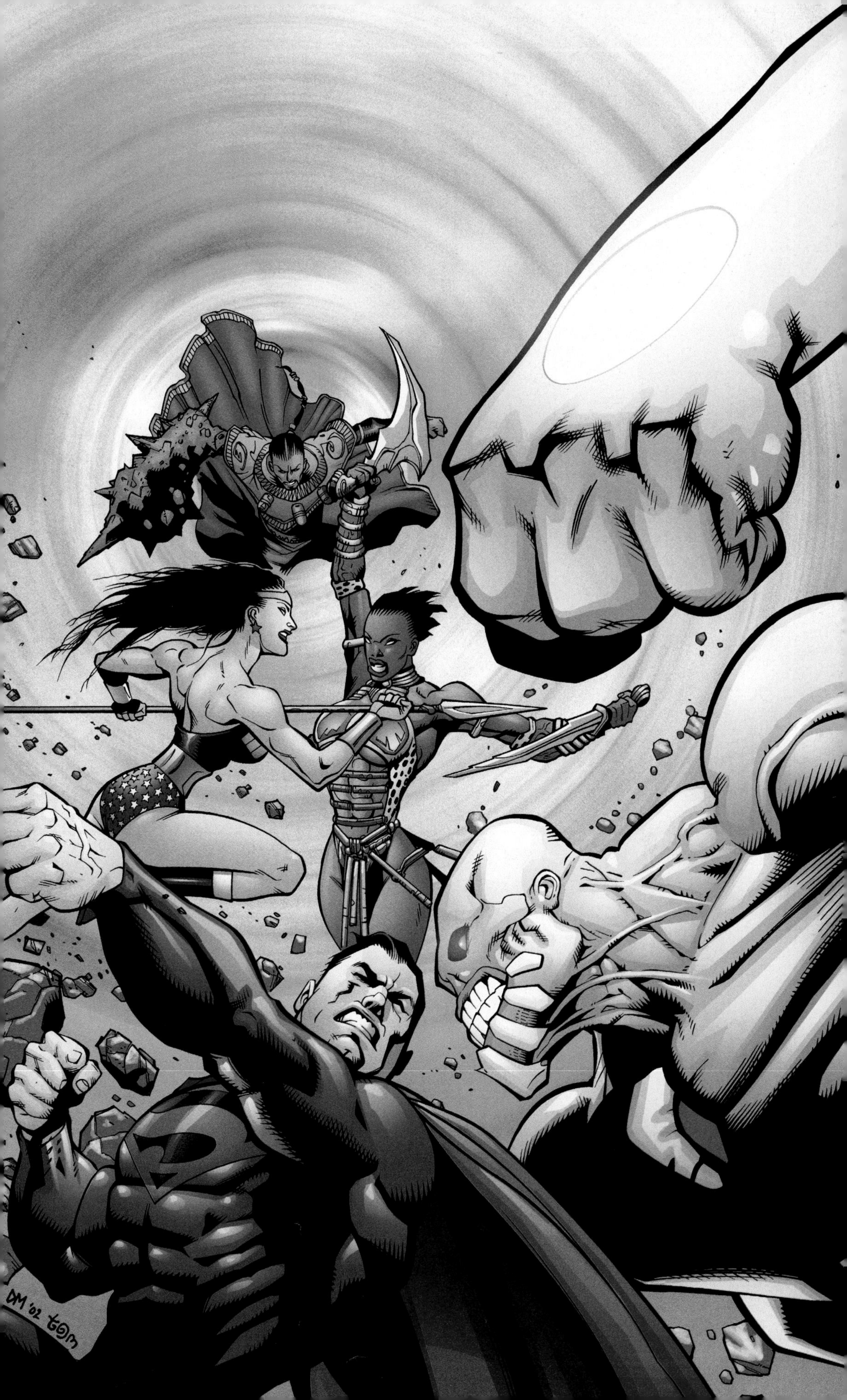

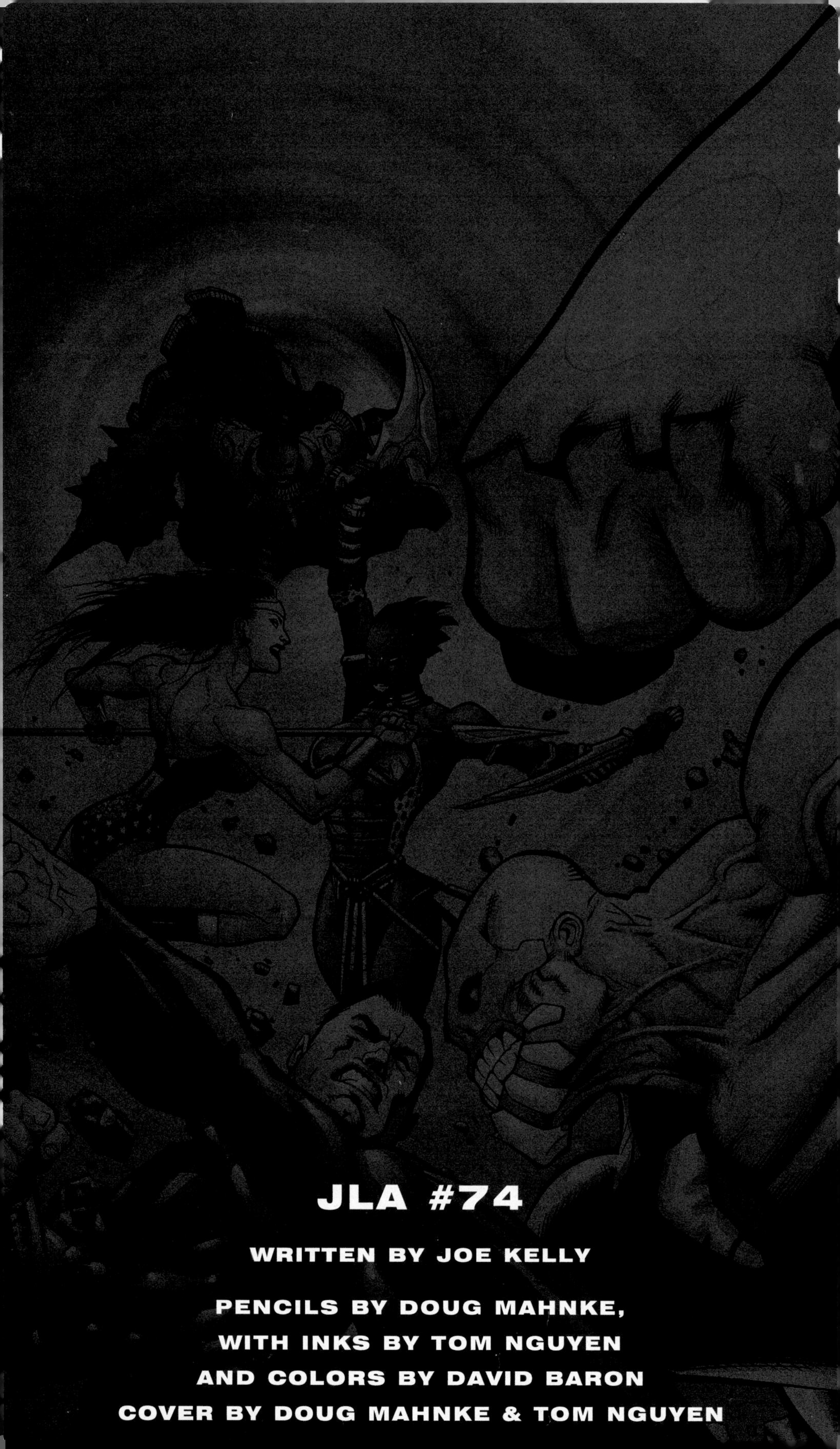

JLA #74

WRITTEN BY JOE KELLY

PENCILS BY DOUG MAHNKE,
WITH INKS BY TOM NGUYEN
AND COLORS BY DAVID BARON
COVER BY DOUG MAHNKE & TOM NGUYEN

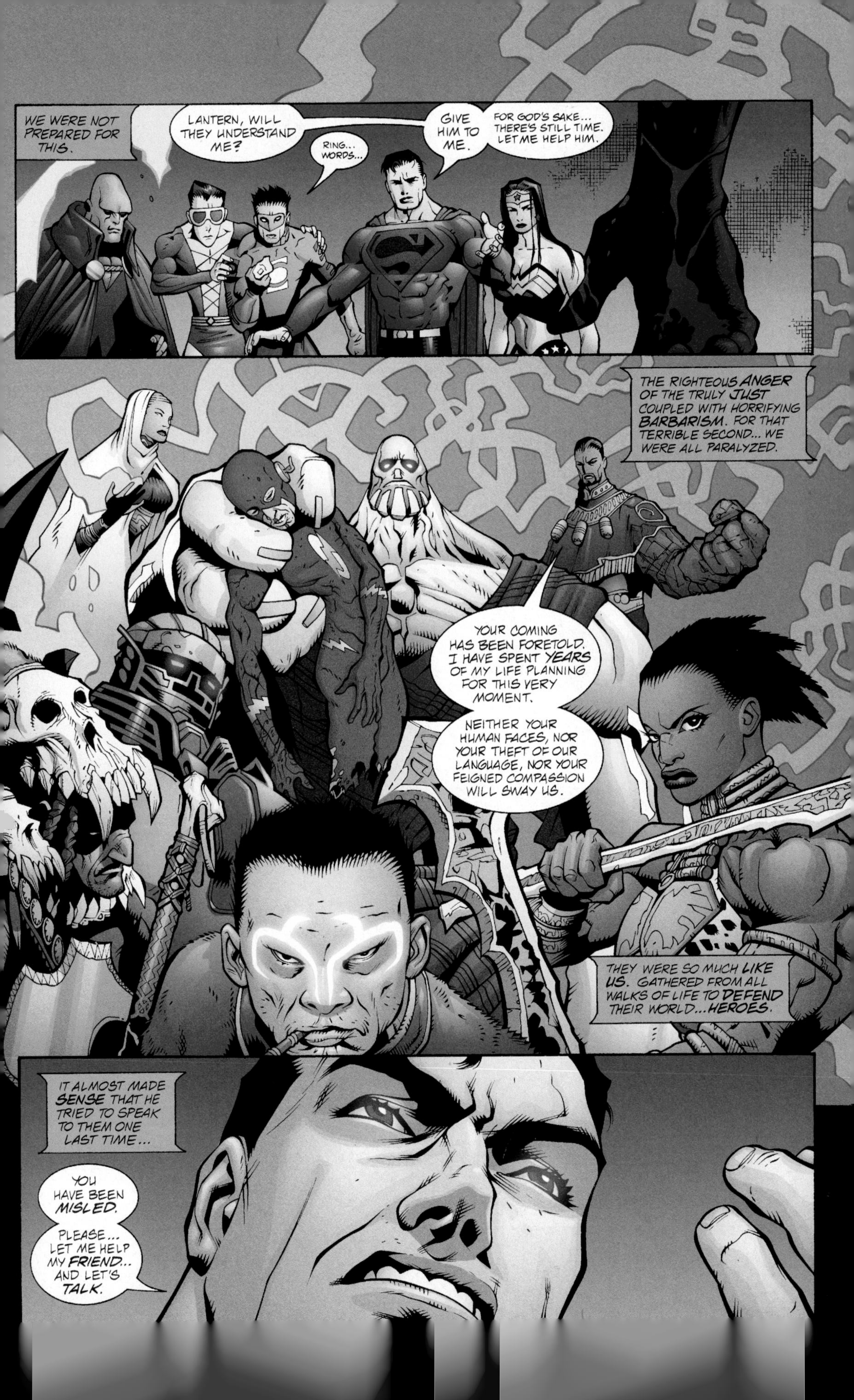
WE WERE NOT PREPARED FOR THIS.
LANTERN, WILL THEY UNDERSTAND ME?
RING... WORDS...
GIVE HIM TO ME.
FOR GOD'S SAKE... THERE'S STILL TIME. LET ME HELP HIM.
THE RIGHTEOUS ANGER OF THE TRULY JUST COUPLED WITH HORRIFYING BARBARISM. FOR THAT TERRIBLE SECOND... WE WERE ALL PARALYZED.
YOUR COMING HAS BEEN FORETOLD. I HAVE SPENT YEARS OF MY LIFE PLANNING FOR THIS VERY MOMENT.
NEITHER YOUR HUMAN FACES, NOR YOUR THEFT OF OUR LANGUAGE, NOR YOUR FEIGNED COMPASSION WILL SWAY US.
THEY WERE SO MUCH LIKE US. GATHERED FROM ALL WALKS OF LIFE TO DEFEND THEIR WORLD... HEROES.
IT ALMOST MADE SENSE THAT HE TRIED TO SPEAK TO THEM ONE LAST TIME...
YOU HAVE BEEN MISLED.
PLEASE... LET ME HELP MY FRIEND... AND LET'S TALK.

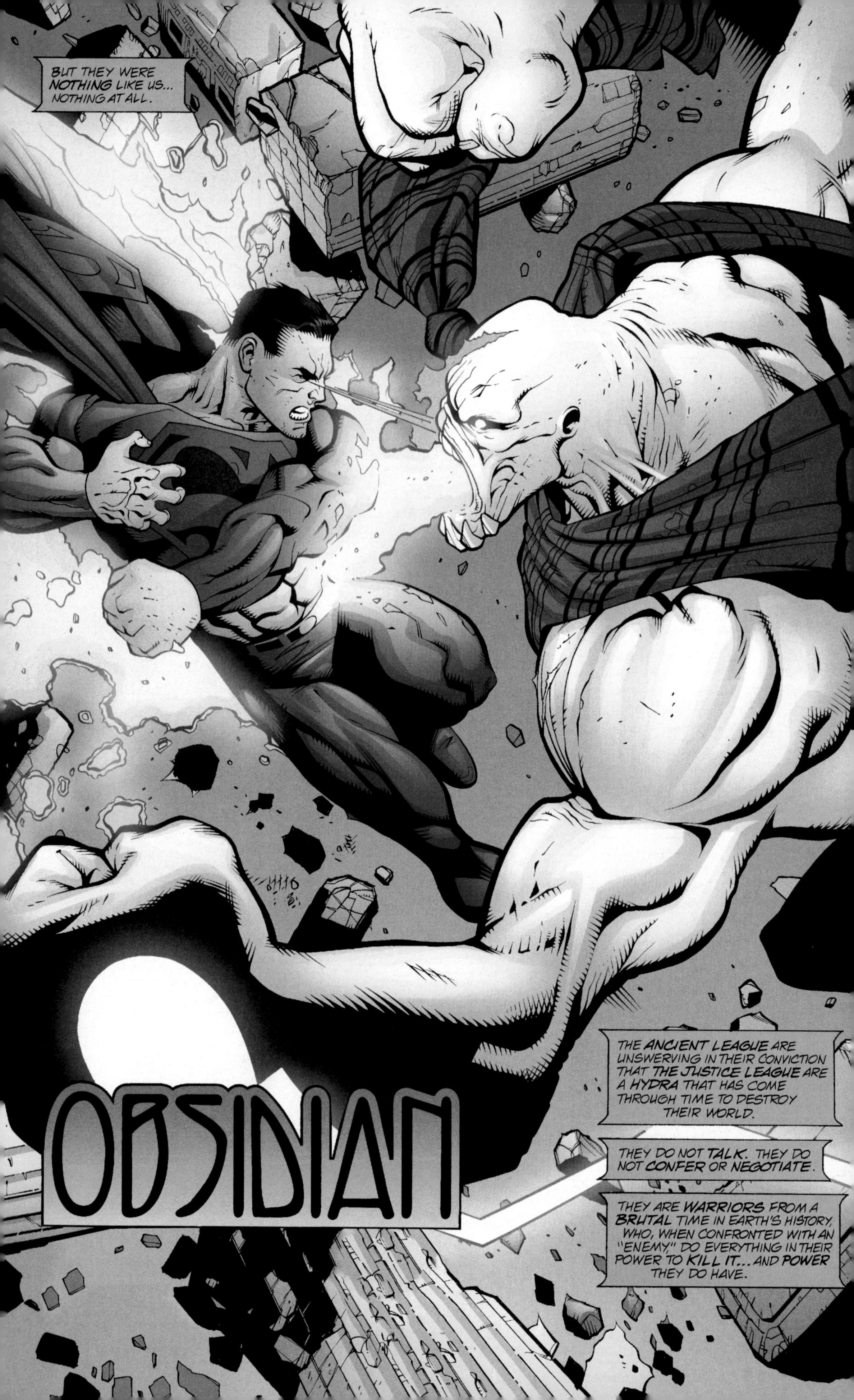
BUT THEY WERE NOTHING LIKE US... NOTHING AT ALL.
THE ANCIENT LEAGUE ARE UNSWERVING IN THEIR CONVICTION THAT THE JUSTICE LEAGUE ARE A HYDRA THAT HAS COME THROUGH TIME TO DESTROY THEIR WORLD.
OBSIDIAN
THEY DO NOT TALK. THEY DO NOT CONFER OR NEGOTIATE.
THEY ARE WARRIORS FROM A BRUTAL TIME IN EARTH'S HISTORY, WHO, WHEN CONFRONTED WITH AN "ENEMY," DO EVERYTHING IN THEIR POWER TO KILL IT... AND POWER THEY DO HAVE.

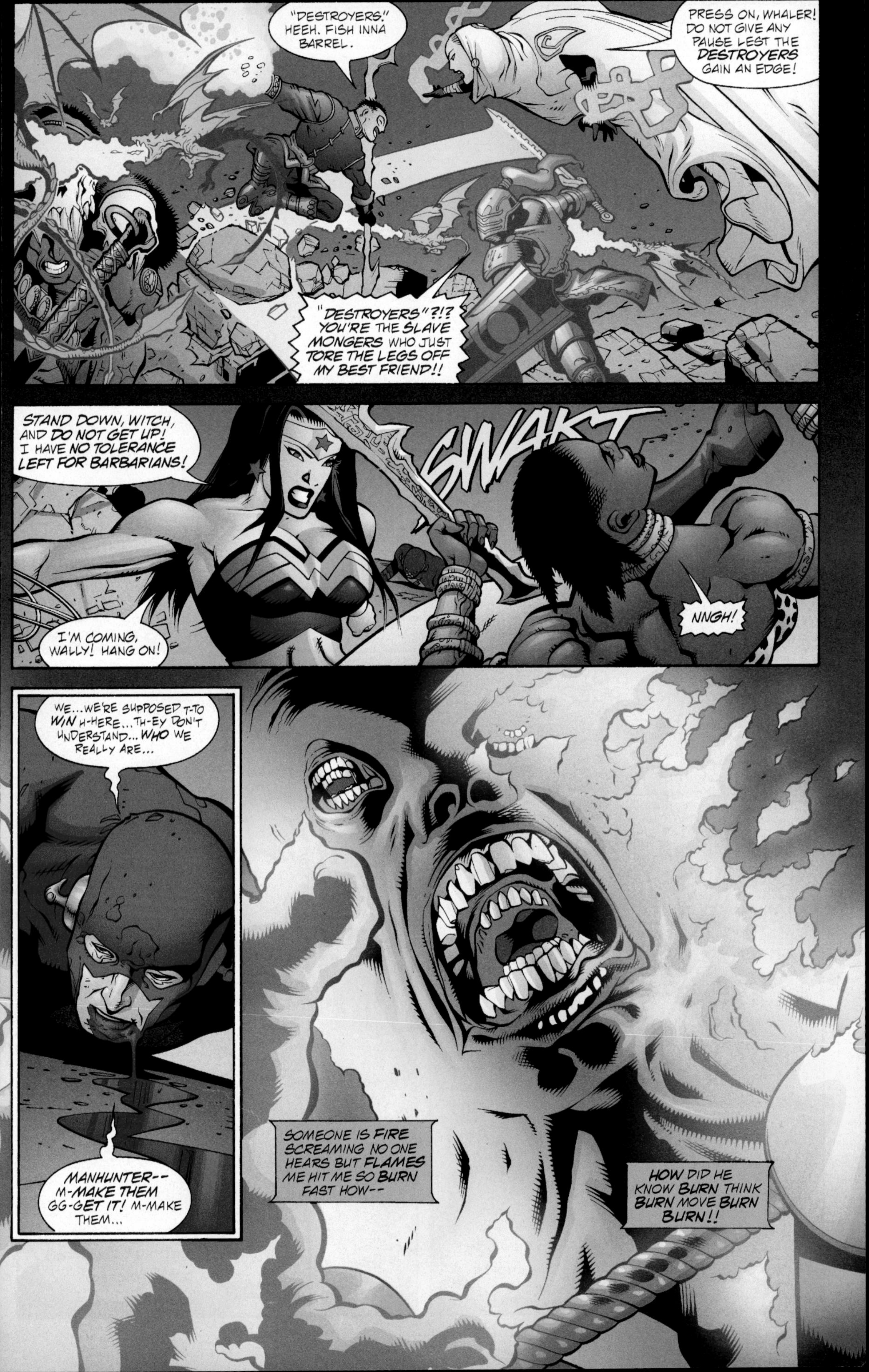
"DESTROYERS." HEEH. FISH INNA BARREL.
PRESS ON, WHALER! DO NOT GIVE ANY PAUSE LEST THE DESTROYERS GAIN AN EDGE!
"DESTROYERS"?!? YOU'RE THE SLAVE MONGERS WHO JUST TORE THE LEGS OFF MY BEST FRIEND!!
STAND DOWN, WITCH, AND DO NOT GET UP! I HAVE NO TOLERANCE LEFT FOR BARBARIANS!
SWAKT
NNGH!
I'M COMING, WALLY! HANG ON!
WE...WE'RE SUPPOSED T-TO WIN H-HERE...TH-EY DON'T UNDERSTAND...WHO WE REALLY ARE...
MANHUNTER-- M-MAKE THEM GG-GET IT! M-MAKE THEM...
SOMEONE IS FIRE SCREAMING NO ONE HEARS BUT FLAMES ME HIT ME SO BURN FAST HOW--
HOW DID HE KNOW BURN THINK BURN MOVE BURN BURN!!

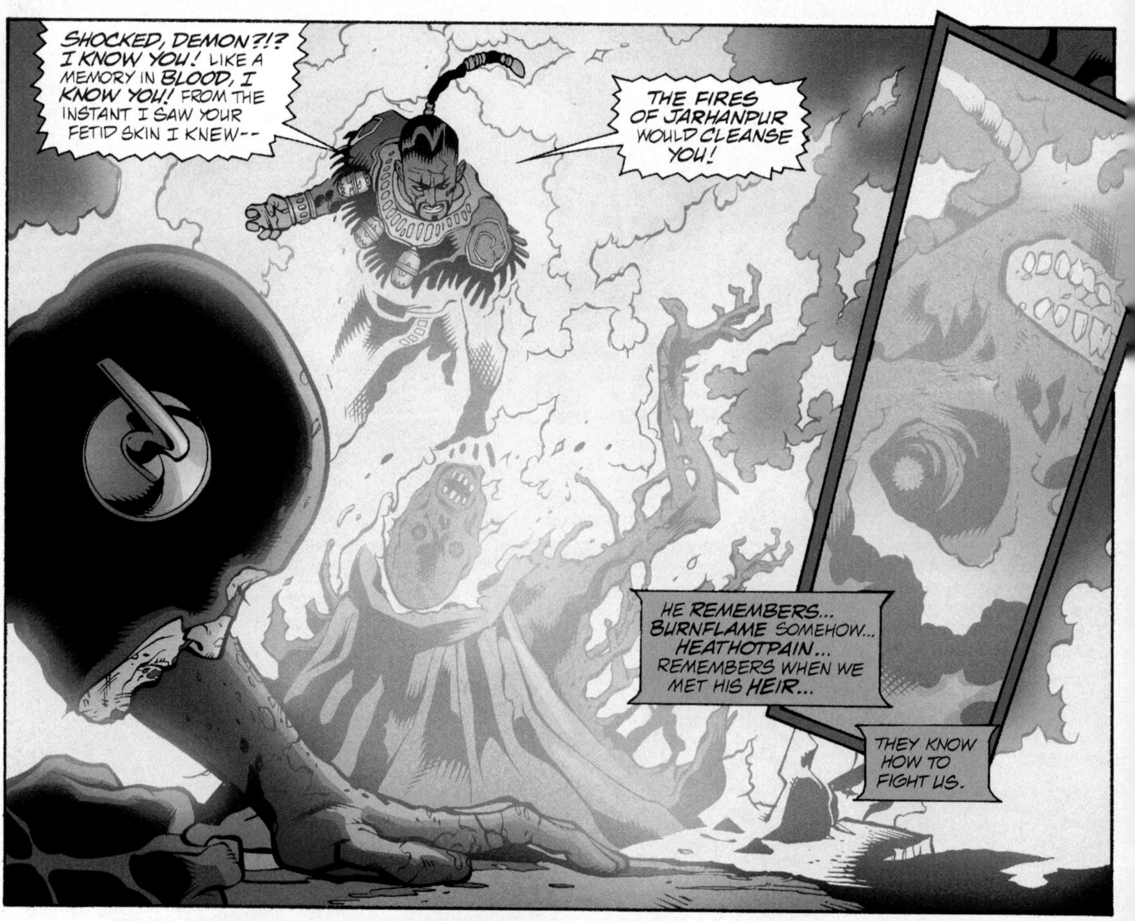
SHOCKED, DEMON?!? I KNOW YOU! LIKE A MEMORY IN BLOOD, I KNOW YOU! FROM THE INSTANT I SAW YOUR FETID SKIN I KNEW--
THE FIRES OF JARHANPUR WOULD CLEANSE YOU!
HE REMEMBERS... BURNFLAME SOMEHOW... HEATHOTPAIN... REMEMBERS WHEN WE MET HIS HEIR...
THEY KNOW HOW TO FIGHT US.

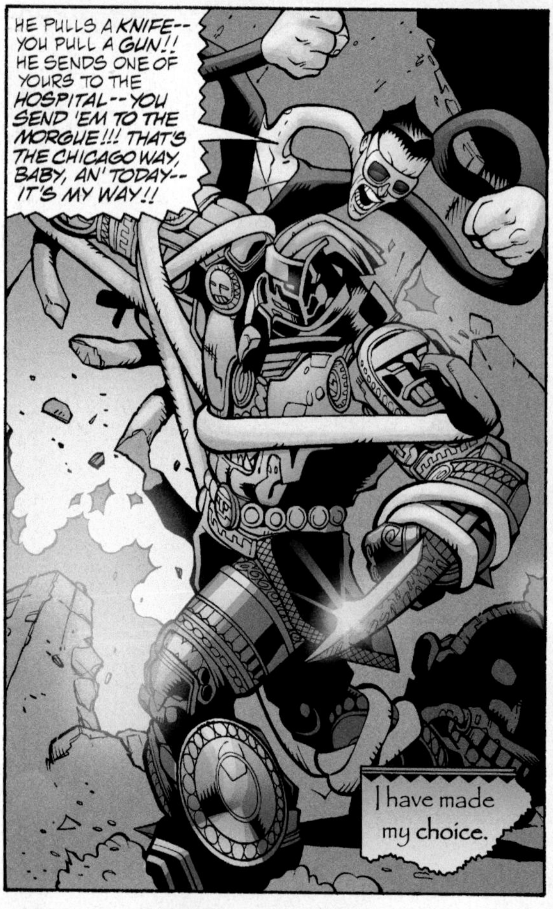
HE PULLS A KNIFE-- YOU PULL A GUN!! HE SENDS ONE OF YOURS TO THE HOSPITAL--YOU SEND 'EM TO THE MORGUE!!! THAT'S THE CHICAGO WAY, BABY, AN' TODAY-- IT'S MY WAY!!
I have made my choice.

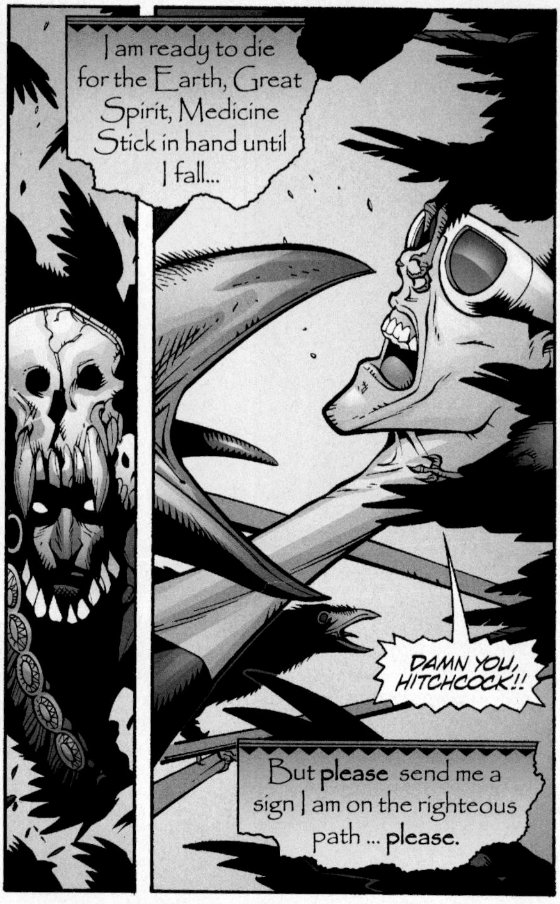
I am ready to die for the Earth, Great Spirit, Medicine Stick in hand until I fall...
DAMN YOU, HITCHCOCK!!
But please send me a sign I am on the righteous path ... please.

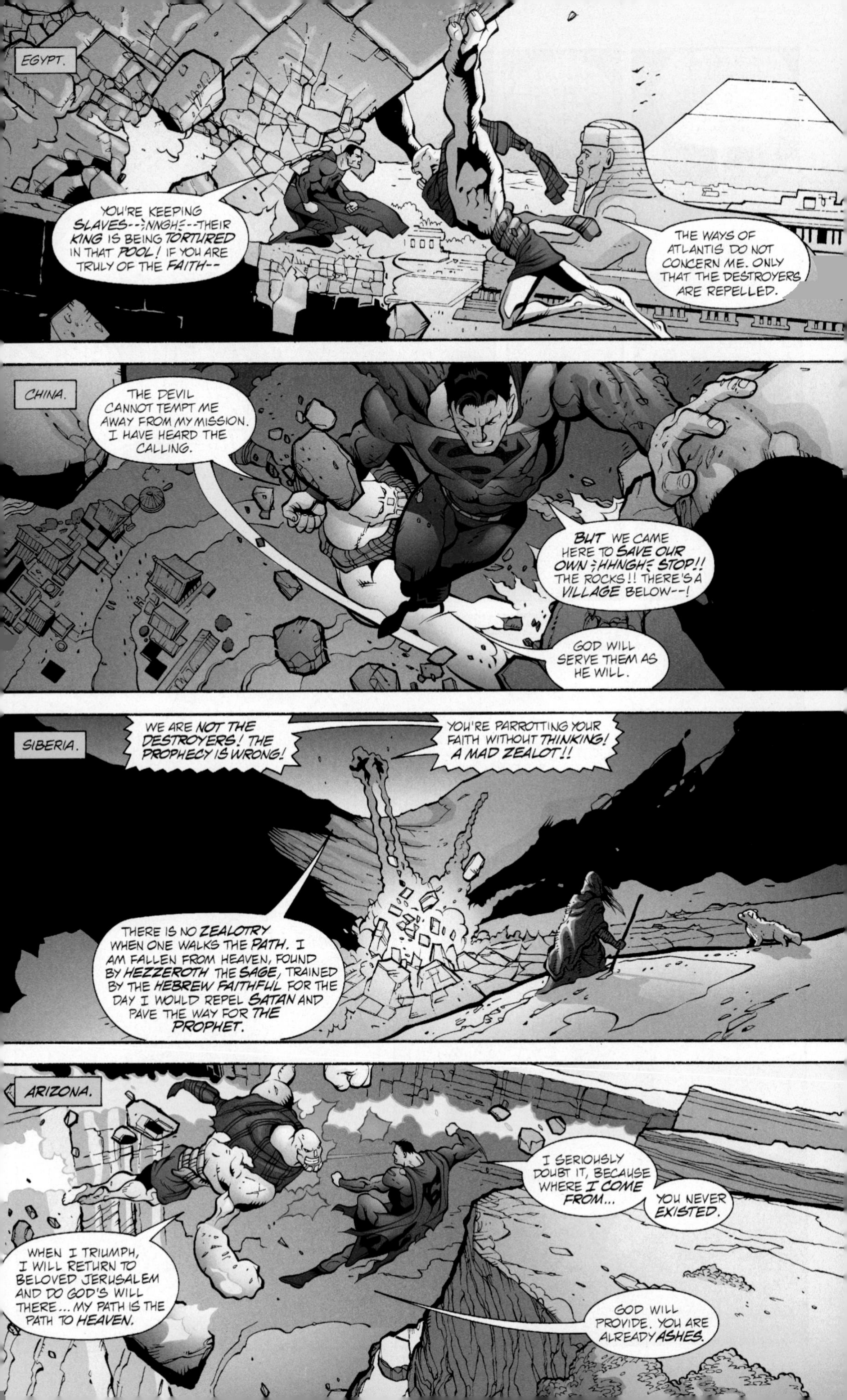
EGYPT.
YOU'RE KEEPING SLAVES--ⱻNNGHⱻ--THEIR KING IS BEING TORTURED IN THAT POOL! IF YOU ARE TRULY OF THE FAITH--
THE WAYS OF ATLANTIS DO NOT CONCERN ME. ONLY THAT THE DESTROYERS ARE REPELLED.
CHINA.
THE DEVIL CANNOT TEMPT ME AWAY FROM MY MISSION. I HAVE HEARD THE CALLING.
BUT WE CAME HERE TO SAVE OUR OWN ⱻHHNGHⱻ STOP!! THE ROCKS!! THERE'S A VILLAGE BELOW--!
GOD WILL SERVE THEM AS HE WILL.
SIBERIA.
WE ARE NOT THE DESTROYERS! THE PROPHECY IS WRONG!
YOU'RE PARROTTING YOUR FAITH WITHOUT THINKING! A MAD ZEALOT!!
THERE IS NO ZEALOTRY WHEN ONE WALKS THE PATH. I AM FALLEN FROM HEAVEN, FOUND BY HEZZEROTH THE SAGE, TRAINED BY THE HEBREW FAITHFUL FOR THE DAY I WOULD REPEL SATAN AND PAVE THE WAY FOR THE PROPHET.
ARIZONA.
I SERIOUSLY DOUBT IT, BECAUSE WHERE I COME FROM...
YOU NEVER EXISTED.
WHEN I TRIUMPH, I WILL RETURN TO BELOVED JERUSALEM AND DO GOD'S WILL THERE... MY PATH IS THE PATH TO HEAVEN.
GOD WILL PROVIDE. YOU ARE ALREADY ASHES.

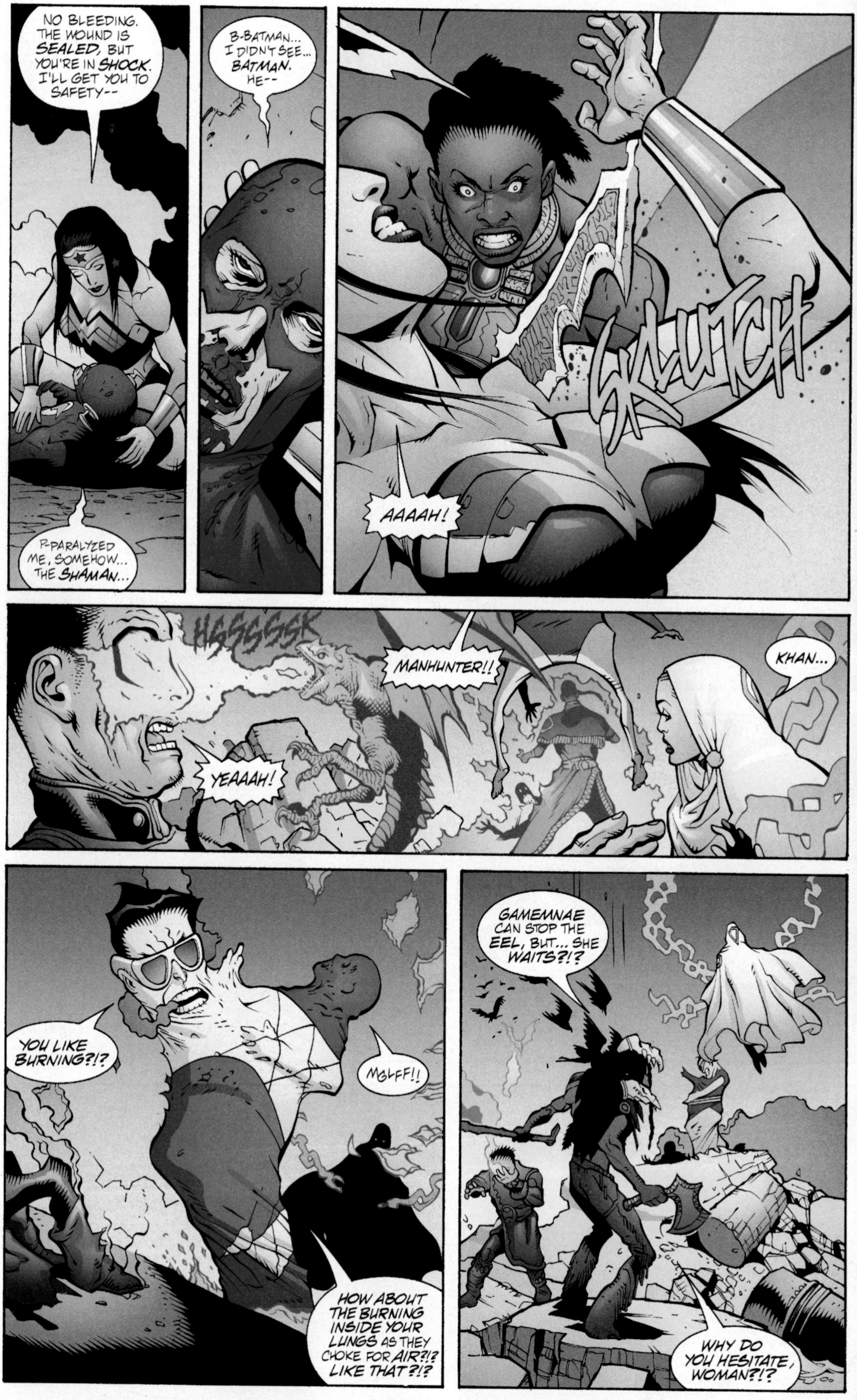
NO BLEEDING. THE WOUND IS SEALED, BUT YOU'RE IN SHOCK. I'LL GET YOU TO SAFETY--
P-PARALYZED ME, SOMEHOW... THE SHAMAN...
B-BATMAN... I DIDN'T SEE... BATMAN. HE--
SKLUTCH
AAAAH!
HSSSSSK
MANHUNTER!!
YEAAAH!
KHAN...
YOU LIKE BURNING?!?
MGLFF!!
HOW ABOUT THE BURNING INSIDE YOUR LUNGS AS THEY CHOKE FOR AIR?!? LIKE THAT?!?
GAMEMNAE CAN STOP THE EEL, BUT... SHE WAITS?!?
WHY DO YOU HESITATE, WOMAN?!?

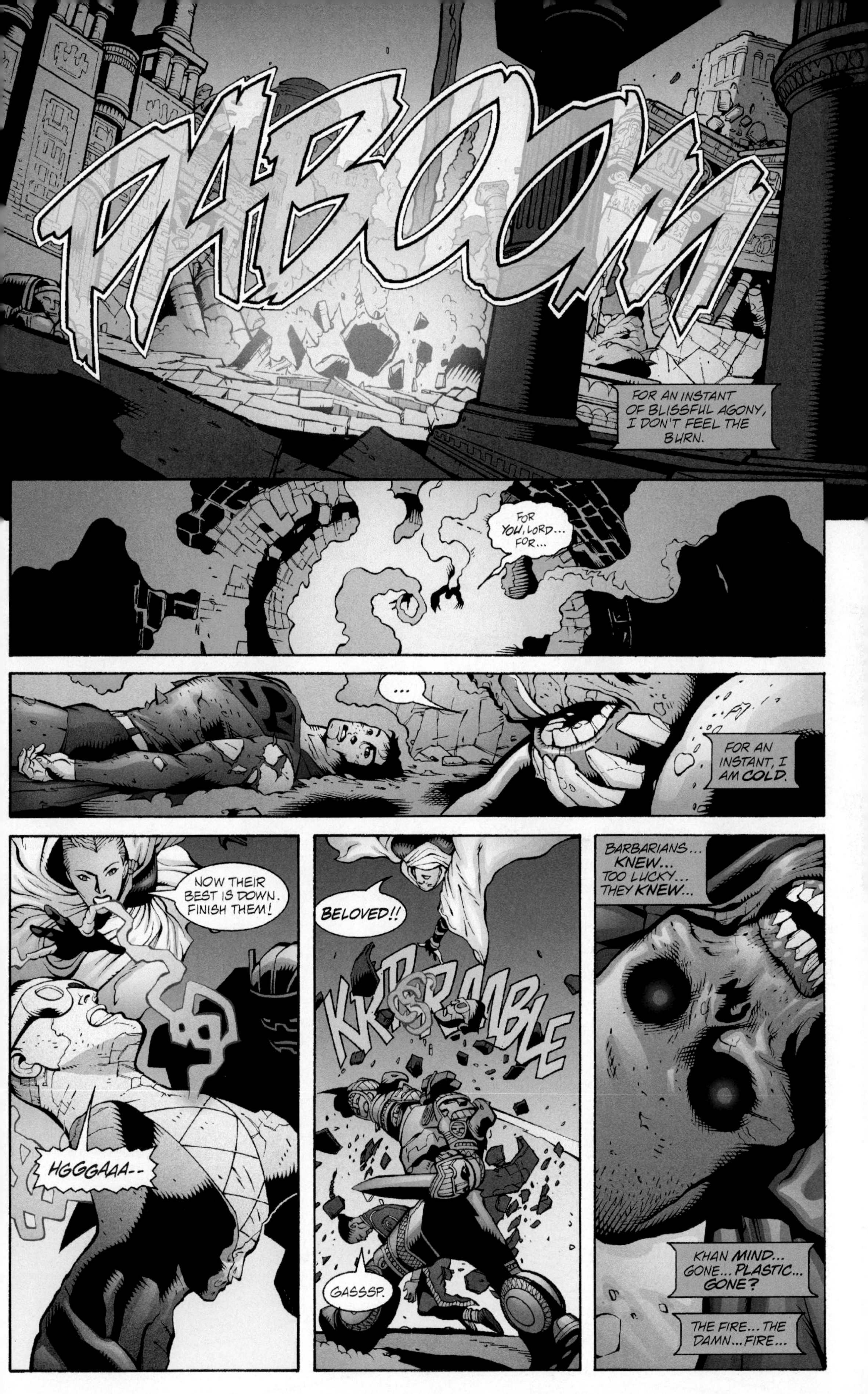
FOR AN INSTANT OF BLISSFUL AGONY, I DON'T FEEL THE BURN.
FOR YOU, LORD... FOR...
...
FOR AN INSTANT, I AM COLD.
NOW THEIR BEST IS DOWN. FINISH THEM!
HGGGAAA--
BELOVED!!
GASSSP.
BARBARIANS... KNEW... TOO LUCKY... THEY KNEW...
KHAN MIND... GONE... PLASTIC... GONE?
THE FIRE... THE DAMN... FIRE...

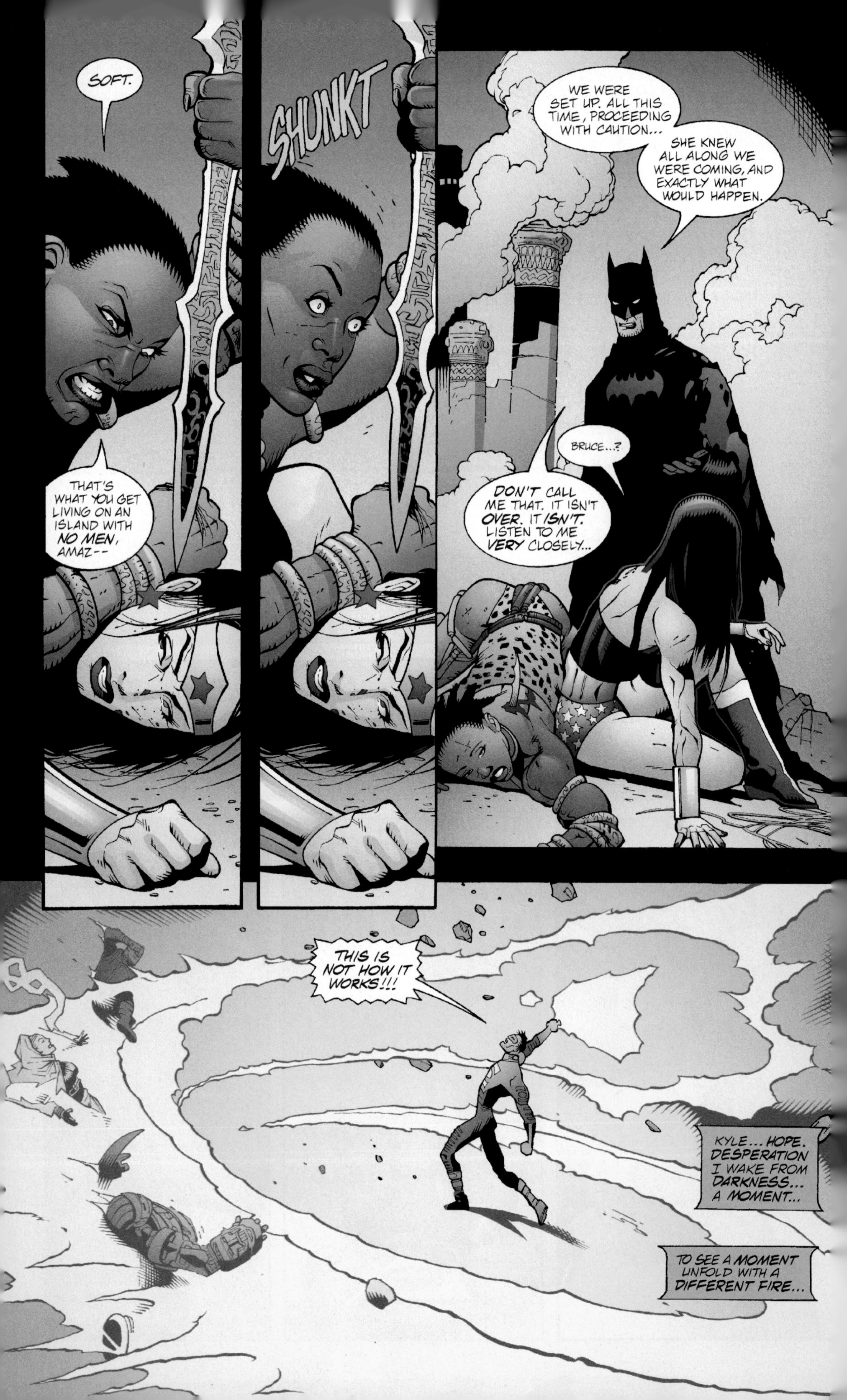
SOFT.
SHUNKT
THAT'S WHAT YOU GET LIVING ON AN ISLAND WITH NO MEN, AMAZ--
WE WERE SET UP. ALL THIS TIME, PROCEEDING WITH CAUTION...
SHE KNEW ALL ALONG WE WERE COMING, AND EXACTLY WHAT WOULD HAPPEN.
BRUCE...?
DON'T CALL ME THAT. IT ISN'T OVER. IT ISN'T. LISTEN TO ME VERY CLOSELY...
THIS IS NOT HOW IT WORKS!!!
KYLE... HOPE. DESPERATION I WAKE FROM DARKNESS... A MOMENT...
TO SEE A MOMENT UNFOLD WITH A DIFFERENT FIRE...

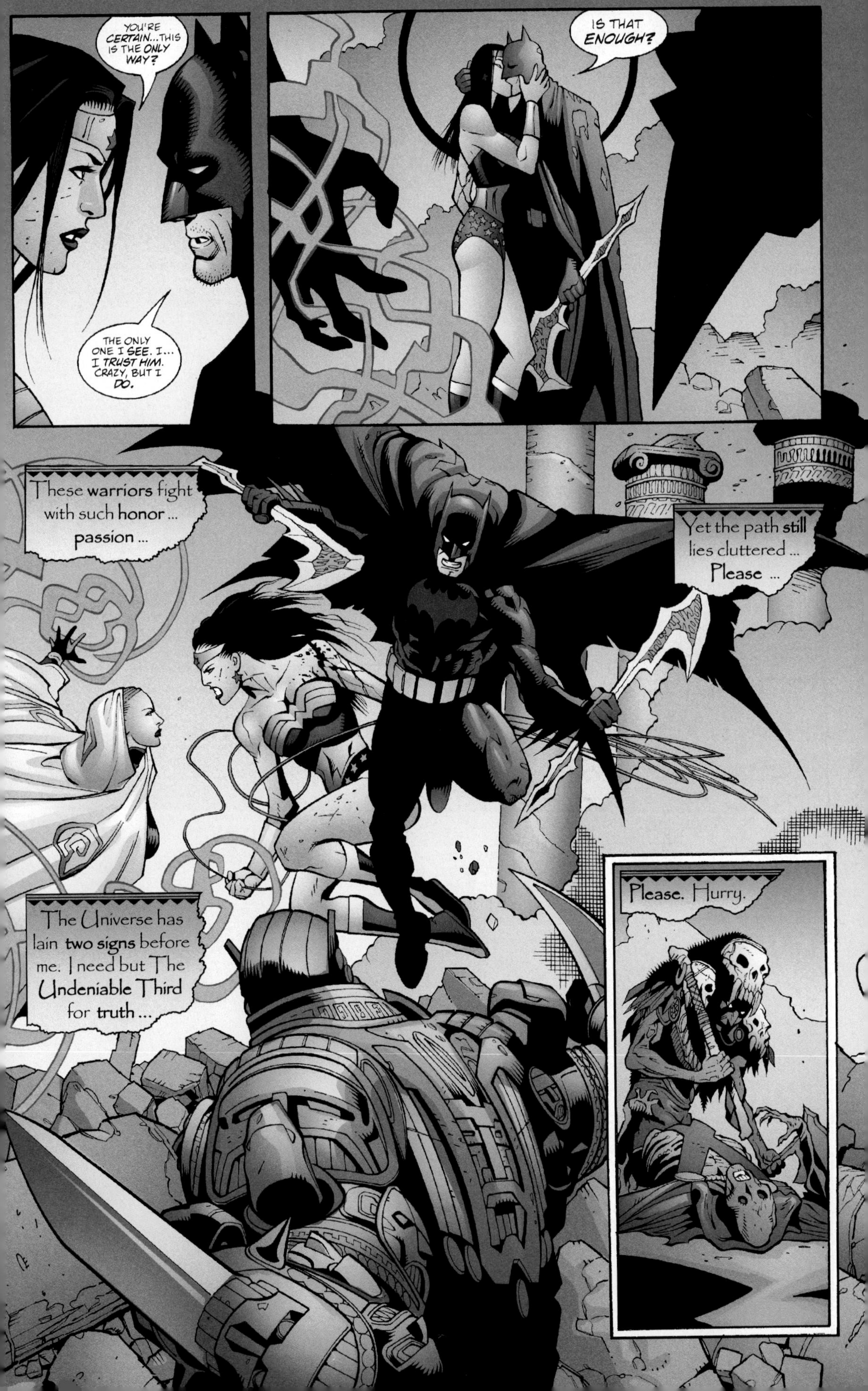

YOU'RE CERTAIN...THIS IS THE ONLY WAY?
THE ONLY ONE I SEE. I... I TRUST HIM. CRAZY, BUT I DO.
IS THAT ENOUGH?
These warriors fight with such honor ... passion ...
Yet the path still lies cluttered ... Please ...
The Universe has lain two signs before me. I need but The Undeniable Third for truth ...
Please. Hurry.

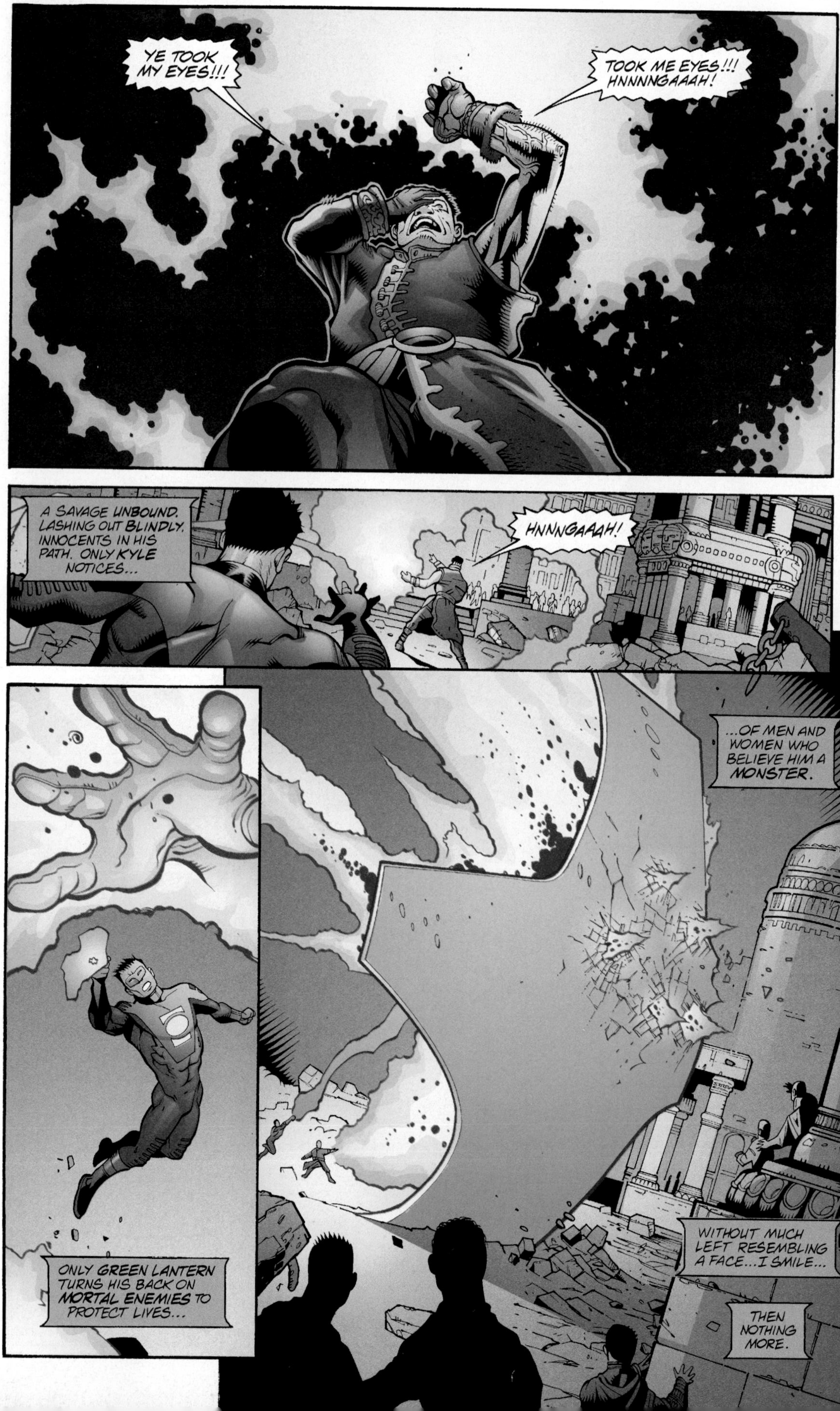
YE TOOK MY EYES!!!
TOOK ME EYES!!! HNNNNGAAAH!
A SAVAGE UNBOUND. LASHING OUT BLINDLY. INNOCENTS IN HIS PATH. ONLY KYLE NOTICES...
HNNNGAAAH!
ONLY GREEN LANTERN TURNS HIS BACK ON MORTAL ENEMIES TO PROTECT LIVES...
...OF MEN AND WOMEN WHO BELIEVE HIM A MONSTER.
WITHOUT MUCH LEFT RESEMBLING A FACE... I SMILE...
THEN NOTHING MORE.

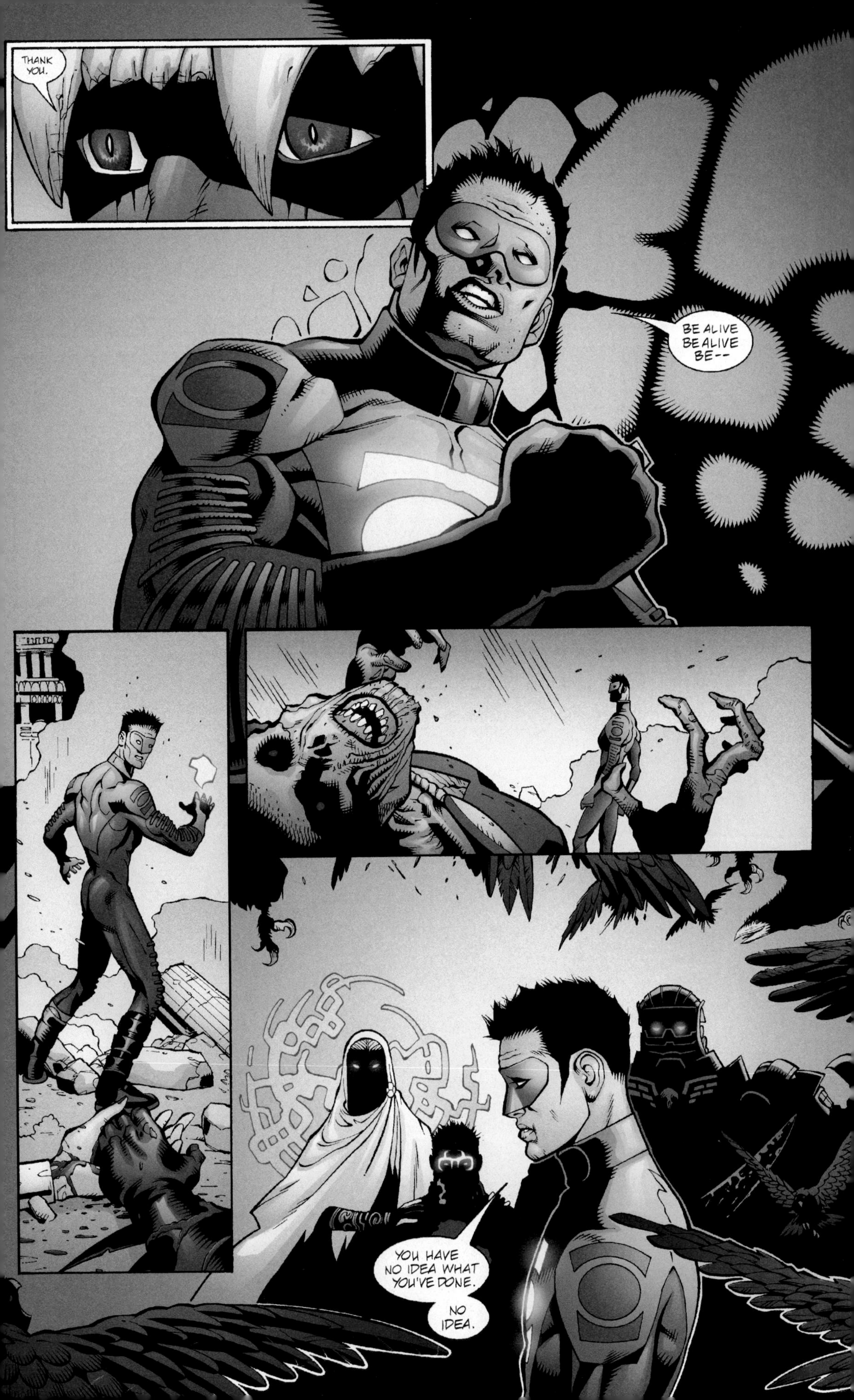
THANK YOU.
BE ALIVE BE ALIVE BE--
YOU HAVE NO IDEA WHAT YOU'VE DONE.
NO IDEA.

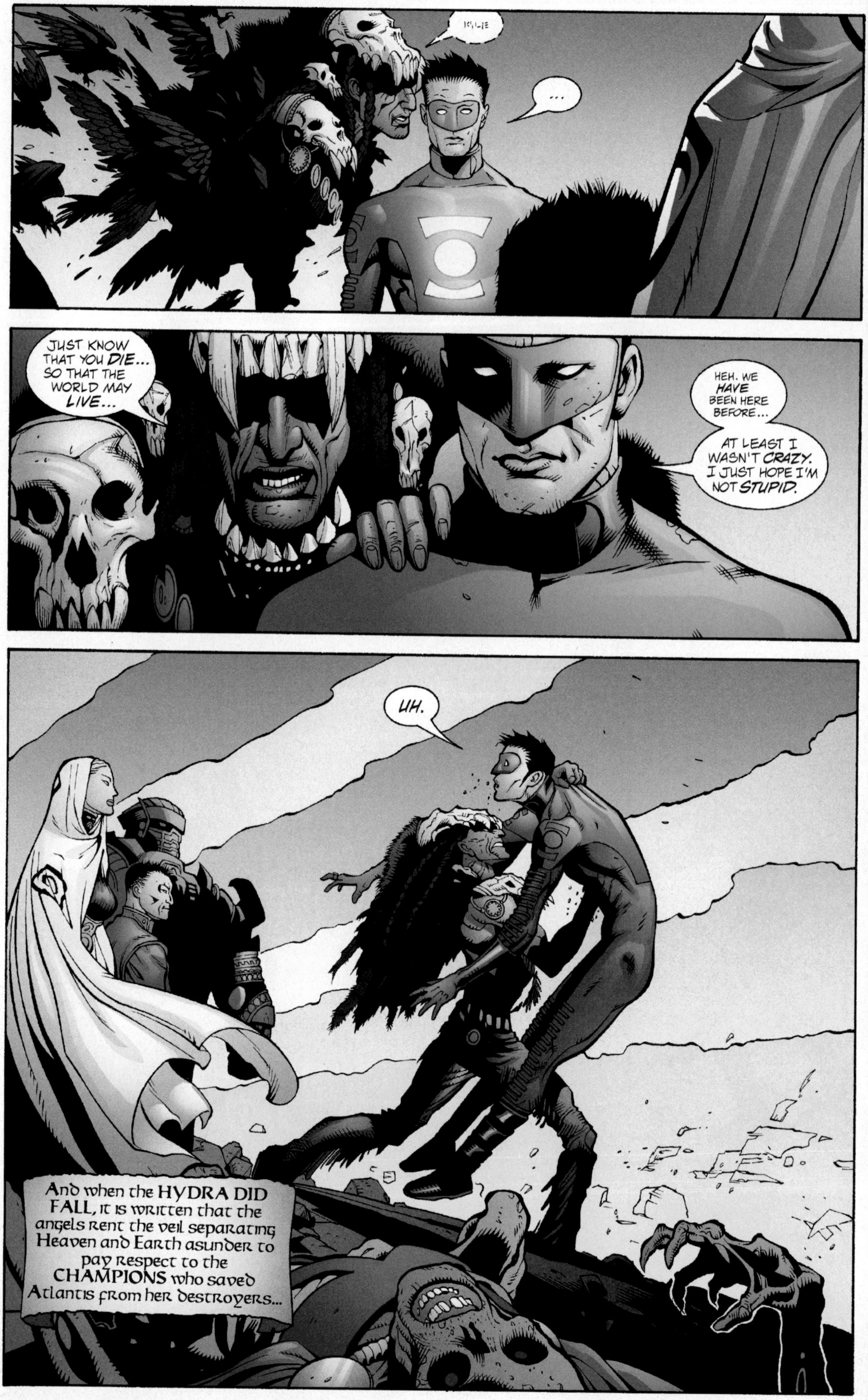
KYLE
...
JUST KNOW THAT YOU DIE... SO THAT THE WORLD MAY LIVE...
HEH. WE HAVE BEEN HERE BEFORE...
AT LEAST I WASN'T CRAZY. I JUST HOPE I'M NOT STUPID.
UH.
And when the HYDRA DID FALL, it is written that the angels rent the veil separating Heaven and Earth asunder to pay respect to the CHAMPIONS who saved Atlantis from her destroyers...

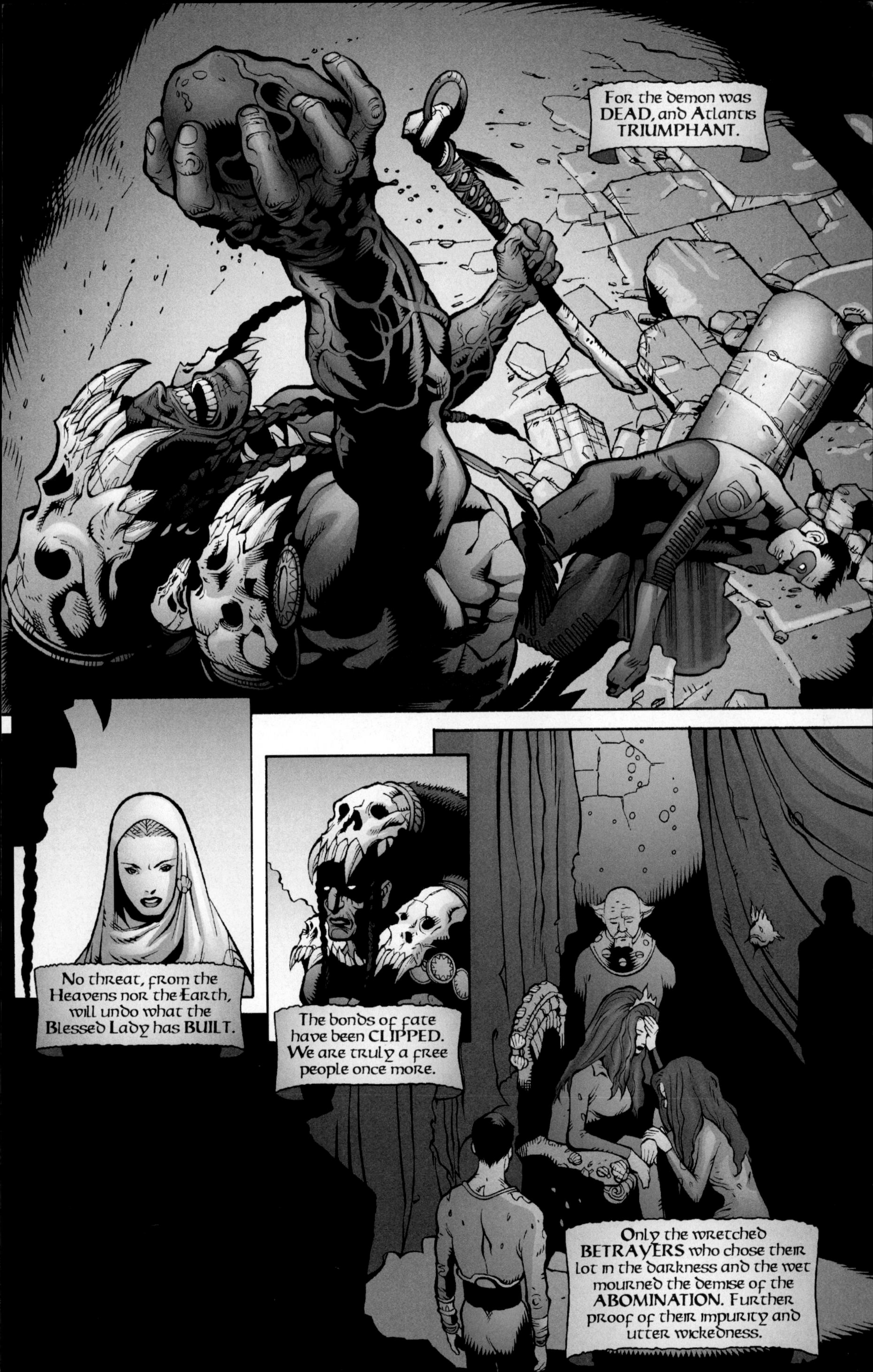
For the demon was DEAD, and Atlantis TRIUMPHANT.
No threat, from the Heavens nor the Earth, will undo what the Blessed Lady has BUILT.
The bonds of fate have been CLIPPED. We are truly a free people once more.
Only the wretched BETRAYERS who chose their lot in the darkness and the wet mourned the demise of the ABOMINATION. Further proof of their impurity and utter wickedness.

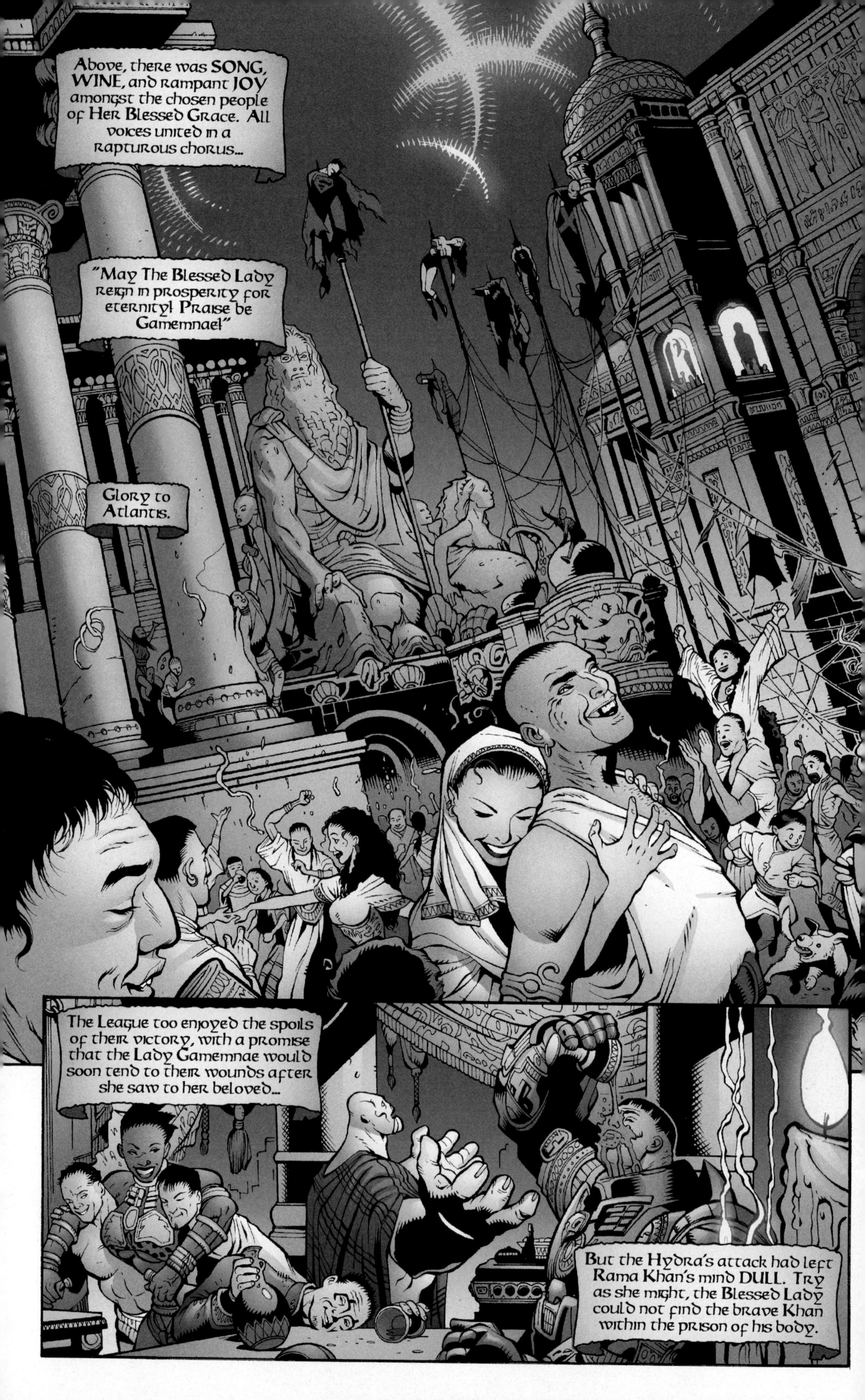
Above, there was SONG, WINE, and rampant JOY amongst the chosen people of Her Blessed Grace. All voices united in a rapturous chorus...
"May The Blessed Lady reign in prosperity for eternity! Praise be Gamemnae!"
Glory to Atlantis.
The League too enjoyed the spoils of their victory, with a promise that the Lady Gamemnae would soon tend to their wounds after she saw to her beloved...
But the Hydra's attack had left Rama Khan's mind DULL. Try as she might, the Blessed Lady could not find the brave Khan within the prison of his body.

Fate can be bitter to those who defy it.

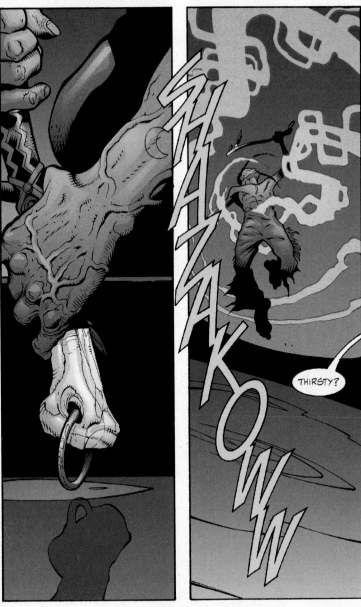

THIRSTY?

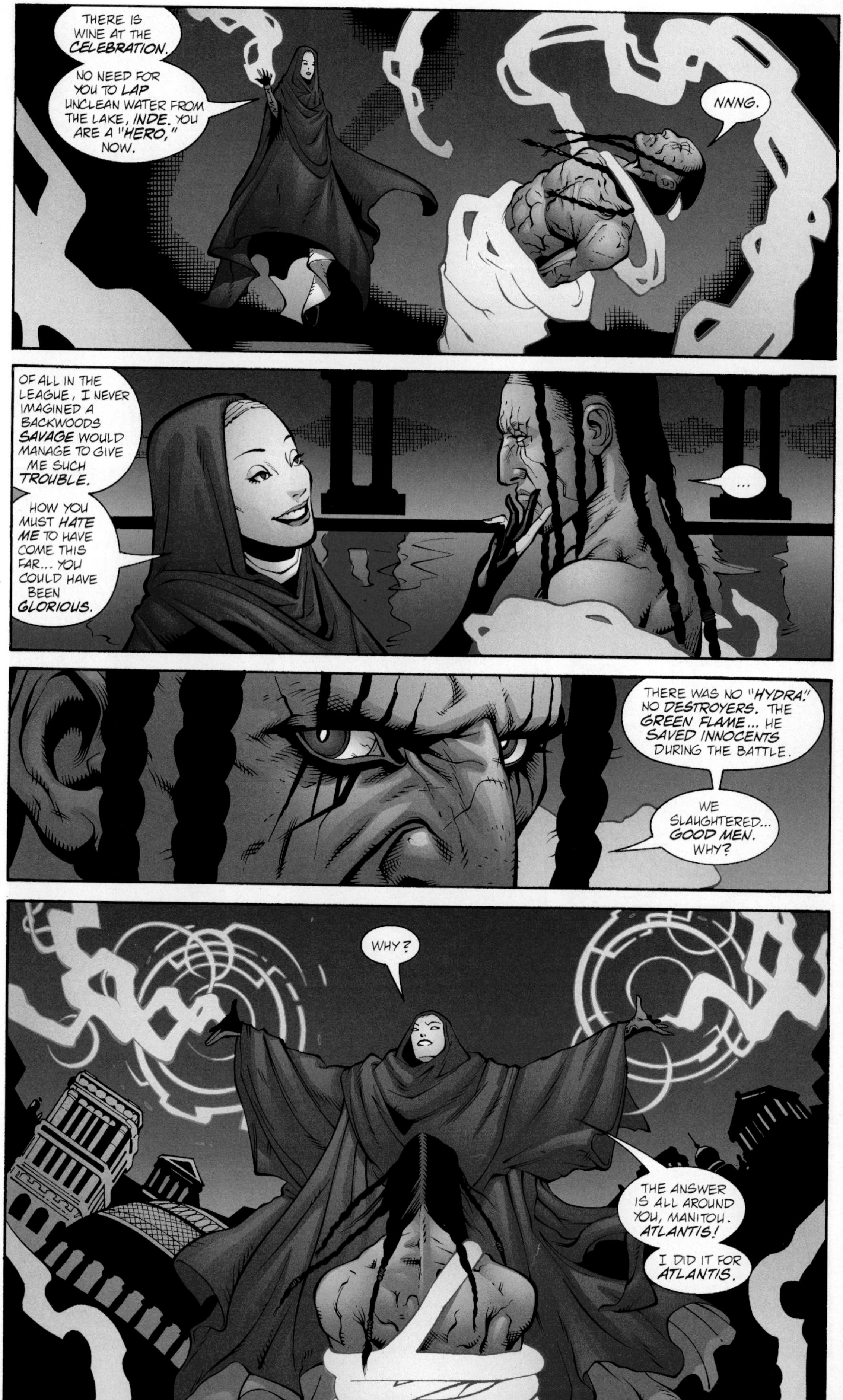
THERE IS WINE AT THE CELEBRATION.
NO NEED FOR YOU TO LAP UNCLEAN WATER FROM THE LAKE, INDE. YOU ARE A "HERO," NOW.
NNNG.
OF ALL IN THE LEAGUE, I NEVER IMAGINED A BACKWOODS SAVAGE WOULD MANAGE TO GIVE ME SUCH TROUBLE.
HOW YOU MUST HATE ME TO HAVE COME THIS FAR... YOU COULD HAVE BEEN GLORIOUS.
...
THERE WAS NO "HYDRA." NO DESTROYERS. THE GREEN FLAME... HE SAVED INNOCENTS DURING THE BATTLE.
WE SLAUGHTERED... GOOD MEN. WHY?
WHY?
THE ANSWER IS ALL AROUND YOU, MANITOU. ATLANTIS!
I DID IT FOR ATLANTIS.

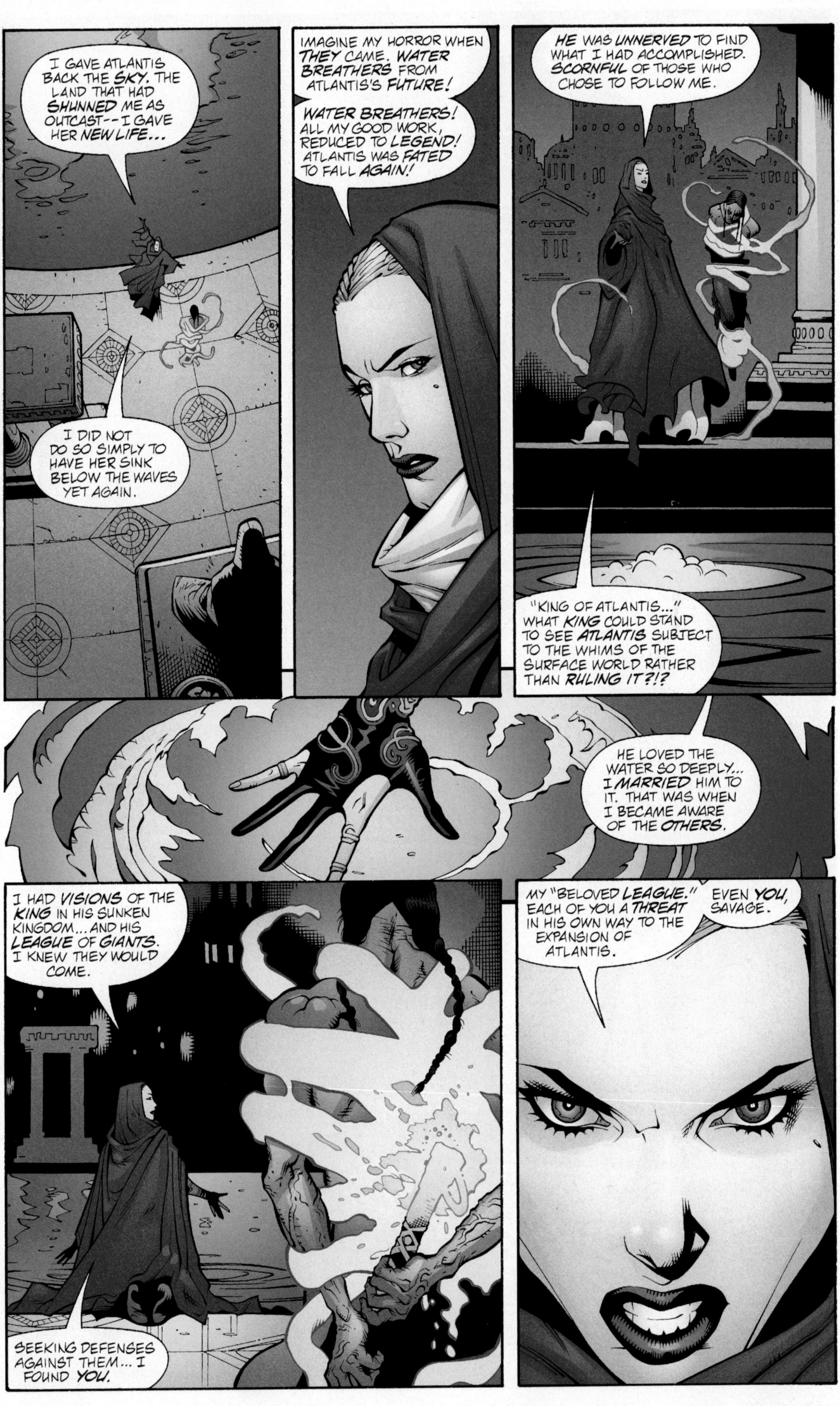
I GAVE ATLANTIS BACK THE SKY. THE LAND THAT HAD SHUNNED ME AS OUTCAST--I GAVE HER NEW LIFE...
I DID NOT DO SO SIMPLY TO HAVE HER SINK BELOW THE WAVES YET AGAIN.
IMAGINE MY HORROR WHEN THEY CAME. WATER BREATHERS FROM ATLANTIS'S FUTURE!
WATER BREATHERS! ALL MY GOOD WORK, REDUCED TO LEGEND! ATLANTIS WAS FATED TO FALL AGAIN!
HE WAS UNNERVED TO FIND WHAT I HAD ACCOMPLISHED. SCORNFUL OF THOSE WHO CHOSE TO FOLLOW ME.
"KING OF ATLANTIS..." WHAT KING COULD STAND TO SEE ATLANTIS SUBJECT TO THE WHIMS OF THE SURFACE WORLD RATHER THAN RULING IT?!?
HE LOVED THE WATER SO DEEPLY... I MARRIED HIM TO IT. THAT WAS WHEN I BECAME AWARE OF THE OTHERS.
I HAD VISIONS OF THE KING IN HIS SUNKEN KINGDOM... AND HIS LEAGUE OF GIANTS. I KNEW THEY WOULD COME.
SEEKING DEFENSES AGAINST THEM... I FOUND YOU.
MY "BELOVED LEAGUE." EACH OF YOU A THREAT IN HIS OWN WAY TO THE EXPANSION OF ATLANTIS.
EVEN YOU, SAVAGE.

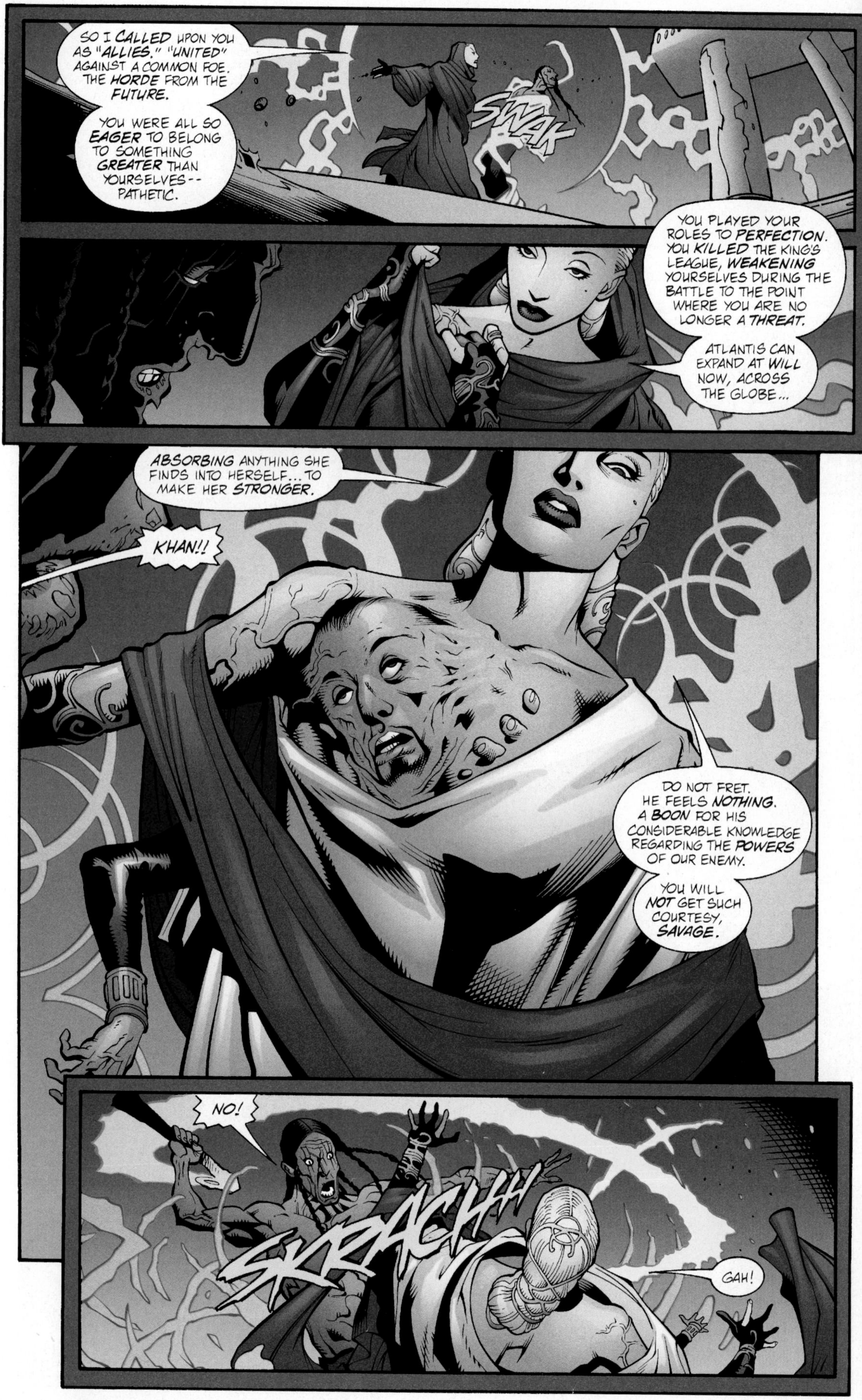

SO I CALLED UPON YOU AS "ALLIES." "UNITED" AGAINST A COMMON FOE. THE HORDE FROM THE FUTURE.
YOU WERE ALL SO EAGER TO BELONG TO SOMETHING GREATER THAN YOURSELVES-- PATHETIC.
SWAK
YOU PLAYED YOUR ROLES TO PERFECTION. YOU KILLED THE KING'S LEAGUE, WEAKENING YOURSELVES DURING THE BATTLE TO THE POINT WHERE YOU ARE NO LONGER A THREAT.
ATLANTIS CAN EXPAND AT WILL NOW, ACROSS THE GLOBE...
ABSORBING ANYTHING SHE FINDS INTO HERSELF... TO MAKE HER STRONGER.
KHAN!!
DO NOT FRET. HE FEELS NOTHING. A BOON FOR HIS CONSIDERABLE KNOWLEDGE REGARDING THE POWERS OF OUR ENEMY.
YOU WILL NOT GET SUCH COURTESY, SAVAGE.
NO!
SKRACHH
GAH!

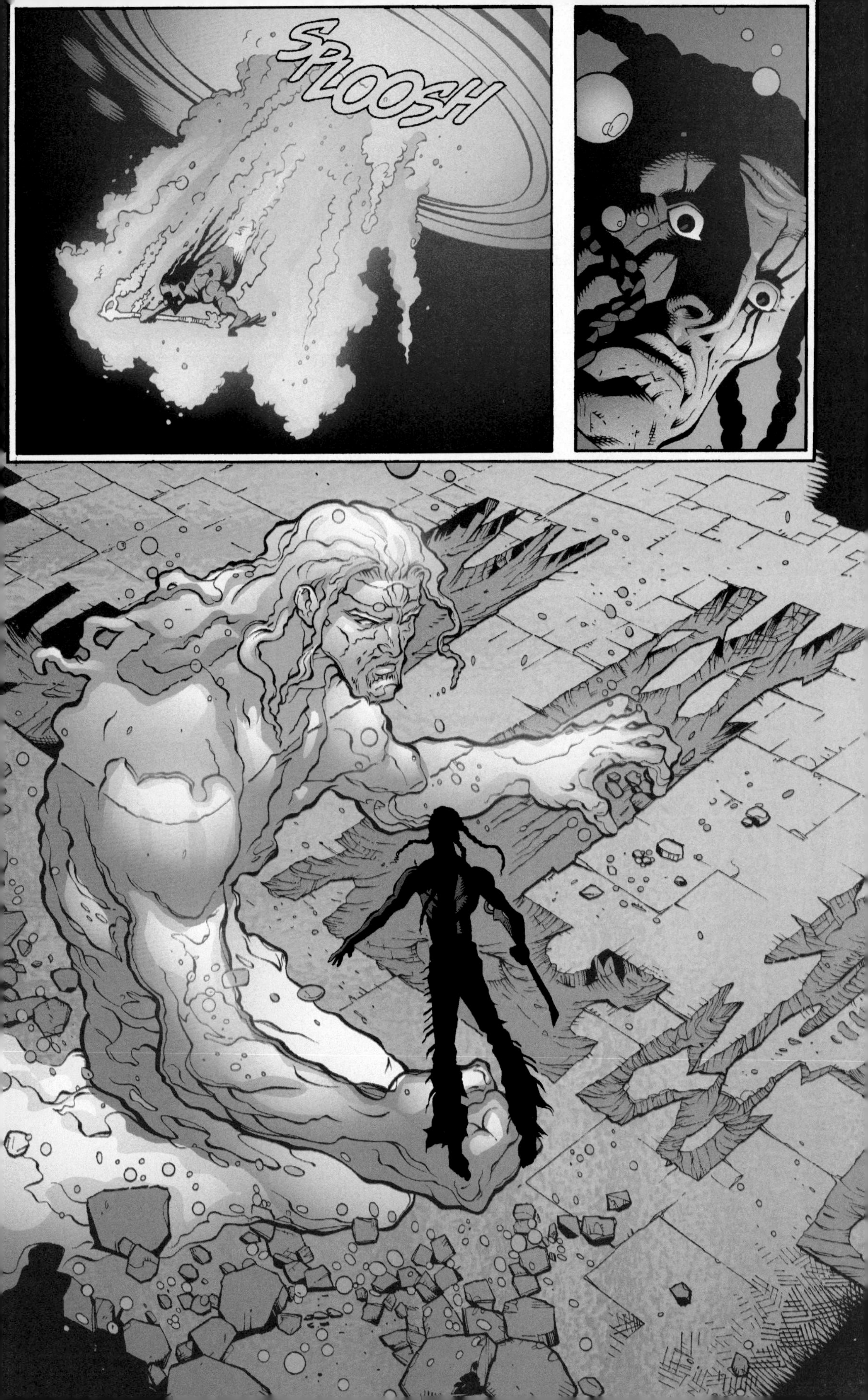
SPLOOSH

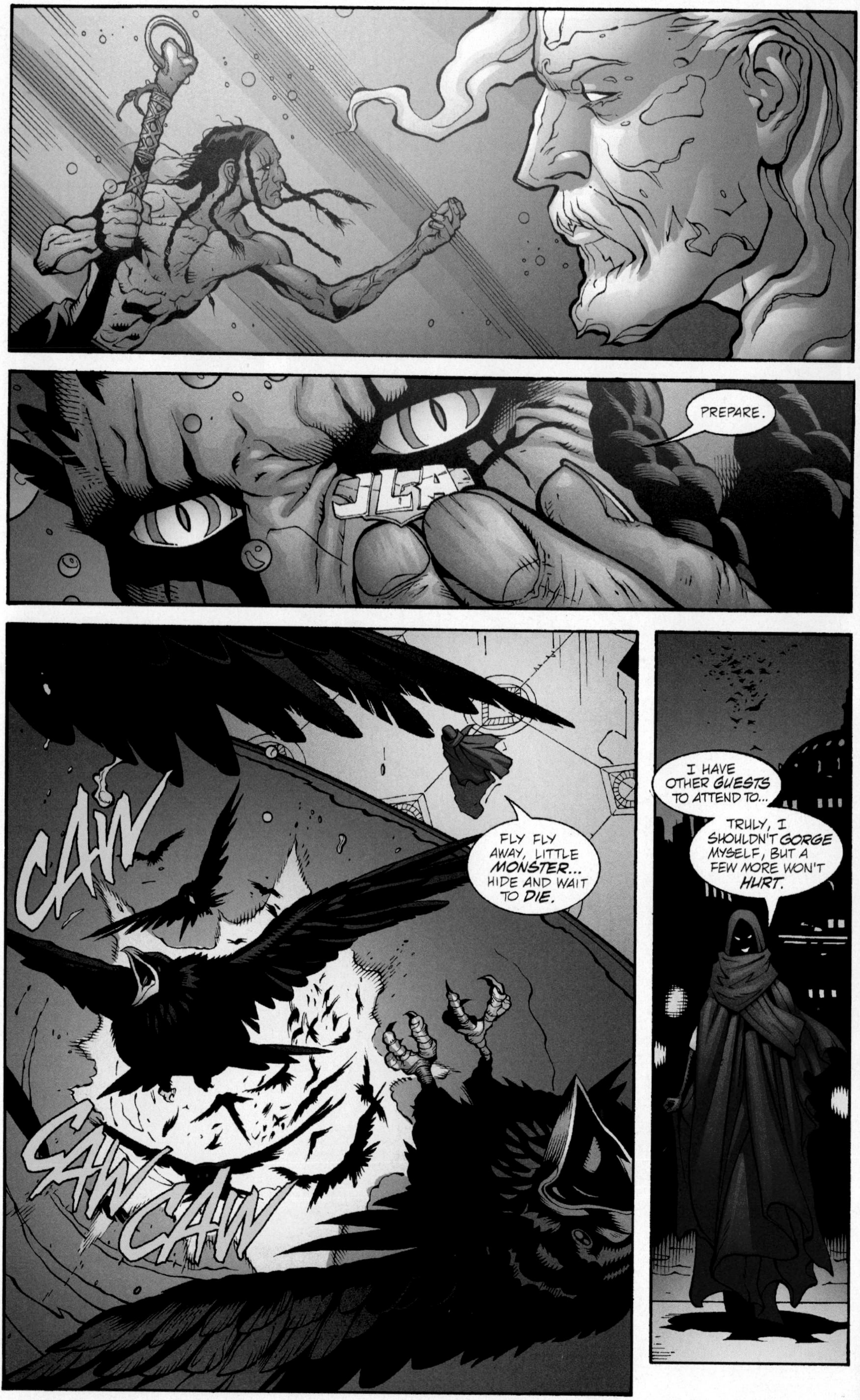
PREPARE.
CAW
FLY FLY AWAY, LITTLE MONSTER... HIDE AND WAIT TO DIE.
CAW CAW
I HAVE OTHER GUESTS TO ATTEND TO...
TRULY, I SHOULDN'T GORGE MYSELF, BUT A FEW MORE WON'T HURT.

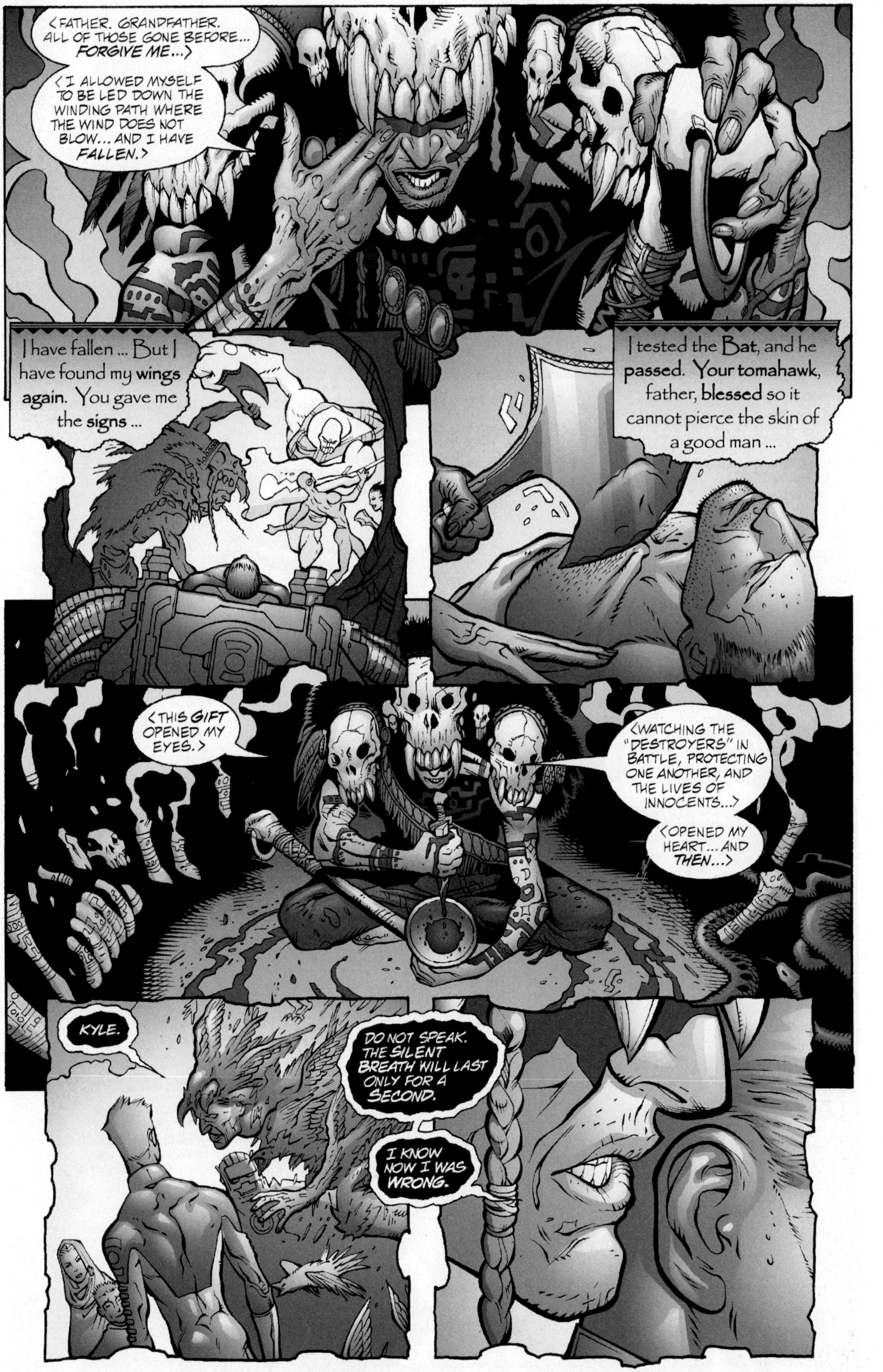

<FATHER. GRANDFATHER. ALL OF THOSE GONE BEFORE... FORGIVE ME...>
<I ALLOWED MYSELF TO BE LED DOWN THE WINDING PATH WHERE THE WIND DOES NOT BLOW... AND I HAVE FALLEN.>
I have fallen ... But I have found my wings again. You gave me the signs ...
I tested the Bat, and he passed. Your tomahawk, father, blessed so it cannot pierce the skin of a good man ...
<THIS GIFT OPENED MY EYES.>
<WATCHING THE "DESTROYERS" IN BATTLE, PROTECTING ONE ANOTHER, AND THE LIVES OF INNOCENTS...>
<OPENED MY HEART... AND THEN...>
KYLE.
DO NOT SPEAK. THE SILENT BREATH WILL LAST ONLY FOR A SECOND.
I KNOW NOW I WAS WRONG.

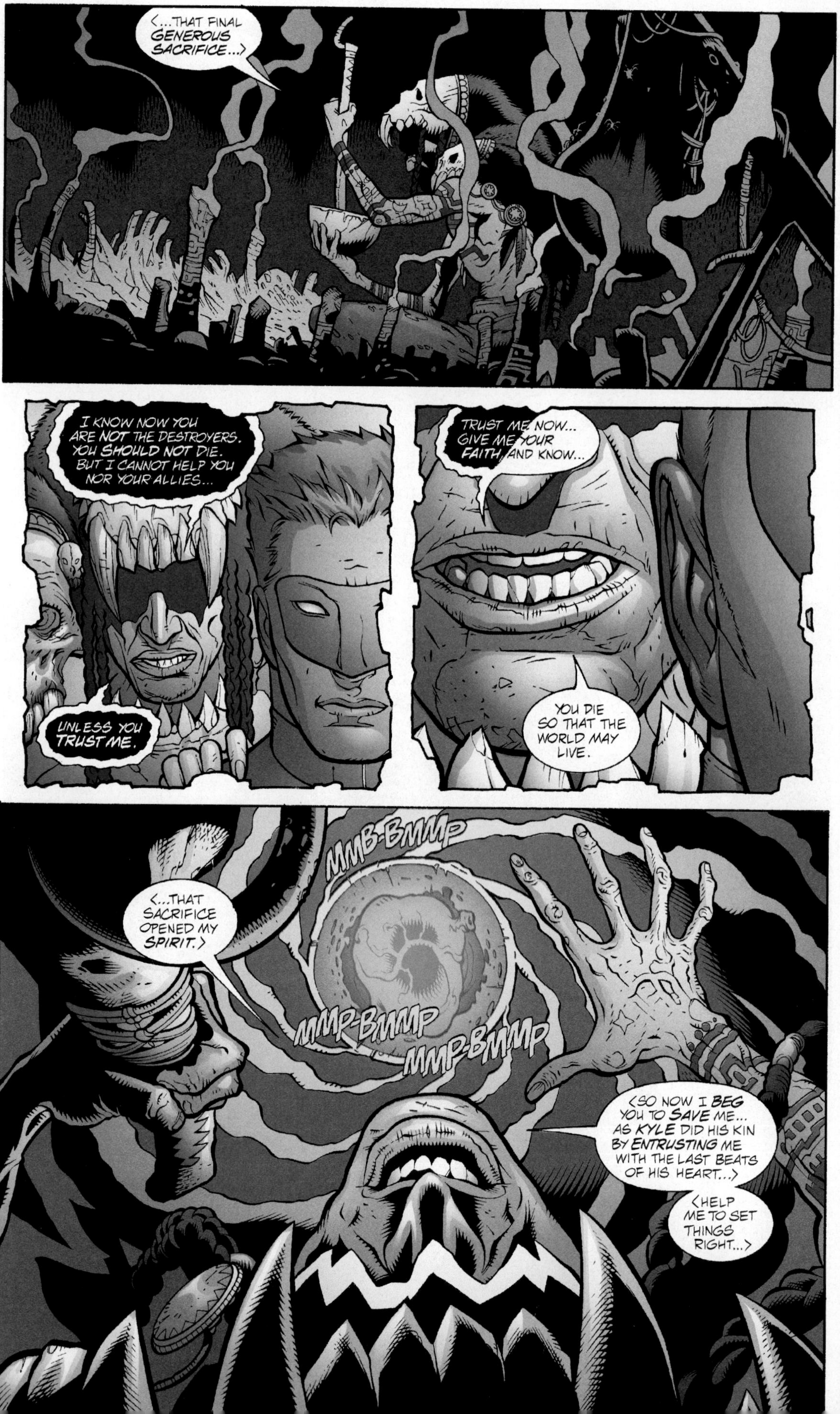
<...THAT FINAL GENEROUS SACRIFICE...>
I KNOW NOW YOU ARE NOT THE DESTROYERS. YOU SHOULD NOT DIE. BUT I CANNOT HELP YOU NOR YOUR ALLIES...
UNLESS YOU TRUST ME.
TRUST ME NOW... GIVE ME YOUR FAITH, AND KNOW...
YOU DIE SO THAT THE WORLD MAY LIVE.
MMB-BMMP
<...THAT SACRIFICE OPENED MY SPIRIT.>
MMP-BMMP
MMP-BMMP
<SO NOW I BEG YOU TO SAVE ME... AS KYLE DID HIS KIN BY ENTRUSTING ME WITH THE LAST BEATS OF HIS HEART...>
<HELP ME TO SET THINGS RIGHT...>

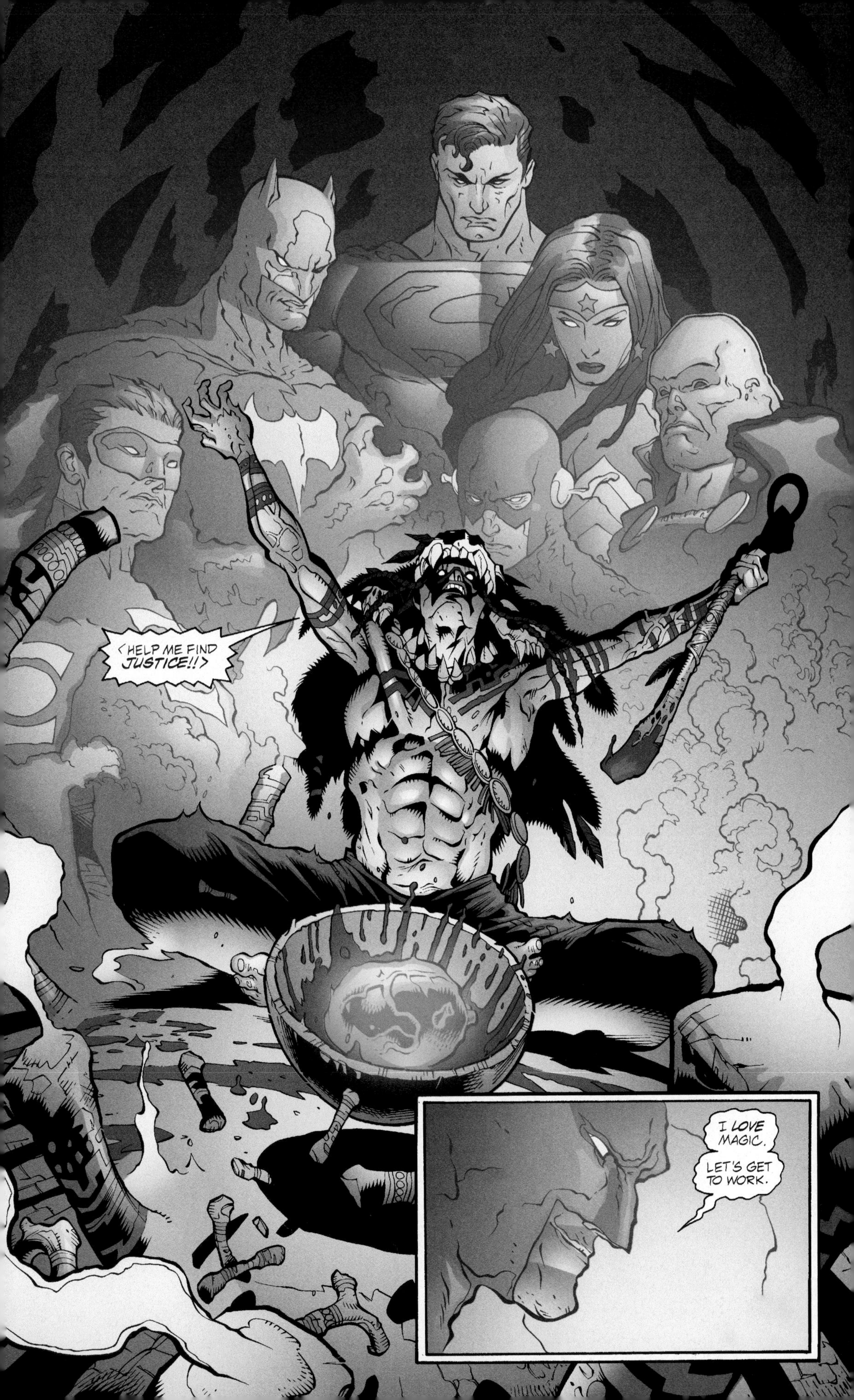
<HELP ME FIND JUSTICE!!>
I LOVE MAGIC.
LET'S GET TO WORK.

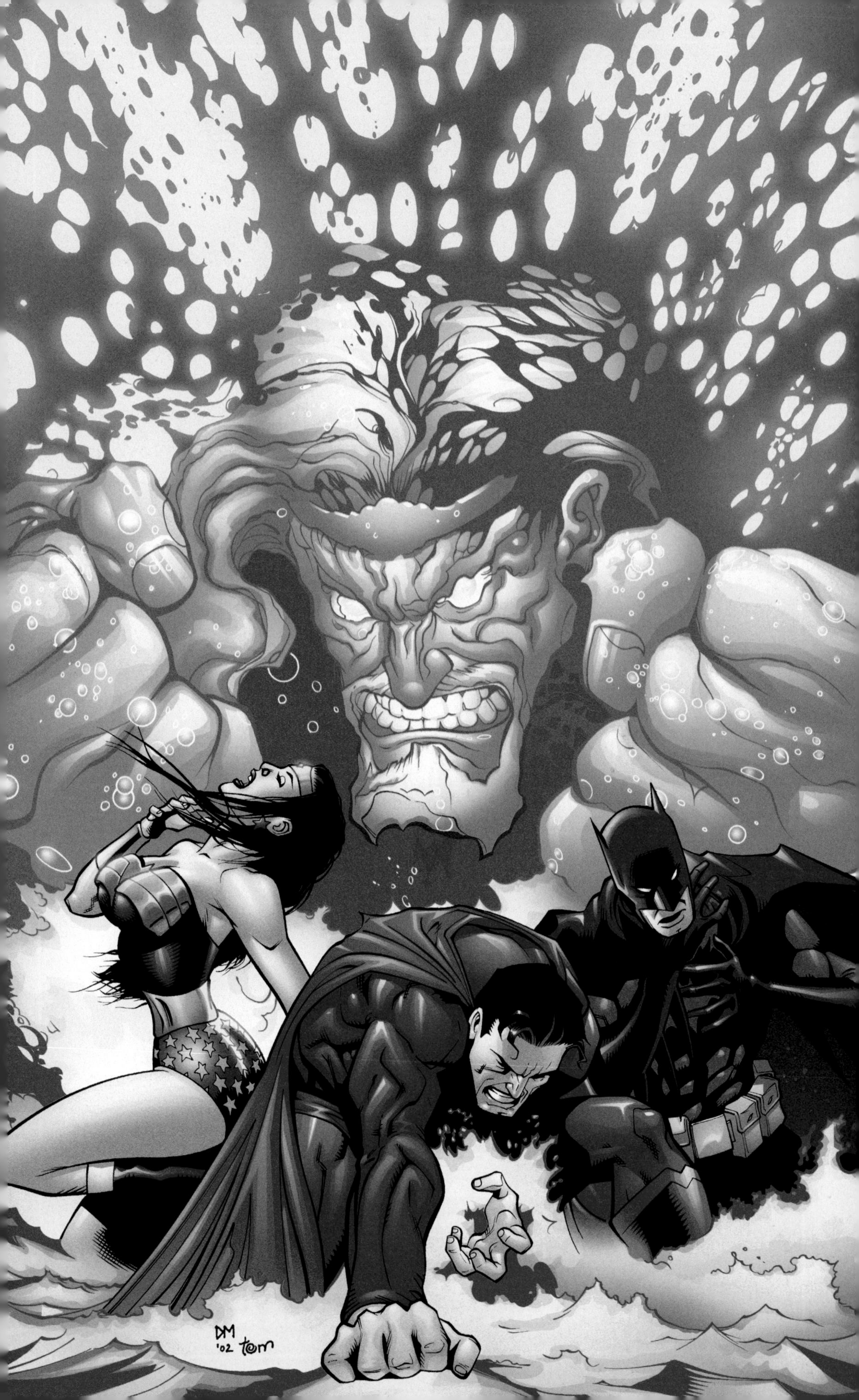

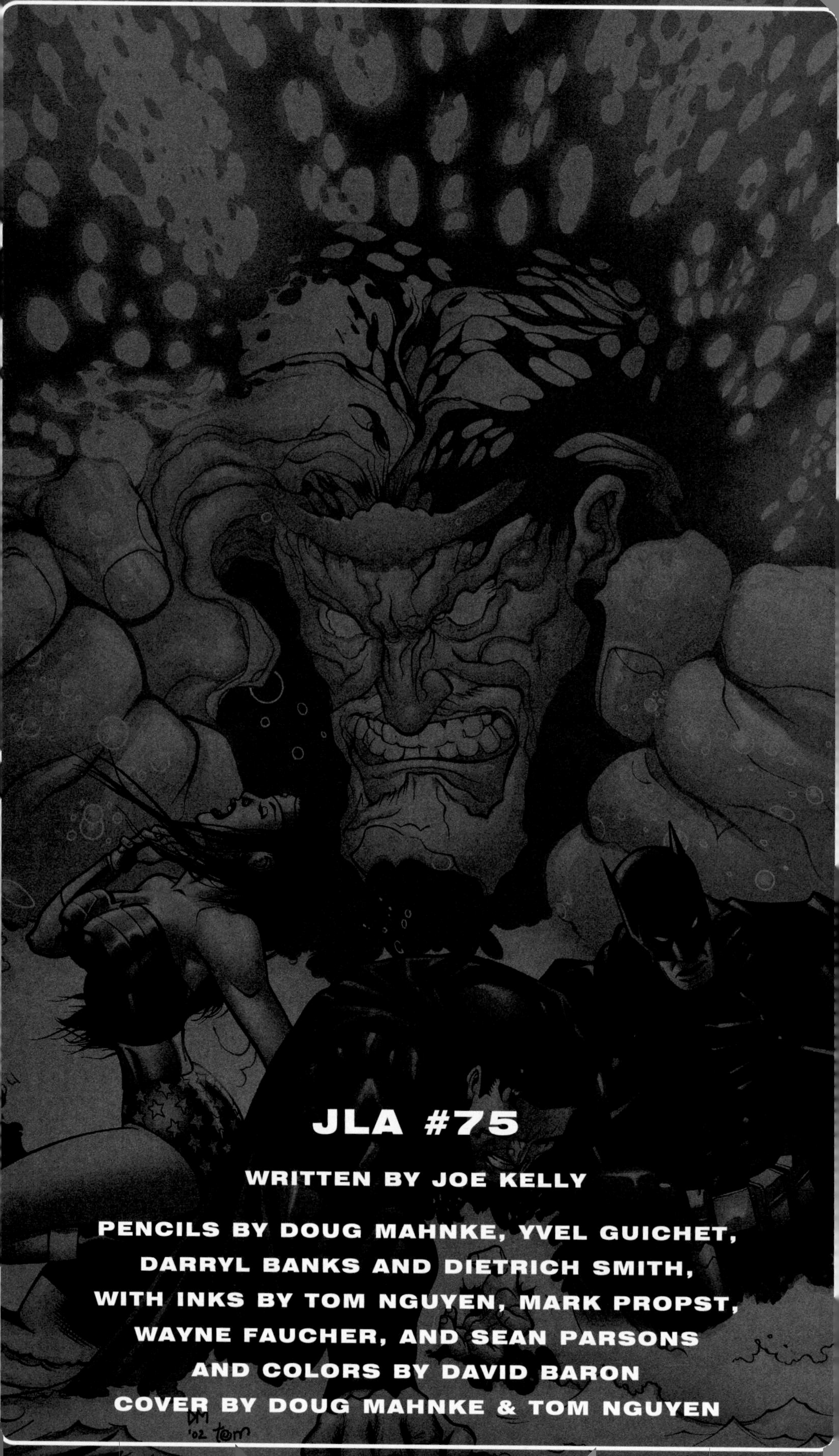

JLA #75

WRITTEN BY JOE KELLY

PENCILS BY DOUG MAHNKE, YVEL GUICHET, DARRYL BANKS AND DIETRICH SMITH, WITH INKS BY TOM NGUYEN, MARK PROPST, WAYNE FAUCHER, AND SEAN PARSONS AND COLORS BY DAVID BARON

COVER BY DOUG MAHNKE & TOM NGUYEN

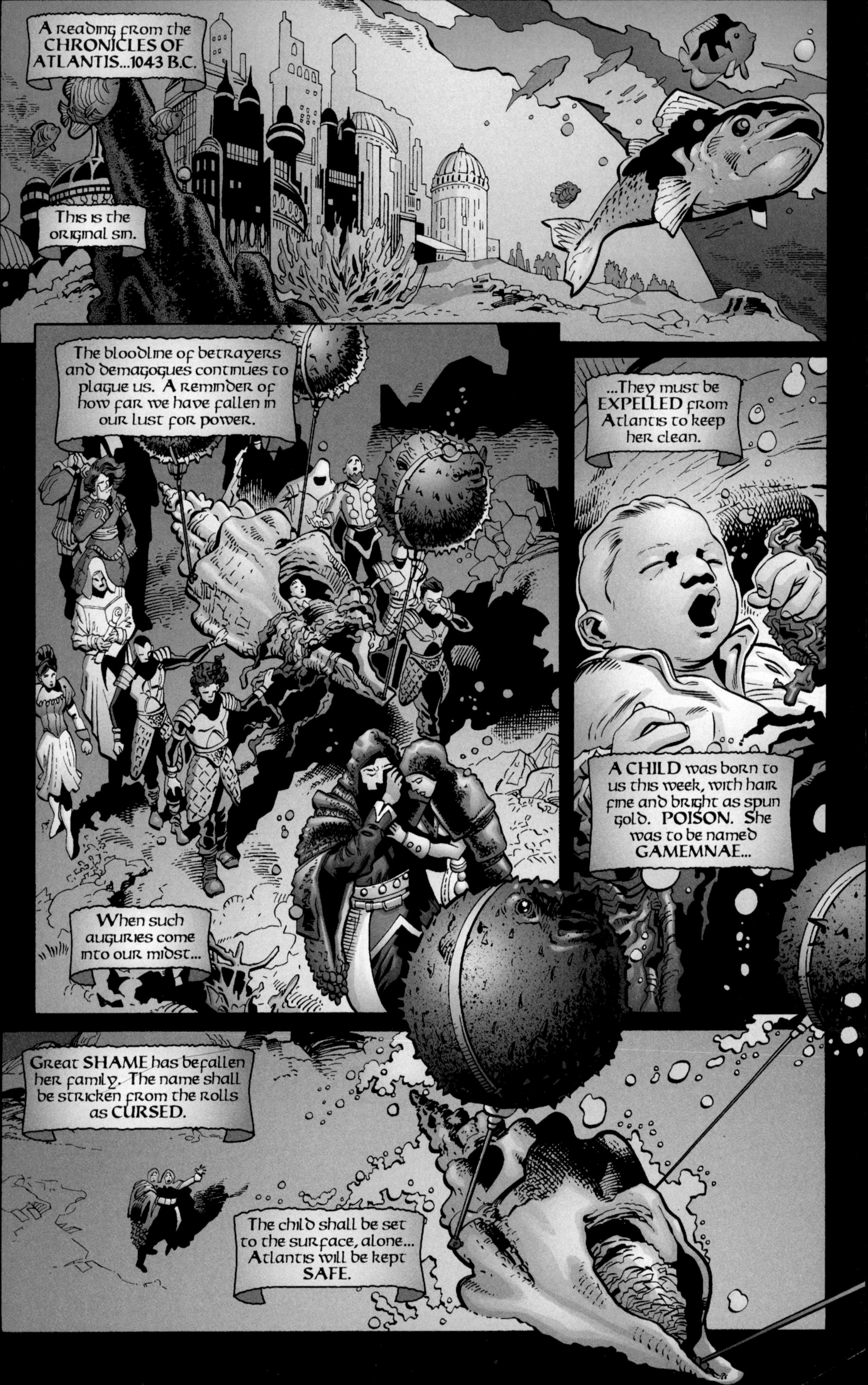
A reading from the CHRONICLES OF ATLANTIS...1043 B.C.
This is the original sin.
The bloodline of betrayers and demagogues continues to plague us. A reminder of how far we have fallen in our lust for power.
When such auguries come into our midst...
...They must be EXPELLED from Atlantis to keep her clean.
A CHILD was born to us this week, with hair fine and bright as spun gold. POISON. She was to be named GAMEMNAE...
Great SHAME has befallen her family. The name shall be stricken from the rolls as CURSED.
The child shall be set to the surface, alone... Atlantis will be kept SAFE.

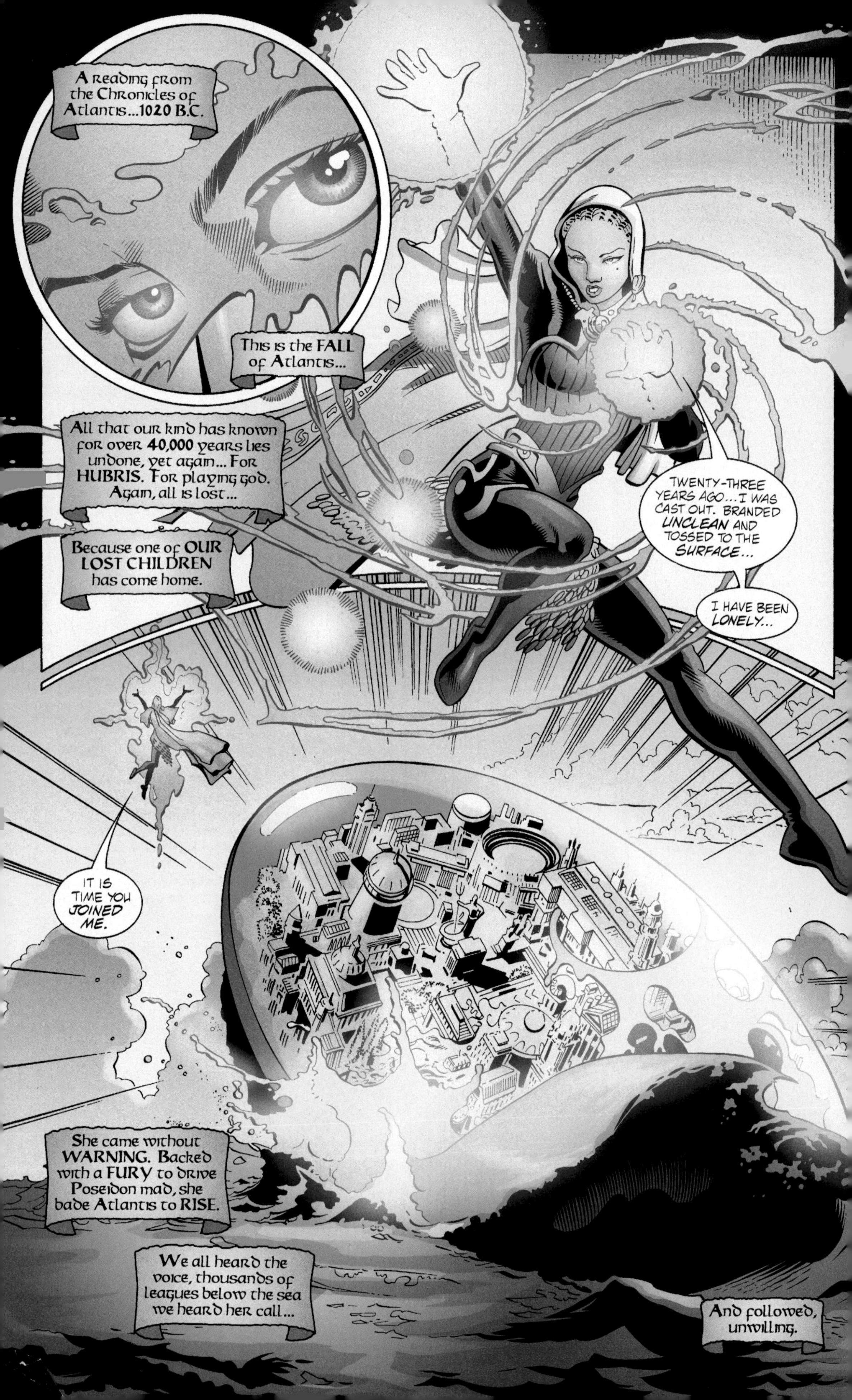
A reading from the Chronicles of Atlantis...1020 B.C.
This is the FALL of Atlantis...
All that our kind has known for over 40,000 years lies undone, yet again... For HUBRIS. For playing god. Again, all is lost...
Because one of OUR LOST CHILDREN has come home.
TWENTY-THREE YEARS AGO... I WAS CAST OUT. BRANDED UNCLEAN AND TOSSED TO THE SURFACE...
I HAVE BEEN LONELY...
IT IS TIME YOU JOINED ME.
She came without WARNING. Backed with a FURY to drive Poseidon mad, she bade Atlantis to RISE.
We all heard the voice, thousands of leagues below the sea we heard her call...
And followed, unwilling.

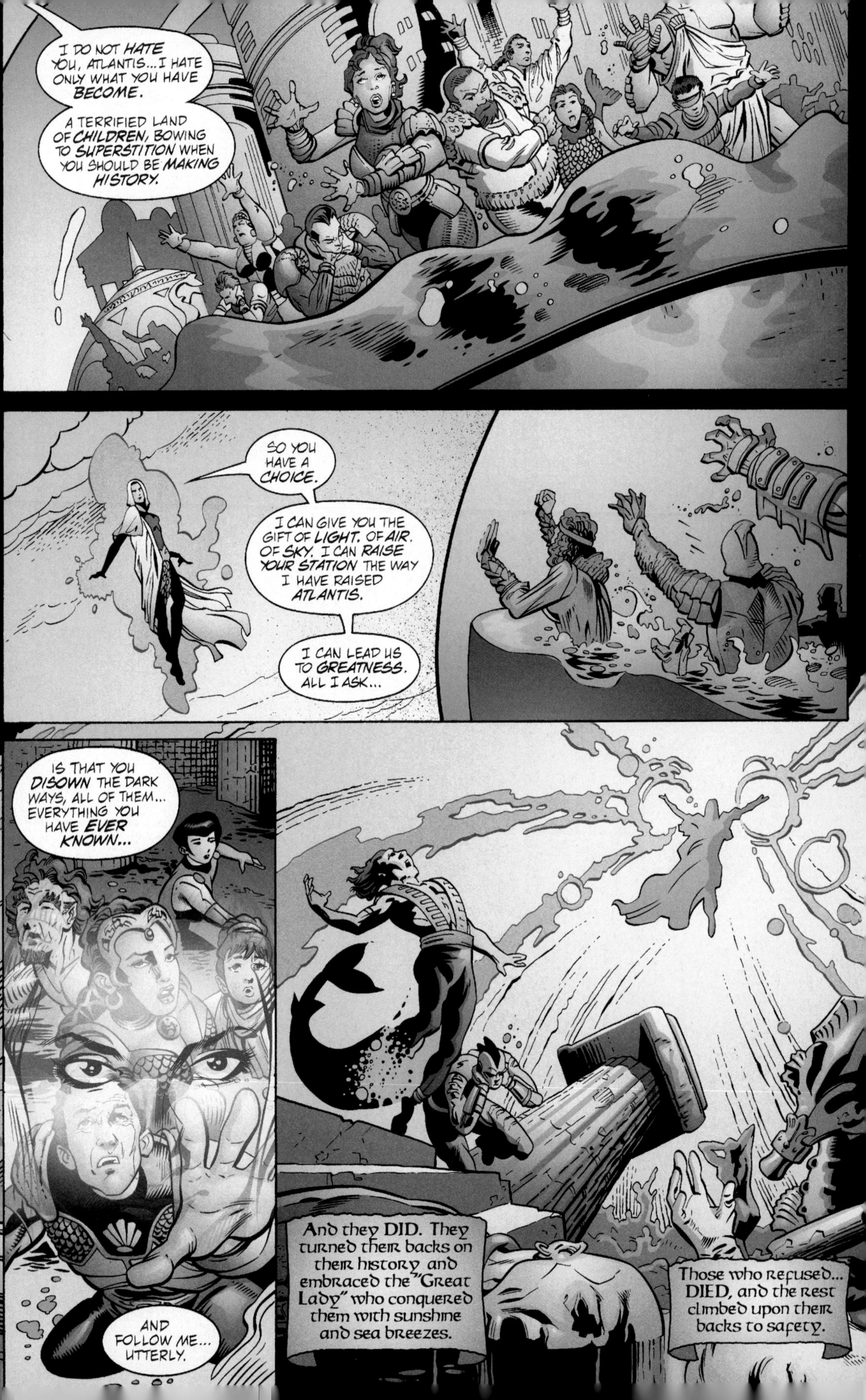

I DO NOT HATE YOU, ATLANTIS... I HATE ONLY WHAT YOU HAVE BECOME.
A TERRIFIED LAND OF CHILDREN, BOWING TO SUPERSTITION WHEN YOU SHOULD BE MAKING HISTORY.
!
SO YOU HAVE A CHOICE.
I CAN GIVE YOU THE GIFT OF LIGHT. OF AIR. OF SKY. I CAN RAISE YOUR STATION THE WAY I HAVE RAISED ATLANTIS.
I CAN LEAD US TO GREATNESS. ALL I ASK...
IS THAT YOU DISOWN THE DARK WAYS, ALL OF THEM... EVERYTHING YOU HAVE EVER KNOWN...
AND FOLLOW ME... UTTERLY.
And they DID. They turned their backs on their history and embraced the "Great Lady" who conquered them with sunshine and sea breezes.
Those who refused... DIED, and the rest climbed upon their backs to safety.

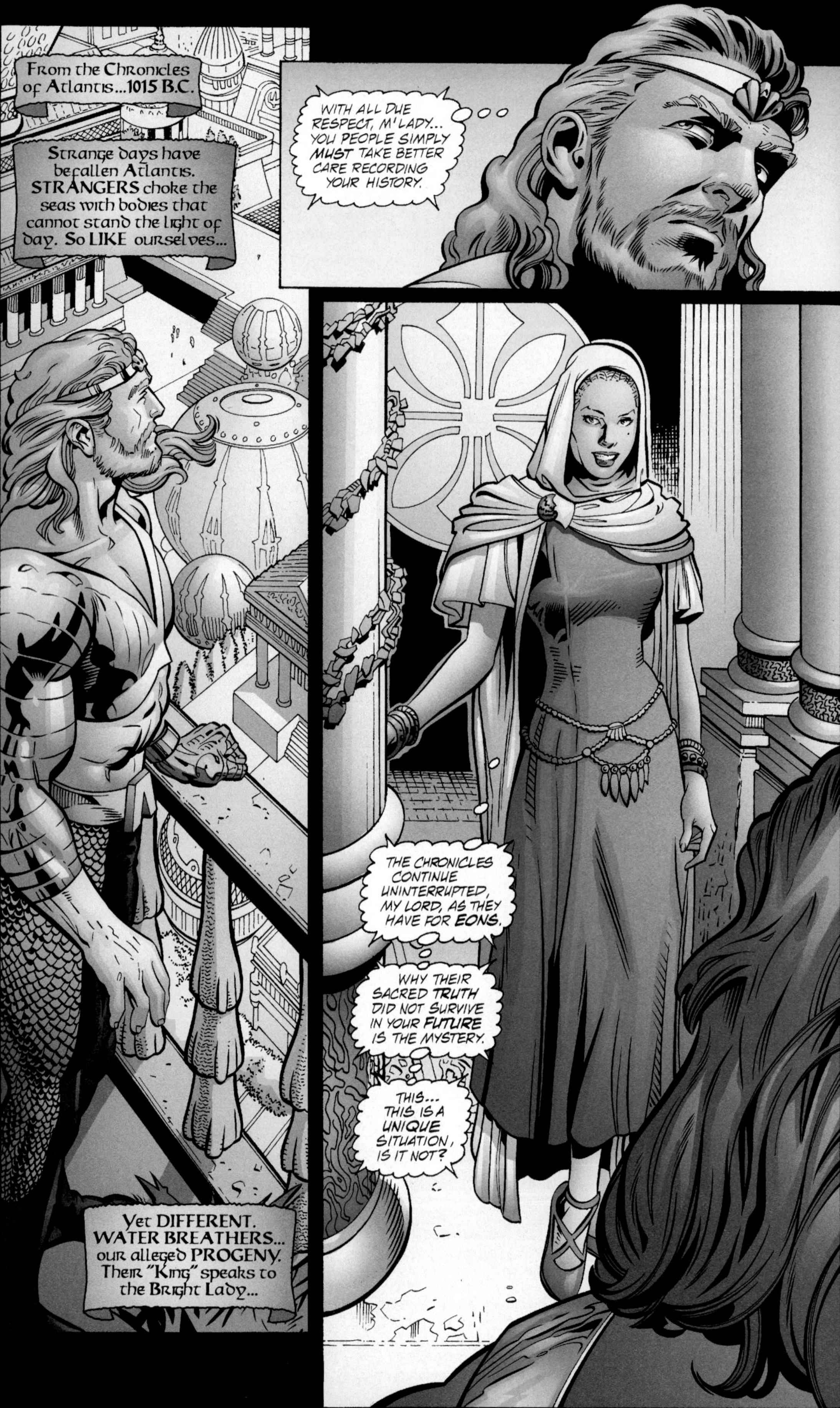
From the Chronicles of Atlantis...1015 B.C.
Strange days have befallen Atlantis. STRANGERS choke the seas with bodies that cannot stand the light of day. So LIKE ourselves...
WITH ALL DUE RESPECT, M'LADY... YOU PEOPLE SIMPLY MUST TAKE BETTER CARE RECORDING YOUR HISTORY.
THE CHRONICLES CONTINUE UNINTERRUPTED, MY LORD, AS THEY HAVE FOR EONS.
WHY THEIR SACRED TRUTH DID NOT SURVIVE IN YOUR FUTURE IS THE MYSTERY.
THIS... THIS IS A UNIQUE SITUATION, IS IT NOT?
Yet DIFFERENT. WATER BREATHERS... our alleged PROGENY. Their "King" speaks to the Bright Lady...

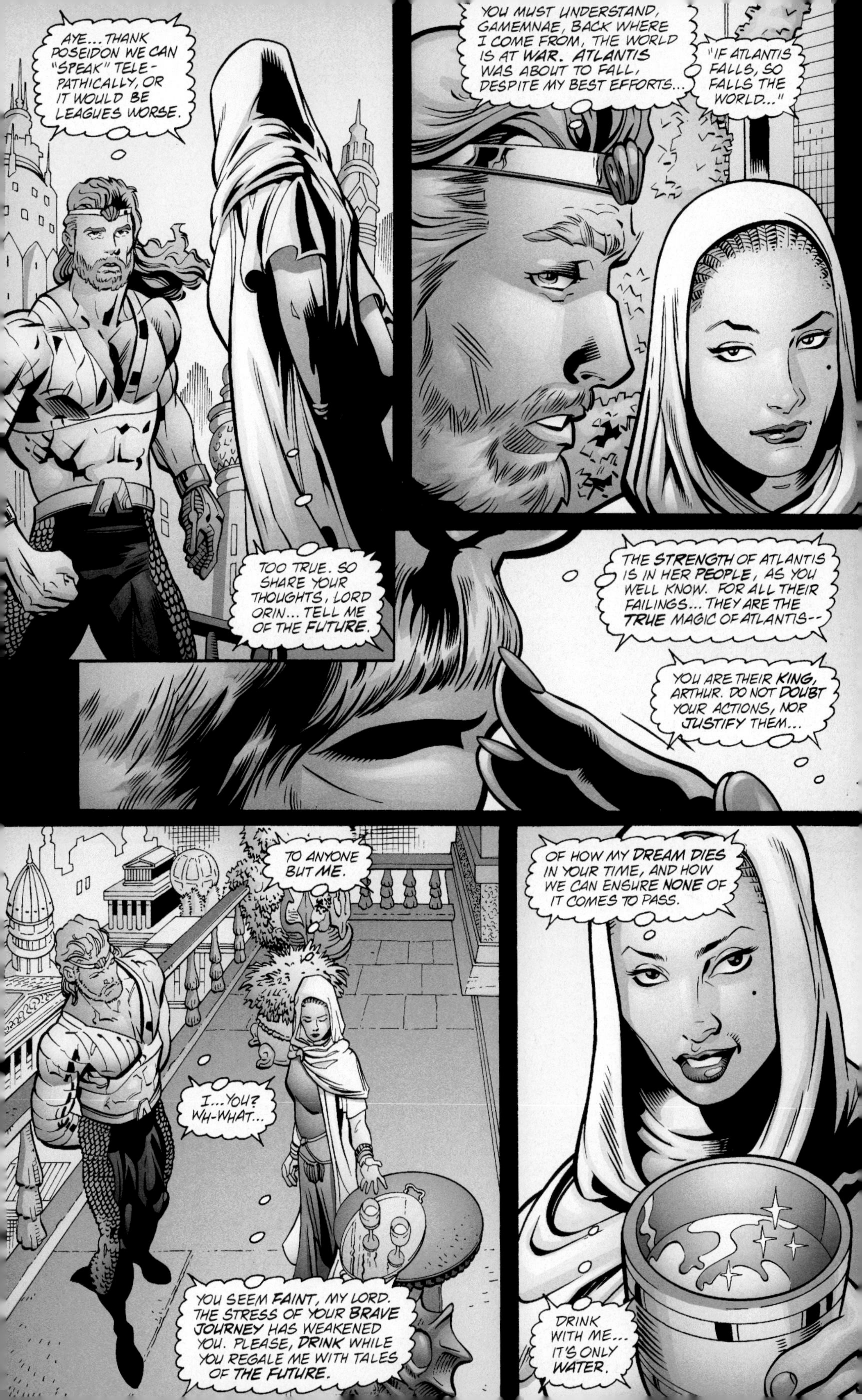
AYE... THANK POSEIDON WE CAN "SPEAK" TELEPATHICALLY, OR IT WOULD BE LEAGUES WORSE.
TOO TRUE. SO SHARE YOUR THOUGHTS, LORD ORIN... TELL ME OF THE FUTURE.
YOU MUST UNDERSTAND, GAMEMNAE, BACK WHERE I COME FROM, THE WORLD IS AT WAR. ATLANTIS WAS ABOUT TO FALL, DESPITE MY BEST EFFORTS...
"IF ATLANTIS FALLS, SO FALLS THE WORLD..."
THE STRENGTH OF ATLANTIS IS IN HER PEOPLE, AS YOU WELL KNOW. FOR ALL THEIR FAILINGS... THEY ARE THE TRUE MAGIC OF ATLANTIS--
YOU ARE THEIR KING, ARTHUR. DO NOT DOUBT YOUR ACTIONS, NOR JUSTIFY THEM...
TO ANYONE BUT ME.
I... YOU? WH-WHAT...
YOU SEEM FAINT, MY LORD. THE STRESS OF YOUR BRAVE JOURNEY HAS WEAKENED YOU. PLEASE, DRINK WHILE YOU REGALE ME WITH TALES OF THE FUTURE.
OF HOW MY DREAM DIES IN YOUR TIME, AND HOW WE CAN ENSURE NONE OF IT COMES TO PASS.
DRINK WITH ME... IT'S ONLY WATER.

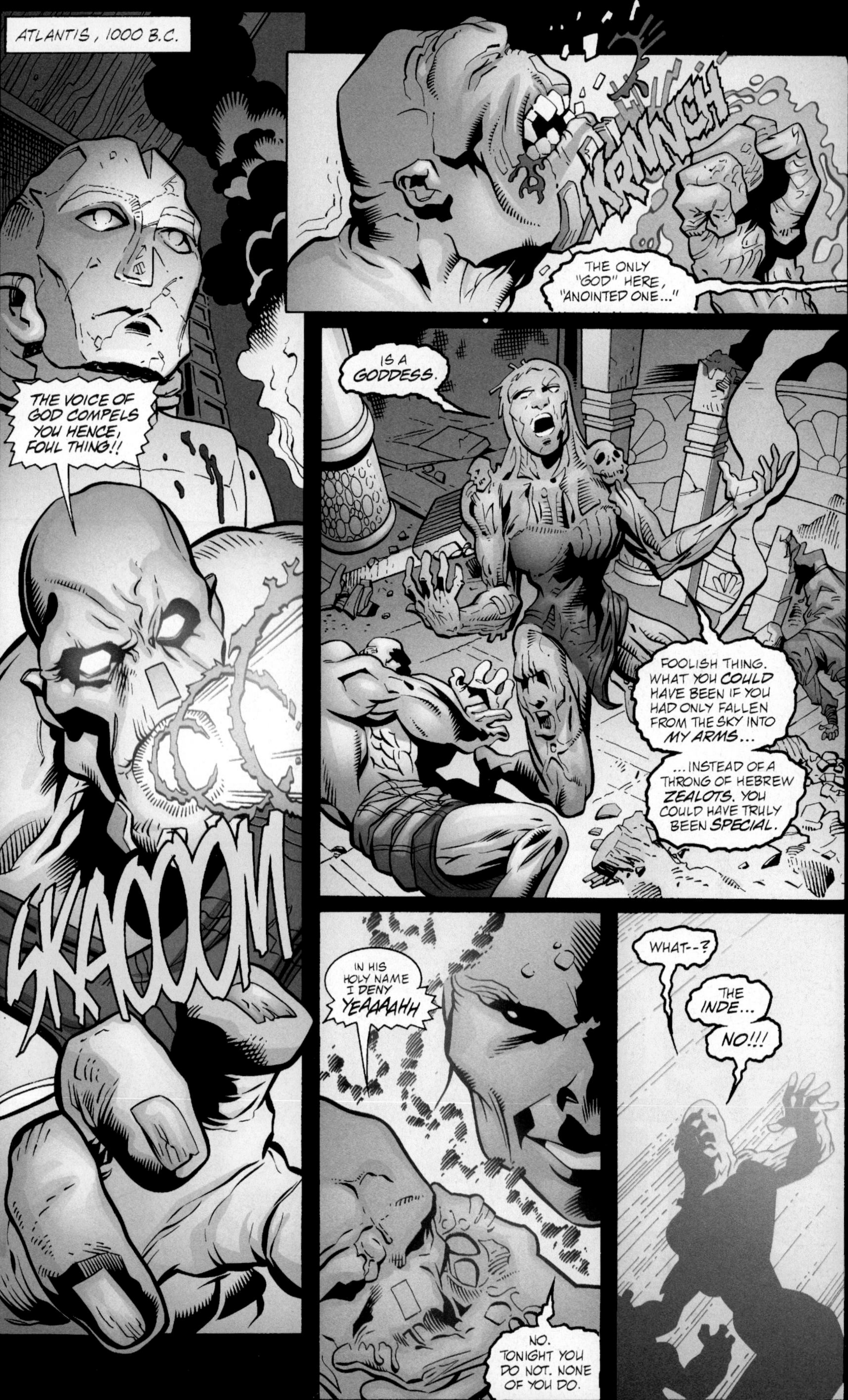
ATLANTIS, 1000 B.C.
KRNNCH
THE ONLY "GOD" HERE, "ANOINTED ONE..."
THE VOICE OF GOD COMPELS YOU HENCE, FOUL THING!!
SKAOOOM
IS A GODDESS.
FOOLISH THING. WHAT YOU COULD HAVE BEEN IF YOU HAD ONLY FALLEN FROM THE SKY INTO MY ARMS...
...INSTEAD OF A THRONG OF HEBREW ZEALOTS. YOU COULD HAVE TRULY BEEN SPECIAL.
IN HIS HOLY NAME I DENY YEAAAAHH
NO. TONIGHT YOU DO NOT. NONE OF YOU DO.
WHAT--?
THE INDE...
NO!!!

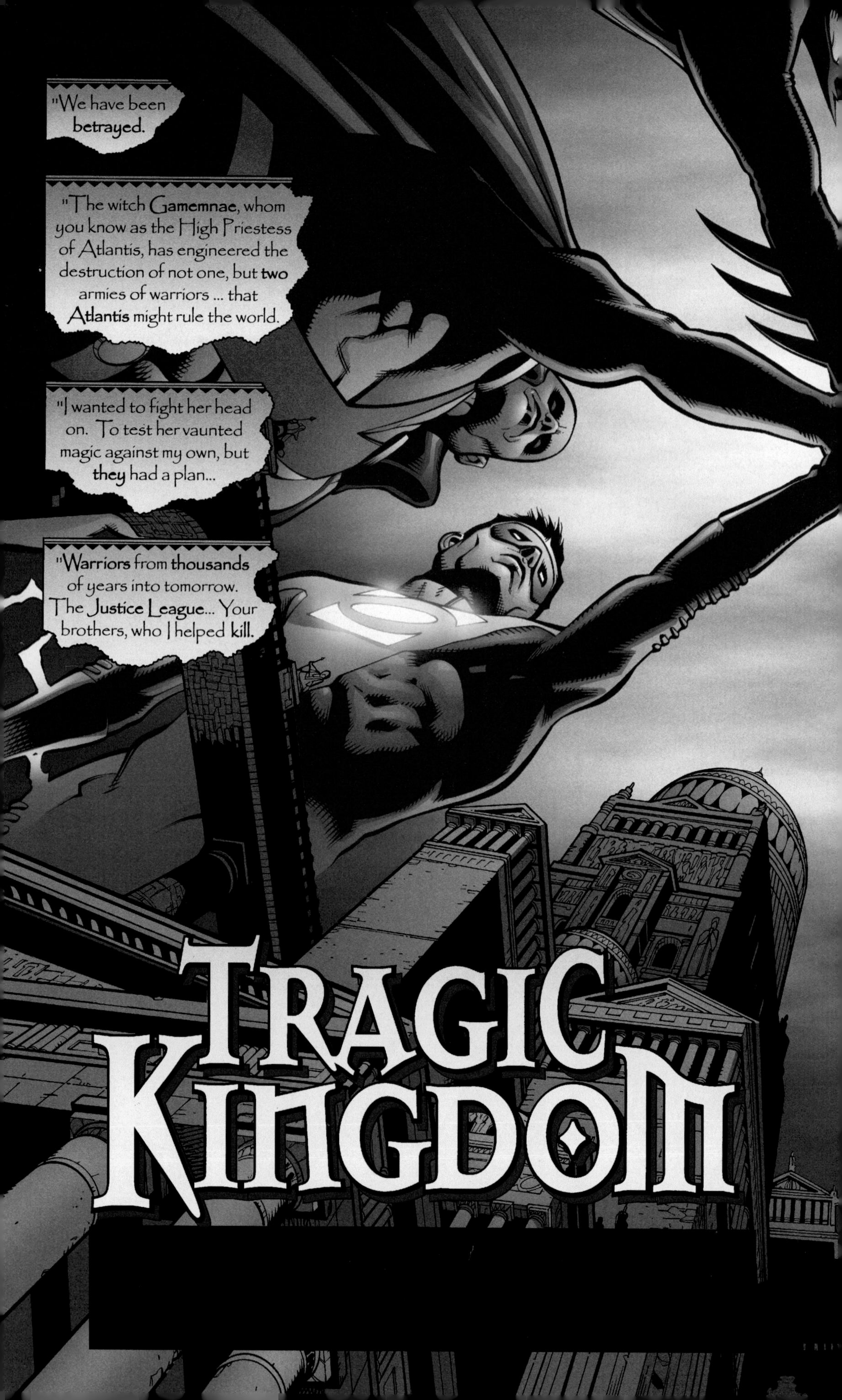
"We have been betrayed.
"The witch Gamemnae, whom you know as the High Priestess of Atlantis, has engineered the destruction of not one, but two armies of warriors ... that Atlantis might rule the world.
"I wanted to fight her head on. To test her vaunted magic against my own, but they had a plan...
"Warriors from thousands of years into tomorrow. The Justice League... Your brothers, who I helped kill.
TRAGIC KINGDOM
[redacted]

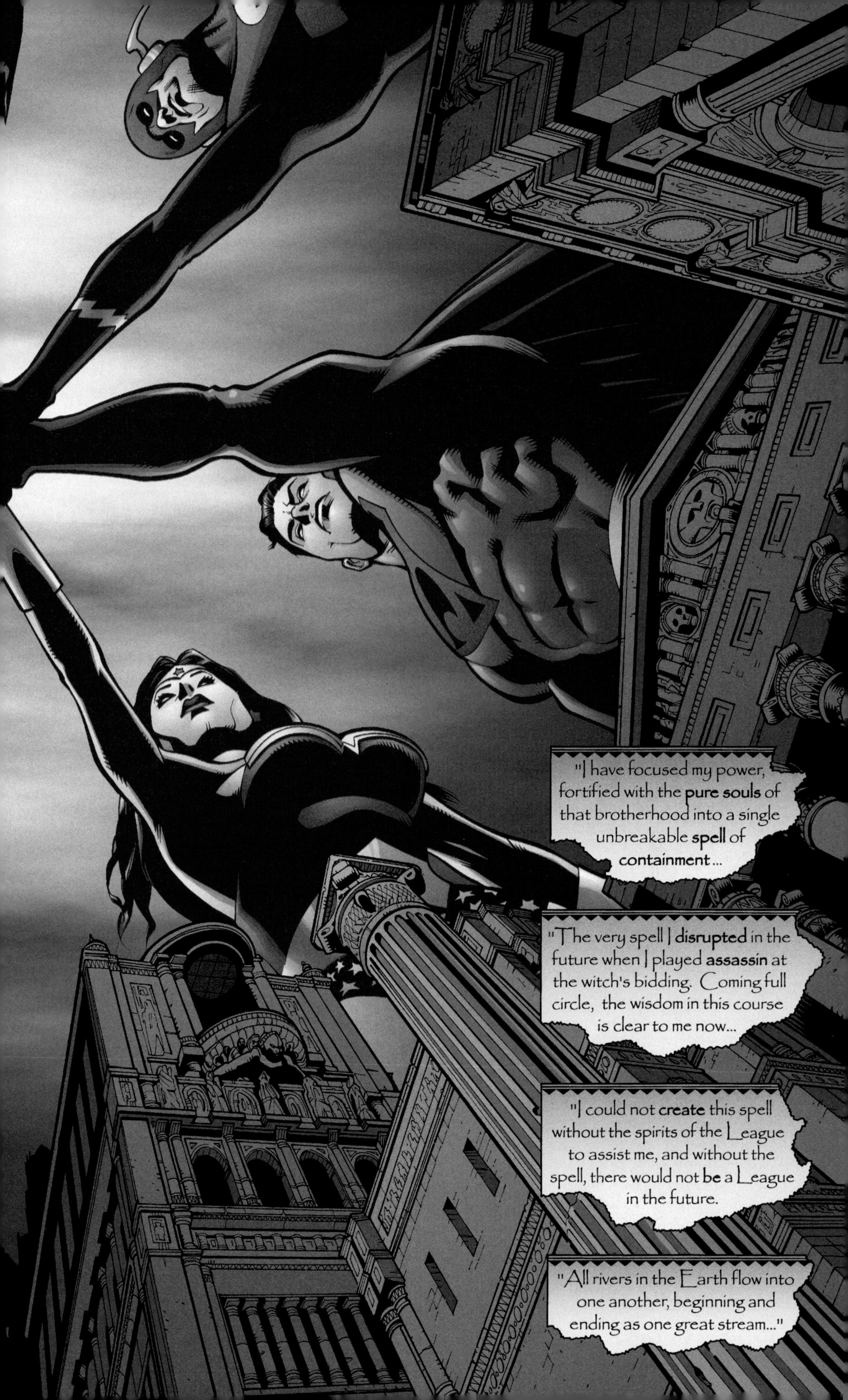
"I have focused my power, fortified with the pure souls of that brotherhood into a single unbreakable spell of containment...
"The very spell I disrupted in the future when I played assassin at the witch's bidding. Coming full circle, the wisdom in this course is clear to me now...
"I could not create this spell without the spirits of the League to assist me, and without the spell, there would not be a League in the future.
"All rivers in the Earth flow into one another, beginning and ending as one great stream..."

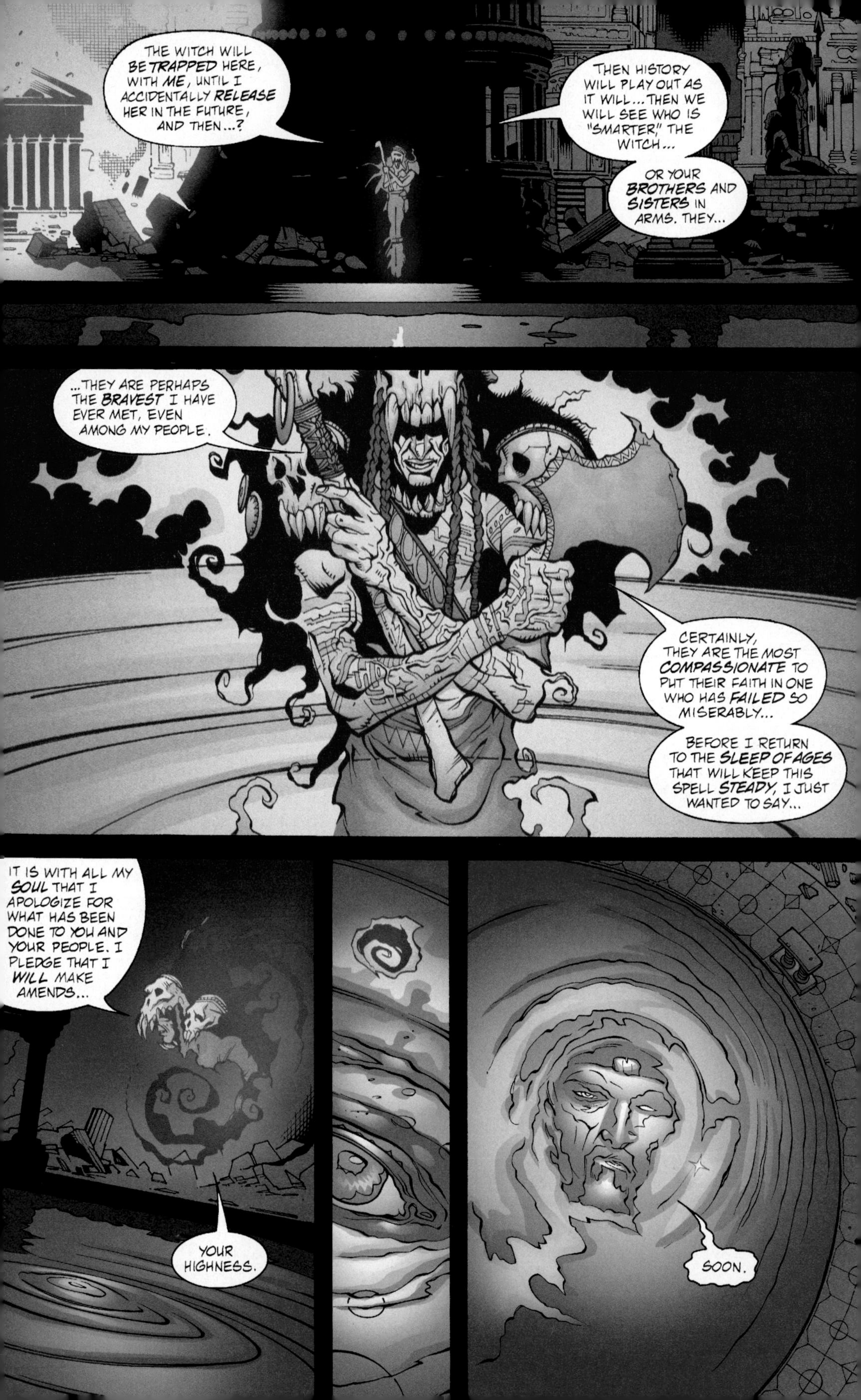
THE WITCH WILL BE TRAPPED HERE, WITH ME, UNTIL I ACCIDENTALLY RELEASE HER IN THE FUTURE, AND THEN...?
THEN HISTORY WILL PLAY OUT AS IT WILL... THEN WE WILL SEE WHO IS "SMARTER," THE WITCH...
OR YOUR BROTHERS AND SISTERS IN ARMS. THEY...
...THEY ARE PERHAPS THE BRAVEST I HAVE EVER MET, EVEN AMONG MY PEOPLE.
CERTAINLY, THEY ARE THE MOST COMPASSIONATE TO PUT THEIR FAITH IN ONE WHO HAS FAILED SO MISERABLY...
BEFORE I RETURN TO THE SLEEP OF AGES THAT WILL KEEP THIS SPELL STEADY, I JUST WANTED TO SAY...
IT IS WITH ALL MY SOUL THAT I APOLOGIZE FOR WHAT HAS BEEN DONE TO YOU AND YOUR PEOPLE. I PLEDGE THAT I WILL MAKE AMENDS...
YOUR HIGHNESS.
SOON.

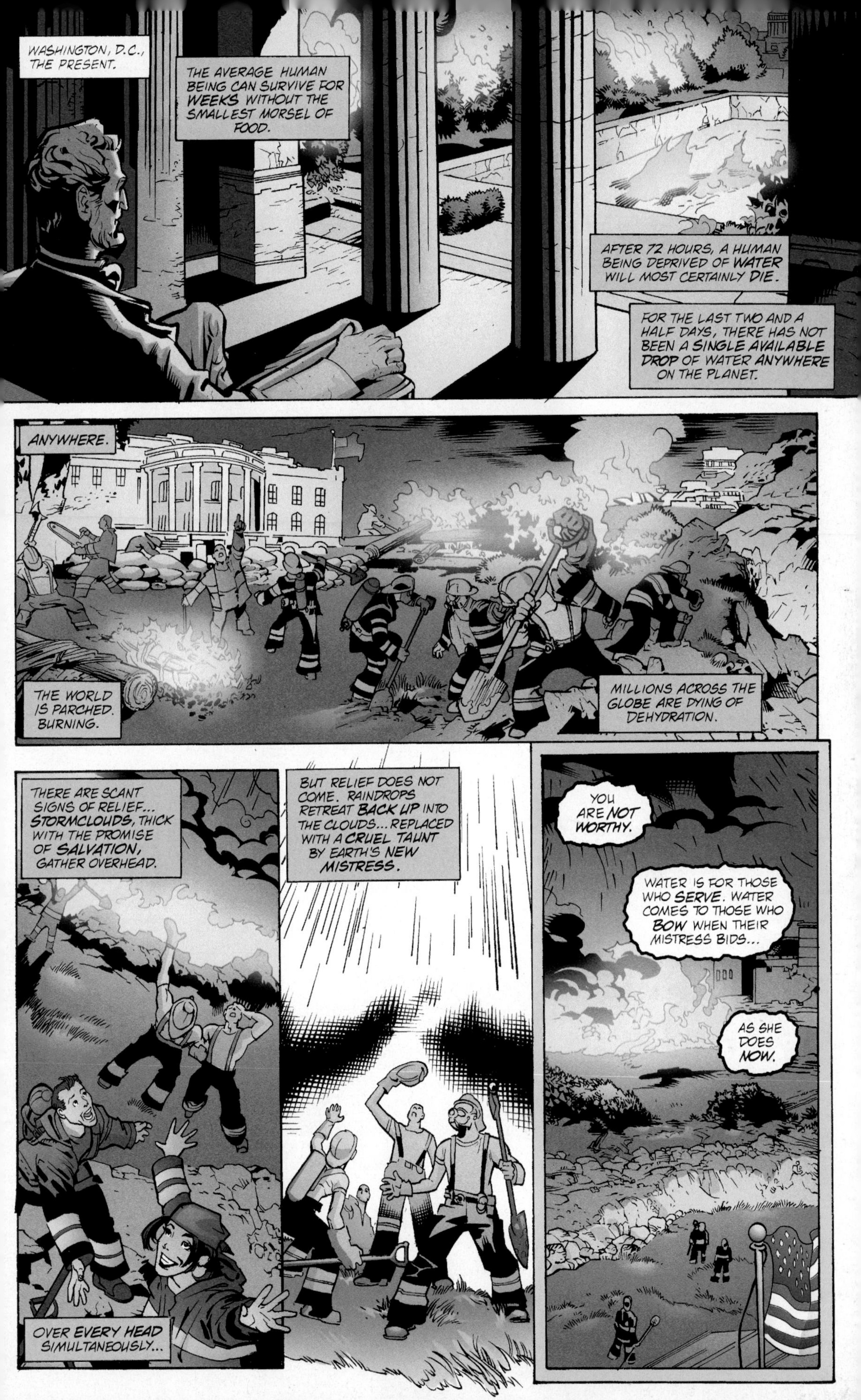

WASHINGTON, D.C., THE PRESENT.
THE AVERAGE HUMAN BEING CAN SURVIVE FOR WEEKS WITHOUT THE SMALLEST MORSEL OF FOOD.
AFTER 72 HOURS, A HUMAN BEING DEPRIVED OF WATER WILL MOST CERTAINLY DIE.
FOR THE LAST TWO AND A HALF DAYS, THERE HAS NOT BEEN A SINGLE AVAILABLE DROP OF WATER ANYWHERE ON THE PLANET.
ANYWHERE.
THE WORLD IS PARCHED. BURNING.
MILLIONS ACROSS THE GLOBE ARE DYING OF DEHYDRATION.
THERE ARE SCANT SIGNS OF RELIEF... STORMCLOUDS, THICK WITH THE PROMISE OF SALVATION, GATHER OVERHEAD.
OVER EVERY HEAD SIMULTANEOUSLY...
BUT RELIEF DOES NOT COME. RAINDROPS RETREAT BACK UP INTO THE CLOUDS... REPLACED WITH A CRUEL TAUNT BY EARTH'S NEW MISTRESS.
YOU ARE NOT WORTHY.
WATER IS FOR THOSE WHO SERVE. WATER COMES TO THOSE WHO BOW WHEN THEIR MISTRESS BIDS...
AS SHE DOES NOW.

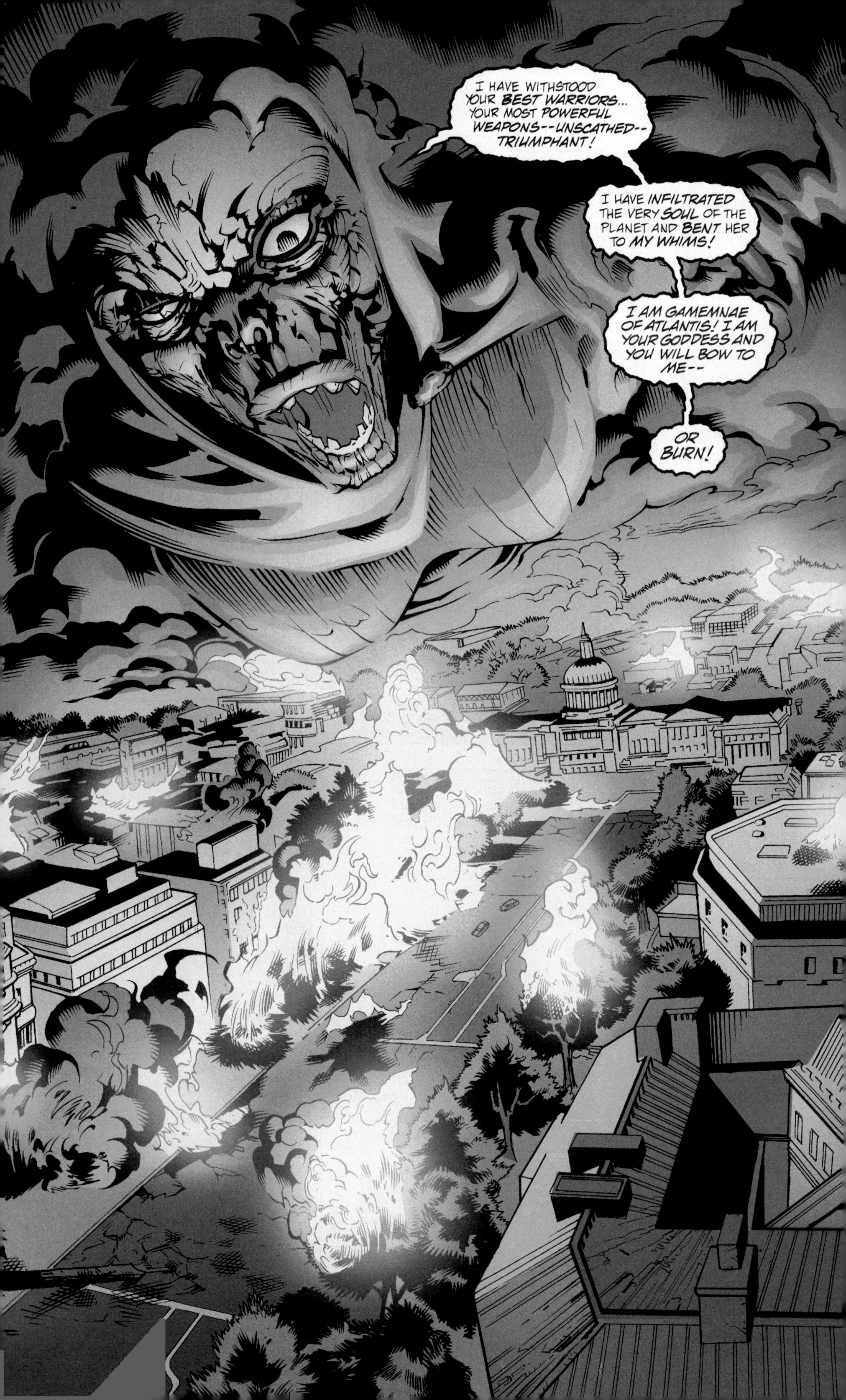
I HAVE WITHSTOOD YOUR BEST WARRIORS... YOUR MOST POWERFUL WEAPONS--UNSCATHED--TRIUMPHANT!
I HAVE INFILTRATED THE VERY SOUL OF THE PLANET AND BENT HER TO MY WHIMS!
I AM GAMEMNAE OF ATLANTIS! I AM YOUR GODDESS AND YOU WILL BOW TO ME--
OR BURN!

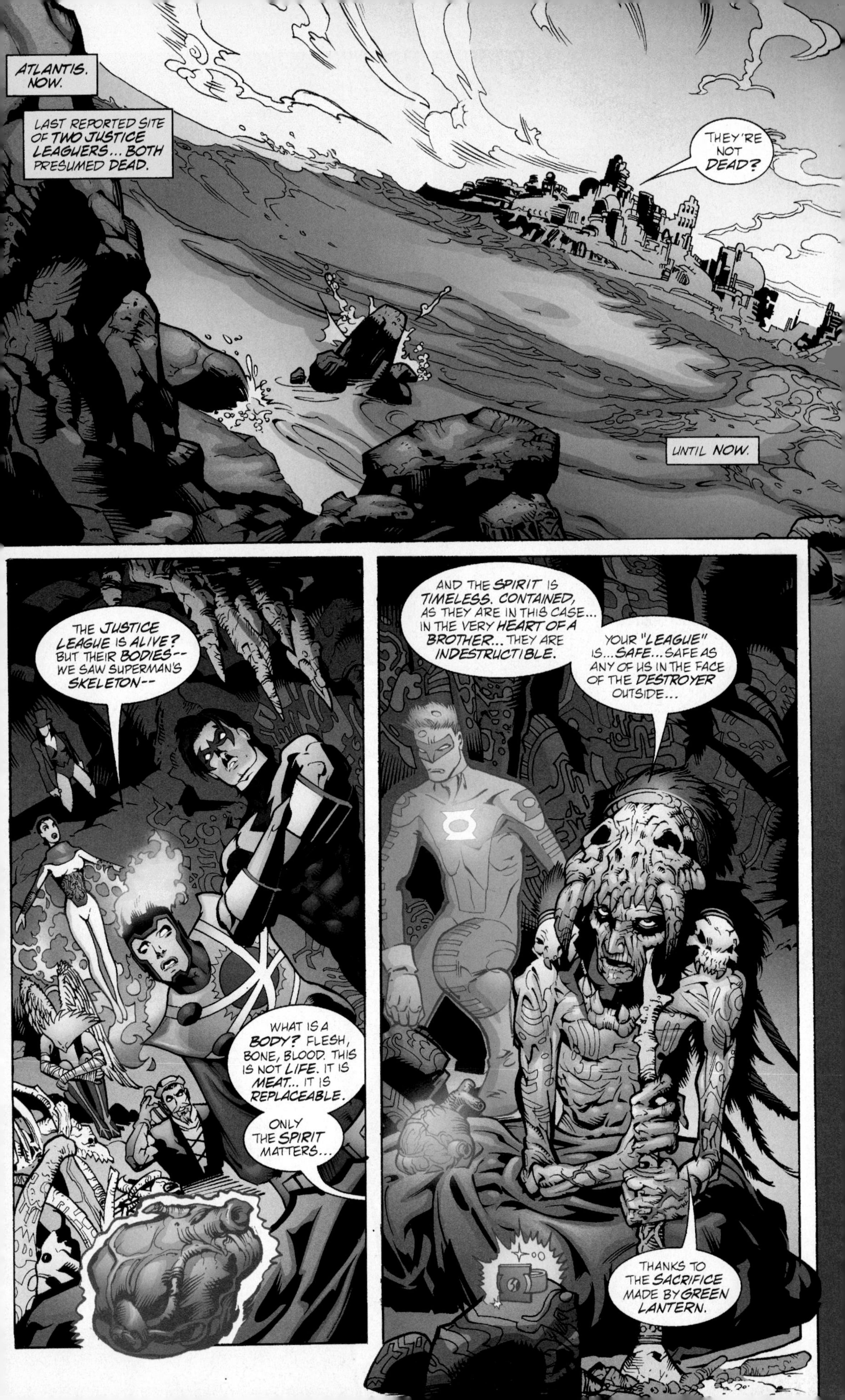
ATLANTIS. NOW.
LAST REPORTED SITE OF TWO JUSTICE LEAGUERS... BOTH PRESUMED DEAD.
THEY'RE NOT DEAD?
UNTIL NOW.
THE JUSTICE LEAGUE IS ALIVE? BUT THEIR BODIES-- WE SAW SUPERMAN'S SKELETON--
WHAT IS A BODY? FLESH, BONE, BLOOD. THIS IS NOT LIFE. IT IS MEAT... IT IS REPLACEABLE.
ONLY THE SPIRIT MATTERS...
AND THE SPIRIT IS TIMELESS. CONTAINED, AS THEY ARE IN THIS CASE... IN THE VERY HEART OF A BROTHER... THEY ARE INDESTRUCTIBLE.
YOUR "LEAGUE" IS... SAFE... SAFE AS ANY OF US IN THE FACE OF THE DESTROYER OUTSIDE...
THANKS TO THE SACRIFICE MADE BY GREEN LANTERN.

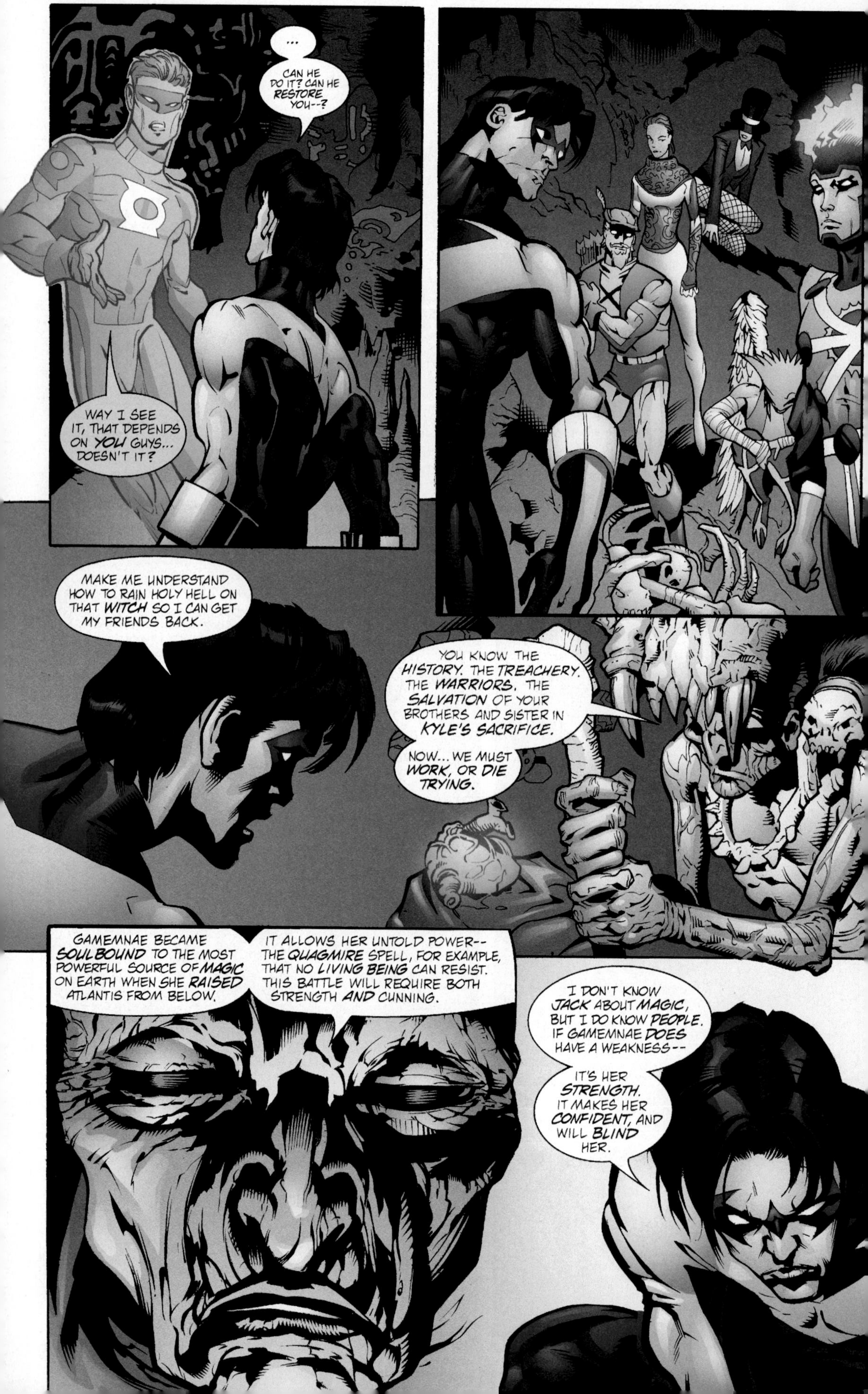
...
CAN HE DO IT? CAN HE RESTORE YOU--?
WAY I SEE IT, THAT DEPENDS ON YOU GUYS... DOESN'T IT?
MAKE ME UNDERSTAND HOW TO RAIN HOLY HELL ON THAT WITCH SO I CAN GET MY FRIENDS BACK.
YOU KNOW THE HISTORY. THE TREACHERY. THE WARRIORS. THE SALVATION OF YOUR BROTHERS AND SISTER IN KYLE'S SACRIFICE.
NOW... WE MUST WORK, OR DIE TRYING.
GAMEMNAE BECAME SOULBOUND TO THE MOST POWERFUL SOURCE OF MAGIC ON EARTH WHEN SHE RAISED ATLANTIS FROM BELOW.
IT ALLOWS HER UNTOLD POWER-- THE QUAGMIRE SPELL, FOR EXAMPLE, THAT NO LIVING BEING CAN RESIST. THIS BATTLE WILL REQUIRE BOTH STRENGTH AND CUNNING.
I DON'T KNOW JACK ABOUT MAGIC, BUT I DO KNOW PEOPLE. IF GAMEMNAE DOES HAVE A WEAKNESS--
IT'S HER STRENGTH. IT MAKES HER CONFIDENT, AND WILL BLIND HER.

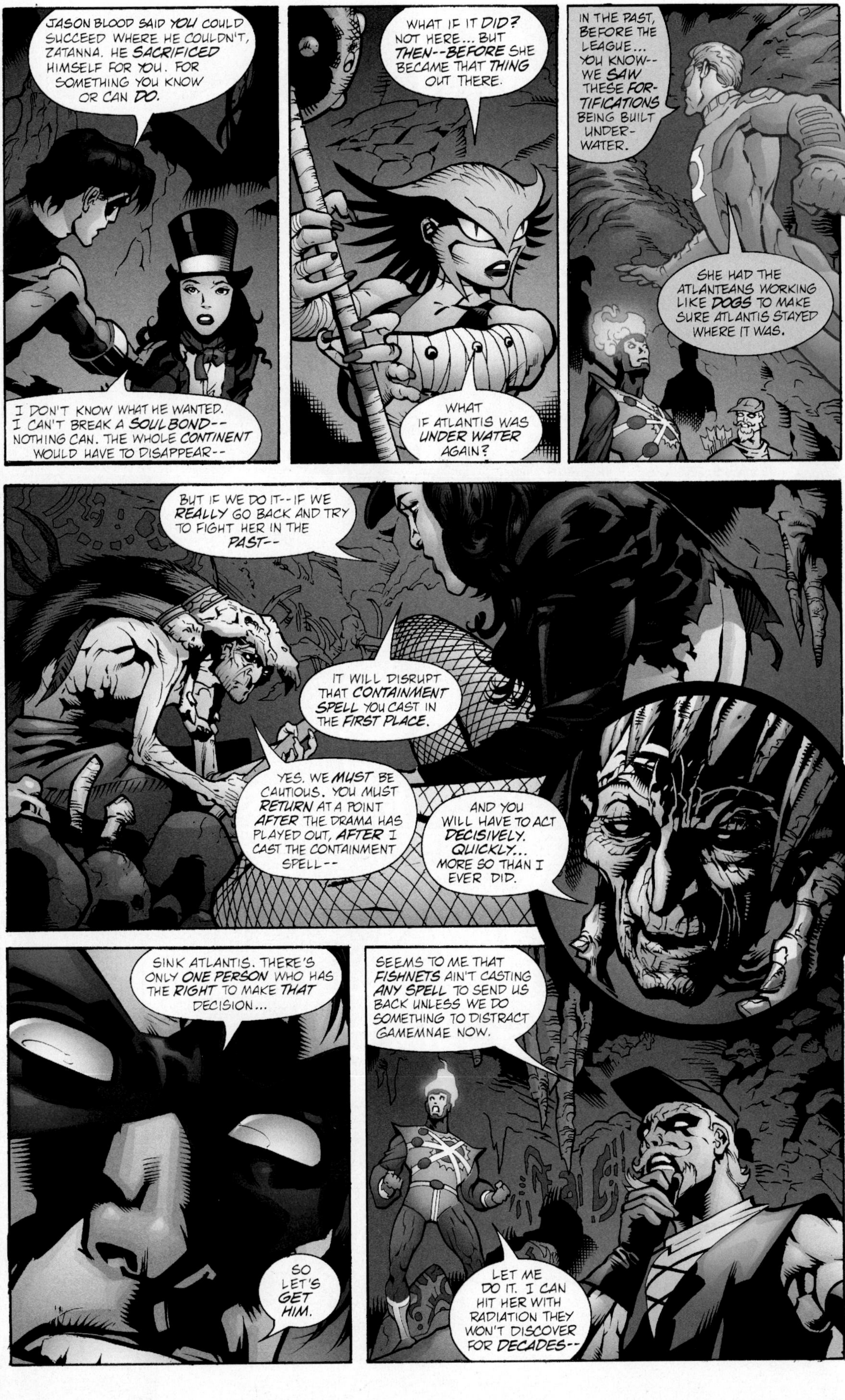
JASON BLOOD SAID YOU COULD SUCCEED WHERE HE COULDN'T, ZATANNA. HE SACRIFICED HIMSELF FOR YOU. FOR SOMETHING YOU KNOW OR CAN DO.
I DON'T KNOW WHAT HE WANTED. I CAN'T BREAK A SOULBOND-- NOTHING CAN. THE WHOLE CONTINENT WOULD HAVE TO DISAPPEAR--
WHAT IF IT DID? NOT HERE... BUT THEN--BEFORE SHE BECAME THAT THING OUT THERE.
WHAT IF ATLANTIS WAS UNDER WATER AGAIN?
IN THE PAST, BEFORE THE LEAGUE... YOU KNOW-- WE SAW THESE FORTIFICATIONS BEING BUILT UNDERWATER.
SHE HAD THE ATLANTEANS WORKING LIKE DOGS TO MAKE SURE ATLANTIS STAYED WHERE IT WAS.
BUT IF WE DO IT--IF WE REALLY GO BACK AND TRY TO FIGHT HER IN THE PAST--
IT WILL DISRUPT THAT CONTAINMENT SPELL YOU CAST IN THE FIRST PLACE.
YES. WE MUST BE CAUTIOUS. YOU MUST RETURN AT A POINT AFTER THE DRAMA HAS PLAYED OUT, AFTER I CAST THE CONTAINMENT SPELL--
AND YOU WILL HAVE TO ACT DECISIVELY. QUICKLY... MORE SO THAN I EVER DID.
SINK ATLANTIS. THERE'S ONLY ONE PERSON WHO HAS THE RIGHT TO MAKE THAT DECISION...
SO LET'S GET HIM.
SEEMS TO ME THAT FISHNETS AIN'T CASTING ANY SPELL TO SEND US BACK UNLESS WE DO SOMETHING TO DISTRACT GAMEMNAE NOW.
LET ME DO IT. I CAN HIT HER WITH RADIATION THEY WON'T DISCOVER FOR DECADES--

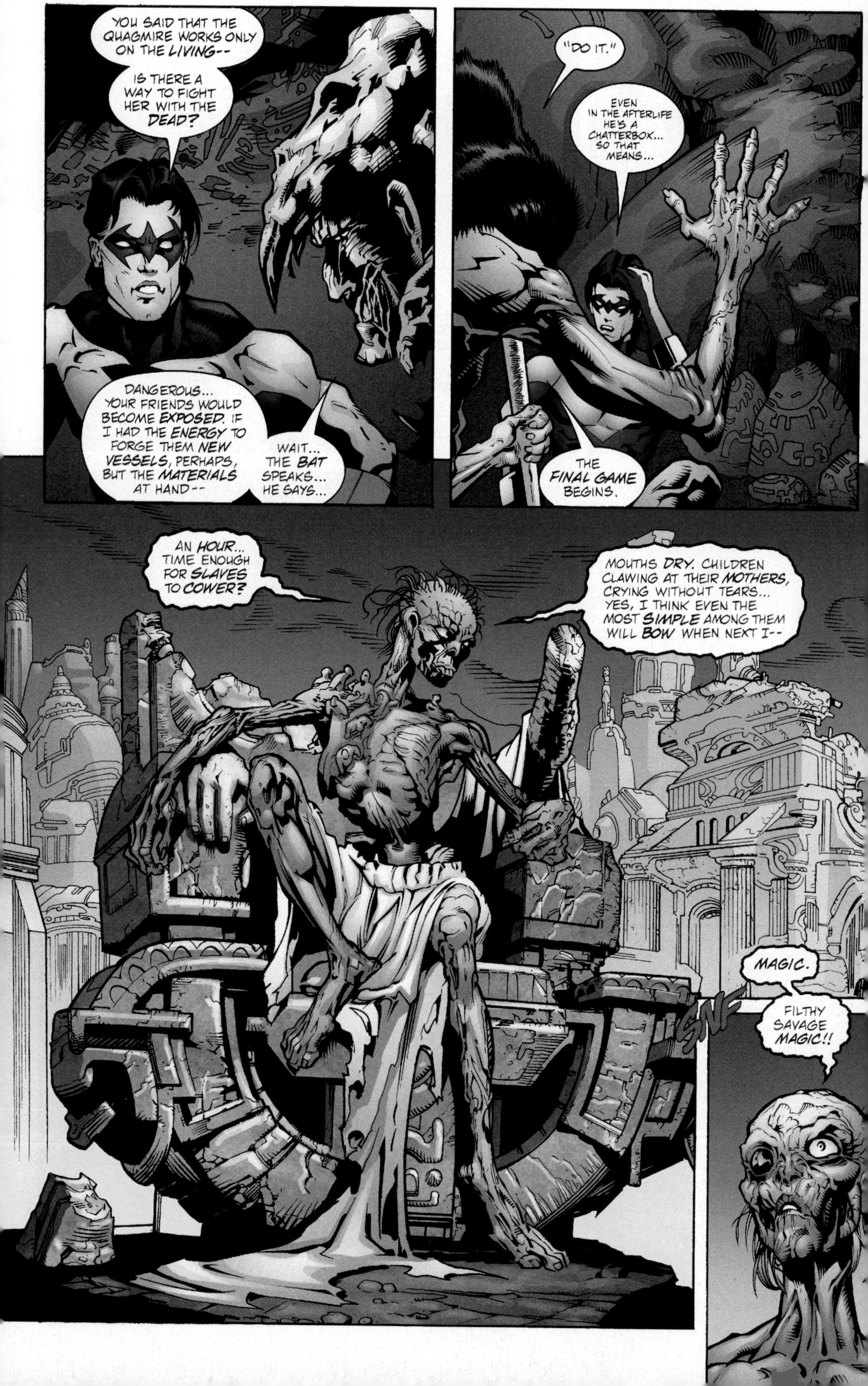
YOU SAID THAT THE QUAGMIRE WORKS ONLY ON THE LIVING--
IS THERE A WAY TO FIGHT HER WITH THE DEAD?
DANGEROUS... YOUR FRIENDS WOULD BECOME EXPOSED. IF I HAD THE ENERGY TO FORGE THEM NEW VESSELS, PERHAPS, BUT THE MATERIALS AT HAND--
WAIT... THE BAT SPEAKS... HE SAYS...
"DO IT."
EVEN IN THE AFTERLIFE HE'S A CHATTERBOX... SO THAT MEANS...
THE FINAL GAME BEGINS.
AN HOUR... TIME ENOUGH FOR SLAVES TO COWER?
MOUTHS DRY. CHILDREN CLAWING AT THEIR MOTHERS, CRYING WITHOUT TEARS... YES, I THINK EVEN THE MOST SIMPLE AMONG THEM WILL BOW WHEN NEXT I--
SNF
MAGIC.
FILTHY SAVAGE MAGIC!!

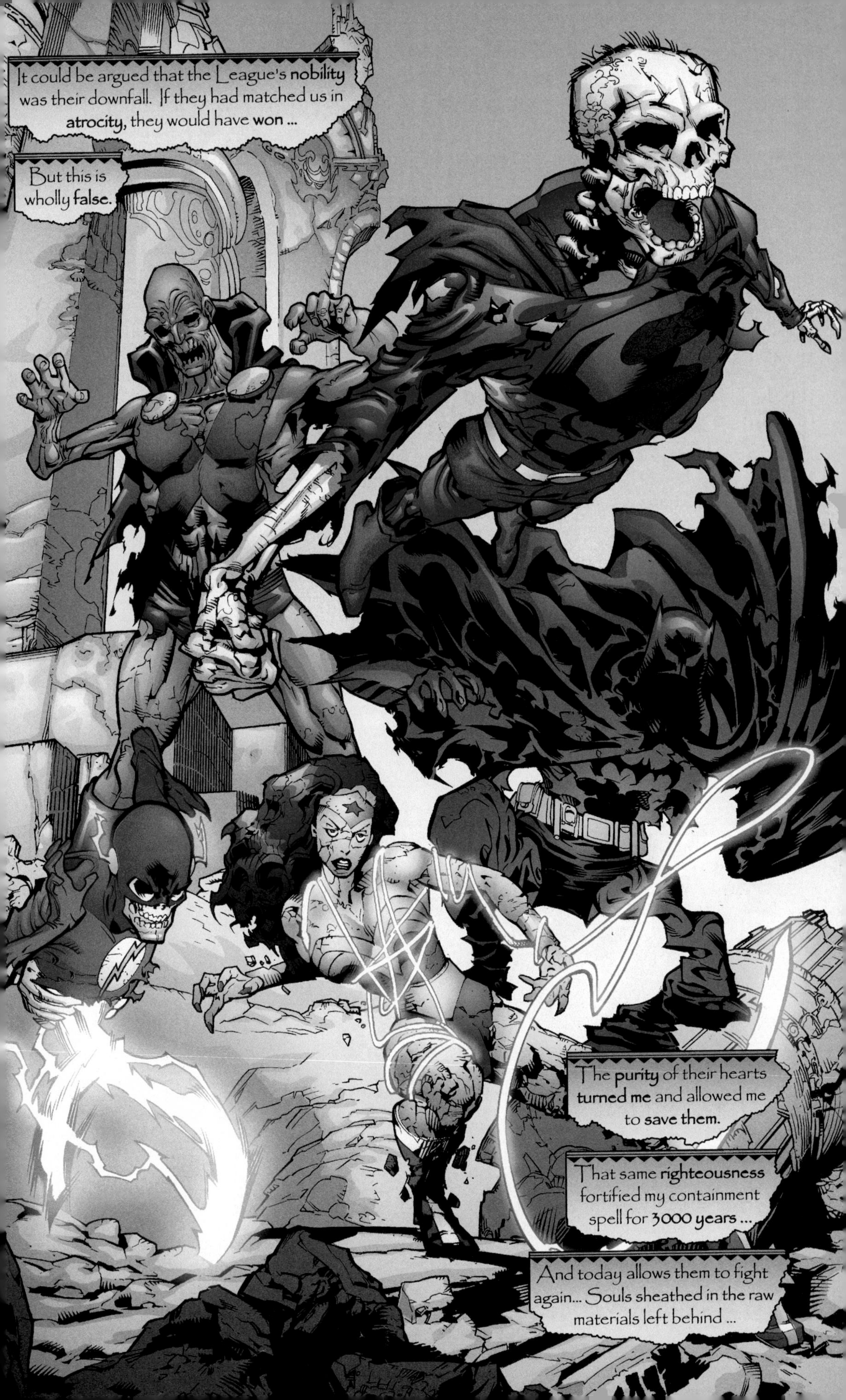
It could be argued that the League's nobility was their downfall. If they had matched us in atrocity, they would have won ...
But this is wholly false.
The purity of their hearts turned me and allowed me to save them.
That same righteousness fortified my containment spell for 3000 years ...
And today allows them to fight again... Souls sheathed in the raw materials left behind ...

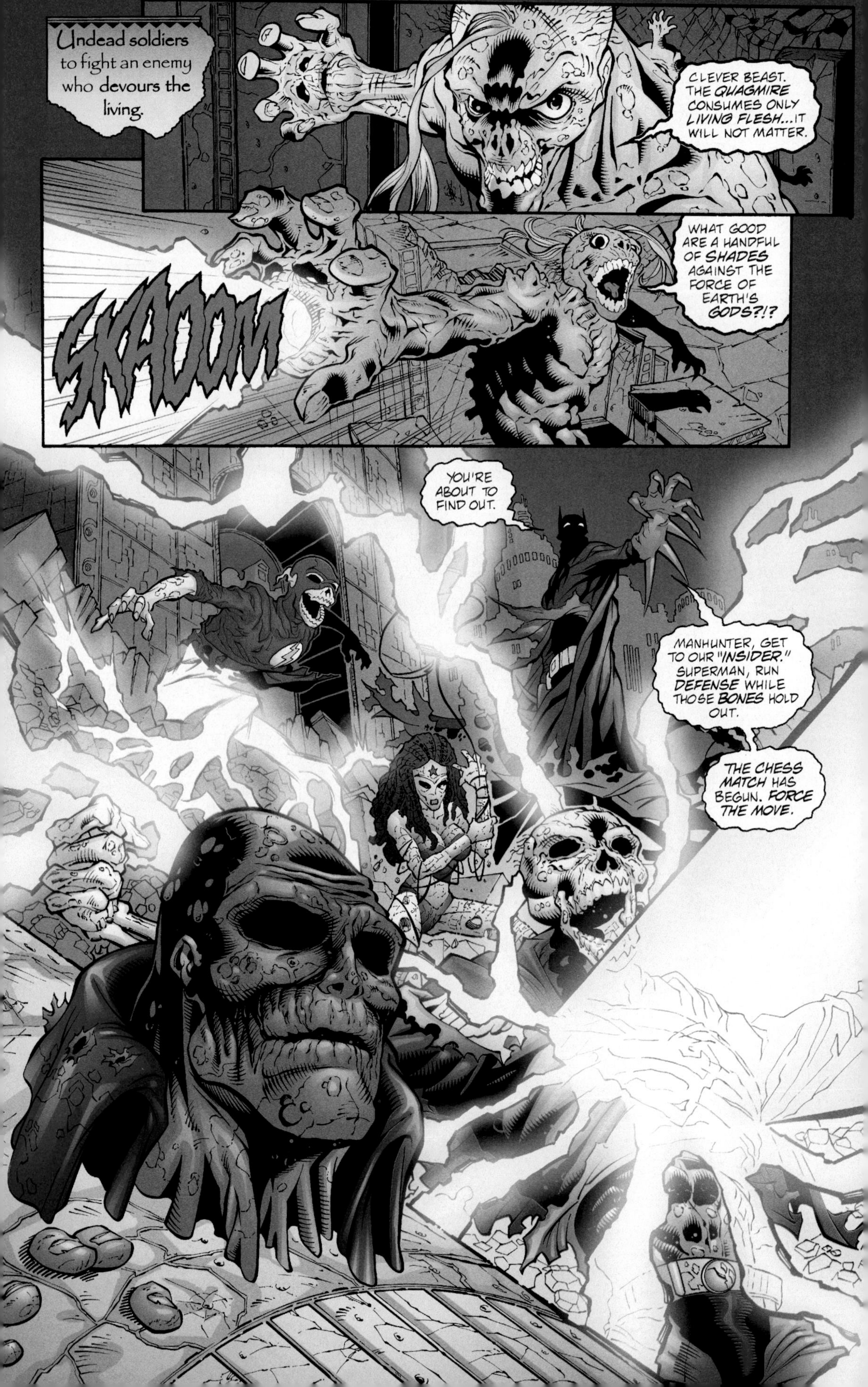
Undead soldiers to fight an enemy who devours the living.
CLEVER BEAST. THE QUAGMIRE CONSUMES ONLY LIVING FLESH...IT WILL NOT MATTER.
WHAT GOOD ARE A HANDFUL OF SHADES AGAINST THE FORCE OF EARTH'S GODS?!?
SKAOOM
YOU'RE ABOUT TO FIND OUT.
MANHUNTER, GET TO OUR "INSIDER." SUPERMAN, RUN DEFENSE WHILE THOSE BONES HOLD OUT.
THE CHESS MATCH HAS BEGUN. FORCE THE MOVE.

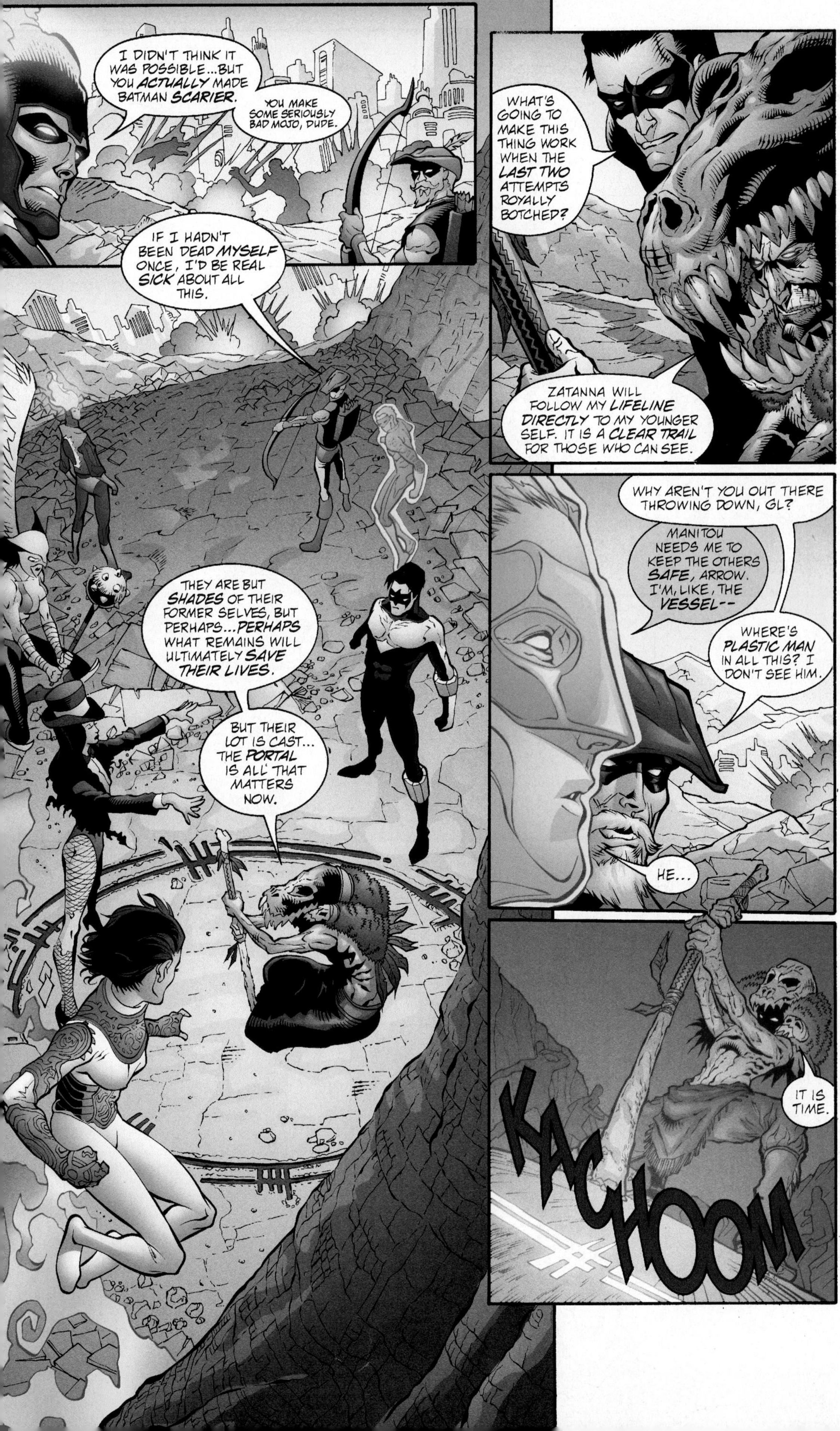
I DIDN'T THINK IT WAS POSSIBLE...BUT YOU ACTUALLY MADE BATMAN SCARIER.
YOU MAKE SOME SERIOUSLY BAD MOJO, DUDE.
IF I HADN'T BEEN DEAD MYSELF ONCE, I'D BE REAL SICK ABOUT ALL THIS.
THEY ARE BUT SHADES OF THEIR FORMER SELVES, BUT PERHAPS...PERHAPS WHAT REMAINS WILL ULTIMATELY SAVE THEIR LIVES.
BUT THEIR LOT IS CAST... THE PORTAL IS ALL THAT MATTERS NOW.
WHAT'S GOING TO MAKE THIS THING WORK WHEN THE LAST TWO ATTEMPTS ROYALLY BOTCHED?
ZATANNA WILL FOLLOW MY LIFELINE DIRECTLY TO MY YOUNGER SELF. IT IS A CLEAR TRAIL FOR THOSE WHO CAN SEE.
WHY AREN'T YOU OUT THERE THROWING DOWN, GL?
MANITOU NEEDS ME TO KEEP THE OTHERS SAFE, ARROW. I'M, LIKE, THE VESSEL--
WHERE'S PLASTIC MAN IN ALL THIS? I DON'T SEE HIM.
HE...
IT IS TIME.
KACHOOM

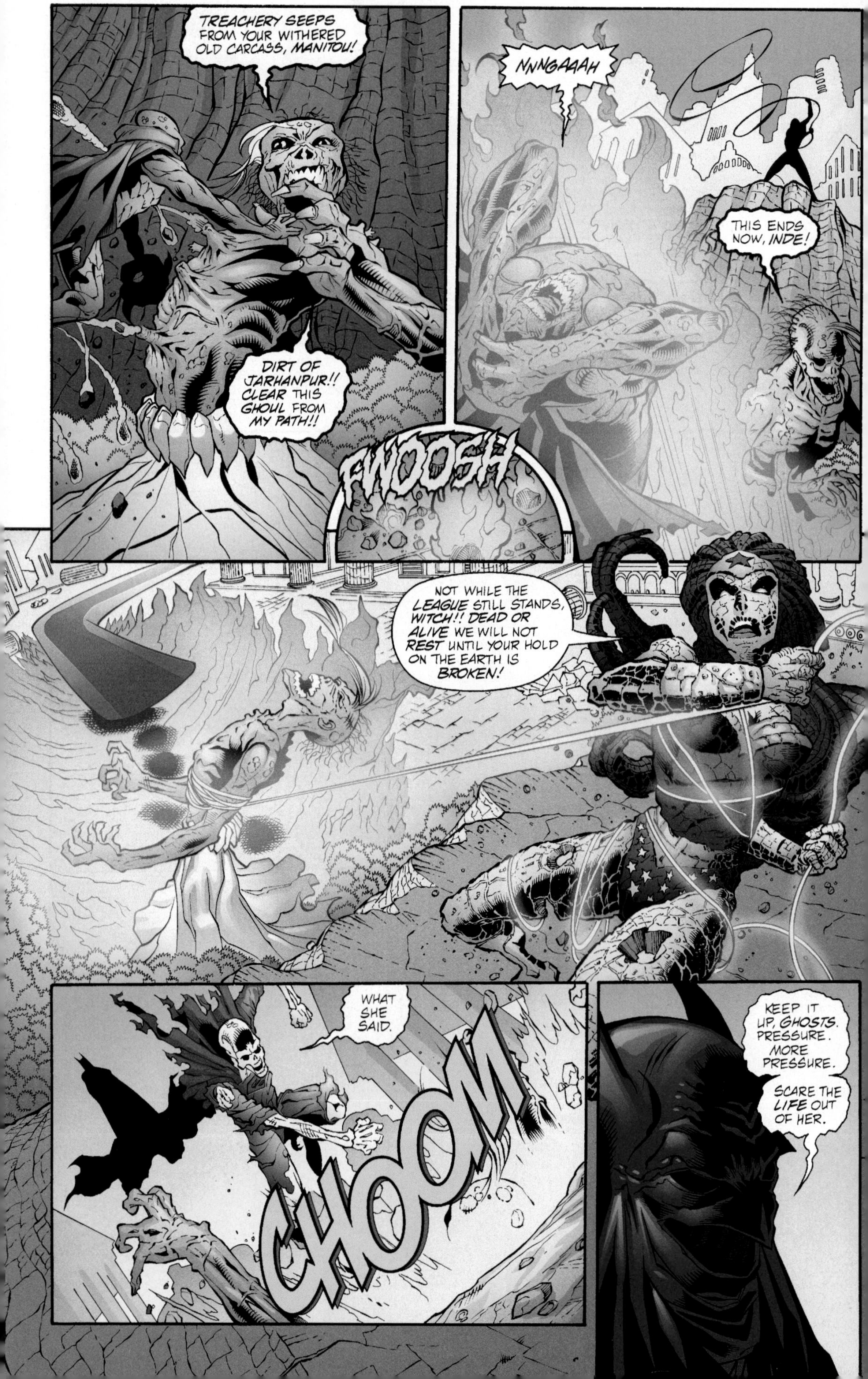
TREACHERY SEEPS FROM YOUR WITHERED OLD CARCASS, MANITOU!
DIRT OF JARHANPUR!! CLEAR THIS GHOUL FROM MY PATH!!
NNNGAAAH
THIS ENDS NOW, INDE!
FWOOSH
NOT WHILE THE LEAGUE STILL STANDS, WITCH!! DEAD OR ALIVE WE WILL NOT REST UNTIL YOUR HOLD ON THE EARTH IS BROKEN!
WHAT SHE SAID.
CHOOM
KEEP IT UP, GHOSTS. PRESSURE. MORE PRESSURE.
SCARE THE LIFE OUT OF HER.

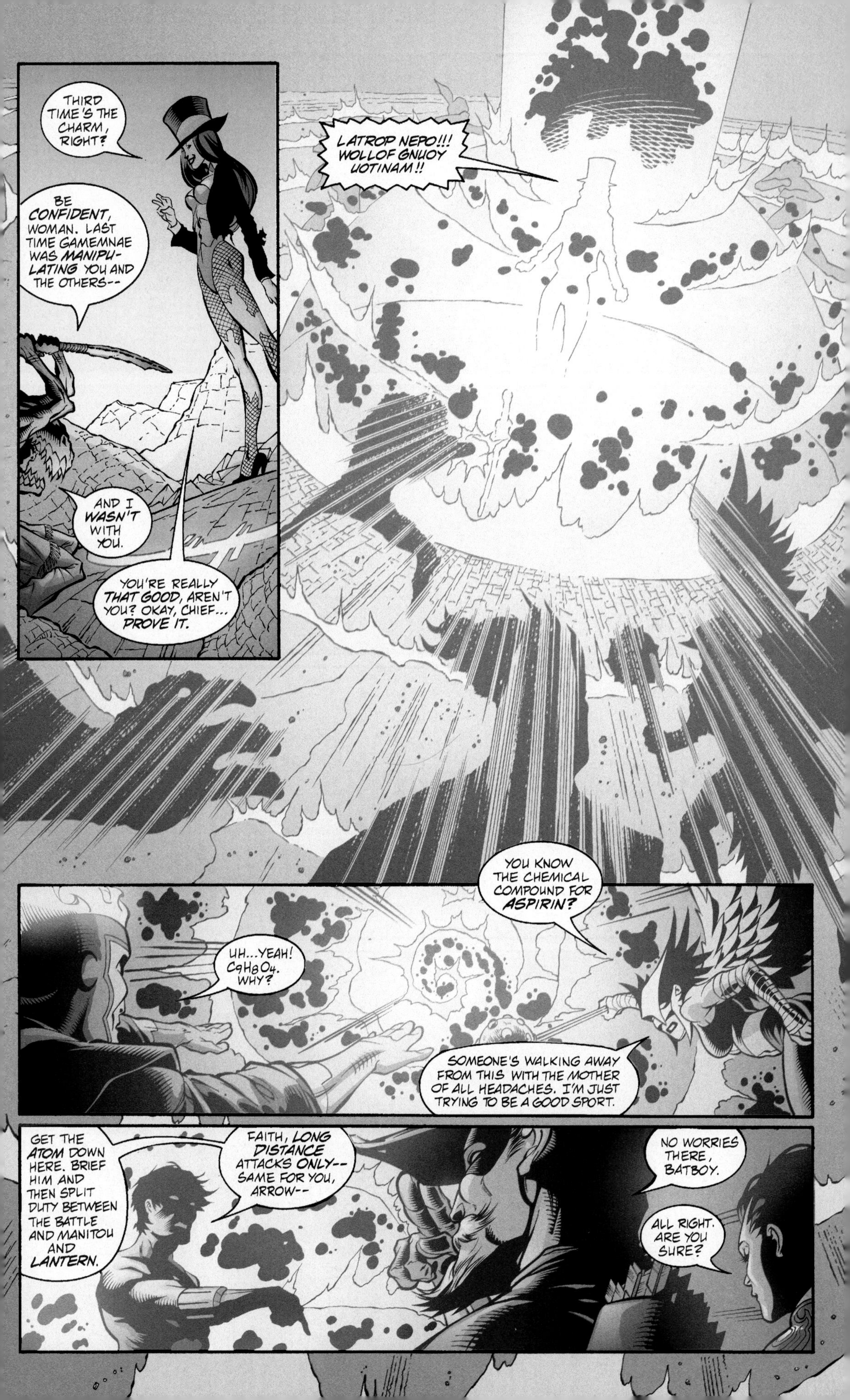
THIRD TIME'S THE CHARM, RIGHT?
BE CONFIDENT, WOMAN. LAST TIME GAMEMNAE WAS MANIPULATING YOU AND THE OTHERS--
AND I WASN'T WITH YOU.
YOU'RE REALLY THAT GOOD, AREN'T YOU? OKAY, CHIEF... PROVE IT.
LATROP NEPO!!! WOLLOF GNUOY UOTINAM!!
YOU KNOW THE CHEMICAL COMPOUND FOR ASPIRIN?
UH...YEAH! C9H8O4. WHY?
SOMEONE'S WALKING AWAY FROM THIS WITH THE MOTHER OF ALL HEADACHES. I'M JUST TRYING TO BE A GOOD SPORT.
GET THE ATOM DOWN HERE. BRIEF HIM AND THEN SPLIT DUTY BETWEEN THE BATTLE AND MANITOU AND LANTERN.
FAITH, LONG DISTANCE ATTACKS ONLY-- SAME FOR YOU, ARROW--
NO WORRIES THERE, BATBOY.
ALL RIGHT. ARE YOU SURE?

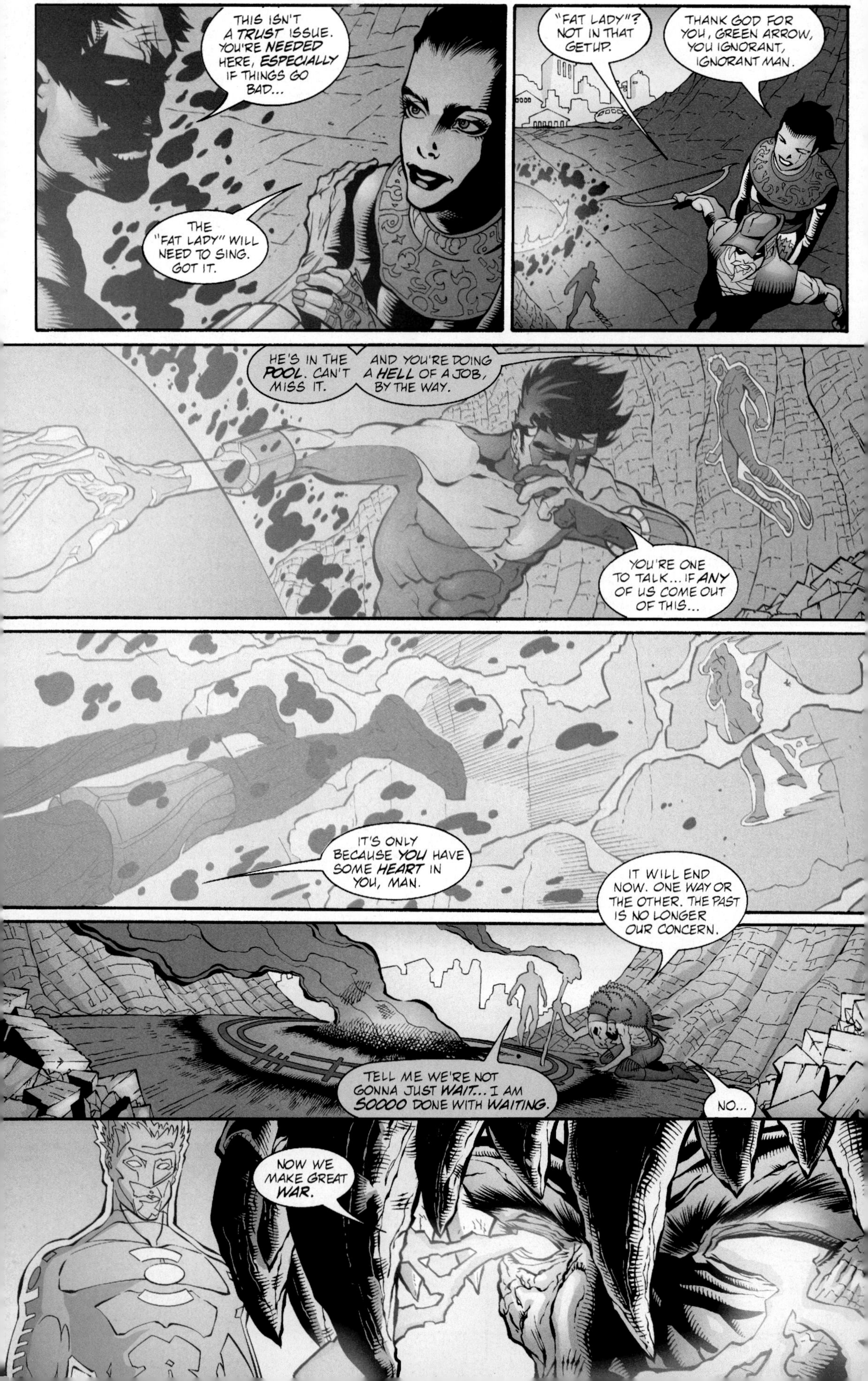
THIS ISN'T A TRUST ISSUE. YOU'RE NEEDED HERE, ESPECIALLY IF THINGS GO BAD...
THE "FAT LADY" WILL NEED TO SING. GOT IT.
"FAT LADY"? NOT IN THAT GETUP.
THANK GOD FOR YOU, GREEN ARROW, YOU IGNORANT, IGNORANT MAN.
HE'S IN THE POOL. CAN'T MISS IT.
AND YOU'RE DOING A HELL OF A JOB, BY THE WAY.
YOU'RE ONE TO TALK... IF ANY OF US COME OUT OF THIS...
IT'S ONLY BECAUSE YOU HAVE SOME HEART IN YOU, MAN.
IT WILL END NOW. ONE WAY OR THE OTHER. THE PAST IS NO LONGER OUR CONCERN.
TELL ME WE'RE NOT GONNA JUST WAIT... I AM SOOOO DONE WITH WAITING.
NO...
NOW WE MAKE GREAT WAR.

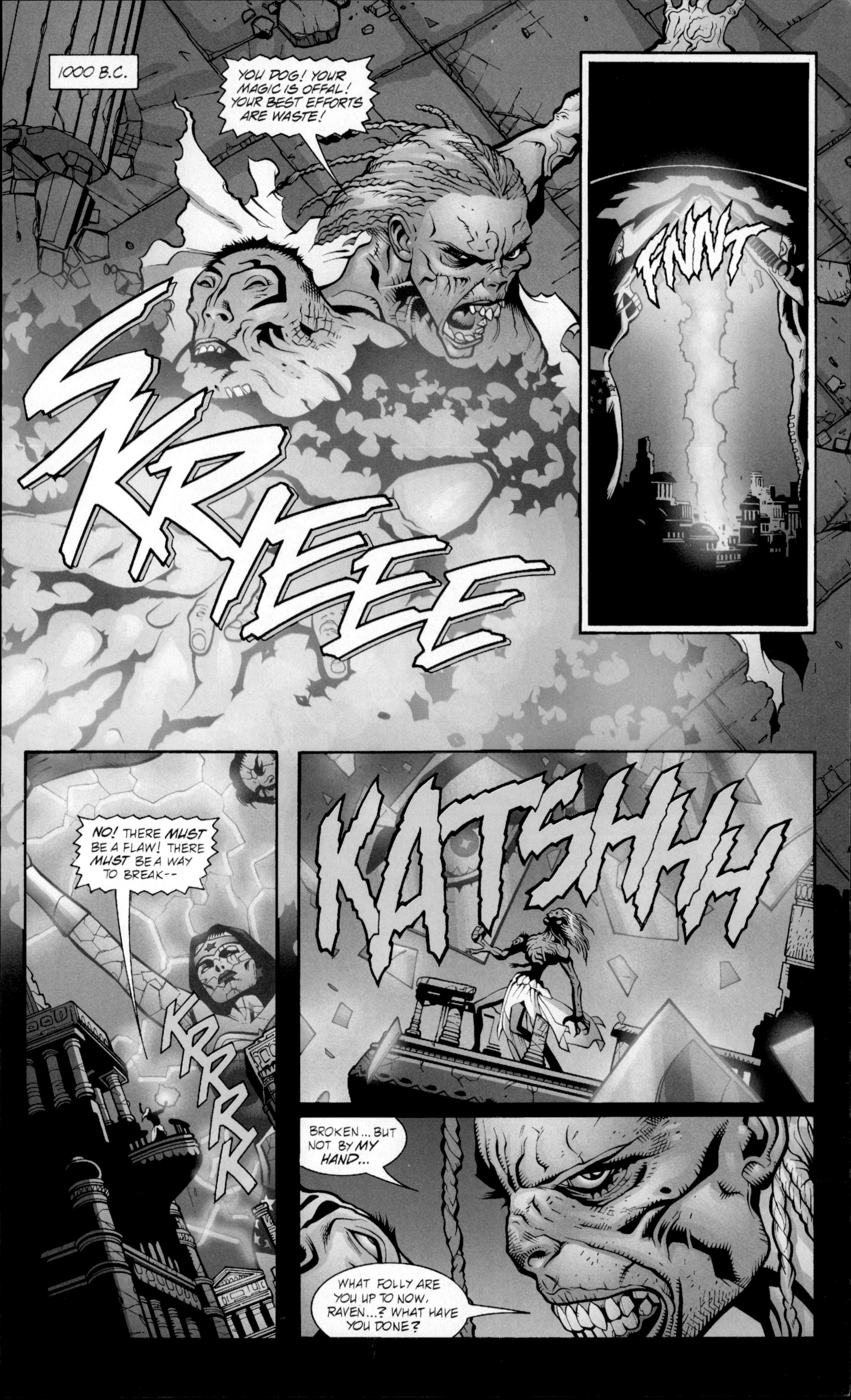
1000 B.C.
YOU DOG! YOUR MAGIC IS OFFAL! YOUR BEST EFFORTS ARE WASTE!
SKRYEEE
FNNT
NO! THERE MUST BE A FLAW! THERE MUST BE A WAY TO BREAK--
KRRRR
KATSHHH
BROKEN... BUT NOT BY MY HAND...
WHAT FOLLY ARE YOU UP TO NOW, RAVEN...? WHAT HAVE YOU DONE?

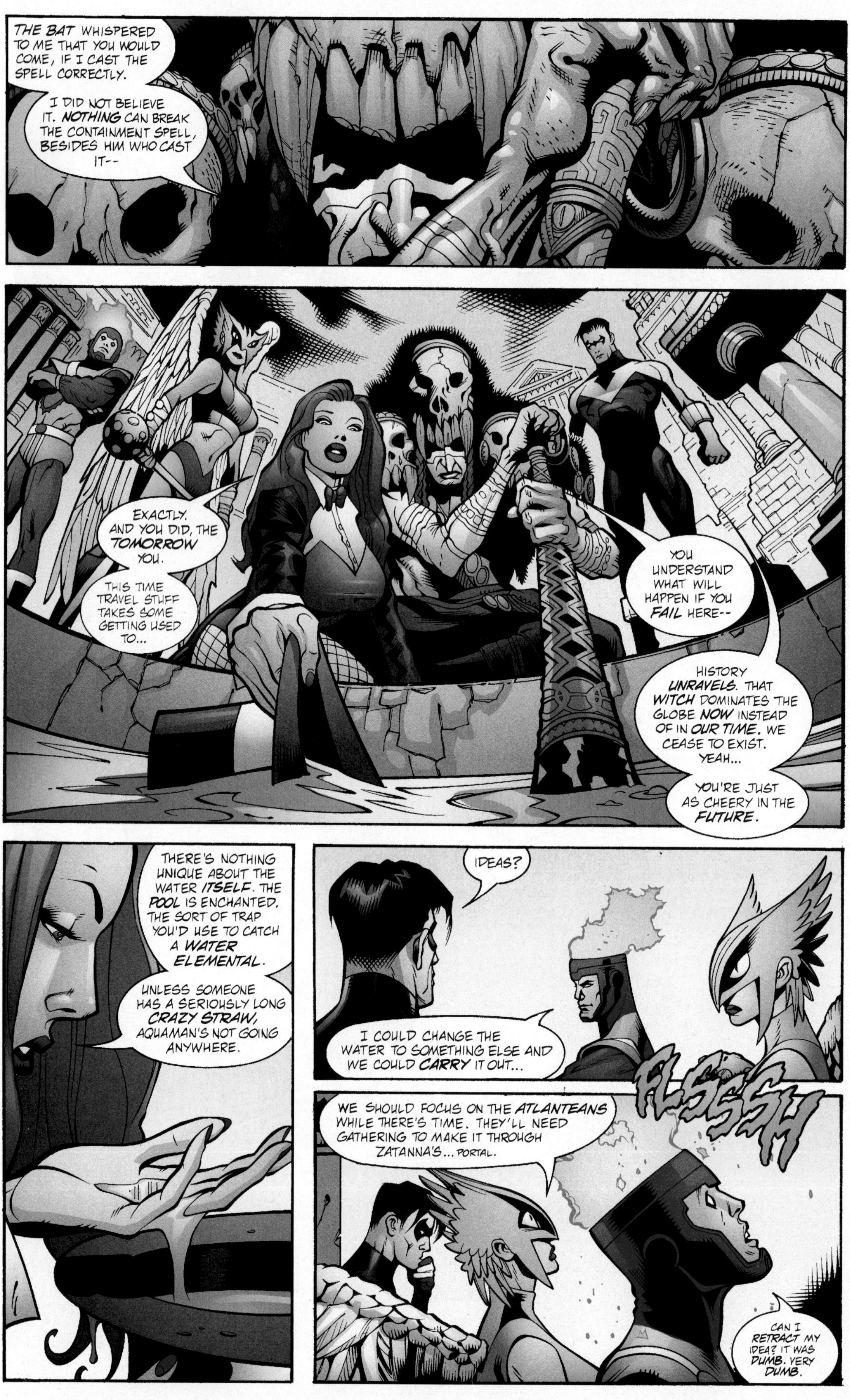
THE BAT WHISPERED TO ME THAT YOU WOULD COME, IF I CAST THE SPELL CORRECTLY.
I DID NOT BELIEVE IT. NOTHING CAN BREAK THE CONTAINMENT SPELL, BESIDES HIM WHO CAST IT--
EXACTLY. AND YOU DID, THE TOMORROW YOU.
THIS TIME TRAVEL STUFF TAKES SOME GETTING USED TO...
YOU UNDERSTAND WHAT WILL HAPPEN IF YOU FAIL HERE--
HISTORY UNRAVELS. THAT WITCH DOMINATES THE GLOBE NOW INSTEAD OF IN OUR TIME. WE CEASE TO EXIST.
YEAH...
YOU'RE JUST AS CHEERY IN THE FUTURE.
THERE'S NOTHING UNIQUE ABOUT THE WATER ITSELF. THE POOL IS ENCHANTED. THE SORT OF TRAP YOU'D USE TO CATCH A WATER ELEMENTAL.
UNLESS SOMEONE HAS A SERIOUSLY LONG CRAZY STRAW, AQUAMAN'S NOT GOING ANYWHERE.
IDEAS?
I COULD CHANGE THE WATER TO SOMETHING ELSE AND WE COULD CARRY IT OUT...
FLSSSH
WE SHOULD FOCUS ON THE ATLANTEANS WHILE THERE'S TIME. THEY'LL NEED GATHERING TO MAKE IT THROUGH ZATANNA'S... PORTAL.
CAN I RETRACT MY IDEA? IT WAS DUMB. VERY DUMB.

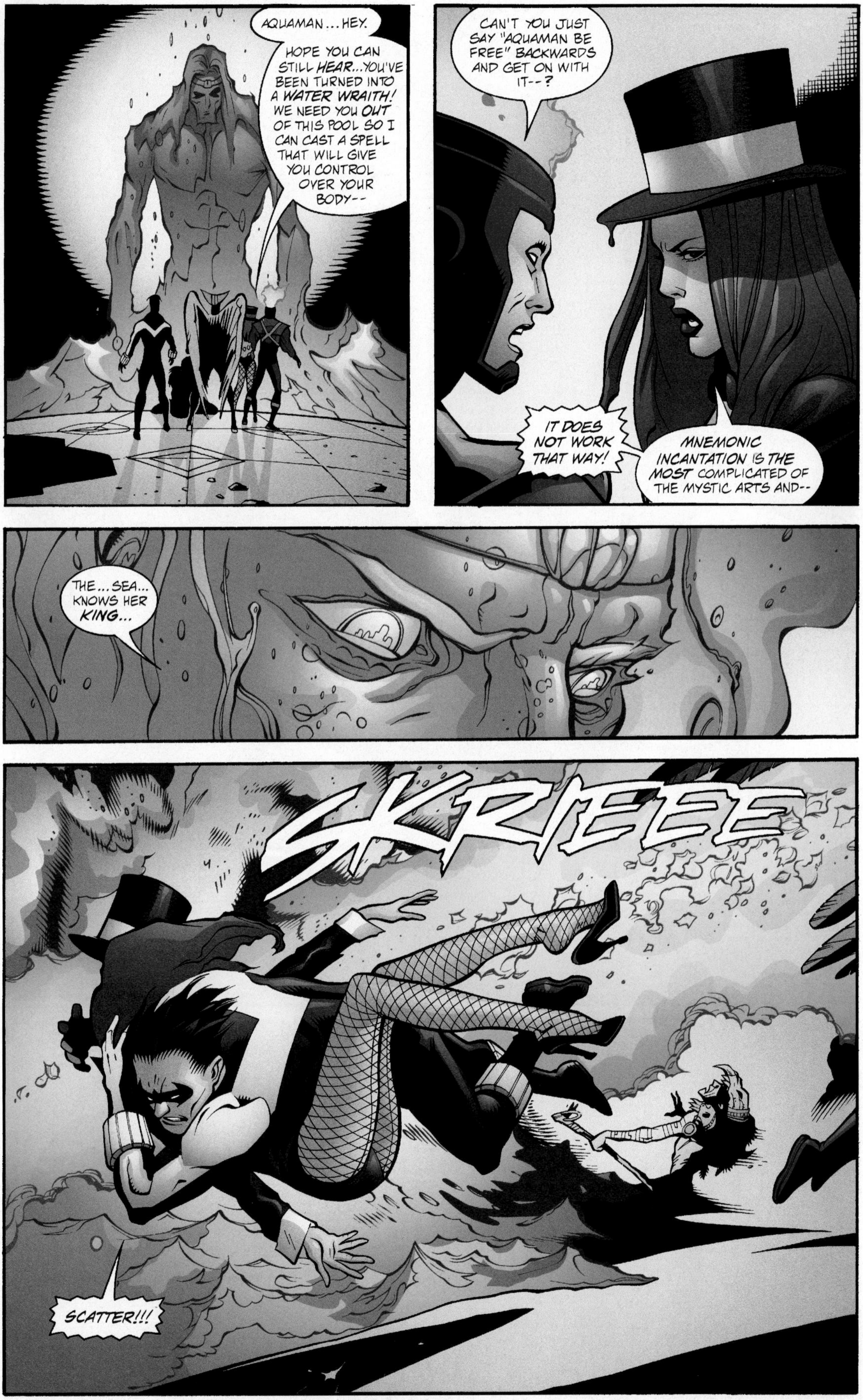
AQUAMAN... HEY.
HOPE YOU CAN STILL HEAR...YOU'VE BEEN TURNED INTO A WATER WRAITH! WE NEED YOU OUT OF THIS POOL SO I CAN CAST A SPELL THAT WILL GIVE YOU CONTROL OVER YOUR BODY--
CAN'T YOU JUST SAY "AQUAMAN BE FREE" BACKWARDS AND GET ON WITH IT--?
IT DOES NOT WORK THAT WAY!
MNEMONIC INCANTATION IS THE MOST COMPLICATED OF THE MYSTIC ARTS AND--
THE... SEA... KNOWS HER KING...
SKRIEEE
SCATTER!!!

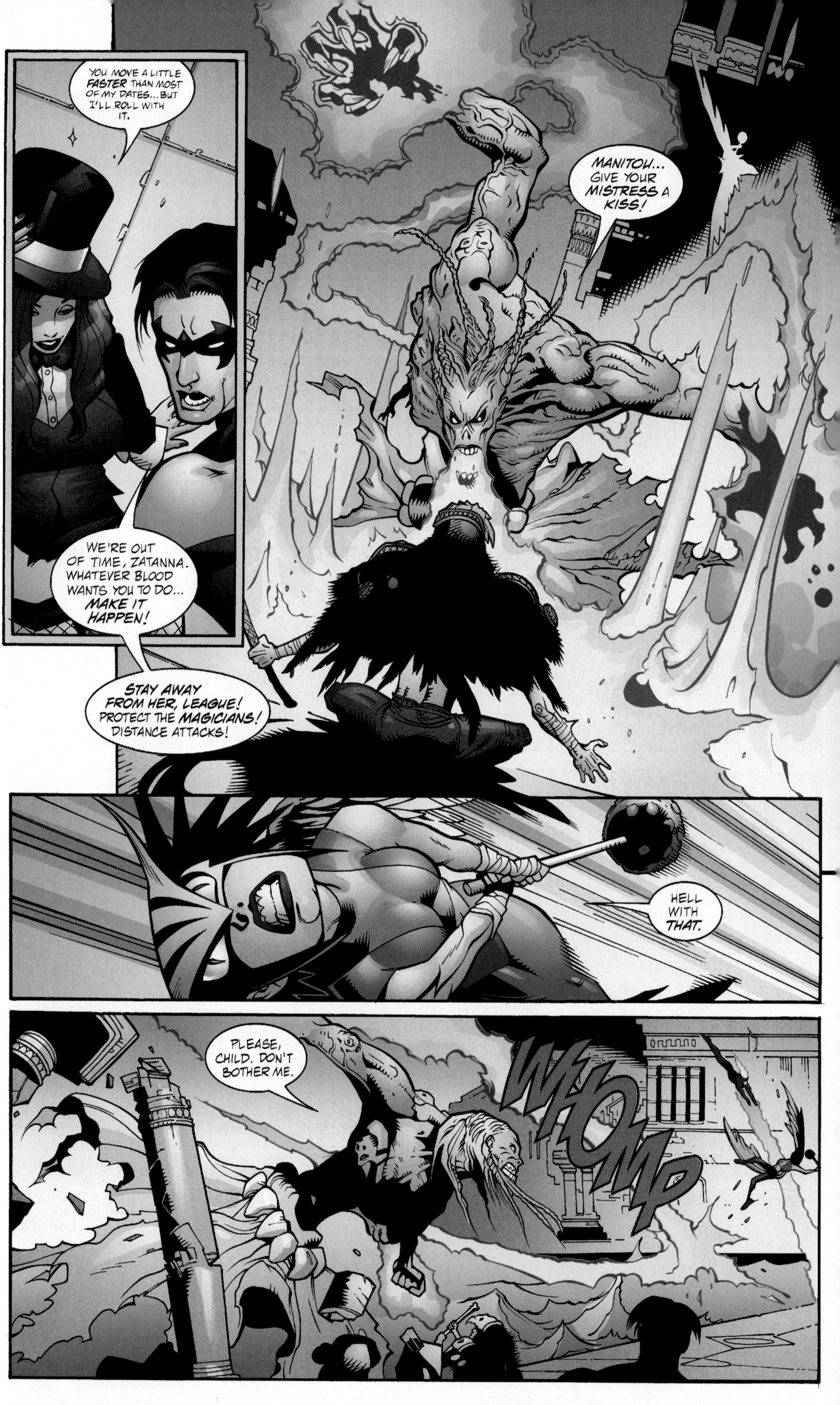

YOU MOVE A LITTLE FASTER THAN MOST OF MY DATES... BUT I'LL ROLL WITH IT.
WE'RE OUT OF TIME, ZATANNA. WHATEVER BLOOD WANTS YOU TO DO... MAKE IT HAPPEN!
MANITOU... GIVE YOUR MISTRESS A KISS!
STAY AWAY FROM HER, LEAGUE! PROTECT THE MAGICIANS! DISTANCE ATTACKS!
HELL WITH THAT.
PLEASE, CHILD. DON'T BOTHER ME.
WHOMP

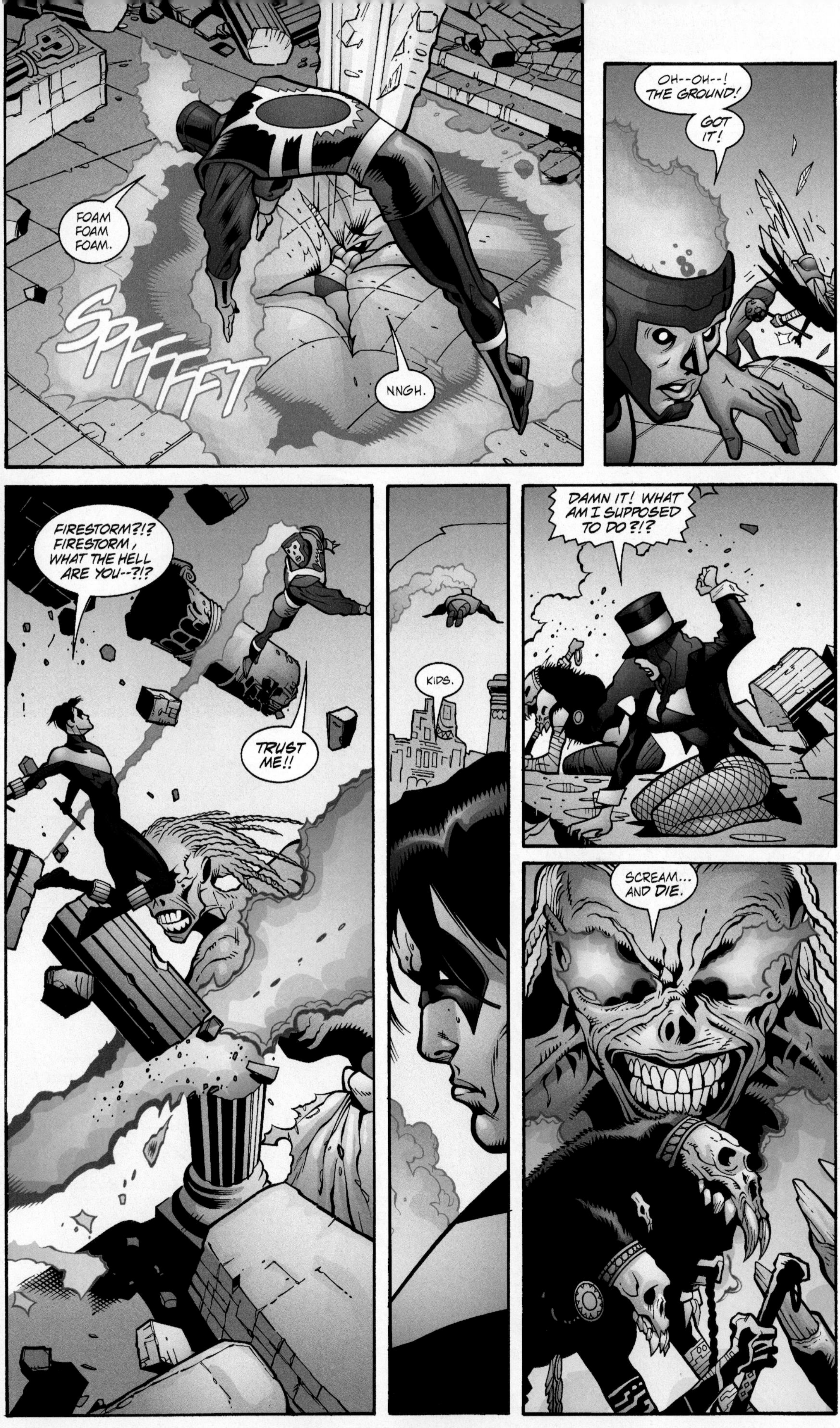
FOAM FOAM FOAM.
SPFFFFFT
NNGH.
OH--OH--! THE GROUND!
GOT IT!
FIRESTORM?!? FIRESTORM, WHAT THE HELL ARE YOU--?!?
TRUST ME!!
KIDS.
DAMN IT! WHAT AM I SUPPOSED TO DO?!?
SCREAM... AND DIE.

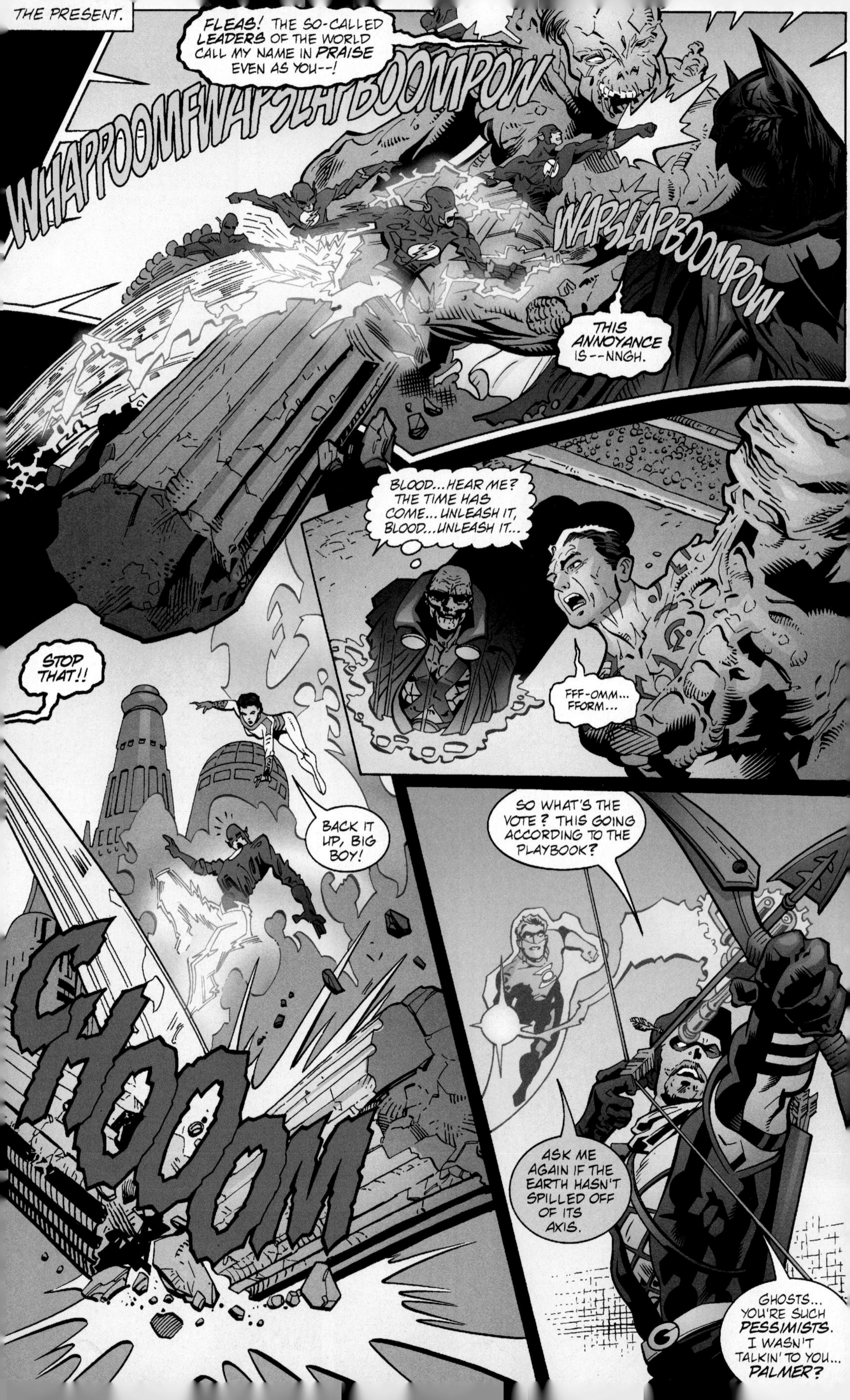
THE PRESENT.
FLEAS! THE SO-CALLED LEADERS OF THE WORLD CALL MY NAME IN PRAISE EVEN AS YOU--!
WHAPPOOMFWAPSLAPBOOMPOW
WAPSLAPBOOMPOW
THIS ANNOYANCE IS--NNGH.
BLOOD...HEAR ME? THE TIME HAS COME...UNLEASH IT, BLOOD...UNLEASH IT...
FFF-OMM... FFORM...
STOP THAT!!
BACK IT UP, BIG BOY!
CHOOOM
SO WHAT'S THE VOTE? THIS GOING ACCORDING TO THE PLAYBOOK?
ASK ME AGAIN IF THE EARTH HASN'T SPILLED OFF OF ITS AXIS.
GHOSTS... YOU'RE SUCH PESSIMISTS. I WASN'T TALKIN' TO YOU... PALMER?

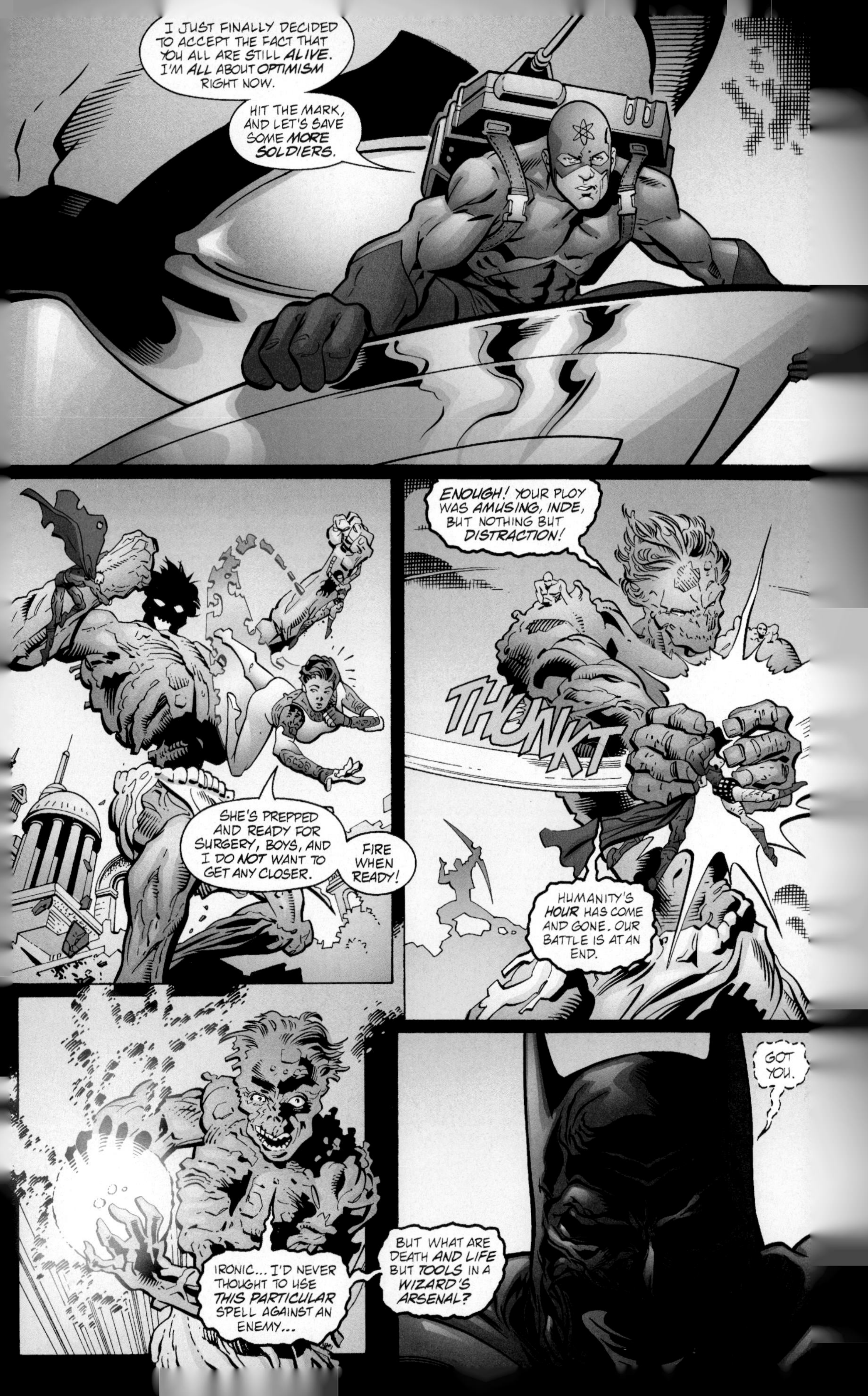
I JUST FINALLY DECIDED TO ACCEPT THE FACT THAT YOU ALL ARE STILL ALIVE. I'M ALL ABOUT OPTIMISM RIGHT NOW.
HIT THE MARK, AND LET'S SAVE SOME MORE SOLDIERS.
SHE'S PREPPED AND READY FOR SURGERY, BOYS, AND I DO NOT WANT TO GET ANY CLOSER.
FIRE WHEN READY!
ENOUGH! YOUR PLOY WAS AMUSING, INDE, BUT NOTHING BUT DISTRACTION!
THUNKT
HUMANITY'S HOUR HAS COME AND GONE. OUR BATTLE IS AT AN END.
IRONIC... I'D NEVER THOUGHT TO USE THIS PARTICULAR SPELL AGAINST AN ENEMY...
BUT WHAT ARE DEATH AND LIFE BUT TOOLS IN A WIZARD'S ARSENAL?
GOT YOU.

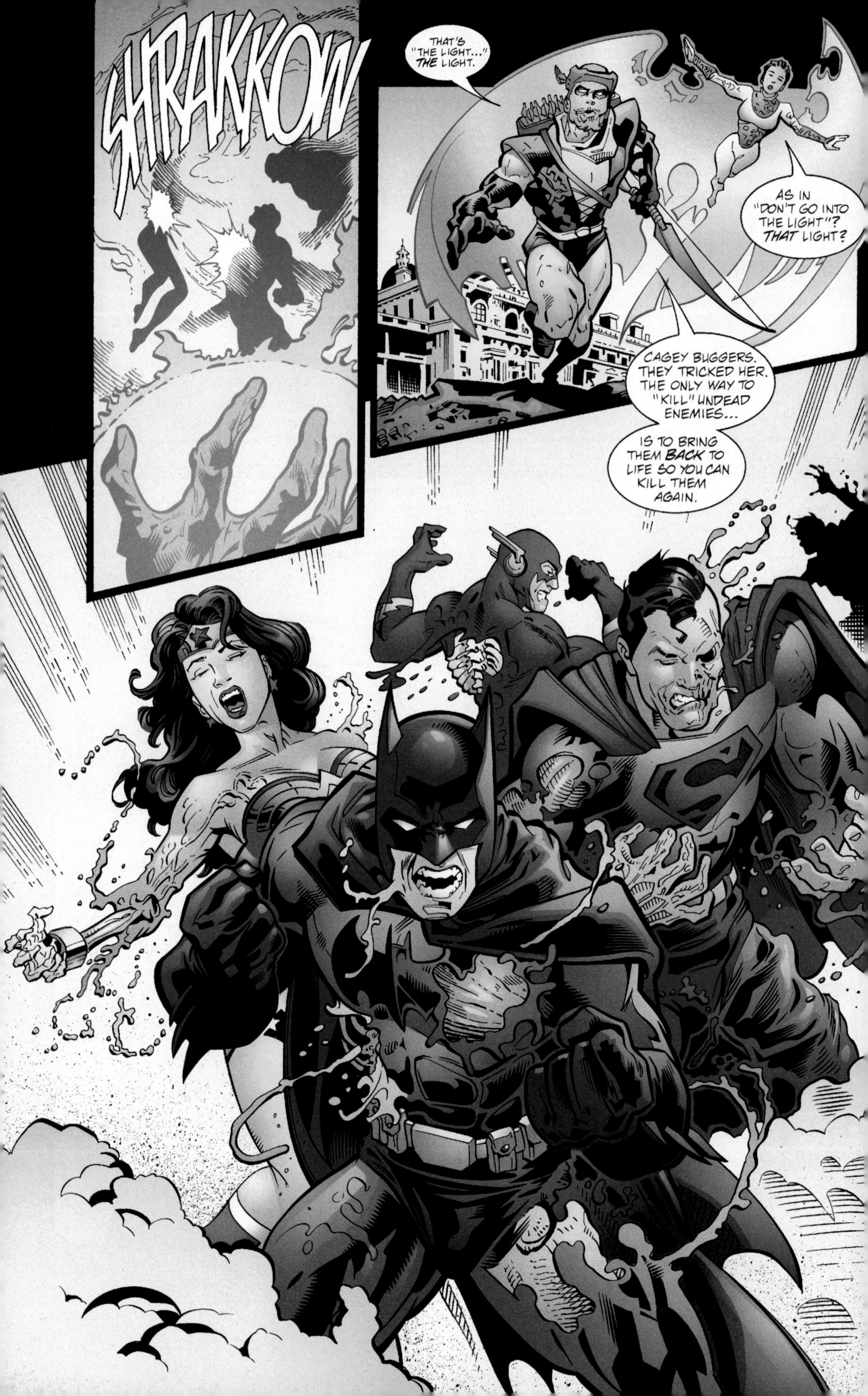
SHRAKKOW
THAT'S "THE LIGHT..." THE LIGHT.
AS IN "DON'T GO INTO THE LIGHT"? THAT LIGHT?
CAGEY BUGGERS. THEY TRICKED HER. THE ONLY WAY TO "KILL" UNDEAD ENEMIES...
IS TO BRING THEM BACK TO LIFE SO YOU CAN KILL THEM AGAIN.

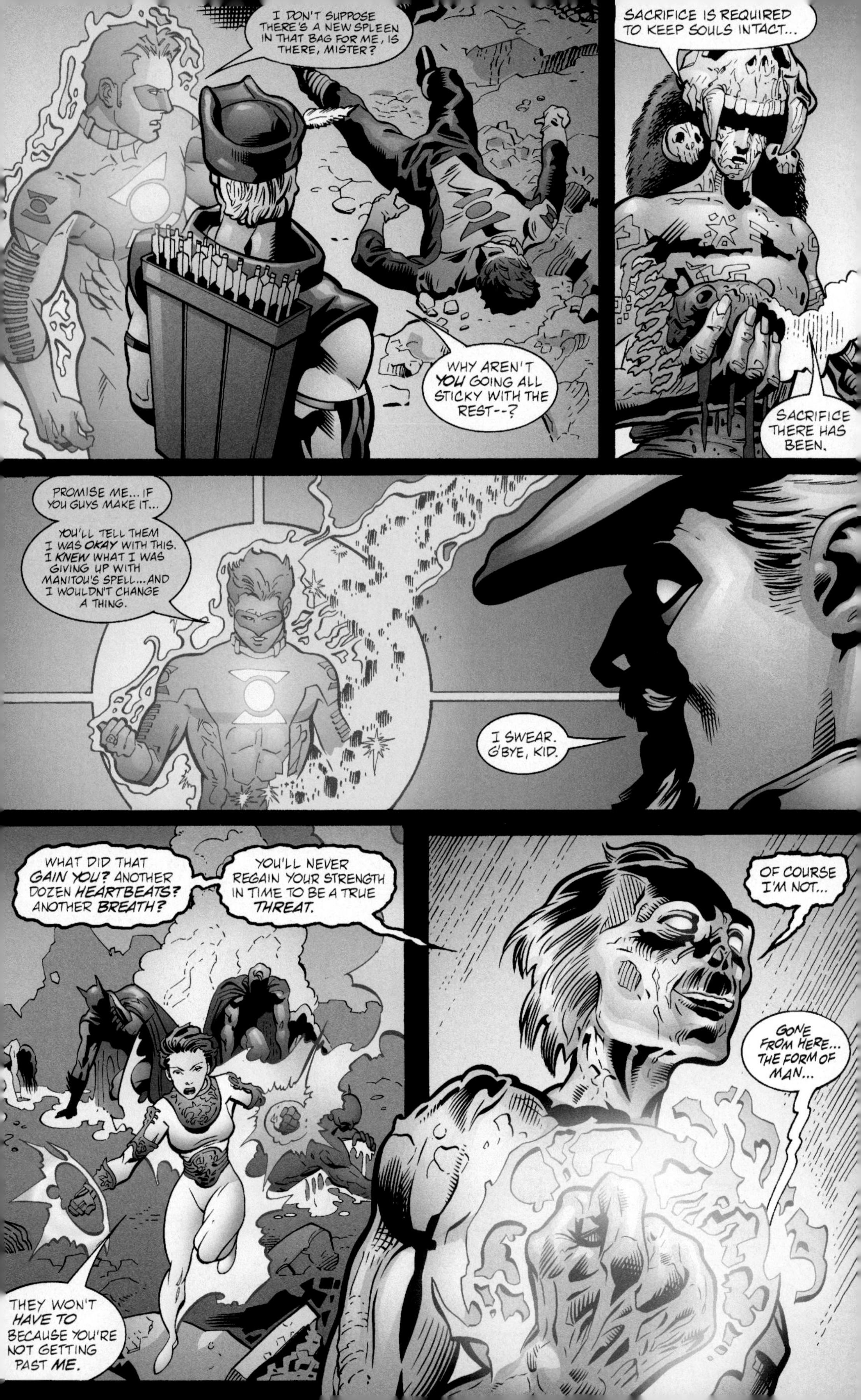

I DON'T SUPPOSE THERE'S A NEW SPLEEN IN THAT BAG FOR ME, IS THERE, MISTER?
WHY AREN'T YOU GOING ALL STICKY WITH THE REST--?
SACRIFICE IS REQUIRED TO KEEP SOULS INTACT...
SACRIFICE THERE HAS BEEN.
PROMISE ME... IF YOU GUYS MAKE IT...
YOU'LL TELL THEM I WAS OKAY WITH THIS. I KNEW WHAT I WAS GIVING UP WITH MANITOU'S SPELL...AND I WOULDN'T CHANGE A THING.
I SWEAR. G'BYE, KID.
WHAT DID THAT GAIN YOU? ANOTHER DOZEN HEARTBEATS? ANOTHER BREATH?
YOU'LL NEVER REGAIN YOUR STRENGTH IN TIME TO BE A TRUE THREAT.
THEY WON'T HAVE TO BECAUSE YOU'RE NOT GETTING PAST ME.
OF COURSE I'M NOT...
GONE FROM HERE... THE FORM OF MAN...

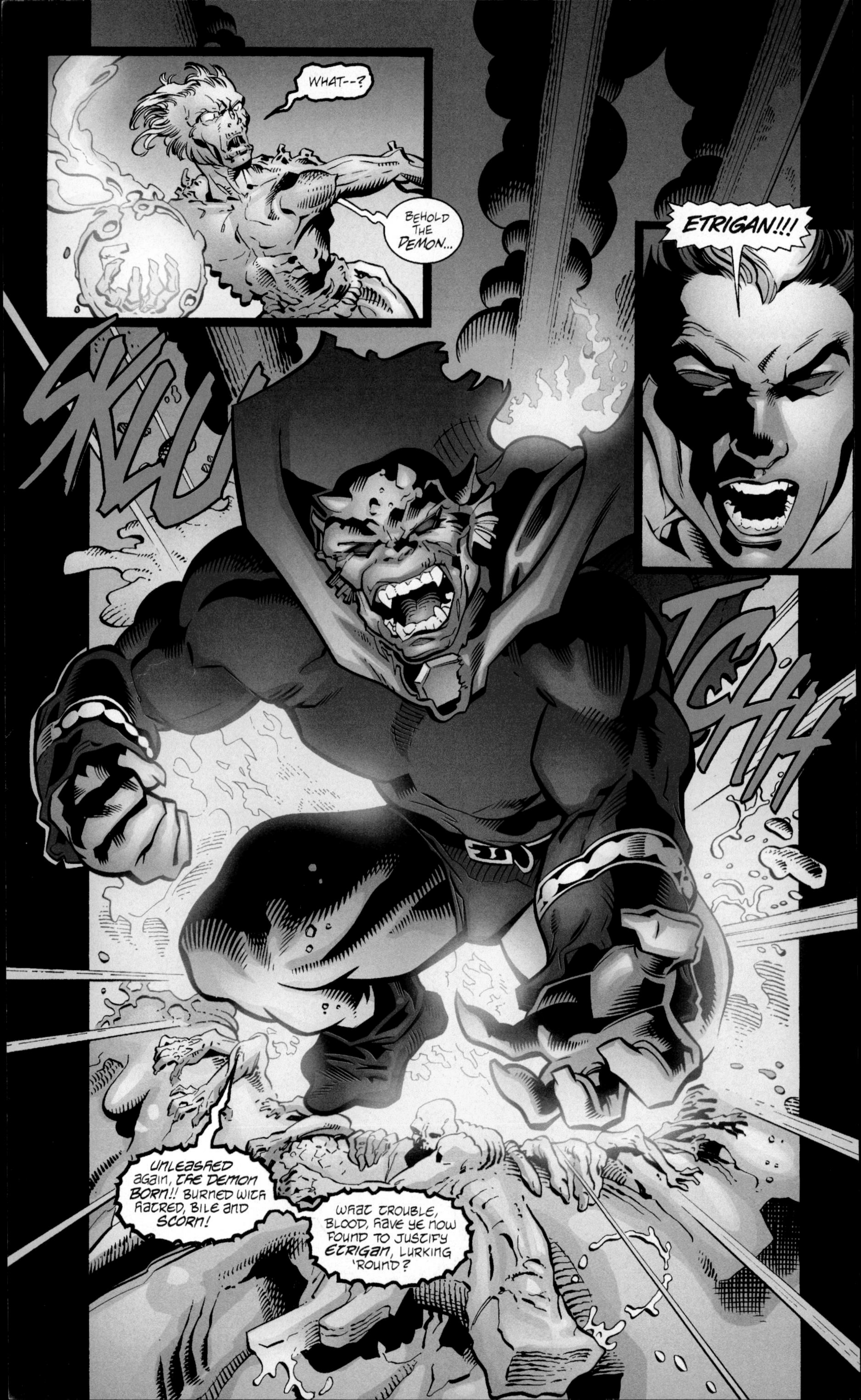
WHAT--?
BEHOLD THE DEMON...
ETRIGAN!!!
SKLU
TCHH
UNLEASHED AGAIN, THE DEMON BORN!! BURNED WITH HATRED, BILE AND SCORN!
WHAT TROUBLE, BLOOD, HAVE YE NOW FOUND TO JUSTIFY ETRIGAN, LURKING 'ROUND?

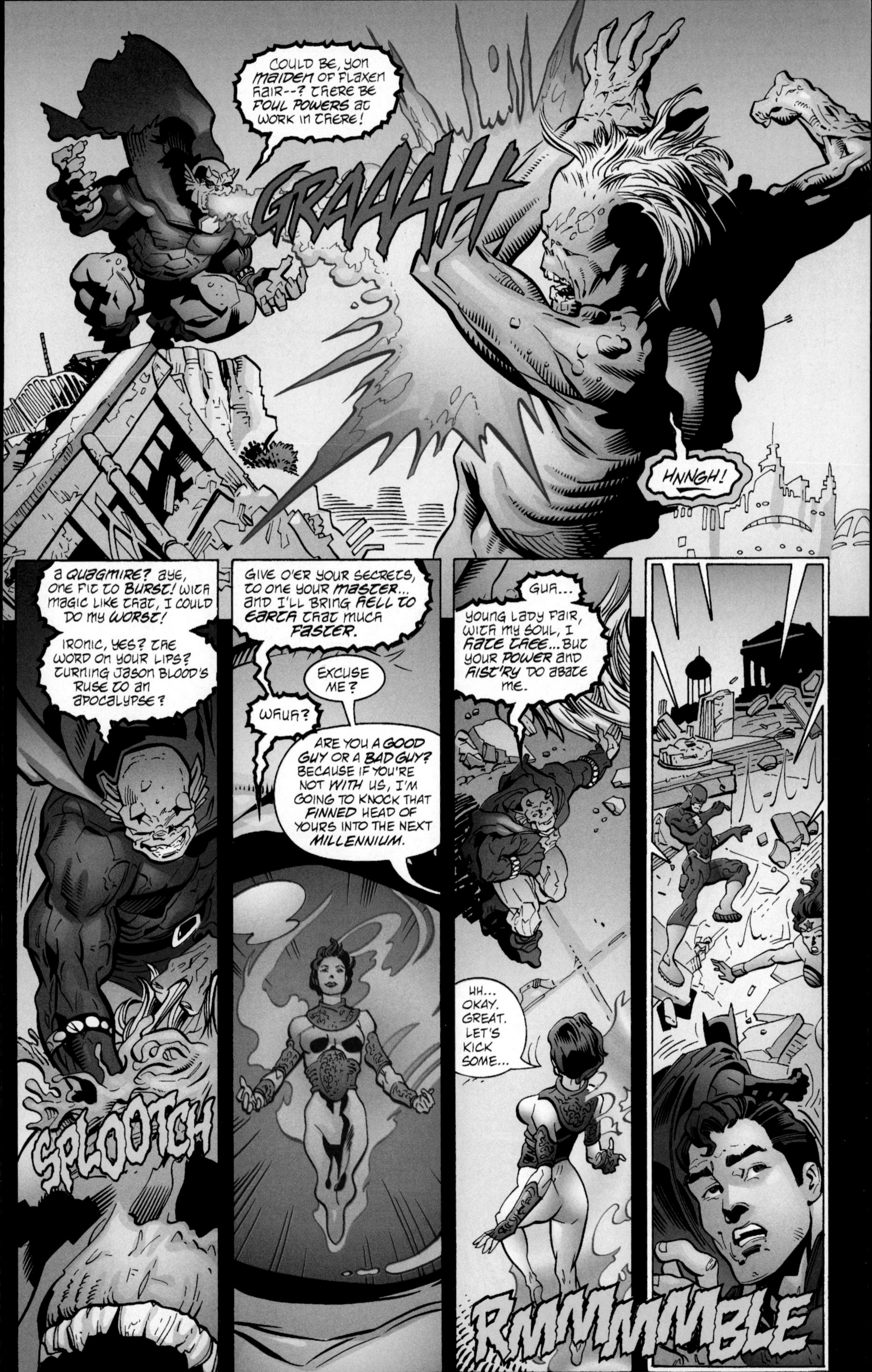
COULD BE, YON MAIDEN OF FLAXEN HAIR--? THERE BE FOUL POWERS AT WORK IN THERE!
GRAAAH
HNNGH!
A QUAGMIRE? AYE, ONE FIT TO BURST! WITH MAGIC LIKE THAT, I COULD DO MY WORST!
IRONIC, YES? THE WORD ON YOUR LIPS? TURNING JASON BLOOD'S RUSE TO AN APOCALYPSE?
SPLOOTCH
GIVE O'ER YOUR SECRETS, TO ONE YOUR MASTER... AND I'LL BRING HELL TO EARTH THAT MUCH FASTER.
WHUH?
EXCUSE ME?
ARE YOU A GOOD GUY OR A BAD GUY? BECAUSE IF YOU'RE NOT WITH US, I'M GOING TO KNOCK THAT FINNED HEAD OF YOURS INTO THE NEXT MILLENNIUM.
GUH...
YOUNG LADY FAIR, WITH MY SOUL, I HATE THEE... BUT YOUR POWER AND FIST'RY DO ABATE ME.
UH... OKAY. GREAT. LET'S KICK SOME...
RMMMMBLE

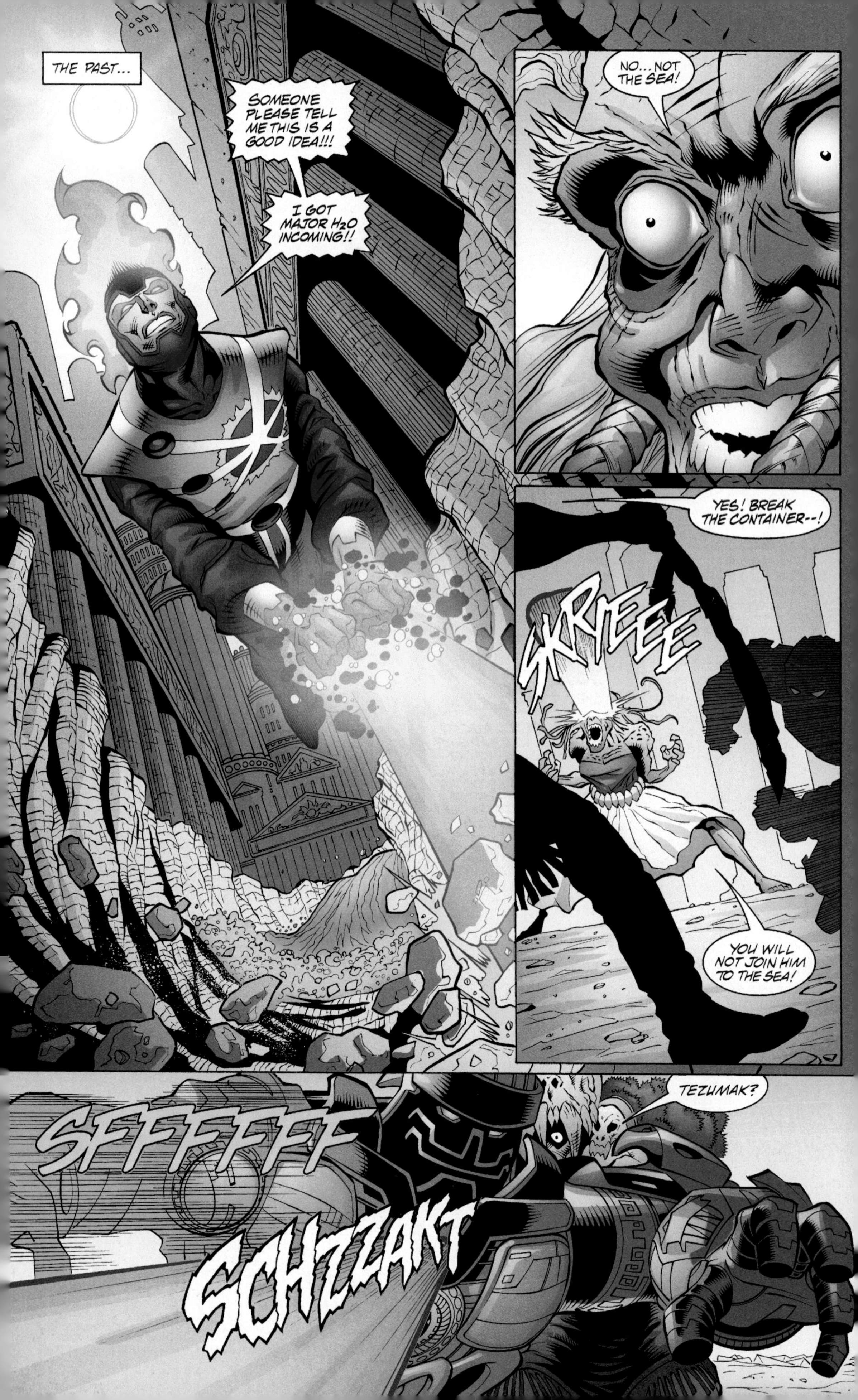
THE PAST...
SOMEONE PLEASE TELL ME THIS IS A GOOD IDEA!!!
I GOT MAJOR H_2O INCOMING!!
NO...NOT THE SEA!
YES! BREAK THE CONTAINER--!
SKRIEEE
YOU WILL NOT JOIN HIM TO THE SEA!
TEZUMAK?
SFFFFFF
SCHZZAKT

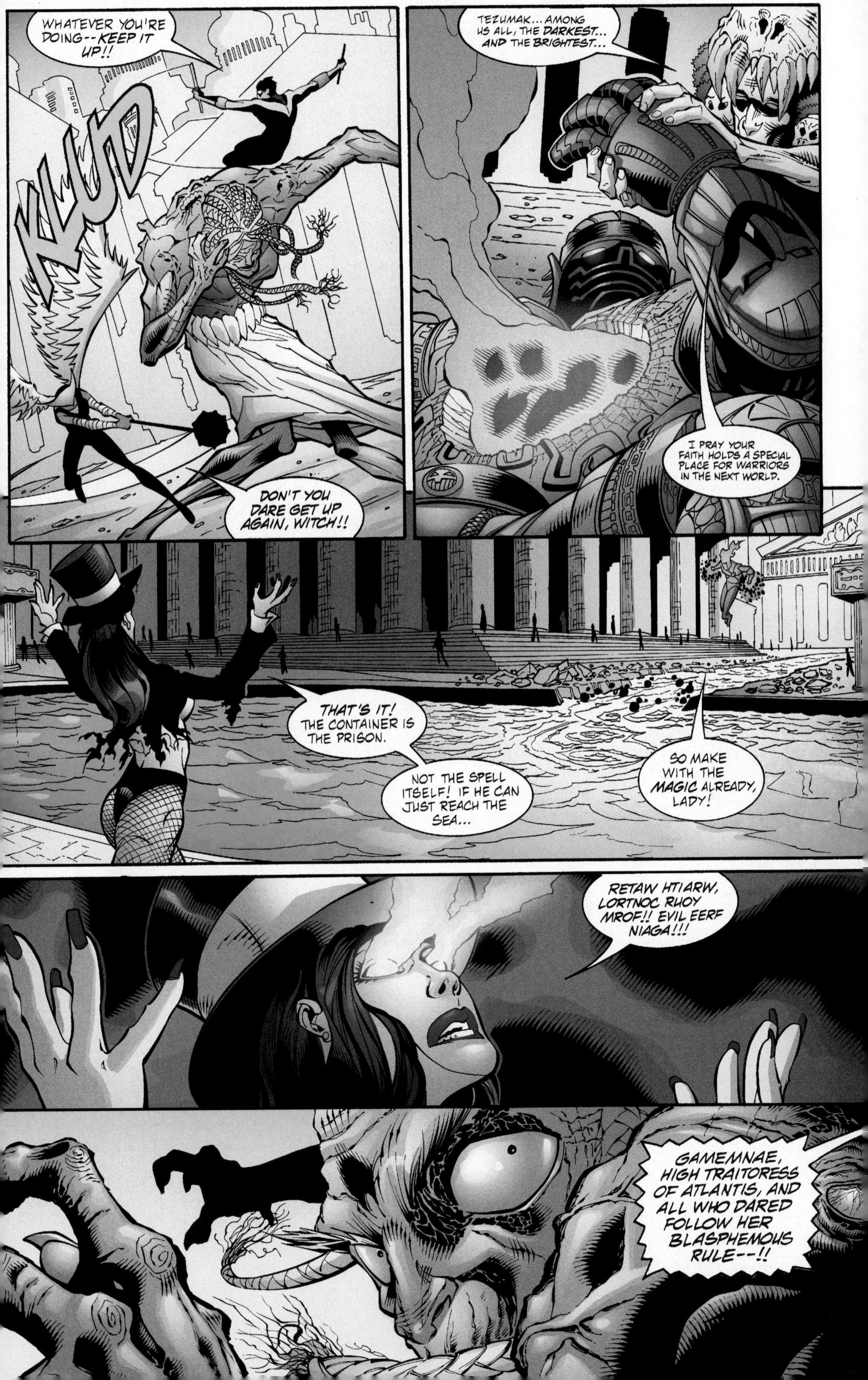
WHATEVER YOU'RE DOING--KEEP IT UP!!
KLUD
DON'T YOU DARE GET UP AGAIN, WITCH!!
TEZUMAK... AMONG US ALL, THE DARKEST... AND THE BRIGHTEST...
I PRAY YOUR FAITH HOLDS A SPECIAL PLACE FOR WARRIORS IN THE NEXT WORLD.
THAT'S IT! THE CONTAINER IS THE PRISON.
NOT THE SPELL ITSELF! IF HE CAN JUST REACH THE SEA...
SO MAKE WITH THE MAGIC ALREADY, LADY!
RETAW HTIARW, LORTNOC RUOY MROF!! EVIL EERF NIAGA!!!
GAMEMNAE, HIGH TRAITORESS OF ATLANTIS, AND ALL WHO DARED FOLLOW HER BLASPHEMOUS RULE--!!

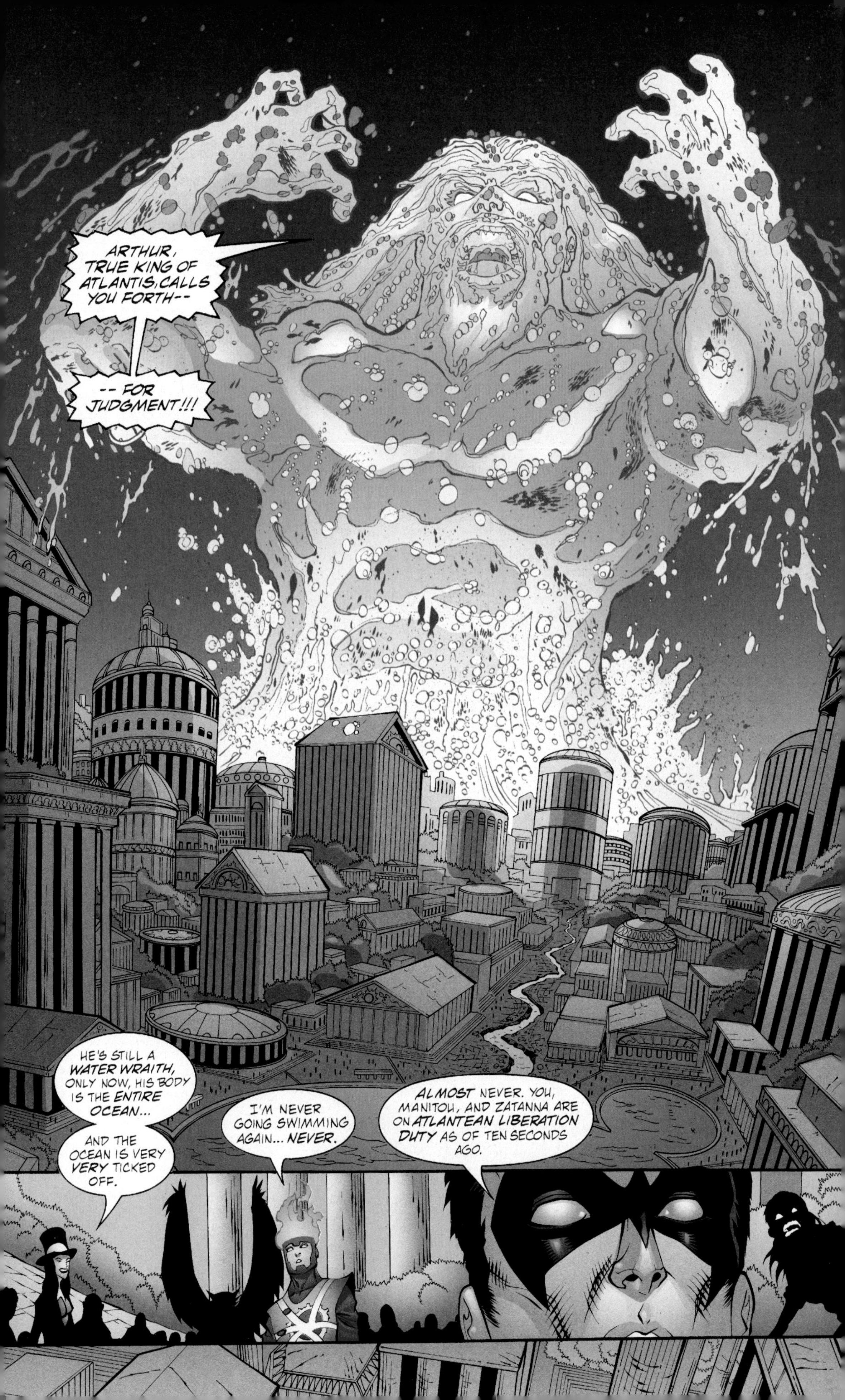
ARTHUR, TRUE KING OF ATLANTIS, CALLS YOU FORTH--
-- FOR JUDGMENT!!!
HE'S STILL A WATER WRAITH, ONLY NOW, HIS BODY IS THE ENTIRE OCEAN...
AND THE OCEAN IS VERY VERY TICKED OFF.
I'M NEVER GOING SWIMMING AGAIN... NEVER.
ALMOST NEVER. YOU, MANITOU, AND ZATANNA ARE ON ATLANTEAN LIBERATION DUTY AS OF TEN SECONDS AGO.

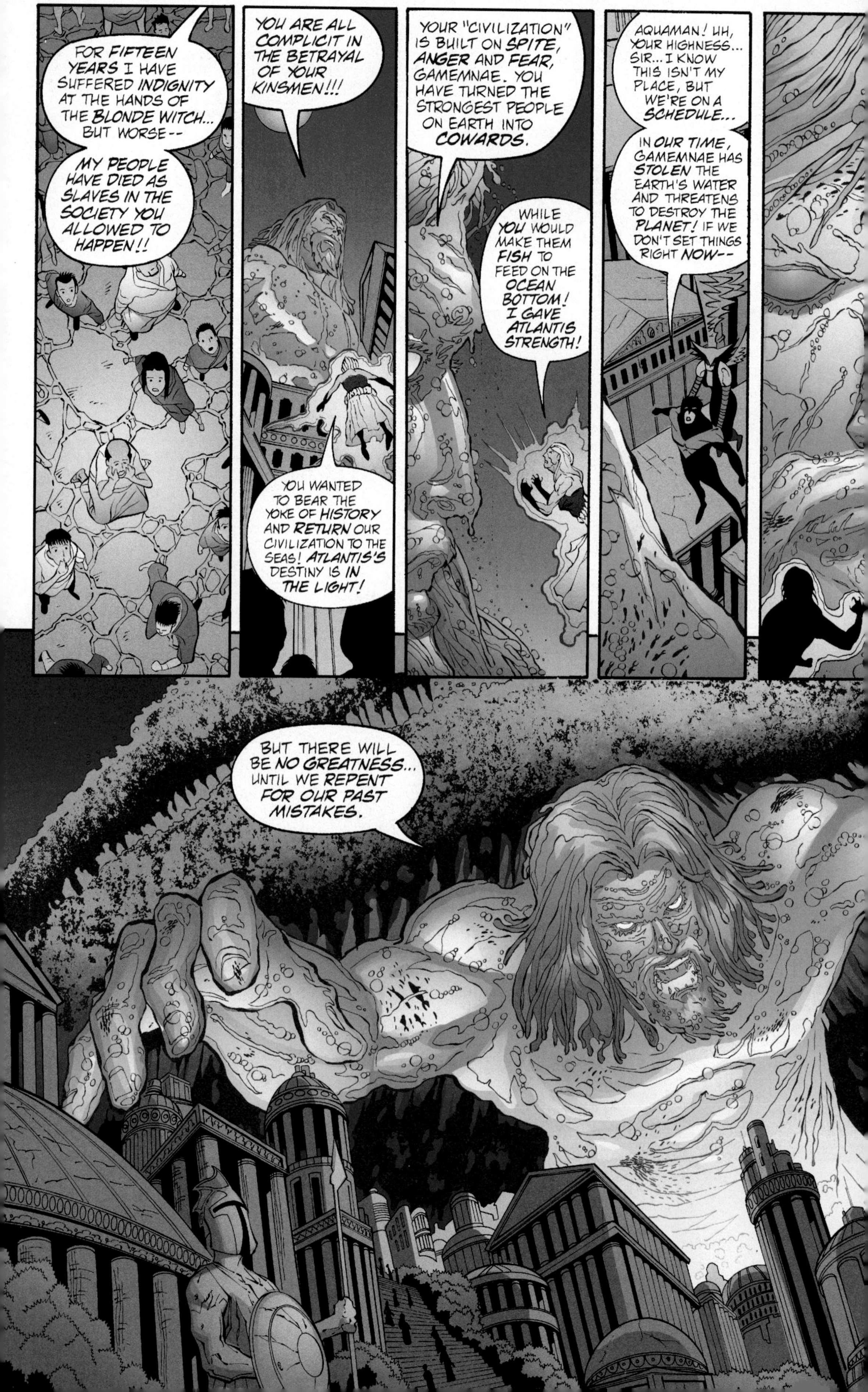
FOR FIFTEEN YEARS I HAVE SUFFERED INDIGNITY AT THE HANDS OF THE BLONDE WITCH... BUT WORSE--
MY PEOPLE HAVE DIED AS SLAVES IN THE SOCIETY YOU ALLOWED TO HAPPEN!!
YOU ARE ALL COMPLICIT IN THE BETRAYAL OF YOUR KINSMEN!!!
YOU WANTED TO BEAR THE YOKE OF HISTORY AND RETURN OUR CIVILIZATION TO THE SEAS! ATLANTIS'S DESTINY IS IN THE LIGHT!
YOUR "CIVILIZATION" IS BUILT ON SPITE, ANGER AND FEAR, GAMEMNAE. YOU HAVE TURNED THE STRONGEST PEOPLE ON EARTH INTO COWARDS.
WHILE YOU WOULD MAKE THEM FISH TO FEED ON THE OCEAN BOTTOM! I GAVE ATLANTIS STRENGTH!
AQUAMAN! UH, YOUR HIGHNESS... SIR... I KNOW THIS ISN'T MY PLACE, BUT WE'RE ON A SCHEDULE...
IN OUR TIME, GAMEMNAE HAS STOLEN THE EARTH'S WATER AND THREATENS TO DESTROY THE PLANET! IF WE DON'T SET THINGS RIGHT NOW--
BUT THERE WILL BE NO GREATNESS... UNTIL WE REPENT FOR OUR PAST MISTAKES.

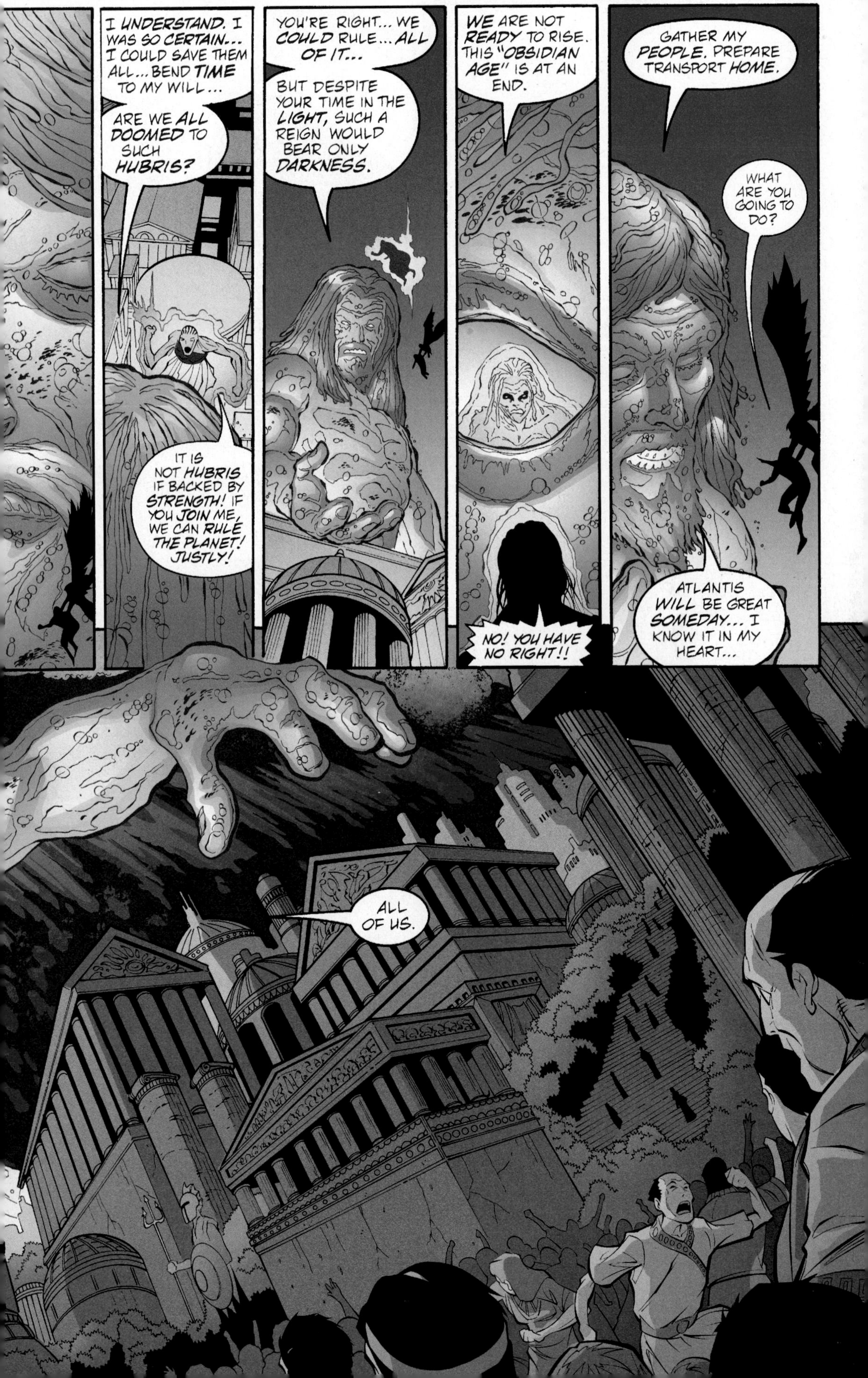
I UNDERSTAND. I WAS SO CERTAIN... I COULD SAVE THEM ALL... BEND TIME TO MY WILL...
ARE WE ALL DOOMED TO SUCH HUBRIS?
IT IS NOT HUBRIS IF BACKED BY STRENGTH! IF YOU JOIN ME, WE CAN RULE THE PLANET! JUSTLY!
YOU'RE RIGHT... WE COULD RULE... ALL OF IT...
BUT DESPITE YOUR TIME IN THE LIGHT, SUCH A REIGN WOULD BEAR ONLY DARKNESS.
WE ARE NOT READY TO RISE. THIS "OBSIDIAN AGE" IS AT AN END.
NO! YOU HAVE NO RIGHT!!
GATHER MY PEOPLE. PREPARE TRANSPORT HOME.
WHAT ARE YOU GOING TO DO?
ATLANTIS WILL BE GREAT SOMEDAY... I KNOW IT IN MY HEART...
ALL OF US.

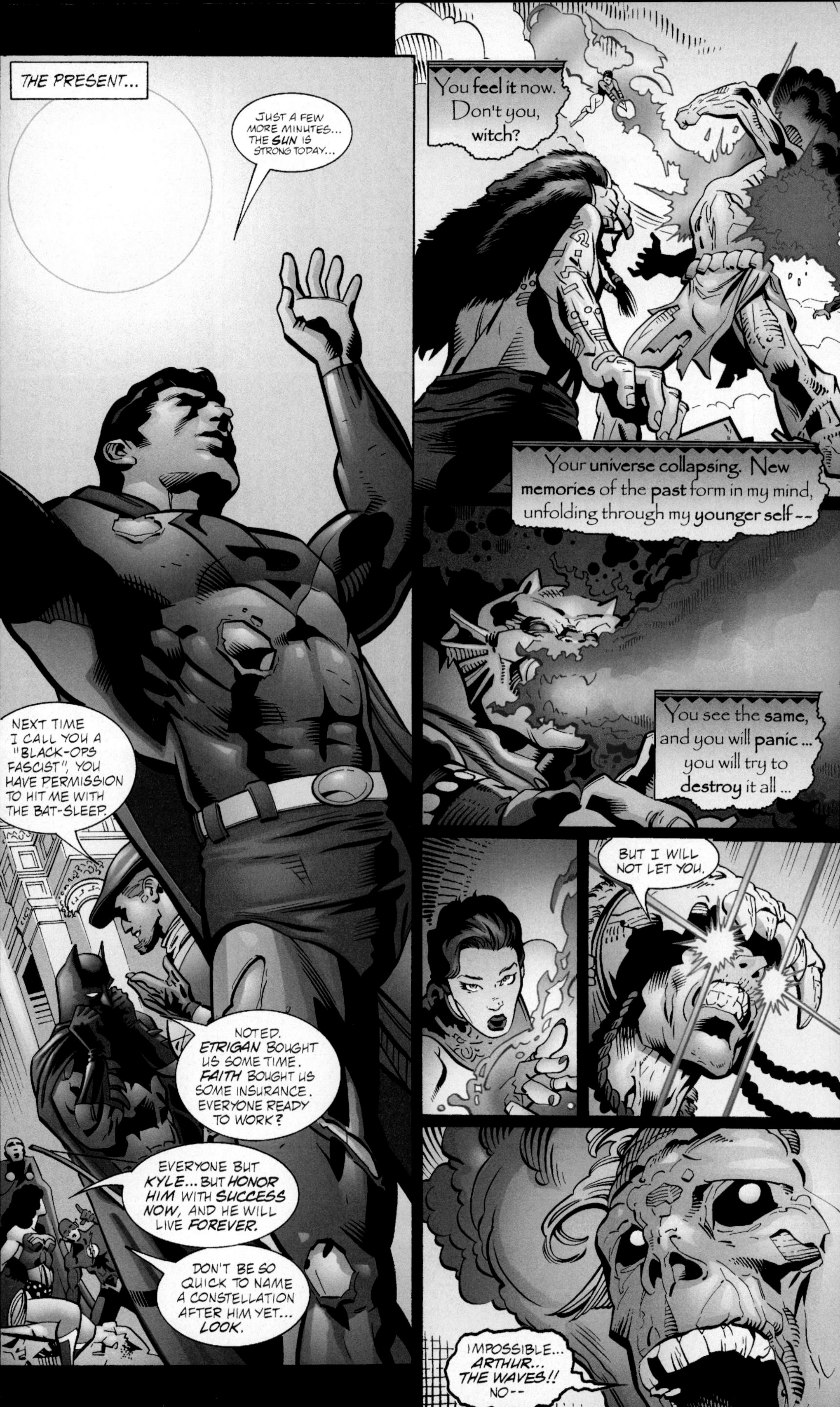
THE PRESENT...
JUST A FEW MORE MINUTES... THE SUN IS STRONG TODAY...
NEXT TIME I CALL YOU A "BLACK-OPS FASCIST", YOU HAVE PERMISSION TO HIT ME WITH THE BAT-SLEEP.
NOTED. ETRIGAN BOUGHT US SOME TIME. FAITH BOUGHT US SOME INSURANCE. EVERYONE READY TO WORK?
EVERYONE BUT KYLE... BUT HONOR HIM WITH SUCCESS NOW, AND HE WILL LIVE FOREVER.
DON'T BE SO QUICK TO NAME A CONSTELLATION AFTER HIM YET... LOOK.
You feel it now. Don't you, witch?
Your universe collapsing. New memories of the past form in my mind, unfolding through my younger self--
You see the same, and you will panic... you will try to destroy it all...
BUT I WILL NOT LET YOU.
IMPOSSIBLE... ARTHUR... THE WAVES!! NO--

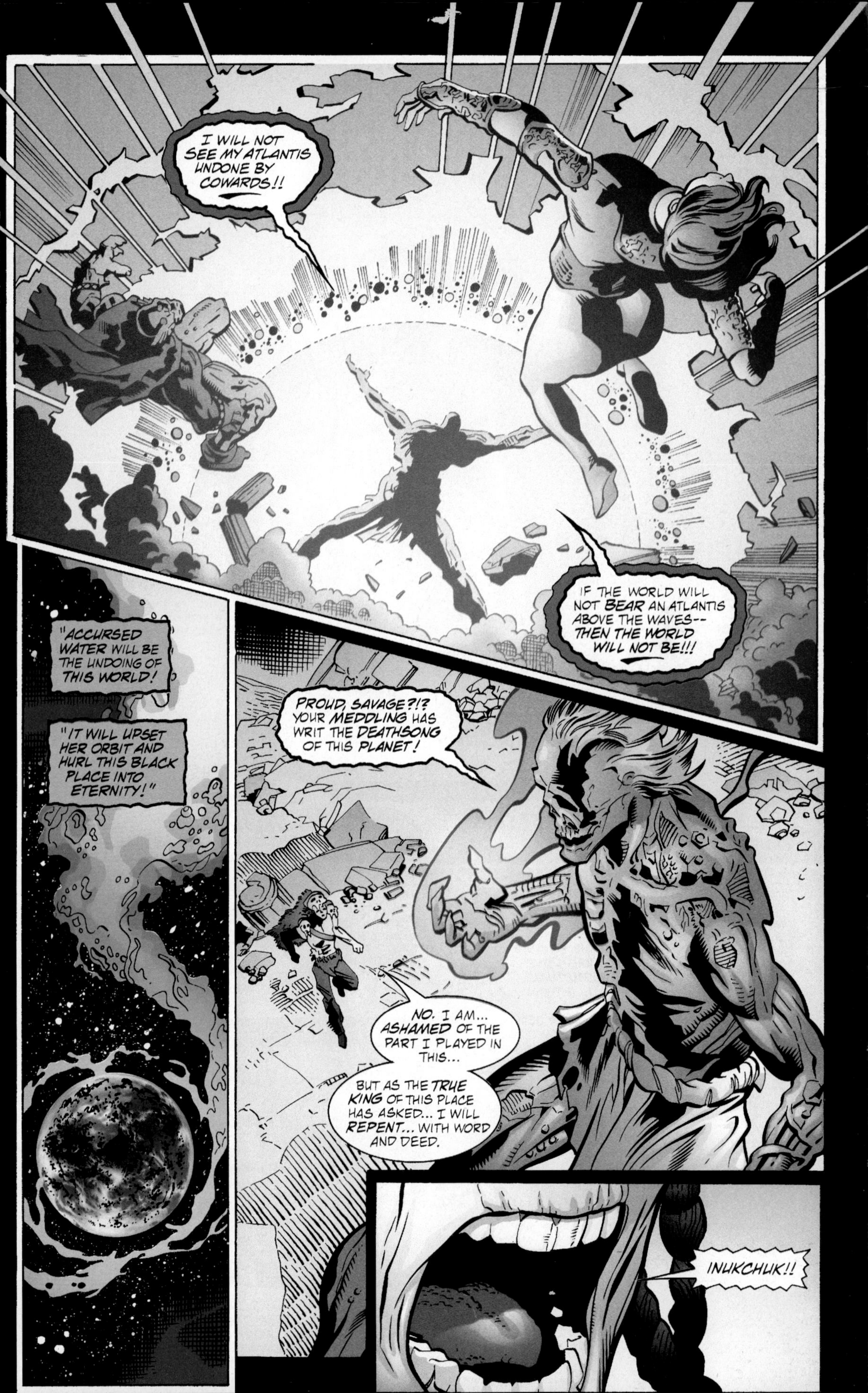

I WILL NOT SEE MY ATLANTIS UNDONE BY COWARDS!!
IF THE WORLD WILL NOT BEAR AN ATLANTIS ABOVE THE WAVES-- THEN THE WORLD WILL NOT BE!!!
"ACCURSED WATER WILL BE THE UNDOING OF THIS WORLD!
"IT WILL UPSET HER ORBIT AND HURL THIS BLACK PLACE INTO ETERNITY!"
PROUD, SAVAGE?!? YOUR MEDDLING HAS WRIT THE DEATHSONG OF THIS PLANET!
NO. I AM... ASHAMED OF THE PART I PLAYED IN THIS...
BUT AS THE TRUE KING OF THIS PLACE HAS ASKED... I WILL REPENT... WITH WORD AND DEED.
INUKCHUK!!

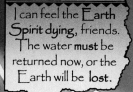

I can feel the Earth Spirit dying, friends. The water **must** be returned now, or the Earth will be **lost**.

Use this time wisely. I cannot maintain this form for long.

DON'T HAVE TO TELL US TWICE. IS THE *LASSO LONG* ENOUGH?

THE SHAMAN HAS *DONE SOMETHING* TO IT... I THINK...

HERA HELP ME, I *KNOW* IT WILL BE AS LONG AS WE *NEED*. THE TRUE QUESTION IS, WILL *WE* BE *STRONG* ENOUGH?

WE'RE CLEAR!! IF ANYONE'S STILL ON COMLINK-- I HAVE *TEMPEST* AND MAJOR DISASTER CLEAR OF THE *QUAGMIRE*--

--AND I JUST PROVED THE THEOREM THAT *MAGIC SPELLS* DON'T WORK ON ANYTHING THE SIZE OF A *THEORETICAL PARTICLE.*

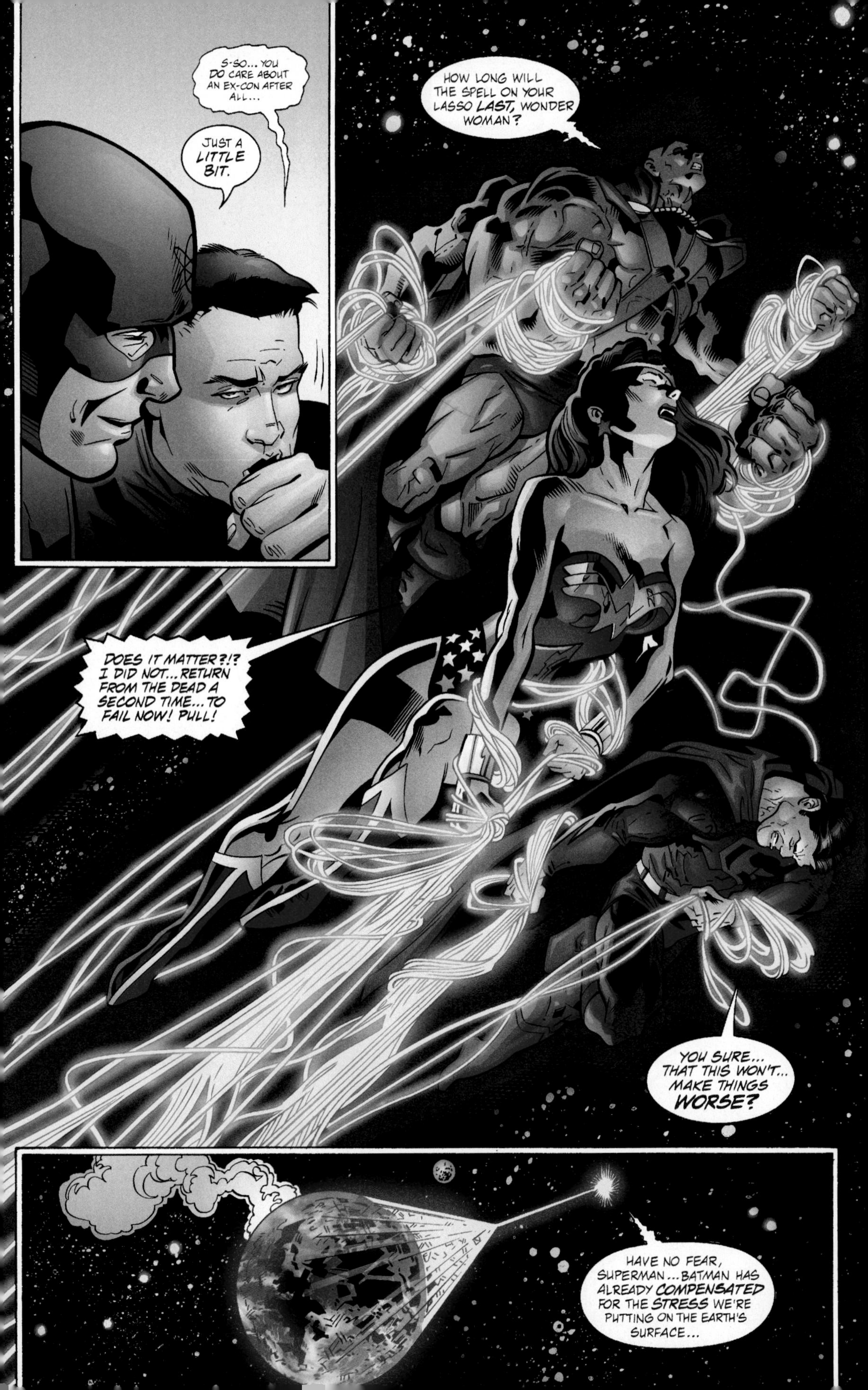
S-SO... YOU DO CARE ABOUT AN EX-CON AFTER ALL...
JUST A LITTLE BIT.
HOW LONG WILL THE SPELL ON YOUR LASSO LAST, WONDER WOMAN?
DOES IT MATTER?!? I DID NOT... RETURN FROM THE DEAD A SECOND TIME... TO FAIL NOW! PULL!
YOU SURE... THAT THIS WON'T... MAKE THINGS WORSE?
HAVE NO FEAR, SUPERMAN... BATMAN HAS ALREADY COMPENSATED FOR THE STRESS WE'RE PUTTING ON THE EARTH'S SURFACE...

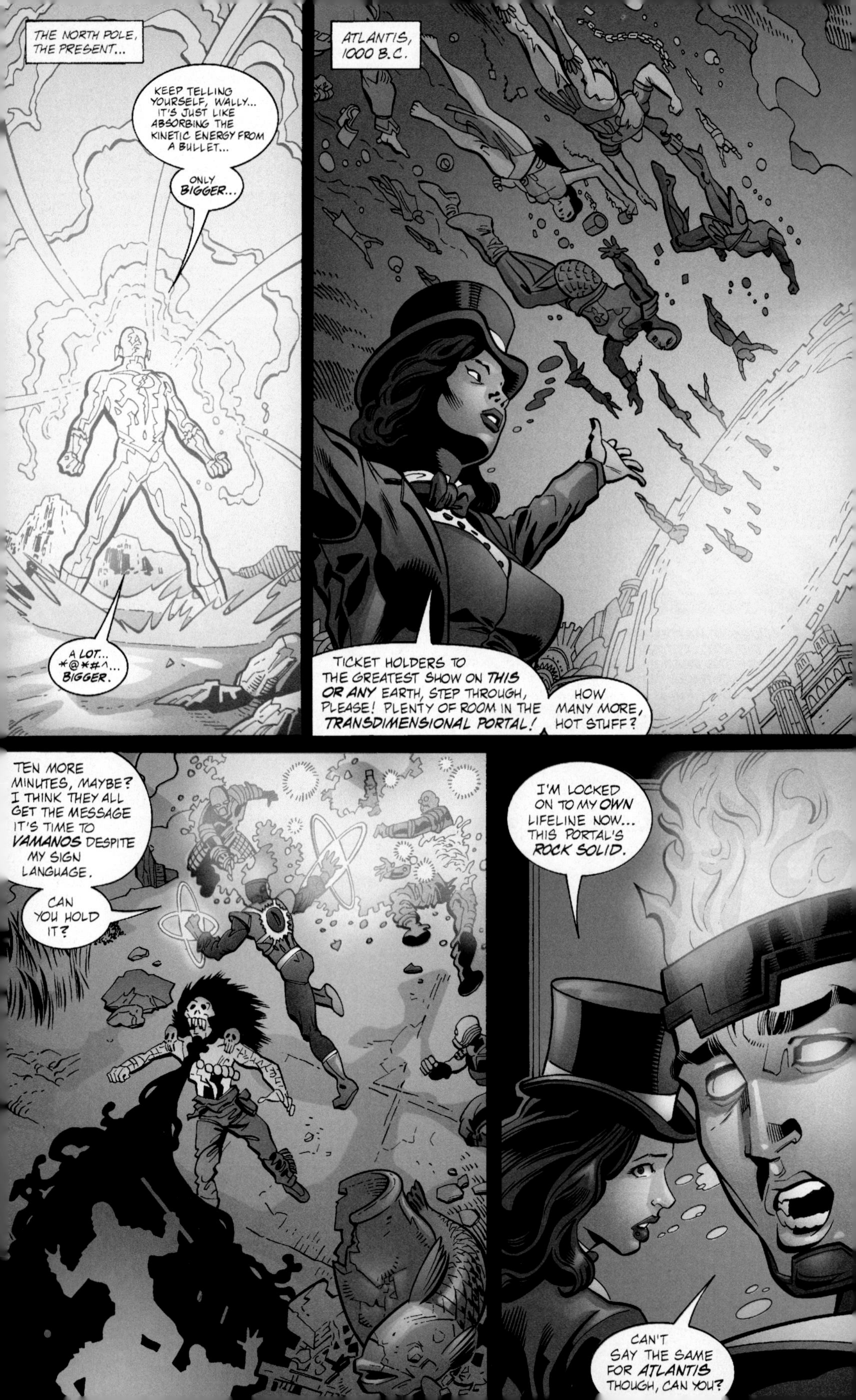
THE NORTH POLE, THE PRESENT...
KEEP TELLING YOURSELF, WALLY... IT'S JUST LIKE ABSORBING THE KINETIC ENERGY FROM A BULLET...
ONLY BIGGER...
A LOT... *@*#^... BIGGER.
ATLANTIS, 1000 B.C.
TICKET HOLDERS TO THE GREATEST SHOW ON THIS OR ANY EARTH, STEP THROUGH, PLEASE! PLENTY OF ROOM IN THE TRANSDIMENSIONAL PORTAL!
HOW MANY MORE, HOT STUFF?
TEN MORE MINUTES, MAYBE? I THINK THEY ALL GET THE MESSAGE IT'S TIME TO VAMANOS DESPITE MY SIGN LANGUAGE.
CAN YOU HOLD IT?
I'M LOCKED ON TO MY OWN LIFELINE NOW... THIS PORTAL'S ROCK SOLID.
CAN'T SAY THE SAME FOR ATLANTIS THOUGH, CAN YOU?

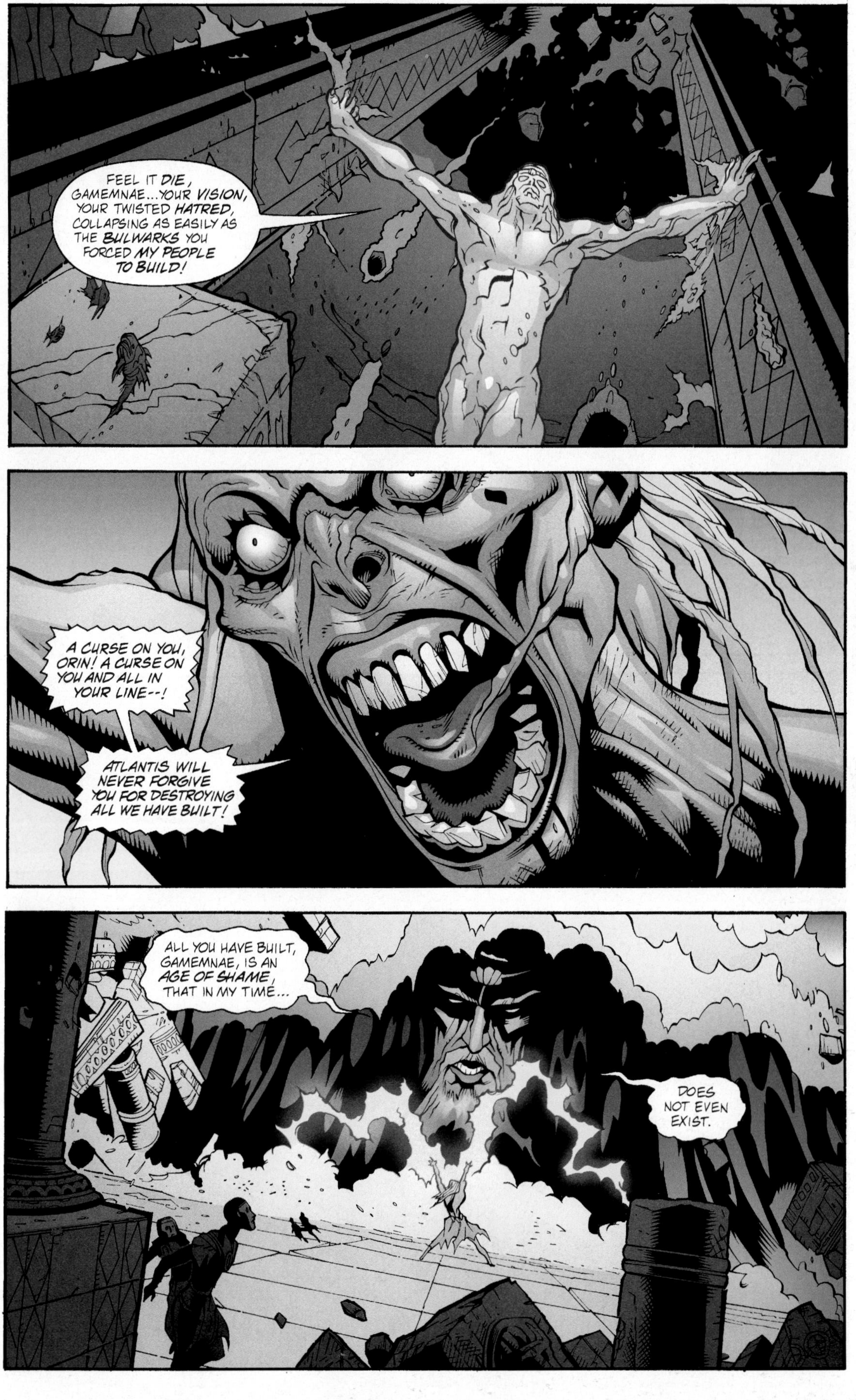
FEEL IT DIE, GAMEMNAE... YOUR VISION, YOUR TWISTED HATRED, COLLAPSING AS EASILY AS THE BULWARKS YOU FORCED MY PEOPLE TO BUILD!
A CURSE ON YOU, ORIN! A CURSE ON YOU AND ALL IN YOUR LINE--!
ATLANTIS WILL NEVER FORGIVE YOU FOR DESTROYING ALL WE HAVE BUILT!
ALL YOU HAVE BUILT, GAMEMNAE, IS AN AGE OF SHAME, THAT IN MY TIME...
DOES NOT EVEN EXIST.

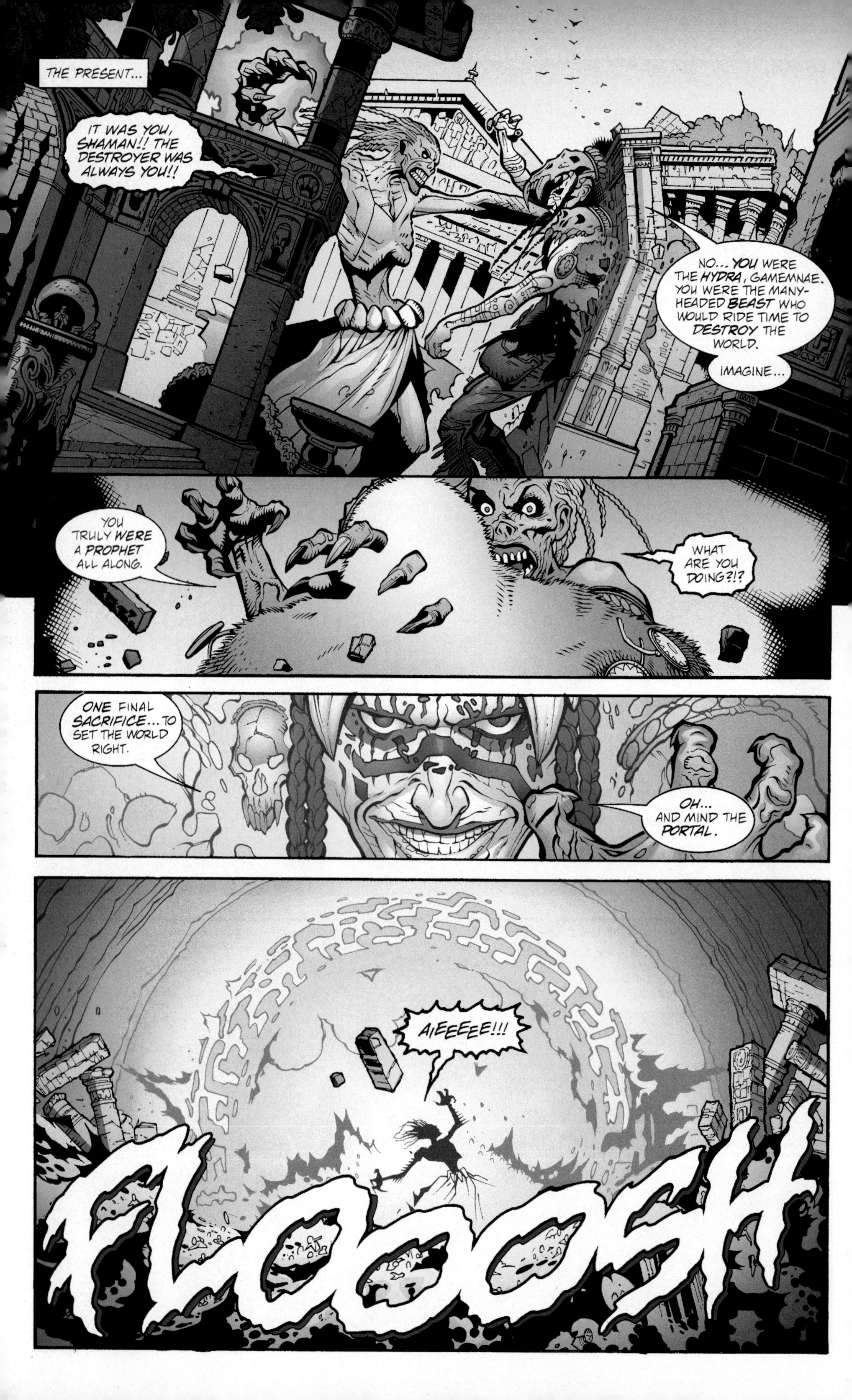
THE PRESENT...
IT WAS YOU, SHAMAN!! THE DESTROYER WAS ALWAYS YOU!!
NO... YOU WERE THE HYDRA, GAMEMNAE. YOU WERE THE MANY-HEADED BEAST WHO WOULD RIDE TIME TO DESTROY THE WORLD.
IMAGINE...
YOU TRULY WERE A PROPHET ALL ALONG.
WHAT ARE YOU DOING?!?
ONE FINAL SACRIFICE... TO SET THE WORLD RIGHT.
OH... AND MIND THE PORTAL.
AIEEEEE!!!
FLOOOSH

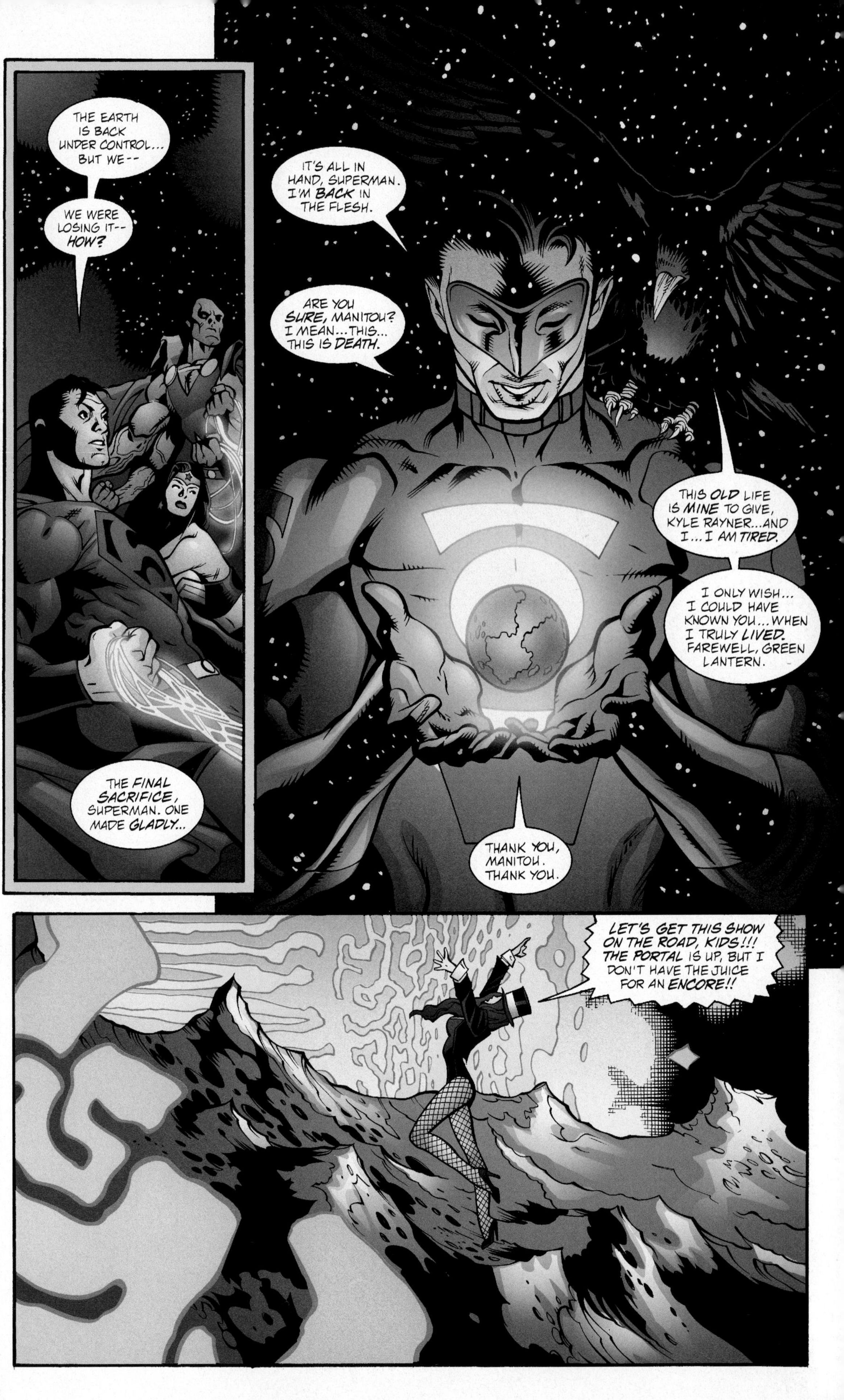
THE EARTH IS BACK UNDER CONTROL... BUT WE--
WE WERE LOSING IT-- HOW?
IT'S ALL IN HAND, SUPERMAN. I'M BACK IN THE FLESH.
ARE YOU SURE, MANITOU? I MEAN... THIS... THIS IS DEATH.
THIS OLD LIFE IS MINE TO GIVE, KYLE RAYNER... AND I... I AM TIRED.
I ONLY WISH... I COULD HAVE KNOWN YOU... WHEN I TRULY LIVED. FAREWELL, GREEN LANTERN.
THE FINAL SACRIFICE, SUPERMAN. ONE MADE GLADLY...
THANK YOU, MANITOU. THANK YOU.
LET'S GET THIS SHOW ON THE ROAD, KIDS!!! THE PORTAL IS UP, BUT I DON'T HAVE THE JUICE FOR AN ENCORE!!

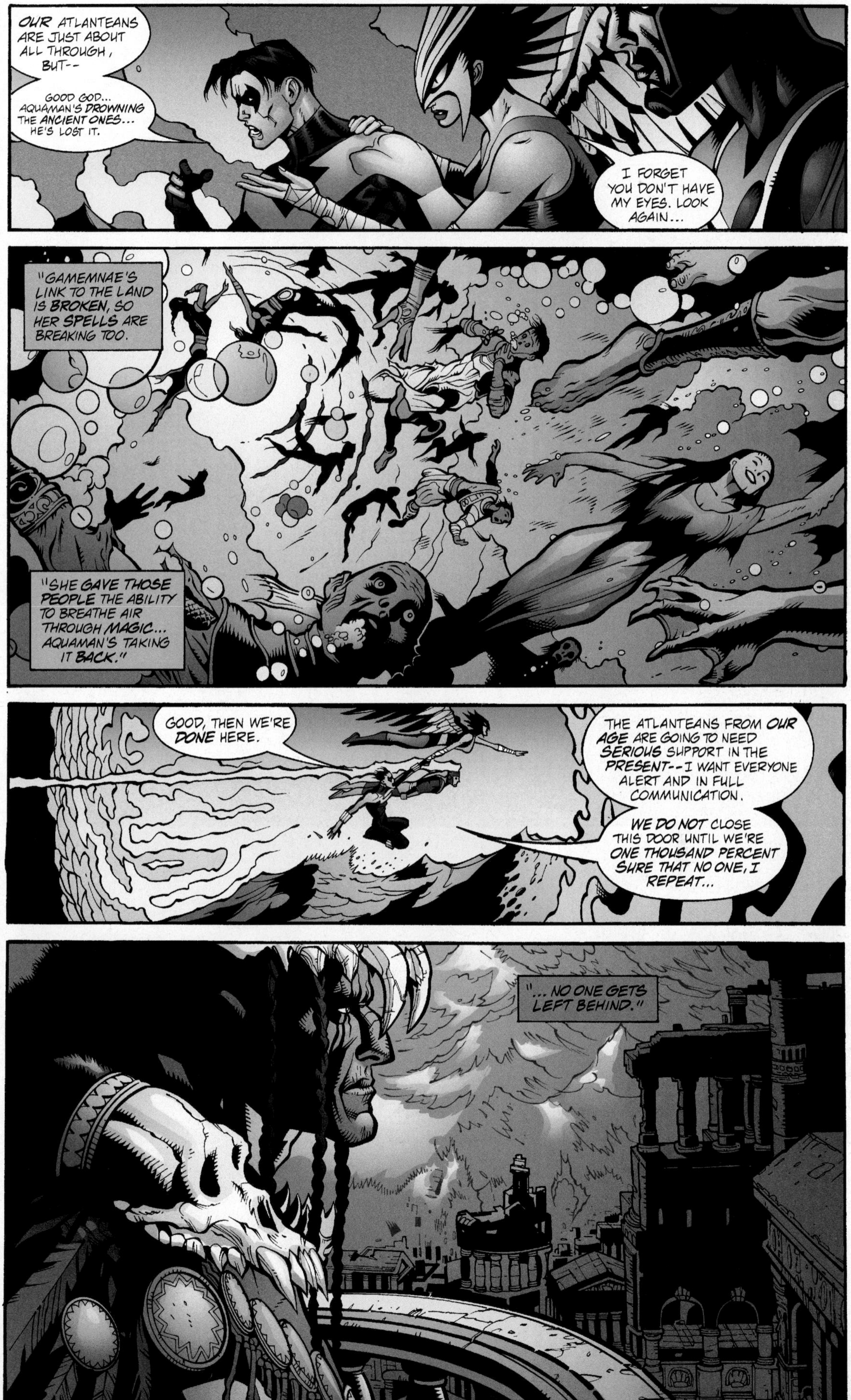
OUR ATLANTEANS ARE JUST ABOUT ALL THROUGH, BUT--
GOOD GOD... AQUAMAN'S DROWNING THE ANCIENT ONES... HE'S LOST IT.
I FORGET YOU DON'T HAVE MY EYES. LOOK AGAIN...
"GAMEMNAE'S LINK TO THE LAND IS BROKEN, SO HER SPELLS ARE BREAKING TOO.
"SHE GAVE THOSE PEOPLE THE ABILITY TO BREATHE AIR THROUGH MAGIC... AQUAMAN'S TAKING IT BACK."
GOOD, THEN WE'RE DONE HERE.
THE ATLANTEANS FROM OUR AGE ARE GOING TO NEED SERIOUS SUPPORT IN THE PRESENT--I WANT EVERYONE ALERT AND IN FULL COMMUNICATION.
WE DO NOT CLOSE THIS DOOR UNTIL WE'RE ONE THOUSAND PERCENT SURE THAT NO ONE, I REPEAT...
"...NO ONE GETS LEFT BEHIND."

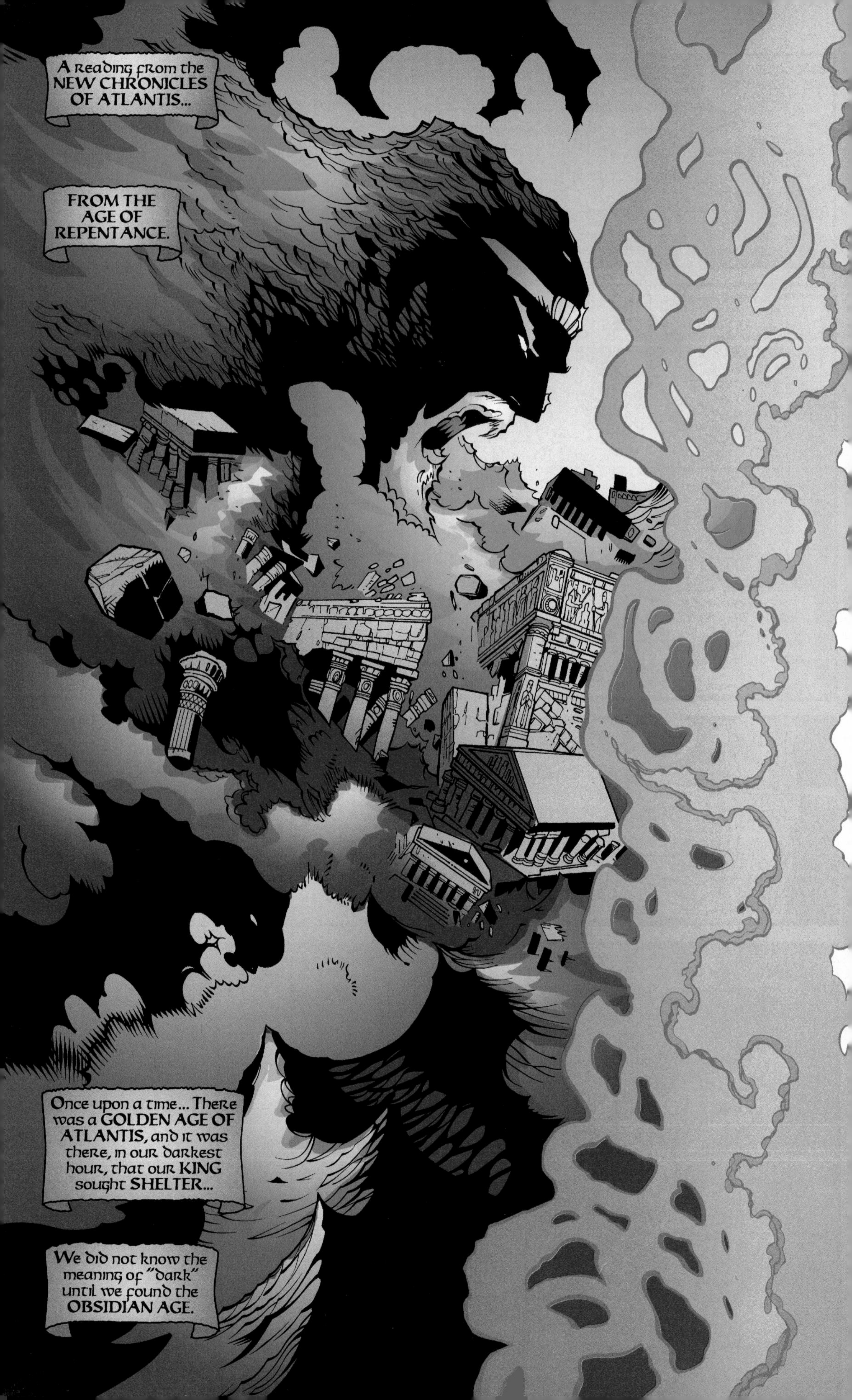
A reading from the NEW CHRONICLES OF ATLANTIS...
FROM THE AGE OF REPENTANCE.
Once upon a time... There was a GOLDEN AGE OF ATLANTIS, and it was there, in our darkest hour, that our KING sought SHELTER...
We did not know the meaning of "dark" until we found the OBSIDIAN AGE.

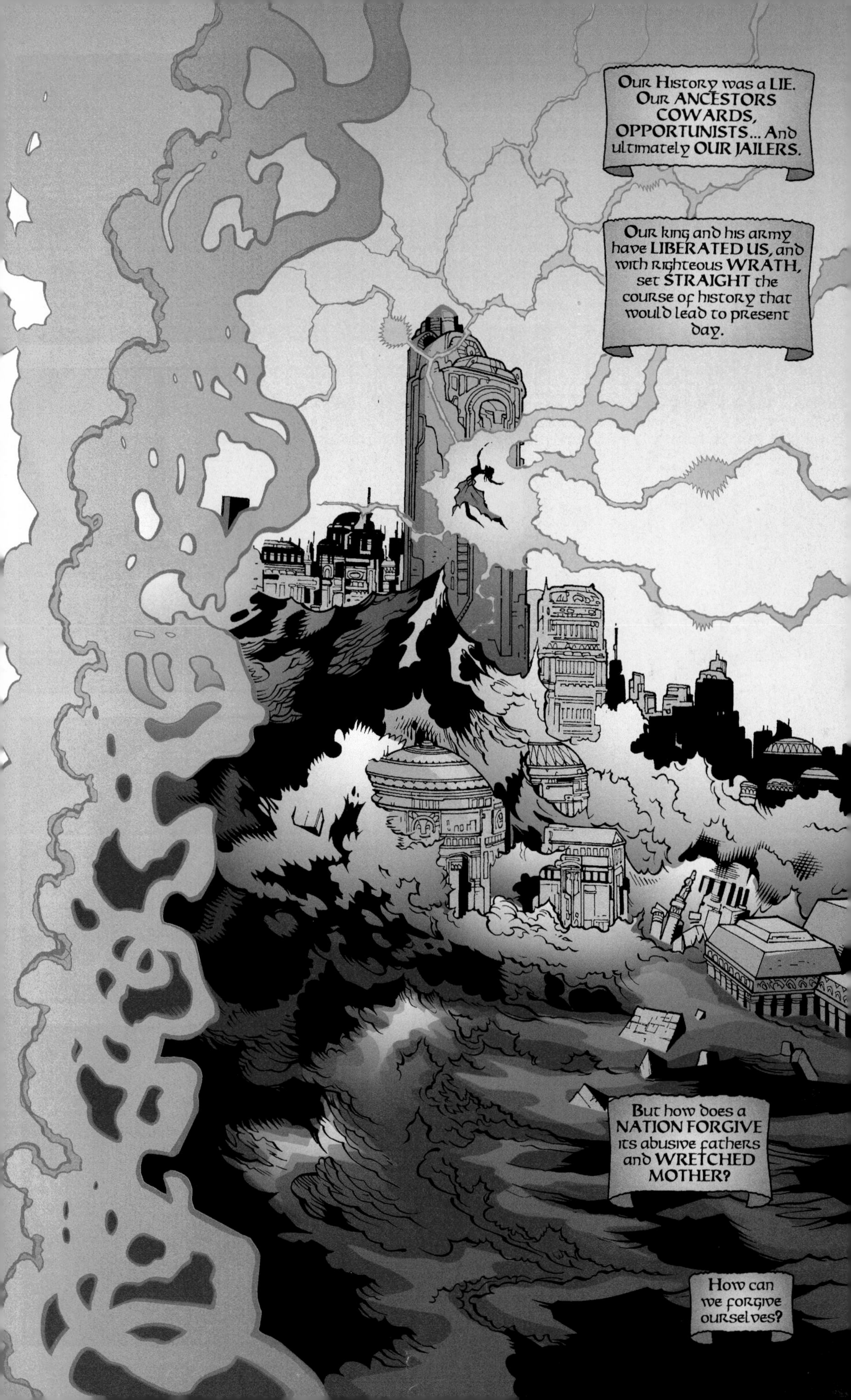
Our History was a LIE. Our ANCESTORS COWARDS, OPPORTUNISTS... And ultimately OUR JAILERS.
Our king and his army have LIBERATED US, and with righteous WRATH, set STRAIGHT the course of history that would lead to present day.
But how does a NATION FORGIVE its abusive fathers and WRETCHED MOTHER?
How can we forgive ourselves?

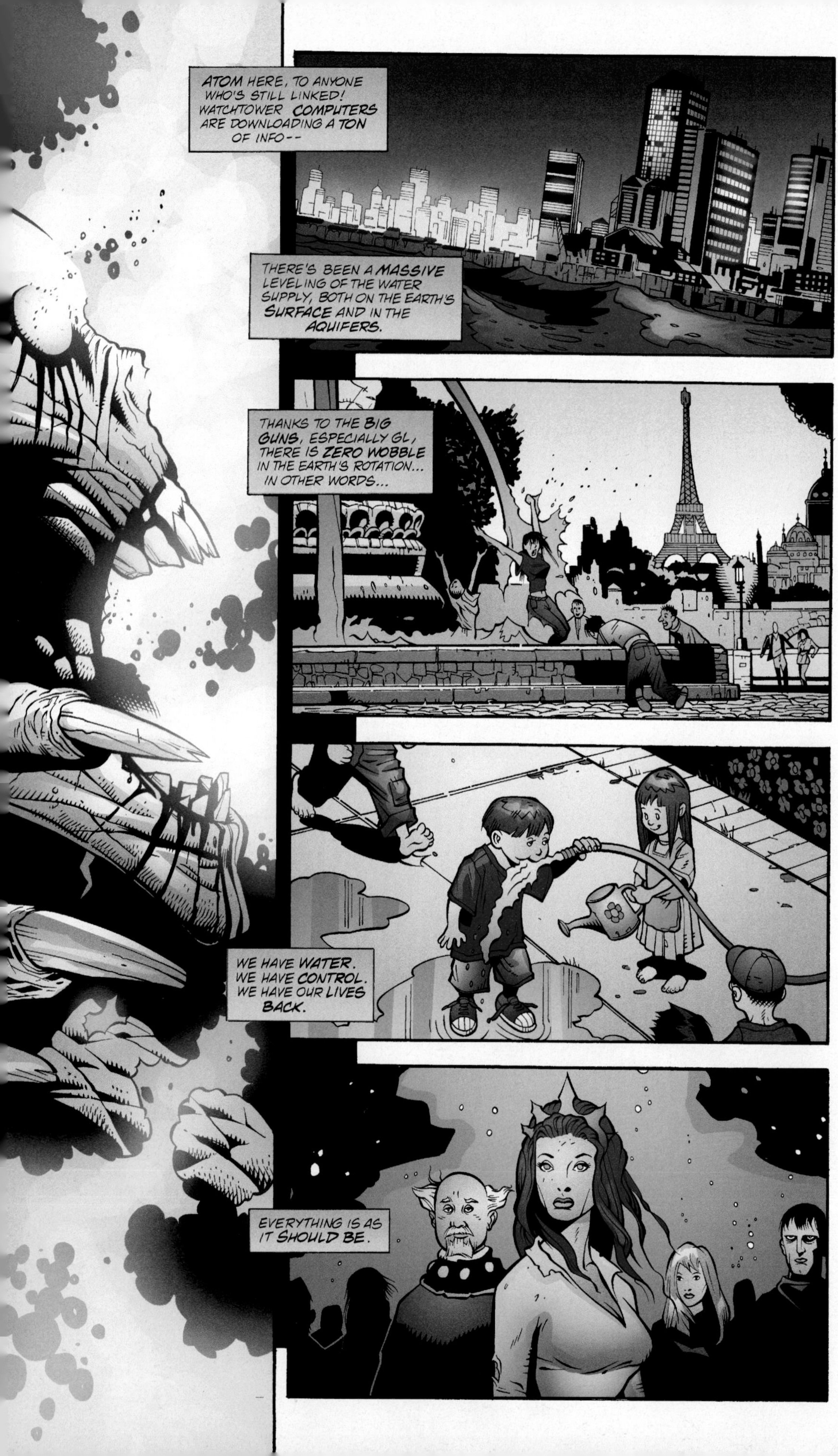
ATOM HERE, TO ANYONE WHO'S STILL LINKED! WATCHTOWER COMPUTERS ARE DOWNLOADING A TON OF INFO--
THERE'S BEEN A MASSIVE LEVELING OF THE WATER SUPPLY, BOTH ON THE EARTH'S SURFACE AND IN THE AQUIFERS.
THANKS TO THE BIG GUNS, ESPECIALLY GL, THERE IS ZERO WOBBLE IN THE EARTH'S ROTATION... IN OTHER WORDS...
WE HAVE WATER. WE HAVE CONTROL. WE HAVE OUR LIVES BACK.
EVERYTHING IS AS IT SHOULD BE.

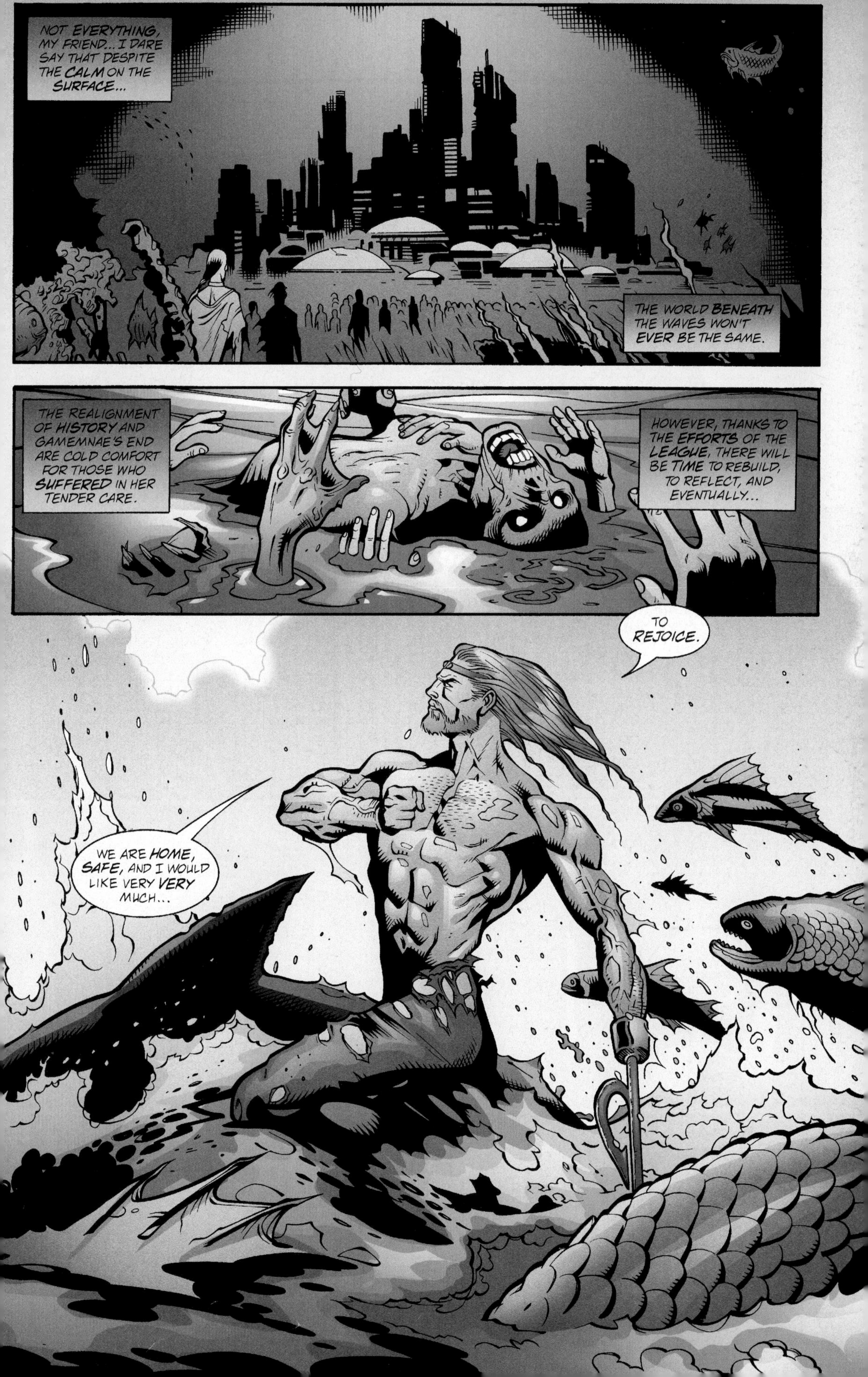
NOT EVERYTHING, MY FRIEND... I DARE SAY THAT DESPITE THE CALM ON THE SURFACE...
THE WORLD BENEATH THE WAVES WON'T EVER BE THE SAME.
THE REALIGNMENT OF HISTORY AND GAMEMNAE'S END ARE COLD COMFORT FOR THOSE WHO SUFFERED IN HER TENDER CARE.
HOWEVER, THANKS TO THE EFFORTS OF THE LEAGUE, THERE WILL BE TIME TO REBUILD, TO REFLECT, AND EVENTUALLY...
WE ARE HOME, SAFE, AND I WOULD LIKE VERY VERY MUCH...
TO REJOICE.

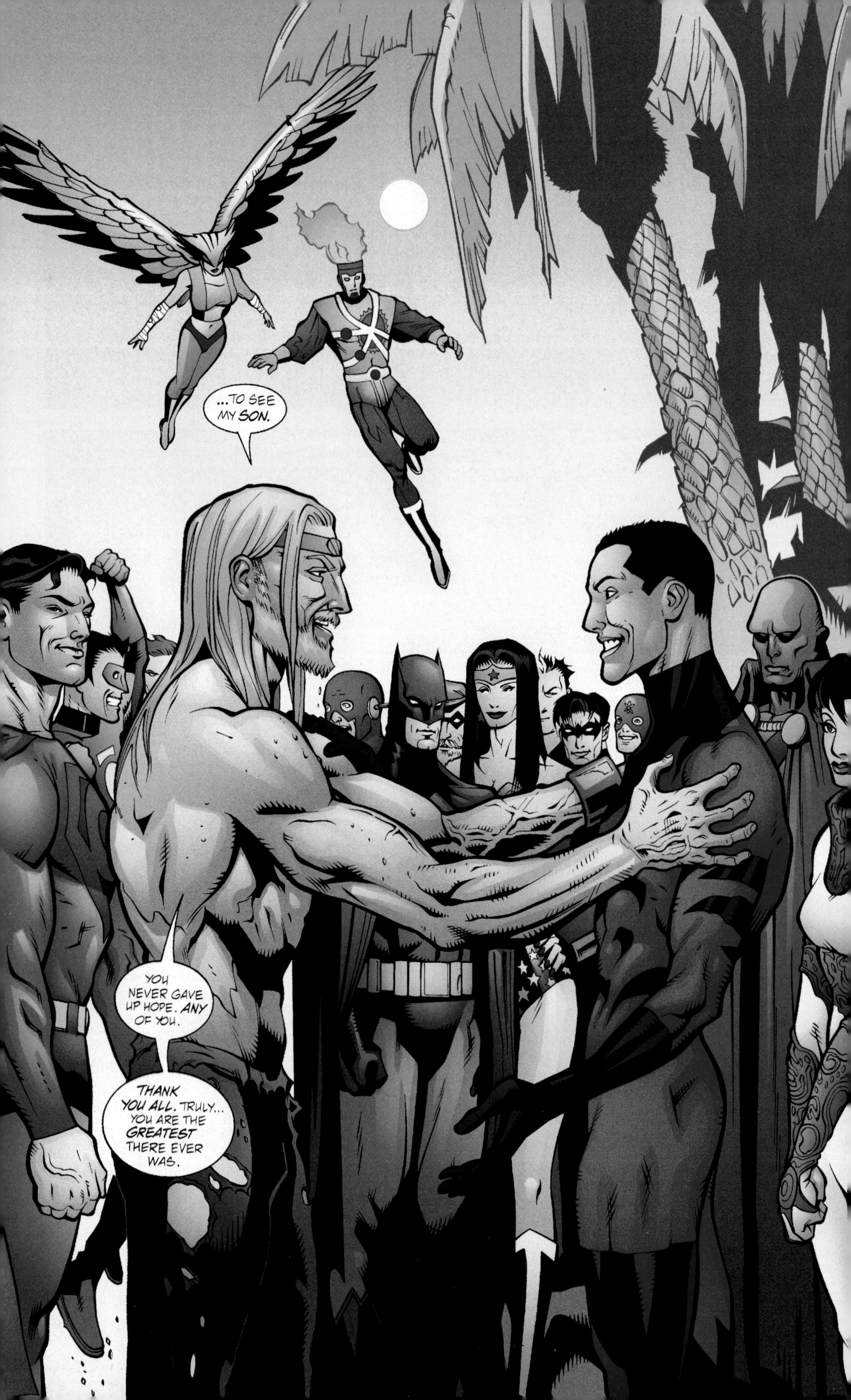

...TO SEE MY SON.
YOU NEVER GAVE UP HOPE. ANY OF YOU.
THANK YOU ALL. TRULY... YOU ARE THE GREATEST THERE EVER WAS.

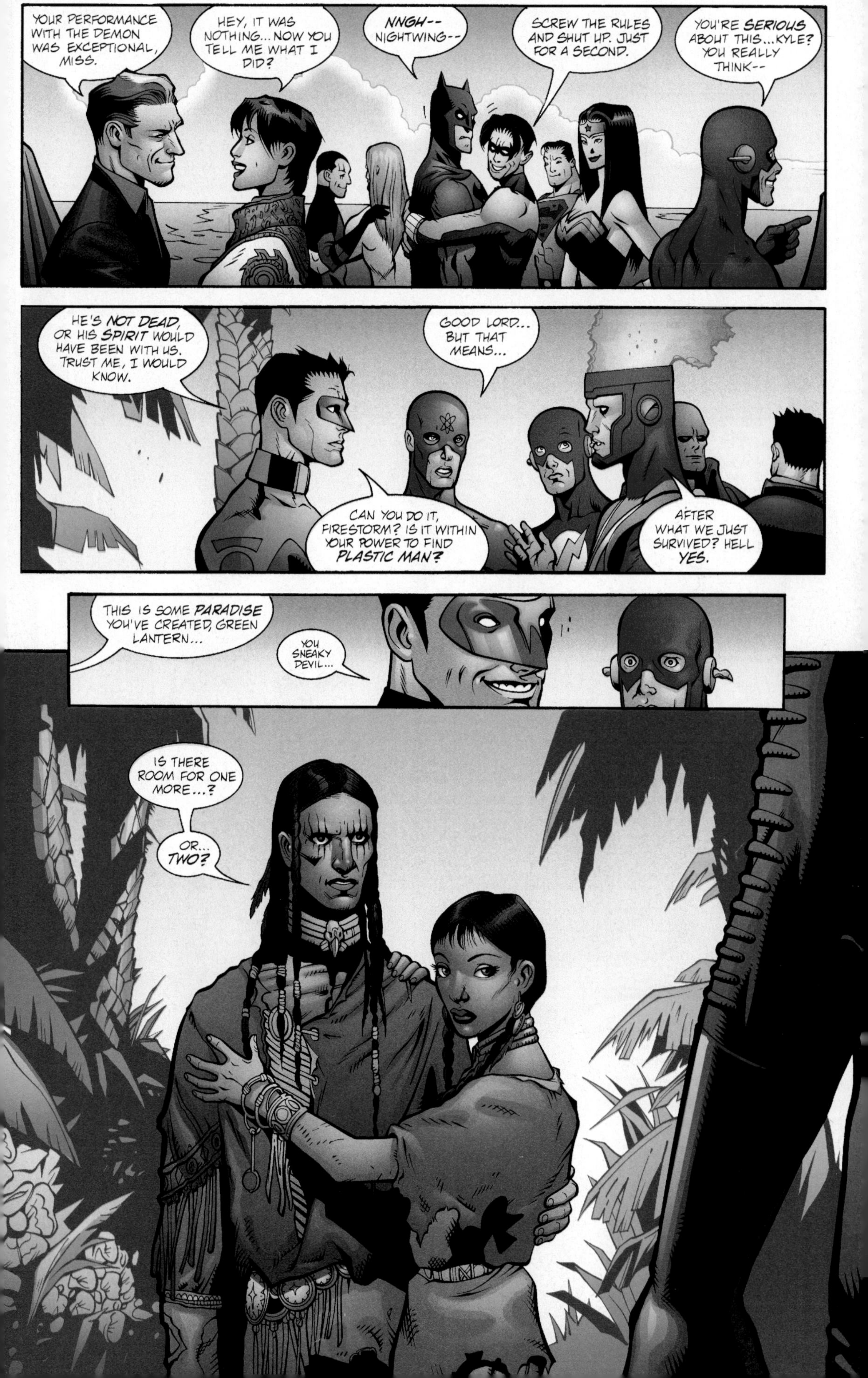
YOUR PERFORMANCE WITH THE DEMON WAS EXCEPTIONAL, MISS.
HEY, IT WAS NOTHING... NOW YOU TELL ME WHAT I DID?
NNGH-- NIGHTWING--
SCREW THE RULES AND SHUT UP. JUST FOR A SECOND.
YOU'RE SERIOUS ABOUT THIS... KYLE? YOU REALLY THINK--
HE'S NOT DEAD, OR HIS SPIRIT WOULD HAVE BEEN WITH US. TRUST ME, I WOULD KNOW.
GOOD LORD... BUT THAT MEANS...
CAN YOU DO IT, FIRESTORM? IS IT WITHIN YOUR POWER TO FIND PLASTIC MAN?
AFTER WHAT WE JUST SURVIVED? HELL YES.
THIS IS SOME PARADISE YOU'VE CREATED, GREEN LANTERN...
YOU SNEAKY DEVIL...
IS THERE ROOM FOR ONE MORE...?
OR... TWO?

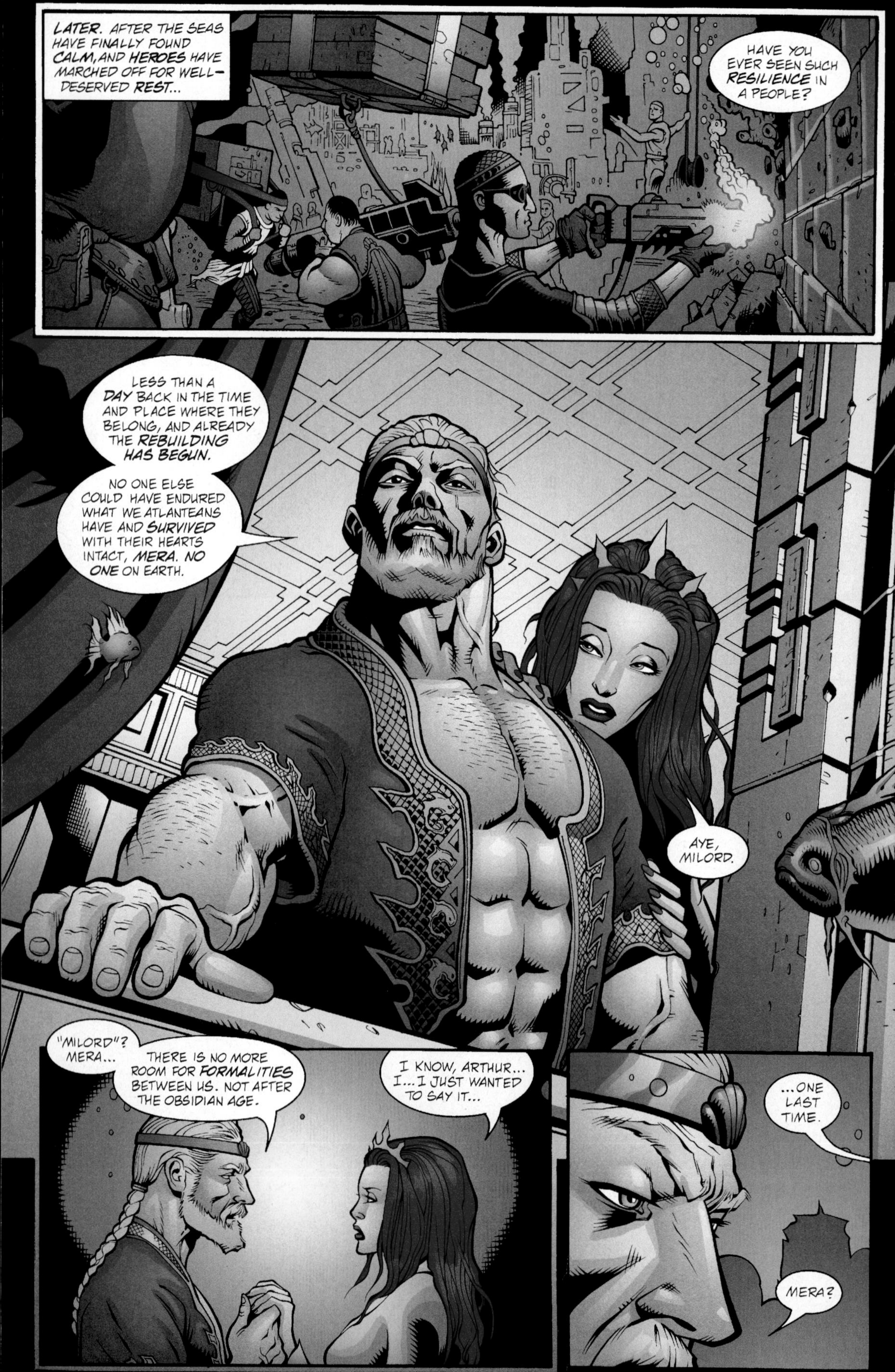
LATER. AFTER THE SEAS HAVE FINALLY FOUND CALM, AND HEROES HAVE MARCHED OFF FOR WELL-DESERVED REST...
HAVE YOU EVER SEEN SUCH RESILIENCE IN A PEOPLE?
LESS THAN A DAY BACK IN THE TIME AND PLACE WHERE THEY BELONG, AND ALREADY THE REBUILDING HAS BEGUN.
NO ONE ELSE COULD HAVE ENDURED WHAT WE ATLANTEANS HAVE AND SURVIVED WITH THEIR HEARTS INTACT, MERA. NO ONE ON EARTH.
AYE, MILORD.
"MILORD"? MERA...
THERE IS NO MORE ROOM FOR FORMALITIES BETWEEN US. NOT AFTER THE OBSIDIAN AGE.
I KNOW, ARTHUR... I... I JUST WANTED TO SAY IT...
...ONE LAST TIME.
MERA?

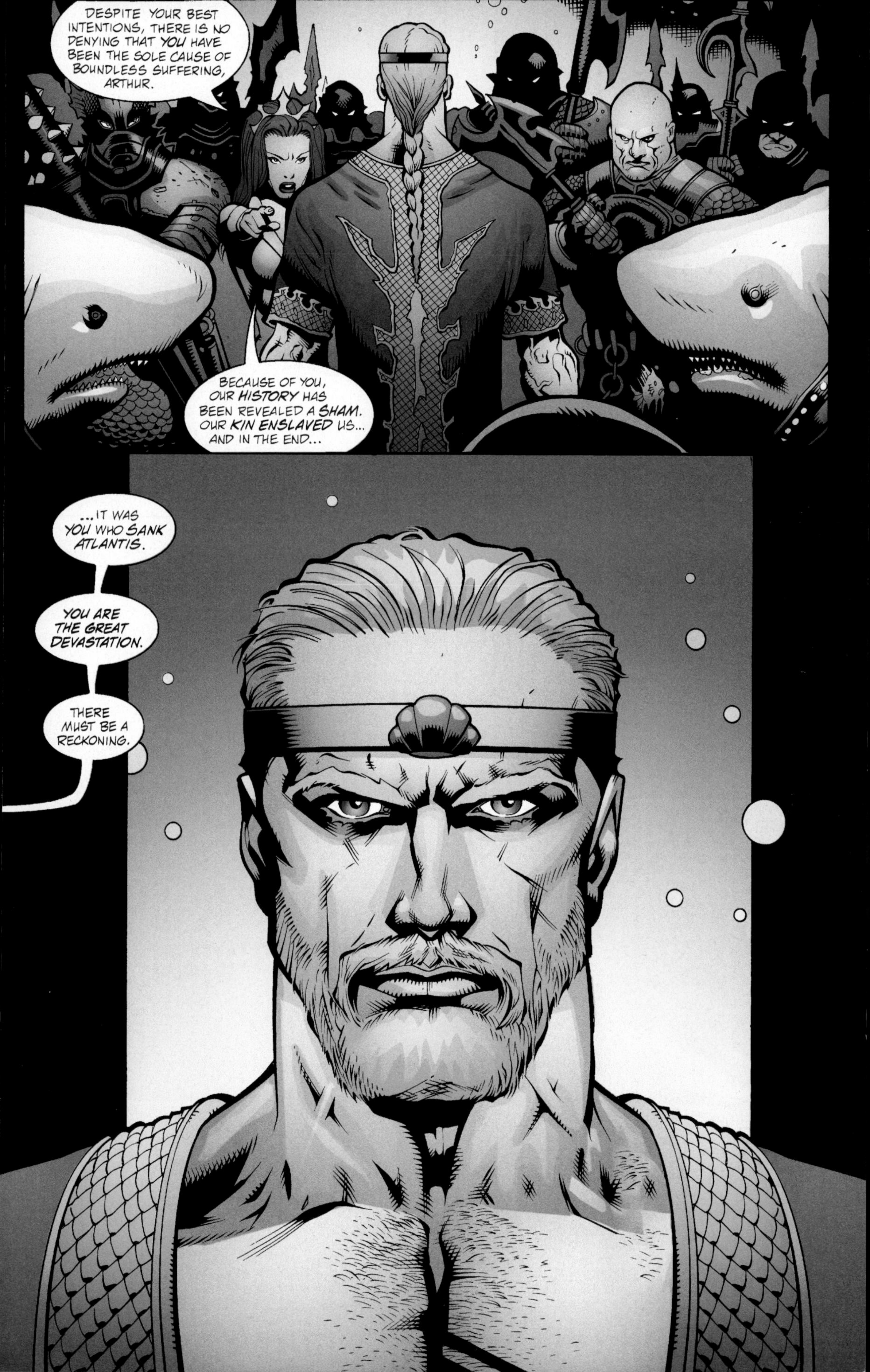
DESPITE YOUR BEST INTENTIONS, THERE IS NO DENYING THAT YOU HAVE BEEN THE SOLE CAUSE OF BOUNDLESS SUFFERING, ARTHUR.
BECAUSE OF YOU, OUR HISTORY HAS BEEN REVEALED A SHAM. OUR KIN ENSLAVED US... AND IN THE END...
...IT WAS YOU WHO SANK ATLANTIS.
YOU ARE THE GREAT DEVASTATION.
THERE MUST BE A RECKONING.

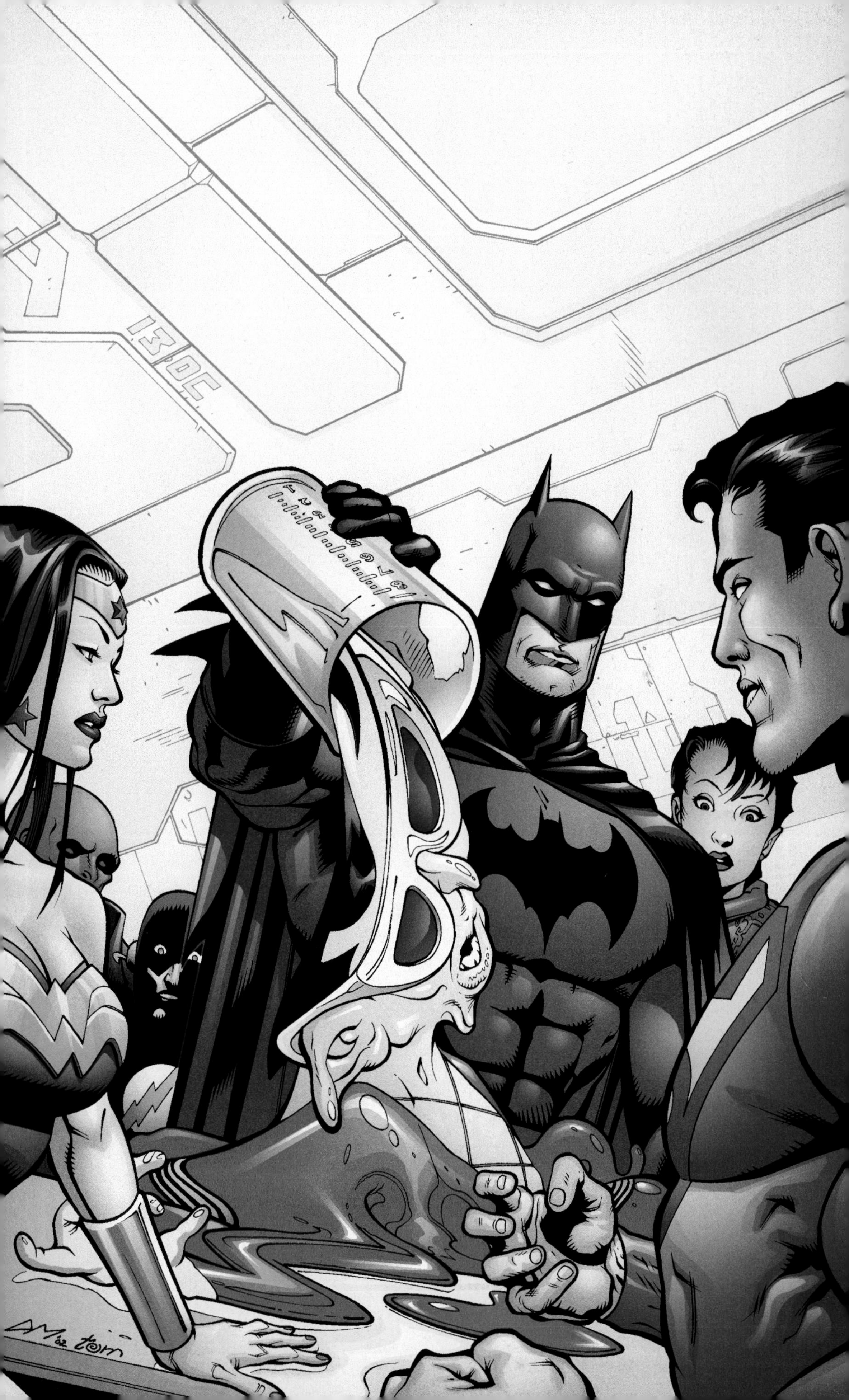

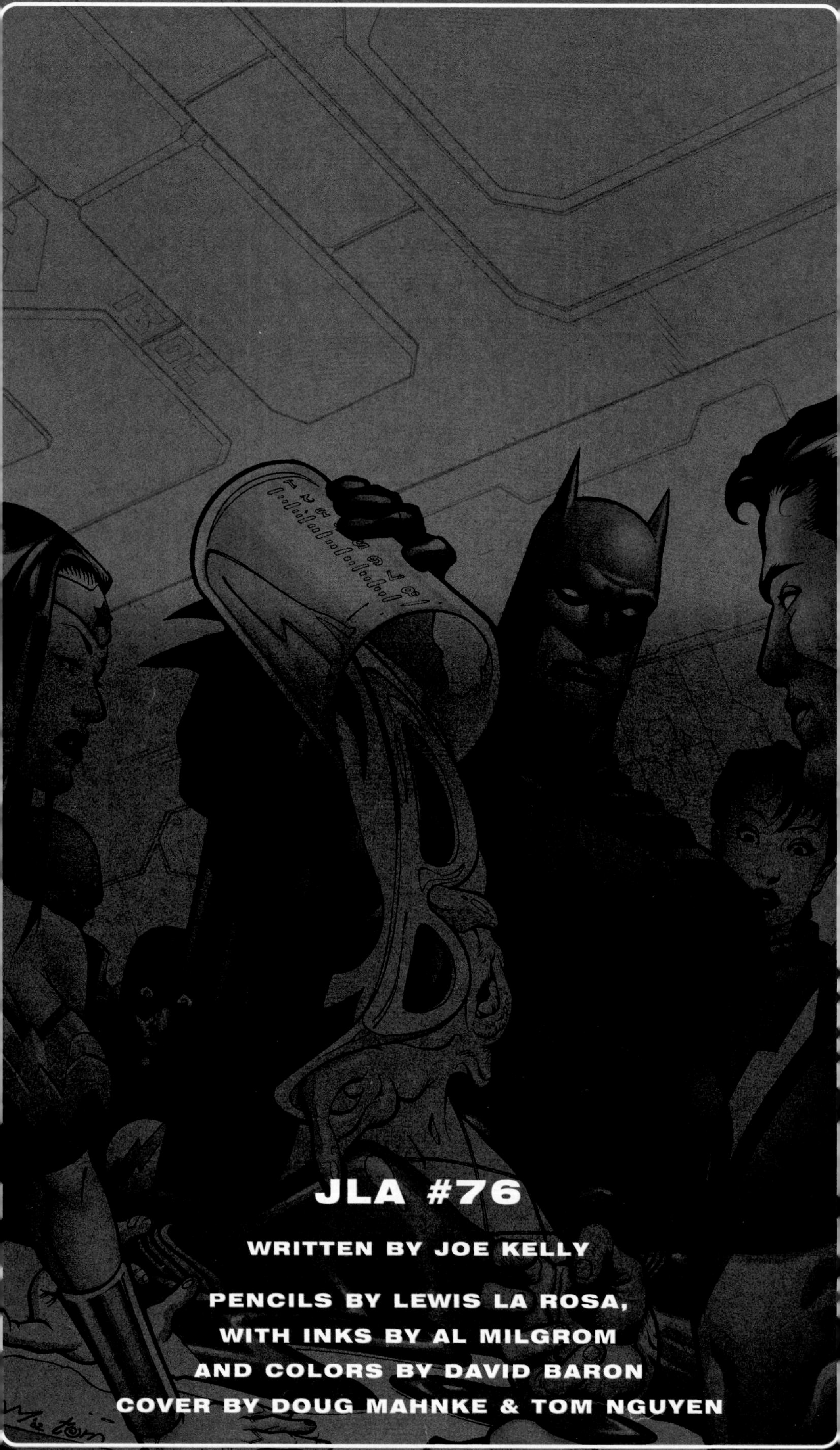

JLA #76

WRITTEN BY JOE KELLY

PENCILS BY LEWIS LA ROSA,
WITH INKS BY AL MILGROM
AND COLORS BY DAVID BARON
COVER BY DOUG MAHNKE & TOM NGUYEN

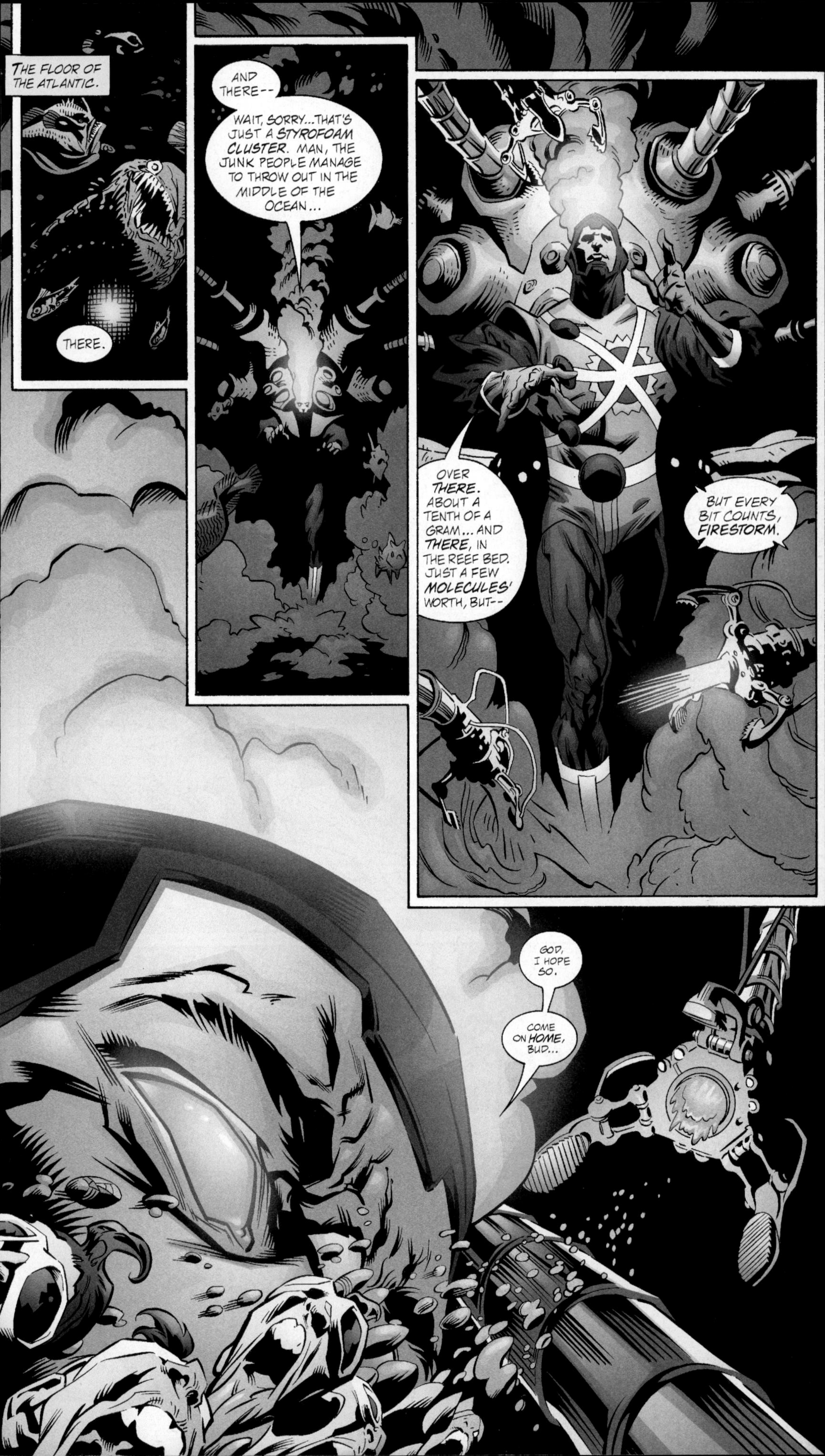
THE FLOOR OF THE ATLANTIC.
THERE.
AND THERE--
WAIT, SORRY...THAT'S JUST A STYROFOAM CLUSTER. MAN, THE JUNK PEOPLE MANAGE TO THROW OUT IN THE MIDDLE OF THE OCEAN...
OVER THERE. ABOUT A TENTH OF A GRAM... AND THERE, IN THE REEF BED. JUST A FEW MOLECULES' WORTH, BUT--
BUT EVERY BIT COUNTS, FIRESTORM.
GOD, I HOPE SO.
COME ON HOME, BUD...

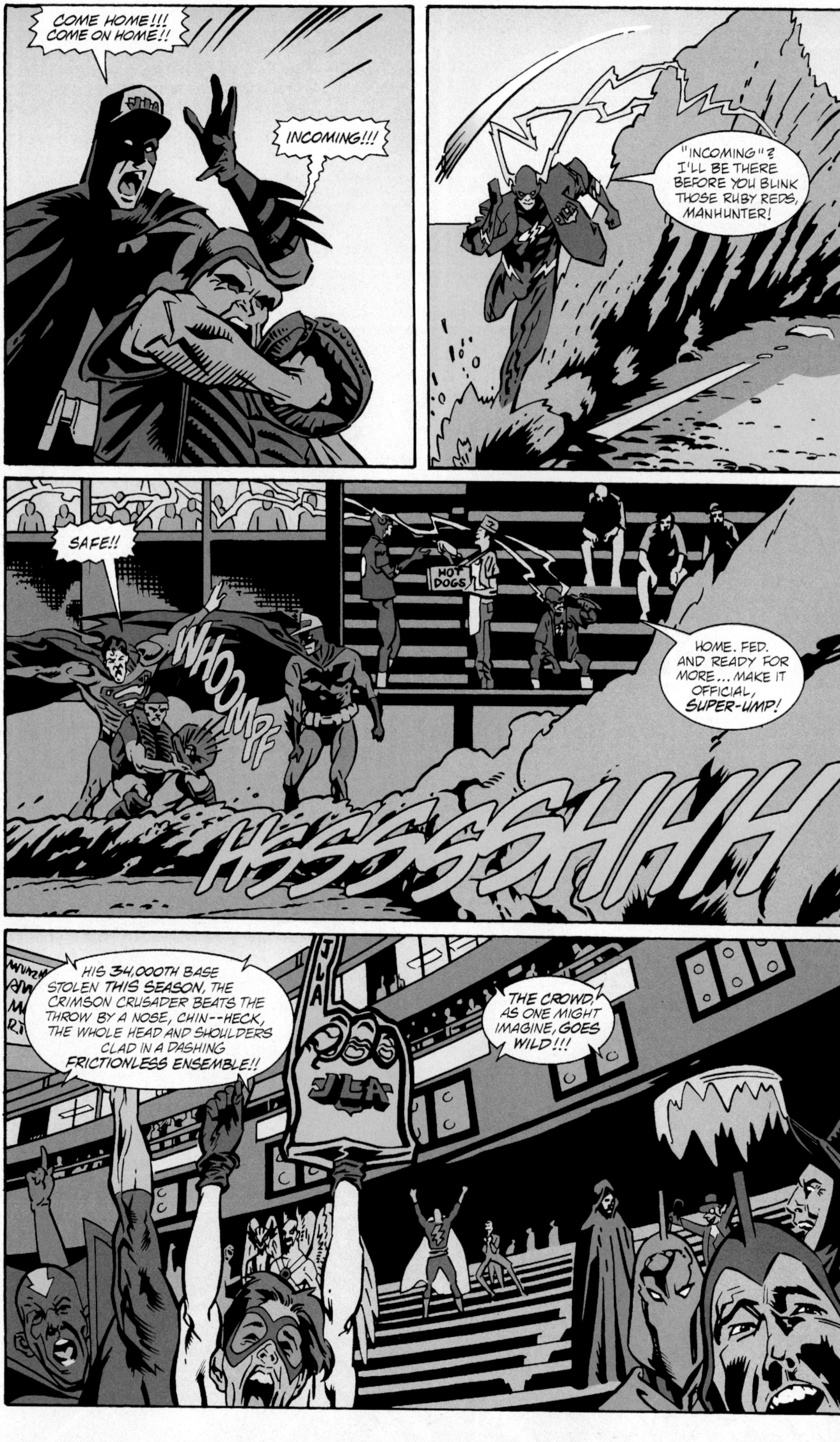
COME HOME!!! COME ON HOME!!
INCOMING!!!
"INCOMING"? I'LL BE THERE BEFORE YOU BLINK THOSE RUBY REDS, MANHUNTER!
SAFE!!
HOT DOGS
WHOOMPF
HOME. FED. AND READY FOR MORE... MAKE IT OFFICIAL, SUPER-UMP!
HSSSSSHHH
HIS 34,000TH BASE STOLEN THIS SEASON, THE CRIMSON CRUSADER BEATS THE THROW BY A NOSE, CHIN--HECK, THE WHOLE HEAD AND SHOULDERS CLAD IN A DASHING FRICTIONLESS ENSEMBLE!!
JLA
THE CROWD, AS ONE MIGHT IMAGINE, GOES WILD!!!
JLA

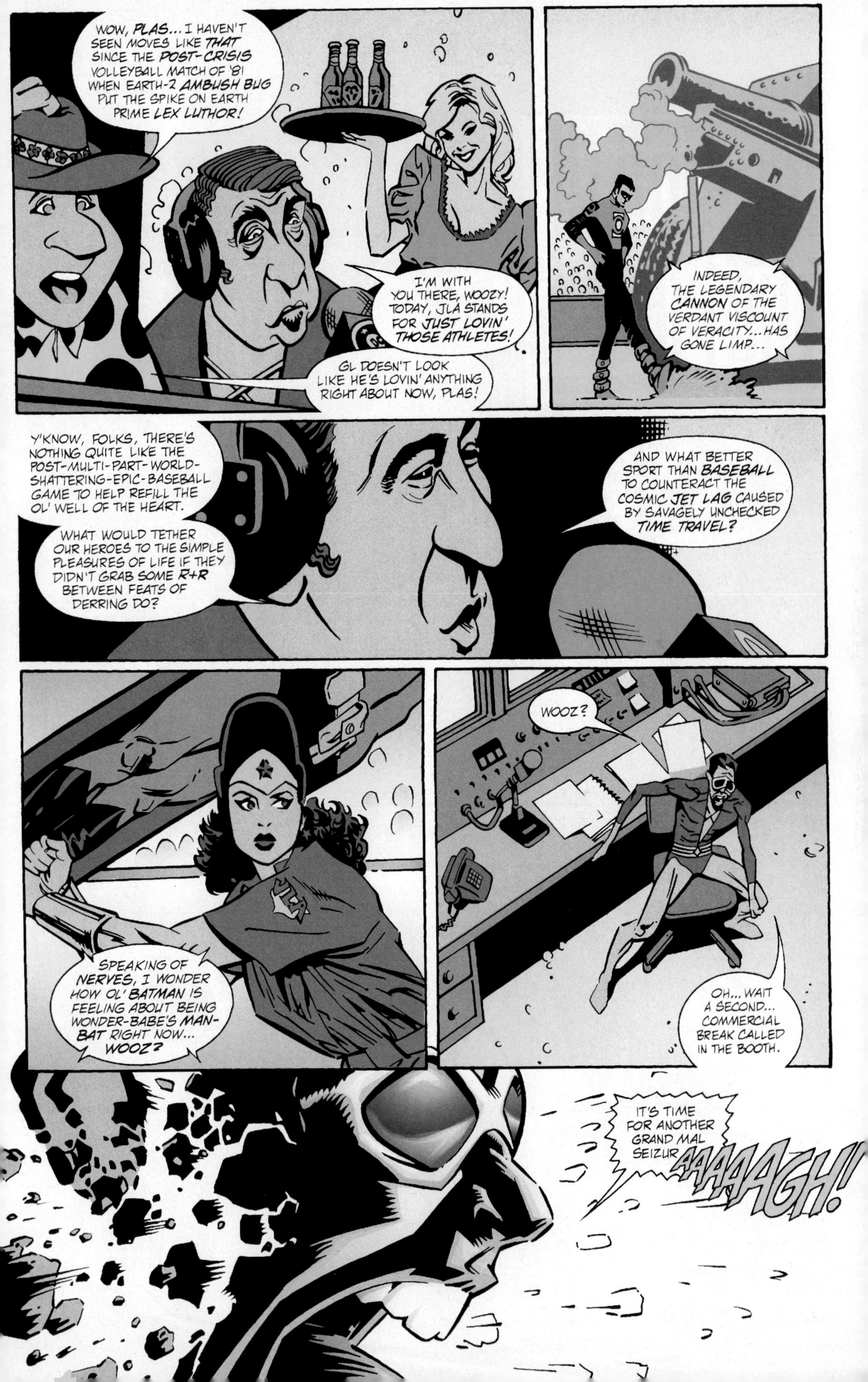
WOW, PLAS... I HAVEN'T SEEN MOVES LIKE THAT SINCE THE POST-CRISIS VOLLEYBALL MATCH OF '81 WHEN EARTH-2 AMBUSH BUG PUT THE SPIKE ON EARTH PRIME LEX LUTHOR!
I'M WITH YOU THERE, WOOZY! TODAY, JLA STANDS FOR JUST LOVIN' THOSE ATHLETES!
GL DOESN'T LOOK LIKE HE'S LOVIN' ANYTHING RIGHT ABOUT NOW, PLAS!
INDEED, THE LEGENDARY CANNON OF THE VERDANT VISCOUNT OF VERACITY... HAS GONE LIMP...
Y'KNOW, FOLKS, THERE'S NOTHING QUITE LIKE THE POST-MULTI-PART-WORLD-SHATTERING-EPIC-BASEBALL GAME TO HELP REFILL THE OL' WELL OF THE HEART.
WHAT WOULD TETHER OUR HEROES TO THE SIMPLE PLEASURES OF LIFE IF THEY DIDN'T GRAB SOME R+R BETWEEN FEATS OF DERRING DO?
AND WHAT BETTER SPORT THAN BASEBALL TO COUNTERACT THE COSMIC JET LAG CAUSED BY SAVAGELY UNCHECKED TIME TRAVEL?
SPEAKING OF NERVES, I WONDER HOW OL' BATMAN IS FEELING ABOUT BEING WONDER-BABE'S MAN-BAT RIGHT NOW... WOOZ?
WOOZ?
OH... WAIT A SECOND... COMMERCIAL BREAK CALLED IN THE BOOTH.
IT'S TIME FOR ANOTHER GRAND MAL SEIZUR
AAAAAGH!

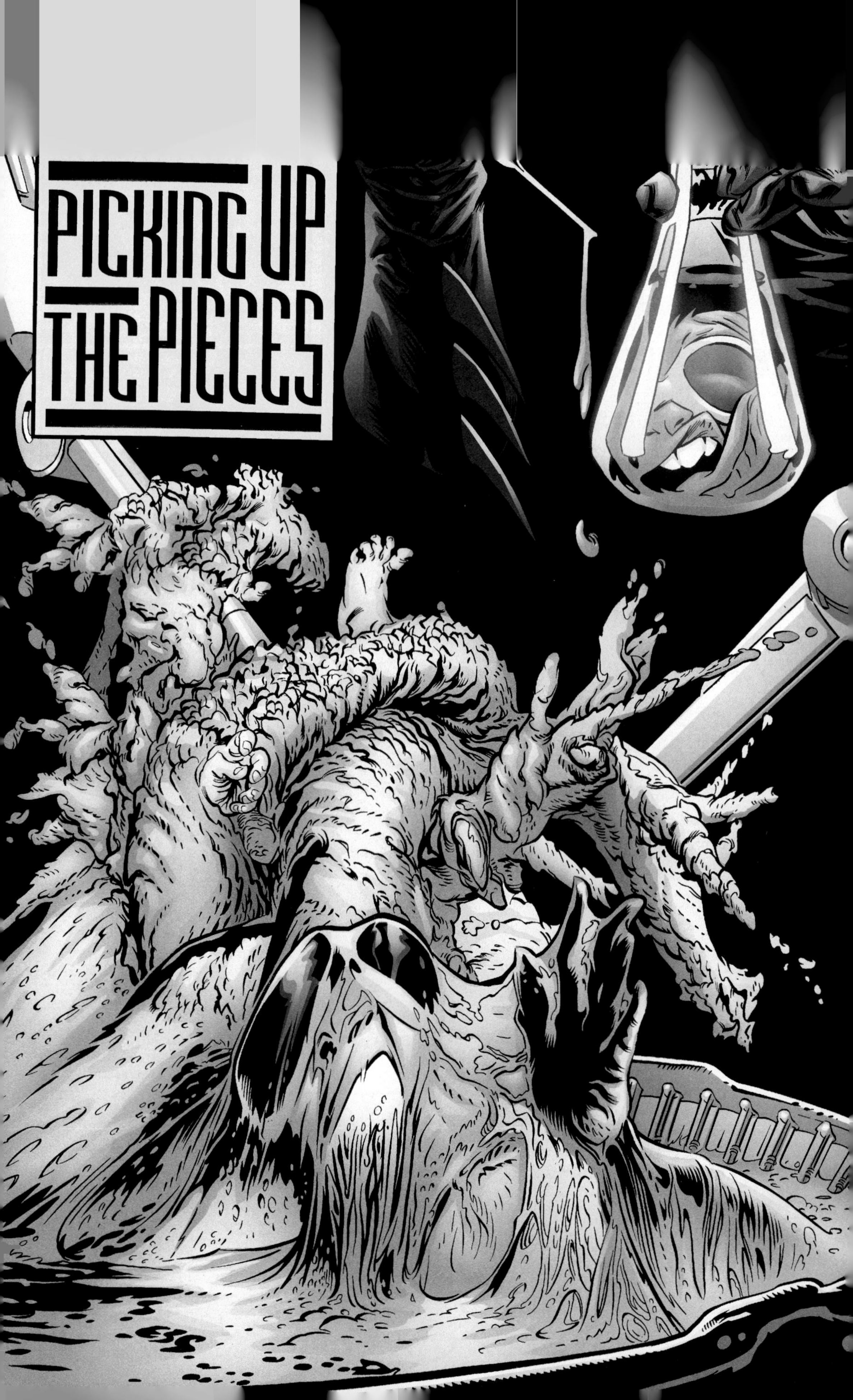
PICKING UP
THE PIECES

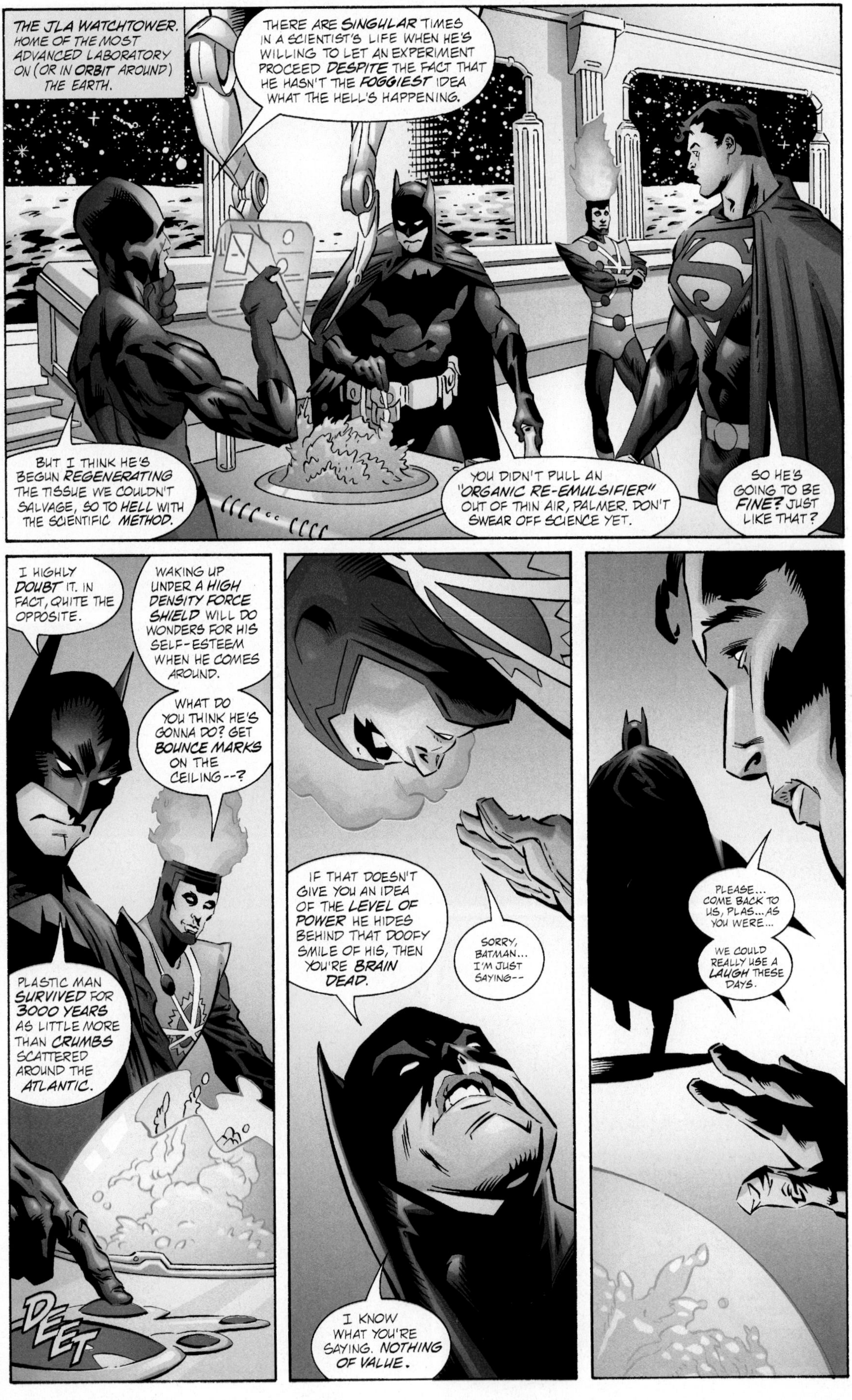
THE JLA WATCHTOWER. HOME OF THE MOST ADVANCED LABORATORY ON (OR IN ORBIT AROUND) THE EARTH.
THERE ARE SINGULAR TIMES IN A SCIENTIST'S LIFE WHEN HE'S WILLING TO LET AN EXPERIMENT PROCEED DESPITE THE FACT THAT HE HASN'T THE FOGGIEST IDEA WHAT THE HELL'S HAPPENING.
BUT I THINK HE'S BEGUN REGENERATING THE TISSUE WE COULDN'T SALVAGE, SO TO HELL WITH THE SCIENTIFIC METHOD.
YOU DIDN'T PULL AN "ORGANIC RE-EMULSIFIER" OUT OF THIN AIR, PALMER. DON'T SWEAR OFF SCIENCE YET.
SO HE'S GOING TO BE FINE? JUST LIKE THAT?
I HIGHLY DOUBT IT. IN FACT, QUITE THE OPPOSITE.
WAKING UP UNDER A HIGH DENSITY FORCE SHIELD WILL DO WONDERS FOR HIS SELF-ESTEEM WHEN HE COMES AROUND.
WHAT DO YOU THINK HE'S GONNA DO? GET BOUNCE MARKS ON THE CEILING--?
PLASTIC MAN SURVIVED FOR 3000 YEARS AS LITTLE MORE THAN CRUMBS SCATTERED AROUND THE ATLANTIC.
DEET
IF THAT DOESN'T GIVE YOU AN IDEA OF THE LEVEL OF POWER HE HIDES BEHIND THAT DOOFY SMILE OF HIS, THEN YOU'RE BRAIN DEAD.
SORRY, BATMAN... I'M JUST SAYING--
I KNOW WHAT YOU'RE SAYING. NOTHING OF VALUE.
PLEASE... COME BACK TO US, PLAS... AS YOU WERE...
WE COULD REALLY USE A LAUGH THESE DAYS.

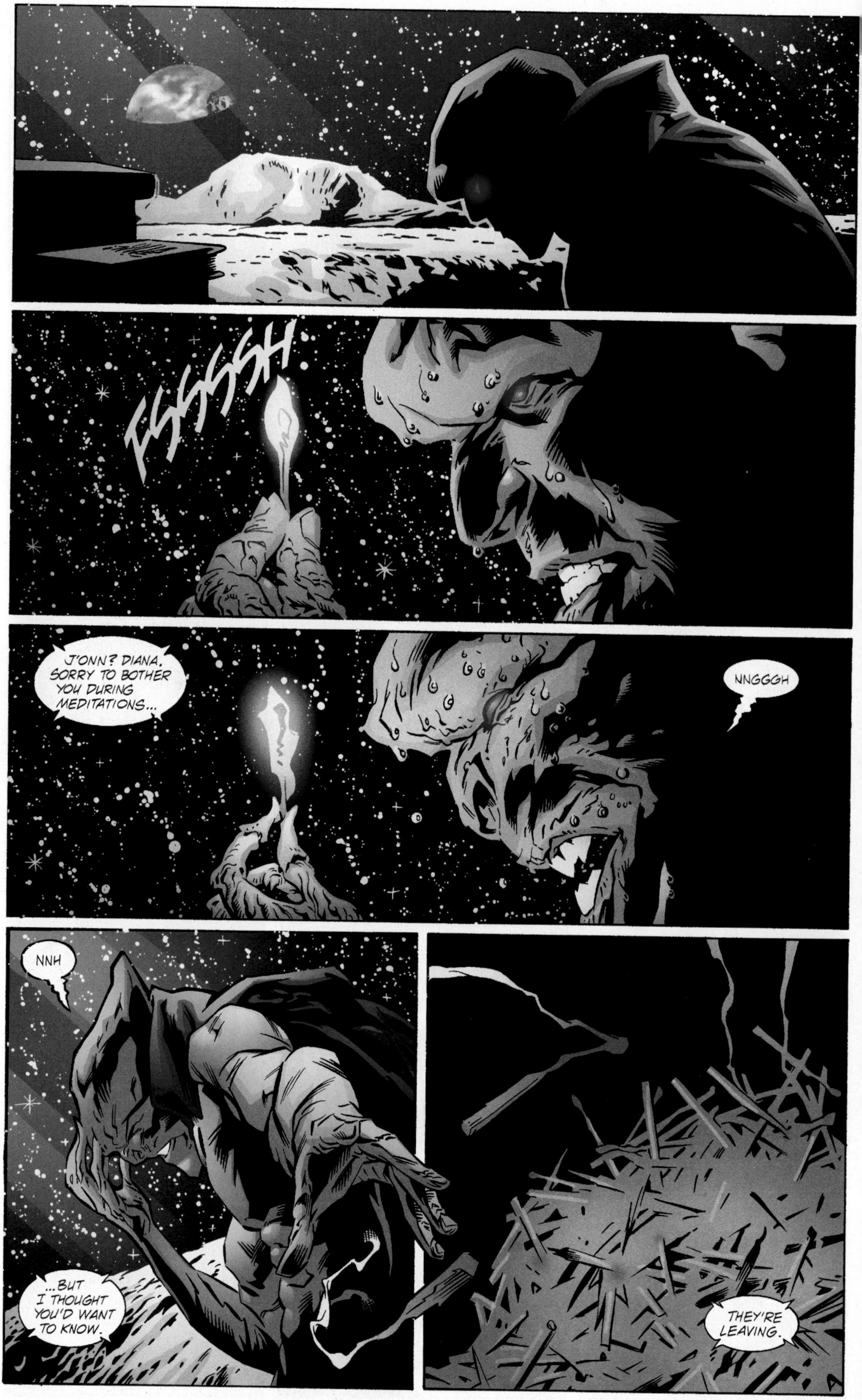
FSSSSH
J'ONN? DIANA. SORRY TO BOTHER YOU DURING MEDITATIONS...
NNGGGH
NNH
...BUT I THOUGHT YOU'D WANT TO KNOW.
THEY'RE LEAVING.

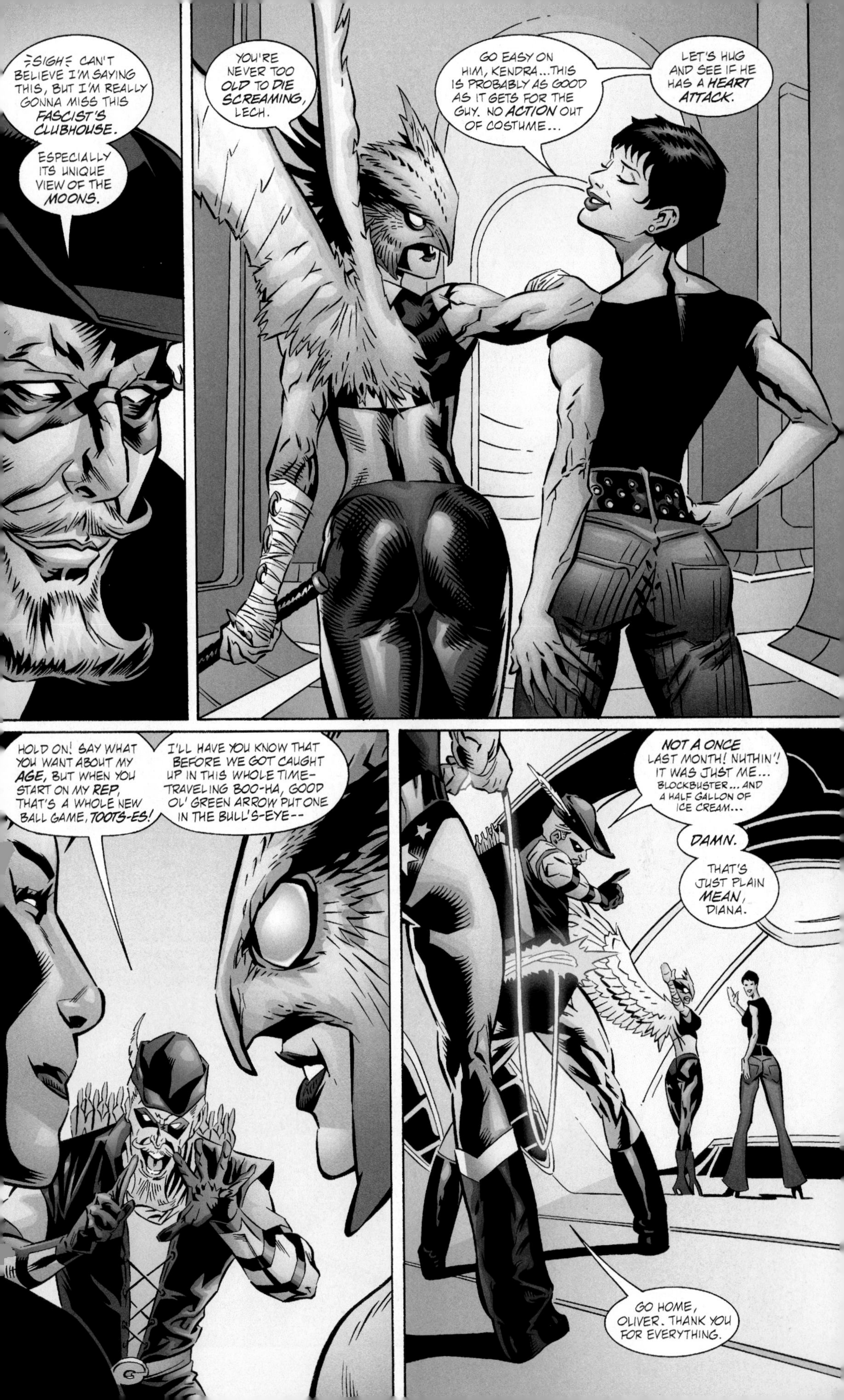

≈SIGH≈ CAN'T BELIEVE I'M SAYING THIS, BUT I'M REALLY GONNA MISS THIS FASCIST'S CLUBHOUSE.
ESPECIALLY ITS UNIQUE VIEW OF THE MOONS.
YOU'RE NEVER TOO OLD TO DIE SCREAMING, LECH.
GO EASY ON HIM, KENDRA... THIS IS PROBABLY AS GOOD AS IT GETS FOR THE GUY. NO ACTION OUT OF COSTUME...
LET'S HUG AND SEE IF HE HAS A HEART ATTACK.
HOLD ON! SAY WHAT YOU WANT ABOUT MY AGE, BUT WHEN YOU START ON MY REP, THAT'S A WHOLE NEW BALL GAME, TOOTS-ES!
I'LL HAVE YOU KNOW THAT BEFORE WE GOT CAUGHT UP IN THIS WHOLE TIME-TRAVELING BOO-HA, GOOD OL' GREEN ARROW PUT ONE IN THE BULL'S-EYE--
NOT A ONCE LAST MONTH! NUTHIN'! IT WAS JUST ME... BLOCKBUSTER... AND A HALF GALLON OF ICE CREAM...
DAMN.
THAT'S JUST PLAIN MEAN, DIANA.
GO HOME, OLIVER. THANK YOU FOR EVERYTHING.

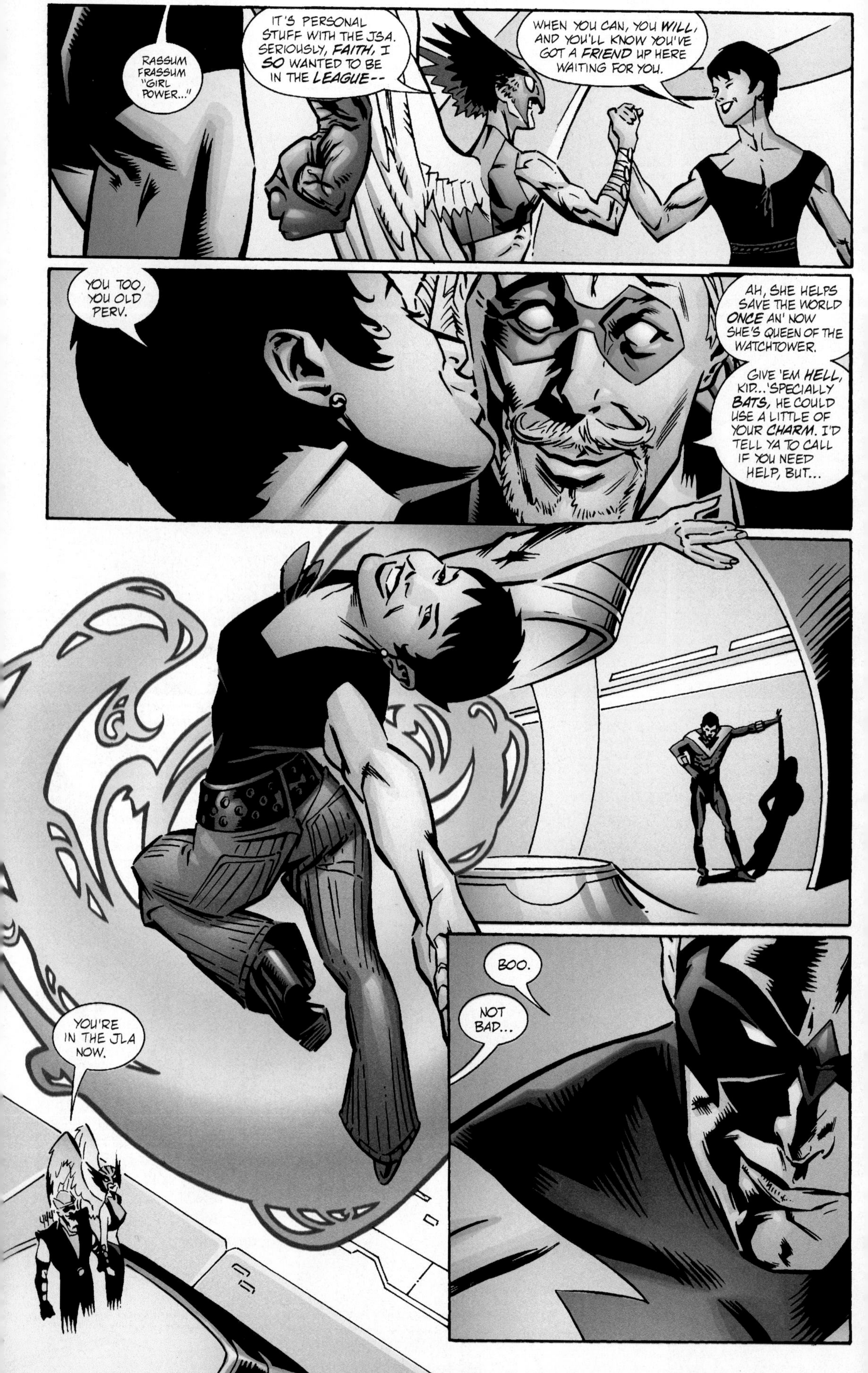
RASSUM FRASSUM "GIRL POWER..."
IT'S PERSONAL STUFF WITH THE JSA. SERIOUSLY, FAITH, I SO WANTED TO BE IN THE LEAGUE--
WHEN YOU CAN, YOU WILL, AND YOU'LL KNOW YOU'VE GOT A FRIEND UP HERE WAITING FOR YOU.
YOU TOO, YOU OLD PERV.
AH, SHE HELPS SAVE THE WORLD ONCE AN' NOW SHE'S QUEEN OF THE WATCHTOWER.
GIVE 'EM HELL, KID...'SPECIALLY BATS, HE COULD USE A LITTLE OF YOUR CHARM. I'D TELL YA TO CALL IF YOU NEED HELP, BUT...
YOU'RE IN THE JLA NOW.
BOO.
NOT BAD...

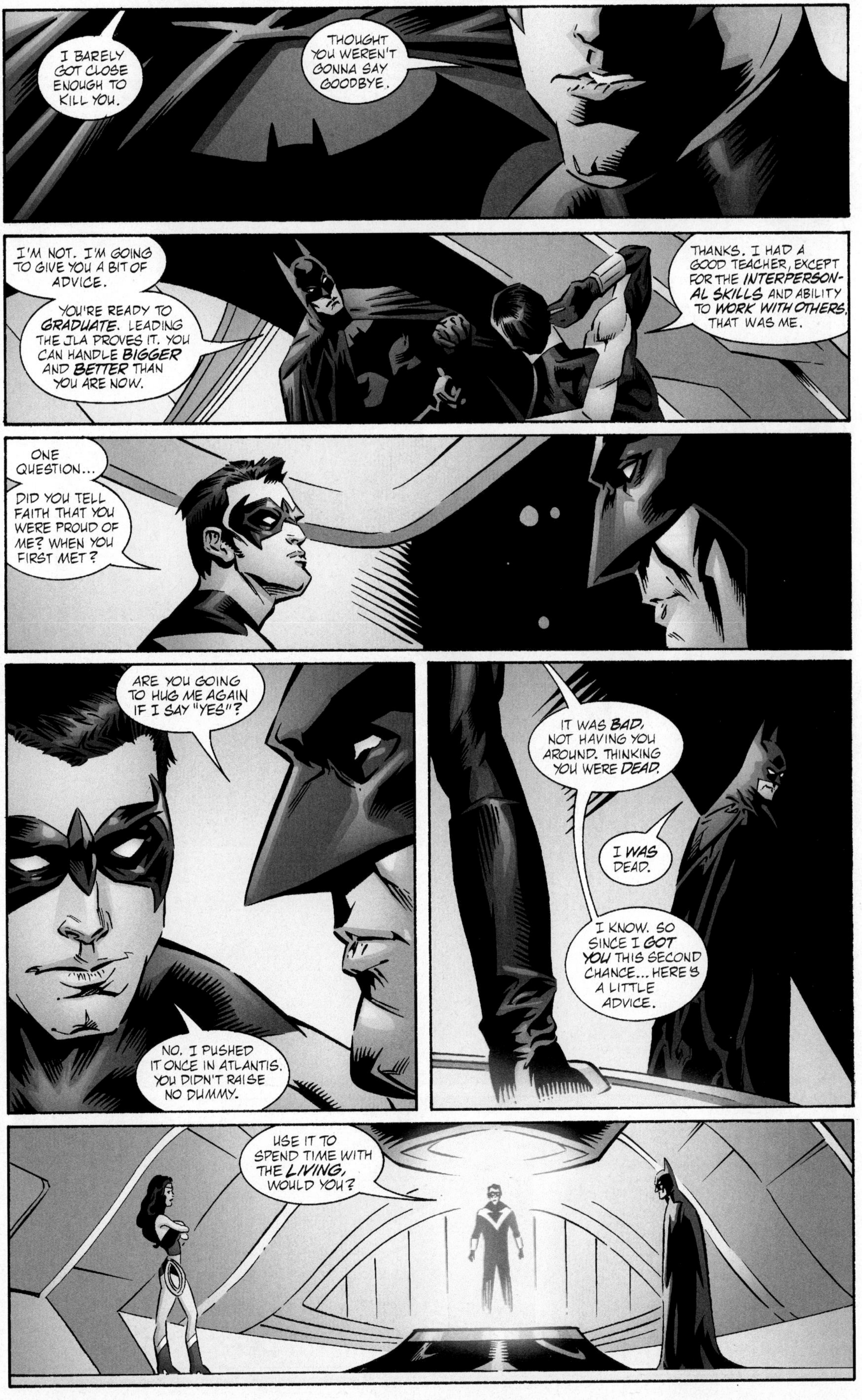

I BARELY GOT CLOSE ENOUGH TO KILL YOU.
THOUGHT YOU WEREN'T GONNA SAY GOODBYE.
I'M NOT. I'M GOING TO GIVE YOU A BIT OF ADVICE.
YOU'RE READY TO GRADUATE. LEADING THE JLA PROVES IT. YOU CAN HANDLE BIGGER AND BETTER THAN YOU ARE NOW.
THANKS. I HAD A GOOD TEACHER, EXCEPT FOR THE INTERPERSONAL SKILLS AND ABILITY TO WORK WITH OTHERS. THAT WAS ME.
ONE QUESTION...
DID YOU TELL FAITH THAT YOU WERE PROUD OF ME? WHEN YOU FIRST MET?
ARE YOU GOING TO HUG ME AGAIN IF I SAY "YES"?
NO. I PUSHED IT ONCE IN ATLANTIS. YOU DIDN'T RAISE NO DUMMY.
IT WAS BAD, NOT HAVING YOU AROUND. THINKING YOU WERE DEAD.
I WAS DEAD.
I KNOW. SO SINCE I GOT YOU THIS SECOND CHANCE... HERE'S A LITTLE ADVICE.
USE IT TO SPEND TIME WITH THE LIVING, WOULD YOU?

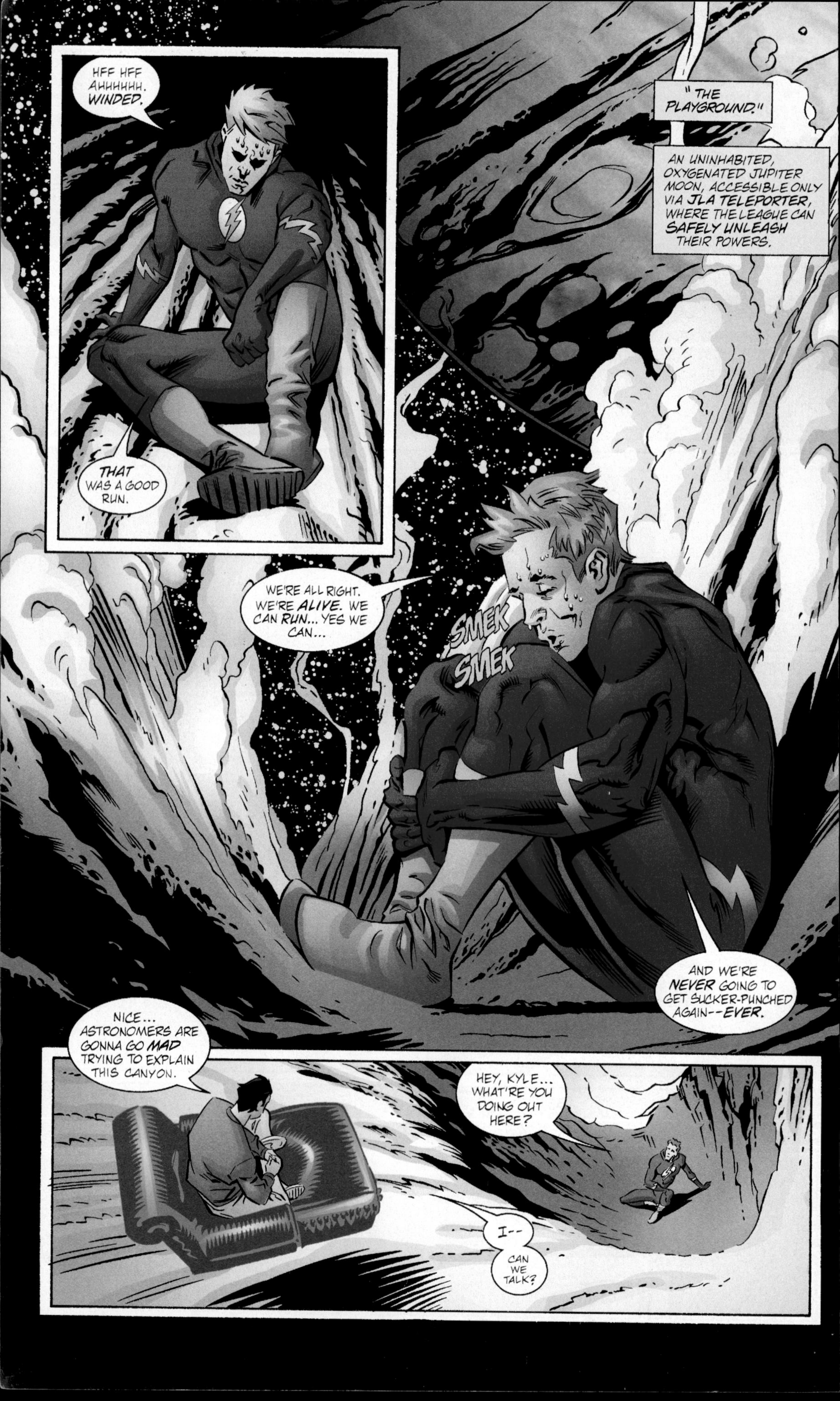

HFF HFF AHHHHHH. WINDED.
THAT WAS A GOOD RUN.
"THE PLAYGROUND."
AN UNINHABITED, OXYGENATED JUPITER MOON, ACCESSIBLE ONLY VIA JLA TELEPORTER, WHERE THE LEAGUE CAN SAFELY UNLEASH THEIR POWERS.
WE'RE ALL RIGHT. WE'RE ALIVE. WE CAN RUN... YES WE CAN...
SMEK
SMEK
AND WE'RE NEVER GOING TO GET SUCKER-PUNCHED AGAIN--EVER.
NICE... ASTRONOMERS ARE GONNA GO MAD TRYING TO EXPLAIN THIS CANYON.
HEY, KYLE... WHAT'RE YOU DOING OUT HERE?
I--
CAN WE TALK?

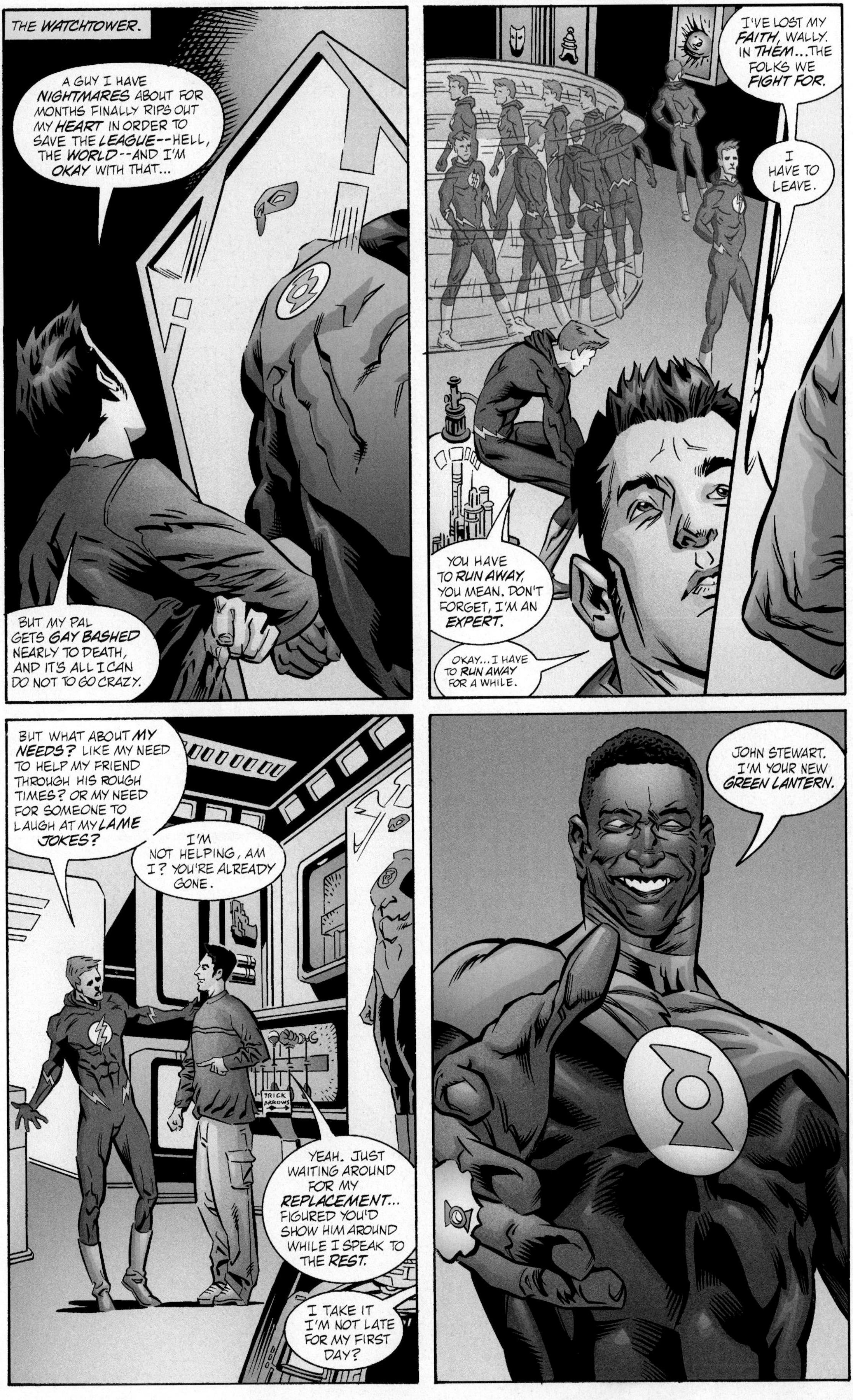
THE WATCHTOWER.
A GUY I HAVE NIGHTMARES ABOUT FOR MONTHS FINALLY RIPS OUT MY HEART IN ORDER TO SAVE THE LEAGUE--HELL, THE WORLD--AND I'M OKAY WITH THAT...
BUT MY PAL GETS GAY BASHED NEARLY TO DEATH, AND IT'S ALL I CAN DO NOT TO GO CRAZY.
I'VE LOST MY FAITH, WALLY. IN THEM...THE FOLKS WE FIGHT FOR.
I HAVE TO LEAVE.
YOU HAVE TO RUN AWAY, YOU MEAN. DON'T FORGET, I'M AN EXPERT.
OKAY...I HAVE TO RUN AWAY FOR A WHILE.
BUT WHAT ABOUT MY NEEDS? LIKE MY NEED TO HELP MY FRIEND THROUGH HIS ROUGH TIMES? OR MY NEED FOR SOMEONE TO LAUGH AT MY LAME JOKES?
I'M NOT HELPING, AM I? YOU'RE ALREADY GONE.
TRICK ARROWS
YEAH. JUST WAITING AROUND FOR MY REPLACEMENT... FIGURED YOU'D SHOW HIM AROUND WHILE I SPEAK TO THE REST.
I TAKE IT I'M NOT LATE FOR MY FIRST DAY?
JOHN STEWART. I'M YOUR NEW GREEN LANTERN.

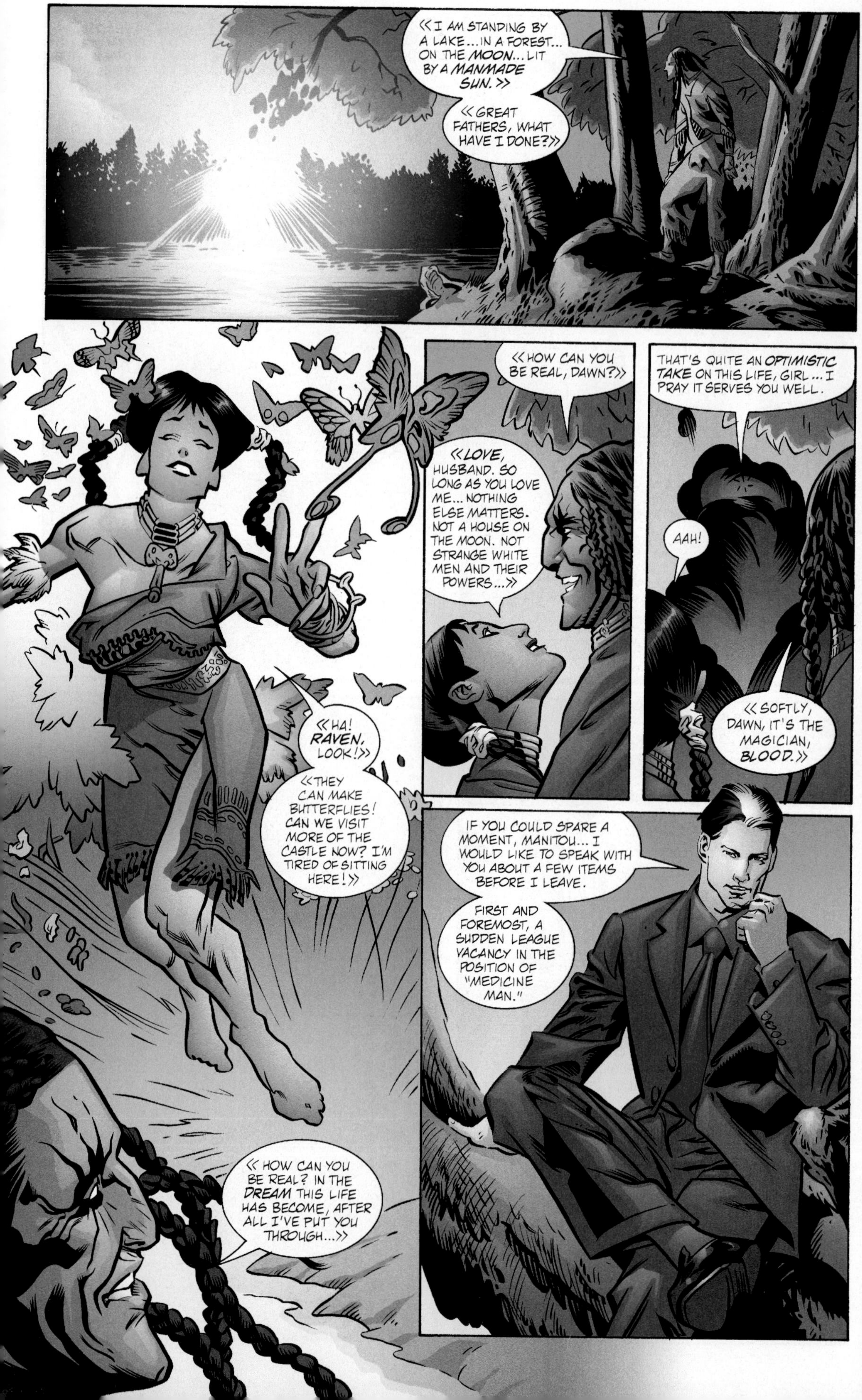

<< I AM STANDING BY A LAKE... IN A FOREST... ON THE MOON... LIT BY A MANMADE SUN. >>
<< GREAT FATHERS, WHAT HAVE I DONE? >>
<< HA! RAVEN, LOOK! >>
<< THEY CAN MAKE BUTTERFLIES! CAN WE VISIT MORE OF THE CASTLE NOW? I'M TIRED OF SITTING HERE! >>
<< HOW CAN YOU BE REAL? IN THE DREAM THIS LIFE HAS BECOME, AFTER ALL I'VE PUT YOU THROUGH... >>
<< HOW CAN YOU BE REAL, DAWN? >>
<< LOVE, HUSBAND. SO LONG AS YOU LOVE ME... NOTHING ELSE MATTERS. NOT A HOUSE ON THE MOON. NOT STRANGE WHITE MEN AND THEIR POWERS... >>
THAT'S QUITE AN OPTIMISTIC TAKE ON THIS LIFE, GIRL... I PRAY IT SERVES YOU WELL.
AAH!
<< SOFTLY, DAWN, IT'S THE MAGICIAN, BLOOD. >>
IF YOU COULD SPARE A MOMENT, MANITOU... I WOULD LIKE TO SPEAK WITH YOU ABOUT A FEW ITEMS BEFORE I LEAVE.
FIRST AND FOREMOST, A SUDDEN LEAGUE VACANCY IN THE POSITION OF "MEDICINE MAN."

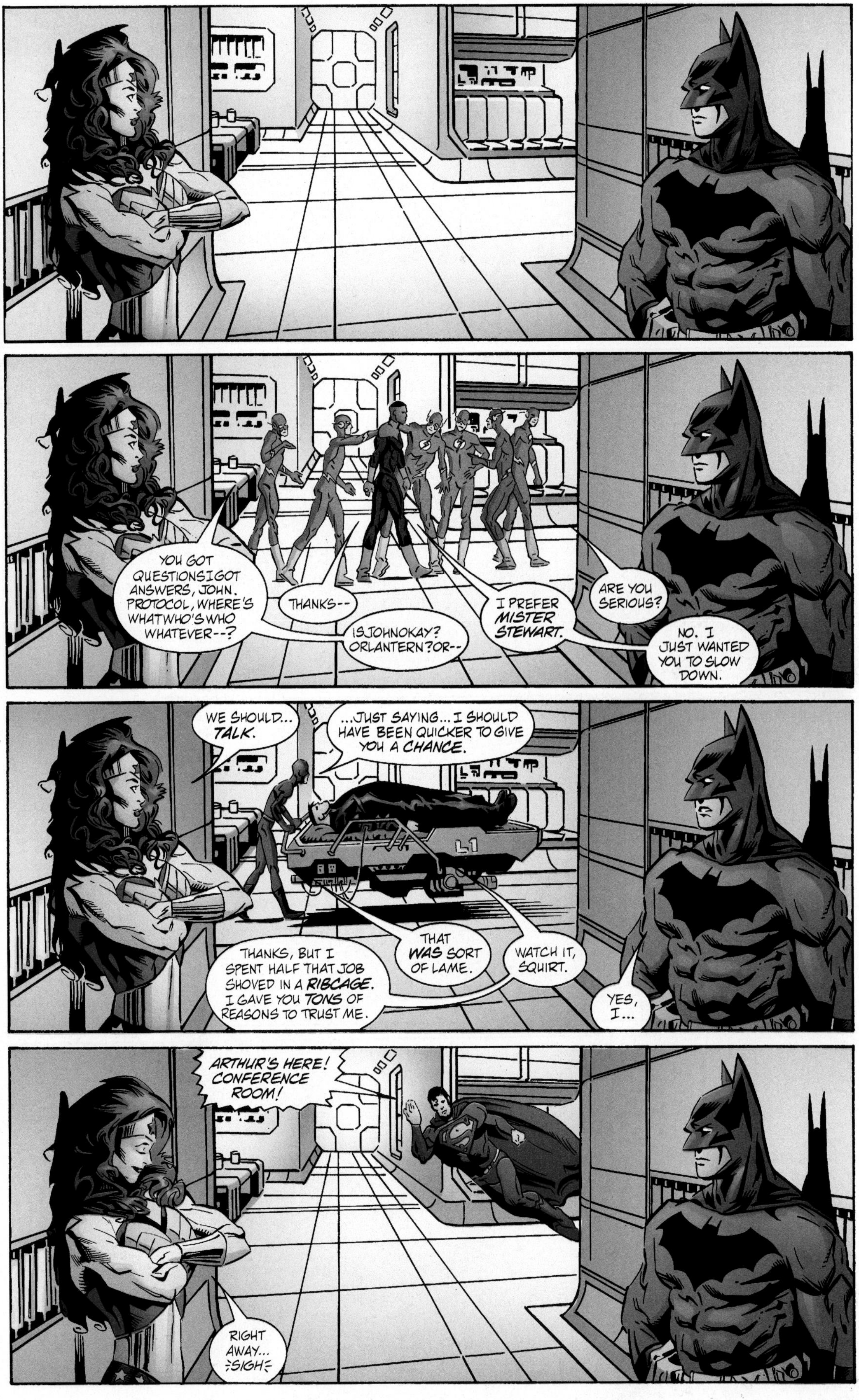
YOU GOT QUESTIONSIGOT ANSWERS, JOHN. PROTOCOL, WHERE'S WHATWHO'S WHO WHATEVER--?
THANKS--
ISJOHNOKAY? ORLANTERN?OR--
I PREFER *MISTER STEWART.*
ARE YOU SERIOUS?
NO. I JUST WANTED YOU TO SLOW DOWN.
WE SHOULD... *TALK.*
...JUST SAYING... I SHOULD HAVE BEEN QUICKER TO GIVE YOU A *CHANCE.*
L1
THANKS, BUT I SPENT HALF THAT JOB SHOVED IN A *RIBCAGE.* I GAVE YOU *TONS* OF REASONS TO TRUST ME.
THAT *WAS* SORT OF LAME.
WATCH IT, SQUIRT.
YES, I...
ARTHUR'S HERE! CONFERENCE ROOM!
RIGHT AWAY... ⁓SIGH⁓

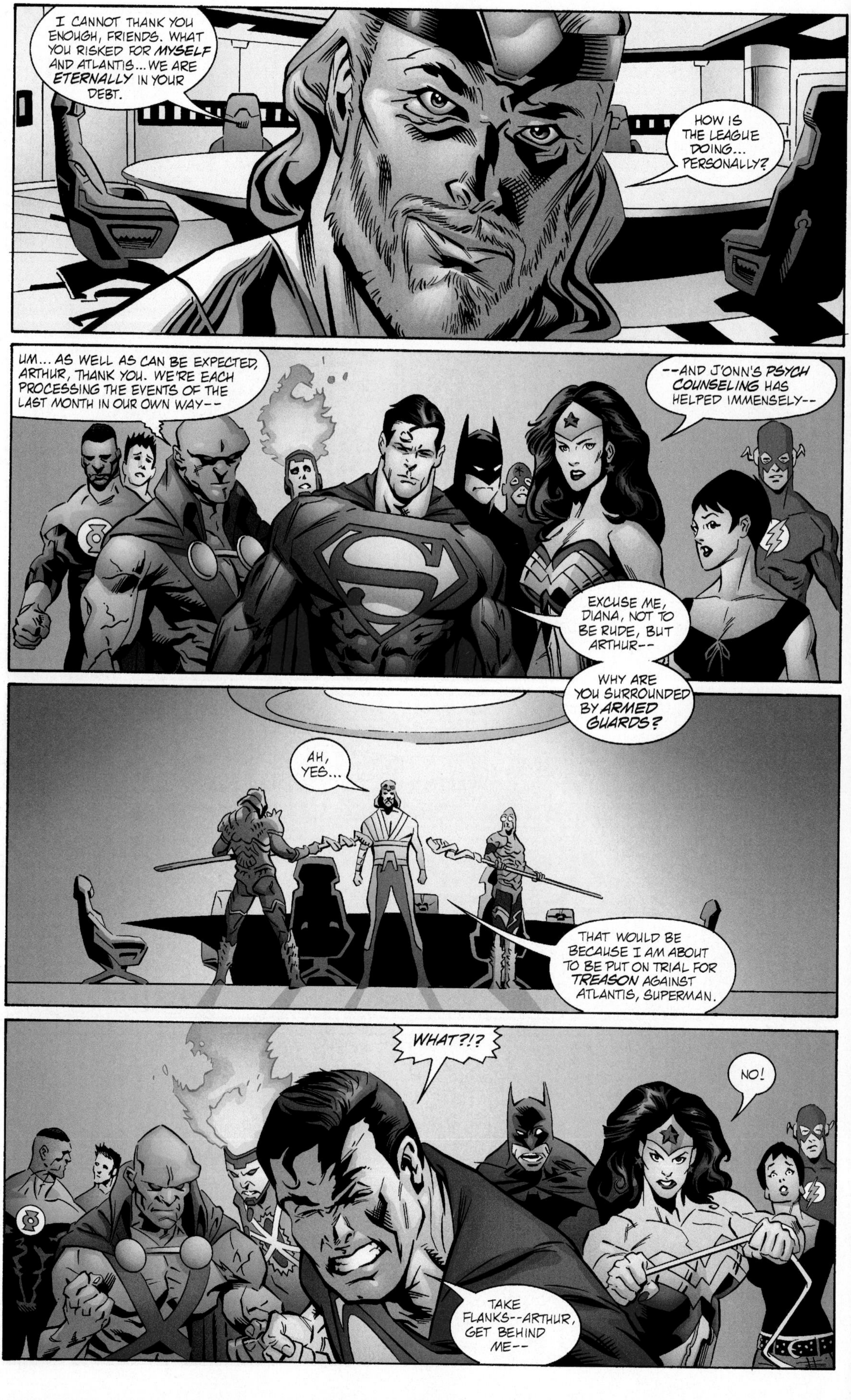
I CANNOT THANK YOU ENOUGH, FRIENDS. WHAT YOU RISKED FOR MYSELF AND ATLANTIS... WE ARE ETERNALLY IN YOUR DEBT.
HOW IS THE LEAGUE DOING... PERSONALLY?
UM... AS WELL AS CAN BE EXPECTED, ARTHUR, THANK YOU. WE'RE EACH PROCESSING THE EVENTS OF THE LAST MONTH IN OUR OWN WAY--
--AND J'ONN'S PSYCH COUNSELING HAS HELPED IMMENSELY--
EXCUSE ME, DIANA, NOT TO BE RUDE, BUT ARTHUR--
WHY ARE YOU SURROUNDED BY ARMED GUARDS?
AH, YES...
THAT WOULD BE BECAUSE I AM ABOUT TO BE PUT ON TRIAL FOR TREASON AGAINST ATLANTIS, SUPERMAN.
WHAT?!?
NO!
TAKE FLANKS--ARTHUR, GET BEHIND ME--

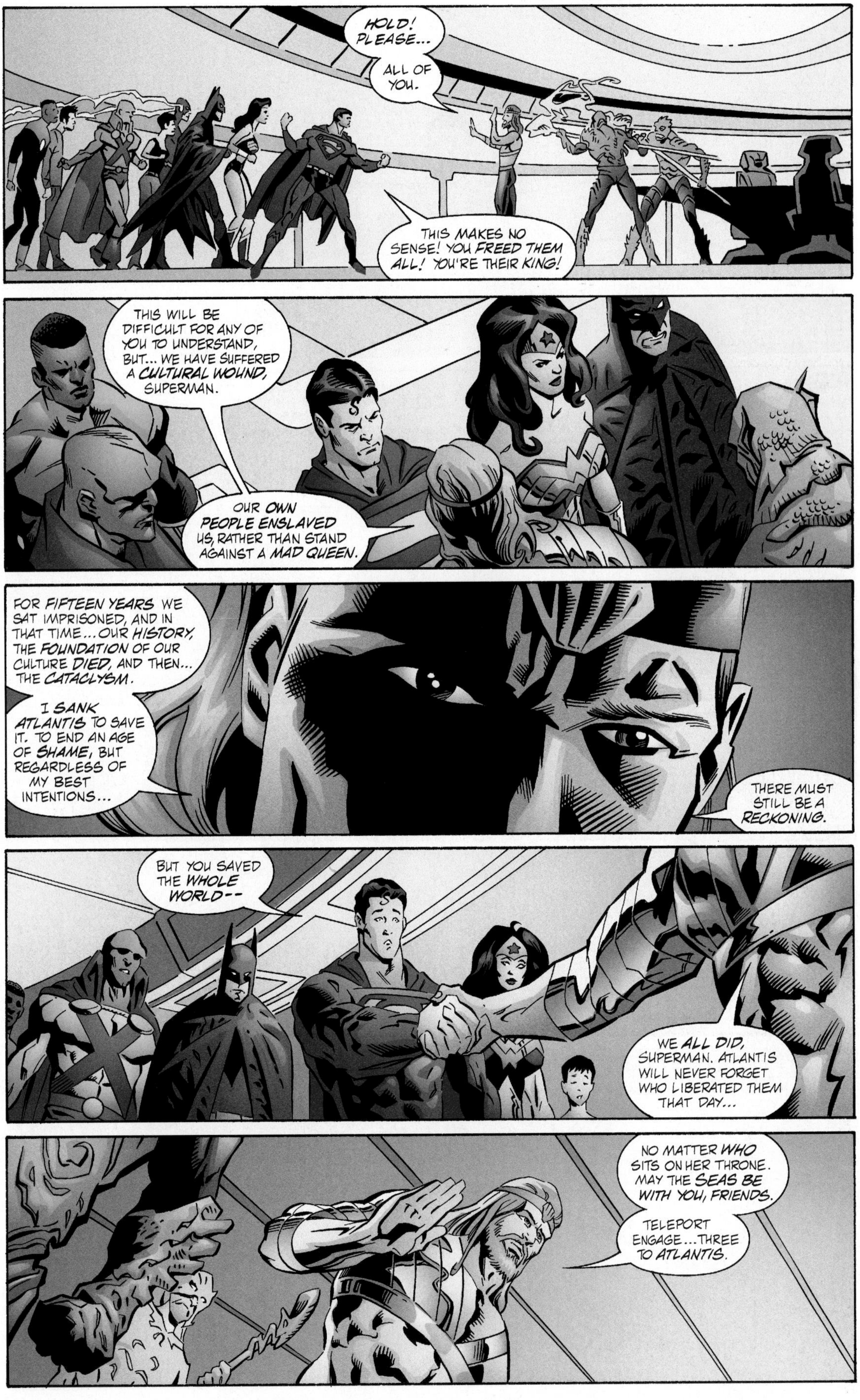
HOLD! PLEASE...
ALL OF YOU.
THIS MAKES NO SENSE! YOU FREED THEM ALL! YOU'RE THEIR KING!
THIS WILL BE DIFFICULT FOR ANY OF YOU TO UNDERSTAND, BUT... WE HAVE SUFFERED A CULTURAL WOUND, SUPERMAN.
OUR OWN PEOPLE ENSLAVED US, RATHER THAN STAND AGAINST A MAD QUEEN.
FOR FIFTEEN YEARS WE SAT IMPRISONED, AND IN THAT TIME... OUR HISTORY, THE FOUNDATION OF OUR CULTURE DIED, AND THEN... THE CATACLYSM.
I SANK ATLANTIS TO SAVE IT. TO END AN AGE OF SHAME, BUT REGARDLESS OF MY BEST INTENTIONS...
THERE MUST STILL BE A RECKONING.
BUT YOU SAVED THE WHOLE WORLD--
WE ALL DID, SUPERMAN. ATLANTIS WILL NEVER FORGET WHO LIBERATED THEM THAT DAY...
NO MATTER WHO SITS ON HER THRONE. MAY THE SEAS BE WITH YOU, FRIENDS.
TELEPORT ENGAGE... THREE TO ATLANTIS.

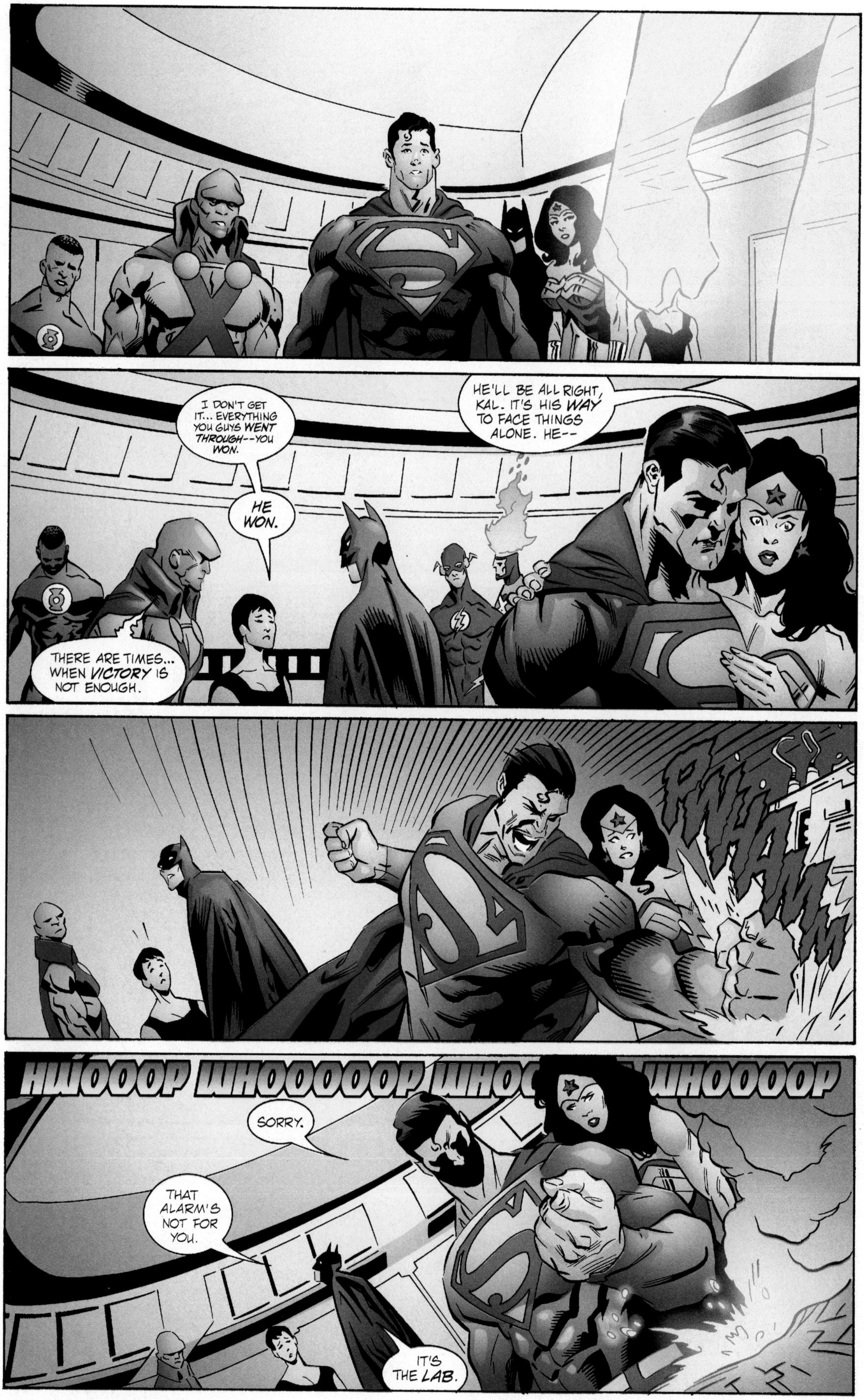
I DON'T GET IT... EVERYTHING YOU GUYS WENT THROUGH--YOU WON.
HE WON.
HE'LL BE ALL RIGHT, KAL. IT'S HIS WAY TO FACE THINGS ALONE. HE--
THERE ARE TIMES... WHEN VICTORY IS NOT ENOUGH.
PWHAMM
WHOOOOOOP
WHOOOOOP
SORRY.
THAT ALARM'S NOT FOR YOU.
IT'S THE LAB.

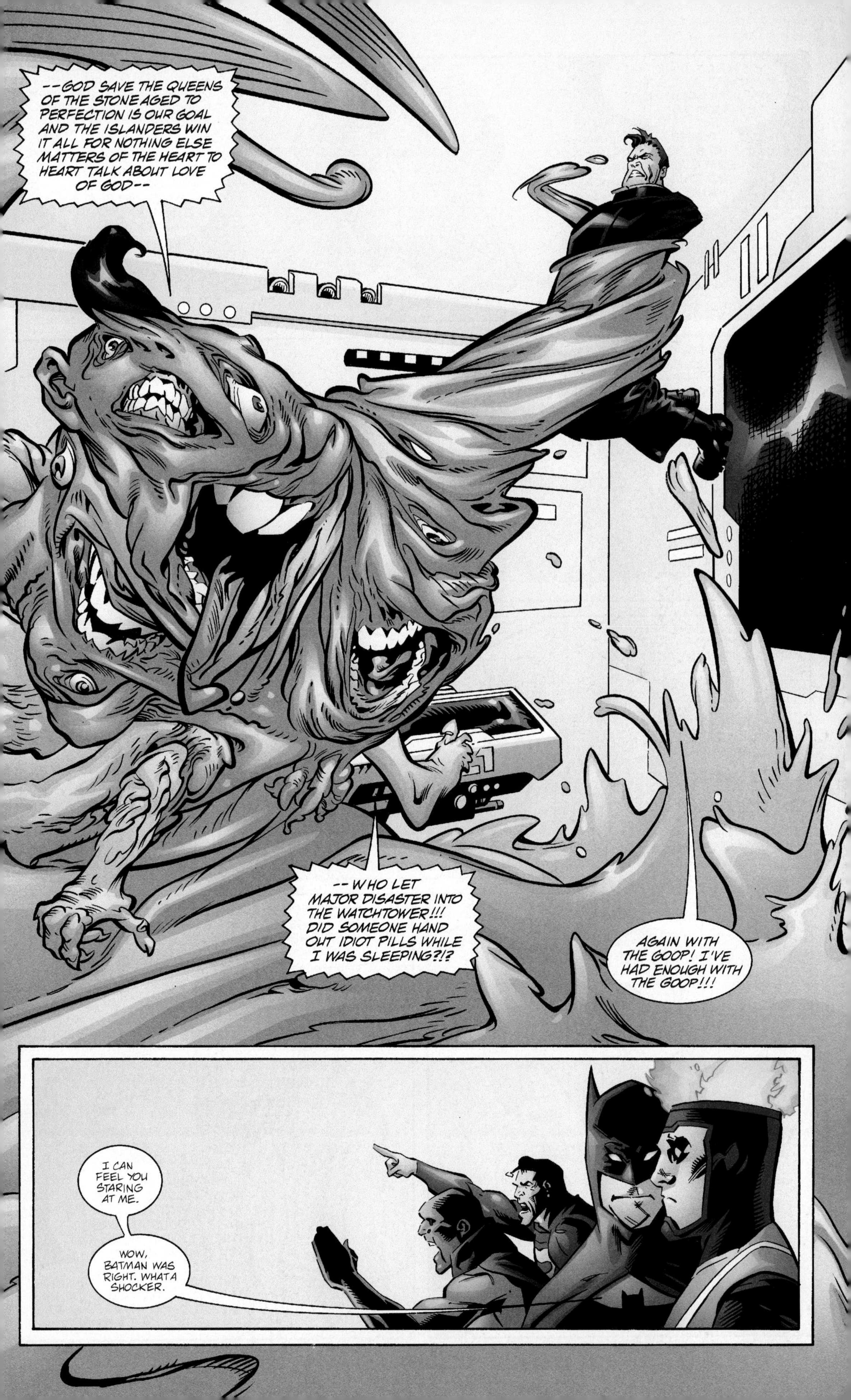
--GOD SAVE THE QUEENS OF THE STONE AGED TO PERFECTION IS OUR GOAL AND THE ISLANDERS WIN IT ALL FOR NOTHING ELSE MATTERS OF THE HEART TO HEART TALK ABOUT LOVE OF GOD--
--WHO LET MAJOR DISASTER INTO THE WATCHTOWER!!! DID SOMEONE HAND OUT IDIOT PILLS WHILE I WAS SLEEPING?!?
AGAIN WITH THE GOOP! I'VE HAD ENOUGH WITH THE GOOP!!!
I CAN FEEL YOU STARING AT ME.
WOW, BATMAN WAS RIGHT. WHAT A SHOCKER.

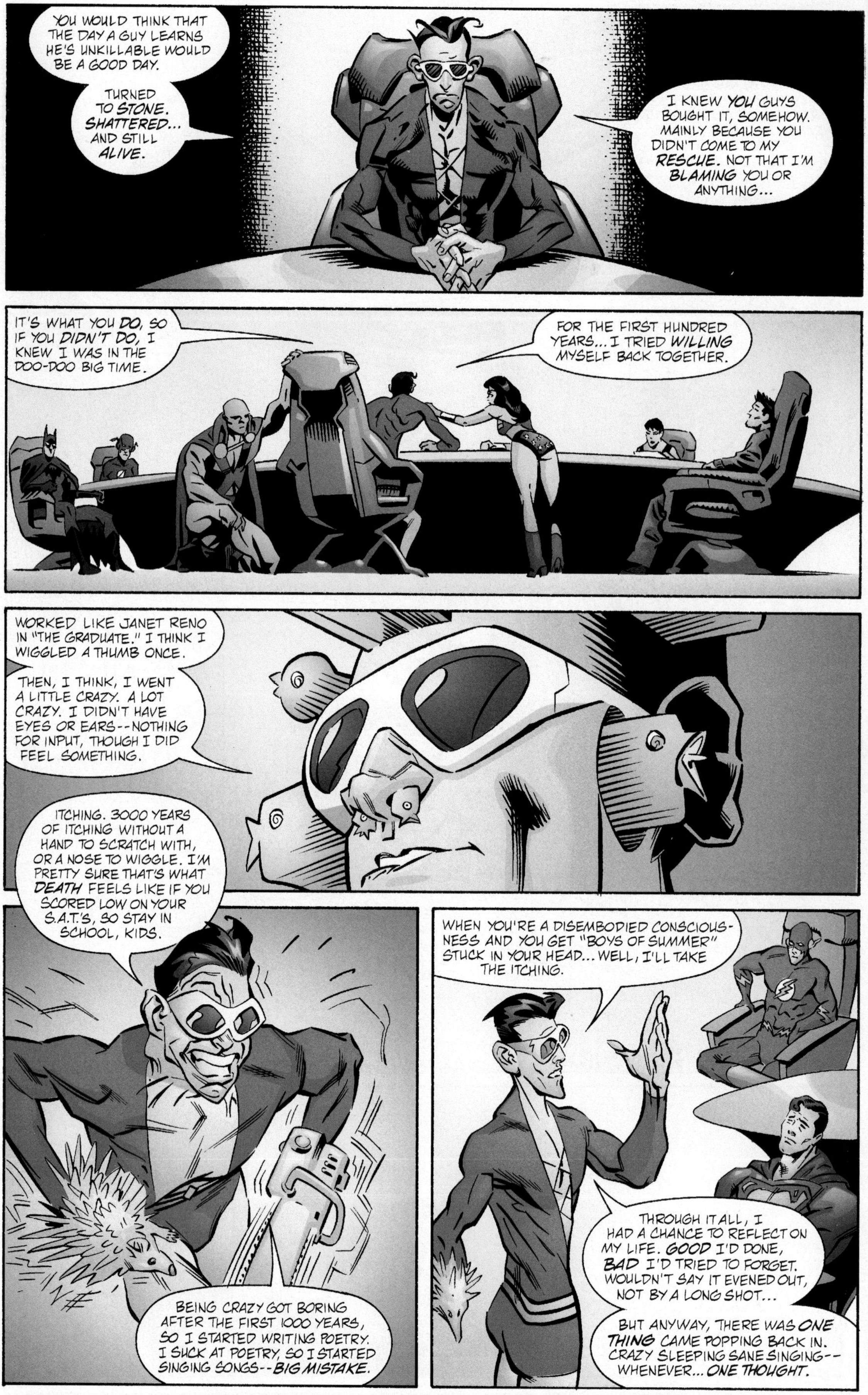

YOU WOULD THINK THAT THE DAY A GUY LEARNS HE'S UNKILLABLE WOULD BE A GOOD DAY.
TURNED TO STONE. SHATTERED... AND STILL ALIVE.
I KNEW YOU GUYS BOUGHT IT, SOMEHOW. MAINLY BECAUSE YOU DIDN'T COME TO MY RESCUE. NOT THAT I'M BLAMING YOU OR ANYTHING...
IT'S WHAT YOU DO, SO IF YOU DIDN'T DO, I KNEW I WAS IN THE DOO-DOO BIG TIME.
FOR THE FIRST HUNDRED YEARS... I TRIED WILLING MYSELF BACK TOGETHER.
WORKED LIKE JANET RENO IN "THE GRADUATE." I THINK I WIGGLED A THUMB ONCE.
THEN, I THINK, I WENT A LITTLE CRAZY. A LOT CRAZY. I DIDN'T HAVE EYES OR EARS--NOTHING FOR INPUT, THOUGH I DID FEEL SOMETHING.
ITCHING. 3000 YEARS OF ITCHING WITHOUT A HAND TO SCRATCH WITH, OR A NOSE TO WIGGLE. I'M PRETTY SURE THAT'S WHAT DEATH FEELS LIKE IF YOU SCORED LOW ON YOUR S.A.T.'S, SO STAY IN SCHOOL, KIDS.
BEING CRAZY GOT BORING AFTER THE FIRST 1000 YEARS, SO I STARTED WRITING POETRY. I SUCK AT POETRY, SO I STARTED SINGING SONGS--BIG MISTAKE.
WHEN YOU'RE A DISEMBODIED CONSCIOUSNESS AND YOU GET "BOYS OF SUMMER" STUCK IN YOUR HEAD... WELL, I'LL TAKE THE ITCHING.
THROUGH IT ALL, I HAD A CHANCE TO REFLECT ON MY LIFE. GOOD I'D DONE, BAD I'D TRIED TO FORGET. WOULDN'T SAY IT EVENED OUT, NOT BY A LONG SHOT...
BUT ANYWAY, THERE WAS ONE THING CAME POPPING BACK IN. CRAZY SLEEPING SANE SINGING--WHENEVER... ONE THOUGHT.

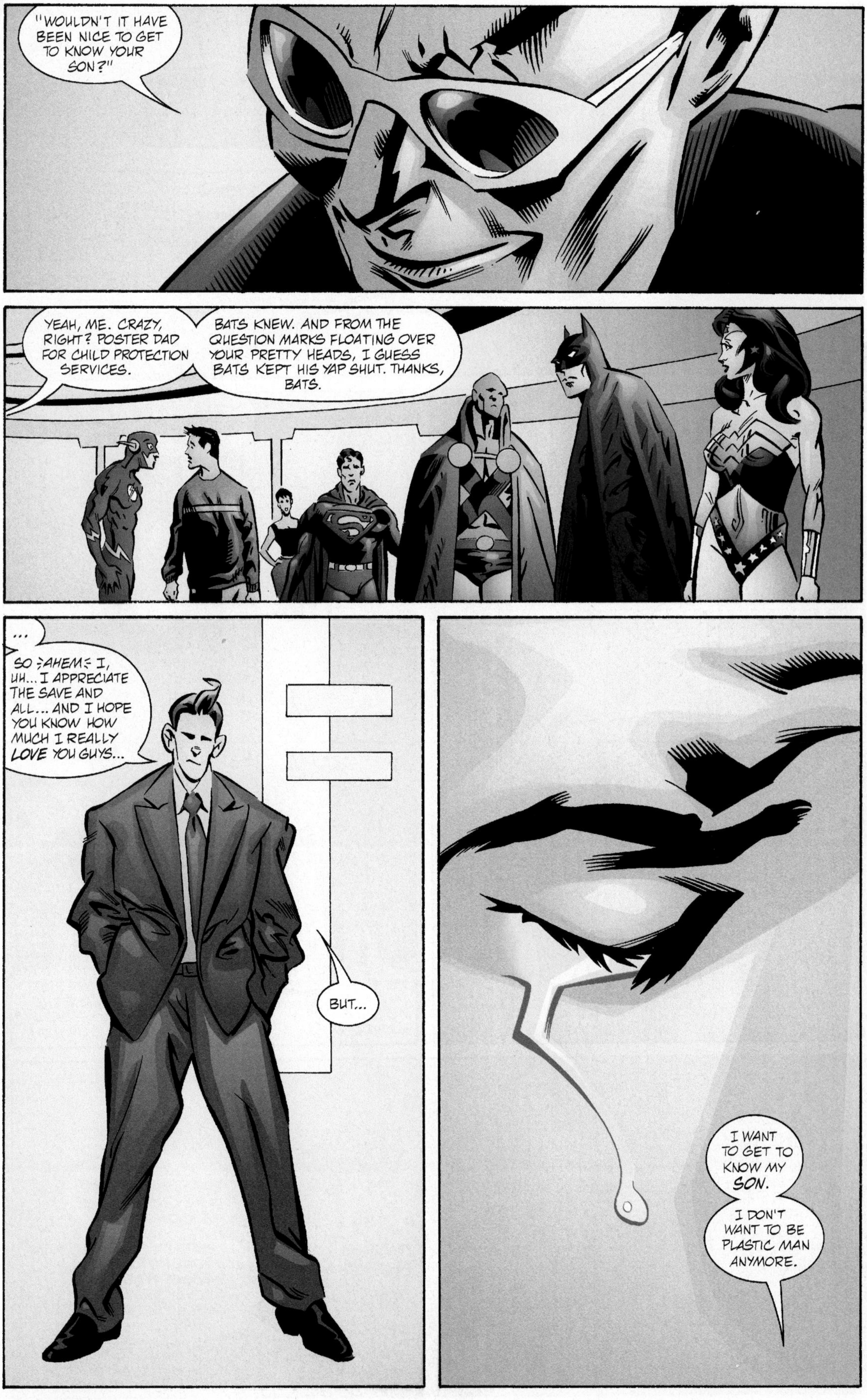
"WOULDN'T IT HAVE BEEN NICE TO GET TO KNOW YOUR SON?"
YEAH, ME. CRAZY, RIGHT? POSTER DAD FOR CHILD PROTECTION SERVICES.
BATS KNEW. AND FROM THE QUESTION MARKS FLOATING OVER YOUR PRETTY HEADS, I GUESS BATS KEPT HIS YAP SHUT. THANKS, BATS.
...
SO *AHEM* I, UH... I APPRECIATE THE SAVE AND ALL... AND I HOPE YOU KNOW HOW MUCH I REALLY LOVE YOU GUYS...
BUT...
I WANT TO GET TO KNOW MY SON.
I DON'T WANT TO BE PLASTIC MAN ANYMORE.

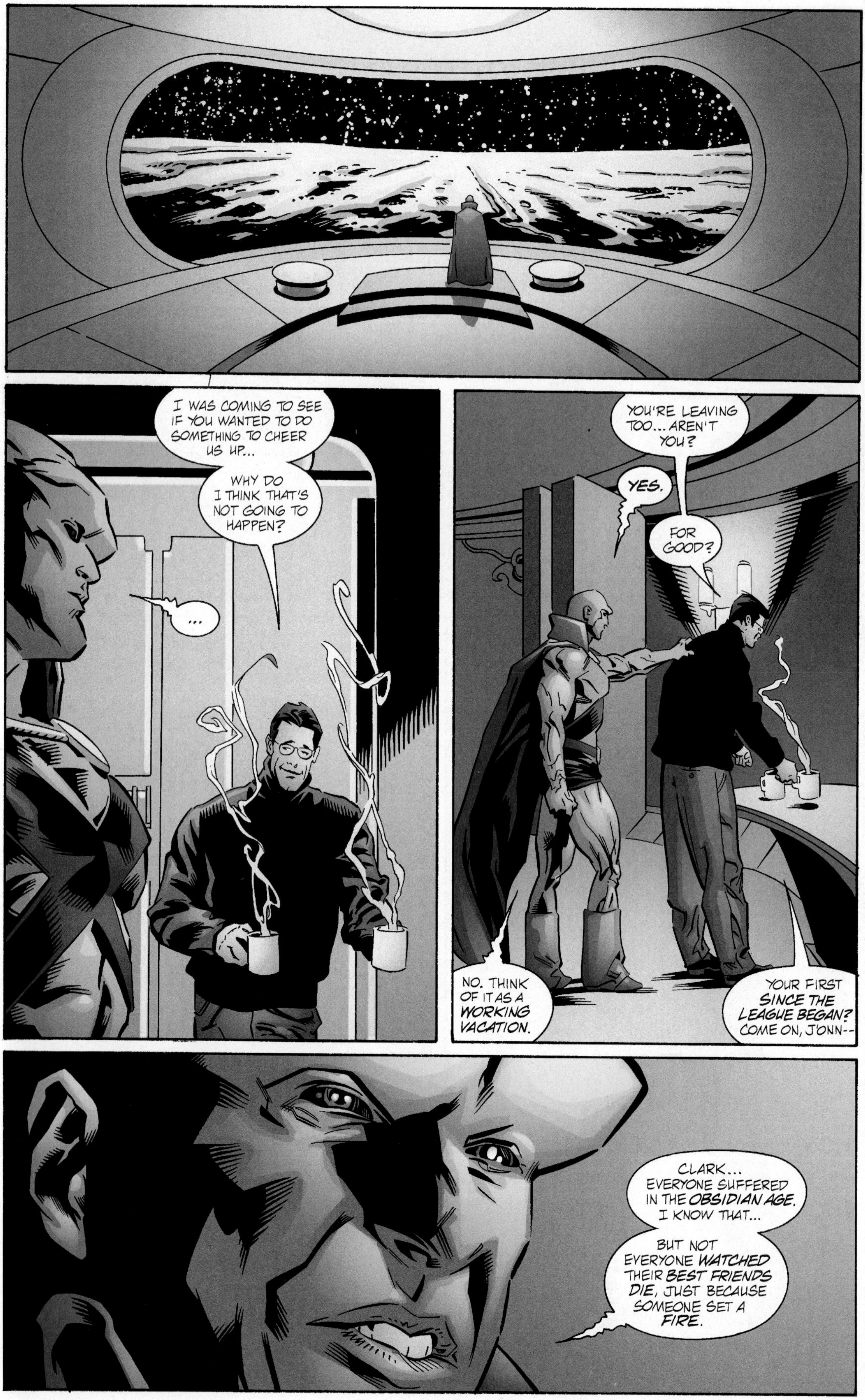
I WAS COMING TO SEE IF YOU WANTED TO DO SOMETHING TO CHEER US UP...
WHY DO I THINK THAT'S NOT GOING TO HAPPEN?
...
YOU'RE LEAVING TOO... AREN'T YOU?
YES.
FOR GOOD?
NO. THINK OF IT AS A WORKING VACATION.
YOUR FIRST SINCE THE LEAGUE BEGAN? COME ON, J'ONN--
CLARK... EVERYONE SUFFERED IN THE OBSIDIAN AGE. I KNOW THAT...
BUT NOT EVERYONE WATCHED THEIR BEST FRIENDS DIE, JUST BECAUSE SOMEONE SET A FIRE.

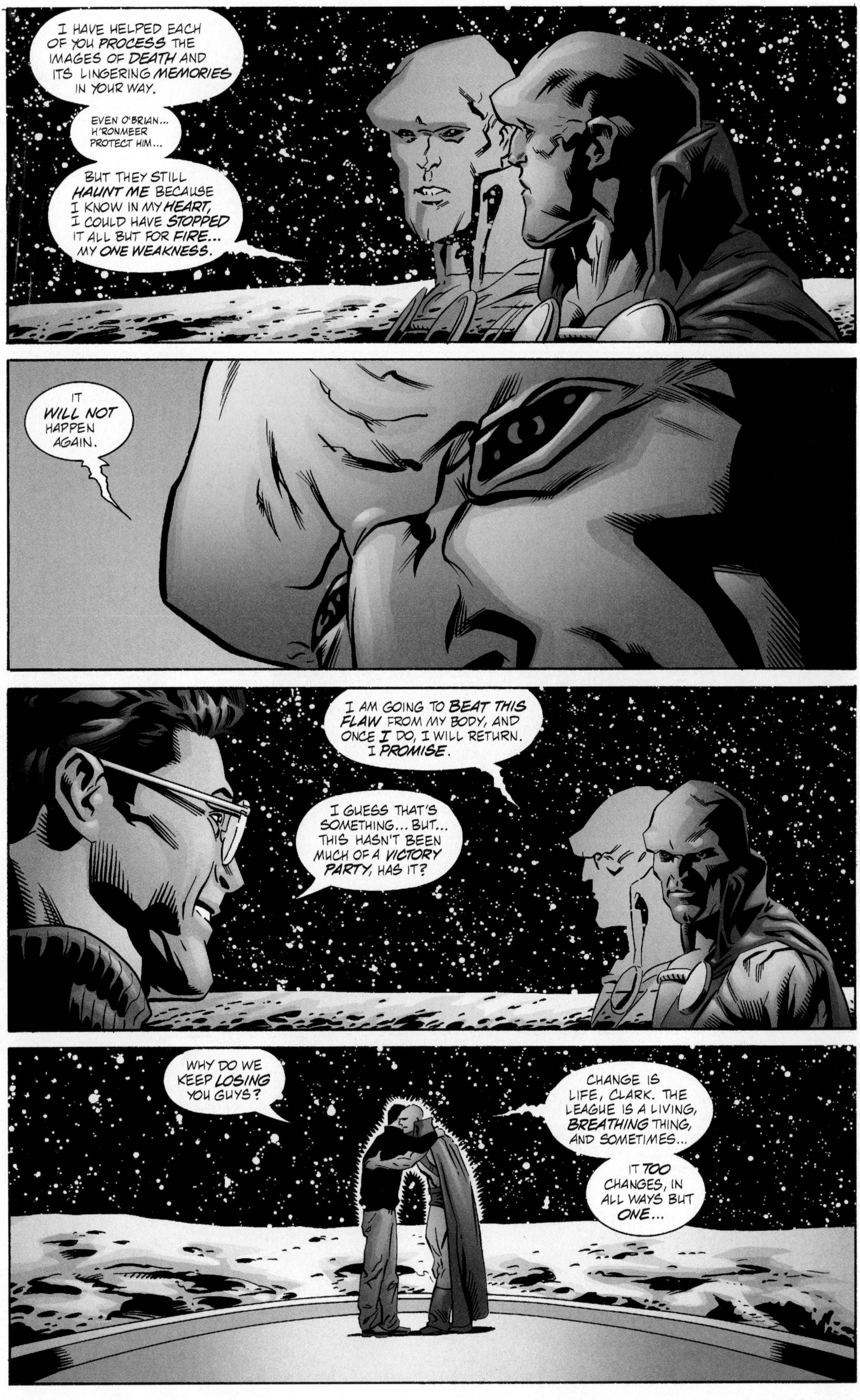
I HAVE HELPED EACH OF YOU PROCESS THE IMAGES OF DEATH AND ITS LINGERING MEMORIES IN YOUR WAY.
EVEN O'BRIAN... H'RONMEER PROTECT HIM...
BUT THEY STILL HAUNT ME BECAUSE I KNOW IN MY HEART, I COULD HAVE STOPPED IT ALL BUT FOR FIRE... MY ONE WEAKNESS.
IT WILL NOT HAPPEN AGAIN.
I AM GOING TO BEAT THIS FLAW FROM MY BODY, AND ONCE I DO, I WILL RETURN. I PROMISE.
I GUESS THAT'S SOMETHING... BUT... THIS HASN'T BEEN MUCH OF A VICTORY PARTY, HAS IT?
WHY DO WE KEEP LOSING YOU GUYS?
CHANGE IS LIFE, CLARK. THE LEAGUE IS A LIVING, BREATHING THING, AND SOMETIMES...
IT TOO CHANGES, IN ALL WAYS BUT ONE...

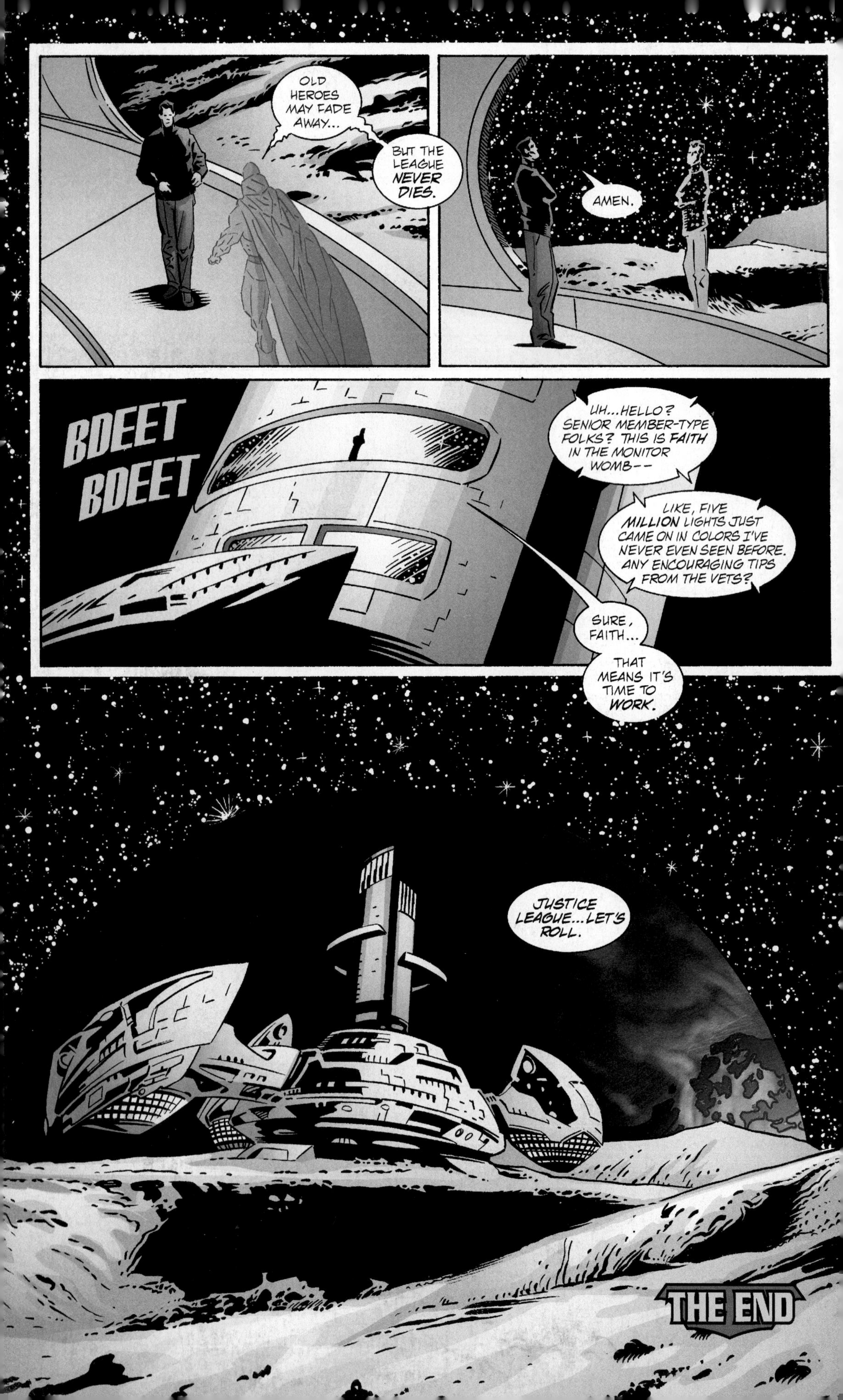
OLD HEROES MAY FADE AWAY...
BUT THE LEAGUE NEVER DIES.
AMEN.
BDEET BDEET
UH...HELLO? SENIOR MEMBER-TYPE FOLKS? THIS IS FAITH IN THE MONITOR WOMB--
LIKE, FIVE MILLION LIGHTS JUST CAME ON IN COLORS I'VE NEVER EVEN SEEN BEFORE. ANY ENCOURAGING TIPS FROM THE VETS?
SURE, FAITH...
THAT MEANS IT'S TIME TO WORK.
JUSTICE LEAGUE...LET'S ROLL.
THE END

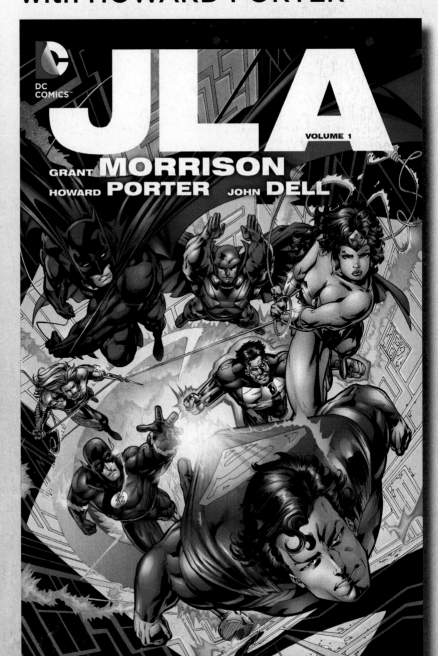

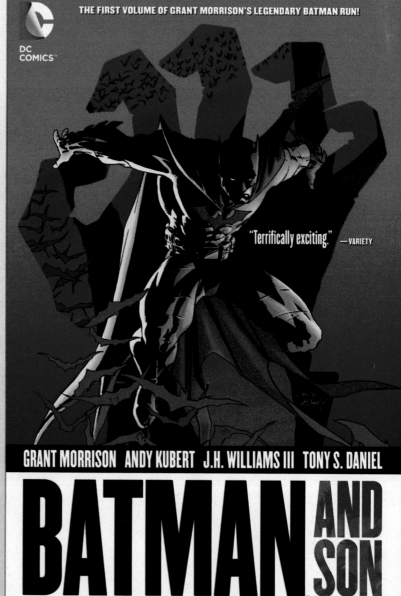

ALEX ROSS
with MARK WAID

JUSTICE

with JIM KRUEGER
& DOUG BRAITHWAITE

THE WORLD'S
GREATEST
SUPER-HEROES

with PAUL DINI

JUSTICE SOCIETY OF AMERICA:
THY KINGDOM COME
PARTS 1-3

with GEOFF JOHNS and
DALE EAGLESHAM

THE GREATEST SUPER-HERO EPIC OF TOMORROW!

KINGDOM COME™

MARK WAID   ALEX ROSS

DC COMICS™